# Best Jobs for the 21st Century

**Sixth Edition**

Part of JIST's Best Jobs® Series

## Laurence Shatkin, Ph.D.

### Also in JIST's *Best Jobs* Series

- 150 Best Federal Jobs
- 200 Best Jobs for College Graduates
- 300 Best Jobs Without a Four-Year Degree
- 200 Best Jobs Through Apprenticeships
- 50 Best Jobs for Your Personality
- 40 Best Fields for Your Career
- 225 Best Jobs for Baby Boomers

- 250 Best-Paying Jobs
- 150 Best Jobs for Your Skills
- 150 Best Jobs for a Better World
- 200 Best Jobs for Introverts
- 10 Best College Majors for Your Personality
- 150 Best Low-Stress Jobs
- 150 Best Jobs for a Secure Future

JIST Works
America's Career Publisher®

# Best Jobs for the 21st Century, Sixth Edition

© 2012 by JIST Publishing

Published by JIST Works, an imprint of JIST Publishing
875 Montreal Way
St. Paul, MN 55102

Email: info@jist.com          Web site: www.jist.com

**Some Other Books by Laurence Shatkin, Ph.D.**

The Sequel

50 Best Jobs for Your Personality

150 Best Jobs for a Secure Future

150 Best Jobs for Your Skills

**Visit www.jist.com** for information on JIST, free job search information, tables of contents, sample pages, and ordering information on our many products.

Acquisitions Editor: Susan Pines
Development Editor: Stephanie Koutek
Cover and Interior Designer: Aleata Halbig
Cover Illustration: Daniel Laflor, iStockphoto®

Interior Layout: Aleata Halbig
Proofreaders: Laura Bowman, Jeanne Clark
Indexer: Cheryl Ann Lenser

Printed in the United States of America
16  15  14  13  12          9  8  7  6  5  4  3  2
Library of Congress Cataloging-in-Publication data is on file with the Library of Congress.

ISBN 978-1-59357-900-5

# This Is a Big Book, But It Is Very Easy to Use

This book is designed to help you explore career options in a variety of interesting ways. The nice thing about it is that you don't have to read it all. Instead, I designed it to allow you to browse and find information that most interests you.

The table of contents will give you a good idea of what's inside and how to use the book, so I suggest you start there. Part I of the book is made up of interesting lists that will help you explore jobs based on pay, education level, personality type, career cluster, and many other criteria. Part II provides descriptions for each job included in the book. Just find a job that interests you in one of the lists in Part I and look up its description in Part II. Simple.

## How I Selected the Best Jobs for the 21st Century

Deciding on the "best" job is a choice that only you can make, but objective criteria can help you identify jobs that are, for example, better paying than other jobs with similar duties. Here is an explanation of the process I used to determine which jobs to include in this book.

I sorted 664 major jobs from highest to lowest in terms of earnings, growth rate through 2018, and number of annual openings, assigning a number to their relative position on each list. I then combined the job position numbers on the three lists, putting the job with the best total score at the top, followed by the job with next-best total score, on down the list. The first list in Part I is called "The Best Jobs Overall," and it contains the 400 jobs with the best combined scores for earnings, growth rate, and openings. You can find descriptions for all 400 best jobs in Part II, plus 221 specializations within these jobs.

I'm not suggesting that the 400 jobs with the best overall scores for earnings, growth, and number of openings are all good ones for you to consider—some will not be. But the jobs that met my criteria present such a wide range of work tasks, work settings, and other features that you are likely to find one or more that will interest you. They also are likely to have higher pay, faster projected growth, and a larger number of openings than most other jobs at similar levels of education and training.

## Some Things You Can Do with This Book

- ❋ Identify more interesting or better-paying jobs that don't require additional training or education.
- ❋ Develop long-term plans that may require additional training, education, or experience.
- ❋ Explore and select a college major or a training or educational program that relates to a career objective.
- ❋ Find reliable earnings information to negotiate pay.
- ❋ Prepare for interviews and the job search.

These are a few of the many ways you can use this book. I hope you find it as interesting to browse as I did to put together. I've tried to make it easy to use and as interesting as occupational information can be.

When you are done with this book, pass it along or tell someone else about it. I wish you well in your career and in your life.

# Table of Contents

## Summary of Major Sections

**Introduction.** A short overview to help you better understand and use the book. *Starts on page 1.*

**Part I: The Best Jobs Lists.** Very useful for exploring career options! Lists are arranged into easy-to-use groups. The first group of lists presents the best overall jobs—jobs with the highest earnings, projected growth, and number of openings. More specialized lists follow, presenting the best jobs for workers age 16–24, workers 55 and over, self-employed workers, women, men, urban workers, and rural workers. Other lists present the best jobs at various levels of education, by career cluster, and by personality type. The column starting at right presents all the list titles within the groups. *Starts on page 15.*

**Part II: The Job Descriptions.** Provides complete descriptions of the 400 jobs that met my criteria for high pay, fast growth, or large number of openings. Each description contains information on earnings, projected growth, job specializations, job duties, skills, education and training required, related knowledge and courses, and many other details. *Starts on page 133.*

**Appendix: Definitions of Skills and Knowledge/Courses Referenced in This Book.** Provides definitions for all skills and knowledge/courses listed in the descriptions in Part II. *Starts on page 582.*

Table of Contents _____

Best Jobs for the 21st Century © JIST Works

# Introduction

I kept this introduction short to encourage you to actually read it. For this reason, I don't provide many details on the technical issues involved in creating the job lists or descriptions. Instead, I give you short explanations to help you understand and use the information the book provides for career exploration or planning. I think this brief and user-oriented approach makes sense for most people who will use this book.

## Who This Book Is For and What It Covers

This book is designed to help students and adults explore their career, education, training, and life options. Employers, educators, program planners, career counselors, and others will also find this book to be of value.

To create it, I started with hundreds of major jobs at all levels of training and education. From these, I selected those with the highest earnings, projected growth rate, and number of job openings. Part I contains lists that rank the jobs according to many criteria, including earnings, growth, openings, education level, and personality type. Part II contains job descriptions for all of the jobs.

I think you will find many of the job lists in Part I interesting and useful for identifying career options to consider. The job descriptions are also packed with useful information.

## Where the Information Comes From

The information I used in creating this book comes from three major government sources: the Bureau of Labor Statistics (BLS), the Census Bureau, and the Office of Vocational and Adult Education.

※ I started with 775 jobs for which the BLS reports economic information. For these jobs, the Occupational Employment Statistics survey provided the most reliable figures on earnings I could obtain, and the Employment Projections program provided the nation's best figures on job growth and openings. These 775 jobs also are linked to about 1,100 job titles in a database called the O*NET (Occupational Information Network), which is the primary source of detailed information on occupations. The Labor Department updates the O*NET on a regular basis, and I used the most recent one available, release 15.1.

❋ The Spring 2010 issue of the *Occupational Outlook Quarterly (OOQ),* a BLS publication, provided the statements about "Considerations for Job Outlook." The *OOQ* is available on the Web at www.bls.gov/opub/ooq.

❋ Information about the level of education or training required for each occupation is taken mostly from a table on the website of the Office of Occupational Statistics and Employment Projections (www.bls.gov/emp/ep_table_111.htm). For recently emerged job specializations not included in that table, I relied on other sources of information, such as professional associations.

❋ Data on the demographic characteristics of workers came from the Current Population Survey (CPS), conducted by the U.S. Census Bureau. This includes the information about the proportion of workers in each job who are men and women or who are within various age brackets.

❋ I used the Classification of Instructional Programs, a system developed by the U.S. Department of Education, for the names of the education and training programs related to each job. I linked programs to jobs by following the crosswalk developed jointly by the BLS and the National Center for Education Statistics.

❋ Information about the career clusters and pathways linked to each occupation is based on materials developed for the U.S. Department of Education's Office of Vocational and Adult Education.

Of course, information in a database format can be boring and even confusing, so I did many things to help make the data useful and present it to you in a form that is easy to understand.

# How the Best Jobs Were Selected

The "This Is a Big Book, But It Is Very Easy to Use" section at the beginning of this book gives a brief description of how I selected the jobs we include in this book. Here are a few more details:

1. I began by creating my own database of information from the government sources listed in the previous section. This database covered 775 job titles at all levels of education and training.

2. I eliminated 3 occupations—Actors, Musicians and Singers, and Dancers—that have such highly variable earnings that no figures are reported for annual earnings. I collapsed 8 specializations of medical doctors into one occupation, Physicians and Surgeons, as explained later in this introduction. I eliminated another 42 occupations because no information is available about their work tasks. I removed 59 more occupations because they are expected to shrink in size and offer fewer than 500 job openings per year and therefore cannot be considered good jobs.

3. I ranked the remaining 664 jobs three times, based on these major criteria: median annual earnings, projected growth through 2018, and number of job openings projected per year.

4. I then added the three numerical rankings for each job to calculate its overall score.

5. To emphasize jobs that tend to pay more, are likely to grow more rapidly, and have more job openings, I selected the 400 job titles with the best total overall scores. These 400 jobs are the basis of all the lists in Part I of this book and are described in Part II, along with 221 O*NET specializations.

Because I rank the jobs by combining scores for earnings, growth, and number of job openings, the top-ranking job—Software Developers, Applications—is listed first even though it is not the best-paying job (which is a tie between two dentistry specializations, Orthodontists and Oral and Maxillofacial Surgeons), the fastest-growing job (which is Biomedical Engineers), or the job with the most openings (which is Retail Salespersons).

# Understand the Limits of the Data in This Book

In this book, I used the most reliable and up-to-date information available on earnings, projected growth, number of openings, and other topics. The earnings data came from the BLS's Occupational Employment Statistics survey. As you look at the figures, keep in mind that they are estimates. They give you a general idea about the number of workers employed, annual earnings, rate of job growth, and annual job openings.

Understand that a problem with such data is that it describes an average. Just as there is no precisely average person, there is no such thing as a statistically average example of a particular job. I say this because data, while helpful, can also be misleading.

Take, for example, the yearly earnings information in this book. This is highly reliable data obtained from a very large U.S. working population sample by the BLS. It reports the average annual pay received as of May 2010 by people in various job titles. (Actually, it is the median annual pay, which means that half earned more and half less.)

This sounds great, except that half of all people in that occupation earned less than that amount. For example, people who are new to the occupation or with only a few years of work experience often earn much less than the median amount. People who live in rural areas or who work for smaller employers typically earn less than those who do similar work in cities (where the cost of living is higher) or for bigger employers. People in certain areas of the country earn less than those in others. Other factors also influence how much you are likely to earn in a given job in your area. For example, dentists in ten metropolitan areas in North Carolina have median earnings of more than $166,400 (compared to a national median of $141,040), mostly because North Carolina had only one dentistry school until 2011. With less competition, dentists there can charge higher fees.

Also keep in mind that the figures for job growth and number of openings are projections by labor economists—their best guesses about what can be expected between now and 2018. Those projections are not guarantees. A catastrophic economic downturn, war, or technological breakthrough could change the actual outcome.

Finally, don't forget that the job market consists of both job openings and job *seekers*. The figures on job growth and openings don't tell you how many people will be competing with you to be hired. The Department of Labor does not publish figures on the supply of job candidates, so I'm unable to tell you about the level of competition you can expect. Competition is an important issue that you should research for any tentative career goal. The *Occupational Outlook Handbook* provides informative statements for many occupations. The "Considerations for Job Outlook" statements in the Part II job descriptions sometimes refer to competition for job entry. You also should speak to people who educate or train tomorrow's workers; they probably have a good idea of how many graduates find rewarding employment and how quickly. People in the workforce can provide insights into this issue as well. Use your critical thinking skills to evaluate what people tell you. For example, educators or trainers may be trying to recruit you, whereas people in the workforce may be trying to discourage you from competing. Get a variety of opinions to balance out possible biases.

So, in reviewing the information in this book, please understand the limitations of the data. You need to use common sense in career decision making as in most other things in life. I hope that, by using that approach, you find the information helpful and interesting.

# Data Complexities

For those of you who like details, I present some of the complexities inherent in our sources of information and what I did to make sense of them here. You don't need to know these things to use the book, so jump to the next section of the introduction if details bore you.

I selected the jobs on the basis of economic data, and I include information on earnings, projected growth, and number of job openings for each job throughout this book. I think this information is important to most people, but getting it for each job is not a simple task.

## Earnings

The employment security agency of each state gathers information on earnings for various jobs and forwards it to the BLS. This information is organized in standardized ways by a BLS program called Occupational Employment Statistics, or OES. To keep the earnings for the various jobs and regions comparable, the OES screens out certain types of earnings and includes others, so the OES earnings I use in this book represent straight-time gross pay exclusive of premium pay. More specifically, the OES earnings include each job's base rate; cost-of-living allowances; guaranteed pay; hazardous-duty pay; incentive pay, including commissions and production bonuses; on-call pay; and tips. The OES earnings do not include back pay, jury duty pay, overtime pay, severance pay, shift differentials, nonproduction bonuses, or tuition reimbursements. Also, self-employed workers are not included in the estimates, and they can be a significant segment in certain occupations. When data on annual earnings for an occupation is highly unreliable, OES does not report a figure, which meant that I reluctantly had to exclude a few occupations, such as Hunters and Trappers, from this book.

For each job, you'll find two facts related to earnings, both based on the OES survey:

❇ The Annual Earnings figure shows the median earnings (half earn more, half earn less).

❇ The Earnings Growth Potential statement represents the gap between the 10th percentile and the median. This information answers the question, "If I compared the wages of the low earners to the median, how much of a pay difference (in percentage terms) would I find?" If the difference is large, the job has great potential for increasing your earnings as you gain experience and skills. If the difference is small, you probably will need to move on to another occupation to improve your earnings substantially. Because a percentage figure, by itself, might be hard to interpret, I precede the figure with an easy-to-understand verbal tag that expresses the Earnings Growth Potential: "very low" when the percentage is less than 25%, "low" for 25%–35%, "medium" for 36%–40%, "high" for 41%–50%, and "very high" for any figure higher than 51%.

The median earnings for all workers in all occupations were $33,840 in May 2010. The 400 jobs in this book were chosen partly on the basis of good earnings, so their average is a respectable $46,991. (This is a weighted average, which means that jobs with larger workforces are given greater weight in the computation. It also is based on the assumption that the two jobs with income reported as "more than $166,400" pay exactly $166,400, so the actual average is a little bit higher.)

# Projected Growth and Number of Job Openings

This information comes from the Office of Occupational Statistics and Employment Projections, a program within the BLS that develops information about projected trends in the nation's labor market for the next ten years. The most recent projections available cover the years from 2008 to 2018. The projections are based on information about people moving into and out of occupations. The BLS uses data from various sources in projecting the growth and number of openings for each job title—some data comes from the Census Bureau's Current Population Survey and some comes from an OES survey. The BLS economists assumed an economy unaffected by a major war, depression, or other upheaval. They also assumed that recessions may occur during the decade covered by these projections, as would be consistent with the pattern of business cycles the United States has experienced for several decades. However, because their projections cover 10 years, the figures for job growth and openings are intended to provide an average of both the good times and the bad times.

The Department of Labor provides a single figure (15.1%) for the projected growth of 38 postsecondary teaching jobs and also provides a single figure (55,290) for the projected annual job openings for these 38 occupations. Because these college-teaching jobs are related to very different interests—from engineering to art to forestry to social work—and because separate *earnings* figures are available for each of the 38 jobs, I thought you'd appreciate having these jobs appear separately in the lists in this book. If the trends of the last several years continue, none of these jobs can be expected to grow or take on workers at a much faster rate than the other 37. Therefore, in preparing the Part I lists and the Part II descriptions, I assumed that all of these college-teaching jobs share the same rate of projected job growth, 15.1%, and I computed a figure for their projected job openings by dividing the total (55,290) into 38 parts, each of which is proportional in size to the current workforce of the job.

I was unable to do the same thing for Physicians and Surgeons. As a group, the occupations of medical doctors are projected to grow at the rate of 21.8% and offer 26,050 job openings each year. However, the specialized jobs within this group have been growing at very different rates over the past several years, so I have no way to estimate how many job openings each of these specializations will offer. Therefore, I treat the group as a single occupation in all the Part I lists.

While salary figures are fairly straightforward, you may not know what to make of job-growth figures. For example, is projected growth of 15% good or bad? Keep in mind that the average (mean) growth projected for all occupations by the BLS is 10.4%. One-quarter of the SOC (Standard Occupational Classification) occupations have a growth projection of 3.2% or lower. Growth of 11.6% is the median, meaning that half of the occupations have more, half less. Only one-quarter of the occupations have growth projected at more than 17.4%.

Because the jobs in this book were selected as "best" partly on the basis of job growth, their mean growth is 14.0%, which compares favorably to the mean for all jobs. Among these 400 jobs, the job ranked 100th by projected growth has a figure of 19.5%, the job ranked 200th (the median) has a projected growth of 15.1%, and the job ranked 300th has a projected growth of 10.9%.

The average number of job openings for the 400 best jobs—8,993—is significantly lower than the national average of about 35,000 openings for all occupations. But you should not be surprised by this; most of the jobs with a very large number of openings are low-skill jobs with rapid turnover, such as fast-food workers. The jobs in this book tend to require higher skills and experience slower turnover. Among them, the job ranked 100th for job openings has a figure of about 9,200 annual openings projected, the job ranked 200th (the median) has about 3,500 openings projected, and the job ranked 300th has about 1,300 openings projected.

Perhaps you're wondering why I present figures on both job growth *and* number of openings. Aren't these two ways of saying the same thing? Actually, you need to know both. Consider the occupation Occupational Therapist Aides, which is projected to grow at the impressive rate of 30.7%. There should be lots of opportunities in such a fast-growing job, right? Not exactly. This is a small occupation, with only about 7,800 people currently employed. So, even though it is growing rapidly, it will not create many new jobs (about 350 per year).

Now consider Team Assemblers. Because most manufacturers are either shifting production overseas or increasing use of automation, this occupation is not growing at all (to be exact, its projected growth rate is .03%). Nevertheless, this is a huge occupation that employs over one million workers. So, even though the workforce size will stay the same, the occupation is expected to take on 25,000 new workers each year through job turnover: new workers will replace existing workers who move on to other jobs, retire, or die. That's why I base my selection of the best jobs on both of these economic indicators and why you should pay attention to both when you scan the lists of best jobs.

## Other Job Characteristics

Like the figures for earnings, some of the other figures used to create the lists of jobs in this book are shared by more than one job title. For example, the BLS does not report separate figures for the percentages of female workers in four clerical occupations: Executive Secretaries and Administrative Assistants; Legal Secretaries; Medical Secretaries; and Secretaries, Except Legal, Medical, and Executive. Instead, the BLS reports one figure, 96.8%, for the combined occupation Secretaries and Administrative Assistants. As a result, you'll find these four occupations ordered alphabetically but otherwise tied in the list of jobs with the highest percentage of female workers. You may notice similar figure-sharing among related jobs where I list the percentages of workers in specific age brackets.

## Information in the Job Descriptions

I used a variety of government sources to compile the job descriptions in Part II. Details on these various sources are mentioned later in this introduction in the section "Part II: The Job Descriptions."

# Part I: The Best Jobs Lists

There are 69 separate lists in Part I of this book—look in the table of contents for a complete list of the lists. The lists are not difficult to understand, because they have clear titles and are organized into groupings of related lists.

Depending on your situation, some of the job lists in Part I will interest you more than others. For example, if you are young, you may be interested to learn the highest-paying jobs that employ high percentages of workers age 16–24. Other lists organize jobs by personality type, by level of education, and in other ways that you might find helpful in exploring your career options.

Whatever your situation, I suggest you use the lists that make sense for you to help explore career options. Following are the names of each group of lists along with short comments on each group. You will find additional information in a brief introduction provided at the beginning of each group of lists in Part I.

Here is an overview of each major group of lists you will find in Part I.

# Best Jobs Overall: Lists of Jobs with the Highest Pay, Fastest Growth, and Most Openings

Four lists are in this group, and they are the ones that most people want to see first. The first list presents all 400 job titles in order of their combined scores for earnings, growth, and number of job openings. Three more lists in this group present the 100 jobs with the highest earnings, the 100 jobs projected to grow most rapidly, and the 100 jobs with the most openings.

# Best Jobs Lists by Demographic

This group of lists presents interesting information for a variety of types of people based on data from the U.S. Census Bureau. The lists are arranged into groups for workers age 16–24, workers age 55 and older, self-employed workers, women, men, urban workers, and rural workers. I created five lists for each group, basing the last four on the information in the first list:

- ❀ Jobs having the highest percentage of people of each type
- ❀ 25 jobs with the best combined scores for earnings, growth, and number of openings
- ❀ 25 jobs with the highest earnings
- ❀ 25 jobs with the highest growth rates
- ❀ 25 jobs with the largest number of openings

# Best Jobs Lists Based on Levels of Education and Experience

I created separate lists for each level of education and training as defined by the U.S. Department of Labor. I put each of the 400 job titles into at least one of the lists based on the education and training required for entry. (Some jobs have specializations requiring different levels of education or training.) Jobs within these lists are presented in order of their total combined scores for earnings, growth, and number of openings. The lists include jobs in these groupings:

- ❀ Short-term on-the-job training
- ❀ Moderate-term on-the-job training
- ❀ Long-term on-the-job training
- ❀ Work experience in a related job
- ❀ Postsecondary vocational training
- ❀ Associate degree
- ❀ Bachelor's degree
- ❀ Work experience plus degree
- ❀ Master's degree

* Doctoral degree
* First professional degree

# Best Jobs Lists Based on Career Clusters

These lists organize the 400 best jobs into the 16 career clusters that were developed by the U.S. Department of Education in 1999 and are used by many educational institutions and career information resources to divide up the world of work and the educational and training programs that prepare for careers. Because a single occupation may be open to people who come out of several different educational or training programs, you will find some jobs that appear on the lists for two or more clusters. Here are the 16 interest career clusters used in these lists: Agriculture and Natural Resources; Architecture and Construction; Arts and Communication; Business and Administration; Education and Training; Finance and Insurance; Government and Public Administration; Health Science; Hospitality, Tourism, and Recreation; Human Service; Information Technology; Law and Public Safety; Manufacturing; Retail and Wholesale Sales and Service; Scientific Research, Engineering, and Mathematics; Transportation, Distribution, and Logistics.

# Best Jobs Lists Based on Personality Types

These lists organize the 400 best jobs into six personality types, which are described in the introduction to the lists: Realistic, Investigative, Artistic, Social, Enterprising, and Conventional. The jobs within each list are presented in order of their total scores for earnings, growth, and number of openings.

# Bonus Lists: Jobs with the Greatest Changes in Outlook Since the Previous Edition

These two lists show the jobs that have had the greatest revisions to their job-growth projections since the previous edition of this book. One lists the 25 jobs with the greatest increase in job-growth projection, and the other lists the 25 jobs with the greatest decrease.

# Part II: The Job Descriptions

This part of the book provides a brief but information-packed description for the jobs that met my criteria for this book. The descriptions in Part II are presented in alphabetical order by job title. This makes it easy to look up any job you find in Part I that you want to learn more about.

I used the most current information from a variety of government sources to create the descriptions. I designed the descriptions to be easy to understand, and the sample that follows—with an explanation of each of its component parts—will help you better understand and use the descriptions.

Job Title →

## Medical and Health Services Managers

Data Elements →

- ❋ Annual Earnings: $84,270
- ❋ Earnings Growth Potential: Medium (39.1%)
- ❋ Growth: 16.0%
- ❋ Annual Job Openings: 9,940
- ❋ Self-Employed: 6.0%

Considerations for Job Outlook →

**Considerations for Job Outlook:** The health-care industry is expected to continue growing and diversifying, requiring managers increasingly to run business operations. Opportunities should be good, especially for jobseekers who have work experience in health care and strong business management skills.

Summary Description and Tasks →

**Plan, direct, or coordinate medicine and health services in hospitals, clinics, managed care organizations, public health agencies, or similar organizations.** Conduct and administer fiscal operations, including accounting, planning budgets, authorizing expenditures, establishing rates for services, and coordinating financial reporting. Direct, supervise, and evaluate work activities of medical, nursing, technical, clerical, service, maintenance, and other personnel. Maintain communication between governing boards, medical staff, and department heads by attending board meetings and coordinating interdepartmental functioning. Review and analyze facility activities and data to aid planning and cash and risk management and to improve service utilization. Plan, implement, and administer programs and services in a health-care or medical facility, including personnel administration, training, and coordination of medical, nursing, and physical plant staff. Direct or conduct recruitment, hiring, and training of personnel. Establish work schedules and assignments for staff, according to workload, space, and equipment availability. Maintain awareness of advances in medicine, computerized diagnostic and treatment equipment, data processing technology, government regulations, health insurance changes, and financing options. Monitor the use of diagnostic services, inpatient beds, facilities, and staff to ensure effective use of resources and assess the need for additional staff, equipment, and services. Develop and maintain computerized record management systems to store and process data such as personnel activities and information and to produce reports. Establish and evaluate objectives and evaluative operational criteria for units they manage. Prepare activity reports to inform management of the status and implementation plans of programs, services, and quality initiatives. Inspect facilities and recommend building or equipment modifications to ensure emergency readiness and compliance with access, safety, and sanitation regulations. Develop and implement organizational policies and procedures for the facility or medical unit.

Education/ Training Required →

**Education/Training Required:** Work experience plus degree.

Education/ Training Programs →

**Education and Training Programs:** Community Health and Preventive Medicine; Health and Medical Administrative Services, Other; Health Information/Medical Records Administration/Administrator; Health Services Administration; Health Unit Manager/Ward Supervisor Training; Health/Health Care Administration/Management; Hospital and Health Care Facilities Administration/Management; Public Health, General.

Knowledge/ Courses →

**Knowledge/Courses**—Economics and Accounting, Personnel and Human Resources, Administration and Management, Sales and Marketing, Medicine and Dentistry, Law and Government.

Personality Type, Career Cluster, Career Pathway, and Other Jobs in This Pathway →

**Personality Type:** Enterprising-Conventional-Social. **Career Cluster:** 08 Health Science. **Career Pathways:** 8.1 Therapeutic Services; 8.2 Diagnostics Services; 8.3 Health Informatics. **Other Jobs in These Pathways:** Cytogenetic Technologists; Cytotechnologists; Dental Assistants; Dental Hygienists; Emergency Medical Technicians and Paramedics; Endoscopy Technicians; Engineers, All Other; Executive Secretaries and Executive Administrative Assistants; First-Line Supervisors of Office and Administrative Support Workers; Healthcare Support Workers, All Other; Histotechnologists and Histologic Technicians; Home Health Aides; Licensed Practical and Licensed Vocational Nurses; Medical and Clinical Laboratory Technologists; Medical Assistants; Medical Records and Health Information Technicians; Medical Secretaries; Pharmacists; Pharmacy Technicians; Physical Therapists; Public Relations Specialists; Radiologic Technologists; Receptionists and Information Clerks; Social and Human Service Assistants; Speech-Language Pathology Assistants; others.

Skills →

**Skills**—Management of Financial Resources, Operations Analysis, Management of Material Resources, Science, Management of Personnel Resources, Systems Evaluation, Coordination, Time Management.

**Work Environment:** Indoors; sitting; exposed to disease or infections.

**Work Environment**

- ❋ **Job Title:** This is the job title for the job as defined by the U.S. Department of Labor and used in its Standard Occupational Classification (SOC).

- ❋ **Data Elements:** The information on education, earnings, earnings growth potential, growth, annual openings, and percentage of self-employed workers comes from various government databases, as explained earlier in this introduction.

- ❋ **Considerations for Job Outlook:** This information, based on the BLS's *Occupational Projections and Training Data*, explains some factors that are expected to affect opportunities for job seekers over the period of time from 2008 to 2018.

- ❋ **Summary Description and Tasks:** The first part of each job description provides a summary of the occupation in bold type. It is followed by a listing of tasks that are generally performed by people who work in the job. This information comes from the O*NET database; where necessary, I edited the tasks to keep them from exceeding 2,200 characters.

- ❋ **Education/Training Required:** Based mostly on information from the BLS, this phrase identifies the most common level of education or training that is required of workers entering the career. Understand that a higher level of preparation than what appears here may sometimes be beneficial, either to make you more competitive against other job seekers or to allow you to enter the job at a more responsible and better-paying level. On the other hand, if the demand for workers is high, it sometimes may be possible for you to enter the career with a lower level of preparation.

- ❋ **Education/Training Program(s):** This part of the job description provides the name of the educational or training program or programs for the job. It will help you identify sources of formal or informal training for a job that interests you. To get this information, I used a crosswalk developed jointly by the BLS and the National Center for Education Statistics (NCES). In 12 cases, I abbreviated the listing of related programs for the sake of space; such entries end with "others." Keep in mind that many jobs are open to people from various backgrounds; the programs listed here are those most commonly recommended, but often they are not the only possible entry routes.

- ❋ **Knowledge/Courses:** This entry can help you understand the most important knowledge areas that are required for a job and the types of courses or programs you will likely need to take to prepare for it. For each job, I identified the highest-rated knowledge area in the O*NET database, so every job for which data is available has at least one listed. I identified any additional knowledge area with a rating that was higher than the average rating for that knowledge area for all jobs. I listed as many as six knowledge areas in descending order.

- ❋ **Personality Type:** The O*NET database assigns each job to a primary personality type and to as many as two secondary types. These job descriptions include the names of the related personality types. You can find more information on the personality types as well as a brief definition of each type in the introduction to the lists of jobs based on personality types in Part I.

❋ **Career Cluster, Career Pathway,** and **Other Jobs in This Pathway:** This information cross-references the 16 career clusters developed by the U.S. Department of Education and used in a variety of educational institutions and career information systems. Here I include the cluster and career pathway that the job fits into, as well as other job titles that have similar interests, require similar skills, or need similar secondary school preparation.

❋ **Skills:** The O*NET database provides data on 35 skills, so I decided to list only those that were most important for each job rather than list pages of unhelpful details. For each job, I identify any skill with a rating for level of mastery that was higher than the average rating for this skill for all jobs and a rating for importance that was higher than very low. I order the skills by the amount by which their ratings exceed the average rating for all occupations, from highest to lowest. If there are more than eight such skills, I include only those eight with the highest ratings. If no skill has a rating higher than the average for all jobs, I say "None met the criteria." Each listed skill is followed by a brief description of that skill.

❋ **Work Environment:** I include any work condition with a rating that exceeds the midpoint of the rating scale. The order does not indicate any condition's frequency on the job. Consider whether you like these conditions and whether any of these conditions would make you uncomfortable. Keep in mind that when hazards are present (for example, contaminants), protective equipment and procedures are provided to keep you safe.

Getting all the information I used in the job descriptions was not a simple process, and it is not always perfect. For some information topics, data is not available. However, I used the best and most recent sources of data I could find, and I think that the results will be helpful to many people.

# Sources of Additional Information

Hundreds of sources of career information exist, so here are a few I consider most helpful in getting additional information on the jobs listed in this book.

## Print References

❋ *O*NET Dictionary of Occupational Titles:* Revised on a regular basis, this book provides good descriptions for all jobs listed in the U.S. Department of Labor's O*NET database. There are 950 job descriptions at all levels of education and training, plus lists of related job titles in other major career information sources, educational programs, and other information. Published by JIST.

❋ *Enhanced Occupational Outlook Handbook:* Updated regularly, this book provides thorough descriptions for 270 major jobs in the current *Occupational Outlook Handbook,* brief descriptions for the O*NET jobs that are related to each, brief descriptions of thousands of more-specialized jobs from the *Dictionary of Occupational Titles,* and other information. Published by JIST.

# Internet Resources

❋ **The U.S. Department of Labor Bureau of Labor Statistics website:** The Department of Labor Bureau of Labor Statistics website (www.bls.gov) provides a lot of career information, including links to other webpages that provide information on the jobs covered in this book. This website is a bit formal and, well, confusing, but it will take you to the major sources of government career information if you explore its options.

❋ **O*NET site:** Go to http://online.onetcenter.org for detailed information on the O*NET job titles presented in Part II of this book.

❋ **My Next Move:** This site, www.mynextmove.org, features the same content as the O*NET site but in a more user-friendly format.

❋ **CareerOneStop:** This site (www.careeronestop.org) is operated by the Minnesota Department of Labor on behalf of the U.S. Department of Labor and provides access to state and local information about occupations. It also can identify a one-stop career center near you that can help you find local job openings and providers of education and training.

# Thanks

Thanks for reading this introduction. You are surely a more thorough person than those who jumped into the book without reading it, and you will probably get more out of the book as a result. I wish you a satisfying career and, more important, a good life.

**Credits and Acknowledgments:** While the author created this book, it is based on the work of many others. The occupational information is based on data obtained from the U.S. Department of Labor, the U.S. Department of Education, and the U.S. Census Bureau. These sources provide the most authoritative occupational information available. The noneconomic job-related information is from the O*NET database, which was developed by researchers and developers under the direction of the U.S. Department of Labor. They, in turn, were assisted by thousands of employers who provided details on the nature of work in the many thousands of job samplings used in the database's development. I used the most recent version of the O*NET database, release 15.1. I appreciate and thank the staff of the U.S. Department of Labor for their efforts and expertise in providing such a rich source of data. The taxonomy of college majors (the Classification of Instructional Programs) is from the U.S. Department of Education.

# PART I

# The Best Jobs Lists

This part contains a lot of interesting lists, and it's a good place for you to start using the book. Here are some suggestions for using the lists to explore career options:

⊛ The table of contents at the beginning of this book presents a complete listing of the list titles in this section. You can browse the lists or use the table of contents to find those that interest you most.

⊛ I gave the lists clear titles, so most require little explanation. I provide comments for each group of lists.

⊛ As you review the lists of jobs, one or more of the jobs may appeal to you enough that you want to seek additional information. As this happens, mark that job (or, if someone else will be using this book, write it on a separate sheet of paper) so that you can look up the description of the job in Part II.

⊛ Keep in mind that all jobs in these lists meet my basic criteria for being included in this book, as explained in the introduction. All lists, therefore, contain jobs that have high pay, high growth, or large numbers of openings. These measures are easily quantified and are often presented in lists of best jobs in the newspapers and other media. Although earnings, growth, and openings are important, you also should consider other factors in your career planning, such as location, liking the people you work with, and having opportunities to be creative. Many other factors that may help define the ideal job for you are difficult or impossible to quantify and thus aren't used in this book, so you will need to consider the importance of these issues yourself.

⊛ All data used to create these lists comes from the U.S. Department of Labor and the Census Bureau. The earnings figures are based on the average annual pay received by full-time workers. Because the earnings represent the national averages, actual pay rates can vary greatly by location, amount of previous work experience, and other factors. Even lists that focus on a particular type of worker (for example, rural workers) use earnings figures based on the national averages.

# Some Details on the Lists

The sources of the information I used in constructing these lists are presented in this book's introduction. Here are some additional details on how I created the lists:

❋ Some jobs have the same scores for one or more data elements. For example, in the category of fastest-growing, two jobs (Cost Estimators and Surgical Technologists) are expected to grow at the same rate, 25.3 percent. Therefore I ordered these two jobs alphabetically, and their order in relation to each other has no other significance. Avoiding these ties was impossible, so understand that the difference of several positions on a list may not mean as much as it seems.

❋ Likewise, it is unwise to place too much emphasis on small differences in outlook information: projections for job growth and job openings. For example, Medical Assistants are projected to have 21,780 job openings per year, whereas 21,770 openings are projected for Clergy. This is a difference of only 10 jobs spread over the entire United States, and, of course, it is only a projection. Before 2007, the Bureau of Labor Statistics rounded these projections to the nearest 1,000 and would have assigned these two occupations the same figure (22,000), which would have given Clergy the higher rank on the basis of alphabetical ordering. So, again, keep in mind that small differences of position on a list aren't very significant.

# Best Jobs Overall: Lists of Jobs with the Highest Pay, Fastest Growth, and Most Openings

The four lists that follow are this book's premier lists. They are the lists that are most often mentioned in the media and the ones that most readers want to see.

To create these lists, I started with a database of 775 jobs, collapsed some specializations, eliminated jobs that lacked information or did not meet my standards for good jobs, and ranked the remaining 664 major jobs according to a combination of their earnings, growth, and openings. I then selected the 400 jobs with the best total scores for use in this book. (The process for ranking the jobs is explained in more detail in the introduction.)

The first list presents all 400 best jobs. Three additional lists present the 100 jobs with the top scores in each of three measures: annual earnings, projected percentage growth through 2018, and number of annual openings. Descriptions for all the jobs in these lists are included in Part II.

# The Best Jobs Overall—Jobs with the Best Combination of Pay, Growth, and Openings

This list arranges all 400 jobs that were selected for this book in order of their overall scores for pay, growth, and number of openings, as explained in the introduction. The job with the best overall score was Software Developers, Applications. Other jobs follow in order of their combined scores for pay, growth, and openings. These 400 jobs are the ones I use throughout this book: in the other lists in Part I and in the descriptions found in Part II.

As you look over the list, remember that jobs near the top of the list are not necessarily "good" jobs—nor are jobs toward the end of the list necessarily "bad" ones for you to consider. Their positions in the list are simply a result of each one's total score based on pay, growth, and number of openings. This means, for example, that some jobs with low pay and modest growth but a high number of openings appear higher on the list than some jobs with higher pay and modest growth but a low number of openings. A "right" job for you could be anywhere on this list.

| The Best Jobs Overall | | | |
|---|---|---|---|
| Job | Annual Earnings | Percent Growth | Annual Openings |
| 1. Software Developers, Applications | $87,790 | 34.0% | 21,840 |
| 2. Physicians and Surgeons | $165,279 | 21.8% | 26,050 |
| 3. Software Developers, Systems Software | $94,180 | 30.4% | 15,340 |
| 4. Management Analysts | $78,160 | 23.9% | 30,650 |
| 5. Computer Systems Analysts | $77,740 | 20.3% | 22,280 |
| 6. Registered Nurses | $64,690 | 22.2% | 103,900 |
| 7. Civil Engineers | $77,560 | 24.3% | 11,460 |
| 8. Medical Scientists, Except Epidemiologists | $76,700 | 40.4% | 6,620 |
| 9. Physical Therapists | $76,310 | 30.3% | 7,860 |
| 10. Dental Hygienists | $68,250 | 36.1% | 9,840 |
| 11. Accountants and Auditors | $61,690 | 21.6% | 49,750 |
| 12. Network and Computer Systems Administrators | $69,160 | 23.2% | 13,550 |
| 13. Pharmacists | $111,570 | 17.0% | 10,580 |
| 14. Computer and Information Systems Managers | $115,780 | 16.9% | 9,710 |
| 15. Physician Assistants | $86,410 | 39.0% | 4,280 |
| 16. Market Research Analysts and Marketing Specialists | $60,570 | 28.1% | 13,730 |
| 17. Construction Managers | $83,860 | 17.2% | 13,770 |
| 18. Personal Financial Advisors | $64,750 | 30.1% | 8,530 |
| 19. Compliance Officers | $58,720 | 31.0% | 10,850 |
| 20. Financial Analysts | $74,350 | 19.8% | 9,520 |

*(continued)*

*(continued)*

## The Best Jobs Overall

| Job | Annual Earnings | Percent Growth | Annual Openings |
|---|---|---|---|
| 21. Lawyers | $112,760 | 13.0% | 24,040 |
| 22. Medical and Health Services Managers | $84,270 | 16.0% | 9,940 |
| 23. Sales Managers | $98,530 | 14.9% | 12,660 |
| 24. Cost Estimators | $57,860 | 25.3% | 10,360 |
| 25. Occupational Therapists | $72,320 | 25.6% | 4,580 |
| 26. Dentists, General | $141,040 | 15.3% | 5,180 |
| 27. Veterinarians | $82,040 | 32.9% | 3,020 |
| 28. Human Resources Specialists | $52,690 | 27.9% | 11,230 |
| 29. Public Relations Specialists | $52,090 | 24.0% | 13,130 |
| 30. Environmental Engineers | $78,740 | 30.6% | 2,790 |
| 31. Training and Development Specialists | $54,160 | 23.3% | 10,710 |
| 32. Environmental Scientists and Specialists, Including Health | $61,700 | 27.9% | 4,840 |
| 33. Supervisors of Construction and Extraction Workers | $58,680 | 15.4% | 24,220 |
| 34. Database Administrators | $73,490 | 20.3% | 4,440 |
| 35. Instructional Coordinators | $58,830 | 23.2% | 6,060 |
| 36. Elementary School Teachers, Except Special Education | $51,660 | 15.8% | 59,650 |
| 37. Compensation, Benefits, and Job Analysis Specialists | $57,000 | 23.6% | 6,050 |
| 38. Logisticians | $70,800 | 19.5% | 4,190 |
| 39. Paralegals and Legal Assistants | $46,680 | 28.1% | 10,400 |
| 40. Optometrists | $94,990 | 24.4% | 2,010 |
| 41. Heating, Air Conditioning, and Refrigeration Mechanics and Installers | $42,530 | 28.1% | 13,620 |
| 42. Industrial Engineers | $76,100 | 14.2% | 8,540 |
| 43. Operations Research Analysts | $70,960 | 22.0% | 3,220 |
| 44. Middle School Teachers, Except Special and Career/Technical Education | $51,960 | 15.3% | 25,110 |
| 45. Architects, Except Landscape and Naval | $72,550 | 16.2% | 4,680 |
| 46. Biochemists and Biophysicists | $79,390 | 37.4% | 1,620 |
| 47. Licensed Practical and Licensed Vocational Nurses | $40,380 | 20.6% | 39,130 |
| 48. Speech-Language Pathologists | $66,920 | 18.5% | 4,380 |
| 49. Biomedical Engineers | $81,540 | 72.0% | 1,490 |
| 50. Health Specialties Teachers, Postsecondary | $85,270 | 15.1% | 4,000 |
| 51. Marketing Managers | $112,800 | 12.5% | 5,970 |
| 52. Computer Occupations, All Other | $79,240 | 13.1% | 7,260 |
| 53. Financial Examiners | $74,940 | 41.2% | 1,600 |
| 54. Social Scientists and Related Workers, All Other | $74,620 | 22.4% | 2,380 |
| 55. Detectives and Criminal Investigators | $68,820 | 16.6% | 4,160 |

## The Best Jobs Overall

| Job | Annual Earnings | Percent Growth | Annual Openings |
|---|---|---|---|
| 56. Managers, All Other | $96,450 | 7.3% | 29,750 |
| 57. Computer and Information Research Scientists | $100,660 | 24.2% | 1,320 |
| 58. Administrative Services Managers | $77,890 | 12.5% | 8,660 |
| 59. Firefighters | $45,250 | 18.5% | 15,280 |
| 60. Business Operations Specialists, All Other | $62,450 | 11.5% | 36,830 |
| 61. Healthcare Social Workers | $47,230 | 22.4% | 6,590 |
| 62. Radiologic Technologists | $54,340 | 17.2% | 6,800 |
| 63. Self-Enrichment Education Teachers | $36,340 | 32.0% | 12,030 |
| 64. Financial Managers | $103,910 | 7.6% | 13,820 |
| 65. Education Administrators, All Other | $75,690 | 23.9% | 1,690 |
| 66. Natural Sciences Managers | $116,020 | 15.5% | 2,010 |
| 67. Sales Representatives, Wholesale and Manufacturing, Technical and Scientific Products | $73,710 | 9.7% | 14,230 |
| 68. Respiratory Therapists | $54,280 | 20.9% | 4,140 |
| 69. Plumbers, Pipefitters, and Steamfitters | $46,660 | 15.3% | 17,550 |
| 70. Dental Assistants | $33,470 | 35.7% | 16,100 |
| 71. Purchasing Agents, Except Wholesale, Retail, and Farm Products | $56,580 | 13.9% | 11,860 |
| 72. Sales Representatives, Services, All Other | $50,620 | 13.9% | 22,810 |
| 73. Physical Therapist Assistants | $49,690 | 33.3% | 3,050 |
| 74. Education Administrators, Elementary and Secondary School | $86,970 | 8.6% | 8,880 |
| 75. Securities, Commodities, and Financial Services Sales Agents | $70,190 | 9.3% | 12,680 |
| 76. Actuaries | $87,650 | 21.4% | 1,000 |
| 77. Commercial Pilots | $67,500 | 18.5% | 2,060 |
| 78. Educational, Guidance, School, and Vocational Counselors | $53,380 | 14.0% | 9,440 |
| 79. Chiropractors | $67,200 | 19.5% | 1,820 |
| 80. Legal Secretaries | $41,500 | 18.4% | 8,380 |
| 81. Real Estate Sales Agents | $40,030 | 16.2% | 12,830 |
| 82. Medical Secretaries | $30,530 | 26.6% | 18,900 |
| 83. Geoscientists, Except Hydrologists and Geographers | $82,500 | 17.5% | 1,540 |
| 84. Medical Assistants | $28,860 | 33.9% | 21,780 |
| 85. Human Resources Managers | $99,180 | 9.6% | 4,140 |
| 86. Probation Officers and Correctional Treatment Specialists | $47,200 | 19.3% | 4,180 |
| 87. Surgical Technologists | $39,920 | 25.3% | 4,630 |
| 88. Electricians | $48,250 | 11.9% | 25,090 |
| 89. General and Operations Managers | $94,400 | −0.1% | 50,220 |
| 90. Writers and Authors | $55,420 | 14.8% | 5,420 |

*(continued)*

*(continued)*

## The Best Jobs Overall

| Job | Annual Earnings | Percent Growth | Annual Openings |
|---|---|---|---|
| 91. Fitness Trainers and Aerobics Instructors | $31,090 | 29.4% | 12,380 |
| 92. Construction and Building Inspectors | $52,360 | 16.8% | 3,970 |
| 93. Mental Health Counselors | $38,150 | 24.0% | 5,010 |
| 94. Petroleum Engineers | $114,080 | 18.4% | 860 |
| 95. Business Teachers, Postsecondary | $73,760 | 15.1% | 2,000 |
| 96. Executive Secretaries and Executive Administrative Assistants | $43,520 | 12.8% | 41,920 |
| 97. Pharmacy Technicians | $28,400 | 30.6% | 18,200 |
| 98. Biological Scientists, All Other | $68,220 | 18.8% | 1,610 |
| 99. First-Line Supervisors of Office and Administrative Support Workers | $47,460 | 11.0% | 48,900 |
| 100. Clinical, Counseling, and School Psychologists | $66,810 | 11.1% | 5,990 |
| 101. Mental Health and Substance Abuse Social Workers | $38,600 | 19.5% | 6,130 |
| 102. Secondary School Teachers, Except Special and Career/Technical Education | $53,230 | 8.9% | 41,240 |
| 103. Social and Community Service Managers | $57,950 | 13.8% | 4,820 |
| 104. Captains, Mates, and Pilots of Water Vessels | $64,180 | 17.3% | 1,950 |
| 105. Customer Service Representatives | $30,460 | 17.7% | 110,840 |
| 106. Water and Wastewater Treatment Plant and System Operators | $40,770 | 19.8% | 4,690 |
| 107. Radiation Therapists | $74,980 | 27.1% | 690 |
| 108. Construction Laborers | $29,280 | 20.5% | 33,940 |
| 109. Kindergarten Teachers, Except Special Education | $48,800 | 15.0% | 6,300 |
| 110. Home Health Aides | $20,560 | 50.0% | 55,270 |
| 111. Interior Designers | $46,280 | 19.4% | 3,590 |
| 112. Public Relations and Fundraising Managers | $91,810 | 12.9% | 2,060 |
| 113. Biological Science Teachers, Postsecondary | $72,700 | 15.1% | 1,700 |
| 114. Clergy | $43,970 | 12.7% | 21,770 |
| 115. Insurance Sales Agents | $46,770 | 11.9% | 15,260 |
| 116. Technical Writers | $63,280 | 18.2% | 1,680 |
| 117. Art, Drama, and Music Teachers, Postsecondary | $62,040 | 15.1% | 2,500 |
| 118. Diagnostic Medical Sonographers | $64,380 | 18.3% | 1,650 |
| 119. Police and Sheriff's Patrol Officers | $53,540 | 8.7% | 22,790 |
| 120. Architectural and Engineering Managers | $119,260 | 6.2% | 4,870 |
| 121. Personal Care Aides | $19,640 | 46.0% | 47,780 |
| 122. Carpenters | $39,530 | 12.9% | 32,540 |
| 123. Urban and Regional Planners | $63,040 | 19.0% | 1,470 |
| 124. Bill and Account Collectors | $31,310 | 19.3% | 15,690 |
| 125. Heavy and Tractor-Trailer Truck Drivers | $37,770 | 12.9% | 55,460 |

## The Best Jobs Overall

| Job | Annual Earnings | Percent Growth | Annual Openings |
|---|---|---|---|
| 126. Engineers, All Other | $90,270 | 6.7% | 5,020 |
| 127. Art Directors | $80,630 | 11.7% | 2,870 |
| 128. Agents and Business Managers of Artists, Performers, and Athletes | $63,130 | 22.4% | 1,010 |
| 129. Cardiovascular Technologists and Technicians | $49,410 | 24.1% | 1,910 |
| 130. First-Line Supervisors of Police and Detectives | $78,260 | 8.1% | 5,050 |
| 131. Engineering Teachers, Postsecondary | $89,670 | 15.1% | 1,000 |
| 132. Budget Analysts | $68,200 | 15.1% | 2,230 |
| 133. Medical and Clinical Laboratory Technologists | $56,130 | 11.9% | 5,330 |
| 134. Cargo and Freight Agents | $37,150 | 23.9% | 4,030 |
| 135. Environmental Science and Protection Technicians, Including Health | $41,380 | 28.9% | 2,520 |
| 136. Mechanical Engineers | $78,160 | 6.0% | 7,570 |
| 137. Medical Equipment Repairers | $44,490 | 27.2% | 2,320 |
| 138. Chief Executives | $165,080 | −1.4% | 11,250 |
| 139. Vocational Education Teachers, Postsecondary | $48,210 | 15.1% | 4,000 |
| 140. Sales Engineers | $87,390 | 8.8% | 3,500 |
| 141. Social and Human Service Assistants | $28,200 | 22.6% | 15,390 |
| 142. Airline Pilots, Copilots, and Flight Engineers | $103,210 | 8.4% | 3,250 |
| 143. First-Line Supervisors of Non-Retail Sales Workers | $68,880 | 4.8% | 12,950 |
| 144. Graphic Designers | $43,500 | 12.9% | 12,480 |
| 145. Orthodontists | $166,400+ | 19.8% | 360 |
| 146. Physicists | $106,370 | 15.9% | 690 |
| 147. English Language and Literature Teachers, Postsecondary | $60,400 | 15.1% | 2,000 |
| 148. Aerospace Engineers | $97,480 | 10.4% | 2,230 |
| 149. Producers and Directors | $68,440 | 9.8% | 4,040 |
| 150. Loan Officers | $56,490 | 10.1% | 6,880 |
| 151. Sales Representatives, Wholesale and Manufacturing, Except Technical and Scientific Products | $52,440 | 6.6% | 45,790 |
| 152. Air Traffic Controllers | $108,040 | 13.1% | 1,230 |
| 153. Prosthodontists | $118,400 | 28.3% | 30 |
| 154. Civil Engineering Technicians | $46,290 | 16.9% | 3,280 |
| 155. Occupational Therapy Assistants | $51,010 | 29.8% | 1,180 |
| 156. Coaches and Scouts | $28,340 | 24.8% | 9,920 |
| 157. First-Line Supervisors of Personal Service Workers | $35,290 | 15.4% | 9,080 |
| 158. Medical Records and Health Information Technicians | $32,350 | 20.3% | 7,030 |
| 159. Multimedia Artists and Animators | $58,510 | 14.2% | 2,890 |
| 160. Substance Abuse and Behavioral Disorder Counselors | $38,120 | 21.0% | 3,550 |

*(continued)*

*(continued)*

## The Best Jobs Overall

| Job | Annual Earnings | Percent Growth | Annual Openings |
|---|---|---|---|
| 161. Biological Technicians | $39,020 | 17.6% | 4,190 |
| 162. Security and Fire Alarm Systems Installers | $38,500 | 24.8% | 2,780 |
| 163. Credit Analysts | $58,850 | 15.0% | 2,430 |
| 164. Landscape Architects | $62,090 | 19.7% | 980 |
| 165. Billing and Posting Clerks | $32,170 | 15.3% | 16,760 |
| 166. Financial Specialists, All Other | $60,980 | 10.5% | 4,320 |
| 167. Veterinary Technologists and Technicians | $29,710 | 35.8% | 4,850 |
| 168. Education Teachers, Postsecondary | $59,140 | 15.1% | 1,800 |
| 169. Audiologists | $66,660 | 25.0% | 580 |
| 170. Interpreters and Translators | $43,300 | 22.2% | 2,340 |
| 171. Claims Adjusters, Examiners, and Investigators | $58,620 | 7.1% | 9,560 |
| 172. Health Educators | $45,830 | 18.2% | 2,600 |
| 173. First-Line Supervisors of Landscaping, Lawn Service, and Groundskeeping Workers | $41,860 | 14.9% | 5,600 |
| 174. Political Scientists | $107,420 | 19.4% | 280 |
| 175. Industrial-Organizational Psychologists | $87,330 | 26.1% | 130 |
| 176. Mathematicians | $99,380 | 22.4% | 150 |
| 177. Refuse and Recyclable Material Collectors | $32,640 | 18.6% | 7,110 |
| 178. Medical and Clinical Laboratory Technicians | $36,280 | 16.1% | 5,460 |
| 179. Operating Engineers and Other Construction Equipment Operators | $40,400 | 12.0% | 11,820 |
| 180. Nursing Instructors and Teachers, Postsecondary | $62,390 | 15.1% | 1,500 |
| 181. Child, Family, and School Social Workers | $40,210 | 12.3% | 10,960 |
| 182. Computer Science Teachers, Postsecondary | $70,300 | 15.1% | 1,000 |
| 183. Preschool Teachers, Except Special Education | $25,700 | 19.0% | 17,830 |
| 184. Transportation Inspectors | $57,640 | 18.3% | 1,130 |
| 185. First-Line Supervisors of Mechanics, Installers, and Repairers | $59,150 | 4.2% | 13,650 |
| 186. Surveying and Mapping Technicians | $37,900 | 20.4% | 2,940 |
| 187. Private Detectives and Investigators | $42,870 | 22.0% | 1,930 |
| 188. Hairdressers, Hairstylists, and Cosmetologists | $22,760 | 20.1% | 21,950 |
| 189. Surveyors | $54,880 | 14.9% | 2,330 |
| 190. Health Technologists and Technicians, All Other | $38,460 | 18.7% | 3,200 |
| 191. Psychology Teachers, Postsecondary | $67,330 | 15.1% | 1,000 |
| 192. Healthcare Practitioners and Technical Workers, All Other | $43,970 | 15.9% | 2,910 |
| 193. Landscaping and Groundskeeping Workers | $23,400 | 18.0% | 36,220 |
| 194. Ship Engineers | $65,880 | 18.6% | 700 |
| 195. Mathematical Science Teachers, Postsecondary | $65,710 | 15.1% | 1,000 |

## The Best Jobs Overall

| Job | Annual Earnings | Percent Growth | Annual Openings |
|---|---|---|---|
| 196. Rehabilitation Counselors | $32,350 | 18.9% | 5,070 |
| 197. Massage Therapists | $34,900 | 18.9% | 3,950 |
| 198. Athletic Trainers | $41,600 | 36.9% | 1,150 |
| 199. Cartographers and Photogrammetrists | $54,510 | 26.8% | 640 |
| 200. Health Diagnosing and Treating Practitioners, All Other | $69,310 | 13.0% | 1,530 |
| 201. Receptionists and Information Clerks | $25,240 | 15.2% | 48,020 |
| 202. Farmers, Ranchers, and Other Agricultural Managers | $60,750 | 5.9% | 6,490 |
| 203. Property, Real Estate, and Community Association Managers | $51,480 | 8.4% | 7,800 |
| 204. Oral and Maxillofacial Surgeons | $166,400+ | 15.3% | 290 |
| 205. Occupational Health and Safety Specialists | $64,660 | 11.2% | 2,490 |
| 206. Tax Examiners and Collectors, and Revenue Agents | $49,360 | 13.0% | 3,520 |
| 207. Training and Development Managers | $89,170 | 11.9% | 1,010 |
| 208. Brickmasons and Blockmasons | $46,930 | 11.5% | 5,000 |
| 209. Correctional Officers and Jailers | $39,040 | 9.4% | 14,360 |
| 210. Environmental Engineering Technicians | $43,390 | 30.1% | 1,040 |
| 211. Geographers | $72,800 | 26.0% | 100 |
| 212. Teachers and Instructors, All Other | $29,820 | 14.7% | 22,570 |
| 213. Nuclear Medicine Technologists | $68,560 | 16.3% | 670 |
| 214. Adult Basic and Secondary Education and Literacy Teachers and Instructors | $46,530 | 15.1% | 2,920 |
| 215. First-Line Supervisors of Fire Fighting and Prevention Workers | $68,240 | 8.2% | 3,250 |
| 216. Police, Fire, and Ambulance Dispatchers | $35,370 | 17.8% | 3,840 |
| 217. Psychologists, All Other | $89,900 | 14.4% | 680 |
| 218. Law Teachers, Postsecondary | $94,260 | 15.1% | 400 |
| 219. Meeting, Convention, and Event Planners | $45,260 | 15.6% | 2,140 |
| 220. Librarians | $54,500 | 7.8% | 5,450 |
| 221. Hydrologists | $75,690 | 18.2% | 380 |
| 222. Physical Scientists, All Other | $94,780 | 11.1% | 1,010 |
| 223. Sociologists | $72,360 | 22.0% | 200 |
| 224. Helpers—Electricians | $27,220 | 24.7% | 4,800 |
| 225. Bookkeeping, Accounting, and Auditing Clerks | $34,030 | 10.3% | 46,040 |
| 226. Career/Technical Education Teachers, Secondary School | $54,310 | 9.6% | 3,850 |
| 227. Nuclear Power Reactor Operators | $75,650 | 18.9% | 270 |
| 228. Education Administrators, Postsecondary | $83,710 | 2.3% | 4,010 |
| 229. Boilermakers | $54,640 | 18.8% | 810 |
| 230. Interviewers, Except Eligibility and Loan | $28,820 | 15.6% | 9,210 |
| 231. Healthcare Support Workers, All Other | $30,280 | 17.1% | 5,670 |
| 232. Electrical Engineers | $84,540 | 1.7% | 3,890 |

*(continued)*

*(continued)*

## The Best Jobs Overall

| Job | Annual Earnings | Percent Growth | Annual Openings |
|---|---|---|---|
| 233. Anthropologists and Archeologists | $54,230 | 28.0% | 450 |
| 234. Economics Teachers, Postsecondary | $83,370 | 15.1% | 400 |
| 235. Statisticians | $72,830 | 13.1% | 960 |
| 236. Chemistry Teachers, Postsecondary | $70,520 | 15.1% | 600 |
| 237. Cement Masons and Concrete Finishers | $35,450 | 12.9% | 7,640 |
| 238. History Teachers, Postsecondary | $64,880 | 15.1% | 700 |
| 239. Life, Physical, and Social Science Technicians, All Other | $43,350 | 13.3% | 3,640 |
| 240. Computer Programmers | $71,380 | −2.9% | 8,030 |
| 241. Food Scientists and Technologists | $60,180 | 16.3% | 690 |
| 242. Foreign Language and Literature Teachers, Postsecondary | $59,080 | 15.1% | 900 |
| 243. Forensic Science Technicians | $51,570 | 19.6% | 800 |
| 244. Mixing and Blending Machine Setters, Operators, and Tenders | $32,870 | 15.5% | 4,610 |
| 245. Survey Researchers | $36,050 | 30.3% | 1,340 |
| 246. Communications Teachers, Postsecondary | $60,300 | 15.1% | 800 |
| 247. Industrial Production Managers | $87,160 | −7.7% | 5,470 |
| 248. Physics Teachers, Postsecondary | $77,610 | 15.1% | 400 |
| 249. Atmospheric, Earth, Marine, and Space Sciences Teachers, Postsecondary | $82,840 | 15.1% | 300 |
| 250. Mining and Geological Engineers, Including Mining Safety Engineers | $82,870 | 15.3% | 260 |
| 251. Electronics Engineers, Except Computer | $90,170 | 0.3% | 3,340 |
| 252. Computer Hardware Engineers | $98,810 | 3.8% | 2,350 |
| 253. Helpers—Pipelayers, Plumbers, Pipefitters, and Steamfitters | $26,740 | 25.7% | 3,730 |
| 254. Political Science Teachers, Postsecondary | $70,540 | 15.1% | 500 |
| 255. Compensation and Benefits Managers | $89,270 | 8.5% | 1,210 |
| 256. Agricultural Sciences Teachers, Postsecondary | $78,370 | 15.1% | 300 |
| 257. Security Guards | $23,920 | 14.2% | 37,390 |
| 258. Curators | $48,450 | 23.0% | 620 |
| 259. Astronomers | $87,260 | 15.6% | 70 |
| 260. Nonfarm Animal Caretakers | $19,550 | 20.7% | 7,360 |
| 261. Soil and Plant Scientists | $57,340 | 15.5% | 700 |
| 262. Real Estate Brokers | $54,910 | 8.6% | 3,080 |
| 263. Office Clerks, General | $26,610 | 11.9% | 77,090 |
| 264. Skincare Specialists | $28,920 | 37.8% | 2,030 |
| 265. Philosophy and Religion Teachers, Postsecondary | $62,330 | 15.1% | 600 |
| 266. Atmospheric and Space Scientists | $87,780 | 14.6% | 330 |
| 267. Food Service Managers | $48,130 | 5.3% | 8,370 |

# The Best Jobs Overall

| Job | Annual Earnings | Percent Growth | Annual Openings |
|---|---|---|---|
| 268. Insulation Workers, Mechanical | $37,650 | 19.4% | 1,550 |
| 269. Graduate Teaching Assistants | $32,750 | 15.1% | 4,000 |
| 270. Electrical Power-Line Installers and Repairers | $58,030 | 4.5% | 4,550 |
| 271. Industrial Machinery Mechanics | $45,420 | 7.3% | 6,240 |
| 272. Drywall and Ceiling Tile Installers | $37,320 | 13.5% | 3,700 |
| 273. Sociology Teachers, Postsecondary | $64,810 | 15.1% | 500 |
| 274. Dietitians and Nutritionists | $53,250 | 9.2% | 2,570 |
| 275. Helpers—Carpenters | $25,760 | 23.3% | 3,530 |
| 276. Tile and Marble Setters | $38,110 | 14.3% | 3,070 |
| 277. Purchasing Managers | $95,070 | 1.5% | 2,110 |
| 278. Subway and Streetcar Operators | $56,880 | 18.8% | 390 |
| 279. Protective Service Workers, All Other | $29,890 | 14.0% | 7,150 |
| 280. Postal Service Mail Carriers | $53,860 | −1.1% | 10,720 |
| 281. Health and Safety Engineers, Except Mining Safety Engineers and Inspectors | $75,430 | 10.3% | 920 |
| 282. Pipelayers | $34,800 | 17.2% | 2,280 |
| 283. Anthropology and Archeology Teachers, Postsecondary | $73,600 | 15.1% | 200 |
| 284. Combined Food Preparation and Serving Workers, Including Fast Food | $17,950 | 14.6% | 96,720 |
| 285. Architecture Teachers, Postsecondary | $73,500 | 15.1% | 200 |
| 286. Forestry and Conservation Science Teachers, Postsecondary | $78,290 | 15.1% | 100 |
| 287. Nuclear Engineers | $99,920 | 10.9% | 540 |
| 288. Court Reporters | $47,700 | 18.3% | 710 |
| 289. Recreation and Fitness Studies Teachers, Postsecondary | $57,650 | 15.1% | 600 |
| 290. Tree Trimmers and Pruners | $30,450 | 26.3% | 1,720 |
| 291. First-Line Supervisors of Retail Sales Workers | $35,820 | 5.2% | 45,010 |
| 292. Architectural and Civil Drafters | $46,430 | 9.1% | 3,620 |
| 293. Materials Engineers | $83,120 | 9.3% | 810 |
| 294. Environmental Science Teachers, Postsecondary | $71,020 | 15.1% | 200 |
| 295. Taxi Drivers and Chauffeurs | $22,440 | 15.5% | 7,730 |
| 296. Chemists | $68,320 | 2.5% | 3,000 |
| 297. Commercial and Industrial Designers | $58,230 | 9.0% | 1,760 |
| 298. Materials Scientists | $84,720 | 11.9% | 440 |
| 299. Microbiologists | $65,920 | 12.2% | 750 |
| 300. Physical Therapist Aides | $23,680 | 36.3% | 2,340 |
| 301. Septic Tank Servicers and Sewer Pipe Cleaners | $33,570 | 23.8% | 1,320 |
| 302. Orthotists and Prosthetists | $65,060 | 15.4% | 210 |

*(continued)*

*(continued)*

## The Best Jobs Overall

| Job | Annual Earnings | Percent Growth | Annual Openings |
|---|---|---|---|
| 303. Area, Ethnic, and Cultural Studies Teachers, Postsecondary | $68,020 | 15.1% | 200 |
| 304. Advertising Sales Agents | $45,350 | 7.2% | 4,510 |
| 305. Criminal Justice and Law Enforcement Teachers, Postsecondary | $59,520 | 15.1% | 400 |
| 306. Pest Control Workers | $30,340 | 15.3% | 3,400 |
| 307. Social Work Teachers, Postsecondary | $63,090 | 15.1% | 300 |
| 308. Mobile Heavy Equipment Mechanics, Except Engines | $44,830 | 8.7% | 3,770 |
| 309. Social Science Research Assistants | $37,230 | 17.8% | 1,270 |
| 310. Gaming Dealers | $18,090 | 19.0% | 5,590 |
| 311. Elevator Installers and Repairers | $70,910 | 9.2% | 920 |
| 312. Structural Iron and Steel Workers | $44,540 | 12.4% | 2,020 |
| 313. First-Line Supervisors of Correctional Officers | $55,910 | 8.5% | 1,940 |
| 314. Home Economics Teachers, Postsecondary | $65,040 | 15.1% | 200 |
| 315. Education Administrators, Preschool and Childcare Center/Program | $42,960 | 11.8% | 2,460 |
| 316. Aircraft Mechanics and Service Technicians | $53,420 | 6.4% | 3,140 |
| 317. Audio and Video Equipment Technicians | $40,540 | 12.6% | 2,370 |
| 318. Bus and Truck Mechanics and Diesel Engine Specialists | $40,850 | 5.7% | 7,530 |
| 319. Zoologists and Wildlife Biologists | $57,430 | 12.8% | 880 |
| 320. First-Line Supervisors of Production and Operating Workers | $53,090 | −5.2% | 9,190 |
| 321. Recreation Workers | $22,260 | 14.7% | 10,720 |
| 322. Eligibility Interviewers, Government Programs | $39,960 | 9.2% | 3,880 |
| 323. Funeral Attendants | $22,990 | 26.3% | 2,550 |
| 324. Automotive Service Technicians and Mechanics | $35,790 | 4.7% | 18,170 |
| 325. Geography Teachers, Postsecondary | $66,700 | 15.1% | 100 |
| 326. Museum Technicians and Conservators | $37,310 | 25.6% | 610 |
| 327. Sheet Metal Workers | $41,710 | 6.5% | 5,170 |
| 328. Morticians, Undertakers, and Funeral Directors | $54,330 | 11.9% | 960 |
| 329. Teacher Assistants | $23,220 | 10.3% | 41,270 |
| 330. Transportation, Storage, and Distribution Managers | $80,210 | −5.3% | 2,740 |
| 331. Gaming Supervisors | $48,530 | 11.8% | 1,410 |
| 332. Hazardous Materials Removal Workers | $37,600 | 14.8% | 1,780 |
| 333. Electrical and Electronics Repairers, Powerhouse, Substation, and Relay | $65,230 | 11.5% | 670 |
| 334. Amusement and Recreation Attendants | $18,450 | 13.3% | 17,120 |
| 335. Installation, Maintenance, and Repair Workers, All Other | $36,420 | 9.2% | 4,180 |
| 336. Podiatrists | $118,030 | 9.0% | 320 |

# The Best Jobs Overall

| Job | Annual Earnings | Percent Growth | Annual Openings |
|---|---|---|---|
| 337. Library Science Teachers, Postsecondary | $62,720 | 15.1% | 100 |
| 338. Painters, Construction and Maintenance | $34,280 | 7.0% | 10,650 |
| 339. Hotel, Motel, and Resort Desk Clerks | $19,930 | 13.7% | 10,950 |
| 340. Childcare Workers | $19,300 | 10.9% | 52,310 |
| 341. Directors, Religious Activities and Education | $36,170 | 12.6% | 2,640 |
| 342. Set and Exhibit Designers | $46,680 | 16.5% | 510 |
| 343. Extruding, Forming, Pressing, and Compacting Machine Setters, Operators, and Tenders | $31,210 | 15.0% | 2,960 |
| 344. Veterinary Assistants and Laboratory Animal Caretakers | $22,040 | 22.8% | 2,550 |
| 345. Marriage and Family Therapists | $45,720 | 14.5% | 950 |
| 346. Highway Maintenance Workers | $34,780 | 8.5% | 5,200 |
| 347. Production, Planning, and Expediting Clerks | $42,220 | 1.5% | 7,410 |
| 348. Credit Counselors | $38,140 | 16.3% | 880 |
| 349. Epidemiologists | $63,010 | 15.1% | 170 |
| 350. Secretaries and Administrative Assistants, Except Legal, Medical, and Executive | $30,830 | 4.6% | 36,550 |
| 351. Animal Trainers | $26,580 | 20.4% | 1,900 |
| 352. Bus Drivers, Transit and Intercity | $35,520 | 8.2% | 4,990 |
| 353. Dishwashers | $18,150 | 11.6% | 27,570 |
| 354. Film and Video Editors | $50,930 | 11.9% | 930 |
| 355. Recreational Therapists | $39,410 | 14.6% | 1,160 |
| 356. Engineering Technicians, Except Drafters, All Other | $58,020 | 5.2% | 1,850 |
| 357. Telecommunications Equipment Installers and Repairers, Except Line Installers | $54,710 | –0.2% | 3,560 |
| 358. Music Directors and Composers | $45,970 | 10.0% | 1,620 |
| 359. Retail Salespersons | $20,670 | 8.3% | 162,690 |
| 360. Emergency Medical Technicians and Paramedics | $30,360 | 9.0% | 6,200 |
| 361. Photographers | $29,130 | 11.5% | 4,800 |
| 362. Ushers, Lobby Attendants, and Ticket Takers | $18,560 | 13.7% | 8,190 |
| 363. Counter Attendants, Cafeteria, Food Concession, and Coffee Shop | $18,370 | 9.3% | 43,490 |
| 364. First-Line Supervisors of Food Preparation and Serving Workers | $29,560 | 6.6% | 13,440 |
| 365. Tapers | $45,490 | 13.0% | 900 |
| 366. Cooks, Institution and Cafeteria | $22,730 | 9.7% | 13,810 |
| 367. Rail-Track Laying and Maintenance Equipment Operators | $45,970 | 14.8% | 650 |
| 368. Arbitrators, Mediators, and Conciliators | $55,800 | 14.0% | 320 |
| 369. Conservation Scientists | $59,310 | 11.9% | 410 |

*(continued)*

*(continued)*

## The Best Jobs Overall

| Job | Annual Earnings | Percent Growth | Annual Openings |
|---|---|---|---|
| 370. Library Technicians | $29,860 | 8.8% | 6,470 |
| 371. Administrative Law Judges, Adjudicators, and Hearing Officers | $85,500 | 8.1% | 380 |
| 372. Gaming Managers | $66,960 | 11.9% | 200 |
| 373. Insurance Underwriters | $59,290 | –4.1% | 3,000 |
| 374. Agricultural Engineers | $71,090 | 11.9% | 90 |
| 375. Court, Municipal, and License Clerks | $34,390 | 8.2% | 4,460 |
| 376. Manicurists and Pedicurists | $19,650 | 18.8% | 2,530 |
| 377. Helpers—Brickmasons, Blockmasons, Stonemasons, and Tile and Marble Setters | $27,780 | 16.4% | 1,890 |
| 378. Railroad Conductors and Yardmasters | $49,770 | 6.9% | 1,700 |
| 379. Electrical and Electronic Engineering Technicians | $56,040 | –2.2% | 3,100 |
| 380. Opticians, Dispensing | $32,940 | 13.4% | 2,020 |
| 381. Stock Clerks and Order Fillers | $21,290 | 7.2% | 56,260 |
| 382. Construction and Related Workers, All Other | $34,500 | 11.1% | 2,660 |
| 383. First-Line Supervisors of Helpers, Laborers, and Material Movers, Hand | $43,800 | 3.6% | 3,850 |
| 384. Economists | $89,450 | 5.8% | 500 |
| 385. Dental Laboratory Technicians | $35,140 | 13.9% | 1,530 |
| 386. Flight Attendants | $37,740 | 8.1% | 3,010 |
| 387. Industrial Engineering Technicians | $48,210 | 6.6% | 1,850 |
| 388. First-Line Supervisors of Transportation and Material-Moving Machine and Vehicle Operators | $52,720 | –3.7% | 3,770 |
| 389. Editors | $51,470 | –0.3% | 3,390 |
| 390. Railroad Brake, Signal, and Switch Operators | $47,670 | 9.4% | 1,070 |
| 391. Excavating and Loading Machine and Dragline Operators | $36,920 | 8.6% | 2,850 |
| 392. Insulation Workers, Floor, Ceiling, and Wall | $31,830 | 15.2% | 1,320 |
| 393. Aircraft Structure, Surfaces, Rigging, and Systems Assemblers | $44,820 | 9.4% | 1,340 |
| 394. Animal Scientists | $58,250 | 13.2% | 180 |
| 395. Reservation and Transportation Ticket Agents and Travel Clerks | $31,740 | 8.1% | 5,150 |
| 396. Sailors and Marine Oilers | $36,260 | 11.7% | 1,790 |
| 397. Advertising and Promotions Managers | $83,890 | –1.7% | 1,050 |
| 398. Tellers | $24,100 | 6.2% | 28,440 |
| 399. Telecommunications Line Installers and Repairers | $50,850 | 0.9% | 2,790 |
| 400. Appraisers and Assessors of Real Estate | $48,500 | 4.6% | 2,100 |

# The 100 Best-Paying Jobs

I sorted all 400 jobs based on their annual median earnings from highest to lowest. *Median earnings* means that half of all workers in each of these jobs earn more than that amount and half earn less. I then selected the 100 jobs with the highest earnings to create the list that follows.

It shouldn't be a big surprise to learn that most of the highest-paying jobs require advanced levels of education, training, or experience. For example, most of the 20 jobs with the highest earnings require a doctoral or professional degree, and others, such as Chief Executives and Engineering Managers, require extensive training and experience beyond the bachelor's degree. Although the top 20 jobs may not appeal to you for various reasons, you are likely to find others that will among the top 100 jobs with the highest earnings.

Keep in mind that the earnings reflect the national average for all workers in the occupation. This is an important consideration, because starting pay in the job is usually much less than the pay that workers can earn with several years of experience. (To get an idea of how much difference this might make, see the statement about earnings growth potential in the Part II description of the job.) Earnings also vary significantly by region of the country, so actual pay in your area could be substantially different.

You'll note that the two dentistry jobs at the top of the list have annual earnings of "$166,400+." The Department of Labor does not report more specific figures when earnings are that high. The American Dental Association reports median 2009 earnings of more than $342,000 for dental specialists.

The figure listed for Physicians and Surgeons is the average for eight medical specializations. The BLS reports earnings of $163,510 for Family and General Practitioners; $155,370 for Pediatricians, General; $164,220 for Psychiatrists; and $166,400+ for Anesthesiologists; Internists, General; Surgeons; and Physicians and Surgeons, All Other.

| The 100 Best-Paying Jobs | |
| --- | --- |
| Job | Annual Earnings |
| 1. Oral and Maxillofacial Surgeons | $166,400+ |
| 2. Orthodontists | $166,400+ |
| 3. Physicians and Surgeons | $165,279 |
| 4. Chief Executives | $165,080 |
| 5. Dentists, General | $141,040 |
| 6. Architectural and Engineering Managers | $119,260 |
| 7. Prosthodontists | $118,400 |
| 8. Podiatrists | $118,030 |
| 9. Natural Sciences Managers | $116,020 |
| 10. Computer and Information Systems Managers | $115,780 |

*(continued)*

*(continued)*

## The 100 Best-Paying Jobs

| Job | Annual Earnings |
|---|---|
| 11. Petroleum Engineers | $114,080 |
| 12. Marketing Managers | $112,800 |
| 13. Lawyers | $112,760 |
| 14. Pharmacists | $111,570 |
| 15. Air Traffic Controllers | $108,040 |
| 16. Political Scientists | $107,420 |
| 17. Physicists | $106,370 |
| 18. Financial Managers | $103,910 |
| 19. Airline Pilots, Copilots, and Flight Engineers | $103,210 |
| 20. Computer and Information Research Scientists | $100,660 |
| 21. Nuclear Engineers | $99,920 |
| 22. Mathematicians | $99,380 |
| 23. Human Resources Managers | $99,180 |
| 24. Computer Hardware Engineers | $98,810 |
| 25. Sales Managers | $98,530 |
| 26. Aerospace Engineers | $97,480 |
| 27. Managers, All Other | $96,450 |
| 28. Purchasing Managers | $95,070 |
| 29. Optometrists | $94,990 |
| 30. Physical Scientists, All Other | $94,780 |
| 31. General and Operations Managers | $94,400 |
| 32. Law Teachers, Postsecondary | $94,260 |
| 33. Software Developers, Systems Software | $94,180 |
| 34. Public Relations and Fundraising Managers | $91,810 |
| 35. Engineers, All Other | $90,270 |
| 36. Electronics Engineers, Except Computer | $90,170 |
| 37. Psychologists, All Other | $89,900 |
| 38. Engineering Teachers, Postsecondary | $89,670 |
| 39. Economists | $89,450 |
| 40. Compensation and Benefits Managers | $89,270 |
| 41. Training and Development Managers | $89,170 |
| 42. Software Developers, Applications | $87,790 |
| 43. Atmospheric and Space Scientists | $87,780 |
| 44. Actuaries | $87,650 |
| 45. Sales Engineers | $87,390 |
| 46. Industrial-Organizational Psychologists | $87,330 |
| 47. Astronomers | $87,260 |

*Best Jobs for the 21st Century © JIST Works*

# The 100 Best-Paying Jobs

| Job | Annual Earnings |
|---|---|
| 48. Industrial Production Managers | $87,160 |
| 49. Education Administrators, Elementary and Secondary School | $86,970 |
| 50. Physician Assistants | $86,410 |
| 51. Administrative Law Judges, Adjudicators, and Hearing Officers | $85,500 |
| 52. Health Specialties Teachers, Postsecondary | $85,270 |
| 53. Materials Scientists | $84,720 |
| 54. Electrical Engineers | $84,540 |
| 55. Medical and Health Services Managers | $84,270 |
| 56. Advertising and Promotions Managers | $83,890 |
| 57. Construction Managers | $83,860 |
| 58. Education Administrators, Postsecondary | $83,710 |
| 59. Economics Teachers, Postsecondary | $83,370 |
| 60. Materials Engineers | $83,120 |
| 61. Mining and Geological Engineers, Including Mining Safety Engineers | $82,870 |
| 62. Atmospheric, Earth, Marine, and Space Sciences Teachers, Postsecondary | $82,840 |
| 63. Geoscientists, Except Hydrologists and Geographers | $82,500 |
| 64. Veterinarians | $82,040 |
| 65. Biomedical Engineers | $81,540 |
| 66. Art Directors | $80,630 |
| 67. Transportation, Storage, and Distribution Managers | $80,210 |
| 68. Biochemists and Biophysicists | $79,390 |
| 69. Computer Occupations, All Other | $79,240 |
| 70. Environmental Engineers | $78,740 |
| 71. Agricultural Sciences Teachers, Postsecondary | $78,370 |
| 72. Forestry and Conservation Science Teachers, Postsecondary | $78,290 |
| 73. First-Line Supervisors of Police and Detectives | $78,260 |
| 74. Management Analysts | $78,160 |
| 75. Mechanical Engineers | $78,160 |
| 76. Administrative Services Managers | $77,890 |
| 77. Computer Systems Analysts | $77,740 |
| 78. Physics Teachers, Postsecondary | $77,610 |
| 79. Civil Engineers | $77,560 |
| 80. Medical Scientists, Except Epidemiologists | $76,700 |
| 81. Physical Therapists | $76,310 |
| 82. Industrial Engineers | $76,100 |
| 83. Education Administrators, All Other | $75,690 |
| 84. Hydrologists | $75,690 |
| 85. Nuclear Power Reactor Operators | $75,650 |

*(continued)*

*(continued)*

## The 100 Best-Paying Jobs

| Job | Annual Earnings |
|---|---|
| 86. Health and Safety Engineers, Except Mining Safety Engineers and Inspectors | $75,430 |
| 87. Radiation Therapists | $74,980 |
| 88. Financial Examiners | $74,940 |
| 89. Social Scientists and Related Workers, All Other | $74,620 |
| 90. Financial Analysts | $74,350 |
| 91. Business Teachers, Postsecondary | $73,760 |
| 92. Sales Representatives, Wholesale and Manufacturing, Technical and Scientific Products | $73,710 |
| 93. Anthropology and Archeology Teachers, Postsecondary | $73,600 |
| 94. Architecture Teachers, Postsecondary | $73,500 |
| 95. Database Administrators | $73,490 |
| 96. Statisticians | $72,830 |
| 97. Geographers | $72,800 |
| 98. Biological Science Teachers, Postsecondary | $72,700 |
| 99. Architects, Except Landscape and Naval | $72,550 |
| 100. Sociologists | $72,360 |

# The 100 Fastest-Growing Jobs

I created this list by sorting all 400 best jobs by their projected growth over the ten-year period from 2008 to 2018. Growth rates are one measure to consider in exploring career options, as jobs with higher growth rates tend to provide more job opportunities.

Jobs in the computer and health-care fields dominate the 20 fastest-growing jobs. Biomedical Engineers is the job with the highest growth rate—the number employed is projected to grow by nearly three-quarters from 2008 to 2018. You can find a wide range of rapidly growing jobs in a variety of fields and at different levels of training and education among the jobs in this list.

# The 100 Fastest-Growing Jobs

| Job | Percent Growth |
|---|---|
| 1. Biomedical Engineers | 72.0% |
| 2. Home Health Aides | 50.0% |
| 3. Personal Care Aides | 46.0% |
| 4. Financial Examiners | 41.2% |
| 5. Medical Scientists, Except Epidemiologists | 40.4% |
| 6. Physician Assistants | 39.0% |
| 7. Skincare Specialists | 37.8% |
| 8. Biochemists and Biophysicists | 37.4% |
| 9. Athletic Trainers | 36.9% |
| 10. Physical Therapist Aides | 36.3% |
| 11. Dental Hygienists | 36.1% |
| 12. Veterinary Technologists and Technicians | 35.8% |
| 13. Dental Assistants | 35.7% |
| 14. Software Developers, Applications | 34.0% |
| 15. Medical Assistants | 33.9% |
| 16. Physical Therapist Assistants | 33.3% |
| 17. Veterinarians | 32.9% |
| 18. Self-Enrichment Education Teachers | 32.0% |
| 19. Compliance Officers | 31.0% |
| 20. Environmental Engineers | 30.6% |
| 21. Pharmacy Technicians | 30.6% |
| 22. Software Developers, Systems Software | 30.4% |
| 23. Survey Researchers | 30.3% |
| 24. Physical Therapists | 30.3% |
| 25. Personal Financial Advisors | 30.1% |
| 26. Environmental Engineering Technicians | 30.1% |
| 27. Occupational Therapy Assistants | 29.8% |
| 28. Fitness Trainers and Aerobics Instructors | 29.4% |
| 29. Environmental Science and Protection Technicians, Including Health | 28.9% |
| 30. Prosthodontists | 28.3% |
| 31. Heating, Air Conditioning, and Refrigeration Mechanics and Installers | 28.1% |
| 32. Paralegals and Legal Assistants | 28.1% |
| 33. Market Research Analysts and Marketing Specialists | 28.1% |
| 34. Anthropologists and Archeologists | 28.0% |
| 35. Human Resources Specialists | 27.9% |
| 36. Environmental Scientists and Specialists, Including Health | 27.9% |
| 37. Medical Equipment Repairers | 27.2% |

*(continued)*

*(continued)*

| The 100 Fastest-Growing Jobs | |
|---|---|
| Job | Percent Growth |
| 38. Radiation Therapists | 27.1% |
| 39. Cartographers and Photogrammetrists | 26.8% |
| 40. Medical Secretaries | 26.6% |
| 41. Tree Trimmers and Pruners | 26.3% |
| 42. Funeral Attendants | 26.3% |
| 43. Industrial-Organizational Psychologists | 26.1% |
| 44. Geographers | 26.0% |
| 45. Helpers—Pipelayers, Plumbers, Pipefitters, and Steamfitters | 25.7% |
| 46. Occupational Therapists | 25.6% |
| 47. Museum Technicians and Conservators | 25.6% |
| 48. Cost Estimators | 25.3% |
| 49. Surgical Technologists | 25.3% |
| 50. Audiologists | 25.0% |
| 51. Security and Fire Alarm Systems Installers | 24.8% |
| 52. Coaches and Scouts | 24.8% |
| 53. Helpers—Electricians | 24.7% |
| 54. Optometrists | 24.4% |
| 55. Civil Engineers | 24.3% |
| 56. Computer and Information Research Scientists | 24.2% |
| 57. Cardiovascular Technologists and Technicians | 24.1% |
| 58. Public Relations Specialists | 24.0% |
| 59. Mental Health Counselors | 24.0% |
| 60. Cargo and Freight Agents | 23.9% |
| 61. Management Analysts | 23.9% |
| 62. Education Administrators, All Other | 23.9% |
| 63. Septic Tank Servicers and Sewer Pipe Cleaners | 23.8% |
| 64. Compensation, Benefits, and Job Analysis Specialists | 23.6% |
| 65. Helpers—Carpenters | 23.3% |
| 66. Training and Development Specialists | 23.3% |
| 67. Network and Computer Systems Administrators | 23.2% |
| 68. Instructional Coordinators | 23.2% |
| 69. Curators | 23.0% |
| 70. Veterinary Assistants and Laboratory Animal Caretakers | 22.8% |
| 71. Social and Human Service Assistants | 22.6% |
| 72. Mathematicians | 22.4% |
| 73. Agents and Business Managers of Artists, Performers, and Athletes | 22.4% |
| 74. Social Scientists and Related Workers, All Other | 22.4% |

## The 100 Fastest-Growing Jobs

| Job | Percent Growth |
|---|---|
| 75. Healthcare Social Workers | 22.4% |
| 76. Registered Nurses | 22.2% |
| 77. Interpreters and Translators | 22.2% |
| 78. Operations Research Analysts | 22.0% |
| 79. Private Detectives and Investigators | 22.0% |
| 80. Sociologists | 22.0% |
| 81. Physicians and Surgeons | 21.8% |
| 82. Accountants and Auditors | 21.6% |
| 83. Actuaries | 21.4% |
| 84. Substance Abuse and Behavioral Disorder Counselors | 21.0% |
| 85. Respiratory Therapists | 20.9% |
| 86. Nonfarm Animal Caretakers | 20.7% |
| 87. Licensed Practical and Licensed Vocational Nurses | 20.6% |
| 88. Construction Laborers | 20.5% |
| 89. Animal Trainers | 20.4% |
| 90. Surveying and Mapping Technicians | 20.4% |
| 91. Medical Records and Health Information Technicians | 20.3% |
| 92. Computer Systems Analysts | 20.3% |
| 93. Database Administrators | 20.3% |
| 94. Hairdressers, Hairstylists, and Cosmetologists | 20.1% |
| 95. Water and Wastewater Treatment Plant and System Operators | 19.8% |
| 96. Financial Analysts | 19.8% |
| 97. Orthodontists | 19.8% |
| 98. Landscape Architects | 19.7% |
| 99. Forensic Science Technicians | 19.6% |
| 100. Logisticians | 19.5% |

# The 100 Jobs with the Most Openings

I created this list by sorting all 400 best jobs by the number of job openings that each is expected to have per year. Many of these occupations, such as Construction Laborers, are not among the highest-paying jobs. But jobs with large numbers of openings often provide easier entry for new workers, make it easier to move from one position to another, or are attractive for other reasons. Some of these jobs may also appeal to people re-entering the labor market, part-time workers, and workers who want to move from one employer to another. And some of these jobs pay quite well, offer good benefits, or have other advantages.

*(continued)*

## The 100 Jobs with the Most Openings

| Job | Annual Openings |
| --- | --- |
| 1. Retail Salespersons | 162,690 |
| 2. Customer Service Representatives | 110,840 |
| 3. Registered Nurses | 103,900 |
| 4. Combined Food Preparation and Serving Workers, Including Fast Food | 96,720 |
| 5. Office Clerks, General | 77,090 |
| 6. Elementary School Teachers, Except Special Education | 59,650 |
| 7. Stock Clerks and Order Fillers | 56,260 |
| 8. Heavy and Tractor-Trailer Truck Drivers | 55,460 |
| 9. Home Health Aides | 55,270 |
| 10. Childcare Workers | 52,310 |
| 11. General and Operations Managers | 50,220 |
| 12. Accountants and Auditors | 49,750 |
| 13. First-Line Supervisors of Office and Administrative Support Workers | 48,900 |
| 14. Receptionists and Information Clerks | 48,020 |
| 15. Personal Care Aides | 47,780 |
| 16. Bookkeeping, Accounting, and Auditing Clerks | 46,040 |
| 17. Sales Representatives, Wholesale and Manufacturing, Except Technical and Scientific Products | 45,790 |
| 18. First-Line Supervisors of Retail Sales Workers | 45,010 |
| 19. Counter Attendants, Cafeteria, Food Concession, and Coffee Shop | 43,490 |
| 20. Executive Secretaries and Executive Administrative Assistants | 41,920 |
| 21. Teacher Assistants | 41,270 |
| 22. Secondary School Teachers, Except Special and Career/Technical Education | 41,240 |
| 23. Licensed Practical and Licensed Vocational Nurses | 39,130 |
| 24. Security Guards | 37,390 |
| 25. Business Operations Specialists, All Other | 36,830 |
| 26. Secretaries and Administrative Assistants, Except Legal, Medical, and Executive | 36,550 |
| 27. Landscaping and Groundskeeping Workers | 36,220 |
| 28. Construction Laborers | 33,940 |
| 29. Carpenters | 32,540 |
| 30. Management Analysts | 30,650 |
| 31. Managers, All Other | 29,750 |
| 32. Tellers | 28,440 |
| 33. Dishwashers | 27,570 |
| 34. Physicians and Surgeons | 26,050 |
| 35. Middle School Teachers, Except Special and Career/Technical Education | 25,110 |
| 36. Electricians | 25,090 |
| 37. Supervisors of Construction and Extraction Workers | 24,220 |

# The 100 Jobs with the Most Openings

| Job | Annual Openings |
|---|---|
| 38. Lawyers | 24,040 |
| 39. Sales Representatives, Services, All Other | 22,810 |
| 40. Police and Sheriff's Patrol Officers | 22,790 |
| 41. Teachers and Instructors, All Other | 22,570 |
| 42. Computer Systems Analysts | 22,280 |
| 43. Hairdressers, Hairstylists, and Cosmetologists | 21,950 |
| 44. Software Developers, Applications | 21,840 |
| 45. Medical Assistants | 21,780 |
| 46. Clergy | 21,770 |
| 47. Medical Secretaries | 18,900 |
| 48. Pharmacy Technicians | 18,200 |
| 49. Automotive Service Technicians and Mechanics | 18,170 |
| 50. Preschool Teachers, Except Special Education | 17,830 |
| 51. Plumbers, Pipefitters, and Steamfitters | 17,550 |
| 52. Amusement and Recreation Attendants | 17,120 |
| 53. Billing and Posting Clerks | 16,760 |
| 54. Dental Assistants | 16,100 |
| 55. Bill and Account Collectors | 15,690 |
| 56. Social and Human Service Assistants | 15,390 |
| 57. Software Developers, Systems Software | 15,340 |
| 58. Firefighters | 15,280 |
| 59. Insurance Sales Agents | 15,260 |
| 60. Correctional Officers and Jailers | 14,360 |
| 61. Sales Representatives, Wholesale and Manufacturing, Technical and Scientific Products | 14,230 |
| 62. Financial Managers | 13,820 |
| 63. Cooks, Institution and Cafeteria | 13,810 |
| 64. Construction Managers | 13,770 |
| 65. Market Research Analysts and Marketing Specialists | 13,730 |
| 66. First-Line Supervisors of Mechanics, Installers, and Repairers | 13,650 |
| 67. Heating, Air Conditioning, and Refrigeration Mechanics and Installers | 13,620 |
| 68. Network and Computer Systems Administrators | 13,550 |
| 69. First-Line Supervisors of Food Preparation and Serving Workers | 13,440 |
| 70. Public Relations Specialists | 13,130 |
| 71. First-Line Supervisors of Non-Retail Sales Workers | 12,950 |
| 72. Real Estate Sales Agents | 12,830 |
| 73. Securities, Commodities, and Financial Services Sales Agents | 12,680 |
| 74. Sales Managers | 12,660 |

*(continued)*

*(continued)*

## The 100 Jobs with the Most Openings

| Job | Annual Openings |
|---|---|
| 75. Graphic Designers | 12,480 |
| 76. Fitness Trainers and Aerobics Instructors | 12,380 |
| 77. Self-Enrichment Education Teachers | 12,030 |
| 78. Purchasing Agents, Except Wholesale, Retail, and Farm Products | 11,860 |
| 79. Operating Engineers and Other Construction Equipment Operators | 11,820 |
| 80. Civil Engineers | 11,460 |
| 81. Chief Executives | 11,250 |
| 82. Human Resources Specialists | 11,230 |
| 83. Child, Family, and School Social Workers | 10,960 |
| 84. Hotel, Motel, and Resort Desk Clerks | 10,950 |
| 85. Compliance Officers | 10,850 |
| 86. Postal Service Mail Carriers | 10,720 |
| 87. Recreation Workers | 10,720 |
| 88. Training and Development Specialists | 10,710 |
| 89. Painters, Construction and Maintenance | 10,650 |
| 90. Pharmacists | 10,580 |
| 91. Paralegals and Legal Assistants | 10,400 |
| 92. Cost Estimators | 10,360 |
| 93. Medical and Health Services Managers | 9,940 |
| 94. Coaches and Scouts | 9,920 |
| 95. Dental Hygienists | 9,840 |
| 96. Computer and Information Systems Managers | 9,710 |
| 97. Claims Adjusters, Examiners, and Investigators | 9,560 |
| 98. Financial Analysts | 9,520 |
| 99. Educational, Guidance, School, and Vocational Counselors | 9,440 |
| 100. Interviewers, Except Eligibility and Loan | 9,210 |

# Best Jobs Lists by Demographic

Different types of jobs attract different types of workers. It's interesting to consider which jobs have the highest percentage of men or young workers. I'm not saying that men or young people should consider these jobs over others based solely on this information, but it is useful information to know.

In some cases, these lists can give you ideas for jobs to consider that you might otherwise overlook. For example, perhaps women should consider some jobs that traditionally have high percentages of men in them. Or older workers might consider some jobs typically held by young people. Although these aren't obvious ways of using these lists, the lists may give you some good ideas of jobs to consider. The lists may also help you identify jobs that work well for others like you—for example, jobs with plentiful opportunities for self-employment, if that's a work arrangement that appeals to you.

All lists in this section were created through a similar process. I began with the 400 best jobs and sorted those jobs in order of the primary criterion for each set of lists. I eliminated jobs that scored low on the primary criterion and created an initial list of jobs ordered from highest to lowest percentage of the criterion. For example, when I sorted the 400 jobs based on the percentage of workers age 16 to 24, I set the cutoff point at 20 percent and produced a list of 37 jobs, ranging from a high of 74.0 percent to a low of 21.5 percent. For other criteria, such as number of self-employed workers or female workers, I used other cutoff levels. From this initial list of jobs with a high percentage of each type of worker, I created four more-specialized lists:

* 25 Best Jobs Overall (the subset of jobs that have the highest combined scores for earnings, growth rate, and number of openings)
* 25 Best-Paying Jobs
* 25 Fastest-Growing Jobs
* 25 Jobs with the Most Openings

Note that the economic figures I used to sort the jobs in these four lists are based on the averages for *all* workers, not just workers who match the particular demographic group. For example, it was not possible to obtain earnings figures that applied specifically to young people, although it is known that they tend to earn less. Similarly, it was not possible to obtain separate percentage figures for job growth in urban or rural areas.

# Best Jobs with the Highest Percentage of Workers Age 16–24

From my list of 400 jobs used in this book, this list contains jobs with the highest percentage (more than 20 percent) of workers age 16 to 24, presented in order of the percentage of these young workers in each job. Younger workers are found in all jobs, but jobs with higher percentages of younger workers may present more opportunities for initial entry or upward mobility. Many jobs with the highest percentages of younger workers are those that don't require extensive training or education, but there is a wide variety of jobs in different fields among these occupations.

## Best Jobs with the Highest Percentage of Workers Age 16–24

| Job | Percent Age 16–24 |
| --- | --- |
| 1. Protective Service Workers, All Other | 74.0% |
| 2. Counter Attendants, Cafeteria, Food Concession, and Coffee Shop | 72.7% |

*(continued)*

## Best Jobs with the Highest Percentage of Workers Age 16–24

| Job | Percent Age 16–24 |
|---|---|
| 3. Amusement and Recreation Attendants | 51.9% |
| 4. Combined Food Preparation and Serving Workers, Including Fast Food | 47.2% |
| 5. Ushers, Lobby Attendants, and Ticket Takers | 46.8% |
| 6. Dishwashers | 44.5% |
| 7. Helpers—Brickmasons, Blockmasons, Stonemasons, and Tile and Marble Setters | 41.7% |
| 8. Helpers—Carpenters | 41.7% |
| 9. Helpers—Electricians | 41.7% |
| 10. Helpers—Pipelayers, Plumbers, Pipefitters, and Steamfitters | 41.7% |
| 11. Coaches and Scouts | 33.7% |
| 12. Tellers | 33.3% |
| 13. Hotel, Motel, and Resort Desk Clerks | 32.8% |
| 14. Cooks, Institution and Cafeteria | 32.1% |
| 15. Stock Clerks and Order Fillers | 31.6% |
| 16. Fitness Trainers and Aerobics Instructors | 30.3% |
| 17. Recreation Workers | 30.3% |
| 18. Nonfarm Animal Caretakers | 29.9% |
| 19. Library Technicians | 29.7% |
| 20. Retail Salespersons | 29.6% |
| 21. Childcare Workers | 27.1% |
| 22. Landscaping and Groundskeeping Workers | 25.9% |
| 23. Tree Trimmers and Pruners | 25.9% |
| 24. Environmental Science and Protection Technicians, Including Health | 23.8% |
| 25. Forensic Science Technicians | 23.8% |
| 26. Life, Physical, and Social Science Technicians, All Other | 23.8% |
| 27. Social Science Research Assistants | 23.8% |
| 28. Receptionists and Information Clerks | 22.6% |
| 29. First-Line Supervisors of Food Preparation and Serving Workers | 22.1% |
| 30. Customer Service Representatives | 21.6% |
| 31. Physical Therapist Aides | 21.6% |
| 32. Physical Therapist Assistants | 21.6% |
| 33. Animal Trainers | 21.5% |
| 34. Pharmacy Technicians | 21.5% |
| 35. Surgical Technologists | 21.5% |
| 36. Veterinary Technologists and Technicians | 21.5% |

The jobs in the following four lists are derived from the preceding list of the jobs with the highest percentage of workers age 16–24.

## Best Jobs Overall with a High Percentage of Workers Age 16–24

| Job | Percent Growth | Annual Earnings | Percent Age 16–24 | Annual Openings |
|---|---|---|---|---|
| 1. Fitness Trainers and Aerobics Instructors | 30.3% | $31,090 | 29.4% | 12,380 |
| 2. Customer Service Representatives | 21.6% | $30,460 | 17.7% | 110,840 |
| 3. Pharmacy Technicians | 21.5% | $28,400 | 30.6% | 18,200 |
| 4. Physical Therapist Assistants | 21.6% | $49,690 | 33.3% | 3,050 |
| 5. Veterinary Technologists and Technicians | 21.5% | $29,710 | 35.8% | 4,850 |
| 6. Surgical Technologists | 21.5% | $39,920 | 25.3% | 4,630 |
| 7. Environmental Science and Protection Technicians, Including Health | 23.8% | $41,380 | 28.9% | 2,520 |
| 8. Coaches and Scouts | 33.7% | $28,340 | 24.8% | 9,920 |
| 9. Receptionists and Information Clerks | 22.6% | $25,240 | 15.2% | 48,020 |
| 10. Landscaping and Groundskeeping Workers | 25.9% | $23,400 | 18.0% | 36,220 |
| 11. Tree Trimmers and Pruners | 25.9% | $30,450 | 26.3% | 1,720 |
| 12. Forensic Science Technicians | 23.8% | $51,570 | 19.6% | 800 |
| 13. Helpers—Electricians | 41.7% | $27,220 | 24.7% | 4,800 |
| 14. Helpers—Pipelayers, Plumbers, Pipefitters, and Steamfitters | 41.7% | $26,740 | 25.7% | 3,730 |
| 15. Protective Service Workers, All Other | 74.0% | $29,890 | 14.0% | 7,150 |
| 16. Physical Therapist Aides | 21.6% | $23,680 | 36.3% | 2,340 |
| 17. Life, Physical, and Social Science Technicians, All Other | 23.8% | $43,350 | 13.3% | 3,640 |
| 18. Social Science Research Assistants | 23.8% | $37,230 | 17.8% | 1,270 |
| 19. Helpers—Carpenters | 41.7% | $25,760 | 23.3% | 3,530 |
| 20. Combined Food Preparation and Serving Workers, Including Fast Food | 47.2% | $17,950 | 14.6% | 96,720 |
| 21. First-Line Supervisors of Food Preparation and Serving Workers | 22.1% | $29,560 | 6.6% | 13,440 |
| 22. Retail Salespersons | 29.6% | $20,670 | 8.3% | 162,690 |
| 23. Nonfarm Animal Caretakers | 29.9% | $19,550 | 20.7% | 7,360 |
| 24. Recreation Workers | 30.3% | $22,260 | 14.7% | 10,720 |
| 25. Animal Trainers | 21.5% | $26,580 | 20.4% | 1,900 |

## Best-Paying Jobs with a High Percentage of Workers Age 16–24

| Job | Percent Age 16–24 | Annual Earnings |
|---|---|---|
| 1. Forensic Science Technicians | 23.8% | $51,570 |
| 2. Physical Therapist Assistants | 21.6% | $49,690 |
| 3. Life, Physical, and Social Science Technicians, All Other | 23.8% | $43,350 |
| 4. Environmental Science and Protection Technicians, Including Health | 23.8% | $41,380 |
| 5. Surgical Technologists | 21.5% | $39,920 |
| 6. Social Science Research Assistants | 23.8% | $37,230 |
| 7. Fitness Trainers and Aerobics Instructors | 30.3% | $31,090 |
| 8. Customer Service Representatives | 21.6% | $30,460 |
| 9. Tree Trimmers and Pruners | 25.9% | $30,450 |
| 10. Protective Service Workers, All Other | 74.0% | $29,890 |
| 11. Library Technicians | 29.7% | $29,860 |
| 12. Veterinary Technologists and Technicians | 21.5% | $29,710 |
| 13. First-Line Supervisors of Food Preparation and Serving Workers | 22.1% | $29,560 |
| 14. Pharmacy Technicians | 21.5% | $28,400 |
| 15. Coaches and Scouts | 33.7% | $28,340 |
| 16. Helpers—Brickmasons, Blockmasons, Stonemasons, and Tile and Marble Setters | 41.7% | $27,780 |
| 17. Helpers—Electricians | 41.7% | $27,220 |
| 18. Helpers—Pipelayers, Plumbers, Pipefitters, and Steamfitters | 41.7% | $26,740 |
| 19. Animal Trainers | 21.5% | $26,580 |
| 20. Helpers—Carpenters | 41.7% | $25,760 |
| 21. Receptionists and Information Clerks | 22.6% | $25,240 |
| 22. Tellers | 33.3% | $24,100 |
| 23. Physical Therapist Aides | 21.6% | $23,680 |
| 24. Landscaping and Groundskeeping Workers | 25.9% | $23,400 |
| 25. Cooks, Institution and Cafeteria | 32.1% | $22,730 |

## Fastest-Growing Jobs with a High Percentage of Workers Age 16–24

| Job | Percent Age 16–24 | Percent Growth |
|---|---|---|
| 1. Physical Therapist Aides | 21.6% | 36.3% |
| 2. Veterinary Technologists and Technicians | 21.5% | 35.8% |
| 3. Physical Therapist Assistants | 21.6% | 33.3% |
| 4. Pharmacy Technicians | 21.5% | 30.6% |
| 5. Fitness Trainers and Aerobics Instructors | 30.3% | 29.4% |

## Fastest-Growing Jobs with a High Percentage of Workers Age 16–24

| Job | Percent Age 16–24 | Percent Growth |
|---|---|---|
| 6. Environmental Science and Protection Technicians, Including Health | 23.8% | 28.9% |
| 7. Tree Trimmers and Pruners | 25.9% | 26.3% |
| 8. Helpers—Pipelayers, Plumbers, Pipefitters, and Steamfitters | 41.7% | 25.7% |
| 9. Surgical Technologists | 21.5% | 25.3% |
| 10. Coaches and Scouts | 33.7% | 24.8% |
| 11. Helpers—Electricians | 41.7% | 24.7% |
| 12. Helpers—Carpenters | 41.7% | 23.3% |
| 13. Nonfarm Animal Caretakers | 29.9% | 20.7% |
| 14. Animal Trainers | 21.5% | 20.4% |
| 15. Forensic Science Technicians | 23.8% | 19.6% |
| 16. Landscaping and Groundskeeping Workers | 25.9% | 18.0% |
| 17. Social Science Research Assistants | 23.8% | 17.8% |
| 18. Customer Service Representatives | 21.6% | 17.7% |
| 19. Helpers—Brickmasons, Blockmasons, Stonemasons, and Tile and Marble Setters | 41.7% | 16.4% |
| 20. Receptionists and Information Clerks | 22.6% | 15.2% |
| 21. Recreation Workers | 30.3% | 14.7% |
| 22. Combined Food Preparation and Serving Workers, Including Fast Food | 47.2% | 14.6% |
| 23. Protective Service Workers, All Other | 74.0% | 14.0% |
| 24. Hotel, Motel, and Resort Desk Clerks | 32.8% | 13.7% |
| 25. Ushers, Lobby Attendants, and Ticket Takers | 46.8% | 13.7% |

## Jobs with the Most Openings with a High Percentage of Workers Age 16–24

| Job | Percent Age 16–24 | Annual Openings |
|---|---|---|
| 1. Retail Salespersons | 29.6% | 162,690 |
| 2. Customer Service Representatives | 21.6% | 110,840 |
| 3. Combined Food Preparation and Serving Workers, Including Fast Food | 47.2% | 96,720 |
| 4. Stock Clerks and Order Fillers | 31.6% | 56,260 |
| 5. Childcare Workers | 27.1% | 52,310 |
| 6. Receptionists and Information Clerks | 22.6% | 48,020 |
| 7. Counter Attendants, Cafeteria, Food Concession, and Coffee Shop | 72.7% | 43,490 |
| 8. Landscaping and Groundskeeping Workers | 25.9% | 36,220 |

*(continued)*

*(continued)*

| Jobs with the Most Openings with a High Percentage of Workers Age 16–24 | | |
| --- | --- | --- |
| Job | Percent Age 16–24 | Annual Openings |
| 9. Tellers | 33.3% | 28,440 |
| 10. Dishwashers | 44.5% | 27,570 |
| 11. Pharmacy Technicians | 21.5% | 18,200 |
| 12. Amusement and Recreation Attendants | 51.9% | 17,120 |
| 13. Cooks, Institution and Cafeteria | 32.1% | 13,810 |
| 14. First-Line Supervisors of Food Preparation and Serving Workers | 22.1% | 13,440 |
| 15. Fitness Trainers and Aerobics Instructors | 30.3% | 12,380 |
| 16. Hotel, Motel, and Resort Desk Clerks | 32.8% | 10,950 |
| 17. Recreation Workers | 30.3% | 10,720 |
| 18. Coaches and Scouts | 33.7% | 9,920 |
| 19. Ushers, Lobby Attendants, and Ticket Takers | 46.8% | 8,190 |
| 20. Nonfarm Animal Caretakers | 29.9% | 7,360 |
| 21. Protective Service Workers, All Other | 74.0% | 7,150 |
| 22. Library Technicians | 29.7% | 6,470 |
| 23. Veterinary Technologists and Technicians | 21.5% | 4,850 |
| 24. Helpers—Electricians | 41.7% | 4,800 |
| 25. Surgical Technologists | 21.5% | 4,630 |

# Best Jobs with a High Percentage of Workers Age 55 and Over

In this set of lists, all the jobs have more than 30 percent of workers age 55 and over. You may be surprised to find Graduate Teaching Assistants listed here, but that's because only one percentage figure was available for all college teaching occupations.

Older workers don't change careers as often as younger ones do, and on average, they tend to have been in their jobs for quite some time. Many of the jobs with the highest percentages of workers age 55 and over require considerable preparation, either through experience or through education and training. The highly skilled workers in these jobs have invested a lot of time and money in lengthy career preparation; they tend to resist career change or retirement so they can recoup more of their investment. Many of these jobs also have modest physical demands that older workers can handle easily.

Highly skilled older workers who are interested in changing careers may also want to consider some of the jobs on the following list. Some would make good "retirement" jobs, particularly if they allow for part-time work or self-employment. Others may be long-term targets for younger workers because the high percentage of workers near retirement age indicates the likelihood of future job openings.

## Best Jobs with the Highest Percentage of Workers Age 55 and Over

| Job | Percent Age 55 and Over |
|---|---|
| 1. Farmers, Ranchers, and Other Agricultural Managers | 54.9% |
| 2. Clinical, Counseling, and School Psychologists | 41.9% |
| 3. Industrial-Organizational Psychologists | 41.9% |
| 4. Psychologists, All Other | 41.9% |
| 5. Librarians | 41.8% |
| 6. Clergy | 41.5% |
| 7. Morticians, Undertakers, and Funeral Directors | 41.4% |
| 8. Construction and Building Inspectors | 40.1% |
| 9. Bus Drivers, Transit and Intercity | 39.4% |
| 10. Curators | 39.0% |
| 11. Museum Technicians and Conservators | 39.0% |
| 12. Funeral Attendants | 37.3% |
| 13. Dentists, General | 36.1% |
| 14. Oral and Maxillofacial Surgeons | 36.1% |
| 15. Orthodontists | 36.1% |
| 16. Prosthodontists | 36.1% |
| 17. Real Estate Brokers | 35.7% |
| 18. Real Estate Sales Agents | 35.7% |
| 19. Chief Executives | 35.5% |
| 20. Property, Real Estate, and Community Association Managers | 35.4% |
| 21. Art Directors | 35.0% |
| 22. Multimedia Artists and Animators | 35.0% |
| 23. Taxi Drivers and Chauffeurs | 34.8% |
| 24. Mining and Geological Engineers, Including Mining Safety Engineers | 34.3% |
| 25. Nuclear Engineers | 34.3% |
| 26. Astronomers | 33.8% |
| 27. Physicists | 33.8% |
| 28. Urban and Regional Planners | 33.8% |
| 29. Directors, Religious Activities and Education | 33.4% |
| 30. Management Analysts | 32.3% |

*(continued)*

*(continued)*

## Best Jobs with the Highest Percentage of Workers Age 55 and Over

| Job | Percent Age 55 and Over |
|---|---|
| 31. Music Directors and Composers | 32.3% |
| 32. Education Administrators, All Other | 32.2% |
| 33. Education Administrators, Elementary and Secondary School | 32.2% |
| 34. Education Administrators, Postsecondary | 32.2% |
| 35. Education Administrators, Preschool and Childcare Center/Program | 32.2% |
| 36. Administrative Services Managers | 31.9% |
| 37. Instructional Coordinators | 31.9% |
| 38. Writers and Authors | 31.9% |
| 39. Appraisers and Assessors of Real Estate | 31.5% |
| 40. Transportation Inspectors | 31.3% |
| 41. Cost Estimators | 30.9% |
| 42. Dental Laboratory Technicians | 30.8% |
| 43. Social and Community Service Managers | 30.8% |
| 44. Optometrists | 30.6% |
| 45. Agricultural Sciences Teachers, Postsecondary | 30.1% |
| 46. Anthropology and Archeology Teachers, Postsecondary | 30.1% |
| 47. Architecture Teachers, Postsecondary | 30.1% |
| 48. Area, Ethnic, and Cultural Studies Teachers, Postsecondary | 30.1% |
| 49. Art, Drama, and Music Teachers, Postsecondary | 30.1% |
| 50. Atmospheric, Earth, Marine, and Space Sciences Teachers, Postsecondary | 30.1% |
| 51. Biological Science Teachers, Postsecondary | 30.1% |
| 52. Business Teachers, Postsecondary | 30.1% |
| 53. Chemistry Teachers, Postsecondary | 30.1% |
| 54. Communications Teachers, Postsecondary | 30.1% |
| 55. Computer Science Teachers, Postsecondary | 30.1% |
| 56. Criminal Justice and Law Enforcement Teachers, Postsecondary | 30.1% |
| 57. Economics Teachers, Postsecondary | 30.1% |
| 58. Education Teachers, Postsecondary | 30.1% |
| 59. Engineering Teachers, Postsecondary | 30.1% |
| 60. English Language and Literature Teachers, Postsecondary | 30.1% |
| 61. Environmental Science Teachers, Postsecondary | 30.1% |
| 62. Foreign Language and Literature Teachers, Postsecondary | 30.1% |
| 63. Forestry and Conservation Science Teachers, Postsecondary | 30.1% |
| 64. Geography Teachers, Postsecondary | 30.1% |
| 65. Graduate Teaching Assistants | 30.1% |

## Best Jobs with the Highest Percentage of Workers Age 55 and Over

| Job | Percent Age 55 and Over |
|---|---|
| 66. Health Specialties Teachers, Postsecondary | 30.1% |
| 67. History Teachers, Postsecondary | 30.1% |
| 68. Home Economics Teachers, Postsecondary | 30.1% |
| 69. Law Teachers, Postsecondary | 30.1% |
| 70. Library Science Teachers, Postsecondary | 30.1% |
| 71. Mathematical Science Teachers, Postsecondary | 30.1% |
| 72. Nursing Instructors and Teachers, Postsecondary | 30.1% |
| 73. Philosophy and Religion Teachers, Postsecondary | 30.1% |
| 74. Physics Teachers, Postsecondary | 30.1% |
| 75. Political Science Teachers, Postsecondary | 30.1% |
| 76. Psychology Teachers, Postsecondary | 30.1% |
| 77. Recreation and Fitness Studies Teachers, Postsecondary | 30.1% |
| 78. Social Work Teachers, Postsecondary | 30.1% |
| 79. Sociology Teachers, Postsecondary | 30.1% |
| 80. Vocational Education Teachers, Postsecondary | 30.1% |

The jobs in the following four lists are derived from the preceding list of the jobs with the highest percentage of workers age 55 and over.

## Best Jobs Overall with a High Percentage of Workers Age 55 and Over

| Job | Percent Age 55 and Over | Annual Earnings | Percent Growth | Annual Openings |
|---|---|---|---|---|
| 1. Management Analysts | 32.3% | $78,160 | 23.9% | 30,650 |
| 2. Dentists, General | 36.1% | $141,040 | 15.3% | 5,180 |
| 3. Optometrists | 30.6% | $94,990 | 24.4% | 2,010 |
| 4. Health Specialties Teachers, Postsecondary | 30.1% | $85,270 | 15.1% | 4,000 |
| 5. Cost Estimators | 30.9% | $57,860 | 25.3% | 10,360 |
| 6. Education Administrators, All Other | 32.2% | $75,690 | 23.9% | 1,690 |
| 7. Physicists | 33.8% | $106,370 | 15.9% | 690 |
| 8. Engineering Teachers, Postsecondary | 30.1% | $89,670 | 15.1% | 1,000 |
| 9. Instructional Coordinators | 31.9% | $58,830 | 23.2% | 6,060 |
| 10. Orthodontists | 36.1% | $166,400+ | 19.8% | 360 |
| 11. Business Teachers, Postsecondary | 30.1% | $73,760 | 15.1% | 2,000 |
| 12. Prosthodontists | 36.1% | $118,400 | 28.3% | 30 |

(continued)

*(continued)*

## Best Jobs Overall with a High Percentage of Workers Age 55 and Over

| Job | Percent Age 55 and Over | Annual Earnings | Percent Growth | Annual Openings |
|---|---|---|---|---|
| 13. Biological Science Teachers, Postsecondary | 30.1% | $72,700 | 15.1% | 1,700 |
| 14. Chief Executives | 35.5% | $165,080 | −1.4% | 11,250 |
| 15. Oral and Maxillofacial Surgeons | 36.1% | $166,400+ | 15.3% | 290 |
| 16. Industrial-Organizational Psychologists | 41.9% | $87,330 | 26.1% | 130 |
| 17. Law Teachers, Postsecondary | 30.1% | $94,260 | 15.1% | 400 |
| 18. Real Estate Sales Agents | 35.7% | $40,030 | 16.2% | 12,830 |
| 19. Education Administrators, Elementary and Secondary School | 32.2% | $86,970 | 8.6% | 8,880 |
| 20. Administrative Services Managers | 31.9% | $77,890 | 12.5% | 8,660 |
| 21. Urban and Regional Planners | 33.8% | $63,040 | 19.0% | 1,470 |
| 22. Art, Drama, and Music Teachers, Postsecondary | 30.1% | $62,040 | 15.1% | 2,500 |
| 23. Computer Science Teachers, Postsecondary | 30.1% | $70,300 | 15.1% | 1,000 |
| 24. Economics Teachers, Postsecondary | 30.1% | $83,370 | 15.1% | 400 |
| 25. Psychology Teachers, Postsecondary | 30.1% | $67,330 | 15.1% | 1,000 |

## Best-Paying Jobs with a High Percentage of Workers Age 55 and Over

| Job | Percent Age 55 and Over | Annual Earnings |
|---|---|---|
| 1. Oral and Maxillofacial Surgeons | 36.1% | $166,400+ |
| 2. Orthodontists | 36.1% | $166,400+ |
| 3. Chief Executives | 35.5% | $165,080 |
| 4. Dentists, General | 36.1% | $141,040 |
| 5. Prosthodontists | 36.1% | $118,400 |
| 6. Physicists | 33.8% | $106,370 |
| 7. Nuclear Engineers | 34.3% | $99,920 |
| 8. Optometrists | 30.6% | $94,990 |
| 9. Law Teachers, Postsecondary | 30.1% | $94,260 |
| 10. Psychologists, All Other | 41.9% | $89,900 |
| 11. Engineering Teachers, Postsecondary | 30.1% | $89,670 |
| 12. Industrial-Organizational Psychologists | 41.9% | $87,330 |
| 13. Astronomers | 33.8% | $87,260 |
| 14. Education Administrators, Elementary and Secondary School | 32.2% | $86,970 |
| 15. Health Specialties Teachers, Postsecondary | 30.1% | $85,270 |

## Best-Paying Jobs with a High Percentage of Workers Age 55 and Over

| Job | Percent Age 55 and Over | Annual Earnings |
|---|---|---|
| 16. Education Administrators, Postsecondary | 32.2% | $83,710 |
| 17. Economics Teachers, Postsecondary | 30.1% | $83,370 |
| 18. Mining and Geological Engineers, Including Mining Safety Engineers | 34.3% | $82,870 |
| 19. Atmospheric, Earth, Marine, and Space Sciences Teachers, Postsecondary | 30.1% | $82,840 |
| 20. Art Directors | 35.0% | $80,630 |
| 21. Agricultural Sciences Teachers, Postsecondary | 30.1% | $78,370 |
| 22. Forestry and Conservation Science Teachers, Postsecondary | 30.1% | $78,290 |
| 23. Management Analysts | 32.3% | $78,160 |
| 24. Administrative Services Managers | 31.9% | $77,890 |
| 25. Physics Teachers, Postsecondary | 30.1% | $77,610 |

## Fastest-Growing Jobs with a High Percentage of Workers Age 55 and Over

| Job | Percent Age 55 and Over | Percent Growth |
|---|---|---|
| 1. Prosthodontists | 36.1% | 28.3% |
| 2. Funeral Attendants | 37.3% | 26.3% |
| 3. Industrial-Organizational Psychologists | 41.9% | 26.1% |
| 4. Museum Technicians and Conservators | 39.0% | 25.6% |
| 5. Cost Estimators | 30.9% | 25.3% |
| 6. Optometrists | 30.6% | 24.4% |
| 7. Education Administrators, All Other | 32.2% | 23.9% |
| 8. Management Analysts | 32.3% | 23.9% |
| 9. Instructional Coordinators | 31.9% | 23.2% |
| 10. Curators | 39.0% | 23.0% |
| 11. Orthodontists | 36.1% | 19.8% |
| 12. Urban and Regional Planners | 33.8% | 19.0% |
| 13. Transportation Inspectors | 31.3% | 18.3% |
| 14. Construction and Building Inspectors | 40.1% | 16.8% |
| 15. Real Estate Sales Agents | 35.7% | 16.2% |
| 16. Physicists | 33.8% | 15.9% |
| 17. Astronomers | 33.8% | 15.6% |
| 18. Taxi Drivers and Chauffeurs | 34.8% | 15.5% |

*(continued)*

*(continued)*

## Fastest-Growing Jobs with a High Percentage of Workers Age 55 and Over

| Job | Percent Age 55 and Over | Percent Growth |
|---|---|---|
| 19. Dentists, General | 36.1% | 15.3% |
| 20. Mining and Geological Engineers, Including Mining Safety Engineers | 34.3% | 15.3% |
| 21. Oral and Maxillofacial Surgeons | 36.1% | 15.3% |
| 22. Agricultural Sciences Teachers, Postsecondary | 30.1% | 15.1% |
| 23. Anthropology and Archeology Teachers, Postsecondary | 30.1% | 15.1% |
| 24. Architecture Teachers, Postsecondary | 30.1% | 15.1% |
| 25. Area, Ethnic, and Cultural Studies Teachers, Postsecondary | 30.1% | 15.1% |

## Jobs with the Most Openings with a High Percentage of Workers Age 55 and Over

| Job | Percent Age 55 and Over | Annual Openings |
|---|---|---|
| 1. Management Analysts | 32.3% | 30,650 |
| 2. Clergy | 41.5% | 21,770 |
| 3. Real Estate Sales Agents | 35.7% | 12,830 |
| 4. Chief Executives | 35.5% | 11,250 |
| 5. Cost Estimators | 30.9% | 10,360 |
| 6. Education Administrators, Elementary and Secondary School | 32.2% | 8,880 |
| 7. Administrative Services Managers | 31.9% | 8,660 |
| 8. Property, Real Estate, and Community Association Managers | 35.4% | 7,800 |
| 9. Taxi Drivers and Chauffeurs | 34.8% | 7,730 |
| 10. Farmers, Ranchers, and Other Agricultural Managers | 54.9% | 6,490 |
| 11. Instructional Coordinators | 31.9% | 6,060 |
| 12. Clinical, Counseling, and School Psychologists | 41.9% | 5,990 |
| 13. Librarians | 41.8% | 5,450 |
| 14. Writers and Authors | 31.9% | 5,420 |
| 15. Dentists, General | 36.1% | 5,180 |
| 16. Bus Drivers, Transit and Intercity | 39.4% | 4,990 |
| 17. Social and Community Service Managers | 30.8% | 4,820 |
| 18. Education Administrators, Postsecondary | 32.2% | 4,010 |
| 19. Graduate Teaching Assistants | 30.1% | 4,000 |

## Jobs with the Most Openings with a High Percentage of Workers Age 55 and Over

| Job | Percent Age 55 and Over | Annual Openings |
|---|---|---|
| 20. Health Specialties Teachers, Postsecondary | 30.1% | 4,000 |
| 21. Vocational Education Teachers, Postsecondary | 30.1% | 4,000 |
| 22. Construction and Building Inspectors | 40.1% | 3,970 |
| 23. Real Estate Brokers | 35.7% | 3,080 |
| 24. Multimedia Artists and Animators | 35.0% | 2,890 |
| 25. Art Directors | 35.0% | 2,870 |

# Best Jobs with a High Percentage of Self-Employed Workers

About 8% of all working people are self-employed. Although you may think of the self-employed as having similar jobs, they actually work in an enormous range of situations, fields, and work environments that you may not have considered.

Among the self-employed are people who own small or large businesses, as many real estate brokers and funeral directors do; professionals who own their own practices, as many lawyers, psychologists, and medical doctors do; people working on a contract basis for one or more employers, as many editors do; people running home consulting or other businesses; and people in many other situations. They may go to the same worksite every day, as most attorneys do; visit multiple employers during the course of a week, as many models do; or do most of their work from home, as many craft artists do. Some work part time, others full time.

The point is that there is an enormous range of situations. One of them could make sense for you now or in the future.

The following list contains jobs in which more than 30% of the workers are self-employed.

## Jobs with the Highest Percentage of Self-Employed Workers

| Job | Percent Self-Employed Workers |
|---|---|
| 1. Writers and Authors | 69.4% |
| 2. Construction Managers | 60.9% |
| 3. Art Directors | 60.2% |

*(continued)*

*(continued)*

## Jobs with the Highest Percentage of Self-Employed Workers

| Job | Percent Self-Employed Workers |
|---|---|
| 4. Multimedia Artists and Animators | 60.1% |
| 5. Photographers | 60.1% |
| 6. Real Estate Sales Agents | 58.3% |
| 7. Real Estate Brokers | 58.3% |
| 8. Massage Therapists | 57.2% |
| 9. Managers, All Other | 57.1% |
| 10. Animal Trainers | 54.3% |
| 11. First-Line Supervisors of Landscaping, Lawn Service, and Groundskeeping Workers | 50.4% |
| 12. Property, Real Estate, and Community Association Managers | 45.9% |
| 13. Agents and Business Managers of Artists, Performers, and Athletes | 45.8% |
| 14. First-Line Supervisors of Non-Retail Sales Workers | 45.6% |
| 15. Painters, Construction and Maintenance | 45.0% |
| 16. Chiropractors | 44.5% |
| 17. Hairdressers, Hairstylists, and Cosmetologists | 43.5% |
| 18. Food Service Managers | 42.0% |
| 19. Gaming Managers | 38.6% |
| 20. First-Line Supervisors of Personal Service Workers | 37.8% |
| 21. Gaming Supervisors | 36.6% |
| 22. Music Directors and Composers | 36.2% |
| 23. Tile and Marble Setters | 35.1% |
| 24. Clinical, Counseling, and School Psychologists | 34.1% |
| 25. Industrial-Organizational Psychologists | 33.6% |
| 26. Psychologists, All Other | 32.8% |
| 27. Childcare Workers | 32.4% |
| 28. Carpenters | 32.0% |
| 29. Manicurists and Pedicurists | 32.0% |
| 30. Skincare Specialists | 31.9% |
| 31. First-Line Supervisors of Retail Sales Workers | 30.6% |

The jobs in the following four lists are derived from the preceding list of jobs with the highest percentage of self-employed workers. Where the following lists give earnings estimates, keep in mind that these figures are based on a survey that *doesn't include self-employed workers*. The median earnings for self-employed workers in these occupations may be significantly higher or lower.

## Best Jobs Overall with a High Percentage of Self-Employed Workers

| Job | Percent Self-Employed Workers | Annual Earnings | Percent Growth | Annual Openings |
|---|---|---|---|---|
| 1. Construction Managers | 60.9% | $83,860 | 17.2% | 13,770 |
| 2. Managers, All Other | 57.1% | $96,450 | 7.3% | 29,750 |
| 3. Industrial-Organizational Psychologists | 33.6% | $87,330 | 26.1% | 130 |
| 4. Real Estate Sales Agents | 58.3% | $40,030 | 16.2% | 12,830 |
| 5. Chiropractors | 44.5% | $67,200 | 19.5% | 1,820 |
| 6. Hairdressers, Hairstylists, and Cosmetologists | 43.5% | $22,760 | 20.1% | 21,950 |
| 7. Carpenters | 32.0% | $39,530 | 12.9% | 32,540 |
| 8. Writers and Authors | 69.4% | $55,420 | 14.8% | 5,420 |
| 9. Agents and Business Managers of Artists, Performers, and Athletes | 45.8% | $63,130 | 22.4% | 1,010 |
| 10. Clinical, Counseling, and School Psychologists | 34.1% | $66,810 | 11.1% | 5,990 |
| 11. First-Line Supervisors of Landscaping, Lawn Service, and Groundskeeping Workers | 50.4% | $41,860 | 14.9% | 5,600 |
| 12. First-Line Supervisors of Non-Retail Sales Workers | 45.6% | $68,880 | 4.8% | 12,950 |
| 13. First-Line Supervisors of Personal Service Workers | 37.8% | $35,290 | 15.4% | 9,080 |
| 14. Psychologists, All Other | 32.8% | $89,900 | 14.4% | 680 |
| 15. Art Directors | 60.2% | $80,630 | 11.7% | 2,870 |
| 16. Multimedia Artists and Animators | 60.1% | $58,510 | 14.2% | 2,890 |
| 17. Massage Therapists | 57.2% | $34,900 | 18.9% | 3,950 |
| 18. Skincare Specialists | 31.9% | $28,920 | 37.8% | 2,030 |
| 19. Property, Real Estate, and Community Association Managers | 45.9% | $51,480 | 8.4% | 7,800 |
| 20. First-Line Supervisors of Retail Sales Workers | 30.6% | $35,820 | 5.2% | 45,010 |
| 21. Childcare Workers | 32.4% | $19,300 | 10.9% | 52,310 |
| 22. Tile and Marble Setters | 35.1% | $38,110 | 14.3% | 3,070 |
| 23. Animal Trainers | 54.3% | $26,580 | 20.4% | 1,900 |
| 24. Food Service Managers | 42.0% | $48,130 | 5.3% | 8,370 |
| 25. Gaming Managers | 38.6% | $66,960 | 11.9% | 200 |

## Best-Paying Jobs with a High Percentage of Self-Employed Workers

| Job | Percent Self-Employed Workers | Annual Earnings |
|---|---|---|
| 1. Managers, All Other | 57.1% | $96,450 |
| 2. Psychologists, All Other | 32.8% | $89,900 |
| 3. Industrial-Organizational Psychologists | 33.6% | $87,330 |
| 4. Construction Managers | 60.9% | $83,860 |
| 5. Art Directors | 60.2% | $80,630 |
| 6. First-Line Supervisors of Non-Retail Sales Workers | 45.6% | $68,880 |
| 7. Chiropractors | 44.5% | $67,200 |
| 8. Gaming Managers | 38.6% | $66,960 |
| 9. Clinical, Counseling, and School Psychologists | 34.1% | $66,810 |
| 10. Agents and Business Managers of Artists, Performers, and Athletes | 45.8% | $63,130 |
| 11. Multimedia Artists and Animators | 60.1% | $58,510 |
| 12. Writers and Authors | 69.4% | $55,420 |
| 13. Real Estate Brokers | 58.3% | $54,910 |
| 14. Property, Real Estate, and Community Association Managers | 45.9% | $51,480 |
| 15. Gaming Supervisors | 36.6% | $48,530 |
| 16. Food Service Managers | 42.0% | $48,130 |
| 17. Music Directors and Composers | 36.2% | $45,970 |
| 18. First-Line Supervisors of Landscaping, Lawn Service, and Groundskeeping Workers | 50.4% | $41,860 |
| 19. Real Estate Sales Agents | 58.3% | $40,030 |
| 20. Carpenters | 32.0% | $39,530 |
| 21. Tile and Marble Setters | 35.1% | $38,110 |
| 22. First-Line Supervisors of Retail Sales Workers | 30.6% | $35,820 |
| 23. First-Line Supervisors of Personal Service Workers | 37.8% | $35,290 |
| 24. Massage Therapists | 57.2% | $34,900 |
| 25. Painters, Construction and Maintenance | 45.0% | $34,280 |

## Fastest-Growing Jobs with a High Percentage of Self-Employed Workers

| Job | Percent Self-Employed Workers | Percent Growth |
|---|---|---|
| 1. Skincare Specialists | 31.9% | 37.8% |
| 2. Industrial-Organizational Psychologists | 33.6% | 26.1% |
| 3. Agents and Business Managers of Artists, Performers, and Athletes | 45.8% | 22.4% |
| 4. Animal Trainers | 54.3% | 20.4% |
| 5. Hairdressers, Hairstylists, and Cosmetologists | 43.5% | 20.1% |

## Fastest-Growing Jobs with a High Percentage of Self-Employed Workers

| Job | Percent Self-Employed Workers | Percent Growth |
|---|---|---|
| 6. Chiropractors | 44.5% | 19.5% |
| 7. Massage Therapists | 57.2% | 18.9% |
| 8. Manicurists and Pedicurists | 32.0% | 18.8% |
| 9. Construction Managers | 60.9% | 17.2% |
| 10. Real Estate Sales Agents | 58.3% | 16.2% |
| 11. First-Line Supervisors of Personal Service Workers | 37.8% | 15.4% |
| 12. First-Line Supervisors of Landscaping, Lawn Service, and Groundskeeping Workers | 50.4% | 14.9% |
| 13. Writers and Authors | 69.4% | 14.8% |
| 14. Psychologists, All Other | 32.8% | 14.4% |
| 15. Tile and Marble Setters | 35.1% | 14.3% |
| 16. Multimedia Artists and Animators | 60.1% | 14.2% |
| 17. Carpenters | 32.0% | 12.9% |
| 18. Gaming Managers | 38.6% | 11.9% |
| 19. Gaming Supervisors | 36.6% | 11.8% |
| 20. Art Directors | 60.2% | 11.7% |
| 21. Photographers | 60.1% | 11.5% |
| 22. Clinical, Counseling, and School Psychologists | 34.1% | 11.1% |
| 23. Childcare Workers | 32.4% | 10.9% |
| 24. Music Directors and Composers | 36.2% | 10.0% |
| 25. Real Estate Brokers | 58.3% | 8.6% |

## Jobs with the Most Openings with a High Percentage of Self-Employed Workers

| Job | Percent Self-Employed Workers | Annual Openings |
|---|---|---|
| 1. Childcare Workers | 32.4% | 52,310 |
| 2. First-Line Supervisors of Retail Sales Workers | 30.6% | 45,010 |
| 3. Carpenters | 32.0% | 32,540 |
| 4. Managers, All Other | 57.1% | 29,750 |
| 5. Hairdressers, Hairstylists, and Cosmetologists | 43.5% | 21,950 |
| 6. Construction Managers | 60.9% | 13,770 |

*(continued)*

*(continued)*

## Jobs with the Most Openings with a High Percentage of Self-Employed Workers

| Job | Percent Self-Employed Workers | Annual Openings |
|---|---|---|
| 7. First-Line Supervisors of Non-Retail Sales Workers | 45.6% | 12,950 |
| 8. Real Estate Sales Agents | 58.3% | 12,830 |
| 9. Painters, Construction and Maintenance | 45.0% | 10,650 |
| 10. First-Line Supervisors of Personal Service Workers | 37.8% | 9,080 |
| 11. Food Service Managers | 42.0% | 8,370 |
| 12. Property, Real Estate, and Community Association Managers | 45.9% | 7,800 |
| 13. Clinical, Counseling, and School Psychologists | 34.1% | 5,990 |
| 14. First-Line Supervisors of Landscaping, Lawn Service, and Groundskeeping Workers | 50.4% | 5,600 |
| 15. Writers and Authors | 69.4% | 5,420 |
| 16. Photographers | 60.1% | 4,800 |
| 17. Massage Therapists | 57.2% | 3,950 |
| 18. Real Estate Brokers | 58.3% | 3,080 |
| 19. Tile and Marble Setters | 35.1% | 3,070 |
| 20. Multimedia Artists and Animators | 60.1% | 2,890 |
| 21. Art Directors | 60.2% | 2,870 |
| 22. Manicurists and Pedicurists | 32.0% | 2,530 |
| 23. Skincare Specialists | 31.9% | 2,030 |
| 24. Animal Trainers | 54.3% | 1,900 |
| 25. Chiropractors | 44.5% | 1,820 |

# Best Jobs Employing a High Percentage of Women

To create the lists that follow, I sorted the 400 best jobs according to the percentages of women and men in the workforce, setting the cutoff level at 80%. (Actually, I sorted the 399 jobs for which I had this information. I had no percentage figure to use for Computer Occupations, All Other, but this job probably is not dominated by either sex.) Similar lists of the best jobs with high percentages of men and women are included in all the books in the *Best Jobs* series. It's important to understand that these lists aren't meant to restrict women or men from considering job options. Actually, my reasoning for including them is exactly the opposite: I hope the lists help people see possibilities that they might not otherwise have considered.

The fact is that jobs with high percentages of women or high percentages of men offer good opportunities for both men and women if they want to do one of these jobs. So I suggest that women browse the lists of jobs that employ high percentages of men and that men browse the lists of jobs with high percentages of women. There are jobs in both sets of lists that pay well, and women or men who are interested in them and who have or can obtain the necessary education and training should consider them.

An interesting and unfortunate tidbit to bring up at your next party is that the average earnings for the jobs with the highest percentage of women is $35,904, compared to average earnings of $46,649 for the jobs with the highest percentage of men. But earnings don't tell the whole story. I computed the average growth and job openings of the jobs with the highest percentage of women and found statistics of 17.3% growth and 23,103 openings, compared to 12.2% growth and 6,628 openings for the jobs with the highest percentage of men. This discrepancy reinforces the idea that men have had more problems than women in adapting to an economy dominated by service and information-based jobs. Many women may simply be better prepared, possessing more appropriate skills for the jobs that are now growing rapidly and have more job openings.

## Best Jobs Employing the Highest Percentage of Women

| Job | Percent Women |
|-----|--------------|
| 1. Kindergarten Teachers, Except Special Education | 98.4% |
| 2. Preschool Teachers, Except Special Education | 98.4% |
| 3. Speech-Language Pathologists | 97.7% |
| 4. Executive Secretaries and Executive Administrative Assistants | 96.8% |
| 5. Legal Secretaries | 96.8% |
| 6. Medical Secretaries | 96.8% |
| 7. Secretaries and Administrative Assistants, Except Legal, Medical, and Executive | 96.8% |
| 8. Dental Assistants | 96.7% |
| 9. Dental Hygienists | 96.1% |
| 10. Childcare Workers | 95.8% |
| 11. Receptionists and Information Clerks | 92.4% |
| 12. Teacher Assistants | 91.5% |
| 13. Licensed Practical and Licensed Vocational Nurses | 91.4% |
| 14. Registered Nurses | 90.7% |
| 15. Healthcare Support Workers, All Other | 90.4% |
| 16. Medical Assistants | 90.4% |
| 17. Veterinary Assistants and Laboratory Animal Caretakers | 90.4% |
| 18. Bookkeeping, Accounting, and Auditing Clerks | 90.0% |
| 19. Billing and Posting Clerks | 89.6% |
| 20. Athletic Trainers | 88.9% |

*(continued)*

*(continued)*

## Best Jobs Employing the Highest Percentage of Women

| Job | Percent Women |
|---|---|
| 21. Healthcare Practitioners and Technical Workers, All Other | 88.9% |
| 22. Occupational Health and Safety Specialists | 88.9% |
| 23. Medical Records and Health Information Technicians | 88.4% |
| 24. Home Health Aides | 88.0% |
| 25. Tellers | 87.1% |
| 26. Hairdressers, Hairstylists, and Cosmetologists | 87.0% |
| 27. Eligibility Interviewers, Government Programs | 86.9% |
| 28. Paralegals and Legal Assistants | 86.7% |
| 29. Interviewers, Except Eligibility and Loan | 84.4% |
| 30. Dietitians and Nutritionists | 83.3% |
| 31. Recreational Therapists | 83.3% |
| 32. Meeting, Convention, and Event Planners | 82.9% |
| 33. Personal Care Aides | 82.7% |
| 34. Office Clerks, General | 82.2% |
| 35. Occupational Therapists | 81.7% |
| 36. Child, Family, and School Social Workers | 81.5% |
| 37. Healthcare Social Workers | 81.5% |
| 38. Mental Health and Substance Abuse Social Workers | 81.5% |
| 39. Elementary School Teachers, Except Special Education | 81.3% |
| 40. Middle School Teachers, Except Special and Career/Technical Education | 81.3% |

The jobs in the following four lists are derived from the preceding list of the jobs employing the highest percentage of women.

## Best Jobs Overall Employing a High Percentage of Women

| Job | Percent Women | Annual Earnings | Percent Growth | Annual Openings |
|---|---|---|---|---|
| 1. Registered Nurses | 90.7% | $64,690 | 22.2% | 103,900 |
| 2. Dental Hygienists | 96.1% | $68,250 | 36.1% | 9,840 |
| 3. Elementary School Teachers, Except Special Education | 81.3% | $51,660 | 15.8% | 59,650 |
| 4. Paralegals and Legal Assistants | 86.7% | $46,680 | 28.1% | 10,400 |
| 5. Licensed Practical and Licensed Vocational Nurses | 91.4% | $40,380 | 20.6% | 39,130 |
| 6. Occupational Therapists | 81.7% | $72,320 | 25.6% | 4,580 |
| 7. Home Health Aides | 88.0% | $20,560 | 50.0% | 55,270 |

## Best Jobs Overall Employing a High Percentage of Women

| Job | Percent Women | Annual Earnings | Percent Growth | Annual Openings |
|---|---|---|---|---|
| 8. Middle School Teachers, Except Special and Career/Technical Education | 81.3% | $51,960 | 15.3% | 25,110 |
| 9. Dental Assistants | 96.7% | $33,470 | 35.7% | 16,100 |
| 10. Healthcare Social Workers | 81.5% | $47,230 | 22.4% | 6,590 |
| 11. Personal Care Aides | 82.7% | $19,640 | 46.0% | 47,780 |
| 12. Medical Assistants | 90.4% | $28,860 | 33.9% | 21,780 |
| 13. Medical Secretaries | 96.8% | $30,530 | 26.6% | 18,900 |
| 14. Executive Secretaries and Executive Administrative Assistants | 96.8% | $43,520 | 12.8% | 41,920 |
| 15. Speech-Language Pathologists | 97.7% | $66,920 | 18.5% | 4,380 |
| 16. Athletic Trainers | 88.9% | $41,600 | 36.9% | 1,150 |
| 17. Legal Secretaries | 96.8% | $41,500 | 18.4% | 8,380 |
| 18. Medical Records and Health Information Technicians | 88.4% | $32,350 | 20.3% | 7,030 |
| 19. Bookkeeping, Accounting, and Auditing Clerks | 90.0% | $34,030 | 10.3% | 46,040 |
| 20. Kindergarten Teachers, Except Special Education | 98.4% | $48,800 | 15.0% | 6,300 |
| 21. Office Clerks, General | 82.2% | $26,610 | 11.9% | 77,090 |
| 22. Hairdressers, Hairstylists, and Cosmetologists | 87.0% | $22,760 | 20.1% | 21,950 |
| 23. Mental Health and Substance Abuse Social Workers | 81.5% | $38,600 | 19.5% | 6,130 |
| 24. Receptionists and Information Clerks | 92.4% | $25,240 | 15.2% | 48,020 |
| 25. Preschool Teachers, Except Special Education | 98.4% | $25,700 | 19.0% | 17,830 |

## Best-Paying Jobs Employing a High Percentage of Women

| Job | Percent Women | Annual Earnings |
|---|---|---|
| 1. Occupational Therapists | 81.7% | $72,320 |
| 2. Dental Hygienists | 96.1% | $68,250 |
| 3. Speech-Language Pathologists | 97.7% | $66,920 |
| 4. Registered Nurses | 90.7% | $64,690 |
| 5. Occupational Health and Safety Specialists | 88.9% | $64,660 |
| 6. Dietitians and Nutritionists | 83.3% | $53,250 |
| 7. Middle School Teachers, Except Special and Career/Technical Education | 81.3% | $51,960 |
| 8. Elementary School Teachers, Except Special Education | 81.3% | $51,660 |
| 9. Kindergarten Teachers, Except Special Education | 98.4% | $48,800 |

*(continued)*

*(continued)*

## Best-Paying Jobs Employing a High Percentage of Women

| Job | Percent Women | Annual Earnings |
|---|---|---|
| 10. Healthcare Social Workers | 81.5% | $47,230 |
| 11. Paralegals and Legal Assistants | 86.7% | $46,680 |
| 12. Meeting, Convention, and Event Planners | 82.9% | $45,260 |
| 13. Healthcare Practitioners and Technical Workers, All Other | 88.9% | $43,970 |
| 14. Executive Secretaries and Executive Administrative Assistants | 96.8% | $43,520 |
| 15. Athletic Trainers | 88.9% | $41,600 |
| 16. Legal Secretaries | 96.8% | $41,500 |
| 17. Licensed Practical and Licensed Vocational Nurses | 91.4% | $40,380 |
| 18. Child, Family, and School Social Workers | 81.5% | $40,210 |
| 19. Eligibility Interviewers, Government Programs | 86.9% | $39,960 |
| 20. Recreational Therapists | 83.3% | $39,410 |
| 21. Mental Health and Substance Abuse Social Workers | 81.5% | $38,600 |
| 22. Bookkeeping, Accounting, and Auditing Clerks | 90.0% | $34,030 |
| 23. Dental Assistants | 96.7% | $33,470 |
| 24. Medical Records and Health Information Technicians | 88.4% | $32,350 |
| 25. Billing and Posting Clerks | 89.6% | $32,170 |

## Fastest-Growing Jobs Employing a High Percentage of Women

| Job | Percent Women | Percent Growth |
|---|---|---|
| 1. Home Health Aides | 88.0% | 50.0% |
| 2. Personal Care Aides | 82.7% | 46.0% |
| 3. Athletic Trainers | 88.9% | 36.9% |
| 4. Dental Hygienists | 96.1% | 36.1% |
| 5. Dental Assistants | 96.7% | 35.7% |
| 6. Medical Assistants | 90.4% | 33.9% |
| 7. Paralegals and Legal Assistants | 86.7% | 28.1% |
| 8. Medical Secretaries | 96.8% | 26.6% |
| 9. Occupational Therapists | 81.7% | 25.6% |
| 10. Veterinary Assistants and Laboratory Animal Caretakers | 90.4% | 22.8% |
| 11. Healthcare Social Workers | 81.5% | 22.4% |
| 12. Registered Nurses | 90.7% | 22.2% |
| 13. Licensed Practical and Licensed Vocational Nurses | 91.4% | 20.6% |
| 14. Medical Records and Health Information Technicians | 88.4% | 20.3% |

## Fastest-Growing Jobs Employing a High Percentage of Women

| Job | Percent Women | Percent Growth |
|---|---|---|
| 15. Hairdressers, Hairstylists, and Cosmetologists | 87.0% | 20.1% |
| 16. Mental Health and Substance Abuse Social Workers | 81.5% | 19.5% |
| 17. Preschool Teachers, Except Special Education | 98.4% | 19.0% |
| 18. Speech-Language Pathologists | 97.7% | 18.5% |
| 19. Legal Secretaries | 96.8% | 18.4% |
| 20. Healthcare Support Workers, All Other | 90.4% | 17.1% |
| 21. Healthcare Practitioners and Technical Workers, All Other | 88.9% | 15.9% |
| 22. Elementary School Teachers, Except Special Education | 81.3% | 15.8% |
| 23. Interviewers, Except Eligibility and Loan | 84.4% | 15.6% |
| 24. Meeting, Convention, and Event Planners | 82.9% | 15.6% |
| 25. Billing and Posting Clerks | 89.6% | 15.3% |

## Jobs with the Most Openings Employing a High Percentage of Women

| Job | Percent Women | Annual Openings |
|---|---|---|
| 1. Registered Nurses | 90.7% | 103,900 |
| 2. Office Clerks, General | 82.2% | 77,090 |
| 3. Elementary School Teachers, Except Special Education | 81.3% | 59,650 |
| 4. Home Health Aides | 88.0% | 55,270 |
| 5. Childcare Workers | 95.8% | 52,310 |
| 6. Receptionists and Information Clerks | 92.4% | 48,020 |
| 7. Personal Care Aides | 82.7% | 47,780 |
| 8. Bookkeeping, Accounting, and Auditing Clerks | 90.0% | 46,040 |
| 9. Executive Secretaries and Executive Administrative Assistants | 96.8% | 41,920 |
| 10. Teacher Assistants | 91.5% | 41,270 |
| 11. Licensed Practical and Licensed Vocational Nurses | 91.4% | 39,130 |
| 12. Secretaries and Administrative Assistants, Except Legal, Medical, and Executive | 96.8% | 36,550 |
| 13. Tellers | 87.1% | 28,440 |
| 14. Middle School Teachers, Except Special and Career/Technical Education | 81.3% | 25,110 |
| 15. Hairdressers, Hairstylists, and Cosmetologists | 87.0% | 21,950 |
| 16. Medical Assistants | 90.4% | 21,780 |
| 17. Medical Secretaries | 96.8% | 18,900 |
| 18. Preschool Teachers, Except Special Education | 98.4% | 17,830 |
| 19. Billing and Posting Clerks | 89.6% | 16,760 |

*(continued)*

*(continued)*

### Jobs with the Most Openings Employing a High Percentage of Women

| Job | Percent Women | Annual Openings |
|---|---|---|
| 20. Dental Assistants | 96.7% | 16,100 |
| 21. Child, Family, and School Social Workers | 81.5% | 10,960 |
| 22. Paralegals and Legal Assistants | 86.7% | 10,400 |
| 23. Dental Hygienists | 96.1% | 9,840 |
| 24. Interviewers, Except Eligibility and Loan | 84.4% | 9,210 |
| 25. Legal Secretaries | 96.8% | 8,380 |

# Best Jobs Employing a High Percentage of Men

If you haven't already read the intro to the previous group of lists, "Best Jobs Employing a High Percentage of Women," consider doing so. Much of the content there applies to these lists as well.

I didn't include these groups of lists with the assumption that men should consider only jobs with high percentages of men or that women should consider only jobs with high percentages of women. Instead, these lists are here because I think they are interesting and perhaps helpful in considering nontraditional career options. For example, some men would do very well in and enjoy some of the jobs with high percentages of women but may not have considered them seriously. Similarly, some women would very much enjoy and do well in some jobs that traditionally have been held by high percentages of men. I hope that these lists help you consider options that you simply didn't seriously consider because of gender stereotypes.

In the jobs on the following lists, more than 80% of the workers are men, but increasing numbers of women are entering many of these jobs. Note that some of the jobs listed as having 100% men probably include a few women but have such a small total workforce that the sample queried by the Census Department's Current Population Survey did not include any female workers.

### Best Jobs Employing the Highest Percentage of Men

| Job | Percent Men |
|---|---|
| 1. Agricultural Engineers | 100.0% |
| 2. Brickmasons and Blockmasons | 100.0% |
| 3. Captains, Mates, and Pilots of Water Vessels | 100.0% |

## Best Jobs Employing the Highest Percentage of Men

| Job | Percent Men |
|---|---|
| 4. Electrical and Electronics Repairers, Powerhouse, Substation, and Relay | 100.0% |
| 5. Elevator Installers and Repairers | 100.0% |
| 6. Nuclear Engineers | 100.0% |
| 7. Railroad Brake, Signal, and Switch Operators | 100.0% |
| 8. Rail-Track Laying and Maintenance Equipment Operators | 100.0% |
| 9. Sailors and Marine Oilers | 100.0% |
| 10. Septic Tank Servicers and Sewer Pipe Cleaners | 100.0% |
| 11. Ship Engineers | 100.0% |
| 12. Subway and Streetcar Operators | 100.0% |
| 13. Bus and Truck Mechanics and Diesel Engine Specialists | 99.7% |
| 14. Cement Masons and Concrete Finishers | 99.6% |
| 15. Heating, Air Conditioning, and Refrigeration Mechanics and Installers | 99.4% |
| 16. Operating Engineers and Other Construction Equipment Operators | 99.1% |
| 17. Pipelayers | 99.0% |
| 18. Plumbers, Pipefitters, and Steamfitters | 99.0% |
| 19. Mobile Heavy Equipment Mechanics, Except Engines | 98.6% |
| 20. Automotive Service Technicians and Mechanics | 98.4% |
| 21. Electrical Power-Line Installers and Repairers | 98.4% |
| 22. Security and Fire Alarm Systems Installers | 98.4% |
| 23. Drywall and Ceiling Tile Installers | 98.2% |
| 24. Tapers | 98.2% |
| 25. Carpenters | 98.1% |
| 26. Highway Maintenance Workers | 98.1% |
| 27. Construction Laborers | 97.7% |
| 28. Pest Control Workers | 97.7% |
| 29. Sheet Metal Workers | 97.6% |
| 30. Electricians | 97.5% |
| 31. Airline Pilots, Copilots, and Flight Engineers | 97.4% |
| 32. Commercial Pilots | 97.4% |
| 33. Supervisors of Construction and Extraction Workers | 97.4% |
| 34. Excavating and Loading Machine and Dragline Operators | 97.0% |
| 35. Industrial Machinery Mechanics | 97.0% |
| 36. Painters, Construction and Maintenance | 97.0% |
| 37. Construction and Related Workers, All Other | 96.6% |
| 38. Telecommunications Line Installers and Repairers | 96.6% |
| 39. Tile and Marble Setters | 96.6% |

*(continued)*

*(continued)*

## Best Jobs Employing the Highest Percentage of Men

| Job | Percent Men |
|---|---|
| 40. Heavy and Tractor-Trailer Truck Drivers | 96.3% |
| 41. Insulation Workers, Floor, Ceiling, and Wall | 96.3% |
| 42. Insulation Workers, Mechanical | 96.3% |
| 43. Structural Iron and Steel Workers | 96.2% |
| 44. Aircraft Mechanics and Service Technicians | 96.1% |
| 45. Landscaping and Groundskeeping Workers | 96.0% |
| 46. Tree Trimmers and Pruners | 96.0% |
| 47. Railroad Conductors and Yardmasters | 95.9% |
| 48. First-Line Supervisors of Landscaping, Lawn Service, and Groundskeeping Workers | 95.8% |
| 49. Boilermakers | 95.7% |
| 50. Firefighters | 95.5% |
| 51. Helpers—Brickmasons, Blockmasons, Stonemasons, and Tile and Marble Setters | 95.2% |
| 52. Helpers—Carpenters | 95.2% |
| 53. Helpers—Electricians | 95.2% |
| 54. Helpers—Pipelayers, Plumbers, Pipefitters, and Steamfitters | 95.2% |
| 55. Mechanical Engineers | 95.0% |
| 56. Nuclear Power Reactor Operators | 94.7% |
| 57. Installation, Maintenance, and Repair Workers, All Other | 94.5% |
| 58. Construction and Building Inspectors | 94.4% |
| 59. Construction Managers | 93.6% |
| 60. Surveying and Mapping Technicians | 93.5% |
| 61. Refuse and Recyclable Material Collectors | 93.2% |
| 62. Water and Wastewater Treatment Plant and System Operators | 93.0% |
| 63. Hazardous Materials Removal Workers | 92.9% |
| 64. First-Line Supervisors of Fire Fighting and Prevention Workers | 92.3% |
| 65. Telecommunications Equipment Installers and Repairers, Except Line Installers | 92.2% |
| 66. Audio and Video Equipment Technicians | 91.8% |
| 67. Civil Engineers | 91.7% |
| 68. Materials Engineers | 91.7% |
| 69. Transportation Inspectors | 91.5% |
| 70. Electrical Engineers | 91.3% |
| 71. Electronics Engineers, Except Computer | 91.3% |
| 72. Architectural and Engineering Managers | 91.2% |
| 73. First-Line Supervisors of Mechanics, Installers, and Repairers | 90.6% |
| 74. Computer Hardware Engineers | 90.4% |
| 75. Sales Engineers | 90.3% |

## Best Jobs Employing the Highest Percentage of Men

| Job | Percent Men |
|---|---|
| 76. Mining and Geological Engineers, Including Mining Safety Engineers | 90.0% |
| 77. Mixing and Blending Machine Setters, Operators, and Tenders | 89.7% |
| 78. Morticians, Undertakers, and Funeral Directors | 89.7% |
| 79. Medical Equipment Repairers | 89.4% |
| 80. Aerospace Engineers | 88.9% |
| 81. Biomedical Engineers | 88.2% |
| 82. First-Line Supervisors of Police and Detectives | 88.0% |
| 83. Farmers, Ranchers, and Other Agricultural Managers | 87.1% |
| 84. Engineers, All Other | 86.4% |
| 85. Clergy | 86.2% |
| 86. Transportation, Storage, and Distribution Managers | 85.8% |
| 87. Film and Video Editors | 85.7% |
| 88. Industrial Production Managers | 85.7% |
| 89. Cost Estimators | 85.6% |
| 90. Police and Sheriff's Patrol Officers | 85.4% |
| 91. Taxi Drivers and Chauffeurs | 84.8% |
| 92. Coaches and Scouts | 84.0% |
| 93. Economists | 83.9% |
| 94. First-Line Supervisors of Production and Operating Workers | 83.7% |
| 95. Dishwashers | 83.6% |
| 96. Civil Engineering Technicians | 83.0% |
| 97. Electrical and Electronic Engineering Technicians | 83.0% |
| 98. Engineering Technicians, Except Drafters, All Other | 83.0% |
| 99. Environmental Engineering Technicians | 83.0% |
| 100. Industrial Engineering Technicians | 83.0% |
| 101. Health and Safety Engineers, Except Mining Safety Engineers and Inspectors | 82.1% |
| 102. Industrial Engineers | 82.1% |
| 103. Extruding, Forming, Pressing, and Compacting Machine Setters, Operators, and Tenders | 80.6% |

The jobs in the following four lists are derived from the preceding list of the jobs employing the highest percentage of men.

## Best Jobs Overall Employing a High Percentage of Men

| Job | Percent Men | Annual Earnings | Percent Growth | Annual Openings |
|---|---|---|---|---|
| 1. Civil Engineers | 91.7% | $77,560 | 24.3% | 11,460 |
| 2. Construction Managers | 93.6% | $83,860 | 17.2% | 13,770 |
| 3. Cost Estimators | 85.6% | $57,860 | 25.3% | 10,360 |
| 4. Supervisors of Construction and Extraction Workers | 97.4% | $58,680 | 15.4% | 24,220 |
| 5. Heating, Air Conditioning, and Refrigeration Mechanics and Installers | 99.4% | $42,530 | 28.1% | 13,620 |
| 6. Industrial Engineers | 82.1% | $76,100 | 14.2% | 8,540 |
| 7. Firefighters | 95.5% | $45,250 | 18.5% | 15,280 |
| 8. Biomedical Engineers | 88.2% | $81,540 | 72.0% | 1,490 |
| 9. Plumbers, Pipefitters, and Steamfitters | 99.0% | $46,660 | 15.3% | 17,550 |
| 10. Electricians | 97.5% | $48,250 | 11.9% | 25,090 |
| 11. Construction Laborers | 97.7% | $29,280 | 20.5% | 33,940 |
| 12. Construction and Building Inspectors | 94.4% | $52,360 | 16.8% | 3,970 |
| 13. Commercial Pilots | 97.4% | $67,500 | 18.5% | 2,060 |
| 14. Clergy | 86.2% | $43,970 | 12.7% | 21,770 |
| 15. Police and Sheriff's Patrol Officers | 85.4% | $53,540 | 8.7% | 22,790 |
| 16. Carpenters | 98.1% | $39,530 | 12.9% | 32,540 |
| 17. Engineers, All Other | 86.4% | $90,270 | 6.7% | 5,020 |
| 18. Water and Wastewater Treatment Plant and System Operators | 93.0% | $40,770 | 19.8% | 4,690 |
| 19. Architectural and Engineering Managers | 91.2% | $119,260 | 6.2% | 4,870 |
| 20. Coaches and Scouts | 84.0% | $28,340 | 24.8% | 9,920 |
| 21. Heavy and Tractor-Trailer Truck Drivers | 96.3% | $37,770 | 12.9% | 55,460 |
| 22. Captains, Mates, and Pilots of Water Vessels | 100.0% | $64,180 | 17.3% | 1,950 |
| 23. First-Line Supervisors of Police and Detectives | 88.0% | $78,260 | 8.1% | 5,050 |
| 24. Landscaping and Groundskeeping Workers | 96.0% | $23,400 | 18.0% | 36,220 |
| 25. Mechanical Engineers | 95.0% | $78,160 | 6.0% | 7,570 |

## Best-Paying Jobs Employing a High Percentage of Men

| Job | Percent Men | Annual Earnings |
|---|---|---|
| 1. Architectural and Engineering Managers | 91.2% | $119,260 |
| 2. Airline Pilots, Copilots, and Flight Engineers | 97.4% | $103,210 |
| 3. Nuclear Engineers | 100.0% | $99,920 |
| 4. Computer Hardware Engineers | 90.4% | $98,810 |

## Best-Paying Jobs Employing a High Percentage of Men

| Job | Percent Men | Annual Earnings |
|---|---|---|
| 5. Aerospace Engineers | 88.9% | $97,480 |
| 6. Engineers, All Other | 86.4% | $90,270 |
| 7. Electronics Engineers, Except Computer | 91.3% | $90,170 |
| 8. Economists | 83.9% | $89,450 |
| 9. Sales Engineers | 90.3% | $87,390 |
| 10. Industrial Production Managers | 85.7% | $87,160 |
| 11. Electrical Engineers | 91.3% | $84,540 |
| 12. Construction Managers | 93.6% | $83,860 |
| 13. Materials Engineers | 91.7% | $83,120 |
| 14. Mining and Geological Engineers, Including Mining Safety Engineers | 90.0% | $82,870 |
| 15. Biomedical Engineers | 88.2% | $81,540 |
| 16. Transportation, Storage, and Distribution Managers | 85.8% | $80,210 |
| 17. First-Line Supervisors of Police and Detectives | 88.0% | $78,260 |
| 18. Mechanical Engineers | 95.0% | $78,160 |
| 19. Civil Engineers | 91.7% | $77,560 |
| 20. Industrial Engineers | 82.1% | $76,100 |
| 21. Nuclear Power Reactor Operators | 94.7% | $75,650 |
| 22. Health and Safety Engineers, Except Mining Safety Engineers and Inspectors | 82.1% | $75,430 |
| 23. Agricultural Engineers | 100.0% | $71,090 |
| 24. Elevator Installers and Repairers | 100.0% | $70,910 |
| 25. First-Line Supervisors of Fire Fighting and Prevention Workers | 92.3% | $68,240 |

## Fastest-Growing Jobs Employing a High Percentage of Men

| Job | Percent Men | Percent Growth |
|---|---|---|
| 1. Biomedical Engineers | 88.2% | 72.0% |
| 2. Environmental Engineering Technicians | 83.0% | 30.1% |
| 3. Heating, Air Conditioning, and Refrigeration Mechanics and Installers | 99.4% | 28.1% |
| 4. Medical Equipment Repairers | 89.4% | 27.2% |
| 5. Tree Trimmers and Pruners | 96.0% | 26.3% |
| 6. Helpers—Pipelayers, Plumbers, Pipefitters, and Steamfitters | 95.2% | 25.7% |
| 7. Cost Estimators | 85.6% | 25.3% |
| 8. Coaches and Scouts | 84.0% | 24.8% |

*(continued)*

*(continued)*

## Fastest-Growing Jobs Employing a High Percentage of Men

| Job | Percent Men | Percent Growth |
|---|---|---|
| 9. Security and Fire Alarm Systems Installers | 98.4% | 24.8% |
| 10. Helpers—Electricians | 95.2% | 24.7% |
| 11. Civil Engineers | 91.7% | 24.3% |
| 12. Septic Tank Servicers and Sewer Pipe Cleaners | 100.0% | 23.8% |
| 13. Helpers—Carpenters | 95.2% | 23.3% |
| 14. Construction Laborers | 97.7% | 20.5% |
| 15. Surveying and Mapping Technicians | 93.5% | 20.4% |
| 16. Water and Wastewater Treatment Plant and System Operators | 93.0% | 19.8% |
| 17. Insulation Workers, Mechanical | 96.3% | 19.4% |
| 18. Nuclear Power Reactor Operators | 94.7% | 18.9% |
| 19. Boilermakers | 95.7% | 18.8% |
| 20. Subway and Streetcar Operators | 100.0% | 18.8% |
| 21. Refuse and Recyclable Material Collectors | 93.2% | 18.6% |
| 22. Ship Engineers | 100.0% | 18.6% |
| 23. Commercial Pilots | 97.4% | 18.5% |
| 24. Firefighters | 95.5% | 18.5% |
| 25. Transportation Inspectors | 91.5% | 18.3% |

## Jobs with the Most Openings Employing a High Percentage of Men

| Job | Percent Men | Annual Openings |
|---|---|---|
| 1. Heavy and Tractor-Trailer Truck Drivers | 96.3% | 55,460 |
| 2. Landscaping and Groundskeeping Workers | 96.0% | 36,220 |
| 3. Construction Laborers | 97.7% | 33,940 |
| 4. Carpenters | 98.1% | 32,540 |
| 5. Dishwashers | 83.6% | 27,570 |
| 6. Electricians | 97.5% | 25,090 |
| 7. Supervisors of Construction and Extraction Workers | 97.4% | 24,220 |
| 8. Police and Sheriff's Patrol Officers | 85.4% | 22,790 |
| 9. Clergy | 86.2% | 21,770 |
| 10. Automotive Service Technicians and Mechanics | 98.4% | 18,170 |
| 11. Plumbers, Pipefitters, and Steamfitters | 99.0% | 17,550 |
| 12. Firefighters | 95.5% | 15,280 |
| 13. Construction Managers | 93.6% | 13,770 |

## Jobs with the Most Openings Employing a High Percentage of Men

| Job | Percent Men | Annual Openings |
|---|---|---|
| 14. First-Line Supervisors of Mechanics, Installers, and Repairers | 90.6% | 13,650 |
| 15. Heating, Air Conditioning, and Refrigeration Mechanics and Installers | 99.4% | 13,620 |
| 16. Operating Engineers and Other Construction Equipment Operators | 99.1% | 11,820 |
| 17. Civil Engineers | 91.7% | 11,460 |
| 18. Painters, Construction and Maintenance | 97.0% | 10,650 |
| 19. Cost Estimators | 85.6% | 10,360 |
| 20. Coaches and Scouts | 84.0% | 9,920 |
| 21. First-Line Supervisors of Production and Operating Workers | 83.7% | 9,190 |
| 22. Industrial Engineers | 82.1% | 8,540 |
| 23. Taxi Drivers and Chauffeurs | 84.8% | 7,730 |
| 24. Cement Masons and Concrete Finishers | 99.6% | 7,640 |
| 25. Mechanical Engineers | 95.0% | 7,570 |

# Best Jobs with a High Percentage of Urban or Rural Workers

Some people have a strong preference for an urban setting. They want to live and work where there's more energy and excitement, more access to the arts, more diversity, more really good restaurants, and better public transportation. On the other hand, some prefer the open spaces, closeness to nature, quiet, and inexpensive housing of rural locations. If you are strongly attracted to either setting, you'll be interested in the following lists.

I identified urban jobs as those for which 40 percent or more of the workforce is located in the 38 most populous metropolitan areas of the United States. These 38 metro areas—the most populous 10 percent of all U.S. metro areas, according to the Census Bureau—consist primarily of built-up communities, unlike smaller metro areas, which consist of a core city surrounded by a lot of countryside. In the following lists of urban jobs, you'll see a figure called the "urban ratio" for each job that represents the percentage of the total U.S. workforce for the job that is located in those 38 huge metro areas.

The Census Bureau also identifies 173 nonmetropolitan areas—areas that have no city of 50,000 people and a total population of less than 100,000. I identified rural jobs as those for which 15 percent or more of the total U.S. workforce is located in these nonmetropolitan areas. In the following lists of rural jobs, you'll see a figure called the "rural ratio" that represents the percentage of the total U.S. workforce for the job that is located in nonmetropolitan areas.

The "best-of" lists of both urban and rural jobs are ordered by the usual three economic measures: earnings, growth, and openings.

## Jobs with the Highest Percentage of Urban Workers

| Job | Urban Ratio |
|---|---|
| 1. Landscape Architects | 58.6% |
| 2. Materials Scientists | 56.9% |
| 3. Biomedical Engineers | 56.0% |
| 4. Actuaries | 54.6% |
| 5. Curators | 54.3% |
| 6. Epidemiologists | 53.7% |
| 7. Medical Equipment Repairers | 50.5% |
| 8. Tapers | 49.6% |
| 9. Political Science Teachers, Postsecondary | 48.7% |
| 10. Psychologists, All Other | 47.9% |
| 11. Hydrologists | 47.8% |
| 12. Podiatrists | 46.7% |
| 13. Environmental Engineering Technicians | 46.5% |
| 14. Training and Development Managers | 46.2% |
| 15. Cartographers and Photogrammetrists | 46.1% |
| 16. Materials Engineers | 46.0% |
| 17. Economics Teachers, Postsecondary | 45.9% |
| 18. Museum Technicians and Conservators | 45.9% |
| 19. Food Scientists and Technologists | 45.7% |
| 20. Physics Teachers, Postsecondary | 45.2% |
| 21. Arbitrators, Mediators, and Conciliators | 44.9% |
| 22. Directors, Religious Activities and Education | 44.4% |
| 23. Nuclear Medicine Technologists | 44.4% |
| 24. Philosophy and Religion Teachers, Postsecondary | 44.1% |
| 25. Skincare Specialists | 43.0% |
| 26. Sociology Teachers, Postsecondary | 43.0% |
| 27. Audiologists | 42.6% |
| 28. Mathematicians | 42.4% |
| 29. Chiropractors | 42.3% |
| 30. Occupational Therapy Assistants | 42.0% |
| 31. Athletic Trainers | 41.6% |
| 32. Law Teachers, Postsecondary | 41.6% |
| 33. Set and Exhibit Designers | 41.6% |
| 34. Chemistry Teachers, Postsecondary | 41.1% |

## Jobs with the Highest Percentage of Urban Workers

| Job | Urban Ratio |
|---|---|
| 35. Elevator Installers and Repairers | 41.1% |
| 36. Animal Trainers | 40.9% |
| 37. Anthropology and Archeology Teachers, Postsecondary | 40.9% |
| 38. Astronomers | 40.8% |
| 39. Economists | 40.6% |
| 40. Sociologists | 40.2% |
| 41. Biological Scientists, All Other | 40.1% |
| 42. Environmental Science and Protection Technicians, Including Health | 40.1% |
| 43. Statisticians | 40.1% |

## Best Jobs Overall Employing a High Percentage of Urban Workers

| Job | Urban Ratio | Annual Earnings | Percent Growth | Annual Openings |
|---|---|---|---|---|
| 1. Biomedical Engineers | 56.0% | $81,540 | 72.0% | 1,490 |
| 2. Actuaries | 54.6% | $87,650 | 21.4% | 1,000 |
| 3. Chiropractors | 42.3% | $67,200 | 19.5% | 1,820 |
| 4. Medical Equipment Repairers | 50.5% | $44,490 | 27.2% | 2,320 |
| 5. Occupational Therapy Assistants | 42.0% | $51,010 | 29.8% | 1,180 |
| 6. Biological Scientists, All Other | 40.1% | $68,220 | 18.8% | 1,610 |
| 7. Environmental Science and Protection Technicians, Including Health | 40.1% | $41,380 | 28.9% | 2,520 |
| 8. Skincare Specialists | 43.0% | $28,920 | 37.8% | 2,030 |
| 9. Athletic Trainers | 41.6% | $41,600 | 36.9% | 1,150 |
| 10. Environmental Engineering Technicians | 46.5% | $43,390 | 30.1% | 1,040 |
| 11. Mathematicians | 42.4% | $99,380 | 22.4% | 150 |
| 12. Training and Development Managers | 46.2% | $89,170 | 11.9% | 1,010 |
| 13. Psychologists, All Other | 47.9% | $89,900 | 14.4% | 680 |
| 14. Landscape Architects | 58.6% | $62,090 | 19.7% | 980 |
| 15. Law Teachers, Postsecondary | 41.6% | $94,260 | 15.1% | 400 |
| 16. Audiologists | 42.6% | $66,660 | 25.0% | 580 |
| 17. Cartographers and Photogrammetrists | 46.1% | $54,510 | 26.8% | 640 |
| 18. Animal Trainers | 40.9% | $26,580 | 20.4% | 1,900 |
| 19. Nuclear Medicine Technologists | 44.4% | $68,560 | 16.3% | 670 |
| 20. Statisticians | 40.1% | $72,830 | 13.1% | 960 |
| 21. Curators | 54.3% | $48,450 | 23.0% | 620 |

*(continued)*

*(continued)*

## Best Jobs Overall Employing a High Percentage of Urban Workers

| Job | Urban Ratio | Annual Earnings | Percent Growth | Annual Openings |
|---|---|---|---|---|
| 22. Economics Teachers, Postsecondary | 45.9% | $83,370 | 15.1% | 400 |
| 23. Chemistry Teachers, Postsecondary | 41.1% | $70,520 | 15.1% | 600 |
| 24. Food Scientists and Technologists | 45.7% | $60,180 | 16.3% | 690 |
| 25. Hydrologists | 47.8% | $75,690 | 18.2% | 380 |

## Jobs with the Highest Percentage of Rural Workers

| Job | Rural Ratio |
|---|---|
| 1. Highway Maintenance Workers | 33.7% |
| 2. Water and Wastewater Treatment Plant and System Operators | 28.1% |
| 3. First-Line Supervisors of Correctional Officers | 27.6% |
| 4. Electrical Power-Line Installers and Repairers | 26.0% |
| 5. Excavating and Loading Machine and Dragline Operators | 25.0% |
| 6. Career/Technical Education Teachers, Secondary School | 22.5% |
| 7. Police, Fire, and Ambulance Dispatchers | 22.4% |
| 8. Extruding, Forming, Pressing, and Compacting Machine Setters, Operators, and Tenders | 22.2% |
| 9. Conservation Scientists | 22.0% |
| 10. Hotel, Motel, and Resort Desk Clerks | 21.2% |
| 11. Court, Municipal, and License Clerks | 20.8% |
| 12. Mining and Geological Engineers, Including Mining Safety Engineers | 20.4% |
| 13. Emergency Medical Technicians and Paramedics | 20.3% |
| 14. Morticians, Undertakers, and Funeral Directors | 19.8% |
| 15. Mobile Heavy Equipment Mechanics, Except Engines | 18.3% |
| 16. Education Administrators, Elementary and Secondary School | 18.2% |
| 17. Refuse and Recyclable Material Collectors | 18.2% |
| 18. Mixing and Blending Machine Setters, Operators, and Tenders | 17.7% |
| 19. Operating Engineers and Other Construction Equipment Operators | 17.4% |
| 20. Zoologists and Wildlife Biologists | 16.7% |
| 21. Bus and Truck Mechanics and Diesel Engine Specialists | 16.6% |
| 22. Cooks, Institution and Cafeteria | 16.6% |
| 23. Industrial Production Managers | 16.6% |
| 24. Kindergarten Teachers, Except Special Education | 16.2% |
| 25. Library Technicians | 16.2% |
| 26. Librarians | 16.1% |

## Jobs with the Highest Percentage of Rural Workers

| Job | Rural Ratio |
|---|---|
| 27. Industrial Machinery Mechanics | 16.0% |
| 28. Postal Service Mail Carriers | 15.9% |
| 29. Surveying and Mapping Technicians | 15.3% |
| 30. Funeral Attendants | 15.2% |

## Best Jobs Overall Employing a High Percentage of Rural Workers

| Job | Rural Ratio | Annual Earnings | Percent Growth | Annual Openings |
|---|---|---|---|---|
| 1. Court, Municipal, and License Clerks | 20.8% | $34,390 | 8.2% | 4,460 |
| 2. Excavating and Loading Machine and Dragline Operators | 25.0% | $36,920 | 8.6% | 2,850 |
| 3. Highway Maintenance Workers | 33.7% | $34,780 | 8.5% | 5,200 |
| 4. Extruding, Forming, Pressing, and Compacting Machine Setters, Operators, and Tenders | 22.2% | $31,210 | 15.0% | 2,960 |
| 5. First-Line Supervisors of Correctional Officers | 27.6% | $55,910 | 8.5% | 1,940 |
| 6. Emergency Medical Technicians and Paramedics | 20.3% | $30,360 | 9.0% | 6,200 |
| 7. Funeral Attendants | 15.2% | $22,990 | 26.3% | 2,550 |
| 8. Mobile Heavy Equipment Mechanics, Except Engines | 18.3% | $44,830 | 8.7% | 3,770 |
| 9. Library Technicians | 16.2% | $29,860 | 8.8% | 6,470 |
| 10. Electrical Power-Line Installers and Repairers | 26.0% | $58,030 | 4.5% | 4,550 |
| 11. Industrial Machinery Mechanics | 16.0% | $45,420 | 7.3% | 6,240 |
| 12. Morticians, Undertakers, and Funeral Directors | 19.8% | $54,330 | 11.9% | 960 |
| 13. Bus and Truck Mechanics and Diesel Engine Specialists | 16.6% | $40,850 | 5.7% | 7,530 |
| 14. Conservation Scientists | 22.0% | $59,310 | 11.9% | 410 |
| 15. Librarians | 16.1% | $54,500 | 7.8% | 5,450 |
| 16. Career/Technical Education Teachers, Secondary School | 22.5% | $54,310 | 9.6% | 3,850 |
| 17. Cooks, Institution and Cafeteria | 16.6% | $22,730 | 9.7% | 13,810 |
| 18. Mixing and Blending Machine Setters, Operators, and Tenders | 17.7% | $32,870 | 15.5% | 4,610 |
| 19. Police, Fire, and Ambulance Dispatchers | 22.4% | $35,370 | 17.8% | 3,840 |
| 20. Zoologists and Wildlife Biologists | 16.7% | $57,430 | 12.8% | 880 |
| 21. Postal Service Mail Carriers | 15.9% | $53,860 | −1.1% | 10,720 |

*(continued)*

*(continued)*

| Best Jobs Overall Employing a High Percentage of Rural Workers | | | | |
|---|---|---|---|---|
| Job | Rural Ratio | Annual Earnings | Percent Growth | Annual Openings |
| 22. Hotel, Motel, and Resort Desk Clerks | 21.2% | $19,930 | 13.7% | 10,950 |
| 23. Industrial Production Managers | 16.6% | $87,160 | –7.7% | 5,470 |
| 24. Surveying and Mapping Technicians | 15.3% | $37,900 | 20.4% | 2,940 |
| 25. Mining and Geological Engineers, Including Mining Safety Engineers | 20.4% | $82,870 | 15.3% | 260 |

# Best Jobs Lists Based on Levels of Education and Experience

The lists in this section organize the 400 best jobs into groups based on the education or training typically required for entry. Unlike in many of the previous sections, here you won't find separate lists for highest pay, growth, or number of openings. Instead, I provide one list that includes all the occupations in my database that fit into each of the education levels and that ranks them by their total combined score for earnings, growth, and number of openings.

These lists can help you identify a job with higher earnings or upward mobility that requires a similar level of education to the job you now hold. For example, you will find jobs within the same level of education that require similar skills, yet one pays significantly better than the other, is projected to grow more rapidly, or has significantly more job openings per year. This information can help you leverage your present skills and experience into jobs that might provide better long-term career opportunities.

You can also use these lists to explore possible job options if you were to get additional training, education, or work experience. For example, you can use these lists to identify occupations that offer high potential and then look into the education or training required to get the jobs that interest you most.

The lists can also help you when you plan your education. For example, you might be thinking about vocational training but you aren't sure what kind of work you want to do. The lists show that Tapers need moderate-term on-the-job training and earn $45,490, while Dental Laboratory Technicians need long-term on-the-job training and earn an average of only $35,140. If you want higher earnings with less training, this information might make a difference in your choice.

## The Education Levels

On average, a clear relationship exists between education and earnings—the more education or training you have, the more you are likely to earn. The lists that follow arrange all the jobs that met my criteria for inclusion in this book (see the Introduction) by level of education, training, and work experience. These are the levels typically required for a new entrant to begin work in each occupation.

I included on each list all the occupations out of the best 400 that fit the education level for that list. Thirty-two of the occupations appear on more than one list. For example, the occupation Statisticians appears on two lists because it is linked to two occupational specializations (O*NET-SOC titles) that usually require a master's degree, Biostatisticians and Statisticians, and one that usually requires only a bachelor's degree, Clinical Data Managers.

Each list is sorted by the combined scores of each occupation on earnings, job growth, and job openings.

The following definitions are used by the federal government to classify jobs based on the minimum level of education or training typically required for entry into a job. I used these definitions to construct the lists in this section. Use the training and education level descriptions as guidelines that can help you understand what is generally required, but understand that you will need to learn more about specific requirements before you make a decision on one career over another.

❋ **Short-term on-the-job training:** It is possible to work in these occupations and achieve an average level of performance within a few days or weeks through on-the-job training.

❋ **Moderate-term on-the-job training:** Occupations requiring this type of training can be performed adequately after a 1- to 12-month period of combined on-the-job and informal training. Typically, untrained workers observe experienced workers performing tasks and are gradually moved into progressively more difficult assignments.

❋ **Long-term on-the-job training:** This training requires more than 12 months of on-the-job training or combined work experience and formal classroom instruction. This includes occupations that use formal apprenticeships for training workers that may take up to four years. It also includes intensive occupation-specific, employer-sponsored training, such as police academies. Furthermore, it includes occupations that require natural talent that must be developed over many years.

❋ **Work experience in a related occupation:** This type of job requires experience in a related occupation. For example, police detectives are selected based on their experience as police patrol officers.

❋ **Postsecondary vocational training:** This requirement usually involves a few months to less than one year of training. In a few instances, as many as four years of training may be required.

❋ **Associate degree:** This degree usually requires two years of full-time academic work beyond high school.

❋ **Bachelor's degree:** This degree requires approximately four to five years of full-time academic work beyond high school.

⟡ **Work experience plus degree:** Many jobs in this category are management-related and require some experience in a related nonmanagerial position. Others require completion of a specific formal training program.

⟡ **Master's degree:** Completion of a master's degree usually requires one to two years of full-time study beyond the bachelor's degree.

⟡ **Doctoral degree:** This degree normally requires two or more years of full-time academic work beyond the bachelor's degree.

⟡ **First professional degree:** This type of degree normally requires a minimum of two years of education beyond the bachelor's degree and frequently requires three years.

# Another Warning About the Data

I warned you in the Introduction to use caution in interpreting the data in this book, and I want to do it again here. The occupational data I use is the most accurate available anywhere, but it has its limitations. The education or training requirements for entry into a job are those typically required as a minimum, but some people working in those jobs may have considerably more or different credentials. For example, although a bachelor's degree is considered the usual requirement for Construction Managers, more than one-third of the people working in this occupation have no formal education beyond high school. On the other hand, Fitness Trainers and Aerobics Instructors usually need to have completed only postsecondary vocational training, but more than half of these workers have college degrees.

You also need to be cautious about assuming that more education or training always leads to higher income. It is true that people with jobs that require long-term on-the-job training typically earn more than people with jobs that require short-term on-the-job training. (For the jobs in this book, the average annual difference is $23,210.) However, some people with short-term on-the-job training earn more than the average for the highest-paying occupations listed in this book; furthermore, some people with long-term on-the-job training earn much less than the average shown in this book—this is particularly true of people just beginning in these careers.

So as you browse the following lists, please use them as a way to be encouraged rather than discouraged. Education and training are very important for success in the labor market of the future, but so are ability, drive, initiative, and—yes—luck.

Having said this, I encourage you to get as much education and training as you can. You used to be able to get your schooling and then close the schoolbooks forever, but this isn't a good attitude to have now. You will probably need to continue learning new things throughout your working life. This can be done by going back to school, which is a good thing for many people. But other workers may learn through workshops, adult education programs, certification programs, employer training, professional conferences, Internet training, or reading related books and magazines. Upgrading your computer skills—and other technical skills—is particularly important in our rapidly changing workplace, and you avoid doing so at your peril.

## Best Jobs Requiring Short-Term On-the-Job Training

| Job | Annual Earnings | Percent Growth | Annual Openings |
|---|---|---|---|
| 1. Bill and Account Collectors | $31,310 | 19.3% | 15,690 |
| 2. Home Health Aides | $20,560 | 50.0% | 55,270 |
| 3. Personal Care Aides | $19,640 | 46.0% | 47,780 |
| 4. Refuse and Recyclable Material Collectors | $32,640 | 18.6% | 7,110 |
| 5. Receptionists and Information Clerks | $25,240 | 15.2% | 48,020 |
| 6. Office Clerks, General | $26,610 | 11.9% | 77,090 |
| 7. Teachers and Instructors, All Other | $29,820 | 14.7% | 22,570 |
| 8. Landscaping and Groundskeeping Workers | $23,400 | 18.0% | 36,220 |
| 9. Interviewers, Except Eligibility and Loan | $28,820 | 15.6% | 9,210 |
| 10. Healthcare Support Workers, All Other | $30,280 | 17.1% | 5,670 |
| 11. Helpers—Electricians | $27,220 | 24.7% | 4,800 |
| 12. Tree Trimmers and Pruners | $30,450 | 26.3% | 1,720 |
| 13. Helpers—Pipelayers, Plumbers, Pipefitters, and Steamfitters | $26,740 | 25.7% | 3,730 |
| 14. Security Guards | $23,920 | 14.2% | 37,390 |
| 15. Helpers—Carpenters | $25,760 | 23.3% | 3,530 |
| 16. Protective Service Workers, All Other | $29,890 | 14.0% | 7,150 |
| 17. Physical Therapist Aides | $23,680 | 36.3% | 2,340 |
| 18. Postal Service Mail Carriers | $53,860 | –1.1% | 10,720 |
| 19. Combined Food Preparation and Serving Workers, Including Fast Food | $17,950 | 14.6% | 96,720 |
| 20. Funeral Attendants | $22,990 | 26.3% | 2,550 |
| 21. Retail Salespersons | $20,670 | 8.3% | 162,690 |
| 22. Helpers—Brickmasons, Blockmasons, Stonemasons, and Tile and Marble Setters | $27,780 | 16.4% | 1,890 |
| 23. Teacher Assistants | $23,220 | 10.3% | 41,270 |
| 24. Taxi Drivers and Chauffeurs | $22,440 | 15.5% | 7,730 |
| 25. Nonfarm Animal Caretakers | $19,550 | 20.7% | 7,360 |
| 26. Court, Municipal, and License Clerks | $34,390 | 8.2% | 4,460 |
| 27. Sailors and Marine Oilers | $36,260 | 11.7% | 1,790 |
| 28. Stock Clerks and Order Fillers | $21,290 | 7.2% | 56,260 |
| 29. Reservation and Transportation Ticket Agents and Travel Clerks | $31,740 | 8.1% | 5,150 |
| 30. Veterinary Assistants and Laboratory Animal Caretakers | $22,040 | 22.8% | 2,550 |
| 31. Childcare Workers | $19,300 | 10.9% | 52,310 |
| 32. Tellers | $24,100 | 6.2% | 28,440 |
| 33. Hotel, Motel, and Resort Desk Clerks | $19,930 | 13.7% | 10,950 |
| 34. Amusement and Recreation Attendants | $18,450 | 13.3% | 17,120 |

*(continued)*

*(continued)*

## Best Jobs Requiring Short-Term On-the-Job Training

| Job | Annual Earnings | Percent Growth | Annual Openings |
|---|---|---|---|
| 35. Counter Attendants, Cafeteria, Food Concession, and Coffee Shop | $18,370 | 9.3% | 43,490 |
| 36. Ushers, Lobby Attendants, and Ticket Takers | $18,560 | 13.7% | 8,190 |
| 37. Dishwashers | $18,150 | 11.6% | 27,570 |

## Best Jobs Requiring Moderate-Term On-the-Job Training

| Job | Annual Earnings | Percent Growth | Annual Openings |
|---|---|---|---|
| 1. Dental Assistants | $33,470 | 35.7% | 16,100 |
| 2. Heavy and Tractor-Trailer Truck Drivers | $37,770 | 12.9% | 55,460 |
| 3. Cargo and Freight Agents | $37,150 | 23.9% | 4,030 |
| 4. Medical Secretaries | $30,530 | 26.6% | 18,900 |
| 5. Medical Assistants | $28,860 | 33.9% | 21,780 |
| 6. Customer Service Representatives | $30,460 | 17.7% | 110,840 |
| 7. Construction Laborers | $29,280 | 20.5% | 33,940 |
| 8. Operating Engineers and Other Construction Equipment Operators | $40,400 | 12.0% | 11,820 |
| 9. Pharmacy Technicians | $28,400 | 30.6% | 18,200 |
| 10. Surveying and Mapping Technicians | $37,900 | 20.4% | 2,940 |
| 11. Correctional Officers and Jailers | $39,040 | 9.4% | 14,360 |
| 12. Subway and Streetcar Operators | $56,880 | 18.8% | 390 |
| 13. Billing and Posting Clerks | $32,170 | 15.3% | 16,760 |
| 14. Life, Physical, and Social Science Technicians, All Other | $43,350 | 13.3% | 3,640 |
| 15. Social and Human Service Assistants | $28,200 | 22.6% | 15,390 |
| 16. Police, Fire, and Ambulance Dispatchers | $35,370 | 17.8% | 3,840 |
| 17. Bookkeeping, Accounting, and Auditing Clerks | $34,030 | 10.3% | 46,040 |
| 18. Insulation Workers, Mechanical | $37,650 | 19.4% | 1,550 |
| 19. Cement Masons and Concrete Finishers | $35,450 | 12.9% | 7,640 |
| 20. Advertising Sales Agents | $45,350 | 7.2% | 4,510 |
| 21. Drywall and Ceiling Tile Installers | $37,320 | 13.5% | 3,700 |
| 22. Mixing and Blending Machine Setters, Operators, and Tenders | $32,870 | 15.5% | 4,610 |
| 23. Production, Planning, and Expediting Clerks | $42,220 | 1.5% | 7,410 |
| 24. Rail-Track Laying and Maintenance Equipment Operators | $45,970 | 14.8% | 650 |
| 25. Eligibility Interviewers, Government Programs | $39,960 | 9.2% | 3,880 |
| 26. Credit Counselors | $38,140 | 16.3% | 880 |

## Best Jobs Requiring Moderate-Term On-the-Job Training

| Job | Annual Earnings | Percent Growth | Annual Openings |
|---|---|---|---|
| 27. Healthcare Support Workers, All Other | $30,280 | 17.1% | 5,670 |
| 28. Pipelayers | $34,800 | 17.2% | 2,280 |
| 29. Tapers | $45,490 | 13.0% | 900 |
| 30. Hazardous Materials Removal Workers | $37,600 | 14.8% | 1,780 |
| 31. Septic Tank Servicers and Sewer Pipe Cleaners | $33,570 | 23.8% | 1,320 |
| 32. Railroad Brake, Signal, and Switch Operators | $47,670 | 9.4% | 1,070 |
| 33. Aircraft Structure, Surfaces, Rigging, and Systems Assemblers | $44,820 | 9.4% | 1,340 |
| 34. Installation, Maintenance, and Repair Workers, All Other | $36,420 | 9.2% | 4,180 |
| 35. Bus Drivers, Transit and Intercity | $35,520 | 8.2% | 4,990 |
| 36. Railroad Conductors and Yardmasters | $49,770 | 6.9% | 1,700 |
| 37. Highway Maintenance Workers | $34,780 | 8.5% | 5,200 |
| 38. Secretaries and Administrative Assistants, Except Legal, Medical, and Executive | $30,830 | 4.6% | 36,550 |
| 39. Painters, Construction and Maintenance | $34,280 | 7.0% | 10,650 |
| 40. Extruding, Forming, Pressing, and Compacting Machine Setters, Operators, and Tenders | $31,210 | 15.0% | 2,960 |
| 41. Pest Control Workers | $30,340 | 15.3% | 3,400 |
| 42. Animal Trainers | $26,580 | 20.4% | 1,900 |
| 43. Construction and Related Workers, All Other | $34,500 | 11.1% | 2,660 |
| 44. Excavating and Loading Machine and Dragline Operators | $36,920 | 8.6% | 2,850 |
| 45. Cooks, Institution and Cafeteria | $22,730 | 9.7% | 13,810 |
| 46. Insulation Workers, Floor, Ceiling, and Wall | $31,830 | 15.2% | 1,320 |

## Best Jobs Requiring Long-Term On-the-Job Training

| Job | Annual Earnings | Percent Growth | Annual Openings |
|---|---|---|---|
| 1. Compliance Officers | $58,720 | 31.0% | 10,850 |
| 2. Purchasing Agents, Except Wholesale, Retail, and Farm Products | $56,580 | 13.9% | 11,860 |
| 3. Plumbers, Pipefitters, and Steamfitters | $46,660 | 15.3% | 17,550 |
| 4. Firefighters | $45,250 | 18.5% | 15,280 |
| 5. Heating, Air Conditioning, and Refrigeration Mechanics and Installers | $42,530 | 28.1% | 13,620 |
| 6. Electricians | $48,250 | 11.9% | 25,090 |
| 7. Police and Sheriff's Patrol Officers | $53,540 | 8.7% | 22,790 |

*(continued)*

*(continued)*

## Best Jobs Requiring Long-Term On-the-Job Training

| Job | Annual Earnings | Percent Growth | Annual Openings |
|---|---|---|---|
| 8. Nuclear Power Reactor Operators | $75,650 | 18.9% | 270 |
| 9. Carpenters | $39,530 | 12.9% | 32,540 |
| 10. Water and Wastewater Treatment Plant and System Operators | $40,770 | 19.8% | 4,690 |
| 11. Coaches and Scouts | $28,340 | 24.8% | 9,920 |
| 12. Producers and Directors | $68,440 | 9.8% | 4,040 |
| 13. Air Traffic Controllers | $108,040 | 13.1% | 1,230 |
| 14. Claims Adjusters, Examiners, and Investigators | $58,620 | 7.1% | 9,560 |
| 15. Brickmasons and Blockmasons | $46,930 | 11.5% | 5,000 |
| 16. Boilermakers | $54,640 | 18.8% | 810 |
| 17. Interpreters and Translators | $43,300 | 22.2% | 2,340 |
| 18. Healthcare Practitioners and Technical Workers, All Other | $43,970 | 15.9% | 2,910 |
| 19. Electrical Power-Line Installers and Repairers | $58,030 | 4.5% | 4,550 |
| 20. Industrial Machinery Mechanics | $45,420 | 7.3% | 6,240 |
| 21. Elevator Installers and Repairers | $70,910 | 9.2% | 920 |
| 22. Tile and Marble Setters | $38,110 | 14.3% | 3,070 |
| 23. Mobile Heavy Equipment Mechanics, Except Engines | $44,830 | 8.7% | 3,770 |
| 24. Structural Iron and Steel Workers | $44,540 | 12.4% | 2,020 |
| 25. Sheet Metal Workers | $41,710 | 6.5% | 5,170 |
| 26. Audio and Video Equipment Technicians | $40,540 | 12.6% | 2,370 |
| 27. Photographers | $29,130 | 11.5% | 4,800 |
| 28. Telecommunications Line Installers and Repairers | $50,850 | 0.9% | 2,790 |
| 29. Installation, Maintenance, and Repair Workers, All Other | $36,420 | 9.2% | 4,180 |
| 30. Dental Laboratory Technicians | $35,140 | 13.9% | 1,530 |
| 31. Opticians, Dispensing | $32,940 | 13.4% | 2,020 |
| 32. Flight Attendants | $37,740 | 8.1% | 3,010 |

## Best Jobs Requiring Work Experience in a Related Job

| Job | Annual Earnings | Percent Growth | Annual Openings |
|---|---|---|---|
| 1. Compliance Officers | $58,720 | 31.0% | 10,850 |
| 2. Managers, All Other | $96,450 | 7.3% | 29,750 |
| 3. Supervisors of Construction and Extraction Workers | $58,680 | 15.4% | 24,220 |
| 4. Business Operations Specialists, All Other | $62,450 | 11.5% | 36,830 |
| 5. Computer Occupations, All Other | $79,240 | 13.1% | 7,260 |

## Best Jobs Requiring Work Experience in a Related Job

| Job | Annual Earnings | Percent Growth | Annual Openings |
|---|---|---|---|
| 6. Sales Representatives, Wholesale and Manufacturing, Technical and Scientific Products | $73,710 | 9.7% | 14,230 |
| 7. Detectives and Criminal Investigators | $68,820 | 16.6% | 4,160 |
| 8. Natural Sciences Managers | $116,020 | 15.5% | 2,010 |
| 9. Sales Representatives, Services, All Other | $50,620 | 13.9% | 22,810 |
| 10. Self-Enrichment Education Teachers | $36,340 | 32.0% | 12,030 |
| 11. Captains, Mates, and Pilots of Water Vessels | $64,180 | 17.3% | 1,950 |
| 12. First-Line Supervisors of Office and Administrative Support Workers | $47,460 | 11.0% | 48,900 |
| 13. Executive Secretaries and Executive Administrative Assistants | $43,520 | 12.8% | 41,920 |
| 14. First-Line Supervisors of Non-Retail Sales Workers | $68,880 | 4.8% | 12,950 |
| 15. First-Line Supervisors of Police and Detectives | $78,260 | 8.1% | 5,050 |
| 16. Ship Engineers | $65,880 | 18.6% | 700 |
| 17. Sales Representatives, Wholesale and Manufacturing, Except Technical and Scientific Products | $52,440 | 6.6% | 45,790 |
| 18. Construction and Building Inspectors | $52,360 | 16.8% | 3,970 |
| 19. Financial Specialists, All Other | $60,980 | 10.5% | 4,320 |
| 20. First-Line Supervisors of Mechanics, Installers, and Repairers | $59,150 | 4.2% | 13,650 |
| 21. Transportation Inspectors | $57,640 | 18.3% | 1,130 |
| 22. Industrial Production Managers | $87,160 | −7.7% | 5,470 |
| 23. First-Line Supervisors of Fire Fighting and Prevention Workers | $68,240 | 8.2% | 3,250 |
| 24. First-Line Supervisors of Personal Service Workers | $35,290 | 15.4% | 9,080 |
| 25. Farmers, Ranchers, and Other Agricultural Managers | $60,750 | 5.9% | 6,490 |
| 26. Vocational Education Teachers, Postsecondary | $48,210 | 15.1% | 4,000 |
| 27. Gaming Managers | $66,960 | 11.9% | 200 |
| 28. First-Line Supervisors of Landscaping, Lawn Service, and Groundskeeping Workers | $41,860 | 14.9% | 5,600 |
| 29. First-Line Supervisors of Retail Sales Workers | $35,820 | 5.2% | 45,010 |
| 30. Private Detectives and Investigators | $42,870 | 22.0% | 1,930 |
| 31. Transportation, Storage, and Distribution Managers | $80,210 | −5.3% | 2,740 |
| 32. First-Line Supervisors of Production and Operating Workers | $53,090 | −5.2% | 9,190 |
| 33. Real Estate Brokers | $54,910 | 8.6% | 3,080 |
| 34. First-Line Supervisors of Food Preparation and Serving Workers | $29,560 | 6.6% | 13,440 |
| 35. Food Service Managers | $48,130 | 5.3% | 8,370 |
| 36. First-Line Supervisors of Correctional Officers | $55,910 | 8.5% | 1,940 |
| 37. Gaming Supervisors | $48,530 | 11.8% | 1,410 |

*(continued)*

*(continued)*

## Best Jobs Requiring Work Experience in a Related Job

| Job | Annual Earnings | Percent Growth | Annual Openings |
|---|---|---|---|
| 38. First-Line Supervisors of Transportation and Material-Moving Machine and Vehicle Operators | $52,720 | –3.7% | 3,770 |
| 39. First-Line Supervisors of Helpers, Laborers, and Material Movers, Hand | $43,800 | 3.6% | 3,850 |

## Best Jobs Requiring Postsecondary Vocational Training

| Job | Annual Earnings | Percent Growth | Annual Openings |
|---|---|---|---|
| 1. Licensed Practical and Licensed Vocational Nurses | $40,380 | 20.6% | 39,130 |
| 2. Business Operations Specialists, All Other | $62,450 | 11.5% | 36,830 |
| 3. Computer Occupations, All Other | $79,240 | 13.1% | 7,260 |
| 4. Fitness Trainers and Aerobics Instructors | $31,090 | 29.4% | 12,380 |
| 5. Surgical Technologists | $39,920 | 25.3% | 4,630 |
| 6. Real Estate Sales Agents | $40,030 | 16.2% | 12,830 |
| 7. Hairdressers, Hairstylists, and Cosmetologists | $22,760 | 20.1% | 21,950 |
| 8. Preschool Teachers, Except Special Education | $25,700 | 19.0% | 17,830 |
| 9. Commercial Pilots | $67,500 | 18.5% | 2,060 |
| 10. Security and Fire Alarm Systems Installers | $38,500 | 24.8% | 2,780 |
| 11. Life, Physical, and Social Science Technicians, All Other | $43,350 | 13.3% | 3,640 |
| 12. Massage Therapists | $34,900 | 18.9% | 3,950 |
| 13. Bus and Truck Mechanics and Diesel Engine Specialists | $40,850 | 5.7% | 7,530 |
| 14. Architectural and Civil Drafters | $46,430 | 9.1% | 3,620 |
| 15. Health Technologists and Technicians, All Other | $38,460 | 18.7% | 3,200 |
| 16. Gaming Dealers | $18,090 | 19.0% | 5,590 |
| 17. Automotive Service Technicians and Mechanics | $35,790 | 4.7% | 18,170 |
| 18. Court Reporters | $47,700 | 18.3% | 710 |
| 19. Electrical and Electronics Repairers, Powerhouse, Substation, and Relay | $65,230 | 11.5% | 670 |
| 20. Skincare Specialists | $28,920 | 37.8% | 2,030 |
| 21. Aircraft Mechanics and Service Technicians | $53,420 | 6.4% | 3,140 |
| 22. Telecommunications Equipment Installers and Repairers, Except Line Installers | $54,710 | –0.2% | 3,560 |
| 23. Emergency Medical Technicians and Paramedics | $30,360 | 9.0% | 6,200 |
| 24. Library Technicians | $29,860 | 8.8% | 6,470 |

## Best Jobs Requiring Postsecondary Vocational Training

| Job | Annual Earnings | Percent Growth | Annual Openings |
|---|---|---|---|
| 25. Engineering Technicians, Except Drafters, All Other | $58,020 | 5.2% | 1,850 |
| 26. Manicurists and Pedicurists | $19,650 | 18.8% | 2,530 |
| 27. Construction and Related Workers, All Other | $34,500 | 11.1% | 2,660 |

## Best Jobs Requiring an Associate Degree

| Job | Annual Earnings | Percent Growth | Annual Openings |
|---|---|---|---|
| 1. Dental Hygienists | $68,250 | 36.1% | 9,840 |
| 2. Registered Nurses | $64,690 | 22.2% | 103,900 |
| 3. Paralegals and Legal Assistants | $46,680 | 28.1% | 10,400 |
| 4. Computer Occupations, All Other | $79,240 | 13.1% | 7,260 |
| 5. Business Operations Specialists, All Other | $62,450 | 11.5% | 36,830 |
| 6. Physical Therapist Assistants | $49,690 | 33.3% | 3,050 |
| 7. Radiologic Technologists | $54,340 | 17.2% | 6,800 |
| 8. Respiratory Therapists | $54,280 | 20.9% | 4,140 |
| 9. Radiation Therapists | $74,980 | 27.1% | 690 |
| 10. Legal Secretaries | $41,500 | 18.4% | 8,380 |
| 11. Occupational Therapy Assistants | $51,010 | 29.8% | 1,180 |
| 12. Veterinary Technologists and Technicians | $29,710 | 35.8% | 4,850 |
| 13. Medical and Clinical Laboratory Technologists | $56,130 | 11.9% | 5,330 |
| 14. Cardiovascular Technologists and Technicians | $49,410 | 24.1% | 1,910 |
| 15. Diagnostic Medical Sonographers | $64,380 | 18.3% | 1,650 |
| 16. Interior Designers | $46,280 | 19.4% | 3,590 |
| 17. Medical Records and Health Information Technicians | $32,350 | 20.3% | 7,030 |
| 18. Medical Equipment Repairers | $44,490 | 27.2% | 2,320 |
| 19. Environmental Science and Protection Technicians, Including Health | $41,380 | 28.9% | 2,520 |
| 20. Environmental Engineering Technicians | $43,390 | 30.1% | 1,040 |
| 21. Civil Engineering Technicians | $46,290 | 16.9% | 3,280 |
| 22. Nuclear Medicine Technologists | $68,560 | 16.3% | 670 |
| 23. Health Technologists and Technicians, All Other | $38,460 | 18.7% | 3,200 |
| 24. Healthcare Support Workers, All Other | $30,280 | 17.1% | 5,670 |
| 25. Electrical and Electronic Engineering Technicians | $56,040 | –2.2% | 3,100 |
| 26. Medical and Clinical Laboratory Technicians | $36,280 | 16.1% | 5,460 |
| 27. Protective Service Workers, All Other | $29,890 | 14.0% | 7,150 |

*(continued)*

*(continued)*

## Best Jobs Requiring an Associate Degree

| Job | Annual Earnings | Percent Growth | Annual Openings |
|---|---|---|---|
| 28. Engineering Technicians, Except Drafters, All Other | $58,020 | 5.2% | 1,850 |
| 29. Life, Physical, and Social Science Technicians, All Other | $43,350 | 13.3% | 3,640 |
| 30. Morticians, Undertakers, and Funeral Directors | $54,330 | 11.9% | 960 |
| 31. Industrial Engineering Technicians | $48,210 | 6.6% | 1,850 |
| 32. Social Science Research Assistants | $37,230 | 17.8% | 1,270 |

## Best Jobs Requiring a Bachelor's Degree

| Job | Annual Earnings | Percent Growth | Annual Openings |
|---|---|---|---|
| 1. Software Developers, Applications | $87,790 | 34.0% | 21,840 |
| 2. Software Developers, Systems Software | $94,180 | 30.4% | 15,340 |
| 3. Computer Systems Analysts | $77,740 | 20.3% | 22,280 |
| 4. Civil Engineers | $77,560 | 24.3% | 11,460 |
| 5. Construction Managers | $83,860 | 17.2% | 13,770 |
| 6. Accountants and Auditors | $61,690 | 21.6% | 49,750 |
| 7. Network and Computer Systems Administrators | $69,160 | 23.2% | 13,550 |
| 8. Market Research Analysts and Marketing Specialists | $60,570 | 28.1% | 13,730 |
| 9. Personal Financial Advisors | $64,750 | 30.1% | 8,530 |
| 10. Financial Analysts | $74,350 | 19.8% | 9,520 |
| 11. Environmental Engineers | $78,740 | 30.6% | 2,790 |
| 12. Database Administrators | $73,490 | 20.3% | 4,440 |
| 13. Cost Estimators | $57,860 | 25.3% | 10,360 |
| 14. Biomedical Engineers | $81,540 | 72.0% | 1,490 |
| 15. Human Resources Specialists | $52,690 | 27.9% | 11,230 |
| 16. Managers, All Other | $96,450 | 7.3% | 29,750 |
| 17. Public Relations Specialists | $52,090 | 24.0% | 13,130 |
| 18. Financial Examiners | $74,940 | 41.2% | 1,600 |
| 19. Instructional Coordinators | $58,830 | 23.2% | 6,060 |
| 20. Logisticians | $70,800 | 19.5% | 4,190 |
| 21. Industrial Engineers | $76,100 | 14.2% | 8,540 |
| 22. Architects, Except Landscape and Naval | $72,550 | 16.2% | 4,680 |
| 23. Computer Occupations, All Other | $79,240 | 13.1% | 7,260 |
| 24. Compensation, Benefits, and Job Analysis Specialists | $57,000 | 23.6% | 6,050 |
| 25. Education Administrators, All Other | $75,690 | 23.9% | 1,690 |

## Best Jobs Requiring a Bachelor's Degree

| Job | Annual Earnings | Percent Growth | Annual Openings |
|---|---|---|---|
| 26. Elementary School Teachers, Except Special Education | $51,660 | 15.8% | 59,650 |
| 27. Petroleum Engineers | $114,080 | 18.4% | 860 |
| 28. Middle School Teachers, Except Special and Career/Technical Education | $51,960 | 15.3% | 25,110 |
| 29. Business Operations Specialists, All Other | $62,450 | 11.5% | 36,830 |
| 30. Healthcare Social Workers | $47,230 | 22.4% | 6,590 |
| 31. Customer Service Representatives | $30,460 | 17.7% | 110,840 |
| 32. Securities, Commodities, and Financial Services Sales Agents | $70,190 | 9.3% | 12,680 |
| 33. Engineers, All Other | $90,270 | 6.7% | 5,020 |
| 34. Airline Pilots, Copilots, and Flight Engineers | $103,210 | 8.4% | 3,250 |
| 35. Mechanical Engineers | $78,160 | 6.0% | 7,570 |
| 36. Technical Writers | $63,280 | 18.2% | 1,680 |
| 37. Sales Engineers | $87,390 | 8.8% | 3,500 |
| 38. Aerospace Engineers | $97,480 | 10.4% | 2,230 |
| 39. Industrial Production Managers | $87,160 | −7.7% | 5,470 |
| 40. Budget Analysts | $68,200 | 15.1% | 2,230 |
| 41. Landscape Architects | $62,090 | 19.7% | 980 |
| 42. Writers and Authors | $55,420 | 14.8% | 5,420 |
| 43. Probation Officers and Correctional Treatment Specialists | $47,200 | 19.3% | 4,180 |
| 44. Social and Community Service Managers | $57,950 | 13.8% | 4,820 |
| 45. Computer Programmers | $71,380 | −2.9% | 8,030 |
| 46. Electrical Engineers | $84,540 | 1.7% | 3,890 |
| 47. Electronics Engineers, Except Computer | $90,170 | 0.3% | 3,340 |
| 48. Secondary School Teachers, Except Special and Career/Technical Education | $53,230 | 8.9% | 41,240 |
| 49. Kindergarten Teachers, Except Special Education | $48,800 | 15.0% | 6,300 |
| 50. Mining and Geological Engineers, Including Mining Safety Engineers | $82,870 | 15.3% | 260 |
| 51. Teachers and Instructors, All Other | $29,820 | 14.7% | 22,570 |
| 52. Computer Hardware Engineers | $98,810 | 3.8% | 2,350 |
| 53. Insurance Sales Agents | $46,770 | 11.9% | 15,260 |
| 54. Physical Scientists, All Other | $94,780 | 11.1% | 1,010 |
| 55. Atmospheric and Space Scientists | $87,780 | 14.6% | 330 |
| 56. Substance Abuse and Behavioral Disorder Counselors | $38,120 | 21.0% | 3,550 |
| 57. Credit Analysts | $58,850 | 15.0% | 2,430 |
| 58. Financial Specialists, All Other | $60,980 | 10.5% | 4,320 |
| 59. Biological Technicians | $39,020 | 17.6% | 4,190 |

*(continued)*

*(continued)*

## Best Jobs Requiring a Bachelor's Degree

| Job | Annual Earnings | Percent Growth | Annual Openings |
|---|---|---|---|
| 60. Multimedia Artists and Animators | $58,510 | 14.2% | 2,890 |
| 61. Cartographers and Photogrammetrists | $54,510 | 26.8% | 640 |
| 62. Medical and Clinical Laboratory Technologists | $56,130 | 11.9% | 5,330 |
| 63. Graphic Designers | $43,500 | 12.9% | 12,480 |
| 64. Athletic Trainers | $41,600 | 36.9% | 1,150 |
| 65. Nuclear Engineers | $99,920 | 10.9% | 540 |
| 66. Statisticians | $72,830 | 13.1% | 960 |
| 67. Health Diagnosing and Treating Practitioners, All Other | $69,310 | 13.0% | 1,530 |
| 68. Loan Officers | $56,490 | 10.1% | 6,880 |
| 69. Recreation Workers | $22,260 | 14.7% | 10,720 |
| 70. Food Scientists and Technologists | $60,180 | 16.3% | 690 |
| 71. Health Educators | $45,830 | 18.2% | 2,600 |
| 72. Child, Family, and School Social Workers | $40,210 | 12.3% | 10,960 |
| 73. Materials Scientists | $84,720 | 11.9% | 440 |
| 74. Occupational Health and Safety Specialists | $64,660 | 11.2% | 2,490 |
| 75. Survey Researchers | $36,050 | 30.3% | 1,340 |
| 76. Surveyors | $54,880 | 14.9% | 2,330 |
| 77. Healthcare Practitioners and Technical Workers, All Other | $43,970 | 15.9% | 2,910 |
| 78. Orthotists and Prosthetists | $65,060 | 15.4% | 210 |
| 79. Adult Basic and Secondary Education and Literacy Teachers and Instructors | $46,530 | 15.1% | 2,920 |
| 80. Materials Engineers | $83,120 | 9.3% | 810 |
| 81. Chemists | $68,320 | 2.5% | 3,000 |
| 82. Forensic Science Technicians | $51,570 | 19.6% | 800 |
| 83. Tax Examiners and Collectors, and Revenue Agents | $49,360 | 13.0% | 3,520 |
| 84. Graduate Teaching Assistants | $32,750 | 15.1% | 4,000 |
| 85. Property, Real Estate, and Community Association Managers | $51,480 | 8.4% | 7,800 |
| 86. Health and Safety Engineers, Except Mining Safety Engineers and Inspectors | $75,430 | 10.3% | 920 |
| 87. Soil and Plant Scientists | $57,340 | 15.5% | 700 |
| 88. Meeting, Convention, and Event Planners | $45,260 | 15.6% | 2,140 |
| 89. Museum Technicians and Conservators | $37,310 | 25.6% | 610 |
| 90. Agricultural Engineers | $71,090 | 11.9% | 90 |
| 91. Insurance Underwriters | $59,290 | –4.1% | 3,000 |
| 92. Zoologists and Wildlife Biologists | $57,430 | 12.8% | 880 |
| 93. Commercial and Industrial Designers | $58,230 | 9.0% | 1,760 |
| 94. Dietitians and Nutritionists | $53,250 | 9.2% | 2,570 |

## Best Jobs Requiring a Bachelor's Degree

| Job | Annual Earnings | Percent Growth | Annual Openings |
|---|---|---|---|
| 95. Set and Exhibit Designers | $46,680 | 16.5% | 510 |
| 96. Credit Counselors | $38,140 | 16.3% | 880 |
| 97. Animal Scientists | $58,250 | 13.2% | 180 |
| 98. Conservation Scientists | $59,310 | 11.9% | 410 |
| 99. Engineering Technicians, Except Drafters, All Other | $58,020 | 5.2% | 1,850 |
| 100. Directors, Religious Activities and Education | $36,170 | 12.6% | 2,640 |
| 101. Recreational Therapists | $39,410 | 14.6% | 1,160 |
| 102. Editors | $51,470 | –0.3% | 3,390 |
| 103. Film and Video Editors | $50,930 | 11.9% | 930 |
| 104. Appraisers and Assessors of Real Estate | $48,500 | 4.6% | 2,100 |

## Best Jobs Requiring Work Experience Plus Degree

| Job | Annual Earnings | Percent Growth | Annual Openings |
|---|---|---|---|
| 1. Computer and Information Systems Managers | $115,780 | 16.9% | 9,710 |
| 2. Sales Managers | $98,530 | 14.9% | 12,660 |
| 3. Management Analysts | $78,160 | 23.9% | 30,650 |
| 4. Marketing Managers | $112,800 | 12.5% | 5,970 |
| 5. Medical and Health Services Managers | $84,270 | 16.0% | 9,940 |
| 6. Financial Managers | $103,910 | 7.6% | 13,820 |
| 7. Natural Sciences Managers | $116,020 | 15.5% | 2,010 |
| 8. Managers, All Other | $96,450 | 7.3% | 29,750 |
| 9. Chief Executives | $165,080 | –1.4% | 11,250 |
| 10. Training and Development Specialists | $54,160 | 23.3% | 10,710 |
| 11. General and Operations Managers | $94,400 | –0.1% | 50,220 |
| 12. Computer Occupations, All Other | $79,240 | 13.1% | 7,260 |
| 13. Architectural and Engineering Managers | $119,260 | 6.2% | 4,870 |
| 14. Human Resources Managers | $99,180 | 9.6% | 4,140 |
| 15. Administrative Services Managers | $77,890 | 12.5% | 8,660 |
| 16. Business Operations Specialists, All Other | $62,450 | 11.5% | 36,830 |
| 17. Detectives and Criminal Investigators | $68,820 | 16.6% | 4,160 |
| 18. Education Administrators, Elementary and Secondary School | $86,970 | 8.6% | 8,880 |
| 19. Public Relations and Fundraising Managers | $91,810 | 12.9% | 2,060 |
| 20. Actuaries | $87,650 | 21.4% | 1,000 |
| 21. Education Administrators, All Other | $75,690 | 23.9% | 1,690 |

*(continued)*

*(continued)*

## Best Jobs Requiring Work Experience Plus Degree

| Job | Annual Earnings | Percent Growth | Annual Openings |
|---|---|---|---|
| 22. Art Directors | $80,630 | 11.7% | 2,870 |
| 23. Training and Development Managers | $89,170 | 11.9% | 1,010 |
| 24. Health Technologists and Technicians, All Other | $38,460 | 18.7% | 3,200 |
| 25. Agents and Business Managers of Artists, Performers, and Athletes | $63,130 | 22.4% | 1,010 |
| 26. Financial Specialists, All Other | $60,980 | 10.5% | 4,320 |
| 27. Purchasing Managers | $95,070 | 1.5% | 2,110 |
| 28. Health Diagnosing and Treating Practitioners, All Other | $69,310 | 13.0% | 1,530 |
| 29. Producers and Directors | $68,440 | 9.8% | 4,040 |
| 30. Compensation and Benefits Managers | $89,270 | 8.5% | 1,210 |
| 31. Education Administrators, Postsecondary | $83,710 | 2.3% | 4,010 |
| 32. Farmers, Ranchers, and Other Agricultural Managers | $60,750 | 5.9% | 6,490 |
| 33. Career/Technical Education Teachers, Secondary School | $54,310 | 9.6% | 3,850 |
| 34. Education Administrators, Preschool and Childcare Center/Program | $42,960 | 11.8% | 2,460 |
| 35. Administrative Law Judges, Adjudicators, and Hearing Officers | $85,500 | 8.1% | 380 |
| 36. Arbitrators, Mediators, and Conciliators | $55,800 | 14.0% | 320 |
| 37. Transportation, Storage, and Distribution Managers | $80,210 | −5.3% | 2,740 |
| 38. Advertising and Promotions Managers | $83,890 | −1.7% | 1,050 |
| 39. Music Directors and Composers | $45,970 | 10.0% | 1,620 |

## Best Jobs Requiring a Master's Degree

| Job | Annual Earnings | Percent Growth | Annual Openings |
|---|---|---|---|
| 1. Physical Therapists | $76,310 | 30.3% | 7,860 |
| 2. Physician Assistants | $86,410 | 39.0% | 4,280 |
| 3. Computer Systems Analysts | $77,740 | 20.3% | 22,280 |
| 4. Registered Nurses | $64,690 | 22.2% | 103,900 |
| 5. Occupational Therapists | $72,320 | 25.6% | 4,580 |
| 6. Environmental Scientists and Specialists, Including Health | $61,700 | 27.9% | 4,840 |
| 7. Instructional Coordinators | $58,830 | 23.2% | 6,060 |
| 8. Social Scientists and Related Workers, All Other | $74,620 | 22.4% | 2,380 |
| 9. Industrial-Organizational Psychologists | $87,330 | 26.1% | 130 |
| 10. Operations Research Analysts | $70,960 | 22.0% | 3,220 |
| 11. Geoscientists, Except Hydrologists and Geographers | $82,500 | 17.5% | 1,540 |

## Best Jobs Requiring a Master's Degree

| Job | Annual Earnings | Percent Growth | Annual Openings |
|---|---|---|---|
| 12. Political Scientists | $107,420 | 19.4% | 280 |
| 13. Mental Health Counselors | $38,150 | 24.0% | 5,010 |
| 14. Speech-Language Pathologists | $66,920 | 18.5% | 4,380 |
| 15. Geographers | $72,800 | 26.0% | 100 |
| 16. Psychologists, All Other | $89,900 | 14.4% | 680 |
| 17. Mental Health and Substance Abuse Social Workers | $38,600 | 19.5% | 6,130 |
| 18. Anthropologists and Archeologists | $54,230 | 28.0% | 450 |
| 19. Sociologists | $72,360 | 22.0% | 200 |
| 20. Urban and Regional Planners | $63,040 | 19.0% | 1,470 |
| 21. Educational, Guidance, School, and Vocational Counselors | $53,380 | 14.0% | 9,440 |
| 22. Hydrologists | $75,690 | 18.2% | 380 |
| 23. Clergy | $43,970 | 12.7% | 21,770 |
| 24. Curators | $48,450 | 23.0% | 620 |
| 25. Economists | $89,450 | 5.8% | 500 |
| 26. Rehabilitation Counselors | $32,350 | 18.9% | 5,070 |
| 27. Statisticians | $72,830 | 13.1% | 960 |
| 28. Librarians | $54,500 | 7.8% | 5,450 |
| 29. Financial Specialists, All Other | $60,980 | 10.5% | 4,320 |
| 30. Epidemiologists | $63,010 | 15.1% | 170 |
| 31. Recreational Therapists | $39,410 | 14.6% | 1,160 |
| 32. Marriage and Family Therapists | $45,720 | 14.5% | 950 |

## Best Jobs Requiring a Doctoral Degree

| Job | Annual Earnings | Percent Growth | Annual Openings |
|---|---|---|---|
| 1. Medical Scientists, Except Epidemiologists | $76,700 | 40.4% | 6,620 |
| 2. Computer and Information Research Scientists | $100,660 | 24.2% | 1,320 |
| 3. Health Specialties Teachers, Postsecondary | $85,270 | 15.1% | 4,000 |
| 4. Biochemists and Biophysicists | $79,390 | 37.4% | 1,620 |
| 5. Engineering Teachers, Postsecondary | $89,670 | 15.1% | 1,000 |
| 6. Business Teachers, Postsecondary | $73,760 | 15.1% | 2,000 |
| 7. Physicists | $106,370 | 15.9% | 690 |
| 8. Biological Science Teachers, Postsecondary | $72,700 | 15.1% | 1,700 |
| 9. Biological Scientists, All Other | $68,220 | 18.8% | 1,610 |
| 10. Computer Science Teachers, Postsecondary | $70,300 | 15.1% | 1,000 |

*(continued)*

*(continued)*

## Best Jobs Requiring a Doctoral Degree

| Job | Annual Earnings | Percent Growth | Annual Openings |
|---|---|---|---|
| 11. Economics Teachers, Postsecondary | $83,370 | 15.1% | 400 |
| 12. Mathematicians | $99,380 | 22.4% | 150 |
| 13. Psychology Teachers, Postsecondary | $67,330 | 15.1% | 1,000 |
| 14. Atmospheric, Earth, Marine, and Space Sciences Teachers, Postsecondary | $82,840 | 15.1% | 300 |
| 15. Art, Drama, and Music Teachers, Postsecondary | $62,040 | 15.1% | 2,500 |
| 16. Physics Teachers, Postsecondary | $77,610 | 15.1% | 400 |
| 17. Agricultural Sciences Teachers, Postsecondary | $78,370 | 15.1% | 300 |
| 18. Chemistry Teachers, Postsecondary | $70,520 | 15.1% | 600 |
| 19. English Language and Literature Teachers, Postsecondary | $60,400 | 15.1% | 2,000 |
| 20. Mathematical Science Teachers, Postsecondary | $65,710 | 15.1% | 1,000 |
| 21. Political Science Teachers, Postsecondary | $70,540 | 15.1% | 500 |
| 22. Nursing Instructors and Teachers, Postsecondary | $62,390 | 15.1% | 1,500 |
| 23. Astronomers | $87,260 | 15.6% | 70 |
| 24. Audiologists | $66,660 | 25.0% | 580 |
| 25. Education Teachers, Postsecondary | $59,140 | 15.1% | 1,800 |
| 26. Anthropology and Archeology Teachers, Postsecondary | $73,600 | 15.1% | 200 |
| 27. Architecture Teachers, Postsecondary | $73,500 | 15.1% | 200 |
| 28. Forestry and Conservation Science Teachers, Postsecondary | $78,290 | 15.1% | 100 |
| 29. History Teachers, Postsecondary | $64,880 | 15.1% | 700 |
| 30. Environmental Science Teachers, Postsecondary | $71,020 | 15.1% | 200 |
| 31. Communications Teachers, Postsecondary | $60,300 | 15.1% | 800 |
| 32. Psychologists, All Other | $89,900 | 14.4% | 680 |
| 33. Area, Ethnic, and Cultural Studies Teachers, Postsecondary | $68,020 | 15.1% | 200 |
| 34. Foreign Language and Literature Teachers, Postsecondary | $59,080 | 15.1% | 900 |
| 35. Philosophy and Religion Teachers, Postsecondary | $62,330 | 15.1% | 600 |
| 36. Sociology Teachers, Postsecondary | $64,810 | 15.1% | 500 |
| 37. Clinical, Counseling, and School Psychologists | $66,810 | 11.1% | 5,990 |
| 38. Health Diagnosing and Treating Practitioners, All Other | $69,310 | 13.0% | 1,530 |
| 39. Home Economics Teachers, Postsecondary | $65,040 | 15.1% | 200 |
| 40. Social Work Teachers, Postsecondary | $63,090 | 15.1% | 300 |
| 41. Recreation and Fitness Studies Teachers, Postsecondary | $57,650 | 15.1% | 600 |
| 42. Geography Teachers, Postsecondary | $66,700 | 15.1% | 100 |
| 43. Criminal Justice and Law Enforcement Teachers, Postsecondary | $59,520 | 15.1% | 400 |
| 44. Library Science Teachers, Postsecondary | $62,720 | 15.1% | 100 |
| 45. Microbiologists | $65,920 | 12.2% | 750 |

## Best Jobs Requiring a First Professional Degree

| Job | Annual Earnings | Percent Growth | Annual Openings |
|---|---|---|---|
| 1. Dentists, General | $141,040 | 15.3% | 5,180 |
| 2. Orthodontists | $166,400+ | 19.8% | 360 |
| 3. Pharmacists | $111,570 | 17.0% | 10,580 |
| 4. Veterinarians | $82,040 | 32.9% | 3,020 |
| 5. Optometrists | $94,990 | 24.4% | 2,010 |
| 6. Lawyers | $112,760 | 13.0% | 24,040 |
| 7. Prosthodontists | $118,400 | 28.3% | 30 |
| 8. Oral and Maxillofacial Surgeons | $166,400+ | 15.3% | 290 |
| 9. Chiropractors | $67,200 | 19.5% | 1,820 |
| 10. Law Teachers, Postsecondary | $94,260 | 15.1% | 400 |
| 11. Podiatrists | $118,030 | 9.0% | 320 |

# Best Jobs Lists Based on Career Clusters

This group of lists organizes the 400 best jobs into 16 career clusters. The U.S. Department of Education's Office of Vocational and Adult Education developed these career clusters in 1999, and many states now use them to organize their career-oriented programs and career information. You can use these lists to identify jobs quickly based on your interests. When you find jobs you want to explore in more detail, look up their descriptions in Part II. You can also review clusters that represent areas in which you've had past experience, education, or training to see whether other jobs in those areas would meet your current requirements.

In this set of lists, you may notice that some occupations appear on multiple lists. This happens when two or more industries commonly employ workers with the same occupational title. For example, Nuclear Technicians may operate nuclear power plants (and thus work in the Manufacturing cluster), aid in scientific research (Science, Technology, Engineering, and Mathematics), or maintain a therapeutic radiation machine (Health Science). If you decide to pursue one of these multiple-cluster occupations, you may have to choose your intended industry early in your education or training pathway, or it may be possible to specialize later or (more rarely) even jump between industries after you have worked for several years.

Within each cluster, jobs are listed by combined score for earnings, job growth, and job openings, from highest to lowest.

# Descriptions for the 16 Interest Areas

Brief descriptions follow for the 16 career clusters, defining them in terms of interests. Some of them refer to jobs (as examples) that aren't included in this book.

- **Agriculture and Natural Resources:** *An interest in working with plants, animals, forests, or mineral resources for agriculture, horticulture, conservation, extraction, and other purposes.* You can satisfy this interest by working in farming, landscaping, forestry, fishing, mining, and related fields. You may like doing physical work outdoors, such as on a farm or ranch, in a forest, or on a drilling rig. If you have a scientific curiosity, you could study plants and animals or analyze biological or rock samples in a lab. If you have management ability, you could own, operate, or manage a fish hatchery, a landscaping business, or a greenhouse.

- **Architecture and Construction:** *An interest in designing, assembling, and maintaining components of buildings and other structures.* You may want to be part of the team of architects, drafters, and others who design buildings and render plans. If construction interests you, you might find fulfillment in the many building projects that are being undertaken at all times. If you like to organize and plan, you can find careers in managing these projects. Or you can play a more direct role in putting up and finishing buildings by doing jobs such as plumbing, carpentry, masonry, painting, or roofing, either as a skilled craftsworker or as a helper. You can prepare the building site by operating heavy equipment or installing, maintaining, and repairing vital building equipment and systems such as electricity and heating.

- **Arts and Communication:** *An interest in creatively expressing feelings or ideas, in communicating news or information, or in performing.* You can satisfy this interest in creative, verbal, or performing activities. For example, if you enjoy literature, perhaps writing or editing would appeal to you. Journalism and public relations are other fields for people who like to use their writing or speaking skills. Do you prefer to work in the performing arts? If so, you could direct or perform in drama, music, or dance. If you especially enjoy the visual arts, you could create paintings, sculpture, or ceramics or design products or visual displays. A flair for technology might lead you to specialize in photography, broadcast production, or dispatching.

- **Business and Administration:** *An interest in making a business organization or function run smoothly.* You can satisfy this interest by working in a position of leadership or by specializing in a function that contributes to the overall effort in a business, a nonprofit organization, or a government agency. If you especially enjoy working with people, you may find fulfillment from working in human resources. An interest in numbers may lead you to consider accounting, finance, budgeting, billing, or financial record-keeping. A job as an administrative assistant may interest you if you like a variety of tasks in a busy environment. If you are good with details and word processing, you may enjoy a job as a secretary or data-entry clerk. Or perhaps you would do well as the manager of a business.

- **Education and Training:** *An interest in helping people learn.* You can satisfy this interest by teaching students, who may be preschoolers, retirees, or any age in between. You may specialize in a particular academic field or work with learners of a particular age, with a particular interest, or with a particular learning problem. Working in a library or museum may give you an opportunity to expand people's understanding of the world.

✳ **Finance and Insurance:** *An interest in helping businesses and people be assured of a financially secure future.* You can satisfy this interest by working in a financial or insurance business in a leadership or support role. If you like gathering and analyzing information, you may find fulfillment as an insurance adjuster or financial analyst. Or you may deal with information at the clerical level as a banking or insurance clerk or in person-to-person situations providing customer service. Another way to interact with people is to sell financial or insurance services that will meet their needs.

✳ **Government and Public Administration:** *An interest in helping a government agency serve the needs of the public.* You can satisfy this interest by working in a position of leadership or by specializing in a function that contributes to the role of government. You may help protect the public by working as an inspector or examiner to enforce standards. If you enjoy using clerical skills, you could work as a clerk in a law court or government office. Or perhaps you prefer the top-down perspective of a government executive or urban planner.

✳ **Health Science:** *An interest in helping people and animals be healthy.* You can satisfy this interest by working on a health-care team as a doctor, therapist, or nurse. You might specialize in one of the many different parts of the body (such as the teeth or eyes) or in one of the many different types of care. Or you may want to be a generalist who deals with the whole patient. If you like technology, you might find satisfaction working with X-rays or new diagnostic methods. You might work with relatively healthy people, helping them to eat better. If you enjoy working with animals, you might care for them and keep them healthy.

✳ **Hospitality, Tourism, and Recreation:** *An interest in catering to the personal wishes and needs of others so that they can enjoy a clean environment, good food and drink, comfortable lodging away from home, and recreation.* You can satisfy this interest by providing services for the convenience, care, and pampering of others in hotels, restaurants, airplanes, beauty parlors, and so on. You may want to use your love of cooking as a chef. If you like working with people, you may want to provide personal services by being a travel guide, a flight attendant, a concierge, a hairdresser, or a waiter. You may want to work in cleaning and building services if you like a clean environment. If you enjoy sports or games, you could work for an athletic team or casino.

✳ **Human Service:** *An interest in improving people's social, mental, emotional, or spiritual well-being.* You can satisfy this interest as a counselor, social worker, or religious worker who helps people sort out their complicated lives or solve personal problems. You may work as a caretaker for very young people or the elderly. Or you may interview people to help identify the social services they need.

✳ **Information Technology:** *An interest in designing, developing, managing, and supporting information systems.* You can satisfy this interest by working with hardware, software, multimedia, or integrated systems. If you like to use your organizational skills, you might work as a systems or database administrator. Or you can solve complex problems as a software engineer or systems analyst. If you enjoy getting your hands on hardware, you might find work servicing computers, peripherals, and information-intense machines such as cash registers and ATMs.

⁕ **Law and Public Safety:** *An interest in upholding people's rights or in protecting people and property by using authority, inspecting, or investigating.* You can satisfy this interest by working in law, law enforcement, fire fighting, the military, and related fields. For example, if you enjoy mental challenge and intrigue, you could investigate crimes or fires for a living. If you enjoy working with verbal skills and research skills, you may want to defend citizens in court or research deeds, wills, and other legal documents. If you want to help people in critical situations, you may want to fight fires, work as a police officer, or become a paramedic. Or, if you want more routine work in public safety, perhaps a job in guarding, patrolling, or inspecting would appeal to you. If you have management ability, you could seek a leadership position in law enforcement and the protective services. Work in the military gives you a chance to use technical and leadership skills while serving your country.

⁕ **Manufacturing:** *An interest in processing materials into intermediate or final products or maintaining and repairing products by using machines or hand tools.* You can satisfy this interest by working in one of many industries that mass-produce goods or by working for a utility that distributes electrical power or other resources. You might enjoy manual work, using your hands or hand tools in highly skilled jobs such as assembling engines or electronic equipment. If you enjoy making machines run efficiently or fixing them when they break down, you could seek a job installing or repairing such devices as copiers, aircraft engines, cars, or watches. Perhaps you prefer to set up or operate machines that are used to manufacture products made of food, glass, or paper. You could enjoy cutting and grinding metal and plastic parts to desired shapes and measurements. Or you may want to operate equipment in systems that provide water and process wastewater. You may like inspecting, sorting, counting, or weighing products. Another option is to work with your hands and machinery to move boxes and freight in a warehouse. If leadership appeals to you, you could manage people engaged in production and repair.

⁕ **Retail and Wholesale Sales and Service:** *An interest in bringing others to a particular point of view by personal persuasion and by sales and promotional techniques.* You can satisfy this interest in various jobs that involve persuasion and selling. If you like using knowledge of science, you may enjoy selling pharmaceutical, medical, or electronic products or services. Real estate offers several kinds of sales jobs as well. If you like speaking on the phone, you could work as a telemarketer. Or you may enjoy selling apparel and other merchandise in a retail setting. If you prefer to help people, you may want a job in customer service.

⁕ **Scientific Research, Engineering, and Mathematics:** *An interest in discovering, collecting, and analyzing information about the natural world; in applying scientific research findings to problems in medicine, the life sciences, human behavior, and the natural sciences; in imagining and manipulating quantitative data; and in applying technology to manufacturing, transportation, and other economic activities.* You can satisfy this interest by working with the knowledge and processes of the sciences. You may enjoy researching and developing new knowledge in mathematics, or perhaps solving problems in the physical, life, or social sciences would appeal to you. You may want to study engineering and help create new machines, processes, and structures. If you want to work with scientific equipment and procedures, you could seek a job in a research or testing laboratory.

✸ **Transportation, Distribution, and Logistics:** *An interest in operations that move people or materials.* You can satisfy this interest by managing a transportation service, by helping vehicles keep on their assigned schedules and routes, or by driving or piloting a vehicle. If you enjoy taking responsibility, perhaps managing a rail line would appeal to you. If you work well with details and can take pressure on the job, you might consider being an air traffic controller. Or would you rather get out on the highway, on the water, or up in the air? If so, you could drive a truck from state to state, be employed on a ship, or fly a crop duster over a cornfield. If you prefer to stay closer to home, you could drive a delivery van, taxi, or school bus. You can use your physical strength to load freight and arrange it so that it gets to its destination in one piece.

## Best Jobs for People Interested in Agriculture and Natural Resources

| Job | Annual Earnings | Percent Growth | Annual Openings |
|---|---|---|---|
| 1. Veterinarians | $82,040 | 32.9% | 3,020 |
| 2. Environmental Scientists and Specialists, Including Health | $61,700 | 27.9% | 4,840 |
| 3. Biochemists and Biophysicists | $79,390 | 37.4% | 1,620 |
| 4. Biological Scientists, All Other | $68,220 | 18.8% | 1,610 |
| 5. Biological Science Teachers, Postsecondary | $72,700 | 15.1% | 1,700 |
| 6. Environmental Science and Protection Technicians, Including Health | $41,380 | 28.9% | 2,520 |
| 7. Water and Wastewater Treatment Plant and System Operators | $40,770 | 19.8% | 4,690 |
| 8. Refuse and Recyclable Material Collectors | $32,640 | 18.6% | 7,110 |
| 9. Landscaping and Groundskeeping Workers | $23,400 | 18.0% | 36,220 |
| 10. Nonfarm Animal Caretakers | $19,550 | 20.7% | 7,360 |
| 11. Environmental Engineering Technicians | $43,390 | 30.1% | 1,040 |
| 12. First-Line Supervisors of Office and Administrative Support Workers | $47,460 | 11.0% | 48,900 |
| 13. Graphic Designers | $43,500 | 12.9% | 12,480 |
| 14. Agricultural Sciences Teachers, Postsecondary | $78,370 | 15.1% | 300 |
| 15. Farmers, Ranchers, and Other Agricultural Managers | $60,750 | 5.9% | 6,490 |
| 16. Food Scientists and Technologists | $60,180 | 16.3% | 690 |
| 17. First-Line Supervisors of Landscaping, Lawn Service, and Groundskeeping Workers | $41,860 | 14.9% | 5,600 |
| 18. Occupational Health and Safety Specialists | $64,660 | 11.2% | 2,490 |

*(continued)*

*(continued)*

## Best Jobs for People Interested in Agriculture and Natural Resources

| Job | Annual Earnings | Percent Growth | Annual Openings |
|---|---|---|---|
| 19. Environmental Science Teachers, Postsecondary | $71,020 | 15.1% | 200 |
| 20. Forestry and Conservation Science Teachers, Postsecondary | $78,290 | 15.1% | 100 |
| 21. Tree Trimmers and Pruners | $30,450 | 26.3% | 1,720 |
| 22. Animal Trainers | $26,580 | 20.4% | 1,900 |
| 23. Soil and Plant Scientists | $57,340 | 15.5% | 700 |
| 24. Life, Physical, and Social Science Technicians, All Other | $43,350 | 13.3% | 3,640 |
| 25. Pest Control Workers | $30,340 | 15.3% | 3,400 |
| 26. Recreation and Fitness Studies Teachers, Postsecondary | $57,650 | 15.1% | 600 |
| 27. Recreation Workers | $22,260 | 14.7% | 10,720 |
| 28. Mobile Heavy Equipment Mechanics, Except Engines | $44,830 | 8.7% | 3,770 |
| 29. Economists | $89,450 | 5.8% | 500 |
| 30. First-Line Supervisors of Retail Sales Workers | $35,820 | 5.2% | 45,010 |
| 31. Retail Salespersons | $20,670 | 8.3% | 162,690 |
| 32. Engineering Technicians, Except Drafters, All Other | $58,020 | 5.2% | 1,850 |
| 33. Hazardous Materials Removal Workers | $37,600 | 14.8% | 1,780 |
| 34. Zoologists and Wildlife Biologists | $57,430 | 12.8% | 880 |
| 35. Conservation Scientists | $59,310 | 11.9% | 410 |
| 36. Animal Scientists | $58,250 | 13.2% | 180 |

## Best Jobs for People Interested in Architecture and Construction

| Job | Annual Earnings | Percent Growth | Annual Openings |
|---|---|---|---|
| 1. Construction Managers | $83,860 | 17.2% | 13,770 |
| 2. Cost Estimators | $57,860 | 25.3% | 10,360 |
| 3. Heating, Air Conditioning, and Refrigeration Mechanics and Installers | $42,530 | 28.1% | 13,620 |
| 4. Supervisors of Construction and Extraction Workers | $58,680 | 15.4% | 24,220 |
| 5. Architects, Except Landscape and Naval | $72,550 | 16.2% | 4,680 |
| 6. Plumbers, Pipefitters, and Steamfitters | $46,660 | 15.3% | 17,550 |
| 7. Construction Laborers | $29,280 | 20.5% | 33,940 |
| 8. Construction and Building Inspectors | $52,360 | 16.8% | 3,970 |
| 9. Electricians | $48,250 | 11.9% | 25,090 |
| 10. Interior Designers | $46,280 | 19.4% | 3,590 |
| 11. Engineers, All Other | $90,270 | 6.7% | 5,020 |
| 12. Landscape Architects | $62,090 | 19.7% | 980 |

## Best Jobs for People Interested in Architecture and Construction

| Job | Annual Earnings | Percent Growth | Annual Openings |
|---|---|---|---|
| 13. Architectural and Engineering Managers | $119,260 | 6.2% | 4,870 |
| 14. Carpenters | $39,530 | 12.9% | 32,540 |
| 15. Cartographers and Photogrammetrists | $54,510 | 26.8% | 640 |
| 16. Civil Engineering Technicians | $46,290 | 16.9% | 3,280 |
| 17. Security and Fire Alarm Systems Installers | $38,500 | 24.8% | 2,780 |
| 18. Helpers—Electricians | $27,220 | 24.7% | 4,800 |
| 19. Engineering Teachers, Postsecondary | $89,670 | 15.1% | 1,000 |
| 20. Brickmasons and Blockmasons | $46,930 | 11.5% | 5,000 |
| 21. Helpers—Pipelayers, Plumbers, Pipefitters, and Steamfitters | $26,740 | 25.7% | 3,730 |
| 22. Surveying and Mapping Technicians | $37,900 | 20.4% | 2,940 |
| 23. Operating Engineers and Other Construction Equipment Operators | $40,400 | 12.0% | 11,820 |
| 24. Boilermakers | $54,640 | 18.8% | 810 |
| 25. Surveyors | $54,880 | 14.9% | 2,330 |
| 26. Electrical Power-Line Installers and Repairers | $58,030 | 4.5% | 4,550 |
| 27. Architecture Teachers, Postsecondary | $73,500 | 15.1% | 200 |
| 28. Cement Masons and Concrete Finishers | $35,450 | 12.9% | 7,640 |
| 29. Helpers—Carpenters | $25,760 | 23.3% | 3,530 |
| 30. Architectural and Civil Drafters | $46,430 | 9.1% | 3,620 |
| 31. Insulation Workers, Mechanical | $37,650 | 19.4% | 1,550 |
| 32. Drywall and Ceiling Tile Installers | $37,320 | 13.5% | 3,700 |
| 33. Pipelayers | $34,800 | 17.2% | 2,280 |
| 34. Septic Tank Servicers and Sewer Pipe Cleaners | $33,570 | 23.8% | 1,320 |
| 35. Tile and Marble Setters | $38,110 | 14.3% | 3,070 |
| 36. Highway Maintenance Workers | $34,780 | 8.5% | 5,200 |
| 37. Painters, Construction and Maintenance | $34,280 | 7.0% | 10,650 |
| 38. Engineering Technicians, Except Drafters, All Other | $58,020 | 5.2% | 1,850 |
| 39. Structural Iron and Steel Workers | $44,540 | 12.4% | 2,020 |
| 40. Rail-Track Laying and Maintenance Equipment Operators | $45,970 | 14.8% | 650 |
| 41. Tapers | $45,490 | 13.0% | 900 |
| 42. Helpers—Brickmasons, Blockmasons, Stonemasons, and Tile and Marble Setters | $27,780 | 16.4% | 1,890 |
| 43. Excavating and Loading Machine and Dragline Operators | $36,920 | 8.6% | 2,850 |
| 44. Insulation Workers, Floor, Ceiling, and Wall | $31,830 | 15.2% | 1,320 |
| 45. Construction and Related Workers, All Other | $34,500 | 11.1% | 2,660 |

## Best Jobs for People Interested in Arts and Communication

| Job | Annual Earnings | Percent Growth | Annual Openings |
|---|---|---|---|
| 1. Public Relations Specialists | $52,090 | 24.0% | 13,130 |
| 2. Computer Occupations, All Other | $79,240 | 13.1% | 7,260 |
| 3. Managers, All Other | $96,450 | 7.3% | 29,750 |
| 4. Art, Drama, and Music Teachers, Postsecondary | $62,040 | 15.1% | 2,500 |
| 5. Technical Writers | $63,280 | 18.2% | 1,680 |
| 6. Writers and Authors | $55,420 | 14.8% | 5,420 |
| 7. Agents and Business Managers of Artists, Performers, and Athletes | $63,130 | 22.4% | 1,010 |
| 8. Art Directors | $80,630 | 11.7% | 2,870 |
| 9. English Language and Literature Teachers, Postsecondary | $60,400 | 15.1% | 2,000 |
| 10. Producers and Directors | $68,440 | 9.8% | 4,040 |
| 11. Interior Designers | $46,280 | 19.4% | 3,590 |
| 12. Multimedia Artists and Animators | $58,510 | 14.2% | 2,890 |
| 13. Communications Teachers, Postsecondary | $60,300 | 15.1% | 800 |
| 14. Graphic Designers | $43,500 | 12.9% | 12,480 |
| 15. Curators | $48,450 | 23.0% | 620 |
| 16. Telecommunications Equipment Installers and Repairers, Except Line Installers | $54,710 | –0.2% | 3,560 |
| 17. Museum Technicians and Conservators | $37,310 | 25.6% | 610 |
| 18. Commercial and Industrial Designers | $58,230 | 9.0% | 1,760 |
| 19. Photographers | $29,130 | 11.5% | 4,800 |
| 20. Editors | $51,470 | –0.3% | 3,390 |
| 21. Set and Exhibit Designers | $46,680 | 16.5% | 510 |
| 22. Audio and Video Equipment Technicians | $40,540 | 12.6% | 2,370 |
| 23. Film and Video Editors | $50,930 | 11.9% | 930 |
| 24. Music Directors and Composers | $45,970 | 10.0% | 1,620 |

## Best Jobs for People Interested in Business and Administration

| Job | Annual Earnings | Percent Growth | Annual Openings |
|---|---|---|---|
| 1. Management Analysts | $78,160 | 23.9% | 30,650 |
| 2. Computer and Information Systems Managers | $115,780 | 16.9% | 9,710 |
| 3. Accountants and Auditors | $61,690 | 21.6% | 49,750 |
| 4. Construction Managers | $83,860 | 17.2% | 13,770 |
| 5. Market Research Analysts and Marketing Specialists | $60,570 | 28.1% | 13,730 |
| 6. Sales Managers | $98,530 | 14.9% | 12,660 |

## Best Jobs for People Interested in Business and Administration

| Job | Annual Earnings | Percent Growth | Annual Openings |
|---|---|---|---|
| 7. Financial Analysts | $74,350 | 19.8% | 9,520 |
| 8. Financial Managers | $103,910 | 7.6% | 13,820 |
| 9. General and Operations Managers | $94,400 | –0.1% | 50,220 |
| 10. Cost Estimators | $57,860 | 25.3% | 10,360 |
| 11. Human Resources Specialists | $52,690 | 27.9% | 11,230 |
| 12. Public Relations Specialists | $52,090 | 24.0% | 13,130 |
| 13. Managers, All Other | $96,450 | 7.3% | 29,750 |
| 14. Natural Sciences Managers | $116,020 | 15.5% | 2,010 |
| 15. Financial Examiners | $74,940 | 41.2% | 1,600 |
| 16. Training and Development Specialists | $54,160 | 23.3% | 10,710 |
| 17. Customer Service Representatives | $30,460 | 17.7% | 110,840 |
| 18. Chief Executives | $165,080 | –1.4% | 11,250 |
| 19. Operations Research Analysts | $70,960 | 22.0% | 3,220 |
| 20. Compensation, Benefits, and Job Analysis Specialists | $57,000 | 23.6% | 6,050 |
| 21. Logisticians | $70,800 | 19.5% | 4,190 |
| 22. Business Operations Specialists, All Other | $62,450 | 11.5% | 36,830 |
| 23. Computer Occupations, All Other | $79,240 | 13.1% | 7,260 |
| 24. Human Resources Managers | $99,180 | 9.6% | 4,140 |
| 25. Administrative Services Managers | $77,890 | 12.5% | 8,660 |
| 26. Public Relations and Fundraising Managers | $91,810 | 12.9% | 2,060 |
| 27. Receptionists and Information Clerks | $25,240 | 15.2% | 48,020 |
| 28. Billing and Posting Clerks | $32,170 | 15.3% | 16,760 |
| 29. Executive Secretaries and Executive Administrative Assistants | $43,520 | 12.8% | 41,920 |
| 30. First-Line Supervisors of Office and Administrative Support Workers | $47,460 | 11.0% | 48,900 |
| 31. Cargo and Freight Agents | $37,150 | 23.9% | 4,030 |
| 32. Technical Writers | $63,280 | 18.2% | 1,680 |
| 33. Agents and Business Managers of Artists, Performers, and Athletes | $63,130 | 22.4% | 1,010 |
| 34. Budget Analysts | $68,200 | 15.1% | 2,230 |
| 35. Business Teachers, Postsecondary | $73,760 | 15.1% | 2,000 |
| 36. Office Clerks, General | $26,610 | 11.9% | 77,090 |
| 37. First-Line Supervisors of Personal Service Workers | $35,290 | 15.4% | 9,080 |
| 38. Economics Teachers, Postsecondary | $83,370 | 15.1% | 400 |
| 39. Social and Community Service Managers | $57,950 | 13.8% | 4,820 |
| 40. Survey Researchers | $36,050 | 30.3% | 1,340 |
| 41. Bookkeeping, Accounting, and Auditing Clerks | $34,030 | 10.3% | 46,040 |

*(continued)*

*(continued)*

## Best Jobs for People Interested in Business and Administration

| Job | Annual Earnings | Percent Growth | Annual Openings |
|---|---|---|---|
| 42. Interviewers, Except Eligibility and Loan | $28,820 | 15.6% | 9,210 |
| 43. Purchasing Managers | $95,070 | 1.5% | 2,110 |
| 44. Industrial Production Managers | $87,160 | −7.7% | 5,470 |
| 45. Training and Development Managers | $89,170 | 11.9% | 1,010 |
| 46. Credit Analysts | $58,850 | 15.0% | 2,430 |
| 47. Compensation and Benefits Managers | $89,270 | 8.5% | 1,210 |
| 48. Statisticians | $72,830 | 13.1% | 960 |
| 49. Secretaries and Administrative Assistants, Except Legal, Medical, and Executive | $30,830 | 4.6% | 36,550 |
| 50. Transportation, Storage, and Distribution Managers | $80,210 | −5.3% | 2,740 |
| 51. Communications Teachers, Postsecondary | $60,300 | 15.1% | 800 |
| 52. Postal Service Mail Carriers | $53,860 | −1.1% | 10,720 |
| 53. Economists | $89,450 | 5.8% | 500 |
| 54. Advertising and Promotions Managers | $83,890 | −1.7% | 1,050 |
| 55. Advertising Sales Agents | $45,350 | 7.2% | 4,510 |
| 56. Court, Municipal, and License Clerks | $34,390 | 8.2% | 4,460 |
| 57. Gaming Supervisors | $48,530 | 11.8% | 1,410 |

## Best Jobs for People Interested in Education and Training

| Job | Annual Earnings | Percent Growth | Annual Openings |
|---|---|---|---|
| 1. Health Specialties Teachers, Postsecondary | $85,270 | 15.1% | 4,000 |
| 2. Education Administrators, All Other | $75,690 | 23.9% | 1,690 |
| 3. Engineering Teachers, Postsecondary | $89,670 | 15.1% | 1,000 |
| 4. Physicists | $106,370 | 15.9% | 690 |
| 5. Business Teachers, Postsecondary | $73,760 | 15.1% | 2,000 |
| 6. Training and Development Specialists | $54,160 | 23.3% | 10,710 |
| 7. Elementary School Teachers, Except Special Education | $51,660 | 15.8% | 59,650 |
| 8. Instructional Coordinators | $58,830 | 23.2% | 6,060 |
| 9. Biological Science Teachers, Postsecondary | $72,700 | 15.1% | 1,700 |
| 10. Middle School Teachers, Except Special and Career/Technical Education | $51,960 | 15.3% | 25,110 |
| 11. Self-Enrichment Education Teachers | $36,340 | 32.0% | 12,030 |
| 12. Law Teachers, Postsecondary | $94,260 | 15.1% | 400 |
| 13. Fitness Trainers and Aerobics Instructors | $31,090 | 29.4% | 12,380 |

## Best Jobs for People Interested in Education and Training

| Job | Annual Earnings | Percent Growth | Annual Openings |
|---|---|---|---|
| 14. Computer Science Teachers, Postsecondary | $70,300 | 15.1% | 1,000 |
| 15. Art, Drama, and Music Teachers, Postsecondary | $62,040 | 15.1% | 2,500 |
| 16. Atmospheric, Earth, Marine, and Space Sciences Teachers, Postsecondary | $82,840 | 15.1% | 300 |
| 17. Psychology Teachers, Postsecondary | $67,330 | 15.1% | 1,000 |
| 18. Agricultural Sciences Teachers, Postsecondary | $78,370 | 15.1% | 300 |
| 19. Coaches and Scouts | $28,340 | 24.8% | 9,920 |
| 20. Preschool Teachers, Except Special Education | $25,700 | 19.0% | 17,830 |
| 21. English Language and Literature Teachers, Postsecondary | $60,400 | 15.1% | 2,000 |
| 22. Education Administrators, Elementary and Secondary School | $86,970 | 8.6% | 8,880 |
| 23. Nursing Instructors and Teachers, Postsecondary | $62,390 | 15.1% | 1,500 |
| 24. Political Science Teachers, Postsecondary | $70,540 | 15.1% | 500 |
| 25. Anthropology and Archeology Teachers, Postsecondary | $73,600 | 15.1% | 200 |
| 26. Education Teachers, Postsecondary | $59,140 | 15.1% | 1,800 |
| 27. History Teachers, Postsecondary | $64,880 | 15.1% | 700 |
| 28. Architecture Teachers, Postsecondary | $73,500 | 15.1% | 200 |
| 29. Vocational Education Teachers, Postsecondary | $48,210 | 15.1% | 4,000 |
| 30. Forestry and Conservation Science Teachers, Postsecondary | $78,290 | 15.1% | 100 |
| 31. Environmental Science Teachers, Postsecondary | $71,020 | 15.1% | 200 |
| 32. Sociology Teachers, Postsecondary | $64,810 | 15.1% | 500 |
| 33. Graduate Teaching Assistants | $32,750 | 15.1% | 4,000 |
| 34. Adult Basic and Secondary Education and Literacy Teachers and Instructors | $46,530 | 15.1% | 2,920 |
| 35. Area, Ethnic, and Cultural Studies Teachers, Postsecondary | $68,020 | 15.1% | 200 |
| 36. Communications Teachers, Postsecondary | $60,300 | 15.1% | 800 |
| 37. Education Administrators, Postsecondary | $83,710 | 2.3% | 4,010 |
| 38. Interpreters and Translators | $43,300 | 22.2% | 2,340 |
| 39. Philosophy and Religion Teachers, Postsecondary | $62,330 | 15.1% | 600 |
| 40. Foreign Language and Literature Teachers, Postsecondary | $59,080 | 15.1% | 900 |
| 41. Home Economics Teachers, Postsecondary | $65,040 | 15.1% | 200 |
| 42. Social Work Teachers, Postsecondary | $63,090 | 15.1% | 300 |
| 43. Training and Development Managers | $89,170 | 11.9% | 1,010 |
| 44. Geography Teachers, Postsecondary | $66,700 | 15.1% | 100 |
| 45. Criminal Justice and Law Enforcement Teachers, Postsecondary | $59,520 | 15.1% | 400 |
| 46. Recreation and Fitness Studies Teachers, Postsecondary | $57,650 | 15.1% | 600 |
| 47. Library Science Teachers, Postsecondary | $62,720 | 15.1% | 100 |

*(continued)*

*(continued)*

## Best Jobs for People Interested in Education and Training

| Job | Annual Earnings | Percent Growth | Annual Openings |
|---|---|---|---|
| 48. Chemists | $68,320 | 2.5% | 3,000 |
| 49. Secondary School Teachers, Except Special and Career/ Technical Education | $53,230 | 8.9% | 41,240 |
| 50. Educational, Guidance, School, and Vocational Counselors | $53,380 | 14.0% | 9,440 |
| 51. Kindergarten Teachers, Except Special Education | $48,800 | 15.0% | 6,300 |
| 52. Teachers and Instructors, All Other | $29,820 | 14.7% | 22,570 |
| 53. Teacher Assistants | $23,220 | 10.3% | 41,270 |
| 54. Librarians | $54,500 | 7.8% | 5,450 |
| 55. Career/Technical Education Teachers, Secondary School | $54,310 | 9.6% | 3,850 |
| 56. Recreation Workers | $22,260 | 14.7% | 10,720 |
| 57. Dietitians and Nutritionists | $53,250 | 9.2% | 2,570 |
| 58. Library Technicians | $29,860 | 8.8% | 6,470 |
| 59. Education Administrators, Preschool and Childcare Center/Program | $42,960 | 11.8% | 2,460 |

## Best Jobs for People Interested in Finance and Insurance

| Job | Annual Earnings | Percent Growth | Annual Openings |
|---|---|---|---|
| 1. Financial Analysts | $74,350 | 19.8% | 9,520 |
| 2. Personal Financial Advisors | $64,750 | 30.1% | 8,530 |
| 3. Financial Managers | $103,910 | 7.6% | 13,820 |
| 4. Actuaries | $87,650 | 21.4% | 1,000 |
| 5. Bill and Account Collectors | $31,310 | 19.3% | 15,690 |
| 6. Securities, Commodities, and Financial Services Sales Agents | $70,190 | 9.3% | 12,680 |
| 7. Business Teachers, Postsecondary | $73,760 | 15.1% | 2,000 |
| 8. Budget Analysts | $68,200 | 15.1% | 2,230 |
| 9. Insurance Sales Agents | $46,770 | 11.9% | 15,260 |
| 10. Financial Specialists, All Other | $60,980 | 10.5% | 4,320 |
| 11. Credit Analysts | $58,850 | 15.0% | 2,430 |
| 12. Claims Adjusters, Examiners, and Investigators | $58,620 | 7.1% | 9,560 |
| 13. Loan Officers | $56,490 | 10.1% | 6,880 |
| 14. Tellers | $24,100 | 6.2% | 28,440 |
| 15. Credit Counselors | $38,140 | 16.3% | 880 |
| 16. Insurance Underwriters | $59,290 | –4.1% | 3,000 |

## Best Jobs for People Interested in Government and Public Administration

| Job | Annual Earnings | Percent Growth | Annual Openings |
|---|---|---|---|
| 1. Accountants and Auditors | $61,690 | 21.6% | 49,750 |
| 2. General and Operations Managers | $94,400 | −0.1% | 50,220 |
| 3. Managers, All Other | $96,450 | 7.3% | 29,750 |
| 4. Chief Executives | $165,080 | −1.4% | 11,250 |
| 5. Compliance Officers | $58,720 | 31.0% | 10,850 |
| 6. Financial Examiners | $74,940 | 41.2% | 1,600 |
| 7. Political Scientists | $107,420 | 19.4% | 280 |
| 8. Administrative Services Managers | $77,890 | 12.5% | 8,660 |
| 9. Social and Community Service Managers | $57,950 | 13.8% | 4,820 |
| 10. Surveying and Mapping Technicians | $37,900 | 20.4% | 2,940 |
| 11. Urban and Regional Planners | $63,040 | 19.0% | 1,470 |
| 12. Political Science Teachers, Postsecondary | $70,540 | 15.1% | 500 |
| 13. Transportation, Storage, and Distribution Managers | $80,210 | −5.3% | 2,740 |
| 14. Tax Examiners and Collectors, and Revenue Agents | $49,360 | 13.0% | 3,520 |

## Best Jobs for People Interested in Health Science

| Job | Annual Earnings | Percent Growth | Annual Openings |
|---|---|---|---|
| 1. Physicians and Surgeons | $165,279 | 21.8% | 26,050 |
| 2. Medical Scientists, Except Epidemiologists | $76,700 | 40.4% | 6,620 |
| 3. Dental Hygienists | $68,250 | 36.1% | 9,840 |
| 4. Physical Therapists | $76,310 | 30.3% | 7,860 |
| 5. Physician Assistants | $86,410 | 39.0% | 4,280 |
| 6. Computer Systems Analysts | $77,740 | 20.3% | 22,280 |
| 7. Registered Nurses | $64,690 | 22.2% | 103,900 |
| 8. Pharmacists | $111,570 | 17.0% | 10,580 |
| 9. Veterinarians | $82,040 | 32.9% | 3,020 |
| 10. Occupational Therapists | $72,320 | 25.6% | 4,580 |
| 11. Home Health Aides | $20,560 | 50.0% | 55,270 |
| 12. Dental Assistants | $33,470 | 35.7% | 16,100 |
| 13. Medical and Health Services Managers | $84,270 | 16.0% | 9,940 |
| 14. Public Relations Specialists | $52,090 | 24.0% | 13,130 |
| 15. Optometrists | $94,990 | 24.4% | 2,010 |
| 16. Dentists, General | $141,040 | 15.3% | 5,180 |

*(continued)*

*(continued)*

## Best Jobs for People Interested in Health Science

| Job | Annual Earnings | Percent Growth | Annual Openings |
|---|---|---|---|
| 17. Medical Assistants | $28,860 | 33.9% | 21,780 |
| 18. Licensed Practical and Licensed Vocational Nurses | $40,380 | 20.6% | 39,130 |
| 19. Medical Secretaries | $30,530 | 26.6% | 18,900 |
| 20. Pharmacy Technicians | $28,400 | 30.6% | 18,200 |
| 21. Prosthodontists | $118,400 | 28.3% | 30 |
| 22. Physical Therapist Assistants | $49,690 | 33.3% | 3,050 |
| 23. Radiation Therapists | $74,980 | 27.1% | 690 |
| 24. Radiologic Technologists | $54,340 | 17.2% | 6,800 |
| 25. Speech-Language Pathologists | $66,920 | 18.5% | 4,380 |
| 26. Industrial-Organizational Psychologists | $87,330 | 26.1% | 130 |
| 27. Health Specialties Teachers, Postsecondary | $85,270 | 15.1% | 4,000 |
| 28. Orthodontists | $166,400+ | 19.8% | 360 |
| 29. Surgical Technologists | $39,920 | 25.3% | 4,630 |
| 30. Respiratory Therapists | $54,280 | 20.9% | 4,140 |
| 31. Veterinary Technologists and Technicians | $29,710 | 35.8% | 4,850 |
| 32. Mental Health Counselors | $38,150 | 24.0% | 5,010 |
| 33. Social and Human Service Assistants | $28,200 | 22.6% | 15,390 |
| 34. Engineers, All Other | $90,270 | 6.7% | 5,020 |
| 35. Medical Records and Health Information Technicians | $32,350 | 20.3% | 7,030 |
| 36. Chiropractors | $67,200 | 19.5% | 1,820 |
| 37. Athletic Trainers | $41,600 | 36.9% | 1,150 |
| 38. Occupational Therapy Assistants | $51,010 | 29.8% | 1,180 |
| 39. Executive Secretaries and Executive Administrative Assistants | $43,520 | 12.8% | 41,920 |
| 40. First-Line Supervisors of Office and Administrative Support Workers | $47,460 | 11.0% | 48,900 |
| 41. Audiologists | $66,660 | 25.0% | 580 |
| 42. Biological Scientists, All Other | $68,220 | 18.8% | 1,610 |
| 43. Clinical, Counseling, and School Psychologists | $66,810 | 11.1% | 5,990 |
| 44. Cardiovascular Technologists and Technicians | $49,410 | 24.1% | 1,910 |
| 45. Oral and Maxillofacial Surgeons | $166,400+ | 15.3% | 290 |
| 46. Substance Abuse and Behavioral Disorder Counselors | $38,120 | 21.0% | 3,550 |
| 47. Rehabilitation Counselors | $32,350 | 18.9% | 5,070 |
| 48. Physical Therapist Aides | $23,680 | 36.3% | 2,340 |
| 49. Receptionists and Information Clerks | $25,240 | 15.2% | 48,020 |
| 50. Medical and Clinical Laboratory Technologists | $56,130 | 11.9% | 5,330 |
| 51. Diagnostic Medical Sonographers | $64,380 | 18.3% | 1,650 |

## Best Jobs for People Interested in Health Science

| Job | Annual Earnings | Percent Growth | Annual Openings |
|---|---|---|---|
| 52. Medical and Clinical Laboratory Technicians | $36,280 | 16.1% | 5,460 |
| 53. Massage Therapists | $34,900 | 18.9% | 3,950 |
| 54. Health Educators | $45,830 | 18.2% | 2,600 |
| 55. Healthcare Support Workers, All Other | $30,280 | 17.1% | 5,670 |
| 56. Health Technologists and Technicians, All Other | $38,460 | 18.7% | 3,200 |
| 57. Nuclear Medicine Technologists | $68,560 | 16.3% | 670 |
| 58. Psychologists, All Other | $89,900 | 14.4% | 680 |
| 59. Physical Scientists, All Other | $94,780 | 11.1% | 1,010 |
| 60. Health Diagnosing and Treating Practitioners, All Other | $69,310 | 13.0% | 1,530 |
| 61. Healthcare Practitioners and Technical Workers, All Other | $43,970 | 15.9% | 2,910 |
| 62. Psychology Teachers, Postsecondary | $67,330 | 15.1% | 1,000 |
| 63. Nursing Instructors and Teachers, Postsecondary | $62,390 | 15.1% | 1,500 |
| 64. Occupational Health and Safety Specialists | $64,660 | 11.2% | 2,490 |
| 65. Podiatrists | $118,030 | 9.0% | 320 |
| 66. Veterinary Assistants and Laboratory Animal Caretakers | $22,040 | 22.8% | 2,550 |
| 67. Life, Physical, and Social Science Technicians, All Other | $43,350 | 13.3% | 3,640 |
| 68. Orthotists and Prosthetists | $65,060 | 15.4% | 210 |
| 69. Communications Teachers, Postsecondary | $60,300 | 15.1% | 800 |
| 70. Cooks, Institution and Cafeteria | $22,730 | 9.7% | 13,810 |
| 71. First-Line Supervisors of Food Preparation and Serving Workers | $29,560 | 6.6% | 13,440 |
| 72. Dietitians and Nutritionists | $53,250 | 9.2% | 2,570 |
| 73. Home Economics Teachers, Postsecondary | $65,040 | 15.1% | 200 |
| 74. Editors | $51,470 | –0.3% | 3,390 |
| 75. Emergency Medical Technicians and Paramedics | $30,360 | 9.0% | 6,200 |
| 76. Recreational Therapists | $39,410 | 14.6% | 1,160 |
| 77. Opticians, Dispensing | $32,940 | 13.4% | 2,020 |
| 78. Dental Laboratory Technicians | $35,140 | 13.9% | 1,530 |

## Best Jobs for People Interested in Hospitality, Tourism, and Recreation

| Job | Annual Earnings | Percent Growth | Annual Openings |
|---|---|---|---|
| 1. Managers, All Other | $96,450 | 7.3% | 29,750 |
| 2. Combined Food Preparation and Serving Workers, Including Fast Food | $17,950 | 14.6% | 96,720 |

*(continued)*

*(continued)*

## Best Jobs for People Interested in Hospitality, Tourism, and Recreation

| Job | Annual Earnings | Percent Growth | Annual Openings |
|---|---|---|---|
| 3. Amusement and Recreation Attendants | $18,450 | 13.3% | 17,120 |
| 4. Cooks, Institution and Cafeteria | $22,730 | 9.7% | 13,810 |
| 5. Counter Attendants, Cafeteria, Food Concession, and Coffee Shop | $18,370 | 9.3% | 43,490 |
| 6. Gaming Managers | $66,960 | 11.9% | 200 |
| 7. Ushers, Lobby Attendants, and Ticket Takers | $18,560 | 13.7% | 8,190 |
| 8. Dishwashers | $18,150 | 11.6% | 27,570 |
| 9. Gaming Dealers | $18,090 | 19.0% | 5,590 |
| 10. Food Service Managers | $48,130 | 5.3% | 8,370 |
| 11. First-Line Supervisors of Food Preparation and Serving Workers | $29,560 | 6.6% | 13,440 |
| 12. Flight Attendants | $37,740 | 8.1% | 3,010 |
| 13. Reservation and Transportation Ticket Agents and Travel Clerks | $31,740 | 8.1% | 5,150 |

## Best Jobs for People Interested in Human Service

| Job | Annual Earnings | Percent Growth | Annual Openings |
|---|---|---|---|
| 1. Public Relations Specialists | $52,090 | 24.0% | 13,130 |
| 2. Sales Managers | $98,530 | 14.9% | 12,660 |
| 3. Healthcare Social Workers | $47,230 | 22.4% | 6,590 |
| 4. Social Scientists and Related Workers, All Other | $74,620 | 22.4% | 2,380 |
| 5. Personal Care Aides | $19,640 | 46.0% | 47,780 |
| 6. Managers, All Other | $96,450 | 7.3% | 29,750 |
| 7. Mental Health Counselors | $38,150 | 24.0% | 5,010 |
| 8. Chief Executives | $165,080 | −1.4% | 11,250 |
| 9. Probation Officers and Correctional Treatment Specialists | $47,200 | 19.3% | 4,180 |
| 10. Hairdressers, Hairstylists, and Cosmetologists | $22,760 | 20.1% | 21,950 |
| 11. Sociologists | $72,360 | 22.0% | 200 |
| 12. Mental Health and Substance Abuse Social Workers | $38,600 | 19.5% | 6,130 |
| 13. Preschool Teachers, Except Special Education | $25,700 | 19.0% | 17,830 |
| 14. Writers and Authors | $55,420 | 14.8% | 5,420 |
| 15. Psychology Teachers, Postsecondary | $67,330 | 15.1% | 1,000 |
| 16. Clergy | $43,970 | 12.7% | 21,770 |

## Best Jobs for People Interested in Human Service

| Job | Annual Earnings | Percent Growth | Annual Openings |
|---|---|---|---|
| 17. Clinical, Counseling, and School Psychologists | $66,810 | 11.1% | 5,990 |
| 18. Interpreters and Translators | $43,300 | 22.2% | 2,340 |
| 19. Health Educators | $45,830 | 18.2% | 2,600 |
| 20. Substance Abuse and Behavioral Disorder Counselors | $38,120 | 21.0% | 3,550 |
| 21. Area, Ethnic, and Cultural Studies Teachers, Postsecondary | $68,020 | 15.1% | 200 |
| 22. Social and Community Service Managers | $57,950 | 13.8% | 4,820 |
| 23. Funeral Attendants | $22,990 | 26.3% | 2,550 |
| 24. Skincare Specialists | $28,920 | 37.8% | 2,030 |
| 25. Home Economics Teachers, Postsecondary | $65,040 | 15.1% | 200 |
| 26. Social Work Teachers, Postsecondary | $63,090 | 15.1% | 300 |
| 27. Philosophy and Religion Teachers, Postsecondary | $62,330 | 15.1% | 600 |
| 28. Psychologists, All Other | $89,900 | 14.4% | 680 |
| 29. Child, Family, and School Social Workers | $40,210 | 12.3% | 10,960 |
| 30. Epidemiologists | $63,010 | 15.1% | 170 |
| 31. First-Line Supervisors of Retail Sales Workers | $35,820 | 5.2% | 45,010 |
| 32. Protective Service Workers, All Other | $29,890 | 14.0% | 7,150 |
| 33. Recreation Workers | $22,260 | 14.7% | 10,720 |
| 34. Childcare Workers | $19,300 | 10.9% | 52,310 |
| 35. Social Science Research Assistants | $37,230 | 17.8% | 1,270 |
| 36. Manicurists and Pedicurists | $19,650 | 18.8% | 2,530 |
| 37. Marriage and Family Therapists | $45,720 | 14.5% | 950 |
| 38. Morticians, Undertakers, and Funeral Directors | $54,330 | 11.9% | 960 |
| 39. Eligibility Interviewers, Government Programs | $39,960 | 9.2% | 3,880 |
| 40. Directors, Religious Activities and Education | $36,170 | 12.6% | 2,640 |
| 41. Music Directors and Composers | $45,970 | 10.0% | 1,620 |

## Best Jobs for People Interested in Information Technology

| Job | Annual Earnings | Percent Growth | Annual Openings |
|---|---|---|---|
| 1. Software Developers, Applications | $87,790 | 34.0% | 21,840 |
| 2. Software Developers, Systems Software | $94,180 | 30.4% | 15,340 |
| 3. Computer and Information Systems Managers | $115,780 | 16.9% | 9,710 |
| 4. Computer Systems Analysts | $77,740 | 20.3% | 22,280 |
| 5. Computer and Information Research Scientists | $100,660 | 24.2% | 1,320 |

*(continued)*

*(continued)*

## Best Jobs for People Interested in Information Technology

| Job | Annual Earnings | Percent Growth | Annual Openings |
|---|---|---|---|
| 6. Network and Computer Systems Administrators | $69,160 | 23.2% | 13,550 |
| 7. Architectural and Engineering Managers | $119,260 | 6.2% | 4,870 |
| 8. Database Administrators | $73,490 | 20.3% | 4,440 |
| 9. Computer Occupations, All Other | $79,240 | 13.1% | 7,260 |
| 10. Engineering Teachers, Postsecondary | $89,670 | 15.1% | 1,000 |
| 11. Computer Hardware Engineers | $98,810 | 3.8% | 2,350 |
| 12. Biological Scientists, All Other | $68,220 | 18.8% | 1,610 |
| 13. Graphic Designers | $43,500 | 12.9% | 12,480 |
| 14. Physical Scientists, All Other | $94,780 | 11.1% | 1,010 |
| 15. Computer Programmers | $71,380 | −2.9% | 8,030 |
| 16. Computer Science Teachers, Postsecondary | $70,300 | 15.1% | 1,000 |
| 17. Multimedia Artists and Animators | $58,510 | 14.2% | 2,890 |
| 18. Life, Physical, and Social Science Technicians, All Other | $43,350 | 13.3% | 3,640 |

## Best Jobs for People Interested in Law and Public Safety

| Job | Annual Earnings | Percent Growth | Annual Openings |
|---|---|---|---|
| 1. Compliance Officers | $58,720 | 31.0% | 10,850 |
| 2. Lawyers | $112,760 | 13.0% | 24,040 |
| 3. Firefighters | $45,250 | 18.5% | 15,280 |
| 4. Paralegals and Legal Assistants | $46,680 | 28.1% | 10,400 |
| 5. Detectives and Criminal Investigators | $68,820 | 16.6% | 4,160 |
| 6. Law Teachers, Postsecondary | $94,260 | 15.1% | 400 |
| 7. Legal Secretaries | $41,500 | 18.4% | 8,380 |
| 8. Psychology Teachers, Postsecondary | $67,330 | 15.1% | 1,000 |
| 9. Forensic Science Technicians | $51,570 | 19.6% | 800 |
| 10. Physical Scientists, All Other | $94,780 | 11.1% | 1,010 |
| 11. Police and Sheriff's Patrol Officers | $53,540 | 8.7% | 22,790 |
| 12. Private Detectives and Investigators | $42,870 | 22.0% | 1,930 |
| 13. First-Line Supervisors of Police and Detectives | $78,260 | 8.1% | 5,050 |
| 14. Security Guards | $23,920 | 14.2% | 37,390 |
| 15. Anthropology and Archeology Teachers, Postsecondary | $73,600 | 15.1% | 200 |
| 16. Criminal Justice and Law Enforcement Teachers, Postsecondary | $59,520 | 15.1% | 400 |

## Best Jobs for People Interested in Law and Public Safety

| Job | Annual Earnings | Percent Growth | Annual Openings |
|---|---|---|---|
| 17. Court Reporters | $47,700 | 18.3% | 710 |
| 18. Police, Fire, and Ambulance Dispatchers | $35,370 | 17.8% | 3,840 |
| 19. Child, Family, and School Social Workers | $40,210 | 12.3% | 10,960 |
| 20. First-Line Supervisors of Fire Fighting and Prevention Workers | $68,240 | 8.2% | 3,250 |
| 21. Correctional Officers and Jailers | $39,040 | 9.4% | 14,360 |
| 22. First-Line Supervisors of Correctional Officers | $55,910 | 8.5% | 1,940 |
| 23. Protective Service Workers, All Other | $29,890 | 14.0% | 7,150 |
| 24. Administrative Law Judges, Adjudicators, and Hearing Officers | $85,500 | 8.1% | 380 |
| 25. Arbitrators, Mediators, and Conciliators | $55,800 | 14.0% | 320 |

## Best Jobs for People Interested in Manufacturing

| Job | Annual Earnings | Percent Growth | Annual Openings |
|---|---|---|---|
| 1. Cost Estimators | $57,860 | 25.3% | 10,360 |
| 2. First-Line Supervisors of Mechanics, Installers, and Repairers | $59,150 | 4.2% | 13,650 |
| 3. Interior Designers | $46,280 | 19.4% | 3,590 |
| 4. Civil Engineering Technicians | $46,290 | 16.9% | 3,280 |
| 5. Nuclear Power Reactor Operators | $75,650 | 18.9% | 270 |
| 6. Biological Technicians | $39,020 | 17.6% | 4,190 |
| 7. Industrial Machinery Mechanics | $45,420 | 7.3% | 6,240 |
| 8. Occupational Health and Safety Specialists | $64,660 | 11.2% | 2,490 |
| 9. Medical Equipment Repairers | $44,490 | 27.2% | 2,320 |
| 10. First-Line Supervisors of Production and Operating Workers | $53,090 | –5.2% | 9,190 |
| 11. Environmental Science and Protection Technicians, Including Health | $41,380 | 28.9% | 2,520 |
| 12. Life, Physical, and Social Science Technicians, All Other | $43,350 | 13.3% | 3,640 |
| 13. Electrical and Electronics Repairers, Powerhouse, Substation, and Relay | $65,230 | 11.5% | 670 |
| 14. Mixing and Blending Machine Setters, Operators, and Tenders | $32,870 | 15.5% | 4,610 |
| 15. Mobile Heavy Equipment Mechanics, Except Engines | $44,830 | 8.7% | 3,770 |
| 16. Aircraft Mechanics and Service Technicians | $53,420 | 6.4% | 3,140 |
| 17. Elevator Installers and Repairers | $70,910 | 9.2% | 920 |
| 18. Environmental Engineering Technicians | $43,390 | 30.1% | 1,040 |
| 19. Surveying and Mapping Technicians | $37,900 | 20.4% | 2,940 |
| 20. Sheet Metal Workers | $41,710 | 6.5% | 5,170 |

*(continued)*

(continued)

## Best Jobs for People Interested in Manufacturing

| Job | Annual Earnings | Percent Growth | Annual Openings |
|---|---|---|---|
| 21. Installation, Maintenance, and Repair Workers, All Other | $36,420 | 9.2% | 4,180 |
| 22. Automotive Service Technicians and Mechanics | $35,790 | 4.7% | 18,170 |
| 23. Electrical and Electronic Engineering Technicians | $56,040 | –2.2% | 3,100 |
| 24. Engineering Technicians, Except Drafters, All Other | $58,020 | 5.2% | 1,850 |
| 25. First-Line Supervisors of Helpers, Laborers, and Material Movers, Hand | $43,800 | 3.6% | 3,850 |
| 26. Industrial Engineering Technicians | $48,210 | 6.6% | 1,850 |
| 27. Extruding, Forming, Pressing, and Compacting Machine Setters, Operators, and Tenders | $31,210 | 15.0% | 2,960 |
| 28. Telecommunications Line Installers and Repairers | $50,850 | 0.9% | 2,790 |
| 29. Hazardous Materials Removal Workers | $37,600 | 14.8% | 1,780 |
| 30. Construction and Related Workers, All Other | $34,500 | 11.1% | 2,660 |

## Best Jobs for People Interested in Retail and Wholesale Sales and Service

| Job | Annual Earnings | Percent Growth | Annual Openings |
|---|---|---|---|
| 1. Sales Managers | $98,530 | 14.9% | 12,660 |
| 2. Business Operations Specialists, All Other | $62,450 | 11.5% | 36,830 |
| 3. Marketing Managers | $112,800 | 12.5% | 5,970 |
| 4. Sales Representatives, Services, All Other | $50,620 | 13.9% | 22,810 |
| 5. Sales Representatives, Wholesale and Manufacturing, Technical and Scientific Products | $73,710 | 9.7% | 14,230 |
| 6. Purchasing Agents, Except Wholesale, Retail, and Farm Products | $56,580 | 13.9% | 11,860 |
| 7. Computer Occupations, All Other | $79,240 | 13.1% | 7,260 |
| 8. Real Estate Sales Agents | $40,030 | 16.2% | 12,830 |
| 9. Business Teachers, Postsecondary | $73,760 | 15.1% | 2,000 |
| 10. Interior Designers | $46,280 | 19.4% | 3,590 |
| 11. Sales Engineers | $87,390 | 8.8% | 3,500 |
| 12. Sales Representatives, Wholesale and Manufacturing, Except Technical and Scientific Products | $52,440 | 6.6% | 45,790 |
| 13. First-Line Supervisors of Non-Retail Sales Workers | $68,880 | 4.8% | 12,950 |
| 14. Meeting, Convention, and Event Planners | $45,260 | 15.6% | 2,140 |
| 15. Retail Salespersons | $20,670 | 8.3% | 162,690 |

## Best Jobs for People Interested in Retail and Wholesale Sales and Service

| Job | Annual Earnings | Percent Growth | Annual Openings |
|---|---|---|---|
| 16. Property, Real Estate, and Community Association Managers | $51,480 | 8.4% | 7,800 |
| 17. Stock Clerks and Order Fillers | $21,290 | 7.2% | 56,260 |
| 18. Survey Researchers | $36,050 | 30.3% | 1,340 |
| 19. First-Line Supervisors of Retail Sales Workers | $35,820 | 5.2% | 45,010 |
| 20. Hotel, Motel, and Resort Desk Clerks | $19,930 | 13.7% | 10,950 |
| 21. Real Estate Brokers | $54,910 | 8.6% | 3,080 |
| 22. Advertising and Promotions Managers | $83,890 | –1.7% | 1,050 |
| 23. Reservation and Transportation Ticket Agents and Travel Clerks | $31,740 | 8.1% | 5,150 |
| 24. Appraisers and Assessors of Real Estate | $48,500 | 4.6% | 2,100 |

## Best Jobs for People Interested in Scientific Research, Engineering, and Mathematics

| Job | Annual Earnings | Percent Growth | Annual Openings |
|---|---|---|---|
| 1. Medical Scientists, Except Epidemiologists | $76,700 | 40.4% | 6,620 |
| 2. Civil Engineers | $77,560 | 24.3% | 11,460 |
| 3. Natural Sciences Managers | $116,020 | 15.5% | 2,010 |
| 4. Environmental Engineers | $78,740 | 30.6% | 2,790 |
| 5. Biochemists and Biophysicists | $79,390 | 37.4% | 1,620 |
| 6. Biomedical Engineers | $81,540 | 72.0% | 1,490 |
| 7. Health Specialties Teachers, Postsecondary | $85,270 | 15.1% | 4,000 |
| 8. Petroleum Engineers | $114,080 | 18.4% | 860 |
| 9. Physicists | $106,370 | 15.9% | 690 |
| 10. Social Scientists and Related Workers, All Other | $74,620 | 22.4% | 2,380 |
| 11. Architectural and Engineering Managers | $119,260 | 6.2% | 4,870 |
| 12. Cost Estimators | $57,860 | 25.3% | 10,360 |
| 13. Engineering Teachers, Postsecondary | $89,670 | 15.1% | 1,000 |
| 14. Geoscientists, Except Hydrologists and Geographers | $82,500 | 17.5% | 1,540 |
| 15. Operations Research Analysts | $70,960 | 22.0% | 3,220 |
| 16. Engineers, All Other | $90,270 | 6.7% | 5,020 |
| 17. Political Scientists | $107,420 | 19.4% | 280 |
| 18. Aerospace Engineers | $97,480 | 10.4% | 2,230 |

*(continued)*

*(continued)*

## Best Jobs for People Interested in Scientific Research, Engineering, and Mathematics

| Job | Annual Earnings | Percent Growth | Annual Openings |
|---|---|---|---|
| 19. Industrial Engineers | $76,100 | 14.2% | 8,540 |
| 20. Mathematicians | $99,380 | 22.4% | 150 |
| 21. Computer Hardware Engineers | $98,810 | 3.8% | 2,350 |
| 22. Electronics Engineers, Except Computer | $90,170 | 0.3% | 3,340 |
| 23. Physical Scientists, All Other | $94,780 | 11.1% | 1,010 |
| 24. Biological Science Teachers, Postsecondary | $72,700 | 15.1% | 1,700 |
| 25. Biological Scientists, All Other | $68,220 | 18.8% | 1,610 |
| 26. Electrical Engineers | $84,540 | 1.7% | 3,890 |
| 27. Mechanical Engineers | $78,160 | 6.0% | 7,570 |
| 28. Psychologists, All Other | $89,900 | 14.4% | 680 |
| 29. Survey Researchers | $36,050 | 30.3% | 1,340 |
| 30. Economics Teachers, Postsecondary | $83,370 | 15.1% | 400 |
| 31. Nuclear Engineers | $99,920 | 10.9% | 540 |
| 32. Atmospheric, Earth, Marine, and Space Sciences Teachers, Postsecondary | $82,840 | 15.1% | 300 |
| 33. Cartographers and Photogrammetrists | $54,510 | 26.8% | 640 |
| 34. Mining and Geological Engineers, Including Mining Safety Engineers | $82,870 | 15.3% | 260 |
| 35. Astronomers | $87,260 | 15.6% | 70 |
| 36. Hydrologists | $75,690 | 18.2% | 380 |
| 37. Mathematical Science Teachers, Postsecondary | $65,710 | 15.1% | 1,000 |
| 38. Physics Teachers, Postsecondary | $77,610 | 15.1% | 400 |
| 39. Atmospheric and Space Scientists | $87,780 | 14.6% | 330 |
| 40. Geographers | $72,800 | 26.0% | 100 |
| 41. Materials Engineers | $83,120 | 9.3% | 810 |
| 42. Anthropologists and Archeologists | $54,230 | 28.0% | 450 |
| 43. Curators | $48,450 | 23.0% | 620 |
| 44. Museum Technicians and Conservators | $37,310 | 25.6% | 610 |
| 45. Sociologists | $72,360 | 22.0% | 200 |
| 46. Statisticians | $72,830 | 13.1% | 960 |
| 47. Chemistry Teachers, Postsecondary | $70,520 | 15.1% | 600 |
| 48. History Teachers, Postsecondary | $64,880 | 15.1% | 700 |
| 49. Materials Scientists | $84,720 | 11.9% | 440 |
| 50. Political Science Teachers, Postsecondary | $70,540 | 15.1% | 500 |
| 51. Economists | $89,450 | 5.8% | 500 |

## Best Jobs for People Interested in Scientific Research, Engineering, and Mathematics

| Job | Annual Earnings | Percent Growth | Annual Openings |
|---|---|---|---|
| 52. Health and Safety Engineers, Except Mining Safety Engineers and Inspectors | $75,430 | 10.3% | 920 |
| 53. Anthropology and Archeology Teachers, Postsecondary | $73,600 | 15.1% | 200 |
| 54. Architecture Teachers, Postsecondary | $73,500 | 15.1% | 200 |
| 55. Chemists | $68,320 | 2.5% | 3,000 |
| 56. Sociology Teachers, Postsecondary | $64,810 | 15.1% | 500 |
| 57. Dietitians and Nutritionists | $53,250 | 9.2% | 2,570 |
| 58. Microbiologists | $65,920 | 12.2% | 750 |
| 59. Zoologists and Wildlife Biologists | $57,430 | 12.8% | 880 |
| 60. Geography Teachers, Postsecondary | $66,700 | 15.1% | 100 |
| 61. Industrial Engineering Technicians | $48,210 | 6.6% | 1,850 |
| 62. Epidemiologists | $63,010 | 15.1% | 170 |
| 63. Agricultural Engineers | $71,090 | 11.9% | 90 |

## Best Jobs for People Interested in Transportation, Distribution, and Logistics

| Job | Annual Earnings | Percent Growth | Annual Openings |
|---|---|---|---|
| 1. Compliance Officers | $58,720 | 31.0% | 10,850 |
| 2. Logisticians | $70,800 | 19.5% | 4,190 |
| 3. Environmental Engineers | $78,740 | 30.6% | 2,790 |
| 4. Environmental Scientists and Specialists, Including Health | $61,700 | 27.9% | 4,840 |
| 5. Managers, All Other | $96,450 | 7.3% | 29,750 |
| 6. Chief Executives | $165,080 | −1.4% | 11,250 |
| 7. Commercial Pilots | $67,500 | 18.5% | 2,060 |
| 8. Airline Pilots, Copilots, and Flight Engineers | $103,210 | 8.4% | 3,250 |
| 9. Air Traffic Controllers | $108,040 | 13.1% | 1,230 |
| 10. Heavy and Tractor-Trailer Truck Drivers | $37,770 | 12.9% | 55,460 |
| 11. Captains, Mates, and Pilots of Water Vessels | $64,180 | 17.3% | 1,950 |
| 12. Operating Engineers and Other Construction Equipment Operators | $40,400 | 12.0% | 11,820 |
| 13. Environmental Science and Protection Technicians, Including Health | $41,380 | 28.9% | 2,520 |

*(continued)*

*(continued)*

| Best Jobs for People Interested in Transportation, Distribution, and Logistics | | | |
|---|---|---|---|
| Job | Annual Earnings | Percent Growth | Annual Openings |
| 14. Ship Engineers | $65,880 | 18.6% | 700 |
| 15. Taxi Drivers and Chauffeurs | $22,440 | 15.5% | 7,730 |
| 16. Transportation Inspectors | $57,640 | 18.3% | 1,130 |
| 17. Health and Safety Engineers, Except Mining Safety Engineers and Inspectors | $75,430 | 10.3% | 920 |
| 18. Subway and Streetcar Operators | $56,880 | 18.8% | 390 |
| 19. Transportation, Storage, and Distribution Managers | $80,210 | −5.3% | 2,740 |
| 20. Aircraft Mechanics and Service Technicians | $53,420 | 6.4% | 3,140 |
| 21. Bus and Truck Mechanics and Diesel Engine Specialists | $40,850 | 5.7% | 7,530 |
| 22. Automotive Service Technicians and Mechanics | $35,790 | 4.7% | 18,170 |
| 23. Installation, Maintenance, and Repair Workers, All Other | $36,420 | 9.2% | 4,180 |
| 24. Production, Planning, and Expediting Clerks | $42,220 | 1.5% | 7,410 |
| 25. Bus Drivers, Transit and Intercity | $35,520 | 8.2% | 4,990 |
| 26. Aircraft Structure, Surfaces, Rigging, and Systems Assemblers | $44,820 | 9.4% | 1,340 |
| 27. First-Line Supervisors of Helpers, Laborers, and Material Movers, Hand | $43,800 | 3.6% | 3,850 |
| 28. First-Line Supervisors of Transportation and Material-Moving Machine and Vehicle Operators | $52,720 | −3.7% | 3,770 |
| 29. Railroad Brake, Signal, and Switch Operators | $47,670 | 9.4% | 1,070 |
| 30. Railroad Conductors and Yardmasters | $49,770 | 6.9% | 1,700 |
| 31. Sailors and Marine Oilers | $36,260 | 11.7% | 1,790 |

# Best Jobs Lists Based on Personality Types

These lists organize the 400 best jobs into groups matching six personality types. Within each personality type, I ranked the jobs based on each one's total combined score for earnings, growth, and annual job openings.

The personality types are Realistic, Investigative, Artistic, Social, Enterprising, and Conventional (RIASEC). This system was developed by John Holland and is used in the *Self-Directed Search (SDS)* and other career assessment inventories and information systems. If you have used one of these career inventories or systems, the lists will help you identify jobs that most closely match these personality types. Even if you have not used one of these systems, the concept of personality types and the jobs that are related to them can help you identify jobs that suit the type of person you are.

Like the set of lists for the career clusters, this set assigns some the jobs to more than one list in order to match the differing characteristics of job specializations. For example, you will find the job Financial Managers on two lists because it is linked to the specializations Treasurers and Controllers (Conventional) and Financial Managers, Branch or Department (Enterprising). In addition, you should be aware that these lists are based on the primary personality type that describes the job, but most jobs also are linked to one or two secondary personality types. The job descriptions in Part II indicate all significant personality types. Consider reviewing the jobs for more than one personality type so you don't overlook possible jobs that would interest you.

The O*NET database, which was my source for RIASEC information about the best jobs, provided no RIASEC information for Construction and Related Workers, All Other, and three others of the best jobs that have "All Other" in their title.

# Descriptions of the Six Personality Types

Following are brief descriptions for each of the six personality types used in the lists. Select the two or three descriptions that most closely describe you and then use the lists to identify jobs that best fit these personality types.

- **Realistic:** These occupations frequently involve work activities that include practical, hands-on problems and solutions. They often deal with plants; animals; and real-world materials such as wood, tools, and machinery. Many of the occupations require working outside and don't involve a lot of paperwork or working closely with others.

- **Investigative:** These occupations frequently involve working with ideas and require an extensive amount of thinking. These occupations can involve searching for facts and figuring out problems mentally.

- **Artistic:** These occupations frequently involve working with forms, designs, and patterns. They often require self-expression, and the work can be done without following a clear set of rules.

- **Social:** These occupations frequently involve working with, communicating with, and teaching people. These occupations often involve helping or providing service to others.

- **Enterprising:** These occupations frequently involve starting up and carrying out projects. These occupations can involve leading people and making many decisions. They sometimes require risk taking and often deal with business.

- **Conventional:** These occupations frequently involve following set procedures and routines. These occupations can include working with data and details more than with ideas. Usually there is a clear line of authority to follow.

## Best Jobs for People with a Realistic Personality Type

| Job | Annual Earnings | Percent Growth | Annual Openings |
|---|---|---|---|
| 1. Civil Engineers | $77,560 | 24.3% | 11,460 |
| 2. Physician Assistants | $86,410 | 39.0% | 4,280 |
| 3. Heating, Air Conditioning, and Refrigeration Mechanics and Installers | $42,530 | 28.1% | 13,620 |
| 4. Firefighters | $45,250 | 18.5% | 15,280 |
| 5. Radiologic Technologists | $54,340 | 17.2% | 6,800 |
| 6. Business Operations Specialists, All Other | $62,450 | 11.5% | 36,830 |
| 7. Plumbers, Pipefitters, and Steamfitters | $46,660 | 15.3% | 17,550 |
| 8. Surgical Technologists | $39,920 | 25.3% | 4,630 |
| 9. Electricians | $48,250 | 11.9% | 25,090 |
| 10. Water and Wastewater Treatment Plant and System Operators | $40,770 | 19.8% | 4,690 |
| 11. Commercial Pilots | $67,500 | 18.5% | 2,060 |
| 12. Construction Laborers | $29,280 | 20.5% | 33,940 |
| 13. Construction and Building Inspectors | $52,360 | 16.8% | 3,970 |
| 14. Medical and Clinical Laboratory Technologists | $56,130 | 11.9% | 5,330 |
| 15. Cardiovascular Technologists and Technicians | $49,410 | 24.1% | 1,910 |
| 16. Medical Equipment Repairers | $44,490 | 27.2% | 2,320 |
| 17. Police and Sheriff's Patrol Officers | $53,540 | 8.7% | 22,790 |
| 18. Captains, Mates, and Pilots of Water Vessels | $64,180 | 17.3% | 1,950 |
| 19. Carpenters | $39,530 | 12.9% | 32,540 |
| 20. Veterinary Technologists and Technicians | $29,710 | 35.8% | 4,850 |
| 21. Heavy and Tractor-Trailer Truck Drivers | $37,770 | 12.9% | 55,460 |
| 22. Cartographers and Photogrammetrists | $54,510 | 26.8% | 640 |
| 23. Engineers, All Other | $90,270 | 6.7% | 5,020 |
| 24. Civil Engineering Technicians | $46,290 | 16.9% | 3,280 |
| 25. Landscaping and Groundskeeping Workers | $23,400 | 18.0% | 36,220 |
| 26. Nuclear Power Reactor Operators | $75,650 | 18.9% | 270 |
| 27. Refuse and Recyclable Material Collectors | $32,640 | 18.6% | 7,110 |
| 28. Security and Fire Alarm Systems Installers | $38,500 | 24.8% | 2,780 |
| 29. Ship Engineers | $65,880 | 18.6% | 700 |
| 30. Biological Technicians | $39,020 | 17.6% | 4,190 |
| 31. Operating Engineers and Other Construction Equipment Operators | $40,400 | 12.0% | 11,820 |
| 32. Environmental Engineering Technicians | $43,390 | 30.1% | 1,040 |
| 33. Helpers—Electricians | $27,220 | 24.7% | 4,800 |
| 34. Transportation Inspectors | $57,640 | 18.3% | 1,130 |
| 35. Brickmasons and Blockmasons | $46,930 | 11.5% | 5,000 |

## Best Jobs for People with a Realistic Personality Type

| Job | Annual Earnings | Percent Growth | Annual Openings |
|---|---|---|---|
| 36. Medical and Clinical Laboratory Technicians | $36,280 | 16.1% | 5,460 |
| 37. Boilermakers | $54,640 | 18.8% | 810 |
| 38. Nonfarm Animal Caretakers | $19,550 | 20.7% | 7,360 |
| 39. Surveyors | $54,880 | 14.9% | 2,330 |
| 40. Surveying and Mapping Technicians | $37,900 | 20.4% | 2,940 |
| 41. Airline Pilots, Copilots, and Flight Engineers | $103,210 | 8.4% | 3,250 |
| 42. Health Technologists and Technicians, All Other | $38,460 | 18.7% | 3,200 |
| 43. Helpers—Pipelayers, Plumbers, Pipefitters, and Steamfitters | $26,740 | 25.7% | 3,730 |
| 44. Subway and Streetcar Operators | $56,880 | 18.8% | 390 |
| 45. Correctional Officers and Jailers | $39,040 | 9.4% | 14,360 |
| 46. Oral and Maxillofacial Surgeons | $166,400+ | 15.3% | 290 |
| 47. Healthcare Support Workers, All Other | $30,280 | 17.1% | 5,670 |
| 48. Security Guards | $23,920 | 14.2% | 37,390 |
| 49. Life, Physical, and Social Science Technicians, All Other | $43,350 | 13.3% | 3,640 |
| 50. Cement Masons and Concrete Finishers | $35,450 | 12.9% | 7,640 |
| 51. Electrical Power-Line Installers and Repairers | $58,030 | 4.5% | 4,550 |
| 52. Industrial Machinery Mechanics | $45,420 | 7.3% | 6,240 |
| 53. Electronics Engineers, Except Computer | $90,170 | 0.3% | 3,340 |
| 54. Helpers—Carpenters | $25,760 | 23.3% | 3,530 |
| 55. Taxi Drivers and Chauffeurs | $22,440 | 15.5% | 7,730 |
| 56. Mixing and Blending Machine Setters, Operators, and Tenders | $32,870 | 15.5% | 4,610 |
| 57. Architectural and Civil Drafters | $46,430 | 9.1% | 3,620 |
| 58. Physical Scientists, All Other | $94,780 | 11.1% | 1,010 |
| 59. Bus and Truck Mechanics and Diesel Engine Specialists | $40,850 | 5.7% | 7,530 |
| 60. Insulation Workers, Mechanical | $37,650 | 19.4% | 1,550 |
| 61. Drywall and Ceiling Tile Installers | $37,320 | 13.5% | 3,700 |
| 62. Mobile Heavy Equipment Mechanics, Except Engines | $44,830 | 8.7% | 3,770 |
| 63. Tree Trimmers and Pruners | $30,450 | 26.3% | 1,720 |
| 64. Museum Technicians and Conservators | $37,310 | 25.6% | 610 |
| 65. Sheet Metal Workers | $41,710 | 6.5% | 5,170 |
| 66. Telecommunications Equipment Installers and Repairers, Except Line Installers | $54,710 | –0.2% | 3,560 |
| 67. Tile and Marble Setters | $38,110 | 14.3% | 3,070 |
| 68. Septic Tank Servicers and Sewer Pipe Cleaners | $33,570 | 23.8% | 1,320 |
| 69. Electrical and Electronics Repairers, Powerhouse, Substation, and Relay | $65,230 | 11.5% | 670 |
| 70. Aircraft Mechanics and Service Technicians | $53,420 | 6.4% | 3,140 |

*(continued)*

*(continued)*

## Best Jobs for People with a Realistic Personality Type

| Job | Annual Earnings | Percent Growth | Annual Openings |
|---|---|---|---|
| 71. Automotive Service Technicians and Mechanics | $35,790 | 4.7% | 18,170 |
| 72. Veterinary Assistants and Laboratory Animal Caretakers | $22,040 | 22.8% | 2,550 |
| 73. Conservation Scientists | $59,310 | 11.9% | 410 |
| 74. Elevator Installers and Repairers | $70,910 | 9.2% | 920 |
| 75. Dishwashers | $18,150 | 11.6% | 27,570 |
| 76. Electrical and Electronic Engineering Technicians | $56,040 | –2.2% | 3,100 |
| 77. Structural Iron and Steel Workers | $44,540 | 12.4% | 2,020 |
| 78. Pest Control Workers | $30,340 | 15.3% | 3,400 |
| 79. Pipelayers | $34,800 | 17.2% | 2,280 |
| 80. Audio and Video Equipment Technicians | $40,540 | 12.6% | 2,370 |
| 81. Counter Attendants, Cafeteria, Food Concession, and Coffee Shop | $18,370 | 9.3% | 43,490 |
| 82. Animal Trainers | $26,580 | 20.4% | 1,900 |
| 83. Cooks, Institution and Cafeteria | $22,730 | 9.7% | 13,810 |
| 84. Rail-Track Laying and Maintenance Equipment Operators | $45,970 | 14.8% | 650 |
| 85. Painters, Construction and Maintenance | $34,280 | 7.0% | 10,650 |
| 86. Stock Clerks and Order Fillers | $21,290 | 7.2% | 56,260 |
| 87. Engineering Technicians, Except Drafters, All Other | $58,020 | 5.2% | 1,850 |
| 88. Manicurists and Pedicurists | $19,650 | 18.8% | 2,530 |
| 89. Tapers | $45,490 | 13.0% | 900 |
| 90. Extruding, Forming, Pressing, and Compacting Machine Setters, Operators, and Tenders | $31,210 | 15.0% | 2,960 |
| 91. Highway Maintenance Workers | $34,780 | 8.5% | 5,200 |
| 92. Telecommunications Line Installers and Repairers | $50,850 | 0.9% | 2,790 |
| 93. Bus Drivers, Transit and Intercity | $35,520 | 8.2% | 4,990 |
| 94. Hazardous Materials Removal Workers | $37,600 | 14.8% | 1,780 |
| 95. Railroad Brake, Signal, and Switch Operators | $47,670 | 9.4% | 1,070 |
| 96. Aircraft Structure, Surfaces, Rigging, and Systems Assemblers | $44,820 | 9.4% | 1,340 |
| 97. Helpers—Brickmasons, Blockmasons, Stonemasons, and Tile and Marble Setters | $27,780 | 16.4% | 1,890 |
| 98. Dental Laboratory Technicians | $35,140 | 13.9% | 1,530 |
| 99. Excavating and Loading Machine and Dragline Operators | $36,920 | 8.6% | 2,850 |
| 100. Insulation Workers, Floor, Ceiling, and Wall | $31,830 | 15.2% | 1,320 |
| 101. Sailors and Marine Oilers | $36,260 | 11.7% | 1,790 |

## Best Jobs for People with an Investigative Personality Type

| Job | Annual Earnings | Percent Growth | Annual Openings |
|---|---|---|---|
| 1. Software Developers, Systems Software | $94,180 | 30.4% | 15,340 |
| 2. Physicians and Surgeons | $165,279 | 21.8% | 26,050 |
| 3. Software Developers, Applications | $87,790 | 34.0% | 21,840 |
| 4. Pharmacists | $111,570 | 17.0% | 10,580 |
| 5. Medical Scientists, Except Epidemiologists | $76,700 | 40.4% | 6,620 |
| 6. Management Analysts | $78,160 | 23.9% | 30,650 |
| 7. Veterinarians | $82,040 | 32.9% | 3,020 |
| 8. Dentists, General | $141,040 | 15.3% | 5,180 |
| 9. Computer Systems Analysts | $77,740 | 20.3% | 22,280 |
| 10. Optometrists | $94,990 | 24.4% | 2,010 |
| 11. Environmental Engineers | $78,740 | 30.6% | 2,790 |
| 12. Biochemists and Biophysicists | $79,390 | 37.4% | 1,620 |
| 13. Computer and Information Research Scientists | $100,660 | 24.2% | 1,320 |
| 14. Biomedical Engineers | $81,540 | 72.0% | 1,490 |
| 15. Network and Computer Systems Administrators | $69,160 | 23.2% | 13,550 |
| 16. Compliance Officers | $58,720 | 31.0% | 10,850 |
| 17. Market Research Analysts and Marketing Specialists | $60,570 | 28.1% | 13,730 |
| 18. Petroleum Engineers | $114,080 | 18.4% | 860 |
| 19. Prosthodontists | $118,400 | 28.3% | 30 |
| 20. Environmental Scientists and Specialists, Including Health | $61,700 | 27.9% | 4,840 |
| 21. Orthodontists | $166,400+ | 19.8% | 360 |
| 22. Social Scientists and Related Workers, All Other | $74,620 | 22.4% | 2,380 |
| 23. Operations Research Analysts | $70,960 | 22.0% | 3,220 |
| 24. Computer Occupations, All Other | $79,240 | 13.1% | 7,260 |
| 25. Industrial Engineers | $76,100 | 14.2% | 8,540 |
| 26. Logisticians | $70,800 | 19.5% | 4,190 |
| 27. Engineers, All Other | $90,270 | 6.7% | 5,020 |
| 28. Physicists | $106,370 | 15.9% | 690 |
| 29. Geoscientists, Except Hydrologists and Geographers | $82,500 | 17.5% | 1,540 |
| 30. Mathematicians | $99,380 | 22.4% | 150 |
| 31. Political Scientists | $107,420 | 19.4% | 280 |
| 32. Engineering Teachers, Postsecondary | $89,670 | 15.1% | 1,000 |
| 33. Aerospace Engineers | $97,480 | 10.4% | 2,230 |
| 34. Industrial-Organizational Psychologists | $87,330 | 26.1% | 130 |
| 35. Environmental Science and Protection Technicians, Including Health | $41,380 | 28.9% | 2,520 |
| 36. Electronics Engineers, Except Computer | $90,170 | 0.3% | 3,340 |

*(continued)*

*(continued)*

## Best Jobs for People with an Investigative Personality Type

| Job | Annual Earnings | Percent Growth | Annual Openings |
|-----|----------------|---------------|----------------|
| 37. Computer Hardware Engineers | $98,810 | 3.8% | 2,350 |
| 38. Mechanical Engineers | $78,160 | 6.0% | 7,570 |
| 39. Electrical Engineers | $84,540 | 1.7% | 3,890 |
| 40. Psychologists, All Other | $89,900 | 14.4% | 680 |
| 41. Biological Scientists, All Other | $68,220 | 18.8% | 1,610 |
| 42. Diagnostic Medical Sonographers | $64,380 | 18.3% | 1,650 |
| 43. Audiologists | $66,660 | 25.0% | 580 |
| 44. Clinical, Counseling, and School Psychologists | $66,810 | 11.1% | 5,990 |
| 45. Survey Researchers | $36,050 | 30.3% | 1,340 |
| 46. Nuclear Engineers | $99,920 | 10.9% | 540 |
| 47. Urban and Regional Planners | $63,040 | 19.0% | 1,470 |
| 48. Computer Programmers | $71,380 | −2.9% | 8,030 |
| 49. Geographers | $72,800 | 26.0% | 100 |
| 50. Atmospheric and Space Scientists | $87,780 | 14.6% | 330 |
| 51. Sociologists | $72,360 | 22.0% | 200 |
| 52. Hydrologists | $75,690 | 18.2% | 380 |
| 53. Mining and Geological Engineers, Including Mining Safety Engineers | $82,870 | 15.3% | 260 |
| 54. Podiatrists | $118,030 | 9.0% | 320 |
| 55. Statisticians | $72,830 | 13.1% | 960 |
| 56. Astronomers | $87,260 | 15.6% | 70 |
| 57. Medical and Clinical Laboratory Technologists | $56,130 | 11.9% | 5,330 |
| 58. Health Diagnosing and Treating Practitioners, All Other | $69,310 | 13.0% | 1,530 |
| 59. Materials Engineers | $83,120 | 9.3% | 810 |
| 60. Materials Scientists | $84,720 | 11.9% | 440 |
| 61. Financial Specialists, All Other | $60,980 | 10.5% | 4,320 |
| 62. Anthropologists and Archeologists | $54,230 | 28.0% | 450 |
| 63. Nuclear Medicine Technologists | $68,560 | 16.3% | 670 |
| 64. Occupational Health and Safety Specialists | $64,660 | 11.2% | 2,490 |
| 65. Surveyors | $54,880 | 14.9% | 2,330 |
| 66. Chemists | $68,320 | 2.5% | 3,000 |
| 67. Economists | $89,450 | 5.8% | 500 |
| 68. Health and Safety Engineers, Except Mining Safety Engineers and Inspectors | $75,430 | 10.3% | 920 |
| 69. Forensic Science Technicians | $51,570 | 19.6% | 800 |
| 70. Food Scientists and Technologists | $60,180 | 16.3% | 690 |
| 71. Microbiologists | $65,920 | 12.2% | 750 |

## Best Jobs for People with an Investigative Personality Type

| Job | Annual Earnings | Percent Growth | Annual Openings |
|---|---|---|---|
| 72. Soil and Plant Scientists | $57,340 | 15.5% | 700 |
| 73. Dietitians and Nutritionists | $53,250 | 9.2% | 2,570 |
| 74. Zoologists and Wildlife Biologists | $57,430 | 12.8% | 880 |
| 75. Engineering Technicians, Except Drafters, All Other | $58,020 | 5.2% | 1,850 |
| 76. Epidemiologists | $63,010 | 15.1% | 170 |
| 77. Agricultural Engineers | $71,090 | 11.9% | 90 |
| 78. Industrial Engineering Technicians | $48,210 | 6.6% | 1,850 |
| 79. Conservation Scientists | $59,310 | 11.9% | 410 |
| 80. Animal Scientists | $58,250 | 13.2% | 180 |

## Best Jobs for People with an Artistic Personality Type

| Job | Annual Earnings | Percent Growth | Annual Openings |
|---|---|---|---|
| 1. Architects, Except Landscape and Naval | $72,550 | 16.2% | 4,680 |
| 2. Writers and Authors | $55,420 | 14.8% | 5,420 |
| 3. Hairdressers, Hairstylists, and Cosmetologists | $22,760 | 20.1% | 21,950 |
| 4. Technical Writers | $63,280 | 18.2% | 1,680 |
| 5. Landscape Architects | $62,090 | 19.7% | 980 |
| 6. Art Directors | $80,630 | 11.7% | 2,870 |
| 7. Interior Designers | $46,280 | 19.4% | 3,590 |
| 8. Multimedia Artists and Animators | $58,510 | 14.2% | 2,890 |
| 9. Graphic Designers | $43,500 | 12.9% | 12,480 |
| 10. Interpreters and Translators | $43,300 | 22.2% | 2,340 |
| 11. Architectural and Civil Drafters | $46,430 | 9.1% | 3,620 |
| 12. Editors | $51,470 | −0.3% | 3,390 |
| 13. Photographers | $29,130 | 11.5% | 4,800 |
| 14. Set and Exhibit Designers | $46,680 | 16.5% | 510 |
| 15. Commercial and Industrial Designers | $58,230 | 9.0% | 1,760 |
| 16. Film and Video Editors | $50,930 | 11.9% | 930 |
| 17. Music Directors and Composers | $45,970 | 10.0% | 1,620 |

## Best Jobs for People with a Social Personality Type

| Job | Annual Earnings | Percent Growth | Annual Openings |
|---|---|---|---|
| 1. Physician Assistants | $86,410 | 39.0% | 4,280 |
| 2. Computer Systems Analysts | $77,740 | 20.3% | 22,280 |
| 3. Physical Therapists | $76,310 | 30.3% | 7,860 |
| 4. Dental Hygienists | $68,250 | 36.1% | 9,840 |
| 5. Registered Nurses | $64,690 | 22.2% | 103,900 |
| 6. Occupational Therapists | $72,320 | 25.6% | 4,580 |
| 7. Compliance Officers | $58,720 | 31.0% | 10,850 |
| 8. Health Specialties Teachers, Postsecondary | $85,270 | 15.1% | 4,000 |
| 9. Training and Development Specialists | $54,160 | 23.3% | 10,710 |
| 10. Speech-Language Pathologists | $66,920 | 18.5% | 4,380 |
| 11. Instructional Coordinators | $58,830 | 23.2% | 6,060 |
| 12. Elementary School Teachers, Except Special Education | $51,660 | 15.8% | 59,650 |
| 13. Home Health Aides | $20,560 | 50.0% | 55,270 |
| 14. Radiation Therapists | $74,980 | 27.1% | 690 |
| 15. Personal Care Aides | $19,640 | 46.0% | 47,780 |
| 16. Self-Enrichment Education Teachers | $36,340 | 32.0% | 12,030 |
| 17. Licensed Practical and Licensed Vocational Nurses | $40,380 | 20.6% | 39,130 |
| 18. Medical Assistants | $28,860 | 33.9% | 21,780 |
| 19. Middle School Teachers, Except Special and Career/Technical Education | $51,960 | 15.3% | 25,110 |
| 20. Business Teachers, Postsecondary | $73,760 | 15.1% | 2,000 |
| 21. Healthcare Social Workers | $47,230 | 22.4% | 6,590 |
| 22. Chiropractors | $67,200 | 19.5% | 1,820 |
| 23. Fitness Trainers and Aerobics Instructors | $31,090 | 29.4% | 12,380 |
| 24. Physical Therapist Assistants | $49,690 | 33.3% | 3,050 |
| 25. Respiratory Therapists | $54,280 | 20.9% | 4,140 |
| 26. Biological Science Teachers, Postsecondary | $72,700 | 15.1% | 1,700 |
| 27. Customer Service Representatives | $30,460 | 17.7% | 110,840 |
| 28. Law Teachers, Postsecondary | $94,260 | 15.1% | 400 |
| 29. Coaches and Scouts | $28,340 | 24.8% | 9,920 |
| 30. Economics Teachers, Postsecondary | $83,370 | 15.1% | 400 |
| 31. Computer Science Teachers, Postsecondary | $70,300 | 15.1% | 1,000 |
| 32. Mental Health Counselors | $38,150 | 24.0% | 5,010 |
| 33. Physics Teachers, Postsecondary | $77,610 | 15.1% | 400 |
| 34. Probation Officers and Correctional Treatment Specialists | $47,200 | 19.3% | 4,180 |
| 35. Atmospheric, Earth, Marine, and Space Sciences Teachers, Postsecondary | $82,840 | 15.1% | 300 |

## Best Jobs for People with a Social Personality Type

| Job | Annual Earnings | Percent Growth | Annual Openings |
|---|---|---|---|
| 36. Mental Health and Substance Abuse Social Workers | $38,600 | 19.5% | 6,130 |
| 37. Psychology Teachers, Postsecondary | $67,330 | 15.1% | 1,000 |
| 38. Agricultural Sciences Teachers, Postsecondary | $78,370 | 15.1% | 300 |
| 39. Occupational Therapy Assistants | $51,010 | 29.8% | 1,180 |
| 40. Preschool Teachers, Except Special Education | $25,700 | 19.0% | 17,830 |
| 41. Art, Drama, and Music Teachers, Postsecondary | $62,040 | 15.1% | 2,500 |
| 42. Chemistry Teachers, Postsecondary | $70,520 | 15.1% | 600 |
| 43. Mathematical Science Teachers, Postsecondary | $65,710 | 15.1% | 1,000 |
| 44. Political Science Teachers, Postsecondary | $70,540 | 15.1% | 500 |
| 45. English Language and Literature Teachers, Postsecondary | $60,400 | 15.1% | 2,000 |
| 46. Athletic Trainers | $41,600 | 36.9% | 1,150 |
| 47. Nursing Instructors and Teachers, Postsecondary | $62,390 | 15.1% | 1,500 |
| 48. Forestry and Conservation Science Teachers, Postsecondary | $78,290 | 15.1% | 100 |
| 49. Vocational Education Teachers, Postsecondary | $48,210 | 15.1% | 4,000 |
| 50. Anthropology and Archeology Teachers, Postsecondary | $73,600 | 15.1% | 200 |
| 51. Architecture Teachers, Postsecondary | $73,500 | 15.1% | 200 |
| 52. Education Teachers, Postsecondary | $59,140 | 15.1% | 1,800 |
| 53. History Teachers, Postsecondary | $64,880 | 15.1% | 700 |
| 54. Rehabilitation Counselors | $32,350 | 18.9% | 5,070 |
| 55. Substance Abuse and Behavioral Disorder Counselors | $38,120 | 21.0% | 3,550 |
| 56. Environmental Science Teachers, Postsecondary | $71,020 | 15.1% | 200 |
| 57. Clinical, Counseling, and School Psychologists | $66,810 | 11.1% | 5,990 |
| 58. Physical Therapist Aides | $23,680 | 36.3% | 2,340 |
| 59. Health Educators | $45,830 | 18.2% | 2,600 |
| 60. Sociology Teachers, Postsecondary | $64,810 | 15.1% | 500 |
| 61. Adult Basic and Secondary Education and Literacy Teachers and Instructors | $46,530 | 15.1% | 2,920 |
| 62. Area, Ethnic, and Cultural Studies Teachers, Postsecondary | $68,020 | 15.1% | 200 |
| 63. Communications Teachers, Postsecondary | $60,300 | 15.1% | 800 |
| 64. Healthcare Practitioners and Technical Workers, All Other | $43,970 | 15.9% | 2,910 |
| 65. Healthcare Support Workers, All Other | $30,280 | 17.1% | 5,670 |
| 66. Massage Therapists | $34,900 | 18.9% | 3,950 |
| 67. Philosophy and Religion Teachers, Postsecondary | $62,330 | 15.1% | 600 |
| 68. Foreign Language and Literature Teachers, Postsecondary | $59,080 | 15.1% | 900 |
| 69. Funeral Attendants | $22,990 | 26.3% | 2,550 |
| 70. Orthotists and Prosthetists | $65,060 | 15.4% | 210 |
| 71. Educational, Guidance, School, and Vocational Counselors | $53,380 | 14.0% | 9,440 |

*(continued)*

*(continued)*

## Best Jobs for People with a Social Personality Type

| Job | Annual Earnings | Percent Growth | Annual Openings |
|---|---|---|---|
| 72. Secondary School Teachers, Except Special and Career/Technical Education | $53,230 | 8.9% | 41,240 |
| 73. Graduate Teaching Assistants | $32,750 | 15.1% | 4,000 |
| 74. Home Economics Teachers, Postsecondary | $65,040 | 15.1% | 200 |
| 75. Social Work Teachers, Postsecondary | $63,090 | 15.1% | 300 |
| 76. Criminal Justice and Law Enforcement Teachers, Postsecondary | $59,520 | 15.1% | 400 |
| 77. Geography Teachers, Postsecondary | $66,700 | 15.1% | 100 |
| 78. Recreation and Fitness Studies Teachers, Postsecondary | $57,650 | 15.1% | 600 |
| 79. Kindergarten Teachers, Except Special Education | $48,800 | 15.0% | 6,300 |
| 80. Clergy | $43,970 | 12.7% | 21,770 |
| 81. Health Diagnosing and Treating Practitioners, All Other | $69,310 | 13.0% | 1,530 |
| 82. Library Science Teachers, Postsecondary | $62,720 | 15.1% | 100 |
| 83. Child, Family, and School Social Workers | $40,210 | 12.3% | 10,960 |
| 84. Career/Technical Education Teachers, Secondary School | $54,310 | 9.6% | 3,850 |
| 85. Teacher Assistants | $23,220 | 10.3% | 41,270 |
| 86. Recreation Workers | $22,260 | 14.7% | 10,720 |
| 87. Childcare Workers | $19,300 | 10.9% | 52,310 |
| 88. Ushers, Lobby Attendants, and Ticket Takers | $18,560 | 13.7% | 8,190 |
| 89. Emergency Medical Technicians and Paramedics | $30,360 | 9.0% | 6,200 |
| 90. Conservation Scientists | $59,310 | 11.9% | 410 |
| 91. Education Administrators, Preschool and Childcare Center/Program | $42,960 | 11.8% | 2,460 |
| 92. Eligibility Interviewers, Government Programs | $39,960 | 9.2% | 3,880 |
| 93. Arbitrators, Mediators, and Conciliators | $55,800 | 14.0% | 320 |
| 94. Marriage and Family Therapists | $45,720 | 14.5% | 950 |
| 95. Recreational Therapists | $39,410 | 14.6% | 1,160 |

## Best Jobs for People with an Enterprising Personality Type

| Job | Annual Earnings | Percent Growth | Annual Openings |
|---|---|---|---|
| 1. Computer and Information Systems Managers | $115,780 | 16.9% | 9,710 |
| 2. Lawyers | $112,760 | 13.0% | 24,040 |
| 3. Registered Nurses | $64,690 | 22.2% | 103,900 |
| 4. Construction Managers | $83,860 | 17.2% | 13,770 |

## Best Jobs for People with an Enterprising Personality Type

| Job | Annual Earnings | Percent Growth | Annual Openings |
|---|---|---|---|
| 5. Sales Managers | $98,530 | 14.9% | 12,660 |
| 6. Medical and Health Services Managers | $84,270 | 16.0% | 9,940 |
| 7. Personal Financial Advisors | $64,750 | 30.1% | 8,530 |
| 8. Supervisors of Construction and Extraction Workers | $58,680 | 15.4% | 24,220 |
| 9. Marketing Managers | $112,800 | 12.5% | 5,970 |
| 10. Public Relations Specialists | $52,090 | 24.0% | 13,130 |
| 11. Managers, All Other | $96,450 | 7.3% | 29,750 |
| 12. Human Resources Specialists | $52,690 | 27.9% | 11,230 |
| 13. Financial Managers | $103,910 | 7.6% | 13,820 |
| 14. Logisticians | $70,800 | 19.5% | 4,190 |
| 15. Customer Service Representatives | $30,460 | 17.7% | 110,840 |
| 16. Natural Sciences Managers | $116,020 | 15.5% | 2,010 |
| 17. Business Operations Specialists, All Other | $62,450 | 11.5% | 36,830 |
| 18. Sales Representatives, Wholesale and Manufacturing, Technical and Scientific Products | $73,710 | 9.7% | 14,230 |
| 19. General and Operations Managers | $94,400 | –0.1% | 50,220 |
| 20. Administrative Services Managers | $77,890 | 12.5% | 8,660 |
| 21. Sales Representatives, Services, All Other | $50,620 | 13.9% | 22,810 |
| 22. Detectives and Criminal Investigators | $68,820 | 16.6% | 4,160 |
| 23. Financial Examiners | $74,940 | 41.2% | 1,600 |
| 24. Education Administrators, Elementary and Secondary School | $86,970 | 8.6% | 8,880 |
| 25. Securities, Commodities, and Financial Services Sales Agents | $70,190 | 9.3% | 12,680 |
| 26. Chief Executives | $165,080 | –1.4% | 11,250 |
| 27. Human Resources Managers | $99,180 | 9.6% | 4,140 |
| 28. Real Estate Sales Agents | $40,030 | 16.2% | 12,830 |
| 29. First-Line Supervisors of Office and Administrative Support Workers | $47,460 | 11.0% | 48,900 |
| 30. Public Relations and Fundraising Managers | $91,810 | 12.9% | 2,060 |
| 31. Air Traffic Controllers | $108,040 | 13.1% | 1,230 |
| 32. Architectural and Engineering Managers | $119,260 | 6.2% | 4,870 |
| 33. Police and Sheriff's Patrol Officers | $53,540 | 8.7% | 22,790 |
| 34. Writers and Authors | $55,420 | 14.8% | 5,420 |
| 35. Insurance Sales Agents | $46,770 | 11.9% | 15,260 |
| 36. Captains, Mates, and Pilots of Water Vessels | $64,180 | 17.3% | 1,950 |
| 37. Social and Community Service Managers | $57,950 | 13.8% | 4,820 |
| 38. Sales Engineers | $87,390 | 8.8% | 3,500 |

*(continued)*

*(continued)*

## Best Jobs for People with an Enterprising Personality Type

| Job | Annual Earnings | Percent Growth | Annual Openings |
|---|---|---|---|
| 39. Agents and Business Managers of Artists, Performers, and Athletes | $63,130 | 22.4% | 1,010 |
| 40. First-Line Supervisors of Non-Retail Sales Workers | $68,880 | 4.8% | 12,950 |
| 41. Amusement and Recreation Attendants | $18,450 | 13.3% | 17,120 |
| 42. First-Line Supervisors of Personal Service Workers | $35,290 | 15.4% | 9,080 |
| 43. First-Line Supervisors of Police and Detectives | $78,260 | 8.1% | 5,050 |
| 44. Producers and Directors | $68,440 | 9.8% | 4,040 |
| 45. Training and Development Managers | $89,170 | 11.9% | 1,010 |
| 46. First-Line Supervisors of Landscaping, Lawn Service, and Groundskeeping Workers | $41,860 | 14.9% | 5,600 |
| 47. Financial Specialists, All Other | $60,980 | 10.5% | 4,320 |
| 48. First-Line Supervisors of Mechanics, Installers, and Repairers | $59,150 | 4.2% | 13,650 |
| 49. Counter Attendants, Cafeteria, Food Concession, and Coffee Shop | $18,370 | 9.3% | 43,490 |
| 50. Retail Salespersons | $20,670 | 8.3% | 162,690 |
| 51. Protective Service Workers, All Other | $29,890 | 14.0% | 7,150 |
| 52. Industrial Production Managers | $87,160 | −7.7% | 5,470 |
| 53. Compensation and Benefits Managers | $89,270 | 8.5% | 1,210 |
| 54. Meeting, Convention, and Event Planners | $45,260 | 15.6% | 2,140 |
| 55. Private Detectives and Investigators | $42,870 | 22.0% | 1,930 |
| 56. Skincare Specialists | $28,920 | 37.8% | 2,030 |
| 57. Curators | $48,450 | 23.0% | 620 |
| 58. Property, Real Estate, and Community Association Managers | $51,480 | 8.4% | 7,800 |
| 59. Farmers, Ranchers, and Other Agricultural Managers | $60,750 | 5.9% | 6,490 |
| 60. First-Line Supervisors of Fire Fighting and Prevention Workers | $68,240 | 8.2% | 3,250 |
| 61. First-Line Supervisors of Retail Sales Workers | $35,820 | 5.2% | 45,010 |
| 62. Purchasing Managers | $95,070 | 1.5% | 2,110 |
| 63. Education Administrators, Postsecondary | $83,710 | 2.3% | 4,010 |
| 64. Gaming Managers | $66,960 | 11.9% | 200 |
| 65. Real Estate Brokers | $54,910 | 8.6% | 3,080 |
| 66. Administrative Law Judges, Adjudicators, and Hearing Officers | $85,500 | 8.1% | 380 |
| 67. First-Line Supervisors of Production and Operating Workers | $53,090 | −5.2% | 9,190 |
| 68. First-Line Supervisors of Food Preparation and Serving Workers | $29,560 | 6.6% | 13,440 |
| 69. Food Service Managers | $48,130 | 5.3% | 8,370 |
| 70. Morticians, Undertakers, and Funeral Directors | $54,330 | 11.9% | 960 |
| 71. Transportation, Storage, and Distribution Managers | $80,210 | −5.3% | 2,740 |

## Best Jobs for People with an Enterprising Personality Type

| Job | Annual Earnings | Percent Growth | Annual Openings |
|---|---|---|---|
| 72. Credit Counselors | $38,140 | 16.3% | 880 |
| 73. Directors, Religious Activities and Education | $36,170 | 12.6% | 2,640 |
| 74. First-Line Supervisors of Correctional Officers | $55,910 | 8.5% | 1,940 |
| 75. Opticians, Dispensing | $32,940 | 13.4% | 2,020 |
| 76. Gaming Supervisors | $48,530 | 11.8% | 1,410 |
| 77. Advertising Sales Agents | $45,350 | 7.2% | 4,510 |
| 78. Advertising and Promotions Managers | $83,890 | –1.7% | 1,050 |
| 79. First-Line Supervisors of Transportation and Material-Moving Machine and Vehicle Operators | $52,720 | –3.7% | 3,770 |
| 80. Flight Attendants | $37,740 | 8.1% | 3,010 |
| 81. First-Line Supervisors of Helpers, Laborers, and Material Movers, Hand | $43,800 | 3.6% | 3,850 |
| 82. Railroad Conductors and Yardmasters | $49,770 | 6.9% | 1,700 |
| 83. Appraisers and Assessors of Real Estate | $48,500 | 4.6% | 2,100 |

## Best Jobs for People with a Conventional Personality Type

| Job | Annual Earnings | Percent Growth | Annual Openings |
|---|---|---|---|
| 1. Accountants and Auditors | $61,690 | 21.6% | 49,750 |
| 2. Compliance Officers | $58,720 | 31.0% | 10,850 |
| 3. Financial Analysts | $74,350 | 19.8% | 9,520 |
| 4. Cost Estimators | $57,860 | 25.3% | 10,360 |
| 5. Dental Assistants | $33,470 | 35.7% | 16,100 |
| 6. Paralegals and Legal Assistants | $46,680 | 28.1% | 10,400 |
| 7. Business Operations Specialists, All Other | $62,450 | 11.5% | 36,830 |
| 8. Database Administrators | $73,490 | 20.3% | 4,440 |
| 9. Managers, All Other | $96,450 | 7.3% | 29,750 |
| 10. Compensation, Benefits, and Job Analysis Specialists | $57,000 | 23.6% | 6,050 |
| 11. Medical Secretaries | $30,530 | 26.6% | 18,900 |
| 12. Pharmacy Technicians | $28,400 | 30.6% | 18,200 |
| 13. Financial Managers | $103,910 | 7.6% | 13,820 |
| 14. Logisticians | $70,800 | 19.5% | 4,190 |
| 15. Actuaries | $87,650 | 21.4% | 1,000 |
| 16. Computer Occupations, All Other | $79,240 | 13.1% | 7,260 |

*(continued)*

*(continued)*

# Best Jobs for People with a Conventional Personality Type

| Job | Annual Earnings | Percent Growth | Annual Openings |
|---|---|---|---|
| 17. Purchasing Agents, Except Wholesale, Retail, and Farm Products | $56,580 | 13.9% | 11,860 |
| 18. Executive Secretaries and Executive Administrative Assistants | $43,520 | 12.8% | 41,920 |
| 19. Detectives and Criminal Investigators | $68,820 | 16.6% | 4,160 |
| 20. Social and Human Service Assistants | $28,200 | 22.6% | 15,390 |
| 21. Bill and Account Collectors | $31,310 | 19.3% | 15,690 |
| 22. Legal Secretaries | $41,500 | 18.4% | 8,380 |
| 23. Billing and Posting Clerks | $32,170 | 15.3% | 16,760 |
| 24. Sales Representatives, Wholesale and Manufacturing, Except Technical and Scientific Products | $52,440 | 6.6% | 45,790 |
| 25. Receptionists and Information Clerks | $25,240 | 15.2% | 48,020 |
| 26. Bookkeeping, Accounting, and Auditing Clerks | $34,030 | 10.3% | 46,040 |
| 27. Medical Records and Health Information Technicians | $32,350 | 20.3% | 7,030 |
| 28. Cargo and Freight Agents | $37,150 | 23.9% | 4,030 |
| 29. Combined Food Preparation and Serving Workers, Including Fast Food | $17,950 | 14.6% | 96,720 |
| 30. Budget Analysts | $68,200 | 15.1% | 2,230 |
| 31. Office Clerks, General | $26,610 | 11.9% | 77,090 |
| 32. Claims Adjusters, Examiners, and Investigators | $58,620 | 7.1% | 9,560 |
| 33. Credit Analysts | $58,850 | 15.0% | 2,430 |
| 34. Financial Specialists, All Other | $60,980 | 10.5% | 4,320 |
| 35. Surveying and Mapping Technicians | $37,900 | 20.4% | 2,940 |
| 36. Loan Officers | $56,490 | 10.1% | 6,880 |
| 37. Statisticians | $72,830 | 13.1% | 960 |
| 38. Interviewers, Except Eligibility and Loan | $28,820 | 15.6% | 9,210 |
| 39. Postal Service Mail Carriers | $53,860 | −1.1% | 10,720 |
| 40. Police, Fire, and Ambulance Dispatchers | $35,370 | 17.8% | 3,840 |
| 41. Court Reporters | $47,700 | 18.3% | 710 |
| 42. Librarians | $54,500 | 7.8% | 5,450 |
| 43. Stock Clerks and Order Fillers | $21,290 | 7.2% | 56,260 |
| 44. Hotel, Motel, and Resort Desk Clerks | $19,930 | 13.7% | 10,950 |
| 45. Secretaries and Administrative Assistants, Except Legal, Medical, and Executive | $30,830 | 4.6% | 36,550 |
| 46. Tax Examiners and Collectors, and Revenue Agents | $49,360 | 13.0% | 3,520 |
| 47. Life, Physical, and Social Science Technicians, All Other | $43,350 | 13.3% | 3,640 |
| 48. Social Science Research Assistants | $37,230 | 17.8% | 1,270 |
| 49. Gaming Dealers | $18,090 | 19.0% | 5,590 |

## Best Jobs for People with a Conventional Personality Type

| Job | Annual Earnings | Percent Growth | Annual Openings |
|---|---|---|---|
| 50. Production, Planning, and Expediting Clerks | $42,220 | 1.5% | 7,410 |
| 51. Tellers | $24,100 | 6.2% | 28,440 |
| 52. Insurance Underwriters | $59,290 | –4.1% | 3,000 |
| 53. Court, Municipal, and License Clerks | $34,390 | 8.2% | 4,460 |
| 54. Library Technicians | $29,860 | 8.8% | 6,470 |
| 55. Reservation and Transportation Ticket Agents and Travel Clerks | $31,740 | 8.1% | 5,150 |
| 56. Appraisers and Assessors of Real Estate | $48,500 | 4.6% | 2,100 |

# Bonus Lists: Jobs with the Greatest Changes in Outlook Since the Previous Edition

The previous edition of this book, which came out in 2009, used job-growth figures from the Bureau of Labor Statistics (BLS) that were projected for the period from 2006 to 2016. Since that edition was prepared, the BLS has updated its projections, based on the latest economic data and improvements to their forecasting models. Some jobs now are expected to have much better job growth than was previously projected; for other jobs, expectations for job growth have been scaled back. Remember that short-term changes in the economy, such as the recession that hit around the time the previous edition came out, don't figure into these projections. The projections represent the average growth over a ten-year period.

I thought you might be interested in seeing which 25 jobs had the greatest *increases* and greatest *decreases* in job-growth projection, so I compiled the following two lists. I based the lists on those 374 jobs that were included in the best jobs in both editions.

## Jobs with the Greatest Increase in Job-Growth Projection

| Job | Projected Job Growth 2006–2016 | Projected Job Growth 2008–2018 | Change in Forecast |
|---|---|---|---|
| 1. Biomedical Engineers | 21.1% | 72.0% | 50.9% |
| 2. Financial Examiners | 10.7% | 41.2% | 30.5% |
| 3. Coroners | 4.9% | 31.0% | 26.1% |
| 4. Environmental Compliance Inspectors | 4.9% | 31.0% | 26.1% |
| 5. Equal Opportunity Representatives and Officers | 4.9% | 31.0% | 26.1% |

*(continued)*

*(continued)*

## Jobs with the Greatest Increase in Job-Growth Projection

| Job | Projected Job Growth 2006–2016 | Projected Job Growth 2008–2018 | Change in Forecast |
|---|---|---|---|
| 6. Government Property Inspectors and Investigators | 4.9% | 31.0% | 26.1% |
| 7. Licensing Examiners and Inspectors | 4.9% | 31.0% | 26.1% |
| 8. Biochemists and Biophysicists | 15.9% | 37.4% | 21.5% |
| 9. Medical Scientists, Except Epidemiologists | 20.2% | 40.4% | 20.2% |
| 10. Heating and Air Conditioning Mechanics and Installers | 8.7% | 28.1% | 19.4% |
| 11. Refrigeration Mechanics and Installers | 8.7% | 28.1% | 19.4% |
| 12. Helpers—Electricians | 6.8% | 24.7% | 17.9% |
| 13. Prosthodontists | 10.7% | 28.3% | 17.6% |
| 14. Tree Trimmers and Pruners | 11.1% | 26.3% | 15.2% |
| 15. Survey Researchers | 15.9% | 30.3% | 14.4% |
| 16. Vocational Education Teachers, Secondary School | −4.6% | 9.6% | 14.2% |
| 17. Political Scientists | 5.3% | 19.4% | 14.1% |
| 18. Helpers—Pipelayers, Plumbers, Pipefitters, and Steamfitters | 11.9% | 25.7% | 13.8% |
| 19. Purchasing Agents, Except Wholesale, Retail, and Farm Products | 0.1% | 13.9% | 13.8% |
| 20. Petroleum Engineers | 5.2% | 18.4% | 13.2% |
| 21. Credit Analysts | 1.9% | 15.0% | 13.1% |
| 22. Optometrists | 11.3% | 24.4% | 13.1% |
| 23. Anthropologists | 15.0% | 28.0% | 13.0% |
| 24. Archeologists | 15.0% | 28.0% | 13.0% |
| 25. Agents and Business Managers of Artists, Performers, and Athletes | 9.6% | 22.4% | 12.8% |

## Jobs with the Greatest Decrease in Job-Growth Projection

| Job | Projected Job Growth 2006–2016 | Projected Job Growth 2008–2018 | Change in Forecast |
|---|---|---|---|
| 1. Sales Agents, Financial Services | 24.8% | 9.3% | −15.5% |
| 2. Marriage and Family Therapists | 29.8% | 14.5% | −15.3% |
| 3. Financial Analysts | 33.8% | 19.8% | −14.0% |
| 4. First-Line Supervisors/Managers of Transportation and Material-Moving Machine and Vehicle Operators | 10.2% | −3.7% | −13.9% |
| 5. Storage and Distribution Managers | 8.3% | −5.3% | −13.6% |
| 6. Transportation Managers | 8.3% | −5.3% | −13.6% |

## Jobs with the Greatest Decrease in Job-Growth Projection

| Job | Projected Job Growth 2006–2016 | Projected Job Growth 2008–2018 | Change in Forecast |
|---|---|---|---|
| 7. Substance Abuse and Behavioral Disorder Counselors | 34.3% | 21.0% | –13.3% |
| 8. Advertising Sales Agents | 20.3% | 7.2% | –13.1% |
| 9. Gaming Managers | 24.4% | 11.9% | –12.5% |
| 10. Appraisers, Real Estate | 16.9% | 4.6% | –12.3% |
| 11. Assessors | 16.9% | 4.6% | –12.3% |
| 12. Education Administrators, Postsecondary | 14.2% | 2.3% | –11.9% |
| 13. Education Administrators, Preschool and Child Care Center/Program | 23.5% | 11.8% | –11.7% |
| 14. Audio and Video Equipment Technicians | 24.2% | 12.6% | –11.6% |
| 15. Gaming Supervisors | 23.4% | 11.8% | –11.6% |
| 16. Multi-Media Artists and Animators | 25.8% | 14.2% | –11.6% |
| 17. Forensic Science Technicians | 30.7% | 19.6% | –11.1% |
| 18. Social and Human Service Assistants | 33.6% | 22.6% | –11.0% |
| 19. Personal Financial Advisors | 41.0% | 30.1% | –10.9% |
| 20. Social and Community Service Managers | 24.7% | 13.8% | –10.9% |
| 21. Insurance Underwriters | 6.3% | –4.1% | –10.4% |
| 22. Mental Health and Substance Abuse Social Workers | 29.9% | 19.5% | –10.4% |
| 23. Emergency Medical Technicians and Paramedics | 19.2% | 9.0% | –10.2% |
| 24. Automotive Master Mechanics | 14.3% | 4.7% | –9.6% |
| 25. Automotive Specialty Technicians | 14.3% | 4.7% | –9.6% |

# PART II

# The Job Descriptions

This part of the book provides descriptions for all the jobs included in the lists in Part I. The Introduction gives more details on how to use and interpret the job descriptions, but here is some additional information:

- Job descriptions are arranged in alphabetical order by job title. This approach allows you to quickly find a description if you know its correct title from one of the lists in Part I.

- If you are using this section to browse for interesting options, I suggest you begin with the Table of Contents. Part I features many interesting lists that will help you identify job titles to explore in more detail. If you have not browsed the lists in Part I, consider spending some time there. The lists are interesting and will help you identify job titles you can find described in the material that follows.

# Accountants and Auditors

- ✻ Annual Earnings: $61,690
- ✻ Earnings Growth Potential: Medium (36.9%)
- ✻ Growth: 21.6%
- ✻ Annual Job Openings: 49,750
- ✻ Self-Employed: 8.1%

**Considerations for Job Outlook:** An increase in the number of businesses, a more stringent regulatory environment, and increased corporate accountability are expected to drive job growth for accountants and auditors. Opportunities should be favorable; job seekers with professional certification, especially a CPA, should have the best prospects.

## Job Specialization: Accountants

**Analyze financial information and prepare financial reports to determine or maintain record of assets, liabilities, profit and loss, tax liability, or other financial activities within an organization.** Prepare, examine, or analyze accounting records, financial statements, or other financial reports to assess accuracy, completeness, and conformance to reporting and procedural standards. Compute taxes owed and prepare tax returns, ensuring compliance with payment, reporting, or other tax requirements. Analyze business operations, trends, costs, revenues, financial commitments, and obligations to project future revenues and expenses or to provide advice. Report to management regarding the finances of establishment. Establish tables of accounts and assign entries to proper accounts. Develop, maintain, and analyze budgets, preparing periodic reports that compare budgeted costs to actual costs. Develop, implement, modify, and document recordkeeping and accounting systems, making use of current computer technology. Prepare forms and manuals for accounting and bookkeeping personnel and direct their work activities. Survey operations to ascertain accounting needs and to recommend, develop, or maintain solutions to business and financial problems. Work as Internal Revenue Service (IRS) agents. Advise management about issues such as resource utilization, tax strategies, and the assumptions underlying budget forecasts. Provide internal and external auditing services for businesses or individuals. Advise clients in areas such as compensation, employee health-care benefits, the design of accounting or data-processing systems, or long-range tax or estate plans. Investigate bankruptcies and other complex financial transactions and prepare reports summarizing the findings. Represent clients before taxing authorities and provide support during litigation involving financial issues. Appraise, evaluate, and inventory real property and equipment, recording information such as the description, value, and location of property. Maintain or examine the records of government agencies. Serve as bankruptcy trustees or business valuators.

**Education/Training Required:** Bachelor's degree. **Education and Training Programs:** Accounting; Accounting and Business/Management; Accounting and Computer Science; Accounting and Finance; Auditing; Taxation. **Knowledge/Courses**—Economics and Accounting, Clerical, Mathematics, Computers and Electronics, Personnel and Human Resources, Administration and Management.

**Personality Type:** Conventional-Enterprising. **Career Cluster:** 04 Business, Management, and Administration. **Career Pathway:** 4.2 Business, Financial Management, and Accounting. **Other Jobs in This Pathway:** Auditors; Billing and Posting Clerks; Billing, Cost, and Rate Clerks; Bookkeeping, Accounting, and Auditing Clerks; Brokerage Clerks; Brownfield Redevelopment Specialists and Site Managers; Budget Analysts; Compliance Managers; Credit Analysts; Financial Analysts; Financial Managers, Branch or Department; Investment Fund Managers; Logistics Managers; Loss Prevention Managers; Managers, All Other; Natural Sciences Managers; Payroll and Timekeeping Clerks; Regulatory Affairs Managers; Security Managers; Statement Clerks; Supply Chain Managers; Tax Preparers; Treasurers and Controllers; Wind Energy Operations Managers; Wind Energy Project Managers; others.

**Skills**—Operations Analysis, Mathematics, Systems Analysis, Management of Financial Resources, Systems Evaluation, Critical Thinking, Judgment and Decision Making, Negotiation.

**Work Environment:** Indoors; sitting; repetitive motions.

## Job Specialization: Auditors

**Examine and analyze accounting records to determine financial status of establishment and prepare financial reports concerning operating procedures.** Collect and analyze data to detect deficient controls; duplicated effort; extravagance; fraud; or non-compliance with laws, regulations, and management policies. Prepare detailed reports on audit findings. Supervise auditing of establishments and determine scope of investigation required. Report to management about asset utilization and audit results and recommend changes in operations and financial activities. Inspect account books and accounting systems for efficiency, effectiveness, and use of accepted accounting procedures to record transactions. Examine records and interview workers to ensure recording of transactions and compliance with laws and regulations. Examine and evaluate financial and information systems, recommending controls to ensure system reliability and data integrity. Review data about material assets, net worth, liabilities, capital stock, surplus, income, and expenditures. Confer with company officials about financial and regulatory matters. Examine whether the organization's objectives are reflected in its management activities and whether employees understand the objectives. Prepare, analyze, and verify annual reports, financial statements, and other records, using accepted accounting and statistical procedures to assess financial condition and facilitate financial planning. Inspect cash on hand, notes receivable and payable, negotiable securities, and canceled checks to confirm records are accurate. Examine inventory to verify journal and ledger entries. Direct activities of personnel engaged in filing, recording, compiling, and transmitting financial records. Conduct pre-implementation audits to determine whether systems and programs under development will work as planned. Audit payroll and personnel records to determine unemployment insurance premiums, workers' compensation coverage, liabilities, and compliance with tax laws.

**Education/Training Required:** Bachelor's degree. **Education and Training Programs:** Accounting; Accounting and Business/Management; Accounting and Computer Science; Accounting and Finance; Auditing; Taxation. **Knowledge/Courses**—Economics and Accounting, Administration and Management, Personnel and Human Resources, Law and Government, Computers and Electronics, Mathematics.

**Personality Type:** Conventional-Enterprising-Investigative. **Career Cluster:** 04 Business, Management, and Administration. **Career Pathway:** 4.2 Business, Financial Management, and Accounting. **Other Jobs in This Pathway:** Accountants; Billing and Posting Clerks; Billing, Cost, and Rate Clerks; Bookkeeping, Accounting, and Auditing Clerks; Brokerage Clerks; Brownfield Redevelopment Specialists and Site Managers; Budget Analysts; Compliance Managers; Credit Analysts; Financial Analysts; Financial Managers, Branch or Department; Investment Fund Managers; Logistics Managers; Loss Prevention Managers; Managers, All Other; Natural Sciences Managers; Payroll and Timekeeping Clerks; Regulatory Affairs Managers; Security Managers; Statement Clerks; Supply Chain Managers; Tax Preparers; Treasurers and Controllers; Wind Energy Operations Managers; Wind Energy Project Managers; others.

**Skills**—Systems Evaluation, Systems Analysis, Management of Financial Resources, Mathematics, Programming, Writing, Operations Analysis, Management of Personnel Resources.

**Work Environment:** Indoors; sitting.

# Actuaries

- ✳ Annual Earnings: $87,650
- ✳ Earnings Growth Potential: Medium (39.4%)
- ✳ Growth: 21.4%
- ✳ Annual Job Openings: 1,000
- ✳ Self-Employed: 0.0%

**Considerations for Job Outlook:** Employment growth is projected as industries not traditionally associated with actuaries, such as financial services and consulting, employ these workers to assess risk. Keen competition is expected.

**Analyze statistical data, such as mortality, accident, sickness, disability, and retirement rates, and construct probability tables to forecast risk and liability for payment of future benefits. May ascertain premium rates required and cash reserves necessary to ensure payment of future benefits.** Ascertain premium rates required and cash reserves and liabilities necessary to ensure payment of future benefits. Analyze statistical information to estimate mortality, accident, sickness, disability, and retirement rates. Design, review, and help administer insurance, annuity, and pension plans, determining financial soundness and calculating premiums. Collaborate with programmers, underwriters, accountants, claims experts, and senior management to help companies develop plans for new lines of business or for improving existing business. Determine or help determine company policy and explain complex technical matters to company executives, government officials, shareholders, policyholders, or the public. Testify before public agencies on proposed legislation affecting businesses. Provide advice to clients on a contract basis, working as a consultant. Testify in court as expert witness or to provide legal evidence on matters such as the value of potential lifetime earnings of a person who is disabled or killed in an accident. Construct probability tables for events such as fires, natural disasters, and unemployment, based on analysis of statistical data and other pertinent information. Determine policy contract provisions for each type of insurance. Manage credit and help price corporate security offerings. Provide expertise to help financial institutions manage risks and maximize returns associated with investment products or credit offerings. Determine equitable basis for distributing surplus earnings under participating insurance and annuity contracts in mutual companies. Explain changes in contract provisions to customers.

**Education/Training Required:** Work experience plus degree. **Education and Training Program:** Actuarial Science. **Knowledge/Courses**—Economics and Accounting, Mathematics, Computers and Electronics, Administration and Management, Personnel and Human Resources, Sales and Marketing.

**Personality Type:** Conventional-Investigative-Enterprising. **Career Cluster:** 06 Finance. **Career Pathway:** 6.4 Insurance Services. **Other Jobs in This Pathway:** Claims Examiners, Property and Casualty Insurance; Insurance Adjusters, Examiners, and Investigators; Insurance Appraisers, Auto Damage; Insurance Sales Agents; Insurance Underwriters; Telemarketers.

**Skills**—Mathematics, Management of Financial Resources, Systems Evaluation, Systems Analysis, Programming, Judgment and Decision Making, Operations Analysis, Complex Problem Solving.

**Work Environment:** Indoors; sitting.

# Administrative Law Judges, Adjudicators, and Hearing Officers

- ❀ Annual Earnings: $85,500
- ❀ Earnings Growth Potential: Very high (53.2%)
- ❀ Growth: 8.1%
- ❀ Annual Job Openings: 380
- ❀ Self-Employed: 0.0%

**Considerations for Job Outlook:** Budget pressures are expected to limit the hiring of new judges, particularly in federal courts. Alternatives to litigation are usually faster and less expensive, spurring employment growth for other judicial workers, such as arbitrators, mediators, and conciliators.

**Conduct hearings to decide or recommend decisions on claims concerning government programs or other government-related matters and prepare decisions. Determine penalties or the existence and the amount of liability or recommend the acceptance or rejection of claims or compromise settlements.** Prepare written opinions and decisions. Review and evaluate data on documents such as claim applications, birth or death certificates, and physician or employer records. Research and analyze laws, regulations, policies, and precedent decisions to prepare for hearings and to determine conclusions. Confer with individuals or organizations involved in cases to obtain relevant information. Recommend the acceptance or rejection of claims or compromise settlements according to laws, regulations, policies, and precedent decisions. Explain to claimants how they can appeal rulings that go against them. Monitor and direct the activities of trials and hearings to ensure that they are conducted fairly and that courts administer justice while safeguarding the legal rights of all involved parties. Authorize payment of valid claims and determine method of payment. Conduct hearings to review and decide claims regarding issues such as social program eligibility, environmental protection, and enforcement of health and safety regulations. Rule on exceptions, motions, and admissibility of evidence. Determine existence and amount of liability according to current laws, administrative and judicial precedents, and available evidence. Issue subpoenas and administer oaths in preparation for formal hearings. Conduct studies of appeals procedures in field agencies to ensure adherence to legal requirements and to facilitate determination of cases.

**Education/Training Required:** Work experience plus degree. **Education and Training Programs:** Law (LL.B., J.D.); Legal Professions and Studies, Other; Legal Studies, General. **Knowledge/Courses**—Law and Government, Medicine and Dentistry, Psychology, Therapy and Counseling, Biology, Customer and Personal Service.

**Personality Type:** Enterprising-Investigative-Social. **Career Cluster:** 12 Law, Public Safety, Corrections, and Security. **Career Pathway:** 12.5 Legal Services. **Other Jobs in This Pathway:** Arbitrators, Mediators, and Conciliators; Court Reporters; Farm and Home Management Advisors; Judges, Magistrate Judges, and Magistrates; Lawyers; Legal Secretaries; Legal Support Workers, All Other; Paralegals and Legal Assistants; Title Examiners, Abstractors, and Searchers.

**Skills**—Active Listening, Critical Thinking, Reading Comprehension, Speaking, Operations Analysis, Writing, Judgment and Decision Making, Negotiation.

**Work Environment:** Indoors; sitting.

# Administrative Services Managers

- ❀ Annual Earnings: $77,890
- ❀ Earnings Growth Potential: High (46.8%)
- ❀ Growth: 12.5%
- ❀ Annual Job Openings: 8,660
- ❀ Self-Employed: 0.2%

**Considerations for Job Outlook:** Employment of these workers is projected to increase as companies strive to maintain, secure, and efficiently operate their facilities. Competition should be keen for top managers; better opportunities are expected at the entry level.

**Plan, direct, or coordinate supportive services of an organization, such as recordkeeping, mail distribution, telephone operator/receptionist, and other office support services. May oversee facilities planning and maintenance and custodial operations.** Monitor the facility to ensure that it remains safe, secure, and well-maintained. Direct or coordinate the supportive services department of a business, agency, or organization. Set goals and deadlines for the department. Prepare and review operational reports and schedules to ensure accuracy and efficiency. Analyze internal processes and recommend and implement procedural or policy changes to improve operations such as supply changes or the disposal of records. Acquire, distribute, and store supplies. Plan, administer, and control budgets for contracts, equipment, and supplies. Oversee construction and renovation projects to improve efficiency and to ensure that facilities meet environmental, health, and security standards and comply with government regulations. Hire and terminate clerical and administrative personnel. Oversee the maintenance and repair of machinery, equipment, and electrical and mechanical systems. Manage leasing of facility space. Participate in architectural and engineering planning and design, including space and installation management. Conduct classes to teach procedures to staff. Dispose of, or oversee the disposal of, surplus or unclaimed property.

**Education/Training Required:** Work experience plus degree. **Education and Training Programs:** Business Administration and Management, General; Business/Commerce, General; Medical Staff Services Technology/Technician; Medical/Health Management and Clinical Assistant/Specialist Training; Public Administration; Purchasing, Procurement/Acquisitions, and Contracts Management; Transportation/Mobility Management. **Knowledge/Courses**—Clerical, Economics and Accounting, Personnel and Human Resources, Customer and Personal Service, Sales and Marketing, Administration and Management.

**Personality Type:** Enterprising-Conventional. **Career Clusters:** 04 Business, Management, and Administration; 07 Government and Public Administration. **Career Pathways:** 4.1 Management; 7.1 Governance. **Other Jobs in These Pathways:** Brownfield Redevelopment Specialists and Site Managers; Business Continuity Planners; Business Operations Specialists, All Other; Chief Executives; Chief Sustainability Officers; Compliance Managers; Computer and Information Systems Managers; Construction Managers; Customs Brokers; Energy Auditors; First-Line Supervisors of Office and Administrative Support Workers; General and Operations Managers; Investment Fund Managers; Loss Prevention Managers; Management Analysts; Managers, All Other; Public Relations Specialists; Regulatory Affairs Managers; Sales Managers; Security Management Specialists; Security Managers; Supply Chain Managers; Sustainability Specialists; Wind Energy Operations Managers; Wind Energy Project Managers; others.

**Skills**—Management of Financial Resources, Management of Material Resources, Management of Personnel Resources, Negotiation, Coordination, Time Management, Social Perceptiveness, Service Orientation.

**Work Environment:** Indoors; sitting.

# Adult Basic and Secondary Education and Literacy Teachers and Instructors

- ✳ Annual Earnings: $46,530
- ✳ Earnings Growth Potential: High (41.8%)
- ✳ Growth: 15.1%
- ✳ Annual Job Openings: 2,920
- ✳ Self-Employed: 20.4%

**Considerations for Job Outlook:** As the need for educated workers increases, so will the need for teachers to instruct them. In addition, there should be employment growth for teachers to help immigrants and others improve their English language skills. Opportunities should be favorable.

**Teach or instruct out-of-school youths and adults in remedial education classes, preparatory classes for the General Educational Development test, literacy, or English as a Second Language. Teaching may or may not take place in a traditional educational institution.** Adapt teaching methods and instructional materials to meet students' varying needs, abilities, and interests. Observe and evaluate students' work to determine progress and make suggestions for improvement. Instruct students individually and in groups, using various teaching methods such as lectures, discussions, and demonstrations. Plan and conduct activities for a balanced program of instruction, demonstration, and work time that provides students with opportunities to observe, question, and investigate. Maintain accurate and complete student records as required by laws or administrative policies. Prepare materials and classrooms for class activities. Establish clear objectives for all lessons, units, and projects and communicate those objectives to students. Conduct classes, workshops, and demonstrations to teach principles, techniques, or methods in subjects such as basic English language skills, life skills, and workforce entry skills. Prepare students for further education by encouraging them to explore learning opportunities and to persevere with challenging tasks. Establish and enforce rules for behavior and procedures for maintaining order among the students for whom they are responsible. Provide information, guidance, and preparation for the General Equivalency Diploma (GED) examination. Assign and grade classwork and homework. Observe students to determine qualifications, limitations, abilities, interests, and other individual characteristics. Register, orient, and assess new students according to standards and procedures. Prepare and implement remedial programs for students requiring extra help. Prepare and administer written, oral, and performance tests and issue grades in accordance with performance. Use computers, audiovisual aids, and other equipment and materials to supplement presentations. Prepare objectives and outlines for courses of study, following curriculum guidelines or requirements of states and schools.

**Education/Training Required:** Bachelor's degree. **Education and Training Programs:** Adult and Continuing Education and Teaching; Adult Literacy Tutor/Instructor Training; Bilingual and Multilingual Education; Multicultural Education; Teaching English as a Second or Foreign Language/ESL Language Instructor. **Knowledge/Courses**—English Language, History and Archeology, Education and Training, Sociology and Anthropology, Geography, Foreign Language.

**Personality Type:** Social-Artistic-Enterprising. **Career Cluster:** 05 Education and Training. **Career Pathway:** 5.3 Teaching/Training. **Other Jobs in This Pathway:** Athletes and Sports Competitors; Audio-Visual and Multimedia Collections Specialists; Career/Technical Education Teachers, Middle School; Career/Technical Education Teachers, Secondary School; Chemists; Coaches and Scouts; Dietitians and Nutritionists; Elementary School Teachers, Except Special Education; Fitness Trainers and Aerobics Instructors; Historians; Instructional Coordinators; Instructional Designers and Technologists; Interpreters and Translators; Kindergarten Teachers, Except Special Education; Librarians; Middle School Teachers, Except Special and Career/Technical Education; Physicists; Preschool Teachers, Except Special Education; Recreation Workers; Secondary School Teachers, Except Special and Career/Technical Education; Self-Enrichment Education Teachers; Teacher Assistants; Teachers and Instructors, All Other; Tutors.

**Skills**—Learning Strategies, Instructing, Writing, Reading Comprehension, Persuasion, Time Management, Social Perceptiveness, Negotiation.

**Work Environment:** Indoors; standing.

# Advertising and Promotions Managers

* Annual Earnings: $83,890
* Earnings Growth Potential: High (50.6%)
* Growth: –1.7%
* Annual Job Openings: 1,050
* Self-Employed: 16.6%

**Considerations for Job Outlook:** Job growth is expected to result from companies' need to distinguish their products and services in an increasingly competitive marketplace. Keen competition is expected.

**Plan and direct advertising policies and programs or produce collateral materials, such as posters, contests, coupons, or giveaways, to create extra interest in the purchase of a product or service for a department, for an entire organization, or on an account basis.** Prepare budgets and submit estimates for program costs as part of campaign plan development. Plan and prepare advertising and promotional material to increase sales of products or services, working with customers, company officials, sales departments, and advertising agencies. Assist with annual budget development. Inspect layouts and advertising copy and edit scripts, audiotapes and videotapes, and other promotional material for adherence to specifications. Coordinate activities of departments such as sales, graphic arts, media, finance, and research. Prepare and negotiate advertising and sales contracts. Identify and develop contacts for promotional campaigns and industry programs that meet identified buyer targets, such as dealers, distributors, or consumers. Gather and organize information to plan advertising campaigns. Confer with department heads or staff to discuss topics such as contracts, selection of advertising media, or product to be advertised. Confer with clients to provide marketing or technical advice. Monitor and analyze sales promotion results to determine cost-effectiveness of promotion campaigns. Read trade journals and professional literature to stay informed on trends, innovations, and changes that affect media planning. Formulate plans to extend business with established accounts and to transact business as agent for advertising accounts. Provide presentation and product demonstration support during the introduction of new products and services to field staff and customers. Direct, motivate, and monitor the mobilization of a campaign team to advance campaign goals. Plan and execute advertising policies and strategies for organizations. Track program budgets and expenses and campaign response rates to evaluate each campaign based on program objectives and industry norms. Assemble and communicate with a strong, diverse coalition of organizations or public figures, securing their cooperation, support, and action to further campaign goals.

**Education/Training Required:** Work experience plus degree. **Education and Training Programs:** Advertising; Marketing/Marketing Management, General; Public Relations/Image Management. **Knowledge/Courses**—Communications and Media, Fine Arts, Sales and Marketing, Telecommunications, English Language, Design.

**Personality Type:** Enterprising-Artistic-Conventional. **Career Clusters:** 04 Business, Management, and Administration; 14 Marketing, Sales, and Service. **Career Pathways:** 4.1 Management; 4.5 Marketing; 14.1 Management and Entrepreneurship. **Other Jobs in These Pathways:** Brownfield Redevelopment Specialists and Site Managers; Business Continuity Planners; Business Operations Specialists, All Other; Chief Executives; Chief Sustainability Officers; Compliance Managers; Computer and Information Systems Managers; Construction Managers; Customs Brokers; Energy Auditors; First-Line Supervisors of Office and Administrative Support Workers; General and Operations Managers; Investment Fund Managers; Loss Prevention Managers; Management Analysts; Managers, All Other; Public Relations Specialists; Regulatory Affairs Managers; Sales Managers; Security Management Specialists; Security Managers; Supply Chain Managers; Sustainability Specialists; Wind Energy Operations Managers; Wind Energy Project Managers; others.

**Skills**—Management of Financial Resources, Management of Personnel Resources, Operations Analysis, Systems Evaluation, Coordination, Management of Material Resources, Negotiation, Speaking.

**Work Environment:** Indoors; sitting.

## Job Specialization: Green Marketers

**Create and implement methods to market green products and services.** Prepare renewable energy communications in response to public relations or promotional inquiries. Monitor energy industry statistics or literature to identify trends. Maintain portfolios of marketing campaigns, strategies, and other marketing products or ideas.

Generate or identify sales leads for green energy. Devise or evaluate methods and procedures for collecting data, such as surveys, opinion polls, and questionnaires. Conduct market simulations for wind, solar, or geothermal energy projects. Write marketing content for green energy websites, brochures, or other communication media. Revise existing marketing plans or campaigns for green products or services. Monitor energy market or regulatory conditions to identify buying or other business opportunities. Identify marketing channels for green energy products or services. Develop communications materials, advertisements, presentations, or public relations initiatives to promote awareness of, and participation in, green energy initiatives. Consult with clients to identify potential energy efficiency opportunities or to promote green energy alternatives. Conduct energy pricing analyses for specific clients or client groups. Conduct research on consumer opinions and marketing strategies related to green energy technologies. Attend or participate in conferences or meetings to promote green energy, environmental protection, or energy conservation. Analyze the effectiveness of marketing tactics or channels. Analyze regional energy markets, including energy pricing, market structures, energy generation competition, and energy transmission constraints. Analyze green energy marketing or sales trends to forecast future conditions. Develop branding or sales initiatives for green energy products. Develop comprehensive marketing strategies, using knowledge of green energy products, markets, and regulations.

**Education/Training Required:** Work experience plus degree. **Education and Training Programs:** Advertising; Marketing/Marketing Management, General; Public Relations/Image Management. **Knowledge/Courses**—No data available.

**Personality Type:** No data available. **Career Clusters:** 04 Business, Management, and Administration; 14 Marketing, Sales, and Service. **Career Pathways:** 4.1 Management; 4.5 Marketing; 14.1 Management and Entrepreneurship. **Other Jobs in These Pathways:** Brownfield Redevelopment Specialists and Site Managers; Business Continuity Planners; Business Operations Specialists, All Other; Chief Executives; Chief Sustainability Officers; Compliance Managers; Computer and Information Systems Managers; Construction Managers; Customs Brokers; Energy Auditors; First-Line Supervisors of Office and Administrative Support Workers; General and Operations Managers; Investment Fund Managers; Loss Prevention Managers; Management Analysts; Managers, All Other; Public Relations Specialists; Regulatory Affairs Managers; Sales Managers; Security Management Specialists; Security Managers; Supply Chain

Managers; Sustainability Specialists; Wind Energy Operations Managers; Wind Energy Project Managers; others.

**Skills**—No data available.

**Work Environment:** No data available.

# Advertising Sales Agents

- ❀ Annual Earnings: $45,350
- ❀ Earnings Growth Potential: High (49.8%)
- ❀ Growth: 7.2%
- ❀ Annual Job Openings: 4,510
- ❀ Self-Employed: 5.0%

**Considerations for Job Outlook:** Continued growth of media outlets is expected to generate demand for advertising sales. Opportunities for entry-level workers should be good, especially for job seekers who have sales experience and a college degree.

**Sell or solicit advertising, including graphic art, advertising space in publications, custom-made signs, or TV and radio advertising time. May obtain leases for outdoor advertising sites or persuade retailer to use sales promotion display items.** Prepare and deliver sales presentations to new and existing customers to sell new advertising programs and to protect and increase existing advertising. Explain to customers how specific types of advertising will help promote their products or services in the most effective way possible. Maintain assigned account bases while developing new accounts. Process all correspondence and paperwork related to accounts. Deliver advertising or illustration proofs to customers for approval. Draw up contracts for advertising work and collect payments due. Locate and contact potential clients to offer advertising services. Provide clients with estimates of the costs of advertising products or services. Recommend appropriate sizes and formats for advertising, depending on medium being used. Inform customers of available options for advertisement artwork and provide samples. Obtain and study information about clients' products, needs, problems, advertising history, and business practices to offer effective sales presentations and appropriate product assistance. Determine advertising medium to be used and prepare sample advertisements within the selected medium for presentation to customers. Consult with company officials, sales departments, and advertising agencies to develop promotional plans. Prepare promotional plans, sales literature, media kits, and sales contracts, using computer. Identify new advertising markets and propose products to serve them. Write copy as part

of layout. Attend sales meetings, industry trade shows, and training seminars to gather information, promote products, expand network of contacts, and increase knowledge. Gather all relevant material for bid processes and coordinate bidding and contract approval. Arrange for commercial taping sessions and accompany clients to sessions. Write sales outlines for use by staff.

**Education/Training Required:** Moderate-term on-the-job training. **Education and Training Program:** Advertising. **Knowledge/Courses**—Sales and Marketing, Communications and Media, Clerical, Customer and Personal Service, Economics and Accounting, Telecommunications.

**Personality Type:** Enterprising-Conventional-Artistic. **Career Cluster:** 04 Business, Management, and Administration. **Career Pathway:** 4.5 Marketing. **Other Jobs in This Pathway:** Technical Writers.

**Skills**—Persuasion, Negotiation, Service Orientation, Speaking, Management of Financial Resources, Mathematics, Social Perceptiveness, Systems Evaluation.

**Work Environment:** More often indoors than outdoors; sitting; noise.

# Aerospace Engineers

- ❀ Annual Earnings: $97,480
- ❀ Earnings Growth Potential: Medium (37.8%)
- ❀ Growth: 10.4%
- ❀ Annual Job Openings: 2,230
- ❀ Self-Employed: 3.3%

**Considerations for Job Outlook:** Aerospace engineers are expected to have 10 percent growth in employment from 2008–2018, about as fast as the average for all occupations. New technologies and new designs for commercial and military aircraft and spacecraft produced during the next decade should spur demand for aerospace engineers. The employment outlook for aerospace engineers appears favorable. Although the number of degrees granted in aerospace engineering has begun to increase after many years of declines, new graduates continue to be needed to replace aerospace engineers who retire or leave the occupation for other reasons.

**Perform a variety of engineering work in designing, constructing, and testing aircraft, missiles, and spacecraft. May conduct basic and applied research to evaluate adaptability of materials and equipment to aircraft**

**design and manufacture. May recommend improvements in testing equipment and techniques.** Formulate conceptual design of aeronautical or aerospace products or systems to meet customer requirements. Direct and coordinate activities of engineering or technical personnel designing, fabricating, modifying, or testing aircraft or aerospace products. Develop design criteria for aeronautical or aerospace products or systems, including testing methods, production costs, quality standards, and completion dates. Plan and conduct experimental, environmental, operational, and stress tests on models and prototypes of aircraft and aerospace systems and equipment. Evaluate product data and design from inspections and reports for conformance to engineering principles, customer requirements, and quality standards. Formulate mathematical models or other methods of computer analysis to develop, evaluate, or modify design according to customer engineering requirements. Write technical reports and other documentation, such as handbooks and bulletins, for use by engineering staff, management, and customers. Analyze project requests and proposals and engineering data to determine feasibility, productibility, cost, and production time of aerospace or aeronautical product. Review performance reports and documentation from customers and field engineers and inspect malfunctioning or damaged products to determine problem. Direct research and development programs. Evaluate and approve selection of vendors by study of past performance and new advertisements. Plan and coordinate activities concerned with investigating and resolving customers' reports of technical problems with aircraft or aerospace vehicles. Maintain records of performance reports for future reference.

**Education/Training Required:** Bachelor's degree. **Education and Training Program:** Aerospace, Aeronautical, and Astronautical/Space Engineering. **Knowledge/Courses—** Engineering and Technology, Physics, Design, Mechanical, Mathematics, Production and Processing.

**Personality Type:** Investigative-Realistic. **Career Cluster:** 15 Science, Technology, Engineering, and Mathematics. **Career Pathway:** 15.1 Engineering and Technology. **Other Jobs in This Pathway:** Architectural and Engineering Managers; Automotive Engineers; Biochemical Engineers; Biofuels/Biodiesel Technology and Product Development Managers; Civil Engineers; Cost Estimators; Electrical Engineers; Electronics Engineers, Except Computer; Energy Engineers; Engineers, All Other; Fuel Cell Engineers; Human Factors Engineers and Ergonomists; Industrial Engineers; Manufacturing Engineers; Mechanical Engineers; Mechatronics Engineers; Microsystems Engineers; Nanosystems Engineers; Photonics Engineers; Radio Frequency Identification Device Specialists; Robotics Engineers; Solar Energy Systems Engineers; Transportation Engineers; Validation Engineers; Wind Energy Engineers; others.

**Skills**—Science, Operations Analysis, Technology Design, Mathematics, Quality Control Analysis, Reading Comprehension, Systems Analysis, Writing.

**Work Environment:** Indoors; sitting.

# Agents and Business Managers of Artists, Performers, and Athletes

- ❋ Annual Earnings: $63,130
- ❋ Earnings Growth Potential: Very high (59.7%)
- ❋ Growth: 22.4%
- ❋ Annual Job Openings: 1,010
- ❋ Self-Employed: 45.8%

**Considerations for Job Outlook:** Much-faster-than-average employment growth is projected.

**Represent and promote artists, performers, and athletes to prospective employers. May handle contract negotiation and other business matters for clients.** Manage business and financial affairs for clients, such as arranging travel and lodging, selling tickets, and directing marketing and advertising activities. Obtain information about and/or inspect performance facilities, equipment, and accommodations to ensure that they meet specifications. Negotiate with managers, promoters, union officials, and other persons regarding clients' contractual rights and obligations. Advise clients on financial and legal matters such as investments and taxes. Hire trainers or coaches to advise clients on performance matters such as training techniques or performance presentations. Prepare periodic accounting statements for clients. Keep informed of industry trends and deals. Develop contacts with individuals and organizations and apply effective strategies and techniques to ensure their clients' success. Confer with clients to develop strategies for their careers and to explain actions taken on their behalf. Conduct auditions or interviews in order to evaluate potential clients. Schedule promotional or performance engagements for clients. Arrange meetings concerning issues involving their clients. Collect fees, commissions, or other payments according to contract terms.

**Education/Training Required:** Work experience plus degree. **Education and Training Program:** Purchasing,

Procurement/Acquisitions, and Contracts Management. **Knowledge/Courses**—Fine Arts, Sales and Marketing, Communications and Media, Clerical, Customer and Personal Service, Economics and Accounting.

**Personality Type:** Enterprising-Social. **Career Clusters:** 03 Arts, Audio/Video Technology, and Communications; 04 Business, Management, and Administration. **Career Pathways:** 3.1 Audio and Video Technology and Film; 4.1 Management. **Other Jobs in These Pathways:** Brownfield Redevelopment Specialists and Site Managers; Business Continuity Planners; Business Operations Specialists, All Other; Chief Executives; Chief Sustainability Officers; Compliance Managers; Computer and Information Systems Managers; Construction Managers; Customs Brokers; Energy Auditors; First-Line Supervisors of Office and Administrative Support Workers; General and Operations Managers; Graphic Designers; Investment Fund Managers; Loss Prevention Managers; Management Analysts; Managers, All Other; Regulatory Affairs Managers; Sales Managers; Security Management Specialists; Security Managers; Supply Chain Managers; Sustainability Specialists; Wind Energy Operations Managers; Wind Energy Project Managers; others.

**Skills**—Negotiation, Persuasion, Management of Financial Resources, Service Orientation, Judgment and Decision Making, Speaking, Management of Personnel Resources, Time Management.

**Work Environment:** Indoors; sitting.

# Agricultural Engineers

- ❋ Annual Earnings: $71,090
- ❋ Earnings Growth Potential: Medium (40.6%)
- ❋ Growth: 11.9%
- ❋ Annual Job Openings: 90
- ❋ Self-Employed: 0.0%

**Considerations for Job Outlook:** Agricultural engineers are expected to have employment growth of 12 percent from 2008–2018, about as fast as the average for all occupations. Employment growth should result from the need to increase crop yields to feed an expanding population and to produce crops used as renewable energy sources. Moreover, engineers will be needed to develop more efficient agricultural production and to conserve resources. In addition, engineers will be needed to meet the increasing demand for biosensors, used to determine the optimal treatment of crops.

**Apply knowledge of engineering technology and biological science to agricultural problems concerned with power and machinery, electrification, structures, soil and water conservation, and processing of agricultural products.** Visit sites to observe environmental problems, to consult with contractors, or to monitor construction activities. Design agricultural machinery components and equipment, using computer-aided design (CAD) technology. Test agricultural machinery and equipment to ensure adequate performance. Design structures for crop storage, animal shelter and loading, and animal and crop processing and supervise their construction. Provide advice on water quality and issues related to pollution management, river control, and ground and surface water resources. Conduct educational programs that provide farmers or farm cooperative members with information that can help them improve agricultural productivity. Discuss plans with clients, contractors, consultants, and other engineers so that they can be evaluated and necessary changes made. Supervise food processing or manufacturing plant operations. Design and supervise environmental and land reclamation projects in agriculture and related industries. Design food processing plants and related mechanical systems. Plan and direct construction of rural electric-power distribution systems and irrigation, drainage, and flood control systems for soil and water conservation. Prepare reports, sketches, working drawings, specifications, proposals, and budgets for proposed sites or systems. Meet with clients, such as district or regional councils, farmers, and developers, to discuss their needs. Design sensing, measuring, and recording devices and other instrumentation used to study plant or animal life.

**Education/Training Required:** Bachelor's degree. **Education and Training Program:** Agricultural Engineering. **Knowledge/Courses**—Engineering and Technology, Design, Physics, Food Production, Building and Construction, Mechanical.

**Personality Type:** Investigative-Realistic-Enterprising. **Career Cluster:** 15 Science, Technology, Engineering, and Mathematics. **Career Pathway:** 15.1 Engineering and Technology. **Other Jobs in This Pathway:** Architectural and Engineering Managers; Automotive Engineers; Biochemical Engineers; Biofuels/Biodiesel Technology and Product Development Managers; Civil Engineers; Cost Estimators; Electrical Engineers; Electronics Engineers, Except Computer; Energy Engineers; Engineers, All Other; Fuel Cell Engineers; Human Factors Engineers and Ergonomists; Industrial Engineers; Manufacturing Engineers; Mechanical Engineers; Mechatronics Engineers; Microsystems Engineers; Nanosystems Engineers; Photonics Engineers; Radio Frequency Identification Device Specialists; Robotics

Engineers; Solar Energy Systems Engineers; Transportation Engineers; Validation Engineers; Wind Energy Engineers; others.

**Skills**—Technology Design, Science, Mathematics, Management of Material Resources, Complex Problem Solving, Systems Evaluation, Systems Analysis, Writing.

**Work Environment:** More often indoors than outdoors; sitting.

# Agricultural Sciences Teachers, Postsecondary

- ❀ Annual Earnings: $78,370
- ❀ Earnings Growth Potential: High (46.9%)
- ❀ Growth: 15.1%
- ❀ Annual Job Openings: 300
- ❀ Self-Employed: 0.2%

**Considerations for Job Outlook:** Enrollments in postsecondary institutions are expected to continue rising as more people attend college and as workers return to school to update their skills. Opportunities for part-time or temporary positions should be favorable, but significant competition exists for tenure-track positions.

**Teach courses in the agricultural sciences, including agronomy, dairy sciences, fisheries management, horticultural sciences, poultry sciences, range management, and agricultural soil conservation.** Prepare course materials such as syllabi, homework assignments, and handouts. Evaluate and grade students' classwork, laboratory work, assignments, and papers. Keep abreast of developments in agriculture by reading current literature, talking with colleagues, and participating in professional conferences. Prepare and deliver lectures to undergraduate and/or graduate students on topics such as crop production, plant genetics, and soil chemistry. Initiate, facilitate, and moderate classroom discussions. Conduct research in a particular field of knowledge and publish findings in professional journals, books, and/or electronic media. Supervise laboratory sessions and fieldwork and coordinate laboratory operations. Supervise undergraduate and/or graduate teaching, internship, and research work. Compile, administer, and grade examinations or assign this work to others. Advise students on academic and vocational curricula and on career issues. Plan, evaluate, and revise curricula, course content, and course materials and methods of instruction. Maintain student attendance records, grades, and other required records. Write grant proposals to procure external research funding.

Collaborate with colleagues to address teaching and research issues. Maintain regularly scheduled office hours in order to advise and assist students. Participate in student recruitment, registration, and placement activities. Select and obtain materials and supplies such as textbooks and laboratory equipment. Act as advisers to student organizations. Participate in campus and community events. Serve on academic or administrative committees that deal with institutional policies, departmental matters, and academic issues. Provide professional consulting services to government and/or industry. Perform administrative duties such as serving as department head. Compile bibliographies of specialized materials for outside reading assignments.

**Education/Training Required:** Doctoral degree. **Education and Training Programs:** Agribusiness/Agricultural Business Operations; Agricultural and Food Products Processing; Agricultural and Horticultural Plant Breeding; Agricultural Animal Breeding; Agricultural Business and Management, General; Agricultural Economics; Agricultural Mechanization, General; Agricultural Power Machinery Operation; Agricultural Production Operations, General; Agricultural Teacher Education; Agricultural/Farm Supplies Retailing and Wholesaling; Agriculture, General; Animal Health; Animal Nutrition; Animal Training; Animal/Livestock Husbandry and Production; Applied Horticulture/Horticulture Operations, General; Aquaculture; Crop Production; Dairy Science; Equestrian/Equine Studies; Farm/Farm and Ranch Management; Food Science; Greenhouse Operations and Management; Horticultural Science; International Agriculture; Landscaping and Groundskeeping; Livestock Management; Ornamental Horticulture; Plant Nursery Operations and Management; Plant Protection and Integrated Pest Management; Plant Sciences, General; Poultry Science; Range Science and Management; Soil Science and Agronomy, General; Turf and Turfgrass Management; others. **Knowledge/Courses**—Biology, Food Production, Education and Training, Geography, Chemistry, Communications and Media.

**Personality Type:** Social-Investigative-Realistic. **Career Clusters:** 01 Agriculture, Food, and Natural Resources; 05 Education and Training. **Career Pathways:** 1.1 Food Products and Processing Systems; 1.2 Plant Systems; 1.3 Animal Systems; 1.4 Power Structure and Technical Systems; 1.7 Agribusiness Systems; 5.3 Teaching/Training. **Other Jobs in These Pathways:** Career/Technical Education Teachers, Secondary School; Coaches and Scouts; Elementary School Teachers, Except Special Education; First-Line Supervisors of Landscaping, Lawn Service, and Groundskeeping Workers; First-Line Supervisors of Office and Administrative Support Workers; First-Line Supervisors of Retail Sales

Workers; Fitness Trainers and Aerobics Instructors; Food Batchmakers; Graphic Designers; Instructional Coordinators; Instructional Designers and Technologists; Kindergarten Teachers, Except Special Education; Landscaping and Groundskeeping Workers; Librarians; Middle School Teachers, Except Special and Career/Technical Education; Mobile Heavy Equipment Mechanics, Except Engines; Nonfarm Animal Caretakers; Preschool Teachers, Except Special Education; Recreation Workers; Retail Salespersons; Secondary School Teachers, Except Special and Career/Technical Education; Self-Enrichment Education Teachers; Teacher Assistants; Tutors; 37 other postsecondary teaching occupations; others.

**Skills**—Instructing, Science, Writing, Speaking, Reading Comprehension, Active Learning, Learning Strategies, Operations Analysis.

**Work Environment:** Indoors; sitting.

# Air Traffic Controllers

- ❋ Annual Earnings: $108,040
- ❋ Earnings Growth Potential: High (49.6%)
- ❋ Growth: 13.1%
- ❋ Annual Job Openings: 1,230
- ❋ Self-Employed: 0.0%

**Considerations for Job Outlook:** More controllers are expected to be needed to handle increasing air traffic. Competition for admission to the FAA Academy—the usual first step in employment as an air traffic controller—is expected to remain keen.

**Control air traffic on and within vicinity of airport and movement of air traffic between altitude sectors and control centers according to established procedures and policies. Authorize, regulate, and control commercial airline flights according to government or company regulations to expedite and ensure flight safety.** Control air traffic on and within vicinity of airport and movement of air traffic between altitude sectors and control centers according to established procedures and policies. Authorize, regulate, and control commercial airline flights according to government or company regulations to expedite and ensure flight safety.

**Education/Training Required:** Long-term on-the-job training. **Education and Training Program:** Air Traffic Controller Training. **Knowledge/Courses**—Transportation, Geography, Telecommunications, Public Safety and Security, Physics, Education and Training.

**Personality Type:** Enterprising-Conventional. **Career Cluster:** 16 Transportation, Distribution, and Logistics. **Career Pathway:** 16.1 Transportation Operations. **Other Jobs in This Pathway:** Airline Pilots, Copilots, and Flight Engineers; Automotive and Watercraft Service Attendants; Automotive Master Mechanics; Bus Drivers, School or Special Client; Bus Drivers, Transit and Intercity; Commercial Pilots; Crane and Tower Operators; First-Line Supervisors of Helpers, Laborers, and Material Movers, Hand; First-Line Supervisors of Transportation and Material-Moving Machine and Vehicle Operators; Freight and Cargo Inspectors; Heavy and Tractor-Trailer Truck Drivers; Laborers and Freight, Stock, and Material Movers, Hand; Light Truck or Delivery Services Drivers; Mates—Ship, Boat, and Barge; Motor Vehicle Operators, All Other; Operating Engineers and Other Construction Equipment Operators; Parking Lot Attendants; Pilots, Ship; Railroad Conductors and Yardmasters; Sailors and Marine Oilers; Ship and Boat Captains; Storage and Distribution Managers; Taxi Drivers and Chauffeurs; Transportation Managers; Transportation Workers, All Other; others.

**Skills**—Complex Problem Solving, Operation Monitoring, Judgment and Decision Making, Operations Analysis, Monitoring, Coordination, Systems Analysis, Systems Evaluation.

**Work Environment:** Indoors; sitting; using hands; repetitive motions; noise.

# Aircraft Mechanics and Service Technicians

- ❋ Annual Earnings: $53,420
- ❋ Earnings Growth Potential: Medium (37.0%)
- ❋ Growth: 6.4%
- ❋ Annual Job Openings: 3,140
- ❋ Self-Employed: 1.1%

**Considerations for Job Outlook:** Air traffic is expected to increase due to an expanding economy and a growing population, leading to employment growth for aircraft mechanics and service technicians. Prospects should be best for job seekers who have experience and professional certification.

**Diagnose, adjust, repair, or overhaul aircraft engines and assemblies such as hydraulic and pneumatic systems.** Read and interpret maintenance manuals, service bulletins, and other specifications to determine the feasibility and method of repairing or replacing malfunctioning or damaged components. Inspect completed work to certify that maintenance meets standards and that aircraft are ready for operation. Maintain repair logs, documenting all preventive and corrective aircraft maintenance. Conduct routine and special inspections as required by regulations. Examine and inspect aircraft components, including landing gear, hydraulic systems, and de-icers, to locate cracks, breaks, leaks, or other problem. Inspect airframes for wear or other defects. Maintain, repair, and rebuild aircraft structures; functional components; and parts such as wings and fuselage, rigging, hydraulic units, oxygen systems, fuel systems, electrical systems, gaskets, and seals. Measure the tension of control cables. Replace or repair worn, defective, or damaged components, using hand tools, gauges, and testing equipment. Measure parts for wear, using precision instruments. Assemble and install electrical, plumbing, mechanical, hydraulic, and structural components and accessories, using hand tools and power tools. Test operation of engines and other systems, using test equipment such as ignition analyzers, compression checkers, distributor timers, and ammeters. Obtain fuel and oil samples and check them for contamination. Reassemble engines following repair or inspection and re-install engines in aircraft. Read and interpret pilots' descriptions of problems to diagnose causes. Modify aircraft structures, space vehicles, systems, or components, following drawings, schematics, charts, engineering orders, and technical publications. Install and align repaired or replacement parts for subsequent riveting or welding, using clamps and wrenches. Locate and mark dimensions and reference lines on defective or replacement parts, using templates, scribes, compasses, and steel rules.

**Education/Training Required:** Postsecondary vocational training. **Education and Training Programs:** Agricultural Mechanics and Equipment/Machine Technology; Aircraft Powerplant Technology/Technician; Airframe Mechanics and Aircraft Maintenance Technology/Technician. **Knowledge/Courses**—Mechanical, Design, Physics, Engineering and Technology, Chemistry, Transportation.

**Personality Type:** Realistic-Conventional-Investigative. **Career Clusters:** 13 Manufacturing; 16 Transportation, Distribution, and Logistics. **Career Pathways:** 13.3 Maintenance, Installation, and Repair; 16.4 Facility and Mobile Equipment Maintenance. **Other Jobs in These Pathways:** Automotive Body and Related Repairers; Automotive Master Mechanics; Automotive Specialty Technicians; Biological Technicians; Bus and Truck Mechanics and Diesel Engine Specialists; Civil Engineering Technicians; Cleaners of Vehicles and Equipment; Computer, Automated Teller, and Office Machine Repairers; Electrical and Electronic Equipment Assemblers; Electrical and Electronics Repairers;

Commercial and Industrial Equipment; Electrical Engineering Technicians; Electrical Engineering Technologists; Electromechanical Engineering Technologists; Electronics Engineering Technicians; Electronics Engineering Technologists; Engineering Technicians, Except Drafters, All Other; Fuel Cell Technicians; Helpers—Installation, Maintenance, and Repair Workers; Industrial Engineering Technologists; Industrial Machinery Mechanics; Installation, Maintenance, and Repair Workers, All Other; Manufacturing Engineering Technologists; Mobile Heavy Equipment Mechanics, Except Engines; Telecommunications Line Installers and Repairers; Tire Repairers and Changers; others.

**Skills**—Equipment Maintenance, Repairing, Troubleshooting, Equipment Selection, Quality Control Analysis, Operation Monitoring, Operation and Control, Installation.

**Work Environment:** Indoors; standing; walking and running; using hands; bending or twisting the body; noise; contaminants; cramped work space; hazardous conditions; hazardous equipment.

# Aircraft Structure, Surfaces, Rigging, and Systems Assemblers

- ❀ Annual Earnings: $44,820
- ❀ Earnings Growth Potential: Medium (39.8%)
- ❀ Growth: 9.4%
- ❀ Annual Job Openings: 1,340
- ❀ Self-Employed: 0.0%

**Considerations for Job Outlook:** Increased production and efficiency in manufacturing, where most of these workers are employed, should stabilize employment. Good job prospects are expected.

**Assemble, fit, fasten, and install parts of airplanes, space vehicles, or missiles, such as tails, wings, fuselage, bulkheads, stabilizers, landing gear, rigging and control equipment, or heating and ventilating systems.** Form loops or splices in cables, using clamps and fittings, or reweave cable strands. Align and fit structural assemblies manually or signal crane operators to position assemblies for joining. Align, fit, assemble, connect, and install system components, using jigs, fixtures, measuring instruments, hand tools, and power tools. Assemble and fit prefabricated parts to form subassemblies. Assemble, install, and connect parts, fittings, and assemblies on aircraft, using layout tools; hand tools; power tools; and fasteners such as bolts, screws, rivets, and clamps. Attach brackets, hinges, or clips to secure or support components and subassemblies, using bolts, screws, rivets, chemical bonding, or welding. Select and install accessories in swaging machines, using hand tools. Fit and fasten sheet metal coverings to surface areas and other sections of aircraft prior to welding or riveting. Lay out and mark reference points and locations for installation of parts and components, using jigs, templates, and measuring and marking instruments. Inspect and test installed units, parts, systems, and assemblies for fit, alignment, performance, defects, and compliance with standards, using measuring instruments and test equipment. Install mechanical linkages and actuators and verify tension of cables, using tensiometers. Join structural assemblies such as wings, tails, and fuselage. Measure and cut cables and tubing, using master templates, measuring instruments, and cable cutters or saws. Read and interpret blueprints, illustrations, and specifications to determine layouts, sequences of operations, or identities and relationships of parts. Prepare and load live ammunition, missiles, and bombs onto aircraft according to established procedures. Adjust, repair, rework, or replace parts and assemblies to eliminate malfunctions and to ensure proper operation.

**Education/Training Required:** Moderate-term on-the-job training. **Education and Training Programs:** Aircraft Powerplant Technology/Technician; Airframe Mechanics and Aircraft Maintenance Technology/Technician; Avionics Maintenance Technology/Technician. **Knowledge/Courses**—Mechanical, Design, Chemistry, Public Safety and Security.

**Personality Type:** Realistic-Conventional. **Career Cluster:** 16 Transportation, Distribution, and Logistics. **Career Pathway:** 16.4 Facility and Mobile Equipment Maintenance. **Other Jobs in This Pathway:** Aircraft Mechanics and Service Technicians; Automotive Body and Related Repairers; Automotive Glass Installers and Repairers; Automotive Master Mechanics; Automotive Specialty Technicians; Bicycle Repairers; Bus and Truck Mechanics and Diesel Engine Specialists; Cleaners of Vehicles and Equipment; Electrical and Electronics Installers and Repairers, Transportation Equipment; Electronic Equipment Installers and Repairers, Motor Vehicles; Engine and Other Machine Assemblers; Gem and Diamond Workers; Installation, Maintenance, and Repair Workers, All Other; Motorboat Mechanics and Service Technicians; Motorcycle Mechanics; Outdoor Power Equipment and Other Small Engine Mechanics; Painters, Transportation Equipment.

**Skills**—Installation, Troubleshooting, Equipment Selection, Repairing, Quality Control Analysis, Equipment Maintenance, Operation and Control, Technology Design.

**Work Environment:** Standing; walking and running; using hands; bending or twisting the body; repetitive motions; noise; very hot or cold; bright or inadequate lighting; contaminants; cramped work space; hazardous conditions; hazardous equipment; minor burns, cuts, bites, or stings.

# Airline Pilots, Copilots, and Flight Engineers

* Annual Earnings: $103,210
* Earnings Growth Potential: High (46.7%)
* Growth: 8.4%
* Annual Job Openings: 3,250
* Self-Employed: 0.0%

**Considerations for Job Outlook:** Population growth and economic expansion are expected to boost demand for air travel. Regional airlines and low-cost carriers should have the best opportunities; pilots vying for jobs with major airlines face strong competition.

**Pilot and navigate the flight of multi-engine aircraft in regularly scheduled service for the transport of passengers and cargo. Requires Federal Air Transport rating and certification in specific aircraft type used.** Use instrumentation to guide flights when visibility is poor. Respond to and report in-flight emergencies and malfunctions. Work as part of a flight team with other crew members, especially during takeoffs and landings. Contact control towers for takeoff clearances, arrival instructions, and other information, using radio equipment. Steer aircraft along planned routes with the assistance of autopilot and flight management computers. Monitor gauges, warning devices, and control panels to verify aircraft performance and to regulate engine speed. Start engines, operate controls, and pilot airplanes to transport passengers, mail, or freight while adhering to flight plans, regulations, and procedures. Inspect aircraft for defects and malfunctions according to pre-flight checklists. Check passenger and cargo distributions and fuel amounts to ensure that weight and balance specifications are met. Monitor engine operation, fuel consumption, and functioning of aircraft systems during flights. Confer with flight dispatchers and weather forecasters to keep abreast of flight conditions. Coordinate flight activities with ground crews and air-traffic control and inform crew members of flight and test procedures. Order changes in fuel supplies, loads, routes, or schedules to ensure safety of flights. Choose routes, altitudes, and speeds that will provide the fastest, safest, and smoothest flights. Direct activities of aircraft crews during flights. Brief crews about flight details such as destinations, duties, and responsibilities. Record in log-books information such as flight times, distances flown, and fuel consumption. Make announcements regarding flights, using public address systems. File instrument flight plans with air traffic control to ensure that flights are coordinated with other air traffic. Perform minor maintenance work or arrange for major maintenance. Instruct other pilots and student pilots in aircraft operations and the principles of flight.

**Education/Training Required:** Bachelor's degree. **Education and Training Programs:** Airline/Commercial/Professional Pilot and Flight Crew Training; Flight Instructor Training. **Knowledge/Courses—**Transportation, Geography, Physics, Public Safety and Security, Psychology, Law and Government.

**Personality Type:** Realistic-Conventional-Investigative. **Career Cluster:** 16 Transportation, Distribution, and Logistics. **Career Pathway:** 16.1 Transportation Operations. **Other Jobs in This Pathway:** Automotive and Watercraft Service Attendants; Automotive Master Mechanics; Bus Drivers, School or Special Client; Bus Drivers, Transit and Intercity; Commercial Pilots; Crane and Tower Operators; First-Line Supervisors of Helpers, Laborers, and Material Movers, Hand; First-Line Supervisors of Transportation and Material-Moving Machine and Vehicle Operators; Freight and Cargo Inspectors; Heavy and Tractor-Trailer Truck Drivers; Laborers and Freight, Stock, and Material Movers, Hand; Light Truck or Delivery Services Drivers; Mates—Ship, Boat, and Barge; Motor Vehicle Operators, All Other; Operating Engineers and Other Construction Equipment Operators; Parking Lot Attendants; Pilots, Ship; Railroad Conductors and Yardmasters; Sailors and Marine Oilers; Ship and Boat Captains; Storage and Distribution Managers; Taxi Drivers and Chauffeurs; Transportation Inspectors; Transportation Managers; Transportation Workers, All Other; others.

**Skills—**Operation and Control, Operation Monitoring, Science, Troubleshooting, Instructing, Judgment and Decision Making, Quality Control Analysis, Mathematics.

**Work Environment:** More often indoors than outdoors; sitting; using hands; noise; very hot or cold; bright or inadequate lighting; contaminants; cramped work space; exposed to radiation.

# Amusement and Recreation Attendants

- ❋ Annual Earnings: $18,450
- ❋ Earnings Growth Potential: Very low (14.5%)
- ❋ Growth: 13.3%
- ❋ Annual Job Openings: 17,120
- ❋ Self-Employed: 0.6%

**Considerations for Job Outlook:** About average employment growth is projected.

**Perform variety of attending duties at amusement or recreation facility. May schedule use of recreation facilities, maintain and provide equipment to participants of sporting events or recreational pursuits, or operate amusement concessions and rides.** Provide information about facilities, entertainment options, and rules and regulations. Record details of attendance, sales, receipts, reservations, or repair activities. Monitor activities to ensure adherence to rules and safety procedures or arrange for the removal of unruly patrons. Sell tickets and collect fees from customers. Clean sporting equipment, vehicles, rides, booths, facilities, or grounds. Keep informed of shut-down and emergency evacuation procedures. Operate machines to clean, smooth, and prepare the ice surfaces of rinks for activities such as skating, hockey, and curling. Announce or describe amusement park attractions to patrons to entice customers to games and other entertainment. Fasten safety devices for patrons or provide them with directions for fastening devices. Inspect equipment to detect wear and damage and perform minor repairs, adjustments, or maintenance tasks such as oiling parts. Operate, drive, or explain the use of mechanical riding devices or other automatic equipment in amusement parks, carnivals, or recreation areas. Rent, sell, or issue sporting equipment and supplies such as bowling shoes, golf balls, swimming suits, and beach chairs. Verify, collect, or punch tickets before admitting patrons to venues such as amusement parks and rides. Direct patrons to rides, seats, or attractions. Tend amusement booths in parks, carnivals, or stadiums, performing duties such as conducting games, photographing patrons, and awarding prizes. Provide assistance to patrons entering or exiting amusement rides, boats, or ski lifts or mounting or dismounting animals. Sell and serve refreshments to customers. Schedule the use of recreation facilities such as golf courses, tennis courts, bowling alleys, and softball diamonds. Maintain inventories of equipment, storing and retrieving items and assembling and disassembling equipment as necessary.

**Education/Training Required:** Short-term on-the-job training. **Education and Training Programs:** No related CIP programs; this job is learned through short-term on-the-job training. **Knowledge/Courses**—Customer and Personal Service, Public Safety and Security.

**Personality Type:** Enterprising-Conventional-Realistic. **Career Cluster:** 09 Hospitality and Tourism. **Career Pathway:** 9.4 Recreation, Amusements, and Attractions. **Other Jobs in This Pathway:** Baggage Porters and Bellhops; Concierges; Costume Attendants; Entertainment Attendants and Related Workers, All Other; Farm and Home Management Advisors; Gaming and Sports Book Writers and Runners; Gaming Dealers; Gaming Service Workers, All Other; Locker Room, Coatroom, and Dressing Room Attendants; Lodging Managers; Motion Picture Projectionists; Personal Care and Service Workers, All Other; Ushers, Lobby Attendants, and Ticket Takers.

**Skills**—Operation and Control, Equipment Maintenance, Quality Control Analysis, Operation Monitoring, Repairing, Service Orientation.

**Work Environment:** More often indoors than outdoors; sitting; using hands; noise.

# Animal Scientists

- ❋ Annual Earnings: $58,250
- ❋ Earnings Growth Potential: High (41.7%)
- ❋ Growth: 13.2%
- ❋ Annual Job Openings: 180
- ❋ Self-Employed: 11.9%

**Considerations for Job Outlook:** Job growth is expected to stem primarily from efforts to increase the quantity and quality of food for a growing population and to balance output with protection and preservation of soil, water, and ecosystems. Opportunities should be good for agricultural and food scientists in almost all fields.

**Conduct research in the genetics, nutrition, reproduction, growth, and development of domestic farm animals.** Conduct research concerning animal nutrition, breeding, or management to improve products or processes. Advise producers about improved products and techniques that could enhance their animal production efforts. Study nutritional requirements of animals and nutritive values of animal feed materials. Study effects of management practices, processing methods, feed, or environmental conditions on quality and quantity of animal products, such as eggs and milk. Develop improved practices in feeding, housing, sanitation,

or parasite and disease control of animals. Research and control animal selection and breeding practices to increase production efficiency and improve animal quality. Determine genetic composition of animal populations and heritability of traits, utilizing principles of genetics. Crossbreed animals with existing strains or cross strains to obtain new combinations of desirable characteristics.

**Education/Training Required:** Bachelor's degree. **Education and Training Programs:** Agricultural Animal Breeding; Agriculture, General; Animal Health; Animal Nutrition; Animal Sciences, Other; Dairy Science; Poultry Science; Range Science and Management. **Knowledge/Courses**—Biology, Food Production, Chemistry, Mathematics, Economics and Accounting, Sales and Marketing.

**Personality Type:** Investigative-Realistic. **Career Cluster:** 01 Agriculture, Food, and Natural Resources. **Career Pathways:** 1.2 Plant Systems; 1.3 Animal Systems. **Other Jobs in These Pathways:** Agricultural Technicians; Animal Breeders; Animal Trainers; Biochemists and Biophysicists; Biologists; Economists; Environmental Economists; Farm and Home Management Advisors; First-Line Supervisors of Landscaping, Lawn Service, and Groundskeeping Workers; First-Line Supervisors of Retail Sales Workers; Floral Designers; Food Science Technicians; Food Scientists and Technologists; Geneticists; Grounds Maintenance Workers, All Other; Landscaping and Groundskeeping Workers; Nonfarm Animal Caretakers; Pesticide Handlers, Sprayers, and Applicators, Vegetation; Precision Agriculture Technicians; Retail Salespersons; Soil and Plant Scientists; Tree Trimmers and Pruners; Veterinarians.

**Skills**—Science, Systems Evaluation, Judgment and Decision Making, Writing, Mathematics, Complex Problem Solving, Active Learning, Systems Analysis.

**Work Environment:** More often outdoors than indoors; sitting; contaminants.

# Animal Trainers

- ❋ Annual Earnings: $26,580
- ❋ Earnings Growth Potential: Low (35.1%)
- ❋ Growth: 20.4%
- ❋ Annual Job Openings: 1,900
- ❋ Self-Employed: 54.3%

**Considerations for Job Outlook:** Pet owners purchasing more services—including grooming, boarding, and training—is expected to lead to employment growth for animal care and service workers. Emphasis on reducing animal abuse should also increase their employment in animal shelters. Excellent opportunities are expected.

**Train animals for riding, harness, security, performance, or obedience or assisting persons with disabilities. Accustom animals to human voice and contact and condition animals to respond to commands. Train animals according to prescribed standards for show or competition. May train animals to carry pack loads or work as part of pack team.** Observe animals' physical conditions to detect illness or unhealthy conditions requiring medical care. Cue or signal animals during performances. Administer prescribed medications to animals. Evaluate animals to determine their temperaments, abilities, and aptitude for training. Feed and exercise animals and provide other general care such as cleaning and maintaining holding and performance areas. Talk to and interact with animals in order to familiarize them to human voices and contact. Conduct training programs to develop and maintain desired animal behaviors for competition, entertainment, obedience, security, riding, and related areas. Keep records documenting animal health, diet, and behavior. Advise animal owners regarding the purchase of specific animals. Instruct jockeys in handling specific horses during races. Train horses or other equines for riding, harness, show, racing, or other work, using knowledge of breed characteristics, training methods, performance standards, and the peculiarities of each animal. Use oral, spur, rein, and hand commands to condition horses to carry riders or to pull horse-drawn equipment. Place tack or harnesses on horses to accustom horses to the feel of equipment. Train dogs in human-assistance or property protection duties. Retrain horses to break bad habits, such as kicking, bolting, and resisting bridling and grooming. Train and rehearse animals, according to scripts, for motion picture, television, film, stage, or circus performances. Organize and conduct animal shows. Arrange for mating of stallions and mares and assist mares during foaling.

**Education/Training Required:** Moderate-term on-the-job training. **Education and Training Programs:** Animal Training; Equestrian/Equine Studies. **Knowledge/Courses**—Sales and Marketing, Biology, Economics and Accounting, Communications and Media, Customer and Personal Service, Clerical.

**Personality Type:** Realistic. **Career Cluster:** 01 Agriculture, Food, and Natural Resources. **Career Pathway:** 1.3 Animal Systems. **Other Jobs in This Pathway:** Agricultural Technicians; Animal Breeders; Animal Scientists; Biologists; Farm and Home Management Advisors; Food Science Technicians; Geneticists; Nonfarm Animal Caretakers; Precision Agriculture Technicians; Veterinarians.

**Skills**—Learning Strategies, Management of Material Resources, Management of Financial Resources, Operation and Control, Instructing, Monitoring, Science, Persuasion.

**Work Environment:** Outdoors; standing; walking and running; using hands; bending or twisting the body; repetitive motions; noise; very hot or cold; contaminants; minor burns, cuts, bites, or stings.

# Anthropologists and Archeologists

- ✳ Annual Earnings: $54,230
- ✳ Earnings Growth Potential: High (42.3%)
- ✳ Growth: 28.0%
- ✳ Annual Job Openings: 450
- ✳ Self-Employed: 1.5%

**Considerations for Job Outlook:** Anthropologists are projected to have significant employment growth in the management, scientific, and technical consulting industry. Expected job growth for archaeologists is associated with large-scale construction projects that must comply with federal laws to preserve archaeological sites. Job competition is expected.

## Job Specialization: Anthropologists

**Research, evaluate, and establish public policy concerning the origins of humans; their physical, social, linguistic, and cultural development; and their behavior, as well as the cultures, organizations, and institutions they have created.** Collect information and make judgments through observation, interviews, and the review of documents. Plan and direct research to characterize and compare the economic, demographic, health-care, social, political, linguistic, and religious institutions of distinct cultural groups, communities, and organizations. Write about and present research findings for a variety of specialized and general audiences. Advise government agencies, private organizations, and communities regarding proposed programs, plans, and policies and their potential impacts on cultural institutions, organizations, and communities. Identify culturally-specific beliefs and practices affecting health status and access to services for distinct populations and communities in collaboration with medical and public health officials. Build and use text-based database management systems to support the analysis of detailed first-hand observational records, or "field notes." Develop intervention procedures, utilizing techniques such as individual and focus group interviews, consultations, and participant observation of social interaction. Construct and test data collection methods. Explain the origins and physical, social, or cultural development of humans, including physical attributes, cultural traditions, beliefs, languages, resource management practices, and settlement patterns. Conduct participatory action research in communities and organizations to assess how work is done and to design work systems, technologies, and environments. Train others in the application of ethnographic research methods to solve problems in organizational effectiveness, communications, technology development, policy-making, and program planning. Formulate general rules that describe and predict the development and behavior of cultures and social institutions.

**Education/Training Required:** Master's degree. **Education and Training Programs:** Anthropology; Archeology; Classics and Classical Languages, Literatures, and Linguistics, General; Physical and Biological Anthropology. **Knowledge/Courses—**Sociology and Anthropology, History and Archeology, Foreign Language, Philosophy and Theology, Geography, Biology.

**Personality Type:** Investigative-Artistic. **Career Cluster:** 15 Science, Technology, Engineering, and Mathematics. **Career Pathway:** 15.2 Science and Mathematics. **Other Jobs in This Pathway:** Architectural and Engineering Managers; Biochemists and Biophysicists; Biofuels/Biodiesel Technology and Product Development Managers; Bioinformatics Scientists; Biological Scientists, All Other; Biologists; Biostatisticians; Chemists; Clinical Data Managers; Clinical Research Coordinators; Community and Social Service Specialists, All Other; Dietitians and Nutritionists; Education, Training, and Library Workers, All Other; Geneticists; Geoscientists, Except Hydrologists and Geographers; Medical Scientists, Except Epidemiologists; Molecular and Cellular Biologists; Natural Sciences Managers; Operations Research Analysts; Physical Scientists, All Other; Social Scientists and Related Workers, All Other; Statisticians; Survey Researchers; Transportation Planners; Water Resource Specialists; others.

**Skills—**Science, Operations Analysis, Systems Analysis, Writing, Systems Evaluation, Speaking, Social Perceptiveness, Reading Comprehension.

**Work Environment:** Indoors; sitting.

## Job Specialization: Archeologists

**Conduct research to reconstruct record of past human life and culture from human remains, artifacts, architectural features, and structures recovered through excavation,** underwater recovery, or other means of discovery. Write, present, and publish reports that record site history, methodology, and artifact analysis results, along with recommendations for conserving and interpreting findings. Compare findings from one site with archeological data from other sites to find similarities or differences. Research, survey, or assess sites of past societies and cultures in search of answers to specific research questions. Study objects and structures recovered by excavation to identify, date, and authenticate them and to interpret their significance. Develop and test theories concerning the origin and development of past cultures. Consult site reports, existing artifacts, and topographic maps to identify archeological sites. Create a grid of each site and draw and update maps of unit profiles, stratum surfaces, features, and findings. Record the exact locations and conditions of artifacts uncovered in diggings or surveys, using drawings and photographs as necessary. Assess archeological sites for resource management, development, or conservation purposes and recommend methods for site protection. Describe artifacts' physical properties or attributes, such as the materials from which artifacts are made and their size, shape, function, and decoration. Teach archeology at colleges and universities. Collect artifacts made of stone, bone, metal, and other materials, placing them in bags and marking them to show where they were found. Create artifact typologies to organize and make sense of past material cultures. Lead field training sites and train field staff, students, and volunteers in excavation methods. Clean, restore, and preserve artifacts.

**Education/Training Required:** Master's degree. **Education and Training Programs:** Anthropology; Archeology; Classics and Classical Languages, Literatures, and Linguistics, General; Physical and Biological Anthropology. **Knowledge/Courses—**History and Archeology, Sociology and Anthropology, Geography, Philosophy and Theology, Foreign Language, English Language.

**Personality Type:** Investigative-Realistic-Artistic. **Career Cluster:** 15 Science, Technology, Engineering, and Mathematics. **Career Pathway:** 15.2 Science and Mathematics. **Other Jobs in This Pathway:** Architectural and Engineering Managers; Biochemists and Biophysicists; Biofuels/Biodiesel Technology and Product Development Managers; Bioinformatics Scientists; Biological Scientists, All Other; Biologists; Biostatisticians; Chemists; Clinical Data Managers; Clinical Research Coordinators; Community and Social Service Specialists, All Other; Dietitians and Nutritionists; Education, Training, and Library Workers, All Other; Geneticists; Geoscientists, Except Hydrologists and Geographers; Medical Scientists, Except Epidemiologists; Molecular and Cellular Biologists; Natural Sciences Managers; Operations

Research Analysts; Physical Scientists, All Other; Social Scientists and Related Workers, All Other; Statisticians; Survey Researchers; Transportation Planners; Water Resource Specialists; others.

**Skills**—Science, Reading Comprehension, Writing, Programming, Learning Strategies, Management of Personnel Resources, Mathematics, Active Learning.

**Work Environment:** More often indoors than outdoors; sitting; using hands.

# Anthropology and Archeology Teachers, Postsecondary

- ❋ Annual Earnings: $73,600
- ❋ Earnings Growth Potential: High (43.9%)
- ❋ Growth: 15.1%
- ❋ Annual Job Openings: 200
- ❋ Self-Employed: 0.2%

**Considerations for Job Outlook:** Enrollments in postsecondary institutions are expected to continue rising as more people attend college and as workers return to school to update their skills. Opportunities for part-time or temporary positions should be favorable, but significant competition exists for tenure-track positions.

**Teach courses in anthropology or archeology.** Conduct research in a particular field of knowledge and publish findings in professional journals, books, and electronic media. Keep abreast of developments in their field by reading current literature, talking with colleagues, and participating in professional conferences. Prepare and deliver lectures to undergraduate and graduate students on topics such as research methods, urban anthropology, and language and culture. Evaluate and grade students' classwork, assignments, and papers. Initiate, facilitate, and moderate classroom discussions. Write grant proposals to procure external research funding. Supervise undergraduate and/or graduate teaching, internship, and research work. Prepare course materials such as syllabi, homework assignments, and handouts. Compile, administer, and grade examinations or assign this work to others. Supervise students' laboratory work or fieldwork. Plan, evaluate, and revise curricula, course content, and course materials and methods of instruction. Advise students on academic and vocational curricula, career issues, and laboratory and field research. Maintain student attendance records, grades, and other required records. Maintain regularly scheduled office hours in order to advise and assist students. Collaborate with colleagues to address teaching and research issues. Compile bibliographies of specialized materials for outside reading assignments. Perform administrative duties such as serving as department head. Select and obtain materials and supplies such as textbooks and laboratory equipment. Serve on academic or administrative committees that deal with institutional policies, departmental matters, and academic issues. Participate in student recruitment, registration, and placement activities. Participate in campus and community events. Provide professional consulting services to government and industry. Act as advisers to student organizations.

**Education/Training Required:** Doctoral degree. **Education and Training Programs:** Anthropology; Archeology; Humanities/Humanistic Studies; Physical and Biological Anthropology; Social Science Teacher Education. **Knowledge/Courses**—Sociology and Anthropology, History and Archeology, Geography, Foreign Language, Philosophy and Theology, English Language.

**Personality Type:** Social-Investigative. **Career Clusters:** 05 Education and Training; 12 Law, Public Safety, Corrections, and Security; 15 Science, Technology, Engineering, and Mathematics. **Career Pathways:** 5.3 Teaching/Training; 12.4 Law Enforcement Services; 15.2 Science and Mathematics. **Other Jobs in These Pathways:** Architectural and Engineering Managers; Biofuels/Biodiesel Technology and Product Development Managers; Coaches and Scouts; Community and Social Service Specialists, All Other; Correctional Officers and Jailers; Criminal Investigators and Special Agents; Education, Training, and Library Workers, All Other; Elementary School Teachers, Except Special Education; Fitness Trainers and Aerobics Instructors; Immigration and Customs Inspectors; Instructional Coordinators; Instructional Designers and Technologists; Intelligence Analysts; Kindergarten Teachers, Except Special Education; Librarians; Middle School Teachers, Except Special and Career/Technical Education; Police Patrol Officers; Preschool Teachers, Except Special Education; Recreation Workers; Secondary School Teachers, Except Special and Career/Technical Education; Self-Enrichment Education Teachers; Sheriffs and Deputy Sheriffs; Teacher Assistants; Tutors; 37 other postsecondary teaching occupations; others.

**Skills**—Science, Writing, Speaking, Judgment and Decision Making, Operations Analysis, Reading Comprehension, Active Listening, Systems Evaluation.

**Work Environment:** Indoors; sitting.

# Appraisers and Assessors of Real Estate

❋ Annual Earnings: $48,500
❋ Earnings Growth Potential: High (46.6%)
❋ Growth: 4.6%
❋ Annual Job Openings: 2,100
❋ Self-Employed: 27.2%

**Considerations for Job Outlook:** Projected employment growth will be driven by economic expansion and population increases, both of which generate demand for real property. Job gains, however, will be limited somewhat by productivity increases related to increased use of computers and other technologies. Opportunities should be best in areas with active real estate markets.

## Job Specialization: Appraisers, Real Estate

**Appraise real property to determine its value for purchase, sales, investment, mortgage, or loan purposes.** Prepare written reports that estimate property values, outline methods by which the estimations were made, and meet appraisal standards. Compute final estimation of property values, taking into account such factors as depreciation, replacement costs, value comparisons of similar properties, and income potential. Search public records for transactions such as sales, leases, and assessments. Inspect properties to evaluate construction, condition, special features, and functional design and to take property measurements. Photograph interiors and exteriors of properties in order to assist in estimating property value, substantiate findings, and complete appraisal reports. Evaluate land and neighborhoods where properties are situated, considering locations and trends or impending changes that could influence future values. Obtain county land values and sales information about nearby properties in order to aid in establishment of property values. Verify legal descriptions of properties by comparing them to county records. Check building codes and zoning bylaws in order to determine any effects on the properties being appraised. Estimate building replacement costs, using building valuation manuals and professional cost estimators. Examine income records and operating costs of income properties. Interview persons familiar with properties and immediate surroundings, such as contractors, homeowners, and realtors, in order to obtain pertinent information. Examine the type and location of nearby services such as shopping centers, schools, parks, and other neighborhood features in order to evaluate their impact on property values. Draw land diagrams that will be used in appraisal reports to support findings. Testify in court as to the value of a piece of real estate property.

**Education/Training Required:** Bachelor's degree. **Education and Training Program:** Real Estate. **Knowledge/Courses**—Building and Construction, Economics and Accounting, Geography, Clerical, Law and Government, Sales and Marketing.

**Personality Type:** Enterprising-Conventional-Realistic. **Career Cluster:** 14 Marketing, Sales, and Service. **Career Pathway:** 14.2 Professional Sales and Marketing. **Other Jobs in This Pathway:** Cashiers; Counter and Rental Clerks; Door-To-Door Sales Workers, News and Street Vendors, and Related Workers; Driver/Sales Workers; Energy Brokers; First-Line Supervisors of Non-Retail Sales Workers; First-Line Supervisors of Retail Sales Workers; Hotel, Motel, and Resort Desk Clerks; Marketing Managers; Marking Clerks; Online Merchants; Order Fillers, Wholesale and Retail Sales; Parts Salespersons; Property, Real Estate, and Community Association Managers; Real Estate Sales Agents; Reservation and Transportation Ticket Agents and Travel Clerks; Retail Salespersons; Sales and Related Workers, All Other; Sales Representatives, Services, All Other; Sales Representatives, Wholesale and Manufacturing, Except Technical and Scientific Products; Sales Representatives, Wholesale and Manufacturing, Technical and Scientific Products; Solar Sales Representatives and Assessors; Stock Clerks—Stockroom, Warehouse, or Storage Yard; Stock Clerks, Sales Floor; Telemarketers; others.

**Skills**—Management of Financial Resources, Mathematics, Management of Material Resources, Active Listening, Writing, Critical Thinking, Judgment and Decision Making, Science.

**Work Environment:** More often outdoors than indoors; sitting.

## Job Specialization: Assessors

**Appraise real and personal property to determine its fair value. May assess taxes in accordance with prescribed schedules.** Determine taxability and value of properties, using methods such as field inspection, structural measurement, calculation, sales analysis, market trend studies, and income and expense analysis. Inspect new construction and major improvements to existing structures to determine values. Explain assessed values to property owners and defend appealed assessments at public hearings. Inspect properties, considering factors such as market value, location, and building or replacement costs to determine appraisal value. Prepare and maintain current data on each parcel assessed, including maps of boundaries, inventories of land and structures, property characteristics, and any applicable exemptions. Identify the ownership of each piece of taxable property. Conduct regular reviews of property within jurisdictions to determine changes in property due to construction or demolition. Complete and maintain assessment rolls that show the assessed values and status of all property in a municipality. Issue notices of assessments and taxes. Review information about transfers of property to ensure its accuracy, checking basic information on buyers, sellers, and sales prices and making corrections as necessary. Maintain familiarity with aspects of local real estate markets. Analyze trends in sales prices, construction costs, and rents to assess property values or determine the accuracy of assessments. Approve applications for property tax exemptions or deductions. Establish uniform and equitable systems for assessing all classes and kinds of property. Write and submit appraisal and tax reports for public record. Serve on assessment review boards. Hire staff members. Provide sales analyses to be used for equalization of school aid. Calculate tax bills for properties by multiplying assessed values by jurisdiction tax rates.

**Education/Training Required:** Bachelor's degree. **Education and Training Program:** Real Estate. **Knowledge/Courses**—Building and Construction, Clerical, Law and Government, Mathematics, Economics and Accounting, Geography.

**Personality Type:** Conventional-Enterprising-Investigative. **Career Cluster:** 14 Marketing, Sales, and Service. **Career Pathway:** 14.2 Professional Sales and Marketing. **Other Jobs in This Pathway:** Cashiers; Counter and Rental Clerks; Door-To-Door Sales Workers, News and Street Vendors, and Related Workers; Driver/Sales Workers; Energy Brokers; First-Line Supervisors of Non-Retail Sales Workers; First-Line Supervisors of Retail Sales Workers; Hotel, Motel, and Resort Desk Clerks; Marketing Managers; Marking Clerks; Online Merchants; Order Fillers, Wholesale and Retail Sales; Parts Salespersons; Property, Real Estate, and Community Association Managers; Real Estate Sales Agents; Reservation and Transportation Ticket Agents and Travel Clerks; Retail Salespersons; Sales and Related Workers, All Other; Sales Representatives, Services, All Other; Sales Representatives, Wholesale and Manufacturing, Except Technical and Scientific Products; Sales Representatives, Wholesale and Manufacturing, Technical and Scientific Products; Solar Sales Representatives and Assessors; Stock Clerks—Stockroom, Warehouse, or Storage Yard; Stock Clerks, Sales Floor; Telemarketers; others.

**Skills**—Mathematics, Speaking, Persuasion, Reading Comprehension, Writing, Active Learning, Critical Thinking, Quality Control Analysis.

**Work Environment:** More often indoors than outdoors; sitting; using hands; repetitive motions.

# Arbitrators, Mediators, and Conciliators

* Annual Earnings: $55,800
* Earnings Growth Potential: High (45.2%)
* Growth: 14.0%
* Annual Job Openings: 320
* Self-Employed: 0.0%

**Considerations for Job Outlook:** Budget pressures are expected to limit the hiring of new judges, particularly in federal courts. Alternatives to litigation are usually faster and less expensive, spurring employment growth for other judicial workers, such as arbitrators, mediators, and conciliators.

**Facilitate negotiation and conflict resolution through dialogue. Resolve conflicts outside of the court system by mutual consent of parties involved.** Conduct studies of appeals procedures in order to ensure adherence to legal requirements and to facilitate disposition of cases. Rule on exceptions, motions, and admissibility of evidence. Review and evaluate information from documents such as claim applications, birth or death certificates, and physician or employer records. Organize and deliver public presentations about mediation to organizations such as community agencies and schools. Prepare written opinions and decisions regarding cases. Prepare settlement agreements for disputants to sign. Use mediation techniques to facilitate communication between disputants, to further parties' understanding of different perspectives, and to guide parties toward mutual agreement. Notify claimants of denied claims and appeal rights. Analyze evidence and apply relevant laws, regulations, policies, and precedents in order to reach conclusions. Conduct initial meetings with disputants to outline the arbitration process, settle procedural matters such as fees, and determine details such as witness numbers and time requirements. Confer with disputants to clarify issues, identify underlying concerns, and develop an understanding of their respective needs and interests. Participate in court proceedings. Arrange and conduct hearings to obtain information and evidence relative to disposition of claims. Recommend acceptance or rejection of compromise settlement offers. Research laws, regulations, policies, and precedent decisions to prepare for hearings. Set up appointments for parties to meet for mediation. Authorize payment of valid claims. Determine existence and amount of liability according to evidence, laws, and administrative and judicial precedents. Issue subpoenas and administer oaths to prepare for formal hearings. Interview claimants, agents, or witnesses to obtain information about disputed issues.

**Education/Training Required:** Work experience plus degree. **Education and Training Programs:** Law (LL.B, J.D.); Legal Professions and Studies, Other; Legal Studies, General. **Knowledge/Courses**—Sociology and Anthropology, Therapy and Counseling, Law and Government, Personnel and Human Resources, Psychology, Philosophy and Theology.

**Personality Type:** Social-Enterprising. **Career Cluster:** 12 Law, Public Safety, Corrections, and Security. **Career Pathway:** 12.5 Legal Services. **Other Jobs in This Pathway:** Administrative Law Judges, Adjudicators, and Hearing Officers; Court Reporters; Farm and Home Management Advisors; Judges, Magistrate Judges, and Magistrates; Lawyers; Legal Secretaries; Legal Support Workers, All Other; Paralegals and Legal Assistants; Title Examiners, Abstractors, and Searchers.

**Skills**—Negotiation, Persuasion, Active Listening, Speaking, Critical Thinking, Operations Analysis, Social Perceptiveness, Reading Comprehension.

**Work Environment:** Indoors; sitting.

# Architects, Except Landscape and Naval

- ❀ Annual Earnings: $72,550
- ❀ Earnings Growth Potential: Medium (40.9%)
- ❀ Growth: 16.2%
- ❀ Annual Job Openings: 4,680
- ❀ Self-Employed: 21.2%

**Considerations for Job Outlook:** Changing demographics, such as the population's aging and shifting to warmer states, should lead to employment growth for architects to design new buildings to accommodate these changes. Job competition should be keen.

**Plan and design structures such as private residences, office buildings, theaters, factories, and other structural property.** Prepare information regarding design, structure specifications, materials, color, equipment, estimated costs, or construction time. Consult with client to determine functional and spatial requirements of structure. Direct activities of workers engaged in preparing drawings and specification documents. Plan layout of project. Prepare contract documents for building contractors. Prepare scale drawings. Integrate engineering element into unified design. Conduct periodic on-site observation of work during construction to monitor compliance with plans. Administer construction contracts. Represent client in obtaining bids and awarding construction contracts. Prepare operating and maintenance manuals, studies, and reports.

**Education/Training Required:** Bachelor's degree. **Education and Training Programs:** Architectural History and Criticism, General; Architecture (BArch, BA/BS, MArch, MA/MS, PhD); Architecture and Related Services, Other; Environmental Design/Architecture. **Knowledge/Courses**—Design, Building and Construction, Engineering and Technology, Fine Arts, Sales and Marketing, Law and Government.

**Personality Type:** Artistic-Investigative. **Career Cluster:** 02 Architecture and Construction. **Career Pathway:** 2.1 Design/Pre-Construction. **Other Jobs in This Pathway:** Architectural and Engineering Managers; Architectural Drafters; Cartographers and Photogrammetrists; Civil Drafters; Civil Engineering Technicians; Drafters, All Other; Electrical Drafters; Electronic Drafters; Engineering Technicians, Except Drafters, All Other; Engineers, All Other; Geodetic Surveyors; Interior Designers; Landscape Architects; Mechanical Drafters; Surveying Technicians.

**Skills**—Operations Analysis, Management of Financial Resources, Management of Material Resources, Mathematics, Science, Judgment and Decision Making, Quality Control Analysis, Negotiation.

**Work Environment:** Indoors; sitting; using hands; repetitive motions.

# Architectural and Civil Drafters

- ❀ Annual Earnings: $46,430
- ❀ Earnings Growth Potential: Low (35.4%)
- ❀ Growth: 9.1%
- ❀ Annual Job Openings: 3,620
- ❀ Self-Employed: 2.9%

**Considerations for Job Outlook:** Employment growth of drafters is expected to fall as computer-aided drafting systems allow other workers to complete tasks previously performed by drafters. Opportunities should be best for job seekers who have at least two years of postsecondary training, strong technical skills, and experience with computer-aided drafting and design systems.

## Job Specialization: Architectural Drafters

**Prepare detailed drawings of architectural designs and plans for buildings and structures according to specifications provided by architect.** Analyze building codes, by-laws, space and site requirements, and other technical documents and reports to determine their effect on architectural designs. Operate computer-aided drafting (CAD) equipment or conventional drafting station to produce designs, working drawings, charts, forms, and records. Coordinate structural, electrical, and mechanical designs and determine a method of presentation to graphically represent building plans. Obtain and assemble data to complete architectural designs, visiting job sites to compile measurements as necessary. Lay out and plan interior room arrangements for commercial buildings, using computer-assisted drafting (CAD) equipment and software. Draw rough and detailed scale plans for foundations, buildings, and structures based on preliminary concepts, sketches, engineering calculations, specification sheets, and other data. Supervise, coordinate, and inspect the work of draftspersons, technicians, and technologists on construction projects. Represent architect on construction site, ensuring builder compliance with design specifications and advising on design corrections under architect's supervision. Check dimensions of materials to be used and assign numbers to lists of materials. Determine procedures and instructions to be followed according to design specifications and quantity of required materials. Analyze technical implications of architect's design concept, calculating weights, volumes, and stress factors. Create freehand drawings and lettering to accompany drawings. Prepare colored drawings of landscape and interior designs for presentation to client. Reproduce drawings on copy machines or trace copies of plans and drawings, using transparent paper or cloth, ink, pencil, and standard drafting instruments. Prepare cost estimates, contracts, bidding documents, and technical reports for specific projects under an architect's supervision.

**Education/Training Required:** Postsecondary vocational training. **Education and Training Programs:** Architectural Drafting and Architectural CAD/CADD; Architectural Technology/Technician; CAD/CADD Drafting and/or Design Technology/Technician; Civil Drafting and Civil Engineering CAD/CADD; Drafting and Design Technology/Technician, General. **Knowledge/Courses**—Design,

Building and Construction, Engineering and Technology, Fine Arts, Computers and Electronics, Law and Government.

**Personality Type:** Artistic-Realistic-Investigative. **Career Cluster:** 02 Architecture and Construction. **Career Pathway:** 2.1 Design/Pre-Construction. **Other Jobs in This Pathway:** Architects, Except Landscape and Naval; Architectural and Engineering Managers; Cartographers and Photogrammetrists; Civil Drafters; Civil Engineering Technicians; Drafters, All Other; Electrical Drafters; Electronic Drafters; Engineering Technicians, Except Drafters, All Other; Engineers, All Other; Geodetic Surveyors; Interior Designers; Landscape Architects; Mechanical Drafters; Surveying Technicians.

**Skills**—Mathematics, Programming, Systems Analysis, Quality Control Analysis, Management of Financial Resources, Operations Analysis, Management of Material Resources, Technology Design.

**Work Environment:** Indoors; sitting; using hands; repetitive motions.

## Job Specialization: Civil Drafters

**Prepare drawings and topographical and relief maps used in civil engineering projects such as highways, bridges, pipelines, flood control projects, and water and sewerage control systems.** Produce drawings by using computer-assisted drafting systems (CAD) or drafting machines or by hand, using compasses, dividers, protractors, triangles, and other drafting devices. Draw maps, diagrams, and profiles, using cross-sections and surveys, to represent elevations, topographical contours, subsurface formations, and structures. Draft plans and detailed drawings for structures, installations, and construction projects such as highways, sewage disposal systems, and dikes, working from sketches or notes. Determine the order of work and method of presentation such as orthographic or isometric drawing. Finish and duplicate drawings and documentation packages according to required mediums and specifications for reproduction, using blueprinting, photography, or other duplication methods. Review rough sketches, drawings, specifications, and other engineering data received from civil engineers to ensure that they conform to design concepts. Calculate excavation tonnage and prepare graphs and fill-hauling diagrams for use in earth-moving operations. Supervise and train other technologists, technicians, and drafters. Correlate, interpret, and modify data obtained from topographical surveys, well logs, and geophysical prospecting reports. Determine quality, cost, strength, and quantity of required materials and enter figures on materials lists. Locate and identify symbols located on topographical surveys to denote geological and geophysical formations or oil field installations. Calculate weights, volumes, and stress factors and their implications for technical aspects of designs. Supervise or conduct field surveys, inspections, or technical investigations to obtain data required to revise construction drawings. Explain drawings to production or construction teams and provide adjustments as necessary.

**Education/Training Required:** Postsecondary vocational training. **Education and Training Programs:** Architectural Drafting and Architectural CAD/CADD; Architectural Technology/Technician; CAD/CADD Drafting and/or Design Technology/Technician; Civil Drafting and Civil Engineering CAD/CADD; Drafting and Design Technology/Technician, General. **Knowledge/Courses**—Design, Engineering and Technology, Building and Construction, Geography, Mathematics, Physics.

**Personality Type:** Realistic-Conventional-Investigative. **Career Cluster:** 02 Architecture and Construction. **Career Pathway:** 2.1 Design/Pre-Construction. **Other Jobs in This Pathway:** Architects, Except Landscape and Naval; Architectural and Engineering Managers; Architectural Drafters; Cartographers and Photogrammetrists; Civil Engineering Technicians; Drafters, All Other; Electrical Drafters; Electronic Drafters; Engineering Technicians, Except Drafters, All Other; Engineers, All Other; Geodetic Surveyors; Interior Designers; Landscape Architects; Mechanical Drafters; Surveying Technicians.

**Skills**—Mathematics, Operations Analysis, Quality Control Analysis, Science, Systems Evaluation, Systems Analysis, Reading Comprehension, Programming.

**Work Environment:** Indoors; sitting; using hands; repetitive motions.

# Architectural and Engineering Managers

- ✹ Annual Earnings: $119,260
- ✹ Earnings Growth Potential: Low (35.1%)
- ✹ Growth: 6.2%
- ✹ Annual Job Openings: 4,870
- ✹ Self-Employed: 0.6%

**Considerations for Job Outlook:** Employment is expected to grow along with that of the scientists and engineers these workers supervise. Prospects should be better in the rapidly growing areas of environmental and biomedical engineering and medical and environmental sciences.

**Plan, direct, or coordinate activities or research and development in such fields as architecture and engineering.** Coordinate and direct projects, making detailed plans to accomplish goals and directing the integration of technical activities. Consult or negotiate with clients to prepare project specifications. Present and explain proposals, reports, and findings to clients. Direct, review, and approve product design and changes. Recruit employees; assign, direct, and evaluate their work; and oversee the development and maintenance of staff competence. Perform administrative functions such as reviewing and writing reports, approving expenditures, enforcing rules, and making decisions about the purchase of materials or services. Prepare budgets, bids, and contracts and direct the negotiation of research contracts. Analyze technology, resource needs, and market demand to plan and assess the feasibility of projects. Confer with management, production, and marketing staff to discuss project specifications and procedures. Review and recommend or approve contracts and cost estimates. Develop and implement policies, standards, and procedures for the engineering and technical work performed in the department, service, laboratory, or firm. Plan and direct the installation, testing, operation, maintenance, and repair of facilities and equipment. Administer highway planning, construction, and maintenance. Confer with and report to officials and the public to provide information and solicit support for projects. Set scientific and technical goals within broad outlines provided by top management. Direct the engineering of water control, treatment, and distribution projects. Plan, direct, and coordinate survey work with other staff activities, certify survey work, and write land legal descriptions.

**Education/Training Required:** Work experience plus degree. **Education and Training Programs:** Aerospace, Aeronautical, and Astronautical/Space Engineering; Agricultural Engineering; Architectural Engineering; Architecture; Bioengineering and Biomedical Engineering; Ceramic Sciences and Engineering; Chemical Engineering; City/Urban, Community and Regional Planning; Civil Engineering, General; Computer Engineering, General; Computer Hardware Engineering; Computer Software Engineering; Construction Engineering; Electrical and Electronics Engineering; Engineering Mechanics; Engineering Physics/Applied Physics; Engineering Science; Engineering, General; Environmental Design; Environmental/Environmental Health Engineering; Forest Engineering; Geological Engineering; Geotechnical and Geoenvironmental Engineering; Industrial Engineering; Interior Architecture; Landscape

Architecture; Manufacturing Engineering; Materials Engineering; Mechanical Engineering; Metallurgical Engineering; Mining and Mineral Engineering; Naval Architecture and Marine Engineering; Nuclear Engineering; Ocean Engineering; Petroleum Engineering; Polymer/Plastics Engineering; Structural Engineering; Surveying Engineering; Systems Engineering; Textile Sciences and Engineering; Transportation and Highway Engineering; Water Resources Engineering; others. **Knowledge/Courses**—Engineering and Technology, Design, Physics, Building and Construction, Computers and Electronics, Mathematics.

**Personality Type:** Enterprising-Realistic-Investigative. **Career Clusters:** 02 Architecture and Construction; 11 Information Technology; 15 Science, Technology, Engineering, and Mathematics. **Career Pathways:** 2.1 Design/Pre-Construction; 11.4 Programming and Software Development; 15.1 Engineering and Technology; 15.2 Science and Mathematics. **Other Jobs in These Pathways:** Architects, Except Landscape and Naval; Automotive Engineers; Biochemical Engineers; Biofuels/Biodiesel Technology and Product Development Managers; Civil Engineers; Cost Estimators; Electrical Engineers; Electronics Engineers, Except Computer; Energy Engineers; Engineers, All Other; Fuel Cell Engineers; Human Factors Engineers and Ergonomists; Industrial Engineers; Manufacturing Engineers; Mechanical Engineers; Mechatronics Engineers; Microsystems Engineers; Nanosystems Engineers; Photonics Engineers; Radio Frequency Identification Device Specialists; Robotics Engineers; Solar Energy Systems Engineers; Transportation Engineers; Validation Engineers; Wind Energy Engineers; others.

**Skills**—Operations Analysis, Management of Financial Resources, Management of Material Resources, Science, Mathematics, Systems Evaluation, Management of Personnel Resources, Systems Analysis.

**Work Environment:** Indoors; sitting; noise.

## Job Specialization: Biofuels/Biodiesel Technology and Product Development Managers

**Define, plan, or execute biofuel/biodiesel research programs that evaluate alternative feedstock and process technologies with near-term commercial potential.** Develop lab scale models of industrial scale processes, such as fermentation. Develop computational tools or approaches to improve biofuels research and development activities. Develop carbohydrates arrays and associated methods for screening enzymes involved in biomass conversion. Provide technical or scientific guidance to technical staff in the conduct of biofuels research or development. Prepare, or oversee the preparation of, experimental plans for biofuels research or development. Prepare biofuels research and development reports for senior management or technical professionals. Perform protein functional analysis and engineering for processing of feedstock and creation of biofuels. Develop separation processes to recover biofuels. Develop methods to recover ethanol or other fuels from complex bioreactor liquid and gas streams. Develop methods to estimate the efficiency of biomass pretreatments. Design or execute solvent or product recovery experiments in laboratory or field settings. Design or conduct applied biodiesel or biofuels research projects on topics such as transport, thermodynamics, mixing, filtration, distillation, fermentation, extraction, and separation. Design chemical conversion processes, such as etherification, esterification, interesterification, transesterification, distillation, hydrogenation, oxidation or reduction of fats and oils, and vegetable oil refining. Conduct experiments on biomass or pretreatment technologies. Conduct experiments to test new or alternate feedstock fermentation processes. Analyze data from biofuels studies, such as fluid dynamics, water treatments, or solvent extraction and recovery processes. Oversee biodiesel/biofuels prototyping or development projects. Propose new biofuels products, processes, technologies or applications based on findings from applied biofuels or biomass research projects.

**Education/Training Required:** Work experience plus degree. **Education and Training Programs:** Agricultural Engineering; Bioengineering and Biomedical Engineering; Chemical Engineering; Engineering, Other; Manufacturing Engineering. **Knowledge/Courses**—No data available.

**Personality Type:** No data available. **Career Cluster:** 15 Science, Technology, Engineering, and Mathematics. **Career Pathways:** 15.1 Engineering and Technology; 15.2 Science and Mathematics. **Other Jobs in These Pathways:** Architectural and Engineering Managers; Automotive Engineers; Biochemical Engineers; Civil Engineers; Community and Social Service Specialists, All Other; Cost Estimators; Electrical Engineers; Electronics Engineers, Except Computer; Energy Engineers; Engineers, All Other; Fuel Cell Engineers; Human Factors Engineers and Ergonomists; Industrial Engineers; Manufacturing Engineers; Mechanical Engineers; Mechatronics Engineers; Microsystems Engineers; Nanosystems Engineers; Photonics Engineers; Radio Frequency Identification Device Specialists; Robotics Engineers; Solar Energy Systems Engineers; Transportation Engineers; Validation Engineers; Wind Energy Engineers; others.

**Skills**—No data available.

**Work Environment:** No data available.

# Architecture Teachers, Postsecondary

* Annual Earnings: $73,500
* Earnings Growth Potential: High (43.2%)
* Growth: 15.1%
* Annual Job Openings: 200
* Self-Employed: 0.2%

**Considerations for Job Outlook:** Enrollments in postsecondary institutions are expected to continue rising as more people attend college and as workers return to school to update their skills. Opportunities for part-time or temporary positions should be favorable, but significant competition exists for tenure-track positions.

**Teach courses in architecture and architectural design, such as architectural environmental design, interior architecture/design, and landscape architecture.** Evaluate and grade students' work, including work performed in design studios. Prepare and deliver lectures to undergraduate and/or graduate students on topics such as architectural design methods, aesthetics and design, and structures and materials. Prepare course materials such as syllabi, homework assignments, and handouts. Initiate, facilitate, and moderate classroom discussions. Plan, evaluate, and revise curricula, course content, and course materials and methods of instruction. Keep abreast of developments in their field by reading current literature, talking with colleagues, and participating in professional conferences. Maintain student attendance records, grades, and other required records. Maintain regularly scheduled office hours to advise and assist students. Compile, administer, and grade examinations or assign this work to others. Conduct research in a particular field of knowledge and publish findings in professional journals, books, and/or electronic media. Supervise undergraduate and/or graduate teaching, internship, and research work. Advise students on academic and vocational curricula and on career issues. Collaborate with colleagues to address teaching and research issues. Compile bibliographies of specialized materials for outside reading assignments. Serve on academic or administrative committees that deal with institutional policies, departmental matters, and academic issues. Participate in student recruitment, registration, and placement activities. Select and obtain materials and supplies such as textbooks and laboratory equipment.

Write grant proposals to procure external research funding. Provide professional consulting services to government and/or industry. Perform administrative duties such as serving as department head. Act as advisers to student organizations. Participate in campus and community events.

**Education/Training Required:** Doctoral degree. **Education and Training Programs:** Architectural Engineering; Architecture (BArch, BA/BS, MArch, MA/MS, PhD); City/Urban, Community and Regional Planning; Environmental Design/Architecture; Interior Architecture; Landscape Architecture (BS, BSLA, BLA, MSLA, MLA, PhD); Teacher Education and Professional Development, Specific Subject Areas, Other. **Knowledge/Courses**—Fine Arts, Building and Construction, Design, History and Archeology, Philosophy and Theology, Geography.

**Personality Type:** Social-Artistic. **Career Clusters:** 02 Architecture and Construction; 05 Education and Training; 15 Science, Technology, Engineering, and Mathematics. **Career Pathways:** 2.1 Design/Pre-Construction; 5.3 Teaching/Training; 15.1 Engineering and Technology. **Other Jobs in These Pathways:** Architectural and Engineering Managers; Automotive Engineers; Biochemical Engineers; Biofuels/Biodiesel Technology and Product Development Managers; Civil Engineers; Coaches and Scouts; Cost Estimators; Elementary School Teachers, Except Special Education; Energy Engineers; Engineers, All Other; Fitness Trainers and Aerobics Instructors; Fuel Cell Engineers; Human Factors Engineers and Ergonomists; Industrial Engineers; Manufacturing Engineers; Mechanical Engineers; Middle School Teachers, Except Special and Career/Technical Education; Preschool Teachers, Except Special Education; Recreation Workers; Secondary School Teachers, Except Special and Career/Technical Education; Self-Enrichment Education Teachers; Teacher Assistants; Transportation Engineers; Tutors; 37 other postsecondary teaching occupations; others.

**Skills**—Writing, Reading Comprehension, Speaking, Instructing, Operations Analysis, Learning Strategies, Active Learning, Critical Thinking.

**Work Environment:** Indoors; sitting.

# Area, Ethnic, and Cultural Studies Teachers, Postsecondary

- ❋ Annual Earnings: $68,020
- ❋ Earnings Growth Potential: High (47.1%)
- ❋ Growth: 15.1%
- ❋ Annual Job Openings: 200
- ❋ Self-Employed: 0.2%

**Considerations for Job Outlook:** Enrollments in postsecondary institutions are expected to continue rising as more people attend college and as workers return to school to update their skills. Opportunities for part-time or temporary positions should be favorable, but significant competition exists for tenure-track positions.

**Teach courses pertaining to the culture and development of an area (e.g., Latin America), an ethnic group, or any other group (e.g., women's studies, urban affairs).** Keep abreast of developments in their field by reading current literature, talking with colleagues, and participating in professional conferences. Conduct research in a particular field of knowledge and publish findings in professional journals, books, and/or electronic media. Evaluate and grade students' classwork, assignments, and papers. Prepare course materials such as syllabi, homework assignments, and handouts. Prepare and deliver lectures to undergraduate and/or graduate students on topics such as race and ethnic relations, gender studies, and cross-cultural perspectives. Initiate, facilitate, and moderate classroom discussions. Compile, administer, and grade examinations or assign this work to others. Maintain regularly scheduled office hours in order to advise and assist students. Plan, evaluate, and revise curricula, course content, and course materials and methods of instruction. Maintain student attendance records, grades, and other required records. Advise students on academic and vocational curricula and on career issues. Supervise undergraduate and/or graduate teaching, internship, and research work. Select and obtain materials and supplies such as textbooks. Collaborate with colleagues to address teaching and research issues. Serve on academic or administrative committees that deal with institutional policies, departmental matters, and academic issues. Compile bibliographies of specialized materials for outside reading assignments. Write grant proposals to procure external research funding. Participate in campus and community events. Participate in student recruitment, registration, and placement activities. Act as advisers to student organizations. Incorporate experiential/site visit components into courses. Perform administrative duties such as serving as department head. Provide professional consulting services to government and/or industry.

**Education/Training Required:** Doctoral degree. **Education and Training Programs:** African Studies; African-American/Black Studies; American Indian/Native American Studies; American Studies; Asian Studies/Civilization; Asian-American Studies; Balkans Studies; Baltic Studies; Canadian Studies; Caribbean Studies; Chinese Studies; Commonwealth Studies; East Asian Studies; European Studies; French Studies; Gay/Lesbian Studies; German Studies; Hispanic-American, Puerto Rican, and Mexican-American/Chicano Studies; Humanities; Intercultural/Multicultural and Diversity Studies; Islamic Studies; Italian Studies; Japanese Studies; Jewish Studies; Korean Studies; Latin American Studies; Near and Middle Eastern Studies; Pacific Area/Pacific Rim Studies; Polish Studies; Regional Studies; Russian Studies; Russian, Central European, East European and Eurasian Studies; Scandinavian Studies; Slavic Studies; Social Studies Teacher Education; South Asian Studies; Southeast Asian Studies; Spanish and Iberian Studies; Tibetan Studies; Ukraine Studies; Ural-Altaic and Central Asian Studies; Western European Studies; Women's Studies; others. **Knowledge/Courses**—History and Archeology, Sociology and Anthropology, Foreign Language, Philosophy and Theology, Geography, Education and Training.

**Personality Type:** Social-Investigative-Artistic. **Career Clusters:** 05 Education and Training; 10 Human Services. **Career Pathways:** 5.3 Teaching/Training; 10.2 Counseling and Mental Health Services. **Other Jobs in These Pathways:** Adult Basic and Secondary Education and Literacy Teachers and Instructors; Career/Technical Education Teachers, Secondary School; Clergy; Clinical Psychologists; Coaches and Scouts; Counseling Psychologists; Elementary School Teachers, Except Special Education; Fitness Trainers and Aerobics Instructors; Healthcare Social Workers; Instructional Coordinators; Instructional Designers and Technologists; Kindergarten Teachers, Except Special Education; Librarians; Mental Health and Substance Abuse Social Workers; Mental Health Counselors; Middle School Teachers, Except Special and Career/Technical Education; Preschool Teachers, Except Special Education; Recreation Workers; School Psychologists; Secondary School Teachers, Except Special and Career/Technical Education; Self-Enrichment Education Teachers; Substance Abuse and Behavioral Disorder Counselors; Teacher Assistants; Tutors; 37 other postsecondary teaching occupations; others.

**Skills**—Science, Writing, Operations Analysis, Learning Strategies, Speaking, Reading Comprehension, Active Learning, Active Listening.

**Work Environment:** Indoors; sitting.

# Art Directors

- ❋ Annual Earnings: $80,630
- ❋ Earnings Growth Potential: High (46.9%)
- ❋ Growth: 11.7%
- ❋ Annual Job Openings: 2,870
- ❋ Self-Employed: 60.2%

**Considerations for Job Outlook:** Demand for digital and multimedia artwork is expected to drive growth. Competition should be keen for certain kinds of jobs.

**Formulate design concepts and presentation approaches and direct workers engaged in art work, layout design, and copy writing for visual communications media, such as magazines, books, newspapers, and packaging.** Formulate basic layout design or presentation approach and specify material details, such as style and size of type, photographs, graphics, animation, video, and sound. Review and approve proofs of printed copy and art and copy materials developed by staff members. Manage own accounts and projects, working within budget and scheduling requirements. Confer with creative, art, copy-writing, or production department heads to discuss client requirements and presentation concepts and to coordinate creative activities. Present final layouts to clients for approval. Confer with clients to determine objectives; budget; background information; and presentation approaches, styles, and techniques. Hire, train, and direct staff members who develop design concepts into art layouts or who prepare layouts for printing. Work with creative directors to develop design solutions. Review illustrative material to determine if it conforms to standards and specifications. Attend photo shoots and printing sessions to ensure that the products needed are obtained. Create custom illustrations or other graphic elements. Mark up, paste, and complete layouts and write typography instructions to prepare materials for typesetting or printing. Negotiate with printers and estimators to determine what services will be performed. Conceptualize and help design interfaces for multimedia games, products, and devices. Prepare detailed storyboards showing sequence and timing of story development for television production.

**Education/Training Required:** Work experience plus degree. **Education and Training Programs:** Graphic Design; Intermedia/Multimedia. **Knowledge/Courses—** Fine Arts, Design, Communications and Media, Production and Processing, Computers and Electronics, Administration and Management.

**Personality Type:** Artistic-Enterprising. **Career Cluster:** 03 Arts, Audio/Video Technology, and Communications.

**Career Pathway:** 3.3 Visual Arts. **Other Jobs in This Pathway:** Artists and Related Workers, All Other; Audio and Video Equipment Technicians; Commercial and Industrial Designers; Craft Artists; Designers, All Other; Fashion Designers; Fine Artists, Including Painters, Sculptors, and Illustrators; Graphic Designers; Interior Designers; Multimedia Artists and Animators; Painting, Coating, and Decorating Workers; Photographers; Set and Exhibit Designers.

**Skills**—Management of Financial Resources, Management of Material Resources, Operations Analysis, Coordination, Management of Personnel Resources, Systems Evaluation, Learning Strategies, Instructing.

**Work Environment:** Indoors; sitting; using hands; repetitive motions.

# Art, Drama, and Music Teachers, Postsecondary

- ❋ Annual Earnings: $62,040
- ❋ Earnings Growth Potential: High (46.5%)
- ❋ Growth: 15.1%
- ❋ Annual Job Openings: 2,500
- ❋ Self-Employed: 0.2%

**Considerations for Job Outlook:** Enrollments in postsecondary institutions are expected to continue rising as more people attend college and as workers return to school to update their skills. Opportunities for part-time or temporary positions should be favorable, but significant competition exists for tenure-track positions.

**Teach courses in drama; music; and the arts, including fine and applied art, such as painting and sculpture, or design and crafts.** Evaluate and grade students' classwork, performances, projects, assignments, and papers. Explain and demonstrate artistic techniques. Prepare students for performances, exams, or assessments. Prepare and deliver lectures to undergraduate or graduate students on topics such as acting techniques, fundamentals of music, and art history. Organize performance groups and direct their rehearsals. Prepare course materials such as syllabi, homework assignments, and handouts. Initiate, facilitate, and moderate classroom discussions. Keep abreast of developments in their field by reading current literature, talking with colleagues, and participating in professional conferences. Advise students on academic and vocational curricula and on career issues. Maintain student attendance records, grades, and other required records. Conduct research in a particular field of knowledge and publish findings in professional journals, books, or electronic media. Supervise undergraduate and/or graduate teaching, internship, and research work. Plan, evaluate, and revise curricula, course content, and course materials and methods of instruction. Maintain regularly scheduled office hours to advise and assist students. Compile, administer, and grade examinations or assign this work to others. Participate in student recruitment, registration, and placement activities. Select and obtain materials and supplies such as textbooks and performance pieces. Collaborate with colleagues to address teaching and research issues. Serve on academic or administrative committees that deal with institutional policies, departmental matters, and academic issues. Participate in campus and community events. Keep students informed of community events such as plays and concerts. Compile bibliographies of specialized materials for outside reading assignments. Display students' work in schools, galleries, and exhibitions. Perform administrative duties such as serving as department head.

**Education/Training Required:** Doctoral degree. **Education and Training Programs:** Art History, Criticism and Conservation; Art, General; Ceramic Arts and Ceramics; Cinematography and Film/Video Production; Commercial Photography; Conducting; Crafts/Craft Design, Folk Art and Artisanry; Dance, General; Design and Visual Communications, General; Directing and Theatrical Production; Drama and Dramatics/Theatre Arts, General; Fashion/Apparel Design; Fiber, Textile and Weaving Arts; Film/Cinema/Video Studies; Fine/Studio Arts, General; Graphic Design; Humanities/Humanistic Studies; Industrial and Product Design; Interior Design; Intermedia/Multimedia; Jazz/Jazz Studies; Keyboard Instruments; Metal and Jewelry Arts; Music History, Literature, and Theory; Music Pedagogy; Music Performance, General; Music Theory and Composition; Musicology and Ethnomusicology; Painting; Photography; Playwriting and Screenwriting; Printmaking; Sculpture; Stringed Instruments; Technical Theatre/Theatre Design and Technology; Theatre Literature, History and Criticism; Visual and Performing Arts, General; Voice and Opera; others. **Knowledge/Courses**—Fine Arts, History and Archeology, Philosophy and Theology, Education and Training, Communications and Media, Sociology and Anthropology.

**Personality Type:** Social-Artistic. **Career Clusters:** 03 Arts, Audio/Video Technology, and Communications; 05 Education and Training. **Career Pathways:** 3.1 Audio and Video Technology and Film; 3.2 Printing Technology; 3.3 Visual Arts; 3.4 Performing Arts; 5.3 Teaching/Training. **Other Jobs in These Pathways:** Career/Technical Education Teachers, Secondary School; Coaches and Scouts; Data Entry Keyers; Directors—Stage, Motion Pictures, Television, and Radio; Elementary School Teachers, Except Special Education; Fitness Trainers and Aerobics Instructors; Graphic Designers; Instructional Coordinators; Instructional Designers and Technologists; Kindergarten Teachers, Except Special Education; Librarians; Managers, All Other; Middle School Teachers, Except Special and Career/Technical Education; Musicians, Instrumental; Photographers; Poets, Lyricists and Creative Writers; Preschool Teachers, Except Special Education; Producers; Recreation Workers; Secondary School Teachers, Except Special and Career/Technical Education; Self-Enrichment Education Teachers; Singers; Teacher Assistants; Tutors; 37 other postsecondary teaching occupations; others.

**Skills**—Instructing, Learning Strategies, Speaking, Reading Comprehension, Monitoring, Writing, Management of Material Resources, Active Learning.

**Work Environment:** Indoors; sitting; noise.

# Astronomers

* Annual Earnings: $87,260
* Earnings Growth Potential: High (44.2%)
* Growth: 15.6%
* Annual Job Openings: 70
* Self-Employed: 0.0%

**Considerations for Job Outlook:** An increased focus on basic research, particularly that related to energy, is expected to drive employment growth for these workers. Prospects should be favorable for astronomers in government and academia.

**Observe, research, and interpret celestial and astronomical phenomena to increase basic knowledge and apply such information to practical problems.** Study celestial phenomena, using a variety of ground-based and space-borne telescopes and scientific instruments. Analyze research data to determine its significance, using computers. Present research findings at scientific conferences and in papers written for scientific journals. Measure radio, infrared, gamma, and X-ray emissions from extraterrestrial sources. Develop theories based on personal observations or on observations and theories of other astronomers. Raise funds for scientific research. Collaborate with other astronomers to carry out research projects. Develop instrumentation and software for astronomical observation and analysis. Teach astronomy or astrophysics. Develop and modify astronomy-related programs for public presentation. Calculate orbits and determine sizes, shapes, brightness, and motions of different celestial bodies. Direct the operations of a planetarium.

**Education/Training Required:** Doctoral degree. **Education and Training Programs:** Astronomy; Astronomy and Astrophysics, Other; Astrophysics; Planetary Astronomy and Science. **Knowledge/Courses**—Physics, Mathematics, Engineering and Technology, Chemistry, Computers and Electronics, Education and Training.

**Personality Type:** Investigative-Artistic-Realistic. **Career Cluster:** 15 Science, Technology, Engineering, and Mathematics. **Career Pathway:** 15.2 Science and Mathematics. **Other Jobs in This Pathway:** Architectural and Engineering Managers; Biochemists and Biophysicists; Biofuels/Biodiesel Technology and Product Development Managers; Bioinformatics Scientists; Biological Scientists, All Other; Biologists; Biostatisticians; Chemists; Clinical Data Managers; Clinical Research Coordinators; Community and Social Service Specialists, All Other; Dietitians and Nutritionists; Education, Training, and Library Workers, All Other; Geneticists; Geoscientists, Except Hydrologists and Geographers; Medical Scientists, Except Epidemiologists; Molecular and Cellular Biologists; Natural Sciences Managers; Operations Research Analysts; Physical Scientists, All Other; Social Scientists and Related Workers, All Other; Statisticians; Survey Researchers; Transportation Planners; Water Resource Specialists; others.

**Skills**—Science, Mathematics, Active Learning, Reading Comprehension, Writing, Management of Financial Resources, Technology Design, Operations Analysis.

**Work Environment:** Indoors; sitting.

# Athletic Trainers

- ❀ Annual Earnings: $41,600
- ❀ Earnings Growth Potential: Medium (38.1%)
- ❀ Growth: 36.9%
- ❀ Annual Job Openings: 1,150
- ❀ Self-Employed: 0.7%

**Considerations for Job Outlook:** Employment growth is expected to be concentrated in the health-care industry, as athletic training is increasingly used to prevent illness and injury. Job prospects for athletic trainers should also be good in high schools. Keen competition is expected for positions with professional and college sports teams.

**Evaluate, advise, and treat athletes to assist recovery from injury, avoid injury, or maintain peak physical fitness.** Conduct an initial assessment of an athlete's injury or illness to provide emergency or continued care and to determine whether he or she should be referred to physicians for definitive diagnosis and treatment. Care for athletic injuries, using physical therapy equipment, techniques, and medication. Evaluate athletes' readiness to play and provide participation clearances when necessary and warranted. Apply protective or injury-preventive devices such as tape, bandages, or braces to body parts such as ankles, fingers, or wrists. Assess and report the progress of recovering athletes to coaches and physicians. Collaborate with physicians to develop and implement comprehensive rehabilitation programs for athletic injuries. Advise athletes on the proper use of equipment. Plan and implement comprehensive athletic injury and illness prevention programs. Develop training programs and routines designed to improve athletic performance. Travel with athletic teams to be available at sporting events. Instruct coaches, athletes, parents, medical personnel, and community members in the care and prevention of athletic injuries. Inspect playing fields to locate any items that could injure players. Conduct research and provide instruction on subject matter related to athletic training or sports medicine. Recommend special diets to improve athletes' health, increase their stamina, or alter their weight. Massage body parts to relieve soreness, strains, and bruises. Confer with coaches to select protective equipment. Accompany injured athletes to hospitals. Perform team-support duties such as running errands, maintaining equipment, and stocking supplies. Lead stretching exercises for team members before games and practices.

**Education/Training Required:** Bachelor's degree. **Education and Training Program:** Athletic Training/Trainer. **Knowledge/Courses**—Medicine and Dentistry, Therapy and Counseling, Biology, Psychology, Customer and Personal Service, Clerical.

**Personality Type:** Social-Realistic-Investigative. **Career Cluster:** 08 Health Science. **Career Pathway:** 8.2 Diagnostics Services. **Other Jobs in This Pathway:** Ambulance Drivers and Attendants, Except Emergency Medical Technicians; Anesthesiologist Assistants; Cardiovascular Technologists and Technicians; Cytogenetic Technologists; Cytotechnologists; Diagnostic Medical Sonographers; Emergency Medical Technicians and Paramedics; Endoscopy Technicians; Health Diagnosing and Treating Practitioners, All Other; Health Technologists and Technicians, All Other; Healthcare Practitioners and Technical Workers, All Other; Histotechnologists and Histologic Technicians; Medical and Clinical Laboratory Technicians; Medical and Clinical Laboratory Technologists; Medical and Health Services Managers; Medical Assistants; Medical Equipment Preparers; Neurodiagnostic Technologists; Ophthalmic Laboratory Technicians; Physical Scientists, All Other;

Physician Assistants; Radiologic Technicians; Radiologic Technologists; Surgical Technologists; Veterinary Assistants and Laboratory Animal Caretakers; others.

**Skills**—Learning Strategies, Quality Control Analysis, Service Orientation, Instructing, Social Perceptiveness, Science, Monitoring, Systems Evaluation.

**Work Environment:** More often indoors than outdoors; standing; using hands; exposed to disease or infections.

# Atmospheric and Space Scientists

- ❋ Annual Earnings: $87,780
- ❋ Earnings Growth Potential: High (48.7%)
- ❋ Growth: 14.6%
- ❋ Annual Job Openings: 330
- ❋ Self-Employed: 0.0%

**Considerations for Job Outlook:** As research leads to continuing improvements in weather forecasting, employment of these workers is projected to grow, especially in private firms that provide weather consulting services to climate-sensitive industries such as farming or insurance. Atmospheric scientists face keen competition.

**Investigate atmospheric phenomena and interpret meteorological data gathered by surface and air stations, satellites, and radar to prepare reports and forecasts for public and other uses.** Study and interpret data, reports, maps, photographs, and charts to predict long- and short-range weather conditions, using computer models and knowledge of climate theory, physics, and mathematics. Broadcast weather conditions, forecasts, and severe weather warnings to the public via television, radio, and the Internet or provide this information to the news media. Gather data from sources such as surface and upper air stations, satellites, weather bureaus, and radar for use in meteorological reports and forecasts. Prepare forecasts and briefings to meet the needs of industry, business, government, and other groups. Apply meteorological knowledge to problems in areas including agriculture, pollution control, and water management and to issues such as global warming or ozone depletion. Conduct basic or applied meteorological research into the processes and determinants of atmospheric phenomena, weather, and climate. Operate computer graphic equipment to produce weather reports and maps for analysis, distribution, or use in weather broadcasts. Measure wind, temperature, and humidity in the upper atmosphere, using weather balloons. Develop and use weather forecasting tools such as mathematical and computer models. Direct

forecasting services at weather stations or at radio or television broadcasting facilities. Research and analyze the impact of industrial projects and pollution on climate, air quality, and weather phenomena. Collect air samples from planes and ships over land and sea to study atmospheric composition. Conduct numerical simulations of climate conditions to understand and predict global and regional weather patterns. Collect and analyze historical climate information such as precipitation and temperature records help predict future weather and climate trends. Consult with agencies, professionals, or researchers regarding the use and interpretation of climatological information.

**Education/Training Required:** Bachelor's degree. **Education and Training Programs:** Atmospheric Chemistry and Climatology; Atmospheric Physics and Dynamics; Atmospheric Sciences and Meteorology, General; Atmospheric Sciences and Meteorology, Other; Meteorology. **Knowledge/Courses**—Geography, Physics, Mathematics, Computers and Electronics, Communications and Media, Customer and Personal Service.

**Personality Type:** Investigative-Realistic. **Career Cluster:** 15 Science, Technology, Engineering, and Mathematics. **Career Pathway:** 15.2 Science and Mathematics. **Other Jobs in This Pathway:** Architectural and Engineering Managers; Biochemists and Biophysicists; Biofuels/Biodiesel Technology and Product Development Managers; Bioinformatics Scientists; Biological Scientists, All Other; Biologists; Biostatisticians; Chemists; Clinical Data Managers; Clinical Research Coordinators; Community and Social Service Specialists, All Other; Dietitians and Nutritionists; Education, Training, and Library Workers, All Other; Geneticists; Geoscientists, Except Hydrologists and Geographers; Medical Scientists, Except Epidemiologists; Molecular and Cellular Biologists; Natural Sciences Managers; Operations Research Analysts; Physical Scientists, All Other; Social Scientists and Related Workers, All Other; Statisticians; Survey Researchers; Transportation Planners; Water Resource Specialists; others.

**Skills**—Science, Operations Analysis, Reading Comprehension, Mathematics, Active Learning, Writing, Systems Analysis, Systems Evaluation.

**Work Environment:** Indoors; sitting; repetitive motions; noise.

# Atmospheric, Earth, Marine, and Space Sciences Teachers, Postsecondary

✳ Annual Earnings: $82,840
✳ Earnings Growth Potential: High (46.9%)
✳ Growth: 15.1%
✳ Annual Job Openings: 300
✳ Self-Employed: 0.2%

**Considerations for Job Outlook:** Enrollments in postsecondary institutions are expected to continue rising as more people attend college and as workers return to school to update their skills. Opportunities for part-time or temporary positions should be favorable, but significant competition exists for tenure-track positions.

**Teach courses in the physical sciences, except chemistry and physics.** Conduct research in a particular field of knowledge and publish findings in professional journals, books, and/or electronic media. Write grant proposals to procure external research funding. Keep abreast of developments in their field by reading current literature, talking with colleagues, and participating in professional conferences. Supervise undergraduate and/or graduate teaching, internships, and research work. Prepare and deliver lectures to undergraduate and/or graduate students on topics such as structural geology, micrometeorology, and atmospheric thermodynamics. Supervise laboratory work and fieldwork. Evaluate and grade students' classwork, assignments, and papers. Prepare course materials such as syllabi, homework assignments, and handouts. Collaborate with colleagues to address teaching and research issues. Compile, administer, and grade examinations or assign this work to others. Plan, evaluate, and revise curricula, course content, course materials, and methods of instruction. Initiate, facilitate, and moderate classroom discussions. Maintain regularly scheduled office hours to advise and assist students. Advise students on academic and vocational curricula and on career issues. Maintain student attendance records, grades, and other required records. Participate in student recruitment, registration, and placement activities. Perform administrative duties such as serving as department head. Select and obtain materials and supplies such as textbooks and laboratory equipment. Serve on academic or administrative committees that deal with institutional policies, departmental matters, and academic issues. Compile bibliographies of specialized materials for outside reading assignments. Provide professional consulting services to government and/or industry. Act as adviser to student organizations. Participate in campus and community events.

**Education/Training Required:** Doctoral degree. **Education and Training Programs:** Acoustics; Astronomy; Astrophysics; Atmospheric Chemistry and Climatology; Atmospheric Physics and Dynamics; Atmospheric Sciences and Meteorology, General; Atmospheric Sciences and Meteorology, Other; Atomic/Molecular Physics; Condensed Matter and Materials Physics; Elementary Particle Physics; Geochemistry; Geochemistry and Petrology; Geological and Earth Sciences/Geosciences, Other; Geology/Earth Science, General; Geophysics and Seismology; Hydrology and Water Resources Science; Meteorology; Nuclear Physics; Oceanography, Chemical and Physical; Optics/Optical Sciences; Paleontology; Physics Teacher Education; Physics, Other; Planetary Astronomy and Science; Plasma and High-Temperature Physics; Science Teacher Education/General Science Teacher Education; Theoretical and Mathematical Physics. **Knowledge/Courses**—Physics, Geography, Chemistry, Biology, Mathematics, Education and Training.

**Personality Type:** Social-Investigative. **Career Clusters:** 05 Education and Training; 15 Science, Technology, Engineering, and Mathematics. **Career Pathways:** 5.3 Teaching/Training; 15.2 Science and Mathematics. **Other Jobs in These Pathways:** Adult Basic and Secondary Education and Literacy Teachers and Instructors; Architectural and Engineering Managers; Biofuels/Biodiesel Technology and Product Development Managers; Biologists; Career/Technical Education Teachers, Secondary School; Chemists; Coaches and Scouts; Community and Social Service Specialists, All Other; Education, Training, and Library Workers, All Other; Elementary School Teachers, Except Special Education; Fitness Trainers and Aerobics Instructors; Instructional Coordinators; Instructional Designers and Technologists; Kindergarten Teachers, Except Special Education; Librarians; Medical Scientists, Except Epidemiologists; Middle School Teachers, Except Special and Career/Technical Education; Operations Research Analysts; Preschool Teachers, Except Special Education; Recreation Workers; Secondary School Teachers, Except Special and Career/Technical Education; Self-Enrichment Education Teachers; Teacher Assistants; Tutors; 37 other postsecondary teaching occupations; others.

**Skills**—Science, Learning Strategies, Writing, Instructing, Reading Comprehension, Speaking, Mathematics, Active Listening.

**Work Environment:** Indoors; sitting.

# Audio and Video Equipment Technicians

* Annual Earnings: $40,540
* Earnings Growth Potential: High (43.6%)
* Growth: 12.6%
* Annual Job Openings: 2,370
* Self-Employed: 12.4%

**Considerations for Job Outlook:** Employment growth is expected to vary. Demand for audio-visual equipment is growing, which should lead to employment increases for audio and video equipment technicians. But labor productivity increases and broadcast industry consolidation are expected to limit growth in broadcasting. Job prospects should be best in small cities and towns.

**Set up or set up and operate audio and video equipment, including microphones, sound speakers, video screens, projectors, video monitors, recording equipment, connecting wires and cables, sound and mixing boards, and related electronic equipment, for concerts, sports events, meetings and conventions, presentations, and news conferences. May also set up and operate associated spotlights and other custom lighting systems.** Notify supervisors when major equipment repairs are needed. Monitor incoming and outgoing pictures and sound feeds to ensure quality; notify directors of any possible problems. Mix and regulate sound inputs and feeds or coordinate audio feeds with television pictures. Install, adjust, and operate electronic equipment used to record, edit, and transmit radio and television programs, cable programs, and motion pictures. Design layouts of audio and video equipment and perform upgrades and maintenance. Perform minor repairs and routine cleaning of audio and video equipment. Diagnose and resolve media system problems in classrooms. Switch sources of video input from one camera or studio to another, from film to live programming, or from network to local programming. Meet with directors and senior members of camera crews to discuss assignments and determine filming sequences, camera movements, and picture composition. Construct and position properties, sets, lighting equipment, and other equipment. Compress, digitize, duplicate, and store audio and video data. Obtain, set up, and load videotapes for scheduled productions or broadcasts. Edit videotapes by erasing and removing portions of programs and adding video or sound as required. Direct and coordinate activities of assistants and other personnel during production. Plan and develop pre-production ideas into outlines, scripts, storyboards, and graphics, using

own ideas or specifications of assignments. Maintain inventories of audiotapes and videotapes and related supplies. Determine formats, approaches, content, levels, and media to effectively meet objectives within budgetary constraints, utilizing research, knowledge, and training. Record and edit audio material such as movie soundtracks, using audio recording and editing equipment. Inform users of audiotaping and videotaping service policies and procedures.

**Education/Training Required:** Long-term on-the-job training. **Education and Training Programs:** Agricultural Communication/Journalism; Photographic and Film/Video Technology/Technician and Assistant; Recording Arts Technology/Technician. **Knowledge/Courses**—Telecommunications, Communications and Media, Fine Arts, Computers and Electronics, Engineering and Technology, Production and Processing.

**Personality Type:** Realistic-Investigative-Conventional. **Career Cluster:** 03 Arts, Audio/Video Technology, and Communications. **Career Pathways:** 3.3 Visual Arts; 3.5 Journalism and Broadcasting. **Other Jobs in These Pathways:** Art Directors; Artists and Related Workers, All Other; Broadcast Technicians; Camera Operators, Television, Video, and Motion Picture; Commercial and Industrial Designers; Copy Writers; Directors—Stage, Motion Pictures, Television, and Radio; Editors; Fashion Designers; Film and Video Editors; Fine Artists, Including Painters, Sculptors, and Illustrators; Graphic Designers; Interior Designers; Media and Communication Workers, All Other; Multimedia Artists and Animators; Painting, Coating, and Decorating Workers; Photographers; Producers; Program Directors; Public Relations Specialists; Radio and Television Announcers; Reporters and Correspondents; Talent Directors; Technical Directors/Managers; Technical Writers; others.

**Skills**—Installation, Troubleshooting, Equipment Selection, Operation and Control, Repairing, Operation Monitoring, Equipment Maintenance, Technology Design.

**Work Environment:** Indoors; sitting; using hands; repetitive motions.

# Audiologists

* Annual Earnings: $66,660
* Earnings Growth Potential: Medium (36.1%)
* Growth: 25.0%
* Annual Job Openings: 580
* Self-Employed: 1.3%

**Considerations for Job Outlook:** Employment of audiologists is expected to grow as the population ages and more care is needed for the elderly, who often have problems with hearing and balance. Job prospects should be favorable for job seekers who have a doctorate in audiology.

**Assess and treat persons with hearing and related disorders. May fit hearing aids and provide auditory training. May perform research related to hearing problems.** Examine and clean patients' ear canals. Educate and supervise audiology students and health care personnel. Develop and supervise hearing screening programs. Counsel and instruct patients and their families in techniques to improve hearing and communication related to hearing loss. Evaluate hearing and balance disorders to determine diagnoses and courses of treatment. Program and monitor cochlear implants to fit the needs of patients. Participate in conferences or training to update or share knowledge of new hearing or balance disorder treatment methods or technologies. Conduct or direct research on hearing or balance topics and report findings to help in the development of procedures, technology, or treatments. Plan and conduct treatment programs for patients' hearing or balance problems, consulting with educators, physicians, nurses, psychologists, speech-language pathologists, and other health care personnel as necessary. Administer hearing tests and examine patients to collect information on type and degree of impairment, using specialized instruments and electronic equipment. Engage in marketing activities, such as developing marketing plans, to promote business for private practices. Recommend assistive devices according to patients' needs or nature of impairments. Fit, dispense, and repair assistive devices, such as hearing aids. Advise educators or other medical staff on hearing or balance topics. Provide information to the public on hearing or balance topics. Instruct patients, parents, teachers, or employers in communication strategies to maximize effective receptive communication. Work with multidisciplinary teams to assess and rehabilitate recipients of implanted hearing devices through auditory training and counseling. Monitor patients' progress and provide ongoing observation of hearing or balance status. Measure noise levels in workplaces and conduct hearing conservation programs in industry, military, schools, and communities.

**Education/Training Required:** Doctoral degree. **Education and Training Programs:** Audiology/Audiologist; Audiology/Audiologist and Speech-Language Pathology/Pathologist; Communication Disorders Sciences and Services, Other; Communication Disorders, General; Communication Sciences and Disorders, General. **Knowledge/Courses**—Therapy and Counseling, Medicine and Dentistry, Sales and Marketing, Psychology, Biology, Sociology and Anthropology.

**Personality Type:** Investigative-Social. **Career Cluster:** 08 Health Science. **Career Pathway:** 8.1 Therapeutic Services. **Other Jobs in This Pathway:** Clinical Psychologists; Community and Social Service Specialists, All Other; Counseling Psychologists; Dental Assistants; Dental Hygienists; Dentists, General; Health Technologists and Technicians, All Other; Healthcare Support Workers, All Other; Home Health Aides; Licensed Practical and Licensed Vocational Nurses; Low Vision Therapists, Orientation and Mobility Specialists, and Vision Rehabilitation Therapists; Massage Therapists; Medical and Clinical Laboratory Technicians; Medical and Health Services Managers; Medical Scientists, Except Epidemiologists; Medical Secretaries; Occupational Therapists; Pharmacists; Pharmacy Technicians; Radiologic Technologists; School Psychologists; Social and Human Service Assistants; Speech-Language Pathologists; Speech-Language Pathology Assistants; Substance Abuse and Behavioral Disorder Counselors; others.

**Skills**—Science, Repairing, Equipment Selection, Reading Comprehension, Technology Design, Troubleshooting, Learning Strategies, Active Learning.

**Work Environment:** Indoors; sitting; using hands; exposed to disease or infections.

# Automotive Service Technicians and Mechanics

- ❈ Annual Earnings: $35,790
- ❈ Earnings Growth Potential: High (43.6%)
- ❈ Growth: 4.7%
- ❈ Annual Job Openings: 18,170
- ❈ Self-Employed: 15.9%

**Considerations for Job Outlook:** Consolidation in the automobile dealer industry, a significant employer of technicians, is expected to limit growth in this occupation. But some opportunities are expected because of the need to service the growing number of vehicles in the United States. Job seekers who complete formal training should have good prospects.

## Job Specialization: Automotive Master Mechanics

**Repair automobiles, trucks, buses, and other vehicles. Master mechanics repair virtually any part on the vehicle**

**or specialize in the transmission system.** Examine vehicles to determine extent of damage or malfunctions. Test-drive vehicles and test components and systems, using equipment such as infrared engine analyzers, compression gauges, and computerized diagnostic devices. Repair, reline, replace, and adjust brakes. Review work orders and discuss work with supervisors. Follow checklists to ensure all important parts are examined, including belts, hoses, steering systems, spark plugs, brake and fuel systems, wheel bearings, and other potentially troublesome areas. Plan work procedures, using charts, technical manuals, and experience. Test and adjust repaired systems to meet manufacturers' performance specifications. Confer with customers to obtain descriptions of vehicle problems and to discuss work to be performed and future repair requirements. Perform routine and scheduled maintenance services such as oil changes, lubrications, and tune-ups. Disassemble units and inspect parts for wear, using micrometers, calipers, and gauges. Overhaul or replace carburetors, blowers, generators, distributors, starters, and pumps. Repair and service air conditioning, heating, engine-cooling, and electrical systems. Repair or replace parts such as pistons, rods, gears, valves, and bearings. Tear down, repair, and rebuild faulty assemblies such as power systems, steering systems, and linkages. Rewire ignition systems, lights, and instrument panels. Repair radiator leaks. Install and repair accessories such as radios, heaters, mirrors, and windshield wipers. Repair manual and automatic transmissions. Repair or replace shock absorbers. Align vehicles' front ends. Rebuild parts such as crankshafts and cylinder blocks. Repair damaged automobile bodies. Replace and adjust headlights.

**Education/Training Required:** Postsecondary vocational training. **Education and Training Programs:** Alternative Fuel Vehicle Technology/Technician; Autobody/Collision and Repair Technology/Technician; Automobile/Automotive Mechanics Technology/Technician; Automotive Engineering Technology/Technician; Medium/Heavy Vehicle and Truck Technology/Technician; Vehicle Emissions Inspection and Maintenance Technology/Technician. **Knowledge/Courses**—Mechanical, Engineering and Technology, Physics, Design, Chemistry, Computers and Electronics.

**Personality Type:** Realistic-Investigative. **Career Cluster:** 16 Transportation, Distribution, and Logistics. **Career Pathways:** 16.1 Transportation Operations; 16.4 Facility and Mobile Equipment Maintenance. **Other Jobs in These Pathways:** Aircraft Mechanics and Service Technicians; Aircraft Structure, Surfaces, Rigging, and Systems Assemblers; Airline Pilots, Copilots, and Flight Engineers; Automotive and Watercraft Service Attendants; Automotive Body and Related Repairers; Automotive Specialty Technicians; Bus and Truck Mechanics and Diesel Engine Specialists; Bus Drivers, School or Special Client; Bus Drivers, Transit and Intercity; Cleaners of Vehicles and Equipment; Crane and Tower Operators; First-Line Supervisors of Helpers, Laborers, and Material Movers, Hand; First-Line Supervisors of Transportation and Material-Moving Machine and Vehicle Operators; Gem and Diamond Workers; Heavy and Tractor-Trailer Truck Drivers; Installation, Maintenance, and Repair Workers, All Other; Laborers and Freight, Stock, and Material Movers, Hand; Light Truck or Delivery Services Drivers; Motor Vehicle Operators, All Other; Operating Engineers and Other Construction Equipment Operators; Painters, Transportation Equipment; Parking Lot Attendants; Storage and Distribution Managers; Taxi Drivers and Chauffeurs; Transportation Managers; others.

**Skills**—Repairing, Equipment Maintenance, Installation, Troubleshooting, Equipment Selection, Operation and Control, Quality Control Analysis, Operation Monitoring.

**Work Environment:** Standing; using hands; bending or twisting the body; repetitive motions; noise; very hot or cold; bright or inadequate lighting; contaminants; cramped work space; hazardous conditions; hazardous equipment; minor burns, cuts, bites, or stings.

## Job Specialization: Automotive Specialty Technicians

**Repair only one system or component on a vehicle, such as brakes, suspension, or radiator.** Examine vehicles, compile estimates of repair costs, and secure customers' approval to perform repairs. Repair, overhaul, and adjust automobile brake systems. Use electronic test equipment to locate and correct malfunctions in fuel, ignition, and emissions control systems. Repair and replace defective ball joint suspensions, brake shoes, and wheel bearings. Inspect and test new vehicles for damage; then record findings so that necessary repairs can be made. Test electronic computer components in automobiles to ensure that they are working properly. Tune automobile engines to ensure proper and efficient functioning. Install and repair air conditioners and service components such as compressors, condensers, and controls. Repair, replace, and adjust defective carburetor parts and gasoline filters. Remove and replace defective mufflers and tailpipes. Repair and replace automobile leaf springs. Rebuild, repair, and test automotive fuel injection units. Align and repair wheels, axles, frames, torsion bars, and steering mechanisms of automobiles, using special alignment equipment and wheel-balancing machines. Repair, install, and adjust hydraulic and electromagnetic automatic lift mechanisms used to raise and lower automobile windows, seats, and tops. Repair and rebuild clutch systems. Convert vehicle fuel systems from gasoline to butane gas operations and repair and service operating butane fuel units.

**Education/Training Required:** Postsecondary vocational training. **Education and Training Programs:** Alternative Fuel Vehicle Technology/Technician; Autobody/Collision and Repair Technology/Technician; Automobile/Automotive Mechanics Technology/Technician; Automotive Engineering Technology/Technician; Medium/Heavy Vehicle and Truck Technology/Technician; Vehicle Emissions Inspection and Maintenance Technology/Technician. **Knowledge/Courses**—Mechanical, Physics, Engineering and Technology, Customer and Personal Service, Sales and Marketing, Administration and Management.

**Personality Type:** Realistic-Investigative-Conventional. **Career Clusters:** 13 Manufacturing; 16 Transportation, Distribution, and Logistics. **Career Pathways:** 13.3 Maintenance, Installation, and Repair; 16.4 Facility and Mobile Equipment Maintenance. **Other Jobs in These Pathways:** Aircraft Mechanics and Service Technicians; Automotive Body and Related Repairers; Automotive Master Mechanics; Biological Technicians; Bus and Truck Mechanics and Diesel Engine Specialists; Civil Engineering Technicians; Cleaners of Vehicles and Equipment; Computer, Automated Teller, and Office Machine Repairers; Electrical and Electronic Equipment Assemblers; Electrical and Electronics Repairers, Commercial and Industrial Equipment; Electrical Engineering Technicians; Electrical Engineering Technologists; Electromechanical Engineering Technologists; Electronics Engineering Technicians; Electronics Engineering Technologists; Engineering Technicians, Except Drafters, All Other; Fuel Cell Technicians; Helpers—Installation, Maintenance, and Repair Workers; Industrial Engineering Technologists; Industrial Machinery Mechanics; Installation, Maintenance, and Repair Workers, All Other; Manufacturing Engineering Technologists; Mobile Heavy Equipment Mechanics, Except Engines; Telecommunications Line Installers and Repairers; Tire Repairers and Changers; others.

**Skills**—Repairing, Equipment Maintenance, Troubleshooting, Operation and Control, Equipment Selection, Installation, Quality Control Analysis, Operation Monitoring.

**Work Environment:** Standing; walking and running; kneeling, crouching, stooping, or crawling; using hands; bending or twisting the body; repetitive motions; noise; very hot or cold; bright or inadequate lighting; contaminants; cramped work space; hazardous conditions; hazardous equipment; minor burns, cuts, bites, or stings.

# Bill and Account Collectors

* Annual Earnings: $31,310
* Earnings Growth Potential: Low (31.9%)
* Growth: 19.3%
* Annual Job Openings: 15,690
* Self-Employed: 0.9%

**Considerations for Job Outlook:** New jobs are projected to be created in industries in which delinquent accounts are common, such as health care and financial services. Opportunities also should be favorable. Job seekers who have related experience should have the best prospects.

**Locate and notify customers of delinquent accounts by mail, telephone, or personal visit to solicit payment. Duties include receiving payment and posting amount to customer's account, preparing statements to credit department if customer fails to respond, initiating repossession proceedings or service disconnection, and keeping records of collection and status of accounts.** Receive payments and post amounts paid to customer accounts. Locate and monitor overdue accounts, using computers and a variety of automated systems. Record information about financial status of customers and status of collection efforts. Locate and notify customers of delinquent accounts by mail, telephone, or personal visits to solicit payment. Confer with customers by telephone or in person to determine reasons for overdue payments and to review the terms of sales, service, or credit contracts. Advise customers of necessary actions and strategies for debt repayment. Persuade customers to pay amounts due on credit accounts, damage claims, or nonpayable checks or to return merchandise. Sort and file correspondence and perform miscellaneous clerical duties such as answering correspondence and writing reports. Perform various administrative functions for assigned accounts, such as recording address changes and purging the records of deceased customers. Arrange for debt repayment or establish repayment schedules based on customers' financial situations. Negotiate credit extensions when necessary. Trace delinquent customers to new addresses by inquiring at post offices, telephone companies, or credit bureaus or through the questioning of neighbors. Notify credit departments, order merchandise repossession or service disconnection, and turn over account records to attorneys when customers fail to respond to collection attempts. Drive vehicles to visit customers, return merchandise to creditors, or deliver bills.

**Education/Training Required:** Short-term on-the-job training. **Education and Training Program:** Banking and Financial Support Services. **Knowledge/Courses**—Clerical, Economics and Accounting, Customer and Personal Service, Law and Government, Computers and Electronics.

**Personality Type:** Conventional-Enterprising. **Career Cluster:** 06 Finance. **Career Pathway:** 6.3 Banking and Related Services. **Other Jobs in This Pathway:** Credit Analysts; Credit Authorizers; Credit Checkers; Loan Counselors; Loan Interviewers and Clerks; New Accounts Clerks; Tellers; Title Examiners, Abstractors, and Searchers.

**Skills**—Persuasion, Negotiation, Speaking, Active Listening, Mathematics, Social Perceptiveness, Writing, Critical Thinking.

**Work Environment:** Indoors; sitting; using hands; repetitive motions; noise.

# Billing and Posting Clerks

- ❋ Annual Earnings: $32,170
- ❋ Earnings Growth Potential: Low (30.8%)
- ❋ Growth: 15.3%
- ❋ Annual Job Openings: 16,760
- ❋ Self-Employed: 1.7%

**Considerations for Job Outlook:** Employment growth is projected to stem from an increasing number of transactions, especially in the rapidly growing health-care industry. Prospects should be good.

**Compile, compute, and record billing, accounting, statistical, and other numerical data for billing purposes. Prepare billing invoices for services rendered or for delivery or shipment of goods.** No task data available.

**Education/Training Required:** Moderate-term on-the-job training. **Education and Training Program:** Accounting Technology/Technician and Bookkeeping. **Knowledge/Courses**—No data available.

**Personality Type:** No data available. **Career Cluster:** 04 Business, Management, and Administration. **Career Pathway:** 4.2 Business, Financial Management, and Accounting. **Other Jobs in This Pathway:** Accountants; Auditors; Billing, Cost, and Rate Clerks; Bookkeeping, Accounting, and Auditing Clerks; Brokerage Clerks; Brownfield Redevelopment Specialists and Site Managers; Budget Analysts; Compliance Managers; Credit Analysts; Financial Analysts; Financial Managers, Branch or Department; Investment

Fund Managers; Logistics Managers; Loss Prevention Managers; Managers, All Other; Natural Sciences Managers; Payroll and Timekeeping Clerks; Regulatory Affairs Managers; Security Managers; Statement Clerks; Supply Chain Managers; Tax Preparers; Treasurers and Controllers; Wind Energy Operations Managers; Wind Energy Project Managers; others.

**Skills**—No data available.

**Work Environment:** No data available.

## Job Specialization: Billing, Cost, and Rate Clerks

**Compile data, compute fees and charges, and prepare invoices for billing purposes. Duties include computing costs and calculating rates for goods, services, and shipment of goods; posting data; and keeping other relevant records. May involve use of computer or typewriter, calculator, and adding and bookkeeping machines.** Verify accuracy of billing data and revise any errors. Operate typing, adding, calculating, and billing machines. Prepare itemized statements, bills, or invoices and record amounts due for items purchased or services rendered. Review documents such as purchase orders, sales tickets, charge slips, or hospital records to compute fees and charges due. Perform bookkeeping work, including posting data and keeping other records concerning costs of goods and services and the shipment of goods. Keep records of invoices and support documents. Resolve discrepancies in accounting records. Type billing documents, shipping labels, credit memorandums, and credit forms, using typewriters or computers. Contact customers to obtain or relay account information. Compute credit terms, discounts, shipment charges, and rates for goods and services to complete billing documents. Answer mail and telephone inquiries regarding rates, routing, and procedures. Track accumulated hours and dollar amounts charged to each client job to calculate client fees for professional services such as legal and accounting services. Review compiled data on operating costs and revenues to set rates. Compile reports of cost factors, such as labor, production, storage, and equipment. Consult sources such as rate books, manuals, and insurance company representatives to determine specific charges and information such as rules, regulations, and government tax and tariff information. Update manuals when rates, rules, or regulations are amended. Estimate market value of products or services.

**Education/Training Required:** Moderate-term on-the-job training. **Education and Training Program:** Accounting

Technology/Technician and Bookkeeping. **Knowledge/ Courses**—Clerical, Economics and Accounting, Computers and Electronics.

**Personality Type:** Conventional-Enterprising. **Career Cluster:** 04 Business, Management, and Administration. **Career Pathway:** 4.2 Business, Financial Management, and Accounting. **Other Jobs in This Pathway:** Accountants; Auditors; Billing and Posting Clerks; Bookkeeping, Accounting, and Auditing Clerks; Brokerage Clerks; Brownfield Redevelopment Specialists and Site Managers; Budget Analysts; Compliance Managers; Credit Analysts; Financial Analysts; Financial Managers, Branch or Department; Investment Fund Managers; Logistics Managers; Loss Prevention Managers; Managers, All Other; Natural Sciences Managers; Payroll and Timekeeping Clerks; Regulatory Affairs Managers; Security Managers; Statement Clerks; Supply Chain Managers; Tax Preparers; Treasurers and Controllers; Wind Energy Operations Managers; Wind Energy Project Managers; others.

**Skills**—Programming, Mathematics, Active Listening, Service Orientation.

**Work Environment:** Indoors; sitting.

## Job Specialization: Statement Clerks

**Prepare and distribute bank statements to customers, answer inquiries, and reconcile discrepancies in records and accounts.** Encode and cancel checks, using bank machines. Take orders for imprinted checks. Compare previously prepared bank statements with canceled checks and reconcile discrepancies. Verify signatures and required information on checks. Post stop-payment notices to prevent payment of protested checks. Maintain files of canceled checks and customers' signatures. Match statements with batches of canceled checks by account numbers. Weigh envelopes containing statements to determine correct postage and affix postage, using stamps or metering equipment. Load machines with statements, cancelled checks, and envelopes to prepare statements for distribution to customers or stuff envelopes by hand. Retrieve checks returned to customers in error, adjusting customer accounts and answering inquiries about errors as necessary. Route statements for mailing or over-the-counter delivery to customers. Monitor equipment to ensure proper operation. Fix minor problems, such as equipment jams, and notify repair personnel of major equipment problems.

**Education/Training Required:** Moderate-term on-the-job training. **Education and Training Program:** Accounting

Technology/Technician and Bookkeeping. **Knowledge/ Courses**—Economics and Accounting, Clerical, Administration and Management.

**Personality Type:** Conventional-Enterprising-Social. **Career Cluster:** 04 Business, Management, and Administration. **Career Pathway:** 4.2 Business, Financial Management, and Accounting. **Other Jobs in This Pathway:** Accountants; Auditors; Billing and Posting Clerks; Billing, Cost, and Rate Clerks; Bookkeeping, Accounting, and Auditing Clerks; Brokerage Clerks; Brownfield Redevelopment Specialists and Site Managers; Budget Analysts; Compliance Managers; Credit Analysts; Financial Analysts; Financial Managers, Branch or Department; Investment Fund Managers; Logistics Managers; Loss Prevention Managers; Managers, All Other; Natural Sciences Managers; Payroll and Timekeeping Clerks; Regulatory Affairs Managers; Security Managers; Supply Chain Managers; Tax Preparers; Treasurers and Controllers; Wind Energy Operations Managers; Wind Energy Project Managers; others.

**Skills**—Programming.

**Work Environment:** Indoors; sitting; repetitive motions.

# Biochemists and Biophysicists

- ❋ Annual Earnings: $79,390
- ❋ Earnings Growth Potential: High (45.8%)
- ❋ Growth: 37.4%
- ❋ Annual Job Openings: 1,620
- ❋ Self-Employed: 2.7%

**Considerations for Job Outlook:** Biotechnological research and development should continue to drive job growth. Doctoral degree holders are expected to face competition for research positions in academia.

**Study the chemical composition and physical principles of living cells and organisms and their electrical and mechanical energy and related phenomena. May conduct research in order to further understanding of the complex chemical combinations and reactions involved in metabolism, reproduction, growth, and heredity. May determine the effects of foods, drugs, serums, hormones, and other substances on tissues and vital processes of living organisms.** Design and perform experiments with equipment such as lasers, accelerators, and mass spectrometers. Analyze brain functions, such as learning, thinking, and memory, and analyze the dynamics of seeing and hearing. Share research findings by writing scientific articles and by making presentations at scientific conferences. Develop and test new drugs and medications intended for commercial distribution. Develop methods to process, store, and use foods, drugs, and chemical compounds. Develop new methods to study the mechanisms of biological processes. Examine the molecular and chemical aspects of immune system functioning. Investigate the nature, composition, and expression of genes and research how genetic engineering can impact these processes. Determine the three-dimensional structure of biological macromolecules. Prepare reports and recommendations based upon research outcomes. Design and build laboratory equipment needed for special research projects. Isolate, analyze, and synthesize vitamins, hormones, allergens, minerals, and enzymes and determine their effects on body functions. Research cancer treatment, using radiation and nuclear particles. Research transformations of substances in cells, using atomic isotopes. Study how light is absorbed in processes such as photosynthesis or vision. Analyze foods to determine their nutritional values and the effects of cooking, canning, and processing on these values. Study spatial configurations of submicroscopic molecules such as proteins, using X-rays and electron microscopes. Teach and advise undergraduate and graduate students and supervise their research. Investigate the transmission of electrical impulses along nerves and muscles. Research how characteristics of plants and animals are carried through successive generations. Investigate damage to cells and tissues caused by X-rays and nuclear particles.

**Education/Training Required:** Doctoral degree. **Education and Training Programs:** Biochemistry; Biochemistry and Molecular Biology; Biophysics; Cell/Cellular Biology and Anatomical Sciences, Other; Molecular Biochemistry; Molecular Biophysics; Soil Chemistry and Physics; Soil Microbiology. **Knowledge/Courses**—Biology, Chemistry, Physics, Engineering and Technology, Medicine and Dentistry, Mechanical.

**Personality Type:** Investigative-Artistic-Realistic. **Career Clusters:** 01 Agriculture, Food, and Natural Resources; 15 Science, Technology, Engineering, and Mathematics. **Career Pathways:** 1.2 Plant Systems; 15.2 Science and Mathematics. **Other Jobs in These Pathways:** Architectural and Engineering Managers; Biofuels/Biodiesel Technology and Product Development Managers; Bioinformatics Scientists; Biological Scientists, All Other; Biologists; Chemists; Clinical Research Coordinators; Community and Social Service Specialists, All Other; Dietitians and Nutritionists; Education, Training, and Library Workers, All Other; First-Line Supervisors of Landscaping, Lawn Service, and Groundskeeping Workers; First-Line Supervisors of Retail Sales Workers; Floral Designers; Geneticists; Geoscientists, Except Hydrologists and Geographers; Landscaping

and Groundskeeping Workers; Medical Scientists, Except Epidemiologists; Natural Sciences Managers; Operations Research Analysts; Precision Agriculture Technicians; Retail Salespersons; Social Scientists and Related Workers, All Other; Transportation Planners; Tree Trimmers and Pruners; Water Resource Specialists; others.

**Skills**—Science, Programming, Active Learning, Technology Design, Mathematics, Learning Strategies, Reading Comprehension, Writing.

**Work Environment:** Indoors; sitting; using hands; exposed to disease or infections.

# Biological Science Teachers, Postsecondary

- ❋ Annual Earnings: $72,700
- ❋ Earnings Growth Potential: High (44.5%)
- ❋ Growth: 15.1%
- ❋ Annual Job Openings: 1,700
- ❋ Self-Employed: 0.2%

**Considerations for Job Outlook:** Enrollments in postsecondary institutions are expected to continue rising as more people attend college and as workers return to school to update their skills. Opportunities for part-time or temporary positions should be favorable, but significant competition exists for tenure-track positions.

**Teach courses in biological sciences.** Prepare and deliver lectures to undergraduate and/or graduate students on topics such as molecular biology, marine biology, and botany. Evaluate and grade students' classwork, laboratory work, assignments, and papers. Prepare course materials such as syllabi, homework assignments, and handouts. Compile, administer, and grade examinations or assign this work to others. Supervise students' laboratory work. Keep abreast of developments in their field by reading current literature, talking with colleagues, and participating in professional conferences. Maintain student attendance records, grades, and other required records. Initiate, facilitate, and moderate classroom discussions. Plan, evaluate, and revise curricula, course content, course materials, and methods of instruction. Advise students on academic and vocational curricula and on career issues. Maintain regularly scheduled office hours to advise and assist students. Supervise undergraduate and/or graduate teaching, internships, and research work. Select and obtain materials and supplies such as textbooks and laboratory equipment. Collaborate with colleagues to address teaching and research issues. Conduct research in a particular field of knowledge and publish findings in professional journals, books, and/or electronic media. Serve on academic or administrative committees that deal with institutional policies, departmental matters, and academic issues. Participate in student recruitment, registration, and placement activities. Write grant proposals to procure external research funding. Perform administrative duties such as serving as department head. Act as advisers to student organizations. Compile bibliographies of specialized materials for outside reading assignments. Participate in campus and community events. Provide professional consulting services to government and/or industry.

**Education/Training Required:** Doctoral degree. **Education and Training Programs:** Anatomy; Animal Physiology; Biochemistry; Biological and Biomedical Sciences, Other; Biology/Biological Sciences, General; Biometry/Biometrics; Biophysics; Biotechnology; Botany/Plant Biology; Cell/Cellular Biology and Histology; Ecology; Ecology, Evolution, Systematics and Population Biology, Other; Entomology; Evolutionary Biology; Immunology; Marine Biology and Biological Oceanography; Microbiology, General; Molecular Biology; Nutrition Sciences; Parasitology; Pathology/Experimental Pathology; Pharmacology; Plant Genetics; Plant Pathology/Phytopathology; Plant Physiology; Radiation Biology/Radiobiology; Toxicology; Virology; Zoology/Animal Biology. **Knowledge/Courses**—Biology, Chemistry, Education and Training, Medicine and Dentistry, Physics, Geography.

**Personality Type:** Social-Investigative. **Career Clusters:** 01 Agriculture, Food, and Natural Resources; 05 Education and Training; 15 Science, Technology, Engineering, and Mathematics. **Career Pathways:** 1.5 Natural Resources Systems; 5.3 Teaching/Training; 15.2 Science and Mathematics. **Other Jobs in These Pathways:** Adult Basic and Secondary Education and Literacy Teachers and Instructors; Architectural and Engineering Managers; Biofuels/Biodiesel Technology and Product Development Managers; Biologists; Career/Technical Education Teachers, Secondary School; Coaches and Scouts; Community and Social Service Specialists, All Other; Education, Training, and Library Workers, All Other; Elementary School Teachers, Except Special Education; Fitness Trainers and Aerobics Instructors; Industrial Truck and Tractor Operators; Instructional Coordinators; Instructional Designers and Technologists; Kindergarten Teachers, Except Special Education; Librarians; Medical Scientists, Except Epidemiologists; Middle School Teachers, Except Special and Career/Technical Education; Preschool Teachers, Except Special Education; Recreation Workers; Refuse and Recyclable Material Collectors;

Secondary School Teachers, Except Special and Career/Technical Education; Self-Enrichment Education Teachers; Teacher Assistants; Tutors; 37 other postsecondary teaching occupations; others.

**Skills**—Science, Instructing, Writing, Learning Strategies, Speaking, Reading Comprehension, Active Learning, Operations Analysis.

**Work Environment:** Indoors; sitting; standing.

# Biological Scientists, All Other

- ❋ Annual Earnings: $68,220
- ❋ Earnings Growth Potential: High (43.2%)
- ❋ Growth: 18.8%
- ❋ Annual Job Openings: 1,610
- ❋ Self-Employed: 2.5%

**Considerations for Job Outlook:** Biotechnological research and development should continue to drive job growth. Doctoral degree holders are expected to face competition for research positions in academia.

**This occupation includes all biological scientists not listed separately.** Because this is a highly diverse occupation, no data is available for some information topics.

**Education/Training Required:** Doctoral degree. **Education and Training Program:** Biological and Biomedical Sciences, Other.

**Career Clusters:** 08 Health Science; 15 Science, Technology, Engineering, and Mathematics. **Career Pathways:** 8.5 Biotechnology Research and Development; 15.2 Science and Mathematics. **Other Jobs in These Pathways:** Architectural and Engineering Managers; Biochemists and Biophysicists; Biofuels/Biodiesel Technology and Product Development Managers; Bioinformatics Scientists; Biologists; Biostatisticians; Chemists; Clinical Data Managers; Clinical Research Coordinators; Community and Social Service Specialists, All Other; Dietitians and Nutritionists; Education, Training, and Library Workers, All Other; Geneticists; Geoscientists, Except Hydrologists and Geographers; Medical Scientists, Except Epidemiologists; Molecular and Cellular Biologists; Natural Sciences Managers; Operations Research Analysts; Pharmacists; Physical Scientists, All Other; Social Scientists and Related Workers, All Other; Statisticians; Survey Researchers; Transportation Planners; Water Resource Specialists; others.

# Job Specialization: Bioinformatics Scientists

**Conduct research using bioinformatics theory and methods in areas such as pharmaceuticals, medical technology, biotechnology, computational biology, proteomics, computer information science, biology and medical informatics. May design databases and develop algorithms for processing and analyzing genomic information, or other biological information.** Recommend new systems and processes to improve operations. Keep abreast of new biochemistries, instrumentation, or software by reading scientific literature and attending professional conferences. Confer with departments such as marketing, business development, and operations to coordinate product development or improvement. Collaborate with software developers in the development and modification of commercial bioinformatics software. Test new and updated bioinformatics tools and software. Provide statistical and computational tools for biologically based activities such as genetic analysis, measurement of gene expression, and gene function determination. Prepare summary statistics of information regarding human genomes. Instruct others in the selection and use of bioinformatics tools. Improve user interfaces to bioinformatics software and databases. Direct the work of technicians and information technology staff applying bioinformatics tools or applications in areas such as proteomics, transcriptomics, metabolomics, and clinical bioinformatics. Develop new software applications or customize existing applications to meet specific scientific project needs. Develop data models and databases. Create or modify web-based bioinformatics tools. Design and apply bioinformatics algorithms including unsupervised and supervised machine learning, dynamic programming, or graphic algorithms. Create novel computational approaches and analytical tools as required by research goals. Compile data for use in activities such as gene expression profiling, genome annotation, and structural bioinformatics. Communicate research results through conference presentations, scientific publications, or project reports. Manipulate publicly accessible, commercial, or proprietary genomic, proteomic, or post-genomic databases. Consult with researchers to analyze problems, recommend technology-based solutions, or determine computational strategies.

**Education/Training Required:** Doctoral degree. **Education and Training Program:** Bioinformatics. **Knowledge/Courses**—No data available.

**Personality Type:** Investigative-Conventional-Realistic. **Career Clusters:** 11 Information Technology; 15 Science, Technology, Engineering, and Mathematics. **Career**

**Pathways:** 11.4 Programming and Software Development; 15.2 Science and Mathematics. **Other Jobs in These Pathways:** Architectural and Engineering Managers; Biochemists and Biophysicists; Biofuels/Biodiesel Technology and Product Development Managers; Biological Scientists, All Other; Biologists; Biostatisticians; Chemists; Clinical Data Managers; Clinical Research Coordinators; Community and Social Service Specialists, All Other; Computer Hardware Engineers; Dietitians and Nutritionists; Education, Training, and Library Workers, All Other; Geneticists; Geoscientists, Except Hydrologists and Geographers; Medical Scientists, Except Epidemiologists; Molecular and Cellular Biologists; Natural Sciences Managers; Operations Research Analysts; Physical Scientists, All Other; Social Scientists and Related Workers, All Other; Statisticians; Survey Researchers; Transportation Planners; Water Resource Specialists; others.

**Skills**—No data available.

**Work Environment:** No data available.

# Job Specialization: Geneticists

**Research and study the inheritance of traits at the molecular, organism, or population level. May evaluate or treat patients with genetic disorders.** Write grants and papers or attend fundraising events to seek research funds. Verify that cytogenetic, molecular genetic, and related equipment and instrumentation is maintained in working condition to ensure accuracy and quality of experimental results. Plan curatorial programs for species collections that include acquisition, distribution, maintenance, or regeneration. Participate in the development of endangered species breeding programs or species survival plans. Maintain laboratory safety programs and train personnel in laboratory safety techniques. Instruct medical students, graduate students, or others in methods or procedures for diagnosis and management of genetic disorders. Evaluate, diagnose, or treat genetic diseases. Design and maintain genetics computer databases. Confer with information technology specialists to develop computer applications for genetic data analysis. Collaborate with biologists and other professionals to conduct appropriate genetic and biochemical analyses. Attend clinical and research conferences and read scientific literature to keep abreast of technological advances and current genetic research findings. Supervise or direct the work of other geneticists, biologists, technicians, or biometricians working on genetics research projects. Review, approve, or interpret genetic laboratory results. Search scientific literature to select and modify methods and procedures most appropriate for genetic research goals. Prepare results of experimental findings for presentation at professional conferences or in scientific journals. Maintain laboratory notebooks that record research methods, procedures, and results. Extract deoxyribonucleic acid (DNA) or perform diagnostic tests involving processes such as gel electrophoresis, Southern blot analysis, and polymerase chain reaction analysis. Evaluate genetic data by performing appropriate mathematical or statistical calculations and analyses.

**Education/Training Required:** Doctoral degree. **Education and Training Programs:** Animal Genetics; Genetics, General; Genetics, Other; Genome Sciences/Genomics; Human/Medical Genetics; Microbial and Eukaryotic Genetics; Molecular Genetics; Plant Genetics. **Knowledge/Courses**—Biology, Chemistry, Medicine and Dentistry, Education and Training, English Language, Mathematics.

**Personality Type:** Investigative-Artistic-Realistic. **Career Clusters:** 01 Agriculture, Food, and Natural Resources; 15 Science, Technology, Engineering, and Mathematics. **Career Pathways:** 1.2 Plant Systems; 1.3 Animal Systems; 15.2 Science and Mathematics. **Other Jobs in These Pathways:** Animal Trainers; Architectural and Engineering Managers; Biofuels/Biodiesel Technology and Product Development Managers; Biologists; Chemists; Clinical Research Coordinators; Community and Social Service Specialists, All Other; Dietitians and Nutritionists; Education, Training, and Library Workers, All Other; First-Line Supervisors of Landscaping, Lawn Service, and Groundskeeping Workers; First-Line Supervisors of Retail Sales Workers; Floral Designers; Geoscientists, Except Hydrologists and Geographers; Landscaping and Groundskeeping Workers; Medical Scientists, Except Epidemiologists; Natural Sciences Managers; Nonfarm Animal Caretakers; Operations Research Analysts; Precision Agriculture Technicians; Retail Salespersons; Social Scientists and Related Workers, All Other; Transportation Planners; Tree Trimmers and Pruners; Veterinarians; Water Resource Specialists; others.

**Skills**—Science, Mathematics, Writing, Reading Comprehension, Learning Strategies, Systems Analysis, Instructing, Management of Material Resources.

**Work Environment:** Indoors; sitting; using hands.

## Job Specialization: Molecular and Cellular Biologists

**Research and study cellular molecules and organelles to understand cell function and organization.** Verify all financial, physical, and human resources assigned to research or development projects are used as planned. Participate in all levels of bio-product development including proposing new products, performing market analyses, designing and performing experiments, and collaborating with operations and quality control teams during product launches. Evaluate new supplies and equipment to ensure operability in specific laboratory settings. Develop guidelines for procedures such as the management of viruses. Coordinate molecular or cellular research activities with scientists specializing in other fields. Confer with vendors to evaluate new equipment or reagents or to discuss the customization of product lines to meet user requirements. Supervise technical personnel and postdoctoral research fellows. Prepare reports, manuscripts, and meeting presentations. Provide scientific direction for project teams regarding the evaluation or handling of devices, drugs, or cells for in vitro and in vivo disease models. Perform laboratory procedures following protocols including deoxyribonucleic acid (DNA) sequencing, cloning and extraction, ribonucleic acid (RNA) purification, or gel electrophoresis. Monitor or operate specialized equipment such as gas chromatographs and high pressure liquid chromatographs, electrophoresis units, thermocyclers, fluorescence activated cell sorters, and phosphoimagers. Maintain accurate laboratory records and data. Instruct undergraduate and graduate students within the areas of cellular or molecular biology. Evaluate new technologies to enhance or complement current research. Direct, coordinate, organize, or prioritize biological laboratory activities. Develop assays that monitor cell characteristics. Design databases such as mutagenesis libraries. Design molecular or cellular laboratory experiments, oversee their execution, and interpret results.

**Education/Training Required:** Doctoral degree. **Education and Training Program:** Cell/Cellular Biology and Histology. **Knowledge/Courses**—Biology, Chemistry, English Language, Medicine and Dentistry, Computers and Electronics, Mathematics.

**Personality Type:** Investigative-Realistic-Artistic. **Career Cluster:** 15 Science, Technology, Engineering, and Mathematics. **Career Pathway:** 15.2 Science and Mathematics. **Other Jobs in This Pathway:** Architectural and Engineering Managers; Biochemists and Biophysicists; Biofuels/Biodiesel Technology and Product Development Managers; Bioinformatics Scientists; Biological Scientists, All Other; Biologists; Biostatisticians; Chemists; Clinical Data Managers; Clinical Research Coordinators; Community and Social Service Specialists, All Other; Dietitians and Nutritionists; Education, Training, and Library Workers, All Other; Geneticists; Geoscientists, Except Hydrologists and Geographers; Medical Scientists, Except Epidemiologists; Natural Sciences Managers; Operations Research Analysts; Physical

B

Scientists, All Other; Social Scientists and Related Workers, All Other; Statisticians; Survey Researchers; Transportation Planners; Water Resource Specialists; Zoologists and Wildlife Biologists; others.

**Skills**—Science, Programming, Reading Comprehension, Active Learning, Mathematics, Management of Financial Resources, Writing, Learning Strategies.

**Work Environment:** Indoors; sitting; using hands; hazardous conditions.

# Biological Technicians

- ❋ Annual Earnings: $39,020
- ❋ Earnings Growth Potential: Medium (36.1%)
- ❋ Growth: 17.6%
- ❋ Annual Job Openings: 4,190
- ❋ Self-Employed: 0.3%

**Considerations for Job Outlook:** The continued growth of scientific and medical research and the development and manufacturing of technical products are expected to drive employment growth for these workers. Opportunities are expected to be best for graduates of applied science technology programs who are knowledgeable about equipment used in laboratories or production facilities.

**Assist biological and medical scientists in laboratories. Set up, operate, and maintain laboratory instruments and equipment; monitor experiments; make observations; and calculate and record results. May analyze organic substances, such as blood, food, and drugs.** Keep detailed logs of all work-related activities. Monitor laboratory work to ensure compliance with set standards. Isolate, identify, and prepare specimens for examination. Use computers, computer-interfaced equipment, robotics, or high-technology industrial applications to perform work duties. Conduct research or assist in the conduct of research, including the collection of information and samples such as blood, water, soil, plants, and animals. Set up, adjust, calibrate, clean, maintain, and troubleshoot laboratory and field equipment. Provide technical support and services for scientists and engineers working in fields such as agriculture, environmental science, resource management, biology, and health sciences. Clean, maintain, and prepare supplies and work areas. Participate in the research, development, or manufacturing of medicinal and pharmaceutical preparations. Conduct standardized biological, microbiological, or biochemical tests and laboratory analyses to evaluate the

quantity or quality of physical or chemical substances in food or other products. Analyze experimental data and interpret results to write reports and summaries of findings. Measure or weigh compounds and solutions for use in testing or animal feed. Monitor and observe experiments, recording production and test data for evaluation by research personnel. Examine animals and specimens to detect the presence of disease or other problems. Conduct or supervise operational programs such as fish hatcheries, greenhouses, and livestock production programs. Feed livestock or laboratory animals.

**Education/Training Required:** Bachelor's degree. **Education and Training Program:** Biology Technician/Biotechnology Laboratory Technician Training. **Knowledge/Courses**—Biology, Chemistry, Computers and Electronics, Mathematics, Mechanical, Engineering and Technology.

**Personality Type:** Realistic-Investigative-Conventional. **Career Cluster:** 13 Manufacturing. **Career Pathway:** 13.3 Maintenance, Installation, and Repair. **Other Jobs in This Pathway:** Aircraft Mechanics and Service Technicians; Automotive Specialty Technicians; Civil Engineering Technicians; Computer, Automated Teller, and Office Machine Repairers; Electrical and Electronic Equipment Assemblers; Electrical and Electronics Repairers, Commercial and Industrial Equipment; Electrical Engineering Technicians; Electrical Engineering Technologists; Electromechanical Engineering Technologists; Electronics Engineering Technicians; Electronics Engineering Technologists; Engineering Technicians, Except Drafters, All Other; Fuel Cell Technicians; Helpers—Installation, Maintenance, and Repair Workers; Industrial Engineering Technologists; Industrial Machinery Mechanics; Installation, Maintenance, and Repair Workers, All Other; Manufacturing Engineering Technologists; Manufacturing Production Technicians; Mapping Technicians; Mechanical Engineering Technologists; Mobile Heavy Equipment Mechanics, Except Engines; Nanotechnology Engineering Technicians; Telecommunications Line Installers and Repairers; Tire Repairers and Changers; others.

**Skills**—Science, Programming, Mathematics, Troubleshooting, Reading Comprehension, Quality Control Analysis, Operation and Control, Technology Design.

**Work Environment:** Indoors; sitting; using hands; repetitive motions; contaminants.

# Biomedical Engineers

- ❋ Annual Earnings: $81,540
- ❋ Earnings Growth Potential: Medium (39.1%)
- ❋ Growth: 72.0%
- ❋ Annual Job Openings: 1,490
- ❋ Self-Employed: 3.3%

**Considerations for Job Outlook:** Biomedical engineers are expected to have employment growth of 72 percent from 2008–2018, much faster than the average for all occupations. The aging of the population and a growing focus on health issues will drive demand for better medical devices and equipment designed by biomedical engineers. Along with the demand for more sophisticated medical equipment and procedures, an increased concern for cost-effectiveness will boost demand for biomedical engineers, particularly in pharmaceutical manufacturing and related industries. Because of the growing interest in this field, the number of degrees granted in biomedical engineering has increased greatly. Many biomedical engineers, particularly those employed in research laboratories, need a graduate degree.

**Apply knowledge of engineering, biology, and biomechanical principles to the design, development, and evaluation of biological and health systems and products, such as artificial organs, prostheses, instrumentation, medical information systems, and health management and care delivery systems.** Evaluate the safety, efficiency, and effectiveness of biomedical equipment. Install, adjust, maintain, and/or repair biomedical equipment. Advise hospital administrators on the planning, acquisition, and use of medical equipment. Advise and assist in the application of instrumentation in clinical environments. Develop models or computer simulations of human bio-behavioral systems in order to obtain data for measuring or controlling life processes. Research new materials to be used for products such as implanted artificial organs. Design and develop medical diagnostic and clinical instrumentation, equipment, and procedures, utilizing the principles of engineering and bio-behavioral sciences. Conduct research, along with life scientists, chemists, and medical scientists, on the engineering aspects of the biological systems of humans and animals. Teach biomedical engineering or disseminate knowledge about field through writing or consulting. Design and deliver technology to assist people with disabilities. Diagnose and interpret bioelectric data, using signal-processing techniques. Adapt or design computer hardware or software for medical science uses. Analyze new medical procedures in order to forecast likely outcomes. Develop new applications for energy sources, such as using nuclear power for biomedical implants.

**Education/Training Required:** Bachelor's degree. **Education and Training Program:** Bioengineering and Biomedical Engineering. **Knowledge/Courses**—Biology, Engineering and Technology, Physics, Design, Medicine and Dentistry, Chemistry.

**Personality Type:** Investigative-Realistic. **Career Cluster:** 15 Science, Technology, Engineering, and Mathematics. **Career Pathway:** 15.1 Engineering and Technology. **Other Jobs in This Pathway:** Architectural and Engineering Managers; Automotive Engineers; Biochemical Engineers; Biofuels/Biodiesel Technology and Product Development Managers; Civil Engineers; Cost Estimators; Electrical Engineers; Electronics Engineers, Except Computer; Energy Engineers; Engineers, All Other; Fuel Cell Engineers; Human Factors Engineers and Ergonomists; Industrial Engineers; Manufacturing Engineers; Mechanical Engineers; Mechatronics Engineers; Microsystems Engineers; Nanosystems Engineers; Photonics Engineers; Radio Frequency Identification Device Specialists; Robotics Engineers; Solar Energy Systems Engineers; Transportation Engineers; Validation Engineers; Wind Energy Engineers; others.

**Skills**—Science, Technology Design, Programming, Installation, Operations Analysis, Mathematics, Troubleshooting, Equipment Selection.

**Work Environment:** Indoors; sitting.

# Boilermakers

- ❋ Annual Earnings: $54,640
- ❋ Earnings Growth Potential: High (44.3%)
- ❋ Growth: 18.8%
- ❋ Annual Job Openings: 810
- ❋ Self-Employed: 0.0%

**Considerations for Job Outlook:** Projected employment growth will be driven by the need to maintain and upgrade existing boilers and install equipment that is less harmful to the environment. Job prospects should be favorable.

**Construct, assemble, maintain, and repair stationary steam boilers and boiler house auxiliaries. Align structures or plate sections to assemble boiler frame tanks or vats, following blueprints. Work involves use of hand and power tools, plumb bobs, levels, wedges, dogs, or**

turnbuckles. **Assist in testing assembled vessels. Direct cleaning of boilers and boiler furnaces. Inspect and repair boiler fittings, such as safety valves, regulators, automatic-control mechanisms, water columns, and auxiliary machines.** Examine boilers, pressure vessels, tanks, and vats to locate defects such as leaks, weak spots, and defective sections so that they can be repaired. Bolt or arc-weld pressure vessel structures and parts together, using wrenches and welding equipment. Inspect assembled vessels and individual components, such as tubes, fittings, valves, controls, and auxiliary mechanisms, to locate any defects. Repair or replace defective pressure vessel parts, such as safety valves and regulators, using torches, jacks, caulking hammers, power saws, threading dies, welding equipment, and metalworking machinery. Attach rigging and signal crane or hoist operators to lift heavy frame and plate sections and other parts into place. Bell, bead with power hammers, or weld pressure vessel tube ends in order to ensure leakproof joints. Lay out plate, sheet steel, or other heavy metal and locate and mark bending and cutting lines, using protractors, compasses, and drawing instruments or templates. Install manholes, handholes, taps, tubes, valves, gauges, and feedwater connections in drums of water tube boilers, using hand tools. Study blueprints to determine locations, relationships, and dimensions of parts. Straighten or reshape bent pressure vessel plates and structure parts, using hammers, jacks, and torches. Shape seams, joints, and irregular edges of pressure vessel sections and structural parts in order to attain specified fit of parts, using cutting torches, hammers, files, and metalworking machines. Position, align, and secure structural parts and related assemblies to boiler frames, tanks, or vats of pressure vessels, following blueprints. Locate and mark reference points for columns or plates on boiler foundations, following blueprints and using straightedges, squares, transits, and measuring instruments.

**Education/Training Required:** Long-term on-the-job training. **Education and Training Program:** Boilermaking/Boilermaker. **Knowledge/Courses**—Building and Construction, Mechanical, Engineering and Technology, Design, Physics, Transportation.

**Personality Type:** Realistic-Conventional. **Career Cluster:** 02 Architecture and Construction. **Career Pathway:** 2.2 Construction. **Other Jobs in This Pathway:** Brickmasons and Blockmasons; Cement Masons and Concrete Finishers; Construction and Building Inspectors; Construction Carpenters; Construction Laborers; Construction Managers; Cost Estimators; Drywall and Ceiling Tile Installers; Electrical Power-Line Installers and Repairers; Electricians; Engineering Technicians, Except Drafters, All Other; First-Line Supervisors of Construction Trades and Extraction Workers; Heating and Air Conditioning Mechanics and Installers; Helpers—Carpenters; Helpers—Electricians; Helpers—Pipelayers, Plumbers, Pipefitters, and Steamfitters; Highway Maintenance Workers; Operating Engineers and Other Construction Equipment Operators; Painters, Construction and Maintenance; Pipe Fitters and Steamfitters; Plumbers; Refrigeration Mechanics and Installers; Roofers; Rough Carpenters; Solar Energy Installation Managers; others.

**Skills**—Repairing, Equipment Maintenance, Operation and Control, Troubleshooting, Equipment Selection, Quality Control Analysis, Operation Monitoring, Installation.

**Work Environment:** Outdoors; standing; using hands; noise; very hot or cold; bright or inadequate lighting; contaminants; cramped work space; high places; hazardous conditions; hazardous equipment; minor burns, cuts, bites, or stings.

# Bookkeeping, Accounting, and Auditing Clerks

- ❋ Annual Earnings: $34,030
- ❋ Earnings Growth Potential: Medium (37.5%)
- ❋ Growth: 10.3%
- ❋ Annual Job Openings: 46,040
- ❋ Self-Employed: 6.3%

**Considerations for Job Outlook:** Overall economic expansion will result in more financial transactions and other activities requiring recordkeeping, leading to expected employment growth for these workers. Job openings will be plentiful, including many opportunities for temporary and part-time work.

**Compute, classify, and record numerical data to keep financial records complete. Perform any combination of routine calculating, posting, and verifying duties to obtain primary financial data for use in maintaining accounting records. May also check the accuracy of figures, calculations, and postings pertaining to business transactions recorded by other workers.** Operate computers programmed with accounting software to record, store, and analyze information. Check figures, postings, and documents for correct entry, mathematical accuracy, and proper codes. Comply with federal, state, and company policies, procedures, and regulations. Debit, credit, and total accounts on computer spreadsheets and databases, using specialized accounting software. Classify, record, and summarize numerical and financial data to compile and keep financial records, using journals and ledgers or computers. Calculate, prepare, and issue bills, invoices, account statements, and other financial statements according to established procedures. Code documents according to company procedures. Compile statistical, financial, accounting, or auditing reports and tables pertaining to such matters as cash receipts, expenditures, accounts payable and receivable, and profits and losses. Operate 10-key calculators, typewriters, and copy machines to perform calculations and produce documents. Access computerized financial information to answer general questions as well as those related to specific accounts. Reconcile or note and report discrepancies found in records. Perform financial calculations such as amounts due, interest charges, balances, discounts, equity, and principal. Perform general office duties such as filing, answering telephones, and handling routine correspondence. Prepare bank deposits by compiling data from cashiers; verifying and balancing receipts; and sending cash, checks, or other forms of payment to banks. Receive, record, and bank cash, checks, and vouchers. Calculate and prepare checks for utilities, taxes, and other payments. Compare computer printouts to manually maintained journals to determine if they match. Reconcile records of bank transactions. Prepare trial balances of books. Monitor status of loans and accounts to ensure that payments are up to date.

**Education/Training Required:** Moderate-term on-the-job training. **Education and Training Programs:** Accounting and Related Services, Other; Accounting Technology/Technician and Bookkeeping. **Knowledge/Courses—**Economics and Accounting, Clerical, Mathematics, Computers and Electronics.

**Personality Type:** Conventional-Enterprising. **Career Cluster:** 04 Business, Management, and Administration. **Career Pathway:** 4.2 Business, Financial Management, and Accounting. **Other Jobs in This Pathway:** Accountants; Auditors; Billing and Posting Clerks; Billing, Cost, and Rate Clerks; Brokerage Clerks; Brownfield Redevelopment Specialists and Site Managers; Budget Analysts; Compliance Managers; Credit Analysts; Financial Analysts; Financial Managers, Branch or Department; Investment Fund Managers; Logistics Managers; Loss Prevention Managers; Managers, All Other; Natural Sciences Managers; Payroll and Timekeeping Clerks; Regulatory Affairs Managers; Security Managers; Statement Clerks; Supply Chain Managers; Tax Preparers; Treasurers and Controllers; Wind Energy Operations Managers; Wind Energy Project Managers; others.

**Skills—**Management of Financial Resources, Mathematics, Active Listening, Reading Comprehension, Time Management, Writing, Speaking.

**Work Environment:** Indoors; sitting; using hands; repetitive motions.

# Brickmasons and Blockmasons

- ❋ Annual Earnings: $46,930
- ❋ Earnings Growth Potential: Medium (38.7%)
- ❋ Growth: 11.5%
- ❋ Annual Job Openings: 5,000
- ❋ Self-Employed: 27.3%

**Considerations for Job Outlook:** Employment growth is expected to be driven by a growing population's need for many types of new structures. These workers will also be needed to renovate older buildings and increase their energy efficiency.

**Lay and bind building materials, such as brick, structural tile, concrete block, cinderblock, glass block, and terra-cotta block, with mortar and other substances to construct or repair walls, partitions, arches, sewers, and other structures.** Construct corners by fastening in plumb position a corner pole or building a corner pyramid of bricks and filling in between the corners, using a line from corner to corner to guide each course, or layer, of brick. Measure distance from reference points and mark guidelines to lay out work, using plumb bobs and levels. Fasten or fuse brick or other building material to structure with wire clamps, anchor holes, torch, or cement. Calculate angles and courses and determine vertical and horizontal alignment of courses. Break or cut bricks, tiles, or blocks to size, using trowel edge, hammer, or power saw. Remove excess mortar with trowels and hand tools and finish mortar joints with jointing tools for a sealed, uniform appearance. Interpret blueprints and drawings to determine specifications and to calculate the materials required. Apply and smooth mortar or other mixture over work surface. Mix specified amounts of sand, clay, dirt, or mortar powder with water to form refractory mixtures. Examine brickwork or structure to determine need for repair. Clean working surface to remove scale, dust, soot, or chips of brick and mortar, using broom, wire brush, or scraper. Lay and align bricks, blocks, or tiles to build or repair structures or high-temperature equipment, such as cupola, kilns, ovens, or furnaces. Remove burned or damaged brick or mortar, using sledgehammer, crowbar, chipping gun, or chisel. Spray or spread refractory material over brickwork to protect against deterioration.

**Education/Training Required:** Long-term on-the-job training. **Education and Training Program:** Masonry/

Mason Training. **Knowledge/Courses**—Building and Construction, Design, Engineering and Technology, Production and Processing, Physics, Public Safety and Security.

**Personality Type:** Realistic-Conventional-Investigative. **Career Cluster:** 02 Architecture and Construction. **Career Pathway:** 2.2 Construction. **Other Jobs in This Pathway:** Cement Masons and Concrete Finishers; Construction and Building Inspectors; Construction Carpenters; Construction Laborers; Construction Managers; Cost Estimators; Drywall and Ceiling Tile Installers; Electrical Power-Line Installers and Repairers; Electricians; Engineering Technicians, Except Drafters, All Other; Excavating and Loading Machine and Dragline Operators; First-Line Supervisors of Construction Trades and Extraction Workers; Heating and Air Conditioning Mechanics and Installers; Helpers—Carpenters; Helpers—Electricians; Helpers—Pipelayers, Plumbers, Pipefitters, and Steamfitters; Highway Maintenance Workers; Operating Engineers and Other Construction Equipment Operators; Painters, Construction and Maintenance; Pipe Fitters and Steamfitters; Plumbers; Refrigeration Mechanics and Installers; Roofers; Rough Carpenters; Solar Energy Installation Managers; others.

**Skills**—Repairing, Mathematics, Equipment Maintenance, Equipment Selection, Quality Control Analysis, Operation and Control, Management of Material Resources, Troubleshooting.

**Work Environment:** Outdoors; standing; walking and running; using hands; bending or twisting the body; repetitive motions; noise; very hot or cold; contaminants; cramped work space; high places; hazardous equipment; minor burns, cuts, bites, or stings.

## Budget Analysts

- ❋ Annual Earnings: $68,200
- ❋ Earnings Growth Potential: Low (34.2%)
- ❋ Growth: 15.1%
- ❋ Annual Job Openings: 2,230
- ❋ Self-Employed: 0.0%

**Considerations for Job Outlook:** Projected employment growth will be driven by the continued demand for financial analysis in both the public and the private sectors. Job seekers with a master's degree should have the best prospects.

**Examine budget estimates for completeness, accuracy, and conformance with procedures and regulations. Analyze budgeting and accounting reports for the purpose of maintaining expenditure controls.** Direct the preparation

of regular and special budget reports. Consult with managers to ensure that budget adjustments are made in accordance with program changes. Match appropriations for specific programs with appropriations for broader programs, including items for emergency funds. Provide advice and technical assistance with cost analysis, fiscal allocation, and budget preparation. Summarize budgets and submit recommendations for the approval or disapproval of funds requests. Seek new ways to improve efficiency and increase profits. Review operating budgets to analyze trends affecting budget needs. Perform cost-benefit analyses to compare operating programs, review financial requests, or explore alternative financing methods. Interpret budget directives and establish policies for carrying out directives. Compile and analyze accounting records and other data to determine the financial resources required to implement a program. Testify before examining and fund-granting authorities, clarifying and promoting the proposed budgets.

**Education/Training Required:** Bachelor's degree. **Education and Training Programs:** Accounting; Finance, General. **Knowledge/Courses**—Economics and Accounting, Clerical, Administration and Management, Mathematics, Personnel and Human Resources, Law and Government.

**Personality Type:** Conventional-Enterprising-Investigative. **Career Clusters:** 04 Business, Management, and Administration; 06 Finance. **Career Pathways:** 4.2 Business, Financial Management, and Accounting; 6.1 Financial and Investment Planning. **Other Jobs in These Pathways:** Accountants; Auditors; Billing and Posting Clerks; Billing, Cost, and Rate Clerks; Bookkeeping, Accounting, and Auditing Clerks; Brownfield Redevelopment Specialists and Site Managers; Compliance Managers; Financial Analysts; Financial Managers, Branch or Department; Investment Fund Managers; Loss Prevention Managers; Managers, All Other; Payroll and Timekeeping Clerks; Personal Financial Advisors; Regulatory Affairs Managers; Sales Agents, Financial Services; Sales Agents, Securities and Commodities; Securities and Commodities Traders; Securities, Commodities, and Financial Services Sales Agents; Security Managers; Statement Clerks; Supply Chain Managers; Treasurers and Controllers; Wind Energy Operations Managers; Wind Energy Project Managers; others.

**Skills**—Management of Financial Resources, Operations Analysis, Systems Analysis, Mathematics, Management of Material Resources, Systems Evaluation, Judgment and Decision Making, Active Learning.

**Work Environment:** Indoors; sitting; repetitive motions.

# Bus and Truck Mechanics and Diesel Engine Specialists

❋ Annual Earnings: $40,850
❋ Earnings Growth Potential: Low (35.0%)
❋ Growth: 5.7%
❋ Annual Job Openings: 7,530
❋ Self-Employed: 5.9%

**Considerations for Job Outlook:** The increasing durability of new diesel engines is expected to hamper growth for the workers who repair them. This factor will be partially offset by the need for these workers due to increased freight shipments and the need to retrofit vehicles to meet environmental regulations. Opportunities should be very good for job seekers with technical skills and formal training.

**Diagnose, adjust, repair, or overhaul trucks, buses, and all types of diesel engines. Includes mechanics working primarily with automobile diesel engines.** Use hand tools such as screwdrivers, pliers, wrenches, pressure gauges, and precision instruments, as well as power tools such as pneumatic wrenches, lathes, welding equipment, and jacks and hoists. Inspect brake systems, steering mechanisms, wheel bearings, and other important parts to ensure that they are in proper operating condition. Perform routine maintenance such as changing oil, checking batteries, and lubricating equipment and machinery. Adjust and reline brakes, align wheels, tighten bolts and screws, and reassemble equipment. Raise trucks, buses, and heavy parts or equipment, using hydraulic jacks or hoists. Test drive trucks and buses to diagnose malfunctions or to ensure that they are working properly. Inspect, test, and listen to defective equipment to diagnose malfunctions, using test instruments such as handheld computers, motor analyzers, chassis charts, and pressure gauges. Examine and adjust protective guards, loose bolts, and specified safety devices. Inspect and verify dimensions and clearances of parts to ensure conformance to factory specifications. Specialize in repairing and maintaining parts of the engine, such as fuel injection systems. Attach test instruments to equipment and read dials and gauges to diagnose malfunctions. Rewire ignition systems, lights, and instrument panels. Recondition and replace parts, pistons, bearings, gears, and valves. Repair and adjust seats, doors, and windows and install and repair accessories. Inspect, repair, and maintain automotive and mechanical equipment and machinery such as pumps and compressors. Disassemble and overhaul internal combustion engines, pumps, generators, transmissions, clutches, and differential units. Rebuild gas or diesel engines. Align front ends and suspension systems. Operate valve-grinding machines to grind and reset valves.

**Education/Training Required:** Postsecondary vocational training. **Education and Training Programs:** Diesel Mechanics Technology/Technician; Medium/Heavy Vehicle and Truck Technology/Technician. **Knowledge/Courses—** Mechanical, Transportation, Physics, Public Safety and Security, Engineering and Technology, Mathematics.

**Personality Type:** Realistic-Conventional. **Career Cluster:** 16 Transportation, Distribution, and Logistics. **Career Pathway:** 16.4 Facility and Mobile Equipment Maintenance. **Other Jobs in This Pathway:** Aircraft Mechanics and Service Technicians; Aircraft Structure, Surfaces, Rigging, and Systems Assemblers; Automotive Body and Related Repairers; Automotive Glass Installers and Repairers; Automotive Master Mechanics; Automotive Specialty Technicians; Bicycle Repairers; Cleaners of Vehicles and Equipment; Electrical and Electronics Installers and Repairers, Transportation Equipment; Electronic Equipment Installers and Repairers, Motor Vehicles; Engine and Other Machine Assemblers; Gem and Diamond Workers; Installation, Maintenance, and Repair Workers, All Other; Motorboat Mechanics and Service Technicians; Motorcycle Mechanics; Outdoor Power Equipment and Other Small Engine Mechanics; Painters, Transportation Equipment.

**Skills—**Repairing, Equipment Maintenance, Troubleshooting, Equipment Selection, Operation and Control, Quality Control Analysis, Operation Monitoring, Installation.

**Work Environment:** Outdoors; standing; walking and running; kneeling, crouching, stooping, or crawling; using hands; bending or twisting the body; repetitive motions; noise; very hot or cold; bright or inadequate lighting; contaminants; cramped work space; hazardous conditions; hazardous equipment; minor burns, cuts, bites, or stings.

# Bus Drivers, Transit and Intercity

❋ Annual Earnings: $35,520
❋ Earnings Growth Potential: Medium (40.8%)
❋ Growth: 8.2%
❋ Annual Job Openings: 4,990
❋ Self-Employed: 1.2%

**Considerations for Job Outlook:** Population growth is expected to create jobs for school bus drivers, and the increased popularity of public transportation as an alternative to driving should create employment growth for transit and intercity bus drivers. Good job prospects are expected.

**Drive bus or motor coach, including regular route operations, charters, and private carriage. May assist passengers with baggage. May collect fares or tickets.** Inspect vehicles and check gas, oil, and water levels prior to departure. Drive vehicles over specified routes or to specified destinations according to time schedules to transport passengers, complying with traffic regulations. Park vehicles at loading areas so that passengers can board. Assist passengers with baggage and collect tickets or cash fares. Report delays or accidents. Advise passengers to be seated and orderly while on vehicles. Regulate heating, lighting, and ventilating systems for passenger comfort. Load and unload baggage in baggage compartments. Record cash receipts and ticket fares. Make minor repairs to vehicle and change tires.

**Education/Training Required:** Moderate-term on-the-job training. **Education and Training Program:** Truck and Bus Driver Training/Commercial Vehicle Operator and Instructor Training. **Knowledge/Courses—**Transportation, Public Safety and Security, Geography, Psychology, Telecommunications, Customer and Personal Service.

**Personality Type:** Realistic-Social. **Career Cluster:** 16 Transportation, Distribution, and Logistics. **Career Pathway:** 16.1 Transportation Operations. **Other Jobs in This Pathway:** Airline Pilots, Copilots, and Flight Engineers; Automotive and Watercraft Service Attendants; Automotive Master Mechanics; Bus Drivers, School or Special Client; Commercial Pilots; Crane and Tower Operators; First-Line Supervisors of Helpers, Laborers, and Material Movers, Hand; First-Line Supervisors of Transportation and Material-Moving Machine and Vehicle Operators; Freight and Cargo Inspectors; Heavy and Tractor-Trailer Truck Drivers; Laborers and Freight, Stock, and Material Movers, Hand; Light Truck or Delivery Services Drivers; Mates—Ship, Boat, and Barge; Motor Vehicle Operators, All Other; Operating Engineers and Other Construction Equipment Operators; Parking Lot Attendants; Pilots, Ship; Railroad Conductors and Yardmasters; Sailors and Marine Oilers; Ship and Boat Captains; Storage and Distribution Managers; Taxi Drivers and Chauffeurs; Transportation Inspectors; Transportation Managers; Transportation Workers, All Other; others.

**Skills—**Operation and Control, Operation Monitoring, Troubleshooting, Equipment Maintenance, Repairing.

**Work Environment:** Outdoors; sitting; using hands; repetitive motions; noise; very hot or cold; bright or inadequate lighting; contaminants; exposed to disease or infections.

# Business Operations Specialists, All Other

- ❀ Annual Earnings: $62,450
- ❀ Earnings Growth Potential: High (45.8%)
- ❀ Growth: 11.5%
- ❀ Annual Job Openings: 36,830
- ❀ Self-Employed: 0.6%

**Considerations for Job Outlook:** About average employment growth is projected.

**This occupation includes all business operations specialists not listed separately.** Because this is a highly diverse occupation, no data is available for some information topics.

**Education/Training Required:** Bachelor's degree. **Education and Training Program:** Business Administration and Management, General.

**Career Cluster:** 04 Business, Management, and Administration. **Career Pathway:** 4.1 Management. **Other Jobs in This Pathway:** Administrative Services Managers; Brownfield Redevelopment Specialists and Site Managers; Business Continuity Planners; Chief Executives; Chief Sustainability Officers; Compliance Managers; Computer and Information Systems Managers; Construction Managers; Customs Brokers; Energy Auditors; First-Line Supervisors of Office and Administrative Support Workers; General and Operations Managers; Investment Fund Managers; Loss Prevention Managers; Management Analysts; Managers, All Other; Public Relations Specialists; Regulatory Affairs Managers; Sales Managers; Security Management Specialists; Security Managers; Supply Chain Managers; Sustainability Specialists; Wind Energy Operations Managers; Wind Energy Project Managers; others.

## Job Specialization: Business Continuity Planners

**Develop, maintain and implement business continuity and disaster recovery strategies and solutions. Perform risk analyses. Act as a coordinator for recovery efforts in emergency situations.** Write reports to summarize testing activities, including descriptions of goals, planning, scheduling, execution, results, analysis, conclusions, and recommendations. Maintain and update organization information technology applications and network systems blueprints. Interpret government regulations and applicable codes to ensure compliance. Identify individual or transaction targets to direct intelligence collection. Establish, maintain, or test call trees to ensure appropriate communication during disaster. Design or implement products and services to mitigate risk or facilitate use of technology-based tools and methods. Create business continuity and disaster recovery budgets. Create or administer training and awareness presentations or materials. Attend professional meetings, read literature, and participate in training or other educational offerings to keep abreast of new developments and technologies related to disaster recovery and business continuity. Test documented disaster recovery strategies and plans. Review existing disaster recovery, crisis management, or business continuity plans. Recommend or implement methods to monitor, evaluate, or enable resolution of safety, operations, or compliance interruptions. Prepare reports summarizing operational results, financial performance, or accomplishments of specified objectives, goals, or plans. Analyze impact on, and risk to, essential business functions or information systems to identify acceptable recovery time periods and resource requirements. Identify opportunities for strategic improvement or mitigation of business interruption and other risks caused by business, regulatory, or industry-specific change initiatives. Develop disaster recovery plans for physical locations with critical assets such as data centers. Create scenarios to re-establish operations from various types of business disruptions. Conduct or oversee contingency plan integration and operation.

**Education/Training Required:** Work experience plus degree. **Education and Training Program:** Business Administration and Management, General. **Knowledge/Courses**—No data available.

**Personality Type:** No data available. **Career Cluster:** 04 Business, Management, and Administration. **Career Pathway:** 4.1 Management. **Other Jobs in This Pathway:** Administrative Services Managers; Brownfield Redevelopment Specialists and Site Managers; Business Operations Specialists, All Other; Chief Executives; Chief Sustainability Officers; Compliance Managers; Computer and Information Systems Managers; Construction Managers; Customs Brokers; Energy Auditors; First-Line Supervisors of Office and Administrative Support Workers; General and Operations Managers; Investment Fund Managers; Loss Prevention Managers; Management Analysts; Managers, All Other; Public Relations Specialists; Regulatory Affairs Managers; Sales Managers; Security Management Specialists; Security Managers; Supply Chain Managers; Sustainability

Specialists; Wind Energy Operations Managers; Wind Energy Project Managers; others.

**Skills**—No data available.

**Work Environment:** No data available.

## Job Specialization: Customs Brokers

**Prepare customs documentation and ensure that shipments meet all applicable laws to facilitate the import and export of goods. Determine and track duties and taxes payable and process payments on behalf of client. Sign documents under a power of attorney. Represent clients in meetings with customs officials and apply for duty refunds and tariff reclassifications. Coordinate transportation and storage of imported goods.** Sign documents on behalf of clients, using powers of attorney. Provide advice on transportation options, types of carriers, or shipping routes. Post bonds for the products being imported or assist clients in obtaining bonds. Insure cargo against loss, damage, or pilferage. Obtain line releases for frequent shippers of low-risk commodities, high-volume entries, or multiple-container loads. Contract with freight forwarders for destination services. Arrange for transportation, warehousing, or product distribution of imported or exported products. Suggest best methods of packaging or labeling products. Request or compile necessary import documentation, such as customs invoices, certificates of origin, and cargo-control documents. Stay abreast of changes in import or export laws or regulations by reading current literature, attending meetings or conferences, or conferring with colleagues. Quote duty and tax rates on goods to be imported, based on federal tariffs and excise taxes. Prepare papers for shippers to appeal duty charges. Pay, or arrange for payment of, taxes and duties on shipments. Monitor or trace the location of goods. Maintain relationships with customs brokers in other ports to expedite clearing of cargo. Inform importers and exporters of steps to reduce duties and taxes. Confer with officials in various agencies to facilitate clearance of goods through customs and quarantine. Classify goods according to tariff coding system. Calculate duty and tariff payments owed on shipments. Apply for tariff concessions or for duty drawbacks and other refunds. Advise customers on import and export restrictions, tariff systems, insurance requirements, quotas, or other customs-related matters. Prepare and process import and export documentation according to customs regulations, laws, or procedures. Clear goods through customs and to their destinations for clients.

**Education/Training Required:** Postsecondary vocational training. **Education and Training Program:** Traffic,

Customs, and Transportation Clerk/Technician Training. **Knowledge/Courses**—No data available.

**Personality Type:** Enterprising-Conventional. **Career Cluster:** 04 Business, Management, and Administration. **Career Pathway:** 4.1 Management. **Other Jobs in This Pathway:** Administrative Services Managers; Brownfield Redevelopment Specialists and Site Managers; Business Continuity Planners; Business Operations Specialists, All Other; Chief Executives; Chief Sustainability Officers; Compliance Managers; Computer and Information Systems Managers; Construction Managers; Energy Auditors; First-Line Supervisors of Office and Administrative Support Workers; General and Operations Managers; Investment Fund Managers; Loss Prevention Managers; Management Analysts; Managers, All Other; Public Relations Specialists; Regulatory Affairs Managers; Sales Managers; Security Management Specialists; Security Managers; Supply Chain Managers; Sustainability Specialists; Wind Energy Operations Managers; Wind Energy Project Managers; others.

**Skills**—No data available.

**Work Environment:** No data available.

## Job Specialization: Energy Auditors

**Conduct energy audits of buildings, building systems, and process systems. May also conduct investment grade audits of buildings or systems.** Identify and prioritize energy saving measures. Prepare audit reports containing energy analysis results and recommendations for energy cost savings. Inspect or evaluate building envelopes, mechanical systems, electrical systems, or process systems to determine the energy consumption of each system. Collect and analyze field data related to energy usage. Perform tests such as blower-door tests to locate air leaks. Calculate potential for energy savings. Educate customers on energy efficiency or answer questions on topics such as the costs of running household appliances and the selection of energy efficient appliances. Recommend energy efficient technologies or alternate energy sources. Prepare job specification sheets for home energy improvements such as attic insulation, window retrofits, and heating system upgrades. Quantify energy consumption to establish baselines for energy use and need. Identify opportunities to improve the operation, maintenance, or energy efficiency of building or process systems. Analyze technical feasibility of energy saving measures using knowledge of engineering, energy production, energy use, construction, maintenance, system operation, or process systems. Analyze energy bills including utility rates or tariffs to gather historical energy usage data. Measure energy usage with devices such as data loggers, universal data recorders, light meters, sling psychrometers, psychrometric charts, flue gas analyzers, amp-probes, watt meters, volt meters, thermometers, and utility meters. Determine patterns of building use to show annual or monthly needs for heating, cooling, lighting, or other energy needs. Compare existing energy consumption levels to normative data. Oversee installation of equipment such as water heater wraps, pipe insulation, weatherstripping, door sweeps, and low flow showerheads to improve energy efficiency.

**Education/Training Required:** Associate degree. **Education and Training Program:** Energy Management and Systems Technology/Technician. **Knowledge/Courses**—Building and Construction, Physics, Sales and Marketing, Design, Clerical, Mechanical.

**Personality Type:** Conventional-Enterprising. **Career Cluster:** 04 Business, Management, and Administration. **Career Pathway:** 4.1 Management. **Other Jobs in This Pathway:** Administrative Services Managers; Brownfield Redevelopment Specialists and Site Managers; Business Continuity Planners; Business Operations Specialists, All Other; Chief Executives; Chief Sustainability Officers; Compliance Managers; Computer and Information Systems Managers; Construction Managers; Customs Brokers; First-Line Supervisors of Office and Administrative Support Workers; General and Operations Managers; Investment Fund Managers; Loss Prevention Managers; Management Analysts; Managers, All Other; Public Relations Specialists; Regulatory Affairs Managers; Sales Managers; Security Management Specialists; Security Managers; Supply Chain Managers; Sustainability Specialists; Wind Energy Operations Managers; Wind Energy Project Managers; others.

**Skills**—Operations Analysis, Science, Systems Evaluation, Systems Analysis, Mathematics, Management of Financial Resources, Operation and Control, Writing.

**Work Environment:** More often outdoors than indoors; standing; using hands; very hot or cold; bright or inadequate lighting; contaminants; cramped work space; high places.

## Job Specialization: Online Merchants

**Plan, direct, or coordinate retail activities of businesses operating online. May perform duties such as preparing business strategies, buying merchandise, managing inventory, implementing marketing activities, fulfilling and shipping online orders, and balancing financial records.** Participate in online forums and conferences to stay abreast of online retailing trends, techniques, and security threats. Upload digital media, such as photos, video, or scanned images to online storefront, auction sites, or other shopping websites. Order or purchase merchandise to maintain optimal inventory levels. Maintain inventory of shipping supplies, such as boxes, labels, tape, bubble wrap, loose packing materials, and tape guns. Integrate online retailing strategy with physical and catalogue retailing operations. Determine and set product prices. Disclose merchant information and terms and policies of transactions in online and offline materials. Deliver e-mail confirmation of completed transactions and shipment. Create, manage, and automate orders and invoices using order management and invoicing software. Create and maintain database of customer accounts. Create and distribute offline promotional material, such as brochures, pamphlets, business cards, stationary, and signage. Collaborate with search engine shopping specialists to place marketing content in desired online locations. Cancel orders based on customer requests or inventory or delivery problems. Transfer digital media, such as music, video, and software, to customers via the Internet. Select and purchase technical web services, such as web hosting services, online merchant accounts, shopping cart software, payment gateway software, and spyware. Promote products in online communities through weblog or discussion-forum postings, e-mail marketing programs, or online advertising. Fill customer orders by packaging sold items and documentation for direct shipping or by transferring order to manufacturer or third-party distributor. Measure and analyze website usage data to maximize search engine returns or refine customer interfaces. Investigate sources, such as auctions, estate sales, liquidators, wholesalers, and trade shows for new items, used items, or collectibles.

**Education/Training Required:** Work experience in a related occupation. **Education and Training Program:** E-commerce/Electronic Commerce. **Knowledge/Courses**—No data available.

**Personality Type:** Enterprising-Conventional-Realistic. **Career Cluster:** 14 Marketing, Sales, and Service. **Career Pathway:** 14.2 Professional Sales and Marketing. **Other Jobs in This Pathway:** Cashiers; Counter and Rental Clerks; Door-To-Door Sales Workers, News and Street Vendors, and Related Workers; Driver/Sales Workers; Energy Brokers; First-Line Supervisors of Non-Retail Sales Workers; First-Line Supervisors of Retail Sales Workers; Hotel, Motel, and Resort Desk Clerks; Marketing Managers; Marking Clerks; Order Fillers, Wholesale and Retail Sales; Parts Salespersons; Property, Real Estate, and Community Association Managers; Real Estate Sales Agents; Reservation and Transportation Ticket Agents and Travel Clerks; Retail Salespersons; Sales and Related Workers, All Other; Sales Representatives, Services, All Other; Sales Representatives, Wholesale and Manufacturing, Except Technical and Scientific Products; Sales Representatives, Wholesale and Manufacturing, Technical and Scientific Products; Solar Sales Representatives and Assessors; Stock Clerks—Stockroom, Warehouse, or Storage Yard; Stock Clerks, Sales Floor; Telemarketers; Wholesale and Retail Buyers, Except Farm Products; others.

**Skills**—No data available.

**Work Environment:** No data available.

# Job Specialization: Security Management Specialists

**Conduct security assessments for organizations, and design security systems and processes. May specialize in areas such as physical security, personnel security, and information security. May work in fields such as health care, banking, gaming, security engineering, or manufacturing.** Prepare documentation for case reports or court proceedings. Review design drawings or technical documents for completeness, correctness, or appropriateness. Monitor tapes or digital recordings to identify the source of losses. Interview witnesses or suspects to identify persons responsible for security breaches, establish losses, pursue prosecutions, or obtain restitution. Budget and schedule security design work. Develop conceptual designs of security systems. Respond to emergency situations on an on-call basis. Train personnel in security procedures or use of security equipment. Prepare, maintain, or update security procedures, security system drawings, or related documentation. Monitor the work of contractors in the design, construction, and startup phases of security systems. Inspect security design features, installations, or programs to ensure compliance with applicable standards or regulations. Inspect fire, intruder detection, or other security systems. Engineer, install, maintain, or repair security systems, programmable logic controls, or other security-related electronic systems. Recommend improvements in security systems or procedures. Develop or review specifications for design or construction of security systems. Design security policies, programs, or practices to ensure adequate security relating to issues such as protection of assets, alarm response, and access card use. Design or implement security systems, video surveillance, motion detection, or closed-circuit television systems to ensure proper installation and operation. Conduct security audits to identify potential problems related to physical security, staff safety, or asset protection.

**Education/Training Required:** Bachelor's degree. **Education and Training Program:** Security and Loss Prevention Services. **Knowledge/Courses**—No data available.

**Personality Type:** Realistic-Investigative-Conventional. **Career Cluster:** 04 Business, Management, and Administration. **Career Pathway:** 4.1 Management. **Other Jobs in This Pathway:** Administrative Services Managers; Brownfield Redevelopment Specialists and Site Managers; Business Continuity Planners; Business Operations Specialists, All Other; Chief Executives; Chief Sustainability Officers; Compliance Managers; Computer and Information Systems Managers; Construction Managers; Customs Brokers; Energy Auditors; First-Line Supervisors of Office and Administrative Support Workers; General and Operations Managers; Investment Fund Managers; Loss Prevention Managers; Management Analysts; Managers, All Other; Public Relations Specialists; Regulatory Affairs Managers; Sales Managers; Security Managers; Supply Chain Managers; Sustainability Specialists; Wind Energy Operations Managers; Wind Energy Project Managers; others.

**Skills**—No data available.

**Work Environment:** No data available.

## Job Specialization: Sustainability Specialists

**Address organizational sustainability issues, such as waste stream management, green building practices, and green procurement plans.** Review and revise sustainability proposals or policies. Research or review regulatory, technical, or market issues related to sustainability. Identify or investigate violations of natural resources, waste management, recycling, or other environmental policies. Identify or create new sustainability indicators. Write grant applications, rebate applications, or project proposals to secure funding for sustainability projects. Provide technical or administrative support for sustainability programs or issues. Identify or procure needed resources to implement sustainability programs or projects. Create or maintain plans or other documents related to sustainability projects. Develop reports or presentations to communicate the effectiveness of sustainability initiatives. Create marketing or outreach media, such as brochures or websites, to communicate sustainability issues, procedures, or objectives. Collect information about waste stream management or green building practices to inform decision-makers. Assess or propose sustainability initiatives, considering factors such as cost effectiveness, technical feasibility, and acceptance. Monitor or track sustainability indicators, such as energy usage, natural resource usage, waste generation, and recycling. Develop sustainability project goals, objectives, initiatives, or strategies in collaboration with other sustainability professionals.

**Education/Training Required:** Bachelor's degree. **Education and Training Program:** Business Administration and Management, General. **Knowledge/Courses**—No data available.

**Personality Type:** No data available. **Career Cluster:** 04 Business, Management, and Administration. **Career Pathway:** 4.1 Management. **Other Jobs in This Pathway:** Administrative Services Managers; Brownfield Redevelopment Specialists and Site Managers; Business Continuity Planners; Business Operations Specialists, All Other; Chief Executives; Chief Sustainability Officers; Compliance Managers; Computer and Information Systems Managers; Construction Managers; Customs Brokers; Energy Auditors; First-Line Supervisors of Office and Administrative Support Workers; General and Operations Managers; Investment Fund Managers; Loss Prevention Managers; Management Analysts; Managers, All Other; Public Relations Specialists; Regulatory Affairs Managers; Sales Managers; Security Management Specialists; Security Managers; Supply Chain Managers; Wind Energy Operations Managers; Wind Energy Project Managers; others.

**Skills**—No data available.

**Work Environment:** No data available.

# Business Teachers, Postsecondary

- ❋ Annual Earnings: $73,760
- ❋ Earnings Growth Potential: Very high (53.0%)
- ❋ Growth: 15.1%
- ❋ Annual Job Openings: 2,000
- ❋ Self-Employed: 0.2%

**Considerations for Job Outlook:** Enrollments in postsecondary institutions are expected to continue rising as more people attend college and as workers return to school to update their skills. Opportunities for part-time or temporary positions should be favorable, but significant competition exists for tenure-track positions.

**Teach courses in business administration and management, such as accounting, finance, human resources, labor relations, marketing, and operations research.** Prepare and deliver lectures to undergraduate and/or graduate students on topics such as financial accounting, principles of marketing, and operations management. Evaluate and grade students' classwork, assignments, and papers. Compile, administer, and grade examinations or assign this work to others. Prepare course materials such as syllabi, homework assignments, and handouts. Maintain student attendance records, grades, and other required records. Initiate, facilitate, and moderate classroom discussions. Plan, evaluate, and revise curricula, course content, and course materials and methods of instruction. Keep abreast of developments in their field by reading current literature, talking with colleagues, and participating in professional organizations and conferences. Maintain regularly scheduled office hours to advise and assist students. Advise students on academic and vocational curricula and on career issues. Select and obtain materials and supplies such as textbooks. Collaborate with colleagues to address teaching and research issues. Collaborate with members of the business community to improve programs, to develop new programs, and to provide student access to learning opportunities such as internships. Participate in student recruitment, registration, and placement activities. Serve on academic or administrative committees that deal with institutional policies, departmental matters, and academic issues. Participate in campus and community events. Compile bibliographies of specialized materials for outside reading assignments. Perform administrative duties such as serving as department head. Supervise undergraduate and/or graduate teaching, internship, and research work. Conduct research in a particular field of knowledge and publish findings in professional journals, books, and/or electronic media. Act as advisers to student organizations. Provide professional consulting services to government and/or industry.

**Education/Training Required:** Doctoral degree. **Education and Training Programs:** Accounting; Actuarial Science; Business Administration and Management, General; Business Statistics; Business Teacher Education; Business/Commerce, General; Business/Corporate Communications; Entrepreneurship/Entrepreneurial Studies; Finance, General; Financial Planning and Services; Franchising and Franchise Operations; Human Resources Management/Personnel Administration, General; Insurance; International Business/Trade/Commerce; International Finance; International Marketing; Investments and Securities; Labor and Industrial Relations; Logistics, Materials, and Supply Chain Management; Management Science; Marketing Research; Marketing/Marketing Management, General; Operations Management and Supervision; Organizational Behavior Studies; Public Finance; Purchasing, Procurement/Acquisitions and Contracts Management. **Knowledge/**

**Courses**—Economics and Accounting, Education and Training, Sociology and Anthropology, Sales and Marketing, Philosophy and Theology, English Language.

**Personality Type:** Social-Enterprising-Investigative. **Career Clusters:** 04 Business, Management, and Administration; 05 Education and Training; 06 Finance; 14 Marketing, Sales, and Service. **Career Pathways:** 4.1 Management; 4.2 Business, Financial Management, and Accounting; 4.3 Human Resources; 4.5 Marketing; 5.3 Teaching/Training; 6.1 Financial and Investment Planning; 6.4 Insurance Services; 14.1 Management and Entrepreneurship; 14.5 Marketing Information Management and Research. **Other Jobs in These Pathways:** Accountants; Auditors; Bookkeeping, Accounting, and Auditing Clerks; Brownfield Redevelopment Specialists and Site Managers; Business Continuity Planners; Business Operations Specialists, All Other; Compliance Managers; Customs Brokers; Elementary School Teachers, Except Special Education; Energy Auditors; First-Line Supervisors of Office and Administrative Support Workers; First-Line Supervisors of Retail Sales Workers; General and Operations Managers; Investment Fund Managers; Loss Prevention Managers; Managers, All Other; Regulatory Affairs Managers; Secondary School Teachers, Except Special and Career/Technical Education; Security Management Specialists; Security Managers; Supply Chain Managers; Sustainability Specialists; Teacher Assistants; Wind Energy Operations Managers; Wind Energy Project Managers; 37 other postsecondary teaching occupations; others.

**Skills**—Learning Strategies, Instructing, Reading Comprehension, Writing, Active Learning, Speaking, Judgment and Decision Making, Systems Analysis.

**Work Environment:** Indoors; sitting.

# Captains, Mates, and Pilots of Water Vessels

- ✳ Annual Earnings: $64,180
- ✳ Earnings Growth Potential: Very high (52.2%)
- ✳ Growth: 17.3%
- ✳ Annual Job Openings: 1,950
- ✳ Self-Employed: 7.2%

**Considerations for Job Outlook:** Job growth is expected to stem from increasing tourism and from growth in offshore oil and gas production. Employment is also projected to increase in and around major port cities due to growing international trade. Opportunities should be excellent as the need to replace workers, particularly officers, generates many job openings.

## Job Specialization: Mates—Ship, Boat, and Barge

**Supervise and coordinate activities of crew aboard ships, boats, barges, or dredges.** Determine geographical position of ship, using lorans, azimuths of celestial bodies, or computers, and use this information to determine the course and speed of the ship. Observe water from ship's masthead to advise on navigational direction. Supervise crews in cleaning and maintaining decks, superstructures, and bridges. Supervise crew members in the repair or replacement of defective gear and equipment. Steer vessels, using navigational devices such as compasses and sextants and navigational aids such as lighthouses and buoys. Inspect equipment such as cargo-handling gear, lifesaving equipment, visual-signaling equipment, and fishing, towing, or dredging gear to detect problems. Arrange for ships to be stocked, fueled, and repaired. Assume command of vessel in the event that ship's master becomes incapacitated. Participate in activities related to maintenance of vessel security. Stand watches on vessel during specified periods while vessel is under way. Observe loading and unloading of cargo and equipment to ensure that handling and storage are performed according to specifications.

**Education/Training Required:** Work experience in a related occupation. **Education and Training Programs:** Commercial Fishing; Marine Science/Merchant Marine Officer; Marine Transportation Services, Other. **Knowledge/Courses—**Transportation, Geography, Public Safety and Security, Telecommunications, Personnel and Human Resources, Mechanical.

**Personality Type:** Enterprising-Realistic-Conventional. **Career Cluster:** 16 Transportation, Distribution, and Logistics. **Career Pathway:** 16.1 Transportation Operations. **Other Jobs in This Pathway:** Airline Pilots, Copilots, and Flight Engineers; Automotive and Watercraft Service Attendants; Automotive Master Mechanics; Bus Drivers, School or Special Client; Bus Drivers, Transit and Intercity; Commercial Pilots; Crane and Tower Operators; First-Line Supervisors of Helpers, Laborers, and Material Movers, Hand; First-Line Supervisors of Transportation and Material-Moving Machine and Vehicle Operators; Freight and Cargo Inspectors; Heavy and Tractor-Trailer Truck Drivers; Laborers and Freight, Stock, and Material Movers, Hand; Light Truck or Delivery Services Drivers; Motor Vehicle

Operators, All Other; Operating Engineers and Other Construction Equipment Operators; Parking Lot Attendants; Pilots, Ship; Railroad Conductors and Yardmasters; Sailors and Marine Oilers; Ship and Boat Captains; Storage and Distribution Managers; Taxi Drivers and Chauffeurs; Transportation Inspectors; Transportation Managers; Transportation Workers, All Other; others.

**Skills—**Repairing, Equipment Maintenance, Operation and Control, Troubleshooting, Operation Monitoring, Equipment Selection, Quality Control Analysis, Management of Personnel Resources.

**Work Environment:** More often outdoors than indoors; standing; balancing; using hands; noise; very hot or cold; bright or inadequate lighting; contaminants; cramped work space; whole-body vibration; high places; hazardous conditions; hazardous equipment; minor burns, cuts, bites, or stings.

## Job Specialization: Pilots, Ship

**Command ships to steer them into and out of harbors, estuaries, straits, and sounds and on rivers, lakes, and bays. Must be licensed by U.S. Coast Guard with limitations indicating class and tonnage of vessels for which licenses are valid and routes and waters that may be piloted.** Maintain and repair boats and equipment. Give directions to crew members who are steering ships. Make nautical maps. Set ships' courses to avoid reefs, outlying shoals, and other hazards, using navigational aids such as lighthouses and buoys. Report to appropriate authorities any violations of federal or state pilotage laws. Relieve crew members on tugs and launches. Provide assistance to vessels approaching or leaving seacoasts, navigating harbors, and docking and undocking. Provide assistance in maritime rescue operations. Prevent ships under their navigational control from engaging in unsafe operations. Operate amphibious craft during troop landings. Maintain ships' logs. Learn to operate new technology systems and procedures, through the use of instruction, simulators, and models. Advise ships' masters on harbor rules and customs procedures. Steer ships into and out of berths or signal tugboat captains to berth and unberth ships. Serve as vessels' docking masters upon arrival at a port and when at a berth. Operate ship-to-shore radios to exchange information needed for ship operations. Consult maps, charts, weather reports, and navigation equipment to determine and direct ship movements. Direct courses and speeds of ships, based on specialized knowledge of local winds, weather, water depths, tides, currents, and hazards. Oversee cargo storage on or below decks.

**Education/Training Required:** Work experience in a related occupation. **Education and Training Programs:** Commercial Fishing; Marine Science/Merchant Marine Officer; Marine Transportation Services, Other. **Knowledge/Courses**—Transportation, Geography, Public Safety and Security, Telecommunications, Mechanical, Law and Government.

**Personality Type:** Realistic-Conventional-Investigative. **Career Cluster:** 16 Transportation, Distribution, and Logistics. **Career Pathway:** 16.1 Transportation Operations. **Other Jobs in This Pathway:** Airline Pilots, Copilots, and Flight Engineers; Automotive and Watercraft Service Attendants; Automotive Master Mechanics; Bus Drivers, School or Special Client; Bus Drivers, Transit and Intercity; Commercial Pilots; Crane and Tower Operators; First-Line Supervisors of Helpers, Laborers, and Material Movers, Hand; First-Line Supervisors of Transportation and Material-Moving Machine and Vehicle Operators; Freight and Cargo Inspectors; Heavy and Tractor-Trailer Truck Drivers; Laborers and Freight, Stock, and Material Movers, Hand; Light Truck or Delivery Services Drivers; Mates—Ship, Boat, and Barge; Motor Vehicle Operators, All Other; Operating Engineers and Other Construction Equipment Operators; Parking Lot Attendants; Railroad Conductors and Yardmasters; Sailors and Marine Oilers; Ship and Boat Captains; Storage and Distribution Managers; Taxi Drivers and Chauffeurs; Transportation Inspectors; Transportation Managers; Transportation Workers, All Other; others.

**Skills**—Operation and Control, Operation Monitoring, Troubleshooting, Equipment Maintenance, Management of Personnel Resources, Repairing, Quality Control Analysis, Complex Problem Solving.

**Work Environment:** More often outdoors than indoors; standing; using hands; noise; very hot or cold; bright or inadequate lighting; contaminants; whole-body vibration; hazardous conditions.

## Job Specialization: Ship and Boat Captains

**Command vessels in oceans, bays, lakes, rivers, and coastal waters.** Assign watches and living quarters to crew members. Sort logs, form log booms, and salvage lost logs. Perform various marine duties such as checking for oil spills or other pollutants around ports and harbors, and patrolling beaches. Contact buyers to sell cargo such as fish. Tow and maneuver barges, or signal for tugboats to tow barges to destinations. Signal passing vessels, using whistles, flashing lights, flags, and radios. Resolve questions or problems with customs officials. Read gauges to verify sufficient levels of hydraulic fluid, air pressure, and oxygen. Purchase supplies and equipment. Measure depths of water, using depth-measuring equipment. Maintain boats and equipment on board, such as engines, winches, navigational systems, fire extinguishers, and life preservers. Collect fares from customers, or signal ferryboat helpers to collect fares. Arrange for ships to be fueled, restocked with supplies, and/or repaired. Signal crew members or deckhands to rig tow lines, open or close gates and ramps, and pull guard chains across entries. Maintain records of daily activities, personnel reports, ship positions and movements, ports of call, weather and sea conditions, pollution control efforts, and/or cargo and passenger statuses. Inspect vessels to ensure efficient and safe operation of vessels and equipment, and conformance to regulations. Direct and coordinate crew members or workers performing activities such as loading and unloading cargo, steering vessels, operating engines, and operating, maintaining, and repairing ship equipment. Compute positions, set courses, and determine speeds by using charts, area plotting sheets, compasses, sextants, and knowledge of local conditions. Calculate sightings of land, using electronic sounding devices, and following contour lines on charts. Monitor the loading and discharging of cargo or passengers. Interview and hire crew members.

**Education/Training Required:** Work experience in a related occupation. **Education and Training Programs:** Commercial Fishing; Marine Science/Merchant Marine Officer; Marine Transportation Services, Other. **Knowledge/Courses**—Transportation, Public Safety and Security, Geography, Telecommunications, Mechanical, Psychology.

**Personality Type:** Enterprising-Realistic. **Career Cluster:** 16 Transportation, Distribution, and Logistics. **Career Pathway:** 16.1 Transportation Operations. **Other Jobs in This Pathway:** Airline Pilots, Copilots, and Flight Engineers; Automotive and Watercraft Service Attendants; Automotive Master Mechanics; Bus Drivers, School or Special Client; Bus Drivers, Transit and Intercity; Commercial Pilots; Crane and Tower Operators; First-Line Supervisors of Helpers, Laborers, and Material Movers, Hand; First-Line Supervisors of Transportation and Material-Moving Machine and Vehicle Operators; Freight and Cargo Inspectors; Heavy and Tractor-Trailer Truck Drivers; Laborers and Freight, Stock, and Material Movers, Hand; Light Truck or Delivery Services Drivers; Mates—Ship, Boat, and Barge; Motor Vehicle Operators, All Other; Operating Engineers and Other Construction Equipment Operators; Parking Lot Attendants; Pilots, Ship; Railroad Conductors and Yardmasters; Sailors and Marine Oilers; Storage and Distribution

Managers; Taxi Drivers and Chauffeurs; Transportation Inspectors; Transportation Managers; Transportation Workers, All Other; others.

**Skills**—Operation and Control, Repairing, Management of Material Resources, Management of Financial Resources, Equipment Maintenance, Troubleshooting, Operation Monitoring, Equipment Selection.

**Work Environment:** More often outdoors than indoors; standing; using hands; repetitive motions; noise; very hot or cold; bright or inadequate lighting; contaminants; whole-body vibration; hazardous equipment; minor burns, cuts, bites, or stings.

# Cardiovascular Technologists and Technicians

- ❀ Annual Earnings: $49,410
- ❀ Earnings Growth Potential: High (46.1%)
- ❀ Growth: 24.1%
- ❀ Annual Job Openings: 1,910
- ❀ Self-Employed: 0.8%

**Considerations for Job Outlook:** An aging population and the continued prevalence of heart disease will drive employment growth for cardiovascular technologists and technicians. Prospects should be the best for job seekers who have multiple credentials.

**Conduct tests on pulmonary or cardiovascular systems of patients for diagnostic purposes. May conduct or assist in electrocardiograms, cardiac catheterizations, pulmonary-functions, lung capacity, and similar tests.** Monitor patients' blood pressures and heart rates, using electrocardiogram (EKG) equipment during diagnostic and therapeutic procedures to notify physicians if something appears wrong. Explain testing procedures to patients to obtain cooperation and reduce anxiety. Observe gauges, recorders, and video screens of data analysis systems during imaging of cardiovascular systems. Monitor patients' comfort and safety during tests, alerting physicians to abnormalities or changes in patient responses. Obtain and record patients' identities, medical histories, or test results. Attach electrodes to patients' chests, arms, and legs; connect electrodes to leads from electrocardiogram (EKG) machines; and operate EKG machines to obtain readings. Adjust equipment and controls according to physicians' orders or established protocol. Prepare and position patients for testing. Check, test, and maintain cardiology equipment, making minor repairs when necessary, to ensure proper operation. Supervise and train

other cardiology technologists and students. Perform general administrative tasks, such as scheduling appointments or ordering supplies and equipment. Maintain a proper sterile field during surgical procedures. Assist physicians in the diagnosis and treatment of cardiac and peripheral vascular treatments, such as implanting pacemakers or assisting with balloon angioplasties to treat blood vessel blockages. Inject contrast medium into patients' blood vessels. Assess cardiac physiology and calculate valve areas from blood flow velocity measurements. Operate diagnostic imaging equipment to produce contrast enhanced radiographs of hearts and cardiovascular systems. Observe ultrasound display screens and listen to signals to record vascular information such as blood pressure, limb volume changes, oxygen saturation, and cerebral circulation. Transcribe, type, and distribute reports of diagnostic procedures for interpretation by physician.

**Education/Training Required:** Associate degree. **Education and Training Programs:** Cardiopulmonary Technology/Technologist; Cardiovascular Technology/Technologist; Electrocardiograph Technology/Technician; Perfusion Technology/Perfusionist. **Knowledge/Courses**—Medicine and Dentistry, Biology, Psychology, Customer and Personal Service, Sociology and Anthropology, Chemistry.

**Personality Type:** Realistic-Investigative-Social. **Career Cluster:** 08 Health Science. **Career Pathway:** 8.2 Diagnostics Services. **Other Jobs in This Pathway:** Ambulance Drivers and Attendants, Except Emergency Medical Technicians; Anesthesiologist Assistants; Cytogenetic Technologists; Cytotechnologists; Diagnostic Medical Sonographers; Emergency Medical Technicians and Paramedics; Endoscopy Technicians; Health Diagnosing and Treating Practitioners, All Other; Health Technologists and Technicians, All Other; Healthcare Practitioners and Technical Workers, All Other; Histotechnologists and Histologic Technicians; Medical and Clinical Laboratory Technicians; Medical and Clinical Laboratory Technologists; Medical and Health Services Managers; Medical Assistants; Medical Equipment Preparers; Neurodiagnostic Technologists; Nuclear Medicine Technologists; Ophthalmic Laboratory Technicians; Physical Scientists, All Other; Physician Assistants; Radiologic Technicians; Radiologic Technologists; Surgical Technologists; Veterinary Assistants and Laboratory Animal Caretakers; others.

**Skills**—Science, Equipment Maintenance, Operation and Control, Repairing, Operation Monitoring, Service Orientation, Equipment Selection, Troubleshooting.

**Work Environment:** Indoors; standing; walking and running; using hands; repetitive motions; exposed to radiation; exposed to disease or infections.

# Career/Technical Education Teachers, Secondary School

❀ Annual Earnings: $54,310
❀ Earnings Growth Potential: Low (33.2%)
❀ Growth: 9.6%
❀ Annual Job Openings: 3,850
❀ Self-Employed: 0.0%

**Considerations for Job Outlook:** Employment growth for these workers should arise from continued increases in school enrollments, but growth will be limited by the focus on traditional academic subjects. Prospects are expected to be favorable as workers leave the occupation permanently.

**Teach or instruct vocational or occupational subjects at the secondary school level.** Prepare materials and classroom for class activities. Maintain accurate and complete student records as required by law, district policy, and administrative regulations. Instruct students individually and in groups, using various teaching methods such as lectures, discussions, and demonstrations. Observe and evaluate students' performance, behavior, social development, and physical health. Establish and enforce rules for behavior and procedures for maintaining order among the students for whom they are responsible. Instruct and monitor students the in use and care of equipment and materials to prevent injury and damage. Plan and conduct activities for a balanced program of instruction, demonstration, and work time that provides students with opportunities to observe, question, and investigate. Prepare, administer, and grade tests and assignments to evaluate students' progress. Enforce all administration policies and rules governing students. Assign and grade classwork and homework. Instruct students in the knowledge and skills required in a specific occupation or occupational field, using a systematic plan of lectures; discussions; audio-visual presentations; and laboratory, shop, and field studies. Establish clear objectives for all lessons, units, and projects and communicate those objectives to students. Use computers, audiovisual aids, and other equipment and materials to supplement presentations. Plan and supervise work-experience programs in businesses, industrial shops, and school laboratories. Prepare students for later grades by encouraging them to explore learning opportunities and to persevere with challenging tasks. Confer with parents or guardians, other teachers, counselors, and administrators in order to resolve students' behavioral and academic problems. Guide and counsel students with adjustment or academic problems or special academic interests.

**Education/Training Required:** Work experience plus degree. **Education and Training Program:** Technology Teacher Education/Industrial Arts Teacher Education. **Knowledge/Courses**—Education and Training, Therapy and Counseling, Sales and Marketing, Psychology, Sociology and Anthropology, Clerical.

**Personality Type:** Social. **Career Cluster:** 05 Education and Training. **Career Pathway:** 5.3 Teaching/Training. **Other Jobs in This Pathway:** Adult Basic and Secondary Education and Literacy Teachers and Instructors; Athletes and Sports Competitors; Audio-Visual and Multimedia Collections Specialists; Career/Technical Education Teachers, Middle School; Chemists; Coaches and Scouts; Dietitians and Nutritionists; Elementary School Teachers, Except Special Education; Fitness Trainers and Aerobics Instructors; Historians; Instructional Coordinators; Instructional Designers and Technologists; Interpreters and Translators; Kindergarten Teachers, Except Special Education; Librarians; Middle School Teachers, Except Special and Career/Technical Education; Physicists; Preschool Teachers, Except Special Education; Recreation Workers; Secondary School Teachers, Except Special and Career/Technical Education; Self-Enrichment Education Teachers; Teacher Assistants; Teachers and Instructors, All Other; Tutors.

**Skills**—Learning Strategies, Instructing, Persuasion, Management of Material Resources, Negotiation, Systems Evaluation, Social Perceptiveness, Coordination.

**Work Environment:** Indoors; standing; walking and running; using hands; noise; contaminants.

# Cargo and Freight Agents

❀ Annual Earnings: $37,150
❀ Earnings Growth Potential: Medium (40.5%)
❀ Growth: 23.9%
❀ Annual Job Openings: 4,030
❀ Self-Employed: 0.3%

**Considerations for Job Outlook:** More agents should be needed to handle the growing number of shipments resulting from expected increases in cargo traffic. Job prospects should be good.

**Expedite and route movement of incoming and outgoing cargo and freight shipments in airline, train, and trucking terminals and shipping docks. Take orders from customers and arrange pickup of freight and cargo for delivery to loading platform. Prepare and examine bills of lading**

**to determine shipping charges and tariffs.** Negotiate and arrange transport of goods with shipping or freight companies. Notify consignees, passengers, or customers of the arrival of freight or baggage and arrange for delivery. Advise clients on transportation and payment methods. Prepare manifests showing baggage, mail, and freight weights and number of passengers on airplanes and transmit data to destinations. Determine method of shipment and prepare bills of lading, invoices, and other shipping documents. Check import/export documentation to determine cargo contents and classify goods into different fee or tariff groups, using a tariff coding system. Estimate freight or postal rates and record shipment costs and weights. Enter shipping information into a computer by hand or by using a hand-held scanner that reads bar codes on goods. Retrieve stored items and trace lost shipments as necessary. Pack goods for shipping, using tools such as staplers, strapping machines, and hammers. Direct delivery trucks to shipping doors or designated marshalling areas and help load and unload goods safely. Inspect and count items received and check them against invoices or other documents, recording shortages and rejecting damaged goods. Install straps, braces, and padding to loads to prevent shifting or damage during shipment. Keep records of all goods shipped, received, and stored. Coordinate and supervise activities of workers engaged in packing and shipping merchandise. Arrange insurance coverage for goods. Direct or participate in cargo loading to ensure completeness of load and even distribution of weight. Open cargo containers and unwrap contents, using steel cutters, crowbars, or other hand tools. Attach address labels, identification codes, and shipping instructions to containers. Contact vendors or claims adjustment departments to resolve problems with shipments or contact service depots to arrange for repairs.

**Education/Training Required:** Moderate-term on-the-job training. **Education and Training Program:** General Office Occupations and Clerical Services. **Knowledge/Courses—**Transportation, Geography, Customer and Personal Service, Clerical, Administration and Management, Computers and Electronics.

**Personality Type:** Conventional-Enterprising-Realistic. **Career Cluster:** 04 Business, Management, and Administration. **Career Pathway:** 4.6 Administrative and Information Support. **Other Jobs in This Pathway:** Couriers and Messengers; Court Clerks; Court, Municipal, and License Clerks; Customer Service Representatives; Data Entry Keyers; Dispatchers, Except Police, Fire, and Ambulance; Executive Secretaries and Executive Administrative Assistants; File Clerks; Human Resources Assistants, Except Payroll and Timekeeping; Information and Record Clerks, All Other; Insurance Claims Clerks; Insurance Policy Processing Clerks; Interviewers, Except Eligibility and Loan; Mail Clerks and Mail Machine Operators, Except Postal Service; Office and Administrative Support Workers, All Other; Office Clerks, General; Order Clerks; Patient Representatives; Postal Service Mail Carriers; Postal Service Mail Sorters, Processors, and Processing Machine Operators; Receptionists and Information Clerks; Secretaries and Administrative Assistants, Except Legal, Medical, and Executive; Shipping, Receiving, and Traffic Clerks; Switchboard Operators, Including Answering Service; Word Processors and Typists; others.

**Skills—**Negotiation, Service Orientation, Time Management, Mathematics, Systems Evaluation, Speaking, Persuasion, Critical Thinking.

**Work Environment:** Indoors; sitting; repetitive motions.

## Job Specialization: Freight Forwarders

**Research rates, routings, or modes of transport for shipment of products. Maintain awareness of regulations affecting the international movement of cargo. Make arrangements for additional services such as storage and inland transportation.** Select shipment routes, based on nature of goods shipped, transit times, or security needs. Determine efficient and cost-effective methods of moving goods from one location to another. Reserve necessary space on ships, aircraft, trains, or trucks. Arrange delivery or storage of goods at destinations. Arrange for special transport of sensitive cargoes, such as livestock, food, and medical supplies. Assist clients in obtaining insurance reimbursements. Calculate weight, volume, or cost of goods to be moved. Complete shipping documentation, such as including bills of lading, packing lists, dock receipts, and certificates of origin. Consolidate loads with a common destination to reduce costs to individual shippers. Inform clients of factors such as shipping options, timelines, transfers, and regulations affecting shipments. Keep records of goods dispatched and received. Maintain current knowledge of relevant legislation, political situations, or other factors that could affect freight shipping. Monitor and record locations of goods in transit. Negotiate shipping rates with freight carriers. Obtain or arrange cargo insurance. Pay, or arrange for payment of, freight and insurance fees, or other charges. Prepare invoices and cost quotations for freight transportation. Recommend or arrange appropriate merchandise packing methods, according to climate, terrain, weight, nature of goods, or costs. Verify proper packaging and labeling of exported goods. Verify adherence of documentation to customs, insurance, or regulatory requirements. Clear goods through customs, arranging for applicable duties and taxes. Complete customs paperwork. Make arrangements with customs brokers to facilitate the passage of goods through customs. Provide detailed port information to importers and exporters. Provide shipment status notification to exporters, consignees, or insurers.

**Education/Training Required:** Moderate-term on-the-job training. **Education and Training Program:** General Office Occupations and Clerical Services. **Knowledge/Courses—** No data available.

**Personality Type:** Conventional-Enterprising. **Career Cluster:** 04 Business, Management, and Administration. **Career Pathway:** 4.6 Administrative and Information Support. **Other Jobs in This Pathway:** Couriers and Messengers; Court Clerks; Court, Municipal, and License Clerks; Customer Service Representatives; Data Entry Keyers; Dispatchers, Except Police, Fire, and Ambulance; Executive Secretaries and Executive Administrative Assistants; File Clerks; Human Resources Assistants, Except Payroll and Timekeeping; Information and Record Clerks, All Other; Insurance Claims Clerks; Insurance Policy Processing Clerks; Interviewers, Except Eligibility and Loan; Mail Clerks and Mail Machine Operators, Except Postal Service; Office and Administrative Support Workers, All Other; Office Clerks, General; Order Clerks; Patient Representatives; Postal Service Mail Carriers; Postal Service Mail Sorters, Processors, and Processing Machine Operators; Receptionists and Information Clerks; Secretaries and Administrative Assistants, Except Legal, Medical, and Executive; Shipping, Receiving, and Traffic Clerks; Switchboard Operators, Including Answering Service; Word Processors and Typists; others.

**Skills—** No data available.

**Work Environment:** No data available.

# Carpenters

- ❀ Annual Earnings: $39,530
- ❀ Earnings Growth Potential: Medium (37.6%)
- ❀ Growth: 12.9%
- ❀ Annual Job Openings: 32,540
- ❀ Self-Employed: 32.0%

**Considerations for Job Outlook:** New construction projects are expected to increase employment for carpenters. Opportunities should be best for job seekers who prepare through an apprenticeship or other formal training.

## Job Specialization: Construction Carpenters

**Construct, erect, install, and repair structures and fixtures of wood, plywood, and wallboard, using carpenter's hand tools and power tools.** Measure and mark cutting lines on materials, using ruler, pencil, chalk, and marking gauge. Follow established safety rules and regulations and maintain a safe and clean environment. Verify trueness of structure, using plumb bob and level. Shape or cut materials to specified measurements, using hand tools, machines, or power saw. Study specifications in blueprints, sketches, or building plans to prepare project layout and determine dimensions and materials required. Assemble and fasten materials to make framework or props, using hand tools and wood screws, nails, dowel pins, or glue. Build or repair cabinets, doors, frameworks, floors, and other wooden fixtures used in buildings, using woodworking machines, carpenter's hand tools, and power tools. Erect scaffolding and ladders for assembling structures above ground level. Remove damaged or defective parts or sections of structures and repair or replace, using hand tools. Install structures and fixtures, such as windows, frames, floorings, and trim, or hardware, using carpenter's hand and power tools. Select and order lumber and other required materials. Maintain records, document actions, and present written progress reports. Finish surfaces of woodwork or wallboard in houses and buildings, using paint, hand tools, and paneling. Prepare cost estimates for clients or employers. Arrange for subcontractors to deal with special areas such as heating and electrical wiring work. Inspect ceiling or floor tile, wall coverings, siding, glass, or woodwork to detect broken or damaged structures. Work with or remove hazardous material. Construct forms and chutes for pouring concrete. Cover subfloors with building paper to keep out moisture and lay hardwood, parquet, and wood-strip-block floors by nailing floors to subfloor or cementing them to mastic or asphalt base. Fill cracks and other defects in plaster or plasterboard and sand patch, using patching plaster, trowel, and sanding tool.

**Education/Training Required:** Long-term on-the-job training. **Education and Training Program:** Carpentry/Carpenter. **Knowledge/Courses—** Building and Construction, Design, Mechanical, Engineering and Technology, Production and Processing, Mathematics.

**Personality Type:** Realistic-Conventional-Investigative. **Career Cluster:** 02 Architecture and Construction. **Career Pathway:** 2.2 Construction. **Other Jobs in This Pathway:** Brickmasons and Blockmasons; Cement Masons and Concrete Finishers; Construction and Building Inspectors; Construction Laborers; Construction Managers; Cost

Estimators; Drywall and Ceiling Tile Installers; Electrical Power-Line Installers and Repairers; Electricians; Engineering Technicians, Except Drafters, All Other; Excavating and Loading Machine and Dragline Operators; First-Line Supervisors of Construction Trades and Extraction Workers; Heating and Air Conditioning Mechanics and Installers; Helpers—Carpenters; Helpers—Electricians; Helpers—Pipelayers, Plumbers, Pipefitters, and Steamfitters; Highway Maintenance Workers; Operating Engineers and Other Construction Equipment Operators; Painters, Construction and Maintenance; Pipe Fitters and Steamfitters; Plumbers; Refrigeration Mechanics and Installers; Roofers; Rough Carpenters; Solar Energy Installation Managers; others.

**Skills**—Repairing, Equipment Selection, Installation, Quality Control Analysis, Equipment Maintenance, Operation and Control, Troubleshooting, Management of Material Resources.

**Work Environment:** Outdoors; standing; walking and running; kneeling, crouching, stooping, or crawling; using hands; bending or twisting the body; repetitive motions; noise; very hot or cold; bright or inadequate lighting; contaminants; cramped work space; high places; hazardous equipment; minor burns, cuts, bites, or stings.

## Job Specialization: Rough Carpenters

**Build rough wooden structures, such as concrete forms, scaffolds, tunnel, bridge, or sewer supports, billboard signs, and temporary frame shelters, according to sketches, blueprints, or oral instructions.** Study blueprints and diagrams to determine dimensions of structure or form to be constructed. Measure materials or distances, using square, measuring tape, or rule to lay out work. Cut or saw boards, timbers, or plywood to required size, using handsaw, power saw, or woodworking machine. Assemble and fasten material together to construct wood or metal framework of structure, using bolts, nails, or screws. Anchor and brace forms and other structures in place, using nails, bolts, anchor rods, steel cables, planks, wedges, and timbers. Mark cutting lines on materials, using pencil and scriber. Erect forms, framework, scaffolds, hoists, roof supports, or chutes, using hand tools, plumb rule, and level. Install rough door and window frames, subflooring, fixtures, or temporary supports in structures undergoing construction or repair. Examine structural timbers and supports to detect decay and replace timbers as required, using hand tools, nuts, and bolts. Bore boltholes in timber, masonry, or concrete walls, using power drill. Fabricate parts, using woodworking and metalworking machines. Dig or direct digging of post holes and set poles to support structures. Build sleds from logs and timbers for use in hauling camp buildings and machinery through wooded areas. Build chutes for pouring concrete.

**Education/Training Required:** Long-term on-the-job training. **Education and Training Program:** Carpentry/Carpenter. **Knowledge/Courses**—Building and Construction, Design, Mechanical, Production and Processing, Public Safety and Security, Mathematics.

**Personality Type:** Realistic-Conventional-Investigative. **Career Cluster:** 02 Architecture and Construction. **Career Pathway:** 2.2 Construction. **Other Jobs in This Pathway:** Brickmasons and Blockmasons; Cement Masons and Concrete Finishers; Construction and Building Inspectors; Construction Carpenters; Construction Laborers; Construction Managers; Cost Estimators; Drywall and Ceiling Tile Installers; Electrical Power-Line Installers and Repairers; Electricians; Engineering Technicians, Except Drafters, All Other; Excavating and Loading Machine and Dragline Operators; First-Line Supervisors of Construction Trades and Extraction Workers; Heating and Air Conditioning Mechanics and Installers; Helpers—Carpenters; Helpers—Electricians; Helpers—Pipelayers, Plumbers, Pipefitters, and Steamfitters; Highway Maintenance Workers; Operating Engineers and Other Construction Equipment Operators; Painters, Construction and Maintenance; Pipe Fitters and Steamfitters; Plumbers; Refrigeration Mechanics and Installers; Roofers; Solar Energy Installation Managers; others.

**Skills**—Repairing, Equipment Maintenance, Troubleshooting, Operation and Control, Installation, Mathematics, Operation Monitoring, Coordination.

**Work Environment:** Outdoors; standing; walking and running; kneeling, crouching, stooping, or crawling; balancing; using hands; bending or twisting the body; repetitive motions; noise; very hot or cold; contaminants; cramped work space; high places; hazardous equipment; minor burns, cuts, bites, or stings.

## Cartographers and Photogrammetrists

- ❈ Annual Earnings: $54,510
- ❈ Earnings Growth Potential: Medium (39.0%)
- ❈ Growth: 26.8%
- ❈ Annual Job Openings: 640
- ❈ Self-Employed: 2.5%

**Considerations for Job Outlook:** Increasing demand for geographic information should be the main source of employment growth. Job seekers with a bachelor's degree and strong technical skills should have favorable prospects.

**Collect, analyze, and interpret geographic information provided by geodetic surveys, aerial photographs, and satellite data. Research, study, and prepare maps and other spatial data in digital or graphic form for legal, social, political, educational, and design purposes. May work with Geographic Information Systems (GIS). May design and evaluate algorithms, data structures, and user interfaces for GIS and mapping systems.** Identify, scale, and orient geodetic points, elevations, and other planimetric or topographic features, applying standard mathematical formulas. Collect information about specific features of the Earth, using aerial photography and other digital remote sensing techniques. Revise existing maps and charts, making all necessary corrections and adjustments. Compile data required for map preparation, including aerial photographs, survey notes, records, reports, and original maps. Inspect final compositions to ensure completeness and accuracy. Determine map content and layout, as well as production specifications such as scale, size, projection, and colors, and direct production to ensure that specifications are followed. Examine and analyze data from ground surveys, reports, aerial photographs, and satellite images to prepare topographic maps, aerial-photograph mosaics, and related charts. Select aerial photographic and remote sensing techniques and plotting equipment needed to meet required standards of accuracy. Delineate aerial photographic detail such as control points, hydrography, topography, and cultural features, using precision stereoplotting apparatus or drafting instruments. Build and update digital databases. Prepare and alter trace maps, charts, tables, detailed drawings, and three-dimensional optical models of terrain, using stereoscopic plotting and computer graphics equipment. Determine guidelines that specify which source material is acceptable for use. Study legal records to establish boundaries of local, national, and international properties. Travel over photographed areas to observe, identify, record, and verify all relevant features.

**Education/Training Required:** Bachelor's degree. **Education and Training Programs:** Geographic Information Science and Cartography; Surveying Technology/Surveying. **Knowledge/Courses**—Geography, Design, Computers and Electronics, Mathematics, Production and Processing, Engineering and Technology.

**Personality Type:** Realistic-Investigative-Conventional. **Career Clusters:** 02 Architecture and Construction; 15

Science, Technology, Engineering, and Mathematics. **Career Pathways:** 2.1 Design/Pre-Construction; 15.2 Science and Mathematics. **Other Jobs in These Pathways:** Architects, Except Landscape and Naval; Architectural and Engineering Managers; Architectural Drafters; Biofuels/Biodiesel Technology and Product Development Managers; Biologists; Chemists; Civil Drafters; Civil Engineering Technicians; Clinical Research Coordinators; Community and Social Service Specialists, All Other; Dietitians and Nutritionists; Education, Training, and Library Workers, All Other; Electrical Drafters; Electronic Drafters; Engineering Technicians, Except Drafters, All Other; Engineers, All Other; Geodetic Surveyors; Geoscientists, Except Hydrologists and Geographers; Interior Designers; Mechanical Drafters; Medical Scientists, Except Epidemiologists; Natural Sciences Managers; Operations Research Analysts; Surveying Technicians; Water Resource Specialists; others.

**Skills**—Mathematics, Systems Analysis, Programming, Writing, Reading Comprehension, Learning Strategies, Instructing, Technology Design.

**Work Environment:** Indoors; sitting; using hands; repetitive motions.

# Cement Masons and Concrete Finishers

- ✳ Annual Earnings: $35,450
- ✳ Earnings Growth Potential: Low (34.8%)
- ✳ Growth: 12.9%
- ✳ Annual Job Openings: 7,640
- ✳ Self-Employed: 4.7%

**Considerations for Job Outlook:** Expected employment growth should result from new construction projects and from the need to repair and renovate existing highways, bridges, and other structures. Entry-level opportunities should be good.

**Smooth and finish surfaces of poured concrete, such as floors, walks, sidewalks, roads, or curbs, using a variety of hand and power tools. Align forms for sidewalks, curbs, or gutters; patch voids; and use saws to cut expansion joints.** Check the forms that hold the concrete to see that they are properly constructed. Set the forms that hold concrete to the desired pitch and depth and align them. Spread, level, and smooth concrete, using rake, shovel, hand or power trowel, hand or power screed, and float. Mold expansion joints and edges, using edging tools, jointers, and straightedge. Monitor how the wind, heat, or cold affect the curing of the concrete throughout the entire process. Signal truck driver to position truck to facilitate pouring concrete and move chute to direct concrete on forms. Produce rough concrete surface, using broom. Operate power vibrator to compact concrete. Direct the casting of the concrete and supervise laborers who use shovels or special tools to spread it. Mix cement, sand, and water to produce concrete, grout, or slurry, using hoe, trowel, tamper, scraper, or concrete-mixing machine. Cut out damaged areas, drill holes for reinforcing rods, and position reinforcing rods to repair concrete, using power saw and drill. Wet surface to prepare for bonding, fill holes and cracks with grout or slurry, and smooth, using trowel. Wet concrete surface and rub with stone to smooth surface and obtain specified finish. Clean chipped area, using wire brush, and feel and observe surface to determine if it is rough or uneven. Apply hardening and sealing compounds to cure surface of concrete and waterproof or restore surface. Chip, scrape, and grind high spots, ridges, and rough projections to finish concrete, using pneumatic chisels, power grinders, or hand tools. Spread roofing paper on surface of foundation and spread concrete onto roofing paper with trowel to form terrazzo base. Build wooden molds and clamp molds around area to be repaired, using hand tools. Sprinkle colored marble or stone chips, powdered steel, or coloring powder over surface to produce prescribed finish. Cut metal division strips and press them into terrazzo base so that top edges form desired design or pattern.

**Education/Training Required:** Moderate-term on-the-job training. **Education and Training Program:** Concrete Finishing/Concrete Finisher. **Knowledge/Courses**—Building and Construction, Mechanical, Engineering and Technology, Design, Chemistry, Physics.

**Personality Type:** Realistic-Enterprising. **Career Cluster:** 02 Architecture and Construction. **Career Pathway:** 2.2 Construction. **Other Jobs in This Pathway:** Brickmasons and Blockmasons; Construction and Building Inspectors; Construction Carpenters; Construction Laborers; Construction Managers; Cost Estimators; Drywall and Ceiling Tile Installers; Electrical Power-Line Installers and Repairers; Electricians; Engineering Technicians, Except Drafters, All Other; Excavating and Loading Machine and Dragline Operators; First-Line Supervisors of Construction Trades and Extraction Workers; Heating and Air Conditioning Mechanics and Installers; Helpers—Carpenters; Helpers—Electricians; Helpers—Pipelayers, Plumbers, Pipefitters, and Steamfitters; Highway Maintenance Workers; Operating Engineers and Other Construction Equipment Operators; Painters, Construction and Maintenance; Pipe Fitters and Steamfitters; Plumbers; Refrigeration Mechanics and

Installers; Roofers; Rough Carpenters; Solar Energy Installation Managers; others.

**Skills**—Operation and Control, Mathematics, Quality Control Analysis, Equipment Selection, Installation, Coordination.

**Work Environment:** Outdoors; standing; walking and running; kneeling, crouching, stooping, or crawling; using hands; bending or twisting the body; repetitive motions; noise; very hot or cold; bright or inadequate lighting; contaminants; whole-body vibration; hazardous equipment; minor burns, cuts, bites, or stings.

# Chemistry Teachers, Postsecondary

- ❋ Annual Earnings: $70,520
- ❋ Earnings Growth Potential: High (41.9%)
- ❋ Growth: 15.1%
- ❋ Annual Job Openings: 600
- ❋ Self-Employed: 0.2%

**Considerations for Job Outlook:** Enrollments in postsecondary institutions are expected to continue rising as more people attend college and as workers return to school to update their skills. Opportunities for part-time or temporary positions should be favorable, but significant competition exists for tenure-track positions.

**Teach courses pertaining to the chemical and physical properties and compositional changes of substances. Work may include instruction in the methods of qualitative and quantitative chemical analysis. Includes both teachers primarily engaged in teaching and those who do a combination of both teaching and research.** Prepare and deliver lectures to undergraduate and/or graduate students on topics such as organic chemistry, analytical chemistry, and chemical separation. Supervise students' laboratory work. Evaluate and grade students' classwork, laboratory performance, assignments, and papers. Compile, administer, and grade examinations or assign this work to others. Maintain student attendance records, grades, and other required records. Prepare course materials such as syllabi, homework assignments, and handouts. Maintain regularly scheduled office hours to advise and assist students. Plan, evaluate, and revise curricula, course content, course materials, and methods of instruction. Supervise undergraduate and/or graduate teaching, internships, and research work. Keep abreast of developments in the field by reading current literature, talking with colleagues, and participating in professional conferences. Initiate, facilitate, and moderate classroom discussions. Select and obtain materials and supplies such as textbooks and laboratory equipment. Conduct research in a particular field of knowledge and publish findings in professional journals, books, and/or electronic media. Advise students on academic and vocational curricula and on career issues. Collaborate with colleagues to address teaching and research issues. Serve on academic or administrative committees that deal with institutional policies, departmental matters, and academic issues. Write grant proposals to procure external research funding. Participate in student recruitment, registration, and placement activities. Prepare and submit required reports related to instruction. Perform administrative duties such as serving as a department head. Act as advisers to student organizations. Compile bibliographies of specialized materials for outside reading assignments. Participate in campus and community events. Provide professional consulting services to government and/or industry.

**Education/Training Required:** Doctoral degree. **Education and Training Programs:** Analytical Chemistry; Chemical Physics; Chemistry, General; Chemistry, Other; Geochemistry; Inorganic Chemistry; Organic Chemistry; Physical Chemistry; Polymer Chemistry. **Knowledge/Courses**—Chemistry, Biology, Physics, Education and Training, Mathematics, English Language.

**Personality Type:** Social-Investigative-Realistic. **Career Cluster:** 15 Science, Technology, Engineering, and Mathematics. **Career Pathway:** 15.2 Science and Mathematics. **Other Jobs in This Pathway:** Architectural and Engineering Managers; Biochemists and Biophysicists; Biofuels/Biodiesel Technology and Product Development Managers; Bioinformatics Scientists; Biological Scientists, All Other; Biologists; Biostatisticians; Chemists; Clinical Data Managers; Clinical Research Coordinators; Community and Social Service Specialists, All Other; Dietitians and Nutritionists; Education, Training, and Library Workers, All Other; Geneticists; Geoscientists, Except Hydrologists and Geographers; Medical Scientists, Except Epidemiologists; Molecular and Cellular Biologists; Natural Sciences Managers; Operations Research Analysts; Physical Scientists, All Other; Social Scientists and Related Workers, All Other; Statisticians; Survey Researchers; Transportation Planners; Water Resource Specialists; 37 other postsecondary teaching occupations; others.

**Skills**—Science, Reading Comprehension, Speaking, Writing, Learning Strategies, Instructing, Operations Analysis, Active Learning.

**Work Environment:** Indoors; sitting; contaminants; hazardous conditions.

# Chemists

- Annual Earnings: $68,320
- Earnings Growth Potential: High (42.5%)
- Growth: 2.5%
- Annual Job Openings: 3,000
- Self-Employed: 0.3%

**Considerations for Job Outlook:** Manufacturing companies' outsourcing of research and development and testing operations is expected to limit employment growth for these scientists. Most entry-level chemists should expect competition for jobs, particularly in declining chemical manufacturing industries.

**Conduct qualitative and quantitative chemical analyses or chemical experiments in laboratories for quality or process control or to develop new products or knowledge.** Analyze organic and inorganic compounds to determine chemical and physical properties, composition, structure, relationships, and reactions, utilizing chromatography, spectroscopy, and spectrophotometry techniques. Maintain laboratory instruments to ensure proper working order and troubleshoot malfunctions when needed. Develop, improve, and customize products, equipment, formulas, processes, and analytical methods. Conduct quality control tests. Direct, coordinate, and advise personnel in test procedures for analyzing components and physical properties of materials. Prepare test solutions, compounds, and reagents for laboratory personnel to conduct test. Compile and analyze test information to determine process or equipment operating efficiency and to diagnose malfunctions. Confer with scientists and engineers to conduct analyses of research projects, interpret test results, or develop nonstandard tests. Write technical papers and reports and prepare standards and specifications for processes, facilities, products, or tests. Induce changes in composition of substances by introducing heat, light, energy, and chemical catalysts for quantitative and qualitative analysis. Study effects of various methods of processing, preserving, and packaging on composition and properties of foods.

**Education/Training Required:** Bachelor's degree. **Education and Training Programs:** Analytical Chemistry; Chemical Physics; Chemistry, General; Chemistry, Other; Inorganic Chemistry; Organic Chemistry; Physical Chemistry; Polymer Chemistry. **Knowledge/Courses**—Chemistry, Physics, Mathematics, Production and Processing, Biology, Clerical.

**Personality Type:** Investigative-Realistic-Conventional. **Career Clusters:** 05 Education and Training; 15 Science,

Technology, Engineering, and Mathematics. **Career Pathways:** 5.3 Teaching/Training; 15.2 Science and Mathematics. **Other Jobs in These Pathways:** Adult Basic and Secondary Education and Literacy Teachers and Instructors; Architectural and Engineering Managers; Biofuels/Biodiesel Technology and Product Development Managers; Biologists; Career/Technical Education Teachers, Secondary School; Coaches and Scouts; Community and Social Service Specialists, All Other; Dietitians and Nutritionists; Education, Training, and Library Workers, All Other; Elementary School Teachers, Except Special Education; Fitness Trainers and Aerobics Instructors; Instructional Coordinators; Instructional Designers and Technologists; Kindergarten Teachers, Except Special Education; Librarians; Medical Scientists, Except Epidemiologists; Middle School Teachers, Except Special and Career/Technical Education; Operations Research Analysts; Preschool Teachers, Except Special Education; Recreation Workers; Secondary School Teachers, Except Special and Career/Technical Education; Self-Enrichment Education Teachers; Teacher Assistants; Teachers and Instructors, All Other; Tutors; others.

**Skills**—Science, Repairing, Equipment Maintenance, Mathematics, Reading Comprehension, Writing, Operations Analysis, Quality Control Analysis.

**Work Environment:** Indoors; sitting; contaminants; hazardous conditions.

# Chief Executives

- ❋ Annual Earnings: $165,080
- ❋ Earnings Growth Potential: Very high (54.5%)
- ❋ Growth: –1.4%
- ❋ Annual Job Openings: 11,250
- ❋ Self-Employed: 21.6%

**Considerations for Job Outlook:** The number of top executives is expected to remain steady, but employment may be adversely affected by consolidation and mergers. Keen competition is expected.

**Determine and formulate policies and provide the overall direction of companies or private and public sector organizations within the guidelines set up by a board of directors or similar governing body. Plan, direct, or coordinate operational activities at the highest level of management with the help of subordinate executives and staff managers.** Direct and coordinate an organization's financial and budget activities in order to fund operations, maximize investments, and increase efficiency. Confer with board members, organization officials, and staff members to discuss issues, coordinate activities, and resolve problems. Analyze operations to evaluate performance of a company and its staff in meeting objectives and to determine areas of potential cost reduction, program improvement, or policy change. Direct, plan, and implement policies, objectives, and activities of organizations or businesses in order to ensure continuing operations, to maximize returns on investments, and to increase productivity. Prepare budgets for approval, including those for funding and implementation of programs. Direct and coordinate activities of businesses or departments concerned with production, pricing, sales, and/or distribution of products. Negotiate or approve contracts and agreements with suppliers, distributors, federal and state agencies, and other organizational entities. Review reports submitted by staff members in order to recommend approval or to suggest changes. Appoint department heads or managers and assign or delegate responsibilities to them. Direct human resources activities, including the approval of human resource plans and activities, the selection of directors and other high-level staff, and establishment and organization of major departments. Preside over or serve on boards of directors, management committees, or other governing boards. Prepare and present reports concerning activities, expenses, budgets, government statutes and rulings, and other items affecting businesses or program services. Establish departmental responsibilities and coordinate functions among departments and sites. Implement corrective action plans to solve organizational or departmental problems.

**Education/Training Required:** Work experience plus degree. **Education and Training Programs:** Business Administration and Management, General; Business/Commerce, General; Entrepreneurship/Entrepreneurial Studies; International Business/Trade/Commerce; International Relations and Affairs; Public Administration; Public Administration and Social Service Professions, Other; Public Policy Analysis, General; Transportation/Mobility Management. **Knowledge/Courses**—Economics and Accounting, Administration and Management, Sales and Marketing, Personnel and Human Resources, Law and Government, Medicine and Dentistry.

**Personality Type:** Enterprising-Conventional. **Career Clusters:** 04 Business, Management, and Administration; 07 Government and Public Administration; 10 Human Services; 16 Transportation, Distribution, and Logistics. **Career Pathways:** 4.1 Management; 7.1 Governance; 7.3 Foreign Service; 7.6 Regulation; 10.3 Family and Community Services; 16.2 Logistics, Planning, and Management

Services. **Other Jobs in These Pathways:** Brownfield Redevelopment Specialists and Site Managers; Business Continuity Planners; Business Operations Specialists, All Other; Chief Sustainability Officers; Childcare Workers; Compliance Managers; Construction Managers; Customs Brokers; Energy Auditors; First-Line Supervisors of Office and Administrative Support Workers; General and Operations Managers; Investment Fund Managers; Loss Prevention Managers; Management Analysts; Managers, All Other; Nannies; Personal Care Aides; Regulatory Affairs Managers; Sales Managers; Security Management Specialists; Security Managers; Supply Chain Managers; Sustainability Specialists; Wind Energy Operations Managers; Wind Energy Project Managers; others.

**Skills**—Management of Financial Resources, Management of Material Resources, Management of Personnel Resources, Systems Evaluation, Systems Analysis, Judgment and Decision Making, Persuasion, Monitoring.

**Work Environment:** Indoors; sitting.

## Job Specialization: Chief Sustainability Officers

**Communicate and coordinate with management, shareholders, customers, and employees to address sustainability issues. Enact or oversee a corporate sustainability strategy.** Identify educational, training, or other development opportunities for sustainability employees or volunteers. Identify and evaluate pilot projects or programs to enhance the sustainability research agenda. Conduct sustainability- or environment-related risk assessments. Create and maintain sustainability program documents, such as schedules and budgets. Write project proposals, grant applications, or other documents to pursue funding for environmental initiatives. Supervise employees or volunteers working on sustainability projects. Write and distribute financial or environmental impact reports. Review sustainability program objectives, progress, or status to ensure compliance with policies, standards, regulations, or laws. Formulate or implement sustainability campaign or marketing strategies. Research environmental sustainability issues, concerns, or stakeholder interests. Evaluate and approve proposals for sustainability projects, considering factors such as cost effectiveness, technical feasibility, and integration with other initiatives. Develop sustainability reports, presentations, or proposals for supplier, employee, academia, media, government, public interest, or other groups. Develop, or oversee the development of, sustainability evaluation or monitoring systems. Develop, or oversee the development of, marketing or outreach media for sustainability projects or events. Develop methodologies to assess the viability or success of sustainability initiatives. Monitor and evaluate effectiveness of sustainability programs. Direct sustainability program operations to ensure compliance with environmental or governmental regulations. Develop or execute strategies to address issues such as energy use, resource conservation, recycling, pollution reduction, waste elimination, transportation, education, and building design.

**Education/Training Required:** Work experience plus degree. **Education and Training Programs:** Business Administration and Management, General; Business/Commerce, General; Entrepreneurship/Entrepreneurial Studies; International Business/Trade/Commerce; International Relations and Affairs; Public Administration; Public Administration and Social Service Professions, Other; Public Policy Analysis, General; Transportation/Mobility Management. **Knowledge/Courses**—No data available.

**Personality Type:** No data available. **Career Clusters:** 04 Business, Management, and Administration; 07 Government and Public Administration; 16 Transportation, Distribution, and Logistics. **Career Pathways:** 4.1 Management; 7.1 Governance; 16.2 Logistics, Planning, and Management Services. **Other Jobs in These Pathways:** Administrative Services Managers; Brownfield Redevelopment Specialists and Site Managers; Business Continuity Planners; Business Operations Specialists, All Other; Chief Executives; Compliance Managers; Computer and Information Systems Managers; Construction Managers; Customs Brokers; Energy Auditors; First-Line Supervisors of Office and Administrative Support Workers; General and Operations Managers; Investment Fund Managers; Loss Prevention Managers; Management Analysts; Managers, All Other; Public Relations Specialists; Regulatory Affairs Managers; Sales Managers; Security Management Specialists; Security Managers; Supply Chain Managers; Sustainability Specialists; Wind Energy Operations Managers; Wind Energy Project Managers; others.

**Skills**—No data available.

**Work Environment:** No data available.

# Child, Family, and School Social Workers

- ✿ Annual Earnings: $40,210
- ✿ Earnings Growth Potential: Low (34.9%)
- ✿ Growth: 12.3%
- ✿ Annual Job Openings: 10,960
- ✿ Self-Employed: 2.2%

**Considerations for Job Outlook:** The rapidly increasing elderly population is expected to spur demand for social services. Job prospects should be favorable because of the need to replace the many workers who are leaving the occupation permanently.

**Provide social services and assistance to improve the social and psychological functioning of children and their families and to maximize the family well-being and the academic functioning of children. May assist single parents, arrange adoptions, and find foster homes for abandoned or abused children. In schools, they address such problems as teenage pregnancy, misbehavior, and truancy. May also advise teachers on how to deal with problem children.** Interview clients individually, in families, or in groups, assessing their situations, capabilities, and problems, to determine what services are required to meet their needs. Counsel individuals, groups, families, or communities regarding issues including mental health, poverty, unemployment, substance abuse, physical abuse, rehabilitation, social adjustment, child care, or medical care. Maintain case history records and prepare reports. Counsel students whose behavior, school progress, or mental or physical impairment indicate a need for assistance, diagnosing students' problems and arranging for needed services. Consult with parents, teachers, and other school personnel to determine causes of problems such as truancy and misbehavior and to implement solutions. Counsel parents with child rearing problems, interviewing the child and family to determine whether further action is required. Develop and review service plans in consultation with clients and perform follow-ups assessing the quantity and quality of services provided. Collect supplementary information needed to assist clients, such as employment records, medical records, or school reports. Address legal issues, such as child abuse and discipline, assisting with hearings and providing testimony to inform custody arrangements. Provide, find, or arrange for support services, such as child care, homemaker service, prenatal care, substance abuse treatment, job training, counseling, or parenting classes, to prevent more serious problems from developing. Refer clients to community resources for services such as job placement, debt counseling, legal aid, housing, medical treatment, or financial assistance and provide concrete information, such as where to go and how to apply. Arrange for medical, psychiatric, and other tests that may disclose causes of difficulties and indicate remedial measures. Work in child and adolescent residential institutions. Administer welfare programs.

**Education/Training Required:** Bachelor's degree. **Education and Training Programs:** Juvenile Corrections; Social Work; Youth Services/Administration. **Knowledge/Courses**—Therapy and Counseling, Psychology, Philosophy and Theology, Sociology and Anthropology, Law and Government, Customer and Personal Service.

**Personality Type:** Social-Enterprising. **Career Clusters:** 10 Human Services; 12 Law, Public Safety, Corrections, and Security. **Career Pathways:** 10.3 Family and Community Services; 12.1 Correction Services. **Other Jobs in These Pathways:** Chief Executives; Childcare Workers; City and Regional Planning Aides; Counselors, All Other; Eligibility Interviewers, Government Programs; Farm and Home Management Advisors; First-Line Supervisors of Correctional Officers; First-Line Supervisors of Police and Detectives; Legislators; Managers, All Other; Marriage and Family Therapists; Nannies; Personal Care Aides; Probation Officers and Correctional Treatment Specialists; Protective Service Workers, All Other; Security Guards; Social and Community Service Managers; Social Science Research Assistants; Social Scientists and Related Workers, All Other; Social Workers, All Other; Sociologists; Supply Chain Managers.

**Skills**—Operations Analysis, Science, Social Perceptiveness, Service Orientation, Negotiation, Active Listening, Persuasion, Speaking.

**Work Environment:** Indoors; sitting.

# Childcare Workers

- ✿ Annual Earnings: $19,300
- ✿ Earnings Growth Potential: Very low (17.6%)
- ✿ Growth: 10.9%
- ✿ Annual Job Openings: 52,310
- ✿ Self-Employed: 32.4%

**Considerations for Job Outlook:** Increased emphasis on early childhood education should lead to employment growth for these workers. But growth is expected to be moderated by relatively slow growth in the population of children under age 5. The need to replace workers who leave the occupation permanently should create good job opportunities.

**Attend to children at schools, businesses, private households, and child care institutions. Perform a variety of tasks, such as dressing, feeding, bathing, and overseeing play.** Support children's emotional and social development, encouraging understanding of others and positive self-concepts. Care for children in institutional setting, such as group homes, nursery schools, private businesses, or schools for the handicapped. Sanitize toys and play equipment. Discipline children and recommend or initiate other measures to control behavior, such as caring for own clothing and picking up toys and books. Identify signs of emotional or developmental problems in children and bring them to parents' or guardians' attention. Observe and monitor children's play activities. Keep records on individual children, including daily observations and information about activities, meals served, and medications administered. Instruct children in health and personal habits such as eating, resting, and toilet habits. Read to children and teach them simple painting, drawing, handicrafts, and songs. Organize and participate in recreational activities, such as games. Assist in preparing food for children, serve meals and refreshments to children, and regulate rest periods. Organize and store toys and materials to ensure order in activity areas. Operate in-house daycare centers within businesses. Sterilize bottles and prepare formulas. Provide counseling or therapy to mentally disturbed, delinquent, or handicapped children. Dress children and change diapers. Help children with homework and school work. Perform housekeeping duties such as laundry, cleaning, dishwashing, and changing of linens. Accompany children to and from school, on outings, and to medical appointments. Place or hoist children into baths or pools.

**Education/Training Required:** Short-term on-the-job training. **Education and Training Program:** Child Care Provider/Assistant Training. **Knowledge/Courses**—Therapy and Counseling, Psychology.

**Personality Type:** Social-Artistic. **Career Cluster:** 10 Human Services. **Career Pathway:** 10.3 Family and Community Services. **Other Jobs in This Pathway:** Chief Executives; Child, Family, and School Social Workers; City and Regional Planning Aides; Counselors, All Other; Eligibility Interviewers, Government Programs; Farm and Home Management Advisors; Legislators; Managers, All Other; Marriage and Family Therapists; Nannies; Personal Care Aides; Probation Officers and Correctional Treatment Specialists; Protective Service Workers, All Other; Social and Community Service Managers; Social Science Research Assistants; Social Scientists and Related Workers, All Other; Social Workers, All Other; Sociologists; Supply Chain Managers.

**Skills**—Social Perceptiveness, Learning Strategies, Technology Design, Negotiation, Service Orientation, Instructing, Persuasion, Time Management.

**Work Environment:** More often indoors than outdoors; standing; walking and running; bending or twisting the body; noise; exposed to disease or infections.

## Job Specialization: Nannies

**Care for children in private households and provide support and expertise to parents in satisfying children's physical, emotional, intellectual, and social needs. Duties may include meal planning and preparation, laundry and clothing care, organization of play activities and outings, discipline, intellectual stimulation, language activities, and transportation.** Perform first aid or CPR when required. Regulate children's rest periods and nap schedules. Meet regularly with parents to discuss children's activities and development. Help prepare and serve nutritionally balanced meals and snacks for children. Instruct children in safe behavior, such as seeking adult assistance when crossing the street and avoiding contact or play with unsafe objects. Organize and conduct age-appropriate recreational activities, such as games, arts and crafts, sports, walks, and play dates. Observe children's behavior for irregularities, take temperature, transport children to doctor, or administer medications as directed to maintain children's health. Model appropriate social behaviors and encourage concern for others to cultivate development of interpersonal relationships and communication skills. Work with parents to develop and implement discipline programs to promote desirable child behavior. Help develop or monitor family schedule. Supervise and assist with homework. Assign appropriate chores and praise targeted behaviors to encourage development of self-control, self-confidence, and responsibility. Transport children to schools, social outings, and medical appointments. Perform housekeeping and cleaning duties related to children's care. Instruct and assist children in the development of health and personal habits, such as eating, resting, and toilet behavior. Keep records of play, meal schedules, and bill payment. Teach and perform age-appropriate activities such as lap play, reading, and arts and crafts to encourage intellectual development of children. Remove hazards and develop appropriate boundaries and rules to create a safe environment for children.

**Education/Training Required:** Short-term on-the-job training. **Education and Training Program:** Child Care

Provider/Assistant Training. **Knowledge/Courses**—Philosophy and Theology, Medicine and Dentistry, Geography, Therapy and Counseling, Sociology and Anthropology, Psychology.

**Personality Type:** Social-Artistic-Enterprising. **Career Cluster:** 10 Human Services. **Career Pathway:** 10.3 Family and Community Services. **Other Jobs in This Pathway:** Chief Executives; Child, Family, and School Social Workers; Childcare Workers; City and Regional Planning Aides; Counselors, All Other; Eligibility Interviewers, Government Programs; Farm and Home Management Advisors; Legislators; Managers, All Other; Marriage and Family Therapists; Personal Care Aides; Probation Officers and Correctional Treatment Specialists; Protective Service Workers, All Other; Social and Community Service Managers; Social Science Research Assistants; Social Scientists and Related Workers, All Other; Social Workers, All Other; Sociologists; Supply Chain Managers.

**Skills**—Service Orientation, Learning Strategies, Persuasion, Social Perceptiveness, Negotiation, Monitoring, Systems Evaluation, Complex Problem Solving.

**Work Environment:** More often indoors than outdoors; standing; using hands; exposed to disease or infections.

# Chiropractors

- ❋ Annual Earnings: $67,200
- ❋ Earnings Growth Potential: Very high (52.0%)
- ❋ Growth: 19.5%
- ❋ Annual Job Openings: 1,820
- ❋ Self-Employed: 44.5%

**Considerations for Job Outlook:** Projected growth stems from increasing consumer demand for alternative health care. Job prospects for new chiropractors are expected to be good, especially for those who enter a multidisciplined practice.

**Adjust spinal column and other articulations of the body to correct abnormalities of the human body believed to be caused by interference with the nervous system. Examine patients to determine nature and extent of disorders. Manipulate spines or other involved areas. May utilize supplementary measures such as exercise, rest, water, light, heat, and nutritional therapy.** Diagnose health problems by reviewing patients' health and medical histories; questioning, observing, and examining patients; and interpreting X-rays. Maintain accurate case histories of

patients. Evaluate the functioning of the neuromuscular-skeletal system and the spine, using systems of chiropractic diagnosis. Perform a series of manual adjustments to spines, or other articulations of the body, to correct musculoskeletal systems. Obtain and record patients' medical histories. Advise patients about recommended courses of treatment. Consult with and refer patients to appropriate health practitioners when necessary. Analyze X-rays to locate the sources of patients' difficulties and to rule out fractures or diseases as sources of problems. Counsel patients about nutrition, exercise, sleeping habits, stress management, and other matters. Arrange for diagnostic X-rays to be taken. Suggest and apply the use of supports such as straps, tapes, bandages, and braces if necessary.

**Education/Training Required:** First professional degree. **Education and Training Program:** Chiropractic (DC). **Knowledge/Courses**—Medicine and Dentistry, Therapy and Counseling, Biology, Psychology, Personnel and Human Resources, Sales and Marketing.

**Personality Type:** Social-Investigative-Realistic. **Career Cluster:** 08 Health Science. **Career Pathway:** 8.1 Therapeutic Services. **Other Jobs in This Pathway:** Clinical Psychologists; Community and Social Service Specialists, All Other; Counseling Psychologists; Dental Assistants; Dental Hygienists; Dentists, General; Health Technologists and Technicians, All Other; Healthcare Support Workers, All Other; Home Health Aides; Licensed Practical and Licensed Vocational Nurses; Low Vision Therapists, Orientation and Mobility Specialists, and Vision Rehabilitation Therapists; Massage Therapists; Medical and Clinical Laboratory Technicians; Medical and Health Services Managers; Medical Scientists, Except Epidemiologists; Medical Secretaries; Occupational Therapists; Pharmacists; Pharmacy Technicians; Radiologic Technologists; School Psychologists; Social and Human Service Assistants; Speech-Language Pathologists; Speech-Language Pathology Assistants; Substance Abuse and Behavioral Disorder Counselors; others.

**Skills**—Science, Service Orientation, Management of Financial Resources, Operations Analysis, Writing, Reading Comprehension, Systems Evaluation, Time Management.

**Work Environment:** Indoors; standing; using hands; bending or twisting the body; repetitive motions; exposed to disease or infections.

# Civil Engineering Technicians

- ❋ Annual Earnings: $46,290
- ❋ Earnings Growth Potential: Medium (37.2%)
- ❋ Growth: 16.9%
- ❋ Annual Job Openings: 3,280
- ❋ Self-Employed: 0.7%

**Considerations for Job Outlook:** Labor-saving efficiencies and the automation of many engineering support activities will limit the need for new engineering technicians. In general, opportunities should be best for job seekers who have an associate degree or other postsecondary training in engineering technology.

**Apply theory and principles of civil engineering in planning, designing, and overseeing construction and maintenance of structures and facilities under the direction of engineering staff or physical scientists.** Calculate dimensions, square footage, profile and component specifications, and material quantities, using calculator or computer. Draft detailed dimensional drawings and design layouts for projects and to ensure conformance to specifications. Analyze proposed site factors and design maps, graphs, tracings, and diagrams to illustrate findings. Read and review project blueprints and structural specifications to determine dimensions of structure or system and material requirements. Prepare reports and document project activities and data. Confer with supervisor to determine project details such as plan preparation, acceptance testing, and evaluation of field conditions. Inspect project site and evaluate contractor work to detect design malfunctions and ensure conformance to design specifications and applicable codes. Plan and conduct field surveys to locate new sites and analyze details of project sites. Develop plans and estimate costs for installation of systems, utilization of facilities, or construction of structures. Report maintenance problems occurring at project site to supervisor and negotiate changes to resolve system conflicts. Conduct materials test and analysis, using tools and equipment and applying engineering knowledge. Respond to public suggestions and complaints. Evaluate facility to determine suitability for occupancy and square footage availability.

**Education/Training Required:** Associate degree. **Education and Training Programs:** Civil Engineering Technology/Technician; Construction Engineering Technology/Technician. **Knowledge/Courses**—Building and Construction, Engineering and Technology, Design, Geography, Transportation, Physics.

**Personality Type:** Realistic-Conventional-Investigative. **Career Clusters:** 02 Architecture and Construction; 13 Manufacturing. **Career Pathways:** 2.1 Design/Pre-Construction; 13.3 Maintenance, Installation, and Repair. **Other Jobs in These Pathways:** Aircraft Mechanics and Service Technicians; Architects, Except Landscape and Naval; Architectural and Engineering Managers; Architectural Drafters; Automotive Specialty Technicians; Biological Technicians; Civil Drafters; Computer, Automated Teller, and Office Machine Repairers; Electrical and Electronic Equipment Assemblers; Electrical and Electronics Repairers, Commercial and Industrial Equipment; Electrical Engineering Technicians; Electrical Engineering Technologists; Electromechanical Engineering Technologists; Electronics Engineering Technicians; Electronics Engineering Technologists; Engineering Technicians, Except Drafters, All Other; Engineers, All Other; Fuel Cell Technicians; Helpers—Installation, Maintenance, and Repair Workers; Industrial Machinery Mechanics; Installation, Maintenance, and Repair Workers, All Other; Mechanical Drafters; Mobile Heavy Equipment Mechanics, Except Engines; Telecommunications Line Installers and Repairers; Tire Repairers and Changers; others.

**Skills**—Operations Analysis, Mathematics, Operation Monitoring, Operation and Control, Science, Management of Financial Resources, Management of Material Resources, Active Listening.

**Work Environment:** More often indoors than outdoors; sitting; using hands; repetitive motions.

# Civil Engineers

- ❋ Annual Earnings: $77,560
- ❋ Earnings Growth Potential: Low (34.8%)
- ❋ Growth: 24.3%
- ❋ Annual Job Openings: 11,460
- ❋ Self-Employed: 4.3%

**Considerations for Job Outlook:** Civil engineers are expected to have employment growth of 24 percent from 2008–2018, much faster than the average for all occupations. Spurred by general population growth and the related need to improve the nation's infrastructure, more civil engineers will be needed to design and construct or expand transportation, water supply, and pollution control systems, and buildings and building complexes. They also will be needed to repair or replace existing roads, bridges, and other public structures. Because construction industries and architectural, engineering, and related services employ many civil engineers, employment opportunities will vary by geographic area and may decrease during economic slowdowns, when construction is often curtailed.

**Perform engineering duties in planning, designing, and overseeing construction and maintenance of building structures and facilities such as roads, railroads, airports, bridges, harbors, channels, dams, irrigation projects, pipelines, power plants, water and sewage systems, and waste disposal units. Includes architectural, structural, traffic, ocean, and geo-technical engineers.** Manage and direct staff members and construction, operations, or maintenance activities at project site. Provide technical advice regarding design, construction, or program modifications and structural repairs to industrial and managerial personnel. Inspect project sites to monitor progress and ensure conformance to design specifications and safety or sanitation standards. Estimate quantities and cost of materials, equipment, or labor to determine project feasibility. Test soils and materials to determine the adequacy and strength of foundations, concrete, asphalt, or steel. Compute load and grade requirements, water flow rates, and material stress factors to determine design specifications. Plan and design transportation or hydraulic systems and structures, following construction and government standards and using design software and drawing tools. Analyze survey reports, maps, drawings, blueprints, aerial photography, and other topographical or geologic data to plan projects. Prepare or present public reports on topics such as bid proposals, deeds, environmental impact statements, or property and right-of-way descriptions. Direct or participate in surveying to lay out installations and establish reference points, grades, and elevations to guide construction. Conduct studies of traffic patterns or environmental conditions to identify engineering problems and assess the potential impact of projects.

**Education/Training Required:** Bachelor's degree. **Education and Training Programs:** Civil Engineering, General; Civil Engineering, Other; Transportation and Highway Engineering; Water Resources Engineering. **Knowledge/Courses**—Engineering and Technology, Building and Construction, Design, Physics, Transportation, Geography.

**Personality Type:** Realistic-Investigative-Conventional. **Career Cluster:** 15 Science, Technology, Engineering, and Mathematics. **Career Pathway:** 15.1 Engineering and Technology. **Other Jobs in This Pathway:** Architectural and Engineering Managers; Automotive Engineers; Biochemical Engineers; Biofuels/Biodiesel Technology and Product Development Managers; Cost Estimators; Education, Training, and Library Workers, All Other; Electrical Engineers; Electronics Engineers, Except Computer; Energy Engineers;

Engineers, All Other; Fuel Cell Engineers; Human Factors Engineers and Ergonomists; Industrial Engineers; Manufacturing Engineers; Mechanical Engineers; Mechatronics Engineers; Microsystems Engineers; Nanosystems Engineers; Photonics Engineers; Radio Frequency Identification Device Specialists; Robotics Engineers; Solar Energy Systems Engineers; Transportation Engineers; Validation Engineers; Wind Energy Engineers; others.

**Skills**—Operations Analysis, Mathematics, Science, Management of Financial Resources, Management of Material Resources, Programming, Systems Evaluation, Systems Analysis.

**Work Environment:** Indoors; sitting.

## Job Specialization: Transportation Engineers

**Develop plans for surface transportation projects according to established engineering standards and state or federal construction policy. Prepare plans, estimates, or specifications to design transportation facilities. Plan alterations and modifications of existing streets, highways, or freeways to improve traffic flow.** Prepare data, maps, or other information at construction-related public hearings and meetings. Review development plans to determine potential traffic impact. Prepare administrative, technical, or statistical reports on traffic-operation matters, such as accidents, safety measures, and pedestrian volume and practices. Evaluate transportation systems or traffic control devices and lighting systems to determine need for modification or expansion. Evaluate traffic control devices or lighting systems to determine need for modification or expansion. Develop, or assist in the development of, transportation-related computer software or computer processes. Prepare project budgets, schedules, or specifications for labor and materials. Prepare final project layout drawings that include details such as stress calculations. Plan alteration and modification of existing transportation structures to improve safety or function. Participate in contract bidding, negotiation, or administration. Model transportation scenarios to evaluate the impacts of activities such as new development or to identify possible solutions to transportation problems. Investigate traffic problems and recommend methods to improve traffic flow and safety. Investigate or test specific construction project materials to determine compliance to specifications or standards. Inspect completed transportation projects to ensure safety or compliance with applicable standards or regulations. Direct the surveying, staking, and laying-out of construction projects. Estimate transportation project costs. Confer with contractors, utility companies, or government agencies to discuss plans, specifications, or work schedules. Check construction plans, design calculations, or cost estimations to ensure completeness, accuracy, and conformity to engineering standards and practices. Analyze environmental impact statements for transportation projects.

**Education/Training Required:** Bachelor's degree. **Education and Training Programs:** Civil Engineering, General; Civil Engineering, Other; Transportation and Highway Engineering; Water Resources Engineering. **Knowledge/ Courses**—No data available.

**Personality Type:** Realistic-Investigative. **Career Cluster:** 15 Science, Technology, Engineering, and Mathematics. **Career Pathway:** 15.1 Engineering and Technology. **Other Jobs in This Pathway:** Architectural and Engineering Managers; Automotive Engineers; Biochemical Engineers; Biofuels/Biodiesel Technology and Product Development Managers; Civil Engineers; Cost Estimators; Education, Training, and Library Workers, All Other; Electrical Engineers; Electronics Engineers, Except Computer; Energy Engineers; Engineers, All Other; Fuel Cell Engineers; Human Factors Engineers and Ergonomists; Industrial Engineers; Manufacturing Engineers; Mechanical Engineers; Mechatronics Engineers; Microsystems Engineers; Nanosystems Engineers; Photonics Engineers; Radio Frequency Identification Device Specialists; Robotics Engineers; Solar Energy Systems Engineers; Validation Engineers; Wind Energy Engineers; others.

**Skills**—No data available.

**Work Environment:** No data available.

# Claims Adjusters, Examiners, and Investigators

- ❀ Annual Earnings: $58,620
- ❀ Earnings Growth Potential: Medium (39.1%)
- ❀ Growth: 7.1%
- ❀ Annual Job Openings: 9,560
- ❀ Self-Employed: 1.6%

**Considerations for Job Outlook:** Job growth for adjusters and claims examiners should grow along with the growth of the healthcare industry. Employment growth for insurance investigators should be tempered by productivity increases associated with the Internet. Keen competition is expected for investigator jobs.

## Job Specialization: Claims Examiners, Property and Casualty Insurance

**Review settled insurance claims to determine that payments and settlements have been made in accordance with company practices and procedures. Report overpayments, underpayments, and other irregularities. Confer with legal counsel on claims requiring litigation.** Investigate, evaluate, and settle claims, applying technical knowledge and human relations skills to effect fair and prompt disposal of cases and to contribute to a reduced loss ratio. Pay and process claims within designated authority level. Adjust reserves or provide reserve recommendations to ensure that reserve activities are consistent with corporate policies. Enter claim payments, reserves, and new claims on computer system, inputting concise yet sufficient file documentation. Resolve complex severe exposure claims, using high-service-oriented file handling. Maintain claim files such as records of settled claims and an inventory of claims requiring detailed analysis. Verify and analyze data used in settling claims to ensure that claims are valid and that settlements are made according to company practices and procedures. Examine claims investigated by insurance adjusters, further investigating questionable claims to determine whether to authorize payments. Present cases and participate in their discussion at claim committee meetings. Contact or interview claimants, doctors, medical specialists, or employers to get additional information. Confer with legal counsel on claims requiring litigation. Report overpayments, underpayments, and other irregularities. Communicate with reinsurance brokers to obtain information necessary for processing claims. Supervise claims adjusters to ensure that adjusters have followed proper methods. Conduct detailed bill reviews to implement sound litigation management and expense control. Prepare reports to be submitted to company's data-processing department.

**Education/Training Required:** Long-term on-the-job training. **Education and Training Programs:** Health/Medical Claims Examiner Training; Insurance. **Knowledge/ Courses**—Customer and Personal Service, Law and Government, Building and Construction, Administration and Management, English Language, Clerical.

**Personality Type:** Conventional-Enterprising. **Career Cluster:** 06 Finance. **Career Pathway:** 6.4 Insurance Services. **Other Jobs in This Pathway:** Actuaries; Insurance Adjusters, Examiners, and Investigators; Insurance Appraisers, Auto Damage; Insurance Sales Agents; Insurance Underwriters; Telemarketers.

Skills—Negotiation, Persuasion, Reading Comprehension, Service Orientation, Writing, Management of Financial Resources, Critical Thinking, Mathematics.

Work Environment: Indoors; sitting; repetitive motions; noise.

## Job Specialization: Insurance Adjusters, Examiners, and Investigators

Investigate, analyze, and determine the extent of insurance company's liability concerning personal, casualty, or property loss or damages and attempt to effect settlement with claimants. Correspond with or interview medical specialists, agents, witnesses, or claimants to compile information. Calculate benefit payments and approve payment of claims within a certain monetary limit. Interview or correspond with claimant and witnesses, consult police and hospital records, and inspect property damage to determine extent of liability. Investigate and assess damage to property. Examine claims forms and other records to determine insurance coverage. Analyze information gathered by investigation and report findings and recommendations. Negotiate claim settlements and recommend litigation when settlement cannot be negotiated. Collect evidence to support contested claims in court. Prepare report of findings of investigation. Interview or correspond with agents and claimants to correct errors or omissions and to investigate questionable claims. Refer questionable claims to investigator or claims adjuster for investigation or settlement. Examine titles to property to determine validity and act as company agent in transactions with property owners. Obtain credit information from banks and other credit services. Communicate with former associates to verify employment record and to obtain background information regarding persons or businesses applying for credit.

Education/Training Required: Long-term on-the-job training. Education and Training Programs: Health/Medical Claims Examiner Training; Insurance. Knowledge/Courses—Customer and Personal Service, Clerical, Building and Construction, English Language, Law and Government, Mathematics.

Personality Type: Conventional-Enterprising. Career Cluster: 06 Finance. Career Pathway: 6.4 Insurance Services. Other Jobs in This Pathway: Actuaries; Claims Examiners, Property and Casualty Insurance; Insurance Appraisers, Auto Damage; Insurance Sales Agents; Insurance Underwriters; Telemarketers.

Skills—Management of Financial Resources, Negotiation, Mathematics, Critical Thinking, Active Listening, Speaking, Reading Comprehension, Writing.

Work Environment: Indoors; sitting; repetitive motions.

## Clergy

- ❋ Annual Earnings: $43,970
- ❋ Earnings Growth Potential: High (44.9%)
- ❋ Growth: 12.7%
- ❋ Annual Job Openings: 21,770
- ❋ Self-Employed: 0.1%

Considerations for Job Outlook: About average employment growth is projected.

Conduct religious worship and perform other spiritual functions associated with beliefs and practices of religious faith or denomination. Provide spiritual and moral guidance and assistance to members. Pray and promote spirituality. Read from sacred texts such as the Bible, Torah, or Koran. Prepare and deliver sermons and other talks. Organize and lead regular religious services. Share information about religious issues by writing articles, giving speeches, or teaching. Instruct people who seek conversion to a particular faith. Visit people in homes, hospitals, and prisons to provide them with comfort and support. Counsel individuals and groups concerning their spiritual, emotional, and personal needs. Train leaders of church, community, and youth groups. Administer religious rites or ordinances. Study and interpret religious laws, doctrines, or traditions. Conduct special ceremonies such as weddings, funerals, and confirmations. Plan and lead religious education programs for congregation. Respond to requests for assistance during emergencies or crises. Devise ways in which congregation membership can be expanded. Collaborate with committees and individuals to address financial and administrative issues pertaining to congregation. Prepare people for participation in religious ceremonies. Perform administrative duties such as overseeing building management, ordering supplies, contracting for services and repairs, and supervising the work of staff members and volunteers. Refer people to community support services, psychologists, and doctors as necessary. Participate in fundraising activities to support congregation activities and facilities. Organize and engage in interfaith, community, civic, educational, and recreational activities sponsored by or related to their religion.

Education/Training Required: Master's degree. Education and Training Programs: Clinical Pastoral Counseling/

Patient Counseling; Divinity/Ministry (BD, MDiv.); Pastoral Counseling and Specialized Ministries, Other; Pastoral Studies/Counseling; Philosophy; Pre-Theology/Pre-Ministerial Studies; Rabbinical Studies (M.H.L./Rav); Religion/Religious Studies; Theological and Ministerial Studies, Other; Theology and Religious Vocations, Other; Theology/Theological Studies; Youth Ministry. **Knowledge/Courses**—Philosophy and Theology, Therapy and Counseling, Sociology and Anthropology, Psychology, Public Safety and Security, Customer and Personal Service.

**Personality Type:** Social-Enterprising-Artistic. **Career Cluster:** 10 Human Services. **Career Pathway:** 10.2 Counseling and Mental Health Services. **Other Jobs in This Pathway:** Clinical Psychologists; Counseling Psychologists; Counselors, All Other; Directors, Religious Activities and Education; Epidemiologists; Health Educators; Healthcare Social Workers; Marriage and Family Therapists; Mental Health and Substance Abuse Social Workers; Mental Health Counselors; Music Directors; Psychologists, All Other; Recreation Workers; Religious Workers, All Other; School Psychologists; Substance Abuse and Behavioral Disorder Counselors.

**Skills**—Management of Financial Resources, Social Perceptiveness, Persuasion, Negotiation, Learning Strategies, Management of Material Resources, Service Orientation, Systems Evaluation.

**Work Environment:** Indoors; sitting.

# Clinical, Counseling, and School Psychologists

- ❊ Annual Earnings: $66,810
- ❊ Earnings Growth Potential: High (41.6%)
- ❊ Growth: 11.1%
- ❊ Annual Job Openings: 5,990
- ❊ Self-Employed: 34.1%

**Considerations for Job Outlook:** Employment growth is expected due to increased emphasis on mental health in a variety of specializations, including school counseling, depression, and substance abuse. Job seekers with a doctoral degree should have the best opportunities.

## Job Specialization: Clinical Psychologists

**Diagnose or evaluate mental and emotional disorders of individuals through observation, interview, and psychological tests and formulate and administer programs of treatment.** Identify psychological, emotional, or behavioral issues and diagnose disorders, using information obtained from interviews, tests, records, and reference materials. Develop and implement individual treatment plans, specifying type, frequency, intensity, and duration of therapy. Interact with clients to assist them in gaining insight, defining goals, and planning action to achieve effective personal, social, educational, and vocational development and adjustment. Discuss the treatment of problems with clients. Utilize a variety of treatment methods such as psychotherapy, hypnosis, behavior modification, stress reduction therapy, psychodrama, and play therapy. Counsel individuals and groups regarding problems such as stress, substance abuse, and family situations to modify behavior or to improve personal, social, and vocational adjustment. Write reports on clients and maintain required paperwork. Evaluate the effectiveness of counseling or treatments and the accuracy and completeness of diagnoses; then modify plans and diagnoses as necessary. Obtain and study medical, psychological, social, and family histories by interviewing individuals, couples, or families and by reviewing records. Consult reference material such as textbooks, manuals, and journals to identify symptoms, make diagnoses, and develop approaches to treatment. Maintain current knowledge of relevant research. Observe individuals at play, in group interactions, or in other contexts to detect indications of mental deficiency, abnormal behavior, or maladjustment. Select, administer, score, and interpret psychological tests to obtain information on individuals' intelligence, achievements, interests, and personalities. Refer clients to other specialists, institutions, or support services as necessary. Develop, direct, and participate in training programs for staff and students.

**Education/Training Required:** Doctoral degree. **Education and Training Programs:** Psychoanalysis and Psychotherapy; Psychology, General. **Knowledge/Courses**—Therapy and Counseling, Psychology, Sociology and Anthropology, Philosophy and Theology, Customer and Personal Service, Medicine and Dentistry.

**Personality Type:** Investigative-Social-Artistic. **Career Clusters:** 08 Health Science; 10 Human Services. **Career Pathways:** 8.1 Therapeutic Services; 8.3 Health Informatics; 10.2 Counseling and Mental Health Services. **Other Jobs in These Pathways:** Clergy; Counseling Psychologists; Dental Assistants; Dental Hygienists; Engineers, All Other; Executive Secretaries and Executive Administrative Assistants; First-Line Supervisors of Office and Administrative Support Workers; Healthcare Support Workers, All Other; Home Health Aides; Licensed Practical and Licensed

Vocational Nurses; Medical and Clinical Laboratory Technicians; Medical and Health Services Managers; Medical Assistants; Medical Records and Health Information Technicians; Medical Secretaries; Pharmacists; Pharmacy Technicians; Physical Therapists; Public Relations Specialists; Radiologic Technologists; Receptionists and Information Clerks; Recreation Workers; School Psychologists; Social and Human Service Assistants; Speech-Language Pathology Assistants; others.

**Skills**—Science, Social Perceptiveness, Active Listening, Operations Analysis, Learning Strategies, Speaking, Reading Comprehension, Service Orientation.

**Work Environment:** Indoors; sitting.

## Job Specialization: Counseling Psychologists

**Assess and evaluate individuals' problems through the use of case history, interview, and observation and provide individual or group counseling services to assist individuals in achieving more effective personal, social, educational, and vocational development and adjustment.** Collect information about individuals or clients, using interviews, case histories, observational techniques, and other assessment methods. Counsel individuals, groups, or families to help them understand problems, define goals, and develop realistic action plans. Develop therapeutic and treatment plans based on clients' interests, abilities, and needs. Consult with other professionals to discuss therapies, treatments, counseling resources, or techniques and to share occupational information. Analyze data such as interview notes, test results, and reference manuals in order to identify symptoms and to diagnose the nature of clients' problems. Advise clients on how they could be helped by counseling. Evaluate the results of counseling methods to determine the reliability and validity of treatments. Provide consulting services to schools, social service agencies, and businesses. Refer clients to specialists or to other institutions for non-counseling treatment of problems. Select, administer, and interpret psychological tests to assess intelligence, aptitudes, abilities, or interests. Conduct research to develop or improve diagnostic or therapeutic counseling techniques.

**Education/Training Required:** Doctoral degree. **Education and Training Programs:** Psychoanalysis and Psychotherapy; Psychology, General. **Knowledge/Courses**—Therapy and Counseling, Philosophy and Theology, Sociology and Anthropology, Psychology, English Language, Customer and Personal Service.

**Personality Type:** Social-Investigative-Artistic. **Career Clusters:** 08 Health Science; 10 Human Services. **Career Pathways:** 8.1 Therapeutic Services; 10.2 Counseling and Mental Health Services. **Other Jobs in These Pathways:** Clergy; Clinical Psychologists; Community and Social Service Specialists, All Other; Dental Assistants; Dental Hygienists; Dentists, General; Healthcare Social Workers; Healthcare Support Workers, All Other; Home Health Aides; Licensed Practical and Licensed Vocational Nurses; Massage Therapists; Medical and Clinical Laboratory Technicians; Medical and Health Services Managers; Medical Scientists, Except Epidemiologists; Medical Secretaries; Mental Health and Substance Abuse Social Workers; Mental Health Counselors; Pharmacists; Pharmacy Technicians; Radiologic Technologists; Recreation Workers; School Psychologists; Social and Human Service Assistants; Speech-Language Pathologists; Speech-Language Pathology Assistants; others.

**Skills**—Social Perceptiveness, Science, Negotiation, Active Listening, Operations Analysis, Service Orientation, Learning Strategies, Speaking.

**Work Environment:** Indoors; sitting.

## Job Specialization: School Psychologists

**Investigate processes of learning and teaching and develop psychological principles and techniques applicable to educational problems.** Compile and interpret students' test results, along with information from teachers and parents, to diagnose conditions and to help assess eligibility for special services. Report any pertinent information to the proper authorities in cases of child endangerment, neglect, or abuse. Assess an individual child's needs, limitations, and potential, using observation, review of school records, and consultation with parents and school personnel. Select, administer, and score psychological tests. Provide consultation to parents, teachers, administrators, and others on topics such as learning styles and behavior modification techniques. Promote an understanding of child development and its relationship to learning and behavior. Collaborate with other educational professionals to develop teaching strategies and school programs. Counsel children and families to help solve conflicts and problems in learning and adjustment. Develop individualized educational plans in collaboration with teachers and other staff members. Maintain student records, including special education reports, confidential records, records of services provided, and behavioral data. Serve as a resource to help families and schools deal with crises, such as separation and loss. Attend workshops, seminars, or professional meetings to remain informed of new developments in school psychology. Design classes and programs to meet the needs of special students. Refer students and their families to appropriate community agencies for medical, vocational, or social services. Initiate and direct efforts to foster tolerance, understanding, and appreciation of diversity in school communities. Collect and analyze data to evaluate the effectiveness of academic programs and other services, such as behavioral management systems. Provide educational programs on topics such as classroom management, teaching strategies, or parenting skills.

**Education/Training Required:** Doctoral degree. **Education and Training Programs:** Psychoanalysis and Psychotherapy; Psychology, General. **Knowledge/Courses**—Therapy and Counseling, Psychology, Sociology and Anthropology, Education and Training, Foreign Language, Mathematics.

**Personality Type:** Investigative-Social. **Career Clusters:** 08 Health Science; 10 Human Services. **Career Pathways:** 8.1 Therapeutic Services; 10.2 Counseling and Mental Health Services. **Other Jobs in These Pathways:** Clergy; Clinical Psychologists; Community and Social Service Specialists, All Other; Counseling Psychologists; Dental Assistants; Dental Hygienists; Dentists, General; Healthcare Social Workers; Healthcare Support Workers, All Other; Home Health Aides; Licensed Practical and Licensed Vocational Nurses; Massage Therapists; Medical and Clinical Laboratory Technicians; Medical and Health Services Managers; Medical Scientists, Except Epidemiologists; Medical Secretaries; Mental Health and Substance Abuse Social Workers; Mental Health Counselors; Pharmacists; Pharmacy Technicians; Radiologic Technologists; Recreation Workers; Social and Human Service Assistants; Speech-Language Pathologists; Speech-Language Pathology Assistants; others.

**Skills**—Social Perceptiveness, Learning Strategies, Writing, Judgment and Decision Making, Reading Comprehension, Negotiation, Active Listening, Systems Evaluation.

**Work Environment:** Indoors; sitting.

# Coaches and Scouts

- ❋ Annual Earnings: $28,340
- ❋ Earnings Growth Potential: High (42.2%)
- ❋ Growth: 24.8%
- ❋ Annual Job Openings: 9,920
- ❋ Self-Employed: 16.2%

**Considerations for Job Outlook:** Employment is expected to grow as more people participate in organized sports. Opportunities should be best for part-time umpires, referees, and other sports officials at the high school level.

**Instruct or coach groups or individuals in the fundamentals of sports. Demonstrate techniques and methods of participation. May evaluate athletes' strengths and weaknesses as possible recruits or to improve the athletes' technique to prepare them for competition.** Plan, organize, and conduct practice sessions. Provide training direction, encouragement, and motivation to prepare athletes for games, competitive events, or tours. Identify and recruit potential athletes, arranging and offering incentives such as athletic scholarships. Plan strategies and choose team members for individual games or sports seasons. Plan and direct physical conditioning programs that will enable athletes to achieve maximum performance. Adjust coaching techniques based on the strengths and weaknesses of athletes. File scouting reports that detail player assessments, provide recommendations on athlete recruitment, and identify locations and individuals to be targeted for future recruitment efforts. Keep records of athlete, team, and opposing team performance. Instruct individuals or groups in sports rules, game strategies, and performance principles such as specific ways of moving the body, hands, and feet in order to achieve desired results. Analyze the strengths and weaknesses of opposing teams to develop game strategies. Evaluate athletes' skills and review performance records to determine their fitness and potential in a particular area of athletics. Keep abreast of changing rules, techniques, technologies, and philosophies relevant to their sport. Monitor athletes' use of equipment to ensure safe and proper use. Explain and enforce safety rules and regulations. Develop and arrange competition schedules and programs. Serve as organizer, leader, instructor, or referee for outdoor and indoor games such as volleyball, football, and soccer. Explain and demonstrate the use of sports and training equipment, such as trampolines or weights. Perform activities that support a team or a specific sport, such as meeting with media representatives and appearing at fundraising events. Arrange and conduct sports-related activities such as training camps, skill-improvement courses, clinics, or pre-season try-outs.

**Education/Training Required:** Long-term on-the-job training. **Education and Training Programs:** Health and Physical Education, General; Physical Education Teaching and Coaching; Sport and Fitness Administration/Management. **Knowledge/Courses**—Psychology, Therapy and Counseling, Education and Training, Sales and Marketing, Personnel and Human Resources, Sociology and Anthropology.

**Personality Type:** Social-Realistic-Enterprising. **Career Cluster:** 05 Education and Training. **Career Pathways:** 5.1 Administration and Administrative Support; 5.3 Teaching/Training. **Other Jobs in These Pathways:** Adult Basic and Secondary Education and Literacy Teachers and Instructors; Career/Technical Education Teachers, Secondary School; Chemists; Dietitians and Nutritionists; Distance Learning Coordinators; Education Administrators, All Other; Education Administrators, Elementary and Secondary School; Education Administrators, Postsecondary; Education Administrators, Preschool and Childcare Center/Program; Elementary School Teachers, Except Special Education; Fitness and Wellness Coordinators; Fitness Trainers and Aerobics Instructors; Instructional Coordinators; Instructional Designers and Technologists; Interpreters and Translators; Kindergarten Teachers, Except Special Education; Librarians; Middle School Teachers, Except Special and Career/Technical Education; Preschool Teachers, Except Special Education; Recreation Workers; Secondary School Teachers, Except Special and Career/Technical Education; Self-Enrichment Education Teachers; Teacher Assistants; Teachers and Instructors, All Other; Tutors; others.

**Skills**—Management of Personnel Resources, Systems Evaluation, Monitoring, Instructing, Management of Material Resources, Learning Strategies, Negotiation, Social Perceptiveness.

**Work Environment:** More often indoors than outdoors; standing; walking and running; noise.

# Combined Food Preparation and Serving Workers, Including Fast Food

* Annual Earnings: $17,950
* Earnings Growth Potential: Very low (12.8%)
* Growth: 14.6%
* Annual Job Openings: 96,720
* Self-Employed: 0.1%

**Considerations for Job Outlook:** Job growth is projected due to an expanding population and the continued popularity of dining out. Opportunities should be excellent.

**Perform duties that combine food preparation and food service.** Accept payment from customers and make change as necessary. Request and record customer orders and compute bills, using cash registers, multicounting machines, or pencil and paper. Clean and organize eating and service areas. Serve customers in eating places that specialize in fast service and inexpensive carry-out food. Prepare and serve cold drinks or frozen milk drinks or desserts, using drink-dispensing, milkshake, or frozen custard machines. Select food items from serving or storage areas and place them in dishes, on serving trays, or in takeout bags. Prepare simple foods and beverages such as sandwiches, salads, and coffee. Notify kitchen personnel of shortages or special orders. Cook or reheat food items such as french fries. Wash dishes, glassware, and silverware after meals. Collect and return dirty dishes to the kitchen for washing. Relay food orders to cooks. Distribute food to servers. Serve food and beverages to guests at banquets or other social functions. Provide caterers with assistance in food preparation or service. Pack food, dishes, utensils, tablecloths, and accessories for transportation from catering or food preparation establishments to locations designated by customers. Arrange tables and decorations according to instructions.

**Education/Training Required:** Short-term on-the-job training. **Education and Training Programs:** Food Preparation/Professional Cooking/Kitchen Assistant Training; Institutional Food Worker Training. **Knowledge/Courses**—Food Production, Sales and Marketing.

**Personality Type:** Conventional-Realistic-Enterprising. **Career Cluster:** 09 Hospitality and Tourism. **Career Pathway:** 9.1 Restaurants and Food/Beverage Services. **Other Jobs in This Pathway:** Bakers; Baristas; Bartenders; Butchers and Meat Cutters; Chefs and Head Cooks; Cooks, All Other; Cooks, Fast Food; Cooks, Institution and Cafeteria; Cooks, Private Household; Cooks, Restaurant; Cooks, Short Order; Counter Attendants, Cafeteria, Food Concession, and Coffee Shop; Dining Room and Cafeteria Attendants and Bartender Helpers; Dishwashers; First-Line Supervisors of Food Preparation and Serving Workers; Food Preparation and Serving Related Workers, All Other; Food Preparation Workers; Food Servers, Nonrestaurant; Food Service Managers; Gaming Managers; Hosts and Hostesses, Restaurant, Lounge, and Coffee Shop; Meat, Poultry, and Fish Cutters and Trimmers; Slaughterers and Meat Packers; Waiters and Waitresses.

**Skills**—Operation and Control.

**Work Environment:** Indoors; standing; walking and running; using hands; repetitive motions; very hot or cold; minor burns, cuts, bites, or stings.

# Commercial and Industrial Designers

- ❋ Annual Earnings: $58,230
- ❋ Earnings Growth Potential: High (43.0%)
- ❋ Growth: 9.0%
- ❋ Annual Job Openings: 1,760
- ❋ Self-Employed: 26.7%

**Considerations for Job Outlook:** An increase in demand for new and upgraded products should lead to job growth for these workers, but this growth is expected to be tempered by the use of design firms abroad. Keen competition is expected.

**Develop and design manufactured products, such as cars, home appliances, and children's toys. Combine artistic talent with research on product use, marketing, and materials to create the most functional and appealing product design.** Prepare sketches of ideas, detailed drawings, illustrations, artwork, or blueprints, using drafting instruments, paints and brushes, or computer-aided design equipment. Direct and coordinate the fabrication of models or samples and the drafting of working drawings and specification sheets from sketches. Modify and refine designs, using working models, to conform with customer specifications, production limitations, or changes in design trends. Coordinate the look and function of product lines. Confer with engineering, marketing, production, or sales departments, or with customers, to establish and evaluate design concepts for manufactured products. Present designs and reports to customers or design committees for approval and discuss need for modification. Evaluate feasibility of design ideas based on factors such as appearance, safety, function, serviceability, budget, production costs/methods, and market characteristics. Read publications, attend showings, and study competing products and design styles and motifs to obtain perspective and generate design concepts. Research production specifications, costs, production materials, and manufacturing methods and provide cost estimates and itemized production requirements. Design graphic material for use as ornamentation, illustration, or advertising on manufactured materials and packaging or containers. Develop manufacturing procedures and monitor the manufacture of their designs in a factory to improve operations and product quality. Supervise assistants' work throughout the design process. Fabricate models or samples in paper, wood, glass, fabric, plastic, metal, or other materials, using hand or power tools. Investigate product characteristics such as the product's safety and handling qualities; its market appeal; how efficiently it can be produced; and ways of distributing, using, and maintaining it. Develop industrial standards and regulatory guidelines.

**Education/Training Required:** Bachelor's degree. **Education and Training Programs:** Commercial and Advertising Art; Design and Applied Arts, Other; Design and Visual Communications, General; Industrial and Product Design. **Knowledge/Courses**—Design, Engineering and Technology, Mechanical, Production and Processing, Physics, Fine Arts.

**Personality Type:** Artistic-Enterprising-Realistic. **Career Cluster:** 03 Arts, Audio/Video Technology, and Communications. **Career Pathways:** 3.1 Audio and Video Technology and Film; 3.3 Visual Arts. **Other Jobs in These Pathways:** Agents and Business Managers of Artists, Performers, and Athletes; Art Directors; Artists and Related Workers, All Other; Audio and Video Equipment Technicians; Broadcast Technicians; Camera Operators, Television, Video, and Motion Picture; Choreographers; Craft Artists; Curators; Dancers; Designers, All Other; Fashion Designers; Film and Video Editors; Fine Artists, Including Painters, Sculptors, and Illustrators; Graphic Designers; Interior Designers; Managers, All Other; Media and Communication Equipment Workers, All Other; Media and Communication Workers, All Other; Multimedia Artists and Animators; Museum Technicians and Conservators; Painting, Coating, and Decorating Workers; Photographers; Set and Exhibit Designers; Technical Directors/Managers; others.

**Skills**—Technology Design, Operations Analysis, Systems Evaluation, Mathematics, Science, Active Learning, Systems Analysis, Quality Control Analysis.

**Work Environment:** Indoors; sitting; using hands; noise.

# Commercial Pilots

- ❋ Annual Earnings: $67,500
- ❋ Earnings Growth Potential: High (48.4%)
- ❋ Growth: 18.5%
- ❋ Annual Job Openings: 2,060
- ❋ Self-Employed: 12.0%

**Considerations for Job Outlook:** Population growth and economic expansion are expected to boost demand for air travel. Regional airlines and low-cost carriers should have the best opportunities; pilots vying for jobs with major airlines face strong competition.

**Pilot and navigate the flight of small fixed- or rotary-winged aircraft primarily for the transport of cargo and passengers. Requires Commercial Rating.** Check aircraft prior to flights to ensure that the engines, controls, instruments, and other systems are functioning properly. Start engines, operate controls, and pilot airplanes to transport passengers, mail, or freight while adhering to flight plans, regulations, and procedures. Contact control towers for takeoff clearances, arrival instructions, and other information, using radio equipment. Monitor engine operation, fuel consumption, and functioning of aircraft systems during flights. Consider airport altitudes, outside temperatures, plane weights, and wind speeds and directions to calculate the speed needed to become airborne. Order changes in fuel supplies, loads, routes, or schedules to ensure safety of flights. Obtain and review data such as load weights, fuel supplies, weather conditions, and flight schedules to determine flight plans and to see if changes might be necessary. Plan flights, following government and company regulations, using aeronautical charts and navigation instruments. Use instrumentation to pilot aircraft when visibility is poor. Check baggage or cargo to ensure that it has been loaded correctly. Request changes in altitudes or routes as circumstances dictate. Choose routes, altitudes, and speeds that will provide the fastest, safest, and smoothest flights. Coordinate flight activities with ground crews and air-traffic control and inform crew members of flight and test procedures. Write specified information in flight records, such as flight times, altitudes flown, and fuel consumption. Teach company regulations and procedures to other pilots. Instruct other pilots and student pilots in aircraft operations. Co-pilot aircraft or perform captain's duties if required. File instrument flight plans with air traffic control so that flights can be coordinated with other air traffic.

**Education/Training Required:** Postsecondary vocational training. **Education and Training Programs:** Airline/Commercial/Professional Pilot and Flight Crew Training; Flight Instructor Training. **Knowledge/Courses—**Transportation, Geography, Mechanical, Physics, Telecommunications, Psychology.

**Personality Type:** Realistic-Investigative-Enterprising. **Career Cluster:** 16 Transportation, Distribution, and Logistics. **Career Pathway:** 16.1 Transportation Operations. **Other Jobs in This Pathway:** Airline Pilots, Copilots, and Flight Engineers; Automotive and Watercraft Service Attendants; Automotive Master Mechanics; Bus Drivers, School or Special Client; Bus Drivers, Transit and Intercity; Crane and Tower Operators; First-Line Supervisors of Helpers, Laborers, and Material Movers, Hand; First-Line Supervisors of Transportation and Material-Moving Machine and Vehicle Operators; Freight and Cargo Inspectors; Heavy and Tractor-Trailer Truck Drivers; Laborers and Freight, Stock, and Material Movers, Hand; Light Truck or Delivery Services Drivers; Mates—Ship, Boat, and Barge; Motor Vehicle Operators, All Other; Operating Engineers and Other Construction Equipment Operators; Parking Lot Attendants; Pilots, Ship; Railroad Conductors and Yardmasters; Sailors and Marine Oilers; Ship and Boat Captains; Storage and Distribution Managers; Taxi Drivers and Chauffeurs; Transportation Inspectors; Transportation Managers; Transportation Workers, All Other; others.

**Skills—**Operation and Control, Operation Monitoring, Science, Instructing, Troubleshooting, Judgment and Decision Making, Operations Analysis, Complex Problem Solving.

**Work Environment:** Outdoors; sitting; using hands; noise; very hot or cold; contaminants; cramped work space.

## Communications Teachers, Postsecondary

- ❋ Annual Earnings: $60,300
- ❋ Earnings Growth Potential: High (44.5%)
- ❋ Growth: 15.1%
- ❋ Annual Job Openings: 800
- ❋ Self-Employed: 0.2%

**Considerations for Job Outlook:** Enrollments in postsecondary institutions are expected to continue rising as more people attend college and as workers return to school to update their skills. Opportunities for part-time or temporary positions should be favorable, but significant competition exists for tenure-track positions.

**Teach courses in communications, such as organizational communications, public relations, radio/television broadcasting, and journalism.** Evaluate and grade students' classwork, assignments, and papers. Prepare course materials such as syllabi, homework assignments, and handouts. Initiate, facilitate, and moderate classroom discussions. Prepare and deliver lectures to undergraduate or graduate students on topics such as public speaking, media criticism, and oral traditions. Compile, administer, and grade examinations or assign this work to others. Maintain student attendance records, grades, and other required records. Plan, evaluate, and revise curricula, course content, and course materials and methods of instruction. Maintain regularly scheduled office hours to advise and assist students. Keep abreast of developments in their field by reading current literature, talking with colleagues, and participating in professional conferences. Advise students on academic and vocational curricula and on career issues. Supervise undergraduate or graduate teaching, internship, and research work. Select and obtain materials and supplies such as textbooks. Collaborate with colleagues to address teaching and research issues. Conduct research in a particular field of knowledge and publish findings in professional journals, books, or electronic media. Participate in student recruitment, registration, and placement activities. Serve on academic or administrative committees that deal with institutional policies, departmental matters, and academic issues. Compile bibliographies of specialized materials for outside reading assignments. Act as advisers to student organizations. Participate in campus and community events. Perform administrative duties such as serving as department head. Write grant proposals to procure external research funding. Provide professional consulting services to government or industry.

**Education/Training Required:** Doctoral degree. **Education and Training Programs:** Advertising; Broadcast Journalism; Communication, Journalism, and Related Programs, Other; Digital Communication and Media/Multimedia; Health Communication; Humanities/Humanistic Studies; Journalism; Journalism, Other; Mass Communication/Media Studies; Political Communication; Public Relations/Image Management; Radio and Television; Speech Communication and Rhetoric. **Knowledge/Courses—** Communications and Media, Education and Training, Philosophy and Theology, Sociology and Anthropology, English Language, History and Archeology.

**Personality Type:** Social-Artistic. **Career Clusters:** 03 Arts, Audio/Video Technology, and Communications; 04 Business, Management, and Administration; 05 Education and Training; 08 Health Science. **Career Pathways:** 3.5 Journalism and Broadcasting; 4.1 Management; 4.5 Marketing; 5.3 Teaching/Training; 8.3 Health Informatics. **Other Jobs in These Pathways:** Brownfield Redevelopment Specialists and Site Managers; Business Continuity Planners; Business Operations Specialists, All Other; Compliance Managers; Customs Brokers; Elementary School Teachers, Except Special Education; Energy Auditors; Executive Secretaries and Executive Administrative Assistants; First-Line Supervisors of Office and Administrative Support Workers; General and Operations Managers; Investment Fund Managers; Loss Prevention Managers; Managers, All Other; Receptionists and Information Clerks; Regulatory Affairs Managers; Secondary School Teachers, Except Special and Career/Technical Education; Security Management Specialists; Security Managers; Supply Chain Managers; Sustainability Specialists; Teacher Assistants; Tutors; Wind Energy Operations

Managers; Wind Energy Project Managers; 37 other post-secondary teaching occupations; others.

**Skills**—Learning Strategies, Instructing, Speaking, Active Learning, Reading Comprehension, Writing, Active Listening, Monitoring.

**Work Environment:** Indoors; sitting.

# Compensation and Benefits Managers

- ❊ Annual Earnings: $89,270
- ❊ Earnings Growth Potential: High (41.6%)
- ❊ Growth: 8.5%
- ❊ Annual Job Openings: 1,210
- ❊ Self-Employed: 0.6%

**Considerations for Job Outlook:** Efforts to recruit and retain employees, the growing importance of employee training, and new legal standards are expected to increase employment of these workers. College graduates and those with certification should have the best opportunities.

**Plan, direct, or coordinate compensation and benefits activities and staff of an organization.** Advise management on such matters as equal employment opportunity, sexual harassment and discrimination. Direct preparation and distribution of written and verbal information to inform employees of benefits, compensation, and personnel policies. Administer, direct, and review employee benefit programs, including the integration of benefit programs following mergers and acquisitions. Plan and conduct new employee orientations to foster positive attitude toward organizational objectives. Plan, direct, supervise, and coordinate work activities of subordinates and staff relating to employment, compensation, labor relations, and employee relations. Identify and implement benefits to increase the quality of life for employees, by working with brokers and researching benefits issues. Design, evaluate and modify benefits policies to ensure that programs are current, competitive and in compliance with legal requirements. Analyze compensation policies, government regulations, and prevailing wage rates to develop competitive compensation plan. Formulate policies, procedures and programs for recruitment, testing, placement, classification, orientation, benefits and compensation, and labor and industrial relations. Mediate between benefits providers and employees, such as by assisting in handling employees' benefits-related questions or taking suggestions. Fulfill all reporting requirements of all relevant government rules and regulations, including the

C

Employee Retirement Income Security Act (ERISA). Maintain records and compile statistical reports concerning personnel-related data such as hires, transfers, performance appraisals, and absenteeism rates. Analyze statistical data and reports to identify and determine causes of personnel problems and develop recommendations for improvement of organization's personnel policies and practices. Develop methods to improve employment policies, processes, and practices, and recommend changes to management.

**Education/Training Required:** Work experience plus degree. **Education and Training Program:** Human Resources Management/Personnel Administration, General. **Knowledge/Courses**—Personnel and Human Resources, Economics and Accounting, Administration and Management, Mathematics, Law and Government, Communications and Media.

**Personality Type:** Enterprising-Conventional-Social. **Career Cluster:** 04 Business, Management, and Administration. **Career Pathway:** 4.3 Human Resources. **Other Jobs in This Pathway:** Human Resources Specialists.

**Skills**—Management of Financial Resources, Operations Analysis, Systems Evaluation, Systems Analysis, Management of Personnel Resources, Time Management, Management of Material Resources, Negotiation.

**Work Environment:** Indoors; sitting.

## Compensation, Benefits, and Job Analysis Specialists

- ❋ Annual Earnings: $57,000
- ❋ Earnings Growth Potential: Medium (37.4%)
- ❋ Growth: 23.6%
- ❋ Annual Job Openings: 6,050
- ❋ Self-Employed: 1.6%

**Considerations for Job Outlook:** Efforts to recruit and retain employees, the growing importance of employee training, and new legal standards are expected to increase employment of these workers. College graduates and those with certification should have the best opportunities.

**Conduct programs of compensation and benefits and job analysis for employer. May specialize in specific areas, such as position classification and pension programs.** Evaluate job positions, determining classification, exempt or non-exempt status, and salary. Ensure company compliance with federal and state laws, including reporting requirements. Advise managers and employees on state and federal employment regulations, collective agreements, benefit and compensation policies, personnel procedures and classification programs. Plan, develop, evaluate, improve, and communicate methods and techniques for selecting, promoting, compensating, evaluating, and training workers. Provide advice on the resolution of classification and salary complaints. Prepare occupational classifications, job descriptions and salary scales. Assist in preparing and maintaining personnel records and handbooks. Prepare reports, such as organization and flow charts, and career path reports, to summarize job analysis and evaluation and compensation analysis information. Administer employee insurance, pension and savings plans, working with insurance brokers and plan carriers. Negotiate collective agreements on behalf of employers or workers, and mediate labor disputes and grievances. Develop, implement, administer and evaluate personnel and labor relations programs, including performance appraisal, affirmative action and employment equity programs. Perform multifactor data and cost analyses that may be used in areas such as support of collective bargaining agreements. Research employee benefit and health and safety practices and recommend changes or modifications to existing policies. Analyze organizational, occupational, and industrial data to facilitate organizational functions and provide technical information to business, industry, and government. Advise staff of individuals' qualifications. Assess need for and develop job analysis instruments and materials.

**Education/Training Required:** Bachelor's degree. **Education and Training Program:** Human Resources Management/Personnel Administration, General. **Knowledge/Courses**—Personnel and Human Resources, Economics and Accounting, Law and Government, Administration and Management, English Language, Mathematics.

**Personality Type:** Conventional-Enterprising. **Career Cluster:** 04 Business, Management, and Administration. **Career Pathway:** 4.3 Human Resources. **Other Jobs in This Pathway:** Human Resources Specialists.

**Skills**—Operations Analysis, Science, Systems Analysis, Mathematics, Programming, Systems Evaluation, Management of Financial Resources, Learning Strategies.

**Work Environment:** Indoors; sitting.

# Compliance Officers

* Annual Earnings: $58,720
* Earnings Growth Potential: High (41.2%)
* Growth: 31.0%
* Annual Job Openings: 10,850
* Self-Employed: 1.4%

**Considerations for Job Outlook:** Much-faster-than-average employment growth is projected.

**Examine, evaluate, and investigate eligibility for or conformity with laws and regulations governing contract compliance of licenses and permits and other compliance and enforcement inspection activities not classified elsewhere.** No task data available.

**Education/Training Required:** Long-term on-the-job training. **Education and Training Program:** Business Administration and Management, General. **Knowledge/Courses**—No data available.

**Personality Type:** No data available. **Career Cluster:** 12 Law, Public Safety, Corrections, and Security. **Career Pathway:** 12.6 Inspection Services. **Other Jobs in This Pathway:** Coroners; Environmental Compliance Inspectors; Equal Opportunity Representatives and Officers; Government Property Inspectors and Investigators; Licensing Examiners and Inspectors; Regulatory Affairs Specialists.

**Skills**—No data available.

**Work Environment:** No data available.

## Job Specialization: Coroners

**Direct activities such as autopsies, pathological and toxicological analyses, and inquests relating to the investigation of deaths occurring within a legal jurisdiction to determine cause of death or to fix responsibility for accidental, violent, or unexplained deaths.** Perform medicolegal examinations and autopsies, conducting preliminary examinations of the body in order to identify victims, to locate signs of trauma, and to identify factors that would indicate time of death. Inquire into the cause, manner, and circumstances of human deaths and establish the identities of deceased persons. Direct activities of workers who conduct autopsies, perform pathological and toxicological analyses, and prepare documents for permanent records. Complete death certificates, including the assignment of a cause and manner of death. Observe and record the positions and conditions of bodies and of related evidence.

Collect and document any pertinent medical history information. Observe, record, and preserve any objects or personal property related to deaths, including objects such as medication containers and suicide notes. Complete reports and forms required to finalize cases. Remove or supervise removal of bodies from death scenes, using the proper equipment and supplies, and arrange for transportation to morgues. Testify at inquests, hearings, and court trials. Interview persons present at death scenes to obtain information useful in determining the manner of death. Provide information concerning the circumstances of death to relatives of the deceased. Locate and document information regarding the next of kin, including their relationship to the deceased and the status of notification attempts. Confer with officials of public health and law enforcement agencies in order to coordinate interdepartmental activities. Inventory personal effects, such as jewelry or wallets, that are recovered from bodies. Coordinate the release of personal effects to authorized persons and facilitate the disposition of unclaimed corpses and personal effects. Arrange for the next of kin to be notified of deaths. Record the disposition of minor children, as well as details of arrangements made for their care.

**Education/Training Required:** Work experience in a related occupation. **Education and Training Program:** Public Administration. **Knowledge/Courses**—Medicine and Dentistry, Biology, Psychology, Therapy and Counseling, Chemistry, Law and Government.

**Personality Type:** Investigative-Realistic-Conventional. **Career Cluster:** 12 Law, Public Safety, Corrections, and Security. **Career Pathway:** 12.6 Inspection Services. **Other Jobs in This Pathway:** Compliance Officers; Environmental Compliance Inspectors; Equal Opportunity Representatives and Officers; Government Property Inspectors and Investigators; Licensing Examiners and Inspectors; Regulatory Affairs Specialists.

**Skills**—Science, Social Perceptiveness, Speaking, Critical Thinking, Writing, Management of Personnel Resources, Learning Strategies, Instructing.

**Work Environment:** More often indoors than outdoors; sitting; using hands; contaminants; exposed to disease or infections; hazardous equipment.

## Job Specialization: Environmental Compliance Inspectors

**Inspect and investigate sources of pollution to protect the public and environment and ensure conformance with federal, state, and local regulations and ordinances.**

Determine the nature of code violations and actions to be taken and issue written notices of violation; participate in enforcement hearings as necessary. Examine permits, licenses, applications, and records to ensure compliance with licensing requirements. Prepare, organize, and maintain inspection records. Interview individuals to determine the nature of suspected violations and to obtain evidence of violations. Prepare written, oral, tabular, and graphic reports summarizing requirements and regulations, including enforcement and chain of custody documentation. Monitor follow-up actions in cases where violations were found and review compliance monitoring reports. Investigate complaints and suspected violations regarding illegal dumping, pollution, pesticides, product quality, or labeling laws. Inspect waste pretreatment, treatment, and disposal facilities and systems for conformance to federal, state, or local regulations. Inform individuals and groups of pollution control regulations and inspection findings and explain how problems can be corrected. Determine sampling locations and methods and collect water or wastewater samples for analysis, preserving samples with appropriate containers and preservation methods. Verify that hazardous chemicals are handled, stored, and disposed of in accordance with regulations. Research and keep informed of pertinent information and developments in areas such as EPA laws and regulations. Determine which sites and violation reports to investigate and coordinate compliance and enforcement activities with other government agencies. Observe and record field conditions, gathering, interpreting, and reporting data such as flow meter readings and chemical levels. Learn and observe proper safety precautions, rules, regulations, and practices so that unsafe conditions can be recognized and proper safety protocols implemented. Evaluate label information for accuracy and conformance to regulatory requirements.

**Education/Training Required:** Long-term on-the-job training. **Education and Training Program:** Natural Resources Management and Policy, Other. **Knowledge/Courses**—Biology, Law and Government, Chemistry, Geography, Physics, Engineering and Technology.

**Personality Type:** Conventional-Investigative-Realistic. **Career Clusters:** 07 Government and Public Administration; 12 Law, Public Safety, Corrections, and Security; 16 Transportation, Distribution, and Logistics. **Career Pathways:** 7.6 Regulation; 12.6 Inspection Services; 16.6 Health, Safety, and Environmental Management. **Other Jobs in These Pathways:** Chief Executives; Compliance Officers; Coroners; Environmental Engineers; Environmental Science and Protection Technicians, Including Health; Environmental Scientists and Specialists, Including Health;

Equal Opportunity Representatives and Officers; Government Property Inspectors and Investigators; Health and Safety Engineers, Except Mining Safety Engineers and Inspectors; Licensing Examiners and Inspectors; Regulatory Affairs Managers; Regulatory Affairs Specialists.

**Skills**—Quality Control Analysis, Science, Programming, Troubleshooting, Mathematics, Reading Comprehension, Writing, Systems Evaluation.

**Work Environment:** More often indoors than outdoors; sitting; contaminants.

## Job Specialization: Equal Opportunity Representatives and Officers

**Monitor and evaluate compliance with equal opportunity laws, guidelines, and policies to ensure that employment practices and contracting arrangements give equal opportunity without regard to race, religion, color, national origin, sex, age, or disability.** Investigate employment practices and alleged violations of laws to document and correct discriminatory factors. Interpret civil rights laws and equal opportunity regulations for individuals and employers. Study equal opportunity complaints to clarify issues. Meet with persons involved in equal opportunity complaints to verify case information and to arbitrate and settle disputes. Coordinate, monitor, and revise complaint procedures to ensure timely processing and review of complaints. Prepare reports of selection, survey, and other statistics and recommendations for corrective action. Conduct surveys and evaluate findings to determine whether systematic discrimination exists. Develop guidelines for non-discriminatory employment practices and monitor their implementation and impact. Review company contracts to determine actions required to meet governmental equal opportunity provisions. Counsel newly hired members of minority and disadvantaged groups, informing them about details of civil rights laws. Provide information, technical assistance, and training to supervisors, managers, and employees on topics such as employee supervision, hiring, grievance procedures, and staff development. Verify that all job descriptions are submitted for review and approval and that descriptions meet regulatory standards. Act as liaisons between minority placement agencies and employers or between job search committees and other equal opportunity administrators. Consult with community representatives to develop technical assistance agreements in accordance with governmental regulations. Meet with job search committees or coordinators to explain the role of the equal opportunity coordinator, to provide resources for advertising, and to explain expectations for future contacts. Participate in the recruitment of employees through job fairs, career days, and advertising plans.

**Education/Training Required:** Long-term on-the-job training. **Education and Training Program:** Public Administration and Social Service Professions, Other. **Knowledge/Courses**—Law and Government, Personnel and Human Resources, Clerical, English Language, Customer and Personal Service, Administration and Management.

**Personality Type:** Social-Enterprising-Conventional. **Career Cluster:** 12 Law, Public Safety, Corrections, and Security. **Career Pathway:** 12.6 Inspection Services. **Other Jobs in This Pathway:** Compliance Officers; Coroners; Environmental Compliance Inspectors; Government Property Inspectors and Investigators; Licensing Examiners and Inspectors; Regulatory Affairs Specialists.

**Skills**—Persuasion, Reading Comprehension, Active Listening, Programming, Active Learning, Negotiation, Writing, Systems Evaluation.

**Work Environment:** Indoors; sitting; repetitive motions.

## Job Specialization: Government Property Inspectors and Investigators

**Investigate or inspect government property to ensure compliance with contract agreements and government regulations.** Prepare correspondence, reports of inspections or investigations, and recommendations for action. Inspect government-owned equipment and materials in the possession of private contractors to ensure compliance with contracts and regulations and to prevent misuse. Examine records, reports, and documents to establish facts and detect discrepancies. Inspect manufactured or processed products to ensure compliance with contract specifications and legal requirements. Locate and interview plaintiffs, witnesses, or representatives of business or government to gather facts relevant to inspections or alleged violations. Recommend legal or administrative action to protect government property. Submit samples of products to government laboratories for testing as required. Coordinate with and assist law enforcement agencies in matters of mutual concern. Testify in court or at administrative proceedings concerning findings of investigations. Collect, identify, evaluate, and preserve case evidence. Monitor investigations of suspected offenders to ensure that they are conducted in accordance with constitutional requirements. Investigate applications for special licenses or permits, as well as alleged violations of licenses or permits.

**Education/Training Required:** Long-term on-the-job training. **Education and Training Program:** Building/Home/Construction Inspection/Inspector. **Knowledge/Courses**—Building and Construction, Engineering and Technology, Public Safety and Security, Mechanical, Transportation, Computers and Electronics.

**Personality Type:** Conventional-Enterprising-Realistic. **Career Cluster:** 12 Law, Public Safety, Corrections, and Security. **Career Pathway:** 12.6 Inspection Services. **Other Jobs in This Pathway:** Compliance Officers; Coroners; Environmental Compliance Inspectors; Equal Opportunity Representatives and Officers; Licensing Examiners and Inspectors; Regulatory Affairs Specialists.

**Skills**—Quality Control Analysis, Programming, Persuasion, Operation and Control, Systems Evaluation, Writing, Speaking, Judgment and Decision Making.

**Work Environment:** More often outdoors than indoors; sitting; noise; very hot or cold; contaminants.

## Job Specialization: Licensing Examiners and Inspectors

**Examine, evaluate, and investigate eligibility for, conformity with, or liability under licenses or permits.** Issue licenses to individuals meeting standards. Evaluate applications, records, and documents in order to gather information about eligibility or liability issues. Administer oral, written, road, or flight tests to license applicants. Score tests and observe equipment operation and control in order to rate ability of applicants. Advise licensees and other individuals or groups concerning licensing, permit, or passport regulations. Warn violators of infractions or penalties. Prepare reports of activities, evaluations, recommendations, and decisions. Prepare correspondence to inform concerned parties of licensing decisions and of appeals processes. Confer with and interview officials, technical or professional specialists, and applicants in order to obtain information or to clarify facts relevant to licensing decisions. Report law or regulation violations to appropriate boards and agencies. Visit establishments to verify that valid licenses and permits are displayed and that licensing standards are being upheld.

**Education/Training Required:** Long-term on-the-job training. **Education and Training Program:** Public Administration and Social Service Professions, Other. **Knowledge/Courses**—Clerical, Customer and Personal Service, Law and Government, Foreign Language, Psychology, Public Safety and Security.

**Personality Type:** Conventional-Enterprising. **Career Cluster:** 12 Law, Public Safety, Corrections, and Security. **Career Pathway:** 12.6 Inspection Services. **Other Jobs in This Pathway:** Compliance Officers; Coroners; Environmental Compliance Inspectors; Equal Opportunity Representatives and Officers; Government Property Inspectors and Investigators; Regulatory Affairs Specialists.

**Skills**—Quality Control Analysis, Judgment and Decision Making, Social Perceptiveness, Speaking, Operation Monitoring, Service Orientation, Systems Evaluation, Reading Comprehension.

**Work Environment:** More often indoors than outdoors; sitting; using hands; repetitive motions; contaminants.

## Job Specialization: Regulatory Affairs Specialists

**Coordinate and document internal regulatory processes, such as internal audits, inspections, license renewals, or registrations. May compile and prepare materials for submission to regulatory agencies.** Coordinate, prepare, or review regulatory submissions for domestic or international projects. Provide technical review of data or reports that will be incorporated into regulatory submissions to assure scientific rigor, accuracy, and clarity of presentation. Review product promotional materials, labeling, batch records, specification sheets, or test methods for compliance with applicable regulations and policies. Maintain current knowledge base of existing and emerging regulations, standards, or guidance documents. Interpret regulatory rules or rule changes and ensure that they are communicated through corporate policies and procedures. Advise project teams on subjects such as premarket regulatory requirements, export and labeling requirements, and clinical study compliance issues. Determine the types of regulatory submissions or internal documentation that are required in situations such as proposed device changes and labeling changes. Prepare or maintain technical files as necessary to obtain and sustain product approval. Coordinate efforts associated with the preparation of regulatory documents or submissions. Prepare or direct the preparation of additional information or responses as requested by regulatory agencies. Analyze product complaints and make recommendations regarding their reportability. Escort government inspectors during inspections and provide post-inspection follow-up information as requested. Communicate with regulatory agencies regarding pre-submission strategies, potential regulatory pathways, compliance test requirements, or clarification and follow-up of submissions under review. Identify relevant guidance documents, international standards, or consensus standards and provide interpretive assistance. Review clinical protocols to ensure collection of data needed for regulatory submissions. Compile and maintain regulatory documentation databases and systems.

**Education/Training Required:** Work experience in a related occupation. **Education and Training Program:** Business Administration and Management, General. **Knowledge/Courses**—Law and Government, Biology, Medicine and Dentistry, Clerical, English Language, Chemistry.

**Personality Type:** Conventional-Enterprising. **Career Cluster:** 12 Law, Public Safety, Corrections, and Security. **Career Pathway:** 12.6 Inspection Services. **Other Jobs in This Pathway:** Compliance Officers; Coroners; Environmental Compliance Inspectors; Equal Opportunity Representatives and Officers; Government Property Inspectors and Investigators; Licensing Examiners and Inspectors.

**Skills**—Systems Analysis, Systems Evaluation, Judgment and Decision Making, Persuasion, Writing, Speaking, Coordination, Reading Comprehension.

**Work Environment:** Indoors; sitting.

## Computer and Information Research Scientists

- ❋ Annual Earnings: $100,660
- ❋ Earnings Growth Potential: High (42.7%)
- ❋ Growth: 24.2%
- ❋ Annual Job Openings: 1,320
- ❋ Self-Employed: 4.6%

**Considerations for Job Outlook:** Employment is expected to increase because of high demand for sophisticated technological research. Job prospects should be excellent.

**Conduct research into fundamental computer and information science as theorists, designers, or inventors. Solve or develop solutions to problems in the field of computer hardware and software.** Analyze problems to develop solutions involving computer hardware and software. Assign or schedule tasks in order to meet work priorities and goals. Evaluate project plans and proposals to assess feasibility issues. Apply theoretical expertise and innovation to create or apply new technology, such as adapting principles for applying computers to new uses. Consult with users, management, vendors, and technicians to determine computing needs and system requirements. Meet with managers, vendors, and others to solicit cooperation and resolve problems.

Conduct logical analyses of business, scientific, engineering, and other technical problems, formulating mathematical models of problems for solution by computers. Develop and interpret organizational goals, policies, and procedures. Participate in staffing decisions and direct training of subordinates. Develop performance standards, and evaluate work in light of established standards. Design computers and the software that runs them. Maintain network hardware and software, direct network security measures, and monitor networks to ensure availability to system users. Participate in multidisciplinary projects in areas such as virtual reality, human-computer interaction, or robotics. Approve, prepare, monitor, and adjust operational budgets. Direct daily operations of departments, coordinating project activities with other departments.

**Education/Training Required:** Doctoral degree. **Education and Training Programs:** Computer Graphics; Computer Science; Computer Software and Media Applications, Other; Computer Systems Networking and Telecommunications; Data Modeling/Warehousing and Database Administration; Modeling, Virtual Environments and Simulation; Web Page, Digital/Multimedia, and Information Resources Design. **Knowledge/Courses**—Computers and Electronics, Telecommunications, Engineering and Technology, Mathematics, Design, Education and Training.

**Personality Type:** Investigative-Realistic-Conventional. **Career Cluster:** 11 Information Technology. **Career Pathways:** 8.3 Health Informatics; 11.1 Network Systems; 11.2 Information Support Services; 11.3 Interactive Media; 11.4 Programming and Software Development. **Other Jobs in These Pathways:** Architectural and Engineering Managers; Clinical Psychologists; Computer and Information Systems Managers; Computer Hardware Engineers; Computer Operators; Editors; Engineers, All Other; Executive Secretaries and Executive Administrative Assistants; First-Line Supervisors of Office and Administrative Support Workers; Graphic Designers; Health Educators; Medical and Health Services Managers; Medical Assistants; Medical Records and Health Information Technicians; Medical Secretaries; Medical Transcriptionists; Mental Health Counselors; Multimedia Artists and Animators; Physical Therapists; Psychiatric Aides; Public Relations Specialists; Receptionists and Information Clerks; Rehabilitation Counselors; Remote Sensing Technicians; Substance Abuse and Behavioral Disorder Counselors; others.

**Skills**—Programming, Technology Design, Systems Evaluation, Management of Financial Resources, Mathematics, Systems Analysis, Operations Analysis, Science.

**Work Environment:** Indoors; sitting; using hands; repetitive motions.

# Computer and Information Systems Managers

- ❋ Annual Earnings: $115,780
- ❋ Earnings Growth Potential: Medium (38.3%)
- ❋ Growth: 16.9%
- ❋ Annual Job Openings: 9,710
- ❋ Self-Employed: 3.3%

**Considerations for Job Outlook:** New applications of technology in the workplace should continue to drive demand for IT services, fueling employment growth of these managers. Job prospects are expected to be excellent.

**Plan, direct, or coordinate activities in such fields as electronic data processing, information systems, systems analysis, and computer programming.** Review project plans to plan and coordinate project activity. Manage backup, security, and user help systems. Develop and interpret organizational goals, policies, and procedures. Develop computer information resources, providing for data security and control, strategic computing, and disaster recovery. Consult with users, management, vendors, and technicians to assess computing needs and system requirements. Stay abreast of advances in technology. Meet with department heads, managers, supervisors, vendors, and others to solicit cooperation and resolve problems. Provide users with technical support for computer problems. Recruit, hire, train, and supervise staff or participate in staffing decisions. Evaluate data processing proposals to assess project feasibility and requirements. Review and approve all systems charts and programs prior to their implementation. Control operational budget and expenditures. Direct daily operations of department, analyzing workflow, establishing priorities, developing standards, and setting deadlines. Assign and review the work of systems analysts, programmers, and other computer-related workers. Evaluate the organization's technology use and needs and recommend improvements such as hardware and software upgrades. Prepare and review operational reports or project progress reports. Purchase necessary equipment.

**Education/Training Required:** Work experience plus degree. **Education and Training Programs:** Computer and Information Sciences, General; Computer Science; Information Resources Management/CIO Training;

Information Science/Studies; Knowledge Management; Management Information Systems, General; Network and System Administration/Administrator; Operations Management and Supervision. **Knowledge/Courses**—Telecommunications, Computers and Electronics, Economics and Accounting, Production and Processing, Personnel and Human Resources, Administration and Management.

**Personality Type:** Enterprising-Conventional-Investigative. **Career Clusters:** 04 Business, Management, and Administration; 11 Information Technology. **Career Pathways:** 4.1 Management; 4.4 Business Analysis; 11.1 Network Systems; 11.2 Information Support Services. **Other Jobs in These Pathways:** Brownfield Redevelopment Specialists and Site Managers; Business Continuity Planners; Business Operations Specialists, All Other; Chief Executives; Chief Sustainability Officers; Compliance Managers; Construction Managers; Customs Brokers; Energy Auditors; First-Line Supervisors of Office and Administrative Support Workers; General and Operations Managers; Graphic Designers; Investment Fund Managers; Loss Prevention Managers; Management Analysts; Managers, All Other; Public Relations Specialists; Regulatory Affairs Managers; Sales Managers; Security Management Specialists; Security Managers; Supply Chain Managers; Sustainability Specialists; Wind Energy Operations Managers; Wind Energy Project Managers; others.

**Skills**—Management of Financial Resources, Management of Material Resources, Programming, Equipment Selection, Systems Evaluation, Troubleshooting, Repairing, Technology Design.

**Work Environment:** Indoors; sitting; using hands.

# Computer Hardware Engineers

- ❋ Annual Earnings: $98,810
- ❋ Earnings Growth Potential: Medium (37.9%)
- ❋ Growth: 3.8%
- ❋ Annual Job Openings: 2,350
- ❋ Self-Employed: 1.3%

**Considerations for Job Outlook:** Computer hardware engineers are expected to have employment growth of 4 percent from 2008–2018, slower than the average for all occupations. Although the use of information technology continues to expand rapidly, the manufacture of computer hardware is expected to be adversely affected by intense foreign competition. As computer and semiconductor

manufacturers contract out more of their engineering needs to both domestic and foreign design firms, much of the growth in employment of hardware engineers is expected to take place in the computer systems design and related services industry.

**Research, design, develop, and test computer or computer-related equipment for commercial, industrial, military, or scientific use. May supervise the manufacturing and installation of computer or computer-related equipment and components.** Update knowledge and skills to keep up with rapid advancements in computer technology. Provide technical support to designers, marketing and sales departments, suppliers, engineers, and other team members throughout the product development and implementation process. Test and verify hardware and support peripherals to ensure that they meet specifications and requirements, analyzing and recording test data. Monitor functioning of equipment and make necessary modifications to ensure system operates in conformance with specifications. Analyze information to determine, recommend, and plan layout, including type of computers and peripheral equipment modifications. Build, test, and modify product prototypes, using working models or theoretical models constructed using computer simulation. Analyze user needs and recommend appropriate hardware. Direct technicians, engineering designers, or other technical support personnel as needed. Confer with engineering staff and consult specifications to evaluate interface between hardware and software and operational and performance requirements of overall system. Select hardware and material, assuring compliance with specifications and product requirements. Store, retrieve, and manipulate data for analysis of system capabilities and requirements. Write detailed functional specifications that document the hardware development process and support hardware introduction. Specify power supply requirements and configuration, drawing on system performance expectations and design specifications. Provide training and support to system designers and users. Assemble and modify existing pieces of equipment to meet special needs. Evaluate factors such as reporting formats required, cost constraints, and need for security restrictions to determine hardware configuration.

**Education/Training Required:** Bachelor's degree. **Education and Training Programs:** Computer Engineering, General; Computer Hardware Engineering. **Knowledge/Courses**—Computers and Electronics, Engineering and Technology, Telecommunications, Design, Physics, Communications and Media.

**Personality Type:** Investigative-Realistic-Conventional. **Career Clusters:** 11 Information Technology; 15 Science, Technology, Engineering, and Mathematics. **Career Pathways:** 11.4 Programming and Software Development; 15.1 Engineering and Technology. **Other Jobs in These Pathways:** Architectural and Engineering Managers; Automotive Engineers; Biochemical Engineers; Biofuels/Biodiesel Technology and Product Development Managers; Civil Engineers; Cost Estimators; Electrical Engineers; Electronics Engineers, Except Computer; Energy Engineers; Engineers, All Other; Fuel Cell Engineers; Human Factors Engineers and Ergonomists; Industrial Engineers; Manufacturing Engineers; Mechanical Engineers; Mechatronics Engineers; Microsystems Engineers; Nanosystems Engineers; Photonics Engineers; Radio Frequency Identification Device Specialists; Robotics Engineers; Solar Energy Systems Engineers; Transportation Engineers; Validation Engineers; Wind Energy Engineers; others.

**Skills**—Troubleshooting, Science, Programming, Operations Analysis, Systems Evaluation, Quality Control Analysis, Equipment Maintenance, Complex Problem Solving.

**Work Environment:** Indoors; sitting.

# Computer Occupations, All Other

- ❋ Annual Earnings: $79,240
- ❋ Earnings Growth Potential: High (47.4%)
- ❋ Growth: 13.1%
- ❋ Annual Job Openings: 7,260
- ❋ Self-Employed: 3.9%

**Considerations for Job Outlook:** Employment of these workers should grow as organizations increasingly use network technologies and collect and organize data. Job prospects are expected to be excellent.

**This occupation includes all computer occupations not listed separately.** Because this is a highly diverse occupation, no data is available for some information topics.

**Education and Training Program:** Computer and Information Sciences and Support Services, Other.

**Career Cluster:** 11 Information Technology. **Career Pathways:** 11.2 Information Support Services; 11.3 Interactive Media; 11.4 Programming and Software Development. **Other Jobs in These Pathways:** Architectural and Engineering Managers; Bioinformatics Scientists; Computer and Information Systems Managers; Computer Hardware Engineers; Computer Numerically Controlled Machine Tool

Programmers, Metal and Plastic; Computer Operators; Remote Sensing Scientists and Technologists; Remote Sensing Technicians.

# Job Specialization: Business Intelligence Analysts

**Produce financial and market intelligence by querying data repositories and generating periodic reports. Devise methods for identifying data patterns and trends in available information sources.** Provide technical support for existing reports, dashboards, or other tools. Maintain library of model documents, templates, or other reusable knowledge assets. Identify or monitor current and potential customers, using business intelligence tools. Create or review technical design documentation to ensure the accurate development of reporting solutions. Communicate with customers, competitors, suppliers, professional organizations, or others to stay abreast of industry or business trends. Maintain or update business intelligence tools, databases, dashboards, systems, or methods. Manage timely flow of business intelligence information to users. Identify and analyze industry or geographic trends with business strategy implications. Document specifications for business intelligence or information technology (IT) reports, dashboards, or other outputs. Disseminate information regarding tools, reports, or metadata enhancements. Create business intelligence tools or systems, including design of related databases, spreadsheets, or outputs. Conduct or coordinate tests to ensure that intelligence is consistent with defined needs. Collect business intelligence data from available industry reports, public information, field reports, or purchased sources. Analyze technology trends to identify markets for future product development or to improve sales of existing products. Analyze competitive market strategies through analysis of related product, market, or share trends. Synthesize current business intelligence or trend data to support recommendations for action. Generate standard or custom reports summarizing business, financial, or economic data for review by executives, managers, clients, and other stakeholders.

**Education/Training Required:** Work experience plus degree. **Education and Training Program:** Computer and Information Sciences and Support Services, Other. **Knowledge/Courses**—No data available.

**Personality Type:** No data available. **Career Cluster:** 04 Business, Management, and Administration. **Career Pathway:** 11.2 Information Support Services. **Other Jobs in This Pathway:** Computer and Information Systems Managers; Computer Numerically Controlled Machine Tool

Programmers, Metal and Plastic; Computer Operators; Remote Sensing Scientists and Technologists; Remote Sensing Technicians.

**Skills**—No data available.

**Work Environment:** No data available.

## Job Specialization: Computer Systems Engineers/Architects

**Design and develop solutions to complex applications problems, system administration issues, or network concerns. Perform systems management and integration functions.** Communicate with staff or clients to understand specific system requirements. Provide advice on project costs, design concepts, or design changes. Document design specifications, installation instructions, and other system-related information. Verify stability, interoperability, portability, security, or scalability of system architecture. Collaborate with engineers or software developers to select appropriate design solutions or ensure the compatibility of system components. Evaluate current or emerging technologies to consider factors such as cost, portability, compatibility, or usability. Provide technical guidance or support for the development or troubleshooting of systems. Identify system data, hardware, or software components required to meet user needs. Provide guidelines for implementing secure systems to customers or installation teams. Monitor system operation to detect potential problems. Direct the analysis, development, and operation of complete computer systems. Investigate system component suitability for specified purposes and make recommendations regarding component use. Perform ongoing hardware and software maintenance operations, including installing or upgrading hardware or software. Configure servers to meet functional specifications. Develop or approve project plans, schedules, or budgets. Define and analyze objectives, scope, issues, or organizational impact of information systems. Develop system engineering, software engineering, system integration, or distributed system architectures. Design and conduct hardware or software tests. Establish functional or system standards to ensure operational requirements, quality requirements, and design constraints are addressed. Evaluate existing systems to determine effectiveness and suggest changes to meet organizational requirements. Research, test, or verify proper functioning of software patches and fixes. Communicate project information through presentations, technical reports or white papers.

**Education/Training Required:** Bachelor's degree. **Education and Training Programs:** Computer Engineering, General; Data Modeling/Warehousing and Database Administration. **Knowledge/Courses**—Computers and Electronics, Engineering and Technology, Telecommunications, Design, Mathematics, Sales and Marketing.

**Personality Type:** Investigative-Realistic-Conventional. **Career Cluster:** 11 Information Technology. **Career Pathway:** 11.4 Programming and Software Development. **Other Jobs in This Pathway:** Architectural and Engineering Managers; Bioinformatics Scientists; Computer Hardware Engineers; Computer Numerically Controlled Machine Tool Programmers, Metal and Plastic.

**Skills**—Programming, Operations Analysis, Science, Systems Evaluation, Quality Control Analysis, Management of Financial Resources, Equipment Maintenance, Equipment Selection.

**Work Environment:** Indoors; sitting; repetitive motions.

## Job Specialization: Data Warehousing Specialists

**Design, model, or implement corporate data warehousing activities. Program and configure warehouses of database information and provide support to warehouse users.** Test software systems or applications for software enhancements or new products. Review designs, codes, test plans, or documentation to ensure quality. Provide or coordinate troubleshooting support for data warehouses. Prepare functional or technical documentation for data warehouses. Write new programs or modify existing programs to meet customer requirements, using current programming languages and technologies. Verify the structure, accuracy, or quality of warehouse data. Select methods, techniques, or criteria for data warehousing evaluative procedures. Perform system analysis, data analysis or programming, using a variety of computer languages and procedures. Map data between source systems, data warehouses, and data marts. Implement business rules via stored procedures, middleware, or other technologies. Develop and implement data extraction procedures from other systems, such as administration, billing, or claims. Develop or maintain standards, such as organization, structure, or nomenclature, for the design of data warehouse elements, such as data architectures, models, tools, and databases. Design and implement warehouse database structures. Create supporting documentation, such as metadata and diagrams of entity relationships, business processes, and process flow. Create plans, test files, and scripts for data warehouse testing, ranging from unit to integration testing. Create or implement metadata processes and frameworks. Develop data warehouse process models, including sourcing, loading, transformation, and extraction. Design, implement, or operate comprehensive data warehouse systems to balance optimization of data access with batch loading and resource utilization factors, according to customer requirements.

**Education/Training Required:** Bachelor's degree. **Education and Training Program:** Data Modeling/Warehousing and Database Administration. **Knowledge/Courses**—No data available.

**Personality Type:** No data available. **Career Cluster:** 11 Information Technology. **Career Pathway:** 11.2 Information Support Services. **Other Jobs in This Pathway:** Computer and Information Systems Managers; Computer Numerically Controlled Machine Tool Programmers, Metal and Plastic; Computer Operators; Remote Sensing Scientists and Technologists; Remote Sensing Technicians.

**Skills**—No data available.

**Work Environment:** No data available.

## Job Specialization: Database Architects

**Design strategies for enterprise database systems and set standards for operations, programming, and security. Design and construct large relational databases. Integrate new systems with existing warehouse structure and refine system performance and functionality.** Test changes to database applications or systems. Provide technical support to junior staff or clients. Set up database clusters, backup, or recovery processes. Identify, evaluate and recommend hardware or software technologies to achieve desired database performance. Plan and install upgrades of database management system software to enhance database performance. Monitor and report systems resource consumption trends to assure production systems meet availability requirements and hardware enhancements are scheduled appropriately. Identify and correct deviations from database development standards. Document and communicate database schemas, using accepted notations. Develop or maintain archived procedures, procedural codes, or queries for applications. Develop load-balancing processes to eliminate down time for backup processes. Develop data models for applications, metadata tables, views or related database structures. Design databases to support business applications, ensuring system scalability, security, performance and reliability. Design database applications, such as interfaces, data transfer mechanisms, global temporary tables, data partitions, and function-based indexes to enable efficient access

of the generic database structure. Demonstrate database technical functionality, such as performance, security and reliability. Create and enforce database development standards. Collaborate with system architects, software architects, design analysts, and others to understand business or industry requirements. Develop database architectural strategies at the modeling, design and implementation stages to address business or industry requirements. Develop and document database architectures.

**Education/Training Required:** Bachelor's degree. **Education and Training Program:** Data Modeling/Warehousing and Database Administration. **Knowledge/Courses**—No data available.

**Personality Type:** No data available. **Career Cluster:** 11 Information Technology. **Career Pathway:** 11.4 Programming and Software Development. **Other Jobs in This Pathway:** Architectural and Engineering Managers; Bioinformatics Scientists; Computer Hardware Engineers; Computer Numerically Controlled Machine Tool Programmers, Metal and Plastic.

**Skills**—No data available.

**Work Environment:** No data available.

## Job Specialization: Document Management Specialists

**Implement and administer enterprise-wide document management procedures for the capture, storage, retrieval, sharing, and destruction of electronic records and documents.** Keep abreast of developments in document management by reviewing current literature, talking with colleagues, participating in educational programs, attending meetings or workshops, or participating in professional organizations or conferences. Monitor regulatory activity to maintain compliance with records and document management laws. Write, review, or execute plans for testing new or established document management systems. Search electronic sources, such as databases or repositories, or manual sources for information. Retrieve electronic assets from repository for distribution to users, collecting and returning to repository, if necessary. Propose recommendations for improving content management system capabilities. Prepare support documentation and training materials for end users of document management systems. Prepare and record changes to official documents and confirm changes with legal and compliance management staff. Exercise security surveillance over document processing, reproduction, distribution, storage, or archiving. Implement scanning or other

C

automated data entry procedures, using imaging devices and document imaging software. Document technical functions and specifications for new or proposed content management systems. Develop, document, or maintain standards, best practices, or system usage procedures. Consult with end users regarding problems in accessing electronic content. Conduct needs assessments to identify document management requirements of departments or end users. Assist in the development of document or content classification taxonomies to facilitate information capture, search, and retrieval. Assist in the assessment, acquisition, or deployment of new electronic document management systems. Assist in determining document management policies to facilitate efficient, legal, and secure access to electronic content. Analyze, interpret, or disseminate system performance data.

**Education/Training Required:** Associate degree. **Education and Training Program:** Computer and Information Sciences and Support Services, Other. **Knowledge/Courses**—No data available.

**Personality Type:** No data available. **Career Cluster:** 11 Information Technology. **Career Pathway:** 11.2 Information Support Services. **Other Jobs in This Pathway:** Computer and Information Systems Managers; Computer Numerically Controlled Machine Tool Programmers, Metal and Plastic; Computer Operators; Remote Sensing Scientists and Technologists; Remote Sensing Technicians.

**Skills**—No data available.

**Work Environment:** No data available.

## Job Specialization: Geographic Information Systems Technicians

**Assist scientists, technologists, and related professionals in building, maintaining, modifying, and using geographic information systems (GIS) databases. May also perform some custom application development and provide user support.** Recommend procedures and equipment or software upgrades to increase data accessibility or ease of use. Provide technical support to users or clients regarding the maintenance, development, or operation of Geographic Information Systems (GIS) databases, equipment, or applications. Read current literature, talk with colleagues, continue education, or participate in professional organizations or conferences to keep abreast of developments in Geographic Information Systems (GIS) technology, equipment, or systems. Confer with users to analyze, configure, or troubleshoot applications. Select cartographic elements needed for effective presentation of information. Transfer or

rescale information from original photographs onto maps or other photographs. Review existing or incoming data for currency, accuracy, usefulness, quality, or completeness of documentation. Interpret aerial or ortho photographs. Analyze Geographic Information Systems (GIS) data to identify spatial relationships or display results of analyses using maps, graphs, or tabular data. Perform geospatial data building, modeling, or analysis using advanced spatial analysis, data manipulation, or cartography software. Maintain or modify existing Geographic Information Systems (GIS) databases. Enter data into Geographic Information Systems (GIS) databases using techniques such as coordinate geometry, keyboard entry of tabular data, manual digitizing of maps, scanning or automatic conversion to vectors, and conversion of other sources of digital data. Design or prepare graphic representations of Geographic Information Systems (GIS) data using GIS hardware or software applications. Design or coordinate the development of integrated Geographic Information Systems (GIS) spatial or non-spatial databases.

**Education/Training Required:** Associate degree. **Education and Training Program:** Geographic Information Science and Cartography. **Knowledge/Courses**—No data available.

**Personality Type:** Investigative-Realistic-Conventional. **Career Cluster:** 11 Information Technology. **Career Pathway:** 11.4 Programming and Software Development. **Other Jobs in This Pathway:** Architectural and Engineering Managers; Bioinformatics Scientists; Computer Hardware Engineers; Computer Numerically Controlled Machine Tool Programmers, Metal and Plastic.

**Skills**—No data available.

**Work Environment:** No data available.

## Job Specialization: Geospatial Information Scientists and Technologists

**Research and develop geospatial technologies. May produce databases, perform applications programming, or coordinate projects. May specialize in areas such as agriculture, mining, health care, retail trade, urban planning or military intelligence.** Perform integrated and computerized Geographic Information Systems (GIS) analyses to address scientific problems. Develop specialized computer software routines, internet-based Geographic Information Systems (GIS) databases or business applications to customize geographic information. Provide technical support for computer-based Geographic Information Systems (GIS) mapping software. Create visual representations of geospatial data using complex procedures such as analytical modeling, three-dimensional renderings, and plot creation. Perform computer programming, data analysis, or software development for Geographic Information Systems (GIS) applications, including the maintenance of existing systems or research and development for future enhancements. Assist users in formulating Geographic Information Systems (GIS) requirements or understanding the implications of alternatives. Collect, compile, or integrate Geographic Information Systems (GIS) data such as remote sensing and cartographic data for inclusion in map manuscripts. Conduct or coordinate research, data analysis, systems design, or support for software such as Geographic Information Systems (GIS) or Global Positioning Systems (GPS) mapping software. Design, program, or model Geographic Information Systems (GIS) applications or procedures. Document, design, code, or test Geographic Information Systems (GIS) models, internet mapping solutions, or other applications. Make recommendations regarding upgrades, considering implications of new or revised Geographic Information Systems (GIS) software, equipment, or applications. Produce data layers, maps, tables, or reports using spatial analysis procedures and Geographic Information Systems (GIS) technology, equipment, or systems. Coordinate the development or administration of Geographic Information Systems (GIS) projects, including the development of technical priorities, client reporting and interface, or coordination and review of schedules and budgets.

**Education/Training Required:** Bachelor's degree. **Education and Training Program:** Geographic Information Science and Cartography. **Knowledge/Courses**—Geography, Computers and Electronics, Design, Engineering and Technology, Mathematics, Education and Training.

**Personality Type:** Investigative-Realistic-Conventional. **Career Cluster:** 11 Information Technology. **Career Pathway:** 11.4 Programming and Software Development. **Other Jobs in This Pathway:** Architectural and Engineering Managers; Bioinformatics Scientists; Computer Hardware Engineers; Computer Numerically Controlled Machine Tool Programmers, Metal and Plastic.

**Skills**—Science, Programming, Operations Analysis, Systems Evaluation, Systems Analysis, Technology Design, Mathematics, Reading Comprehension.

**Work Environment:** Indoors; sitting; using hands; repetitive motions.

# Job Specialization: Information Technology Project Managers

**Plan, initiate, and manage information technology (IT) projects. Lead and guide the work of technical staff. Serve as liaison between business and technical aspects of projects. Plan project stages and assess business implications for each stage. Monitor progress to assure deadlines, standards, and cost targets are met.** Perform risk assessments to develop response strategies. Submit project deliverables, ensuring adherence to quality standards. Monitor the performance of project team members, providing and documenting performance feedback. Confer with project personnel to identify and resolve problems. Assess current or future customer needs and priorities through communicating directly with customers, conducting surveys, or other methods. Schedule and facilitate meetings related to information technology projects. Monitor or track project milestones and deliverables. Negotiate with project stakeholders or suppliers to obtain resources or materials. Initiate, review, or approve modifications to project plans. Identify, review, or select vendors or consultants to meet project needs. Establish and execute a project communication plan. Identify need for initial or supplemental project resources. Direct or coordinate activities of project personnel. Develop implementation plans that include analyses such as cost-benefit or return on investment (ROI). Coordinate recruitment or selection of project personnel. Develop and manage annual budgets for information technology projects. Assign duties, responsibilities, and spans of authority to project personnel. Prepare project status reports by collecting, analyzing, and summarizing information and trends. Manage project execution to ensure adherence to budget, schedule, and scope. Develop or update project plans for information technology projects including information such as project objectives, technologies, systems, information specifications, schedules, funding, and staffing. Develop and manage work breakdown structure (WBS) of information technology projects.

**Education/Training Required:** Work experience in a related occupation. **Education and Training Program:** Information Technology Project Management. **Knowledge/Courses**—No data available.

**Personality Type:** No data available. **Career Clusters:** 04 Business, Management, and Administration; 11 Information Technology. **Career Pathway:** 11.4 Programming and Software Development. **Other Jobs in This Pathway:** Architectural and Engineering Managers; Bioinformatics Scientists; Computer Hardware Engineers; Computer Numerically Controlled Machine Tool Programmers, Metal and Plastic.

**Skills**—No data available.

**Work Environment:** No data available.

## Job Specialization: Search Marketing Strategists

**Employ search marketing tactics to increase visibility and engagement with content, products, or services in Internet-enabled devices or interfaces. Examine search query behaviors on general or specialty search engines or other Internet-based content. Analyze research, data, or technology to understand user intent and measure outcomes for ongoing optimization.** Keep abreast of government regulations and emerging web technology to ensure regulatory compliance by reviewing current literature, talking with colleagues, participating in educational programs, attending meetings or workshops, or participate in professional organizations or conferences. Resolve product availability problems in collaboration with customer service staff. Implement online customer service processes to ensure positive and consistent user experiences. Identify, evaluate, or procure hardware or software for implementing online marketing campaigns. Identify methods for interfacing web application technologies with enterprise resource planning or other system software. Define product requirements based on market research analysis in collaboration with design and engineering staff. Assist in the evaluation and negotiation of contracts with vendors and online partners. Propose online or multiple-sales-channel campaigns to marketing executives. Assist in the development of online transactional and security policies. Prepare electronic commerce designs and prototypes, such as storyboards, mock-ups, and other content, using graphics design software. Participate in the development of online marketing strategy. Identify and develop commercial or technical specifications to promote transactional web site functionality, including usability, pricing, checkout, or data security. Develop transactional web applications, using web programming software and knowledge of programming languages, such as hypertext markup language (HTML) and extensible markup language (XML). Coordinate sales or other promotional strategies with merchandising, operations, or inventory control staff to ensure product catalogs are current and accurate. Conduct market research analysis to identify electronic commerce trends, market opportunities, or competitor performance. Conduct financial modeling for online marketing programs or website revenue forecasting.

**Education/Training Required:** Bachelor's degree. **Education and Training Program:** Web Page, Digital/ Multimedia, and Information Resources Design. **Knowledge/Courses**—No data available.

**Personality Type:** No data available. **Career Clusters:** 11 Information Technology; 14 Marketing, Sales, and Service. **Career Pathway:** 14.2 Professional Sales and Marketing. **Other Jobs in This Pathway:** Cashiers; Counter and Rental Clerks; Door-To-Door Sales Workers, News and Street Vendors, and Related Workers; Driver/Sales Workers; Energy Brokers; First-Line Supervisors of Non-Retail Sales Workers; First-Line Supervisors of Retail Sales Workers; Hotel, Motel, and Resort Desk Clerks; Marketing Managers; Marking Clerks; Online Merchants; Order Fillers, Wholesale and Retail Sales; Parts Salespersons; Property, Real Estate, and Community Association Managers; Real Estate Sales Agents; Reservation and Transportation Ticket Agents and Travel Clerks; Retail Salespersons; Sales and Related Workers, All Other; Sales Representatives, Services, All Other; Sales Representatives, Wholesale and Manufacturing, Except Technical and Scientific Products; Sales Representatives, Wholesale and Manufacturing, Technical and Scientific Products; Solar Sales Representatives and Assessors; Stock Clerks—Stockroom, Warehouse, or Storage Yard; Stock Clerks, Sales Floor; Telemarketers; others.

**Skills**—No data available.

**Work Environment:** No data available.

## Job Specialization: Software Quality Assurance Engineers and Testers

**Develop and execute software test plans in order to identify software problems and their causes.** Design test plans, scenarios, scripts, or procedures. Test system modifications to prepare for implementation. Develop testing programs that address areas such as database impacts, software scenarios, regression testing, negative testing, error or bug retests, or usability. Document software defects, using a bug tracking system, and report defects to software developers. Identify, analyze, and document problems with program function, output, online screen, or content. Monitor bug resolution efforts and track successes. Create or maintain databases of known test defects. Plan test schedules or strategies in accordance with project scope or delivery dates. Participate in product design reviews to provide input on functional requirements, product designs, schedules, or potential problems. Review software documentation to ensure technical accuracy, compliance, or completeness, or to mitigate risks. Document test procedures to ensure replicability and compliance with standards. Develop or specify standards, methods, or procedures to determine product quality or release readiness. Update automated test scripts to ensure currency. Investigate customer problems referred by technical support. Install, maintain, or use software testing programs. Provide feedback and recommendations to developers on software usability and functionality. Monitor program performance to ensure efficient and problem-free operations. Conduct software compatibility tests with programs, hardware, operating systems, or network environments. Install and configure re-creations of software production environments to allow testing of software performance. Collaborate with field staff or customers to evaluate or diagnose problems and recommend possible solutions. Identify program deviance from standards, and suggest modifications to ensure compliance. Design or develop automated testing tools. Coordinate user or third party testing.

**Education/Training Required:** Bachelor's degree. **Education and Training Program:** Computer Engineering, General. **Knowledge/Courses**—Computers and Electronics, Engineering and Technology, Design, English Language, Mathematics, Clerical.

**Personality Type:** Investigative-Conventional-Realistic. **Career Cluster:** 11 Information Technology. **Career Pathway:** 11.4 Programming and Software Development. **Other Jobs in This Pathway:** Architectural and Engineering Managers; Bioinformatics Scientists; Computer Hardware Engineers; Computer Numerically Controlled Machine Tool Programmers, Metal and Plastic.

**Skills**—Programming, Installation, Technology Design, Operations Analysis, Troubleshooting, Science, Quality Control Analysis, Systems Evaluation.

**Work Environment:** Indoors; sitting; using hands; repetitive motions.

# Job Specialization: Video Game Designers

**Design core features of video games. Specify innovative game and role-play mechanics, storylines, and character biographies. Create and maintain design documentation. Guide and collaborate with production staff to produce games as designed.** Review or evaluate competitive products, film, music, television, and other art forms to generate new game design ideas. Provide test specifications to quality assurance staff. Keep abreast of game design technology and techniques, industry trends, or audience interests, reactions, and needs by reviewing current literature, talking with colleagues, participating in educational programs, attending meetings or workshops, or participating

in professional organizations or conferences. Create gameplay test plans for internal and external test groups. Provide feedback to designers and other colleagues regarding game design features. Balance and adjust gameplay experiences to ensure the critical and commercial success of the product. Write or supervise the writing of game text and dialogue. Solicit, obtain, and integrate feedback from design and technical staff into original game design. Provide feedback to production staff regarding technical game qualities or adherence to original design. Prepare two-dimensional concept layouts or three-dimensional mock-ups. Present new game design concepts to management and technical colleagues, including artists, animators, and programmers. Prepare and revise initial game sketches using two- and three-dimensional graphical design software. Oversee gameplay testing to ensure intended gaming experience and game adherence to original vision. Guide design discussions between development teams. Devise missions, challenges, or puzzles to be encountered in game play. Develop and maintain design level documentation, including mechanics, guidelines, and mission outlines. Determine supplementary virtual features, such as currency, item catalog, menu design, and audio direction. Create gameplay prototypes for presentation to creative and technical staff and management. Create and manage documentation, production schedules, prototyping goals, and communication plans in collaboration with production staff.

**Education/Training Required:** Postsecondary vocational training. **Education and Training Program:** Game and Interactive Media Design. **Knowledge/Courses**—No data available.

**Personality Type:** No data available. **Career Clusters:** 03 Arts, Audio/Video Technology, and Communications; 11 Information Technology. **Career Pathway:** 11.4 Programming and Software Development. **Other Jobs in This Pathway:** Architectural and Engineering Managers; Bioinformatics Scientists; Computer Hardware Engineers; Computer Numerically Controlled Machine Tool Programmers, Metal and Plastic.

**Skills**—No data available.

**Work Environment:** No data available.

# Job Specialization: Web Administrators

**Manage Web environment design, deployment, development, and maintenance activities. Perform testing and quality assurance of websites and Web applications.** Back up or modify applications and related data to provide for disaster recovery. Determine sources of web page or server problems, and take action to correct such problems. Review or update web page content or links in a timely manner, using appropriate tools. Monitor systems for intrusions or denial of service attacks, and report security breaches to appropriate personnel. Implement web site security measures, such as firewalls or message encryption. Administer internet/intranet infrastructure, including components such as web, file transfer protocol (FTP), news and mail servers. Collaborate with development teams to discuss, analyze, or resolve usability issues. Test backup or recovery plans regularly and resolve any problems. Monitor web developments through continuing education, reading, or participation in professional conferences, workshops, or groups. Implement updates, upgrades, and patches in a timely manner to limit loss of service. Identify or document backup or recovery plans. Collaborate with web developers to create and operate internal and external websites, or to manage projects, such as e-marketing campaigns. Install or configure web server software or hardware to ensure that directory structure is well-defined, logical, secure, and that files are named properly. Gather, analyze, or document user feedback to locate or resolve sources of problems. Develop web site performance metrics. Identify or address interoperability requirements. Document installation or configuration procedures to allow maintenance and repetition. Identify, standardize, and communicate levels of access and security. Track, compile, and analyze web site usage data. Test issues such as system integration, performance, and system security on a regular schedule or after any major program modifications. Recommend web site improvements, and develop budgets to support recommendations. Inform web site users of problems, problem resolutions or application changes and updates.

**Education/Training Required:** Bachelor's degree. **Education and Training Programs:** Computer and Information Systems Security/Information Assurance; Network and System Administration/Administrator; System, Networking, and LAN/WAN Management/Manager; Web/Multimedia Management and Webmaster Training. **Knowledge/Courses**—Computers and Electronics, Telecommunications, Design, Communications and Media, Sales and Marketing, Clerical.

**Personality Type:** Conventional-Enterprising-Investigative. **Career Cluster:** 11 Information Technology. **Career Pathway:** 11.4 Programming and Software Development. **Other Jobs in This Pathway:** Architectural and Engineering Managers; Bioinformatics Scientists; Computer Hardware

Engineers; Computer Numerically Controlled Machine Tool Programmers, Metal and Plastic.

**Skills**—Programming, Operations Analysis, Troubleshooting, Science, Technology Design, Quality Control Analysis, Installation, Systems Evaluation.

**Work Environment:** Indoors; sitting; using hands; repetitive motions.

# Computer Programmers

- ❊ Annual Earnings: $71,380
- ❊ Earnings Growth Potential: High (42.8%)
- ❊ Growth: –2.9%
- ❊ Annual Job Openings: 8,030
- ❊ Self-Employed: 5.5%

**Considerations for Job Outlook:** Employment is expected to increase as businesses and other organizations continue to demand newer, more sophisticated software products. As a result of rapid growth, job prospects for software engineers should be excellent. The need to replace workers who leave the occupation is expected to generate numerous openings for programmers.

**Convert project specifications and statements of problems and procedures to detailed logical flow charts for coding into computer language. Develop and write computer programs to store, locate, and retrieve specific documents, data, and information. May program websites.** Correct errors by making appropriate changes and rechecking the program to ensure that the desired results are produced. Conduct trial runs of programs and software applications to be sure they will produce the desired information and that the instructions are correct. Compile and write documentation of program development and subsequent revisions, inserting comments in the coded instructions so others can understand the program. Write, update, and maintain computer programs or software packages to handle specific jobs such as tracking inventory, storing or retrieving data, or controlling other equipment. Consult with managerial, engineering, and technical personnel to clarify program intent, identify problems, and suggest changes. Perform or direct revision, repair, or expansion of existing programs to increase operating efficiency or adapt to new requirements. Write, analyze, review, and rewrite programs, using workflow chart and diagram, and applying knowledge of computer capabilities, subject matter, and symbolic logic. Write or contribute to instructions or manuals to guide end users. Investigate whether networks, workstations, the central processing unit of the system, or peripheral equipment are responding to a program's instructions. Prepare detailed workflow charts and diagrams that describe input, output, and logical operation, and convert them into a series of instructions coded in a computer language. Perform systems analysis and programming tasks to maintain and control the use of computer systems software as a systems programmer. Consult with and assist computer operators or system analysts to define and resolve problems in running computer programs. Assign, coordinate, and review work and activities of programming personnel. Collaborate with computer manufacturers and other users to develop new programming methods. Train subordinates in programming and program coding.

**Education/Training Required:** Bachelor's degree. **Education and Training Programs:** Computer Programming, Other; Computer Programming, Specific Applications; Computer Programming, Vendor/Product Certification; Computer Programming/Programmer Training, General; Computer Science. **Knowledge/Courses**—Computers and Electronics, Mathematics, Design, Administration and Management, English Language, Communications and Media.

**Personality Type:** Investigative-Conventional. **Career Cluster:** 11 Information Technology. **Career Pathways:** 8.3 Health Informatics; 11.1 Network Systems; 11.3 Interactive Media; 11.4 Programming and Software Development; 15.2 Science and Mathematics. **Other Jobs in These Pathways:** Architectural and Engineering Managers; Biofuels/Biodiesel Technology and Product Development Managers; Biologists; Chemists; Clinical Psychologists; Community and Social Service Specialists, All Other; Computer and Information Systems Managers; Editors; Education, Training, and Library Workers, All Other; Engineers, All Other; Executive Secretaries and Executive Administrative Assistants; First-Line Supervisors of Office and Administrative Support Workers; Graphic Designers; Medical and Health Services Managers; Medical Assistants; Medical Records and Health Information Technicians; Medical Scientists, Except Epidemiologists; Medical Secretaries; Medical Transcriptionists; Mental Health Counselors; Physical Therapists; Public Relations Specialists; Receptionists and Information Clerks; Rehabilitation Counselors; Substance Abuse and Behavioral Disorder Counselors; others.

**Skills**—Programming, Quality Control Analysis, Operations Analysis, Technology Design, Systems Evaluation, Science, Mathematics, Systems Analysis.

**Work Environment:** Indoors; sitting; using hands; repetitive motions.

# Computer Science Teachers, Postsecondary

* Annual Earnings: $70,300
* Earnings Growth Potential: High (48.5%)
* Growth: 15.1%
* Annual Job Openings: 1,000
* Self-Employed: 0.2%

**Considerations for Job Outlook:** Enrollments in postsecondary institutions are expected to continue rising as more people attend college and as workers return to school to update their skills. Opportunities for part-time or temporary positions should be favorable, but significant competition exists for tenure-track positions.

**Teach courses in computer science. May specialize in a field of computer science, such as the design and function of computers or operations and research analysis.** Evaluate and grade students' classwork, laboratory work, assignments, and papers. Maintain student attendance records, grades, and other required records. Prepare and deliver lectures to undergraduate and/or graduate students on topics such as programming, data structures, and software design. Prepare course materials such as syllabi, homework assignments, and handouts. Compile, administer, and grade examinations or assign this work to others. Keep abreast of developments in their field by reading current literature, talking with colleagues, and participating in professional conferences. Initiate, facilitate, and moderate classroom discussions. Plan, evaluate, and revise curricula, course content, and course materials and methods of instruction. Supervise students' laboratory work. Maintain regularly scheduled office hours to advise and assist students. Select and obtain materials and supplies such as textbooks and laboratory equipment. Advise students on academic and vocational curricula and on career issues. Participate in student recruitment, registration, and placement activities. Collaborate with colleagues to address teaching and research issues. Serve on academic or administrative committees that deal with institutional policies, departmental matters, and academic issues. Act as advisers to student organizations. Supervise undergraduate and/or graduate teaching, internship, and research work. Perform administrative duties such as serving as department head. Conduct research in a particular field of knowledge and publish findings in professional journals, books, and/or electronic media. Direct research of other teachers or of graduate students working for advanced academic degrees. Provide professional consulting services to government and/or industry. Participate in campus and

C

community events. Compile bibliographies of specialized materials for outside reading assignments. Write grant proposals to procure external research funding.

**Education/Training Required:** Doctoral degree. **Education and Training Programs:** Computer and Information Sciences, General; Computer Programming/Programmer, General; Computer Science; Computer Systems Analysis/Analyst; Information Science/Studies. **Knowledge/Courses**—Computers and Electronics, Education and Training, Telecommunications, Mathematics, Engineering and Technology, English Language.

**Personality Type:** Social-Investigative-Conventional. **Career Clusters:** 05 Education and Training; 11 Information Technology. **Career Pathways:** 5.3 Teaching/Training; 11.1 Network Systems; 11.2 Information Support Services; 11.4 Programming and Software Development. **Other Jobs in These Pathways:** Adult Basic and Secondary Education and Literacy Teachers and Instructors; Architectural and Engineering Managers; Career/Technical Education Teachers, Secondary School; Chemists; Coaches and Scouts; Computer and Information Systems Managers; Computer Hardware Engineers; Computer Operators; Elementary School Teachers, Except Special Education; Fitness Trainers and Aerobics Instructors; Graphic Designers; Instructional Coordinators; Instructional Designers and Technologists; Kindergarten Teachers, Except Special Education; Librarians; Middle School Teachers, Except Special and Career/Technical Education; Multimedia Artists and Animators; Preschool Teachers, Except Special Education; Recreation Workers; Remote Sensing Technicians; Secondary School Teachers, Except Special and Career/Technical Education; Self-Enrichment Education Teachers; Teacher Assistants; Tutors; 37 other postsecondary teaching occupations; others.

**Skills**—Programming, Writing, Learning Strategies, Instructing, Reading Comprehension, Active Learning, Speaking, Systems Analysis.

**Work Environment:** Indoors; sitting.

# Computer Systems Analysts

- ❋ Annual Earnings: $77,740
- ❋ Earnings Growth Potential: Medium (37.8%)
- ❋ Growth: 20.3%
- ❋ Annual Job Openings: 22,280
- ❋ Self-Employed: 5.7%

**Considerations for Job Outlook:** Employment growth is projected as organizations continue to adopt the most efficient technologies and as the need for information security grows. Job prospects should be excellent.

**Analyze science, engineering, business, and all other data-processing problems for application to electronic data-processing systems. Analyze user requirements, procedures, and problems to automate or improve existing systems and review computer system capabilities, workflow, and scheduling limitations. May analyze or recommend commercially available software. May supervise computer programmers.** Provide staff and users with assistance solving computer related problems, such as malfunctions and program problems. Test, maintain, and monitor computer programs and systems, including coordinating the installation of computer programs and systems. Use object-oriented programming languages, as well as client and server applications development processes and multimedia and Internet technology. Confer with clients regarding the nature of the information processing or computation needs a computer program is to address. Coordinate and link the computer systems within an organization to increase compatibility and so information can be shared. Consult with management to ensure agreement on system principles. Expand or modify system to serve new purposes or improve work flow. Interview or survey workers, observe job performance or perform the job to determine what information is processed and how it is processed. Determine computer software or hardware needed to set up or alter system. Train staff and users to work with computer systems and programs. Analyze information processing or computation needs and plan and design computer systems, using techniques such as structured analysis, data modeling and information engineering. Assess the usefulness of pre-developed application packages and adapt them to a user environment. Define the goals of the system and devise flow charts and diagrams describing logical operational steps of programs. Develop, document and revise system design procedures, test procedures, and quality standards. Review and analyze computer printouts and performance indicators to locate code problems, and correct errors by correcting codes. Recommend new equipment or software packages. Read manuals, periodicals, and technical reports to learn how to develop programs that meet staff and user requirements. Supervise computer programmers or other systems analysts or serve as project leaders for particular systems projects.

**Education/Training Required:** Bachelor's degree. **Education and Training Programs:** Computer Systems Analysis/Analyst; Information Science/Studies. **Knowledge/**

**Courses**—Computers and Electronics, Engineering and Technology, Mathematics, Clerical, Telecommunications, English Language.

**Personality Type:** Investigative-Conventional-Realistic. **Career Cluster:** 11 Information Technology. **Career Pathways:** 11.2 Information Support Services; 11.3 Interactive Media; 11.4 Programming and Software Development. **Other Jobs in These Pathways:** Architectural and Engineering Managers; Bioinformatics Scientists; Computer and Information Systems Managers; Computer Hardware Engineers; Computer Numerically Controlled Machine Tool Programmers, Metal and Plastic; Computer Operators; Remote Sensing Scientists and Technologists; Remote Sensing Technicians.

**Skills**—Programming, Technology Design, Troubleshooting, Quality Control Analysis, Systems Evaluation, Operations Analysis, Systems Analysis, Mathematics.

**Work Environment:** Indoors; sitting; using hands; repetitive motions; noise.

## Job Specialization: Informatics Nurse Specialists

**Apply knowledge of nursing and informatics to assist in the design, development, and ongoing modification of computerized health-care systems. May educate staff and assist in problem solving to promote the implementation of the health-care system.** Design, develop, select, test, implement, and evaluate new or modified informatics solutions, data structures, and decision-support mechanisms to support patients, health care professionals, and their information management and human-computer and human-technology interactions within health care contexts. Disseminate information about nursing informatics science and practice to the profession, other health care professions, nursing students, and the public. Translate nursing practice information between nurses and systems engineers, analysts, or designers using object-oriented models or other techniques. Plan, install, repair or troubleshoot telehealth technology applications or systems in homes. Use informatics science to design or implement health information technology applications to resolve clinical or health care administrative problems. Develop, implement or evaluate health information technology applications, tools, processes or structures to assist nurses with data management. Analyze and interpret patient, nursing, or information systems data to improve nursing services. Analyze computer and information technologies to determine applicability to nursing practice, education, administration and research. Apply knowledge of computer science, information science, nursing, and informatics theory to nursing practice, education, administration, or research, in collaboration with other health informatics specialists. Develop or implement policies or practices to ensure the privacy, confidentiality, or security of patient information. Design, conduct, or provide support to nursing informatics research. Develop or deliver training programs for health information technology, creating operating manuals as needed. Develop strategies, policies or procedures for introducing, evaluating or modifying information technology applied to nursing practice, administration, education, or research.

**Education/Training Required:** Master's degree. **Education and Training Programs:** Computer Systems Analysis/Analyst; Information Science/Studies. **Knowledge/Courses**—Medicine and Dentistry, Sociology and Anthropology, Education and Training, Engineering and Technology, Computers and Electronics, Clerical.

**Personality Type:** Social-Investigative. **Career Clusters:** 08 Health Science; 11 Information Technology. **Career Pathway:** 8.1 Therapeutic Services. **Other Jobs in This Pathway:** Clinical Psychologists; Community and Social Service Specialists, All Other; Counseling Psychologists; Dental Assistants; Dental Hygienists; Dentists, General; Health Technologists and Technicians, All Other; Healthcare Support Workers, All Other; Home Health Aides; Licensed Practical and Licensed Vocational Nurses; Low Vision Therapists, Orientation and Mobility Specialists, and Vision Rehabilitation Therapists; Massage Therapists; Medical and Clinical Laboratory Technicians; Medical and Health Services Managers; Medical Scientists, Except Epidemiologists; Medical Secretaries; Occupational Therapists; Pharmacists; Pharmacy Technicians; Radiologic Technologists; School Psychologists; Social and Human Service Assistants; Speech-Language Pathologists; Speech-Language Pathology Assistants; Substance Abuse and Behavioral Disorder Counselors; others.

**Skills**—Programming, Technology Design, Science, Systems Evaluation, Systems Analysis, Operations Analysis, Equipment Selection, Active Learning.

**Work Environment:** Indoors; sitting; using hands; repetitive motions.

# Conservation Scientists

- ❋ Annual Earnings: $59,310
- ❋ Earnings Growth Potential: Medium (39.2%)
- ❋ Growth: 11.9%
- ❋ Annual Job Openings: 410
- ❋ Self-Employed: 1.8%

**Considerations for Job Outlook:** Increased conservation efforts and continued pressure to maximize efficient use of natural resources are expected to lead to more jobs for conservation scientists. Job seekers with a bachelor's degree should have the best prospects.

## Job Specialization: Park Naturalists

**Plan, develop, and conduct programs to inform public of historical, natural, and scientific features of national, state, or local park.** Provide visitor services by explaining regulations; answering visitor requests, needs, and complaints; and providing information about the park and surrounding areas. Conduct field trips to point out scientific, historic, and natural features of parks, forests, historic sites, or other attractions. Prepare and present illustrated lectures and interpretive talks about park features. Perform emergency duties to protect human life, government property, and natural features of park. Confer with park staff to determine subjects and schedules for park programs. Assist with operations of general facilities, such as visitor centers. Plan, organize, and direct activities of seasonal staff members. Perform routine maintenance on park structures. Prepare brochures and write newspaper articles. Construct historical, scientific, and nature visitor-center displays. Research stories regarding the area's natural history or environment. Interview specialists in desired fields to obtain and develop data for park information programs. Compile and maintain official park photographic and information files. Take photographs and motion pictures for use in lectures and publications and to develop displays. Survey park to determine forest conditions and distribution and abundance of fauna and flora. Plan and develop audiovisual devices for public programs.

**Education/Training Required:** Bachelor's degree. **Education and Training Programs:** Forest Management/Forest Resources Management; Forest Sciences and Biology; Forestry, General; Forestry, Other; Land Use Planning and Management/Development; Natural Resources and Conservation, Other; Natural Resources Management and Policy; Natural Resources Management and Policy, Other; Natural Resources/Conservation, General; Water, Wetlands, and Marine Resources Management; Wildlife, Fish, and Wildlands Science and Management. **Knowledge/Courses—** Biology, History and Archeology, Geography, Sociology and Anthropology, Communications and Media, Customer and Personal Service.

**Personality Type:** Social-Realistic-Artistic. **Career Cluster:** 01 Agriculture, Food, and Natural Resources. **Career Pathway:** 1.5 Natural Resources Systems. **Other Jobs in This Pathway:** Climate Change Analysts; Conveyor Operators and Tenders; Derrick Operators, Oil and Gas; Engineering Technicians, Except Drafters, All Other; Environmental Economists; Environmental Restoration Planners; Environmental Science and Protection Technicians, Including Health; Environmental Scientists and Specialists, Including Health; Fishers and Related Fishing Workers; Forest and Conservation Technicians; Geological Sample Test Technicians; Geophysical Data Technicians; Helpers—Extraction Workers; Industrial Ecologists; Industrial Truck and Tractor Operators; Logging Equipment Operators; Mechanical Engineering Technicians; Range Managers; Recreation Workers; Refuse and Recyclable Material Collectors; Rotary Drill Operators, Oil and Gas; Service Unit Operators, Oil, Gas, and Mining; Soil and Water Conservationists; Wellhead Pumpers; Zoologists and Wildlife Biologists; others.

**Skills—**Operations Analysis, Equipment Maintenance, Equipment Selection, Science, Repairing, Writing, Learning Strategies, Troubleshooting.

**Work Environment:** More often indoors than outdoors; sitting; using hands; very hot or cold; minor burns, cuts, bites, or stings.

## Job Specialization: Range Managers

**Research or study range land management practices to provide sustained production of forage, livestock, and wildlife.** Regulate grazing and help ranchers plan and organize grazing systems to manage, improve, and protect rangelands and maximize their use. Measure and assess vegetation resources for biological assessment companies, environmental impact statements, and rangeland monitoring programs. Maintain soil stability and vegetation for non-grazing uses, such as wildlife habitats and outdoor recreation. Mediate agreements among rangeland users and preservationists as to appropriate land use and management. Study rangeland management practices and research range problems to provide sustained production of forage, livestock, and wildlife. Manage forage resources through fire, herbicide use, or revegetation to maintain a sustainable yield from the land.

Offer advice to rangeland users on water management, forage production methods, and control of brush. Plan and direct construction and maintenance of range improvements such as fencing, corrals, stock-watering reservoirs, and soil-erosion control structures. Tailor conservation plans to landowners' goals, such as livestock support, wildlife, or recreation. Develop technical standards and specifications used to manage, protect, and improve the natural resources of rangelands and related grazing lands. Study grazing patterns to determine number and kind of livestock that can be most profitably grazed and to determine the best grazing seasons. Plan and implement revegetation of disturbed sites. Study forage plants and their growth requirements to determine varieties best suited to particular range. Develop methods for protecting range from fire and rodent damage and for controlling poisonous plants. Manage private livestock operations. Develop new and improved instruments and techniques for activities such as range reseeding.

**Education/Training Required:** Bachelor's degree. **Education and Training Programs:** Forest Management/Forest Resources Management; Forest Sciences and Biology; Forestry, General; Forestry, Other; Land Use Planning and Management/Development; Natural Resources and Conservation, Other; Natural Resources Management and Policy; Natural Resources Management and Policy, Other; Natural Resources/Conservation, General; Water, Wetlands, and Marine Resources Management; Wildlife, Fish, and Wildlands Science and Management. **Knowledge/Courses**—Biology, Geography, Food Production, History and Archeology, Law and Government, Engineering and Technology.

**Personality Type:** Realistic-Investigative-Enterprising. **Career Cluster:** 01 Agriculture, Food, and Natural Resources. **Career Pathway:** 1.5 Natural Resources Systems. **Other Jobs in This Pathway:** Climate Change Analysts; Conveyor Operators and Tenders; Derrick Operators, Oil and Gas; Engineering Technicians, Except Drafters, All Other; Environmental Economists; Environmental Restoration Planners; Environmental Science and Protection Technicians, Including Health; Environmental Scientists and Specialists, Including Health; Fishers and Related Fishing Workers; Forest and Conservation Technicians; Geological Sample Test Technicians; Geophysical Data Technicians; Helpers—Extraction Workers; Industrial Ecologists; Industrial Truck and Tractor Operators; Logging Equipment Operators; Mechanical Engineering Technicians; Park Naturalists; Recreation Workers; Refuse and Recyclable Material Collectors; Rotary Drill Operators, Oil and Gas; Service Unit Operators, Oil, Gas, and Mining; Soil and Water Conservationists; Wellhead Pumpers; Zoologists and Wildlife Biologists; others.

**Skills**—Science, Operations Analysis, Systems Analysis, Negotiation, Mathematics, Complex Problem Solving, Management of Material Resources, Operation and Control.

**Work Environment:** More often outdoors than indoors; sitting; noise; very hot or cold; minor burns, cuts, bites, or stings.

## Job Specialization: Soil and Water Conservationists

**Plan and develop coordinated practices for soil erosion control, soil and water conservation, and sound land use.** Develop and maintain working relationships with local government staff and board members. Advise land users such as farmers and ranchers on conservation plans, problems, and alternative solutions and provide technical and planning assistance. Apply principles of specialized fields of science, such as agronomy, soil science, forestry, or agriculture, to achieve conservation objectives. Plan soil management and conservation practices, such as crop rotation, reforestation, permanent vegetation, contour plowing, or terracing, to maintain soil and conserve water. Visit areas affected by erosion problems to seek sources and solutions. Monitor projects during and after construction to ensure projects conform to design specifications. Compute design specifications for implementation of conservation practices, using survey and field information technical guides, engineering manuals, and calculator. Revisit land users to view implemented land use practices and plans. Coordinate and implement technical, financial, and administrative assistance programs for local government units to ensure efficient program implementation and timely responses to requests for assistance. Analyze results of investigations to determine measures needed to maintain or restore proper soil management. Participate on work teams to plan, develop, and implement water and land management programs and policies. Develop, conduct, and/or participate in surveys, studies, and investigations of various land uses, gathering information for use in developing corrective action plans. Survey property to mark locations and measurements, using surveying instruments. Compute cost estimates of different conservation practices based on needs of land users, maintenance requirements, and life expectancy of practices. Provide information, knowledge, expertise, and training to government agencies at all levels to solve water and soil management problems and to assure coordination of resource protection activities.

**Education/Training Required:** Bachelor's degree. **Education and Training Programs:** Forest Management/Forest Resources Management; Forest Sciences and Biology; Forestry, General; Forestry, Other; Land Use Planning and Management/Development; Natural Resources and Conservation, Other; Natural Resources Management and Policy; Natural Resources Management and Policy, Other; Natural Resources/Conservation, General; Water, Wetlands, and Marine Resources Management; Wildlife, Fish, and Wildlands Science and Management. **Knowledge/Courses**— Geography, Biology, Engineering and Technology, Design, History and Archeology, Food Production.

**Personality Type:** Investigative-Realistic-Enterprising. **Career Cluster:** 01 Agriculture, Food, and Natural Resources. **Career Pathway:** 1.5 Natural Resources Systems. **Other Jobs in This Pathway:** Climate Change Analysts; Conveyor Operators and Tenders; Derrick Operators, Oil and Gas; Engineering Technicians, Except Drafters, All Other; Environmental Economists; Environmental Restoration Planners; Environmental Science and Protection Technicians, Including Health; Environmental Scientists and Specialists, Including Health; Fishers and Related Fishing Workers; Forest and Conservation Technicians; Geological Sample Test Technicians; Geophysical Data Technicians; Helpers—Extraction Workers; Industrial Ecologists; Industrial Truck and Tractor Operators; Logging Equipment Operators; Mechanical Engineering Technicians; Park Naturalists; Range Managers; Recreation Workers; Refuse and Recyclable Material Collectors; Rotary Drill Operators, Oil and Gas; Service Unit Operators, Oil, Gas, and Mining; Wellhead Pumpers; Zoologists and Wildlife Biologists; others.

**Skills**—Science, Operations Analysis, Mathematics, Management of Financial Resources, Systems Evaluation, Persuasion, Systems Analysis, Quality Control Analysis.

**Work Environment:** More often outdoors than indoors; sitting; contaminants.

# Construction and Building Inspectors

- ❋ Annual Earnings: $52,360
- ❋ Earnings Growth Potential: Medium (38.9%)
- ❋ Growth: 16.8%
- ❋ Annual Job Openings: 3,970
- ❋ Self-Employed: 7.5%

**Considerations for Job Outlook:** Employment growth is expected to be driven by desires for safety and improved quality of construction. Prospects should be best for workers who have some college education, certification, and construction experience.

**Inspect structures using engineering skills to determine structural soundness and compliance with specifications, building codes, and other regulations. Inspections may be general in nature or may be limited to a specific area, such as electrical systems or plumbing.** Issue violation notices and stop-work orders, conferring with owners, violators, and authorities to explain regulations and recommend rectifications. Inspect bridges, dams, highways, buildings, wiring, plumbing, electrical circuits, sewers, heating systems, and foundations during and after construction for structural quality, general safety, and conformance to specifications and codes. Approve and sign plans that meet required specifications. Review and interpret plans, blueprints, site layouts, specifications, and construction methods to ensure compliance to legal requirements and safety regulations. Monitor installation of plumbing, wiring, equipment, and appliances to ensure that installation is performed properly and is in compliance with applicable regulations. Inspect and monitor construction sites to ensure adherence to safety standards, building codes, and specifications. Measure dimensions and verify level, alignment, and elevation of structures and fixtures to ensure compliance to building plans and codes. Maintain daily logs and supplement inspection records with photographs. Use survey instruments, metering devices, tape measures, and test equipment such as concrete strength measurers to perform inspections. Train, direct, and supervise other construction inspectors. Issue permits for construction, relocation, demolition, and occupancy. Examine lifting and conveying devices such as elevators, escalators, moving sidewalks, lifts and hoists, inclined railways, ski lifts, and amusement rides to ensure safety and proper functioning. Compute estimates of work completed or of needed renovations or upgrades and approve payment for contractors. Evaluate premises for cleanliness, including proper garbage disposal and lack of vermin infestation.

**Education/Training Required:** Work experience in a related occupation. **Education and Training Program:** Building/Home/Construction Inspection/Inspector. **Knowledge/Courses**—Building and Construction, Engineering and Technology, Design, Physics, Public Safety and Security, Mechanical.

**Personality Type:** Realistic-Conventional-Investigative. **Career Cluster:** 02 Architecture and Construction. **Career**

**Pathway:** 2.2 Construction. **Other Jobs in This Pathway:** Brickmasons and Blockmasons; Cement Masons and Concrete Finishers; Construction Carpenters; Construction Laborers; Construction Managers; Cost Estimators; Drywall and Ceiling Tile Installers; Electrical Power-Line Installers and Repairers; Electricians; Engineering Technicians, Except Drafters, All Other; Excavating and Loading Machine and Dragline Operators; First-Line Supervisors of Construction Trades and Extraction Workers; Heating and Air Conditioning Mechanics and Installers; Helpers—Carpenters; Helpers—Electricians; Helpers—Pipelayers, Plumbers, Pipefitters, and Steamfitters; Highway Maintenance Workers; Operating Engineers and Other Construction Equipment Operators; Painters, Construction and Maintenance; Pipe Fitters and Steamfitters; Plumbers; Refrigeration Mechanics and Installers; Roofers; Rough Carpenters; Solar Energy Installation Managers; others.

**Skills**—Science, Quality Control Analysis, Operation and Control, Systems Evaluation, Mathematics, Systems Analysis, Operation Monitoring, Troubleshooting.

**Work Environment:** More often outdoors than indoors; standing; noise; very hot or cold; bright or inadequate lighting; contaminants; cramped work space; high places.

# Construction and Related Workers, All Other

- ❋ Annual Earnings: $34,500
- ❋ Earnings Growth Potential: Medium (39.1%)
- ❋ Growth: 11.1%
- ❋ Annual Job Openings: 2,660
- ❋ Self-Employed: 8.5%

**Considerations for Job Outlook:** About average employment growth is projected.

**This occupation includes all construction and related workers not listed separately.** Because this is a highly diverse occupation, no data is available for some information topics.

**Education/Training Required:** Moderate-term on-the-job training. **Education and Training Programs:** No related CIP programs; this job is learned through informal short-term on-the-job training.

**Career Clusters:** 02 Architecture and Construction; 13 Manufacturing. **Career Pathways:** 2.2 Construction; 13.3 Maintenance, Installation, and Repair. **Other Jobs**

**in These Pathways:** Automotive Specialty Technicians; Cement Masons and Concrete Finishers; Computer, Automated Teller, and Office Machine Repairers; Construction Carpenters; Construction Laborers; Construction Managers; Cost Estimators; Drywall and Ceiling Tile Installers; Electrical and Electronic Equipment Assemblers; Electrical Engineering Technicians; Electricians; Electronics Engineering Technicians; First-Line Supervisors of Construction Trades and Extraction Workers; Heating and Air Conditioning Mechanics and Installers; Helpers—Installation, Maintenance, and Repair Workers; Industrial Machinery Mechanics; Installation, Maintenance, and Repair Workers, All Other; Operating Engineers and Other Construction Equipment Operators; Painters, Construction and Maintenance; Pipe Fitters and Steamfitters; Plumbers; Refrigeration Mechanics and Installers; Rough Carpenters; Solar Energy Installation Managers; Telecommunications Line Installers and Repairers; others.

## Job Specialization: Solar Thermal Installers and Technicians

**Install or repair solar energy systems designed to collect, store, and circulate solar-heated water for residential, commercial or industrial use.** Design active direct or indirect, passive direct or indirect, or pool solar systems. Perform routine maintenance or repairs to restore solar thermal systems to baseline operating conditions. Apply operation or identification tags or labels to system components, as required. Assess collector sites to ensure structural integrity of potential mounting surfaces or the best orientation and tilt for solar collectors. Connect water heaters and storage tanks to power and water sources. Determine locations for installing solar subsystem components, including piping, water heaters, valves, and ancillary equipment. Fill water tanks and check tanks, pipes, and fittings for leaks. Identify plumbing, electrical, environmental, or safety hazards associated with solar thermal installations. Install circulating pumps using pipe, fittings, soldering equipment, electrical supplies, and hand tools. Install copper or plastic plumbing using pipes, fittings, pipe cutters, acetylene torches, solder, wire brushes, sand cloths, flux, plastic pipe cleaners, or plastic glue. Install flat-plat, evacuated glass, or concentrating solar collectors on mounting devices, using brackets or struts. Install heat exchangers and heat exchanger fluids according to installation manuals and schematics. Install monitoring system components, such as flow meters, temperature gauges, and pressure gauges, according to system design and manufacturer specifications. Install plumbing, such as dip tubes, port fittings, drain tank valves, pressure temperature relief valves, or tanks, according to manufacturer specifications and building codes. Install solar collector mounting devices on tile, asphalt, shingle, or built-up gravel roofs, using appropriate materials and penetration methods. Install solar thermal system controllers and sensors. Test operation or functionality of mechanical, plumbing, electrical, and control systems. Apply ultraviolet radiation protection to prevent degradation of plumbing.

**Education/Training Required:** Postsecondary vocational training. **Education and Training Program:** Construction Trades, Other. **Knowledge/Courses**—No data available.

**Personality Type:** No data available. **Career Cluster:** 13 Manufacturing. **Career Pathway:** 13.3 Maintenance, Installation, and Repair. **Other Jobs in This Pathway:** Aircraft Mechanics and Service Technicians; Automotive Specialty Technicians; Biological Technicians; Civil Engineering Technicians; Computer, Automated Teller, and Office Machine Repairers; Electrical and Electronic Equipment Assemblers; Electrical and Electronics Repairers, Commercial and Industrial Equipment; Electrical Engineering Technicians; Electrical Engineering Technologists; Electromechanical Engineering Technologists; Electronics Engineering Technicians; Electronics Engineering Technologists; Engineering Technicians, Except Drafters, All Other; Fuel Cell Technicians; Helpers—Installation, Maintenance, and Repair Workers; Industrial Engineering Technologists; Industrial Machinery Mechanics; Installation, Maintenance, and Repair Workers, All Other; Manufacturing Engineering Technologists; Manufacturing Production Technicians; Mapping Technicians; Mechanical Engineering Technologists; Mobile Heavy Equipment Mechanics, Except Engines; Telecommunications Line Installers and Repairers; Tire Repairers and Changers; others.

**Skills**—No data available.

**Work Environment:** No data available.

## Job Specialization: Weatherization Installers and Technicians

**Perform a variety of activities to weatherize homes and make them more energy efficient. Duties include repairing windows, insulating ducts, and performing heating, ventilating, and air-conditioning (HVAC) work. May perform energy audits and advise clients on energy conservation measures.** Inspect buildings to identify required weatherization measures, including repair work, modification, or replacement. Recommend weatherization techniques to clients in accordance with needs and applicable energy regulations, codes, policies, or statutes. Test and diagnose air flow systems, using furnace efficiency analysis equipment. Apply insulation materials such as loose, blanket, board, and foam insulation to attics, crawl spaces, basements, or walls. Explain energy conservation measures, such as the use of low flow showerheads and energy efficient lighting. Install and seal air ducts, combustion air openings, or ventilation openings to improve heating and cooling efficiency. Install storm windows or storm doors and verify proper fit. Make minor repairs using basic hand or power tools and materials, such as glass, lumber, and drywall. Prepare and apply weather-stripping, glazing, caulking, or door sweeps to reduce energy losses. Prepare cost estimates or specifications for rehabilitation or weatherization services. Wrap air ducts and water lines with insulating materials, such as duct wrap and pipe insulation. Wrap water heaters with water heater blankets. Apply spackling, compounding, or other materials to repair holes in walls. Clean and maintain tools and equipment. Contact residents or building owners to schedule appointments. Explain recommendations, policies, procedures, requirements, or other related information to residents or building owners. Maintain activity logs, financial transaction logs, or other records of weatherization work performed. Prepare or assist in the preparation of bids, contracts, or written reports related to weatherization work.

**Education/Training Required:** Moderate-term on-the-job training. **Education and Training Program:** Insulator Training. **Knowledge/Courses**—No data available.

**Personality Type:** No data available. **Career Cluster:** 13 Manufacturing. **Career Pathway:** 13.3 Maintenance, Installation, and Repair. **Other Jobs in This Pathway:** Aircraft Mechanics and Service Technicians; Automotive Specialty Technicians; Biological Technicians; Civil Engineering Technicians; Computer, Automated Teller, and Office Machine Repairers; Electrical and Electronic Equipment Assemblers; Electrical and Electronics Repairers, Commercial and Industrial Equipment; Electrical Engineering Technicians; Electrical Engineering Technologists; Electromechanical Engineering Technologists; Electronics Engineering Technicians; Electronics Engineering Technologists; Engineering Technicians, Except Drafters, All Other; Fuel Cell Technicians; Helpers—Installation, Maintenance, and Repair Workers; Industrial Engineering Technologists; Industrial Machinery Mechanics; Installation, Maintenance, and Repair Workers, All Other; Manufacturing Engineering Technologists; Manufacturing Production Technicians; Mapping Technicians; Mechanical Engineering Technologists; Mobile Heavy Equipment Mechanics,

Except Engines; Telecommunications Line Installers and Repairers; Tire Repairers and Changers; others.

**Skills**—No data available.

**Work Environment:** No data available.

# Construction Laborers

- ❋ Annual Earnings: $29,280
- ❋ Earnings Growth Potential: Medium (36.6%)
- ❋ Growth: 20.5%
- ❋ Annual Job Openings: 33,940
- ❋ Self-Employed: 21.3%

**Considerations for Job Outlook:** Employment of these workers is projected to increase because of additional government spending on infrastructure repair and reconstruction. Opportunities will vary based on job seekers' experience, training, and willingness to relocate.

**Perform tasks involving physical labor at building, highway, and heavy construction projects; tunnel and shaft excavations; and demolition sites. May operate hand and power tools of all types: air hammers, earth tampers, cement mixers, small mechanical hoists, surveying and measuring equipment, and various other types of equipment and instruments. May clean and prepare sites; dig trenches; set braces to support the sides of excavations; erect scaffolding; clean up rubble and debris; and remove asbestos, lead, and other hazardous waste materials. May assist other craft workers.** Clean and prepare construction sites to eliminate possible hazards. Read and interpret plans, instructions, and specifications to determine work activities. Control traffic passing near, in, and around work zones. Signal equipment operators to facilitate alignment, movement, and adjustment of machinery, equipment, and materials. Dig ditches or trenches, backfill excavations, and compact and level earth to grade specifications, using picks, shovels, pneumatic tampers, and rakes. Measure, mark, and record openings and distances to lay out areas where construction work will be performed. Position, join, align, and seal structural components, such as concrete wall sections and pipes. Load, unload, and identify building materials, machinery, and tools and distribute them to the appropriate locations according to project plans and specifications. Erect and disassemble scaffolding, shoring, braces, traffic barricades, ramps, and other temporary structures. Build and position forms for pouring concrete and dismantle forms after use, using saws, hammers, nails, or bolts. Lubricate, clean, and repair machinery, equipment, and tools. Operate jackhammers and drills to break up concrete or pavement. Smooth and finish freshly poured cement or concrete, using floats, trowels, screeds, or powered cement finishing tools. Operate, read, and maintain air monitoring and other sampling devices in confined or hazardous environments. Install sewer, water, and storm drain pipes, using pipe-laying machinery and laser guidance equipment. Transport and set explosives for tunnel, shaft, and road construction. Provide assistance to craft workers, such as carpenters, plasterers, and masons. Tend pumps, compressors, and generators to provide power for tools, machinery, and equipment or to heat and move materials such as asphalt. Mop, brush, or spread paints, cleaning solutions, or other compounds over surfaces to clean them or to provide protection.

**Education/Training Required:** Moderate-term on-the-job training. **Education and Training Program:** Construction Trades, Other. **Knowledge/Courses**—Building and Construction, Design, Mechanical, Transportation, Public Safety and Security, Engineering and Technology.

**Personality Type:** Realistic-Conventional. **Career Cluster:** 02 Architecture and Construction. **Career Pathway:** 2.2 Construction. **Other Jobs in This Pathway:** Brickmasons and Blockmasons; Cement Masons and Concrete Finishers; Construction and Building Inspectors; Construction Carpenters; Construction Managers; Cost Estimators; Drywall and Ceiling Tile Installers; Electrical Power-Line Installers and Repairers; Electricians; Engineering Technicians, Except Drafters, All Other; Excavating and Loading Machine and Dragline Operators; First-Line Supervisors of Construction Trades and Extraction Workers; Heating and Air Conditioning Mechanics and Installers; Helpers—Carpenters; Helpers—Electricians; Helpers—Pipelayers, Plumbers, Pipefitters, and Steamfitters; Highway Maintenance Workers; Operating Engineers and Other Construction Equipment Operators; Painters, Construction and Maintenance; Pipe Fitters and Steamfitters; Plumbers; Refrigeration Mechanics and Installers; Roofers; Rough Carpenters; Solar Energy Installation Managers; others.

**Skills**—Operation and Control, Equipment Selection, Installation, Equipment Maintenance, Operation Monitoring, Troubleshooting, Repairing, Quality Control Analysis.

**Work Environment:** Outdoors; standing; using hands; bending or twisting the body; repetitive motions; noise; very hot or cold; bright or inadequate lighting; contaminants; whole-body vibration; hazardous equipment; minor burns, cuts, bites, or stings.

# Construction Managers

- ❀ Annual Earnings: $83,860
- ❀ Earnings Growth Potential: Medium (40.1%)
- ❀ Growth: 17.2%
- ❀ Annual Job Openings: 13,770
- ❀ Self-Employed: 60.9%

**Considerations for Job Outlook:** As population and the number of businesses grow, building activity is expected to increase, which in turn will boost employment of construction managers. Prospects should be best for jobseekers who have a bachelor's or higher degree in a construction-related discipline, plus construction experience.

**Plan, direct, coordinate, or budget, usually through subordinate supervisory personnel, activities concerned with the construction and maintenance of structures, facilities, and systems. Participate in the conceptual development of a construction project and oversee its organization, scheduling, and implementation.** Schedule the project in logical steps and budget time required to meet deadlines. Confer with supervisory personnel, owners, contractors, and design professionals to discuss and resolve matters such as work procedures, complaints, and construction problems. Prepare contracts and negotiate revisions, changes, and additions to contractual agreements with architects, consultants, clients, suppliers, and subcontractors. Prepare and submit budget estimates and progress and cost tracking reports. Interpret and explain plans and contract terms to administrative staff, workers, and clients, representing the owner or developer. Plan, organize, and direct activities concerned with the construction and maintenance of structures, facilities, and systems. Take actions to deal with the results of delays, bad weather, or emergencies at construction sites. Inspect and review projects to monitor compliance with building and safety codes and other regulations. Study job specifications to determine appropriate construction methods. Select, contract, and oversee workers who complete specific pieces of the project, such as painting or plumbing. Obtain all necessary permits and licenses. Direct and supervise workers. Develop and implement quality control programs. Investigate damage, accidents, or delays at construction sites to ensure that proper procedures are being carried out. Determine labor requirements and dispatch workers to construction sites. Evaluate construction methods and determine cost-effectiveness of plans, using computers. Requisition supplies and materials to complete construction projects. Direct acquisition of land for construction projects.

**Education/Training Required:** Bachelor's degree. **Education and Training Programs:** Business Administration and Management, General; Business/Commerce, General; Construction Engineering Technology/Technician; Operations Management and Supervision. **Knowledge/Courses—** Building and Construction, Design, Engineering and Technology, Mechanical, Administration and Management, Personnel and Human Resources.

**Personality Type:** Enterprising-Realistic-Conventional. **Career Clusters:** 02 Architecture and Construction; 04 Business, Management, and Administration. **Career Pathways:** 2.2 Construction; 4.1 Management. **Other Jobs in These Pathways:** Brownfield Redevelopment Specialists and Site Managers; Business Continuity Planners; Business Operations Specialists, All Other; Compliance Managers; Construction Carpenters; Construction Laborers; Customs Brokers; Electricians; Energy Auditors; First-Line Supervisors of Construction Trades and Extraction Workers; First-Line Supervisors of Office and Administrative Support Workers; General and Operations Managers; Investment Fund Managers; Loss Prevention Managers; Management Analysts; Managers, All Other; Regulatory Affairs Managers; Rough Carpenters; Security Management Specialists; Security Managers; Solar Energy Installation Managers; Supply Chain Managers; Sustainability Specialists; Wind Energy Operations Managers; Wind Energy Project Managers; others.

**Skills—**Management of Financial Resources, Management of Material Resources, Operations Analysis, Management of Personnel Resources, Mathematics, Negotiation, Persuasion, Systems Evaluation.

**Work Environment:** More often outdoors than indoors; sitting; noise; contaminants; hazardous equipment.

# Cooks, Institution and Cafeteria

- ❀ Annual Earnings: $22,730
- ❀ Earnings Growth Potential: Low (27.5%)
- ❀ Growth: 9.7%
- ❀ Annual Job Openings: 13,810
- ❀ Self-Employed: 1.4%

**Considerations for Job Outlook:** New jobs are expected to arise as people continue to eat out and purchase ready-made food, but growth will be tempered as restaurants and quick-service eating places find more efficient ways to prepare meals. Opportunities should be good.

**Prepare and cook large quantities of food for institutions, such as schools, hospitals, or cafeterias.** Clean and inspect galley equipment, kitchen appliances, and work areas to ensure cleanliness and functional operation. Apportion and serve food to facility residents, employees, or patrons. Cook foodstuffs according to menus, special dietary or nutritional restrictions, and numbers of portions to be served. Clean, cut, and cook meat, fish, and poultry. Monitor use of government food commodities to ensure that proper procedures are followed. Wash pots, pans, dishes, utensils, and other cooking equipment. Compile and maintain records of food use and expenditures. Direct activities of one or more workers who assist in preparing and serving meals. Bake breads, rolls, and other pastries. Train new employees. Take inventory of supplies and equipment. Monitor menus and spending to ensure that meals are prepared economically. Plan menus that are varied, nutritionally balanced, and appetizing, taking advantage of foods in season and local availability. Requisition food supplies, kitchen equipment, and appliances based on estimates of future needs. Determine meal prices based on calculations of ingredient prices.

**Education/Training Required:** Moderate-term on-the-job training. **Education and Training Programs:** Culinary Arts and Related Services, Other; Food Preparation/Professional Cooking/Kitchen Assistant Training; Foodservice Systems Administration/Management; Institutional Food Worker Training. **Knowledge/Courses**—Food Production.

**Personality Type:** Realistic-Conventional. **Career Clusters:** 08 Health Science; 09 Hospitality and Tourism. **Career Pathways:** 8.4 Support Services; 9.1 Restaurants and Food/Beverage Services. **Other Jobs in These Pathways:** Bakers; Baristas; Bartenders; Butchers and Meat Cutters; Chefs and Head Cooks; Combined Food Preparation and Serving Workers, Including Fast Food; Cooks, All Other; Cooks, Fast Food; Cooks, Restaurant; Cooks, Short Order; Counter Attendants, Cafeteria, Food Concession, and Coffee Shop; Dietetic Technicians; Dietitians and Nutritionists; Dining Room and Cafeteria Attendants and Bartender Helpers; Dishwashers; First-Line Supervisors of Food Preparation and Serving Workers; Food Batchmakers; Food Preparation and Serving Related Workers, All Other; Food Preparation Workers; Food Servers, Nonrestaurant; Food Service Managers; Hosts and Hostesses, Restaurant, Lounge, and Coffee Shop; Meat, Poultry, and Fish Cutters and Trimmers; Slaughterers and Meat Packers; Waiters and Waitresses; others.

**Skills**—Management of Financial Resources, Management of Material Resources, Operation and Control, Management

of Personnel Resources, Quality Control Analysis, Time Management, Mathematics, Operation Monitoring.

**Work Environment:** Indoors; standing; walking and running; using hands; bending or twisting the body; repetitive motions; noise; very hot or cold; minor burns, cuts, bites, or stings.

# Correctional Officers and Jailers

- ❀ Annual Earnings: $39,040
- ❀ Earnings Growth Potential: Low (33.3%)
- ❀ Growth: 9.4%
- ❀ Annual Job Openings: 14,360
- ❀ Self-Employed: 0.0%

**Considerations for Job Outlook:** Employment growth is expected to stem from population increases and a corresponding rise in the prison population. Favorable job opportunities are expected.

**Guard inmates in penal or rehabilitative institution in accordance with established regulations and procedures. May guard prisoners in transit between jail, courtroom, prison, or other point. Includes deputy sheriffs and police who spend the majority of their time guarding prisoners in correctional institutions.** Conduct head counts to ensure that each prisoner is present. Monitor conduct of prisoners in housing unit or during work or recreational activities according to established policies, regulations, and procedures to prevent escape or violence. Inspect conditions of locks, window bars, grills, doors, and gates at correctional facilities to ensure security and help prevent escapes. Record information such as prisoner identification, charges, and incidences of inmate disturbance and keep daily logs of prisoner activities. Search prisoners and vehicles and conduct shakedowns of cells for valuables and contraband, such as weapons or drugs. Use weapons, handcuffs, and physical force to maintain discipline and order among prisoners. Guard facility entrances to screen visitors. Inspect mail for the presence of contraband. Maintain records of prisoners' identification and charges. Process or book convicted individuals into prison. Settle disputes between inmates. Conduct fire, safety, and sanitation inspections. Provide to supervisors oral and written reports of the quality and quantity of work performed by inmates, inmate disturbances and rule violations, and unusual occurrences. Participate in required job training. Take prisoners into custody and escort to locations within and outside of facility, such as visiting room, courtroom, or airport. Serve meals, distribute commissary items, and dispense prescribed medication to prisoners. Counsel inmates and respond to legitimate questions, concerns, and requests. Drive passenger vehicles and trucks used to transport inmates to other institutions, courtrooms, hospitals, and work sites. Use non-disciplinary tools and equipment such as a computer. Assign duties to inmates, providing instructions as needed. Investigate crimes that have occurred within an institution or assist police in their investigations of crimes and inmates. Issue clothing, tools, and other authorized items to inmates.

**Education/Training Required:** Moderate-term on-the-job training. **Education and Training Programs:** Corrections; Corrections and Criminal Justice, Other; Juvenile Corrections. **Knowledge/Courses**—Public Safety and Security, Psychology, Therapy and Counseling, Law and Government, Medicine and Dentistry, Sociology and Anthropology.

**Personality Type:** Realistic-Enterprising-Conventional. **Career Cluster:** 12 Law, Public Safety, Corrections, and Security. **Career Pathways:** 12.2 Emergency and Fire Management Services; 12.4 Law Enforcement Services. **Other Jobs in These Pathways:** Bailiffs; Criminal Investigators and Special Agents; Fire Inspectors; Fire Investigators; First-Line Supervisors of Police and Detectives; Forensic Science Technicians; Forest Fire Fighting and Prevention Supervisors; Forest Fire Inspectors and Prevention Specialists; Forest Firefighters; Immigration and Customs Inspectors; Intelligence Analysts; Municipal Fire Fighting and Prevention Supervisors; Municipal Firefighters; Police Detectives; Police Identification and Records Officers; Police Patrol Officers; Remote Sensing Scientists and Technologists; Sheriffs and Deputy Sheriffs.

**Skills**—Negotiation, Persuasion, Social Perceptiveness, Service Orientation, Monitoring, Instructing, Coordination, Operation Monitoring.

**Work Environment:** Indoors; more often sitting than standing; walking and running; using hands; repetitive motions; noise; bright or inadequate lighting; contaminants; exposed to disease or infections.

# Cost Estimators

- ❀ Annual Earnings: $57,860
- ❀ Earnings Growth Potential: High (41.1%)
- ❀ Growth: 25.3%
- ❀ Annual Job Openings: 10,360
- ❀ Self-Employed: 2.0%

**Considerations for Job Outlook:** Projected employment gains will be driven primarily by increased construction and repair activity, particularly that related to infrastructure. Job seekers with a degree or extensive experience should have the best opportunities. In manufacturing, job seekers who have a degree and are familiar with cost estimation software should have the best prospects.

**Prepare cost estimates for product manufacturing, construction projects, or services to aid management in bidding on or determining prices of products or services. May specialize according to particular service performed or type of product manufactured.** Consult with clients, vendors, personnel in other departments, or construction foremen to discuss and formulate estimates and resolve issues. Analyze blueprints and other documentation to prepare time, cost, materials, and labor estimates. Prepare estimates for use in selecting vendors or subcontractors. Confer with engineers, architects, owners, contractors, and subcontractors on changes and adjustments to cost estimates. Prepare estimates used by management for purposes such as planning, organizing, and scheduling work. Prepare cost and expenditure statements and other necessary documentation at regular intervals for the duration of the project. Assess cost-effectiveness of products, projects, or services, tracking actual costs relative to bids as projects develop. Set up cost-monitoring and cost-reporting systems and procedures. Conduct special studies to develop and establish standard hour and related cost data or to effect cost reductions. Review material and labor requirements to decide whether it is more cost-effective to produce or purchase components. Prepare and maintain a directory of suppliers, contractors, and subcontractors. Establish and maintain tendering processes and conduct negotiations. Visit sites and record information about access, drainage and topography, and availability of services such as water and electricity.

**Education/Training Required:** Bachelor's degree. **Education and Training Programs:** Business Administration and Management, General; Business/Commerce, General; Construction Engineering; Construction Engineering Technology/Technician; Manufacturing Engineering; Materials Engineering; Mechanical Engineering. **Knowledge/Courses**—Engineering and Technology, Mathematics, Economics and Accounting, Building and Construction, Design, Computers and Electronics.

**Personality Type:** Conventional-Enterprising. **Career Clusters:** 02 Architecture and Construction; 04 Business, Management, and Administration; 13 Manufacturing; 15 Science, Technology, Engineering, and Mathematics. **Career Pathways:** 2.2 Construction; 4.1 Management; 13.1

Production; 15.1 Engineering and Technology. **Other Jobs in These Pathways:** Brownfield Redevelopment Specialists and Site Managers; Business Continuity Planners; Business Operations Specialists, All Other; Compliance Managers; Construction Carpenters; Construction Laborers; Customs Brokers; Energy Auditors; First-Line Supervisors of Construction Trades and Extraction Workers; First-Line Supervisors of Office and Administrative Support Workers; General and Operations Managers; Investment Fund Managers; Loss Prevention Managers; Management Analysts; Managers, All Other; Packers and Packagers, Hand; Regulatory Affairs Managers; Rough Carpenters; Security Management Specialists; Security Managers; Supply Chain Managers; Sustainability Specialists; Team Assemblers; Wind Energy Operations Managers; Wind Energy Project Managers; others.

**Skills**—Management of Financial Resources, Management of Material Resources, Mathematics, Programming, Systems Analysis, Persuasion, Active Learning, Complex Problem Solving.

**Work Environment:** Indoors; sitting.

# Counter Attendants, Cafeteria, Food Concession, and Coffee Shop

- ❊ Annual Earnings: $18,370
- ❊ Earnings Growth Potential: Very low (14.2%)
- ❊ Growth: 9.3%
- ❊ Annual Job Openings: 43,490
- ❊ Self-Employed: 0.2%

**Considerations for Job Outlook:** Job growth is projected due to an expanding population and the continued popularity of dining out. Opportunities should be excellent.

**Serve food to diners at counter or from a steam table.** Scrub and polish counters, steam tables, and other equipment and clean glasses, dishes, and fountain equipment. Serve food, beverages, or desserts to customers in such settings as take-out counters of restaurants or lunchrooms, business or industrial establishments, hotel rooms, and cars. Replenish foods at serving stations. Take customers' orders and write ordered items on tickets, giving ticket stubs to customers when needed to identify filled orders. Prepare food such as sandwiches, salads, and ice cream dishes, using standard formulas or following directions. Wrap menu item such as sandwiches, hot entrees, and desserts for serving or for takeout. Prepare bills for food, using cash registers,

calculators, or adding machines, and accept payment or make change. Deliver orders to kitchens and pick up and serve food when it is ready. Serve salads, vegetables, meat, breads, and cocktails; ladle soups and sauces; portion desserts; and fill beverage cups and glasses. Add relishes and garnishes to food orders according to instructions. Carve meat. Order items needed to replenish supplies. Set up dining areas for meals and clear them following meals. Brew coffee and tea and fill containers with requested beverages. Balance receipts and payments in cash registers. Arrange reservations for patrons of dining establishments.

**Education/Training Required:** Short-term on-the-job training. **Education and Training Program:** Food Service, Waiter/Waitress, and Dining Room Management/Manager. **Knowledge/Courses**—Food Production.

**Personality Type:** Realistic-Social-Enterprising. **Career Cluster:** 09 Hospitality and Tourism. **Career Pathway:** 9.1 Restaurants and Food/Beverage Services. **Other Jobs in This Pathway:** Bakers; Baristas; Bartenders; Butchers and Meat Cutters; Chefs and Head Cooks; Combined Food Preparation and Serving Workers, Including Fast Food; Cooks, All Other; Cooks, Fast Food; Cooks, Institution and Cafeteria; Cooks, Private Household; Cooks, Restaurant; Cooks, Short Order; Dining Room and Cafeteria Attendants and Bartender Helpers; Dishwashers; First-Line Supervisors of Food Preparation and Serving Workers; Food Preparation and Serving Related Workers, All Other; Food Preparation Workers; Food Servers, Nonrestaurant; Food Service Managers; Gaming Managers; Hosts and Hostesses, Restaurant, Lounge, and Coffee Shop; Meat, Poultry, and Fish Cutters and Trimmers; Slaughterers and Meat Packers; Waiters and Waitresses.

**Skills**—Service Orientation.

**Work Environment:** Indoors; standing; walking and running; using hands; repetitive motions; minor burns, cuts, bites, or stings.

## Job Specialization: Baristas

**Prepare or serve specialty coffee or other beverages. Serve food such as baked goods or sandwiches to patrons.** Prepare or serve hot or cold beverages, such as coffee, espresso drinks, blended coffees and teas. Clean or sanitize work areas, utensils or equipment. Clean service or seating areas. Check temperatures of freezers, refrigerators, or heating equipment to ensure proper functioning. Describe menu items to customers or suggest products that might appeal to them. Order, receive, or stock supplies or retail products.

Provide customers with product details, such as coffee blend and preparation descriptions. Receive and process customer payments. Serve prepared foods, such as muffins, biscotti and bagels. Stock customer service stations with paper products or beverage preparation items. Take customer orders and convey them to other employees for preparation. Take out garbage. Weigh, grind, or pack coffee beans for customers. Wrap, label, or date food items for sale. Create signs to advertise store products or events. Demonstrate the use of retail equipment, such as espresso machines. Prepare or serve menu items, such as sandwiches and salads. Set up or restock product displays. Slice fruits, vegetables, desserts, or meats for use in food service.

**Education/Training Required:** Short-term on-the-job training. **Education and Training Program:** Food Service, Waiter/Waitress, and Dining Room Management/Manager. **Knowledge/Courses—**No data available.

**Personality Type:** Enterprising-Conventional-Realistic. **Career Cluster:** 09 Hospitality and Tourism. **Career Pathway:** 9.1 Restaurants and Food/Beverage Services. **Other Jobs in This Pathway:** Bakers; Bartenders; Butchers and Meat Cutters; Chefs and Head Cooks; Combined Food Preparation and Serving Workers, Including Fast Food; Cooks, All Other; Cooks, Fast Food; Cooks, Institution and Cafeteria; Cooks, Private Household; Cooks, Restaurant; Cooks, Short Order; Counter Attendants, Cafeteria, Food Concession, and Coffee Shop; Dining Room and Cafeteria Attendants and Bartender Helpers; Dishwashers; First-Line Supervisors of Food Preparation and Serving Workers; Food Preparation and Serving Related Workers, All Other; Food Preparation Workers; Food Servers, Nonrestaurant; Food Service Managers; Gaming Managers; Hosts and Hostesses, Restaurant, Lounge, and Coffee Shop; Meat, Poultry, and Fish Cutters and Trimmers; Slaughterers and Meat Packers; Waiters and Waitresses.

**Skills—**No data available.

**Work Environment:** No data available.

## Court, Municipal, and License Clerks

- ❋ Annual Earnings: $34,390
- ❋ Earnings Growth Potential: Low (35.0%)
- ❋ Growth: 8.2%
- ❋ Annual Job Openings: 4,460
- ❋ Self-Employed: 1.5%

**Considerations for Job Outlook:** About average employment growth is projected.

**Perform clerical duties in courts of law, municipalities, and governmental licensing agencies and bureaus. May prepare docket of cases to be called, secure information for judges and court, prepare draft agendas or bylaws for town or city council, answer official correspondence, keep fiscal records and accounts, issue licenses or permits, record data, administer tests, or collect fees.** No task data available.

**Education/Training Required:** Short-term on-the-job training. **Education and Training Program:** General Office Occupations and Clerical Services. **Knowledge/Courses—** No data available.

**Personality Type:** No data available. **Career Cluster:** 04 Business, Management, and Administration. **Career Pathway:** 4.6 Administrative and Information Support. **Other Jobs in This Pathway:** Couriers and Messengers; Court Clerks; Customer Service Representatives; Data Entry Keyers; Dispatchers, Except Police, Fire, and Ambulance; Executive Secretaries and Executive Administrative Assistants; File Clerks; Human Resources Assistants, Except Payroll and Timekeeping; Information and Record Clerks, All Other; Insurance Claims Clerks; Insurance Policy Processing Clerks; Interviewers, Except Eligibility and Loan; License Clerks; Mail Clerks and Mail Machine Operators, Except Postal Service; Office and Administrative Support Workers, All Other; Office Clerks, General; Order Clerks; Patient Representatives; Postal Service Mail Carriers; Postal Service Mail Sorters, Processors, and Processing Machine Operators; Receptionists and Information Clerks; Secretaries and Administrative Assistants, Except Legal, Medical, and Executive; Shipping, Receiving, and Traffic Clerks; Switchboard Operators, Including Answering Service; Word Processors and Typists; others.

**Skills—**No data available.

**Work Environment:** No data available.

## Job Specialization: Court Clerks

**Perform clerical duties in court of law; prepare docket of cases to be called; secure information for judges; and contact witnesses, attorneys, and litigants to obtain information for court.** Prepare dockets or calendars of cases to be called, using typewriters or computers. Record case dispositions, court orders, and arrangements made for payment of court fees. Answer inquiries from the general public regarding judicial procedures, court appearances, trial dates, adjournments, outstanding warrants, summonses, subpoenas, witness fees, and payment of fines. Prepare and issue orders of the court, including probation orders, release documentation, sentencing information, and summonses. Prepare documents recording the outcomes of court proceedings. Instruct parties about timing of court appearances. Explain procedures or forms to parties in cases or to the general public. Search files and contact witnesses, attorneys, and litigants to obtain information for the court. Follow procedures to secure courtrooms and exhibits such as money, drugs, and weapons. Amend indictments when necessary and endorse indictments with pertinent information. Read charges and related information to the court and, if necessary, record defendants' pleas. Swear in jury members, interpreters, witnesses, and defendants. Collect court fees or fines and record amounts collected. Direct support staff in handling of paperwork processed by clerks' offices. Examine legal documents submitted to courts for adherence to laws or court procedures. Prepare and mark all applicable court exhibits and evidence. Record court proceedings, using recording equipment, or record minutes of court proceedings, using stenotype machines or shorthand. Prepare courtrooms with paper, pens, water, easels, and electronic equipment and ensure that recording equipment is working. Conduct roll calls and poll jurors. Meet with judges, lawyers, parole officers, police, and social agency officials to coordinate the functions of the court. Open courts, calling them to order and announcing judges.

**Education/Training Required:** Short-term on-the-job training. **Education and Training Program:** General Office Occupations and Clerical Services. **Knowledge/Courses—** Clerical, Law and Government, Computers and Electronics.

**Personality Type:** Conventional-Enterprising-Realistic. **Career Cluster:** 04 Business, Management, and Administration. **Career Pathway:** 4.6 Administrative and Information Support. **Other Jobs in This Pathway:** Couriers and Messengers; Court, Municipal, and License Clerks; Customer Service Representatives; Data Entry Keyers; Dispatchers, Except Police, Fire, and Ambulance; Executive Secretaries and Executive Administrative Assistants; File Clerks; Human Resources Assistants, Except Payroll and Timekeeping; Information and Record Clerks, All Other; Insurance Claims Clerks; Insurance Policy Processing Clerks; Interviewers, Except Eligibility and Loan; License Clerks; Mail Clerks and Mail Machine Operators, Except Postal Service; Office and Administrative Support Workers, All Other; Office Clerks, General; Order Clerks; Patient Representatives; Postal Service Mail Carriers; Postal Service Mail Sorters, Processors, and Processing Machine

Operators; Receptionists and Information Clerks; Secretaries and Administrative Assistants, Except Legal, Medical, and Executive; Shipping, Receiving, and Traffic Clerks; Switchboard Operators, Including Answering Service; Word Processors and Typists; others.

**Skills—**Reading Comprehension, Writing, Negotiation, Active Listening, Time Management, Speaking, Service Orientation.

**Work Environment:** Indoors; sitting; using hands; repetitive motions; noise.

## Job Specialization: License Clerks

**Issue licenses or permits to qualified applicants. Obtain necessary information, record data, advise applicants on requirements, collect fees, and issue licenses. May conduct oral, written, visual, or performance testing.** Collect prescribed fees for licenses. Code information on license applications for entry into computers. Evaluate information on applications to verify completeness and accuracy and to determine whether applicants are qualified to obtain desired licenses. Answer questions and provide advice to the public regarding licensing policies, procedures, and regulations. Maintain records of applications made and licensing fees collected. Question applicants to obtain required information, such as name, address, and age, and record data on prescribed forms. Update operational records and licensing information, using computer terminals. Inform customers by mail or telephone of additional steps they need to take to obtain licenses. Perform routine data entry and other office support activities, including creating, sorting, photocopying, distributing, and filing documents. Stock counters with adequate supplies of forms, film, licenses, and other required materials. Enforce canine licensing regulations, contacting non-compliant owners in person or by mail to inform them of the required regulations and potential enforcement actions. Assemble photographs with printed license information to produce completed documents. Prepare bank deposits and take them to banks. Operate specialized photographic equipment to obtain photographs for drivers' licenses and photo identification cards. Instruct customers in the completion of drivers' license application forms and other forms such as voter registration cards and organ donor forms. Conduct and score oral, visual, written, or performance tests to determine applicant qualifications and notify applicants of their scores. Send by mail drivers' licenses to out-of-county or out-of-state applicants. Perform record checks on past and current licensees as required by investigations. Respond to correspondence from insurance companies regarding the licensure of agents, brokers, and adjusters.

**Education/Training Required:** Short-term on-the-job training. **Education and Training Program:** General Office Occupations and Clerical Services. **Knowledge/Courses—** Clerical, Customer and Personal Service, Law and Government, Computers and Electronics.

**Personality Type:** Conventional-Enterprising. **Career Cluster:** 04 Business, Management, and Administration. **Career Pathway:** 4.6 Administrative and Information Support. **Other Jobs in This Pathway:** Couriers and Messengers; Court Clerks; Court, Municipal, and License Clerks; Customer Service Representatives; Data Entry Keyers; Dispatchers, Except Police, Fire, and Ambulance; Executive Secretaries and Executive Administrative Assistants; File Clerks; Human Resources Assistants, Except Payroll and Timekeeping; Information and Record Clerks, All Other; Insurance Claims Clerks; Insurance Policy Processing Clerks; Interviewers, Except Eligibility and Loan; Mail Clerks and Mail Machine Operators, Except Postal Service; Office and Administrative Support Workers, All Other; Office Clerks, General; Order Clerks; Patient Representatives; Postal Service Mail Carriers; Postal Service Mail Sorters, Processors, and Processing Machine Operators; Receptionists and Information Clerks; Secretaries and Administrative Assistants, Except Legal, Medical, and Executive; Shipping, Receiving, and Traffic Clerks; Switchboard Operators, Including Answering Service; Word Processors and Typists; others.

**Skills—**Service Orientation.

**Work Environment:** Indoors; sitting; using hands; repetitive motions; noise.

## Job Specialization: Municipal Clerks

**Draft agendas and bylaws for town or city council, record minutes of council meetings, answer official correspondence, keep fiscal records and accounts, and prepare reports on civic needs.** Participate in the administration of municipal elections, including preparation and distribution of ballots, appointment and training of election officers, and tabulation and certification of results. Record and edit the minutes of meetings; then distribute them to appropriate officials and staff members. Plan and direct the maintenance, filing, safekeeping, and computerization of all municipal documents. Issue public notification of all official activities and meetings. Maintain and update documents such as municipal codes and city charters. Prepare

meeting agendas and packets of related information. Prepare ordinances, resolutions, and proclamations so that they can be executed, recorded, archived, and distributed. Respond to requests for information from the public, other municipalities, state officials, and state and federal legislative offices. Maintain fiscal records and accounts. Perform budgeting duties, including assisting in budget preparation, expenditure review, and budget administration. Perform general office duties such as taking and transcribing dictation, typing and proofreading correspondence, distributing and filing official forms, and scheduling appointments. Coordinate and maintain office-tracking systems for correspondence and follow-up actions. Research information in the municipal archives upon request of public officials and private citizens. Perform contract administration duties, assisting with bid openings and the awarding of contracts. Collaborate with other staff to assist in the development and implementation of goals, objectives, policies, and priorities. Represent municipalities at community events and serve as liaisons on community committees. Serve as a notary of the public. Issue various permits and licenses, including marriage, fishing, hunting, and dog licenses, and collect appropriate fees. Provide assistance to persons with disabilities in reaching less-accessible areas of municipal facilities.

**Education/Training Required:** Short-term on-the-job training. **Education and Training Program:** General Office Occupations and Clerical Services. **Knowledge/Courses—** Clerical, Law and Government, Economics and Accounting, English Language, Personnel and Human Resources, Administration and Management.

**Personality Type:** Conventional-Enterprising. **Career Cluster:** 04 Business, Management, and Administration. **Career Pathway:** 4.6 Administrative and Information Support. **Other Jobs in This Pathway:** Couriers and Messengers; Court Clerks; Court, Municipal, and License Clerks; Customer Service Representatives; Data Entry Keyers; Dispatchers, Except Police, Fire, and Ambulance; Executive Secretaries and Executive Administrative Assistants; File Clerks; Human Resources Assistants, Except Payroll and Timekeeping; Information and Record Clerks, All Other; Insurance Claims Clerks; Insurance Policy Processing Clerks; Interviewers, Except Eligibility and Loan; Mail Clerks and Mail Machine Operators, Except Postal Service; Office and Administrative Support Workers, All Other; Office Clerks, General; Order Clerks; Patient Representatives; Postal Service Mail Carriers; Postal Service Mail Sorters, Processors, and Processing Machine Operators; Receptionists and Information Clerks; Secretaries and Administrative Assistants, Except Legal, Medical, and Executive; Shipping, Receiving, and Traffic Clerks; Switchboard

Operators, Including Answering Service; Word Processors and Typists; others.

**Skills**—Management of Financial Resources, Writing, Reading Comprehension, Speaking, Active Listening, Critical Thinking, Service Orientation, Coordination.

**Work Environment:** Indoors; sitting.

# Court Reporters

- ❋ Annual Earnings: $47,700
- ❋ Earnings Growth Potential: High (46.1%)
- ❋ Growth: 18.3%
- ❋ Annual Job Openings: 710
- ❋ Self-Employed: 14.0%

**Considerations for Job Outlook:** The continuing need for transcripts of legal proceedings, the growing demand for TV and other broadcast captioning, and the need to provide translating services for the deaf and the hard of hearing are expected to create jobs. Prospects should be excellent.

**Use verbatim methods and equipment to capture, store, retrieve, and transcribe pretrial and trial proceedings or other information. Includes stenocaptioners who operate computerized stenographic captioning equipment to provide captions of live or prerecorded broadcasts for hearing-impaired viewers.** Take notes in shorthand or use a stenotype or shorthand machine that prints letters on a paper tape. Provide transcripts of proceedings upon request of judges, lawyers, or the public. Record verbatim proceedings of courts, legislative assemblies, committee meetings, and other proceedings, using computerized recording equipment, electronic stenograph machines, or stenomasks. Transcribe recorded proceedings in accordance with established formats. Ask speakers to clarify inaudible statements. File a legible transcript of records of a court case with the court clerk's office. File and store shorthand notes of court session. Respond to requests during court sessions to read portions of the proceedings already recorded. Record depositions and other proceedings for attorneys. Verify accuracy of transcripts by checking copies against original records of proceedings and accuracy of rulings by checking with judges. Record symbols on computer disks or CD-ROM; then translate and display them as text in computer-aided transcription process.

**Education/Training Required:** Postsecondary vocational training. **Education and Training Program:** Court Reporting/Court Reporter. **Knowledge/Courses**—Clerical, English Language, Law and Government, Computers and Electronics, Production and Processing, Customer and Personal Service.

**Personality Type:** Conventional-Enterprising. **Career Cluster:** 12 Law, Public Safety, Corrections, and Security. **Career Pathway:** 12.5 Legal Services. **Other Jobs in This Pathway:** Administrative Law Judges, Adjudicators, and Hearing Officers; Arbitrators, Mediators, and Conciliators; Farm and Home Management Advisors; Judges, Magistrate Judges, and Magistrates; Lawyers; Legal Secretaries; Legal Support Workers, All Other; Paralegals and Legal Assistants; Title Examiners, Abstractors, and Searchers.

**Skills**—Operation and Control, Writing.

**Work Environment:** Indoors; sitting; using hands; repetitive motions; noise.

# Credit Analysts

- ❋ Annual Earnings: $58,850
- ❋ Earnings Growth Potential: Medium (39.2%)
- ❋ Growth: 15.0%
- ❋ Annual Job Openings: 2,430
- ❋ Self-Employed: 0.0%

**Considerations for Job Outlook:** Faster–than-average employment growth is projected.

**Analyze current credit data and financial statements of individuals or firms to determine the degree of risk involved in extending credit or lending money. Prepare reports with this credit information for use in decision-making.** Evaluate customer records and recommend payment plans based on earnings, savings data, payment history, and purchase activity. Confer with credit association and other business representatives to exchange credit information. Complete loan applications, including credit analyses and summaries of loan requests, and submit to loan committees for approval. Generate financial ratios, using computer programs, to evaluate customers' financial status. Review individual or commercial customer files to identify and select delinquent accounts for collection. Compare liquidity, profitability, and credit histories of establishments being evaluated with those of similar establishments in the same industries and geographic locations. Consult with customers to resolve complaints and verify financial and credit transactions. Analyze financial data such as income growth, quality of management, and market share to determine expected profitability of loans.

**Education/Training Required:** Bachelor's degree. **Education and Training Programs:** Accounting; Credit Management; Finance, General. **Knowledge/Courses**—Economics and Accounting, Clerical, Mathematics, Law and Government, English Language.

**Personality Type:** Conventional-Enterprising. **Career Clusters:** 04 Business, Management, and Administration; 06 Finance. **Career Pathways:** 4.2 Business, Financial Management, and Accounting; 6.1 Financial and Investment Planning; 6.2 Business Financial Management; 6.3 Banking and Related Services. **Other Jobs in These Pathways:** Accountants; Auditors; Bill and Account Collectors; Billing and Posting Clerks; Billing, Cost, and Rate Clerks; Bookkeeping, Accounting, and Auditing Clerks; Brownfield Redevelopment Specialists and Site Managers; Compliance Managers; Financial Analysts; Financial Managers, Branch or Department; Investment Fund Managers; Loss Prevention Managers; Managers, All Other; Regulatory Affairs Managers; Sales Agents, Financial Services; Sales Agents, Securities and Commodities; Securities and Commodities Traders; Securities, Commodities, and Financial Services Sales Agents; Security Managers; Statement Clerks; Supply Chain Managers; Tellers; Treasurers and Controllers; Wind Energy Operations Managers; Wind Energy Project Managers; others.

**Skills**—Mathematics, Programming, Systems Evaluation, Management of Financial Resources, Critical Thinking, Operations Analysis, Active Learning, Systems Analysis.

**Work Environment:** Indoors; sitting; repetitive motions.

# Credit Counselors

- ❀ Annual Earnings: $38,140
- ❀ Earnings Growth Potential: Low (29.5%)
- ❀ Growth: 16.3%
- ❀ Annual Job Openings: 880
- ❀ Self-Employed: 3.4%

**Considerations for Job Outlook:** Faster-than-average employment growth is projected.

**Advise and educate individuals or organizations on acquiring and managing debt. May provide guidance in determining the best type of loan and explaining loan requirements or restrictions. May help develop debt management plans, advise on credit issues, or provide budget, mortgage, and bankruptcy counseling.** Assess clients' overall financial situation by reviewing income, assets, debts, expenses, credit reports, or other financial information. Calculate clients' available monthly income to meet debt obligations. Create debt management plans, spending plans, or budgets to assist clients to meet financial goals. Estimate time for debt repayment given amount of debt, interest rates, and available funds. Explain services or policies to clients, such as debt management program rules, the advantages and disadvantages of using services, or creditor concession policies. Interview clients by telephone or in person to gather financial information. Maintain or update records of client account activity, including financial transactions, counseling session notes, correspondence, document images, or client inquiries. Negotiate with creditors on behalf of clients to arrange for payment adjustments, interest rate reductions, time extensions, or to set up payment plans. Prepare written documents to establish contracts with or communicate financial recommendations to clients. Prioritize client debt repayment to avoid dire consequences, such as bankruptcy or foreclosure or to reduce overall costs, such as by paying high-interest or short-term loans first. Recommend educational materials or resources to clients on matters such as financial planning, budgeting, or credit. Recommend strategies for clients to meet their financial goals, such as borrowing money through loans or loan programs, declaring bankruptcy, making budget adjustments, or enrolling in debt management plans. Refer clients to social service or community resources for needs beyond those of credit or debt counseling. Review changes to financial, family, or employment situations to determine whether changes to existing debt management plans, spending plans, or budgets are needed. Advise clients on housing matters, such as housing rental, homeownership, mortgage delinquency, or foreclosure prevention.

**Education/Training Required:** Bachelor's degree. **Education and Training Programs:** Banking and Financial Support Services; Finance and Financial Management Services, Other. **Knowledge/Courses**—No data available.

**Personality Type:** No data available. **Career Cluster:** 06 Finance. **Career Pathway:** 4.2 Business, Financial Management, and Accounting. **Other Jobs in This Pathway:** Accountants; Auditors; Billing and Posting Clerks; Billing, Cost, and Rate Clerks; Bookkeeping, Accounting, and Auditing Clerks; Brokerage Clerks; Brownfield Redevelopment Specialists and Site Managers; Budget Analysts; Compliance Managers; Credit Analysts; Financial Analysts; Financial Managers, Branch or Department; Investment Fund Managers; Logistics Managers; Loss Prevention Managers; Managers, All Other; Payroll and Timekeeping Clerks; Regulatory Affairs Managers; Security Managers; Statement Clerks; Supply Chain Managers; Tax Preparers;

Treasurers and Controllers; Wind Energy Operations Managers; Wind Energy Project Managers; others.

**Skills**—No data available.

**Work Environment:** No data available.

## Job Specialization: Loan Counselors

**Provide guidance to prospective loan applicants who have problems qualifying for traditional loans. Guidance may include determining the best type of loan and explaining loan requirements or restrictions.** Check loan agreements to ensure that they are complete and accurate, according to policies. Refer loans to loan committees for approval. Approve loans within specified limits. Submit applications to credit analysts for verification and recommendation. Analyze applicants' financial status, credit, and property evaluations to determine feasibility of granting loans. Interview applicants and request specified information for loan applications. Establish payment priorities according to credit terms and interest rates to reduce clients' overall costs. Contact applicants or creditors to resolve questions about applications or to assist with completion of paperwork. Maintain current knowledge of credit regulations. Calculate amount of debt and funds available to plan methods of payoff and to estimate time for debt liquidation. Analyze potential loan markets to find opportunities to promote loans and financial services. Review billing for accuracy. Supervise loan personnel. Maintain and review account records, updating and recategorizing them according to status changes. Assist in selection of financial award candidates using electronic databases to certify loan eligibility. Confer with underwriters to resolve mortgage application problems. Inform individuals and groups about the financial assistance available to college or university students. Match students' needs and eligibility with available financial aid programs to provide informed recommendations. Contact creditors to explain clients' financial situations and to arrange for payment adjustments so that payments are feasible for clients and agreeable to creditors. Petition courts to transfer titles and deeds of collateral to banks. Contact borrowers with delinquent accounts to obtain payment in full or to negotiate repayment plans. Compare data on student aid applications with eligibility requirements of assistance programs.

**Education/Training Required:** Moderate-term on-the-job training. **Education and Training Programs:** Banking and Financial Support Services; Finance and Financial Management Services, Other. **Knowledge/Courses**—Economics and Accounting, Law and Government, Clerical,

Customer and Personal Service, Fine Arts, Administration and Management.

**Personality Type:** Enterprising-Social-Conventional. **Career Cluster:** 06 Finance. **Career Pathways:** 6.1 Financial and Investment Planning; 6.3 Banking and Related Services. **Other Jobs in These Pathways:** Bill and Account Collectors; Budget Analysts; Credit Analysts; Credit Authorizers; Credit Checkers; Financial Analysts; Financial Managers, Branch or Department; Financial Quantitative Analysts; Financial Specialists, All Other; Fraud Examiners, Investigators and Analysts; Investment Underwriters; Loan Interviewers and Clerks; New Accounts Clerks; Personal Financial Advisors; Risk Management Specialists; Sales Agents, Financial Services; Sales Agents, Securities and Commodities; Securities and Commodities Traders; Securities, Commodities, and Financial Services Sales Agents; Tellers; Title Examiners, Abstractors, and Searchers; Treasurers and Controllers.

**Skills**—Service Orientation, Learning Strategies, Mathematics, Instructing, Persuasion, Judgment and Decision Making, Time Management, Social Perceptiveness.

**Work Environment:** More often indoors than outdoors; sitting; noise.

# Criminal Justice and Law Enforcement Teachers, Postsecondary

* Annual Earnings: $59,520
* Earnings Growth Potential: High (43.7%)
* Growth: 15.1%
* Annual Job Openings: 400
* Self-Employed: 0.2%

**Considerations for Job Outlook:** Enrollments in postsecondary institutions are expected to continue rising as more people attend college and as workers return to school to update their skills. Opportunities for part-time or temporary positions should be favorable, but significant competition exists for tenure-track positions.

**Teach courses in criminal justice, corrections, and law enforcement administration.** Initiate, facilitate, and moderate classroom discussions. Keep abreast of developments in their field by reading current literature, talking with colleagues, and participating in professional conferences. Evaluate and grade students' classwork, assignments, and papers. Compile, administer, and grade examinations or assign this work to others. Prepare and deliver lectures to undergraduate or graduate students on topics such as criminal law, defensive policing, and investigation techniques. Prepare course materials such as syllabi, homework assignments, and handouts. Conduct research in a particular field of knowledge and publish findings in professional journals, books, and/or electronic media. Plan, evaluate, and revise curricula, course content, and course materials and methods of instruction. Supervise undergraduate and/or graduate teaching, internship, and research work. Maintain student attendance records, grades, and other required records. Select and obtain materials and supplies such as textbooks. Advise students on academic and vocational curricula and on career issues. Maintain regularly scheduled office hours to advise and assist students. Collaborate with colleagues to address teaching and research issues. Write grant proposals to procure external research funding. Serve on academic or administrative committees that deal with institutional policies, departmental matters, and academic issues. Compile bibliographies of specialized materials for outside reading assignments. Participate in student recruitment, registration, and placement activities. Provide professional consulting services to government and/or industry. Perform administrative duties such as serving as department head. Participate in campus and community events. Act as advisers to student organizations.

**Education/Training Required:** Doctoral degree. **Education and Training Programs:** Corrections; Corrections Administration; Corrections and Criminal Justice, Other; Criminal Justice/Law Enforcement Administration; Criminal Justice/Police Science; Criminal Justice/Safety Studies; Criminalistics and Criminal Science; Forensic Science and Technology; Juvenile Corrections; Security and Loss Prevention Services; Teacher Education and Professional Development, Specific Subject Areas, Other. **Knowledge/Courses**—Sociology and Anthropology, Philosophy and Theology, History and Archeology, Law and Government, English Language, Education and Training.

**Personality Type:** Social-Investigative. **Career Clusters:** 05 Education and Training; 12 Law, Public Safety, Corrections, and Security. **Career Pathways:** 5.3 Teaching/Training; 12.1 Correction Services; 12.3 Security and Protective Services; 12.4 Law Enforcement Services. **Other Jobs in These Pathways:** Child, Family, and School Social Workers; Coaches and Scouts; Correctional Officers and Jailers; Criminal Investigators and Special Agents; Elementary School Teachers, Except Special Education; Fitness Trainers and Aerobics Instructors; Forest Firefighters; Immigration and Customs Inspectors; Instructional Coordinators; Instructional Designers and Technologists; Intelligence Analysts; Kindergarten Teachers, Except Special Education; Librarians; Lifeguards, Ski Patrol, and Other Recreational Protective Service Workers; Middle School Teachers, Except Special and Career/Technical Education; Police Patrol Officers; Preschool Teachers, Except Special Education; Recreation Workers; Secondary School Teachers, Except Special and Career/Technical Education; Security Guards; Self-Enrichment Education Teachers; Sheriffs and Deputy Sheriffs; Teacher Assistants; Tutors; 37 other postsecondary teaching occupations; others.

**Skills**—Writing, Learning Strategies, Speaking, Reading Comprehension, Instructing, Active Listening, Active Learning, Systems Analysis.

**Work Environment:** Indoors; sitting.

# Curators

- ❋ Annual Earnings: $48,450
- ❋ Earnings Growth Potential: High (43.0%)
- ❋ Growth: 23.0%
- ❋ Annual Job Openings: 620
- ❋ Self-Employed: 1.9%

**Considerations for Job Outlook:** Employment growth for curators should be strong as museum attendance levels remain high. Keen competition is expected.

**Administer affairs of museum and conduct research programs. Direct instructional, research, and public service activities of institution.** Plan and organize the acquisition, storage, and exhibition of collections and related materials, including the selection of exhibition themes and designs. Develop and maintain an institution's registration, cataloging, and basic recordkeeping systems, using computer databases. Provide information from the institution's holdings to other curators and to the public. Inspect premises to assess the need for repairs and to ensure that climate and pest-control issues are addressed. Train and supervise curatorial, fiscal, technical, research, and clerical staff, as well as volunteers or interns. Negotiate and authorize purchase, sale, exchange, or loan of collections. Plan and conduct special research projects in area of interest or expertise. Conduct or organize tours, workshops, and instructional sessions to acquaint individuals with an institution's facilities and materials. Confer with the board of directors to formulate and interpret policies, to determine budget requirements, and to plan overall operations. Attend meetings, conventions, and civic events to promote use of institution's services, to seek financing, and to maintain community alliances. Schedule events and organize details, including refreshment, entertainment, decorations, and the collection of any fees. Write and review grant proposals, journal articles, institutional reports, and publicity materials. Study, examine, and test acquisitions to authenticate their origin, composition, and history and to assess their current value. Arrange insurance coverage for objects on loan or for special exhibits and recommend changes in coverage for the entire collection. Establish specifications for reproductions and oversee their manufacture or select items from commercially available replica sources.

**Education/Training Required:** Master's degree. **Education and Training Programs:** Art History, Criticism and Conservation; History, General; Museology/Museum Studies; Public/Applied History. **Knowledge/Courses**—History and Archeology, Fine Arts, Geography, Sociology and Anthropology, Philosophy and Theology, English Language.

**Personality Type:** Enterprising-Conventional. **Career Clusters:** 03 Arts, Audio/Video Technology, and Communications; 15 Science, Technology, Engineering, and Mathematics. **Career Pathways:** 3.1 Audio and Video Technology and Film; 15.2 Science and Mathematics. **Other Jobs in These Pathways:** Architectural and Engineering Managers; Biofuels/Biodiesel Technology and Product Development Managers; Bioinformatics Scientists; Biological Scientists, All Other; Biologists; Broadcast Technicians; Chemists; Clinical Research Coordinators; Commercial and Industrial Designers; Community and Social Service Specialists, All Other; Dietitians and Nutritionists; Education, Training, and Library Workers, All Other; Geoscientists, Except Hydrologists and Geographers; Graphic Designers; Managers, All Other; Media and Communication Workers, All Other; Medical Scientists, Except Epidemiologists; Multimedia Artists and Animators; Natural Sciences Managers; Operations Research Analysts; Photographers; Social Scientists and Related Workers, All Other; Technical Directors/Managers; Transportation Planners; Water Resource Specialists; others.

**Skills**—Management of Financial Resources, Management of Material Resources, Writing, Systems Evaluation, Management of Personnel Resources, Active Learning, Systems Analysis, Speaking.

**Work Environment:** Indoors; sitting.

# Customer Service Representatives

- ❋ Annual Earnings: $30,460
- ❋ Earnings Growth Potential: Low (35.8%)
- ❋ Growth: 17.7%
- ❋ Annual Job Openings: 110,840
- ❋ Self-Employed: 0.4%

**Considerations for Job Outlook:** Businesses are expected to place increasing emphasis on customer relations, resulting in increased employment for these workers. Prospects are expected to be good, particularly for job seekers who are fluent in more than one language.

**Interact with customers to provide information in response to inquiries about products and services and to handle and resolve complaints.** Confer with customers by telephone or in person to provide information about products and services, to take orders or cancel accounts, or to obtain details of complaints. Keep records of customer interactions and transactions, recording details of inquiries, complaints, and comments, as well as actions taken. Resolve customers' service or billing complaints by performing activities such as exchanging merchandise, refunding money, and adjusting bills. Check to ensure that appropriate changes were made to resolve customers' problems. Contact customers to respond to inquiries or to notify them of claim investigation results and any planned adjustments. Refer unresolved customer grievances to designated departments for further investigation. Determine charges for services requested, collect deposits or payments, or arrange for billing. Complete contract forms, prepare change of address records, and issue service discontinuance orders, using computers. Obtain and examine all relevant information to assess validity of complaints and to determine possible causes, such as extreme weather conditions, that could increase utility bills. Solicit sale of new or additional services or products. Review insurance policy terms to determine whether a particular loss is covered by insurance. Review claims adjustments with dealers, examining parts claimed to be defective and approving or disapproving dealers' claims. Compare disputed merchandise with original requisitions and information from invoices and prepare invoices for returned goods. Order tests that could determine the causes of product malfunctions. Recommend improvements in products, packaging, shipping, service, or billing methods and procedures to prevent future problems.

**Education/Training Required:** Moderate-term on-the-job training. **Education and Training Programs:** Customer Service Support/Call Center/Teleservice Operation;

Receptionist Training. **Knowledge/Courses**—Clerical, Customer and Personal Service, English Language.

**Personality Type:** Enterprising-Social-Conventional. **Career Cluster:** 04 Business, Management, and Administration. **Career Pathway:** 4.6 Administrative and Information Support. **Other Jobs in This Pathway:** Couriers and Messengers; Court Clerks; Court, Municipal, and License Clerks; Data Entry Keyers; Dispatchers, Except Police, Fire, and Ambulance; Executive Secretaries and Executive Administrative Assistants; File Clerks; Human Resources Assistants, Except Payroll and Timekeeping; Information and Record Clerks, All Other; Insurance Claims Clerks; Insurance Policy Processing Clerks; Interviewers, Except Eligibility and Loan; License Clerks; Mail Clerks and Mail Machine Operators, Except Postal Service; Office and Administrative Support Workers, All Other; Office Clerks, General; Order Clerks; Patient Representatives; Postal Service Mail Carriers; Postal Service Mail Sorters, Processors, and Processing Machine Operators; Receptionists and Information Clerks; Secretaries and Administrative Assistants, Except Legal, Medical, and Executive; Shipping, Receiving, and Traffic Clerks; Switchboard Operators, Including Answering Service; Word Processors and Typists; others.

**Skills**—Service Orientation, Persuasion, Negotiation, Active Listening, Speaking, Reading Comprehension, Programming.

**Work Environment:** Indoors; sitting; using hands; repetitive motions; noise.

## Job Specialization: Patient Representatives

**Assist patients in obtaining services, understanding policies, and making health care decisions.** Explain policies, procedures, or services to patients using medical or administrative knowledge. Coordinate communication between patients, family members, medical staff, administrative staff, or regulatory agencies. Investigate and direct patient inquiries or complaints to appropriate medical staff members and follow up to ensure satisfactory resolution. Interview patients or their representatives to identify problems relating to care. Refer patients to appropriate health care services or resources. Analyze patients' abilities to pay to determine charges on a sliding scale. Collect and report data on topics such as patient encounters and inter-institutional problems, making recommendations for change when appropriate. Develop and distribute newsletters, brochures, or other printed materials to share information with patients or medical staff. Teach patients to use home health care equipment.

Identify and share research, recommendations, or other information regarding legal liabilities, risk management, or quality of care. Read current literature, talk with colleagues, continue education, or participate in professional organizations or conferences to keep abreast of developments in the field. Maintain knowledge of community services and resources available to patients. Provide consultation or training to volunteers or staff on topics such as guest relations, patients' rights, and medical issues.

**Education/Training Required:** Bachelor's degree. **Education and Training Programs:** Customer Service Support/ Call Center/Teleservice Operation; Receptionist Training. **Knowledge/Courses**—No data available.

**Personality Type:** Social-Enterprising. **Career Cluster:** 04 Business, Management, and Administration. **Career Pathway:** 4.6 Administrative and Information Support. **Other Jobs in This Pathway:** Couriers and Messengers; Court Clerks; Court, Municipal, and License Clerks; Customer Service Representatives; Data Entry Keyers; Dispatchers, Except Police, Fire, and Ambulance; Executive Secretaries and Executive Administrative Assistants; File Clerks; Human Resources Assistants, Except Payroll and Timekeeping; Information and Record Clerks, All Other; Insurance Claims Clerks; Insurance Policy Processing Clerks; Interviewers, Except Eligibility and Loan; License Clerks; Mail Clerks and Mail Machine Operators, Except Postal Service; Office and Administrative Support Workers, All Other; Office Clerks, General; Order Clerks; Postal Service Mail Carriers; Postal Service Mail Sorters, Processors, and Processing Machine Operators; Receptionists and Information Clerks; Secretaries and Administrative Assistants, Except Legal, Medical, and Executive; Shipping, Receiving, and Traffic Clerks; Switchboard Operators, Including Answering Service; Word Processors and Typists; others.

**Skills**—No data available.

**Work Environment:** No data available.

## Database Administrators

- ✺ Annual Earnings: $73,490
- ✺ Earnings Growth Potential: High (43.4%)
- ✺ Growth: 20.3%
- ✺ Annual Job Openings: 4,440
- ✺ Self-Employed: 0.6%

**Considerations for Job Outlook:** Employment of these workers should grow as organizations increasingly collect and organize data. Job prospects are expected to be excellent.

Coordinate changes to computer databases; test and implement the databases, applying knowledge of database management systems. May plan, coordinate, and implement security measures to safeguard computer databases. Develop standards and guidelines to guide the use and acquisition of software and to protect vulnerable information. Modify existing databases and database management systems or direct programmers and analysts to make changes. Test programs or databases, correct errors and make necessary modifications. Plan, coordinate, and implement security measures to safeguard information in computer files against accidental or unauthorized damage, modification, or disclosure. Approve, schedule, plan, and supervise the installation and testing of new products and improvements to computer systems such as the installation of new databases. Train users and answer questions. Establish and calculate optimum values for database parameters, using manuals and calculator. Specify users and user access levels for each segment of database. Develop data model describing data elements and how they are used, following procedures and using pen, template or computer software. Develop methods for integrating different products so they work properly together such as customizing commercial databases to fit specific needs. Review project requests describing database user needs to estimate time and cost required to accomplish project. Review procedures in database management system manuals for making changes to database. Work as part of a project team to coordinate database development and determine project scope and limitations. Select and enter codes to monitor database performance and to create production database. Identify and evaluate industry trends in database systems to serve as a source of information and advice for upper management. Write and code logical and physical database descriptions and specify identifiers of database to management system or direct others in coding descriptions. Review workflow charts developed by programmer analyst to understand tasks computer will perform, such as updating records. Revise company definition of data as defined in data dictionary.

**Education/Training Required:** Bachelor's degree. **Education and Training Program:** Data Modeling/Warehousing and Database Administration. **Knowledge/Courses**—Computers and Electronics, Telecommunications, Clerical, Communications and Media, Engineering and Technology, Mathematics.

**Personality Type:** Conventional-Investigative. **Career Cluster:** 11 Information Technology. **Career Pathways:** 4.4 Business Analysis; 11.2 Information Support Services; 11.4 Programming and Software Development. **Other Jobs in These Pathways:** Architectural and Engineering Managers;

Bioinformatics Scientists; Computer and Information Systems Managers; Computer Hardware Engineers; Computer Numerically Controlled Machine Tool Programmers, Metal and Plastic; Computer Operators; Natural Sciences Managers; Operations Research Analysts; Remote Sensing Scientists and Technologists; Remote Sensing Technicians.

**Skills**—Programming, Technology Design, Troubleshooting, Systems Evaluation, Management of Financial Resources, Operations Analysis, Systems Analysis, Mathematics.

**Work Environment:** Indoors; sitting; using hands; repetitive motions; noise.

# Dental Assistants

- ❋ Annual Earnings: $33,470
- ❋ Earnings Growth Potential: Low (32.2%)
- ❋ Growth: 35.7%
- ❋ Annual Job Openings: 16,100
- ❋ Self-Employed: 0.0%

**Considerations for Job Outlook:** An aging population and increased emphasis on preventative dental care will create more demand for dental services, and dentists are expected to hire more assistants to perform routine tasks. Job prospects should be excellent.

**Assist dentist, set up patient and equipment, and keep records.** Prepare patient, sterilize and disinfect instruments, set up instrument trays, prepare materials, and assist dentist during dental procedures. Expose dental diagnostic X-rays. Record treatment information in patient records. Take and record medical and dental histories and vital signs of patients. Provide postoperative instructions prescribed by dentist. Assist dentist in management of medical and dental emergencies. Pour, trim, and polish study casts. Instruct patients in oral hygiene and plaque control programs. Make preliminary impressions for study casts and occlusal registrations for mounting study casts. Clean and polish removable appliances. Clean teeth, using dental instruments. Apply protective coating of fluoride to teeth. Fabricate temporary restorations and custom impressions from preliminary impressions. Schedule appointments, prepare bills, and receive payment for dental services; complete insurance forms; and maintain records, manually or using computer.

**Education/Training Required:** Moderate-term on-the-job training. **Education and Training Program:** Dental Assisting/Assistant. **Knowledge/Courses**—Medicine and Dentistry, Customer and Personal Service, Psychology, Sales and Marketing.

**Personality Type:** Conventional-Realistic-Social. **Career Cluster:** 08 Health Science. **Career Pathway:** 8.1 Therapeutic Services. **Other Jobs in This Pathway:** Clinical Psychologists; Community and Social Service Specialists, All Other; Counseling Psychologists; Dental Hygienists; Dentists, General; Health Technologists and Technicians, All Other; Healthcare Support Workers, All Other; Home Health Aides; Licensed Practical and Licensed Vocational Nurses; Low Vision Therapists, Orientation and Mobility Specialists, and Vision Rehabilitation Therapists; Massage Therapists; Medical and Clinical Laboratory Technicians; Medical and Health Services Managers; Medical Scientists, Except Epidemiologists; Medical Secretaries; Occupational Therapists; Ophthalmic Medical Technologists; Pharmacists; Pharmacy Technicians; Radiologic Technologists; School Psychologists; Social and Human Service Assistants; Speech-Language Pathologists; Speech-Language Pathology Assistants; Substance Abuse and Behavioral Disorder Counselors; others.

**Skills**—Repairing, Equipment Maintenance, Operation Monitoring, Equipment Selection, Service Orientation, Science, Operation and Control, Quality Control Analysis.

**Work Environment:** Indoors; standing; walking and running; using hands; bending or twisting the body; repetitive motions; contaminants; exposed to radiation; exposed to disease or infections; hazardous conditions.

# Dental Hygienists

- ❋ Annual Earnings: $68,250
- ❋ Earnings Growth Potential: Low (34.1%)
- ❋ Growth: 36.1%
- ❋ Annual Job Openings: 9,840
- ❋ Self-Employed: 0.1%

**Considerations for Job Outlook:** An increase in the number of older people and a growing emphasis on preventative dental care are expected to create jobs. To meet increased demand, dental hygienists will perform some services previously done by dentists. Job prospects should be favorable but will vary by geographic location.

**Clean teeth and examine oral areas, head, and neck for signs of oral disease. May educate patients on oral hygiene, take and develop X-rays, or apply fluoride or sealants.** Clean calcareous deposits, accretions, and stains from teeth and beneath margins of gums, using dental instruments. Feel and visually examine gums for sores and signs of disease. Chart conditions of decay and disease

for diagnosis and treatment by dentist. Feel lymph nodes under patient's chin to detect swelling or tenderness that could indicate presence of oral cancer. Apply fluorides and other cavity-preventing agents to arrest dental decay. Examine gums, using probes, to locate periodontal recessed gums and signs of gum disease. Expose and develop X-ray film. Provide clinical services and health education to improve and maintain oral health of schoolchildren. Remove excess cement from coronal surfaces of teeth. Make impressions for study casts. Place, carve, and finish amalgam restorations. Administer local anesthetic agents. Conduct dental health clinics for community groups to augment services of dentist. Remove sutures and dressings. Place and remove rubber dams, matrices, and temporary restorations.

**Education/Training Required:** Associate degree. **Education and Training Program:** Dental Hygiene/Hygienist. **Knowledge/Courses**—Medicine and Dentistry, Psychology, Therapy and Counseling, Chemistry, Biology, Sales and Marketing.

**Personality Type:** Social-Realistic-Conventional. **Career Cluster:** 08 Health Science. **Career Pathway:** 8.1 Therapeutic Services. **Other Jobs in This Pathway:** Clinical Psychologists; Community and Social Service Specialists, All Other; Counseling Psychologists; Dental Assistants; Dentists, General; Health Technologists and Technicians, All Other; Healthcare Support Workers, All Other; Home Health Aides; Licensed Practical and Licensed Vocational Nurses; Low Vision Therapists, Orientation and Mobility Specialists, and Vision Rehabilitation Therapists; Massage Therapists; Medical and Clinical Laboratory Technicians; Medical and Health Services Managers; Medical Scientists, Except Epidemiologists; Medical Secretaries; Occupational Therapists; Ophthalmic Medical Technologists; Pharmacists; Pharmacy Technicians; Radiologic Technologists; School Psychologists; Social and Human Service Assistants; Speech-Language Pathologists; Speech-Language Pathology Assistants; Substance Abuse and Behavioral Disorder Counselors; others.

**Skills**—Science, Troubleshooting, Service Orientation, Writing, Instructing, Coordination, Operation Monitoring, Active Learning.

**Work Environment:** Indoors; sitting; using hands; bending or twisting the body; repetitive motions; noise; contaminants; exposed to radiation; exposed to disease or infections.

# Dental Laboratory Technicians

- ❀ Annual Earnings: $35,140
- ❀ Earnings Growth Potential: Medium (40.4%)
- ❀ Growth: 13.9%
- ❀ Annual Job Openings: 1,530
- ❀ Self-Employed: 6.2%

**Considerations for Job Outlook:** The ongoing prevalence of chronic diseases—which often necessitate the use of medical devices—is expected to increase employment of medical appliance technicians. And an aging population and increased demand for cosmetic dental procedures should create more jobs for dental and ophthalmic laboratory technicians. Favorable job prospects are expected.

**Construct and repair full or partial dentures or dental appliances.** Read prescriptions or specifications and examine models and impressions to determine the design of dental products to be constructed. Fabricate, alter, and repair dental devices such as dentures, crowns, bridges, inlays, and appliances for straightening teeth. Place tooth models on apparatus that mimics bite and movement of patient's jaw to evaluate functionality of model. Test appliances for conformance to specifications and accuracy of occlusion, using articulators and micrometers. Melt metals or mix plaster, porcelain, or acrylic pastes and pour materials into molds or over frameworks to form dental prostheses or apparatus. Prepare metal surfaces for bonding with porcelain to create artificial teeth, using small hand tools. Remove excess metal or porcelain and polish surfaces of prostheses or frameworks, using polishing machines. Create a model of patient's mouth by pouring plaster into a dental impression and allowing plaster to set. Load newly constructed teeth into porcelain furnaces to bake the porcelain onto the metal framework. Build and shape wax teeth, using small hand instruments and information from observations or dentists' specifications. Apply porcelain paste or wax over prosthesis frameworks or setups, using brushes and spatulas. Fill chipped or low spots in surfaces of devices, using acrylic resins. Prepare wax bite-blocks and impression trays for use. Mold wax over denture set-ups to form the full contours of artificial gums. Train and supervise other dental technicians or dental laboratory bench workers. Rebuild or replace linings, wire sections, and missing teeth to repair dentures. Shape and solder wire and metal frames or bands for dental products, using soldering irons and hand tools.

**Education/Training Required:** Long-term on-the-job training. **Education and Training Program:** Dental Laboratory Technology/Technician. **Knowledge/Courses**—Medicine and Dentistry, Design, Production and Processing, Chemistry, Mechanical, Physics.

**Personality Type:** Realistic-Investigative-Conventional. **Career Cluster:** 08 Health Science. **Career Pathway:** 8.3 Health Informatics. **Other Jobs in This Pathway:** Clinical Psychologists; Editors; Engineers, All Other; Executive Secretaries and Executive Administrative Assistants; Fine Artists, Including Painters, Sculptors, and Illustrators; First-Line Supervisors of Office and Administrative Support Workers; Health Educators; Medical and Health Services Managers; Medical Appliance Technicians; Medical Assistants; Medical Records and Health Information Technicians; Medical Secretaries; Medical Transcriptionists; Mental Health Counselors; Occupational Health and Safety Specialists; Occupational Health and Safety Technicians; Physical Therapists; Psychiatric Aides; Psychiatric Technicians; Public Relations Specialists; Receptionists and Information Clerks; Recreational Therapists; Rehabilitation Counselors; Substance Abuse and Behavioral Disorder Counselors; Therapists, All Other; others.

**Skills**—Quality Control Analysis, Equipment Selection, Operation and Control, Technology Design, Repairing, Equipment Maintenance, Operation Monitoring, Management of Material Resources.

**Work Environment:** Indoors; sitting; using hands; repetitive motions; noise; contaminants; exposed to disease or infections; minor burns, cuts, bites, or stings.

# Dentists, General

- ❀ Annual Earnings: $141,040
- ❀ Earnings Growth Potential: High (49.4%)
- ❀ Growth: 15.3%
- ❀ Annual Job Openings: 5,180
- ❀ Self-Employed: 28.0%

**Considerations for Job Outlook:** An increase in the elderly population—who often need complicated dental work—and expanded insurance coverage for dental procedures are expected to create job growth. Good prospects are expected from the need to replace the large number of dentists who are retiring.

**Diagnose and treat diseases, injuries, and malformations of teeth and gums and related oral structures. May treat diseases of nerve, pulp, and other dental tissues affecting vitality of teeth.** Use masks, gloves, and safety glasses to protect themselves and their patients from infectious diseases. Administer anesthetics to limit the amount of pain experienced by patients during procedures. Examine teeth, gums, and related tissues, using dental instruments, X-rays, and other diagnostic equipment, to evaluate dental health, diagnose diseases or abnormalities, and plan appropriate treatments. Formulate plan of treatment for patient's teeth and mouth tissue. Use air turbine and hand instruments, dental appliances, and surgical implements. Advise and instruct patients regarding preventive dental care, the causes and treatment of dental problems, and oral healthcare services. Design, make, and fit prosthodontic appliances such as space maintainers, bridges, and dentures or write fabrication instructions or prescriptions for denturists and dental technicians. Diagnose and treat diseases, injuries, and malformations of teeth, gums, and related oral structures and provide preventive and corrective services. Fill pulp chamber and canal with endodontic materials. Write prescriptions for antibiotics and other medications. Analyze and evaluate dental needs to determine changes and trends in patterns of dental disease. Treat exposure of pulp by pulp capping, removal of pulp from pulp chamber, or root canal, using dental instruments. Eliminate irritating margins of fillings and correct occlusions, using dental instruments. Perform oral and periodontal surgery on the jaw or mouth. Remove diseased tissue, using surgical instruments. Apply fluoride and sealants to teeth. Manage business, employing and supervising staff and handling paperwork and insurance claims. Bleach, clean, or polish teeth to restore natural color. Plan, organize, and maintain dental health programs. Produce and evaluate dental health educational materials.

**Education/Training Required:** First professional degree. **Education and Training Programs:** Advanced General Dentistry (Cert., MS, PhD); Dental Public Health and Education (Cert., MS/MPH, PhD/DPH); Dental Public Health Specialty; Dentistry (DDS, DMD); Pediatric Dentistry Residency Program; Pediatric Dentistry/Pedodontics (Cert., MS, PhD). **Knowledge/Courses**—Medicine and Dentistry, Biology, Psychology, Chemistry, Economics and Accounting, Customer and Personal Service.

**Personality Type:** Investigative-Realistic-Social. **Career Cluster:** 08 Health Science. **Career Pathway:** 8.1 Therapeutic Services. **Other Jobs in This Pathway:** Clinical Psychologists; Counseling Psychologists; Dental Assistants; Dental Hygienists; Dentists, All Other Specialists; Home Health Aides; Licensed Practical and Licensed Vocational Nurses; Low Vision Therapists, Orientation and Mobility Specialists, and Vision Rehabilitation Therapists; Massage Therapists; Medical and Clinical Laboratory Technicians; Medical and Health Services Managers; Medical Scientists, Except Epidemiologists; Medical Secretaries; Occupational Therapists; Ophthalmic Medical Technologists; Oral and Maxillofacial Surgeons; Orthodontists; Pharmacists; Pharmacy Technicians; Prosthodontists; Radiologic Technologists; School Psychologists; Social and Human Service Assistants; Speech-Language Pathologists; Substance Abuse and Behavioral Disorder Counselors; others.

**Skills**—Science, Management of Financial Resources, Management of Material Resources, Active Learning, Reading Comprehension, Operation and Control, Judgment and Decision Making, Complex Problem Solving.

**Work Environment:** Indoors; sitting; using hands; bending or twisting the body; repetitive motions; noise; contaminants; exposed to disease or infections.

# Detectives and Criminal Investigators

- ❋ Annual Earnings: $68,820
- ❋ Earnings Growth Potential: High (43.5%)
- ❋ Growth: 16.6%
- ❋ Annual Job Openings: 4,160
- ❋ Self-Employed: 1.1%

**Considerations for Job Outlook:** Population growth is the main source of demand for police services. Overall, opportunities in local police departments should be favorable for qualified applicants.

## Job Specialization: Criminal Investigators and Special Agents

**Investigate alleged or suspected criminal violations of federal, state, or local laws to determine if evidence is sufficient to recommend prosecution.** Record evidence and documents, using equipment such as cameras and photocopy machines. Obtain and verify evidence by interviewing and observing suspects and witnesses or by analyzing records. Examine records to locate links in chains of evidence or information. Prepare reports that detail investigation findings. Determine scope, timing, and direction of investigations. Collaborate with other offices and agencies to exchange information and coordinate activities. Testify before grand juries concerning criminal activity investigations. Analyze evidence in laboratories or in the field. Investigate organized crime, public corruption, financial crime, copyright infringement, civil rights violations, bank robbery, extortion, kidnapping, and other violations of federal or state statutes. Identify case issues and evidence needed, based on analysis of charges, complaints, or allegations of law violations. Obtain and use search and arrest warrants. Serve subpoenas or other official papers. Collaborate with other authorities on activities such as surveillance, transcription, and research. Develop relationships with informants to obtain information related to cases. Search for and collect evidence such as fingerprints, using investigative equipment. Collect and record physical information about arrested suspects, including fingerprints, height and weight measurements, and photographs. Compare crime scene fingerprints with those from suspects or fingerprint files to identify perpetrators, using computers. Administer counter-terrorism and counter-narcotics reward programs. Provide protection for individuals such as government leaders, political candidates, and visiting foreign dignitaries. Perform undercover assignments and maintain surveillance, including monitoring authorized wiretaps. Manage security programs designed to protect personnel, facilities, and information. Issue security clearances.

**Education/Training Required:** Work experience in a related occupation. **Education and Training Programs:** Criminal Justice/Police Science; Criminalistics and Criminal Science. **Knowledge/Courses**—Law and Government, Psychology, Geography, Public Safety and Security, Clerical, Telecommunications.

**Personality Type:** Enterprising-Investigative. **Career Cluster:** 12 Law, Public Safety, Corrections, and Security. **Career Pathway:** 12.4 Law Enforcement Services. **Other Jobs in This Pathway:** Bailiffs; Correctional Officers and Jailers; First-Line Supervisors of Police and Detectives; Forensic Science Technicians; Immigration and Customs Inspectors; Intelligence Analysts; Police Detectives; Police Identification and Records Officers; Police Patrol Officers; Remote Sensing Scientists and Technologists; Sheriffs and Deputy Sheriffs.

**Skills**—Science, Persuasion, Negotiation, Active Listening, Speaking, Critical Thinking, Operation and Control, Writing.

**Work Environment:** More often outdoors than indoors; standing; noise; very hot or cold.

## Job Specialization: Immigration and Customs Inspectors

**Investigate and inspect persons, common carriers, goods, and merchandise arriving in or departing from the United States or moving between states to detect violations of immigration and customs laws and regulations.** Examine immigration applications, visas, and passports and interview persons to determine eligibility for admission, residence, and travel in U.S. Detain persons found to be in violation of customs or immigration laws and arrange for legal action such as deportation. Locate and seize contraband or undeclared merchandise and vehicles, aircraft, or boats that contain such merchandise. Interpret and explain laws and regulations to travelers, prospective immigrants, shippers, and manufacturers. Inspect cargo, baggage, and personal articles entering or leaving U.S. for compliance with revenue laws and U.S. Customs Service regulations. Record and report job-related activities, findings, transactions, violations, discrepancies, and decisions. Institute civil and criminal prosecutions and cooperate with other law enforcement agencies in the investigation and prosecution of those in violation of immigration or customs laws. Testify regarding decisions at immigration appeals or in federal court. Determine duty and taxes to be paid on goods. Collect samples of merchandise for examination, appraisal, or testing. Investigate applications for duty refunds and petition for remission or mitigation of penalties when warranted.

**Education/Training Required:** Work experience in a related occupation. **Education and Training Programs:** Criminal Justice/Police Science; Criminalistics and Criminal Science. **Knowledge/Courses**—Public Safety and Security, Law and Government, Foreign Language, Geography, Customer and Personal Service, Philosophy and Theology.

**Personality Type:** Conventional-Enterprising-Realistic. **Career Cluster:** 12 Law, Public Safety, Corrections, and Security. **Career Pathway:** 12.4 Law Enforcement Services. **Other Jobs in This Pathway:** Bailiffs; Correctional Officers and Jailers; Criminal Investigators and Special Agents; First-Line Supervisors of Police and Detectives; Forensic Science Technicians; Intelligence Analysts; Police Detectives; Police Identification and Records Officers; Police Patrol Officers; Remote Sensing Scientists and Technologists; Sheriffs and Deputy Sheriffs.

**Skills**—Active Listening, Persuasion, Negotiation, Operation and Control, Speaking, Social Perceptiveness, Time Management, Judgment and Decision Making.

**Work Environment:** More often outdoors than indoors; more often sitting than standing; using hands; repetitive motions; noise; very hot or cold; bright or inadequate lighting; contaminants; cramped work space; exposed to radiation; hazardous equipment.

D

## Job Specialization: Intelligence Analysts

**Gather, analyze, and evaluate information from a variety of sources, such as law enforcement databases, surveillance, intelligence networks and geographic information systems. Use data to anticipate and prevent organized crime activities, such as terrorism.** Predict future gang, organized crime, or terrorist activity, using analyses of intelligence data. Study activities relating to narcotics, money laundering, gangs, auto theft rings, terrorism, or other national security threats. Design, use, or maintain databases and software applications, such as geographic information systems (GIS) mapping and artificial intelligence tools. Establish criminal profiles to aid in connecting criminal organizations with their members. Evaluate records of communications, such as telephone calls, to plot activity and determine the size and location of criminal groups and members. Gather and evaluate information, using tools such as aerial photographs, radar equipment, or sensitive radio equipment. Gather intelligence information by field observation, confidential information sources, or public records. Gather, analyze, correlate, or evaluate information from a variety of resources, such as law enforcement databases. Link or chart suspects to criminal organizations or events to determine activities and interrelationships. Operate cameras, radios, or other surveillance equipment to intercept communications or document activities. Prepare comprehensive written reports, presentations, maps, or charts based on research, collection, and analysis of intelligence data. Prepare plans to intercept foreign communications transmissions. Study the assets of criminal suspects to determine the flow of money from or to targeted groups. Validate known intelligence with data from other sources. Collaborate with representatives from other government and intelligence organizations to share information or coordinate intelligence activities. Develop defense plans or tactics, using intelligence and other information. Interview, interrogate, or interact with witnesses or crime suspects to collect human intelligence. Study communication code languages or foreign languages to translate intelligence.

**Education/Training Required:** Work experience plus degree. **Education and Training Programs:** Criminal Justice/Police Science; Criminalistics and Criminal Science. **Knowledge/Courses**—No data available.

**Personality Type:** No data available. **Career Cluster:** 12 Law, Public Safety, Corrections, and Security. **Career Pathway:** 12.4 Law Enforcement Services. **Other Jobs in This Pathway:** Bailiffs; Correctional Officers and Jailers; Criminal Investigators and Special Agents; First-Line Supervisors of Police and Detectives; Forensic Science Technicians; Immigration and Customs Inspectors; Police Detectives; Police Identification and Records Officers; Police Patrol Officers; Remote Sensing Scientists and Technologists; Sheriffs and Deputy Sheriffs.

**Skills**—No data available.

**Work Environment:** No data available.

## Job Specialization: Police Detectives

**Conduct investigations to prevent crimes or solve criminal cases.** Provide testimony as witnesses in court. Secure deceased bodies and obtain evidence from them, preventing bystanders from tampering with bodies prior to medical examiners' arrival. Examine crime scenes to obtain clues and evidence such as loose hairs, fibers, clothing, or weapons. Obtain evidence from suspects. Record progress of investigations, maintain informational files on suspects, and submit reports to commanding officers or magistrates to authorize warrants. Check victims for signs of life such as breathing and pulse. Prepare charges or responses to charges, or information for court cases, according to formalized procedures. Obtain facts or statements from complainants, witnesses, and accused persons and record interviews, using recording devices. Prepare and serve search and arrest warrants. Note, mark, and photograph locations of objects found such as footprints, tire tracks, bullets, and bloodstains, and take measurements of each scene. Question individuals or observe persons and establishments to confirm information given to patrol officers. Preserve, process, and analyze items of evidence obtained from crime scenes and suspects, placing them in proper containers and destroying evidence no longer needed. Secure persons at scenes, keeping witnesses from conversing or leaving scenes before investigators arrive. Take photographs from all angles of relevant parts of crime scenes, including entrance and exit routes and streets and intersections. Analyze completed police reports to determine what additional information and investigative work is needed. Obtain summary of incidents from officers in charge at crime scenes, taking care to avoid disturbing evidence. Provide information to lab personnel concerning the source of each item of evidence and tests to be performed. Examine records and governmental agency files to find identifying data about suspects. Block or rope off scenes and check perimeters to ensure that scenes are completely secured.

**Education/Training Required:** Work experience in a related occupation. **Education and Training Programs:** Criminal Justice/Police Science; Criminalistics and Criminal Science.

**Knowledge/Courses**—Public Safety and Security, Law and Government, Psychology, Therapy and Counseling, Customer and Personal Service, Philosophy and Theology.

**Personality Type:** Enterprising-Investigative. **Career Cluster:** 12 Law, Public Safety, Corrections, and Security. **Career Pathway:** 12.4 Law Enforcement Services. **Other Jobs in This Pathway:** Bailiffs; Correctional Officers and Jailers; Criminal Investigators and Special Agents; First-Line Supervisors of Police and Detectives; Forensic Science Technicians; Immigration and Customs Inspectors; Intelligence Analysts; Police Identification and Records Officers; Police Patrol Officers; Remote Sensing Scientists and Technologists; Sheriffs and Deputy Sheriffs.

**Skills**—Science, Negotiation, Operation and Control, Social Perceptiveness, Operation Monitoring, Service Orientation, Active Learning, Systems Analysis.

**Work Environment:** More often outdoors than indoors; sitting; noise; very hot or cold; contaminants; exposed to disease or infections.

## Job Specialization: Police Identification and Records Officers

**Collect evidence at crime scene, classify and identify fingerprints, and photograph evidence for use in criminal and civil cases.** Photograph crime or accident scenes for evidence records. Analyze and process evidence at crime scenes and in the laboratory, wearing protective equipment and using powders and chemicals. Look for trace evidence, such as fingerprints, hairs, fibers, or shoe impressions, using alternative light sources when necessary. Dust selected areas of crime scene and lift latent fingerprints, adhering to proper preservation procedures. Testify in court and present evidence. Package, store, and retrieve evidence. Serve as technical advisor and coordinate with other law enforcement workers to exchange information on crime scene collection activities. Perform emergency work during off-hours. Submit evidence to supervisors. Process film and prints from crime or accident scenes. Identify, classify, and file fingerprints, using systems such as the Henry Classification system.

**Education/Training Required:** Work experience in a related occupation. **Education and Training Programs:** Criminal Justice/Police Science; Criminalistics and Criminal Science. **Knowledge/Courses**—Public Safety and Security, Law and Government, Chemistry, Customer and Personal Service, Clerical, Telecommunications.

**Personality Type:** Conventional-Realistic-Investigative. **Career Cluster:** 12 Law, Public Safety, Corrections, and Security. **Career Pathway:** 12.4 Law Enforcement Services. **Other Jobs in This Pathway:** Bailiffs; Correctional Officers and Jailers; Criminal Investigators and Special Agents; First-Line Supervisors of Police and Detectives; Forensic Science Technicians; Immigration and Customs Inspectors; Intelligence Analysts; Police Detectives; Police Patrol Officers; Remote Sensing Scientists and Technologists; Sheriffs and Deputy Sheriffs.

**Skills**—Operation and Control, Speaking, Operation Monitoring, Negotiation, Critical Thinking, Active Listening, Persuasion, Technology Design.

**Work Environment:** Indoors; sitting; using hands; noise; contaminants; exposed to disease or infections; hazardous conditions.

# Diagnostic Medical Sonographers

- ❋ Annual Earnings: $64,380
- ❋ Earnings Growth Potential: Low (30.3%)
- ❋ Growth: 18.3%
- ❋ Annual Job Openings: 1,650
- ❋ Self-Employed: 0.8%

**Considerations for Job Outlook:** The aging population's need for safe and cost-effective diagnostic imaging treatment is expected to spur employment growth. Prospects should be good for job seekers who have multiple professional credentials.

**Produce ultrasonic recordings of internal organs for use by physicians.** Provide sonograms and oral or written summaries of technical findings to physicians for use in medical diagnosis. Decide which images to include, looking for differences between healthy and pathological areas. Operate ultrasound equipment to produce and record images of the motion, shape, and composition of blood, organs, tissues, and bodily masses such as fluid accumulations. Select appropriate equipment settings and adjust patient positions to obtain the best sites and angles. Observe screens during scans to ensure that images produced are satisfactory for diagnostic purposes, making adjustments to equipment as required. Prepare patients for exams by explaining procedures, transferring them to ultrasound tables, scrubbing skin and applying gel, and positioning them properly. Observe and care for patients throughout examinations to ensure their safety and comfort. Obtain and record accurate patient histories, including prior test results and information from physical examinations. Determine whether scope of exams should be extended, based on findings. Maintain records that include patient information; sonographs and interpretations; files of correspondence; publications and regulations; or quality assurance records such as pathology, biopsy, or post-operative reports. Record and store suitable images, using camera unit connected to the ultrasound equipment. Coordinate work with physicians and other health-care team members, including providing assistance during invasive procedures. Perform clerical duties such as scheduling exams and special procedures, keeping records, and archiving computerized images. Perform legal and ethical duties, including preparing safety and accident reports, obtaining written consent from patients to perform invasive procedures, and reporting symptoms of abuse and neglect. Clean, check, and maintain sonographic equipment, submitting maintenance requests or performing minor repairs as necessary.

**Education/Training Required:** Associate degree. **Education and Training Programs:** Allied Health Diagnostic, Intervention, and Treatment Professions, Other; Diagnostic Medical Sonography/Sonographer and Ultrasound Technician Training. **Knowledge/Courses**—Medicine and Dentistry, Physics, Biology, Customer and Personal Service, Psychology, Clerical.

**Personality Type:** Investigative-Social-Realistic. **Career Cluster:** 08 Health Science. **Career Pathways:** 8.1 Therapeutic Services; 8.2 Diagnostics Services. **Other Jobs in These Pathways:** Clinical Psychologists; Counseling Psychologists; Cytogenetic Technologists; Cytotechnologists; Dental Assistants; Dental Hygienists; Dentists, General; Emergency Medical Technicians and Paramedics; Endoscopy Technicians; Healthcare Support Workers, All Other; Histotechnologists and Histologic Technicians; Home Health Aides; Licensed Practical and Licensed Vocational Nurses; Massage Therapists; Medical and Clinical Laboratory Technicians; Medical and Clinical Laboratory Technologists; Medical and Health Services Managers; Medical Assistants; Medical Secretaries; Pharmacists; Pharmacy Technicians; Radiologic Technologists; School Psychologists; Social and Human Service Assistants; Speech-Language Pathology Assistants; others.

**Skills**—Science, Equipment Maintenance, Equipment Selection, Repairing, Operation and Control, Troubleshooting, Operation Monitoring, Quality Control Analysis.

**Work Environment:** Indoors; more often sitting than standing; using hands; bending or twisting the body; repetitive motions; contaminants; exposed to disease or infections.

# Dietitians and Nutritionists

- ❋ Annual Earnings: $53,250
- ❋ Earnings Growth Potential: Medium (37.4%)
- ❋ Growth: 9.2%
- ❋ Annual Job Openings: 2,570
- ❋ Self-Employed: 8.8%

**Considerations for Job Outlook:** Employment growth is expected to result from an increasing emphasis on disease prevention through improved diet. Job opportunities should be best for dietitians and nutritionists with specialized training, an advanced degree, or certifications beyond minimum state requirements.

**Plan and conduct food service or nutritional programs to assist in the promotion of health and control of disease. May supervise activities of a department providing quantity food services, counsel individuals, or conduct nutritional research.** Assess nutritional needs, diet restrictions, and current health plans to develop and implement dietary-care plans and provide nutritional counseling. Consult with physicians and health-care personnel to determine nutritional needs and diet restrictions of patient or client. Advise patients and their families on nutritional principles, dietary plans and diet modifications, and food selection and preparation. Counsel individuals and groups on basic rules of good nutrition, healthy eating habits, and nutrition monitoring to improve their quality of life. Monitor food service operations to ensure conformance to nutritional, safety, sanitation, and quality standards. Coordinate recipe development and standardization and develop new menus for independent food service operations. Develop policies for food service or nutritional programs to assist in health promotion and disease control. Inspect meals served for conformance to prescribed diets and standards of palatability and appearance. Develop curriculum and prepare manuals, visual aids, course outlines, and other materials used in teaching. Prepare and administer budgets for food, equipment, and supplies. Purchase food in accordance with health and safety codes. Select, train, and supervise workers who plan, prepare, and serve meals. Manage quantity food service departments or clinical and community nutrition services. Coordinate diet counseling services. Advise food service managers and organizations on sanitation, safety procedures, menu development, budgeting, and planning to assist with the establishment, operation, and evaluation of food service facilities and nutrition programs. Organize, develop, analyze, test, and prepare special meals such as low-fat, low-cholesterol, and chemical-free meals. Plan, conduct, and evaluate dietary, nutritional, and epidemiological research.

**Education/Training Required:** Bachelor's degree. **Education and Training Programs:** Clinical Nutrition/Nutritionist; Dietetics and Clinical Nutrition Services, Other; Dietetics/Dietitian (RD); Foods, Nutrition, and Related Services, Other; Foods, Nutrition, and Wellness Studies, General; Foodservice Systems Administration/Management; Human Nutrition; Nutrition Sciences. **Knowledge/Courses**—Therapy and Counseling, Biology, Sociology and Anthropology, Food Production, Medicine and Dentistry, Chemistry.

**Personality Type:** Investigative-Social. **Career Clusters:** 05 Education and Training; 08 Health Science; 15 Science, Technology, Engineering, and Mathematics. **Career Pathways:** 5.3 Teaching/Training; 8.1 Therapeutic Services; 8.4 Support Services; 15.2 Science and Mathematics. **Other Jobs in These Pathways:** Architectural and Engineering Managers; Coaches and Scouts; Cooks, Institution and Cafeteria; Dental Assistants; Elementary School Teachers, Except Special Education; First-Line Supervisors of Food Preparation and Serving Workers; Fitness Trainers and Aerobics Instructors; Healthcare Support Workers, All Other; Home Health Aides; Licensed Practical and Licensed Vocational Nurses; Medical and Health Services Managers; Medical Secretaries; Middle School Teachers, Except Special and Career/Technical Education; Pharmacists; Pharmacy Technicians; Preschool Teachers, Except Special Education; Radiologic Technologists; Recreation Workers; Secondary School Teachers, Except Special and Career/Technical Education; Self-Enrichment Education Teachers; Social and Human Service Assistants; Speech-Language Pathology Assistants; Teacher Assistants; Teachers and Instructors, All Other; Tutors; others.

**Skills**—Management of Financial Resources, Science, Management of Material Resources, Operations Analysis, Social Perceptiveness, Learning Strategies, Writing, Systems Evaluation.

**Work Environment:** Indoors; sitting; noise; exposed to disease or infections.

# Directors, Religious Activities and Education

- ❋ Annual Earnings: $36,170
- ❋ Earnings Growth Potential: High (48.8%)
- ❋ Growth: 12.6%
- ❋ Annual Job Openings: 2,640
- ❋ Self-Employed: 0.0%

**Considerations for Job Outlook:** About average employment growth is projected.

**Direct and coordinate activities of their chosen denominational groups to meet religious needs of students. Plan, direct, or coordinate church school programs designed to promote religious education among church membership. May provide counseling and guidance relative to marital, health, financial, and religious problems.** Analyze member participation and changes in congregation emphasis to determine needs for religious education. Collaborate with other ministry members to establish goals and objectives for religious education programs and to develop ways to encourage program participation. Interpret religious education activities to the public through speaking, leading discussions, and writing articles for local and national publications. Implement program plans by ordering needed materials, scheduling speakers, reserving spaces, and handling other administrative details. Confer with clergy members, congregation officials, and congregation organizations to encourage support of and participation in religious education activities. Develop and direct study courses and religious education programs within congregations. Locate and distribute resources such as periodicals and curricula in order to enhance the effectiveness of educational programs. Visit congregation members' homes, or arrange for pastoral visits, in order to provide information and resources regarding religious education programs. Identify and recruit potential volunteer workers. Participate in denominational activities aimed at goals such as promoting interfaith understanding or providing aid to new or small congregations. Publicize programs through sources such as newsletters, bulletins, and mailings. Counsel individuals regarding interpersonal, health, financial, and religious problems. Attend workshops, seminars, and conferences to obtain program ideas, information, and resources. Analyze revenue and program cost data to determine budget priorities. Train and supervise religious education instructional staffs. Select appropriate curricula and class structures for educational programs. Schedule special events such as camps, conferences, meetings, seminars, and retreats. Plan and conduct conferences dealing with the interpretation of religious ideas and convictions.

**Education/Training Required:** Bachelor's degree. **Education and Training Programs:** Bible/Biblical Studies; Missions/Missionary Studies and Missiology; Philosophy; Religious Education; Youth Ministry. **Knowledge/Courses**—Philosophy and Theology, Education and Training, Therapy and Counseling, Sales and Marketing, History and Archeology, Economics and Accounting.

**Personality Type:** Enterprising-Social-Conventional. **Career Cluster:** 10 Human Services. **Career Pathway:** 10.2 Counseling and Mental Health Services. **Other Jobs in This Pathway:** Clergy; Clinical Psychologists; Counseling Psychologists; Counselors, All Other; Epidemiologists; Health Educators; Healthcare Social Workers; Marriage and Family Therapists; Mental Health and Substance Abuse Social Workers; Mental Health Counselors; Music Directors; Psychologists, All Other; Recreation Workers; Religious Workers, All Other; School Psychologists; Substance Abuse and Behavioral Disorder Counselors.

**Skills**—Management of Financial Resources, Social Perceptiveness, Management of Material Resources, Management of Personnel Resources, Learning Strategies, Persuasion, Systems Evaluation, Operations Analysis.

**Work Environment:** Indoors; standing.

# Dishwashers

- ❋ Annual Earnings: $18,150
- ❋ Earnings Growth Potential: Very low (13.3%)
- ❋ Growth: 11.6%
- ❋ Annual Job Openings: 27,570
- ❋ Self-Employed: 0.1%

**Considerations for Job Outlook:** Job growth is projected due to an expanding population and the continued popularity of dining out. Opportunities should be excellent.

**Clean dishes, kitchen, food preparation equipment, or utensils.** Wash dishes, glassware, flatware, pots, and pans by hand or using dishwashers . Place clean dishes, utensils, and cooking equipment in storage areas. Maintain kitchen work areas, equipment, and utensils in clean and orderly condition. Stock supplies such as food and utensils in serving stations, cupboards, refrigerators, and salad bars. Sweep and scrub floors. Clean garbage cans with water or steam.

Sort and remove trash, placing it in designated pickup areas. Clean and prepare various foods for cooking or serving. Set up banquet tables. Transfer supplies and equipment between storage and work areas by hand or using hand trucks. Receive and store supplies. Prepare and package individual place settings. Load or unload trucks that deliver or pick up food and supplies.

**Education/Training Required:** Short-term on-the-job training. **Education and Training Program:** Food Preparation/Professional Cooking/Kitchen Assistant Training.

**Personality Type:** Realistic-Conventional. **Career Cluster:** 09 Hospitality and Tourism. **Career Pathway:** 9.1 Restaurants and Food/Beverage Services. **Other Jobs in This Pathway:** Bakers; Baristas; Bartenders; Butchers and Meat Cutters; Chefs and Head Cooks; Combined Food Preparation and Serving Workers, Including Fast Food; Cooks, All Other; Cooks, Fast Food; Cooks, Institution and Cafeteria; Cooks, Private Household; Cooks, Restaurant; Cooks, Short Order; Counter Attendants, Cafeteria, Food Concession, and Coffee Shop; Dining Room and Cafeteria Attendants and Bartender Helpers; First-Line Supervisors of Food Preparation and Serving Workers; Food Preparation and Serving Related Workers, All Other; Food Preparation Workers; Food Servers, Nonrestaurant; Food Service Managers; Gaming Managers; Hosts and Hostesses, Restaurant, Lounge, and Coffee Shop; Meat, Poultry, and Fish Cutters and Trimmers; Slaughterers and Meat Packers; Waiters and Waitresses.

**Skills**—Equipment Maintenance, Repairing, Equipment Selection, Troubleshooting, Operation and Control.

**Work Environment:** Indoors; standing; walking and running; using hands; bending or twisting the body; repetitive motions; noise; contaminants; minor burns, cuts, bites, or stings.

# Drywall and Ceiling Tile Installers

- ❋ Annual Earnings: $37,320
- ❋ Earnings Growth Potential: Low (34.4%)
- ❋ Growth: 13.5%
- ❋ Annual Job Openings: 3,700
- ❋ Self-Employed: 18.8%

**Considerations for Job Outlook:** Projected employment growth is likely to stem from increases in new construction and remodeling. Overall job prospects are expected to be good, especially for experienced workers.

**Apply plasterboard or other wallboard to ceilings or interior walls of buildings. Apply or mount acoustical tiles or blocks, strips, or sheets of shock-absorbing materials to ceilings and walls of buildings to reduce or reflect sound. Materials may be of decorative quality. Includes lathers who fasten wooden, metal, or rockboard lath to walls, ceilings, or partitions of buildings to provide support base for plaster, fireproofing, or acoustical material.** Inspect furrings, mechanical mountings, and masonry surface for plumbness and level, using spirit or water levels. Install metal lath where plaster applications will be exposed to weather or water or for curved or irregular surfaces. Install blanket insulation between studs and tack plastic moisture barriers over insulation. Coordinate work with drywall finishers who cover the seams between drywall panels. Trim rough edges from wallboard to maintain even joints, using knives. Seal joints between ceiling tiles and walls. Scribe and cut edges of tile to fit walls where wall molding is not specified. Read blueprints and other specifications to determine methods of installation, work procedures, and material and tool requirements. Nail channels or wood furring strips to surfaces to provide mounting for tile. Mount tile by using adhesives or by nailing, screwing, stapling, or wire-tying lath directly to structural frameworks. Measure and mark surfaces to lay out work according to blueprints and drawings, using tape measures, straightedges or squares, and marking devices. Hang drywall panels on metal frameworks of walls and ceilings in offices, schools, and other large buildings, using lifts or hoists to adjust panel heights when necessary. Install horizontal and vertical metal or wooden studs to frames so that wallboard can be attached to interior walls. Fasten metal or rockboard lath to the structural framework of walls, ceilings, and partitions of buildings, using nails, screws, staples, or wire-ties. Apply or mount acoustical tile or blocks, strips, or sheets of shock-absorbing materials to ceilings and walls of buildings to reduce reflection of sound or to decorate rooms. Apply cement to backs of tiles and press tiles into place, aligning them with layout marks or joints of previously laid tile. Hang dry lines (stretched string) to wall moldings in order to guide positioning of main runners.

**Education/Training Required:** Moderate-term on-the-job training. **Education and Training Program:** Drywall Installation/Drywaller. **Knowledge/Courses**—Building and Construction, Design, Mechanical, Mathematics, Production and Processing, Public Safety and Security.

**Personality Type:** Realistic-Conventional. **Career Cluster:** 02 Architecture and Construction. **Career Pathway:** 2.2 Construction. **Other Jobs in This Pathway:** Brickmasons and Blockmasons; Cement Masons and Concrete Finishers; Construction and Building Inspectors; Construction Carpenters; Construction Laborers; Construction Managers; Cost Estimators; Electrical Power-Line Installers and Repairers; Electricians; Engineering Technicians, Except Drafters, All Other; Excavating and Loading Machine and Dragline Operators; First-Line Supervisors of Construction Trades and Extraction Workers; Heating and Air Conditioning Mechanics and Installers; Helpers—Carpenters; Helpers—Electricians; Helpers—Pipelayers, Plumbers, Pipefitters, and Steamfitters; Highway Maintenance Workers; Operating Engineers and Other Construction Equipment Operators; Painters, Construction and Maintenance; Pipe Fitters and Steamfitters; Plumbers; Refrigeration Mechanics and Installers; Roofers; Rough Carpenters; Solar Energy Installation Managers; others.

**Skills**—Repairing, Equipment Maintenance, Installation, Operation and Control, Troubleshooting, Equipment Selection, Operation Monitoring, Quality Control Analysis.

**Work Environment:** More often outdoors than indoors; standing; climbing; walking and running; kneeling, crouching, stooping, or crawling; balancing; using hands; bending or twisting the body; repetitive motions; noise; very hot or cold; bright or inadequate lighting; contaminants; cramped work space; high places; hazardous equipment; minor burns, cuts, bites, or stings.

# Economics Teachers, Postsecondary

- Annual Earnings: $83,370
- Earnings Growth Potential: High (50.5%)
- Growth: 15.1%
- Annual Job Openings: 400
- Self-Employed: 0.2%

**Considerations for Job Outlook:** Enrollments in postsecondary institutions are expected to continue rising as more people attend college and as workers return to school to update their skills. Opportunities for part-time or temporary positions should be favorable, but significant competition exists for tenure-track positions.

**Teach courses in economics.** Prepare and deliver lectures to undergraduate and/or graduate students on topics such as econometrics, price theory, and macroeconomics. Prepare course materials such as syllabi, homework assignments, and handouts. Evaluate and grade students' classwork, assignments, and papers. Compile, administer, and grade examinations or assign this work to others. Keep abreast of developments in their field by reading current literature, talking with colleagues, and participating in professional conferences. Maintain student attendance records, grades, and other required records. Initiate, facilitate, and moderate classroom discussions. Maintain regularly scheduled office hours in order to advise and assist students. Select and obtain materials and supplies such as textbooks. Plan, evaluate, and revise curricula, course content, and course materials and methods of instruction. Conduct research in a particular field of knowledge and publish findings in professional journals, books, and/or electronic media. Supervise undergraduate and/or graduate teaching, internship, and research work. Advise students on academic and vocational curricula and on career issues. Serve on academic or administrative committees that deal with institutional policies, departmental matters, and academic issues. Collaborate with colleagues to address teaching and research issues. Compile bibliographies of specialized materials for outside reading assignments. Participate in student recruitment, registration, and placement activities. Perform administrative duties such as serving as department head. Write grant proposals to procure external research funding. Participate in campus and community events. Provide professional consulting services to government and/or industry. Act as advisers to student organizations.

**Education/Training Required:** Doctoral degree. **Education and Training Programs:** Applied Economics; Business/Managerial Economics; Development Economics and International Development; Econometrics and Quantitative Economics; Economics, General; Economics, Other; Humanities/Humanistic Studies; International Economics; Social Science Teacher Education. **Knowledge/Courses—** Economics and Accounting, History and Archeology, Mathematics, Philosophy and Theology, Education and Training, English Language.

**Personality Type:** Social-Investigative. **Career Clusters:** 04 Business, Management, and Administration; 15 Science, Technology, Engineering, and Mathematics. **Career Pathways:** 4.1 Management; 15.2 Science and Mathematics. **Other Jobs in These Pathways:** Brownfield Redevelopment Specialists and Site Managers; Business Continuity Planners; Business Operations Specialists, All Other; Chief Executives; Chief Sustainability Officers; Compliance Managers; Computer and Information Systems Managers; Construction Managers; Customs Brokers; Energy Auditors; First-Line Supervisors of Office and Administrative Support Workers; General and Operations Managers; Investment Fund Managers; Loss Prevention Managers; Management Analysts; Managers, All Other; Public Relations Specialists;

Regulatory Affairs Managers; Sales Managers; Security Management Specialists; Security Managers; Supply Chain Managers; Sustainability Specialists; Wind Energy Operations Managers; Wind Energy Project Managers; 37 other postsecondary teaching occupations; others.

**Skills**—Science, Operations Analysis, Learning Strategies, Instructing, Writing, Speaking, Programming, Mathematics,

**Work Environment:** Indoors; sitting.

## Economists

* Annual Earnings: $89,450
* Earnings Growth Potential: High (46.1%)
* Growth: 5.8%
* Annual Job Openings: 500
* Self-Employed: 7.9%

**Considerations for Job Outlook:** Although demand for economic analysis will grow, projected employment declines for economists in government sectors will temper overall growth. Job seekers who have a graduate degree in economics should have the best prospects.

**Conduct research, prepare reports, or formulate plans to aid in solution of economic problems arising from production and distribution of goods and services. May collect and process economic and statistical data, using econometric and sampling techniques.** Study economic and statistical data in area of specialization, such as finance, labor, or agriculture. Provide advice and consultation on economic relationships to businesses, public and private agencies, and other employers. Compile, analyze, and report data to explain economic phenomena and forecast market trends, applying mathematical models and statistical techniques. Formulate recommendations, policies, or plans to solve economic problems or to interpret markets. Develop economic guidelines and standards and prepare points of view used in forecasting trends and formulating economic policy. Testify at regulatory or legislative hearings concerning the estimated effects of changes in legislation or public policy and present recommendations based on cost-benefit analyses. Supervise research projects and students' study projects. Forecast production and consumption of renewable resources and supply, consumption, and depletion of non-renewable resources. Teach theories, principles, and methods of economics.

**Education/Training Required:** Master's degree. **Education and Training Programs:** Agricultural Economics; Applied Economics; Business/Managerial Economics; Development

Economics and International Development; Econometrics and Quantitative Economics; Economics, General; Economics, Other; International Economics. **Knowledge/Courses**—Economics and Accounting, Mathematics, Geography, Sales and Marketing, Computers and Electronics, English Language.

**Personality Type:** Investigative-Conventional-Enterprising. **Career Clusters:** 01 Agriculture, Food, and Natural Resources; 04 Business, Management, and Administration; 15 Science, Technology, Engineering, and Mathematics. **Career Pathways:** 1.2 Plant Systems; 4.1 Management; 15.2 Science and Mathematics. **Other Jobs in These Pathways:** Brownfield Redevelopment Specialists and Site Managers; Business Continuity Planners; Business Operations Specialists, All Other; Chief Executives; Chief Sustainability Officers; Compliance Managers; Construction Managers; Customs Brokers; Energy Auditors; First-Line Supervisors of Office and Administrative Support Workers; First-Line Supervisors of Retail Sales Workers; General and Operations Managers; Investment Fund Managers; Landscaping and Groundskeeping Workers; Loss Prevention Managers; Management Analysts; Managers, All Other; Regulatory Affairs Managers; Retail Salespersons; Security Management Specialists; Security Managers; Supply Chain Managers; Sustainability Specialists; Wind Energy Operations Managers; Wind Energy Project Managers; others.

**Skills**—Mathematics, Systems Analysis, Operations Analysis, Complex Problem Solving, Systems Evaluation, Writing, Speaking, Critical Thinking.

**Work Environment:** Indoors; sitting.

# Job Specialization: Environmental Economists

**Assess and quantify the benefits of environmental alternatives, such as use of renewable energy resources.** Prepare and deliver presentations to communicate economic and environmental study results, to present policy recommendations, or to raise awareness of environmental consequences. Monitor or analyze market and environmental trends. Interpret indicators to ascertain the overall health of an environment. Identify and recommend environmentally-friendly business practices. Demonstrate or promote the economic benefits of sound environmental regulations. Write technical documents or academic articles to communicate study results or economic forecasts. Write social, legal, or economic impact statements to inform decision-makers for natural resource policies, standards, or programs. Write

research proposals and grant applications to obtain private or public funding for environmental and economic studies. Examine the exhaustibility of natural resources or the long-term costs of environmental rehabilitation. Develop systems for collecting, analyzing, and interpreting environmental and economic data. Develop programs or policy recommendations to achieve economic and environmental sustainability. Develop environmental research project plans, including information on budgets, goals, deliverables, timelines, and resource requirements. Develop economic models, forecasts, or scenarios to predict future economic and environmental outcomes. Collect and analyze data to compare the environmental implications of economic policy or practice alternatives. Assess the environmental costs and benefits of various economic activities, policies, or regulations. Assess the economic costs and benefits of environmental events or activities. Perform complex, dynamic, and integrated mathematical modeling of ecological, environmental, or economic systems. Conduct research to study the relationships among environmental problems and patterns of economic production and consumption.

**Education/Training Required:** Master's degree. **Education and Training Programs:** Agricultural Economics; Applied Economics; Business/Managerial Economics; Development Economics and International Development; Econometrics and Quantitative Economics; Economics, General; Economics, Other; International Economics. **Knowledge/Courses**—No data available.

**Personality Type:** No data available. **Career Clusters:** 01 Agriculture, Food, and Natural Resources; 04 Business, Management, and Administration; 15 Science, Technology, Engineering, and Mathematics. **Career Pathways:** 1.2 Plant Systems; 1.5 Natural Resources Systems; 4.1 Management; 15.2 Science and Mathematics. **Other Jobs in These Pathways:** Brownfield Redevelopment Specialists and Site Managers; Business Continuity Planners; Business Operations Specialists, All Other; Chief Executives; Compliance Managers; Construction Managers; Customs Brokers; Energy Auditors; First-Line Supervisors of Office and Administrative Support Workers; First-Line Supervisors of Retail Sales Workers; General and Operations Managers; Industrial Truck and Tractor Operators; Investment Fund Managers; Landscaping and Groundskeeping Workers; Loss Prevention Managers; Management Analysts; Managers, All Other; Regulatory Affairs Managers; Retail Salespersons; Security Management Specialists; Security Managers; Supply Chain Managers; Sustainability Specialists; Wind Energy Operations Managers; Wind Energy Project Managers; others.

E

**Skills**—No data available.

**Work Environment:** No data available.

# Editors

- ❇ Annual Earnings: $51,470
- ❇ Earnings Growth Potential: High (43.9%)
- ❇ Growth: –0.3%
- ❇ Annual Job Openings: 3,390
- ❇ Self-Employed: 12.1%

**Considerations for Job Outlook:** Projected job growth for these workers stems from increased use of online media and growing demand for Web-based information. But print publishing is expected to continue weakening. Job competition should be keen.

**Perform variety of editorial duties, such as laying out, indexing, and revising content of written materials, in preparation for final publication.** Prepare, rewrite, and edit copy to improve readability or supervise others who do this work. Read copy or proof to detect and correct errors in spelling, punctuation, and syntax. Allocate print space for story text, photos, and illustrations according to space parameters and copy significance, using knowledge of layout principles. Plan the contents of publications according to the publication's style, editorial policy, and publishing requirements. Verify facts, dates, and statistics, using standard reference sources. Review and approve proofs submitted by composing room prior to publication production. Develop story or content ideas, considering reader or audience appeal. Oversee publication production, including artwork, layout, computer typesetting, and printing, ensuring adherence to deadlines and budget requirements. Confer with management and editorial staff members regarding placement and emphasis of developing news stories. Assign topics, events, and stories to individual writers or reporters for coverage. Read, evaluate, and edit manuscripts or other materials submitted for publication and confer with authors regarding changes in content, style or organization, or publication. Monitor news-gathering operations to ensure utilization of all news sources, such as press releases, telephone contacts, radio, television, wire services, and other reporters. Meet frequently with artists, typesetters, layout personnel, marketing directors, and production managers to discuss projects and resolve problems. Supervise and coordinate work of reporters and other editors. Make manuscript acceptance or revision recommendations to the publisher. Select local, state, national, and international news items received from wire services based on assessment of items'

significance and interest value. Interview and hire writers and reporters or negotiate contracts, royalties, and payments for authors or freelancers.

**Education/Training Required:** Bachelor's degree. **Education and Training Programs:** Broadcast Journalism; Business/Corporate Communications; Communication, Journalism, and Related Programs, Other; English Language and Literature, General; Family and Consumer Sciences/Human Sciences Communication; Journalism; Mass Communication/Media Studies; Publishing. **Knowledge/Courses**—Communications and Media, History and Archeology, Geography, Fine Arts, English Language, Clerical.

**Personality Type:** Artistic-Enterprising-Conventional. **Career Clusters:** 03 Arts, Audio/Video Technology, and Communications; 08 Health Science. **Career Pathways:** 3.5 Journalism and Broadcasting; 8.3 Health Informatics. **Other Jobs in These Pathways:** Clinical Psychologists; Copy Writers; Directors—Stage, Motion Pictures, Television, and Radio; Engineers, All Other; Executive Secretaries and Executive Administrative Assistants; First-Line Supervisors of Office and Administrative Support Workers; Health Educators; Medical and Health Services Managers; Medical Assistants; Medical Records and Health Information Technicians; Medical Secretaries; Medical Transcriptionists; Mental Health Counselors; Photographers; Physical Therapists; Producers; Program Directors; Psychiatric Aides; Public Relations Specialists; Receptionists and Information Clerks; Rehabilitation Counselors; Reporters and Correspondents; Substance Abuse and Behavioral Disorder Counselors; Talent Directors; Technical Directors/Managers; others.

**Skills**—Writing, Reading Comprehension, Quality Control Analysis, Negotiation, Management of Personnel Resources, Time Management, Persuasion, Active Learning.

**Work Environment:** Indoors; sitting; using hands; repetitive motions; noise.

# Education Administrators, All Other

- ❇ Annual Earnings: $75,690
- ❇ Earnings Growth Potential: High (44.6%)
- ❇ Growth: 23.9%
- ❇ Annual Job Openings: 1,690
- ❇ Self-Employed: 4.4%

**Considerations for Job Outlook:** Increasing student enrollments are expected to drive employment growth for these workers. Prospects are expected to be good.

This occupation includes all education administrators not listed separately. Because this is a highly diverse occupation, no data is available for some information topics.

**Education/Training Required:** Work experience plus degree. **Education and Training Program:** Adult and Continuing Education Administration.

**Career Cluster:** 05 Education and Training. **Career Pathway:** 5.1 Administration and Administrative Support. **Other Jobs in This Pathway:** Coaches and Scouts; Distance Learning Coordinators; Education Administrators, Elementary and Secondary School; Education Administrators, Postsecondary; Education Administrators, Preschool and Childcare Center/Program; Fitness and Wellness Coordinators; Fitness Trainers and Aerobics Instructors; Instructional Coordinators; Instructional Designers and Technologists; Umpires, Referees, and Other Sports Officials.

## Job Specialization: Distance Learning Coordinators

**Coordinate day-to-day operations of distance learning programs and schedule courses.** Write and submit grant applications or proposals to secure funding for distance learning programs. Review distance learning content to ensure compliance with copyright, licensing, or other requirements. Conduct inventories of distance learning equipment, summarizing equipment usage data. Communicate technical or marketing information about distance learning via podcasts, webinars, and other technologies. Train instructors and distance learning staff in the use or support of distance learning applications, such as course management software. Troubleshoot and resolve problems with distance learning equipment or applications. Supervise distance learning support staff. Purchase equipment or services in accordance with distance learning plans and budget constraints. Select, direct, and monitor the work of vendors that provide products or services for distance learning programs. Prepare and manage distance learning program budgets. Prepare reports summarizing distance learning statistical data or describing distance learning program objectives and accomplishments. Negotiate with academic units or instructors and vendors to ensure cost-effective and high-quality distance learning programs, services, or courses. Monitor technological developments in distance learning for technological means to educational or outreach goals. Evaluate the effectiveness of distance learning programs in promoting knowledge or skill acquisition. Direct and support the technical operation of distance learning classrooms or equipment. Develop distance learning program goals

or plans, including equipment replacement, quality assurance, or course offering plans. Create and maintain websites or databases that support distance learning programs. Assess distance-learning technological or educational needs and goals. Communicate to faculty, students, or other users availability of, or changes to, distance learning courses or materials, programs, services, or applications.

**Education/Training Required:** Work experience plus degree. **Education and Training Program:** Adult and Continuing Education Administration. **Knowledge/Courses—** No data available.

**Personality Type:** No data available. **Career Cluster:** 05 Education and Training. **Career Pathway:** 5.1 Administration and Administrative Support. **Other Jobs in This Pathway:** Coaches and Scouts; Education Administrators, All Other; Education Administrators, Elementary and Secondary School; Education Administrators, Postsecondary; Education Administrators, Preschool and Childcare Center/Program; Fitness and Wellness Coordinators; Fitness Trainers and Aerobics Instructors; Instructional Coordinators; Instructional Designers and Technologists; Umpires, Referees, and Other Sports Officials.

**Skills—**No data available.

**Work Environment:** No data available.

## Job Specialization: Fitness and Wellness Coordinators

**Manage fitness and wellness programs and services. Direct and train staff of health educators, fitness instructors, or recreation workers.** Track attendance, participation, or performance data related to wellness events. Provide individual support or counseling in general wellness or nutrition. Maintain or arrange for maintenance of fitness equipment and facilities. Develop marketing campaigns to promote a healthy lifestyle or participation in fitness and wellness programs. Conduct surveys to determine interest in, or satisfaction with, wellness and fitness programs, events, or services. Teach fitness classes to improve strength, flexibility, cardiovascular conditioning, or general fitness of participants. Select and supervise contractors, such as event hosts or health, fitness, and wellness practitioners. Respond to customer, public, or media requests for information about wellness programs and services. Recommend or approve new program or service offerings to promote wellness and fitness, produce revenues, and minimize costs. Prepare and implement budgets and strategic, operational, purchasing, and maintenance plans. Organize and oversee health screenings, such as flu, mammography, blood pressure, and cholesterol screenings. Organize and oversee fitness or wellness events or programs, such as information presentations, blood drives, cardiopulmonary resuscitation (CPR) or first aid training, or organized runs or walks. Operate, and instruct others in, proper operation of fitness equipment, such as weight machines, exercise bicycles, benches, hand weights, and fitness assessment devices. Manage or oversee fitness or recreation facilities, ensuring safe and clean facilities and equipment. Maintain wellness- and fitness-related schedules, records, or reports. Conduct or facilitate training sessions or seminars for wellness and fitness staff. Develop fitness or wellness classes, such as yoga, aerobics, weightlifting, and aquatics, ensuring a diversity of class offerings. Supervise fitness or wellness workers, such as fitness instructors, recreation workers, nutritionists, and health educators.

**Education/Training Required:** Bachelor's degree. **Education and Training Program:** Sport and Fitness Administration/Management. **Knowledge/Courses**—No data available.

**Personality Type:** No data available. **Career Cluster:** 05 Education and Training. **Career Pathway:** 5.1 Administration and Administrative Support. **Other Jobs in This Pathway:** Coaches and Scouts; Distance Learning Coordinators; Education Administrators, All Other; Education Administrators, Elementary and Secondary School; Education Administrators, Postsecondary; Education Administrators, Preschool and Childcare Center/Program; Fitness Trainers and Aerobics Instructors; Instructional Coordinators; Instructional Designers and Technologists; Umpires, Referees, and Other Sports Officials.

**Skills**—No data available.

**Work Environment:** No data available.

# Education Administrators, Elementary and Secondary School

- ❋ Annual Earnings: $86,970
- ❋ Earnings Growth Potential: Low (33.0%)
- ❋ Growth: 8.6%
- ❋ Annual Job Openings: 8,880
- ❋ Self-Employed: 4.7%

**Considerations for Job Outlook:** Increasing student enrollments are expected to drive employment growth for these workers. Prospects are expected to be good.

**Plan, direct, or coordinate the academic, clerical, or auxiliary activities of public or private elementary or secondary-level schools.** Review and approve new programs or recommend modifications to existing programs, submitting program proposals for school board approval as necessary. Prepare, maintain, or oversee the preparation and maintenance of attendance, activity, planning, or personnel reports and records. Confer with parents and staff to discuss educational activities, policies, and student behavioral or learning problems. Prepare and submit budget requests and recommendations or grant proposals to solicit program funding. Direct and coordinate school maintenance services and the use of school facilities. Counsel and provide guidance to students regarding personal, academic, vocational, or behavioral issues. Organize and direct committees of specialists, volunteers, and staff to provide technical and advisory assistance for programs. Teach classes or courses to students. Advocate for new schools to be built or for existing facilities to be repaired or remodeled. Plan and develop instructional methods and content for educational, vocational, or student activity programs. Develop partnerships with businesses, communities, and other organizations to help meet identified educational needs and to provide school-to-work programs. Direct and coordinate activities of teachers, administrators, and support staff at schools, public agencies, and institutions. Evaluate curricula, teaching methods, and programs to determine their effectiveness, efficiency, and utilization and to ensure that school activities comply with federal, state, and local regulations. Set educational standards and goals and help establish policies and procedures to carry them out. Recruit, hire, train, and evaluate primary and supplemental staff. Enforce discipline and attendance rules. Observe teaching methods and examine learning materials to evaluate and standardize curricula and teaching techniques and to determine areas where improvement is needed.

**Education/Training Required:** Work experience plus degree. **Education and Training Programs:** Educational Administration and Supervision, Other; Educational Leadership and Administration, General; Educational, Instructional, and Curriculum Supervision; Elementary and Middle School Administration/Principalship; Secondary School Administration/Principalship. **Knowledge/Courses**—Therapy and Counseling, Education and Training, Philosophy and Theology, Sociology and Anthropology, Personnel and Human Resources, History and Archeology.

**Personality Type:** Enterprising-Social-Conventional. **Career Cluster:** 05 Education and Training. **Career Pathway:** 5.1 Administration and Administrative Support.

**Other Jobs in This Pathway:** Coaches and Scouts; Distance Learning Coordinators; Education Administrators, All Other; Education Administrators, Postsecondary; Education Administrators, Preschool and Childcare Center/Program; Fitness and Wellness Coordinators; Fitness Trainers and Aerobics Instructors; Instructional Coordinators; Instructional Designers and Technologists; Umpires, Referees, and Other Sports Officials.

**Skills**—Management of Financial Resources, Management of Material Resources, Learning Strategies, Management of Personnel Resources, Systems Evaluation, Systems Analysis, Persuasion, Negotiation.

**Work Environment:** Indoors; sitting; noise.

# Education Administrators, Postsecondary

- ❈ Annual Earnings: $83,710
- ❈ Earnings Growth Potential: High (43.7%)
- ❈ Growth: 2.3%
- ❈ Annual Job Openings: 4,010
- ❈ Self-Employed: 3.9%

**Considerations for Job Outlook:** Increasing student enrollments are expected to drive employment growth for these workers. Prospects are expected to be good.

**Plan, direct, or coordinate research, instructional, student administration and services, and other educational activities at postsecondary institutions, including universities, colleges, and junior and community colleges.** Recruit, hire, train, and terminate departmental personnel. Plan, administer, and control budgets; maintain financial records; and produce financial reports. Represent institutions at community and campus events, in meetings with other institution personnel, and during accreditation processes. Participate in faculty and college committee activities. Provide assistance to faculty and staff in duties such as teaching classes, conducting orientation programs, issuing transcripts, and scheduling events. Establish operational policies and procedures and make any necessary modifications, based on analysis of operations, demographics, and other research information. Confer with other academic staff to explain and formulate admission requirements and course credit policies. Appoint individuals to faculty positions and evaluate their performance. Direct activities of administrative departments such as admissions, registration, and career services. Develop curricula and recommend curricula revisions and additions. Determine course schedules and coordinate teaching assignments and room assignments to ensure optimum use of buildings and equipment. Consult with government regulatory and licensing agencies to ensure the institution's conformance with applicable standards. Direct, coordinate, and evaluate the activities of personnel engaged in administering academic institutions, departments, and/or alumni organizations. Teach courses within their department. Participate in student recruitment, selection, and admission, making admissions recommendations when required to do so. Review student misconduct reports requiring disciplinary action and counsel students regarding such reports. Supervise coaches. Assess and collect tuition and fees. Direct scholarship, fellowship, and loan programs, performing activities such as selecting recipients and distributing aid. Coordinate the production and dissemination of university publications such as course catalogs and class schedules.

**Education/Training Required:** Work experience plus degree. **Education and Training Programs:** Community College Education; Educational Administration and Supervision, Other; Educational Leadership and Administration, General; Educational, Instructional, and Curriculum Supervision; Higher Education/Higher Education Administration. **Knowledge/Courses**—Therapy and Counseling, Sociology and Anthropology, Psychology, Personnel and Human Resources, Education and Training, Philosophy and Theology.

**Personality Type:** Enterprising-Conventional-Social. **Career Cluster:** 05 Education and Training. **Career Pathway:** 5.1 Administration and Administrative Support. **Other Jobs in This Pathway:** Coaches and Scouts; Distance Learning Coordinators; Education Administrators, All Other; Education Administrators, Elementary and Secondary School; Education Administrators, Preschool and Childcare Center/Program; Fitness and Wellness Coordinators; Fitness Trainers and Aerobics Instructors; Instructional Coordinators; Instructional Designers and Technologists; Umpires, Referees, and Other Sports Officials.

**Skills**—Management of Material Resources, Management of Financial Resources, Management of Personnel Resources, Negotiation, Systems Evaluation, Systems Analysis, Instructing, Time Management.

**Work Environment:** Indoors; sitting.

E

# Education Administrators, Preschool and Childcare Center/ Program

- ❋ Annual Earnings: $42,960
- ❋ Earnings Growth Potential: Medium (36.7%)
- ❋ Growth: 11.8%
- ❋ Annual Job Openings: 2,460
- ❋ Self-Employed: 4.2%

**Considerations for Job Outlook:** Job losses resulting from a declining number of eating and drinking places will be partially offset by the creation of new jobs in grocery and convenience stores, healthcare and elder care facilities, and other establishments. Opportunities for new managers should be good because of the need to replace workers who leave the occupation.

**Plan, direct, or coordinate the academic and nonacademic activities of preschool and child care centers or programs.** Confer with parents and staff to discuss educational activities and policies and students' behavioral or learning problems. Prepare and maintain attendance, activity, planning, accounting, or personnel reports and records for officials and agencies or direct preparation and maintenance activities. Set educational standards and goals and help establish policies, procedures, and programs to carry them out. Monitor students' progress and provide students and teachers with assistance in resolving any problems. Determine allocations of funds for staff, supplies, materials, and equipment and authorize purchases. Recruit, hire, train, and evaluate primary and supplemental staff and recommend personnel actions for programs and services. Direct and coordinate activities of teachers or administrators at daycare centers, schools, public agencies, or institutions. Plan, direct, and monitor instructional methods and content of educational, vocational, or student activity programs. Review and interpret government codes and develop procedures to meet codes and to ensure facility safety, security, and maintenance. Determine the scope of educational program offerings and prepare drafts of program schedules and descriptions to estimate staffing and facility requirements. Review and evaluate new and current programs to determine their efficiency; effectiveness; and compliance with state, local, and federal regulations, and recommend any necessary modifications. Teach classes or courses or provide direct care to children. Prepare and submit budget requests or grant proposals to solicit program funding.

Write articles, manuals, and other publications and assist in the distribution of promotional literature about programs and facilities. Collect and analyze survey data, regulatory information, and demographic and employment trends to forecast enrollment patterns and the need for curriculum changes.

**Education/Training Required:** Work experience plus degree. **Education and Training Programs:** Educational Administration and Supervision, Other; Educational Leadership and Administration, General; Educational, Instructional, and Curriculum Supervision; Elementary and Middle School Administration/Principalship. **Knowledge/ Courses**—Philosophy and Theology, Therapy and Counseling, Personnel and Human Resources, Sociology and Anthropology, Education and Training, Clerical.

**Personality Type:** Social-Enterprising-Conventional. **Career Cluster:** 05 Education and Training. **Career Pathway:** 5.1 Administration and Administrative Support. **Other Jobs in This Pathway:** Coaches and Scouts; Distance Learning Coordinators; Education Administrators, All Other; Education Administrators, Elementary and Secondary School; Education Administrators, Postsecondary; Fitness and Wellness Coordinators; Fitness Trainers and Aerobics Instructors; Instructional Coordinators; Instructional Designers and Technologists; Umpires, Referees, and Other Sports Officials.

**Skills**—Management of Material Resources, Management of Financial Resources, Management of Personnel Resources, Learning Strategies, Negotiation, Systems Evaluation, Time Management, Judgment and Decision Making.

**Work Environment:** Indoors; sitting; exposed to disease or infections.

# Education Teachers, Postsecondary

- ❋ Annual Earnings: $59,140
- ❋ Earnings Growth Potential: High (45.0%)
- ❋ Growth: 15.1%
- ❋ Annual Job Openings: 1,800
- ❋ Self-Employed: 0.2%

**Considerations for Job Outlook:** Enrollments in postsecondary institutions are expected to continue rising as more people attend college and as workers return to school to update their skills. Opportunities for part-time or temporary positions should be favorable, but significant competition exists for tenure-track positions.

**Teach courses pertaining to education, such as counseling, curriculum, guidance, instruction, teacher education, and teaching English as a second language.** Prepare course materials such as syllabi, homework assignments, and handouts. Prepare and deliver lectures to undergraduate and/or graduate students on topics such as children's literature, learning and development, and reading instruction. Initiate, facilitate, and moderate classroom discussions. Evaluate and grade students' classwork, assignments, and papers. Plan, evaluate, and revise curricula, course content, and course materials and methods of instruction. Supervise students' fieldwork, internship, and research work. Keep abreast of developments in their field by reading current literature, talking with colleagues, and participating in professional conferences. Advise students on academic and vocational curricula and on career issues. Maintain regularly scheduled office hours to advise and assist students. Maintain student attendance records, grades, and other required records. Collaborate with colleagues to address teaching and research issues. Compile, administer, and grade examinations or assign this work to others. Conduct research in a particular field of knowledge and publish findings in professional journals, books, or electronic media. Select and obtain materials and supplies such as textbooks. Participate in student recruitment, registration, and placement activities. Advise and instruct teachers employed in school systems by providing activities such as in-service seminars. Serve on academic or administrative committees that deal with institutional policies, departmental matters, and academic issues. Compile bibliographies of specialized materials for outside reading assignments. Write grant proposals to procure external research funding. Participate in campus and community events. Perform administrative duties such as serving as department head. Act as advisers to student organizations. Provide professional consulting services to government and/or industry.

**Education/Training Required:** Doctoral degree. **Education and Training Programs:** Agricultural Teacher Education; Art Teacher Education; Biology Teacher Education; Business Teacher Education; Chemistry Teacher Education; Computer Teacher Education; Drama and Dance Teacher Education; Driver and Safety Teacher Education; Education, General; English/Language Arts Teacher Education; Family and Consumer Sciences/Home Economics Teacher Education; Foreign Language Teacher Education; French Language Teacher Education; Geography Teacher Education; German Language Teacher Education; Health Occupations Teacher Education; Health Teacher Education; History Teacher Education; Humanities; Mathematics Teacher Education; Music Teacher Education; Physical Education Teaching and Coaching; Physics Teacher Education; Reading Teacher Education; Marketing and Distribution Teacher Education; Science Teacher Education; Social Science Teacher Education; Social Studies Teacher Education; Spanish Language Teacher Education; Speech Teacher Education; Technical Teacher Education; Technology Teacher Education/Industrial Arts Teacher Education; Trade and Industrial Teacher Education; others. **Knowledge/Courses**—Therapy and Counseling, Education and Training, Sociology and Anthropology, Philosophy and Theology, Psychology, English Language.

**Personality Type:** Social-Artistic-Investigative. **Career Cluster:** 05 Education and Training. **Career Pathway:** 5.3 Teaching/Training. **Other Jobs in This Pathway:** Adult Basic and Secondary Education and Literacy Teachers and Instructors; Athletes and Sports Competitors; Audio-Visual and Multimedia Collections Specialists; Career/Technical Education Teachers, Middle School; Career/Technical Education Teachers, Secondary School; Chemists; Coaches and Scouts; Dietitians and Nutritionists; Elementary School Teachers, Except Special Education; Fitness Trainers and Aerobics Instructors; Historians; Instructional Coordinators; Instructional Designers and Technologists; Interpreters and Translators; Kindergarten Teachers, Except Special Education; Librarians; Middle School Teachers, Except Special and Career/Technical Education; Physicists; Preschool Teachers, Except Special Education; Recreation Workers; Secondary School Teachers, Except Special and Career/Technical Education; Self-Enrichment Education Teachers; Teacher Assistants; Tutors; 37 other postsecondary teaching occupations.

**Skills**—Learning Strategies, Writing, Speaking, Active Learning, Instructing, Reading Comprehension, Science, Active Listening.

**Work Environment:** Indoors; sitting.

# Educational, Guidance, School, and Vocational Counselors

- ✳ Annual Earnings: $53,380
- ✳ Earnings Growth Potential: Medium (40.7%)
- ✳ Growth: 14.0%
- ✳ Annual Job Openings: 9,440
- ✳ Self-Employed: 5.8%

**Considerations for Job Outlook:** Increasing demand for services provided by counselors is expected to result in employment growth. But growth will vary by specialty and will be faster for mental health, substance abuse and behavioral disorder, and rehabilitation counselors than for counselors of other specialties. Opportunities should be favorable, particularly in rural areas.

**Counsel individuals and provide group educational and vocational guidance services.** Counsel students regarding educational issues such as course and program selection, class scheduling, school adjustment, truancy, study habits, and career planning. Counsel individuals to help them understand and overcome personal, social, or behavioral problems affecting their educational or vocational situations. Maintain accurate and complete student records as required by laws, district policies, and administrative regulations. Confer with parents or guardians, teachers, other counselors, and administrators to resolve students' behavioral, academic, and other problems. Provide crisis intervention to students when difficult situations occur at schools. Identify cases involving domestic abuse or other family problems affecting students' development. Meet with parents and guardians to discuss their children's progress and to determine their priorities for their children and their resource needs. Prepare students for later educational experiences by encouraging them to explore learning opportunities and to persevere with challenging tasks. Encourage students and/or parents to seek additional assistance from mental health professionals when necessary. Observe and evaluate students' performance, behavior, social development, and physical health. Enforce all administration policies and rules governing students. Meet with other professionals to discuss individual students' needs and progress. Provide students with information on such topics as college degree programs and admission requirements, financial aid opportunities, trade and technical schools, and apprenticeship programs. Evaluate individuals' abilities, interests, and personality characteristics, using tests, records, interviews, and professional sources. Collaborate with teachers and administrators in the development, evaluation, and revision of school programs. Establish and enforce behavioral rules and procedures to maintain order among students.

**Education/Training Required:** Master's degree. **Education and Training Programs:** College Student Counseling and Personnel Services; Counselor Education/School Counseling and Guidance Services. **Knowledge/Courses**—Therapy and Counseling, Psychology, Sociology and Anthropology, Education and Training, Philosophy and Theology, Clerical.

**Personality Type:** Social. **Career Cluster:** 05 Education and Training. **Career Pathway:** 5.2 Professional Support Services. **Other Jobs in This Pathway:** Librarians; Library Assistants, Clerical; Library Technicians.

**Skills**—Social Perceptiveness, Service Orientation, Learning Strategies, Writing, Systems Evaluation, Active Listening, Systems Analysis, Persuasion.

**Work Environment:** Indoors; sitting.

# Electrical and Electronic Engineering Technicians

- ❋ Annual Earnings: $56,040
- ❋ Earnings Growth Potential: Medium (39.2%)
- ❋ Growth: –2.2%
- ❋ Annual Job Openings: 3,100
- ❋ Self-Employed: 0.7%

**Considerations for Job Outlook:** Labor-saving efficiencies and the automation of many engineering support activities will limit the need for new engineering technicians. In general, opportunities should be best for job seekers who have an associate degree or other postsecondary training in engineering technology.

## Job Specialization: Electrical Engineering Technicians

**Apply electrical theory and related knowledge to test and modify developmental or operational electrical machinery and electrical control equipment and circuitry in industrial or commercial plants and laboratories. Usually work under direction of engineering staff.** Assemble electrical and electronic systems and prototypes according to engineering data and knowledge of electrical principles, using hand tools and measuring instruments. Provide technical assistance and resolution when electrical or engineering problems are encountered before, during, and after construction. Install and maintain electrical control systems and solid state equipment. Modify electrical prototypes, parts, assemblies, and systems to correct functional deviations. Set up and operate test equipment to evaluate performance of developmental parts, assemblies, or systems under simulated operating conditions and record results. Collaborate with electrical engineers and other personnel to identify, define, and solve developmental problems. Build, calibrate, maintain, troubleshoot, and repair electrical instruments or testing equipment. Analyze and interpret test information to resolve design-related problems. Write commissioning procedures for electrical installations. Prepare project cost and work-time estimates. Evaluate engineering proposals, shop drawings, and design comments for sound electrical engineering practice and conformance with established safety and design criteria and recommend approval or disapproval. Draw or modify diagrams and write engineering specifications to clarify design details and functional criteria of experimental electronics units. Conduct inspections for quality control and assurance programs, reporting findings and recommendations. Prepare contracts and initiate, review, and coordinate modifications to contract specifications and plans throughout the construction process. Plan, schedule, and monitor work of support personnel to assist supervisor. Review existing electrical engineering criteria to identify necessary revisions, deletions, or amendments to outdated material. Perform supervisory duties such as recommending work assignments, approving leaves, and completing performance evaluations.

**Education/Training Required:** Associate degree. **Education and Training Programs:** Computer Engineering Technology/Technician; Computer Technology/Computer Systems Technology; Electrical and Electronic Engineering Technologies/Technicians, Other; Electrical, Electronic, and Communications Engineering Technology/Technician; Telecommunications Technology/Technician. **Knowledge/Courses**—Computers and Electronics, Design, Engineering and Technology, Mechanical, Production and Processing, Physics.

**Personality Type:** Realistic-Investigative-Conventional. **Career Cluster:** 13 Manufacturing. **Career Pathways:** 13.2 Manufacturing Production Process Development; 13.3 Maintenance, Installation, and Repair. **Other Jobs in These Pathways:** Aircraft Mechanics and Service Technicians; Automotive Specialty Technicians; Biological Technicians; Civil Engineering Technicians; Computer, Automated Teller, and Office Machine Repairers; Electrical and Electronic Equipment Assemblers; Electrical and Electronics Repairers, Commercial and Industrial Equipment; Electrical Engineering Technologists; Electromechanical Engineering Technologists; Electronics Engineering Technicians; Electronics Engineering Technologists; Engineering Technicians, Except Drafters, All Other; Fuel Cell Technicians; Helpers—Installation, Maintenance, and Repair Workers; Industrial Engineering Technologists; Industrial Machinery Mechanics; Installation, Maintenance, and Repair Workers, All Other; Manufacturing Engineering Technologists; Manufacturing Production Technicians; Mapping Technicians; Mechanical Engineering Technologists; Mobile Heavy Equipment Mechanics, Except Engines; Nanotechnology

Engineering Technicians; Telecommunications Line Installers and Repairers; Tire Repairers and Changers; others.

**Skills**—Installation, Technology Design, Repairing, Equipment Maintenance, Equipment Selection, Troubleshooting, Quality Control Analysis, Operation Monitoring.

**Work Environment:** Indoors; sitting; using hands; noise.

# Job Specialization: Electronics Engineering Technicians

**Lay out, build, test, troubleshoot, repair, and modify developmental and production electronic components, parts, equipment, and systems, such as computer equipment, missile control instrumentation, electron tubes, test equipment, and machine tool numerical controls, applying principles and theories of electronics, electrical circuitry, engineering mathematics, electronic and electrical testing, and physics. Usually work under direction of engineering staff.** Read blueprints, wiring diagrams, schematic drawings, and engineering instructions for assembling electronics units, applying knowledge of electronic theory and components. Test electronics units, using standard test equipment, and analyze results to evaluate performance and determine need for adjustment. Perform preventative maintenance and calibration of equipment and systems. Assemble, test, and maintain circuitry or electronic components according to engineering instructions, technical manuals, and knowledge of electronics, using hand and power tools. Adjust and replace defective or improperly functioning circuitry and electronics components, using hand tools and soldering iron. Write reports and record data on testing techniques, laboratory equipment, and specifications to assist engineers. Identify and resolve equipment malfunctions, working with manufacturers and field representatives as necessary to procure replacement parts. Provide user applications and engineering support and recommendations for new and existing equipment with regard to installation, upgrades, and enhancement. Maintain system logs and manuals to document testing and operation of equipment. Provide customer support and education, working with users to identify needs, determine sources of problems, and provide information on product use. Maintain working knowledge of state-of-the-art tools or software by reading or by attending conferences, workshops, or other training. Build prototypes from rough sketches or plans. Design basic circuitry and draft sketches for clarification of details and design documentation under engineers' direction, using drafting instruments and computer-aided design (CAD) equipment. Procure parts and maintain inventory and related documentation. Research equipment and component needs, sources, competitive prices, delivery times, and ongoing operational costs. Write computer or microprocessor software programs.

**Education/Training Required:** Associate degree. **Education and Training Programs:** Computer Engineering Technology/Technician; Computer Technology/Computer Systems Technology; Electrical and Electronic Engineering Technologies/Technicians, Other; Electrical, Electronic, and Communications Engineering Technology/Technician; Telecommunications Technology/Technician. **Knowledge/Courses**—Telecommunications, Engineering and Technology, Design, Mechanical, Computers and Electronics, Physics.

**Personality Type:** Realistic-Investigative. **Career Cluster:** 13 Manufacturing. **Career Pathway:** 13.3 Maintenance, Installation, and Repair. **Other Jobs in This Pathway:** Aircraft Mechanics and Service Technicians; Automotive Specialty Technicians; Biological Technicians; Civil Engineering Technicians; Computer, Automated Teller, and Office Machine Repairers; Electrical and Electronic Equipment Assemblers; Electrical and Electronics Repairers, Commercial and Industrial Equipment; Electrical Engineering Technicians; Electrical Engineering Technologists; Electromechanical Engineering Technologists; Electronics Engineering Technologists; Engineering Technicians, Except Drafters, All Other; Fuel Cell Technicians; Helpers—Installation, Maintenance, and Repair Workers; Industrial Engineering Technologists; Industrial Machinery Mechanics; Installation, Maintenance, and Repair Workers, All Other; Manufacturing Engineering Technologists; Manufacturing Production Technicians; Mapping Technicians; Mechanical Engineering Technologists; Mobile Heavy Equipment Mechanics, Except Engines; Nanotechnology Engineering Technicians; Telecommunications Line Installers and Repairers; Tire Repairers and Changers; others.

**Skills**—Repairing, Equipment Maintenance, Troubleshooting, Equipment Selection, Operations Analysis, Science, Programming, Quality Control Analysis.

**Work Environment:** Indoors; sitting; using hands; noise.

# Electrical and Electronics Repairers, Powerhouse, Substation, and Relay

* Annual Earnings: $65,230
* Earnings Growth Potential: Low (30.9%)
* Growth: 11.5%
* Annual Job Openings: 670
* Self-Employed: 0.0%

**Considerations for Job Outlook:** Employment growth for these workers is expected to be limited as improvements in the quality of electrical and electronic equipment result in less need for repairs. The best prospects are expected for job seekers who have certification, an associate degree, and relevant experience.

**Inspect, test, repair, or maintain electrical equipment in generating stations, substations, and in-service relays.** Construct, test, maintain, and repair substation relay and control systems. Inspect and test equipment and circuits to identify malfunctions or defects, using wiring diagrams and testing devices such as ohmmeters, voltmeters, or ammeters. Consult manuals, schematics, wiring diagrams, and engineering personnel to troubleshoot and solve equipment problems and to determine optimum equipment functioning. Notify facility personnel of equipment shutdowns. Open and close switches to isolate defective relays; then perform adjustments or repairs. Prepare and maintain records detailing tests, repairs, and maintenance. Analyze test data to diagnose malfunctions, to determine performance characteristics of systems, and to evaluate effects of system modifications. Test insulators and bushings of equipment by inducing voltage across insulation, testing current, and calculating insulation loss. Repair, replace, and clean equipment and components such as circuit breakers, brushes, and commutators. Disconnect voltage regulators, bolts, and screws and connect replacement regulators to high-voltage lines. Schedule and supervise the construction and testing of special devices and the implementation of unique monitoring or control systems. Run signal quality and connectivity tests for individual cables and record results. Schedule and supervise splicing or termination of cables in color-code order. Test oil in circuit breakers and transformers for dielectric strength, refilling oil periodically. Maintain inventories of spare parts for all equipment, requisitioning parts as necessary. Set forms and pour concrete footings for installation of heavy equipment.

**Education/Training Required:** Postsecondary vocational training. **Education and Training Programs:** Electrical and Power Transmission Installers, Other; Mechanic and Repair Technologies/Technicians, Other. **Knowledge/Courses—** Mechanical, Design, Telecommunications, Building and Construction, Physics, Public Safety and Security.

**Personality Type:** Realistic-Conventional. **Career Cluster:** 13 Manufacturing. **Career Pathway:** 13.3 Maintenance, Installation, and Repair. **Other Jobs in This Pathway:** Aircraft Mechanics and Service Technicians; Automotive Specialty Technicians; Biological Technicians; Civil Engineering Technicians; Computer, Automated Teller, and Office Machine Repairers; Electrical and Electronic Equipment Assemblers; Electrical and Electronics Repairers, Commercial and Industrial Equipment; Electrical Engineering Technicians; Electrical Engineering Technologists; Electromechanical Engineering Technologists; Electronics Engineering Technicians; Electronics Engineering Technologists; Engineering Technicians, Except Drafters, All Other; Fuel Cell Technicians; Helpers—Installation, Maintenance, and Repair Workers; Industrial Engineering Technologists; Industrial Machinery Mechanics; Installation, Maintenance, and Repair Workers, All Other; Manufacturing Engineering Technologists; Manufacturing Production Technicians; Mapping Technicians; Mechanical Engineering Technologists; Mobile Heavy Equipment Mechanics, Except Engines; Telecommunications Line Installers and Repairers; Tire Repairers and Changers; others.

**Skills—**Equipment Maintenance, Repairing, Troubleshooting, Operation and Control, Quality Control Analysis, Science, Operation Monitoring, Equipment Selection.

**Work Environment:** More often outdoors than indoors; standing; using hands; noise; very hot or cold; bright or inadequate lighting; contaminants; hazardous conditions; hazardous equipment; minor burns, cuts, bites, or stings.

# Electrical Engineers

- ❀ Annual Earnings: $84,540
- ❀ Earnings Growth Potential: Medium (36.1%)
- ❀ Growth: 1.7%
- ❀ Annual Job Openings: 3,890
- ❀ Self-Employed: 1.6%

**Considerations for Job Outlook:** Electrical engineers are expected to have employment growth of 2 percent from 2008–2018. Although strong demand for electrical devices—including electric power generators, wireless phone transmitters, high-density batteries, and navigation systems—should spur job growth, international competition and the use of engineering services performed in other countries will limit employment growth. Electrical engineers working in firms providing engineering expertise and design services to manufacturers should have better job prospects.

**Design, develop, test, or supervise the manufacturing and installation of electrical equipment, components, or systems for commercial, industrial, military, or scientific use.** Confer with engineers, customers, and others to discuss existing or potential engineering projects and products. Design, implement, maintain, and improve electrical instruments, equipment, facilities, components, products, and systems for commercial, industrial, and domestic purposes. Operate computer-assisted engineering and design software and equipment to perform engineering tasks. Direct and coordinate manufacturing, construction, installation, maintenance, support, documentation, and testing activities to ensure compliance with specifications, codes, and customer requirements. Perform detailed calculations to compute and establish manufacturing, construction, and installation standards and specifications. Inspect completed installations and observe operations to ensure conformance to design and equipment specifications and compliance with operational and safety standards. Plan and implement research methodology and procedures to apply principles of electrical theory to engineering projects. Prepare specifications for purchase of materials and equipment. Supervise and train project team members as necessary. Investigate and test vendors' and competitors' products. Oversee project production efforts to assure projects are completed satisfactorily, on time, and within budget. Prepare and study technical drawings, specifications of electrical systems, and topographical maps to ensure that installation and operations conform to standards and customer requirements. Investigate customer or public complaints, determine nature and extent of problem, and recommend remedial measures. Plan layout of electric-power-generating plants and distribution lines and stations. Assist in developing capital project programs for new equipment and major repairs. Develop budgets, estimating labor, material, and construction costs. Compile data and write reports regarding existing and potential engineering studies and projects.

**Education/Training Required:** Bachelor's degree. **Education and Training Program:** Electrical and Electronics Engineering. **Knowledge/Courses—**Design, Engineering and Technology, Physics, Computers and Electronics, Mechanical, Mathematics.

**Personality Type:** Investigative-Realistic. **Career Cluster:** 15 Science, Technology, Engineering, and Mathematics. **Career Pathway:** 15.1 Engineering and Technology. **Other Jobs in This Pathway:** Architectural and Engineering Managers; Automotive Engineers; Biochemical Engineers; Biofuels/Biodiesel Technology and Product Development Managers; Civil Engineers; Cost Estimators; Education, Training, and Library Workers, All Other; Electronics Engineers, Except Computer; Energy Engineers; Engineers, All Other; Fuel Cell Engineers; Human Factors Engineers and Ergonomists; Industrial Engineers; Manufacturing Engineers; Mechanical Engineers; Mechatronics Engineers; Microsystems Engineers; Nanosystems Engineers; Photonics Engineers; Radio Frequency Identification Device Specialists; Robotics Engineers; Solar Energy Systems Engineers; Transportation Engineers; Validation Engineers; Wind Energy Engineers; others.

**Skills**—Science, Troubleshooting, Repairing, Operations Analysis, Mathematics, Equipment Maintenance, Operation Monitoring, Technology Design.

**Work Environment:** Indoors; sitting; noise.

# Electrical Power-Line Installers and Repairers

- ❋ Annual Earnings: $58,030
- ❋ Earnings Growth Potential: High (42.0%)
- ❋ Growth: 4.5%
- ❋ Annual Job Openings: 4,550
- ❋ Self-Employed: 1.4%

**Considerations for Job Outlook:** Slow decline in employment is projected.

**Install or repair cables or wires used in electrical power or distribution systems. May erect poles and light- or heavy-duty transmission towers.** Adhere to safety practices and procedures, such as checking equipment regularly and erecting barriers around work areas. Open switches or attach grounding devices to remove electrical hazards from disturbed or fallen lines or to facilitate repairs. Climb poles or use truck-mounted buckets to access equipment. Place insulating or fireproofing materials over conductors and joints. Install, maintain, and repair electrical distribution and transmission systems, including conduits; cables; wires; and related equipment such as transformers, circuit breakers, and switches. Identify defective sectionalizing devices, circuit breakers, fuses, voltage regulators, transformers, switches, relays, or wiring, using wiring diagrams

and electrical-testing instruments. Drive vehicles equipped with tools and materials to job sites. Coordinate work assignment preparation and completion with other workers. String wire conductors and cables between poles, towers, trenches, pylons, and buildings, setting lines in place and using winches to adjust tension. Inspect and test power lines and auxiliary equipment to locate and identify problems, using reading and testing instruments. Test conductors according to electrical diagrams and specifications to identify corresponding conductors and to prevent incorrect connections. Replace damaged poles with new poles and straighten the poles. Install watt-hour meters and connect service drops between power lines and consumers' facilities. Attach crossarms, insulators, and auxiliary equipment to poles prior to installing them. Travel in trucks, helicopters, and airplanes to inspect lines for freedom from obstruction and adequacy of insulation. Dig holes, using augers, and set poles, using cranes and power equipment. Trim trees that could be hazardous to the functioning of cables or wires.

**Education/Training Required:** Long-term on-the-job training. **Education and Training Programs:** Electrical and Power Transmission Installation/Installer, General; Electrical and Power Transmission Installers, Other; Lineworker. **Knowledge/Courses**—Building and Construction, Mechanical, Customer and Personal Service, Engineering and Technology, Transportation, Design.

**Personality Type:** Realistic-Investigative-Conventional. **Career Cluster:** 02 Architecture and Construction. **Career Pathway:** 2.2 Construction. **Other Jobs in This Pathway:** Brickmasons and Blockmasons; Cement Masons and Concrete Finishers; Construction and Building Inspectors; Construction Carpenters; Construction Laborers; Construction Managers; Cost Estimators; Drywall and Ceiling Tile Installers; Electricians; Engineering Technicians, Except Drafters, All Other; Excavating and Loading Machine and Dragline Operators; First-Line Supervisors of Construction Trades and Extraction Workers; Heating and Air Conditioning Mechanics and Installers; Helpers—Carpenters; Helpers—Electricians; Helpers—Pipelayers, Plumbers, Pipefitters, and Steamfitters; Highway Maintenance Workers; Operating Engineers and Other Construction Equipment Operators; Painters, Construction and Maintenance; Pipe Fitters and Steamfitters; Plumbers; Refrigeration Mechanics and Installers; Roofers; Rough Carpenters; Solar Energy Installation Managers; others.

**Skills**—Repairing, Troubleshooting, Equipment Maintenance, Operation and Control, Quality Control Analysis, Operation Monitoring, Installation, Equipment Selection.

**Work Environment:** Outdoors; standing; walking and running; using hands; bending or twisting the body; repetitive motions; noise; very hot or cold; bright or inadequate lighting; contaminants; cramped work space; high places; hazardous conditions; hazardous equipment; minor burns, cuts, bites, or stings.

# Electricians

* Annual Earnings: $48,250
* Earnings Growth Potential: Medium (39.1%)
* Growth: 11.9%
* Annual Job Openings: 25,090
* Self-Employed: 9.3%

**Considerations for Job Outlook:** Population growth is expected to spur increases in construction, which in turn will increase employment of electricians. The need to update the electrical systems of existing buildings should also drive employment growth. Opportunities should be good.

**Install, maintain, and repair electrical wiring, equipment, and fixtures. Ensure that work is in accordance with relevant codes. May install or service street lights, intercom systems, or electrical control systems.** Maintain current electrician's license or identification card to meet governmental regulations. Connect wires to circuit breakers, transformers, or other components. Repair or replace wiring, equipment, and fixtures, using hand tools and power tools. Assemble, install, test, and maintain electrical or electronic wiring, equipment, appliances, apparatus, and fixtures, using hand tools and power tools. Test electrical systems and continuity of circuits in electrical wiring, equipment, and fixtures, using testing devices such as ohmmeters, voltmeters, and oscilloscopes, to ensure compatibility and safety of system. Use a variety of tools and equipment such as power construction equipment, measuring devices, power tools, and testing equipment, including oscilloscopes, ammeters, and test lamps. Plan layout and installation of electrical wiring, equipment, and fixtures based on job specifications and local codes. Inspect electrical systems, equipment, and components to identify hazards, defects, and the need for adjustment or repair and to ensure compliance with codes. Direct and train workers to install, maintain, or repair electrical wiring, equipment, and fixtures. Diagnose malfunctioning systems, apparatus, and components, using test equipment and hand tools, to locate the cause of a breakdown and correct the problem. Prepare sketches or follow blueprints to determine the location of wiring and equipment and to ensure conformance to building and safety codes. Install ground leads and connect power cables to equipment such as motors. Work from ladders, scaffolds, and roofs to install, maintain, or repair electrical wiring, equipment, and fixtures. Perform business management duties such as maintaining records and files, preparing reports, and ordering supplies and equipment. Fasten small metal or plastic boxes to walls to house electrical switches or outlets.

**Education/Training Required:** Long-term on-the-job training. **Education and Training Program:** Electrician. **Knowledge/Courses**—Building and Construction, Mechanical, Design, Physics, Telecommunications, Engineering and Technology.

**Personality Type:** Realistic-Investigative-Conventional. **Career Cluster:** 02 Architecture and Construction. **Career Pathway:** 2.2 Construction. **Other Jobs in This Pathway:** Brickmasons and Blockmasons; Cement Masons and Concrete Finishers; Construction and Building Inspectors; Construction Carpenters; Construction Laborers; Construction Managers; Cost Estimators; Drywall and Ceiling Tile Installers; Electrical Power-Line Installers and Repairers; Engineering Technicians, Except Drafters, All Other; Excavating and Loading Machine and Dragline Operators; First-Line Supervisors of Construction Trades and Extraction Workers; Heating and Air Conditioning Mechanics and Installers; Helpers—Carpenters; Helpers—Electricians; Helpers—Pipelayers, Plumbers, Pipefitters, and Steamfitters; Highway Maintenance Workers; Operating Engineers and Other Construction Equipment Operators; Painters, Construction and Maintenance; Pipe Fitters and Steamfitters; Plumbers; Refrigeration Mechanics and Installers; Roofers; Rough Carpenters; Solar Energy Installation Managers; others.

**Skills**—Installation, Repairing, Equipment Maintenance, Troubleshooting, Equipment Selection, Quality Control Analysis, Operation and Control, Management of Financial Resources.

**Work Environment:** More often outdoors than indoors; standing; climbing; walking and running; using hands; bending or twisting the body; repetitive motions; noise; very hot or cold; bright or inadequate lighting; contaminants; cramped work space; high places; hazardous conditions; hazardous equipment; minor burns, cuts, bites, or stings.

E

# Electronics Engineers, Except Computer

- ❀ Annual Earnings: $90,170
- ❀ Earnings Growth Potential: Low (35.8%)
- ❀ Growth: 0.3%
- ❀ Annual Job Openings: 3,340
- ❀ Self-Employed: 1.6%

**Considerations for Job Outlook:** Electronics engineers, except computer, are expected to experience little to no employment change from 2008–2018. Although rising demand for electronic goods—including communications equipment, defense-related equipment, medical electronics, and consumer products—should continue to increase demand for electronics engineers, foreign competition in electronic products development and the use of engineering services performed in other countries will limit employment growth. Growth is expected to be fastest in service-providing industries—particularly in firms that provide engineering and design services.

**Research, design, develop, and test electronic components and systems for commercial, industrial, military, or scientific use, utilizing knowledge of electronic theory and materials properties. Design electronic circuits and components for use in fields such as telecommunications, aerospace guidance and propulsion control, acoustics, or instruments and controls.** Design electronic components, software, products, or systems for commercial, industrial, medical, military, or scientific applications. Provide technical support and instruction to staff or customers regarding equipment standards, assisting with specific, difficult in-service engineering. Operate computer-assisted engineering and design software and equipment to perform engineering tasks. Analyze system requirements, capacity, cost, and customer needs to determine feasibility of project and develop system plan. Confer with engineers, customers, vendors, or others to discuss existing and potential engineering projects or products. Review and evaluate work of others inside and outside the organization to ensure effectiveness, technical adequacy, and compatibility in the resolution of complex engineering problems. Determine material and equipment needs and order supplies. Inspect electronic equipment, instruments, products, and systems to ensure conformance to specifications, safety standards, and applicable codes and regulations. Evaluate operational systems, prototypes, and proposals and recommend repair or design modifications based on factors such as environment, service, cost, and system capabilities. Prepare documentation containing information such as confidential descriptions and specifications of proprietary hardware and software, product development and introduction schedules, product costs, and information about product performance weaknesses. Direct and coordinate activities concerned with manufacture, construction, installation, maintenance, operation, and modification of electronic equipment, products, and systems. Develop and perform operational, maintenance, and testing procedures for electronic products, components, equipment, and systems. Plan and develop applications and modifications for electronic properties used in components, products, and systems to improve technical performance.

**Education/Training Required:** Bachelor's degree. **Education and Training Program:** Electrical and Electronics Engineering. **Knowledge/Courses**—Design, Engineering and Technology, Physics, Computers and Electronics, Mathematics, Production and Processing.

**Personality Type:** Investigative-Realistic. **Career Cluster:** 15 Science, Technology, Engineering, and Mathematics. **Career Pathway:** 15.1 Engineering and Technology. **Other Jobs in This Pathway:** Architectural and Engineering Managers; Automotive Engineers; Biochemical Engineers; Biofuels/Biodiesel Technology and Product Development Managers; Civil Engineers; Cost Estimators; Education, Training, and Library Workers, All Other; Electrical Engineers; Energy Engineers; Engineers, All Other; Fuel Cell Engineers; Human Factors Engineers and Ergonomists; Industrial Engineers; Manufacturing Engineers; Mechanical Engineers; Mechatronics Engineers; Microsystems Engineers; Nanosystems Engineers; Photonics Engineers; Radio Frequency Identification Device Specialists; Robotics Engineers; Solar Energy Systems Engineers; Transportation Engineers; Validation Engineers; Wind Energy Engineers; others.

**Skills**—Programming, Repairing, Technology Design, Equipment Selection, Equipment Maintenance, Troubleshooting, Operation and Control, Quality Control Analysis.

**Work Environment:** Indoors; sitting; using hands.

## Job Specialization: Radio Frequency Identification Device Specialists

**Design and implement radio frequency identification device (RFID) systems used to track shipments or goods.** Verify compliance of developed applications with architectural standards and established practices. Read current literature, attend meetings or conferences, or talk with colleagues to stay abreast of industry research about new technologies. Provide technical support for radio frequency identification device (RFID) technology. Perform systems analysis or programming of radio frequency identification device (RFID) technology. Document equipment or process details of radio frequency identification device (RFID) technology. Train users in details of system operation. Analyze radio frequency identification device (RFID)-related supply chain data. Test tags or labels to ensure readability. Test radio frequency identification device (RFID) software to ensure proper functioning. Select appropriate radio frequency identification device (RFID) tags and determine placement locations. Perform site analyses to determine system configurations, processes to be impacted, or on-site obstacles to technology implementation. Perform acceptance testing on newly installed or updated systems. Identify operational requirements for new systems to inform selection of technological solutions. Determine usefulness of new radio frequency identification device (RFID) technologies. Develop process flows, work instructions, or standard operating procedures for radio frequency identification device (RFID) systems. Determine means of integrating radio frequency identification device (RFID) into other applications. Define and compare possible radio frequency identification device (RFID) solutions to inform selection for specific projects. Create simulations or models of radio frequency identification device (RFID) systems to provide information for selection and configuration. Install, test, or maintain radio frequency identification device (RFID) systems. Integrate tags, readers, or software in radio frequency identification device (RFID) designs.

**Education/Training Required:** Bachelor's degree. **Education and Training Program:** Electrical and Electronics Engineering. **Knowledge/Courses**—No data available.

**Personality Type:** Realistic-Investigative-Conventional. **Career Cluster:** 15 Science, Technology, Engineering, and Mathematics. **Career Pathway:** 15.1 Engineering and Technology. **Other Jobs in This Pathway:** Architectural and Engineering Managers; Automotive Engineers; Biochemical Engineers; Biofuels/Biodiesel Technology and Product Development Managers; Civil Engineers; Cost Estimators; Education, Training, and Library Workers, All Other; Electrical Engineers; Electronics Engineers, Except Computer; Energy Engineers; Engineers, All Other; Fuel Cell Engineers; Human Factors Engineers and Ergonomists; Industrial Engineers; Manufacturing Engineers; Mechanical Engineers; Mechatronics Engineers; Microsystems Engineers; Nanosystems Engineers; Photonics Engineers; Robotics Engineers; Solar Energy Systems Engineers; Transportation Engineers; Validation Engineers; Wind Energy Engineers; others.

**Skills**—No data available.

**Work Environment:** No data available.

# Elementary School Teachers, Except Special Education

- ❋ Annual Earnings: $51,660
- ❋ Earnings Growth Potential: Low (33.4%)
- ❋ Growth: 15.8%
- ❋ Annual Job Openings: 59,650
- ❋ Self-Employed: 0.0%

**Considerations for Job Outlook:** Enrollment from 2008–2018 is expected to grow more slowly than in recent years. Prospects are usually better in urban and rural areas, for bilingual teachers, and for math and science teachers.

**Teach pupils in public or private schools at the elementary level basic academic, social, and other formative skills.** Establish and enforce rules for behavior and procedures for maintaining order among the students for whom they are responsible. Observe and evaluate students' performance, behavior, social development, and physical health. Prepare materials and classrooms for class activities. Adapt teaching methods and instructional materials to meet students' varying needs and interests. Plan and conduct activities for a balanced program of instruction, demonstration, and work time that provides students with opportunities to observe, question, and investigate. Instruct students individually and in groups, using various teaching methods such as lectures, discussions, and demonstrations. Establish clear objectives for all lessons, units, and projects and communicate those objectives to students. Assign and grade classwork and homework. Read books to entire classes or small groups. Prepare, administer, and grade tests and assignments in order to evaluate students' progress. Confer with parents or guardians, teachers, counselors, and administrators to resolve students' behavioral and academic problems. Meet with parents and guardians to discuss their children's progress and to determine their priorities for their children and their resource needs. Prepare students for later grades by encouraging them to explore learning opportunities and to persevere with challenging tasks. Maintain accurate and complete student records as required by laws, district policies, and administrative regulations. Guide and counsel students with adjustment or academic problems or special academic interests. Prepare and implement remedial programs for students requiring extra help. Prepare objectives and outlines for courses of study, following curriculum guidelines or requirements of states and schools. Provide a variety of materials and resources for children to explore, manipulate, and use, both in learning activities and in imaginative play. Enforce administration policies and rules governing students.

**Education/Training Required:** Bachelor's degree. **Education and Training Programs:** Elementary Education and Teaching; Teacher Education, Multiple Levels. **Knowledge/Courses**—History and Archeology, Geography, Philosophy and Theology, Sociology and Anthropology, Therapy and Counseling, Fine Arts.

**Personality Type:** Social-Artistic-Conventional. **Career Cluster:** 05 Education and Training. **Career Pathway:** 5.3 Teaching/Training. **Other Jobs in This Pathway:** Adult Basic and Secondary Education and Literacy Teachers and Instructors; Athletes and Sports Competitors; Audio-Visual and Multimedia Collections Specialists; Career/Technical Education Teachers, Middle School; Career/Technical Education Teachers, Secondary School; Chemists; Coaches and Scouts; Dietitians and Nutritionists; Fitness Trainers and Aerobics Instructors; Historians; Instructional Coordinators; Instructional Designers and Technologists; Interpreters and Translators; Kindergarten Teachers, Except Special Education; Librarians; Middle School Teachers, Except Special and Career/Technical Education; Physicists; Preschool Teachers, Except Special Education; Recreation Workers; Secondary School Teachers, Except Special and Career/Technical Education; Self-Enrichment Education Teachers; Teacher Assistants; Teachers and Instructors, All Other; Tutors.

**Skills**—Learning Strategies, Social Perceptiveness, Monitoring, Systems Evaluation, Service Orientation, Writing, Systems Analysis, Instructing.

**Work Environment:** Indoors; standing; noise.

# Elevator Installers and Repairers

* Annual Earnings: $70,910
* Earnings Growth Potential: High (44.9%)
* Growth: 9.2%
* Annual Job Openings: 920
* Self-Employed: 0.1%

**Considerations for Job Outlook:** The need to install new equipment and to maintain, update, and repair old equipment should lead to employment growth for these workers. Entry-level workers should have excellent opportunities.

**Assemble, install, repair, or maintain electric or hydraulic freight or passenger elevators, escalators, or dumbwaiters.** Assemble, install, repair, and maintain elevators, escalators, moving sidewalks, and dumbwaiters, using hand and power tools and testing devices such as test lamps, ammeters, and voltmeters. Test newly installed equipment to ensure that it meets specifications such as stopping at floors for set amounts of time. Check that safety regulations and building codes are met and complete service reports verifying conformance to standards. Locate malfunctions in brakes, motors, switches, and signal and control systems, using test equipment. Connect electrical wiring to control panels and electric motors. Read and interpret blueprints to determine the layout of system components, frameworks, and foundations and to select installation equipment. Adjust safety controls; counterweights; door mechanisms; and components such as valves, ratchets, seals, and brake linings. Inspect wiring connections, control panel hookups, door installations, and alignments and clearances of cars and hoistways to ensure that equipment will operate properly. Disassemble defective units and repair or replace parts such as locks, gears, cables, and electric wiring. Maintain log books that detail all repairs and checks performed. Participate in additional training to keep skills up to date. Attach guide shoes and rollers to minimize the lateral motion of cars as they travel through shafts. Connect car frames to counterweights, using steel cables. Bolt or weld steel rails to the walls of shafts to guide elevators, working from scaffolding or platforms. Assemble elevator cars, installing each car's platform, walls, and doors. Install outer doors and door frames at elevator entrances on each floor of a structure. Install electrical wires and controls by attaching conduit along shaft walls from floor to floor and then pulling plastic-covered wires through the conduit. Cut prefabricated sections of framework, rails, and other components to specified dimensions.

**Education/Training Required:** Long-term on-the-job training. **Education and Training Program:** Industrial Mechanics and Maintenance Technology. **Knowledge/Courses**—Building and Construction, Mechanical, Physics, Design, Engineering and Technology, Public Safety and Security.

**Personality Type:** Realistic-Investigative-Conventional. **Career Cluster:** 13 Manufacturing. **Career Pathway:** 13.3 Maintenance, Installation, and Repair. **Other Jobs in This Pathway:** Aircraft Mechanics and Service Technicians; Automotive Specialty Technicians; Biological Technicians; Civil Engineering Technicians; Computer, Automated Teller, and Office Machine Repairers; Electrical and Electronic Equipment Assemblers; Electrical and Electronics Repairers, Commercial and Industrial Equipment; Electrical

Engineering Technicians; Electrical Engineering Technologists; Electromechanical Engineering Technologists; Electronics Engineering Technicians; Electronics Engineering Technologists; Engineering Technicians, Except Drafters, All Other; Fuel Cell Technicians; Helpers—Installation, Maintenance, and Repair Workers; Industrial Engineering Technologists; Industrial Machinery Mechanics; Installation, Maintenance, and Repair Workers, All Other; Manufacturing Engineering Technologists; Manufacturing Production Technicians; Mapping Technicians; Mechanical Engineering Technologists; Mobile Heavy Equipment Mechanics, Except Engines; Telecommunications Line Installers and Repairers; Tire Repairers and Changers; others.

**Skills**—Repairing, Equipment Maintenance, Installation, Troubleshooting, Equipment Selection, Operation and Control, Quality Control Analysis, Operation Monitoring.

**Work Environment:** More often indoors than outdoors; standing; walking and running; using hands; bending or twisting the body; noise; very hot or cold; bright or inadequate lighting; contaminants; cramped work space; high places; hazardous conditions; hazardous equipment; minor burns, cuts, bites, or stings.

# Eligibility Interviewers, Government Programs

- ❋ Annual Earnings: $39,960
- ❋ Earnings Growth Potential: Low (30.5%)
- ❋ Growth: 9.2%
- ❋ Annual Job Openings: 3,880
- ❋ Self-Employed: 0.0%

**Considerations for Job Outlook:** As the population ages, retires, and becomes eligible for benefits and programs, employment in this occupation is expected to increase. But employment growth may be tempered by a trend toward automated services, such as online application. Job opportunities are expected to be favorable.

**Determine eligibility of persons applying to receive assistance from government programs and agency resources, such as welfare, unemployment benefits, social security, and public housing.** Answer applicants' questions about benefits and claim procedures. Interview benefits recipients at specified intervals to certify their eligibility for continuing benefits. Interpret and explain information such as eligibility requirements, application details, payment methods, and applicants' legal rights. Initiate procedures to grant, modify, deny, or terminate assistance or refer applicants to other agencies for assistance. Compile, record, and evaluate personal and financial data to verify completeness and accuracy and to determine eligibility status. Interview and investigate applicants for public assistance to gather information pertinent to their applications. Check with employers or other references to verify answers and obtain further information. Keep records of assigned cases and prepare required reports. Schedule benefits claimants for adjudication interviews to address questions of eligibility. Prepare applications and forms for applicants for such purposes as school enrollment, employment, and medical services. Refer applicants to job openings or to interviews with other staff in accordance with administrative guidelines or office procedures. Provide social workers with pertinent information gathered during applicant interviews. Compute and authorize amounts of assistance for programs such as grants, monetary payments, and food stamps. Monitor the payments of benefits throughout the duration of a claim. Provide applicants with assistance in completing application forms such as those for job referrals or unemployment compensation claims. Investigate claimants for the possibility of fraud or abuse. Conduct annual, interim, and special housing reviews and home visits to ensure conformance to regulations.

**Education/Training Required:** Moderate-term on-the-job training. **Education and Training Program:** Community Organization and Advocacy. **Knowledge/Courses**—Clerical, Customer and Personal Service, Law and Government, Psychology, Sociology and Anthropology, Computers and Electronics.

**Personality Type:** Social-Conventional-Enterprising. **Career Cluster:** 10 Human Services. **Career Pathway:** 10.3 Family and Community Services. **Other Jobs in This Pathway:** Chief Executives; Child, Family, and School Social Workers; Childcare Workers; City and Regional Planning Aides; Counselors, All Other; Farm and Home Management Advisors; Legislators; Managers, All Other; Marriage and Family Therapists; Nannies; Personal Care Aides; Probation Officers and Correctional Treatment Specialists; Protective Service Workers, All Other; Social and Community Service Managers; Social Science Research Assistants; Social Scientists and Related Workers, All Other; Social Workers, All Other; Sociologists; Supply Chain Managers.

**Skills**—Service Orientation, Speaking, Active Listening, Social Perceptiveness, Reading Comprehension, Negotiation, Writing, Critical Thinking.

**Work Environment:** Indoors; sitting; using hands; repetitive motions; contaminants.

# Emergency Medical Technicians and Paramedics

- ❀ Annual Earnings: $30,360
- ❀ Earnings Growth Potential: Low (35.1%)
- ❀ Growth: 9.0%
- ❀ Annual Job Openings: 6,200
- ❀ Self-Employed: 0.4%

**Considerations for Job Outlook:** An aging population is expected to drive employment growth in these occupations. Opportunities should be favorable, especially for job seekers with advanced certification.

**Assess injuries, administer emergency medical care, and extricate trapped individuals. Transport injured or sick persons to medical facilities.** Administer first-aid treatment and life-support care to sick or injured persons in prehospital setting. Perform emergency diagnostic and treatment procedures, such as stomach suction, airway management, or heart monitoring, during ambulance ride. Observe, record, and report to physician the patient's condition or injury, the treatment provided, and reactions to drugs and treatment. Immobilize patient for placement on stretcher and ambulance transport, using backboard or other spinal immobilization device. Maintain vehicles and medical and communication equipment and replenish first-aid equipment and supplies. Assess nature and extent of illness or injury to establish and prioritize medical procedures. Communicate with dispatchers and treatment center personnel to provide information about situation, to arrange reception of victims, and to receive instructions for further treatment. Comfort and reassure patients. Decontaminate ambulance interior following treatment of patient with infectious disease and report case to proper authorities. Operate equipment such as electrocardiograms (EKGs), external defibrillators, and bag-valve mask resuscitators in advanced life-support environments. Drive mobile intensive care unit to specified location, following instructions from emergency medical dispatcher. Coordinate with treatment center personnel to obtain patients' vital statistics and medical history, to determine the circumstances of the emergency, and to administer emergency treatment. Coordinate work with other emergency medical team members and police and fire department personnel. Attend training classes to maintain certification licensure, keep abreast of new developments in the field, or maintain existing knowledge. Administer drugs orally or by injection and perform intravenous procedures under a physician's direction.

**Education/Training Required:** Postsecondary vocational training. **Education and Training Programs:** Emergency Care Attendant (EMT Ambulance) Training; Emergency Medical Technology/Technician (EMT Paramedic). **Knowledge/Courses**—Medicine and Dentistry, Customer and Personal Service, Therapy and Counseling, Psychology, Transportation, Education and Training.

**Personality Type:** Social-Investigative-Realistic. **Career Cluster:** 08 Health Science. **Career Pathway:** 8.2 Diagnostics Services. **Other Jobs in This Pathway:** Ambulance Drivers and Attendants, Except Emergency Medical Technicians; Anesthesiologist Assistants; Cardiovascular Technologists and Technicians; Cytogenetic Technologists; Cytotechnologists; Diagnostic Medical Sonographers; Endoscopy Technicians; Health Diagnosing and Treating Practitioners, All Other; Health Technologists and Technicians, All Other; Healthcare Practitioners and Technical Workers, All Other; Histotechnologists and Histologic Technicians; Medical and Clinical Laboratory Technicians; Medical and Clinical Laboratory Technologists; Medical and Health Services Managers; Medical Assistants; Medical Equipment Preparers; Neurodiagnostic Technologists; Nuclear Medicine Technologists; Ophthalmic Laboratory Technicians; Physical Scientists, All Other; Physician Assistants; Radiologic Technicians; Radiologic Technologists; Surgical Technologists; Veterinary Assistants and Laboratory Animal Caretakers; others.

**Skills**—Science, Operation and Control, Service Orientation, Coordination, Operation Monitoring, Active Learning, Troubleshooting, Equipment Selection.

**Work Environment:** More often outdoors than indoors; standing; using hands; bending or twisting the body; repetitive motions; noise; very hot or cold; bright or inadequate lighting; contaminants; cramped work space; exposed to disease or infections; hazardous conditions; hazardous equipment; minor burns, cuts, bites, or stings.

# Engineering Teachers, Postsecondary

- ❀ Annual Earnings: $89,670
- ❀ Earnings Growth Potential: High (49.0%)
- ❀ Growth: 15.1%
- ❀ Annual Job Openings: 1,000
- ❀ Self-Employed: 0.2%

**Considerations for Job Outlook:** Enrollments in postsecondary institutions are expected to continue rising as more people attend college and as workers return to school to update their skills. Opportunities for part-time or temporary positions should be favorable, but significant competition exists for tenure-track positions.

**Teach courses pertaining to the application of physical laws and principles of engineering for the development of machines, materials, instruments, processes, and services. Includes teachers of subjects such as chemical, civil, electrical, industrial, mechanical, mineral, and petroleum engineering. Includes both teachers primarily engaged in teaching and those who do a combination of both teaching and research.** Prepare and deliver lectures to undergraduate and/or graduate students on topics such as mechanics, hydraulics, and robotics. Keep abreast of developments in their field by reading current literature, talking with colleagues, and participating in professional conferences. Supervise undergraduate and/or graduate teaching, internship, and research work. Evaluate and grade students' classwork, laboratory work, assignments, and papers. Conduct research in a particular field of knowledge and publish findings in professional journals, books, and/or electronic media. Prepare course materials such as syllabi, homework assignments, and handouts. Compile, administer, and grade examinations or assign this work to others. Write grant proposals to procure external research funding. Supervise students' laboratory work. Initiate, facilitate, and moderate class discussions. Maintain regularly scheduled office hours to advise and assist students. Plan, evaluate, and revise curricula, course content, and course materials and methods of instruction. Advise students on academic and vocational curricula and on career issues. Maintain student attendance records, grades, and other required records. Collaborate with colleagues to address teaching and research issues. Select and obtain materials and supplies such as textbooks and laboratory equipment. Participate in student recruitment, registration, and placement activities. Serve on academic or administrative committees that deal with institutional policies, departmental matters, and academic issues. Perform administrative duties such as serving as department head. Provide professional consulting services to government and/ or industry. Compile bibliographies of specialized materials for outside reading assignments. Act as advisers to student organizations. Participate in campus and community events.

**Education/Training Required:** Doctoral degree. **Education and Training Programs:** Aerospace, Aeronautical, and Astronautical/Space Engineering; Agricultural Engineering; Architectural Engineering; Bioengineering and Biomedical Engineering; Ceramic Sciences and Engineering; Chemical Engineering; Civil Engineering, General; Computer Engineering, General; Computer Hardware Engineering; Computer Software Engineering; Construction Engineering; Electrical and Electronics Engineering; Engineering Mechanics; Engineering Physics/Applied Physics; Engineering Science; Engineering, General; Environmental/Environmental Health Engineering; Forest Engineering; Geological/Geophysical Engineering; Geotechnical and Geoenvironmental Engineering; Industrial Engineering; Manufacturing Engineering; Materials Engineering; Mechanical Engineering; Metallurgical Engineering; Mining and Mineral Engineering; Naval Architecture and Marine Engineering; Nuclear Engineering; Ocean Engineering; Petroleum Engineering; Polymer/Plastics Engineering; Structural Engineering; Surveying Engineering; Systems Engineering; Textile Sciences and Engineering; Transportation and Highway Engineering; Water Resources Engineering; others. **Knowledge/Courses**—Engineering and Technology, Physics, Design, Mathematics, Education and Training, Telecommunications.

**Personality Type:** Investigative-Realistic-Social. **Career Clusters:** 02 Architecture and Construction; 05 Education and Training; 11 Information Technology; 15 Science, Technology, Engineering, and Mathematics. **Career Pathways:** 2.1 Design/Pre-Construction; 5.3 Teaching/Training; 11.4 Programming and Software Development; 15.1 Engineering and Technology; 15.2 Science and Mathematics. **Other Jobs in These Pathways:** Architectural and Engineering Managers; Automotive Engineers; Biochemical Engineers; Biofuels/Biodiesel Technology and Product Development Managers; Civil Engineers; Coaches and Scouts; Cost Estimators; Elementary School Teachers, Except Special Education; Energy Engineers; Engineers, All Other; Fitness Trainers and Aerobics Instructors; Fuel Cell Engineers; Human Factors Engineers and Ergonomists; Industrial Engineers; Manufacturing Engineers; Mechanical Engineers; Middle School Teachers, Except Special and Career/Technical Education; Preschool Teachers, Except Special Education; Recreation Workers; Secondary School Teachers, Except Special and Career/Technical Education; Self-Enrichment Education Teachers; Teacher Assistants; Transportation Engineers; Tutors; 37 other postsecondary teaching occupations; others.

**Skills**—Instructing, Mathematics, Operations Analysis, Science, Programming, Writing, Speaking, Reading Comprehension.

**Work Environment:** Indoors; sitting.

E

# Engineering Technicians, Except Drafters, All Other

- ❋ Annual Earnings: $58,020
- ❋ Earnings Growth Potential: High (46.1%)
- ❋ Growth: 5.2%
- ❋ Annual Job Openings: 1,850
- ❋ Self-Employed: 0.7%

**Considerations for Job Outlook:** Labor-saving efficiencies and the automation of many engineering support activities will limit the need for new engineering technicians. In general, opportunities should be best for job seekers who have an associate degree or other postsecondary training in engineering technology.

**This occupation includes all engineering technicians, except drafters, not listed separately.** Because this is a highly diverse occupation, no data is available for some information topics.

**Education/Training Required:** Associate degree. **Education and Training Program:** Drafting/Design Engineering Technologies/Technicians, Other.

**Career Clusters:** 01 Agriculture, Food, and Natural Resources; 02 Architecture and Construction; 13 Manufacturing. **Career Pathways:** 1.5 Natural Resources Systems; 2.1 Design/Pre-Construction; 2.2 Construction; 13.3 Maintenance, Installation, and Repair. **Other Jobs in These Pathways:** Architectural and Engineering Managers; Automotive Specialty Technicians; Cement Masons and Concrete Finishers; Construction Carpenters; Construction Laborers; Construction Managers; Cost Estimators; Electrical and Electronic Equipment Assemblers; Electrical Engineering Technicians; Electricians; Engineers, All Other; First-Line Supervisors of Construction Trades and Extraction Workers; Heating and Air Conditioning Mechanics and Installers; Industrial Machinery Mechanics; Industrial Truck and Tractor Operators; Installation, Maintenance, and Repair Workers, All Other; Operating Engineers and Other Construction Equipment Operators; Painters, Construction and Maintenance; Pipe Fitters and Steamfitters; Plumbers; Recreation Workers; Refrigeration Mechanics and Installers; Rough Carpenters; Solar Energy Installation Managers; Telecommunications Line Installers and Repairers; others.

# Job Specialization: Electrical Engineering Technologists

Apply engineering theory and technical skills to support electrical engineering activities such as process control, electrical power distribution, and instrumentation design. Prepare layouts of machinery and equipment, plan the flow of work, conduct statistical studies and analyze production costs. Participate in training and continuing education activities to stay abreast of engineering and industry advances. Assist engineers and scientists in conducting applied research in electrical engineering. Diagnose, test, or analyze the performance of electrical components, assemblies, and systems. Set up and operate standard and specialized testing equipment. Review installation and quality assurance documentation. Review, develop and prepare maintenance standards. Compile and maintain records documenting engineering schematics, installed equipment, installation and operational problems, resources used, and repairs or corrective action performed. Supervise the construction and testing of electrical prototypes according to general instructions and established standards. Review electrical engineering plans to ensure adherence to design specifications and compliance with applicable electrical codes and standards. Install or maintain electrical control systems, industrial automation systems, and electrical equipment including control circuits, variable speed drives, or programmable logic controllers. Design or modify engineering schematics for electrical transmission and distribution systems or for electrical installation in residential, commercial, or industrial buildings, using computer-aided design (CAD) software. Calculate design specifications or cost, material, and resource estimates, and prepare project schedules and budgets.

**Education/Training Required:** Bachelor's degree. **Education and Training Program:** Electrical, Electronic, and Communications Engineering Technology/Technician. **Knowledge/Courses**—No data available.

**Personality Type:** Realistic-Investigative-Conventional. **Career Cluster:** 13 Manufacturing. **Career Pathway:** 13.3 Maintenance, Installation, and Repair. **Other Jobs in This Pathway:** Aircraft Mechanics and Service Technicians; Automotive Specialty Technicians; Biological Technicians; Civil Engineering Technicians; Computer, Automated Teller, and Office Machine Repairers; Electrical and Electronic Equipment Assemblers; Electrical and Electronics Repairers, Commercial and Industrial Equipment; Electrical Engineering Technicians; Electromechanical Engineering Technologists; Electronics Engineering Technicians; Electronics Engineering Technologists; Engineering Technicians, Except

Drafters, All Other; Fuel Cell Technicians; Helpers—Installation, Maintenance, and Repair Workers; Industrial Engineering Technologists; Industrial Machinery Mechanics; Installation, Maintenance, and Repair Workers, All Other; Manufacturing Engineering Technologists; Manufacturing Production Technicians; Mapping Technicians; Mechanical Engineering Technologists; Mobile Heavy Equipment Mechanics, Except Engines; Nanotechnology Engineering Technicians; Telecommunications Line Installers and Repairers; Tire Repairers and Changers; others.

**Skills**—No data available.

**Work Environment:** No data available.

## Job Specialization: Electromechanical Engineering Technologists

**Apply engineering theory and technical skills to support electromechanical engineering activities such as computer-based process control, instrumentation, and machine design. Prepare layouts of machinery and equipment, plan the flow of work, conduct statistical studies and analyze production costs.** Modify, maintain, or repair electrical, electronic, and mechanical components, equipment, and systems to ensure proper functioning. Specify, coordinate, and conduct quality-control and quality-assurance programs and procedures. Establish and maintain inventory, records, and documentation systems. Fabricate or assemble mechanical, electrical, and electronic components and assemblies. Select electromechanical equipment, materials, components, and systems to meet functional specifications. Select and use laboratory, operational, and diagnostic techniques and test equipment to assess electromechanical circuits, equipment, processes, systems, and subsystems. Produce electrical, electronic, and mechanical drawings and other related documents or graphics necessary for electromechanical design using computer-aided design (CAD) software. Install and program computer hardware and machine and instrumentation software in microprocessor-based systems. Consult with machinists and technicians to ensure that electromechanical equipment and systems meet design specifications. Translate electromechanical drawings into design specifications, applying principles of engineering, thermal and fluid sciences, mathematics, and statistics. Collaborate with engineers to implement electromechanical designs in industrial or other settings. Analyze engineering designs of logic and digital circuitry, motor controls, instrumentation, and data acquisition for implementation into new or existing automated, servomechanical, or other electromechanical systems.

**Education/Training Required:** Bachelor's degree. **Education and Training Program:** Electrical, Electronic, and Communications Engineering Technology/Technician. **Knowledge/Courses**—No data available.

**Personality Type:** Realistic-Investigative-Conventional. **Career Cluster:** 13 Manufacturing. **Career Pathway:** 13.3 Maintenance, Installation, and Repair. **Other Jobs in This Pathway:** Aircraft Mechanics and Service Technicians; Automotive Specialty Technicians; Biological Technicians; Civil Engineering Technicians; Computer, Automated Teller, and Office Machine Repairers; Electrical and Electronic Equipment Assemblers; Electrical and Electronics Repairers, Commercial and Industrial Equipment; Electrical Engineering Technicians; Electrical Engineering Technologists; Electronics Engineering Technicians; Electronics Engineering Technologists; Engineering Technicians, Except Drafters, All Other; Fuel Cell Technicians; Helpers—Installation, Maintenance, and Repair Workers; Industrial Engineering Technologists; Industrial Machinery Mechanics; Installation, Maintenance, and Repair Workers, All Other; Manufacturing Engineering Technologists; Manufacturing Production Technicians; Mapping Technicians; Mechanical Engineering Technologists; Mobile Heavy Equipment Mechanics, Except Engines; Nanotechnology Engineering Technicians; Telecommunications Line Installers and Repairers; Tire Repairers and Changers; others.

**Skills**—No data available.

**Work Environment:** No data available.

## Job Specialization: Electronics Engineering Technologists

**Apply engineering theory and technical skills to support electronics engineering activities such as electronics systems and instrumentation design and digital signal processing.** Provide support to technical sales staff regarding product characteristics. Educate equipment operators on the proper use of equipment. Modify, maintain, and repair electronics equipment and systems to ensure that they function properly. Assist scientists and engineers in conducting applied research in electronics engineering. Assemble circuitry for electronic systems according to engineering instructions, production specifications, and technical manuals. Specify, coordinate, or conduct quality control and quality assurance programs and procedures. Prepare and maintain design, testing, or operational records and documentation. Write software programs for microcontrollers and computers in machine, assembly, and other languages. Troubleshoot microprocessors and electronic instruments, equipment, and systems using electronic test equipment such as logic analyzers. Set up and operate specialized and standard test equipment to diagnose, test, and analyze the performance of electronic components, assemblies, and systems. Select electronics equipment, components, and systems to meet functional specifications. Replace defective components and parts using hand tools and precision instruments. Produce electronics drawings and other graphics representing industrial control, instrumentation, sensors, or analog and digital telecommunications networks using computer-aided design (CAD) software. Inspect newly installed equipment to adjust or correct operating problems. Integrate software and hardware components using computer, microprocessor, and control architecture. Supervise the building and testing of prototypes of electronics circuits, equipment, and systems. Evaluate machine and process control requirements and develop device and controller specifications suited to operating environments. Conduct or supervise the installation and operation of electronic equipment and systems.

**Education/Training Required:** Associate degree. **Education and Training Program:** Electrical, Electronic, and Communications Engineering Technology/Technician. **Knowledge/Courses**—Engineering and Technology, Telecommunications, Physics, Computers and Electronics, Design, Mathematics.

**Personality Type:** Realistic-Investigative-Conventional. **Career Cluster:** 13 Manufacturing. **Career Pathway:** 13.3 Maintenance, Installation, and Repair. **Other Jobs in This Pathway:** Aircraft Mechanics and Service Technicians; Automotive Specialty Technicians; Biological Technicians; Civil Engineering Technicians; Computer, Automated Teller, and Office Machine Repairers; Electrical and Electronic Equipment Assemblers; Electrical and Electronics Repairers, Commercial and Industrial Equipment; Electrical Engineering Technicians; Electrical Engineering Technologists; Electromechanical Engineering Technologists; Electronics Engineering Technicians; Engineering Technicians, Except Drafters, All Other; Fuel Cell Technicians; Helpers—Installation, Maintenance, and Repair Workers; Industrial Engineering Technologists; Industrial Machinery Mechanics; Installation, Maintenance, and Repair Workers, All Other; Manufacturing Engineering Technologists; Manufacturing Production Technicians; Mapping Technicians; Mechanical Engineering Technologists; Mobile Heavy Equipment Mechanics, Except Engines; Nanotechnology Engineering Technicians; Telecommunications Line Installers and Repairers; Tire Repairers and Changers; others.

**Skills**—Repairing, Equipment Maintenance, Equipment Selection, Troubleshooting, Technology Design, Installation, Programming, Science.

**Work Environment:** Indoors; sitting; using hands; noise; hazardous conditions.

## Job Specialization: Fuel Cell Technicians

**Install, operate, and maintain integrated fuel cell systems in transportation, stationary, or portable applications.** Troubleshoot test equipment. Recommend improvements to fuel cell design and performance. Perform routine vehicle maintenance procedures, such as part replacements and tune-ups. Build or test power plant systems, including pumps, blowers, heat exchangers, or sensors. Order testing materials. Build or test electrical systems, making electrical calculations as needed. Report results of fuel cell test results. Perform routine and preventive maintenance on test equipment. Document or analyze fuel cell test data using spreadsheets or other computer software. Collect and maintain fuel cell test data. Calibrate equipment used for fuel cell testing. Build prototypes, following engineering specifications. Test fuel cells or fuel cell stacks, using complex electronic equipment. Assemble fuel cells or fuel cell stacks according to mechanical or electrical assembly documents or schematics.

**Education/Training Required:** Associate degree. **Education and Training Program:** Manufacturing Engineering Technology/Technician. **Knowledge/Courses**—No data available.

**Personality Type:** No data available. **Career Cluster:** 13 Manufacturing. **Career Pathway:** 13.3 Maintenance, Installation, and Repair. **Other Jobs in This Pathway:** Aircraft Mechanics and Service Technicians; Automotive Specialty Technicians; Biological Technicians; Civil Engineering Technicians; Computer, Automated Teller, and Office Machine Repairers; Electrical and Electronic Equipment Assemblers; Electrical and Electronics Repairers, Commercial and Industrial Equipment; Electrical Engineering Technicians; Electrical Engineering Technologists; Electromechanical Engineering Technologists; Electronics Engineering Technicians; Electronics Engineering Technologists; Engineering Technicians, Except Drafters, All Other; Helpers—Installation, Maintenance, and Repair Workers; Industrial Engineering Technologists; Industrial Machinery Mechanics; Installation, Maintenance, and Repair Workers, All Other; Manufacturing Engineering Technologists; Manufacturing Production Technicians; Mapping Technicians;

Mechanical Engineering Technologists; Mobile Heavy Equipment Mechanics, Except Engines; Nanotechnology Engineering Technicians; Telecommunications Line Installers and Repairers; Tire Repairers and Changers; others.

**Skills**—No data available.

**Work Environment:** No data available.

# Job Specialization: Industrial Engineering Technologists

**Apply engineering theory and technical skills to support industrial engineering activities such as quality control, inventory control and material flow methods. May conduct statistical studies and analyze production costs.** Interpret engineering drawings, sketches, or diagrams. Prepare schedules for equipment use or routine maintenance. Request equipment upgrades or purchases. Supervise production workers. Create computer applications for manufacturing processes or operations using computer-aided design (CAD) or computer-assisted manufacturing (CAM) tools. Oversee and inspect production processes. Prepare reports regarding inventories of raw materials and finished products. Modify equipment or processes to improve resource or cost efficiency. Develop and conduct quality control tests to ensure consistent production quality. Compile operational data to develop cost or time estimates, schedules, or specifications. Collect and analyze data related to quality or industrial health and safety programs. Analyze operational, production, economic, or other data using statistical procedures. Prepare layouts of machinery and equipment using drafting equipment or computer-aided design (CAD) software. Plan the flow of work or materials to maximize efficiency. Monitor and control inventory. Conduct time and motion studies to identify opportunities to improve worker efficiency. Design plant or production facility layouts. Develop and implement programs to address problems related to production, materials, safety, or quality. Analyze, estimate, or report production costs.

**Education/Training Required:** Bachelor's degree. **Education and Training Program:** Quality Control Technology/ Technician. **Knowledge/Courses**—No data available.

**Personality Type:** Investigative-Realistic-Conventional. **Career Cluster:** 13 Manufacturing. **Career Pathway:** 13.3 Maintenance, Installation, and Repair. **Other Jobs in This Pathway:** Aircraft Mechanics and Service Technicians; Automotive Specialty Technicians; Biological Technicians; Civil Engineering Technicians; Computer, Automated Teller, and Office Machine Repairers; Electrical and Electronic

Equipment Assemblers; Electrical and Electronics Repairers, Commercial and Industrial Equipment; Electrical Engineering Technicians; Electrical Engineering Technologists; Electromechanical Engineering Technologists; Electronics Engineering Technicians; Electronics Engineering Technologists; Engineering Technicians, Except Drafters, All Other; Fuel Cell Technicians; Helpers—Installation, Maintenance, and Repair Workers; Industrial Machinery Mechanics; Installation, Maintenance, and Repair Workers, All Other; Manufacturing Engineering Technologists; Manufacturing Production Technicians; Mapping Technicians; Mechanical Engineering Technologists; Mobile Heavy Equipment Mechanics, Except Engines; Nanotechnology Engineering Technicians; Telecommunications Line Installers and Repairers; Tire Repairers and Changers; others.

**Skills**—No data available.

**Work Environment:** No data available.

# Job Specialization: Manufacturing Engineering Technologists

**Apply engineering theory and technical skills to support manufacturing engineering activities. Develop tools, implement designs, and integrate machinery, equipment, and computer technologies to ensure effective manufacturing processes.** Recommend corrective or preventive actions to assure or improve product quality or reliability. Prepare layouts, drawings, or sketches of machinery and equipment such as shop tooling, scale layouts, and new equipment design using drafting equipment or computer-aided design software. Identify and implement new manufacturing technologies, processes, or equipment. Identify opportunities for improvements in quality, cost, or efficiency of automation equipment. Monitor or measure manufacturing processes to identify ways to reduce losses, decrease time requirements, or improve quality. Ensure adherence to safety rules and practices. Coordinate equipment purchases, installations, or transfers. Plan, estimate, or schedule production work. Select material quantities and processing methods needed to achieve efficient production. Develop or maintain programs associated with automated production equipment. Estimate manufacturing costs. Install and evaluate manufacturing equipment, materials, or components. Oversee equipment start-up, characterization, qualification, or release. Develop production, inventory, or quality assurance programs. Create computer applications for manufacturing processes or operations using computer-aided design (CAD) or computer-assisted manufacturing (CAM) tools. Develop manufacturing infrastructure to integrate or

E

deploy new manufacturing processes. Verify weights, measurements, counts, or calculations and record results on batch records. Design plant layouts and production facilities. Operate complex processing equipment. Train manufacturing technicians on topics such as safety, health, fire prevention, and quality. Erect manufacturing engineering equipment. Perform routine equipment maintenance.

**Education/Training Required:** Bachelor's degree. **Education and Training Program:** Manufacturing Engineering Technology/Technician. **Knowledge/Courses**—Engineering and Technology, Design, Mechanical, Physics, Production and Processing, Computers and Electronics.

**Personality Type:** Realistic-Investigative-Conventional. **Career Cluster:** 13 Manufacturing. **Career Pathway:** 13.3 Maintenance, Installation, and Repair. **Other Jobs in This Pathway:** Aircraft Mechanics and Service Technicians; Automotive Specialty Technicians; Biological Technicians; Civil Engineering Technicians; Computer, Automated Teller, and Office Machine Repairers; Electrical and Electronic Equipment Assemblers; Electrical and Electronics Repairers, Commercial and Industrial Equipment; Electrical Engineering Technicians; Electrical Engineering Technologists; Electromechanical Engineering Technologists; Electronics Engineering Technicians; Electronics Engineering Technologists; Engineering Technicians, Except Drafters, All Other; Fuel Cell Technicians; Helpers—Installation, Maintenance, and Repair Workers; Industrial Engineering Technologists; Industrial Machinery Mechanics; Installation, Maintenance, and Repair Workers, All Other; Manufacturing Production Technicians; Mapping Technicians; Mechanical Engineering Technologists; Mobile Heavy Equipment Mechanics, Except Engines; Nanotechnology Engineering Technicians; Telecommunications Line Installers and Repairers; Tire Repairers and Changers; others.

**Skills**—Equipment Selection, Installation, Technology Design, Equipment Maintenance, Programming, Management of Financial Resources, Mathematics, Troubleshooting.

**Work Environment:** Indoors; sitting; noise; contaminants.

# Job Specialization: Manufacturing Production Technicians

**Apply knowledge of manufacturing engineering systems and tools to set up, test, and adjust manufacturing machinery and equipment, using any combination of electrical, electronic, mechanical, hydraulic, pneumatic, and computer technologies.** Adhere to all applicable regulations, policies, and procedures for health, safety, and environmental compliance. Inspect finished products for quality and adherence to customer specifications. Set up and operate production equipment in accordance with current good manufacturing practices and standard operating procedures. Calibrate or adjust equipment to ensure quality production using tools such as calipers, micrometers, height gauges, protractors, and ring gauges. Set up and verify the functionality of safety equipment. Troubleshoot problems with equipment, devices, or products. Monitor and adjust production processes or equipment for quality and productivity. Test products or subassemblies for functionality or quality. Plan and lay out work to meet production and schedule requirements. Start up and shut down processing equipment. Prepare and assemble materials. Provide advice or training to other technicians. Measure and record data associated with operating equipment. Assist engineers in developing, building, or testing prototypes and new products, processes, or procedures. Prepare production documents such as standard operating procedures, manufacturing batch records, inventory reports, and productivity reports. Install new equipment. Keep production logs. Clean production equipment and work areas. Provide production, progress, or changeover reports to shift supervisors. Collect hazardous or non-hazardous waste in correctly labeled barrels or other containers and transfer them to collection areas. Select cleaning materials, tools, and equipment. Build product subassemblies or final assemblies. Ship packages following carrier specifications. Maintain inventory of job materials. Build packaging for finished products. Package finished products.

**Education/Training Required:** Postsecondary vocational training. **Education and Training Program:** Manufacturing Engineering Technology/Technician. **Knowledge/Courses**—Mechanical, Design, Engineering and Technology, Production and Processing, Physics, Chemistry.

**Personality Type:** Realistic-Investigative. **Career Cluster:** 13 Manufacturing. **Career Pathway:** 13.3 Maintenance, Installation, and Repair. **Other Jobs in This Pathway:** Aircraft Mechanics and Service Technicians; Automotive Specialty Technicians; Biological Technicians; Civil Engineering Technicians; Computer, Automated Teller, and Office Machine Repairers; Electrical and Electronic Equipment Assemblers; Electrical and Electronics Repairers, Commercial and Industrial Equipment; Electrical Engineering Technicians; Electrical Engineering Technologists; Electromechanical Engineering Technologists; Electronics Engineering Technicians; Electronics Engineering Technologists; Engineering Technicians, Except Drafters, All Other; Fuel Cell Technicians; Helpers—Installation, Maintenance, and Repair Workers; Industrial Engineering Technologists;

Industrial Machinery Mechanics; Installation, Maintenance, and Repair Workers, All Other; Manufacturing Engineering Technologists; Mapping Technicians; Mechanical Engineering Technologists; Mobile Heavy Equipment Mechanics, Except Engines; Nanotechnology Engineering Technicians; Telecommunications Line Installers and Repairers; Tire Repairers and Changers; others.

**Skills**—Equipment Maintenance, Repairing, Troubleshooting, Installation, Operation and Control, Quality Control Analysis, Operation Monitoring, Equipment Selection.

**Work Environment:** Indoors; standing; using hands; noise; contaminants; hazardous equipment.

## Job Specialization: Mechanical Engineering Technologists

**Apply engineering theory and technical skills to support mechanical engineering activities such as generation, transmission and use of mechanical and fluid energy. Prepare layouts of machinery and equipment and plan the flow of work. May conduct statistical studies and analyze production costs.** Prepare equipment inspection schedules, reliability schedules, work plans, and other records. Prepare cost and materials estimates and project schedules. Provide technical support to other employees regarding mechanical design, fabrication, testing, or documentation. Interpret engineering sketches, specifications, and drawings. Perform routine maintenance on equipment such as leak detectors, glove boxes, and mechanical pumps. Design specialized or customized equipment, machines, or structures. Design molds, tools, dies, jigs, or fixtures for use in manufacturing processes. Conduct failure analyses, document results, and recommend corrective actions. Assist engineers to design, develop, test, or manufacture industrial machinery, consumer products, or other equipment. Analyze or estimate production costs such as labor, equipment, and plant space. Apply testing or monitoring apparatus to operating equipment. Test machines, components, materials, or products to determine characteristics such as performance, strength, and response to stress. Prepare specifications, designs, or sketches for machines, components, and systems related to the generation, transmission, or use of mechanical and fluid energy. Prepare layouts of machinery, tools, plants, and equipment. Inspect and test mechanical equipment. Oversee, monitor, or inspect mechanical installations or construction projects. Assist mechanical engineers in product testing through activities such as setting up instrumentation for automobile crash tests. Assemble or disassemble complex mechanical systems.

**Education/Training Required:** Bachelor's degree. **Education and Training Program:** Mechanical Engineering/Mechanical Technology/Technician. **Knowledge/Courses**—No data available.

**Personality Type:** Realistic-Investigative-Conventional. **Career Cluster:** 13 Manufacturing. **Career Pathway:** 13.3 Maintenance, Installation, and Repair. **Other Jobs in This Pathway:** Aircraft Mechanics and Service Technicians; Automotive Specialty Technicians; Biological Technicians; Civil Engineering Technicians; Computer, Automated Teller, and Office Machine Repairers; Electrical and Electronic Equipment Assemblers; Electrical and Electronics Repairers, Commercial and Industrial Equipment; Electrical Engineering Technicians; Electrical Engineering Technologists; Electromechanical Engineering Technologists; Electronics Engineering Technicians; Electronics Engineering Technologists; Engineering Technicians, Except Drafters, All Other; Fuel Cell Technicians; Helpers—Installation, Maintenance, and Repair Workers; Industrial Engineering Technologists; Industrial Machinery Mechanics; Installation, Maintenance, and Repair Workers, All Other; Manufacturing Engineering Technologists; Manufacturing Production Technicians; Mapping Technicians; Mobile Heavy Equipment Mechanics, Except Engines; Nanotechnology Engineering Technicians; Telecommunications Line Installers and Repairers; Tire Repairers and Changers; others.

**Skills**—No data available.

**Work Environment:** No data available.

## Job Specialization: Nanotechnology Engineering Technologists

**Implement production processes for nanoscale designs to produce and modify materials, devices, and systems of unique molecular or macromolecular composition. Operate advanced microscopy equipment to manipulate nanoscale objects. Work under the supervision of engineering staff.** Supervise or provide technical direction to technicians engaged in nanotechnology research or production. Install nanotechnology production equipment at customer or manufacturing sites. Contribute written material or data for grant or patent applications. Produce images and measurements, using tools and techniques such as atomic force microscopy, scanning electron microscopy, optical microscopy, particle size analysis, and zeta potential analysis. Prepare detailed verbal or written presentations for scientists, engineers, project managers, or upper management. Prepare capability data, training materials, or other documentation for transfer of processes to production. Develop or modify wet chemical or industrial laboratory experimental techniques for nanoscale use. Collect and compile nanotechnology research and engineering data. Inspect or measure thin films of carbon nanotubes, polymers, or inorganic coatings, using a variety of techniques and analytical tools. Implement new or enhanced methods and processes for the processing, testing, or manufacture of nanotechnology materials or products. Design or conduct experiments in collaboration with scientists or engineers supportive of the development of nanotechnology materials, components, devices, or systems.

**Education/Training Required:** Bachelor's degree. **Education and Training Program:** Nanotechnology. **Knowledge/Courses**—No data available.

**Personality Type:** No data available. **Career Cluster:** 13 Manufacturing. **Career Pathway:** 13.3 Maintenance, Installation, and Repair. **Other Jobs in This Pathway:** Aircraft Mechanics and Service Technicians; Automotive Specialty Technicians; Biological Technicians; Civil Engineering Technicians; Computer, Automated Teller, and Office Machine Repairers; Electrical and Electronic Equipment Assemblers; Electrical and Electronics Repairers, Commercial and Industrial Equipment; Electrical Engineering Technicians; Electrical Engineering Technologists; Electromechanical Engineering Technologists; Electronics Engineering Technicians; Electronics Engineering Technologists; Engineering Technicians, Except Drafters, All Other; Fuel Cell Technicians; Helpers—Installation, Maintenance, and Repair Workers; Industrial Engineering Technologists; Industrial Machinery Mechanics; Installation, Maintenance, and Repair Workers, All Other; Manufacturing Engineering Technologists; Manufacturing Production Technicians; Mapping Technicians; Mechanical Engineering Technologists; Mobile Heavy Equipment Mechanics, Except Engines; Telecommunications Line Installers and Repairers; Tire Repairers and Changers; others.

**Skills**—No data available.

**Work Environment:** No data available.

## Job Specialization: Nanotechnology Engineering Technicians

**Operate commercial-scale production equipment to produce, test, and modify materials, devices, and systems of molecular or macromolecular composition. Work under the supervision of engineering staff.** Track inventory and order new supplies, as needed. Repair nanotechnology processing or testing equipment, or submit work orders for equipment repair. Maintain work area according to cleanroom and other processing standards. Set up and execute experiments according to detailed instructions. Compile information and prepare reports. Record test results in logs, laboratory notebooks, or spreadsheet software. Produce detailed images and measurement of objects, using tools such as scanning tunneling microscopes and oscilloscopes. Perform functional tests of nano-enhanced assemblies, components or systems, using equipment such as torque gauges and conductivity meters. Operate computer-controlled machine tools. Monitor equipment during operation to ensure adherence to specifications for characteristics such as pressure, temperature, and flow. Measure or mix chemicals or compounds in accordance with detailed instructions or formulas. Calibrate nanotechnology equipment, such as weighing, testing and production equipment. Inspect work products to ensure quality and adherence to specifications. Maintain accurate production record or batch record documentation. Assist scientists, engineers, or technologists in writing process specifications or documentation. Assist scientists, engineers or technologists in processing or characterizing materials according to physical and chemical properties. Assemble components, using techniques such as interference fitting, solvent bonding, adhesive bonding, heat sealing, and ultrasonic welding. Operate nanotechnology compounding, testing, processing, or production equipment, following appropriate standard operating procedures, good manufacturing practices, hazardous material restrictions, or health and safety requirements.

**Education/Training Required:** Associate degree. **Education and Training Program:** Nanotechnology. **Knowledge/Courses**—No data available.

**Personality Type:** No data available. **Career Cluster:** 13 Manufacturing. **Career Pathway:** 13.3 Maintenance, Installation, and Repair. **Other Jobs in This Pathway:** Aircraft Mechanics and Service Technicians; Automotive Specialty Technicians; Biological Technicians; Civil Engineering Technicians; Computer, Automated Teller, and Office Machine Repairers; Electrical and Electronic Equipment Assemblers; Electrical and Electronics Repairers, Commercial and Industrial Equipment; Electrical Engineering Technicians; Electrical Engineering Technologists; Electromechanical Engineering Technologists; Electronics Engineering Technicians; Electronics Engineering Technologists; Engineering Technicians, Except Drafters, All Other; Fuel Cell Technicians; Helpers—Installation, Maintenance, and Repair Workers; Industrial Engineering Technologists; Industrial Machinery Mechanics; Installation, Maintenance, and Repair Workers, All Other; Manufacturing Engineering Technologists; Manufacturing Production

Technicians; Mapping Technicians; Mechanical Engineering Technologists; Mobile Heavy Equipment Mechanics, Except Engines; Telecommunications Line Installers and Repairers; Tire Repairers and Changers; others.

**Skills**—No data available.

**Work Environment:** No data available.

## Job Specialization: Non-Destructive Testing Specialists

**Test the safety of structures, vehicles, or vessels using X-ray, ultrasound, fiber optic or related equipment.** Supervise or direct the work of non-destructive testing (NDT) trainees or staff. Produce images of objects on film using radiographic techniques. Evaluate material properties using radio astronomy, voltage and amperage measurement, or rheometric flow measurement. Develop or use new non-destructive testing (NDT) methods such as acoustic emission testing, leak testing, and thermal or infrared testing. Document non-destructive testing (NDT) methods, processes, or results. Map the presence of imperfections within objects using sonic measurements. Make radiographic images to detect flaws in objects while leaving objects intact. Visually examine materials, structures, or components using tools and equipment such as endoscopes, closed circuit television systems, and fiber optics for signs of corrosion, metal fatigue, cracks, or other flaws. Interpret or evaluate test results in accordance with applicable codes, standards, specifications, or procedures. Identify defects in concrete or other building materials using thermal or infrared testing. Identify defects in solid materials using ultrasonic testing techniques. Select, calibrate, or operate equipment used in the non-destructive testing (NDT) of products or materials. Conduct liquid penetrant tests to locate surface cracks by coating objects with fluorescent dyes, cleaning excess penetrant, and applying developer. Prepare reports on non-destructive testing (NDT) results. Interpret the results of all methods of non-destructive testing (NDT) such as acoustic emission, electromagnetic, leak, liquid penetrant, magnetic particle, neutron radiographic, radiographic, thermal or infrared, ultrasonic, vibration analysis, and visual testing. Examine structures or vehicles such as aircraft, trains, nuclear reactors, bridges, dams, and pipelines using non-destructive testing (NDT) techniques.

**Education/Training Required:** Associate degree. **Education and Training Program:** Industrial Radiologic Technology/Technician. **Knowledge/Courses**—No data available.

**Personality Type:** Realistic-Investigative-Conventional. **Career Cluster:** 13 Manufacturing. **Career Pathway:** 13.3 Maintenance, Installation, and Repair. **Other Jobs in This Pathway:** Aircraft Mechanics and Service Technicians; Automotive Specialty Technicians; Biological Technicians; Civil Engineering Technicians; Computer, Automated Teller, and Office Machine Repairers; Electrical and Electronic Equipment Assemblers; Electrical and Electronics Repairers, Commercial and Industrial Equipment; Electrical Engineering Technicians; Electrical Engineering Technologists; Electromechanical Engineering Technologists; Electronics Engineering Technicians; Electronics Engineering Technologists; Engineering Technicians, Except Drafters, All Other; Fuel Cell Technicians; Helpers—Installation, Maintenance, and Repair Workers; Industrial Engineering Technologists; Industrial Machinery Mechanics; Installation, Maintenance, and Repair Workers, All Other; Manufacturing Engineering Technologists; Manufacturing Production Technicians; Mapping Technicians; Mechanical Engineering Technologists; Mobile Heavy Equipment Mechanics, Except Engines; Telecommunications Line Installers and Repairers; Tire Repairers and Changers; others.

**Skills**—No data available.

**Work Environment:** No data available.

## Job Specialization: Photonics Technicians

**Build, install, test, and maintain optical and fiber-optic equipment such as lasers, lenses, and mirrors, using spectrometers, interferometers, or related equipment.** Recommend design or material changes to reduce costs or processing times. Monitor inventory levels and order supplies as necessary. Maintain clean working environments according to clean room standards. Document procedures such as calibration. Maintain activity logs. Record test results and compute test data. Test and perform failure analysis for optomechanical or optoelectrical products according to test plans. Assist scientists or engineers in the conduct of photonic experiments. Perform diagnostic analyses of processing steps, using analytical or metrological tools such as microscopy, profilometry, and ellipsometry devices. Optimize process parameters by making prototype and production devices. Mix, pour, and use processing chemicals or gases according to safety standards and established operating procedures. Design, build, or modify fixtures used to assemble parts. Lay out cutting lines for machining using drafting tools. Assist engineers in the development of new products, fixtures, tools, or processes. Assemble and adjust parts

E

or related electrical units of prototypes to prepare for testing. Splice fibers, using fusion splicing or other techniques. Terminate, cure, polish, or test fiber cables with mechanical connectors. Set up or operate prototype or test apparatus such as control consoles, collimators, recording equipment, and cables. Set up or operate assembly or processing equipment such as lasers, cameras, die bonders, wire bonders, dispensers, reflow ovens, soldering irons, die shears, wire pull testers, temperature or humidity chambers, and optical spectrum analyzers. Repair or calibrate products such as surgical lasers. Perform laser seam welding, heat treatment, or hard facing operations. Fabricate devices such as optoelectronic and semiconductor devices. Build prototype optomechanical devices for use in equipment such as aerial cameras, gun sights, and telescopes.

**Education/Training Required:** Associate degree. **Education and Training Program:** Engineering-Related Technologies, Other. **Knowledge/Courses**—No data available.

**Personality Type:** Realistic-Investigative-Conventional. **Career Cluster:** 13 Manufacturing. **Career Pathway:** 13.3 Maintenance, Installation, and Repair. **Other Jobs in This Pathway:** Aircraft Mechanics and Service Technicians; Automotive Specialty Technicians; Biological Technicians; Civil Engineering Technicians; Computer, Automated Teller, and Office Machine Repairers; Electrical and Electronic Equipment Assemblers; Electrical and Electronics Repairers, Commercial and Industrial Equipment; Electrical Engineering Technicians; Electrical Engineering Technologists; Electromechanical Engineering Technologists; Electronics Engineering Technicians; Electronics Engineering Technologists; Engineering Technicians, Except Drafters, All Other; Fuel Cell Technicians; Helpers—Installation, Maintenance, and Repair Workers; Industrial Engineering Technologists; Industrial Machinery Mechanics; Installation, Maintenance, and Repair Workers, All Other; Manufacturing Engineering Technologists; Manufacturing Production Technicians; Mapping Technicians; Mechanical Engineering Technologists; Mobile Heavy Equipment Mechanics, Except Engines; Telecommunications Line Installers and Repairers; Tire Repairers and Changers; others.

**Skills**—No data available.

**Work Environment:** No data available.

# Engineers, All Other

- Annual Earnings: $90,270
- Earnings Growth Potential: High (45.1%)
- Growth: 6.7%
- Annual Job Openings: 5,020
- Self-Employed: 6.4%

**Considerations for Job Outlook:** Competitive pressures and advancing technology are expected to result in businesses hiring more engineers. Overall, job opportunities are expected to be good. Professional, scientific, and technical services industries should generate most of the employment growth.

**This occupation includes all engineers not listed separately.** Because this is a highly diverse occupation, no data is available for some information topics.

**Education/Training Required:** Bachelor's degree. **Education and Training Program:** Engineering, Other.

**Career Clusters:** 02 Architecture and Construction; 08 Health Science; 15 Science, Technology, Engineering, and Mathematics. **Career Pathways:** 2.1 Design/Pre-Construction; 8.3 Health Informatics; 15.1 Engineering and Technology. **Other Jobs in These Pathways:** Architectural and Engineering Managers; Automotive Engineers; Biochemical Engineers; Biofuels/Biodiesel Technology and Product Development Managers; Civil Engineers; Cost Estimators; Energy Engineers; Executive Secretaries and Executive Administrative Assistants; First-Line Supervisors of Office and Administrative Support Workers; Fuel Cell Engineers; Human Factors Engineers and Ergonomists; Industrial Engineers; Manufacturing Engineers; Mechanical Engineers; Mechatronics Engineers; Medical and Health Services Managers; Medical Assistants; Medical Secretaries; Microsystems Engineers; Nanosystems Engineers; Photonics Engineers; Physical Therapists; Public Relations Specialists; Receptionists and Information Clerks; Transportation Engineers; others.

# Job Specialization: Biochemical Engineers

**Apply knowledge of biology, chemistry, and engineering to develop usable, tangible products. Solve problems related to materials, systems and processes that interact with humans, plants, animals, microorganisms, and biological materials.** Read current scientific and trade literature to stay abreast of scientific, industrial, or technological advances. Prepare technical reports, data summary documents, or research articles for scientific publication, regulatory submissions, or patent applications. Prepare project plans for equipment or facility improvements, including time lines, budgetary estimates, or capital spending requests. Participate in equipment or process validation activities. Communicate with suppliers regarding the design and specifications of production equipment, instrumentation, or materials. Communicate with regulatory authorities regarding licensing or compliance responsibilities, such as good manufacturing practices. Collaborate in the development or delivery of biochemical manufacturing training materials. Prepare piping and instrumentation diagrams or other schematics for proposed process improvements, using computer-aided design software. Modify and control biological systems to replace, augment, or sustain chemical and mechanical processes. Maintain databases of experiment characteristics and results. Lead studies to examine or recommend changes in process sequences, operation protocols. Direct experimental or developmental activities at contracted laboratories. Develop statistical models or simulations of biochemical production, using statistical or modeling software. Consult with chemists and biologists to develop or evaluate novel technologies. Confer with research and manufacturing personnel to ensure the compatibility of design and production. Collaborate with manufacturing or quality assurance staff to prepare product specification and safety sheets, standard operating procedures, user manuals, or qualification and validation reports. Advise manufacturing staff regarding problems with fermentation, filtration, or other production processes. Review existing manufacturing processes to identify opportunities for yield improvement or reduced process variation.

**Education/Training Required:** Bachelor's degree. **Education and Training Program:** Biochemical Engineering. **Knowledge/Courses**—No data available.

**Personality Type:** Investigative-Realistic. **Career Cluster:** 15 Science, Technology, Engineering, and Mathematics. **Career Pathway:** 15.1 Engineering and Technology. **Other Jobs in This Pathway:** Architectural and Engineering Managers; Automotive Engineers; Biofuels/Biodiesel Technology and Product Development Managers; Civil Engineers; Cost Estimators; Education, Training, and Library Workers, All Other; Electrical Engineers; Electronics Engineers, Except Computer; Energy Engineers; Engineers, All Other; Fuel Cell Engineers; Human Factors Engineers and Ergonomists; Industrial Engineers; Manufacturing Engineers; Mechanical Engineers; Mechatronics Engineers; Microsystems Engineers; Nanosystems Engineers; Photonics Engineers; Radio Frequency Identification Device Specialists;

Robotics Engineers; Solar Energy Systems Engineers; Transportation Engineers; Validation Engineers; Wind Energy Engineers; others.

**Skills**—No data available.

**Work Environment:** No data available.

# Job Specialization: Energy Engineers

**Design, develop, and evaluate energy-related projects and programs to reduce energy costs or improve energy efficiency during the designing, building, or remodeling stages of construction. May specialize in electrical systems; heating, ventilation, and air-conditioning (HVAC) systems; green buildings; lighting; air quality; or energy procurement.** Identify energy savings opportunities and make recommendations to achieve more energy efficient operation. Manage the development, design, or construction of energy conservation projects to ensure acceptability of budgets and time lines, conformance to federal and state laws, or adherence to approved specifications. Conduct energy audits to evaluate energy use, costs, or conservation measures. Monitor and analyze energy consumption. Perform energy modeling, measurement, verification, commissioning, or retro-commissioning. Oversee design or construction aspects related to energy such as energy engineering, energy management, and sustainable design. Conduct jobsite observations, field inspections, or sub-metering to collect data for energy conservation analyses. Review architectural, mechanical, or electrical plans and specifications to evaluate energy efficiency or determine economic, service, or engineering feasibility. Inspect or monitor energy systems including heating, ventilation and air conditioning (HVAC), or daylighting systems to determine energy use or potential energy savings. Evaluate construction design information such as detail and assembly drawings, design calculations, system layouts and sketches, or specifications. Direct the work of contractors or staff in the implementation of energy management projects. Prepare project reports and other program or technical documentation. Make recommendations regarding energy fuel selection. Analyze, interpret, and create graphical representations of data using engineering software. Train personnel or clients on topics such as energy management. Provide consultation to clients or other engineers on topics such as climate control systems, energy modeling, data logging, energy management control systems, lighting or daylighting design, sustainable design, and energy auditing. Review and negotiate energy purchase agreements. Promote awareness or use of alternative and renewable energy sources.

**Education/Training Required:** Bachelor's degree. **Education and Training Program:** Engineering, Other. **Knowledge/Courses**—Engineering and Technology, Building and Construction, Physics, Design, Economics and Accounting, Mechanical.

**Personality Type:** Investigative-Realistic. **Career Cluster:** 15 Science, Technology, Engineering, and Mathematics. **Career Pathway:** 15.1 Engineering and Technology. **Other Jobs in This Pathway:** Architectural and Engineering Managers; Automotive Engineers; Biochemical Engineers; Biofuels/Biodiesel Technology and Product Development Managers; Civil Engineers; Cost Estimators; Education, Training, and Library Workers, All Other; Electrical Engineers; Electronics Engineers, Except Computer; Engineers, All Other; Fuel Cell Engineers; Human Factors Engineers and Ergonomists; Industrial Engineers; Manufacturing Engineers; Mechanical Engineers; Mechatronics Engineers; Microsystems Engineers; Nanosystems Engineers; Photonics Engineers; Radio Frequency Identification Device Specialists; Robotics Engineers; Solar Energy Systems Engineers; Transportation Engineers; Validation Engineers; Wind Energy Engineers; others.

**Skills**—Science, Operations Analysis, Systems Analysis, Mathematics, Reading Comprehension, Complex Problem Solving, Writing, Systems Evaluation.

**Work Environment:** Indoors; sitting.

## Job Specialization: Manufacturing Engineers

**Apply knowledge of materials and engineering theory and methods to design, integrate, and improve manufacturing systems or related processes. May work with commercial or industrial designers to refine product designs to increase producibility and decrease costs.** Identify opportunities or implement changes to improve products or reduce costs using knowledge of fabrication processes, tooling and production equipment, assembly methods, quality control standards, or product design, materials and parts. Provide technical expertise or support related to manufacturing. Determine root causes of failures using statistical methods and recommend changes in designs, tolerances, or processing methods. Incorporate new methods and processes to improve existing operations. Supervise technicians, technologists, analysts, administrative staff, or other engineers. Troubleshoot new and existing product problems involving designs, materials, or processes. Review product designs for manufacturability and completeness. Train production personnel in new or existing methods. Communicate

manufacturing capabilities, production schedules, or other information to facilitate production processes. Design, install, or troubleshoot manufacturing equipment. Prepare documentation for new manufacturing processes or engineering procedures. Apply continuous improvement methods such as lean manufacturing to enhance manufacturing quality, reliability, or cost-effectiveness. Investigate or resolve operational problems such as material use variances and bottlenecks. Estimate costs, production times, or staffing requirements for new designs. Evaluate manufactured products according to specifications and quality standards. Purchase equipment, materials, or parts. Design layout of equipment or workspaces to achieve maximum efficiency. Design testing methods and test finished products or process capabilities to establish standards or validate process requirements. Read current literature, talk with colleagues, participate in educational programs, attend meetings, attend workshops, or participate in professional organizations or conferences to keep abreast of developments in the field.

**Education/Training Required:** Bachelor's degree. **Education and Training Program:** Manufacturing Engineering. **Knowledge/Courses**—Engineering and Technology, Design, Physics, Production and Processing, Mechanical, Chemistry.

**Personality Type:** Realistic-Investigative. **Career Cluster:** 15 Science, Technology, Engineering, and Mathematics. **Career Pathway:** 15.1 Engineering and Technology. **Other Jobs in This Pathway:** Architectural and Engineering Managers; Automotive Engineers; Biochemical Engineers; Biofuels/Biodiesel Technology and Product Development Managers; Civil Engineers; Cost Estimators; Education, Training, and Library Workers, All Other; Electrical Engineers; Electronics Engineers, Except Computer; Energy Engineers; Engineers, All Other; Fuel Cell Engineers; Human Factors Engineers and Ergonomists; Industrial Engineers; Mechanical Engineers; Mechatronics Engineers; Microsystems Engineers; Nanosystems Engineers; Photonics Engineers; Radio Frequency Identification Device Specialists; Robotics Engineers; Solar Energy Systems Engineers; Transportation Engineers; Validation Engineers; Wind Energy Engineers; others.

**Skills**—Technology Design, Equipment Selection, Installation, Troubleshooting, Management of Financial Resources, Equipment Maintenance, Programming, Management of Material Resources.

**Work Environment:** Indoors; sitting; noise; contaminants; hazardous equipment.

## Job Specialization: Mechatronics Engineers

**Apply knowledge of mechanical, electrical, and computer engineering theory and methods to the design of automation, intelligent systems, smart devices, or industrial systems control.** Publish engineering reports documenting design details and qualification test results. Provide consultation or training on topics such as mechatronics and automated control. Oversee the work of contractors in accordance with project requirements. Create mechanical design documents for parts, assemblies, or finished products. Maintain technical project files. Analyze existing development or manufacturing procedures and suggest improvements. Implement and test design solutions. Research, select, and apply sensors, communication technologies, or control devices for motion control, position sensing, pressure sensing, or electronic communication. Identify and select materials appropriate for mechatronic system designs. Design, develop, or implement control circuits and algorithms for electromechanical and pneumatic devices or systems. Design engineering systems for the automation of industrial tasks. Design advanced electronic control systems for mechanical systems. Create embedded software design programs. Create mechanical models and tolerance analyses to simulate mechatronic design concepts. Conduct studies to determine the feasibility, costs, or performance benefits of new mechatronic equipment. Upgrade the design of existing devices by adding mechatronic elements. Develop electronic, mechanical, or computerized processes to perform tasks in dangerous situations such as underwater exploration and extraterrestrial mining. Design mechatronics components for computer-controlled products such as cameras, video recorders, automobiles, and airplanes. Design advanced precision equipment for accurate and controlled applications. Apply mechatronic or automated solutions to the transfer of materials, components, or finished goods.

**Education/Training Required:** Bachelor's degree. **Education and Training Program:** Mechatronics, Robotics, and Automation Engineering. **Knowledge/Courses**—No data available.

**Personality Type:** Investigative-Realistic-Conventional. **Career Cluster:** 15 Science, Technology, Engineering, and Mathematics. **Career Pathway:** 15.1 Engineering and Technology. **Other Jobs in This Pathway:** Architectural and Engineering Managers; Automotive Engineers; Biochemical Engineers; Biofuels/Biodiesel Technology and Product Development Managers; Civil Engineers; Cost Estimators; Education, Training, and Library Workers, All Other; Electrical Engineers; Electronics Engineers, Except Computer;

Energy Engineers; Engineers, All Other; Fuel Cell Engineers; Human Factors Engineers and Ergonomists; Industrial Engineers; Manufacturing Engineers; Mechanical Engineers; Microsystems Engineers; Nanosystems Engineers; Photonics Engineers; Radio Frequency Identification Device Specialists; Robotics Engineers; Solar Energy Systems Engineers; Transportation Engineers; Validation Engineers; Wind Energy Engineers; others.

**Skills**—No data available.

**Work Environment:** No data available.

## Job Specialization: Microsystems Engineers

**Apply knowledge of electronic and mechanical engineering theory and methods, as well as specialized manufacturing technologies, to design and develop microelectromechanical systems (MEMS) devices.** Manage new product introduction projects to ensure effective deployment of microelectromechanical systems (MEMS) devices and applications. Plan or schedule engineering research or development projects involving microelectromechanical systems (MEMS) technology. Develop or implement microelectromechanical systems (MEMS) processing tools, fixtures, gages, dies, molds, and trays. Identify, procure, or develop test equipment, instrumentation, and facilities for characterization of microelectromechanical systems (MEMS) applications. Develop and verify customer documentation, such as performance specifications, training manuals, and operating instructions. Develop and file intellectual property and patent disclosure or application documents related to microelectromechanical systems (MEMS) devices, products, and systems. Develop and communicate operating characteristics or performance experience to other engineers and designers for training or new product development purposes. Demonstrate miniaturized systems that contain components such as microsensors, microactuators, or integrated electronic circuits fabricated on silicon or silicon carbide wafers. Create or maintain formal engineering documents, such as schematics, bill of materials, components and materials specifications, and packaging requirements. Conduct acceptance tests, vendor-qualification protocols, surveys, audits, corrective-action reviews, or performance monitoring of incoming materials and components to ensure conformance to specifications. Refine final microelectromechanical systems (MEMS) design to optimize design for target dimensions, physical tolerances, and processing constraints. Propose product designs involving microelectromechanical systems (MEMS) technology considering market data or customer requirements. Operate or maintain microelectromechanical systems (MEMS) fabrication and assembly equipment, such as handling, singulation, assembly, wire-bonding, soldering, and package sealing.

**Education/Training Required:** Bachelor's degree. **Education and Training Program:** Nanotechnology. **Knowledge/Courses**—No data available.

**Personality Type:** Investigative-Realistic-Conventional. **Career Cluster:** 15 Science, Technology, Engineering, and Mathematics. **Career Pathway:** 15.1 Engineering and Technology. **Other Jobs in This Pathway:** Architectural and Engineering Managers; Automotive Engineers; Biochemical Engineers; Biofuels/Biodiesel Technology and Product Development Managers; Civil Engineers; Cost Estimators; Education, Training, and Library Workers, All Other; Electrical Engineers; Electronics Engineers, Except Computer; Energy Engineers; Engineers, All Other; Fuel Cell Engineers; Human Factors Engineers and Ergonomists; Industrial Engineers; Manufacturing Engineers; Mechanical Engineers; Mechatronics Engineers; Nanosystems Engineers; Photonics Engineers; Radio Frequency Identification Device Specialists; Robotics Engineers; Solar Energy Systems Engineers; Transportation Engineers; Validation Engineers; Wind Energy Engineers; others.

**Skills**—No data available.

**Work Environment:** No data available.

## Job Specialization: Nanosystems Engineers

**Design, develop, and supervise the production of materials, devices, and systems of unique molecular or macromolecular composition, applying principles of nanoscale physics and electrical, chemical, and biological engineering.** Write proposals to secure external funding or to partner with other companies. Supervise technologists or technicians engaged in nanotechnology research or production. Synthesize, process, or characterize nanomaterials, using advanced tools and techniques. Identify new applications for existing nanotechnologies. Provide technical guidance and support to customers on topics such as nanosystem start-up, maintenance, or use. Generate high-resolution images or measure force-distance curves, using techniques such as atomic force microscopy. Prepare reports, deliver presentations, or participate in program review activities to communicate engineering results and recommendations. Prepare nanotechnology-related invention disclosures

or patent applications. Develop processes or identify equipment needed for pilot or commercial nanoscale scale production. Provide scientific or technical guidance and expertise to scientists, engineers, technologists, technicians, or others using knowledge of chemical, analytical, or biological processes as applied to micro and nanoscale systems. Engineer production processes for specific nanotechnology applications, such as electroplating, nanofabrication, or epoxy. Design or conduct tests of new nanotechnology products, processes, or systems. Coordinate or supervise the work of suppliers or vendors in the designing, building, or testing of nanosystem devices, such as lenses or probes. Design or engineer nanomaterials, nanodevices, nano-enabled products, or nanosystems, using three-dimensional computer-aided design (CAD) software. Create designs or prototypes for nanosystem applications, such as biomedical delivery systems and atomic force microscopes. Conduct research related to a range of nanotechnology topics, such as packaging, heat-transfer, fluorescence detection, nanoparticle dispersion, hybrid systems, liquid systems, nanocomposites, nanofabrication, optoelectronics, and nanolithography.

**Education/Training Required:** Bachelor's degree. **Education and Training Program:** Nanotechnology. **Knowledge/Courses**—No data available.

**Personality Type:** No data available. **Career Cluster:** 15 Science, Technology, Engineering, and Mathematics. **Career Pathway:** 15.1 Engineering and Technology. **Other Jobs in This Pathway:** Architectural and Engineering Managers; Automotive Engineers; Biochemical Engineers; Biofuels/Biodiesel Technology and Product Development Managers; Civil Engineers; Cost Estimators; Education, Training, and Library Workers, All Other; Electrical Engineers; Electronics Engineers, Except Computer; Energy Engineers; Engineers, All Other; Fuel Cell Engineers; Human Factors Engineers and Ergonomists; Industrial Engineers; Manufacturing Engineers; Mechanical Engineers; Mechatronics Engineers; Microsystems Engineers; Photonics Engineers; Radio Frequency Identification Device Specialists; Robotics Engineers; Solar Energy Systems Engineers; Transportation Engineers; Validation Engineers; Wind Energy Engineers; others.

**Skills**—No data available.

**Work Environment:** No data available.

# Job Specialization: Photonics Engineers

**Apply knowledge of engineering and mathematical theory and methods to design technologies specializing in light information and light energy.** Design, integrate, or test photonics systems and components. Develop optical or imaging systems such as optical imaging products, optical components, image processes, signal process technologies, and optical systems. Analyze system performance or operational requirements. Write reports or research proposals. Assist in the transition of photonic prototypes to production. Develop and test photonic prototypes or models. Conduct testing to determine functionality and optimization or to establish limits of photonics systems or components. Design electro-optical sensing or imaging systems. Read current literature, talk with colleagues, continue education, or participate in professional organizations or conferences to keep abreast of developments in the field. Conduct research on new photonics technologies. Determine applications of photonics appropriate to meet product objectives and features. Document design processes including objectives, issues, and outcomes. Oversee or provide expertise on manufacturing, assembly, or fabrication processes. Train operators, engineers, or other personnel. Determine commercial, industrial, scientific, or other uses for electro-optical applications or devices. Design gas lasers, solid state lasers, infrared, or other light emitting or light sensitive devices. Analyze, fabricate, or test fiber-optic links. Create or maintain photonic design histories. Develop laser-processed designs such as laser-cut medical devices. Design laser-machining equipment for purposes such as high speed ablation. Select, purchase, set up, operate, or troubleshoot state-of-the-art laser cutting equipment.

**Education/Training Required:** Bachelor's degree. **Education and Training Program:** Engineering, Other. **Knowledge/Courses**—Physics, Engineering and Technology, Design, Mathematics, Computers and Electronics, Mechanical.

**Personality Type:** Investigative-Realistic-Conventional. **Career Cluster:** 15 Science, Technology, Engineering, and Mathematics. **Career Pathway:** 15.1 Engineering and Technology. **Other Jobs in This Pathway:** Architectural and Engineering Managers; Automotive Engineers; Biochemical Engineers; Biofuels/Biodiesel Technology and Product Development Managers; Civil Engineers; Cost Estimators; Education, Training, and Library Workers, All Other; Electrical Engineers; Electronics Engineers, Except Computer; Energy Engineers; Engineers, All Other; Fuel Cell Engineers; Human Factors Engineers and Ergonomists; Industrial Engineers; Manufacturing Engineers; Mechanical Engineers; Mechatronics Engineers; Microsystems Engineers; Nanosystems Engineers; Radio Frequency Identification Device Specialists; Robotics Engineers; Solar Energy Systems Engineers; Transportation Engineers; Validation Engineers; Wind Energy Engineers; others.

**Skills**—Technology Design, Equipment Selection, Mathematics, Science, Programming, Repairing, Quality Control Analysis, Troubleshooting.

**Work Environment:** Indoors; sitting.

# Job Specialization: Robotics Engineers

**Research, design, develop, and test robotic applications.** Supervise technicians, technologists, or other engineers. Integrate robotics with peripherals such as welders, controllers, or other equipment. Provide technical support for robotic systems. Review or approve designs, calculations, or cost estimates. Make system device lists and event timing charts. Document robotic application development, maintenance, or changes. Write algorithms and programming code for ad hoc robotic applications. Create back-ups of robot programs or parameters. Process and interpret signals or sensor data. Plan mobile robot paths and teach path plans to robots. Investigate mechanical failures or unexpected maintenance problems. Install, calibrate, operate, or maintain robots. Debug robotics programs. Design end-of-arm tooling. Conduct research on robotic technology to create new robotic systems or system capabilities. Automate assays on laboratory robotics. Conduct research into the feasibility, design, operation, or performance of robotic mechanisms, components, or systems such as planetary rovers, multiple mobile robots, reconfigurable robots, and man-machine interactions. Analyze and evaluate robotic systems or prototypes. Design automated robotic systems to increase production volume and precision in high-throughput operations such as automated ribonucleic acid (RNA) analysis; or sorting, moving, and stacking production materials. Design software to control robotic systems for applications such as military defense and manufacturing. Build, configure, and test robots. Design robotic systems such as automatic vehicle control, autonomous vehicles, advanced displays, advanced sensing, robotic platforms, computer vision, and telematics systems.

**Education/Training Required:** Bachelor's degree. **Education and Training Program:** Mechatronics, Robotics, and Automation Engineering. **Knowledge/Courses**—Engineering and Technology, Design, Physics, Mechanical, Computers and Electronics, Production and Processing.

**Personality Type:** Investigative-Realistic-Conventional. **Career Cluster:** 15 Science, Technology, Engineering, and Mathematics. **Career Pathway:** 15.1 Engineering and Technology. **Other Jobs in This Pathway:** Architectural and Engineering Managers; Automotive Engineers; Biochemical Engineers; Biofuels/Biodiesel Technology and Product Development Managers; Civil Engineers; Cost Estimators; Education, Training, and Library Workers, All Other; Electrical Engineers; Electronics Engineers, Except Computer; Energy Engineers; Engineers, All Other; Fuel Cell Engineers; Human Factors Engineers and Ergonomists; Industrial Engineers; Manufacturing Engineers; Mechanical Engineers; Mechatronics Engineers; Microsystems Engineers; Nanosystems Engineers; Photonics Engineers; Radio Frequency Identification Device Specialists; Solar Energy Systems Engineers; Transportation Engineers; Validation Engineers; Wind Energy Engineers; others.

**Skills**—Programming, Equipment Selection, Installation, Technology Design, Equipment Maintenance, Repairing, Mathematics, Troubleshooting.

**Work Environment:** Indoors; sitting; using hands; noise; hazardous equipment.

## Job Specialization: Solar Energy Systems Engineers

**Perform site-specific engineering analysis or evaluation of energy efficiency and solar projects involving residential, commercial, or industrial customers. Design solar domestic hot water and space heating systems for new and existing structures, applying knowledge of structural energy requirements, local climates, solar technology, and thermodynamics.** Test or evaluate photovoltaic (PV) cells or modules. Review specifications and recommend engineering or manufacturing changes to achieve solar design objectives. Perform thermal, stress, or cost reduction analyses for solar systems. Develop standard operation procedures and quality or safety standards for solar installation work. Design or develop vacuum tube collector systems for solar applications. Provide technical direction or support to installation teams during installation, start-up, testing, system commissioning, or performance monitoring. Perform computer simulation of solar photovoltaic (PV) generation system performance or energy production to optimize efficiency. Develop design specifications and functional requirements for residential, commercial, or industrial solar energy systems or components. Create plans for solar energy system development, monitoring, and evaluation activities. Create electrical single-line diagrams, panel schedules, or connection diagrams for solar electric systems using computer-aided design (CAD) software. Create checklists for review or inspection of completed solar installation projects. Design or coordinate design of photovoltaic (PV) or solar thermal systems, including system components, for residential and commercial buildings. Conduct engineering site audits to collect structural, electrical, and related site information for use in the design of residential or commercial solar power systems.

**Education/Training Required:** Bachelor's degree. **Education and Training Program:** Engineering, Other. **Knowledge/Courses**—No data available.

**Personality Type:** No data available. **Career Cluster:** 15 Science, Technology, Engineering, and Mathematics. **Career Pathway:** 15.1 Engineering and Technology. **Other Jobs in This Pathway:** Architectural and Engineering Managers; Automotive Engineers; Biochemical Engineers; Biofuels/Biodiesel Technology and Product Development Managers; Civil Engineers; Cost Estimators; Education, Training, and Library Workers, All Other; Electrical Engineers; Electronics Engineers, Except Computer; Energy Engineers; Engineers, All Other; Fuel Cell Engineers; Human Factors Engineers and Ergonomists; Industrial Engineers; Manufacturing Engineers; Mechanical Engineers; Mechatronics Engineers; Microsystems Engineers; Nanosystems Engineers; Photonics Engineers; Radio Frequency Identification Device Specialists; Robotics Engineers; Transportation Engineers; Validation Engineers; Wind Energy Engineers; others.

**Skills**—No data available.

**Work Environment:** No data available.

## Job Specialization: Validation Engineers

**Design and plan protocols for equipment and processes to produce products meeting internal and external purity, safety, and quality requirements.** Analyze validation test data to determine whether systems or processes have met validation criteria and to identify root causes of production problems. Prepare validation and performance qualification protocols for new or modified manufacturing processes, systems, or equipment for pharmaceutical, electronics, and other types of production. Coordinate the implementation or scheduling of validation testing with affected departments and personnel. Study product characteristics or customer requirements and confer with management to determine validation objectives and standards.

Prepare, maintain, or review validation and compliance documentation such as engineering change notices, schematics, and protocols. Resolve testing problems by modifying testing methods or revising test objectives and standards. Create, populate, or maintain databases for tracking validation activities, test results, or validated systems. Prepare detailed reports and design statements based on results of validation and qualification tests or reviews of procedures and protocols. Identify deviations from established product or process standards and provide recommendations for resolving deviations. Direct validation activities such as protocol creation or testing. Develop validation master plans, process flow diagrams, test cases, or standard operating procedures. Communicate with regulatory agencies regarding compliance documentation or validation results. Conduct validation and qualification tests of new or existing processes, equipment, or software in accordance with internal protocols or external standards. Design validation study features such as sampling, testing, and analytical methodologies. Participate in internal or external training programs to maintain knowledge of validation principles, industry trends, or novel technologies. Conduct audits of validation or performance qualification processes to ensure compliance with internal or regulatory requirements.

**Education/Training Required:** Bachelor's degree. **Education and Training Program:** Engineering, Other. **Knowledge/Courses**—Engineering and Technology, Design, Production and Processing, Chemistry, Physics, Mathematics.

**Personality Type:** Investigative-Realistic-Conventional. **Career Cluster:** 15 Science, Technology, Engineering, and Mathematics. **Career Pathway:** 15.1 Engineering and Technology. **Other Jobs in This Pathway:** Architectural and Engineering Managers; Automotive Engineers; Biochemical Engineers; Biofuels/Biodiesel Technology and Product Development Managers; Civil Engineers; Cost Estimators; Education, Training, and Library Workers, All Other; Electrical Engineers; Electronics Engineers, Except Computer; Energy Engineers; Engineers, All Other; Fuel Cell Engineers; Human Factors Engineers and Ergonomists; Industrial Engineers; Manufacturing Engineers; Mechanical Engineers; Mechatronics Engineers; Microsystems Engineers; Nanosystems Engineers; Photonics Engineers; Radio Frequency Identification Device Specialists; Robotics Engineers; Solar Energy Systems Engineers; Transportation Engineers; Wind Energy Engineers; others.

**Skills**—Science, Operations Analysis, Mathematics, Systems Analysis, Operation Monitoring, Systems Evaluation, Reading Comprehension, Writing.

**Work Environment:** Indoors; sitting.

# Job Specialization: Wind Energy Engineers

**Design underground or overhead wind farm collector systems and prepare and develop site specifications.** Write reports to document wind farm collector system test results. Oversee the work activities of wind farm consultants or subcontractors. Recommend process or infrastructure changes to improve wind turbine performance, reduce operational costs, or comply with regulations. Investigate experimental wind turbines or wind turbine technologies for properties such as aerodynamics, production, noise, and load. Test wind turbine equipment to determine effects of stress or fatigue. Test wind turbine components, using mechanical or electronic testing equipment. Provide engineering technical support to designers of prototype wind turbines. Perform root cause analysis on wind turbine tower component failures. Monitor wind farm construction to ensure compliance with regulatory standards or environmental requirements. Direct balance of plant (BOP) construction, generator installation, testing, commissioning, or supervisory control and data acquisition (SCADA) to ensure compliance with specifications. Develop specifications for wind technology components, such as gearboxes, blades, generators, frequency converters, and pad transformers. Develop active control algorithms, electronics, software, electromechanical, or electrohydraulic systems for wind turbines. Create or maintain wind farm layouts, schematics, or other visual documentation for wind farms. Create models to optimize the layout of wind farm access roads, crane pads, crane paths, collection systems, substations, switchyards, or transmission lines. Design underground or overhead wind farm collector systems. Analyze operation of wind farms or wind farm components to determine reliability, performance, and compliance with specifications.

**Education/Training Required:** Bachelor's degree. **Education and Training Program:** Engineering, Other. **Knowledge/Courses**—No data available.

**Personality Type:** No data available. **Career Cluster:** 15 Science, Technology, Engineering, and Mathematics. **Career Pathway:** 15.1 Engineering and Technology. **Other Jobs in This Pathway:** Architectural and Engineering Managers; Automotive Engineers; Biochemical Engineers; Biofuels/Biodiesel Technology and Product Development Managers; Civil Engineers; Cost Estimators; Education, Training, and Library Workers, All Other; Electrical Engineers; Electronics Engineers, Except Computer; Energy Engineers;

Engineers, All Other; Fuel Cell Engineers; Human Factors Engineers and Ergonomists; Industrial Engineers; Manufacturing Engineers; Mechanical Engineers; Mechatronics Engineers; Microsystems Engineers; Nanosystems Engineers; Photonics Engineers; Radio Frequency Identification Device Specialists; Robotics Engineers; Solar Energy Systems Engineers; Transportation Engineers; Validation Engineers; others.

**Skills**—No data available.

**Work Environment:** No data available.

# English Language and Literature Teachers, Postsecondary

- ❋ Annual Earnings: $60,400
- ❋ Earnings Growth Potential: High (45.6%)
- ❋ Growth: 15.1%
- ❋ Annual Job Openings: 2,000
- ❋ Self-Employed: 0.2%

**Considerations for Job Outlook:** Enrollments in postsecondary institutions are expected to continue rising as more people attend college and as workers return to school to update their skills. Opportunities for part-time or temporary positions should be favorable, but significant competition exists for tenure-track positions.

**Teach courses in English language and literature, including linguistics and comparative literature.** Initiate, facilitate, and moderate classroom discussions. Evaluate and grade students' classwork, assignments, and papers. Prepare course materials such as syllabi, homework assignments, and handouts. Prepare and deliver lectures to undergraduate and graduate students on topics such as poetry, novel structure, and translation and adaptation. Maintain student attendance records, grades, and other required records. Plan, evaluate, and revise curricula, course content, and course materials and methods of instruction. Compile, administer, and grade examinations or assign this work to others. Maintain regularly scheduled office hours in order to advise and assist students. Keep abreast of developments in their field by reading current literature, talking with colleagues, and participating in professional conferences. Select and obtain materials and supplies such as textbooks. Advise students on academic and vocational curricula and on career issues. Conduct research in a particular field of knowledge and publish findings in professional journals, books, or electronic media. Collaborate with colleagues to address teaching and research issues. Serve on academic or administrative committees that deal with institutional policies, departmental matters, and academic issues. Participate in campus and community events. Participate in student recruitment, registration, and placement activities. Compile bibliographies of specialized materials for outside reading assignments. Supervise undergraduate and/or graduate teaching, internship, and research work. Provide assistance to students in college writing centers. Perform administrative duties such as serving as department head. Recruit, train, and supervise student writing instructors. Act as advisers to student organizations. Write grant proposals to procure external research funding. Provide professional consulting services to government or industry.

**Education/Training Required:** Doctoral degree. **Education and Training Programs:** Comparative Literature; English Language and Literature, General; English Language and Literature/Letters, Other; Humanities/Humanistic Studies. **Knowledge/Courses**—Philosophy and Theology, History and Archeology, English Language, Education and Training, Fine Arts, Sociology and Anthropology.

**Personality Type:** Social-Artistic-Investigative. **Career Clusters:** 03 Arts, Audio/Video Technology, and Communications; 05 Education and Training. **Career Pathways:** 3.5 Journalism and Broadcasting; 5.3 Teaching/Training. **Other Jobs in These Pathways:** Career/Technical Education Teachers, Secondary School; Coaches and Scouts; Copy Writers; Directors- Stage, Motion Pictures, Television, and Radio; Editors; Elementary School Teachers, Except Special Education; Fitness Trainers and Aerobics Instructors; Instructional Coordinators; Instructional Designers and Technologists; Kindergarten Teachers, Except Special Education; Librarians; Middle School Teachers, Except Special and Career/Technical Education; Photographers; Preschool Teachers, Except Special Education; Producers; Program Directors; Public Relations Specialists; Recreation Workers; Secondary School Teachers, Except Special and Career/Technical Education; Self-Enrichment Education Teachers; Talent Directors; Teacher Assistants; Technical Directors/Managers; Tutors; 37 other postsecondary teaching occupations; others.

**Skills**—Learning Strategies, Writing, Instructing, Reading Comprehension, Speaking, Active Listening, Monitoring, Active Learning.

**Work Environment:** Indoors; sitting.

# Environmental Engineering Technicians

* ❋ Annual Earnings: $43,390
* ❋ Earnings Growth Potential: Low (35.5%)
* ❋ Growth: 30.1%
* ❋ Annual Job Openings: 1,040
* ❋ Self-Employed: 0.7%

**Considerations for Job Outlook:** Labor-saving efficiencies and the automation of many engineering support activities will limit the need for new engineering technicians. In general, opportunities should be best for job seekers who have an associate degree or other postsecondary training in engineering technology.

**Apply theory and principles of environmental engineering to modify, test, and operate equipment and devices used in the prevention, control, and remediation of environmental pollution, including waste treatment and site remediation. May assist in the development of environmental pollution remediation devices under direction of engineer.** Receive, set up, test, and decontaminate equipment. Maintain project logbook records and computer program files. Perform environmental quality work in field and office settings. Conduct pollution surveys, collecting and analyzing samples such as air and groundwater. Review technical documents to ensure completeness and conformance to requirements. Perform laboratory work such as logging numerical and visual observations, preparing and packaging samples, recording test results, and performing photo documentation. Review work plans to schedule activities. Obtain product information, identify vendors and suppliers, and order materials and equipment to maintain inventory. Arrange for the disposal of lead, asbestos, and other hazardous materials. Inspect facilities to monitor compliance with regulations governing substances such as asbestos, lead, and wastewater. Provide technical engineering support in the planning of projects such as wastewater treatment plants to ensure compliance with environmental regulations and policies. Improve chemical processes to reduce toxic emissions. Oversee support staff. Assist in the cleanup of hazardous material spills. Produce environmental assessment reports, tabulating data and preparing charts, graphs, and sketches. Maintain process parameters and evaluate process anomalies. Work with customers to assess the environmental impact of proposed construction and to develop pollution prevention programs. Perform statistical analysis and correction of air or water pollution data submitted by industry and other agencies. Develop work plans, including writing specifications and establishing material, manpower, and facilities needs.

**Education/Training Required:** Associate degree. **Education and Training Programs:** Environmental Engineering Technology/Environmental Technology; Hazardous Materials Information Systems Technology/Technician. **Knowledge/Courses**—Engineering and Technology, Building and Construction, Physics, Design, Biology, Mechanical.

**Personality Type:** Realistic-Investigative-Conventional. **Career Clusters:** 01 Agriculture, Food, and Natural Resources; 13 Manufacturing. **Career Pathways:** 1.6 Environmental Service Systems; 13.4 Quality Assurance. **Other Jobs in These Pathways:** Hazardous Materials Removal Workers; Inspectors, Testers, Sorters, Samplers, and Weighers; Occupational Health and Safety Specialists; Water and Wastewater Treatment Plant and System Operators.

**Skills**—Mathematics, Reading Comprehension, Programming, Management of Material Resources, Quality Control Analysis, Science, Equipment Selection, Operation Monitoring.

**Work Environment:** More often indoors than outdoors; standing; contaminants; hazardous conditions; hazardous equipment.

# Environmental Engineers

* ❋ Annual Earnings: $78,740
* ❋ Earnings Growth Potential: Medium (37.8%)
* ❋ Growth: 30.6%
* ❋ Annual Job Openings: 2,790
* ❋ Self-Employed: 0.6%

**Considerations for Job Outlook:** Environmental engineers are expected to have employment growth of 31 percent from 2008–2018, much faster than the average for all occupations. More environmental engineers will be needed to help companies comply with environmental regulations and to develop methods of cleaning up environmental hazards. A shift in emphasis toward preventing problems rather than controlling those which already exist, as well as increasing public health concerns resulting from population growth, also are expected to spur demand for environmental engineers. Because of this employment growth, job opportunities should be favorable.

**Design, plan, or perform engineering duties in the prevention, control, and remediation of environmental**

**health hazards, using various engineering disciplines. Work may include waste treatment, site remediation, or pollution control technology.** Collaborate with environmental scientists, planners, hazardous waste technicians, engineers, and other specialists and experts in law and business to address environmental problems. Inspect industrial and municipal facilities and programs to evaluate operational effectiveness and ensure compliance with environmental regulations. Prepare, review, and update environmental investigation and recommendation reports. Design and supervise the development of systems processes or equipment for control, management, or remediation of water, air, or soil quality. Provide environmental engineering assistance in network analysis, regulatory analysis, and planning or reviewing database development. Obtain, update, and maintain plans, permits, and standard operating procedures. Provide technical-level support for environmental remediation and litigation projects, including remediation system design and determination of regulatory applicability. Monitor progress of environmental improvement programs. Inform company employees and other interested parties of environmental issues. Advise corporations and government agencies of procedures to follow in cleaning up contaminated sites to protect people and the environment. Develop proposed project objectives and targets and report to management on progress in attaining them. Request bids from suppliers or consultants. Advise industries and government agencies about environmental policies and standards. Assess the existing or potential environmental impact of land use projects on air, water, and land. Assist in budget implementation, forecasts, and administration. Serve on teams conducting multimedia inspections at complex facilities, providing assistance with planning, quality assurance, safety inspection protocols, and sampling. Coordinate and manage environmental protection programs and projects, assigning and evaluating work. Maintain, write, and revise quality assurance documentation and procedures.

**Education/Training Required:** Bachelor's degree. **Education and Training Program:** Environmental/Environmental Health Engineering. **Knowledge/Courses**—Engineering and Technology, Physics, Design, Chemistry, Building and Construction, Biology.

**Personality Type:** Investigative-Realistic-Conventional. **Career Clusters:** 15 Science, Technology, Engineering, and Mathematics; 16 Transportation, Distribution, and Logistics. **Career Pathways:** 15.1 Engineering and Technology; 16.6 Health, Safety, and Environmental Management. **Other Jobs in These Pathways:** Architectural and Engineering Managers; Automotive Engineers; Biochemical Engineers; Biofuels/Biodiesel Technology and Product

Development Managers; Civil Engineers; Cost Estimators; Electrical Engineers; Electronics Engineers, Except Computer; Energy Engineers; Engineers, All Other; Environmental Compliance Inspectors; Fuel Cell Engineers; Human Factors Engineers and Ergonomists; Industrial Engineers; Manufacturing Engineers; Mechanical Engineers; Mechatronics Engineers; Microsystems Engineers; Nanosystems Engineers; Photonics Engineers; Robotics Engineers; Solar Energy Systems Engineers; Transportation Engineers; Validation Engineers; Wind Energy Engineers; others.

**Skills**—Mathematics, Science, Systems Analysis, Management of Financial Resources, Operations Analysis, Programming, Quality Control Analysis, Systems Evaluation.

**Work Environment:** More often indoors than outdoors; sitting; using hands; noise; contaminants.

## Job Specialization: Water/Wastewater Engineers

**Design or oversee projects involving provision of fresh water, disposal of wastewater and sewage, or prevention of flood-related damage. Prepare environmental documentation for water resources, regulatory program compliance, data management and analysis, and fieldwork. Perform hydraulic modeling and pipeline design.** Write technical reports or publications related to water resources development or water use efficiency. Review and critique proposals, plans, or designs related to water and wastewater treatment systems. Provide technical support on water resource or treatment issues to government agencies. Provide technical direction or supervision to junior engineers, engineering or computer-aided design (CAD) technicians, or other technical personnel. Identify design alternatives for the development of new water resources. Develop plans for new water resources or water efficiency programs. Design or select equipment for use in wastewater processing to ensure compliance with government standards. Conduct water quality studies to identify and characterize water pollutant sources. Perform mathematical modeling of underground or surface water resources, such as floodplains, ocean coastlines, streams, rivers, and wetlands. Perform hydrological analyses, using three-dimensional simulation software, to model the movement of water or forecast the dispersion of chemical pollutants in the water supply. Perform hydraulic analyses of water supply systems or water distribution networks to model flow characteristics, test for pressure losses, or to identify opportunities to mitigate risks and improve operational efficiency. Oversee the construction of decentralized and on-site wastewater treatment systems, including reclaimed water facilities. Gather and analyze water use data to forecast water demand. Conduct feasibility studies for the construction of facilities, such as water supply systems, run-off collection networks, water and wastewater treatment plants, or wastewater collection systems. Conduct environmental impact studies related to water and wastewater collection, treatment, or distribution. Conduct cost-benefit analyses for the construction of water supply systems, run-off collection networks, water and wastewater treatment plants, or wastewater collection systems.

**Education/Training Required:** Bachelor's degree. **Education and Training Program:** Environmental/Environmental Health Engineering. **Knowledge/Courses**—No data available.

**Personality Type:** No data available. **Career Cluster:** 15 Science, Technology, Engineering, and Mathematics. **Career Pathway:** 15.1 Engineering and Technology. **Other Jobs in This Pathway:** Architectural and Engineering Managers; Automotive Engineers; Biochemical Engineers; Biofuels/Biodiesel Technology and Product Development Managers; Civil Engineers; Cost Estimators; Electrical Engineers; Electronics Engineers, Except Computer; Energy Engineers; Engineers, All Other; Fuel Cell Engineers; Human Factors Engineers and Ergonomists; Industrial Engineers; Manufacturing Engineers; Mechanical Engineers; Mechatronics Engineers; Microsystems Engineers; Nanosystems Engineers; Photonics Engineers; Radio Frequency Identification Device Specialists; Robotics Engineers; Solar Energy Systems Engineers; Transportation Engineers; Validation Engineers; Wind Energy Engineers; others.

**Skills**—No data available.

**Work Environment:** No data available.

# Environmental Science and Protection Technicians, Including Health

- ❋ Annual Earnings: $41,380
- ❋ Earnings Growth Potential: Low (35.7%)
- ❋ Growth: 28.9%
- ❋ Annual Job Openings: 2,520
- ❋ Self-Employed: 1.7%

**Considerations for Job Outlook:** The continued growth of scientific and medical research and the development and manufacturing of technical products are expected to drive employment growth for these workers. Opportunities are expected to be best for graduates of applied science technology programs who are knowledgeable about equipment used in laboratories or production facilities.

**Perform laboratory and field tests to monitor the environment and investigate sources of pollution, including those that affect health. Under direction of environmental scientists or specialists, may collect samples of gases, soil, water, and other materials for testing and take corrective actions as assigned.** Collect samples of gases, soils, water, industrial wastewater, and asbestos products to conduct tests on pollutant levels and identify sources of pollution. Record test data and prepare reports, summaries, and charts that interpret test results. Develop and implement programs for monitoring of environmental pollution and radiation. Discuss test results and analyses with customers. Set up equipment or stations to monitor and collect pollutants from sites such as smokestacks, manufacturing plants, or mechanical equipment. Maintain files, such as hazardous waste databases, chemical usage data, personnel exposure information, and diagrams showing equipment locations. Develop testing procedures or direct activities of workers in laboratory. Prepare samples or photomicrographs for testing and analysis. Calibrate microscopes and test instruments. Examine and analyze material for presence and concentration of contaminants such as asbestos, using variety of microscopes. Calculate amount of pollutant in samples or compute air pollution or gas flow in industrial processes, using chemical and mathematical formulas. Make recommendations to control or eliminate unsafe conditions at workplaces or public facilities. Weigh, analyze, and measure collected sample particles such as lead, coal dust, or rock to determine concentration of pollutants. Provide information and technical and program assistance to government representatives, employers, and the general public on the issues of public health, environmental protection, or workplace safety. Conduct standardized tests to ensure materials and supplies used throughout power supply systems meet processing and safety specifications. Perform statistical analysis of environmental data. Respond to and investigate hazardous conditions or spills or outbreaks of disease or food poisoning, collecting samples for analysis.

**Education/Training Required:** Associate degree. **Education and Training Programs:** Environmental Science; Environmental Studies; Physical Science Technologies/Technicians, Other; Science Technologies/Technicians, Other. **Knowledge/Courses**—Biology, Chemistry, Geography, Physics, Computers and Electronics, Building and Construction.

**Personality Type:** Investigative-Realistic-Conventional. **Career Clusters:** 01 Agriculture, Food, and Natural Resources; 13 Manufacturing; 16 Transportation, Distribution, and Logistics. **Career Pathways:** 1.5 Natural Resources Systems; 13.2 Manufacturing Production Process Development; 16.6 Health, Safety, and Environmental Management. **Other Jobs in These Pathways:** Chemical Plant and System Operators; Chemical Technicians; Climate Change Analysts; Conveyor Operators and Tenders; Electrical Engineering Technicians; Electromechanical Equipment Assemblers; Engineering Technicians, Except Drafters, All Other; Environmental Compliance Inspectors; Environmental Engineers; Environmental Restoration Planners; Environmental Scientists and Specialists, Including Health; Fishers and Related Fishing Workers; Forest and Conservation Technicians; Health and Safety Engineers, Except Mining Safety Engineers and Inspectors; Helpers—Extraction Workers; Industrial Ecologists; Industrial Truck and Tractor Operators; Life, Physical, and Social Science Technicians, All Other; Logging Equipment Operators; Mechanical Engineering Technicians; Quality Control Analysts; Recreation Workers; Refuse and Recyclable Material Collectors; Rotary Drill Operators, Oil and Gas; Service Unit Operators, Oil, Gas, and Mining; others.

**Skills**—Science, Equipment Maintenance, Troubleshooting, Operation and Control, Repairing, Operations Analysis, Equipment Selection, Mathematics.

**Work Environment:** More often outdoors than indoors; standing; using hands; noise; very hot or cold; bright or inadequate lighting; contaminants; hazardous conditions; hazardous equipment; minor burns, cuts, bites, or stings.

# Environmental Science Teachers, Postsecondary

* Annual Earnings: $71,020
* Earnings Growth Potential: High (48.4%)
* Growth: 15.1%
* Annual Job Openings: 200
* Self-Employed: 0.2%

**Considerations for Job Outlook:** Enrollments in postsecondary institutions are expected to continue rising as more people attend college and as workers return to school to update their skills. Opportunities for part-time or temporary positions should be favorable, but significant competition exists for tenure-track positions.

**Teach courses in environmental science.** Supervise undergraduate and/or graduate teaching, internship, and research work. Conduct research in a particular field of knowledge and publish findings in professional journals, books, and/or electronic media. Keep abreast of developments in their field by reading current literature, talking with colleagues, and participating in professional conferences. Evaluate and grade students' classwork, laboratory work, assignments, and papers. Write grant proposals to procure external research funding. Supervise students' laboratory work and fieldwork. Prepare course materials such as syllabi, homework assignments, and handouts. Plan, evaluate, and revise curricula, course content, and course materials and methods of instruction. Compile, administer, and grade examinations or assign this work to others. Initiate, facilitate, and moderate classroom discussions. Advise students on academic and vocational curricula and on career issues. Prepare and deliver lectures to undergraduate and/or graduate students on topics such as hazardous waste management, industrial safety, and environmental toxicology. Maintain student attendance records, grades, and other required records. Select and obtain materials and supplies such as textbooks and laboratory equipment. Maintain regularly scheduled office hours in order to advise and assist students. Collaborate with colleagues to address teaching and research issues. Perform administrative duties such as serving as department head. Participate in student recruitment, registration, and placement activities. Provide professional consulting services to government and/or industry. Serve on academic or administrative committees that deal with institutional policies, departmental matters, and academic issues. Compile bibliographies of specialized materials for outside reading assignments. Participate in campus and community events. Act as advisers to student organizations.

**Education/Training Required:** Doctoral degree. **Education and Training Programs:** Environmental Science; Environmental Studies; Science Teacher Education/General Science Teacher Education. **Knowledge/Courses**—Biology, Geography, Chemistry, Education and Training, History and Archeology, Physics.

**Personality Type:** Social-Investigative-Artistic. **Career Clusters:** 01 Agriculture, Food, and Natural Resources; 05 Education and Training. **Career Pathways:** 1.5 Natural Resources Systems; 5.3 Teaching/Training. **Other Jobs in These Pathways:** Adult Basic and Secondary Education and Literacy Teachers and Instructors; Career/Technical Education Teachers, Secondary School; Chemists; Climate Change Analysts; Coaches and Scouts; Elementary School Teachers, Except Special Education; Engineering Technicians, Except Drafters, All Other; Environmental Restoration Planners;

Environmental Scientists and Specialists, Including Health; Fitness Trainers and Aerobics Instructors; Industrial Ecologists; Industrial Truck and Tractor Operators; Instructional Coordinators; Instructional Designers and Technologists; Kindergarten Teachers, Except Special Education; Librarians; Middle School Teachers, Except Special and Career/Technical Education; Preschool Teachers, Except Special Education; Recreation Workers; Refuse and Recyclable Material Collectors; Secondary School Teachers, Except Special and Career/Technical Education; Self-Enrichment Education Teachers; Teacher Assistants; Tutors; 37 other postsecondary teaching occupations; others.

**Skills**—Science, Writing, Reading Comprehension, Operations Analysis, Learning Strategies, Active Learning, Instructing, Systems Evaluation.

**Work Environment:** Indoors; sitting.

# Environmental Scientists and Specialists, Including Health

❋ Annual Earnings: $61,700
❋ Earnings Growth Potential: Medium (38.7%)
❋ Growth: 27.9%
❋ Annual Job Openings: 4,840
❋ Self-Employed: 2.4%

**Considerations for Job Outlook:** A growing population and increased awareness of environmental concerns are expected to increase employment of environmental scientists. These workers should have good job prospects, particularly in state and local governments.

**Conduct research or perform investigation for the purpose of identifying, abating, or eliminating sources of pollutants or hazards that affect either the environment or the health of the population. Using knowledge of various scientific disciplines, may collect, synthesize, study, report, and take action based on data derived from measurements or observations of air, food, soil, water, and other sources.** Collect, synthesize, analyze, manage, and report environmental data such as pollution emission measurements, atmospheric monitoring measurements, meteorological and mineralogical information, and soil or water samples. Analyze data to determine validity, quality, and scientific significance, and to interpret correlations between human activities and environmental effects. Communicate scientific and technical information to the public, organizations, or internal audiences through oral briefings, written

documents, workshops, conferences, training sessions, or public hearings. Provide scientific and technical guidance, support, coordination, and oversight to governmental agencies, environmental programs, industry, or the public. Process and review environmental permits, licenses, and related materials. Review and implement environmental technical standards, guidelines, policies, and formal regulations that meet all appropriate requirements. Prepare charts or graphs from data samples, providing summary information on the environmental relevance of the data. Determine data collection methods to be employed in research projects and surveys. Investigate and report on accidents affecting the environment. Research sources of pollution to determine their effects on the environment and to develop theories or methods of pollution abatement or control. Provide advice on proper standards and regulations or the development of policies, strategies, and codes of practice for environmental management. Monitor effects of pollution and land degradation, and recommend means of prevention or control. Supervise or train students, environmental technologists, technicians, or other related staff. Evaluate violations or problems discovered during inspections to determine appropriate regulatory actions or to provide advice on the development and prosecution of regulatory cases. Conduct environmental audits and inspections, and investigations of violations.

**Education/Training Required:** Master's degree. **Education and Training Programs:** Environmental Science; Environmental Studies. **Knowledge/Courses**—Biology, Geography, Chemistry, Physics, Law and Government, Engineering and Technology.

**Personality Type:** Investigative-Realistic-Conventional. **Career Clusters:** 01 Agriculture, Food, and Natural Resources; 16 Transportation, Distribution, and Logistics. **Career Pathways:** 1.5 Natural Resources Systems; 16.6 Health, Safety, and Environmental Management. **Other Jobs in These Pathways:** Climate Change Analysts; Conveyor Operators and Tenders; Derrick Operators, Oil and Gas; Engineering Technicians, Except Drafters, All Other; Environmental Compliance Inspectors; Environmental Engineers; Environmental Restoration Planners; Environmental Science and Protection Technicians, Including Health; Fishers and Related Fishing Workers; Forest and Conservation Technicians; Health and Safety Engineers, Except Mining Safety Engineers and Inspectors; Helpers—Extraction Workers; Industrial Ecologists; Industrial Truck and Tractor Operators; Logging Equipment Operators; Mechanical Engineering Technicians; Park Naturalists; Range Managers; Recreation Workers; Refuse and Recyclable Material Collectors; Rotary Drill Operators, Oil and

Gas; Service Unit Operators, Oil, Gas, and Mining; Soil and Water Conservationists; Wellhead Pumpers; Zoologists and Wildlife Biologists; others.

**Skills**—Science, Programming, Mathematics, Reading Comprehension, Operations Analysis, Writing, Systems Analysis, Complex Problem Solving.

**Work Environment:** More often indoors than outdoors; sitting; noise.

## Job Specialization: Climate Change Analysts

**Research and analyze policy developments related to climate change. Make climate-related recommendations for actions such as legislation, awareness campaigns, or fundraising approaches.** Write reports or academic papers to communicate findings of climate-related studies. Promote initiatives to mitigate climate change with government or environmental groups. Present climate-related information at public interest, governmental, or other meetings. Present and defend proposals for climate change research projects. Prepare grant applications to obtain funding for programs related to climate change, environmental management, or sustainability. Gather and review climate-related studies from government agencies, research laboratories, and other organizations. Develop, or contribute to the development of, educational or outreach programs on the environment or climate change. Review existing policies or legislation to identify environmental impacts. Provide analytical support for policy briefs related to renewable energy, energy efficiency, or climate change. Prepare study reports, memoranda, briefs, testimonies, or other written materials to inform government or environmental groups on environmental issues such as climate change. Make legislative recommendations related to climate change or environmental management, based on climate change policies, principles, programs, practices, and processes. Research policies, practices, or procedures for climate or environmental management. Propose new or modified policies involving use of traditional and alternative fuels, transportation of goods, and other factors relating to climate and climate change. Analyze and distill climate-related research findings to inform legislators, regulatory agencies, or other stakeholders.

**Education/Training Required:** Master's degree. **Education and Training Programs:** Environmental Science; Environmental Studies. **Knowledge/Courses**—No data available.

**Personality Type:** No data available. **Career Cluster:** 01 Agriculture, Food, and Natural Resources. **Career Pathway:**

1.5 Natural Resources Systems. **Other Jobs in This Pathway:** Conveyor Operators and Tenders; Derrick Operators, Oil and Gas; Engineering Technicians, Except Drafters, All Other; Environmental Economists; Environmental Restoration Planners; Environmental Science and Protection Technicians, Including Health; Environmental Scientists and Specialists, Including Health; Fishers and Related Fishing Workers; Forest and Conservation Technicians; Geological Sample Test Technicians; Geophysical Data Technicians; Helpers—Extraction Workers; Industrial Ecologists; Industrial Truck and Tractor Operators; Logging Equipment Operators; Mechanical Engineering Technicians; Park Naturalists; Range Managers; Recreation Workers; Refuse and Recyclable Material Collectors; Rotary Drill Operators, Oil and Gas; Service Unit Operators, Oil, Gas, and Mining; Soil and Water Conservationists; Wellhead Pumpers; Zoologists and Wildlife Biologists; others.

**Skills**—No data available.

**Work Environment:** No data available.

## Job Specialization: Environmental Restoration Planners

**Collaborate with field and biology staff to oversee the implementation of restoration projects and to develop new products. Process and synthesize complex scientific data into practical strategies for restoration, monitoring or management.** Notify regulatory or permitting agencies of deviations from implemented remediation plans. Develop environmental restoration project schedules and budgets. Develop and communicate recommendations for landowners to maintain or restore environmental conditions. Create diagrams to communicate environmental remediation planning using geographic information systems (GIS), computer-aided design (CAD), or other mapping or diagramming software. Apply for permits required for the implementation of environmental remediation projects. Review existing environmental remediation designs. Supervise and provide technical guidance, training, or assistance to employees working in the field to restore habitats. Provide technical direction on environmental planning to energy engineers, biologists, geologists, or other professionals working to develop restoration plans or strategies. Plan or supervise environmental studies to achieve compliance with environmental regulations in construction, modification, operation, acquisition, or divestiture of facilities such as power plants. Inspect active remediation sites to ensure compliance with environmental or safety policies, standards, or regulations. Plan environmental restoration projects, using biological databases, environmental strategies, and planning software. Identify short- and long-term impacts of environmental remediation activities. Identify environmental mitigation alternatives, ensuring compliance with applicable standards, laws, or regulations. Create environmental models or simulations, using geographic information system (GIS) data and knowledge of particular ecosystems or ecological regions. Conduct feasibility and cost-benefit studies for environmental remediation projects. Conduct environmental impact studies to examine the ecological effects of pollutants, disease, human activities, nature, and climate change.

**Education/Training Required:** Master's degree. **Education and Training Programs:** Environmental Science; Environmental Studies. **Knowledge/Courses**—No data available.

**Personality Type:** No data available. **Career Cluster:** 01 Agriculture, Food, and Natural Resources. **Career Pathway:** 1.5 Natural Resources Systems. **Other Jobs in This Pathway:** Climate Change Analysts; Conveyor Operators and Tenders; Derrick Operators, Oil and Gas; Engineering Technicians, Except Drafters, All Other; Environmental Economists; Environmental Science and Protection Technicians, Including Health; Environmental Scientists and Specialists, Including Health; Fishers and Related Fishing Workers; Forest and Conservation Technicians; Geological Sample Test Technicians; Geophysical Data Technicians; Helpers—Extraction Workers; Industrial Ecologists; Industrial Truck and Tractor Operators; Logging Equipment Operators; Mechanical Engineering Technicians; Park Naturalists; Range Managers; Recreation Workers; Refuse and Recyclable Material Collectors; Rotary Drill Operators, Oil and Gas; Service Unit Operators, Oil, Gas, and Mining; Soil and Water Conservationists; Wellhead Pumpers; Zoologists and Wildlife Biologists; others.

**Skills**—No data available.

**Work Environment:** No data available.

# Job Specialization: Industrial Ecologists

**Study or investigate industrial production and natural ecosystems to achieve high production, sustainable resources, and environmental safety or protection. May apply principles and activities of natural ecosystems to develop models for industrial systems.** Write ecological reports and other technical documents for publication in the research literature or in industrial or government reports. Recommend methods to protect the environment

or minimize environmental damage. Investigate accidents affecting the environment to assess ecological impact. Investigate the adaptability of various animal and plant species to changed environmental conditions. Review industrial practices, such as the methods and materials used in construction or production, to identify potential liabilities and environmental hazards. Research sources of pollution to determine environmental impact or to develop methods of pollution abatement or control. Provide industrial managers with technical materials on environmental issues, regulatory guidelines, or compliance actions. Plan or conduct studies of the ecological implications of historic or projected changes in industrial processes or development. Plan or conduct field research on topics such as industrial production, industrial ecology, population ecology, and environmental production or sustainability. Monitor the environmental impact of development activities, pollution, or land degradation. Model alternative energy investment scenarios to compare economic and environmental costs and benefits. Identify or develop strategies or methods to minimize the environmental impact of industrial production processes. Investigate the impact of changed land management or land use practices on ecosystems. Develop or test protocols to monitor ecosystem components and ecological processes. Create complex and dynamic mathematical models of population, community, or ecological systems. Conduct scientific protection, mitigation, or restoration projects to prevent resource damage, maintain the integrity of critical habitats, and minimize the impact of human activities. Carry out environmental assessments in accordance with applicable standards, regulations, or laws.

**Education/Training Required:** Master's degree. **Education and Training Programs:** Environmental Science; Environmental Studies. **Knowledge/Courses**—No data available.

**Personality Type:** No data available. **Career Cluster:** 01 Agriculture, Food, and Natural Resources. **Career Pathway:** 1.5 Natural Resources Systems. **Other Jobs in This Pathway:** Climate Change Analysts; Conveyor Operators and Tenders; Derrick Operators, Oil and Gas; Engineering Technicians, Except Drafters, All Other; Environmental Economists; Environmental Restoration Planners; Environmental Science and Protection Technicians, Including Health; Environmental Scientists and Specialists, Including Health; Fishers and Related Fishing Workers; Forest and Conservation Technicians; Geological Sample Test Technicians; Geophysical Data Technicians; Helpers—Extraction Workers; Industrial Truck and Tractor Operators; Logging Equipment Operators; Mechanical Engineering Technicians; Park Naturalists; Range Managers; Recreation Workers; Refuse and Recyclable Material Collectors; Rotary Drill

E

Operators, Oil and Gas; Service Unit Operators, Oil, Gas, and Mining; Soil and Water Conservationists; Wellhead Pumpers; Zoologists and Wildlife Biologists; others.

**Skills**—No data available.

**Work Environment:** No data available.

# Epidemiologists

- ❈ Annual Earnings: $63,010
- ❈ Earnings Growth Potential: Low (32.8%)
- ❈ Growth: 15.1%
- ❈ Annual Job Openings: 170
- ❈ Self-Employed: 2.5%

**Considerations for Job Outlook:** Heightened awareness of bioterrorism and rare but infectious diseases are expected to spur employment growth for these workers. Excellent opportunities are expected.

**Investigate and describe the determinants and distribution of disease, disability, and other health outcomes and develop the means for prevention and control.** Monitor and report incidents of infectious diseases to local and state health agencies. Plan and direct studies to investigate human or animal disease, preventive methods, and treatments for disease. Communicate research findings on various types of diseases to health practitioners, policy makers, and the public. Provide expertise in the design, management, and evaluation of study protocols and health status questionnaires, sample selection, and analysis. Oversee public health programs, including statistical analysis, health care planning, surveillance systems, and public health improvement. Investigate diseases or parasites to determine cause and risk factors, progress, life cycle, or mode of transmission. Educate healthcare workers, patients, and the public about infectious and communicable diseases, including disease transmission and prevention. Conduct research to develop methodologies, instrumentation, and procedures for medical application, analyzing data and presenting findings. Identify and analyze public health issues related to foodborne parasitic diseases and their impact on public policies or scientific studies or surveys. Supervise professional, technical, and clerical personnel. Plan, administer, and evaluate health safety standards and programs to improve public health, conferring with health department, industry personnel, physicians, and others. Prepare and analyze samples to study effects of drugs, gases, pesticides, or microorganisms on cell structure and tissue. Consult with and advise physicians, educators, researchers, government health officials, and others regarding medical applications of sciences such as physics, biology, and chemistry. Teach principles of medicine and medical and laboratory procedures to physicians, residents, students, and technicians. Standardize drug dosages, methods of immunization, and procedures for manufacture of drugs and medicinal compounds.

**Education/Training Required:** Master's degree. **Education and Training Programs:** Cell/Cellular Biology and Histology; Epidemiology; Medical Science. **Knowledge/Courses**—Biology, Medicine and Dentistry, Sociology and Anthropology, Geography, Mathematics, Education and Training.

**Personality Type:** Investigative-Social. **Career Clusters:** 10 Human Services; 15 Science, Technology, Engineering, and Mathematics. **Career Pathways:** 10.2 Counseling and Mental Health Services; 15.2 Science and Mathematics. **Other Jobs in These Pathways:** Architectural and Engineering Managers; Biofuels/Biodiesel Technology and Product Development Managers; Biologists; Chemists; Clergy; Clinical Psychologists; Clinical Research Coordinators; Community and Social Service Specialists, All Other; Counseling Psychologists; Dietitians and Nutritionists; Directors, Religious Activities and Education; Education, Training, and Library Workers, All Other; Geoscientists, Except Hydrologists and Geographers; Health Educators; Healthcare Social Workers; Medical Scientists, Except Epidemiologists; Mental Health and Substance Abuse Social Workers; Mental Health Counselors; Music Directors; Natural Sciences Managers; Operations Research Analysts; Recreation Workers; School Psychologists; Substance Abuse and Behavioral Disorder Counselors; Water Resource Specialists; others.

**Skills**—Science, Operations Analysis, Mathematics, Reading Comprehension, Systems Analysis, Systems Evaluation, Complex Problem Solving, Active Learning.

**Work Environment:** Indoors; sitting.

# Excavating and Loading Machine and Dragline Operators

- ❈ Annual Earnings: $36,920
- ❈ Earnings Growth Potential: Low (33.1%)
- ❈ Growth: 8.6%
- ❈ Annual Job Openings: 2,850
- ❈ Self-Employed: 15.9%

**Considerations for Job Outlook:** Improvements in technology are expected to increase productivity, holding employment stable. Good job prospects are expected from the need to replace the many workers leaving these occupations.

**Operate or tend machinery equipped with scoops, shovels, or buckets to excavate and load loose materials.** Move levers, depress foot pedals, and turn dials to operate power machinery such as power shovels, stripping shovels, scraper loaders, and backhoes. Set up and inspect equipment prior to operation. Observe hand signals, grade stakes, and other markings when operating machines so that work can be performed to specifications. Become familiar with digging plans, with machine capabilities and limitations, and with efficient and safe digging procedures in a given application. Operate machinery to perform activities such as backfilling excavations, vibrating or breaking rock or concrete, and making winter roads. Lubricate, adjust, and repair machinery and replace parts such as gears, bearings, and bucket teeth. Create and maintain inclines and ramps. Handle slides, mud, and pit cleanings and maintenance. Move materials over short distances, such as around a construction site, factory, or warehouse. Measure and verify levels of rock, gravel, bases, and other excavated material. Receive written or oral instructions regarding material movement or excavation. Adjust dig face angles for varying overburden depths and set lengths. Drive machines to work sites. Perform manual labor, such as shoveling materials by hand, to prepare or finish sites. Direct ground workers engaged in activities such as moving stakes or markers or changing positions of towers. Direct workers engaged in placing blocks and outriggers to prevent capsizing of machines used to lift heavy loads.

**Education/Training Required:** Moderate-term on-the-job training. **Education and Training Program:** Construction/Heavy Equipment/Earthmoving Equipment Operation. **Knowledge/Courses**—Building and Construction, Mechanical, Transportation, Production and Processing, Public Safety and Security, Engineering and Technology.

**Personality Type:** Realistic. **Career Cluster:** 02 Architecture and Construction. **Career Pathway:** 2.2 Construction. **Other Jobs in This Pathway:** Brickmasons and Blockmasons; Cement Masons and Concrete Finishers; Construction and Building Inspectors; Construction Carpenters; Construction Laborers; Construction Managers; Cost Estimators; Drywall and Ceiling Tile Installers; Electrical Power-Line Installers and Repairers; Electricians; Engineering Technicians, Except Drafters, All Other; First-Line Supervisors of Construction Trades and Extraction Workers; Heating and Air Conditioning Mechanics and Installers; Helpers—Carpenters; Helpers—Electricians; Helpers—Pipelayers, Plumbers, Pipefitters, and Steamfitters; Highway

Maintenance Workers; Operating Engineers and Other Construction Equipment Operators; Painters, Construction and Maintenance; Pipe Fitters and Steamfitters; Plumbers; Refrigeration Mechanics and Installers; Roofers; Rough Carpenters; Solar Energy Installation Managers; others.

**Skills**—Repairing, Equipment Maintenance, Operation and Control, Equipment Selection, Troubleshooting, Operation Monitoring, Quality Control Analysis, Coordination.

**Work Environment:** Outdoors; sitting; using hands; repetitive motions; noise; very hot or cold; contaminants; whole-body vibration; hazardous equipment.

# Executive Secretaries and Executive Administrative Assistants

- ❋ Annual Earnings: $43,520
- ❋ Earnings Growth Potential: Low (34.0%)
- ❋ Growth: 12.8%
- ❋ Annual Job Openings: 41,920
- ❋ Self-Employed: 1.3%

**Considerations for Job Outlook:** Projected employment growth varies by occupational specialty. Faster-than-average growth is expected for medical secretaries and legal secretaries; average growth for executive secretaries and administrative assistants; and slower than average growth for secretaries other than legal, medical, or executive, who account for most of the workers in these specialties. Many opportunities are expected.

**Provide high-level administrative support by conducting research; preparing statistical reports; handling information requests; and performing clerical functions such as preparing correspondence, receiving visitors, arranging conference calls, and scheduling meetings. May also train and supervise lower-level clerical staff.** Manage and maintain executives' schedules. Prepare invoices, reports, memos, letters, financial statements, and other documents, using word-processing, spreadsheet, database, or presentation software. Open, sort, and distribute incoming correspondence, including faxes and e-mail. Read and analyze incoming memos, submissions, and reports to determine their significance and plan their distribution. File and retrieve corporate documents, records, and reports. Greet visitors and determine whether they should be given access to specific individuals. Prepare responses to correspondence containing routine inquiries. Perform general office duties such as ordering supplies, maintaining records management systems, and performing basic bookkeeping work. Prepare agendas and make arrangements for committee, board, and other meetings. Make travel arrangements for executives. Conduct research, compile data, and prepare papers for consideration and presentation by executives, committees, and boards of directors. Compile, transcribe, and distribute minutes of meetings. Attend meetings to record minutes. Coordinate and direct office services, such as records and budget preparation, personnel, and housekeeping, to aid executives. Meet with individuals, special-interest groups, and others on behalf of executives, committees, and boards of directors. Set up and oversee administrative policies and procedures for offices or organizations. Supervise and train other clerical staff. Review operating practices and procedures to determine whether improvements can be made in areas such as workflow, reporting procedures, or expenditures. Interpret administrative and operating policies and procedures for employees.

**Education/Training Required:** Work experience in a related occupation. **Education and Training Programs:** Administrative Assistant and Secretarial Science, General; Executive Assistant/Executive Secretary Training; Medical Administrative/Executive Assistant and Medical Secretary Training. **Knowledge/Courses**—Clerical, Personnel and Human Resources.

**Personality Type:** Conventional-Enterprising. **Career Clusters:** 04 Business, Management, and Administration; 08 Health Science. **Career Pathways:** 4.6 Administrative and Information Support; 8.3 Health Informatics. **Other Jobs in These Pathways:** Customer Service Representatives; Data Entry Keyers; Dispatchers, Except Police, Fire, and Ambulance; Engineers, All Other; File Clerks; First-Line Supervisors of Office and Administrative Support Workers; Information and Record Clerks, All Other; Insurance Claims Clerks; Insurance Policy Processing Clerks; Interviewers, Except Eligibility and Loan; Medical and Health Services Managers; Medical Assistants; Medical Records and Health Information Technicians; Medical Secretaries; Office and Administrative Support Workers, All Other; Office Clerks, General; Order Clerks; Patient Representatives; Physical Therapists; Postal Service Mail Carriers; Postal Service Mail Sorters, Processors, and Processing Machine Operators; Public Relations Specialists; Receptionists and Information Clerks; Secretaries and Administrative Assistants, Except Legal, Medical, and Executive; Shipping, Receiving, and Traffic Clerks; others.

**Skills**—Service Orientation, Programming, Active Listening, Writing, Speaking, Time Management, Reading Comprehension, Monitoring.

**Work Environment:** Indoors; sitting; repetitive motions; noise.

# Extruding, Forming, Pressing, and Compacting Machine Setters, Operators, and Tenders

- ❁ Annual Earnings: $31,210
- ❁ Earnings Growth Potential: Low (33.1%)
- ❁ Growth: 15.0%
- ❁ Annual Job Openings: 2,960
- ❁ Self-Employed: 0.0%

**Considerations for Job Outlook:** Faster-than-average employment growth is projected.

**Set up, operate, or tend machines, such as glass-forming machines, plodder machines, and tuber machines, to shape and form products such as glassware, food, rubber, soap, brick, tile, clay, wax, tobacco, or cosmetics.** Adjust machine components to regulate speeds, pressures, and temperatures and amounts, dimensions, and flow of materials or ingredients. Examine, measure, and weigh materials or products to verify conformance to standards, using measuring devices such as templates, micrometers, or scales. Monitor machine operations and observe lights and gauges to detect malfunctions. Press control buttons to activate machinery and equipment. Turn controls to adjust machine functions, such as regulating air pressure, creating vacuums, and adjusting coolant flow. Review work orders, specifications, or instructions to determine materials, ingredients, procedures, components, settings, and adjustments for extruding, forming, pressing, or compacting machines. Select and install machine components such as dies, molds, and cutters according to specifications, using hand tools and measuring devices. Record and maintain production data such as meter readings and quantities, types, and dimensions of materials produced. Notify supervisors when extruded filaments fail to meet standards. Synchronize speeds of sections of machines when producing products involving several steps or processes. Feed products into machines by hand or conveyor. Clear jams and remove defective or substandard materials or products. Move materials, supplies, components, and finished products between storage and work areas, using work aids such as racks, hoists, and handtrucks.

Swab molds with solutions to prevent products from sticking. Complete work tickets and place them with products. Activate machines to shape or form products such as candy bars, light bulbs, balloons, or insulation panels. Remove molds, mold components, and feeder tubes from machinery after production is complete. Remove materials or products from molds or from extruding, forming, pressing, or compacting machines and stack or store them for additional processing.

**Education/Training Required:** Moderate-term on-the-job training. **Education and Training Programs:** No related CIP programs; this job is learned through informal moderate-term on-the-job training. **Knowledge/Courses**—Production and Processing, Mechanical.

**Personality Type:** Realistic-Conventional-Investigative. **Career Cluster:** 13 Manufacturing. **Career Pathway:** 13.1 Production. **Other Jobs in This Pathway:** Assemblers and Fabricators, All Other; Cabinetmakers and Bench Carpenters; Coating, Painting, and Spraying Machine Setters, Operators, and Tenders; Computer-Controlled Machine Tool Operators, Metal and Plastic; Cost Estimators; Cutting, Punching, and Press Machine Setters, Operators, and Tenders, Metal and Plastic; First-Line Supervisors of Mechanics, Installers, and Repairers; First-Line Supervisors of Production and Operating Workers; Geothermal Technicians; Helpers—Production Workers; Machine Feeders and Offbearers; Machinists; Mixing and Blending Machine Setters, Operators, and Tenders; Molding, Coremaking, and Casting Machine Setters, Operators, and Tenders, Metal and Plastic; Packaging and Filling Machine Operators and Tenders; Packers and Packagers, Hand; Paper Goods Machine Setters, Operators, and Tenders; Production Workers, All Other; Recycling and Reclamation Workers; Recycling Coordinators; Sheet Metal Workers; Solderers and Brazers; Structural Metal Fabricators and Fitters; Team Assemblers; Welders, Cutters, and Welder Fitters; others.

**Skills**—Operation and Control, Repairing, Equipment Maintenance, Operation Monitoring, Equipment Selection, Installation, Troubleshooting, Quality Control Analysis.

**Work Environment:** Standing; walking and running; using hands; bending or twisting the body; repetitive motions; noise; very hot or cold; bright or inadequate lighting; contaminants; minor burns, cuts, bites, or stings.

# Farmers, Ranchers, and Other Agricultural Managers

- ❀ Annual Earnings: $60,750
- ❀ Earnings Growth Potential: Very high (51.8%)
- ❀ Growth: 5.9%
- ❀ Annual Job Openings: 6,490
- ❀ Self-Employed: 0.0%

**Considerations for Job Outlook:** As farm productivity increases and consolidation continues, a decline in the number of farmers and ranchers is expected. Agricultural managers at larger, well-financed operations should have better prospects. Small, local farming offers the best entry-level opportunities.

## Job Specialization: Aquacultural Managers

**Direct and coordinate, through subordinate supervisory personnel, activities of workers engaged in fish hatchery production for corporations, cooperatives, or other owners.** Grow fish and shellfish as cash crops or for release into freshwater or saltwater. Supervise and train aquaculture and fish hatchery support workers. Collect and record growth, production, and environmental data. Conduct and supervise stock examinations in order to identify diseases or parasites. Account for and disburse funds. Devise and participate in activities to improve fish hatching and growth rates, and to prevent disease in hatcheries. Monitor environments to ensure maintenance of optimum conditions for aquatic life. Direct and monitor trapping and spawning of fish, egg incubation, and fry rearing, applying knowledge of management and fish culturing techniques. Coordinate the selection and maintenance of brood stock. Direct and monitor the transfer of mature fish to lakes, ponds, streams, or commercial tanks. Determine, administer, and execute policies relating to operations administration and standards, and facility maintenance. Collect information regarding techniques for fish collection and fertilization, spawn incubation, and treatment of spawn and fry. Determine how to allocate resources, and how to respond to unanticipated problems such as insect infestation, drought, and fire. Operate and maintain cultivating and harvesting equipment. Confer with biologists, fish pathologists, and other fishery personnel to obtain data concerning fish habits, diseases, food, and environmental requirements. Prepare reports required by state and federal laws. Identify environmental requirements of a particular species, and select and oversee the preparation of sites for species cultivation. Scuba dive in order to inspect sea farm operations. Design and construct pens, floating stations, and collector strings or fences for sea farms.

**Education/Training Required:** Work experience plus degree. **Education and Training Program:** Aquaculture. **Knowledge/Courses**—Food Production, Biology, Engineering and Technology, Building and Construction, Chemistry, Mechanical.

**Personality Type:** Enterprising-Realistic-Conventional. **Career Cluster:** 01 Agriculture, Food, and Natural Resources. **Career Pathways:** 1.1 Food Products and Processing Systems; 1.2 Plant Systems; 1.3 Animal Systems. **Other Jobs in These Pathways:** Agricultural Technicians; Animal Trainers; Biochemists and Biophysicists; Biologists; Chemical Technicians; First-Line Supervisors of Landscaping, Lawn Service, and Groundskeeping Workers; First-Line Supervisors of Office and Administrative Support Workers; First-Line Supervisors of Retail Sales Workers; Floral Designers; Food and Tobacco Roasting, Baking, and Drying Machine Operators and Tenders; Food Batchmakers; Food Cooking Machine Operators and Tenders; Food Science Technicians; Geneticists; Graders and Sorters, Agricultural Products; Grounds Maintenance Workers, All Other; Landscaping and Groundskeeping Workers; Nonfarm Animal Caretakers; Office Machine Operators, Except Computer; Pest Control Workers; Pesticide Handlers, Sprayers, and Applicators, Vegetation; Precision Agriculture Technicians; Retail Salespersons; Tree Trimmers and Pruners; Veterinarians; others.

**Skills**—Science, Management of Financial Resources, Equipment Maintenance, Operations Analysis, Systems Analysis, Repairing, Management of Material Resources, Quality Control Analysis.

**Work Environment:** More often outdoors than indoors; standing; using hands; noise; very hot or cold; contaminants.

## Job Specialization: Farm and Ranch Managers

**Plan, direct, or coordinate the management or operation of farms, ranches, greenhouses, aquacultural operations, nurseries, timber tracts, or other agricultural establishments. May hire, train, or supervise farm workers or contract for services to carry out the day-to-day activities of the managed operation. May engage in or supervise planting, cultivating, harvesting, financial, or marketing activities.** Change processes such as drying, grading, storing,

or shipping to improve efficiency or profitability. Determine types or quantities of crops or livestock to be raised, according to factors such as market conditions, federal programs or incentives, or soil conditions. Direct crop production operations, such as planning, tilling, planting, fertilizing, cultivating, spraying, or harvesting. Direct the breeding or raising of stock, such as cattle, poultry, or honeybees, using recognized breeding practices to ensure stock improvement. Evaluate marketing or sales alternatives for farm or ranch products. Hire, train, or supervise workers engaged in planting, cultivating, irrigating, harvesting, or marketing crops, or in raising livestock. Inspect farm or ranch structures, such as buildings, fences, or roads, ordering repair or maintenance activities, as needed. Maintain financial, operational, production, or employment records for farms or ranches. Monitor activities such as irrigation, chemical application, harvesting, milking, breeding, or grading to ensure adherence to safety regulations or standards. Monitor pasture or grazing land use to ensure that livestock are properly fed or that conservation methods, such as rotational grazing, are used. Negotiate with buyers for the sale, storage, or shipment of crops or livestock. Obtain financing necessary for purchases of machinery, land, supplies, or livestock. Operate or oversee the operations of dairy farms that produce bulk milk. Operate or oversee the operations of poultry or swine farms producing meat, eggs, or breeding stock. Plan crop activities based on factors such as crop maturity or weather conditions. Prepare budgets or financial reports for farm or ranch operations. Select or purchase machinery, equipment, livestock, or supplies, such as seed, feed, fertilizer, or chemicals. Supervise the construction of farm or ranch structures, such as buildings, fences, drainage systems, wells, or roads.

**Education/Training Required:** Work experience in a related occupation. **Education and Training Program:** Farm/Farm and Ranch Management. **Knowledge/Courses**—No data available.

**Personality Type:** No data available. **Career Cluster:** 01 Agriculture, Food, and Natural Resources. **Career Pathways:** 1.2 Plant Systems; 1.3 Animal Systems. **Other Jobs in These Pathways:** Agricultural Technicians; Animal Breeders; Animal Scientists; Animal Trainers; Biochemists and Biophysicists; Biologists; Economists; Environmental Economists; Farm and Home Management Advisors; First-Line Supervisors of Landscaping, Lawn Service, and Groundskeeping Workers; First-Line Supervisors of Retail Sales Workers; Floral Designers; Food Science Technicians; Food Scientists and Technologists; Geneticists; Grounds Maintenance Workers, All Other; Landscaping and Groundskeeping Workers; Nonfarm Animal Caretakers; Pesticide Handlers, Sprayers, and Applicators, Vegetation; Precision

Agriculture Technicians; Retail Salespersons; Soil and Plant Scientists; Tree Trimmers and Pruners; Veterinarians.

**Skills**—No data available.

**Work Environment:** No data available.

## Job Specialization: Nursery and Greenhouse Managers

**Plan, organize, direct, control, and coordinate activities of workers engaged in propagating, cultivating, and harvesting horticultural specialties, such as trees, shrubs, flowers, mushrooms, and other plants.** Manage nurseries that grow horticultural plants for sale to trade or retail customers, for display or exhibition, or for research. Identify plants as well as problems such as diseases, weeds, and insect pests. Tour work areas to observe work being done, to inspect crops, and to evaluate plant and soil conditions. Assign work schedules and duties to nursery or greenhouse staff, and supervise their work. Determine plant growing conditions, such as greenhouses, hydroponics, or natural settings, and set planting and care schedules. Apply pesticides and fertilizers to plants. Hire employees, and train them in gardening techniques. Select and purchase seeds, plant nutrients, disease control chemicals, and garden and lawn care equipment. Determine types and quantities of horticultural plants to be grown, based on budgets, projected sales volumes, and/or executive directives. Explain and enforce safety regulations and policies. Position and regulate plant irrigation systems, and program environmental and irrigation control computers. Inspect facilities and equipment for signs of disrepair, and perform necessary maintenance work. Coordinate clerical, recordkeeping, inventory, requisitioning, and marketing activities. Prepare soil for planting, and plant or transplant seeds, bulbs, and cuttings. Confer with horticultural personnel in order to plan facility renovations or additions. Cut and prune trees, shrubs, flowers, and plants. Provide information to customers on the care of trees, shrubs, flowers, plants, and lawns. Construct structures and accessories such as greenhouses and benches. Negotiate contracts such as those for land leases or tree purchases. Graft plants.

**Education/Training Required:** Work experience plus degree. **Education and Training Programs:** Greenhouse Operations and Management; Landscaping and Groundskeeping; Ornamental Horticulture; Plant Nursery Operations and Management. **Knowledge/Courses**—Biology, Production and Processing, Sales and Marketing, Chemistry, Personnel and Human Resources, Design.

**Personality Type:** Enterprising-Realistic-Conventional. **Career Cluster:** 01 Agriculture, Food, and Natural Resources. **Career Pathway:** 1.2 Plant Systems. **Other Jobs in This Pathway:** Agricultural Technicians; Animal Scientists; Biochemists and Biophysicists; Biologists; Economists; Environmental Economists; Farm and Home Management Advisors; First-Line Supervisors of Landscaping, Lawn Service, and Groundskeeping Workers; First-Line Supervisors of Retail Sales Workers; Floral Designers; Food Science Technicians; Food Scientists and Technologists; Geneticists; Grounds Maintenance Workers, All Other; Landscaping and Groundskeeping Workers; Pesticide Handlers, Sprayers, and Applicators, Vegetation; Precision Agriculture Technicians; Retail Salespersons; Soil and Plant Scientists; Tree Trimmers and Pruners.

**Skills**—Management of Material Resources, Management of Financial Resources, Science, Management of Personnel Resources, Instructing, Negotiation, Operation and Control, Persuasion.

**Work Environment:** More often outdoors than indoors; standing; walking and running; kneeling, crouching, stooping, or crawling; noise; very hot or cold; contaminants; hazardous conditions; minor burns, cuts, bites, or stings.

## Film and Video Editors

- Annual Earnings: $50,930
- Earnings Growth Potential: High (49.0%)
- Growth: 11.9%
- Annual Job Openings: 930
- Self-Employed: 26.3%

**Considerations for Job Outlook:** Projected employment growth will be driven by increases in the motion picture and video industry; however, that growth should be tempered by automation in broadcasting. Competition is expected to be keen.

**Edit motion picture soundtracks, film, and video.** Cut shot sequences to different angles at specific points in scenes, making each individual cut as fluid and seamless as possible. Study scripts to become familiar with production concepts and requirements. Edit films and videotapes to insert music, dialogue, and sound effects; to arrange films into sequences; and to correct errors, using editing equipment. Select and combine the most effective shots of each scene to form a logical and smoothly running story. Mark frames where a particular shot or piece of sound is to begin or end. Determine the specific audio and visual effects and music necessary to complete films. Verify key numbers and time codes on materials. Organize and string together raw footage into a continuous whole according to scripts or the instructions of directors and producers. Review assembled films or edited videotapes on screens or monitors to determine if corrections are necessary. Program computerized graphic effects. Review footage sequence by sequence to become familiar with it before assembling it into a final product. Set up and operate computer editing systems, electronic titling systems, video switching equipment, and digital video effects units to produce a final product. Record needed sounds or obtain them from sound effects libraries. Confer with producers and directors concerning layout or editing approaches needed to increase dramatic or entertainment value of productions. Manipulate plot, score, sound, and graphics to make the parts into a continuous whole, working closely with people in audio, visual, music, optical, or special effects departments. Supervise and coordinate activities of workers engaged in film editing, assembling, and recording activities. Trim film segments to specified lengths and reassemble segments in sequences that present stories with maximum effect. Develop post-production models for films. Piece sounds together to develop film soundtracks.

**Education/Training Required:** Bachelor's degree. **Education and Training Programs:** Audiovisual Communications Technologies/Technicians, Other; Cinematography and Film/Video Production; Communications Technology/Technician; Photojournalism; Radio and Television; Radio and Television Broadcasting Technology/Technician. **Knowledge/Courses**—Communications and Media, Fine Arts, Computers and Electronics, Production and Processing, Telecommunications, Sales and Marketing.

**Personality Type:** Artistic-Enterprising-Investigative. **Career Cluster:** 03 Arts, Audio/Video Technology, and Communications. **Career Pathways:** 3.1 Audio and Video Technology and Film; 3.5 Journalism and Broadcasting; 3.6 Telecommunications. **Other Jobs in These Pathways:** Agents and Business Managers of Artists, Performers, and Athletes; Artists and Related Workers, All Other; Audio and Video Equipment Technicians; Broadcast Technicians; Camera Operators, Television, Video, and Motion Picture; Commercial and Industrial Designers; Copy Writers; Directors- Stage, Motion Pictures, Television, and Radio; Editors; Electronic Home Entertainment Equipment Installers and Repairers; Fine Artists, Including Painters, Sculptors, and Illustrators; Graphic Designers; Managers, All Other; Media and Communication Workers, All Other; Multimedia Artists and Animators; Photographers; Producers; Program Directors; Public Relations Specialists; Radio and Television Announcers; Reporters and Correspondents; Talent

Directors; Technical Directors/Managers; Technical Writers; Telecommunications Equipment Installers and Repairers, Except Line Installers; others.

**Skills**—Technology Design, Programming, Time Management, Active Listening, Systems Evaluation, Systems Analysis, Persuasion, Operations Analysis.

**Work Environment:** Indoors; sitting; using hands; repetitive motions.

# Financial Analysts

- ❊ Annual Earnings: $74,350
- ❊ Earnings Growth Potential: Medium (40.2%)
- ❊ Growth: 19.8%
- ❊ Annual Job Openings: 9,520
- ❊ Self-Employed: 4.6%

**Considerations for Job Outlook:** As investments become more numerous and complex, these workers will be needed for their expertise. Keen competition for openings is expected; job seekers with a graduate degree and certification should have the best opportunities.

**Conduct quantitative analyses of information affecting investment programs of public or private institutions.** Assemble spreadsheets and draw charts and graphs used to illustrate technical reports, using computer. Analyze financial information to produce forecasts of business, industry, and economic conditions for use in making investment decisions. Maintain knowledge and stay abreast of developments in the fields of industrial technology, business, finance, and economic theory. Interpret data affecting investment programs, such as price, yield, stability, future trends in investment risks, and economic influences. Monitor fundamental economic, industrial, and corporate developments through the analysis of information obtained from financial publications and services, investment banking firms, government agencies, trade publications, company sources, and personal interviews. Recommend investments and investment timing to companies, investment firm staff, or the investing public. Determine the prices at which securities should be syndicated and offered to the public. Prepare plans of action for investment based on financial analyses. Evaluate and compare the relative quality of various securities in a given industry. Present oral and written reports on general economic trends, individual corporations, and entire industries. Contact brokers and purchase investments for companies according to company policy. Collaborate with investment bankers to attract new corporate clients to securities firms.

**Education/Training Required:** Bachelor's degree. **Education and Training Programs:** Accounting and Business/Management; Accounting and Finance; Finance, General. **Knowledge/Courses**—Economics and Accounting, Mathematics, Law and Government, Clerical, Administration and Management, English Language.

**Personality Type:** Conventional-Investigative-Enterprising. **Career Clusters:** 04 Business, Management, and Administration; 06 Finance. **Career Pathways:** 4.2 Business, Financial Management, and Accounting; 6.1 Financial and Investment Planning; 6.2 Business Financial Management. **Other Jobs in These Pathways:** Accountants; Auditors; Billing and Posting Clerks; Billing, Cost, and Rate Clerks; Bookkeeping, Accounting, and Auditing Clerks; Brownfield Redevelopment Specialists and Site Managers; Compliance Managers; Financial Managers, Branch or Department; Financial Quantitative Analysts; Investment Fund Managers; Loss Prevention Managers; Managers, All Other; Payroll and Timekeeping Clerks; Personal Financial Advisors; Regulatory Affairs Managers; Sales Agents, Financial Services; Sales Agents, Securities and Commodities; Securities and Commodities Traders; Securities, Commodities, and Financial Services Sales Agents; Security Managers; Statement Clerks; Supply Chain Managers; Treasurers and Controllers; Wind Energy Operations Managers; Wind Energy Project Managers; others.

**Skills**—Systems Analysis, Mathematics, Systems Evaluation, Management of Financial Resources, Operations Analysis, Writing, Active Learning, Judgment and Decision Making.

**Work Environment:** Indoors; sitting.

# Financial Examiners

- ❋ Annual Earnings: $74,940
- ❋ Earnings Growth Potential: High (42.4%)
- ❋ Growth: 41.2%
- ❋ Annual Job Openings: 1,600
- ❋ Self-Employed: 0.0%

**Considerations for Job Outlook:** Much-faster-than-average employment growth is projected.

**Enforce or ensure compliance with laws and regulations governing financial and securities institutions and financial and real estate transactions. May examine, verify correctness of, or establish authenticity of records.** Investigate activities of institutions in order to enforce laws and regulations and to ensure legality of transactions and operations or financial solvency. Review and analyze new, proposed, or revised laws, regulations, policies, and procedures in order to interpret their meaning and determine their impact. Plan, supervise, and review work of assigned subordinates. Recommend actions to ensure compliance with laws and regulations or to protect solvency of institutions. Examine the minutes of meetings of directors, stockholders, and committees in order to investigate the specific authority extended at various levels of management. Prepare reports, exhibits, and other supporting schedules that detail an institution's safety and soundness, compliance with laws and regulations, and recommended solutions to questionable financial conditions. Review balance sheets, operating income and expense accounts, and loan documentation in order to confirm institution assets and liabilities. Review audit reports of internal and external auditors in order to monitor adequacy of scope of reports or to discover specific weaknesses in internal routines. Train other examiners in the financial examination process. Establish guidelines for procedures and policies that comply with new and revised regulations and direct their implementation. Direct and participate in formal and informal meetings with bank directors, trustees, senior management, counsels, outside accountants, and consultants in order to gather information and discuss findings. Verify and inspect cash reserves, assigned collateral, and bank-owned securities in order to check internal control procedures. Review applications for mergers, acquisitions, establishment of new institutions, acceptance in Federal Reserve System, or registration of securities sales in order to determine their public interest value and conformance to regulations and recommend acceptance or rejection.

**Education/Training Required:** Bachelor's degree. **Education and Training Programs:** Accounting; Taxation. **Knowledge/Courses**—Economics and Accounting, Law and Government, Clerical, Mathematics, English Language, Administration and Management.

**Personality Type:** Enterprising-Conventional. **Career Clusters:** 04 Business, Management, and Administration; 07 Government and Public Administration. **Career Pathways:** 4.2 Business, Financial Management, and Accounting; 7.5 Revenue and Taxation. **Other Jobs in These Pathways:** Accountants; Auditors; Billing and Posting Clerks; Billing, Cost, and Rate Clerks; Bookkeeping, Accounting, and Auditing Clerks; Brokerage Clerks; Brownfield Redevelopment Specialists and Site Managers; Compliance Managers; Credit Analysts; Financial Analysts; Financial Managers, Branch or Department; Investment Fund Managers; Logistics Managers; Loss Prevention Managers; Managers, All Other; Payroll and Timekeeping Clerks; Regulatory Affairs Managers; Security Managers; Statement Clerks; Supply

Chain Managers; Tax Examiners and Collectors, and Revenue Agents; Tax Preparers; Treasurers and Controllers; Wind Energy Operations Managers; Wind Energy Project Managers; others.

**Skills**—Management of Personnel Resources, Systems Evaluation, Active Learning, Learning Strategies, Systems Analysis, Mathematics, Programming, Writing.

**Work Environment:** Indoors; sitting.

# Financial Managers

- ❋ Annual Earnings: $103,910
- ❋ Earnings Growth Potential: High (46.0%)
- ❋ Growth: 7.6%
- ❋ Annual Job Openings: 13,820
- ❋ Self-Employed: 5.3%

**Considerations for Job Outlook:** Business expansion and globalization will require financial expertise, which is expected to drive employment growth for these managers. Job growth, however, is expected to be tempered by mergers and downsizing. Keen competition is expected.

## Job Specialization: Financial Managers, Branch or Department

**Direct and coordinate financial activities of workers in a branch, office, or department of an establishment, such as branch bank, brokerage firm, risk and insurance department, or credit department.** Establish and maintain relationships with individual and business customers and provide assistance with problems these customers may encounter. Examine, evaluate, and process loan applications. Plan, direct, and coordinate the activities of workers in branches, offices, or departments of such establishments as branch banks, brokerage firms, risk and insurance departments, or credit departments. Oversee the flow of cash and financial instruments. Recruit staff members and oversee training programs. Network within communities to find and attract new business. Approve or reject, or coordinate the approval and rejection of, lines of credit and commercial, real estate, and personal loans. Prepare financial and regulatory reports required by laws, regulations, and boards of directors. Establish procedures for custody and control of assets, records, loan collateral, and securities in order to ensure safekeeping. Review collection reports to determine the status of collections and the amounts of outstanding balances. Prepare operational and risk reports for management

analysis. Evaluate financial reporting systems, accounting and collection procedures, and investment activities and make recommendations for changes to procedures, operating systems, budgets, and other financial control functions. Plan, direct, and coordinate risk and insurance programs of establishments to control risks and losses. Submit delinquent accounts to attorneys or outside agencies for collection. Communicate with stockholders and other investors to provide information and to raise capital. Evaluate data pertaining to costs in order to plan budgets. Analyze and classify risks and investments to determine their potential impacts on companies. Review reports of securities transactions and price lists in order to analyze market conditions. Develop and analyze information to assess the current and future financial status of firms.

**Education/Training Required:** Work experience plus degree. **Education and Training Programs:** Accounting and Business/Management; Accounting and Finance; Credit Management; Finance and Financial Management Services, Other; Finance, General; International Finance; Public Finance. **Knowledge/Courses**—Economics and Accounting, Sales and Marketing, Personnel and Human Resources, Clerical, Customer and Personal Service, Mathematics.

**Personality Type:** Enterprising-Conventional. **Career Clusters:** 04 Business, Management, and Administration; 06 Finance. **Career Pathways:** 4.2 Business, Financial Management, and Accounting; 6.1 Financial and Investment Planning. **Other Jobs in These Pathways:** Accountants; Auditors; Billing and Posting Clerks; Billing, Cost, and Rate Clerks; Bookkeeping, Accounting, and Auditing Clerks; Brownfield Redevelopment Specialists and Site Managers; Compliance Managers; Financial Analysts; Financial Quantitative Analysts; Investment Fund Managers; Loss Prevention Managers; Managers, All Other; Payroll and Timekeeping Clerks; Personal Financial Advisors; Regulatory Affairs Managers; Sales Agents, Financial Services; Sales Agents, Securities and Commodities; Securities and Commodities Traders; Securities, Commodities, and Financial Services Sales Agents; Security Managers; Statement Clerks; Supply Chain Managers; Treasurers and Controllers; Wind Energy Operations Managers; Wind Energy Project Managers; others.

**Skills**—Management of Financial Resources, Management of Personnel Resources, Persuasion, Service Orientation, Systems Evaluation, Learning Strategies, Time Management, Monitoring.

**Work Environment:** Indoors; sitting.

# Job Specialization: Treasurers and Controllers

**Direct financial activities, such as planning, procurement, and investments, for all or part of an organization.** Prepare and file annual tax returns or prepare financial information so that outside accountants can complete tax returns. Prepare or direct preparation of financial statements, business activity reports, financial position forecasts, annual budgets, and/or reports required by regulatory agencies. Supervise employees performing financial reporting, accounting, billing, collections, payroll, and budgeting duties. Delegate authority for the receipt, disbursement, banking, protection, and custody of funds, securities, and financial instruments. Maintain current knowledge of organizational policies and procedures, federal and state policies and directives, and current accounting standards. Conduct or coordinate audits of company accounts and financial transactions to ensure compliance with state and federal requirements and statutes. Receive and record requests for disbursements; authorize disbursements in accordance with policies and procedures. Monitor financial activities and details such as reserve levels to ensure that all legal and regulatory requirements are met. Monitor and evaluate the performance of accounting and other financial staff; recommend and implement personnel actions such as promotions and dismissals. Develop and maintain relationships with banking, insurance, and non-organizational accounting personnel in order to facilitate financial activities. Coordinate and direct the financial planning, budgeting, procurement, or investment activities of all or part of an organization. Develop internal control policies, guidelines, and procedures for activities such as budget administration, cash and credit management, and accounting. Analyze the financial details of past, present, and expected operations in order to identify development opportunities and areas where improvement is needed. Advise management on short-term and long-term financial objectives, policies, and actions.

**Education/Training Required:** Work experience plus degree. **Education and Training Programs:** Accounting and Business/Management; Accounting and Finance; Credit Management; Finance and Financial Management Services, Other; Finance, General; International Finance; Public Finance. **Knowledge/Courses**—Economics and Accounting, Administration and Management, Personnel and Human Resources, Law and Government, Mathematics, English Language.

**Personality Type:** Conventional-Enterprising. **Career Clusters:** 04 Business, Management, and Administration; 06 Finance. **Career Pathways:** 4.2 Business, Financial Management, and Accounting; 6.1 Financial and Investment Planning. **Other Jobs in These Pathways:** Accountants; Auditors; Billing and Posting Clerks; Billing, Cost, and Rate Clerks; Bookkeeping, Accounting, and Auditing Clerks; Brownfield Redevelopment Specialists and Site Managers; Compliance Managers; Financial Analysts; Financial Managers, Branch or Department; Financial Quantitative Analysts; Investment Fund Managers; Loss Prevention Managers; Managers, All Other; Payroll and Timekeeping Clerks; Personal Financial Advisors; Regulatory Affairs Managers; Sales Agents, Financial Services; Sales Agents, Securities and Commodities; Securities and Commodities Traders; Securities, Commodities, and Financial Services Sales Agents; Security Managers; Statement Clerks; Supply Chain Managers; Wind Energy Operations Managers; Wind Energy Project Managers; others.

**Skills**—Management of Financial Resources, Management of Material Resources, Systems Analysis, Operations Analysis, Judgment and Decision Making, Systems Evaluation, Management of Personnel Resources, Mathematics.

**Work Environment:** Indoors; sitting.

# Financial Specialists, All Other

* Annual Earnings: $60,980
* Earnings Growth Potential: High (41.0%)
* Growth: 10.5%
* Annual Job Openings: 4,320
* Self-Employed: 0.9%

**Considerations for Job Outlook:** About average employment growth is projected.

**This occupation includes all financial specialists not listed separately.** Because this is a highly diverse occupation, no data is available for some information topics.

**Education/Training Required:** Bachelor's degree. **Education and Training Program:** Finance and Financial Management Services, Other.

**Career Cluster:** 06 Finance. **Career Pathway:** 6.1 Financial and Investment Planning. **Other Jobs in This Pathway:** Budget Analysts; Credit Analysts; Financial Analysts; Financial Managers, Branch or Department; Financial Quantitative Analysts; Fraud Examiners, Investigators and Analysts; Investment Underwriters; Loan Counselors; Personal Financial Advisors; Risk Management Specialists; Sales Agents, Financial Services; Sales Agents, Securities and

Commodities; Securities and Commodities Traders; Securities, Commodities, and Financial Services Sales Agents; Treasurers and Controllers.

## Job Specialization: Financial Quantitative Analysts

**Develop quantitative financial products used to inform individuals and financial institutions engaged in saving, lending, investing, borrowing, or managing risk. Investigate methods for financial analysis to create mathematical models used to develop improved analytical tools and advanced financial investment instruments.** Write requirements documentation for use by software developers. Provide application or analytical support to researchers and traders on such issues as valuations and data. Identify, track, and maintain metrics for trading system operations. Collaborate in the development and testing of new analytical software to ensure compliance with user requirements, specification, or scope. Research new products or analytics to determine their usefulness. Maintain and modify all analytic models in use. Produce written summaries of research results. Interpret results of analytical procedures. Develop core analytical capabilities or model libraries, using advanced statistical, quantitative, and econometric techniques. Define and recommend model specifications or data collection methods. Consult financial industry personnel, such as traders, to determine the need for new or improved analytical applications. Confer with other financial engineers and analysts to understand trading strategies, market dynamics, and trading system performance to inform development of quantitative techniques. Collaborate with product development teams to research, model, validate, or implement quantitative structured solutions for new or expanded markets. Research and develop analytical tools to address issues such as portfolio construction and optimization, performance measurement, attribution, profit-and-loss measurement, and pricing models. Devise or apply independent models and tools to help verify results of analytical systems. Apply mathematical and statistical techniques to address practical issues in finance, such as derivative valuation, securities trading, risk management, or financial market regulation.

**Education/Training Required:** Master's degree. **Education and Training Program:** Financial Planning and Services. **Knowledge/Courses**—No data available.

**Personality Type:** Investigative-Conventional. **Career Cluster:** 06 Finance. **Career Pathway:** 6.1 Financial and Investment Planning. **Other Jobs in This Pathway:** Budget Analysts; Credit Analysts; Financial Analysts; Financial

Managers, Branch or Department; Financial Specialists, All Other; Fraud Examiners, Investigators and Analysts; Investment Underwriters; Loan Counselors; Personal Financial Advisors; Risk Management Specialists; Sales Agents, Financial Services; Sales Agents, Securities and Commodities; Securities and Commodities Traders; Securities, Commodities, and Financial Services Sales Agents; Treasurers and Controllers.

**Skills**—No data available.

**Work Environment:** No data available.

## Job Specialization: Fraud Examiners, Investigators, and Analysts

**Obtain evidence, take statements, produce reports, and testify to findings regarding resolution of fraud allegations. May coordinate fraud detection and prevention activities.** Maintain knowledge of current events and trends in such areas as money laundering and criminal tools and techniques. Train others in fraud detection and prevention techniques. Research or evaluate new technologies for use in fraud detection systems. Prepare evidence for presentation in court. Obtain and serve subpoenas. Negotiate with responsible parties to arrange for recovery of losses due to fraud. Conduct field surveillance to gather case-related information. Arrest individuals to be charged with fraud. Testify in court regarding investigation findings. Advise businesses or agencies on ways to improve fraud detection. Review reports of suspected fraud to determine need for further investigation. Prepare written reports of investigation findings. Recommend actions in fraud cases. Lead, or participate in, fraud investigation teams. Interview witnesses or suspects and take statements. Design, implement, or maintain fraud detection tools or procedures. Gather financial documents related to investigations. Evaluate business operations to identify risk areas for fraud. Document all investigative activities. Create and maintain logs, records, or databases of information about fraudulent activity. Coordinate investigative efforts with law enforcement officers and attorneys. Conduct in-depth investigations of suspicious financial activity, such as suspected money-laundering efforts. Analyze financial data to detect irregularities in areas such as billing trends, financial relationships, and regulatory compliance procedures.

**Education/Training Required:** Work experience plus degree. **Education and Training Program:** Financial Forensics and Fraud Investigation. **Knowledge/Courses**— Law and Government, Economics and Accounting, Psychology, Personnel and Human Resources, Sociology and Anthropology, Public Safety and Security.

**Personality Type:** Enterprising-Investigative-Conventional. **Career Cluster:** 06 Finance. **Career Pathway:** 6.1 Financial and Investment Planning. **Other Jobs in This Pathway:** Budget Analysts; Credit Analysts; Financial Analysts; Financial Managers, Branch or Department; Financial Quantitative Analysts; Financial Specialists, All Other; Investment Underwriters; Loan Counselors; Personal Financial Advisors; Risk Management Specialists; Sales Agents, Financial Services; Sales Agents, Securities and Commodities; Securities and Commodities Traders; Securities, Commodities, and Financial Services Sales Agents; Treasurers and Controllers.

**Skills**—Writing, Negotiation, Active Listening, Speaking, Reading Comprehension, Systems Evaluation, Systems Analysis, Management of Financial Resources.

**Work Environment:** Indoors; sitting.

## Job Specialization: Investment Underwriters

**Intermediate between corporate issuers of securities and clients regarding private equity investments. Underwrite the issuance of securities to provide capital for client growth. Negotiate and structure the terms of mergers and acquisitions.** Structure marketing campaigns to find buyers for new securities. Supervise, train, or mentor junior team members. Assess companies as investments for clients by examining company facilities. Prepare all materials for transactions and execution of deals. Perform securities valuation and pricing. Determine desirability of deals to develop solutions to financial problems or to assess the financial and capital impact of transactions, using financial modeling. Develop and maintain client relationships. Evaluate capital needs of clients and assess market conditions to inform structuring of financial packages. Create client presentations of plan details. Coordinate due diligence processes and the negotiation and execution of purchase and sale agreements. Collaborate on projects with teams of other professionals, such as lawyers, accountants, and public relations experts. Confer with clients to restructure debt, refinance debt, or raise new debt. Analyze financial and operational performance of companies facing financial difficulties to identify and recommend remedies. Advise clients on aspects of capitalization, such as amounts, sources, and timing. Intermediate between corporate issuers of new securities and the general public. Structure and negotiate deals, such as corporate mergers, sales, and acquisitions. Arrange financing of deals from sources such as financial institutions, agencies, and public or private companies.

**Education/Training Required:** Work experience in a related occupation. **Education and Training Program:** Financial Planning and Services. **Knowledge/Courses**—No data available.

**Personality Type:** Conventional-Enterprising. **Career Cluster:** 06 Finance. **Career Pathway:** 6.1 Financial and Investment Planning. **Other Jobs in This Pathway:** Budget Analysts; Credit Analysts; Financial Analysts; Financial Managers, Branch or Department; Financial Quantitative Analysts; Financial Specialists, All Other; Fraud Examiners, Investigators and Analysts; Loan Counselors; Personal Financial Advisors; Risk Management Specialists; Sales Agents, Financial Services; Sales Agents, Securities and Commodities; Securities and Commodities Traders; Securities, Commodities, and Financial Services Sales Agents; Treasurers and Controllers.

**Skills**—No data available.

**Work Environment:** No data available.

## Job Specialization: Risk Management Specialists

**Analyze and make decisions on risk management issues by identifying, measuring and managing operational and enterprise risks for an organization.** Provide statistical modeling advice to other departments. Review and draft risk disclosures for offer documents. Meet with clients to answer queries on such subjects as risk exposure, market scenarios, and values-at-risk calculations. Maintain input and data quality of risk management systems. Develop contingency plans to deal with emergencies. Devise scenario analyses reflecting possible severe market events. Consult financial literature to ensure use of the latest models and statistical techniques. Track, measure, and report on aspects of market risk for traded issues. Analyze new legislation to determine impact on risk exposure. Recommend ways to control or reduce risk. Produce reports and presentations that outline findings, explain risk positions, and recommend changes. Plan, and contribute to development of, risk management systems. Gather risk-related data from internal or external resources. Develop and implement risk-assessment models and methodologies. Document, and ensure communication of, key risks. Devise systems and processes to monitor validity of risk modeling outputs. Conduct statistical analyses to quantify risk, using statistical analysis software and econometric models. Identify key risks and mitigating factors of potential investments, such as asset types and values, legal and ownership structures, professional reputations, customer bases, or industry segments. Identify and analyze areas of potential risk to the assets, earning capacity, or success of organizations. Confer with traders to identify and communicate risks associated with specific trading strategies and positions.

**Education/Training Required:** Work experience plus degree. **Education and Training Program:** Financial Planning and Services. **Knowledge/Courses**—No data available.

**Personality Type:** Conventional-Enterprising-Investigative. **Career Cluster:** 06 Finance. **Career Pathway:** 6.1 Financial and Investment Planning. **Other Jobs in This Pathway:** Budget Analysts; Credit Analysts; Financial Analysts; Financial Managers, Branch or Department; Financial Quantitative Analysts; Financial Specialists, All Other; Fraud Examiners, Investigators and Analysts; Investment Underwriters; Loan Counselors; Personal Financial Advisors; Sales Agents, Financial Services; Sales Agents, Securities and Commodities; Securities and Commodities Traders; Securities, Commodities, and Financial Services Sales Agents; Treasurers and Controllers.

**Skills**—No data available.

**Work Environment:** No data available.

# Firefighters

* Annual Earnings: $45,250
* Earnings Growth Potential: High (49.1%)
* Growth: 18.5%
* Annual Job Openings: 15,280
* Self-Employed: 0.2%

**Considerations for Job Outlook:** Most job growth will stem from the conversion of volunteer fire fighting positions into paid positions. Job seekers are expected to face keen competition. Those who have completed some fire fighter education at a community college and have EMT or paramedic certification should have the best prospects.

## Job Specialization: Forest Firefighters

**Control and suppress fires in forests or vacant public land.** Maintain contact with fire dispatchers at all times to notify them of the need for additional firefighters and supplies or to detail any difficulties encountered. Rescue fire victims and administer emergency medical aid. Collaborate with other firefighters as a member of a firefighting crew. Patrol burned areas after fires to locate and eliminate hot spots that may restart fires. Extinguish flames and embers to suppress fires, using shovels or engine- or hand-driven water or chemical pumps. Fell trees, cut and clear brush, and dig trenches to create firelines, using axes, chain saws, or shovels. Maintain knowledge of current firefighting practices by participating in drills and by attending seminars, conventions, and conferences. Operate pumps connected to high-pressure hoses. Participate in physical training to maintain high levels of physical fitness. Establish water supplies, connect hoses, and direct water onto fires. Maintain fire equipment and firehouse living quarters. Inform and educate the public about fire prevention. Take action to contain any hazardous chemicals that could catch fire, leak, or spill. Organize fire caches, positioning equipment for the most effective response. Transport personnel and cargo to and from fire areas. Participate in fire prevention and inspection programs. Perform forest maintenance and improvement tasks such as cutting brush, planting trees, building trails, and marking timber. Test and maintain tools, equipment, jump gear, and parachutes to ensure readiness for fire-suppression activities. Observe forest areas from fire lookout towers to spot potential problems. Orient self in relation to fire, using compass and map, and collect supplies and equipment dropped by parachute. Serve as fully trained lead helicopter crewmember and as helispot manager. Drop weighted paper streamers from aircraft to determine the speed and direction of the wind at fire sites.

**Education/Training Required:** Long-term on-the-job training. **Education and Training Programs:** Fire Protection, Other; Fire Science/Firefighting. **Knowledge/Courses**—Geography, Building and Construction, Telecommunications, Public Safety and Security, Mechanical, Customer and Personal Service.

**Personality Type:** Realistic-Social. **Career Cluster:** 12 Law, Public Safety, Corrections, and Security. **Career Pathways:** 12.2 Emergency and Fire Management Services; 12.3 Security and Protective Services. **Other Jobs in These Pathways:** Animal Control Workers; Correctional Officers and Jailers; Crossing Guards; Fire Inspectors; Fire Investigators; First-Line Supervisors of Protective Service Workers, All Other; Forest Fire Fighting and Prevention Supervisors; Forest Fire Inspectors and Prevention Specialists; Gaming Surveillance Officers and Gaming Investigators; Lifeguards, Ski Patrol, and Other Recreational Protective Service Workers; Municipal Fire Fighting and Prevention Supervisors; Municipal Firefighters; Parking Enforcement Workers; Police, Fire, and Ambulance Dispatchers; Private Detectives and Investigators; Retail Loss Prevention Specialists; Security Guards; Sheriffs and Deputy Sheriffs; Transit and Railroad Police.

**Skills**—Repairing, Equipment Maintenance, Equipment Selection, Operation and Control, Troubleshooting, Quality Control Analysis, Operation Monitoring, Coordination.

**Work Environment:** Outdoors; standing; walking and running; using hands; bending or twisting the body; repetitive motions; noise; very hot or cold; bright or inadequate lighting; contaminants; hazardous conditions; hazardous equipment; minor burns, cuts, bites, or stings.

## Job Specialization: Municipal Firefighters

**Control and extinguish municipal fires, protect life and property, and conduct rescue efforts.** Administer first aid and cardiopulmonary resuscitation to injured persons. Rescue victims from burning buildings and accident sites. Search burning buildings to locate fire victims. Drive and operate fire fighting vehicles and equipment. Move toward the source of a fire, using knowledge of types of fires, construction design, building materials, and physical layout of properties. Dress with equipment such as fire-resistant clothing and breathing apparatus. Position and climb ladders to gain access to upper levels of buildings or to rescue individuals from burning structures. Take action to contain hazardous chemicals that might catch fire, leak, or spill. Assess fires and situations and report conditions to superiors to receive instructions, using two-way radios. Respond to fire alarms and other calls for assistance, such as automobile and industrial accidents. Operate pumps connected to high-pressure hoses. Select and attach hose nozzles, depending on fire type, and direct streams of water or chemicals onto fires. Create openings in buildings for ventilation or entrance, using axes, chisels, crowbars, electric saws, or core cutters. Inspect fire sites after flames have been extinguished to ensure that there is no further danger. Lay hose lines and connect them to water supplies. Protect property from water and smoke, using waterproof salvage covers, smoke ejectors, and deodorants. Participate in physical training activities to maintain a high level of physical fitness. Salvage property by removing broken glass, pumping out water, and ventilating buildings to remove smoke. Participate in fire drills and demonstrations of fire fighting techniques. Clean and maintain fire stations and fire fighting equipment and apparatus. Collaborate with police to respond to accidents, disasters, and arson investigation calls. Establish firelines to prevent unauthorized persons from entering areas near fires. Inform and educate the public on fire prevention.

**Education/Training Required:** Long-term on-the-job training. **Education and Training Programs:** Fire Protection, Other; Fire Science/Firefighting. **Knowledge/Courses**—Building and Construction, Public Safety and Security, Mechanical, Customer and Personal Service, Physics, Geography.

**Personality Type:** Realistic-Social-Enterprising. **Career Cluster:** 12 Law, Public Safety, Corrections, and Security. **Career Pathway:** 12.2 Emergency and Fire Management Services. **Other Jobs in This Pathway:** Correctional Officers and Jailers; Fire Inspectors; Fire Investigators; Forest Fire Fighting and Prevention Supervisors; Forest Fire Inspectors and Prevention Specialists; Forest Firefighters; Municipal Fire Fighting and Prevention Supervisors.

**Skills**—Equipment Maintenance, Repairing, Troubleshooting, Operation and Control, Equipment Selection, Science, Operation Monitoring, Quality Control Analysis.

**Work Environment:** More often outdoors than indoors; standing; using hands; noise; very hot or cold; bright or inadequate lighting; contaminants; cramped work space; exposed to disease or infections; hazardous conditions; hazardous equipment; minor burns, cuts, bites, or stings.

# First-Line Supervisors of Correctional Officers

* Annual Earnings: $55,910
* Earnings Growth Potential: Medium (37.9%)
* Growth: 8.5%
* Annual Job Openings: 1,940
* Self-Employed: 0.0%

**Considerations for Job Outlook:** Employment growth is expected to stem from population increases and a corresponding rise in the prison population. Favorable job opportunities are expected.

**Supervise and coordinate activities of correctional officers and jailers.** Take, receive, and check periodic inmate counts. Maintain order, discipline, and security within assigned areas in accordance with relevant rules, regulations, policies, and laws. Respond to emergencies such as escapes. Maintain knowledge of, comply with, and enforce all institutional policies, rules, procedures, and regulations. Supervise and direct the work of correctional officers to ensure the safe custody, discipline, and welfare of inmates. Restrain, secure, and control offenders, using chemical agents, firearms, and other weapons of force as necessary. Supervise and perform searches of inmates and their quarters to locate contraband items. Monitor behavior of subordinates to ensure alert, courteous, and professional behavior toward inmates, parolees, fellow employees, visitors, and the public. Complete administrative paperwork and supervise the preparation and maintenance of records, forms, and reports. Instruct employees and provide on-the-job training. Conduct roll calls of correctional officers. Supervise activities such as searches, shakedowns, riot control, and institutional tours. Carry injured offenders or employees to safety and provide emergency first aid when necessary. Supervise and provide security for offenders performing tasks such as construction, maintenance, laundry, food service, and other industrial or agricultural operations. Develop work and security procedures. Set up employee work schedules. Resolve problems between inmates. Read and review offender information to identify issues that require special attention. Rate behavior of inmates, promoting acceptable attitudes and behaviors to those with low ratings. Transfer and transport offenders on foot or by driving vehicles such as trailers, vans, and buses. Examine incoming and outgoing mail to ensure conformance with regulations. Convey correctional officers' and inmates' complaints to superiors.

**Education/Training Required:** Work experience in a related occupation. **Education and Training Programs:** Corrections; Corrections Administration. **Knowledge/Courses**—Public Safety and Security, Psychology, Therapy and Counseling, Personnel and Human Resources, Clerical, Law and Government.

**Personality Type:** Enterprising-Conventional-Realistic. **Career Cluster:** 12 Law, Public Safety, Corrections, and Security. **Career Pathway:** 12.1 Correction Services. **Other Jobs in This Pathway:** Child, Family, and School Social Workers; First-Line Supervisors of Police and Detectives; Protective Service Workers, All Other; Security Guards.

**Skills**—Management of Personnel Resources, Negotiation, Persuasion, Time Management, Social Perceptiveness, Coordination, Systems Evaluation, Learning Strategies.

**Work Environment:** More often indoors than outdoors; more often sitting than standing; walking and running; using hands; noise; very hot or cold; bright or inadequate lighting; contaminants; exposed to disease or infections.

# First-Line Supervisors of Fire Fighting and Prevention Workers

❈ Annual Earnings: $68,240
❈ Earnings Growth Potential: Medium (39.3%)
❈ Growth: 8.2%
❈ Annual Job Openings: 3,250
❈ Self-Employed: 0.0%

**Considerations for Job Outlook:** Most job growth will stem from the conversion of volunteer fire fighting positions into paid positions. Job seekers are expected to face keen competition. Those who have completed some fire fighter education at a community college and have EMT or paramedic certification should have the best prospects.

## Job Specialization: Forest Fire Fighting and Prevention Supervisors

**Supervise fire fighters who control and suppress fires in forests or vacant public land.** Communicate fire details to superiors, subordinates, and interagency dispatch centers, using two-way radios. Serve as working leader of an engine, hand, helicopter, or prescribed fire crew of three or more firefighters. Maintain fire suppression equipment in good condition, checking equipment periodically to ensure that it is ready for use. Evaluate size, location, and condition of forest fires in order to request and dispatch crews and position equipment so fires can be contained safely and effectively. Operate wildland fire engines and hoselays. Direct and supervise prescribed burn projects and prepare post-burn reports analyzing burn conditions and results. Monitor prescribed burns to ensure that they are conducted safely and effectively. Identify staff training and development needs to ensure that appropriate training can be arranged. Maintain knowledge of forest fire laws and fire prevention techniques and tactics. Recommend equipment modifications or new equipment purchases. Perform administrative duties such as compiling and maintaining records, completing forms, preparing reports, and composing correspondence. Recruit and hire forest fire-fighting personnel. Train workers in such skills as parachute jumping, fire suppression, aerial observation, and radio communication, both in the classroom and on the job. Review and evaluate employee performance. Observe fires and crews from air to determine fire-fighting force requirements and to note changing conditions that will affect fire-fighting efforts. Inspect all stations, uniforms, equipment, and recreation areas to ensure compliance with safety standards, taking corrective action as necessary. Schedule employee work assignments and set work priorities. Regulate open burning by issuing burning permits, inspecting problem sites, issuing citations for violations of laws and ordinances, and educating the public in proper burning practices.

**Education/Training Required:** Work experience in a related occupation. **Education and Training Programs:** Fire Prevention and Safety Technology/Technician; Fire Services Administration. **Knowledge/Courses**—Public Safety and Security, Building and Construction, Mechanical, Customer and Personal Service, Personnel and Human Resources, Transportation.

**Personality Type:** Enterprising-Realistic-Conventional. **Career Cluster:** 12 Law, Public Safety, Corrections, and Security. **Career Pathway:** 12.2 Emergency and Fire Management Services. **Other Jobs in This Pathway:** Correctional Officers and Jailers; Fire Inspectors; Fire Investigators; Forest Fire Inspectors and Prevention Specialists; Forest Firefighters; Municipal Fire Fighting and Prevention Supervisors; Municipal Firefighters.

**Skills**—Operations Analysis, Equipment Maintenance, Operation and Control, Management of Personnel Resources, Coordination, Operation Monitoring, Monitoring, Equipment Selection.

**Work Environment:** Outdoors; standing; walking and running; using hands; noise; very hot or cold; bright or inadequate lighting; contaminants; cramped work space; hazardous equipment; minor burns, cuts, bites, or stings.

## Job Specialization: Municipal Fire Fighting and Prevention Supervisors

**Supervise fire fighters who control and extinguish municipal fires, protect life and property, and conduct rescue efforts.** Assign firefighters to jobs at strategic locations to facilitate rescue of persons and maximize application of extinguishing agents. Provide emergency medical services as required and perform light to heavy rescue functions at emergencies. Assess nature and extent of fire, condition of building, danger to adjacent buildings, and water supply status to determine crew or company requirements. Instruct and drill fire department personnel in assigned duties, including firefighting, medical care, hazardous materials response, fire prevention, and related subjects. Evaluate the performance of assigned firefighting personnel. Direct the training of firefighters, assigning of instructors

to training classes, and providing of supervisors with reports on training progress and status. Prepare activity reports listing fire call locations, actions taken, fire types and probable causes, damage estimates, and situation dispositions. Maintain required maps and records. Attend in-service training classes to remain current in knowledge of codes, laws, ordinances, and regulations. Evaluate fire station procedures to ensure efficiency and enforcement of departmental regulations. Direct firefighters in station maintenance duties and participate in these duties. Compile and maintain equipment and personnel records, including accident reports. Direct investigation of cases of suspected arson, hazards, and false alarms and submit reports outlining findings. Recommend personnel actions related to disciplinary procedures, performance, leaves of absence, and grievances. Supervise and participate in the inspection of properties to ensure that they are in compliance with applicable fire codes, ordinances, laws, regulations, and standards. Write and submit proposals for repair, modification, or replacement of firefighting equipment. Coordinate the distribution of fire prevention promotional materials.

**Education/Training Required:** Work experience in a related occupation. **Education and Training Programs:** Fire Prevention and Safety Technology/Technician; Fire Services Administration. **Knowledge/Courses**—Building and Construction, Public Safety and Security, Medicine and Dentistry, Mechanical, Chemistry, Personnel and Human Resources.

**Personality Type:** Enterprising-Realistic-Social. **Career Cluster:** 12 Law, Public Safety, Corrections, and Security. **Career Pathway:** 12.2 Emergency and Fire Management Services. **Other Jobs in This Pathway:** Correctional Officers and Jailers; Fire Inspectors; Fire Investigators; Forest Fire Fighting and Prevention Supervisors; Forest Fire Inspectors and Prevention Specialists; Forest Firefighters; Municipal Firefighters.

**Skills**—Operation and Control, Science, Equipment Selection, Repairing, Equipment Maintenance, Quality Control Analysis, Management of Personnel Resources, Systems Analysis.

**Work Environment:** More often outdoors than indoors; standing; using hands; noise; very hot or cold; bright or inadequate lighting; contaminants; cramped work space; exposed to disease or infections; high places; hazardous conditions; hazardous equipment; minor burns, cuts, bites, or stings.

# First-Line Supervisors of Food Preparation and Serving Workers

❋ Annual Earnings: $29,560
❋ Earnings Growth Potential: Low (33.9%)
❋ Growth: 6.6%
❋ Annual Job Openings: 13,440
❋ Self-Employed: 3.2%

**Considerations for Job Outlook:** Consumer demand for convenience and a growing variety of dining venues are expected to create some jobs, but most openings are expected to arise from the need to replace workers who leave the occupation. Competition should be keen for jobs at upscale restaurants.

**Supervise workers engaged in preparing and serving food.** Compile and balance cash receipts at the end of the day or shift. Resolve customer complaints regarding food service. Inspect supplies, equipment, and work areas to ensure efficient service and conformance to standards. Train workers in food preparation and in service, sanitation, and safety procedures. Control inventories of food, equipment, smallware, and liquor and report shortages to designated personnel. Observe and evaluate workers and work procedures to ensure quality standards and service. Assign duties, responsibilities, and workstations to employees in accordance with work requirements. Estimate ingredients and supplies required to prepare a recipe. Perform personnel actions such as hiring and firing staff, consulting with other managers as necessary. Analyze operational problems, such as theft and wastage, and establish procedures to alleviate these problems. Specify food portions and courses, production and time sequences, and workstation and equipment arrangements. Recommend measures for improving work procedures and worker performance to increase service quality and enhance job safety. Greet and seat guests and present menus and wine lists. Present bills and accept payments. Forecast staff, equipment, and supply requirements based on a master menu. Record production and operational data on specified forms. Perform serving duties such as carving meat, preparing flambé dishes, or serving wine and liquor. Purchase or requisition supplies and equipment needed to ensure quality and timely delivery of services. Collaborate with other personnel to plan menus, serving arrangements, and related details. Supervise and check the assembly of regular and special diet trays and the delivery of food trolleys to hospital patients. Schedule parties and take reservations. Develop departmental objectives, budgets, policies, procedures, and strategies. Develop equipment maintenance schedules and arrange for repairs. Evaluate new products for usefulness and suitability.

**Education/Training Required:** Work experience in a related occupation. **Education and Training Programs:** Foodservice Systems Administration/Management; Restaurant, Culinary, and Catering Management/Manager. **Knowledge/Courses**—Food Production, Economics and Accounting, Administration and Management, Production and Processing, Personnel and Human Resources, Sales and Marketing.

**Personality Type:** Enterprising-Conventional-Realistic. **Career Clusters:** 08 Health Science; 09 Hospitality and Tourism. **Career Pathways:** 8.4 Support Services; 9.1 Restaurants and Food/Beverage Services. **Other Jobs in These Pathways:** Bakers; Baristas; Bartenders; Butchers and Meat Cutters; Chefs and Head Cooks; Combined Food Preparation and Serving Workers, Including Fast Food; Cooks, All Other; Cooks, Fast Food; Cooks, Institution and Cafeteria; Cooks, Restaurant; Cooks, Short Order; Counter Attendants, Cafeteria, Food Concession, and Coffee Shop; Dietetic Technicians; Dietitians and Nutritionists; Dining Room and Cafeteria Attendants and Bartender Helpers; Dishwashers; Food Batchmakers; Food Preparation and Serving Related Workers, All Other; Food Preparation Workers; Food Servers, Nonrestaurant; Food Service Managers; Hosts and Hostesses, Restaurant, Lounge, and Coffee Shop; Meat, Poultry, and Fish Cutters and Trimmers; Slaughterers and Meat Packers; Waiters and Waitresses; others.

**Skills**—Management of Financial Resources, Management of Material Resources, Systems Evaluation, Management of Personnel Resources, Coordination, Service Orientation, Time Management, Social Perceptiveness.

**Work Environment:** Indoors; standing; walking and running; using hands; bending or twisting the body; repetitive motions; noise; very hot or cold; contaminants; minor burns, cuts, bites, or stings.

# First-Line Supervisors of Helpers, Laborers, and Material Movers, Hand

* ❀ Annual Earnings: $43,800
* ❀ Earnings Growth Potential: Medium (37.3%)
* ❀ Growth: 3.6%
* ❀ Annual Job Openings: 3,850
* ❀ Self-Employed: 0.8%

**Considerations for Job Outlook:** Slower than average employment growth is projected.

**Supervise and coordinate the activities of helpers, laborers, or material movers.** Plan work schedules and assign duties to maintain adequate staffing levels, to ensure that activities are performed effectively, and to respond to fluctuating workloads. Collaborate with workers and managers to solve work-related problems. Review work throughout the work process and at completion to ensure that it has been performed properly. Transmit and explain work orders to laborers. Check specifications of materials loaded or unloaded against information contained in work orders. Inform designated employees or departments of items loaded and problems encountered. Examine freight to determine loading sequences. Evaluate employee performance and prepare performance appraisals. Perform the same work duties as those whom they supervise or perform more difficult or skilled tasks or assist in their performance. Prepare and maintain work records and reports that include information such as employee time and wages, daily receipts, and inspection results. Counsel employees in work-related activities, personal growth, and career development. Conduct staff meetings to relay general information or to address specific topics such as safety. Inspect equipment for wear and for conformance to specifications. Resolve personnel problems, complaints, and formal grievances when possible or refer them to higher-level supervisors for resolution. Recommend or initiate personnel actions such as promotions, transfers, and disciplinary measures. Assess training needs of staff; then arrange for or provide appropriate instruction. Schedule times of shipment and modes of transportation for materials. Quote prices to customers. Estimate material, time, and staffing requirements for a given project based on work orders, job specifications, and experience. Provide assistance in balancing books; tracking, monitoring, and projecting a unit's budget needs; and developing unit policies and procedures. Inspect job sites to determine the extent of maintenance or repairs needed.

**Education/Training Required:** Work experience in a related occupation. **Education and Training Programs:** No related CIP programs; this job is learned through work experience in a related occupation. **Knowledge/Courses—** Production and Processing, Transportation, Personnel and Human Resources, Administration and Management, Public Safety and Security, Psychology.

**Personality Type:** Enterprising-Realistic-Conventional. **Career Cluster:** 16 Transportation, Distribution, and Logistics. **Career Pathway:** 16.1 Transportation Operations. **Other Jobs in This Pathway:** Airline Pilots, Copilots, and Flight Engineers; Automotive and Watercraft Service Attendants; Automotive Master Mechanics; Bus Drivers, School or Special Client; Bus Drivers, Transit and Intercity; Commercial Pilots; Crane and Tower Operators; First-Line Supervisors of Transportation and Material-Moving Machine and Vehicle Operators; Freight and Cargo Inspectors; Heavy and Tractor-Trailer Truck Drivers; Laborers and Freight, Stock, and Material Movers, Hand; Light Truck or Delivery Services Drivers; Mates—Ship, Boat, and Barge; Motor Vehicle Operators, All Other; Operating Engineers and Other Construction Equipment Operators; Parking Lot Attendants; Pilots, Ship; Railroad Conductors and Yardmasters; Sailors and Marine Oilers; Ship and Boat Captains; Storage and Distribution Managers; Taxi Drivers and Chauffeurs; Transportation Inspectors; Transportation Managers; Transportation Workers, All Other; others.

**Skills—**Management of Material Resources, Management of Financial Resources, Management of Personnel Resources, Negotiation, Persuasion, Operations Analysis, Time Management, Systems Evaluation.

**Work Environment:** Indoors; standing; walking and running; noise; very hot or cold; contaminants.

## Job Specialization: Recycling Coordinators

**Supervise curbside and drop-off recycling programs for municipal governments or private firms.** Oversee recycling pick-up or drop-off programs to ensure compliance with community ordinances. Supervise recycling technicians, community service workers, or other recycling operations employees or volunteers. Assign truck drivers or recycling technicians to routes. Coordinate recycling collection schedules to optimize service and efficiency. Coordinate shipments of recycling materials with shipping brokers or processing companies. Create or manage recycling operations budgets. Design community solid and hazardous waste management programs. Develop community or corporate recycling plans and goals to minimize waste and conform to resource constraints. Implement grant-funded projects, monitoring and reporting progress in accordance with sponsoring agency requirements. Investigate violations of solid waste or recycling ordinances. Make presentations to educate the public on how to recycle or on the environmental advantages of recycling. Negotiate contracts with waste management or other firms. Operate fork lifts, skid loaders, or trucks to move or store recyclable materials. Operate recycling processing equipment, such as sorters, balers, crushers, and granulators to sort and process materials. Oversee campaigns to promote recycling or waste reduction programs in communities or private companies. Prepare grant applications to fund recycling programs or program enhancements. Schedule movement of recycling materials into and out of storage areas. Identify or investigate new opportunities for materials to be collected and recycled. Inspect physical condition of recycling or hazardous waste facility for compliance with safety, quality, and service standards. Maintain logs of recycling materials received or shipped to processing companies. Prepare bills of lading, statements of shipping records, or customer receipts related to recycling or hazardous material services.

**Education/Training Required:** Work experience in a related occupation. **Education and Training Programs:** No related CIP programs; this job is learned through work experience in a related occupation. **Knowledge/Courses—** No data available.

**Personality Type:** No data available. **Career Cluster:** 13 Manufacturing. **Career Pathway:** 13.1 Production. **Other Jobs in This Pathway:** Assemblers and Fabricators, All Other; Cabinetmakers and Bench Carpenters; Coating, Painting, and Spraying Machine Setters, Operators, and Tenders; Computer-Controlled Machine Tool Operators, Metal and Plastic; Cost Estimators; Cutting, Punching, and Press Machine Setters, Operators, and Tenders, Metal and Plastic; First-Line Supervisors of Mechanics, Installers, and Repairers; First-Line Supervisors of Production and Operating Workers; Geothermal Technicians; Grinding, Lapping, Polishing, and Buffing Machine Tool Setters, Operators, and Tenders, Metal and Plastic; Helpers—Production Workers; Machine Feeders and Offbearers; Machinists; Mixing and Blending Machine Setters, Operators, and Tenders; Molding, Coremaking, and Casting Machine Setters, Operators, and Tenders, Metal and Plastic; Packaging and Filling Machine Operators and Tenders; Packers and Packagers, Hand; Paper Goods Machine Setters, Operators, and Tenders; Production Workers, All Other; Recycling and Reclamation Workers; Sheet Metal Workers; Solderers

and Brazers; Structural Metal Fabricators and Fitters; Team Assemblers; Welders, Cutters, and Welder Fitters; others.

**Skills**—No data available.

**Work Environment:** No data available.

# First-Line Supervisors of Landscaping, Lawn Service, and Groundskeeping Workers

- ❋ Annual Earnings: $41,860
- ❋ Earnings Growth Potential: Low (35.6%)
- ❋ Growth: 14.9%
- ❋ Annual Job Openings: 5,600
- ❋ Self-Employed: 50.4%

**Considerations for Job Outlook:** Demand for lawn care and landscaping services is expected to grow, resulting in employment growth for these workers. Job prospects are expected to be good. Opportunities for year-round work should be best in regions with temperate climates.

**Plan, organize, direct, or coordinate activities of workers engaged in landscaping or groundskeeping activities such as planting and maintaining ornamental trees, shrubs, flowers, and lawns and applying fertilizers, pesticides, and other chemicals, according to contract specifications. May also coordinate activities of workers engaged in terracing hillsides, building retaining walls, constructing pathways, installing patios, and similar activities in following a landscape design plan. Work may involve reviewing contracts to ascertain service, machine, and work force requirements; answering inquiries from potential customers regarding methods, material, and price ranges; and preparing estimates according to labor, material, and machine costs.** Establish and enforce operating procedures and work standards that will ensure adequate performance and personnel safety. Inspect completed work to ensure conformance to specifications, standards, and contract requirements. Direct activities of workers who perform duties such as landscaping, cultivating lawns, or pruning trees and shrubs. Schedule work for crews depending on work priorities, crew and equipment availability, and weather conditions. Plant and maintain vegetation through activities such as mulching, fertilizing, watering, mowing, and pruning. Monitor project activities to ensure that instructions are followed, deadlines are met, and schedules are maintained. Train workers in tasks such as transplanting and pruning trees and shrubs, finishing cement, using equipment, and caring for turf. Provide workers with assistance in performing duties as necessary to meet deadlines. Inventory supplies of tools, equipment, and materials to ensure that sufficient supplies are available and items are in usable condition. Confer with other supervisors to coordinate work activities with those of other departments or units. Perform personnel-related activities such as hiring workers, evaluating staff performance, and taking disciplinary actions when performance problems occur. Direct or perform mixing and application of fertilizers, insecticides, herbicides, and fungicides. Review contracts or work assignments to determine service, machine, and workforce requirements for jobs. Maintain required records such as personnel information and project records. Prepare and maintain required records such as work activity and personnel reports. Order the performance of corrective work when problems occur, and recommend procedural changes to avoid such problems. Identify diseases and pests affecting landscaping, and order appropriate treatments. Investigate work-related complaints in order to verify problems, and to determine responses.

**Education/Training Required:** Work experience in a related occupation. **Education and Training Programs:** Landscaping and Groundskeeping; Ornamental Horticulture; Turf and Turfgrass Management. **Knowledge/ Courses**—Mechanical, Building and Construction, Design, Biology, Chemistry, Education and Training.

**Personality Type:** Enterprising-Realistic-Conventional. **Career Cluster:** 01 Agriculture, Food, and Natural Resources. **Career Pathway:** 1.2 Plant Systems. **Other Jobs in This Pathway:** Agricultural Technicians; Animal Scientists; Biochemists and Biophysicists; Biologists; Economists; Environmental Economists; Farm and Home Management Advisors; First-Line Supervisors of Retail Sales Workers; Floral Designers; Food Science Technicians; Food Scientists and Technologists; Geneticists; Grounds Maintenance Workers, All Other; Landscaping and Groundskeeping Workers; Pesticide Handlers, Sprayers, and Applicators, Vegetation; Precision Agriculture Technicians; Retail Salespersons; Soil and Plant Scientists; Tree Trimmers and Pruners.

**Skills**—Operation and Control, Repairing, Equipment Maintenance, Operation Monitoring, Management of Financial Resources, Management of Material Resources, Troubleshooting, Quality Control Analysis.

**Work Environment:** More often outdoors than indoors; standing; walking and running; using hands; noise; very hot or cold; bright or inadequate lighting; contaminants; hazardous equipment; minor burns, cuts, bites, or stings.

# First-Line Supervisors of Mechanics, Installers, and Repairers

* Annual Earnings: $59,150
* Earnings Growth Potential: Medium (39.2%)
* Growth: 4.2%
* Annual Job Openings: 13,650
* Self-Employed: 0.4%

**Considerations for Job Outlook:** Slower than average employment growth is projected.

**Supervise and coordinate the activities of mechanics, installers, and repairers.** Determine schedules, sequences, and assignments for work activities, based on work priority, quantity of equipment, and skill of personnel. Monitor employees' work levels and review work performance. Monitor tool and part inventories and the condition and maintenance of shops to ensure adequate working conditions. Recommend or initiate personnel actions such as hires, promotions, transfers, discharges, and disciplinary measures. Investigate accidents and injuries, and prepare reports of findings. Compile operational and personnel records such as time and production records, inventory data, repair and maintenance statistics, and test results. Develop, implement, and evaluate maintenance policies and procedures. Counsel employees about work-related issues and assist employees to correct job-skill deficiencies. Examine objects, systems, or facilities, and analyze information to determine needed installations, services, or repairs. Conduct or arrange for worker training in safety, repair, and maintenance techniques, operational procedures, or equipment use. Inspect and monitor work areas, examine tools and equipment, and provide employee safety training to prevent, detect, and correct unsafe conditions or violations of procedures and safety rules. Inspect, test, and measure completed work, using devices such as hand tools and gauges to verify conformance to standards and repair requirements. Requisition materials and supplies such as tools, equipment, and replacement parts. Participate in budget preparation and administration, coordinating purchasing and documentation, and monitoring departmental expenditures. Perform skilled repair and maintenance operations, using equipment such as hand and power tools, hydraulic presses and shears, and welding equipment. Meet with vendors and suppliers to discuss products used in repair work. Compute estimates and actual costs of factors such as materials, labor, and outside contractors.

**Education/Training Required:** Work experience in a related occupation. **Education and Training Program:** Operations Management and Supervision. **Knowledge/Courses**—Mechanical, Personnel and Human Resources, Production and Processing, Building and Construction, Engineering and Technology, Economics and Accounting.

**Personality Type:** Enterprising-Conventional-Realistic. **Career Cluster:** 13 Manufacturing. **Career Pathway:** 13.1 Production. **Other Jobs in This Pathway:** Assemblers and Fabricators, All Other; Cabinetmakers and Bench Carpenters; Coating, Painting, and Spraying Machine Setters, Operators, and Tenders; Computer-Controlled Machine Tool Operators, Metal and Plastic; Cost Estimators; Cutting, Punching, and Press Machine Setters, Operators, and Tenders, Metal and Plastic; First-Line Supervisors of Production and Operating Workers; Geothermal Technicians; Grinding, Lapping, Polishing, and Buffing Machine Tool Setters, Operators, and Tenders, Metal and Plastic; Helpers—Production Workers; Machine Feeders and Offbearers; Machinists; Mixing and Blending Machine Setters, Operators, and Tenders; Molding, Coremaking, and Casting Machine Setters, Operators, and Tenders, Metal and Plastic; Packaging and Filling Machine Operators and Tenders; Packers and Packagers, Hand; Paper Goods Machine Setters, Operators, and Tenders; Production Workers, All Other; Recycling and Reclamation Workers; Recycling Coordinators; Sheet Metal Workers; Solderers and Brazers; Structural Metal Fabricators and Fitters; Team Assemblers; Welders, Cutters, and Welder Fitters; others.

**Skills**—Repairing, Management of Financial Resources, Equipment Maintenance, Troubleshooting, Management of Material Resources, Equipment Selection, Quality Control Analysis, Operation and Control.

**Work Environment:** More often indoors than outdoors; standing; noise; contaminants; hazardous conditions.

# First-Line Supervisors of Non-Retail Sales Workers

- ❀ Annual Earnings: $68,880
- ❀ Earnings Growth Potential: High (46.2%)
- ❀ Growth: 4.8%
- ❀ Annual Job Openings: 12,950
- ❀ Self-Employed: 45.6%

**Considerations for Job Outlook:** Limited job growth is expected as retailers increase the responsibilities of existing sales worker supervisors and as the retail industry grows

slowly overall. Competition is expected. Job seekers with college degrees and retail experience should have the best prospects.

**Directly supervise and coordinate activities of sales workers other than retail sales workers. May perform duties such as budgeting, accounting, and personnel work in addition to supervisory duties.** Listen to and resolve customer complaints regarding services, products, or personnel. Monitor sales staff performance to ensure that goals are met. Hire, train, and evaluate personnel. Confer with company officials to develop methods and procedures to increase sales, expand markets, and promote business. Direct and supervise employees engaged in sales, inventory-taking, reconciling cash receipts, or performing specific services such as pumping gasoline for customers. Provide staff with assistance in performing difficult or complicated duties. Plan and prepare work schedules and assign employees to specific duties. Attend company meetings to exchange product information and coordinate work activities with other departments. Prepare sales and inventory reports for management and budget departments. Formulate pricing policies on merchandise according to profitability requirements. Examine merchandise to ensure correct pricing and display and ensure that it functions as advertised. Analyze details of sales territories to assess their growth potential and to set quotas. Visit retailers and sales representatives to promote products and gather information. Keep records pertaining to purchases, sales, and requisitions. Coordinate sales promotion activities and prepare merchandise displays and advertising copy. Prepare rental or lease agreements, specifying charges and payment procedures for use of machinery, tools, or other items. Inventory stock and reorder when inventories drop to specified levels. Examine products purchased for resale or received for storage to determine product condition.

**Education/Training Required:** Work experience in a related occupation. **Education and Training Programs:** Business, Management, Marketing, and Related Support Services, Other; General Merchandising, Sales, and Related Marketing Operations, Other; Special Products Marketing Operations; Specialized Merchandising, Sales, and Marketing Operations, Other. **Knowledge/Courses**—Sales and Marketing, Economics and Accounting, Personnel and Human Resources, Administration and Management, Mathematics, Clerical.

**Personality Type:** Enterprising-Conventional-Social. **Career Cluster:** 14 Marketing, Sales, and Service. **Career Pathway:** 14.2 Professional Sales and Marketing. **Other Jobs in This Pathway:** Cashiers; Counter and Rental

Clerks; Door-To-Door Sales Workers, News and Street Vendors, and Related Workers; Driver/Sales Workers; Energy Brokers; First-Line Supervisors of Retail Sales Workers; Hotel, Motel, and Resort Desk Clerks; Marketing Managers; Marking Clerks; Online Merchants; Order Fillers, Wholesale and Retail Sales; Parts Salespersons; Property, Real Estate, and Community Association Managers; Real Estate Sales Agents; Reservation and Transportation Ticket Agents and Travel Clerks; Retail Salespersons; Sales and Related Workers, All Other; Sales Representatives, Services, All Other; Sales Representatives, Wholesale and Manufacturing, Except Technical and Scientific Products; Sales Representatives, Wholesale and Manufacturing, Technical and Scientific Products; Solar Sales Representatives and Assessors; Stock Clerks—Stockroom, Warehouse, or Storage Yard; Stock Clerks, Sales Floor; Telemarketers; Wholesale and Retail Buyers, Except Farm Products; others.

**Skills**—Management of Financial Resources, Management of Material Resources, Systems Evaluation, Instructing, Negotiation, Management of Personnel Resources, Persuasion, Monitoring.

**Work Environment:** Indoors; noise.

# First-Line Supervisors of Office and Administrative Support Workers

- ❋ Annual Earnings: $47,460
- ❋ Earnings Growth Potential: Medium (39.2%)
- ❋ Growth: 11.0%
- ❋ Annual Job Openings: 48,900
- ❋ Self-Employed: 1.4%

**Considerations for Job Outlook:** Employment growth is expected to be tempered by technological advances that increase the productivity of—and thus decrease the need for—these workers and the workers they supervise. Keen competition is expected.

**Supervise and coordinate the activities of clerical and administrative support workers.** Resolve customer complaints and answer customers' questions regarding policies and procedures. Supervise the work of office, administrative, or customer service employees to ensure adherence to quality standards, deadlines, and proper procedures, correcting errors or problems. Provide employees with guidance in handling difficult or complex problems and in resolving escalated complaints or disputes. Implement corporate and departmental policies, procedures, and service standards in conjunction with management. Discuss job performance problems with employees to identify causes and issues and to work on resolving problems. Train and instruct employees in job duties and company policies or arrange for training to be provided. Evaluate employees' job performance and conformance to regulations and recommend appropriate personnel action. Recruit, interview, and select employees. Review records and reports pertaining to activities such as production, payroll, and shipping to verify details, monitor work activities, and evaluate performance. Interpret and communicate work procedures and company policies to staff. Prepare and issue work schedules, deadlines, and duty assignments of office or administrative staff. Maintain records pertaining to inventory, personnel, orders, supplies, and machine maintenance. Compute figures such as balances, totals, and commissions. Research, compile, and prepare reports, manuals, correspondence, and other information required by management or governmental agencies. Coordinate activities with other supervisory personnel and with other work units or departments. Analyze financial activities of establishments or departments and provide input into budget planning and preparation processes. Develop or update procedures, policies, and standards. Make recommendations to management concerning such issues as staffing decisions and procedural changes.

**Education/Training Required:** Work experience in a related occupation. **Education and Training Programs:** Agricultural Business Technology; Customer Service Management; Medical Staff Services Technology/Technician; Medical/Health Management and Clinical Assistant/Specialist Training; Office Management and Supervision. **Knowledge/Courses**—Clerical, Economics and Accounting, Administration and Management, Personnel and Human Resources, Customer and Personal Service, Education and Training.

**Personality Type:** Enterprising-Conventional-Social. **Career Clusters:** 01 Agriculture, Food, and Natural Resources; 04 Business, Management, and Administration; 08 Health Science. **Career Pathways:** 1.1 Food Products and Processing Systems; 4.1 Management; 8.3 Health Informatics. **Other Jobs in These Pathways:** Brownfield Redevelopment Specialists and Site Managers; Business Continuity Planners; Business Operations Specialists, All Other; Chief Executives; Chief Sustainability Officers; Compliance Managers; Construction Managers; Customs Brokers; Energy Auditors; Executive Secretaries and Executive Administrative Assistants; General and Operations Managers; Investment Fund Managers; Loss Prevention Managers; Management Analysts; Managers, All Other; Medical Assistants; Medical Secretaries; Receptionists and

Information Clerks; Regulatory Affairs Managers; Security Management Specialists; Security Managers; Supply Chain Managers; Sustainability Specialists; Wind Energy Operations Managers; Wind Energy Project Managers; others.

**Skills**—Management of Financial Resources, Management of Material Resources, Negotiation, Monitoring, Learning Strategies, Management of Personnel Resources, Persuasion, Time Management.

**Work Environment:** Indoors; sitting; noise.

# First-Line Supervisors of Personal Service Workers

- ❋ Annual Earnings: $35,290
- ❋ Earnings Growth Potential: Medium (37.9%)
- ❋ Growth: 15.4%
- ❋ Annual Job Openings: 9,080
- ❋ Self-Employed: 37.8%

**Considerations for Job Outlook:** Faster-than-average employment growth is projected.

**Supervise and coordinate activities of personal service workers such as flight attendants, hairdressers, or caddies.** Requisition necessary supplies, equipment, and services. Inform workers about interests and special needs of specific groups. Participate in continuing education to stay abreast of industry trends and developments. Meet with managers and other supervisors to stay informed of changes affecting operations. Collaborate with staff members to plan and develop programs of events, schedules of activities, or menus. Train workers in proper operational procedures and functions, and explain company policies. Furnish customers with information on events and activities. Resolve customer complaints regarding worker performance and services rendered. Analyze and record personnel and operational data, and write related activity reports. Observe and evaluate workers' appearance and performance to ensure quality service and compliance with specifications. Inspect work areas and operating equipment to ensure conformance to established standards in areas such as cleanliness and maintenance. Direct and coordinate the activities of workers such as flight attendants, hotel staff, or hair stylists. Assign work schedules, following work requirements, to ensure quality and timely delivery of service. Apply customer/guest feedback to service improvement efforts. Direct marketing, advertising, and other customer recruitment efforts.

Take disciplinary action to address performance problems. Recruit and hire staff members.

**Education/Training Required:** Work experience in a related occupation. **Education and Training Program:** Business, Management, Marketing, and Related Support Services, Other. **Knowledge/Courses**—Psychology, Therapy and Counseling, Education and Training, Philosophy and Theology, Public Safety and Security, Medicine and Dentistry.

**Personality Type:** Enterprising-Conventional-Social. **Career Cluster:** 04 Business, Management, and Administration. **Career Pathway:** 4.1 Management. **Other Jobs in This Pathway:** Brownfield Redevelopment Specialists and Site Managers; Business Continuity Planners; Business Operations Specialists, All Other; Chief Executives; Chief Sustainability Officers; Compliance Managers; Computer and Information Systems Managers; Construction Managers; Customs Brokers; Energy Auditors; First-Line Supervisors of Office and Administrative Support Workers; General and Operations Managers; Investment Fund Managers; Loss Prevention Managers; Management Analysts; Managers, All Other; Public Relations Specialists; Regulatory Affairs Managers; Sales Managers; Security Management Specialists; Security Managers; Supply Chain Managers; Sustainability Specialists; Wind Energy Operations Managers; Wind Energy Project Managers; others.

**Skills**—Management of Personnel Resources, Time Management, Management of Financial Resources, Operation Monitoring, Negotiation, Management of Material Resources, Service Orientation, Systems Evaluation.

**Work Environment:** Indoors; standing; walking and running; using hands; noise; contaminants.

## Job Specialization: Spa Managers

**Plan, direct, or coordinate activities of a spa facility. Coordinate programs, schedule and direct staff, and oversee financial activities.** Inform staff of job responsibilities, performance expectations, client service standards, or corporate policies and guidelines. Plan or direct spa services and programs. Train staff in the use or sale of products, programs, or activities. Assess employee performance and suggest ways to improve work. Check spa equipment to ensure proper functioning. Coordinate facility schedules to maximize usage and efficiency. Develop staff service or retail goals and guide staff in goal achievement. Establish spa budgets and financial goals. Inventory products and order new supplies. Monitor operations to ensure compliance with applicable health, safety, or hygiene standards. Perform accounting duties, such as recording daily cash flow, preparing bank deposits, or generating financial statements. Recruit, interview, or hire employees. Respond to customer inquiries or complaints. Schedule staff or supervise scheduling. Verify staff credentials, such as educational and certification requirements. Develop or implement marketing strategies. Direct facility maintenance or repair. Maintain client databases. Participate in continuing education classes to maintain current knowledge of industry. Schedule guest appointments. Sell products, services, or memberships.

**Education/Training Required:** Work experience in a related occupation. **Education and Training Program:** Resort Management. **Knowledge/Courses**—No data available.

**Personality Type:** Enterprising-Conventional-Social. **Career Cluster:** 04 Business, Management, and Administration. **Career Pathway:** 4.1 Management. **Other Jobs in This Pathway:** Brownfield Redevelopment Specialists and Site Managers; Business Continuity Planners; Business Operations Specialists, All Other; Chief Executives; Chief Sustainability Officers; Compliance Managers; Computer and Information Systems Managers; Construction Managers; Customs Brokers; Energy Auditors; First-Line Supervisors of Office and Administrative Support Workers; General and Operations Managers; Investment Fund Managers; Loss Prevention Managers; Management Analysts; Managers, All Other; Public Relations Specialists; Regulatory Affairs Managers; Sales Managers; Security Management Specialists; Security Managers; Supply Chain Managers; Sustainability Specialists; Wind Energy Operations Managers; Wind Energy Project Managers; others.

**Skills**—No data available.

**Work Environment:** No data available.

# First-Line Supervisors of Police and Detectives

- ❋ Annual Earnings: $78,260
- ❋ Earnings Growth Potential: Medium (40.4%)
- ❋ Growth: 8.1%
- ❋ Annual Job Openings: 5,050
- ❋ Self-Employed: 0.0%

**Considerations for Job Outlook:** Population growth is the main source of demand for police services. Overall, opportunities in local police departments should be favorable for qualified applicants.

**Supervise and coordinate activities of members of police force.** Supervise and coordinate the investigation of criminal cases, offering guidance and expertise to investigators, and ensuring that procedures are conducted in accordance with laws and regulations. Maintain logs, prepare reports, and direct the preparation, handling, and maintenance of departmental records. Explain police operations to subordinates to assist them in performing their job duties. Cooperate with court personnel and officials from other law enforcement agencies and testify in court as necessary. Review contents of written orders to ensure adherence to legal requirements. Investigate and resolve personnel problems within organization and charges of misconduct against staff. Direct collection, preparation, and handling of evidence and personal property of prisoners. Inform personnel of changes in regulations and policies, implications of new or amended laws, and new techniques of police work. Train staff in proper police work procedures. Monitor and evaluate the job performance of subordinates, and authorize promotions and transfers. Prepare work schedules and assign duties to subordinates. Conduct raids and order detention of witnesses and suspects for questioning. Discipline staff for violation of departmental rules and regulations. Develop, implement, and revise departmental policies and procedures. Inspect facilities, supplies, vehicles, and equipment to ensure conformance to standards. Requisition and issue equipment and supplies. Meet with civic, educational, and community groups to develop community programs and events, and to discuss law enforcement subjects. Prepare news releases and respond to police correspondence. Prepare budgets and manage expenditures of department funds. Direct release or transfer of prisoners.

**Education/Training Required:** Work experience in a related occupation. **Education and Training Programs:** Corrections; Criminal Justice/Law Enforcement Administration; Criminal Justice/Safety Studies. **Knowledge/Courses**—Public Safety and Security, Law and Government, Psychology, Sociology and Anthropology, Therapy and Counseling, Personnel and Human Resources.

**Personality Type:** Enterprising-Social-Conventional. **Career Cluster:** 12 Law, Public Safety, Corrections, and Security. **Career Pathways:** 12.1 Correction Services; 12.4 Law Enforcement Services. **Other Jobs in These Pathways:** Bailiffs; Child, Family, and School Social Workers; Correctional Officers and Jailers; Criminal Investigators and Special Agents; First-Line Supervisors of Correctional Officers; Forensic Science Technicians; Immigration and Customs

Inspectors; Intelligence Analysts; Police Detectives; Police Identification and Records Officers; Police Patrol Officers; Protective Service Workers, All Other; Remote Sensing Scientists and Technologists; Security Guards; Sheriffs and Deputy Sheriffs.

**Skills**—Management of Financial Resources, Management of Personnel Resources, Persuasion, Management of Material Resources, Monitoring, Learning Strategies, Time Management, Instructing.

**Work Environment:** More often indoors than outdoors; sitting; noise; very hot or cold; bright or inadequate lighting; contaminants; hazardous equipment.

# First-Line Supervisors of Production and Operating Workers

- ❋ Annual Earnings: $53,090
- ❋ Earnings Growth Potential: Medium (39.2%)
- ❋ Growth: –5.2%
- ❋ Annual Job Openings: 9,190
- ❋ Self-Employed: 4.6%

**Considerations for Job Outlook:** Slow decline in employment is projected.

**Supervise and coordinate the activities of production and operating workers, such as inspectors, precision workers, machine setters and operators, assemblers, fabricators, and plant and system operators.** Enforce safety and sanitation regulations. Direct and coordinate the activities of employees engaged in the production or processing of goods, such as inspectors, machine setters, and fabricators. Read and analyze charts, work orders, production schedules, and other records and reports to determine production requirements and to evaluate current production estimates and outputs. Confer with other supervisors to coordinate operations and activities within or between departments. Plan and establish work schedules, assignments, and production sequences to meet production goals. Inspect materials, products, or equipment to detect defects or malfunctions. Demonstrate equipment operations and work and safety procedures to new employees or assign employees to experienced workers for training. Observe work and monitor gauges, dials, and other indicators to ensure that operators conform to production or processing standards. Interpret specifications, blueprints, job orders, and company policies and procedures for workers. Confer with

management or subordinates to resolve worker problems, complaints, or grievances. Maintain operations data such as time, production, and cost records and prepare management reports of production results. Recommend or implement measures to motivate employees and to improve production methods, equipment performance, product quality, or efficiency. Determine standards, budgets, production goals, and rates based on company policies, equipment and labor availability, and workloads. Requisition materials, supplies, equipment parts, or repair services. Recommend personnel actions such as hirings and promotions. Set up and adjust machines and equipment. Calculate labor and equipment requirements and production specifications, using standard formulas. Plan and develop new products and production processes.

**Education/Training Required:** Work experience in a related occupation. **Education and Training Program:** Operations Management and Supervision. **Knowledge/Courses**—Production and Processing, Mechanical, Personnel and Human Resources, Engineering and Technology, Administration and Management, Psychology.

**Personality Type:** Enterprising-Realistic-Conventional. **Career Cluster:** 13 Manufacturing. **Career Pathway:** 13.1 Production. **Other Jobs in This Pathway:** Assemblers and Fabricators, All Other; Cabinetmakers and Bench Carpenters; Coating, Painting, and Spraying Machine Setters, Operators, and Tenders; Computer-Controlled Machine Tool Operators, Metal and Plastic; Cost Estimators; Cutting, Punching, and Press Machine Setters, Operators, and Tenders, Metal and Plastic; First-Line Supervisors of Mechanics, Installers, and Repairers; Geothermal Technicians; Grinding, Lapping, Polishing, and Buffing Machine Tool Setters, Operators, and Tenders, Metal and Plastic; Helpers—Production Workers; Machine Feeders and Offbearers; Machinists; Mixing and Blending Machine Setters, Operators, and Tenders; Molding, Coremaking, and Casting Machine Setters, Operators, and Tenders, Metal and Plastic; Packaging and Filling Machine Operators and Tenders; Packers and Packagers, Hand; Paper Goods Machine Setters, Operators, and Tenders; Production Workers, All Other; Recycling and Reclamation Workers; Recycling Coordinators; Sheet Metal Workers; Solderers and Brazers; Structural Metal Fabricators and Fitters; Team Assemblers; Welders, Cutters, and Welder Fitters; others.

**Skills**—Management of Financial Resources, Management of Personnel Resources, Management of Material Resources, Operations Analysis, Negotiation, Troubleshooting, Systems Analysis, Repairing.

**Work Environment:** Indoors; standing; walking and running; noise; contaminants; hazardous equipment; minor burns, cuts, bites, or stings.

# First-Line Supervisors of Retail Sales Workers

- ❊ Annual Earnings: $35,820
- ❊ Earnings Growth Potential: Medium (37.5%)
- ❊ Growth: 5.2%
- ❊ Annual Job Openings: 45,010
- ❊ Self-Employed: 30.6%

**Considerations for Job Outlook:** Limited job growth is expected as retailers increase the responsibilities of existing sales worker supervisors and as the retail industry grows slowly overall. Competition is expected. Job seekers with college degrees and retail experience should have the best prospects.

**Directly supervise sales workers in a retail establishment or department. Duties may include management functions, such as purchasing, budgeting, accounting, and personnel work, in addition to supervisory duties.** Provide customer service by greeting and assisting customers and responding to customer inquiries and complaints. Assign employees to specific duties. Monitor sales activities to ensure that customers receive satisfactory service and quality goods. Direct and supervise employees engaged in sales, inventory-taking, reconciling cash receipts, or performing services for customers. Inventory stock and reorder when inventory drops to a specified level. Keep records of purchases, sales, and requisitions. Enforce safety, health, and security rules. Examine products purchased for resale or received for storage to assess the condition of each product or item. Hire, train, and evaluate personnel in sales or marketing establishments, promoting or firing workers when appropriate. Perform work activities of subordinates, such as cleaning and organizing shelves and displays and selling merchandise. Establish and implement policies, goals, objectives, and procedures for their department. Instruct staff on how to handle difficult and complicated sales. Formulate pricing policies for merchandise according to profitability requirements. Estimate consumer demand and determine the types and amounts of goods to be sold. Examine merchandise to ensure that it is correctly priced and displayed and that it functions as advertised. Plan and prepare work schedules and keep records of employees' work schedules and time cards. Review inventory and sales records to prepare reports for management and budget departments. Plan and coordinate advertising campaigns and sales promotions and prepare merchandise displays and advertising copy. Confer with company officials to develop methods and procedures to increase sales, expand markets, and promote business. Establish credit policies and operating procedures. Plan budgets and authorize payments and merchandise returns.

**Education/Training Required:** Work experience in a related occupation. **Education and Training Programs:** Business, Management, Marketing, and Related Support Services, Other; Consumer Merchandising/Retailing Management; E-Commerce/Electronic Commerce; Floriculture/Floristry Operations and Management; Retailing and Retail Operations; Selling Skills and Sales Operations; Special Products Marketing Operations; Specialized Merchandising, Sales, and Marketing Operations, Other. **Knowledge/Courses**—Sales and Marketing, Customer and Personal Service, Personnel and Human Resources, Administration and Management, Economics and Accounting, Education and Training.

**Personality Type:** Enterprising-Conventional-Social. **Career Clusters:** 01 Agriculture, Food, and Natural Resources; 10 Human Services; 14 Marketing, Sales, and Service. **Career Pathways:** 1.2 Plant Systems; 10.5 Consumer Services Career; 14.2 Professional Sales and Marketing; 14.5 Marketing Information Management and Research. **Other Jobs in These Pathways:** Cashiers; Counter and Rental Clerks; Door-To-Door Sales Workers, News and Street Vendors, and Related Workers; Driver/Sales Workers; Energy Brokers; First-Line Supervisors of Landscaping, Lawn Service, and Groundskeeping Workers; First-Line Supervisors of Non-Retail Sales Workers; Hotel, Motel, and Resort Desk Clerks; Landscaping and Groundskeeping Workers; Marking Clerks; Online Merchants; Order Fillers, Wholesale and Retail Sales; Parts Salespersons; Property, Real Estate, and Community Association Managers; Public Relations Specialists; Real Estate Sales Agents; Retail Salespersons; Sales Managers; Sales Representatives, Services, All Other; Sales Representatives, Wholesale and Manufacturing, Except Technical and Scientific Products; Sales Representatives, Wholesale and Manufacturing, Technical and Scientific Products; Solar Sales Representatives and Assessors; Stock Clerks-Stockroom, Warehouse, or Storage Yard; Stock Clerks, Sales Floor; Telemarketers; others.

**Skills**—Management of Financial Resources, Management of Material Resources, Negotiation, Management of Personnel Resources, Persuasion, Systems Evaluation, Learning Strategies, Instructing.

**Work Environment:** Indoors; standing; walking and running; using hands; repetitive motions; noise.

# First-Line Supervisors of Transportation and Material-Moving Machine and Vehicle Operators

* ❈ Annual Earnings: $52,720
* ❈ Earnings Growth Potential: Medium (39.1%)
* ❈ Growth: –3.7%
* ❈ Annual Job Openings: 3,770
* ❈ Self-Employed: 0.8%

**Considerations for Job Outlook:** Slow decline in employment is projected.

**Directly supervise and coordinate activities of transportation and material-moving machine and vehicle operators and helpers.** Enforce safety rules and regulations. Plan work assignments and equipment allocations to meet transportation, operations, or production goals. Confer with customers, supervisors, contractors, and other personnel to exchange information and to resolve problems. Direct workers in transportation or related services, such as pumping, moving, storing, and loading and unloading of materials or people. Resolve worker problems or collaborate with employees to assist in problem resolution. Review orders, production schedules, blueprints, and shipping and receiving notices to determine work sequences and material shipping dates, types, volumes, and destinations. Monitor fieldwork to ensure that it is being performed properly and that materials are being used as they should be. Recommend and implement measures to improve worker motivation, equipment performance, work methods, and customer services. Maintain or verify records of time, materials, expenditures, and crew activities. Interpret transportation and tariff regulations, shipping orders, safety regulations, and company policies and procedures for workers. Explain and demonstrate work tasks to new workers or assign workers to more experienced workers for further training. Prepare, compile, and submit reports on work activities, operations, production, and work-related accidents. Recommend or implement personnel actions such as employee selection, evaluation, and rewards or disciplinary actions. Requisition needed personnel, supplies, equipment, parts, or repair services. Inspect or test materials, stock, vehicles, equipment, and facilities to ensure that they are safe, are free of defects, and meet specifications. Plan and establish transportation routes. Compute and estimate cash, payroll, transportation, personnel, and storage requirements. Dispatch personnel and vehicles in response to telephone or radio reports of emergencies. Perform or schedule repairs and preventive maintenance of vehicles and other equipment.

**Education/Training Required:** Work experience in a related occupation. **Education and Training Programs:** No related CIP programs; this job is learned through work experience in a related occupation. **Knowledge/Courses—** Transportation, Production and Processing, Personnel and Human Resources, Customer and Personal Service, Public Safety and Security, Administration and Management.

**Personality Type:** Enterprising-Conventional-Realistic. **Career Cluster:** 16 Transportation, Distribution, and Logistics. **Career Pathway:** 16.1 Transportation Operations. **Other Jobs in This Pathway:** Airline Pilots, Copilots, and Flight Engineers; Automotive and Watercraft Service Attendants; Automotive Master Mechanics; Bus Drivers, School or Special Client; Bus Drivers, Transit and Intercity; Commercial Pilots; Crane and Tower Operators; First-Line Supervisors of Helpers, Laborers, and Material Movers, Hand; Freight and Cargo Inspectors; Heavy and Tractor-Trailer Truck Drivers; Laborers and Freight, Stock, and Material Movers, Hand; Light Truck or Delivery Services Drivers; Mates-Ship, Boat, and Barge; Motor Vehicle Operators, All Other; Operating Engineers and Other Construction Equipment Operators; Parking Lot Attendants; Pilots, Ship; Railroad Conductors and Yardmasters; Sailors and Marine Oilers; Ship and Boat Captains; Storage and Distribution Managers; Taxi Drivers and Chauffeurs; Transportation Inspectors; Transportation Managers; Transportation Workers, All Other; others.

**Skills—**Management of Material Resources, Management of Financial Resources, Management of Personnel Resources, Systems Evaluation, Systems Analysis, Time Management, Operations Analysis, Negotiation.

**Work Environment:** Indoors; sitting; noise; contaminants.

# Fitness Trainers and Aerobics Instructors

* ❈ Annual Earnings: $31,090
* ❈ Earnings Growth Potential: High (45.1%)
* ❈ Growth: 29.4%
* ❈ Annual Job Openings: 12,380
* ❈ Self-Employed: 9.2%

**Considerations for Job Outlook:** Employment growth for these workers is expected due to increased concern about health and physical fitness. People who have degrees in fitness-related subjects should have better opportunities, and trainers who incorporate new technology and wellness issues as part of their services may be more sought after.

**Instruct or coach groups or individuals in exercise activities and the fundamentals of sports. Demonstrate techniques and methods of participation. Observe participants and inform them of corrective measures necessary to improve their skills.** Explain and enforce safety rules and regulations governing sports, recreational activities, and the use of exercise equipment. Offer alternatives during classes to accommodate different levels of fitness. Plan routines, choose appropriate music, and choose different movements for each set of muscles, depending on participants' capabilities and limitations. Observe participants and inform them of corrective measures necessary for skill improvement. Teach proper breathing techniques used during physical exertion. Teach and demonstrate use of gymnastic and training equipment such as trampolines and weights. Instruct participants in maintaining exertion levels to maximize benefits from exercise routines. Maintain fitness equipment. Conduct therapeutic, recreational, or athletic activities. Monitor participants' progress and adapt programs as needed. Evaluate individuals' abilities, needs, and physical conditions and develop suitable training programs to meet any special requirements. Plan physical education programs to promote development of participants' physical attributes and social skills. Provide students with information and resources regarding nutrition, weight control, and lifestyle issues. Administer emergency first aid, wrap injuries, treat minor chronic disabilities, or refer injured persons to physicians. Advise clients about proper clothing and shoes. Wrap ankles, fingers, wrists, or other body parts with synthetic skin, gauze, or adhesive tape to support muscles and ligaments. Teach individual and team sports to participants through instruction and demonstration, utilizing knowledge of sports techniques and of participants' physical capabilities. Promote health clubs through membership sales and record member information. Organize, lead, and referee indoor and outdoor games such as volleyball, baseball, and basketball. Maintain equipment inventories and select, store, or issue equipment as needed. Organize and conduct competitions and tournaments.

**Education/Training Required:** Postsecondary vocational training. **Education and Training Programs:** Health and Physical Education, General; Physical Education Teaching and Coaching; Sport and Fitness Administration/Management. **Knowledge/Courses—**Education and Training,

Therapy and Counseling, Customer and Personal Service, Psychology, Medicine and Dentistry, Biology.

**Personality Type:** Social-Realistic-Enterprising. **Career Cluster:** 05 Education and Training. **Career Pathways:** 5.1 Administration and Administrative Support; 5.3 Teaching/Training. **Other Jobs in These Pathways:** Adult Basic and Secondary Education and Literacy Teachers and Instructors; Career/Technical Education Teachers, Secondary School; Chemists; Coaches and Scouts; Dietitians and Nutritionists; Distance Learning Coordinators; Education Administrators, All Other; Education Administrators, Elementary and Secondary School; Education Administrators, Postsecondary; Education Administrators, Preschool and Childcare Center/Program; Elementary School Teachers, Except Special Education; Fitness and Wellness Coordinators; Instructional Coordinators; Instructional Designers and Technologists; Interpreters and Translators; Kindergarten Teachers, Except Special Education; Librarians; Middle School Teachers, Except Special and Career/Technical Education; Preschool Teachers, Except Special Education; Recreation Workers; Secondary School Teachers, Except Special and Career/Technical Education; Self-Enrichment Education Teachers; Teacher Assistants; Teachers and Instructors, All Other; Tutors; others.

**Skills—**Learning Strategies, Service Orientation, Instructing, Operations Analysis, Social Perceptiveness, Technology Design, Systems Evaluation, Persuasion.

**Work Environment:** Indoors; standing; walking and running; bending or twisting the body; repetitive motions.

# Flight Attendants

- ❋ Annual Earnings: $37,740
- ❋ Earnings Growth Potential: Low (33.9%)
- ❋ Growth: 8.1%
- ❋ Annual Job Openings: 3,010
- ❋ Self-Employed: 0.0%

**Considerations for Job Outlook:** As the population grows and the economy expands, expected increases in the volume of air passenger traffic will lead to employment growth for flight attendants. Competition is expected to be keen. Job seekers who have a bachelor's degree and relevant experience should have the best prospects.

**Provide personal services to ensure the safety and comfort of airline passengers during flight. Greet passengers, verify tickets, explain use of safety equipment, and serve food or beverages.** Direct and assist passengers in emergency procedures, such as evacuating a plane following an emergency landing. Announce and demonstrate safety and emergency procedures, such as the use of oxygen masks, seat belts, and life jackets. Walk aisles of planes to verify that passengers have complied with federal regulations prior to takeoffs and landings. Verify that first aid kits and other emergency equipment, including fire extinguishers and oxygen bottles, are in working order. Administer first aid to passengers in distress. Attend preflight briefings concerning weather, altitudes, routes, emergency procedures, crew coordination, lengths of flights, food and beverage services offered, and numbers of passengers. Prepare passengers and aircraft for landing, following procedures. Determine special assistance needs of passengers such as small children, the elderly, or disabled persons. Check to ensure that food, beverages, blankets, reading material, emergency equipment, and other supplies are aboard and are in adequate supply. Reassure passengers when situations such as turbulence are encountered. Announce flight delays and descent preparations. Inspect passenger tickets to verify information and to obtain destination information. Answer passengers' questions about flights, aircraft, weather, travel routes and services, arrival times, or schedules. Assist passengers entering or disembarking the aircraft. Inspect and clean cabins, checking for any problems and making sure that cabins are in order. Greet passengers boarding aircraft and direct them to assigned seats. Conduct periodic trips through the cabin to ensure passenger comfort and to distribute reading material, headphones, pillows, playing cards, and blankets. Take inventory of headsets, alcoholic beverages, and money collected. Operate audio and video systems. Assist passengers in placing carry-on luggage in overhead, garment, or under-seat storage.

**Education/Training Required:** Long-term on-the-job training. **Education and Training Program:** Airline Flight Attendant Training. **Knowledge/Courses**—Customer and Personal Service, Psychology, Geography, Transportation, Philosophy and Theology, Public Safety and Security.

**Personality Type:** Enterprising-Social-Conventional. **Career Cluster:** 09 Hospitality and Tourism. **Career Pathway:** 2.2 Construction. **Other Jobs in This Pathway:** Brickmasons and Blockmasons; Cement Masons and Concrete Finishers; Construction and Building Inspectors; Construction Carpenters; Construction Laborers; Construction Managers; Cost Estimators; Drywall and Ceiling Tile Installers; Electrical Power-Line Installers and Repairers; Electricians; Engineering Technicians, Except Drafters, All Other; First-Line Supervisors of Construction Trades and Extraction Workers; Heating and Air Conditioning Mechanics and Installers; Helpers—Carpenters; Helpers—Electricians; Helpers—Pipelayers, Plumbers, Pipefitters, and Steamfitters; Highway Maintenance Workers; Operating Engineers and Other Construction Equipment Operators; Painters, Construction and Maintenance; Pipe Fitters and Steamfitters; Plumbers; Refrigeration Mechanics and Installers; Roofers; Rough Carpenters; Solar Energy Installation Managers; others.

**Skills**—Service Orientation, Negotiation, Critical Thinking, Coordination, Quality Control Analysis, Troubleshooting, Persuasion, Technology Design.

**Work Environment:** Indoors; standing; walking and running; balancing; using hands; bending or twisting the body; repetitive motions; noise; contaminants; cramped work space; exposed to disease or infections; high places.

# Food Scientists and Technologists

* ❋ Annual Earnings: $60,180
* ❋ Earnings Growth Potential: High (43.0%)
* ❋ Growth: 16.3%
* ❋ Annual Job Openings: 690
* ❋ Self-Employed: 12.5%

**Considerations for Job Outlook:** Job growth is expected to stem primarily from efforts to increase the quantity and quality of food for a growing population and to balance output with protection and preservation of soil, water, and ecosystems. Opportunities should be good for agricultural and food scientists in almost all fields.

**Use chemistry, microbiology, engineering, and other sciences to study the principles underlying the processing and deterioration of foods; analyze food content to determine levels of vitamins, fat, sugar, and protein; discover new food sources; research ways to make processed foods safe, palatable, and healthful; and apply food science knowledge to determine the best ways to process, package, preserve, store, and distribute food.** Test new products for flavor, texture, color, nutritional content, and adherence to government and industry standards. Check raw ingredients for maturity or stability for processing and finished products for safety, quality, and nutritional value. Confer with process engineers, plant operators, flavor experts, and packaging and marketing specialists in order to resolve problems in product development. Evaluate food processing and storage operations and assist in the development of quality assurance programs for such operations. Study methods to improve aspects of foods such as chemical composition, flavor, color, texture, nutritional value, and convenience. Study the structure and composition of food or the changes foods undergo in storage and processing. Develop new or improved ways of preserving, processing, packaging, storing, and delivering foods, using knowledge of chemistry, microbiology, and other sciences. Develop food standards and production specifications, safety and sanitary regulations, and waste management and water supply specifications. Demonstrate products to clients. Inspect food processing areas in order to ensure compliance with government regulations and standards for sanitation, safety, quality, and waste management standards. Search for substitutes for harmful or undesirable additives, such as nitrites.

**Education/Training Required:** Bachelor's degree. **Education and Training Programs:** Agriculture, General; Food Science; Food Technology and Processing; International Agriculture. **Knowledge/Courses**—Food Production, Biology, Chemistry, Production and Processing, Physics, Engineering and Technology.

**Personality Type:** Investigative-Realistic-Conventional. **Career Cluster:** 01 Agriculture, Food, and Natural Resources. **Career Pathways:** 1.1 Food Products and Processing Systems; 1.2 Plant Systems; 1.7 Agribusiness Systems. **Other Jobs in These Pathways:** Agricultural Technicians; Biochemists and Biophysicists; Biologists; Chemical Technicians; First-Line Supervisors of Landscaping, Lawn Service, and Groundskeeping Workers; First-Line Supervisors of Office and Administrative Support Workers; First-Line Supervisors of Retail Sales Workers; Floral Designers; Food and Tobacco Roasting, Baking, and Drying Machine Operators and Tenders; Food Batchmakers; Food Cooking Machine Operators and Tenders; Food Science Technicians; Geneticists; Graders and Sorters, Agricultural Products; Graphic Designers; Grounds Maintenance Workers, All Other; Landscaping and Groundskeeping Workers; Nonfarm Animal Caretakers; Office Machine Operators, Except Computer; Pest Control Workers; Pesticide Handlers, Sprayers, and Applicators, Vegetation; Precision Agriculture Technicians; Reporters and Correspondents; Retail Salespersons; Tree Trimmers and Pruners; others.

**Skills**—Science, Quality Control Analysis, Systems Evaluation, Systems Analysis, Negotiation, Complex Problem Solving, Writing, Active Learning.

**Work Environment:** Indoors; sitting; noise.

# Food Service Managers

- ❋ Annual Earnings: $48,130
- ❋ Earnings Growth Potential: Medium (36.7%)
- ❋ Growth: 5.3%
- ❋ Annual Job Openings: 8,370
- ❋ Self-Employed: 42.0%

**Considerations for Job Outlook:** Job losses resulting from a declining number of eating and drinking places will be partially offset by the creation of new jobs in grocery and convenience stores, health-care and elder care facilities, and other establishments. Opportunities for new managers should be good because of the need to replace workers who leave the occupation.

**Plan, direct, or coordinate activities of an organization or department that serves food and beverages.** Monitor compliance with health and fire regulations regarding food preparation and serving and building maintenance for lodging and dining facilities. Monitor food preparation methods, portion sizes, and garnishing and presentation of food to ensure that food is prepared and presented in an acceptable manner. Count money and make bank deposits. Investigate and resolve complaints regarding food quality, service, or accommodations. Coordinate assignments of cooking personnel to ensure economical use of food and timely preparation. Schedule and receive food and beverage deliveries, checking delivery contents to verify product quality and quantity. Monitor budgets and payroll records and review financial transactions to ensure that expenditures are authorized and budgeted. Schedule staff hours and assign duties. Maintain food and equipment inventories and keep inventory records. Establish standards for personnel performance and customer service. Perform some food preparation or service tasks such as cooking, clearing tables, and serving food and drinks, when necessary. Plan menus and food utilization based on anticipated number of guests, nutritional value, palatability, popularity, and costs. Keep records required by government agencies regarding sanitation and, when appropriate, food subsidies. Test cooked food by tasting and smelling it to ensure palatability and flavor conformity. Organize and direct worker training programs, resolve personnel problems, hire new staff, and evaluate employee performance in dining and lodging facilities. Order and purchase equipment and supplies. Review work procedures and operational problems to determine ways to improve service, performance, or safety. Assess staffing needs and recruit staff, using methods such as newspaper advertisements or attendance at job fairs. Arrange for equipment maintenance and repairs and coordinate a variety of services such as waste removal and pest control.

**Education/Training Required:** Work experience in a related occupation. **Education and Training Programs:** Hospitality Administration/Management, General; Hotel/Motel Administration/Management; Restaurant, Culinary, and Catering Management/Manager; Restaurant/Food Services Management. **Knowledge/Courses**—Food Production, Sales and Marketing, Personnel and Human Resources, Production and Processing, Education and Training, Administration and Management.

**Personality Type:** Enterprising-Conventional-Realistic. **Career Cluster:** 09 Hospitality and Tourism. **Career Pathways:** 9.1 Restaurants and Food/Beverage Services; 9.2 Lodging; 9.3 Travel and Tourism. **Other Jobs in These Pathways:** Bakers; Baristas; Bartenders; Butchers and Meat Cutters; Chefs and Head Cooks; Combined Food Preparation and Serving Workers, Including Fast Food; Cooks, Fast Food; Cooks, Institution and Cafeteria; Cooks, Restaurant; Cooks, Short Order; Counter Attendants, Cafeteria, Food Concession, and Coffee Shop; Dining Room and Cafeteria Attendants and Bartender Helpers; Dishwashers; First-Line Supervisors of Food Preparation and Serving Workers; First-Line Supervisors of Housekeeping and Janitorial Workers; Food Preparation Workers; Food Servers, Nonrestaurant; Hosts and Hostesses, Restaurant, Lounge, and Coffee Shop; Janitors and Cleaners, Except Maids and Housekeeping Cleaners; Maids and Housekeeping Cleaners; Managers, All Other; Meat, Poultry, and Fish Cutters and Trimmers; Reservation and Transportation Ticket Agents and Travel Clerks; Supply Chain Managers; Waiters and Waitresses; others.

**Skills**—Management of Financial Resources, Management of Material Resources, Operations Analysis, Management of Personnel Resources, Negotiation, Equipment Maintenance, Service Orientation, Repairing.

**Work Environment:** Indoors; standing; walking and running; using hands; repetitive motions; noise; contaminants; minor burns, cuts, bites, or stings.

# Foreign Language and Literature Teachers, Postsecondary

* Annual Earnings: $59,080
* Earnings Growth Potential: High (42.8%)
* Growth: 15.1%
* Annual Job Openings: 900
* Self-Employed: 0.2%

**Considerations for Job Outlook:** Enrollments in postsecondary institutions are expected to continue rising as more people attend college and as workers return to school to update their skills. Opportunities for part-time or temporary positions should be favorable, but significant competition exists for tenure-track positions.

**Teach courses in foreign (i.e., other than English) languages and literature.** Evaluate and grade students' classwork, assignments, and papers. Prepare course materials such as syllabi, homework assignments, and handouts. Initiate, facilitate, and moderate classroom discussions. Maintain student attendance records, grades, and other required records. Compile, administer, and grade examinations or assign this work to others. Plan, evaluate, and revise curricula, course content, and course materials and methods of instruction. Prepare and deliver lectures to undergraduate and graduate students on topics such as how to speak and write a foreign language and the cultural aspects of areas where a particular language is used. Maintain regularly scheduled office hours to advise and assist students. Select and obtain materials and supplies such as textbooks. Keep abreast of developments in their field by reading current literature, talking with colleagues, and participating in professional organizations and activities. Advise students on academic and vocational curricula and on career issues. Conduct research in a particular field of knowledge and publish findings in scholarly journals, books, and/or electronic media. Collaborate with colleagues to address teaching and research issues. Serve on academic or administrative committees that deal with institutional policies, departmental matters, and academic issues. Participate in student recruitment, registration, and placement activities. Compile bibliographies of specialized materials for outside reading assignments. Participate in campus and community events. Act as advisers to student organizations. Perform administrative duties such as serving as department head. Supervise undergraduate and graduate teaching, internship, and research work. Write grant proposals to procure external research funding. Provide professional consulting services to government or industry.

**Education/Training Required:** Doctoral degree. **Education and Training Programs:** Ancient Near Eastern and Biblical Languages, Literatures, and Linguistics; Ancient/ Classical Greek Language and Literature; Arabic Language and Literature; Celtic Languages, Literatures, and Linguistics; Chinese Language and Literature; Classics and Classical Languages, Literatures, and Linguistics, General; East Asian Languages, Literatures, and Linguistics, Other; Filipino/Tagalog Language and Literature; Foreign Languages and Literatures, General; Foreign Languages, Literatures, and Linguistics, Other; French Language and Literature; German Language and Literature; Germanic Languages, Literatures, and Linguistics, Other; Hebrew Language and Literature; Hindi Language and Literature; Italian Language and Literature; Japanese Language and Literature; Language Interpretation and Translation; Latin Language and Literature; Linguistics; Middle/Near Eastern and Semitic Languages, Literatures, and Linguistics, Other; others. **Knowledge/Courses**—Foreign Language, Philosophy and Theology, History and Archeology, Sociology and Anthropology, Geography, English Language.

**Personality Type:** Social-Artistic-Investigative. **Career Cluster:** 05 Education and Training. **Career Pathway:** 5.3 Teaching/Training. **Other Jobs in This Pathway:** Adult Basic and Secondary Education and Literacy Teachers and Instructors; Athletes and Sports Competitors; Audio-Visual and Multimedia Collections Specialists; Career/Technical Education Teachers, Middle School; Career/Technical Education Teachers, Secondary School; Chemists; Coaches and Scouts; Dietitians and Nutritionists; Elementary School Teachers, Except Special Education; Fitness Trainers and Aerobics Instructors; Historians; Instructional Coordinators; Instructional Designers and Technologists; Interpreters and Translators; Kindergarten Teachers, Except Special Education; Librarians; Middle School Teachers, Except Special and Career/Technical Education; Physicists; Preschool Teachers, Except Special Education; Recreation Workers; Secondary School Teachers, Except Special and Career/ Technical Education; Self-Enrichment Education Teachers; Teacher Assistants; Tutors; 37 other postsecondary teaching occupations.

**Skills**—Writing, Learning Strategies, Instructing, Speaking, Reading Comprehension, Operations Analysis, Active Listening, Active Learning.

**Work Environment:** Indoors; sitting.

# Forensic Science Technicians

- ❋ Annual Earnings: $51,570
- ❋ Earnings Growth Potential: Medium (36.2%)
- ❋ Growth: 19.6%
- ❋ Annual Job Openings: 800
- ❋ Self-Employed: 1.7%

**Considerations for Job Outlook:** The continued growth of scientific and medical research and the development and manufacturing of technical products are expected to drive employment growth for these workers. Opportunities are expected to be best for graduates of applied science technology programs who are knowledgeable about equipment used in laboratories or production facilities.

**Collect, identify, classify, and analyze physical evidence related to criminal investigations. Perform tests on weapons or substances such as fiber, hair, and tissue to determine significance to investigation. May testify as expert witnesses on evidence or crime laboratory techniques. May serve as specialists in area of expertise, such as ballistics, fingerprinting, handwriting, or biochemistry.** Testify in court about investigative and analytical methods and findings. Keep records and prepare reports detailing findings, investigative methods, and laboratory techniques. Interpret laboratory findings and test results to identify and classify substances, materials, and other evidence collected at crime scenes. Operate and maintain laboratory equipment and apparatus. Prepare solutions, reagents, and sample formulations needed for laboratory work. Analyze and classify biological fluids, using DNA typing or serological techniques. Collect evidence from crime scenes, storing it in conditions that preserve its integrity. Identify and quantify drugs and poisons found in biological fluids and tissues, in foods, and at crime scenes. Analyze handwritten and machine-produced textual evidence to decipher altered or obliterated text or to determine authorship, age, or source. Reconstruct crime scenes to determine relationships among pieces of evidence. Examine DNA samples to determine if they match other samples. Collect impressions of dust from surfaces to obtain and identify fingerprints. Analyze gunshot residue and bullet paths to determine how shootings occurred. Visit morgues, examine scenes of crimes, or contact other sources to obtain evidence or information to be used in investigations. Examine physical evidence such as hair, fiber, wood, or soil residues to obtain information about its source and composition. Determine types of bullets used in shooting and whether they were fired from a specific weapon. Examine firearms to determine mechanical condition and legal status, performing restoration work on damaged firearms to obtain information such as serial numbers. Confer with ballistics, fingerprinting, handwriting, document, electronics, medical, chemical, or metallurgical experts concerning evidence and its interpretation. Interpret the pharmacological effects of a drug or a combination of drugs on an individual.

**Education/Training Required:** Bachelor's degree. **Education and Training Program:** Forensic Science and Technology. **Knowledge/Courses**—Chemistry, Biology, Clerical, Law and Government, Design, Customer and Personal Service.

**Personality Type:** Investigative-Realistic-Conventional. **Career Cluster:** 12 Law, Public Safety, Corrections, and Security. **Career Pathway:** 12.4 Law Enforcement Services. **Other Jobs in This Pathway:** Bailiffs; Correctional Officers and Jailers; Criminal Investigators and Special Agents; First-Line Supervisors of Police and Detectives; Immigration and Customs Inspectors; Intelligence Analysts; Police Detectives; Police Identification and Records Officers; Police Patrol Officers; Remote Sensing Scientists and Technologists; Sheriffs and Deputy Sheriffs.

**Skills**—Science, Instructing, Speaking, Writing, Critical Thinking, Mathematics, Reading Comprehension, Operation and Control.

**Work Environment:** More often indoors than outdoors; sitting; using hands; contaminants; hazardous conditions.

# Forestry and Conservation Science Teachers, Postsecondary

* Annual Earnings: $78,290
* Earnings Growth Potential: High (44.5%)
* Growth: 15.1%
* Annual Job Openings: 100
* Self-Employed: 0.2%

**Considerations for Job Outlook:** Enrollments in postsecondary institutions are expected to continue rising as more people attend college and as workers return to school to update their skills. Opportunities for part-time or temporary positions should be favorable, but significant competition exists for tenure-track positions.

**Teach courses in environmental and conservation science.** Conduct research in a particular field of knowledge and publish findings in books, professional journals, and/ or electronic media. Keep abreast of developments in their field by reading current literature, talking with colleagues, and participating in professional conferences. Prepare and deliver lectures to undergraduate and/or graduate students on topics such as forest resource policy, forest pathology, and mapping. Evaluate and grade students' classwork, assignments, and papers. Write grant proposals to procure external research funding. Supervise undergraduate and/ or graduate teaching, internship, and research work. Plan, evaluate, and revise curricula, course content, and course materials and methods of instruction. Prepare course materials such as syllabi, homework assignments, and handouts. Compile, administer, and grade examinations or assign this work to others. Advise students on academic and vocational curricula and on career issues. Initiate, facilitate, and moderate classroom discussions. Supervise students' laboratory work and fieldwork. Maintain student attendance records, grades, and other required records. Collaborate with colleagues to address teaching and research issues. Maintain regularly scheduled office hours in order to advise and assist students. Select and obtain materials and supplies such as textbooks and laboratory equipment. Participate in student recruitment, registration, and placement activities. Serve on academic or administrative committees that deal with institutional policies, departmental matters, and academic issues. Provide professional consulting services to government and/or industry. Perform administrative duties such as serving as department head. Compile bibliographies of specialized materials for outside reading assignments. Act as advisers to student organizations. Participate in campus and community events.

**Education/Training Required:** Doctoral degree. **Education and Training Program:** Science Teacher Education/General Science Teacher Education. **Knowledge/Courses**—Biology, Geography, Education and Training, Mathematics, History and Archeology, Chemistry.

**Personality Type:** Social-Investigative-Realistic. **Career Clusters:** 01 Agriculture, Food, and Natural Resources; 05 Education and Training. **Career Pathways:** 1.5 Natural Resources Systems; 5.3 Teaching/Training. **Other Jobs in These Pathways:** Adult Basic and Secondary Education and Literacy Teachers and Instructors; Career/Technical Education Teachers, Secondary School; Chemists; Climate Change Analysts; Coaches and Scouts; Elementary School Teachers, Except Special Education; Engineering Technicians, Except Drafters, All Other; Environmental Restoration Planners; Environmental Scientists and Specialists, Including Health; Fitness Trainers and Aerobics Instructors; Industrial Ecologists; Industrial Truck and Tractor Operators; Instructional Coordinators; Instructional Designers and Technologists; Kindergarten Teachers, Except Special

Education; Librarians; Middle School Teachers, Except Special and Career/Technical Education; Preschool Teachers, Except Special Education; Recreation Workers; Refuse and Recyclable Material Collectors; Secondary School Teachers, Except Special and Career/Technical Education; Self-Enrichment Education Teachers; Teacher Assistants; Tutors; 37 other postsecondary teaching occupations; others.

**Skills**—Writing, Science, Learning Strategies, Instructing, Reading Comprehension, Active Learning, Speaking, Operations Analysis.

**Work Environment:** Indoors; sitting.

# Funeral Attendants

- ❋ Annual Earnings: $22,990
- ❋ Earnings Growth Potential: Low (27.9%)
- ❋ Growth: 26.3%
- ❋ Annual Job Openings: 2,550
- ❋ Self-Employed: 2.5%

**Considerations for Job Outlook:** Much-faster-than-average employment growth is projected.

**Perform variety of tasks during funeral, such as placing casket in parlor or chapel prior to service, arranging floral offerings or lights around casket, directing or escorting mourners, closing casket, and issuing and storing funeral equipment.** Perform a variety of tasks during funerals to assist funeral directors and to ensure that services run smoothly and as planned. Greet people at the funeral home. Offer assistance to mourners as they enter or exit limousines. Close caskets at appropriate point in services. Transfer the deceased to funeral homes. Obtain burial permits and register deaths. Direct or escort mourners to parlors or chapels in which wakes or funerals are being held. Place caskets in parlors or chapels prior to wakes or funerals. Clean and drive funeral vehicles such as cars or hearses in funeral processions. Carry flowers to hearses or limousines for transportation to places of interment. Clean funeral parlors and chapels. Arrange floral offerings or lights around caskets. Provide advice to mourners on how to make charitable donations in honor of the deceased. Perform general maintenance duties for funeral homes. Issue and store funeral equipment. Assist with cremations and with the processing and packaging of cremated remains. Act as pallbearers.

**Education/Training Required:** Short-term on-the-job training. **Education and Training Program:** Funeral Service and Mortuary Science, General. **Knowledge/Courses**—Philosophy and Theology, Transportation,

Customer and Personal Service, Psychology, Law and Government, Clerical.

**Personality Type:** Social-Enterprising-Realistic. **Career Cluster:** 10 Human Services. **Career Pathway:** 10.4 Personal Care Services. **Other Jobs in This Pathway:** Barbers; Embalmers; Funeral Service Managers; Hairdressers, Hairstylists, and Cosmetologists; Laundry and Dry-Cleaning Workers; Makeup Artists, Theatrical and Performance; Manicurists and Pedicurists; Pressers, Textile, Garment, and Related Materials; Sewers, Hand; Sewing Machine Operators; Shampooers; Skincare Specialists; Tailors, Dressmakers, and Custom Sewers; Textile Bleaching and Dyeing Machine Operators and Tenders.

**Skills**—Equipment Maintenance, Social Perceptiveness, Service Orientation.

**Work Environment:** More often indoors than outdoors; standing.

# Gaming Dealers

- ❋ Annual Earnings: $18,090
- ❋ Earnings Growth Potential: Very low (13.5%)
- ❋ Growth: 19.0%
- ❋ Annual Job Openings: 5,590
- ❋ Self-Employed: 0.9%

**Considerations for Job Outlook:** Expansion of existing facilities and easing of state government restrictions on gaming facilities are expected to drive employment growth in gaming occupations. Keen competition is expected. Prospects should be best for job seekers who have experience, postsecondary training, and customer service skills.

**Operate table games. Stand or sit behind table and operate games of chance by dispensing the appropriate number of cards or blocks to players or operating other gaming equipment. Compare the house's hand against players' hands and pay off or collect players' money or chips.** Exchange paper currency for playing chips or coin money. Pay winnings or collect losing bets as established by the rules and procedures of a specific game. Deal cards to house hands and compare these with players' hands to determine winners, as in blackjack. Conduct gambling games such as dice, roulette, cards, or keno, following all applicable rules and regulations. Check to ensure that all players have placed bets before play begins. Stand behind a gaming table and deal the appropriate number of cards to each player. Inspect cards and equipment to be used in games to ensure that they are in good condition. Start and control games and gaming equipment and announce winning numbers or colors. Open and close cash floats and game tables. Compute amounts of players' wins or losses or scan winning tickets presented by patrons to calculate the amount of money won. Apply rule variations to card games such as poker, in which players bet on the value of their hands. Receive, verify, and record patrons' cash wagers. Answer questions about game rules and casino policies. Refer patrons to gaming cashiers to collect winnings. Work as part of a team of dealers in games such as baccarat or craps. Participate in games for gambling establishments to provide the minimum complement of players at a table. Seat patrons at gaming tables. Prepare collection reports for submission to supervisors. Monitor gambling tables and supervise staff. Train new dealers.

**Education/Training Required:** Postsecondary vocational training. **Education and Training Programs:** No related CIP programs; this job is learned through specialized training, often at a dealer school. **Knowledge/Courses**—Psychology, Mathematics, Customer and Personal Service, Sales and Marketing.

**Personality Type:** Conventional-Enterprising-Realistic. **Career Cluster:** 09 Hospitality and Tourism. **Career Pathway:** 9.4 Recreation, Amusements, and Attractions. **Other Jobs in This Pathway:** Amusement and Recreation Attendants; Baggage Porters and Bellhops; Concierges; Costume Attendants; Entertainment Attendants and Related Workers, All Other; Farm and Home Management Advisors; Gaming and Sports Book Writers and Runners; Gaming Service Workers, All Other; Locker Room, Coatroom, and Dressing Room Attendants; Lodging Managers; Motion Picture Projectionists; Personal Care and Service Workers, All Other; Ushers, Lobby Attendants, and Ticket Takers.

**Skills**—Service Orientation, Negotiation.

**Work Environment:** Indoors; standing; using hands; bending or twisting the body; repetitive motions; noise.

# Gaming Managers

- ❋ Annual Earnings: $66,960
- ❋ Earnings Growth Potential: Medium (39.2%)
- ❋ Growth: 11.9%
- ❋ Annual Job Openings: 200
- ❋ Self-Employed: 38.6%

**Considerations for Job Outlook:** About average employment growth is projected.

**Plan, organize, direct, control, or coordinate gaming operations in a casino. Formulate gaming policies for their area of responsibility.** Resolve customer complaints regarding problems such as payout errors. Remove suspected cheaters, such as card counters and other players who may have systems that shift the odds of winning to their favor. Maintain familiarity with all games used at a facility, as well as strategies and tricks employed in those games. Train new workers and evaluate their performance. Circulate among gaming tables to ensure that operations are conducted properly, that dealers follow house rules, and that players are not cheating. Explain and interpret house rules, such as game rules and betting limits. Monitor staffing levels to ensure that games and tables are adequately staffed for each shift, arranging for staff rotations and breaks and locating substitute employees as necessary. Interview and hire workers. Prepare work schedules and station assignments and keep attendance records. Direct the distribution of complimentary hotel rooms, meals, and other discounts or free items given to players based on their length of play and betting totals. Establish policies on issues such as the type of gambling offered and the odds, the extension of credit, and the serving of food and beverages. Track supplies of money to tables and perform any required paperwork. Set and maintain a bank and table limit for each game. Monitor credit extended to players. Review operational expenses, budget estimates, betting accounts, and collection reports for accuracy. Record, collect, and pay off bets, issuing receipts as necessary. Direct workers compiling summary sheets that show wager amounts and payoffs for races and events. Notify board attendants of table vacancies so that waiting patrons can play.

**Education/Training Required:** Work experience in a related occupation. **Education and Training Program:** Casino Management. **Knowledge/Courses**—Sales and Marketing, Personnel and Human Resources, Customer and Personal Service, Administration and Management, Economics and Accounting, Mathematics.

**Personality Type:** Enterprising-Conventional. **Career Cluster:** 09 Hospitality and Tourism. **Career Pathway:** 9.1 Restaurants and Food/Beverage Services. **Other Jobs in This Pathway:** Bakers; Baristas; Bartenders; Butchers and Meat Cutters; Chefs and Head Cooks; Combined Food Preparation and Serving Workers, Including Fast Food; Cooks, All Other; Cooks, Fast Food; Cooks, Institution and Cafeteria; Cooks, Private Household; Cooks, Restaurant; Cooks, Short Order; Counter Attendants, Cafeteria, Food Concession, and Coffee Shop; Dining Room and Cafeteria Attendants and Bartender Helpers; Dishwashers; First-Line Supervisors of Food Preparation and Serving Workers;

Food Preparation and Serving Related Workers, All Other; Food Preparation Workers; Food Servers, Nonrestaurant; Food Service Managers; Hosts and Hostesses, Restaurant, Lounge, and Coffee Shop; Meat, Poultry, and Fish Cutters and Trimmers; Slaughterers and Meat Packers; Waiters and Waitresses.

**Skills**—Management of Financial Resources, Persuasion, Service Orientation, Negotiation, Management of Personnel Resources, Monitoring, Systems Evaluation, Time Management.

**Work Environment:** Indoors; standing; walking and running; noise; contaminants.

# Gaming Supervisors

- ❀ Annual Earnings: $48,530
- ❀ Earnings Growth Potential: Medium (36.7%)
- ❀ Growth: 11.8%
- ❀ Annual Job Openings: 1,410
- ❀ Self-Employed: 36.6%

**Considerations for Job Outlook:** Expansion of existing facilities and easing of state government restrictions on gaming facilities are expected to drive employment growth in gaming occupations. Keen competition is expected. Prospects should be best for job seekers who have experience, postsecondary training, and customer service skills.

**Supervise gaming operations and personnel in an assigned area. Circulate among tables and observe operations. Ensure that stations and games are covered for each shift. May explain and interpret operating rules of house to patrons. May plan and organize activities and create friendly atmosphere for guests in hotels/casinos. May adjust service complaints.** Monitor game operations to ensure that house rules are followed, that tribal, state, and federal regulations are adhered to, and that employees provide prompt and courteous service. Observe gamblers' behavior for signs of cheating such as marking, switching, or counting cards; notify security staff of suspected cheating. Maintain familiarity with the games at a facility and with strategies and tricks used by cheaters at such games. Perform paperwork required for monetary transactions. Resolve customer and employee complaints. Greet customers and ask about the quality of service they are receiving. Establish and maintain banks and table limits for each game. Report customer-related incidents occurring in gaming areas to supervisors. Monitor stations and games and move dealers from game to game to ensure adequate staffing. Explain and interpret house rules, such as game rules and betting limits, for patrons. Supervise the distribution of complimentary meals, hotel rooms, discounts, and other items given to players based on length of play and amount bet. Evaluate workers' performance and prepare written performance evaluations. Monitor patrons for signs of compulsive gambling, offering assistance if necessary. Record, issue receipts for, and pay off bets. Monitor and verify the counting, wrapping, weighing, and distribution of currency and coins. Direct workers compiling summary sheets for each race or event to record amounts wagered and amounts to be paid to winners. Determine how many gaming tables to open each day and schedule staff accordingly. Establish policies on types of gambling offered, odds, and extension of credit. Interview, hire, and train workers. Provide fire protection and first-aid assistance when necessary. Review operational expenses, budget estimates, betting accounts, and collection reports for accuracy.

**Education/Training Required:** Work experience in a related occupation. **Education and Training Program:** Casino Management. **Knowledge/Courses**—Customer and Personal Service, Psychology, Mathematics, Law and Government, Sales and Marketing, Personnel and Human Resources.

**Personality Type:** Enterprising-Conventional. **Career Cluster:** 04 Business, Management, and Administration. **Career Pathway:** 4.1 Management. **Other Jobs in This Pathway:** Brownfield Redevelopment Specialists and Site Managers; Business Continuity Planners; Business Operations Specialists, All Other; Chief Executives; Chief Sustainability Officers; Compliance Managers; Computer and Information Systems Managers; Construction Managers; Customs Brokers; Energy Auditors; First-Line Supervisors of Office and Administrative Support Workers; General and Operations Managers; Investment Fund Managers; Loss Prevention Managers; Management Analysts; Managers, All Other; Public Relations Specialists; Regulatory Affairs Managers; Sales Managers; Security Management Specialists; Security Managers; Supply Chain Managers; Sustainability Specialists; Wind Energy Operations Managers; Wind Energy Project Managers; others.

**Skills**—Management of Financial Resources, Management of Personnel Resources, Social Perceptiveness, Negotiation, Time Management, Service Orientation, Systems Evaluation, Monitoring.

**Work Environment:** Indoors; standing; walking and running; noise; contaminants.

# General and Operations Managers

- ❈ Annual Earnings: $94,400
- ❈ Earnings Growth Potential: High (49.9%)
- ❈ Growth: –0.1%
- ❈ Annual Job Openings: 50,220
- ❈ Self-Employed: 0.9%

**Considerations for Job Outlook:** The number of top executives is expected to remain steady, but employment may be adversely affected by consolidation and mergers. Keen competition is expected.

**Plan, direct, or coordinate the operations of companies or public- and private-sector organizations. Duties and responsibilities include formulating policies, managing daily operations, and planning the use of materials and human resources, but are too diverse and general in nature to be classified in any one functional area of management or administration, such as personnel, purchasing, or administrative services. Includes owners and managers who head small business establishments whose duties are primarily managerial.** Oversee activities directly related to making products or providing services. Direct and coordinate activities of businesses or departments concerned with the production, pricing, sales, or distribution of products. Review financial statements, sales and activity reports, and other performance data to measure productivity and goal achievement and to determine areas needing cost reduction and program improvement. Manage staff, preparing work schedules and assigning specific duties. Direct and coordinate organization's financial and budget activities to fund operations, maximize investments and increase efficiency. Establish and implement departmental policies, goals, objectives, and procedures, conferring with board members, organization officials, and staff members as necessary. Determine staffing requirements, and interview, hire, and train new employees, or oversee those personnel processes. Plan and direct activities such as sales promotions, coordinating with other department heads as required. Determine goods and services to be sold and set prices and credit terms based on forecasts of customer demand. Monitor businesses and agencies to ensure that they efficiently and effectively provide needed services while staying within budgetary limits. Locate, select, and procure merchandise for resale, representing management in purchase negotiations. Perform sales floor work such as greeting and assisting customers, stocking shelves, and taking inventory. Manage the movement of goods into and out of production facilities. Develop and implement product marketing strategies, including advertising campaigns and sales promotions. Recommend locations for new facilities or oversee the remodeling of current facilities. Direct non-merchandising departments of businesses such as advertising and purchasing. Plan store layouts and design displays.

**Education/Training Required:** Work experience plus degree. **Education and Training Programs:** Business Administration and Management, General; Entrepreneurship/Entrepreneurial Studies; International Business/Trade/Commerce; Public Administration. **Knowledge/Courses—** Economics and Accounting, Personnel and Human Resources, Administration and Management, Sales and Marketing, Clerical, Building and Construction.

**Personality Type:** Enterprising-Conventional-Social. **Career Clusters:** 04 Business, Management, and Administration; 07 Government and Public Administration. **Career Pathways:** 4.1 Management; 7.1 Governance. **Other Jobs in These Pathways:** Administrative Services Managers; Brownfield Redevelopment Specialists and Site Managers; Business Continuity Planners; Business Operations Specialists, All Other; Chief Executives; Chief Sustainability Officers; Compliance Managers; Computer and Information Systems Managers; Construction Managers; Customs Brokers; Energy Auditors; First-Line Supervisors of Office and Administrative Support Workers; Investment Fund Managers; Loss Prevention Managers; Management Analysts; Managers, All Other; Public Relations Specialists; Regulatory Affairs Managers; Sales Managers; Security Management Specialists; Security Managers; Supply Chain Managers; Sustainability Specialists; Wind Energy Operations Managers; Wind Energy Project Managers; others.

**Skills—**Management of Material Resources, Management of Financial Resources, Operations Analysis, Management of Personnel Resources, Negotiation, Systems Analysis, Coordination, Systems Evaluation.

**Work Environment:** Indoors; more often sitting than standing; noise.

# Geographers

- ❈ Annual Earnings: $72,800
- ❈ Earnings Growth Potential: High (41.7%)
- ❈ Growth: 26.0%
- ❈ Annual Job Openings: 100
- ❈ Self-Employed: 1.5%

**Considerations for Job Outlook:** Social scientists, other, are expected to have employment growth of 22 percent from 2008–2018, much faster than the average for all occupations. Job competition is expected.

**Study nature and use of areas of Earth's surface, relating and interpreting interactions of physical and cultural phenomena. Conduct research on physical aspects of a region, including land forms, climates, soils, plants, and animals, and conduct research on the spatial implications of human activities within a given area, including social characteristics, economic activities, and political organization, as well as researching interdependence between regions at scales ranging from local to global.** Create and modify maps, graphs, or diagrams, using geographical information software and related equipment and principles of cartography such as coordinate systems, longitude, latitude, elevation, topography, and map scales. Write and present reports of research findings. Develop, operate, and maintain geographical information (GIS) computer systems, including hardware, software, plotters, digitizers, printers, and video cameras. Locate and obtain existing geographic information databases. Analyze geographic distributions of physical and cultural phenomena on local, regional, continental, or global scales. Teach geography. Gather and compile geographic data from sources including censuses, field observations, satellite imagery, aerial photographs, and existing maps. Conduct fieldwork at outdoor sites. Study the economic, political, and cultural characteristics of a specific region's population. Provide consulting services in fields including resource development and management, business location and market area analysis, environmental hazards, regional cultural history, and urban social planning. Collect data on physical characteristics of specified areas, such as geological formations, climates, and vegetation, using surveying or meteorological equipment. Provide geographical information systems support to the private and public sectors.

**Education/Training Required:** Master's degree. **Education and Training Program:** Geography. **Knowledge/Courses**—Geography, Sociology and Anthropology, History and Archeology, Philosophy and Theology, Foreign Language, Biology.

**Personality Type:** Investigative-Realistic-Artistic. **Career Cluster:** 15 Science, Technology, Engineering, and Mathematics. **Career Pathway:** 15.2 Science and Mathematics. **Other Jobs in This Pathway:** Architectural and Engineering Managers; Biochemists and Biophysicists; Biofuels/Biodiesel Technology and Product Development Managers; Bioinformatics Scientists; Biological Scientists, All Other; Biologists; Biostatisticians; Chemists; Clinical Data Managers; Clinical Research Coordinators; Community and Social Service Specialists, All Other; Dietitians and Nutritionists;

Education, Training, and Library Workers, All Other; Geneticists; Geoscientists, Except Hydrologists and Geographers; Medical Scientists, Except Epidemiologists; Molecular and Cellular Biologists; Natural Sciences Managers; Operations Research Analysts; Physical Scientists, All Other; Social Scientists and Related Workers, All Other; Statisticians; Survey Researchers; Transportation Planners; Water Resource Specialists; others.

**Skills**—Science, Writing, Systems Analysis, Systems Evaluation, Operations Analysis, Reading Comprehension, Active Learning, Instructing.

**Work Environment:** Indoors; sitting.

# Geography Teachers, Postsecondary

- ✹ Annual Earnings: $66,700
- ✹ Earnings Growth Potential: High (42.0%)
- ✹ Growth: 15.1%
- ✹ Annual Job Openings: 100
- ✹ Self-Employed: 0.2%

**Considerations for Job Outlook:** Enrollments in postsecondary institutions are expected to continue rising as more people attend college and as workers return to school to update their skills. Opportunities for part-time or temporary positions should be favorable, but significant competition exists for tenure-track positions.

**Teach courses in geography.** Prepare and deliver lectures to undergraduate and/or graduate students on topics such as urbanization, environmental systems, and cultural geography. Evaluate and grade students' classwork, assignments, and papers. Compile, administer, and grade examinations or assign this work to others. Initiate, facilitate, and moderate classroom discussions. Maintain student attendance records, grades, and other required records. Prepare course materials such as syllabi, homework assignments, and handouts. Keep abreast of developments in their field by reading current literature, talking with colleagues, and participating in professional conferences. Supervise undergraduate and/or graduate teaching, internship, and research work. Plan, evaluate, and revise curricula, course content, and course materials and methods of instruction. Maintain regularly scheduled office hours to advise and assist students. Supervise students' laboratory work and fieldwork. Conduct research in a particular field of knowledge and publish findings in professional journals, books, and electronic media. Collaborate with colleagues to address teaching and research issues. Select and obtain materials and supplies such as textbooks. Advise students on academic and vocational curricula and on career issues. Serve on academic or administrative committees that deal with institutional policies, departmental matters, and academic issues. Participate in student recruitment, registration, and placement activities. Participate in campus and community events. Compile bibliographies of specialized materials for outside reading assignments. Perform administrative duties such as serving as department head. Write grant proposals to procure external research funding. Maintain geographic information systems laboratories, performing duties such as updating software. Perform spatial analysis and modeling, using geographic information system techniques. Act as advisers to student organizations.

**Education/Training Required:** Doctoral degree. **Education and Training Programs:** Geography; Geography Teacher Education; Humanities/Humanistic Studies. **Knowledge/Courses**—Geography, Sociology and Anthropology, History and Archeology, Philosophy and Theology, Education and Training, Communications and Media.

**Personality Type:** Social-Investigative. **Career Clusters:** 05 Education and Training; 15 Science, Technology, Engineering, and Mathematics. **Career Pathways:** 5.3 Teaching/Training; 15.2 Science and Mathematics. **Other Jobs in These Pathways:** Adult Basic and Secondary Education and Literacy Teachers and Instructors; Architectural and Engineering Managers; Biofuels/Biodiesel Technology and Product Development Managers; Biologists; Career/Technical Education Teachers, Secondary School; Chemists; Coaches and Scouts; Community and Social Service Specialists, All Other; Education, Training, and Library Workers, All Other; Elementary School Teachers, Except Special Education; Fitness Trainers and Aerobics Instructors; Instructional Coordinators; Instructional Designers and Technologists; Kindergarten Teachers, Except Special Education; Librarians; Medical Scientists, Except Epidemiologists; Middle School Teachers, Except Special and Career/Technical Education; Operations Research Analysts; Preschool Teachers, Except Special Education; Recreation Workers; Secondary School Teachers, Except Special and Career/Technical Education; Self-Enrichment Education Teachers; Teacher Assistants; Tutors; 37 other postsecondary teaching occupations; others.

**Skills**—Science, Instructing, Writing, Learning Strategies, Active Learning, Operations Analysis, Speaking, Reading Comprehension.

**Work Environment:** Indoors; sitting.

# Geoscientists, Except Hydrologists and Geographers

* Annual Earnings: $82,500
* Earnings Growth Potential: High (46.9%)
* Growth: 17.5%
* Annual Job Openings: 1,540
* Self-Employed: 2.4%

**Considerations for Job Outlook:** The need for energy services, environmental protection services, and responsible land and water management is expected to spur employment growth for these workers. Job seekers who have a master's degree in geoscience should have excellent opportunities.

**Study the composition, structure, and other physical aspects of Earth. May use knowledge of geology, physics, and mathematics in exploration for oil, gas, minerals, or underground water or in waste disposal, land reclamation, or other environmental problems. May study Earth's internal composition, atmospheres, and oceans and its magnetic, electrical, and gravitational forces. Includes mineralogists, crystallographers, paleontologists, stratigraphers, geodesists, and seismologists.** Analyze and interpret geological, geochemical, and geophysical information from sources such as survey data, well logs, bore holes, and aerial photos. Locate and estimate probable natural gas, oil, and mineral ore deposits and underground water resources, using aerial photographs, charts, or research and survey results. Plan and conduct geological, geochemical, and geophysical field studies and surveys, sample collection, or drilling and testing programs used to collect data for research or application. Analyze and interpret geological data, using computer software. Search for and review research articles or environmental, historical, and technical reports. Assess ground and surface water movement to provide advice regarding issues such as waste management, route and site selection, and the restoration of contaminated sites. Prepare geological maps, cross-sectional diagrams, charts, and reports concerning mineral extraction, land use, and resource management, using results of field work and laboratory research. Investigate the composition, structure, and history of the Earth's crust through the collection, examination, measurement, and classification of soils, minerals, rocks, or fossil remains. Conduct geological and geophysical studies to provide information for use in regional development, site selection, and development of public works projects. Measure characteristics of the Earth, such as gravity and magnetic fields, using equipment such as seismographs, gravimeters, torsion balances, and magnetometers. Inspect construction projects to analyze engineering problems, applying geological knowledge and using test equipment and drilling machinery. Design geological mine maps, monitor mine structural integrity, or advise and monitor mining crews. Identify risks for natural disasters such as mudslides, earthquakes, and volcanic eruptions, providing advice on mitigation of potential damage.

**Education/Training Required:** Master's degree. **Education and Training Programs:** Geochemistry; Geochemistry and Petrology; Geological and Earth Sciences/Geosciences, Other; Geology/Earth Science, General; Geophysics and Seismology; Oceanography, Chemical and Physical; Paleontology. **Knowledge/Courses**—Geography, Engineering and Technology, Physics, Chemistry, Mathematics, Design.

**Personality Type:** Investigative-Realistic. **Career Cluster:** 15 Science, Technology, Engineering, and Mathematics. **Career Pathway:** 15.2 Science and Mathematics. **Other Jobs in This Pathway:** Architectural and Engineering Managers; Biochemists and Biophysicists; Biofuels/Biodiesel Technology and Product Development Managers; Bioinformatics Scientists; Biological Scientists, All Other; Biologists; Biostatisticians; Chemists; Clinical Data Managers; Clinical Research Coordinators; Community and Social Service Specialists, All Other; Dietitians and Nutritionists; Education, Training, and Library Workers, All Other; Geneticists; Medical Scientists, Except Epidemiologists; Molecular and Cellular Biologists; Natural Sciences Managers; Operations Research Analysts; Physical Scientists, All Other; Social Scientists and Related Workers, All Other; Statisticians; Survey Researchers; Transportation Planners; Water Resource Specialists; Zoologists and Wildlife Biologists; others.

**Skills**—Science, Reading Comprehension, Operations Analysis, Mathematics, Writing, Systems Evaluation, Systems Analysis, Active Listening.

**Work Environment:** Indoors; sitting.

# Graduate Teaching Assistants

- ❋ Annual Earnings: $32,750
- ❋ Earnings Growth Potential: High (46.8%)
- ❋ Growth: 15.1%
- ❋ Annual Job Openings: 4,000
- ❋ Self-Employed: 0.2%

**Considerations for Job Outlook:** Enrollments in postsecondary institutions are expected to continue rising as more people attend college and as workers return to school to update their skills. Opportunities for part-time or temporary

positions should be favorable, but significant competition exists for tenure-track positions.

**Assist department chairperson, faculty members, or other professional staff members in colleges or universities by performing teaching or teaching-related duties such as teaching lower-level courses, developing teaching materials, preparing and giving examinations, and grading examinations or papers. Graduate assistants must be enrolled in graduate school programs. Graduate assistants who primarily perform non-teaching duties such as laboratory research, should be reported in the occupational category related to the work performed.** Lead discussion sections, tutorials, and laboratory sections. Evaluate and grade examinations, assignments, and papers, and record grades. Return assignments to students in accordance with established deadlines. Schedule and maintain regular office hours to meet with students. Inform students of the procedures for completing and submitting class work such as lab reports. Prepare and proctor examinations. Notify instructors of errors or problems with assignments. Meet with supervisors to discuss students' grades, and to complete required grade-related paperwork. Copy and distribute classroom materials. Demonstrate use of laboratory equipment, and enforce laboratory rules. Teach undergraduate level courses. Complete laboratory projects prior to assigning them to students so that any needed modifications can be made. Develop teaching materials such as syllabi, visual aids, answer keys, supplementary notes, and course websites. Provide assistance to faculty members or staff with laboratory or field research. Arrange for supervisors to conduct teaching observations; meet with supervisors to receive feedback about teaching performance. Attend lectures given by the instructors whom they are assisting. Order or obtain materials needed for classes. Provide instructors with assistance in the use of audiovisual equipment. Assist faculty members or staff with student conferences.

**Education/Training Required:** Bachelor's degree. **Education and Training Program:** Humanities/Humanistic Studies. **Knowledge/Courses**—Sociology and Anthropology, Education and Training, Philosophy and Theology, English Language, Communications and Media, Psychology.

**Personality Type:** Social-Conventional. **Career Cluster:** 05 Education and Training. **Career Pathway:** 5.3 Teaching/Training. **Other Jobs in This Pathway:** Adult Basic and Secondary Education and Literacy Teachers and Instructors; Athletes and Sports Competitors; Audio-Visual and Multimedia Collections Specialists; Career/Technical Education Teachers, Middle School; Career/Technical Education Teachers, Secondary School; Chemists; Coaches and Scouts;

Dietitians and Nutritionists; Elementary School Teachers, Except Special Education; Fitness Trainers and Aerobics Instructors; Historians; Instructional Coordinators; Instructional Designers and Technologists; Interpreters and Translators; Kindergarten Teachers, Except Special Education; Librarians; Middle School Teachers, Except Special and Career/Technical Education; Physicists; Preschool Teachers, Except Special Education; Recreation Workers; Secondary School Teachers, Except Special and Career/Technical Education; Self-Enrichment Education Teachers; Teacher Assistants; Tutors; 37 other postsecondary teaching occupations.

**Skills**—Instructing, Reading Comprehension, Service Orientation, Active Listening, Writing, Learning Strategies, Speaking, Operations Analysis.

**Work Environment:** Indoors; sitting.

# Graphic Designers

- ❋ Annual Earnings: $43,500
- ❋ Earnings Growth Potential: Medium (39.8%)
- ❋ Growth: 12.9%
- ❋ Annual Job Openings: 12,480
- ❋ Self-Employed: 26.3%

**Considerations for Job Outlook:** Advertising firms that specialize in digital and interactive designs are expected to drive growth, but declines in print publishing will temper this growth. Competition is expected to be keen.

**Design or create graphics to meet specific commercial or promotional needs such as packaging, displays, or logos. May use a variety of media to achieve artistic or decorative effects.** Create designs, concepts, and sample layouts based on knowledge of layout principles and esthetic design concepts. Determine size and arrangement of illustrative material and copy; and select style and size of type. Confer with clients to discuss and determine layout designs. Develop graphics and layouts for product illustrations, company logos, and Internet websites. Review final layouts and suggest improvements as needed. Prepare illustrations or rough sketches of material, discussing them with clients or supervisors and making necessary changes. Use computer software to generate new images. Key information into computer equipment to create layouts for client or supervisor. Maintain archive of images, photos, or previous work products. Prepare notes and instructions for workers who assemble and prepare final layouts for printing. Draw and print charts, graphs, illustrations, and other artwork, using

computer. Study illustrations and photographs to plan presentations of materials, products, or services. Research new software or design concepts. Mark up, paste, and assemble final layouts to prepare layouts for printer. Produce still and animated graphics for on-air and taped portions of television news broadcasts, using electronic video equipment. Photograph layouts, using cameras, to make layout prints for supervisors or clients. Develop negatives and prints to produce layout photographs, using negative and print developing equipment and tools.

**Education/Training Required:** Bachelor's degree. **Education and Training Programs:** Agricultural Communication/Journalism; Commercial and Advertising Art; Computer Graphics; Design and Visual Communications, General; Graphic Design; Industrial and Product Design; Web Page, Digital/Multimedia and Information Resources Design. **Knowledge/Courses**—Fine Arts, Design, Communications and Media, Sales and Marketing, Sociology and Anthropology, Computers and Electronics.

**Personality Type:** Artistic-Realistic-Enterprising. **Career Clusters:** 01 Agriculture, Food, and Natural Resources; 03 Arts, Audio/Video Technology, and Communications; 11 Information Technology. **Career Pathways:** 1.7 Agribusiness Systems; 3.1 Audio and Video Technology and Film; 3.3 Visual Arts; 11.1 Network Systems. **Other Jobs in These Pathways:** Agents and Business Managers of Artists, Performers, and Athletes; Art Directors; Artists and Related Workers, All Other; Audio and Video Equipment Technicians; Broadcast Technicians; Camera Operators, Television, Video, and Motion Picture; Choreographers; Commercial and Industrial Designers; Computer and Information Systems Managers; Craft Artists; Dancers; Designers, All Other; Farm and Home Management Advisors; Fashion Designers; Film and Video Editors; Fine Artists, Including Painters, Sculptors, and Illustrators; Interior Designers; Managers, All Other; Media and Communication Equipment Workers, All Other; Media and Communication Workers, All Other; Multimedia Artists and Animators; Painting, Coating, and Decorating Workers; Photographers; Reporters and Correspondents; Technical Directors/Managers; others.

**Skills**—Operations Analysis, Technology Design, Negotiation, Management of Financial Resources, Time Management, Complex Problem Solving, Reading Comprehension, Writing.

**Work Environment:** Indoors; sitting; using hands; repetitive motions.

# Hairdressers, Hairstylists, and Cosmetologists

- ❋ Annual Earnings: $22,760
- ❋ Earnings Growth Potential: Low (28.2%)
- ❋ Growth: 20.1%
- ❋ Annual Job Openings: 21,950
- ❋ Self-Employed: 43.5%

**Considerations for Job Outlook:** A larger population and increasing demand for personal appearance services, especially skin care, are expected to create jobs for these workers. Prospects should be good, especially for job seekers who have formal training.

**Provide beauty services, such as shampooing, cutting, coloring, and styling hair and massaging and treating scalp. May also apply makeup, dress wigs, perform hair removal, and provide nail and skin care services.** Keep work stations clean and sanitize tools such as scissors and combs. Cut, trim, and shape hair or hairpieces based on customers' instructions, hair type, and facial features, using clippers, scissors, trimmers, and razors. Analyze patrons' hair and other physical features to determine and recommend beauty treatment or suggest hairstyles. Schedule client appointments. Bleach, dye, or tint hair, using applicator or brush. Update and maintain customer information records, such as beauty services provided. Shampoo, rinse, condition, and dry hair and scalp or hairpieces with water, liquid soap, or other solutions. Operate cash registers to receive payments from patrons. Demonstrate and sell hair care products and cosmetics. Apply water, setting, straightening, or waving solutions to hair and use curlers, rollers, hot combs, and curling irons to press and curl hair. Develop new styles and techniques. Comb, brush, and spray hair or wigs to set style. Shape eyebrows and remove facial hair, using depilatory cream, tweezers, electrolysis, or wax. Administer therapeutic medication and advise patron to seek medical treatment for chronic or contagious scalp conditions. Massage and treat scalp for hygienic and remedial purposes, using hands, fingers, or vibrating equipment. Shave, trim, and shape beards and moustaches. Train or supervise other hairstylists, hairdressers, and assistants. Recommend and explain the use of cosmetics, lotions, and creams to soften and lubricate skin and enhance and restore natural appearance. Give facials to patrons, using special compounds such as lotions and creams. Clean, shape, and polish fingernails and toenails, using files and nail polish. Apply artificial fingernails. Attach wigs or hairpieces to model heads and dress wigs and hairpieces according to instructions, samples, sketches, or photographs.

**Education/Training Required:** Postsecondary vocational training. **Education and Training Programs:** Cosmetology and Related Personal Grooming Arts, Other; Cosmetology, Barber/Styling, and Nail Instructor; Cosmetology/Cosmetologist Training, General; Electrolysis/Electrology and Electrolysis Technician Training; Hair Styling/Stylist and Hair Design; Make-Up Artist/Specialist Training; Permanent Cosmetics/Makeup and Tattooing; Salon/Beauty Salon Management/Manager Training. **Knowledge/Courses**—Chemistry, Sales and Marketing.

**Personality Type:** Artistic-Enterprising-Social. **Career Cluster:** 10 Human Services. **Career Pathway:** 10.4 Personal Care Services. **Other Jobs in This Pathway:** Barbers; Embalmers; Funeral Attendants; Funeral Service Managers; Laundry and Dry-Cleaning Workers; Makeup Artists, Theatrical and Performance; Manicurists and Pedicurists; Pressers, Textile, Garment, and Related Materials; Sewers, Hand; Sewing Machine Operators; Shampooers; Skincare Specialists; Tailors, Dressmakers, and Custom Sewers; Textile Bleaching and Dyeing Machine Operators and Tenders.

**Skills**—Service Orientation, Learning Strategies, Instructing, Equipment Selection, Operations Analysis.

**Work Environment:** Indoors; standing; using hands; bending or twisting the body; repetitive motions; contaminants; hazardous conditions; minor burns, cuts, bites, or stings.

# Hazardous Materials Removal Workers

- ❋ Annual Earnings: $37,600
- ❋ Earnings Growth Potential: Low (34.3%)
- ❋ Growth: 14.8%
- ❋ Annual Job Openings: 1,780
- ❋ Self-Employed: 0.1%

**Considerations for Job Outlook:** Employment growth is expected due to increased calls for ecofriendly electric generation facilities and production of nuclear power. Job opportunities are expected to be good.

**Identify, remove, pack, transport, or dispose of hazardous materials, including asbestos, lead-based paint, waste oil, fuel, transmission fluid, radioactive materials, contaminated soil, and so on. Specialized training and certification in hazardous materials handling or a**

confined entry permit are generally required. May operate earth-moving equipment or trucks. Follow prescribed safety procedures, and comply with federal laws regulating waste disposal methods. Record numbers of containers stored at disposal sites, and specify amounts and types of equipment and waste disposed. Drive trucks or other heavy equipment to convey contaminated waste to designated sea or ground locations. Operate machines and equipment to remove, package, store, or transport loads of waste materials. Load and unload materials into containers and onto trucks, using hoists or forklifts. Clean contaminated equipment or areas for reuse, using detergents and solvents, sandblasters, filter pumps, and steam cleaners. Construct scaffolding or build containment areas prior to beginning abatement or decontamination work. Remove asbestos and/or lead from surfaces, using hand and power tools such as scrapers, vacuums, and high-pressure sprayers. Unload baskets of irradiated elements onto packaging machines that automatically insert fuel elements into canisters and secure lids. Apply chemical compounds to lead-based paint, allow compounds to dry, then scrape the hazardous material into containers for removal and/or storage. Identify asbestos, lead, or other hazardous materials that need to be removed, using monitoring devices. Pull tram cars along underwater tracks, and position cars to receive irradiated fuel elements; then pull loaded cars to mechanisms that automatically unload elements onto underwater tables. Package, store, and move irradiated fuel elements in the underwater storage basin of a nuclear reactor plant, using machines and equipment. Organize and track the locations of hazardous items in landfills. Operate cranes to move and load baskets, casks, and canisters. Manipulate handgrips of mechanical arms to place irradiated fuel elements into baskets. Mix and pour concrete into forms to encase waste material for disposal.

**Education/Training Required:** Moderate-term on-the-job training. **Education and Training Programs:** Construction Trades, Other; Hazardous Materials Management and Waste Technology/Technician; Mechanic and Repair Technologies/Technicians, Other. **Knowledge/Courses—** Chemistry, Building and Construction, Mechanical, Transportation, Physics, Public Safety and Security.

**Personality Type:** Realistic-Conventional. **Career Clusters:** 01 Agriculture, Food, and Natural Resources; 13 Manufacturing. **Career Pathways:** 1.6 Environmental Service Systems; 13.1 Production; 13.3 Maintenance, Installation, and Repair. **Other Jobs in These Pathways:** Assemblers and Fabricators, All Other; Automotive Specialty Technicians; Computer, Automated Teller, and Office Machine Repairers; Cost Estimators; Cutting, Punching, and Press

Machine Setters, Operators, and Tenders, Metal and Plastic; Electrical and Electronic Equipment Assemblers; Electrical Engineering Technicians; Electronics Engineering Technicians; First-Line Supervisors of Mechanics, Installers, and Repairers; First-Line Supervisors of Production and Operating Workers; Geothermal Technicians; Helpers—Production Workers; Industrial Machinery Mechanics; Installation, Maintenance, and Repair Workers, All Other; Machinists; Packaging and Filling Machine Operators and Tenders; Packers and Packagers, Hand; Production Workers, All Other; Recycling and Reclamation Workers; Recycling Coordinators; Sheet Metal Workers; Solderers and Brazers; Team Assemblers; Telecommunications Line Installers and Repairers; Welders, Cutters, and Welder Fitters; others.

**Skills—**Equipment Maintenance, Operation and Control, Repairing, Troubleshooting, Equipment Selection, Operation Monitoring, Quality Control Analysis, Installation.

**Work Environment:** More often outdoors than indoors; standing; using hands; bending or twisting the body; repetitive motions; noise; very hot or cold; contaminants; high places; hazardous conditions; hazardous equipment.

# Health and Safety Engineers, Except Mining Safety Engineers and Inspectors

- ❋ Annual Earnings: $75,430
- ❋ Earnings Growth Potential: Medium (39.6%)
- ❋ Growth: 10.3%
- ❋ Annual Job Openings: 920
- ❋ Self-Employed: 0.7%

**Considerations for Job Outlook:** Health and safety engineers, except mining safety engineers and inspectors, are expected to have employment growth of 10 percent from 2008–2018, about as fast as the average for all occupations. Because health and safety engineers make production processes and products as safe as possible, their services should be in demand as concern increases for health and safety within work environments. As new technologies for production or processing are developed, health and safety engineers will be needed to ensure that they are safe.

**Promote worksite or product safety by applying knowledge of industrial processes, mechanics, chemistry, psychology, and industrial health and safety laws.** No task data available.

**Education/Training Required:** Bachelor's degree. **Education and Training Program:** Environmental/Environmental Health Engineering. **Knowledge/Courses**—No data available.

**Personality Type:** No data available. **Career Clusters:** 15 Science, Technology, Engineering, and Mathematics; 16 Transportation, Distribution, and Logistics. **Career Pathways:** 15.1 Engineering and Technology; 16.6 Health, Safety, and Environmental Management. **Other Jobs in These Pathways:** Architectural and Engineering Managers; Automotive Engineers; Biochemical Engineers; Biofuels/Biodiesel Technology and Product Development Managers; Civil Engineers; Cost Estimators; Electrical Engineers; Electronics Engineers, Except Computer; Energy Engineers; Engineers, All Other; Environmental Compliance Inspectors; Fuel Cell Engineers; Human Factors Engineers and Ergonomists; Industrial Engineers; Manufacturing Engineers; Mechanical Engineers; Mechatronics Engineers; Microsystems Engineers; Nanosystems Engineers; Photonics Engineers; Robotics Engineers; Solar Energy Systems Engineers; Transportation Engineers; Validation Engineers; Wind Energy Engineers; others.

**Skills**—No data available.

**Work Environment:** No data available.

# Job Specialization: Industrial Safety and Health Engineers

**Plan, implement, and coordinate safety programs requiring application of engineering principles and technology to prevent or correct unsafe environmental working conditions.** Investigate industrial accidents, injuries, or occupational diseases to determine causes and preventive measures. Report or review findings from accident investigations, facilities inspections, or environmental testing. Maintain and apply knowledge of current policies, regulations, and industrial processes. Inspect facilities, machinery, and safety equipment to identify and correct potential hazards and to ensure safety regulation compliance. Conduct or coordinate worker training in areas such as safety laws and regulations, hazardous condition monitoring, and use of safety equipment. Review employee safety programs to determine their adequacy. Interview employers and employees to obtain information about work environments and workplace incidents. Review plans and specifications for construction of new machinery or equipment to determine whether all safety requirements have been met. Compile, analyze, and interpret statistical data related to occupational illnesses and accidents. Interpret safety regulations for others interested in industrial safety, such as safety engineers, labor representatives, and safety inspectors. Recommend process and product safety features that will reduce employees' exposure to chemical, physical, and biological work hazards. Conduct or direct testing of air quality, noise, temperature, or radiation levels to verify compliance with health and safety regulations. Provide technical advice and guidance to organizations on how to handle health-related problems and make needed changes. Confer with medical professionals to assess health risks and to develop ways to manage health issues and concerns. Install safety devices on machinery or direct device installation. Maintain liaisons with outside organizations such as fire departments, mutual aid societies, and rescue teams so that emergency responses can be facilitated. Evaluate adequacy of actions taken to correct health inspection violations. Write and revise safety regulations and codes.

**Education/Training Required:** Bachelor's degree. **Education and Training Program:** Environmental/Environmental Health Engineering. **Knowledge/Courses**—Chemistry, Biology, Physics, Engineering and Technology, Design, Building and Construction.

**Personality Type:** Investigative-Conventional-Realistic. **Career Cluster:** 15 Science, Technology, Engineering, and Mathematics. **Career Pathway:** 15.1 Engineering and Technology. **Other Jobs in This Pathway:** Architectural and Engineering Managers; Automotive Engineers; Biochemical Engineers; Biofuels/Biodiesel Technology and Product Development Managers; Civil Engineers; Cost Estimators; Electrical Engineers; Electronics Engineers, Except Computer; Energy Engineers; Engineers, All Other; Fuel Cell Engineers; Human Factors Engineers and Ergonomists; Industrial Engineers; Manufacturing Engineers; Mechanical Engineers; Mechatronics Engineers; Microsystems Engineers; Nanosystems Engineers; Photonics Engineers; Radio Frequency Identification Device Specialists; Robotics Engineers; Solar Energy Systems Engineers; Transportation Engineers; Validation Engineers; Wind Energy Engineers; others.

**Skills**—Installation, Science, Technology Design, Mathematics, Systems Evaluation, Active Learning, Systems Analysis, Operations Analysis.

**Work Environment:** More often indoors than outdoors; noise; contaminants; hazardous conditions; hazardous equipment.

## Job Specialization: Fire-Prevention and Protection Engineers

**Research causes of fires, determine fire protection methods, and design or recommend materials or equipment such as structural components or fire-detection equipment to assist organizations in safeguarding life and property against fire, explosion, and related hazards.** Design fire detection equipment, alarm systems, and fire extinguishing devices and systems. Inspect buildings or building designs to determine fire protection system requirements and potential problems in areas such as water supplies, exit locations, and construction materials. Advise architects, builders, and other construction personnel on fire prevention equipment and techniques and on fire code and standard interpretation and compliance. Prepare and write reports detailing specific fire prevention and protection issues, such as work performed and proposed review schedules. Determine causes of fires and ways in which they could have been prevented. Direct the purchase, modification, installation, maintenance, and operation of fire protection systems. Consult with authorities to discuss safety regulations and to recommend changes as necessary. Develop plans for the prevention of destruction by fire, wind, and water. Study the relationships between ignition sources and materials to determine how fires start. Attend workshops, seminars, or conferences to present or obtain information regarding fire prevention and protection. Develop training materials and conduct training sessions on fire protection. Evaluate fire department performance and the laws and regulations affecting fire prevention or fire safety. Conduct research on fire retardants and the fire safety of materials and devices.

**Education/Training Required:** Bachelor's degree. **Education and Training Program:** Environmental/Environmental Health Engineering. **Knowledge/Courses**—Design, Engineering and Technology, Building and Construction, Physics, Chemistry, Public Safety and Security.

**Personality Type:** Investigative-Realistic-Enterprising. **Career Cluster:** 15 Science, Technology, Engineering, and Mathematics. **Career Pathway:** 15.1 Engineering and Technology. **Other Jobs in This Pathway:** Architectural and Engineering Managers; Automotive Engineers; Biochemical Engineers; Biofuels/Biodiesel Technology and Product Development Managers; Civil Engineers; Cost Estimators; Electrical Engineers; Electronics Engineers, Except Computer; Energy Engineers; Engineers, All Other; Fuel Cell Engineers; Human Factors Engineers and Ergonomists; Industrial Engineers; Manufacturing Engineers; Mechanical Engineers; Mechatronics Engineers; Microsystems Engineers; Nanosystems Engineers; Photonics Engineers; Radio Frequency Identification Device Specialists; Robotics Engineers; Solar Energy Systems Engineers; Transportation Engineers; Validation Engineers; Wind Energy Engineers; others.

**Skills**—Science, Technology Design, Operations Analysis, Management of Financial Resources, Management of Material Resources, Troubleshooting, Systems Evaluation, Systems Analysis.

**Work Environment:** Indoors; sitting.

## Job Specialization: Product Safety Engineers

**Develop and conduct tests to evaluate product safety levels and recommend measures to reduce or eliminate hazards.** Report accident investigation findings. Conduct research to evaluate safety levels for products. Evaluate potential health hazards or damage that could occur from product misuse. Investigate causes of accidents, injuries, or illnesses related to product usage in order to develop solutions to minimize or prevent recurrence. Recommend procedures for detection, prevention, and elimination of physical, chemical, or other product hazards. Participate in preparation of product usage and precautionary label instructions.

**Education/Training Required:** Bachelor's degree. **Education and Training Program:** Environmental/Environmental Health Engineering. **Knowledge/Courses**—Engineering and Technology, Design, Physics, Mechanical, Chemistry, Public Safety and Security.

**Personality Type:** Investigative-Realistic-Conventional. **Career Cluster:** 15 Science, Technology, Engineering, and Mathematics. **Career Pathway:** 15.1 Engineering and Technology. **Other Jobs in This Pathway:** Architectural and Engineering Managers; Automotive Engineers; Biochemical Engineers; Biofuels/Biodiesel Technology and Product Development Managers; Civil Engineers; Cost Estimators; Electrical Engineers; Electronics Engineers, Except Computer; Energy Engineers; Engineers, All Other; Fuel Cell Engineers; Human Factors Engineers and Ergonomists; Industrial Engineers; Manufacturing Engineers; Mechanical Engineers; Mechatronics Engineers; Microsystems Engineers; Nanosystems Engineers; Photonics Engineers; Radio Frequency Identification Device Specialists; Robotics Engineers; Solar Energy Systems Engineers; Transportation Engineers; Validation Engineers; Wind Energy Engineers; others.

**Skills**—Science, Operations Analysis, Quality Control Analysis, Troubleshooting, Operation Monitoring, Writing, Reading Comprehension, Speaking.

**Work Environment:** Indoors; sitting.

# Health Diagnosing and Treating Practitioners, All Other

- ❋ Annual Earnings: $69,310
- ❋ Earnings Growth Potential: High (44.5%)
- ❋ Growth: 13.0%
- ❋ Annual Job Openings: 1,530
- ❋ Self-Employed: 25.4%

**Considerations for Job Outlook:** About average employment growth is projected.

**This occupation includes all health diagnosing and treating practitioners not listed separately.** Because this is a highly diverse occupation, no data is available for some information topics.

**Education/Training Required:** Bachelor's degree. **Education and Training Program:** Allied Health Diagnostic, Intervention, and Treatment Professions, Other.

**Career Cluster:** 08 Health Science. **Career Pathways:** 8.1 Therapeutic Services; 8.2 Diagnostics Services. **Other Jobs in These Pathways:** Clinical Psychologists; Counseling Psychologists; Cytogenetic Technologists; Cytotechnologists; Dental Assistants; Dental Hygienists; Dentists, General; Emergency Medical Technicians and Paramedics; Endoscopy Technicians; Healthcare Support Workers, All Other; Histotechnologists and Histologic Technicians; Home Health Aides; Licensed Practical and Licensed Vocational Nurses; Massage Therapists; Medical and Clinical Laboratory Technicians; Medical and Clinical Laboratory Technologists; Medical and Health Services Managers; Medical Assistants; Medical Secretaries; Pharmacists; Pharmacy Technicians; Radiologic Technologists; School Psychologists; Social and Human Service Assistants; Speech-Language Pathology Assistants; others.

## Job Specialization: Acupuncturists

**Provide treatment of symptoms and disorders using needles and small electrical currents. May provide massage treatment. May also provide preventive treatments.** Formulate herbal preparations to treat conditions considering herbal properties such as taste, toxicity, effects of preparation, contraindications, and incompatibilities. Maintain and follow standard quality, safety, environmental and infection control policies and procedures. Maintain detailed and complete records of health care plans and prognoses. Dispense herbal formulas and inform patients of dosages and frequencies, treatment duration, possible side effects and drug interactions. Consider Western medical procedures in health assessment, health care team communication, and care referrals. Adhere to local, state and federal laws, regulations and statutes. Treat patients using tools such as needles, cups, ear balls, seeds, pellets, and nutritional supplements. Educate patients on topics such as meditation, ergonomics, stretching, exercise, nutrition, the healing process, breathing, and relaxation techniques. Evaluate treatment outcomes and recommend new or altered treatments as necessary to further promote, restore, or maintain health. Assess patients' general physical appearance to make diagnoses. Collect medical histories and general health and life style information from patients. Apply moxibustion directly or indirectly to patients using Chinese, non-scarring, stick, or pole moxa. Apply heat or cold therapy to patients using materials such as heat pads, hydrocollator packs, warm compresses, cold compresses, heat lamps, and vapor coolants. Analyze physical findings and medical histories to make diagnoses according to Oriental medicine traditions. Develop individual treatment plans and strategies. Treat medical conditions using techniques such as acupressure, shiatsu, and tuina. Insert needles to provide acupuncture treatment. Identify correct anatomical and proportional point locations based on patients' anatomy and positions, contraindications, and precautions related to treatments such as intradermal needles, moxibustion, electricity, guasha, and bleeding.

**Education/Training Required:** Work experience plus degree. **Education and Training Program:** Acupuncture and Oriental Medicine. **Knowledge/Courses**—No data available.

**Personality Type:** Social-Realistic-Investigative. **Career Cluster:** 08 Health Science. **Career Pathway:** 8.1 Therapeutic Services. **Other Jobs in This Pathway:** Clinical Psychologists; Community and Social Service Specialists, All Other; Counseling Psychologists; Dental Assistants; Dental Hygienists; Dentists, General; Health Technologists and Technicians, All Other; Healthcare Support Workers, All Other; Home Health Aides; Licensed Practical and Licensed Vocational Nurses; Low Vision Therapists, Orientation and Mobility Specialists, and Vision Rehabilitation Therapists; Massage Therapists; Medical and Clinical Laboratory Technicians; Medical and Health Services Managers; Medical Scientists, Except Epidemiologists; Medical Secretaries; Occupational Therapists; Pharmacists; Pharmacy

Technicians; Radiologic Technologists; School Psychologists; Social and Human Service Assistants; Speech-Language Pathologists; Speech-Language Pathology Assistants; Substance Abuse and Behavioral Disorder Counselors; others.

**Skills**—No data available.

**Work Environment:** No data available.

## Job Specialization: Naturopathic Physicians

**Diagnose, treat, and help prevent diseases using a system of practice that is based on the natural healing capacity of individuals. May use physiological, psychological or mechanical methods. May also use natural medicines, prescription or legend drugs, foods, herbs, or other natural remedies.** Interview patients to document symptoms and health histories. Advise patients about therapeutic exercise and nutritional medicine regimens. Administer, dispense, or prescribe natural medicines such as food or botanical extracts, herbs, dietary supplements, vitamins, nutraceuticals, and amino acids. Document patients' histories, including identifying data, chief complaints, illnesses, previous medical or family histories, or psychosocial characteristics. Educate patients about health care management. Diagnose health conditions based on patients' symptoms and health histories, laboratory and diagnostic radiology test results, or other physiological measurements, such as electrocardiograms and electroencephalographs. Conduct physical examinations and physiological function tests for diagnostic purposes. Maintain professional development through activities such as post-graduate education, continuing education, preceptorships, and residency programs. Order diagnostic imaging procedures such as radiographs (X-rays), ultrasounds, mammograms, and bone densitometry tests, or refer patients to other health professionals for these procedures. Administer treatments or therapies, such as homeopathy, hydrotherapy, Oriental or Ayurvedic medicine, electrotherapy and diathermy, using physical agents including air, heat, cold, water, sound, or ultraviolet light to catalyze the body to heal itself.

**Education/Training Required:** Doctoral degree. **Education and Training Program:** Naturopathic Medicine/Naturopathy (ND). **Knowledge/Courses**—Medicine and Dentistry, Therapy and Counseling, Biology, Psychology, Chemistry, Sociology and Anthropology.

**Personality Type:** Investigative-Social. **Career Cluster:** 08 Health Science. **Career Pathway:** 8.1 Therapeutic Services.

**Other Jobs in This Pathway:** Clinical Psychologists; Community and Social Service Specialists, All Other; Counseling Psychologists; Dental Assistants; Dental Hygienists; Dentists, General; Health Technologists and Technicians, All Other; Healthcare Support Workers, All Other; Home Health Aides; Licensed Practical and Licensed Vocational Nurses; Low Vision Therapists, Orientation and Mobility Specialists, and Vision Rehabilitation Therapists; Massage Therapists; Medical and Clinical Laboratory Technicians; Medical and Health Services Managers; Medical Scientists, Except Epidemiologists; Medical Secretaries; Occupational Therapists; Pharmacists; Pharmacy Technicians; Radiologic Technologists; School Psychologists; Social and Human Service Assistants; Speech-Language Pathologists; Speech-Language Pathology Assistants; Substance Abuse and Behavioral Disorder Counselors; others.

**Skills**—Science, Social Perceptiveness, Operations Analysis, Reading Comprehension, Judgment and Decision Making, Service Orientation, Systems Evaluation, Active Learning.

**Work Environment:** Indoors; sitting; exposed to disease or infections.

## Job Specialization: Orthoptists

**Diagnose and treat visual system disorders such as binocular vision and eye movement impairments.** Perform diagnostic tests or measurements such as motor testing, visual acuity testing, lensometry, retinoscopy, and color vision testing. Examine patients with problems related to ocular motility, binocular vision, amblyopia, or strabismus. Evaluate, diagnose, or treat disorders of the visual system with an emphasis on binocular vision or abnormal eye movements. Develop non-surgical treatment plans for patients with conditions such as strabismus, nystagmus, and other visual disorders. Provide instructions to patients or family members concerning diagnoses or treatment plans. Provide non-surgical interventions, including corrective lenses, patches, drops, fusion exercises, or stereograms, to treat conditions such as strabismus, heterophoria, and convergence insufficiency. Develop or use special test and communication techniques to facilitate diagnosis and treatment of children or disabled patients. Interpret clinical or diagnostic test results. Refer patients to ophthalmic surgeons or other physicians. Provide training related to clinical methods or orthoptics to students, resident physicians, or other health professionals. Prepare diagnostic or treatment reports for other medical practitioners or therapists. Collaborate with ophthalmologists, optometrists, or other specialists in the diagnosis, treatment, or management of conditions such as glaucoma, cataracts, and retinal diseases. Assist ophthalmologists in diagnostic ophthalmic procedures such as ultrasonography, fundus photography, and tonometry. Perform vision screening of children in schools or community health centers. Participate in clinical research projects. Present or publish scientific papers.

**Education/Training Required:** Work experience plus degree. **Education and Training Program:** Orthoptics/Orthoptist. **Knowledge/Courses**—Medicine and Dentistry, Biology, Therapy and Counseling, Psychology, English Language, Customer and Personal Service.

**Personality Type:** Investigative-Social-Realistic. **Career Cluster:** 08 Health Science. **Career Pathway:** 8.1 Therapeutic Services. **Other Jobs in This Pathway:** Clinical Psychologists; Community and Social Service Specialists, All Other; Counseling Psychologists; Dental Assistants; Dental Hygienists; Dentists, General; Health Technologists and Technicians, All Other; Healthcare Support Workers, All Other; Home Health Aides; Licensed Practical and Licensed Vocational Nurses; Low Vision Therapists, Orientation and Mobility Specialists, and Vision Rehabilitation Therapists; Massage Therapists; Medical and Clinical Laboratory Technicians; Medical and Health Services Managers; Medical Scientists, Except Epidemiologists; Medical Secretaries; Occupational Therapists; Pharmacists; Pharmacy Technicians; Radiologic Technologists; School Psychologists; Social and Human Service Assistants; Speech-Language Pathologists; Speech-Language Pathology Assistants; Substance Abuse and Behavioral Disorder Counselors; others.

**Skills**—Science, Operations Analysis, Reading Comprehension, Service Orientation, Instructing, Systems Evaluation, Active Learning, Learning Strategies.

**Work Environment:** Indoors; sitting; using hands; repetitive motions; exposed to disease or infections.

# Health Educators

- ❊ Annual Earnings: $45,830
- ❊ Earnings Growth Potential: High (41.7%)
- ❊ Growth: 18.2%
- ❊ Annual Job Openings: 2,600
- ❊ Self-Employed: 0.3%

**Considerations for Job Outlook:** As health-care costs rise, insurance companies, businesses, and governments are expected to hire health educators to teach the public how to avoid and detect illnesses. Opportunities should be favorable, especially for those who have gained experience through volunteer work or internships.

**Promote, maintain, and improve individual and community health by assisting individuals and communities to adopt healthy behaviors. Collect and analyze data to identify community needs prior to planning, implementing, monitoring, and evaluating programs designed to encourage healthy lifestyles, policies, and environments. May also serve as a resource to assist individuals, other professionals, or the community and may administer fiscal resources for health education programs.** Document activities, recording information such as the numbers of applications completed, presentations conducted, and persons assisted. Develop and present health education and promotion programs such as training workshops, conferences, and school or community presentations. Develop and maintain cooperative working relationships with agencies and organizations interested in public health care. Prepare and distribute health education materials, including reports; bulletins; and visual aids such as films, videotapes, photographs, and posters. Develop operational plans and policies necessary to achieve health education objectives and services. Collaborate with health specialists and civic groups to determine community health needs and the availability of services and to develop goals for meeting needs. Maintain databases, mailing lists, telephone networks, and other information to facilitate the functioning of health education programs. Supervise professional and technical staff in implementing health programs, objectives, and goals. Design and conduct evaluations and diagnostic studies to assess the quality and performance of health education programs. Provide program information to the public by preparing and presenting press releases, conducting media campaigns, and/or maintaining program-related websites. Develop, prepare, and coordinate grant applications and grant-related activities to obtain funding for health education programs and related work. Provide guidance to agencies and organizations in the assessment of health education needs and in the development and delivery of health education programs. Develop and maintain health education libraries to provide resources for staff and community agencies. Develop, conduct, or coordinate health needs assessments and other public health surveys.

**Education/Training Required:** Bachelor's degree. **Education and Training Programs:** Community Health Services/Liaison/Counseling; Health Communication; International Public Health/International Health; Maternal and Child Health; Public Health Education and Promotion. **Knowledge/Courses**—Sociology and Anthropology, Customer and Personal Service, Education and Training, Personnel and Human Resources, Therapy and Counseling, Psychology.

**Personality Type:** Social-Enterprising. **Career Clusters:** 08 Health Science; 10 Human Services. **Career Pathways:** 8.3 Health Informatics; 10.2 Counseling and Mental Health Services. **Other Jobs in These Pathways:** Clergy; Clinical Psychologists; Counseling Psychologists; Directors, Religious Activities and Education; Editors; Engineers, All Other; Executive Secretaries and Executive Administrative Assistants; First-Line Supervisors of Office and Administrative Support Workers; Healthcare Social Workers; Medical and Health Services Managers; Medical Assistants; Medical Records and Health Information Technicians; Medical Secretaries; Medical Transcriptionists; Mental Health and Substance Abuse Social Workers; Mental Health Counselors; Physical Therapists; Psychiatric Aides; Psychiatric Technicians; Public Relations Specialists; Receptionists and Information Clerks; Recreation Workers; Rehabilitation Counselors; School Psychologists; Substance Abuse and Behavioral Disorder Counselors; others.

**Skills**—Operations Analysis, Science, Writing, Learning Strategies, Speaking, Persuasion, Social Perceptiveness, Service Orientation.

**Work Environment:** Indoors; sitting; using hands; exposed to disease or infections.

# Health Specialties Teachers, Postsecondary

- ❋ Annual Earnings: $85,270
- ❋ Earnings Growth Potential: Very high (52.7%)
- ❋ Growth: 15.1%
- ❋ Annual Job Openings: 4,000
- ❋ Self-Employed: 0.2%

**Considerations for Job Outlook:** Enrollments in postsecondary institutions are expected to continue rising as more people attend college and as workers return to school to update their skills. Opportunities for part-time or temporary positions should be favorable, but significant competition exists for tenure-track positions.

**Teach courses in health specialties, such as veterinary medicine, dentistry, pharmacy, therapy, laboratory technology, and public health.** Initiate, facilitate, and moderate classroom discussions. Keep abreast of developments in their field by reading current literature, talking with colleagues, and participating in professional conferences.

Compile, administer, and grade examinations or assign this work to others. Evaluate and grade students' classwork, assignments, and papers. Prepare course materials such as syllabi, homework assignments, and handouts. Prepare and deliver lectures to undergraduate or graduate students on topics such as public health, stress management, and worksite health promotion. Plan, evaluate, and revise curricula, course content, and course materials and methods of instruction. Supervise undergraduate or graduate teaching, internship, and research work. Conduct research in a particular field of knowledge and publish findings in professional journals, books, or electronic media. Collaborate with colleagues to address teaching and research issues. Supervise laboratory sessions. Maintain student attendance records, grades, and other required records. Maintain regularly scheduled office hours in order to advise and assist students. Advise students on academic and vocational curricula and on career issues. Participate in student recruitment, registration, and placement activities. Write grant proposals to procure external research funding. Serve on academic or administrative committees that deal with institutional policies, departmental matters, and academic issues. Select and obtain materials and supplies such as textbooks and laboratory equipment. Act as advisers to student organizations. Perform administrative duties such as serving as department head. Compile bibliographies of specialized materials for outside reading assignments. Provide professional consulting services to government and industry. Participate in campus and community events.

**Education/Training Required:** Doctoral degree. **Education and Training Programs:** Art Therapy; Asian Bodywork Therapy; Audiology and Speech-Language Pathology; Biostatistics; Blood Bank Technology Specialist Training; Cardiovascular Technology; Chiropractic; Clinical Laboratory Science/Medical Technology; Clinical Laboratory Assistant Training; Clinical Laboratory Technician; Cytotechnology; Dance Therapy; Dental Assisting; Dental Hygiene; Dental Laboratory Technology; Dentistry; Diagnostic Medical Sonography and Ultrasound Technician Training; Electrocardiograph Technology; Emergency Medical Technology; Environmental Health; Medical Radiologic Technology; Music Therapy; Nuclear Medical Technology; Occupational Health and Industrial Hygiene; Occupational Therapist Assistant Training; Occupational Therapy; Orthotist/Prosthetist; Pharmacy; Pharmacy Technician Training; Physical Therapy Assistant Training; Physical Therapy; Physician Assistant Training; Respiratory Care Therapy; Speech-Language Pathology; Surgical Technology; Therapeutic Recreation/Recreational Therapy; Veterinary Medicine; Veterinary Clinical Sciences, General; Veterinary Technology;

Vocational Rehabilitation Counseling; others. **Knowledge/Courses**—Biology, Medicine and Dentistry, Education and Training, Therapy and Counseling, Sociology and Anthropology, Psychology.

**Personality Type:** Social-Investigative. **Career Clusters:** 05 Education and Training; 08 Health Science; 15 Science, Technology, Engineering, and Mathematics. **Career Pathways:** 5.3 Teaching/Training; 8.1 Therapeutic Services; 8.2 Diagnostics Services; 8.3 Health Informatics; 8.5 Biotechnology Research and Development; 15.2 Science and Mathematics. **Other Jobs in These Pathways:** Coaches and Scouts; Dental Assistants; Elementary School Teachers, Except Special Education; Executive Secretaries and Executive Administrative Assistants; First-Line Supervisors of Office and Administrative Support Workers; Fitness Trainers and Aerobics Instructors; Home Health Aides; Licensed Practical and Licensed Vocational Nurses; Medical and Health Services Managers; Medical Assistants; Medical Secretaries; Middle School Teachers, Except Special and Career/Technical Education; Pharmacists; Pharmacy Technicians; Preschool Teachers, Except Special Education; Public Relations Specialists; Radiologic Technologists; Receptionists and Information Clerks; Recreation Workers; Secondary School Teachers, Except Special and Career/Technical Education; Self-Enrichment Education Teachers; Social and Human Service Assistants; Teacher Assistants; Tutors; 37 other postsecondary teaching occupations; others.

**Skills**—Instructing, Learning Strategies, Reading Comprehension, Writing, Science, Active Learning, Speaking, Active Listening.

**Work Environment:** Indoors; sitting.

# Health Technologists and Technicians, All Other

- ❈ Annual Earnings: $38,460
- ❈ Earnings Growth Potential: Low (33.5%)
- ❈ Growth: 18.7%
- ❈ Annual Job Openings: 3,200
- ❈ Self-Employed: 5.7%

**Considerations for Job Outlook:** Faster-than-average employment growth is projected.

**This occupation includes all health technologists and technicians not listed separately.** Because this is a highly diverse occupation, no data is available for some information topics.

**Education/Training Required:** Postsecondary vocational training. **Education and Training Program:** Allied Health Diagnostic, Intervention, and Treatment Professions, Other.

**Career Cluster:** 08 Health Science. **Career Pathways:** 8.1 Therapeutic Services; 8.2 Diagnostics Services. **Other Jobs in These Pathways:** Clinical Psychologists; Counseling Psychologists; Cytogenetic Technologists; Cytotechnologists; Dental Assistants; Dental Hygienists; Dentists, General; Emergency Medical Technicians and Paramedics; Endoscopy Technicians; Healthcare Support Workers, All Other; Histotechnologists and Histologic Technicians; Home Health Aides; Licensed Practical and Licensed Vocational Nurses; Massage Therapists; Medical and Clinical Laboratory Technicians; Medical and Clinical Laboratory Technologists; Medical and Health Services Managers; Medical Assistants; Medical Secretaries; Pharmacists; Pharmacy Technicians; Radiologic Technologists; School Psychologists; Social and Human Service Assistants; Speech-Language Pathology Assistants; others.

# Job Specialization: Neurodiagnostic Technologists

**Conduct electroneurodiagnostic (END) tests such as electroencephalograms, evoked potentials, polysomnograms, or electronystagmograms. May perform nerve conduction studies.** Attach electrodes to patients using adhesives. Summarize technical data to assist physicians to diagnose brain, sleep, or nervous system disorders. Conduct tests or studies such as electroencephalography (EEG), polysomnography (PSG), nerve conduction studies (NCS), electromyography (EMG), and intraoperative monitoring (IOM). Calibrate, troubleshoot, or repair equipment and correct malfunctions as needed. Conduct tests to determine cerebral death, the absence of brain activity, or the probability of recovery from a coma. Measure visual, auditory, or somatosensory evoked potentials (EPs) to determine responses to stimuli. Indicate artifacts or interferences derived from sources outside of the brain, such as poor electrode contact or patient movement, on electroneurodiagnostic recordings. Measure patients' body parts and mark locations where electrodes are to be placed. Monitor patients during tests or surgeries, using electroencephalographs (EEG), evoked potential (EP) instruments, or video recording equipment. Set up, program, or record montages or electrical combinations when testing peripheral nerve, spinal cord, subcortical, or cortical responses. Adjust equipment to optimize viewing of the nervous system. Collect patients' medical information needed to customize tests. Submit reports to physicians summarizing test results. Assist in training technicians, medical students, residents or other staff members. Explain testing procedures to patients, answering questions or reassuring patients as needed. Participate in research projects, conferences, or technical meetings.

**Education/Training Required:** Associate degree. **Education and Training Program:** Electroneurodiagnostic/Electroencephalographic Technology/Technologist. **Knowledge/Courses—**Medicine and Dentistry, Biology, Psychology, Computers and Electronics, Customer and Personal Service, Clerical.

**Personality Type:** Realistic-Investigative. **Career Cluster:** 08 Health Science. **Career Pathway:** 8.2 Diagnostics Services. **Other Jobs in This Pathway:** Ambulance Drivers and Attendants, Except Emergency Medical Technicians; Anesthesiologist Assistants; Cardiovascular Technologists and Technicians; Cytogenetic Technologists; Cytotechnologists; Diagnostic Medical Sonographers; Emergency Medical Technicians and Paramedics; Endoscopy Technicians; Health Diagnosing and Treating Practitioners, All Other; Health Technologists and Technicians, All Other; Healthcare Practitioners and Technical Workers, All Other; Histotechnologists and Histologic Technicians; Medical and Clinical Laboratory Technicians; Medical and Clinical Laboratory Technologists; Medical and Health Services Managers; Medical Assistants; Medical Equipment Preparers; Nuclear Medicine Technologists; Ophthalmic Laboratory Technicians; Physical Scientists, All Other; Physician Assistants; Radiologic Technicians; Radiologic Technologists; Surgical Technologists; Veterinary Assistants and Laboratory Animal Caretakers; others.

**Skills—**Repairing, Troubleshooting, Equipment Maintenance, Operation and Control, Operation Monitoring, Quality Control Analysis, Science, Learning Strategies.

**Work Environment:** Indoors; sitting; using hands; contaminants; exposed to disease or infections.

# Job Specialization: Ophthalmic Medical Technologists

**Assist ophthalmologists by performing ophthalmic clinical functions and ophthalmic photography. Provide instruction and supervision to other ophthalmic personnel. Assist with minor surgical procedures, applying aseptic techniques and preparing instruments. May perform eye exams, administer eye medications, and instruct patients in care and use of corrective lenses.** Administer topical ophthalmic or oral medications. Assess abnormalities of color vision, such as amblyopia. Assess refractive condition of eyes, using retinoscope. Assist physicians in performing ophthalmic procedures, including surgery. Calculate corrections for refractive errors. Collect ophthalmic measurements or other diagnostic information, using ultrasound equipment, such as A-scan ultrasound biometry or B-scan ultrasonography equipment. Conduct binocular disparity tests to assess depth perception. Conduct ocular motility tests to measure function of eye muscles. Conduct tests, such as the Amsler Grid test, to measure central visual field used in the early diagnosis of macular degeneration, glaucoma, or diseases of the eye. Conduct tonometry or tonography tests to measure intraocular pressure. Conduct visual field tests to measure field of vision. Create three-dimensional images of the eye, using computed tomography (CT). Measure and record lens power, using lensometers. Measure corneal curvature with keratometers or ophthalmometers to aid in the diagnosis of conditions, such as astigmatism. Measure corneal thickness, using pachymeter or contact ultrasound methods. Measure the thickness of the retinal nerve, using scanning laser polarimetry techniques to aid in diagnosis of glaucoma. Measure visual acuity, including near, distance, pinhole, or dynamic visual acuity, using appropriate tests. Perform advanced ophthalmic procedures, including electrophysiological, electrophysical, or microbial procedures. Perform flourescein angiography of the eye. Perform slit lamp biomicroscopy procedures to diagnose disorders of the eye, such as retinitis, presbyopia, cataracts, or retinal detachment. Photograph patients' eye areas, using clinical photography techniques, to document retinal or corneal defects. Supervise or instruct ophthalmic staff. Take anatomical or functional ocular measurements of the eye or surrounding tissue, such as axial length measurements.

**Education/Training Required:** Associate degree. **Education and Training Program:** Ophthalmic Technician/Technologist Training. **Knowledge/Courses—**No data available.

**Personality Type:** No data available. **Career Cluster:** 08 Health Science. **Career Pathway:** 8.1 Therapeutic Services. **Other Jobs in This Pathway:** Clinical Psychologists; Community and Social Service Specialists, All Other; Counseling Psychologists; Dental Assistants; Dental Hygienists; Dentists, General; Health Technologists and Technicians, All Other; Healthcare Support Workers, All Other; Home Health Aides; Licensed Practical and Licensed Vocational Nurses; Low Vision Therapists, Orientation and Mobility Specialists, and Vision Rehabilitation Therapists; Massage Therapists; Medical and Clinical Laboratory Technicians; Medical and Health Services Managers; Medical Scientists, Except Epidemiologists; Medical Secretaries; Occupational Therapists; Pharmacists; Pharmacy Technicians; Radiologic

Technologists; School Psychologists; Social and Human Service Assistants; Speech-Language Pathologists; Speech-Language Pathology Assistants; Substance Abuse and Behavioral Disorder Counselors; others.

**Skills**—No data available.

**Work Environment:** No data available.

## Job Specialization: Radiologic Technicians

**Maintain and use equipment and supplies necessary to demonstrate portions of the human body on X-ray film or fluoroscopic screen for diagnostic purposes.** Use beam-restrictive devices and patient-shielding techniques to minimize radiation exposure to patient and staff. Position X-ray equipment and adjust controls to set exposure factors, such as time and distance. Position patient on examining table and set up and adjust equipment to obtain optimum view of specific body area as requested by physician. Determine patients' X-ray needs by reading requests or instructions from physicians. Make exposures necessary for the requested procedures, rejecting and repeating work that does not meet established standards. Process exposed radiographs using film processors or computer generated methods. Explain procedures to patients to reduce anxieties and obtain cooperation. Perform procedures such as linear tomography, mammography, sonograms, joint and cyst aspirations, routine contrast studies, routine fluoroscopy and examinations of the head, trunk, and extremities under supervision of physician. Prepare and set up X-ray room for patient. Provide assistance to physicians or other technologists in the performance of more complex procedures. Provide students and other technologists with suggestions of additional views, alternate positioning or improved techniques to ensure the images produced are of the highest quality. Coordinate work of other technicians or technologists when procedures require more than one person. Assist with on-the-job training of new employees and students, and provide input to supervisors regarding training performance. Maintain a current file of examination protocols. Operate mobile X-ray equipment in operating room, emergency room, or at patient's bedside. Provide assistance in radiopharmaceutical administration, monitoring patients' vital signs and notifying the radiologist of any relevant changes. Prepare contrast material, radiopharmaceuticals and anesthetic or antispasmodic drugs under the direction of a radiologist. Operate digital picture archiving communications systems.

**Education/Training Required:** Associate degree. **Education and Training Program:** Medical Radiologic Technology/Science—Radiation Therapist. **Knowledge/Courses**—Physics, Medicine and Dentistry, Psychology, Biology, Chemistry, Customer and Personal Service.

**Personality Type:** Realistic-Conventional-Social. **Career Cluster:** 08 Health Science. **Career Pathways:** 8.1 Therapeutic Services; 8.2 Diagnostics Services. **Other Jobs in These Pathways:** Clinical Psychologists; Counseling Psychologists; Cytogenetic Technologists; Cytotechnologists; Dental Assistants; Dental Hygienists; Dentists, General; Emergency Medical Technicians and Paramedics; Endoscopy Technicians; Healthcare Support Workers, All Other; Histotechnologists and Histologic Technicians; Home Health Aides; Licensed Practical and Licensed Vocational Nurses; Massage Therapists; Medical and Clinical Laboratory Technicians; Medical and Clinical Laboratory Technologists; Medical and Health Services Managers; Medical Assistants; Medical Secretaries; Pharmacists; Pharmacy Technicians; Radiologic Technologists; School Psychologists; Social and Human Service Assistants; Speech-Language Pathology Assistants; others.

**Skills**—Operation and Control, Science, Operation Monitoring, Service Orientation, Troubleshooting, Technology Design, Coordination, Quality Control Analysis.

**Work Environment:** Indoors; standing; walking and running; using hands; bending or twisting the body; repetitive motions; contaminants; exposed to radiation; exposed to disease or infections.

## Job Specialization: Surgical Assistants

**Assist surgeons during surgery by performing duties such as tissue retraction, insertion of tubes and intravenous lines, or closure of surgical wounds. Perform preoperative and postoperative duties to facilitate patient care.** Adjust and maintain operating room temperature, humidity, or lighting, according to surgeon's specifications. Apply sutures, staples, clips, or other materials to close skin, facia, or subcutaneous wound layers. Assess skin integrity or other body conditions upon completion of the procedure to determine if damage has occurred from body positioning. Assist in the insertion, positioning, or suturing of closed-wound drainage systems. Assist members of surgical team with gowning or gloving. Clamp, ligate, or cauterize blood vessels to control bleeding during surgical entry, using hemostatic clamps, suture ligatures, or electrocautery equipment. Coordinate or participate in the positioning of patients, using body stabilizing equipment or protective padding to provide appropriate exposure for the procedure or to protect against nerve damage or circulation impairment. Coordinate with anesthesia personnel to maintain patient temperature. Discuss with surgeon the nature of the surgical procedure, including operative consent, methods of operative exposure, diagnostic or laboratory data, or patient-advanced directives or other needs. Incise tissue layers in lower extremities to harvest veins. Maintain an unobstructed operative field, using surgical retractors, sponges, or suctioning and irrigating equipment. Monitor and maintain aseptic technique throughout procedures. Monitor patient intra-operative status, including patient position, vital signs, or volume or color of blood. Postoperatively inject a subcutaneous local anesthetic agent to reduce pain. Prepare and apply sterile wound dressings. Assist in applying casts, splints, braces, or similar devices. Assist in volume replacement or autotransfusion techniques. Assist with patient resuscitation during cardiac arrest or other life-threatening events. Cover patients with surgical drapes to create and maintain a sterile operative field. Determine availability of necessary equipment or supplies for operative procedures.

**Education/Training Required:** Work experience plus degree. **Education and Training Program:** Surgical Technology/Technologist. **Knowledge/Courses**—No data available.

**Personality Type:** No data available. **Career Cluster:** 08 Health Science. **Career Pathway:** 8.1 Therapeutic Services. **Other Jobs in This Pathway:** Clinical Psychologists; Community and Social Service Specialists, All Other; Counseling Psychologists; Dental Assistants; Dental Hygienists; Dentists, General; Health Technologists and Technicians, All Other; Healthcare Support Workers, All Other; Home Health Aides; Licensed Practical and Licensed Vocational Nurses; Low Vision Therapists, Orientation and Mobility Specialists, and Vision Rehabilitation Therapists; Massage Therapists; Medical and Clinical Laboratory Technicians; Medical and Health Services Managers; Medical Scientists, Except Epidemiologists; Medical Secretaries; Occupational Therapists; Pharmacists; Pharmacy Technicians; Radiologic Technologists; School Psychologists; Social and Human Service Assistants; Speech-Language Pathologists; Speech-Language Pathology Assistants; Substance Abuse and Behavioral Disorder Counselors; others.

**Skills**—No data available.

**Work Environment:** No data available.

# Healthcare Practitioners and Technical Workers, All Other

- ❋ Annual Earnings: $43,970
- ❋ Earnings Growth Potential: High (44.6%)
- ❋ Growth: 15.9%
- ❋ Annual Job Openings: 2,910
- ❋ Self-Employed: 0.7%

**Considerations for Job Outlook:** Faster-than-average employment growth is projected.

**This occupation includes all health-care practitioners and technical workers not listed separately.** Because this is a highly diverse occupation, no data is available for some information topics.

**Education/Training Required:** Bachelor's degree. **Education and Training Program:** Allied Health Diagnostic, Intervention, and Treatment Professions, Other.

**Career Cluster:** 08 Health Science. **Career Pathways:** 8.1 Therapeutic Services; 8.2 Diagnostics Services. **Other Jobs in These Pathways:** Clinical Psychologists; Counseling Psychologists; Cytogenetic Technologists; Cytotechnologists; Dental Assistants; Dental Hygienists; Dentists, General; Emergency Medical Technicians and Paramedics; Endoscopy Technicians; Healthcare Support Workers, All Other; Histotechnologists and Histologic Technicians; Home Health Aides; Licensed Practical and Licensed Vocational Nurses; Massage Therapists; Medical and Clinical Laboratory Technicians; Medical and Clinical Laboratory Technologists; Medical and Health Services Managers; Medical Assistants; Medical Secretaries; Pharmacists; Pharmacy Technicians; Radiologic Technologists; School Psychologists; Social and Human Service Assistants; Speech-Language Pathology Assistants; others.

# Job Specialization: Midwives

**Provide prenatal care and childbirth assistance.** Assist maternal patients to find physical positions that will facilitate childbirth. Monitor maternal condition during labor by checking vital signs, monitoring uterine contractions, or performing physical examinations. Provide comfort and relaxation measures for mothers in labor through interventions such as massage, breathing techniques, hydrotherapy, and music. Set up or monitor the administration of oxygen or medications. Assess birthing environments to ensure cleanliness, safety, and the availability of appropriate supplies. Assess the status of post-date pregnancies to determine treatments and interventions. Collect specimens for use in laboratory tests. Conduct ongoing prenatal health assessments, tracking changes in physical and emotional health. Develop, implement, or evaluate individualized plans for midwifery care. Establish and follow emergency or contingency plans for mothers and newborns. Estimate patients' due dates and re-evaluate as necessary based on examination results. Evaluate patients' laboratory and medical records, requesting assistance from other practitioners when necessary. Respond to breech birth presentations by applying methods such as exercises and external version. Identify, monitor, or treat pregnancy-related problems such as hypertension, gestational diabetes, pre-term labor, and retarded fetal growth. Identify tubal and ectopic pregnancies and refer patients for treatments. Inform patients of how to prepare and supply birth sites. Monitor fetal growth and well-being through heartbeat detection, body measurement, and palpation. Maintain documentation of all patients' contacts, reviewing and updating records as necessary. Obtain complete health and medical histories from patients including medical, surgical, reproductive, or mental health histories. Perform post-partum health assessments of mothers and babies at regular intervals.

**Education/Training Required:** Long-term on-the-job training. **Education and Training Program:** Direct Entry Midwifery (LM, CPM). **Knowledge/Courses**—No data available.

**Personality Type:** Social-Realistic. **Career Cluster:** 08 Health Science. **Career Pathway:** 8.1 Therapeutic Services. **Other Jobs in This Pathway:** Clinical Psychologists; Community and Social Service Specialists, All Other; Counseling Psychologists; Dental Assistants; Dental Hygienists; Dentists, General; Health Technologists and Technicians, All Other; Healthcare Support Workers, All Other; Home Health Aides; Licensed Practical and Licensed Vocational Nurses; Low Vision Therapists, Orientation and Mobility Specialists, and Vision Rehabilitation Therapists; Massage Therapists; Medical and Clinical Laboratory Technicians; Medical and Health Services Managers; Medical Scientists, Except Epidemiologists; Medical Secretaries; Occupational Therapists; Pharmacists; Pharmacy Technicians; Radiologic Technologists; School Psychologists; Social and Human Service Assistants; Speech-Language Pathologists; Speech-Language Pathology Assistants; Substance Abuse and Behavioral Disorder Counselors; others.

**Skills**—No data available.

**Work Environment:** No data available.

# Healthcare Social Workers

- Annual Earnings: $47,230
- Earnings Growth Potential: Medium (37.6%)
- Growth: 22.4%
- Annual Job Openings: 6,590
- Self-Employed: 2.2%

**Considerations for Job Outlook:** The rapidly increasing elderly population is expected to spur demand for social services. Job prospects should be favorable because of the need to replace the many workers who are leaving the occupation permanently.

**Provide persons, families, or vulnerable populations with the psychosocial support needed to cope with chronic, acute, or terminal illnesses such as Alzheimer's, cancer, or AIDS. Services include advising family caregivers, providing patient education and counseling, and making necessary referrals for other social services.** Advocate for clients or patients to resolve crises. Collaborate with other professionals to evaluate patients' medical or physical condition and to assess client needs. Refer patients, clients, or families to community resources to assist in recovery from mental or physical illnesses and to provide access to services such as financial assistance, legal aid, housing, job placement, or education. Counsel clients and patients in individual and group sessions to help them overcome dependencies, recover from illnesses, and adjust to life. Use consultation data and social work experience to plan and coordinate client or patient care and rehabilitation, following through to ensure service efficacy. Plan discharge from care facility to home or other care facility. Organize support groups or counsel family members to assist them in understanding, dealing with, and supporting clients or patients. Modify treatment plans to comply with changes in clients' statuses. Monitor, evaluate, and record client progress according to measurable goals described in treatment and care plans. Identify environmental impediments to client or patient progress through interviews and review of patient records. Supervise and direct other workers providing services to clients or patients. Develop or advise on social policy and assist in community development. Investigate child abuse or neglect cases and take authorized protective action when necessary. Oversee Medicaid- and Medicare-related paperwork and recordkeeping in hospitals. Plan and conduct programs to combat social problems, prevent substance abuse, or improve community health and counseling services. Conduct social research to advance knowledge in the social work field.

**Education/Training Required:** Bachelor's degree. **Education and Training Program:** Clinical/Medical Social Work. **Knowledge/Courses**—Therapy and Counseling, Sociology and Anthropology, Psychology, Philosophy and Theology, Customer and Personal Service, Medicine and Dentistry.

**Personality Type:** Social-Investigative. **Career Cluster:** 10 Human Services. **Career Pathway:** 10.2 Counseling and Mental Health Services. **Other Jobs in This Pathway:** Clergy; Clinical Psychologists; Counseling Psychologists; Counselors, All Other; Directors, Religious Activities and Education; Epidemiologists; Health Educators; Marriage and Family Therapists; Mental Health and Substance Abuse Social Workers; Mental Health Counselors; Music Directors; Psychologists, All Other; Recreation Workers; Religious Workers, All Other; School Psychologists; Substance Abuse and Behavioral Disorder Counselors.

**Skills**—Social Perceptiveness, Science, Operations Analysis, Service Orientation, Learning Strategies, Active Listening, Writing, Systems Evaluation.

**Work Environment:** Indoors; sitting; noise; exposed to disease or infections.

# Healthcare Support Workers, All Other

- ❋ Annual Earnings: $30,280
- ❋ Earnings Growth Potential: Low (32.2%)
- ❋ Growth: 17.1%
- ❋ Annual Job Openings: 5,670
- ❋ Self-Employed: 3.0%

**Considerations for Job Outlook:** Faster–than-average employment growth is projected.

**This occupation includes all health-care support workers not listed separately.** Because this is a highly diverse occupation, no data is available for some information topics.

**Education/Training Required:** Short-term on-the-job training. **Education and Training Program:** Allied Health Diagnostic, Intervention, and Treatment Professions, Other.

**Career Cluster:** 08 Health Science. **Career Pathway:** 8.1 Therapeutic Services. **Other Jobs in This Pathway:** Clinical Psychologists; Community and Social Service Specialists, All Other; Counseling Psychologists; Dental Assistants; Dental Hygienists; Dentists, General; Health Technologists and Technicians, All Other; Home Health Aides; Licensed Practical and Licensed Vocational Nurses; Low Vision

Therapists, Orientation and Mobility Specialists, and Vision Rehabilitation Therapists; Massage Therapists; Medical and Clinical Laboratory Technicians; Medical and Health Services Managers; Medical Scientists, Except Epidemiologists; Medical Secretaries; Occupational Therapists; Ophthalmic Medical Technologists; Pharmacists; Pharmacy Technicians; Radiologic Technologists; School Psychologists; Social and Human Service Assistants; Speech-Language Pathologists; Speech-Language Pathology Assistants; Substance Abuse and Behavioral Disorder Counselors; others.

# Job Specialization: Endoscopy Technicians

**Maintain a sterile field to provide support for physicians and nurses during endoscopy procedures. Prepare and maintain instruments and equipment. May obtain specimens.** Clean, disinfect, or calibrate scopes or other endoscopic instruments according to manufacturer recommendations and facility standards. Maintain inventories of endoscopic equipment and supplies. Perform safety checks to verify proper equipment functioning. Prepare suites or rooms according to endoscopic procedure requirements. Maintain or repair endoscopic equipment. Position or transport patients in accordance with instructions from medical personnel. Assist physicians or registered nurses in the conduct of endoscopic procedures. Attend in-service training to validate or refresh basic professional skills. Collect specimens from patients using standard medical procedures. Conduct in-service training sessions to disseminate information regarding equipment or instruments. Read current literature, talk with colleagues, or participate in professional organizations or conferences to keep abreast of developments in endoscopy. Place devices, such as blood pressure cuffs, pulse oximeter sensors, nasal cannulas, surgical cautery pads, and cardiac monitoring electrodes, on patients to monitor vital signs.

**Education/Training Required:** Moderate-term on-the-job training. **Education and Training Program:** Allied Health Diagnostic, Intervention, and Treatment Professions, Other. **Knowledge/Courses**—Medicine and Dentistry, Customer and Personal Service, Mechanical, Psychology, Public Safety and Security, Education and Training.

**Personality Type:** Realistic-Investigative-Conventional. **Career Cluster:** 08 Health Science. **Career Pathway:** 8.2 Diagnostics Services. **Other Jobs in This Pathway:** Ambulance Drivers and Attendants, Except Emergency Medical Technicians; Anesthesiologist Assistants; Cardiovascular Technologists and Technicians; Cytogenetic Technologists;

Cytotechnologists; Diagnostic Medical Sonographers; Emergency Medical Technicians and Paramedics; Health Diagnosing and Treating Practitioners, All Other; Health Technologists and Technicians, All Other; Healthcare Practitioners and Technical Workers, All Other; Histotechnologists and Histologic Technicians; Medical and Clinical Laboratory Technicians; Medical and Clinical Laboratory Technologists; Medical and Health Services Managers; Medical Assistants; Medical Equipment Preparers; Neurodiagnostic Technologists; Nuclear Medicine Technologists; Ophthalmic Laboratory Technicians; Physical Scientists, All Other; Physician Assistants; Radiologic Technicians; Radiologic Technologists; Surgical Technologists; Veterinary Assistants and Laboratory Animal Caretakers; others.

**Skills**—Equipment Maintenance, Repairing, Operation Monitoring, Equipment Selection, Troubleshooting, Operation and Control, Quality Control Analysis, Service Orientation.

**Work Environment:** Indoors; standing; walking and running; using hands; repetitive motions; contaminants; exposed to disease or infections; hazardous conditions.

## Job Specialization: Speech-Language Pathology Assistants

**Assist speech-language pathologists in the assessment and treatment of speech, language, voice, and fluency disorders. Implement speech and language programs or activities as planned and directed by speech-language pathologists. Monitor the use of alternative communication devices and systems.** Assist speech-language pathologists in the conduct of client screenings or assessments of language, voice, fluency, articulation, or hearing. Implement treatment plans or protocols as directed by speech-language pathologists. Assist speech-language pathologists in the remediation or development of speech and language skills. Collect and compile data to document clients' performance or assess program quality. Document clients' progress toward meeting established treatment objectives. Test or maintain equipment to ensure correct performance. Assist speech-language pathologists in the conduct of speech-language research projects. Conduct in-service training sessions, or family and community education programs. Perform support duties such as preparing materials, keeping records, maintaining supplies, and scheduling activities. Prepare charts, graphs, or other visual displays to communicate clients' performance information. Select or prepare speech-language instructional materials.

**Education/Training Required:** Associate degree. **Education and Training Program:** Speech-Language Pathology Assistant Training. **Knowledge/Courses**—No data available.

**Personality Type:** Social-Conventional. **Career Cluster:** 08 Health Science. **Career Pathway:** 8.1 Therapeutic Services. **Other Jobs in This Pathway:** Clinical Psychologists; Community and Social Service Specialists, All Other; Counseling Psychologists; Dental Assistants; Dental Hygienists; Dentists, General; Health Technologists and Technicians, All Other; Healthcare Support Workers, All Other; Home Health Aides; Licensed Practical and Licensed Vocational Nurses; Low Vision Therapists, Orientation and Mobility Specialists, and Vision Rehabilitation Therapists; Massage Therapists; Medical and Clinical Laboratory Technicians; Medical and Health Services Managers; Medical Scientists, Except Epidemiologists; Medical Secretaries; Occupational Therapists; Ophthalmic Medical Technologists; Pharmacists; Pharmacy Technicians; Radiologic Technologists; School Psychologists; Social and Human Service Assistants; Speech-Language Pathologists; Substance Abuse and Behavioral Disorder Counselors; others.

**Skills**—No data available.

**Work Environment:** No data available.

# Heating, Air Conditioning, and Refrigeration Mechanics and Installers

* Annual Earnings: $42,530
* Earnings Growth Potential: Medium (37.7%)
* Growth: 28.1%
* Annual Job Openings: 13,620
* Self-Employed: 15.5%

**Considerations for Job Outlook:** Demand for better energy management is expected to create jobs for workers who replace older systems in existing homes and buildings with newer, more efficient units. Prospects should be excellent, particularly for job seekers who have completed accredited training programs or formal apprenticeships.

## Job Specialization: Heating and Air Conditioning Mechanics and Installers

**Install, service, and repair heating and air conditioning systems in residences and commercial establishments.** Obtain and maintain required certifications. Comply with all applicable standards, policies, and procedures, including safety procedures and the maintenance of a clean work area. Repair or replace defective equipment, components, or wiring. Test electrical circuits and components for continuity, using electrical test equipment. Reassemble and test equipment following repairs. Inspect and test system to verify system compliance with plans and specifications and to detect and locate malfunctions. Discuss heating-cooling system malfunctions with users to isolate problems or to verify that malfunctions have been corrected. Test pipe or tubing joints and connections for leaks, using pressure gauge or soap-and-water solution. Record and report all faults, deficiencies, and other unusual occurrences, as well as the time and materials expended on work orders. Adjust system controls to setting recommended by manufacturer to balance system, using hand tools. Recommend, develop, and perform preventive and general maintenance procedures such as cleaning, power-washing, and vacuuming equipment; oiling parts; and changing filters. Lay out and connect electrical wiring between controls and equipment according to wiring diagram, using electrician's hand tools. Install auxiliary components to heating-cooling equipment, such as expansion and discharge valves, air ducts, pipes, blowers, dampers, flues, and stokers, following blueprints. Assist with other work in coordination with repair and maintenance teams. Install, connect, and adjust thermostats, humidistats, and timers, using hand tools. Generate work orders that address deficiencies in need of correction. Join pipes or tubing to equipment and to fuel, water, or refrigerant source to form complete circuit. Assemble, position, and mount heating or cooling equipment, following blueprints.

**Education/Training Required:** Long-term on-the-job training. **Education and Training Programs:** Heating, Air Conditioning, Ventilation, and Refrigeration Maintenance Technology/Technician (HAC, HACR, HVAC, HVACR); Heating, Ventilation, Air Conditioning, and Refrigeration Engineering Technology/Technician; Solar Energy Technology/Technician. **Knowledge/Courses**—Mechanical, Building and Construction, Physics, Chemistry, Design, Engineering and Technology.

**Personality Type:** Realistic-Conventional-Investigative. **Career Cluster:** 02 Architecture and Construction. **Career Pathways:** 2.2 Construction; 2.3 Maintenance/Operations. **Other Jobs in These Pathways:** Brickmasons and Blockmasons; Cement Masons and Concrete Finishers; Construction and Building Inspectors; Construction Carpenters; Construction Laborers; Construction Managers; Cost Estimators; Drywall and Ceiling Tile Installers; Electrical Power-Line Installers and Repairers; Electricians; Engineering Technicians, Except Drafters, All Other; Excavating and Loading Machine and Dragline Operators; First-Line Supervisors of Construction Trades and Extraction Workers; Helpers—Carpenters; Helpers—Electricians; Helpers—Pipelayers, Plumbers, Pipefitters, and Steamfitters; Highway Maintenance Workers; Operating Engineers and Other Construction Equipment Operators; Painters, Construction and Maintenance; Pipe Fitters and Steamfitters; Plumbers; Refrigeration Mechanics and Installers; Roofers; Rough Carpenters; Solar Energy Installation Managers; others.

**Skills**—Installation, Repairing, Equipment Maintenance, Troubleshooting, Equipment Selection, Operation and Control, Quality Control Analysis, Mathematics.

**Work Environment:** More often outdoors than indoors; standing; walking and running; kneeling, crouching, stooping, or crawling; using hands; bending or twisting the body; noise; very hot or cold; bright or inadequate lighting; contaminants; cramped work space; high places; hazardous conditions; hazardous equipment; minor burns, cuts, bites, or stings.

## Job Specialization: Refrigeration Mechanics and Installers

**Install and repair industrial and commercial refrigerating systems.** Braze or solder parts to repair defective joints and leaks. Observe and test system operation, using gauges and instruments. Test lines, components, and connections for leaks. Dismantle malfunctioning systems and test components, using electrical, mechanical, and pneumatic testing equipment. Adjust or replace worn or defective mechanisms and parts and reassemble repaired systems. Read blueprints to determine location, size, capacity, and type of components needed to build refrigeration system. Supervise and instruct assistants. Perform mechanical overhauls and refrigerant reclaiming. Install wiring to connect components to an electric power source. Cut, bend, thread, and connect pipe to functional components and water, power, or refrigeration system. Adjust valves according to specifications and charge system with proper type of refrigerant by pumping the specified gas or fluid into the system. Estimate, order, pick up, deliver, and install materials and supplies needed to maintain equipment in good working condition. Install expansion and control valves, using acetylene torches and wrenches. Mount compressor, condenser, and other components in specified locations on frames, using hand tools and acetylene welding equipment. Keep records of repairs and replacements made and causes of malfunctions. Schedule work with customers and initiate work orders, house requisitions, and orders from stock. Lay out reference points for installation of structural and functional components, using measuring instruments. Fabricate and assemble structural and functional components of refrigeration system, using hand tools, power tools, and welding equipment. Lift and align components into position, using hoist or block and tackle. Drill holes and install mounting brackets and hangers into floor and walls of building. Insulate shells and cabinets of systems.

**Education/Training Required:** Long-term on-the-job training. **Education and Training Programs:** Heating, Air Conditioning, Ventilation, and Refrigeration Maintenance Technology/Technician (HAC, HACR, HVAC, HVACR); Heating, Ventilation, Air Conditioning, and Refrigeration Engineering Technology/Technician. **Knowledge/Courses**—Mechanical, Physics, Building and Construction, Engineering and Technology, Design, Chemistry.

**Personality Type:** Realistic-Conventional-Enterprising. **Career Cluster:** 02 Architecture and Construction. **Career Pathways:** 2.2 Construction; 2.3 Maintenance/Operations. **Other Jobs in These Pathways:** Brickmasons and Blockmasons; Cement Masons and Concrete Finishers; Construction and Building Inspectors; Construction Carpenters; Construction Laborers; Construction Managers; Cost Estimators; Drywall and Ceiling Tile Installers; Electrical Power-Line Installers and Repairers; Electricians; Engineering Technicians, Except Drafters, All Other; Excavating and Loading Machine and Dragline Operators; First-Line Supervisors of Construction Trades and Extraction Workers; Heating and Air Conditioning Mechanics and Installers; Helpers—Carpenters; Helpers—Electricians; Helpers—Pipelayers, Plumbers, Pipefitters, and Steamfitters; Highway Maintenance Workers; Operating Engineers and Other Construction Equipment Operators; Painters, Construction and Maintenance; Pipe Fitters and Steamfitters; Plumbers; Roofers; Rough Carpenters; Solar Energy Installation Managers; others.

**Skills**—Installation, Repairing, Equipment Maintenance, Troubleshooting, Equipment Selection, Operation and Control, Quality Control Analysis, Management of Material Resources.

**Work Environment:** More often outdoors than indoors; standing; walking and running; kneeling, crouching, stooping, or crawling; using hands; bending or twisting the body; repetitive motions; noise; very hot or cold; bright or inadequate lighting; contaminants; cramped work space; high places; hazardous conditions; hazardous equipment; minor burns, cuts, bites, or stings.

# Heavy and Tractor-Trailer Truck Drivers

* Annual Earnings: $37,770
* Earnings Growth Potential: Low (34.5%)
* Growth: 12.9%
* Annual Job Openings: 55,460
* Self-Employed: 8.3%

**Considerations for Job Outlook:** Employment growth for these workers is expected to correspond to overall economic growth. Job opportunities should be favorable, especially for long-haul drivers.

**Drive a tractor-trailer combination or a truck with a capacity of at least 26,000 GVW to transport and deliver goods, livestock, or materials in liquid, loose, or packaged form. May be required to unload truck. May require use of automated routing equipment. Requires commercial drivers' license.** Follow appropriate safety procedures when transporting dangerous goods. Check vehicles before driving them to ensure that mechanical, safety, and emergency equipment is in good working order. Maintain logs of working hours and of vehicle service and repair status, following applicable state and federal regulations. Obtain receipts or signatures when loads are delivered and collect payment for services when required. Check all load-related documentation to ensure that it is complete and accurate. Maneuver trucks into loading or unloading positions, following signals from loading crew as needed; check that vehicle position is correct and any special loading equipment is properly positioned. Drive trucks with capacities greater than 3 tons, including tractor-trailer combinations, to transport and deliver products, livestock, or other materials. Secure cargo for transport, using ropes, blocks, chain, binders, or covers. Read bills of lading to determine assignment details. Report vehicle defects, accidents, traffic violations, or damage to the vehicles. Read and interpret maps to determine vehicle routes. Couple and uncouple trailers by changing trailer jack positions, connecting or disconnecting air and electrical lines, and manipulating fifth-wheel locks. Collect delivery instructions from appropriate sources, verifying instructions and routes. Drive trucks to weigh stations before and after loading and along routes to document weights and to comply with state regulations. Operate equipment such as truck cab computers, CB radios, and telephones to exchange necessary information with bases, supervisors, or other drivers. Check conditions of trailers after contents have been unloaded to ensure that there has been no damage. Crank trailer landing gear up and down to safely secure vehicles. Wrap goods, using pads, packing paper, and containers, and secure loads to trailer walls, using straps.

**Education/Training Required:** Moderate-term on-the-job training. **Education and Training Program:** Truck and Bus Driver Training/Commercial Vehicle Operator and Instructor Training. **Knowledge/Courses**—Transportation, Geography, Public Safety and Security, Law and Government, Mechanical.

**Personality Type:** Realistic-Conventional. **Career Cluster:** 16 Transportation, Distribution, and Logistics. **Career Pathway:** 16.1 Transportation Operations. **Other Jobs in This Pathway:** Airline Pilots, Copilots, and Flight Engineers; Automotive and Watercraft Service Attendants; Automotive Master Mechanics; Bus Drivers, School or Special Client; Bus Drivers, Transit and Intercity; Commercial Pilots; Crane and Tower Operators; First-Line Supervisors of Helpers, Laborers, and Material Movers, Hand; First-Line Supervisors of Transportation and Material-Moving Machine and Vehicle Operators; Freight and Cargo Inspectors; Laborers and Freight, Stock, and Material Movers, Hand; Light Truck or Delivery Services Drivers; Mates—Ship, Boat, and Barge; Motor Vehicle Operators, All Other; Operating Engineers and Other Construction Equipment Operators; Parking Lot Attendants; Pilots, Ship; Railroad Conductors and Yardmasters; Sailors and Marine Oilers; Ship and Boat Captains; Storage and Distribution Managers; Taxi Drivers and Chauffeurs; Transportation Inspectors; Transportation Managers; Transportation Workers, All Other; others.

**Skills**—Operation and Control, Repairing, Equipment Maintenance, Troubleshooting, Operation Monitoring, Quality Control Analysis, Installation, Equipment Selection.

**Work Environment:** Outdoors; sitting; using hands; repetitive motions; very hot or cold; contaminants.

# Helpers—Brickmasons, Blockmasons, Stonemasons, and Tile and Marble Setters

* Annual Earnings: $27,780
* Earnings Growth Potential: Low (30.7%)
* Growth: 16.4%
* Annual Job Openings: 1,890
* Self-Employed: 2.2%

**Considerations for Job Outlook:** Faster-than-average employment growth is projected.

**Help brickmasons, blockmasons, stonemasons, or tile and marble setters by performing duties of lesser skill. Duties include using, supplying, or holding materials or tools and cleaning work area and equipment.** Transport materials, tools, and machines to installation sites, manually or using conveyance equipment. Move or position materials such as marble slabs, using cranes, hoists, or dollies. Modify material moving, mixing, grouting, grinding, polishing, or cleaning procedures according to installation or material requirements. Correct surface imperfections or fill chipped, cracked, or broken bricks or tiles, using fillers, adhesives, and grouting materials. Arrange and store materials, machines, tools, and equipment. Apply caulk, sealants, or other agents to installed surfaces. Select or locate and supply materials to masons for installation, following drawings or numbered sequences. Remove excess grout and residue from tile or brick joints, using sponges or trowels. Remove damaged tile, brick, or mortar and clean and prepare surfaces, using pliers, hammers, chisels, drills, wire brushes, and metal wire anchors. Provide assistance in the preparation, installation, repair, and/or rebuilding of tile, brick, or stone surfaces. Mix mortar, plaster, and grout, manually or using machines, according to standard formulas. Erect scaffolding or other installation structures. Cut materials to specified sizes for installation, using power saws or tile cutters. Clean installation surfaces, equipment, tools, work sites, and storage areas, using water, chemical solutions, oxygen lances, or polishing machines. Apply grout between joints of bricks or tiles, using grouting trowels.

**Education/Training Required:** Short-term on-the-job training. **Education and Training Program:** Masonry/Mason Training. **Knowledge/Courses**—Building and Construction, Chemistry, Transportation, Production and Processing, Mechanical, Design.

**Personality Type:** Realistic. **Career Cluster:** 02 Architecture and Construction. **Career Pathway:** 2.2 Construction. **Other Jobs in This Pathway:** Brickmasons and Blockmasons; Cement Masons and Concrete Finishers; Construction and Building Inspectors; Construction Carpenters; Construction Laborers; Construction Managers; Cost Estimators; Drywall and Ceiling Tile Installers; Electrical Power-Line Installers and Repairers; Electricians; Engineering Technicians, Except Drafters, All Other; First-Line Supervisors of Construction Trades and Extraction Workers; Heating and Air Conditioning Mechanics and Installers; Helpers—Carpenters; Helpers—Electricians; Helpers—Pipelayers, Plumbers, Pipefitters, and Steamfitters; Highway Maintenance Workers; Operating Engineers and Other Construction Equipment Operators; Painters, Construction and Maintenance; Pipe Fitters and Steamfitters; Plumbers; Refrigeration Mechanics and Installers; Roofers; Rough Carpenters; Solar Energy Installation Managers; others.

**Skills**—Equipment Maintenance, Repairing, Equipment Selection, Troubleshooting, Operation and Control, Technology Design, Operation Monitoring, Quality Control Analysis.

**Work Environment:** Outdoors; standing; climbing; walking and running; using hands; bending or twisting the body; repetitive motions; noise; very hot or cold; contaminants; high places; hazardous equipment; minor burns, cuts, bites, or stings.

# Helpers—Carpenters

- ❀ Annual Earnings: $25,760
- ❀ Earnings Growth Potential: Low (31.6%)
- ❀ Growth: 23.3%
- ❀ Annual Job Openings: 3,530
- ❀ Self-Employed: 2.1%

**Considerations for Job Outlook:** Much-faster-than-average employment growth is projected.

**Help carpenters by performing duties of lesser skill. Duties include using, supplying, or holding materials or tools and cleaning work area and equipment.** Position and hold timbers, lumber, and paneling in place for fastening or cutting. Erect scaffolding, shoring, and braces. Select tools, equipment, and materials from storage and transport items to worksite. Fasten timbers or lumber with glue, screws, pegs, or nails and install hardware. Clean work areas, machines, and equipment to maintain a clean and safe jobsite. Align, straighten, plumb, and square forms for

installation. Hold plumb bobs, sighting rods, and other equipment to aid in establishing reference points and lines. Cut timbers, lumber, or paneling to specified dimensions and drill holes in timbers or lumber. Smooth and sand surfaces to remove ridges, tool marks, glue, or caulking. Perform tie spacing layout; then measure, mark, drill, and cut. Secure stakes to grids for constructions of footings, nail scabs to footing forms, and vibrate and float concrete. Construct forms; then assist in raising them to the required elevation. Install handrails under the direction of a carpenter. Glue and clamp edges or joints of assembled parts. Cut and install insulating or sound-absorbing material. Cut tile or linoleum to fit and spread adhesives on flooring to install tile or linoleum. Cover surfaces with laminated-plastic covering material.

**Education/Training Required:** Short-term on-the-job training. **Education and Training Program:** Carpentry/Carpenter. **Knowledge/Courses**—Building and Construction, Design, Engineering and Technology.

**Personality Type:** Realistic-Conventional. **Career Cluster:** 02 Architecture and Construction. **Career Pathway:** 2.2 Construction. **Other Jobs in This Pathway:** Brickmasons and Blockmasons; Cement Masons and Concrete Finishers; Construction and Building Inspectors; Construction Carpenters; Construction Laborers; Construction Managers; Cost Estimators; Drywall and Ceiling Tile Installers; Electrical Power-Line Installers and Repairers; Electricians; Engineering Technicians, Except Drafters, All Other; Excavating and Loading Machine and Dragline Operators; First-Line Supervisors of Construction Trades and Extraction Workers; Heating and Air Conditioning Mechanics and Installers; Helpers—Electricians; Helpers—Pipelayers, Plumbers, Pipefitters, and Steamfitters; Highway Maintenance Workers; Operating Engineers and Other Construction Equipment Operators; Painters, Construction and Maintenance; Pipe Fitters and Steamfitters; Plumbers; Refrigeration Mechanics and Installers; Roofers; Rough Carpenters; Solar Energy Installation Managers; others.

**Skills**—Equipment Selection, Installation, Repairing, Equipment Maintenance, Operation and Control, Quality Control Analysis, Troubleshooting, Technology Design.

**Work Environment:** Outdoors; standing; walking and running; kneeling, crouching, stooping, or crawling; using hands; bending or twisting the body; repetitive motions; noise; very hot or cold; bright or inadequate lighting; contaminants; cramped work space; hazardous equipment; minor burns, cuts, bites, or stings.

# Helpers—Electricians

- ❀ Annual Earnings: $27,220
- ❀ Earnings Growth Potential: Low (28.1%)
- ❀ Growth: 24.7%
- ❀ Annual Job Openings: 4,800
- ❀ Self-Employed: 2.1%

**Considerations for Job Outlook:** Much-faster-than-average employment growth is projected.

**Help electricians by performing duties of lesser skill. Duties include using, supplying, or holding materials or tools and cleaning work area and equipment.** Trace out short circuits in wiring, using test meter. Measure, cut, and bend wire and conduit, using measuring instruments and hand tools. Maintain tools, vehicles, and equipment and keep parts and supplies in order. Drill holes and pull or push wiring through openings, using hand and power tools. Perform semi-skilled and unskilled laboring duties related to the installation, maintenance, and repair of a wide variety of electrical systems and equipment. Disassemble defective electrical equipment, replace defective or worn parts, and reassemble equipment, using hand tools. Transport tools, materials, equipment, and supplies to worksite by hand; handtruck; or heavy, motorized truck. Examine electrical units for loose connections and broken insulation and tighten connections, using hand tools. Strip insulation from wire ends, using wire-stripping pliers, and attach wires to terminals for subsequent soldering. Construct controllers and panels, using power drills, drill presses, taps, saws, and punches. Thread conduit ends, connect couplings, and fabricate and secure conduit support brackets, using hand tools. String transmission lines or cables through ducts or conduits, under the ground, through equipment, or to towers. Clean work area and wash parts. Erect electrical system components and barricades and rig scaffolds, hoists, and shoring. Install copper-clad ground rods, using a manual post driver. Raise, lower, or position equipment, tools, and materials, using hoist, hand line, or block and tackle. Dig trenches or holes for installation of conduit or supports. Requisition materials, using warehouse requisition or release forms. Bolt component parts together to form tower assemblies, using hand tools. Paint a variety of objects related to electrical functions. Operate cutting torches and welding equipment while working with conduit and metal components to construct devices associated with electrical functions.

**Education/Training Required:** Short-term on-the-job training. **Education and Training Program:** Electrician.

**Knowledge/Courses**—Building and Construction, Mechanical, Design, Engineering and Technology, Mathematics, Public Safety and Security.

**Personality Type:** Realistic-Conventional. **Career Cluster:** 02 Architecture and Construction. **Career Pathway:** 2.2 Construction. **Other Jobs in This Pathway:** Brickmasons and Blockmasons; Cement Masons and Concrete Finishers; Construction and Building Inspectors; Construction Carpenters; Construction Laborers; Construction Managers; Cost Estimators; Drywall and Ceiling Tile Installers; Electrical Power-Line Installers and Repairers; Electricians; Engineering Technicians, Except Drafters, All Other; Excavating and Loading Machine and Dragline Operators; First-Line Supervisors of Construction Trades and Extraction Workers; Heating and Air Conditioning Mechanics and Installers; Helpers—Carpenters; Helpers—Pipelayers, Plumbers, Pipefitters, and Steamfitters; Highway Maintenance Workers; Operating Engineers and Other Construction Equipment Operators; Painters, Construction and Maintenance; Pipe Fitters and Steamfitters; Plumbers; Refrigeration Mechanics and Installers; Roofers; Rough Carpenters; Solar Energy Installation Managers; others.

**Skills**—Installation, Repairing, Equipment Maintenance, Operation and Control, Troubleshooting, Equipment Selection, Quality Control Analysis, Coordination.

**Work Environment:** More often outdoors than indoors; standing; climbing; walking and running; kneeling, crouching, stooping, or crawling; balancing; using hands; bending or twisting the body; repetitive motions; noise; very hot or cold; bright or inadequate lighting; contaminants; cramped work space; high places; hazardous conditions; hazardous equipment; minor burns, cuts, bites, or stings.

# Helpers—Pipelayers, Plumbers, Pipefitters, and Steamfitters

- ❀ Annual Earnings: $26,740
- ❀ Earnings Growth Potential: Low (31.7%)
- ❀ Growth: 25.7%
- ❀ Annual Job Openings: 3,730
- ❀ Self-Employed: 2.1%

**Considerations for Job Outlook:** Much-faster-than-average employment growth is projected.

**Help plumbers, pipefitters, steamfitters, or pipelayers by performing duties of lesser skill. Duties include using, supplying, or holding materials or tools and cleaning**

work area and equipment. Assist plumbers by performing rough-ins, repairing and replacing fixtures, and locating and repairing leaking or broken pipes. Cut or drill holes in walls or floors to accommodate the passage of pipes. Measure, cut, thread, and assemble new pipe, placing the assembled pipe in hangers or other supports. Mount brackets and hangers on walls and ceilings to hold pipes and set sleeves or inserts to provide support for pipes. Requisition tools and equipment, select type and size of pipe, and collect and transport materials and equipment to worksite. Fit or assist in fitting valves, couplings, or assemblies to tanks, pumps, or systems, using hand tools. Assist pipe fitters in the layout, assembly, and installation of piping for air, ammonia, gas, and water systems. Excavate and grade ditches and lay and join pipe for water and sewer service. Cut pipe and lift up to fitters. Disassemble and remove damaged or worn pipe. Clean shop, work area, and machines, using solvent and rags. Install gas burners to convert furnaces from wood, coal, or oil. Immerse pipe in chemical solution to remove dirt, oil, and scale. Clean and renew steam traps. Fill pipes with sand or resin to prevent distortion and hold pipes during bending and installation.

Education/Training Required: Short-term on-the-job training. Education and Training Program: Plumbing Technology/Plumber. Knowledge/Courses—Building and Construction, Mechanical, Design, Public Safety and Security, Engineering and Technology, Law and Government.

Personality Type: Realistic. Career Cluster: 02 Architecture and Construction. Career Pathway: 2.2 Construction. Other Jobs in This Pathway: Brickmasons and Blockmasons; Cement Masons and Concrete Finishers; Construction and Building Inspectors; Construction Carpenters; Construction Laborers; Construction Managers; Cost Estimators; Drywall and Ceiling Tile Installers; Electrical Power-Line Installers and Repairers; Electricians; Engineering Technicians, Except Drafters, All Other; Excavating and Loading Machine and Dragline Operators; First-Line Supervisors of Construction Trades and Extraction Workers; Heating and Air Conditioning Mechanics and Installers; Helpers—Carpenters; Helpers—Electricians; Highway Maintenance Workers; Operating Engineers and Other Construction Equipment Operators; Painters, Construction and Maintenance; Pipe Fitters and Steamfitters; Plumbers; Refrigeration Mechanics and Installers; Roofers; Rough Carpenters; Solar Energy Installation Managers; others.

Skills—Repairing, Installation, Equipment Selection, Equipment Maintenance, Troubleshooting, Operation and Control, Quality Control Analysis.

Work Environment: Outdoors; standing; walking and running; kneeling, crouching, stooping, or crawling; using hands; bending or twisting the body; repetitive motions; noise; very hot or cold; bright or inadequate lighting; contaminants; cramped work space; whole-body vibration; high places; hazardous equipment; minor burns, cuts, bites, or stings.

# Highway Maintenance Workers

❋ Annual Earnings: $34,780
❋ Earnings Growth Potential: Medium (37.1%)
❋ Growth: 8.5%
❋ Annual Job Openings: 5,200
❋ Self-Employed: 2.6%

Considerations for Job Outlook: About average employment growth is projected.

Maintain highways, municipal and rural roads, airport runways, and rights-of-way. Duties include patching broken or eroded pavement and repairing guardrails, highway markers, and snow fences. May also mow or clear brush from along road or plow snow from roadway. Flag motorists to warn them of obstacles or repair work ahead. Set out signs and cones around work areas to divert traffic. Drive trucks or tractors with adjustable attachments to sweep debris from paved surfaces, mow grass and weeds, and remove snow and ice. Dump, spread, and tamp asphalt, using pneumatic tampers, to repair joints and patch broken pavement. Drive trucks to transport crews and equipment to worksites. Inspect, clean, and repair drainage systems, bridges, tunnels, and other structures. Haul and spread sand, gravel, and clay to fill washouts and repair road shoulders. Erect, install, or repair guardrails, road shoulders, berms, highway markers, warning signals, and highway lighting, using hand tools and power tools. Remove litter and debris from roadways, including debris from rock slides and mudslides. Clean and clear debris from culverts, catch basins, drop inlets, ditches, and other drain structures. Perform roadside landscaping work, such as clearing weeds and brush and planting and trimming trees. Paint traffic control lines and place pavement traffic messages by hand or using machines. Inspect markers to verify accurate installation. Apply poisons along roadsides and in animal burrows to eliminate unwanted roadside vegetation and rodents. Measure and mark locations for installation of markers, using tape, string, or chalk. Apply oil to road surfaces, using sprayers. Blend compounds to form adhesive mixtures used for marker installation. Place and remove snow fences used to prevent the accumulation of drifting snow on highways.

**Education/Training Required:** Moderate-term on-the-job training. **Education and Training Program:** Construction/Heavy Equipment/Earthmoving Equipment Operation. **Knowledge/Courses**—Building and Construction, Transportation, Public Safety and Security, Mechanical, Law and Government, Telecommunications.

**Personality Type:** Realistic-Conventional. **Career Cluster:** 02 Architecture and Construction. **Career Pathway:** 2.2 Construction. **Other Jobs in This Pathway:** Brickmasons and Blockmasons; Cement Masons and Concrete Finishers; Construction and Building Inspectors; Construction Carpenters; Construction Laborers; Construction Managers; Cost Estimators; Drywall and Ceiling Tile Installers; Electrical Power-Line Installers and Repairers; Electricians; Engineering Technicians, Except Drafters, All Other; Excavating and Loading Machine and Dragline Operators; First-Line Supervisors of Construction Trades and Extraction Workers; Heating and Air Conditioning Mechanics and Installers; Helpers—Carpenters; Helpers—Electricians; Helpers—Pipelayers, Plumbers, Pipefitters, and Steamfitters; Operating Engineers and Other Construction Equipment Operators; Painters, Construction and Maintenance; Pipe Fitters and Steamfitters; Plumbers; Refrigeration Mechanics and Installers; Roofers; Rough Carpenters; Solar Energy Installation Managers; others.

**Skills**—Repairing, Equipment Maintenance, Operation and Control, Troubleshooting, Operation Monitoring, Quality Control Analysis, Equipment Selection, Coordination.

**Work Environment:** Outdoors; standing; using hands; bending or twisting the body; repetitive motions; noise; very hot or cold; contaminants; cramped work space; whole-body vibration; hazardous equipment; minor burns, cuts, bites, or stings.

# History Teachers, Postsecondary

* Annual Earnings: $64,880
* Earnings Growth Potential: High (48.4%)
* Growth: 15.1%
* Annual Job Openings: 700
* Self-Employed: 0.2%

**Considerations for Job Outlook:** Enrollments in postsecondary institutions are expected to continue rising as more people attend college and as workers return to school to update their skills. Opportunities for part-time or temporary positions should be favorable, but significant competition exists for tenure-track positions.

**Teach courses in human history and historiography.** Prepare and deliver lectures to undergraduate and/or graduate students on topics such as ancient history, postwar civilizations, and the history of third-world countries. Evaluate and grade students' classwork, assignments, and papers. Prepare course materials such as syllabi, homework assignments, and handouts. Compile, administer, and grade examinations or assign this work to others. Initiate, facilitate, and moderate classroom discussions. Keep abreast of developments in their field by reading current literature, talking with colleagues, and participating in professional conferences. Plan, evaluate, and revise curricula, course content, and course materials and methods of instruction. Maintain student attendance records, grades, and other required records. Maintain regularly scheduled office hours to advise and assist students. Conduct research in a particular field of knowledge and publish findings in professional journals, books, or electronic media. Select and obtain materials and supplies such as textbooks. Advise students on academic and vocational curricula and on career issues. Collaborate with colleagues to address teaching and research issues. Serve on academic or administrative committees that deal with institutional policies, departmental matters, and academic issues. Participate in campus and community events. Act as advisers to student organizations. Participate in student recruitment, registration, and placement activities. Compile bibliographies of specialized materials for outside reading assignments. Supervise undergraduate and graduate teaching, internship, and research work. Perform administrative duties such as serving as department head. Write grant proposals to procure external research funding. Provide professional consulting services to government, educational institutions, and industry.

**Education/Training Required:** Doctoral degree. **Education and Training Programs:** American History (United States); Asian History; Canadian History; European History; History and Philosophy of Science and Technology; History, General; History, Other; Humanities/Humanistic Studies; Public/Applied History. **Knowledge/Courses**—History and Archeology, Philosophy and Theology, Geography, Sociology and Anthropology, Education and Training, English Language.

**Personality Type:** Social-Investigative-Artistic. **Career Clusters:** 05 Education and Training; 15 Science, Technology, Engineering, and Mathematics. **Career Pathways:** 5.3 Teaching/Training; 15.2 Science and Mathematics. **Other**

**Jobs in These Pathways:** Adult Basic and Secondary Education and Literacy Teachers and Instructors; Architectural and Engineering Managers; Biofuels/Biodiesel Technology and Product Development Managers; Biologists; Career/Technical Education Teachers, Secondary School; Chemists; Coaches and Scouts; Community and Social Service Specialists, All Other; Education, Training, and Library Workers, All Other; Elementary School Teachers, Except Special Education; Fitness Trainers and Aerobics Instructors; Instructional Coordinators; Instructional Designers and Technologists; Kindergarten Teachers, Except Special Education; Librarians; Medical Scientists, Except Epidemiologists; Middle School Teachers, Except Special and Career/Technical Education; Operations Research Analysts; Preschool Teachers, Except Special Education; Recreation Workers; Secondary School Teachers, Except Special and Career/Technical Education; Self-Enrichment Education Teachers; Teacher Assistants; Tutors; 37 other postsecondary teaching occupations; others.

**Skills**—Learning Strategies, Writing, Speaking, Operations Analysis, Reading Comprehension, Active Learning, Instructing, Science.

**Work Environment:** Indoors; sitting.

# Home Economics Teachers, Postsecondary

- ❋ Annual Earnings: $65,040
- ❋ Earnings Growth Potential: High (50.6%)
- ❋ Growth: 15.1%
- ❋ Annual Job Openings: 200
- ❋ Self-Employed: 0.2%

**Considerations for Job Outlook:** Enrollments in postsecondary institutions are expected to continue rising as more people attend college and as workers return to school to update their skills. Opportunities for part-time or temporary positions should be favorable, but significant competition exists for tenure-track positions.

**Teach courses in child care, family relations, finance, nutrition, and related subjects as pertaining to home management.** Evaluate and grade students' classwork, laboratory work, projects, assignments, and papers. Initiate, facilitate, and moderate classroom discussions. Prepare and deliver lectures to undergraduate or graduate students on topics such as food science, nutrition, and child care. Prepare course materials such as syllabi, homework assignments, and handouts. Keep abreast of developments in their field by reading current literature, talking with colleagues, and participating in professional conferences. Maintain student attendance records, grades, and other required records. Plan, evaluate, and revise curricula, course content, and course materials and methods of instruction. Compile, administer, and grade examinations or assign this work to others. Advise students on academic and vocational curricula and on career issues. Maintain regularly scheduled office hours to advise and assist students. Supervise undergraduate or graduate teaching, internship, and research work. Select and obtain materials and supplies such as textbooks. Conduct research in a particular field of knowledge and publish findings in professional journals, books, and/or electronic media. Collaborate with colleagues to address teaching and research issues. Act as advisers to student organizations. Participate in student recruitment, registration, and placement activities. Serve on academic or administrative committees that deal with institutional policies, departmental matters, and academic issues. Participate in campus and community events. Compile bibliographies of specialized materials for outside reading assignments. Perform administrative duties such as serving as department head. Write grant proposals to procure external research funding. Provide professional consulting services to government and industry.

**Education/Training Required:** Doctoral degree. **Education and Training Programs:** Business Family and Consumer Sciences/Human Sciences; Child Care and Support Services Management; Family and Consumer Sciences/Human Sciences, General; Foodservice Systems Administration/Management; Human Development and Family Studies, General. **Knowledge/Courses**—Sociology and Anthropology, Philosophy and Theology, Education and Training, Therapy and Counseling, Psychology, English Language.

**Personality Type:** Social-Investigative-Artistic. **Career Clusters:** 05 Education and Training; 08 Health Science; 10 Human Services. **Career Pathways:** 5.3 Teaching/Training; 8.4 Support Services; 10.1 Early Childhood Development and Services; 10.3 Family and Community Services; 10.5 Consumer Services Career. **Other Jobs in These Pathways:** Chief Executives; Child, Family, and School Social Workers; Childcare Workers; Coaches and Scouts; Cooks, Institution and Cafeteria; Elementary School Teachers, Except Special Education; First-Line Supervisors of Food Preparation and Serving Workers; First-Line Supervisors of Retail Sales Workers; Fitness Trainers and Aerobics Instructors; Kindergarten Teachers, Except Special Education; Librarians; Managers, All Other; Middle School Teachers, Except Special and Career/Technical Education; Nannies; Personal Care Aides; Preschool Teachers, Except Special Education; Public

Relations Specialists; Recreation Workers; Sales Managers; Secondary School Teachers, Except Special and Career/Technical Education; Self-Enrichment Education Teachers; Supply Chain Managers; Teacher Assistants; Tutors; 37 other postsecondary teaching occupations; others.

**Skills**—Learning Strategies, Instructing, Writing, Active Learning, Speaking, Reading Comprehension, Active Listening, Systems Evaluation.

**Work Environment:** Indoors; sitting.

## Home Health Aides

- ❋ Annual Earnings: $20,560
- ❋ Earnings Growth Potential: Very low (20.7%)
- ❋ Growth: 50.0%
- ❋ Annual Job Openings: 55,270
- ❋ Self-Employed: 1.8%

**Considerations for Job Outlook:** Growth is expected to stem from a rise in the number of elderly people, an age group that relies increasingly on home care for assistance with daily activities. This growth, together with the need to replace workers who leave the occupation permanently, should result in excellent job prospects.

**Provide routine personal health care, such as bathing, dressing, or grooming, to elderly, convalescent, or disabled persons in the home of patients or in a residential care facility.** Maintain records of patient care, condition, progress, or problems to report and discuss observations with supervisor or case manager. Provide patients with help moving in and out of beds, baths, wheelchairs, or automobiles and with dressing and grooming. Provide patients and families with emotional support and instruction in areas such as caring for infants, preparing healthy meals, living independently, or adapting to disability or illness. Change bed linens, wash and iron patients' laundry, and clean patients' quarters. Entertain, converse with, or read aloud to patients to keep them mentally healthy and alert. Plan, purchase, prepare, or serve meals to patients or other family members according to prescribed diets. Direct patients in simple prescribed exercises or in the use of braces or artificial limbs. Check patients' pulse, temperature, and respiration. Change dressings. Perform a variety of duties as requested by client, such as obtaining household supplies or running errands. Accompany clients to doctors' offices and on other trips outside the home, providing transportation, assistance, and companionship. Administer prescribed oral medications under written direction of physician or as directed by home care nurse and aide. Care for children who are disabled or who have sick or disabled parents. Massage patients and apply preparations and treatments such as liniment, alcohol rubs, and heat-lamp stimulation.

**Education/Training Required:** Short-term on-the-job training. **Education and Training Program:** Home Health Aide/Home Attendant Training. **Knowledge/Courses**—Psychology, Medicine and Dentistry, Therapy and Counseling, Philosophy and Theology, Customer and Personal Service, Personnel and Human Resources.

**Personality Type:** Social-Realistic. **Career Cluster:** 08 Health Science. **Career Pathway:** 8.1 Therapeutic Services. **Other Jobs in This Pathway:** Clinical Psychologists; Community and Social Service Specialists, All Other; Counseling Psychologists; Dental Assistants; Dental Hygienists; Dentists, General; Health Technologists and Technicians, All Other; Healthcare Support Workers, All Other; Licensed Practical and Licensed Vocational Nurses; Low Vision Therapists, Orientation and Mobility Specialists, and Vision Rehabilitation Therapists; Massage Therapists; Medical and Clinical Laboratory Technicians; Medical and Health Services Managers; Medical Scientists, Except Epidemiologists; Medical Secretaries; Occupational Therapists; Ophthalmic Medical Technologists; Pharmacists; Pharmacy Technicians; Radiologic Technologists; School Psychologists; Social and Human Service Assistants; Speech-Language Pathologists; Speech-Language Pathology Assistants; Substance Abuse and Behavioral Disorder Counselors; others.

**Skills**—Service Orientation, Social Perceptiveness, Negotiation, Instructing, Active Listening, Monitoring, Learning Strategies.

**Work Environment:** Indoors; standing; walking and running; kneeling, crouching, stooping, or crawling; balancing; using hands; bending or twisting the body; repetitive motions; contaminants; exposed to disease or infections.

## Hotel, Motel, and Resort Desk Clerks

- ❋ Annual Earnings: $19,930
- ❋ Earnings Growth Potential: Very low (19.3%)
- ❋ Growth: 13.7%
- ❋ Annual Job Openings: 10,950
- ❋ Self-Employed: 0.0%

**Considerations for Job Outlook:** As the economy improves, travel is expected to increase and developers are expected to open more hotels. Job prospects for these clerks should be favorable.

**Accommodate hotel, motel, and resort patrons by registering and assigning rooms to guests, issuing room keys, transmitting and receiving messages, keeping records of occupied rooms and guests' accounts, making and confirming reservations, and presenting statements to and collecting payments from departing guests.** Greet, register, and assign rooms to guests of hotels or motels. Verify customers' credit and establish how the customer will pay for the accommodation. Keep records of room availability and guests' accounts manually or using computers. Compute bills, collect payments, and make change for guests. Perform simple bookkeeping activities, such as balancing cash accounts. Issue room keys and escort instructions to bellhops. Review accounts and charges with guests during the checkout process. Post charges, such as those for rooms, food, liquor, or telephone calls, to ledgers manually or by using computers. Transmit and receive messages, using telephones or telephone switchboards. Contact housekeeping or maintenance staff when guests report problems. Make and confirm reservations. Answer inquiries pertaining to hotel services; registration of guests; and shopping, dining, entertainment, and travel directions. Record guest comments or complaints, referring customers to managers as necessary. Advise housekeeping staff when rooms have been vacated and are ready for cleaning. Arrange tours, taxis, or restaurant reservations for customers. Deposit guests' valuables in hotel safes or safe-deposit boxes. Date-stamp, sort, and rack incoming mail and messages.

**Education/Training Required:** Short-term on-the-job training. **Education and Training Program:** Selling Skills and Sales Operations. **Knowledge/Courses**—Customer and Personal Service, Clerical, Sales and Marketing, Computers and Electronics.

**Personality Type:** Conventional-Enterprising-Social. **Career Cluster:** 14 Marketing, Sales, and Service. **Career Pathway:** 14.2 Professional Sales and Marketing. **Other Jobs in This Pathway:** Cashiers; Counter and Rental Clerks; Door-To-Door Sales Workers, News and Street Vendors, and Related Workers; Driver/Sales Workers; Energy Brokers; First-Line Supervisors of Non-Retail Sales Workers; First-Line Supervisors of Retail Sales Workers; Marketing Managers; Marking Clerks; Online Merchants; Order Fillers, Wholesale and Retail Sales; Parts Salespersons; Property, Real Estate, and Community Association Managers; Real Estate Sales Agents; Reservation and Transportation Ticket Agents and Travel Clerks; Retail Salespersons; Sales and Related Workers, All Other; Sales Representatives, Services, All Other; Sales Representatives, Wholesale and Manufacturing, Except Technical and Scientific Products; Sales Representatives, Wholesale and Manufacturing, Technical and Scientific Products; Solar Sales Representatives and Assessors; Stock Clerks—Stockroom, Warehouse, or Storage Yard; Stock Clerks, Sales Floor; Telemarketers; Wholesale and Retail Buyers, Except Farm Products; others.

**Skills**—Service Orientation, Programming, Management of Personnel Resources, Persuasion, Reading Comprehension, Systems Evaluation, Instructing.

**Work Environment:** Indoors; standing; using hands.

# Human Resources Managers

* Annual Earnings: $99,180
* Earnings Growth Potential: Medium (37.9%)
* Growth: 9.6%
* Annual Job Openings: 4,140
* Self-Employed: 0.6%

**Considerations for Job Outlook:** Efforts to recruit and retain employees, the growing importance of employee training, and new legal standards are expected to increase employment of these workers. College graduates and those with certification should have the best opportunities.

**Plan, direct, and coordinate human resource management activities of an organization to maximize the strategic use of human resources and maintain functions such as employee compensation, recruitment, personnel policies, and regulatory compliance.** Administer compensation, benefits and performance management systems, and safety and recreation programs. Identify staff vacancies and recruit, interview and select applicants. Allocate human resources, ensuring appropriate matches between personnel. Provide current and prospective employees with information about policies, job duties, working conditions, wages, opportunities for promotion and employee benefits. Perform difficult staffing duties, including dealing with understaffing, refereeing disputes, firing employees, and administering disciplinary procedures. Advise managers on organizational policy matters such as equal employment opportunity and sexual harassment, and recommend needed changes. Analyze and modify compensation and benefits policies to establish competitive programs and ensure compliance with legal requirements. Plan and conduct new employee orientation to foster positive attitude toward organizational objectives. Serve as a link between management and employees by handling questions, interpreting and administering contracts and helping resolve work-related problems. Plan, direct, supervise, and coordinate work activities of subordinates and staff relating to employment, compensation, labor relations, and employee relations. Analyze training needs to design employee development, language training and health and safety programs. Maintain records and compile statistical reports concerning personnel-related data such as hires, transfers, performance appraisals, and absenteeism rates. Analyze statistical data and reports to identify and determine causes of personnel problems and develop recommendations for improvement of organization's personnel policies and practices. Plan, organize, direct, control or coordinate the personnel, training, or labor relations activities of an organization. Conduct exit interviews to identify reasons for employee termination. Investigate and report on industrial accidents for insurance carriers.

**Education/Training Required:** Work experience plus degree. **Education and Training Program:** Human Resources Management/Personnel Administration, General. **Knowledge/Courses**—Personnel and Human Resources, Therapy and Counseling, Sociology and Anthropology, Psychology, Clerical, Administration and Management.

**Personality Type:** Enterprising-Social-Conventional. **Career Cluster:** 04 Business, Management, and Administration. **Career Pathway:** 4.3 Human Resources. **Other Jobs in This Pathway:** Human Resources Specialists.

**Skills**—Management of Financial Resources, Management of Personnel Resources, Management of Material Resources, Systems Evaluation, Negotiation, Systems Analysis, Persuasion, Learning Strategies.

**Work Environment:** Indoors; sitting.

# Human Resources Specialists

- ❀ Annual Earnings: $52,690
- ❀ Earnings Growth Potential: High (44.9%)
- ❀ Growth: 27.9%
- ❀ Annual Job Openings: 11,230
- ❀ Self-Employed: 1.6%

**Considerations for Job Outlook:** Efforts to recruit and retain employees, the growing importance of employee training, and new legal standards are expected to increase employment of these workers. College graduates and those with certification should have the best opportunities.

**Recruit and place workers.** Address employee relations issues, such as harassment allegations, work complaints, or other employee concerns. Analyze employment-related data and prepare required reports. Conduct exit interviews and ensure that necessary employment termination paperwork is completed. Conduct reference or background checks on job applicants. Confer with management to develop or implement personnel policies or procedures. Contact job applicants to inform them of the status of their applications. Develop or implement recruiting strategies to meet current or anticipated staffing needs. Hire employees and process hiring-related paperwork. Inform job applicants of details such as duties and responsibilities, compensation, benefits, schedules, working conditions, or promotion opportunities. Interpret and explain human resources policies, procedures, laws, standards, or regulations. Interview job applicants to obtain information on work history, training, education, or job skills. Maintain and update human resources documents, such as organizational charts, employee handbooks or directories, or performance evaluation forms. Maintain current knowledge of Equal Employment Opportunity (EEO) and affirmative action guidelines and laws, such as the Americans with Disabilities Act (ADA). Perform searches for qualified job candidates, using sources such as computer databases, networking, Internet recruiting resources, media advertisements, job fairs, recruiting firms, or employee referrals. Prepare or maintain employment records related to events such as hiring, termination, leaves, transfers, or promotions, using human resources management system software. Provide management with information or training related to interviewing, performance appraisals, counseling techniques, or documentation of performance issues. Review employment applications and job orders to match applicants with job requirements.

**Education/Training Required:** Bachelor's degree. **Education and Training Programs:** Human Resources Management/Personnel Administration, General; Labor and Industrial Relations. **Knowledge/Courses**—Personnel and Human Resources, Sales and Marketing, Clerical, Law and Government, Customer and Personal Service, Communications and Media.

**Personality Type:** Enterprising-Social-Conventional. **Career Cluster:** 04 Business, Management, and Administration. **Career Pathway:** 4.3 Human Resources. **Other Jobs in This Pathway:** Business Teachers, Postsecondary; Compensation, Benefits, and Job Analysis Specialists; Employment, Recruitment, and Placement Specialists; Labor Relations Specialists; Training and Development Specialists.

**Skills**—Science, Service Orientation, Social Perceptiveness, Speaking, Operations Analysis, Management of Personnel Resources, Writing, Active Listening.

**Work Environment:** Indoors; sitting; repetitive motions.

# Hydrologists

- ❋ Annual Earnings: $75,690
- ❋ Earnings Growth Potential: Medium (36.2%)
- ❋ Growth: 18.2%
- ❋ Annual Job Openings: 380
- ❋ Self-Employed: 2.4%

**Considerations for Job Outlook:** The need for energy services, environmental protection services, and responsible land and water management is expected to spur employment growth for these workers. Job seekers who have a master's degree in geoscience should have excellent opportunities.

**Research the distribution, circulation, and physical properties of underground and surface waters; study the form and intensity of precipitation and its rate of infiltration into the soil, its movement through the earth, and return to the ocean and atmosphere.** Study and document quantities, distribution, disposition, and development of underground and surface waters. Draft final reports describing research results, including illustrations, appendices, maps, and other attachments. Coordinate and supervise the work of professional and technical staff, including research assistants, technologists, and technicians. Prepare hydrogeologic evaluations of known or suspected hazardous waste sites and land treatment and feedlot facilities. Design and conduct scientific hydrogeological investigations to ensure that accurate and appropriate information is available for use in water resource management decisions. Study public water supply issues, including flood and drought risks, water quality, wastewater, and impacts on wetland habitats. Collect and analyze water samples as part of field investigations and/or to validate data from automatic monitors. Apply research findings to help minimize the environmental impacts of pollution, water-borne diseases, erosion, and sedimentation. Measure and graph phenomena such as lake levels, stream flows, and changes in water volumes. Investigate complaints or conflicts related to the alteration of public waters, gathering information, recommending alternatives, informing participants of progress, and preparing draft orders. Develop or modify methods of conducting hydrologic studies. Answer questions and provide technical assistance and information to contractors and/or the public regarding issues such as well drilling, code requirements, hydrology, and geology. Install, maintain, and calibrate instruments such as those that monitor water levels, rainfall, and sediments. Evaluate data and provide recommendations regarding the feasibility of municipal projects such as hydroelectric power plants, irrigation systems, flood warning systems, and waste treatment facilities. Conduct short-term and long-term climate assessments and study storm occurrences.

**Education/Training Required:** Master's degree. **Education and Training Programs:** Geology/Earth Science, General; Hydrology and Water Resources Science; Oceanography, Chemical and Physical. **Knowledge/Courses**—Geography, Biology, Engineering and Technology, Physics, Chemistry, Design.

**Personality Type:** Investigative-Realistic. **Career Cluster:** 15 Science, Technology, Engineering, and Mathematics. **Career Pathway:** 15.2 Science and Mathematics. **Other Jobs in This Pathway:** Architectural and Engineering Managers; Biochemists and Biophysicists; Biofuels/Biodiesel Technology and Product Development Managers; Bioinformatics Scientists; Biological Scientists, All Other; Biologists; Biostatisticians; Chemists; Clinical Data Managers; Clinical Research Coordinators; Community and Social Service Specialists, All Other; Dietitians and Nutritionists; Education, Training, and Library Workers, All Other; Geneticists; Geoscientists, Except Hydrologists and Geographers; Medical Scientists, Except Epidemiologists; Molecular and Cellular Biologists; Natural Sciences Managers; Operations Research Analysts; Physical Scientists, All Other; Social Scientists and Related Workers, All Other; Statisticians; Survey Researchers; Transportation Planners; Water Resource Specialists; others.

**Skills**—Science, Programming, Mathematics, Installation, Systems Analysis, Writing, Systems Evaluation, Active Learning.

**Work Environment:** More often indoors than outdoors; sitting.

# Industrial Engineering Technicians

- ❋ Annual Earnings: $48,210
- ❋ Earnings Growth Potential: Low (34.5%)
- ❋ Growth: 6.6%
- ❋ Annual Job Openings: 1,850
- ❋ Self-Employed: 0.7%

**Considerations for Job Outlook:** Labor-saving efficiencies and the automation of many engineering support activities will limit the need for new engineering technicians. In general, opportunities should be best for job seekers who have an associate degree or other postsecondary training in engineering technology.

**Apply engineering theory and principles to problems of industrial layout or manufacturing production, usually under the direction of engineering staff. May study and record time, motion, method, and speed involved in performance of production, maintenance, clerical, and other worker operations for such purposes as establishing standard production rates or improving efficiency.** Recommend revision to methods of operation, material handling, equipment layout, or other changes to increase production or improve standards. Study time, motion, methods, and speed involved in maintenance, production, and other operations to establish standard production rate and improve efficiency. Interpret engineering drawings, schematic diagrams, or formulas and confer with management or engineering staff to determine quality and reliability standards. Recommend modifications to existing quality or production standards to achieve optimum quality within limits of equipment capability. Aid in planning work assignments in accordance with worker performance, machine capacity, production schedules, and anticipated delays. Observe workers using equipment to verify that equipment is being operated and maintained according to quality assurance standards. Observe workers operating equipment or performing tasks to determine time involved and fatigue rate, using timing devices. Prepare charts, graphs, and diagrams to illustrate workflow, routing, floor layouts, material handling, and machine utilization. Evaluate data and write reports to validate or indicate deviations from existing standards. Read worker logs, product processing sheets, and specification sheets to verify that records adhere to quality assurance specifications. Prepare graphs or charts of data or enter data into computer for analysis. Record test data, applying statistical quality control procedures. Select products for tests at specified stages in production process and test products for performance characteristics and adherence to specifications. Compile and evaluate statistical data to determine and maintain quality and reliability of products.

**Education/Training Required:** Associate degree. **Education and Training Programs:** Engineering/Industrial Management; Industrial Production Technologies/Technicians, Other; Industrial Technology/Technician; Manufacturing Engineering Technology/Technician. **Knowledge/Courses**—Production and Processing, Engineering and Technology, Design, Clerical, Mathematics, Mechanical.

**Personality Type:** Investigative-Realistic-Conventional. **Career Clusters:** 13 Manufacturing; 15 Science, Technology, Engineering, and Mathematics. **Career Pathways:** 13.3 Maintenance, Installation, and Repair; 15.1 Engineering and Technology. **Other Jobs in These Pathways:** Architectural and Engineering Managers; Automotive Engineers; Automotive Specialty Technicians; Biochemical Engineers; Biofuels/Biodiesel Technology and Product Development Managers; Civil Engineers; Cost Estimators; Electrical and Electronic Equipment Assemblers; Energy Engineers; Engineers, All Other; Fuel Cell Engineers; Human Factors Engineers and Ergonomists; Industrial Engineers; Industrial Machinery Mechanics; Manufacturing Engineers; Mechanical Engineers; Mechatronics Engineers; Microsystems Engineers; Nanosystems Engineers; Photonics Engineers; Robotics Engineers; Solar Energy Systems Engineers; Transportation Engineers; Validation Engineers; Wind Energy Engineers; others.

**Skills**—Technology Design, Mathematics, Systems Evaluation, Monitoring, Programming, Systems Analysis, Quality Control Analysis, Judgment and Decision Making.

**Work Environment:** Indoors; standing; walking and running; noise; contaminants; hazardous equipment.

# Industrial Engineers

- ✱ Annual Earnings: $76,100
- ✱ Earnings Growth Potential: Low (34.7%)
- ✱ Growth: 14.2%
- ✱ Annual Job Openings: 8,540
- ✱ Self-Employed: 0.7%

**Considerations for Job Outlook:** Industrial engineers are expected to have employment growth of 14 percent from 2008–2018, faster than the average for all occupations. As firms look for new ways to reduce costs and raise productivity, they increasingly will turn to industrial engineers to develop more efficient processes and reduce costs, delays, and waste. This focus should lead to job growth for these engineers, even in some manufacturing industries with declining employment overall. Because their work is similar to that done in management occupations, many industrial engineers leave the occupation to become managers. Numerous openings will be created by the need to replace industrial engineers who transfer to other occupations or leave the labor force.

**Design, develop, test, and evaluate integrated systems for managing industrial production processes, including**

**human work factors, quality control, inventory control, logistics and material flow, cost analysis, and production coordination.** Analyze statistical data and product specifications to determine standards and establish quality and reliability objectives of finished product. Develop manufacturing methods, labor utilization standards, and cost analysis systems to promote efficient staff and facility utilization. Recommend methods for improving utilization of personnel, material, and utilities. Plan and establish sequence of operations to fabricate and assemble parts or products and to promote efficient utilization. Apply statistical methods and perform mathematical calculations to determine manufacturing processes, staff requirements, and production standards. Coordinate quality control objectives and activities to resolve production problems, maximize product reliability, and minimize cost. Confer with vendors, staff, and management personnel regarding purchases, procedures, product specifications, manufacturing capabilities, and project status. Draft and design layout of equipment, materials, and workspace to illustrate maximum efficiency, using drafting tools and computer. Review production schedules, engineering specifications, orders, and related information to obtain knowledge of manufacturing methods, procedures, and activities. Communicate with management and user personnel to develop production and design standards. Estimate production cost and effect of product design changes for management review, action, and control. Formulate sampling procedures and designs and develop forms and instructions for recording, evaluating, and reporting quality and reliability data. Record or oversee recording of information to ensure currency of engineering drawings and documentation of production problems. Study operations sequence, material flow, functional statements, organization charts, and project information to determine worker functions and responsibilities. Direct workers engaged in product measurement, inspection, and testing activities to ensure quality control and reliability.

**Education/Training Required:** Bachelor's degree. **Education and Training Program:** Industrial Engineering. **Knowledge/Courses**—Engineering and Technology, Design, Production and Processing, Mechanical, Physics, Mathematics.

**Personality Type:** Investigative-Conventional-Enterprising. **Career Cluster:** 15 Science, Technology, Engineering, and Mathematics. **Career Pathway:** 15.1 Engineering and Technology. **Other Jobs in This Pathway:** Architectural and Engineering Managers; Automotive Engineers; Biochemical Engineers; Biofuels/Biodiesel Technology and Product Development Managers; Civil Engineers; Cost Estimators; Education, Training, and Library Workers, All Other;

Electrical Engineers; Electronics Engineers, Except Computer; Energy Engineers; Engineers, All Other; Fuel Cell Engineers; Human Factors Engineers and Ergonomists; Manufacturing Engineers; Mechanical Engineers; Mechatronics Engineers; Microsystems Engineers; Nanosystems Engineers; Photonics Engineers; Radio Frequency Identification Device Specialists; Robotics Engineers; Solar Energy Systems Engineers; Transportation Engineers; Validation Engineers; Wind Energy Engineers; others.

**Skills**—Management of Material Resources, Management of Financial Resources, Mathematics, Systems Evaluation, Systems Analysis, Reading Comprehension, Complex Problem Solving, Technology Design.

**Work Environment:** Indoors; sitting; noise; contaminants; hazardous equipment.

## Job Specialization: Human Factors Engineers and Ergonomists

**Design objects, facilities, and environments to optimize human well-being and overall system performance, applying theory, principles, and data regarding the relationship between humans and respective technology. Investigate and analyze characteristics of human behavior and performance as it relates to the use of technology.** Write, review, or comment on documents such as proposals, test plans, and procedures. Train users in task techniques or ergonomic principles. Review health, safety, accident, or worker compensation records to evaluate safety program effectiveness or to identify jobs with high incidents of injury. Provide human factors technical expertise on topics such as advanced user-interface technology development and the role of human users in automated or autonomous sub-systems in advanced vehicle systems. Investigate theoretical or conceptual issues, such as the human design considerations of lunar landers or habitats. Estimate time and resource requirements for ergonomic or human factors research or development projects. Conduct interviews or surveys of users or customers to collect information on topics such as requirements, needs, fatigue, ergonomics and interface. Recommend workplace changes to improve health and safety, using knowledge of potentially harmful factors, such as heavy loads and repetitive motions. Provide technical support to clients through activities such as rearranging workplace fixtures to reduce physical hazards or discomfort and modifying task sequences to reduce cycle time. Prepare reports or presentations summarizing results or conclusions of human factors engineering or ergonomics activities, such as testing, investigation, and validation. Perform statistical analyses, such as social network pattern analysis, network modeling, discrete event simulation, agent-based modeling, statistical natural language processing, computational sociology, mathematical optimization, and systems dynamics. Perform functional, task or anthropometric analysis, using tools such as checklists, surveys, videotaping and force measurement. Operate testing equipment such as heat stress meters, octave band analyzers, motion analysis equipment, inclinometers, light meters, velometers, sling psychrometers, and colormetric detection tubes.

**Education/Training Required:** Bachelor's degree. **Education and Training Program:** Industrial Engineering. **Knowledge/Courses**—No data available.

**Personality Type:** No data available. **Career Cluster:** 15 Science, Technology, Engineering, and Mathematics. **Career Pathway:** 15.1 Engineering and Technology. **Other Jobs in This Pathway:** Architectural and Engineering Managers; Automotive Engineers; Biochemical Engineers; Biofuels/Biodiesel Technology and Product Development Managers; Civil Engineers; Cost Estimators; Education, Training, and Library Workers, All Other; Electrical Engineers; Electronics Engineers, Except Computer; Energy Engineers; Engineers, All Other; Fuel Cell Engineers; Industrial Engineers; Manufacturing Engineers; Mechanical Engineers; Mechatronics Engineers; Microsystems Engineers; Nanosystems Engineers; Photonics Engineers; Radio Frequency Identification Device Specialists; Robotics Engineers; Solar Energy Systems Engineers; Transportation Engineers; Validation Engineers; Wind Energy Engineers; others.

**Skills**—No data available.

**Work Environment:** No data available.

# Industrial Machinery Mechanics

- ❋ Annual Earnings: $45,420
- ❋ Earnings Growth Potential: Low (34.2%)
- ❋ Growth: 7.3%
- ❋ Annual Job Openings: 6,240
- ❋ Self-Employed: 2.2%

**Considerations for Job Outlook:** The increasing reliance on machinery in manufacturing is expected to lead to employment growth for these maintenance and installation workers. Favorable job prospects are expected.

**Repair, install, adjust, or maintain industrial production and processing machinery or refinery and pipeline distribution systems.** Disassemble machinery and equipment to remove parts and make repairs. Repair and replace broken or malfunctioning components of machinery and equipment. Repair and maintain the operating condition of industrial production and processing machinery and equipment. Examine parts for defects such as breakage and excessive wear. Reassemble equipment after completion of inspections, testing, or repairs. Observe and test the operation of machinery and equipment to diagnose malfunctions, using voltmeters and other testing devices. Operate newly repaired machinery and equipment to verify the adequacy of repairs. Clean, lubricate, and adjust parts, equipment, and machinery. Analyze test results, machine error messages, and information obtained from operators to diagnose equipment problems. Record repairs and maintenance performed. Study blueprints and manufacturers' manuals to determine correct installation and operation of machinery. Record parts and materials used, ordering or requisitioning new parts and materials as necessary. Cut and weld metal to repair broken metal parts, fabricate new parts, and assemble new equipment. Demonstrate equipment functions and features to machine operators. Enter codes and instructions to program computer-controlled machinery.

**Education/Training Required:** Long-term on-the-job training. **Education and Training Programs:** Heavy/Industrial Equipment Maintenance Technologies, Other; Industrial Mechanics and Maintenance Technology. **Knowledge/Courses**—Mechanical, Engineering and Technology, Building and Construction, Design, Chemistry, Physics.

**Personality Type:** Realistic-Investigative-Conventional. **Career Cluster:** 13 Manufacturing. **Career Pathway:** 13.3 Maintenance, Installation, and Repair. **Other Jobs in This Pathway:** Aircraft Mechanics and Service Technicians; Automotive Specialty Technicians; Biological Technicians; Civil Engineering Technicians; Computer, Automated Teller, and Office Machine Repairers; Electrical and Electronic Equipment Assemblers; Electrical and Electronics Repairers, Commercial and Industrial Equipment; Electrical Engineering Technicians; Electrical Engineering Technologists; Electromechanical Engineering Technologists; Electronics Engineering Technicians; Electronics Engineering Technologists; Engineering Technicians, Except Drafters, All Other; Fuel Cell Technicians; Helpers—Installation, Maintenance, and Repair Workers; Industrial Engineering Technologists; Installation, Maintenance, and Repair Workers, All Other; Manufacturing Engineering Technologists; Manufacturing Production Technicians; Mapping Technicians; Mechanical Engineering Technologists; Mobile Heavy Equipment Mechanics, Except Engines; Nanotechnology Engineering Technicians; Telecommunications Line Installers and Repairers; Tire Repairers and Changers; others.

**Skills**—Repairing, Equipment Maintenance, Troubleshooting, Installation, Operation Monitoring, Equipment Selection, Operation and Control, Quality Control Analysis.

**Work Environment:** Standing; walking and running; kneeling, crouching, stooping, or crawling; using hands; bending or twisting the body; repetitive motions; noise; very hot or cold; contaminants; cramped work space; high places; hazardous conditions; hazardous equipment; minor burns, cuts, bites, or stings.

# Industrial Production Managers

- ❋ Annual Earnings: $87,160
- ❋ Earnings Growth Potential: Medium (39.6%)
- ❋ Growth: –7.7%
- ❋ Annual Job Openings: 5,470
- ❋ Self-Employed: 1.3%

**Considerations for Job Outlook:** Moderate decline. Increased domestic labor productivity and rising imports are expected to reduce the need for these managers. Job-seekers who have experience in production occupations—along with a degree in industrial engineering, management, or business administration—should have the best job prospects.

**Plan, direct, or coordinate the work activities and resources necessary for manufacturing products in accordance with specifications for cost, quality, and quantity.** Direct and coordinate production, processing, distribution, and marketing activities of industrial organization. Review processing schedules and production orders to make decisions concerning inventory requirements, staffing requirements, work procedures, and duty assignments, considering budgetary limitations and time constraints. Review operations and confer with technical or administrative staff to resolve production or processing problems. Develop and implement production tracking and quality control systems, analyzing reports on production, quality control, maintenance, and other aspects of operations to detect problems. Hire, train, evaluate, and discharge staff, and resolve personnel grievances. Set and monitor product standards, examining samples of raw products or directing testing during processing, to ensure finished products are of prescribed quality. Prepare and maintain production reports and personnel records. Coordinate and recommend procedures for maintenance or modification of facilities and equipment, including the replacement of machines. Initiate and coordinate inventory and cost control programs. Institute

employee suggestion or involvement programs. Maintain current knowledge of the quality control field, relying on current literature pertaining to materials use, technological advances, and statistical studies. Review plans and confer with research and support staff to develop new products and processes. Develop budgets and approve expenditures for supplies, materials, and human resources, ensuring that materials, labor, and equipment are used efficiently to meet production targets. Negotiate prices of materials with suppliers.

**Education/Training Required:** Work experience in a related occupation. **Education and Training Programs:** Business Administration and Management, General; Business/Commerce, General; Operations Management and Supervision. **Knowledge/Courses**—Production and Processing, Mechanical, Administration and Management, Design, Personnel and Human Resources, Engineering and Technology.

**Personality Type:** Enterprising-Conventional. **Career Cluster:** 04 Business, Management, and Administration. **Career Pathway:** 4.1 Management. **Other Jobs in This Pathway:** Brownfield Redevelopment Specialists and Site Managers; Business Continuity Planners; Business Operations Specialists, All Other; Chief Executives; Chief Sustainability Officers; Compliance Managers; Computer and Information Systems Managers; Construction Managers; Customs Brokers; Energy Auditors; First-Line Supervisors of Office and Administrative Support Workers; General and Operations Managers; Investment Fund Managers; Loss Prevention Managers; Management Analysts; Managers, All Other; Public Relations Specialists; Regulatory Affairs Managers; Sales Managers; Security Management Specialists; Security Managers; Supply Chain Managers; Sustainability Specialists; Wind Energy Operations Managers; Wind Energy Project Managers; others.

**Skills**—Management of Financial Resources, Management of Material Resources, Management of Personnel Resources, Monitoring, Systems Analysis, Operation Monitoring, Judgment and Decision Making, Systems Evaluation.

**Work Environment:** Indoors; standing; walking and running; noise; very hot or cold; contaminants; hazardous equipment; minor burns, cuts, bites, or stings.

# Job Specialization: Biofuels Production Managers

**Manage operations at biofuel power-generation facilities. Collect and process information on plant performance,**

diagnose problems, and design corrective procedures. Provide training to subordinate or new employees to improve biofuels plant safety or increase the production of biofuels. Provide direction to employees to ensure compliance with biofuels plant safety, environmental, or operational standards and regulations. Monitor transportation and storage of flammable or other potentially dangerous feedstocks or products to ensure adherence to safety guidelines. Draw samples of biofuels products or secondary by-products for quality control testing. Confer with technical and supervisory personnel to report or resolve conditions affecting biofuels plant safety, operational efficiency, and product quality. Supervise production employees in the manufacturing of biofuels, such as biodiesel or ethanol. Shut down and restart biofuels plant or equipment in emergency situations or for equipment maintenance, repairs, or replacements. Review logs, datasheets, or reports to ensure adequate production levels or to identify abnormalities with biofuels production equipment or processes. Prepare and manage biofuels plant or unit budgets. Monitor meters, flow gauges, or other real-time data to ensure proper operation of biofuels production equipment, implementing corrective measures as needed. Conduct cost, material, and efficiency studies for biofuels production plants or operations. Approve proposals for the acquisition, replacement, or repair of biofuels processing equipment or the implementation of new production processes. Adjust temperature, pressure, vacuum, level, flow rate, or transfer of biofuels to maintain processes at required levels. Manage operations at biofuels power generation facilities, including production, shipping, maintenance, or quality assurance activities.

**Education/Training Required:** Work experience in a related occupation. **Education and Training Programs:** Business Administration and Management, General; Business/Commerce, General; Operations Management and Supervision. **Knowledge/Courses**—No data available.

**Personality Type:** No data available. **Career Cluster:** 04 Business, Management, and Administration. **Career Pathway:** 4.1 Management. **Other Jobs in This Pathway:** Brownfield Redevelopment Specialists and Site Managers; Business Continuity Planners; Business Operations Specialists, All Other; Chief Executives; Chief Sustainability Officers; Compliance Managers; Computer and Information Systems Managers; Construction Managers; Customs Brokers; Energy Auditors; First-Line Supervisors of Office and Administrative Support Workers; General and Operations Managers; Investment Fund Managers; Loss Prevention Managers; Management Analysts; Managers, All Other; Public Relations Specialists; Regulatory Affairs Managers; Sales Managers; Security Management Specialists; Security

Managers; Supply Chain Managers; Sustainability Specialists; Wind Energy Operations Managers; Wind Energy Project Managers; others.

**Skills**—No data available.

**Work Environment:** No data available.

## Job Specialization: Biomass Power Plant Managers

**Manage operations at biomass power-generation facilities. Direct work activities at plant, including supervision of operations and maintenance staff.** Test, maintain, or repair electrical power distribution machinery or equipment, using hand tools, power tools, and testing devices. Manage parts and supply inventories for biomass plants. Monitor and operate communications systems, such as mobile radios. Compile and record operational data on forms or in log books. Adjust equipment controls to generate specified amounts of electrical power. Supervise operations or maintenance employees in the production of power from biomass such as wood, coal, paper sludge, or other waste or refuse. Shut down and restart biomass power plants or equipment in emergency situations or for equipment maintenance, repairs, or replacements. Review logs, datasheets, or reports to ensure adequate production levels and safe production environments or to identify abnormalities with power production equipment or processes. Review biomass operations performance specifications to ensure compliance with regulatory requirements. Prepare reports on biomass plant operations, status, maintenance, and other information. Prepare and manage biomass plant budgets. Plan and schedule plant activities such as wood, waste, or refuse fuel deliveries, ash removal, and regular maintenance. Operate controls to start, stop, or regulate biomass-fueled generators, generator units, boilers, engines, or auxiliary systems. Inspect biomass gasification processes, equipment, and facilities for ways to maximize capacity and minimize operating costs. Evaluate power production or demand trends to identify opportunities for improved operations. Supervise biomass plant or substation operations, maintenance, repair, or testing activities. Monitor the operating status of biomass plants by observing control system parameters, distributed control systems, switchboard gauges, dials, or other indicators. Conduct field inspections of biomass plants, stations, or substations to ensure normal and safe operating conditions.

**Education/Training Required:** Work experience in a related occupation. **Education and Training Programs:** Business Administration and Management, General;

Business/Commerce, General; Operations Management and Supervision. **Knowledge/Courses**—No data available.

**Personality Type:** No data available. **Career Cluster:** 04 Business, Management, and Administration. **Career Pathway:** 4.1 Management. **Other Jobs in This Pathway:** Brownfield Redevelopment Specialists and Site Managers; Business Continuity Planners; Business Operations Specialists, All Other; Chief Executives; Chief Sustainability Officers; Compliance Managers; Computer and Information Systems Managers; Construction Managers; Customs Brokers; Energy Auditors; First-Line Supervisors of Office and Administrative Support Workers; General and Operations Managers; Investment Fund Managers; Loss Prevention Managers; Management Analysts; Managers, All Other; Public Relations Specialists; Regulatory Affairs Managers; Sales Managers; Security Management Specialists; Security Managers; Supply Chain Managers; Sustainability Specialists; Wind Energy Operations Managers; Wind Energy Project Managers; others.

**Skills**—No data available.

**Work Environment:** No data available.

## Job Specialization: Geothermal Production Managers

**Manage operations at geothermal power generation facilities. Maintain and monitor geothermal plant equipment for efficient and safe plant operations.** Conduct well field site assessments. Select and implement corrosion control or mitigation systems for geothermal plants. Communicate geothermal plant conditions to employees. Troubleshoot and make minor repairs to geothermal plant instrumentation or electrical systems. Record, review, or maintain daily logs, reports, maintenance, and other records associated with geothermal operations. Prepare environmental permit applications or compliance reports. Obtain permits for constructing, upgrading, or operating geothermal power plants. Perform or direct the performance of preventative maintenance on geothermal plant equipment. Negotiate interconnection agreements with other utilities. Monitor geothermal operations, using programmable logic controllers. Identify opportunities to improve plant electrical equipment, controls, or process control methodologies. Identify and evaluate equipment, procedural, or conditional inefficiencies involving geothermal plant systems. Develop operating plans and schedules for geothermal operations. Develop or manage budgets for geothermal operations. Supervise employees in geothermal power plants or well fields. Oversee geothermal plant operations, maintenance, and repairs

to ensure compliance with applicable standards or regulations. Inspect geothermal plant or injection well fields to verify proper equipment operations.

**Education/Training Required:** Work experience in a related occupation. **Education and Training Programs:** Business Administration and Management, General; Business/Commerce, General; Operations Management and Supervision. **Knowledge/Courses**—No data available.

**Personality Type:** No data available. **Career Cluster:** 04 Business, Management, and Administration. **Career Pathway:** 4.1 Management. **Other Jobs in This Pathway:** Brownfield Redevelopment Specialists and Site Managers; Business Continuity Planners; Business Operations Specialists, All Other; Chief Executives; Chief Sustainability Officers; Compliance Managers; Computer and Information Systems Managers; Construction Managers; Customs Brokers; Energy Auditors; First-Line Supervisors of Office and Administrative Support Workers; General and Operations Managers; Investment Fund Managers; Loss Prevention Managers; Management Analysts; Managers, All Other; Public Relations Specialists; Regulatory Affairs Managers; Sales Managers; Security Management Specialists; Security Managers; Supply Chain Managers; Sustainability Specialists; Wind Energy Operations Managers; Wind Energy Project Managers; others.

**Skills**—No data available.

**Work Environment:** No data available.

## Job Specialization: Hydroelectric Production Managers

**Manage operations at hydroelectric power-generation facilities. Maintain and monitor hydroelectric plant equipment for efficient and safe plant operations.** Develop or implement policy evaluation procedures for hydroelectric generation activities. Provide technical direction in the erection and commissioning of hydroelectric equipment and supporting electrical or mechanical systems. Develop and implement projects to improve efficiency, economy, or effectiveness of hydroelectric plant operations. Supervise hydropower plant equipment installations, upgrades, or maintenance. Respond to problems related to ratepayers, water users, power users, government agencies, educational institutions, and other private and public power resource interests. Plan or manage hydroelectric plant upgrades. Plan and coordinate hydroelectric production operations to meet customer requirements. Perform or direct preventive or corrective containment and cleanup to protect the environment. Operate energized high- and low-voltage hydroelectric power transmission system substations according to procedures and safety requirements. Negotiate power generation contracts with other public or private utilities. Maintain records of hydroelectric facility operations, maintenance, or repairs. Monitor or inspect hydroelectric equipment, such as hydro-turbines, generators, and control systems. Inspect hydroelectric facilities, including switchyards, control houses, or relay houses, for normal operation and adherence to safety standards. Identify and communicate power system emergencies. Develop or review budgets, annual plans, power contracts, power rates, standing operating procedures, power reviews, or engineering studies. Create and enforce hydrostation voltage schedules. Check hydroelectric operations for compliance with prescribed operating limits, such as loads, voltages, temperatures, lines, and equipment. Supervise or monitor hydroelectric facility operations to ensure that generation and mechanical equipment conform to applicable regulations or standards. Direct operations, maintenance, or repair of hydroelectric power facilities.

**Education/Training Required:** Work experience in a related occupation. **Education and Training Programs:** Business Administration and Management, General; Business/Commerce, General; Operations Management and Supervision. **Knowledge/Courses**—No data available.

**Personality Type:** No data available. **Career Cluster:** 04 Business, Management, and Administration. **Career Pathway:** 4.1 Management. **Other Jobs in This Pathway:** Brownfield Redevelopment Specialists and Site Managers; Business Continuity Planners; Business Operations Specialists, All Other; Chief Executives; Chief Sustainability Officers; Compliance Managers; Computer and Information Systems Managers; Construction Managers; Customs Brokers; Energy Auditors; First-Line Supervisors of Office and Administrative Support Workers; General and Operations Managers; Investment Fund Managers; Loss Prevention Managers; Management Analysts; Managers, All Other; Public Relations Specialists; Regulatory Affairs Managers; Sales Managers; Security Management Specialists; Security Managers; Supply Chain Managers; Sustainability Specialists; Wind Energy Operations Managers; Wind Energy Project Managers; others.

**Skills**—No data available.

**Work Environment:** No data available.

## Job Specialization: Methane/Landfill Gas Collection System Operators

**Direct daily operations, maintenance, or repair of landfill gas projects, including maintenance of daily logs, determination of service priorities, and compliance with reporting requirements.** Track volume and weight of landfill waste. Recommend or implement practices to reduce turnaround time for trucks in and out of landfill site. Prepare reports on landfill operations and gas collection system productivity or efficiency. Diagnose or troubleshoot gas collection equipment and programmable logic controller (PLC) systems. Coordinate the repair, overhaul, or routine maintenance of diesel engines used in landfill operations. Read meters, gauges, or automatic recording devices at specified intervals to verify gas collection systems operating conditions. Supervise landfill, well field, and other subordinate employees. Prepare and manage landfill gas collection system budgets. Prepare soil reports as required by regulatory or permitting agencies. Oversee landfill gas collection system construction, maintenance, and repair activities. Optimize gas collection landfill operational costs and productivity consistent with safety and environmental rules and regulations. Monitor landfill permit requirements for updates. Operate computerized control panels to manage gas compression operations. Monitor gas collection systems emissions data, including biomethane or nitrous oxide levels. Maintain records for landfill gas collection systems to demonstrate compliance with safety and environmental laws, regulations, or policies. Inspect landfill or conduct site audits to ensure adherence to safety and environmental regulations. Implement landfill operational and emergency procedures. Develop or enforce procedures for normal operation, start-up, or shut-down of methane gas collection systems. Evaluate landfill gas collection service requirements to meet operational plans and productivity goals. Oversee gas collection landfill operations, including leachate and gas management or rail operations. Monitor and control liquid or gas landfill extraction systems.

**Education/Training Required:** Work experience in a related occupation. **Education and Training Programs:** Business Administration and Management, General; Business/Commerce, General; Operations Management and Supervision. **Knowledge/Courses**—No data available.

**Personality Type:** No data available. **Career Cluster:** 04 Business, Management, and Administration. **Career Pathway:** 4.1 Management. **Other Jobs in This Pathway:** Brownfield Redevelopment Specialists and Site Managers; Business Continuity Planners; Business Operations Specialists, All Other; Chief Executives; Chief Sustainability

Officers; Compliance Managers; Computer and Information Systems Managers; Construction Managers; Customs Brokers; Energy Auditors; First-Line Supervisors of Office and Administrative Support Workers; General and Operations Managers; Investment Fund Managers; Loss Prevention Managers; Management Analysts; Managers, All Other; Public Relations Specialists; Regulatory Affairs Managers; Sales Managers; Security Management Specialists; Security Managers; Supply Chain Managers; Sustainability Specialists; Wind Energy Operations Managers; Wind Energy Project Managers; others.

**Skills**—No data available.

**Work Environment:** No data available.

## Job Specialization: Quality Control Systems Managers

**Plan, direct, or coordinate quality assurance programs. Formulate quality control policies and control quality of laboratory and production efforts.** Stop production if serious product defects are present. Review and approve quality plans submitted by contractors. Review statistical studies, technological advances, or regulatory standards and trends to stay abreast of issues in the field of quality control. Generate and maintain quality control operating budgets. Evaluate new testing and sampling methodologies or technologies to determine usefulness. Coordinate the selection and implementation of quality control equipment such as inspection gauges. Collect and analyze production samples to evaluate quality. Audit and inspect subcontractor facilities including external laboratories. Verify that raw materials, purchased parts or components, in-process samples, and finished products meet established testing and inspection standards. Review quality documentation necessary for regulatory submissions and inspections. Review and update standard operating procedures or quality assurance manuals. Produce reports regarding nonconformance of products or processes, daily production quality, root cause analyses, or quality trends. Participate in the development of product specifications. Monitor development of new products to help identify possible problems for mass production. Instruct vendors or contractors on quality guidelines, testing procedures, or ways to eliminate deficiencies. Identify quality problems or areas for improvement and recommend solutions. Instruct staff in quality control and analytical procedures. Identify critical points in the manufacturing process and specify sampling procedures to be used at these points. Document testing procedures, methodologies, or criteria. Direct the tracking of defects, test results, or other

regularly reported quality control data. Create and implement inspection and testing criteria or procedures. Confer with marketing and sales departments to define client requirements and expectations.

**Education/Training Required:** Bachelor's degree. **Education and Training Programs:** Business Administration and Management, General; Business/Commerce, General; Operations Management and Supervision. **Knowledge/Courses**—No data available.

**Personality Type:** Enterprising-Conventional-Realistic. **Career Cluster:** 04 Business, Management, and Administration. **Career Pathway:** 4.1 Management. **Other Jobs in This Pathway:** Brownfield Redevelopment Specialists and Site Managers; Business Continuity Planners; Business Operations Specialists, All Other; Chief Executives; Chief Sustainability Officers; Compliance Managers; Computer and Information Systems Managers; Construction Managers; Customs Brokers; Energy Auditors; First-Line Supervisors of Office and Administrative Support Workers; General and Operations Managers; Investment Fund Managers; Loss Prevention Managers; Management Analysts; Managers, All Other; Public Relations Specialists; Regulatory Affairs Managers; Sales Managers; Security Management Specialists; Security Managers; Supply Chain Managers; Sustainability Specialists; Wind Energy Operations Managers; Wind Energy Project Managers; others.

**Skills**—No data available.

**Work Environment:** No data available.

# Industrial-Organizational Psychologists

- ❋ Annual Earnings: $87,330
- ❋ Earnings Growth Potential: High (43.6%)
- ❋ Growth: 26.1%
- ❋ Annual Job Openings: 130
- ❋ Self-Employed: 33.6%

**Considerations for Job Outlook:** Employment growth is expected due to increased emphasis on mental health in a variety of specializations, including school counseling, depression, and substance abuse. Job seekers with a doctoral degree should have the best opportunities.

**Apply principles of psychology to personnel, administration, management, sales, and marketing problems. Activities may include policy planning; employee screening, training, and development; and organizational**

**development and analysis. May work with management to reorganize the work setting to improve worker productivity.** Develop and implement employee selection and placement programs. Analyze job requirements and content to establish criteria for classification, selection, training, and other related personnel functions. Develop interview techniques, rating scales, and psychological tests used to assess skills, abilities, and interests for the purpose of employee selection, placement, and promotion. Advise management concerning personnel, managerial, and marketing policies and practices and their potential effects on organizational effectiveness and efficiency. Analyze data, using statistical methods and applications, to evaluate the outcomes and effectiveness of workplace programs. Assess employee performance. Observe and interview workers to obtain information about the physical, mental, and educational requirements of jobs as well as information about aspects such as job satisfaction. Write reports on research findings and implications to contribute to general knowledge and to suggest potential changes in organizational functioning. Facilitate organizational development and change. Identify training and development needs. Formulate and implement training programs, applying principles of learning and individual differences. Study organizational effectiveness, productivity, and efficiency, including the nature of workplace supervision and leadership. Conduct research studies of physical work environments, organizational structures, communication systems, group interactions, morale, and motivation to assess organizational functioning. Counsel workers about job and career-related issues. Study consumers' reactions to new products and package designs, and to advertising efforts, using surveys and tests. Participate in mediation and dispute resolution.

**Education/Training Required:** Master's degree. **Education and Training Program:** Psychology, General. **Knowledge/ Courses**—Personnel and Human Resources, Psychology, Sociology and Anthropology, Education and Training, Therapy and Counseling, Mathematics.

**Personality Type:** Investigative-Enterprising-Artistic. **Career Cluster:** 08 Health Science. **Career Pathway:** 8.1 Therapeutic Services. **Other Jobs in This Pathway:** Clinical Psychologists; Community and Social Service Specialists, All Other; Counseling Psychologists; Dental Assistants; Dental Hygienists; Dentists, General; Health Technologists and Technicians, All Other; Healthcare Support Workers, All Other; Home Health Aides; Licensed Practical and Licensed Vocational Nurses; Low Vision Therapists, Orientation and Mobility Specialists, and Vision Rehabilitation Therapists; Massage Therapists; Medical and Clinical Laboratory Technicians; Medical and Health Services Managers; Medical Scientists, Except Epidemiologists; Medical Secretaries; Occupational Therapists; Pharmacists; Pharmacy Technicians; Radiologic Technologists; School Psychologists; Social and Human Service Assistants; Speech-Language Pathologists; Speech-Language Pathology Assistants; Substance Abuse and Behavioral Disorder Counselors; others.

**Skills**—Programming, Science, Mathematics, Systems Evaluation, Learning Strategies, Management of Personnel Resources, Systems Analysis, Operations Analysis.

**Work Environment:** Indoors; sitting.

# Installation, Maintenance, and Repair Workers, All Other

- ❀ Annual Earnings: $36,420
- ❀ Earnings Growth Potential: High (43.5%)
- ❀ Growth: 9.2%
- ❀ Annual Job Openings: 4,180
- ❀ Self-Employed: 17.4%

**Considerations for Job Outlook:** About average employment growth is projected.

**This occupation includes all mechanical, installation, and repair workers and helpers not listed separately.** Because this is a highly diverse occupation, no data is available for some information topics.

**Education/Training Required:** Moderate-term on-the-job training. **Education and Training Programs:** No related CIP programs; this job is learned through moderate-term on-the-job training.

**Career Clusters:** 13 Manufacturing; 16 Transportation, Distribution, and Logistics. **Career Pathways:** 13.3 Maintenance, Installation, and Repair; 16.4 Facility and Mobile Equipment Maintenance. **Other Jobs in These Pathways:** Aircraft Mechanics and Service Technicians; Automotive Body and Related Repairers; Automotive Master Mechanics; Automotive Specialty Technicians; Biological Technicians; Bus and Truck Mechanics and Diesel Engine Specialists; Civil Engineering Technicians; Cleaners of Vehicles and Equipment; Computer, Automated Teller, and Office Machine Repairers; Electrical and Electronic Equipment Assemblers; Electrical and Electronics Repairers, Commercial and Industrial Equipment; Electrical Engineering Technicians; Electrical Engineering Technologists; Electromechanical Engineering Technologists; Electronics Engineering Technicians; Electronics Engineering Technologists;

Engineering Technicians, Except Drafters, All Other; Fuel Cell Technicians; Helpers—Installation, Maintenance, and Repair Workers; Industrial Engineering Technologists; Industrial Machinery Mechanics; Manufacturing Engineering Technologists; Mobile Heavy Equipment Mechanics, Except Engines; Telecommunications Line Installers and Repairers; Tire Repairers and Changers; others.

## Job Specialization: Geothermal Technicians

**Perform technical activities at power plants or individual installations necessary for the generation of power from geothermal energy sources. Monitor and control operating activities at geothermal power generation facilities and perform maintenance and repairs as necessary. Install, test, and maintain residential and commercial geothermal heat pumps.** Identify and correct malfunctions of geothermal plant equipment, electrical systems, instrumentation, or controls. Install, maintain, or repair ground or water source-coupled heat pumps to heat and cool residential or commercial building air or water. Monitor and adjust operations of geothermal power plant equipment or systems. Adjust power production systems to meet load and distribution demands. Backfill piping trenches to protect pipes from damage. Calculate heat loss and heat gain factors for residential properties to determine heating and cooling required by installed geothermal systems. Design and lay out geothermal heat systems according to property characteristics, heating and cooling requirements, piping and equipment requirements, applicable regulations, or other factors. Determine the type of geothermal loop system most suitable to a specific property and its heating and cooling needs. Dig trenches for system piping to appropriate depths and lay piping in trenches. Prepare newly installed geothermal heat systems for operation by flushing, purging, or other actions. Identify equipment options, such as compressors, and make appropriate selections. Install and maintain geothermal system instrumentation or controls. Maintain electrical switchgear, process controls, transmitters, gauges, and control equipment in accordance with geothermal plant procedures. Maintain, calibrate, or repair plant instrumentation, control, and electronic devices in geothermal plants. Perform pre- and post-installation pressure, flow, and related tests of vertical and horizontal geothermal loop piping. Place geothermal system pipes in bodies of water, weighting them to allow them to sink into position. Verify that piping placed in bodies of water is situated to prevent damage to aquaculture and away from potential sources of harm, such as boat anchors. Apply coatings or operate systems to mitigate corrosion of geothermal plant equipment or structures.

**Education/Training Required:** Long-term on-the-job training. **Education and Training Program:** Heating, Air Conditioning, Ventilation, and Refrigeration Maintenance Technology/Technician (HAC, HACR, HVAC, HVACR). **Knowledge/Courses**—No data available.

**Personality Type:** No data available. **Career Cluster:** 13 Manufacturing. **Career Pathway:** 13.1 Production. **Other Jobs in This Pathway:** Assemblers and Fabricators, All Other; Cabinetmakers and Bench Carpenters; Coating, Painting, and Spraying Machine Setters, Operators, and Tenders; Computer-Controlled Machine Tool Operators, Metal and Plastic; Cost Estimators; Cutting, Punching, and Press Machine Setters, Operators, and Tenders, Metal and Plastic; First-Line Supervisors of Mechanics, Installers, and Repairers; First-Line Supervisors of Production and Operating Workers; Grinding, Lapping, Polishing, and Buffing Machine Tool Setters, Operators, and Tenders, Metal and Plastic; Helpers—Production Workers; Machine Feeders and Offbearers; Machinists; Mixing and Blending Machine Setters, Operators, and Tenders; Molding, Coremaking, and Casting Machine Setters, Operators, and Tenders, Metal and Plastic; Packaging and Filling Machine Operators and Tenders; Packers and Packagers, Hand; Paper Goods Machine Setters, Operators, and Tenders; Production Workers, All Other; Recycling and Reclamation Workers; Recycling Coordinators; Sheet Metal Workers; Solderers and Brazers; Structural Metal Fabricators and Fitters; Team Assemblers; Welders, Cutters, and Welder Fitters; others.

**Skills**—No data available.

**Work Environment:** No data available.

# Instructional Coordinators

- ❋ Annual Earnings: $58,830
- ❋ Earnings Growth Potential: High (43.1%)
- ❋ Growth: 23.2%
- ❋ Annual Job Openings: 6,060
- ❋ Self-Employed: 2.9%

**Considerations for Job Outlook:** Continued efforts to improve educational standards are expected to result in more new jobs for these workers. Opportunities should be best for job seekers who train teachers to use classroom technology and who have experience in reading, mathematics, and science.

**Develop instructional material, coordinate educational content, and incorporate current technology in specialized fields that provide guidelines to educators and**

**instructors for developing curricula and conducting courses.** Conduct or participate in workshops, committees, and conferences designed to promote the intellectual, social, and physical welfare of students. Plan and conduct teacher training programs and conferences dealing with new classroom procedures, instructional materials and equipment, and teaching aids. Advise teaching and administrative staff in curriculum development, use of materials and equipment, and implementation of state and federal programs and procedures. Recommend, order, or authorize purchase of instructional materials, supplies, equipment, and visual aids designed to meet student educational needs and district standards. Interpret and enforce provisions of state education codes and rules and regulations of state education boards. Confer with members of educational committees and advisory groups to obtain knowledge of subject areas and to relate curriculum materials to specific subjects, individual student needs, and occupational areas. Organize production and design of curriculum materials. Research, evaluate, and prepare recommendations on curricula, instructional methods, and materials for school systems. Observe work of teaching staff to evaluate performance and to recommend changes that could strengthen teaching skills. Develop instructional materials to be used by educators and instructors. Prepare grant proposals, budgets, and program policies and goals or assist in their preparation. Develop tests, questionnaires, and procedures that measure the effectiveness of curricula and use these tools to determine whether program objectives are being met. Update the content of educational programs to ensure that students are being trained with equipment and processes that are technologically current. Address public audiences to explain program objectives and to elicit support. Advise and teach students. Prepare or approve manuals, guidelines, and reports on state educational policies and practices for distribution to school districts.

**Education/Training Required:** Master's degree. **Education and Training Programs:** Curriculum and Instruction; Educational/Instructional Technology. **Knowledge/Courses**—Education and Training, Therapy and Counseling, Philosophy and Theology, Sociology and Anthropology, Personnel and Human Resources, Psychology.

**Personality Type:** Social-Investigative-Enterprising. **Career Cluster:** 05 Education and Training. **Career Pathways:** 5.1 Administration and Administrative Support; 5.3 Teaching/Training. **Other Jobs in These Pathways:** Adult Basic and Secondary Education and Literacy Teachers and Instructors; Career/Technical Education Teachers, Secondary School; Chemists; Coaches and Scouts; Dietitians and Nutritionists; Distance Learning Coordinators; Education Administrators, All Other; Education Administrators, Elementary and Secondary School; Education Administrators, Postsecondary; Education Administrators, Preschool and Childcare Center/Program; Elementary School Teachers, Except Special Education; Fitness and Wellness Coordinators; Fitness Trainers and Aerobics Instructors; Instructional Designers and Technologists; Interpreters and Translators; Kindergarten Teachers, Except Special Education; Librarians; Middle School Teachers, Except Special and Career/Technical Education; Preschool Teachers, Except Special Education; Recreation Workers; Secondary School Teachers, Except Special and Career/Technical Education; Self-Enrichment Education Teachers; Teacher Assistants; Teachers and Instructors, All Other; Tutors; others.

**Skills**—Learning Strategies, Systems Evaluation, Instructing, Management of Material Resources, Negotiation, Writing, Management of Personnel Resources, Systems Analysis.

**Work Environment:** Indoors; standing.

## Job Specialization: Instructional Designers and Technologists

**Develop instructional materials and products and assist in the technology-based redesign of courses. Assist faculty in learning about, becoming proficient in, and applying instructional technology.** Observe and provide feedback on instructional techniques, presentation methods, or instructional aids. Edit instructional materials, such as books, simulation exercises, lesson plans, instructor guides, and tests. Develop measurement tools to evaluate the effectiveness of instruction or training interventions. Develop instructional materials, such as lesson plans, handouts, or examinations. Define instructional, learning, or performance objectives. Assess effectiveness and efficiency of instruction according to ease of instructional technology use and student learning, knowledge transfer, and satisfaction. Analyze performance data to determine effectiveness of instructional systems, courses, or instructional materials. Research and evaluate emerging instructional technologies or methods. Recommend instructional methods, such as individual or group instruction, self-study, lectures, demonstrations, simulation exercises, and role-playing, appropriate for content and learner characteristics. Recommend changes to curricula or delivery methods, based on information such as instructional effectiveness data, current or future performance requirements, feasibility, and costs. Provide technical support to clients in the implementation of designed instruction or in task analyses and instructional systems design. Provide technical advice on the use of current instructional technologies, including computer-based training, desktop videoconferencing, multimedia, and distance learning technologies. Provide analytical support for the design and development of training curricula, learning strategies, educational policies, or courseware standards. Present and make recommendations regarding course design, technology, and instruction delivery options. Interview subject matter experts or conduct other research to develop instructional content. Develop master course documentation or manuals according to applicable accreditation, certification, or other requirements.

**Education/Training Required:** Bachelor's degree. **Education and Training Programs:** Curriculum and Instruction; Educational/Instructional Technology. **Knowledge/Courses**—No data available.

**Personality Type:** No data available. **Career Cluster:** 05 Education and Training. **Career Pathways:** 5.1 Administration and Administrative Support; 5.3 Teaching/Training. **Other Jobs in These Pathways:** Adult Basic and Secondary Education and Literacy Teachers and Instructors; Career/Technical Education Teachers, Secondary School; Chemists; Coaches and Scouts; Dietitians and Nutritionists; Distance Learning Coordinators; Education Administrators, All Other; Education Administrators, Elementary and Secondary School; Education Administrators, Postsecondary; Education Administrators, Preschool and Childcare Center/Program; Elementary School Teachers, Except Special Education; Fitness and Wellness Coordinators; Fitness Trainers and Aerobics Instructors; Instructional Coordinators; Interpreters and Translators; Kindergarten Teachers, Except Special Education; Librarians; Middle School Teachers, Except Special and Career/Technical Education; Preschool Teachers, Except Special Education; Recreation Workers; Secondary School Teachers, Except Special and Career/Technical Education; Self-Enrichment Education Teachers; Teacher Assistants; Teachers and Instructors, All Other; Tutors; others.

**Skills**—No data available.

**Work Environment:** No data available.

# Insulation Workers, Floor, Ceiling, and Wall

- ❀ Annual Earnings: $31,830
- ❀ Earnings Growth Potential: Medium (36.0%)
- ❀ Growth: 15.2%
- ❀ Annual Job Openings: 1,320
- ❀ Self-Employed: 1.5%

**Considerations for Job Outlook:** Expected employment increases for insulation workers are spurred by the need to make existing buildings more energy efficient. Anticipated construction of new power plants should also lead to employment gains. Opportunities are expected to be excellent, particularly for job seekers with knowledge of weatherization.

**Line and cover structures with insulating materials. May work with batt, roll, or blown insulation materials.** Move controls, buttons, or levers to start blowers and regulate flow of materials through nozzles. Cover and line structures with blown or rolled forms of materials to insulate against cold, heat, or moisture, using saws, knives, rasps, trowels, blowers, and other tools and implements. Cover, seal, or finish insulated surfaces or access holes with plastic covers, canvas strips, sealants, tape, cement, or asphalt mastic. Distribute insulating materials evenly into small spaces within floors, ceilings, or walls, using blowers and hose attachments or cement mortars. Fill blower hoppers with insulating materials. Fit, wrap, staple, or glue insulating materials to structures or surfaces, using hand tools or wires. Read blueprints and select appropriate insulation based on space characteristics and the heat-retaining or -excluding characteristics of the material. Remove old insulation such as asbestos, following safety procedures. Measure and cut insulation for covering surfaces, using tape measures, handsaws, power saws, knives, or scissors. Prepare surfaces for insulation application by brushing or spreading on adhesives, cement, or asphalt or by attaching metal pins to surfaces.

**Education/Training Required:** Moderate-term on-the-job training. **Education and Training Program:** Construction Trades, Other. **Knowledge/Courses**—Building and Construction, Production and Processing, Transportation, Personnel and Human Resources, Design, Economics and Accounting.

**Personality Type:** Realistic. **Career Cluster:** 02 Architecture and Construction. **Career Pathway:** 2.2 Construction. **Other Jobs in This Pathway:** Brickmasons and

Blockmasons; Cement Masons and Concrete Finishers; Construction and Building Inspectors; Construction Carpenters; Construction Laborers; Construction Managers; Cost Estimators; Drywall and Ceiling Tile Installers; Electrical Power-Line Installers and Repairers; Electricians; Engineering Technicians, Except Drafters, All Other; First-Line Supervisors of Construction Trades and Extraction Workers; Heating and Air Conditioning Mechanics and Installers; Helpers—Carpenters; Helpers—Electricians; Helpers—Pipelayers, Plumbers, Pipefitters, and Steamfitters; Highway Maintenance Workers; Operating Engineers and Other Construction Equipment Operators; Painters, Construction and Maintenance; Pipe Fitters and Steamfitters; Plumbers; Refrigeration Mechanics and Installers; Roofers; Rough Carpenters; Solar Energy Installation Managers; others.

**Skills**—Repairing, Equipment Maintenance, Operation and Control, Equipment Selection, Troubleshooting, Quality Control Analysis, Operation Monitoring.

**Work Environment:** Outdoors; standing; climbing; walking and running; kneeling, crouching, stooping, or crawling; balancing; using hands; bending or twisting the body; repetitive motions; noise; very hot or cold; contaminants; cramped work space; high places; minor burns, cuts, bites, or stings.

# Insulation Workers, Mechanical

- ❋ Annual Earnings: $37,650
- ❋ Earnings Growth Potential: Low (33.5%)
- ❋ Growth: 19.4%
- ❋ Annual Job Openings: 1,550
- ❋ Self-Employed: 1.5%

**Considerations for Job Outlook:** Expected employment increases for insulation workers are spurred by the need to make existing buildings more energy efficient. Anticipated construction of new power plants should also lead to employment gains. Opportunities are expected to be excellent, particularly for job seekers with knowledge of weatherization.

**Apply insulating materials to pipes or ductwork or other mechanical systems to help control and maintain temperature.** Cover, seal, or finish insulated surfaces or access holes with plastic covers, canvas strips, sealants, tape, cement, or asphalt mastic. Measure and cut insulation for covering surfaces, using tape measures, handsaws, knives, and scissors. Prepare surfaces for insulation application by brushing or spreading on adhesives, cement, or asphalt, or

by attaching metal pins to surfaces. Select appropriate insulation such as fiberglass, Styrofoam, or cork, based on the heat-retaining or -excluding characteristics of the material. Read blueprints and specifications to determine job requirements. Install sheet metal around insulated pipes with screws to protect the insulation from weather conditions or physical damage. Determine the amounts and types of insulation needed, and methods of installation, based on factors such as location, surface shape, and equipment use. Apply, remove, and repair insulation on industrial equipment, pipes, ductwork, or other mechanical systems, such as heat exchangers, tanks, and vessels, to help control noise and maintain temperatures. Remove or seal off old asbestos insulation, following safety procedures. Move controls, buttons, or levers to start blowers and to regulate flow of materials through nozzles. Fill blower hoppers with insulating materials. Distribute insulating materials evenly into small spaces within floors, ceilings, or walls, using blowers and hose attachments or cement mortar. Fit insulation around obstructions, and shape insulating materials and protective coverings as required.

**Education/Training Required:** Moderate-term on-the-job training. **Education and Training Program:** Construction Trades, Other. **Knowledge/Courses**—Building and Construction, Design, Mechanical, Transportation, Education and Training, Public Safety and Security.

**Personality Type:** Realistic-Conventional-Investigative. **Career Cluster:** 02 Architecture and Construction. **Career Pathway:** 2.2 Construction. **Other Jobs in This Pathway:** Brickmasons and Blockmasons; Cement Masons and Concrete Finishers; Construction and Building Inspectors; Construction Carpenters; Construction Laborers; Construction Managers; Cost Estimators; Drywall and Ceiling Tile Installers; Electrical Power-Line Installers and Repairers; Electricians; Engineering Technicians, Except Drafters, All Other; First-Line Supervisors of Construction Trades and Extraction Workers; Heating and Air Conditioning Mechanics and Installers; Helpers—Carpenters; Helpers—Electricians; Helpers—Pipelayers, Plumbers, Pipefitters, and Steamfitters; Highway Maintenance Workers; Operating Engineers and Other Construction Equipment Operators; Painters, Construction and Maintenance; Pipe Fitters and Steamfitters; Plumbers; Refrigeration Mechanics and Installers; Roofers; Rough Carpenters; Solar Energy Installation Managers; others.

**Skills**—Operation and Control, Installation, Operation Monitoring, Troubleshooting, Management of Material Resources.

**Work Environment:** Outdoors; standing; climbing; walking and running; kneeling, crouching, stooping, or crawling; using hands; bending or twisting the body; repetitive motions; noise; very hot or cold; bright or inadequate lighting; contaminants; cramped work space; high places; hazardous conditions; hazardous equipment; minor burns, cuts, bites, or stings.

# Insurance Sales Agents

- ❋ Annual Earnings: $46,770
- ❋ Earnings Growth Potential: High (44.5%)
- ❋ Growth: 11.9%
- ❋ Annual Job Openings: 15,260
- ❋ Self-Employed: 22.4%

**Considerations for Job Outlook:** Projected employment increases stem from the growth and aging of the population. But these increases will be tempered by insurance carriers attempting to contain costs by relying on independent agents rather than employees. Job opportunities should be best for college graduates with good interpersonal skills.

**Sell life, property, casualty, health, automotive, or other types of insurance. May refer clients to independent brokers, work as independent broker, or be employed by an insurance company.** Call on policyholders to deliver and explain policy, to analyze insurance program and suggest additions or changes, or to change beneficiaries. Calculate premiums and establish payment method. Customize insurance programs to suit individual customers, often covering a variety of risks. Sell various types of insurance policies to businesses and individuals on behalf of insurance companies, including automobile, fire, life, property, medical, and dental insurance or specialized policies such as marine, farm/crop, and medical malpractice. Interview prospective clients to obtain data about their financial resources and needs and the physical condition of the person or property to be insured and to discuss any existing coverage. Seek out new clients and develop clientele by networking to find new customers and generate lists of prospective clients. Explain features, advantages, and disadvantages of various policies to promote sale of insurance plans. Contact underwriter and submit forms to obtain binder coverage. Ensure that policy requirements are fulfilled, including any necessary medical examinations and the completion of appropriate forms. Confer with clients to obtain and provide information when claims are made on a policy. Perform administrative tasks, such as maintaining records and handling policy renewals. Select company that offers type of coverage requested by client to underwrite policy. Monitor insurance claims to ensure that they are settled equitably for both the client and the insurer. Develop marketing strategies to compete with other individuals or companies who sell insurance. Attend meetings, seminars, and programs to learn about new products and services, learn new skills, and receive technical assistance in developing new accounts. Inspect property, examining its general condition, type of construction, age, and other characteristics, to decide if it is a good insurance risk. Install bookkeeping systems and resolve system problems.

**Education/Training Required:** Bachelor's degree. **Education and Training Program:** Insurance. **Knowledge/Courses**—Sales and Marketing, Economics and Accounting, Customer and Personal Service, Clerical, Law and Government, Computers and Electronics.

**Personality Type:** Enterprising-Conventional-Social. **Career Cluster:** 06 Finance. **Career Pathway:** 6.4 Insurance Services. **Other Jobs in This Pathway:** Actuaries; Claims Examiners, Property and Casualty Insurance; Insurance Adjusters, Examiners, and Investigators; Insurance Appraisers, Auto Damage; Insurance Underwriters; Telemarketers.

**Skills**—Negotiation, Persuasion, Service Orientation, Active Listening, Systems Analysis, Speaking, Systems Evaluation, Active Learning.

**Work Environment:** Indoors; sitting.

# Insurance Underwriters

- ❋ Annual Earnings: $59,290
- ❋ Earnings Growth Potential: Medium (38.1%)
- ❋ Growth: –4.1%
- ❋ Annual Job Openings: 3,000
- ❋ Self-Employed: 0.0%

**Considerations for Job Outlook:** Productivity increases, such as automatic underwriting, have limited employment of these workers. But this factor should be partially offset by an increased emphasis on underwriting to boost revenues and counteract decreasing returns on investments. Good job prospects are expected.

**Review individual applications for insurance to evaluate degree of risk involved and determine acceptance of applications.** Examine documents to determine degree of risk from such factors as applicant financial standing and value and condition of property. Decline excessive risks.

Write to field representatives, medical personnel, and others to obtain further information, quote rates, or explain company underwriting policies. Evaluate possibility of losses due to catastrophe or excessive insurance. Decrease value of policy when risk is substandard and specify applicable endorsements or apply rating to ensure safe profitable distribution of risks, using reference materials. Review company records to determine amount of insurance in force on single risk or group of closely related risks. Authorize reinsurance of policy when risk is high.

**Education/Training Required:** Bachelor's degree. **Education and Training Program:** Insurance. **Knowledge/Courses**—Medicine and Dentistry, Economics and Accounting, Clerical, Therapy and Counseling, Sales and Marketing, Biology.

**Personality Type:** Conventional-Enterprising-Investigative. **Career Cluster:** 06 Finance. **Career Pathway:** 6.4 Insurance Services. **Other Jobs in This Pathway:** Actuaries; Claims Examiners, Property and Casualty Insurance; Insurance Adjusters, Examiners, and Investigators; Insurance Appraisers, Auto Damage; Insurance Sales Agents; Telemarketers.

**Skills**—Judgment and Decision Making, Writing, Active Listening, Mathematics, Service Orientation, Systems Evaluation, Speaking, Systems Analysis.

**Work Environment:** Indoors; sitting; repetitive motions.

# Interior Designers

- ❋ Annual Earnings: $46,280
- ❋ Earnings Growth Potential: High (43.0%)
- ❋ Growth: 19.4%
- ❋ Annual Job Openings: 3,590
- ❋ Self-Employed: 26.7%

**Considerations for Job Outlook:** A growing interest in interior design by both homeowners and businesses is expected to lead to employment increases in this occupation. Competition is expected to be keen, and job seekers with formal training should have the best opportunities.

**Plan, design, and furnish interiors of residential, commercial, or industrial buildings. Formulate design that is practical, aesthetic, and conducive to intended purposes, such as raising productivity, selling merchandise, or improving lifestyle. May specialize in a particular field, style, or phase of interior design.** Estimate material requirements and costs and present design to client for approval. Confer with client to determine factors affecting planning interior environments, such as budget, architectural preferences, and purpose and function. Advise client on interior design factors such as space planning, layout, and utilization of furnishings or equipment and color coordination. Select or design and purchase furnishings, artwork, and accessories. Formulate environmental plan to be practical, esthetic, and conducive to intended purposes such as raising productivity or selling merchandise. Subcontract fabrication, installation, and arrangement of carpeting, fixtures, accessories, draperies, paint and wall coverings, artwork, furniture, and related items. Render design ideas in form of paste-ups or drawings. Plan and design interior environments for boats, planes, buses, trains, and other enclosed spaces.

**Education/Training Required:** Associate degree. **Education and Training Programs:** Facilities Planning and Management; Interior Architecture; Interior Design; Textile Science. **Knowledge/Courses**—Design, Fine Arts, Building and Construction, Sales and Marketing, History and Archeology, Psychology.

**Personality Type:** Artistic-Enterprising. **Career Clusters:** 02 Architecture and Construction; 03 Arts, Audio/Video Technology, and Communications; 13 Manufacturing; 14 Marketing, Sales, and Service. **Career Pathways:** 2.1 Design/Pre-Construction; 3.3 Visual Arts; 13.3 Maintenance, Installation, and Repair; 14.2 Professional Sales and Marketing. **Other Jobs in These Pathways:** Automotive Specialty Technicians; Cashiers; Counter and Rental Clerks; Driver/Sales Workers; Electrical and Electronic Equipment Assemblers; Energy Brokers; First-Line Supervisors of Non-Retail Sales Workers; First-Line Supervisors of Retail Sales Workers; Graphic Designers; Hotel, Motel, and Resort Desk Clerks; Industrial Machinery Mechanics; Marking Clerks; Online Merchants; Order Fillers, Wholesale and Retail Sales; Parts Salespersons; Property, Real Estate, and Community Association Managers; Real Estate Sales Agents; Retail Salespersons; Sales Representatives, Services, All Other; Sales Representatives, Wholesale and Manufacturing, Except Technical and Scientific Products; Sales Representatives, Wholesale and Manufacturing, Technical and Scientific Products; Solar Sales Representatives and Assessors; Stock Clerks—Stockroom, Warehouse, or Storage Yard; Stock Clerks, Sales Floor; Telemarketers; others.

**Skills**—Management of Financial Resources, Operations Analysis, Management of Material Resources, Negotiation, Persuasion, Service Orientation, Coordination, Mathematics.

**Work Environment:** Indoors; sitting.

# Interpreters and Translators

❋ Annual Earnings: $43,300
❋ Earnings Growth Potential: High (47.0%)
❋ Growth: 22.2%
❋ Annual Job Openings: 2,340
❋ Self-Employed: 26.1%

**Considerations for Job Outlook:** Globalization and large increases in the number of nonnative English speakers in the United States are expected to lead to employment increases for these workers. Job prospects vary by specialty and language.

**Translate or interpret written, oral, or sign language text into another language for others.** Follow ethical codes that protect the confidentiality of information. Identify and resolve conflicts related to the meanings of words, concepts, practices, or behaviors. Proofread, edit, and revise translated materials. Translate messages simultaneously or consecutively into specified languages orally or by using hand signs, maintaining message content, context, and style as much as possible. Check translations of technical terms and terminology to ensure that they are accurate and remain consistent throughout translation revisions. Read written materials such as legal documents, scientific works, or news reports and rewrite material into specified languages. Refer to reference materials such as dictionaries, lexicons, encyclopedias, and computerized terminology banks as needed to ensure translation accuracy. Compile terminology and information to be used in translations, including technical terms such as those for legal or medical material. Adapt translations to students' cognitive and grade levels, collaborating with educational team members as necessary. Listen to speakers' statements to determine meanings and to prepare translations, using electronic listening systems as necessary. Check original texts or confer with authors to ensure that translations retain the content, meaning, and feeling of the original material. Compile information about the content and context of information to be translated, as well as details of the groups for whom translation or interpretation is being performed. Discuss translation requirements with clients and determine any fees to be charged for services provided. Adapt software and accompanying technical documents to another language and culture. Educate students, parents, staff, and teachers about the roles and functions of educational interpreters. Train and supervise other translators/interpreters. Travel with or guide tourists who speak another language.

**Education/Training Required:** Long-term on-the-job training. **Education and Training Programs:** American Sign Language (ASL); Ancient Near Eastern and Biblical Languages, Literatures, and Linguistics; Ancient/Classical Greek Language and Literature; Arabic Language and Literature; Celtic Languages, Literatures, and Linguistics; Chinese Language and Literature; Classics and Classical Languages, Literatures, and Linguistics, General; East Asian Languages, Literatures, and Linguistics, Other; Education/Teaching of Individuals with Hearing Impairments, Including Deafness; Foreign Languages and Literatures, General; Foreign Languages, Literatures, and Linguistics, Other; French Language and Literature; German Language and Literature; Germanic Languages, Literatures, and Linguistics, Other; Hebrew Language and Literature; Hindi Language and Literature; Italian Language and Literature; Japanese Language and Literature; Language Interpretation and Translation; Latin Language and Literature; Linguistics; Middle/Near Eastern and Semitic Languages, Literatures, and Linguistics, Other; others. **Knowledge/Courses—**Foreign Language, English Language, Geography, Sociology and Anthropology, Communications and Media, Computers and Electronics.

**Personality Type:** Artistic-Social. **Career Clusters:** 05 Education and Training; 10 Human Services. **Career Pathways:** 5.3 Teaching/Training; 10.5 Consumer Services Career. **Other Jobs in These Pathways:** Adult Basic and Secondary Education and Literacy Teachers and Instructors; Athletes and Sports Competitors; Career/Technical Education Teachers, Middle School; Career/Technical Education Teachers, Secondary School; Chemists; Coaches and Scouts; Dietitians and Nutritionists; Elementary School Teachers, Except Special Education; First-Line Supervisors of Retail Sales Workers; Fitness Trainers and Aerobics Instructors; Instructional Coordinators; Instructional Designers and Technologists; Kindergarten Teachers, Except Special Education; Librarians; Middle School Teachers, Except Special and Career/Technical Education; Physicists; Preschool Teachers, Except Special Education; Public Relations Specialists; Recreation Workers; Sales Managers; Secondary School Teachers, Except Special and Career/Technical Education; Self-Enrichment Education Teachers; Teacher Assistants; Teachers and Instructors, All Other; Tutors; others.

**Skills—**Writing, Reading Comprehension, Active Listening, Speaking, Social Perceptiveness, Service Orientation, Learning Strategies, Monitoring.

**Work Environment:** Indoors; sitting; repetitive motions.

# Interviewers, Except Eligibility and Loan

* Annual Earnings: $28,820
* Earnings Growth Potential: Low (33.6%)
* Growth: 15.6%
* Annual Job Openings: 9,210
* Self-Employed: 0.6%

**Considerations for Job Outlook:** Growth in market research and health-care industries is expected to generate jobs for interviewers. Prospects should be good.

**Interview persons by telephone, by mail, in person, or by other means for the purpose of completing forms, applications, or questionnaires. Ask specific questions, record answers, and assist persons with completing form. May sort, classify, and file forms.** Ask questions in accordance with instructions to obtain various specified information such as person's name, address, age, religious preference, and state of residency. Identify and resolve inconsistencies in interviewees' responses by means of appropriate questioning or explanation. Compile, record, and code results and data from interview or survey, using computer or specified form. Review data obtained from interview for completeness and accuracy. Contact individuals to be interviewed at home, place of business, or field location by telephone, by mail, or in person. Assist individuals in filling out applications or questionnaires. Ensure payment for services by verifying benefits with the person's insurance provider or working out financing options. Identify and report problems in obtaining valid data. Explain survey objectives and procedures to interviewees and interpret survey questions to help interviewees' comprehension. Perform patient services, such as answering the telephone and assisting patients with financial and medical questions. Prepare reports to provide answers in response to specific problems. Locate and list addresses and households. Perform other office duties as needed, such as telemarketing and customer service inquiries, billing patients, and receiving payments. Meet with supervisor daily to submit completed assignments and discuss progress. Collect and analyze data, such as studying old records; tallying the number of outpatients entering each day or week; or participating in federal, state, or local population surveys as a census enumerator.

**Education/Training Required:** Short-term on-the-job training. **Education and Training Program:** Receptionist Training. **Knowledge/Courses**—Clerical, Customer and Personal Service, Communications and Media, Computers and Electronics.

**Personality Type:** Conventional-Enterprising-Social. **Career Cluster:** 04 Business, Management, and Administration. **Career Pathway:** 4.6 Administrative and Information Support. **Other Jobs in This Pathway:** Couriers and Messengers; Court Clerks; Court, Municipal, and License Clerks; Customer Service Representatives; Data Entry Keyers; Dispatchers, Except Police, Fire, and Ambulance; Executive Secretaries and Executive Administrative Assistants; File Clerks; Human Resources Assistants, Except Payroll and Timekeeping; Information and Record Clerks, All Other; Insurance Claims Clerks; Insurance Policy Processing Clerks; License Clerks; Mail Clerks and Mail Machine Operators, Except Postal Service; Office and Administrative Support Workers, All Other; Office Clerks, General; Order Clerks; Patient Representatives; Postal Service Mail Carriers; Postal Service Mail Sorters, Processors, and Processing Machine Operators; Receptionists and Information Clerks; Secretaries and Administrative Assistants, Except Legal, Medical, and Executive; Shipping, Receiving, and Traffic Clerks; Switchboard Operators, Including Answering Service; Word Processors and Typists; others.

**Skills**—Active Listening, Speaking, Programming, Writing, Instructing, Persuasion, Social Perceptiveness, Reading Comprehension.

**Work Environment:** Indoors; sitting; using hands; repetitive motions; noise.

# Kindergarten Teachers, Except Special Education

* Annual Earnings: $48,800
* Earnings Growth Potential: Low (35.0%)
* Growth: 15.0%
* Annual Job Openings: 6,300
* Self-Employed: 1.6%

**Considerations for Job Outlook:** Enrollment from 2008–2018 is expected to grow more slowly than in recent years. Prospects are usually better in urban and rural areas, for bilingual teachers, and for math and science teachers.

**Teach elemental natural and social science, personal hygiene, music, art, and literature to children from 4 to 6 years of age. Promote physical, mental, and social development. May be required to hold state certification.** Teach basic skills such as color, shape, number, and letter recognition; personal hygiene; and social skills. Establish and enforce rules for behavior and policies and procedures to maintain order among students. Observe and evaluate children's performance, behavior, social development, and physical health. Instruct students individually and in groups, adapting teaching methods to meet students' varying needs and interests. Read books to entire classes or to small groups. Demonstrate activities to children. Provide a variety of materials and resources for children to explore, manipulate, and use, both in learning activities and in imaginative play. Plan and conduct activities for a balanced program of instruction, demonstration, and work time that provides students with opportunities to observe, question, and investigate. Confer with parents or guardians, other teachers, counselors, and administrators to resolve students' behavioral and academic problems. Prepare children for later grades by encouraging them to explore learning opportunities and to persevere with challenging tasks. Establish clear objectives for all lessons, units, and projects and communicate those objectives to children. Prepare and implement remedial programs for students requiring extra help. Meet with parents and guardians to discuss their children's progress and to determine their priorities for their children and their resource needs. Prepare objectives and outlines for courses of study, following curriculum guidelines or requirements of states and schools. Organize and lead activities designed to promote physical, mental, and social development such as games, arts and crafts, music, and storytelling. Guide and counsel students with adjustment or academic problems or special academic interests. Identify children showing signs of emotional, developmental, or health-related problems and discuss them with supervisors, parents or guardians, and child development specialists.

**Education/Training Required:** Bachelor's degree. **Education and Training Program:** Early Childhood Education and Teaching. **Knowledge/Courses**—Philosophy and Theology, Fine Arts, Geography, Sociology and Anthropology, Psychology, Education and Training.

**Personality Type:** Social-Artistic. **Career Cluster:** 05 Education and Training. **Career Pathway:** 5.3 Teaching/Training. **Other Jobs in This Pathway:** Adult Basic and Secondary Education and Literacy Teachers and Instructors; Athletes and Sports Competitors; Audio-Visual and Multimedia Collections Specialists; Career/Technical Education Teachers, Middle School; Career/Technical Education Teachers, Secondary School; Chemists; Coaches and Scouts; Dietitians and Nutritionists; Elementary School Teachers, Except Special Education; Fitness Trainers and Aerobics Instructors; Historians; Instructional Coordinators; Instructional Designers and Technologists; Interpreters and Translators; Librarians; Middle School Teachers, Except Special and Career/Technical Education; Physicists; Preschool Teachers, Except Special Education; Recreation Workers; Secondary

School Teachers, Except Special and Career/Technical Education; Self-Enrichment Education Teachers; Teacher Assistants; Teachers and Instructors, All Other; Tutors.

**Skills**—Learning Strategies, Negotiation, Social Perceptiveness, Technology Design, Service Orientation, Active Listening, Management of Personnel Resources, Active Learning.

**Work Environment:** Indoors; standing.

# Landscape Architects

- ❋ Annual Earnings: $62,090
- ❋ Earnings Growth Potential: Medium (40.6%)
- ❋ Growth: 19.7%
- ❋ Annual Job Openings: 980
- ❋ Self-Employed: 21.3%

**Considerations for Job Outlook:** Employment should grow as new construction and redevelopment create more opportunities for these workers. Opportunities should be good, but entry-level job seekers should expect keen competition for openings in large firms.

**Plan and design land areas for such projects as parks and other recreational facilities; airports; highways; hospitals; schools; land subdivisions; and commercial, industrial, and residential sites.** Prepare site plans, specifications, and cost estimates for land development, coordinating arrangement of existing and proposed land features and structures. Confer with clients, engineering personnel, and architects on overall program. Compile and analyze data on conditions such as location, drainage, and location of structures for environmental reports and landscaping plans. Inspect landscape work to ensure compliance with specifications, approve quality of materials and work, and advise client and construction personnel.

**Education/Training Required:** Bachelor's degree. **Education and Training Programs:** Environmental Design/Architecture; Landscape Architecture (BS, BSLA, BLA, MSLA, MLA, PhD). **Knowledge/Courses**—Design, Geography, Building and Construction, Fine Arts, Biology, Engineering and Technology.

**Personality Type:** Artistic-Investigative-Realistic. **Career Cluster:** 02 Architecture and Construction. **Career Pathway:** 2.1 Design/Pre-Construction. **Other Jobs in This Pathway:** Architects, Except Landscape and Naval; Architectural and Engineering Managers; Architectural Drafters; Cartographers and Photogrammetrists; Civil Drafters;

Civil Engineering Technicians; Drafters, All Other; Electrical Drafters; Electronic Drafters; Engineering Technicians, Except Drafters, All Other; Engineers, All Other; Geodetic Surveyors; Interior Designers; Mechanical Drafters; Surveying Technicians.

**Skills**—Operations Analysis, Science, Management of Financial Resources, Systems Evaluation, Management of Material Resources, Management of Personnel Resources, Systems Analysis, Persuasion.

**Work Environment:** More often indoors than outdoors; sitting.

# Landscaping and Groundskeeping Workers

* Annual Earnings: $23,400
* Earnings Growth Potential: Low (27.5%)
* Growth: 18.0%
* Annual Job Openings: 36,220
* Self-Employed: 22.0%

**Considerations for Job Outlook:** Demand for lawn care and landscaping services is expected to grow, resulting in employment growth for these workers. Job prospects are expected to be good. Opportunities for year-round work should be best in regions with temperate climates.

**Landscape or maintain grounds of property, using hand or power tools or equipment. Workers typically perform a variety of tasks, which may include any combination of the following: sod laying, mowing, trimming, planting, watering, fertilizing, digging, raking, sprinkler installation, and installation of mortarless segmental concrete masonry wall units.** Operate powered equipment such as mowers, tractors, twin-axle vehicles, snowblowers, chain saws, electric clippers, sod cutters, and pruning saws. Mow and edge lawns, using power mowers and edgers. Shovel snow from walks, driveways, and parking lots and spread salt in those areas. Care for established lawns by mulching; aerating; weeding; grubbing and removing thatch; and trimming and edging around flower beds, walks, and walls. Use hand tools such as shovels, rakes, pruning saws, saws, hedge and brush trimmers, and axes. Prune and trim trees, shrubs, and hedges, using shears, pruners, or chain saws. Maintain and repair tools; equipment; and structures such as buildings, greenhouses, fences, and benches, using hand and power tools. Gather and remove litter. Mix and spray or spread fertilizers, herbicides, or insecticides onto grass, shrubs, and trees, using hand or automatic sprayers or spreaders. Provide proper upkeep of sidewalks, driveways, parking lots, fountains, planters, burial sites, and other grounds features. Water lawns, trees, and plants, using portable sprinkler systems, hoses, or watering cans. Trim and pick flowers and clean flowerbeds. Rake, mulch, and compost leaves. Plant seeds, bulbs, foliage, flowering plants, grass, ground covers, trees, and shrubs and apply mulch for protection, using gardening tools. Follow planned landscaping designs to determine where to lay sod, sow grass, or plant flowers and foliage. Decorate gardens with stones and plants. Maintain irrigation systems, including winterizing the systems and starting them up in spring. Care for natural turf fields, making sure the underlying soil has the required composition to allow proper drainage and to support the grasses used on the fields. Use irrigation methods to adjust the amount of water consumption and to prevent waste. Haul or spread topsoil and spread straw over seeded soil to hold soil in place. Advise customers on plant selection and care.

**Education/Training Required:** Short-term on-the-job training. **Education and Training Programs:** Landscaping and Groundskeeping; Turf and Turfgrass Management. **Knowledge/Courses**—Mechanical.

**Personality Type:** Realistic-Conventional. **Career Cluster:** 01 Agriculture, Food, and Natural Resources. **Career Pathway:** 1.2 Plant Systems. **Other Jobs in This Pathway:** Agricultural Technicians; Animal Scientists; Biochemists and Biophysicists; Biologists; Economists; Environmental Economists; Farm and Home Management Advisors; First-Line Supervisors of Landscaping, Lawn Service, and Groundskeeping Workers; First-Line Supervisors of Retail Sales Workers; Floral Designers; Food Science Technicians; Food Scientists and Technologists; Geneticists; Grounds Maintenance Workers, All Other; Pesticide Handlers, Sprayers, and Applicators, Vegetation; Precision Agriculture Technicians; Retail Salespersons; Soil and Plant Scientists; Tree Trimmers and Pruners.

**Skills**—Operation and Control, Repairing, Equipment Maintenance, Operation Monitoring, Troubleshooting, Equipment Selection, Quality Control Analysis.

**Work Environment:** Outdoors; standing; walking and running; using hands; bending or twisting the body; repetitive motions; noise; very hot or cold; bright or inadequate lighting; contaminants; hazardous equipment; minor burns, cuts, bites, or stings.

# Law Teachers, Postsecondary

- ❋ Annual Earnings: $94,260
- ❋ Earnings Growth Potential: Very high (65.0%)
- ❋ Growth: 15.1%
- ❋ Annual Job Openings: 400
- ❋ Self-Employed: 0.2%

**Considerations for Job Outlook:** Enrollments in postsecondary institutions are expected to continue rising as more people attend college and as workers return to school to update their skills. Opportunities for part-time or temporary positions should be favorable, but significant competition exists for tenure-track positions.

**Teach courses in law.** Evaluate and grade students' classwork, assignments, papers, and oral presentations. Compile, administer, and grade examinations or assign this work to others. Prepare and deliver lectures to undergraduate or graduate students on topics such as civil procedure, contracts, and torts. Initiate, facilitate, and moderate classroom discussions. Prepare course materials such as syllabi, homework assignments, and handouts. Keep abreast of developments in their field by reading current literature, talking with colleagues, and participating in professional conferences. Plan, evaluate, and revise curricula, course content, and course materials and methods of instruction. Maintain regularly scheduled office hours to advise and assist students. Conduct research in a particular field of knowledge and publish findings in professional journals, books, or electronic media. Advise students on academic and vocational curricula and on career issues. Supervise undergraduate and/or graduate teaching, internship, and research work. Select and obtain materials and supplies such as textbooks. Maintain student attendance records, grades, and other required records. Serve on academic or administrative committees that deal with institutional policies, departmental matters, and academic issues. Perform administrative duties such as serving as department head. Collaborate with colleagues to address teaching and research issues. Participate in student recruitment, registration, and placement activities. Compile bibliographies of specialized materials for outside reading assignments. Participate in campus and community events. Act as advisers to student organizations. Assign cases for students to hear and try. Provide professional consulting services to government or industry. Write grant proposals to procure external research funding.

**Education/Training Required:** First professional degree. **Education and Training Program:** Law (LL.B., J.D.).

**Knowledge/Courses**—Law and Government, English Language, History and Archeology, Philosophy and Theology, Education and Training, Communications and Media.

**Personality Type:** Social-Investigative-Enterprising. **Career Clusters:** 05 Education and Training; 12 Law, Public Safety, Corrections, and Security. **Career Pathways:** 5.3 Teaching/Training; 12.5 Legal Services. **Other Jobs in These Pathways:** Adult Basic and Secondary Education and Literacy Teachers and Instructors; Career/Technical Education Teachers, Secondary School; Chemists; Coaches and Scouts; Dietitians and Nutritionists; Elementary School Teachers, Except Special Education; Fitness Trainers and Aerobics Instructors; Instructional Coordinators; Instructional Designers and Technologists; Interpreters and Translators; Kindergarten Teachers, Except Special Education; Lawyers; Legal Secretaries; Legal Support Workers, All Other; Librarians; Middle School Teachers, Except Special and Career/Technical Education; Paralegals and Legal Assistants; Preschool Teachers, Except Special Education; Recreation Workers; Secondary School Teachers, Except Special and Career/Technical Education; Self-Enrichment Education Teachers; Teacher Assistants; Title Examiners, Abstractors, and Searchers; Tutors; 37 other postsecondary teaching occupations; others.

**Skills**—Reading Comprehension, Speaking, Writing, Active Learning, Instructing, Learning Strategies, Critical Thinking, Active Listening.

**Work Environment:** Indoors; sitting.

# Lawyers

- ❋ Annual Earnings: $112,760
- ❋ Earnings Growth Potential: Very high (52.0%)
- ❋ Growth: 13.0%
- ❋ Annual Job Openings: 24,040
- ❋ Self-Employed: 26.2%

**Considerations for Job Outlook:** Growth in both population and business activity is expected to result in more civil disputes and criminal cases and, thus, employment growth for lawyers. This growth is expected to be constrained, however, as paralegals and other workers perform some of the tasks previously done by lawyers. Keen competition is expected.

**Represent clients in criminal and civil litigation and other legal proceedings, draw up legal documents, and manage or advise clients on legal transactions. May specialize in a**

**single area or may practice broadly in many areas of law.** Advise clients concerning business transactions, claim liability, advisability of prosecuting or defending lawsuits, or legal rights and obligations. Interpret laws, rulings, and regulations for individuals and businesses. Analyze the probable outcomes of cases, using knowledge of legal precedents. Present and summarize cases to judges and juries. Gather evidence to formulate defense or to initiate legal actions by such means as interviewing clients and witnesses to ascertain the facts of a case. Evaluate findings and develop strategies and arguments in preparation for presentation of cases. Represent clients in court or before government agencies. Examine legal data to determine advisability of defending or prosecuting lawsuit. Select jurors, argue motions, meet with judges, and question witnesses during the course of a trial. Present evidence to defend clients or prosecute defendants in criminal or civil litigation. Study Constitution, statutes, decisions, regulations, and ordinances of quasi-judicial bodies to determine ramifications for cases. Prepare and draft legal documents, such as wills, deeds, patent applications, mortgages, leases, and contracts. Prepare legal briefs and opinions and file appeals in state and federal courts of appeal. Negotiate settlements of civil disputes. Confer with colleagues with specialties in appropriate areas of legal issue to establish and verify bases for legal proceedings. Search for and examine public and other legal records to write opinions or establish ownership. Supervise legal assistants. Perform administrative and management functions related to the practice of law. Act as agent, trustee, guardian, or executor for businesses or individuals. Probate wills and represent and advise executors and administrators of estates. Help develop federal and state programs, draft and interpret laws and legislation, and establish enforcement procedures.

**Education/Training Required:** First professional degree. **Education and Training Programs:** Advanced Legal Research/Studies, General (LL.M., M.C.L., M.L.I., M.S.L., J.S.D./S.J.D.); American/U.S. Law/Legal Studies/Jurisprudence (LL.M., M.C.J., J.S.D./S.J.D.); Banking, Corporate, Finance, and Securities Law (LL.M., J.S.D./S.J.D.); Canadian Law/Legal Studies/Jurisprudence (LL.M., M.C.J., J.S.D./S.J.D.); Comparative Law (LL.M., M.C.L., J.S.D./S.J.D.); Energy, Environment, and Natural Resources Law (LL.M., M.S., J.S.D./S.J.D.); Health Law (LL.M., M.J., J.S.D./S.J.D.); International Business, Trade, and Tax Law (LL.M., J.S.D./S.J.D.); International Law and Legal Studies (LL.M., J.S.D./S.J.D.); Law (LL.B., J.D.); Legal Professions and Studies, Other; Legal Research and Advanced Professional Studies, Other; Legal Studies, General; Pre-Law Studies; Programs for Foreign Lawyers (LL.M., M.C.L.); Tax Law/Taxation (LL.M., J.S.D./S.J.D.). **Knowledge/**

**Courses**—Law and Government, English Language, Personnel and Human Resources, Customer and Personal Service, Economics and Accounting, Administration and Management.

**Personality Type:** Enterprising-Investigative. **Career Cluster:** 12 Law, Public Safety, Corrections, and Security. **Career Pathway:** 12.5 Legal Services. **Other Jobs in This Pathway:** Administrative Law Judges, Adjudicators, and Hearing Officers; Arbitrators, Mediators, and Conciliators; Court Reporters; Farm and Home Management Advisors; Judges, Magistrate Judges, and Magistrates; Legal Secretaries; Legal Support Workers, All Other; Paralegals and Legal Assistants; Title Examiners, Abstractors, and Searchers.

**Skills**—Persuasion, Negotiation, Speaking, Writing, Critical Thinking, Judgment and Decision Making, Active Learning, Active Listening.

**Work Environment:** Indoors; sitting.

# Legal Secretaries

- ❀ Annual Earnings: $41,500
- ❀ Earnings Growth Potential: Medium (36.5%)
- ❀ Growth: 18.4%
- ❀ Annual Job Openings: 8,380
- ❀ Self-Employed: 1.4%

**Considerations for Job Outlook:** Projected employment growth varies by occupational specialty. Faster-than-average growth is expected for medical secretaries and legal secretaries; average growth for executive secretaries and administrative assistants; and slower-than-average growth for secretaries other than legal, medical, or executive, who account for most of the workers in these specialties. Many opportunities are expected.

**Perform secretarial duties, utilizing legal terminology, procedures, and documents. Prepare legal papers and correspondence, such as summonses, complaints, motions, and subpoenas. May also assist with legal research.** Prepare and process legal documents and papers, such as summonses, subpoenas, complaints, appeals, motions, and pretrial agreements. Mail, fax, or arrange for delivery of legal correspondence to clients, witnesses, and court officials. Receive and place telephone calls. Schedule and make appointments. Make photocopies of correspondence, documents, and other printed matter. Organize and maintain law libraries, documents, and case files. Assist attorneys in collecting information such as employment, medical, and other records. Attend legal meetings, such as client interviews, hearings, or depositions, and take notes. Draft and type office memos. Review legal publications and perform database searches to identify laws and court decisions relevant to pending cases. Submit articles and information from searches to attorneys for review and approval for use. Complete various forms such as accident reports, trial and courtroom requests, and applications for clients.

**Education/Training Required:** Associate degree. **Education and Training Program:** Legal Administrative Assistant/Secretary Training. **Knowledge/Courses**—Clerical, Law and Government, Computers and Electronics, English Language, Customer and Personal Service.

**Personality Type:** Conventional-Enterprising. **Career Cluster:** 12 Law, Public Safety, Corrections, and Security. **Career Pathway:** 12.5 Legal Services. **Other Jobs in This Pathway:** Administrative Law Judges, Adjudicators, and Hearing Officers; Arbitrators, Mediators, and Conciliators; Court Reporters; Farm and Home Management Advisors; Judges, Magistrate Judges, and Magistrates; Lawyers; Legal Support Workers, All Other; Paralegals and Legal Assistants; Title Examiners, Abstractors, and Searchers.

**Skills**—Writing, Reading Comprehension, Active Listening, Programming, Service Orientation, Speaking.

**Work Environment:** Indoors; sitting; using hands; repetitive motions.

# Librarians

- ❋ Annual Earnings: $54,500
- ❋ Earnings Growth Potential: Medium (38.4%)
- ❋ Growth: 7.8%
- ❋ Annual Job Openings: 5,450
- ❋ Self-Employed: 0.3%

**Considerations for Job Outlook:** Growth in the number of librarians is expected to be limited by government budget constraints and the increasing use of electronic resources. Although many openings are expected, there will be competition for jobs in some regions.

**Administer libraries and perform related library services. Work in a variety of settings, including public libraries, schools, colleges and universities, museums, corporations, government agencies, law firms, non-profit organizations, and health-care providers. Tasks may include selecting, acquiring, cataloguing, classifying, circulating, and maintaining library materials and furnishing reference, bibliographical, and readers' advisory services. May perform in-depth, strategic research and synthesize, analyze, edit, and filter information. May set up or work with databases and information systems to catalogue and access information.** Search standard reference materials, including online sources and the Internet, to answer patrons' reference questions. Analyze patrons' requests to determine needed information and assist in furnishing or locating that information. Teach library patrons to search for information by using databases. Keep records of circulation and materials. Supervise budgeting, planning, and personnel activities. Check books in and out of the library. Explain use of library facilities, resources, equipment, and services and provide information about library policies. Review and evaluate resource material, such as book reviews and catalogs, to select and order print, audiovisual, and electronic resources. Code, classify, and catalog books, publications, films, audiovisual aids, and other library materials based on subject matter or standard library classification systems. Locate unusual or unique information in response to specific requests. Direct and train library staff in duties such as receiving, shelving, researching, cataloging, and equipment use. Respond to customer complaints, taking action as necessary. Organize collections of books, publications, documents, audiovisual aids, and other reference materials for convenient access. Develop library policies and procedures. Evaluate materials to determine outdated or unused items to be discarded. Develop information access aids such as indexes and annotated bibliographies, Web pages, electronic pathfinders, and online tutorials. Plan and deliver client-centered programs and services such as special services for corporate clients, storytelling for children, newsletters, or programs for special groups. Compile lists of books, periodicals, articles, and audiovisual materials on particular subjects. Arrange for interlibrary loans of materials not available in a particular library. Assemble and arrange display materials.

**Education/Training Required:** Master's degree. **Education and Training Programs:** Library and Information Science; Library Science, Other; School Librarian/School Library Media Specialist. **Knowledge/Courses**—History and Archeology, Sociology and Anthropology, Clerical, Philosophy and Theology, Education and Training, English Language.

**Personality Type:** Conventional-Social-Enterprising. **Career Cluster:** 05 Education and Training. **Career Pathways:** 5.2 Professional Support Services; 5.3 Teaching/Training. **Other Jobs in These Pathways:** Adult Basic and Secondary Education and Literacy Teachers and Instructors;

Athletes and Sports Competitors; Career/Technical Education Teachers, Middle School; Career/Technical Education Teachers, Secondary School; Chemists; Coaches and Scouts; Dietitians and Nutritionists; Educational, Guidance, School, and Vocational Counselors; Elementary School Teachers, Except Special Education; Fitness Trainers and Aerobics Instructors; Instructional Coordinators; Instructional Designers and Technologists; Interpreters and Translators; Kindergarten Teachers, Except Special Education; Library Assistants, Clerical; Library Technicians; Middle School Teachers, Except Special and Career/Technical Education; Physicists; Preschool Teachers, Except Special Education; Recreation Workers; Secondary School Teachers, Except Special and Career/Technical Education; Self-Enrichment Education Teachers; Teacher Assistants; Teachers and Instructors, All Other; Tutors; others.

**Skills**—Management of Material Resources, Service Orientation, Instructing, Operations Analysis, Negotiation, Management of Financial Resources, Writing, Systems Evaluation.

**Work Environment:** Indoors; sitting; repetitive motions.

# Library Science Teachers, Postsecondary

- ❀ Annual Earnings: $62,720
- ❀ Earnings Growth Potential: Low (35.7%)
- ❀ Growth: 15.1%
- ❀ Annual Job Openings: 100
- ❀ Self-Employed: 0.2%

**Considerations for Job Outlook:** Enrollments in postsecondary institutions are expected to continue rising as more people attend college and as workers return to school to update their skills. Opportunities for part-time or temporary positions should be favorable, but significant competition exists for tenure-track positions.

**Teach courses in library science.** Prepare course materials such as syllabi, homework assignments, and handouts. Prepare and deliver lectures to undergraduate or graduate students on topics such as collection development, archival methods, and indexing and abstracting. Evaluate and grade students' classwork, assignments, and papers. Keep abreast of developments in their field by reading current literature, talking with colleagues, and participating in professional conferences. Initiate, facilitate, and moderate classroom discussions. Plan, evaluate, and revise curricula, course content, and course materials and methods of instruction.

Conduct research in a particular field of knowledge and publish findings in professional journals, books, and/or electronic media. Maintain student attendance records, grades, and other required records. Collaborate with colleagues to address teaching and research issues. Advise students on academic and vocational curricula and on career issues. Compile, administer, and grade examinations or assign this work to others. Supervise undergraduate or graduate teaching, internship, and research work. Maintain regularly scheduled office hours in order to advise and assist students. Write grant proposals to procure external research funding. Select and obtain materials and supplies such as textbooks. Serve on academic or administrative committees that deal with institutional policies, departmental matters, and academic issues. Compile bibliographies of specialized materials for outside reading assignments. Participate in student recruitment, registration, and placement activities. Perform administrative duties such as serving as department head. Participate in campus and community events. Act as advisers to student organizations. Provide professional consulting services to government and/or industry.

**Education/Training Required:** Doctoral degree. **Education and Training Programs:** Humanities/Humanistic Studies; Library and Information Science; Teacher Education and Professional Development, Specific Subject Areas, Other. **Knowledge/Courses**—Education and Training, Sociology and Anthropology, Communications and Media, English Language, History and Archeology, Philosophy and Theology.

**Personality Type:** Social-Investigative-Conventional. **Career Cluster:** 05 Education and Training. **Career Pathways:** 5.2 Professional Support Services; 5.3 Teaching/Training. **Other Jobs in These Pathways:** Adult Basic and Secondary Education and Literacy Teachers and Instructors; Athletes and Sports Competitors; Career/Technical Education Teachers, Middle School; Career/Technical Education Teachers, Secondary School; Chemists; Coaches and Scouts; Dietitians and Nutritionists; Educational, Guidance, School, and Vocational Counselors; Elementary School Teachers, Except Special Education; Fitness Trainers and Aerobics Instructors; Instructional Coordinators; Instructional Designers and Technologists; Interpreters and Translators; Kindergarten Teachers, Except Special Education; Librarians; Library Assistants, Clerical; Library Technicians; Middle School Teachers, Except Special and Career/Technical Education; Preschool Teachers, Except Special Education; Recreation Workers; Secondary School Teachers, Except Special and Career/Technical Education; Self-Enrichment Education Teachers; Teacher Assistants; Tutors; 37 other postsecondary teaching occupations; others.

**Skills**—Writing, Instructing, Learning Strategies, Systems Analysis, Speaking, Reading Comprehension, Active Listening, Active Learning.

**Work Environment:** Indoors; sitting.

# Library Technicians

- ❋ Annual Earnings: $29,860
- ❋ Earnings Growth Potential: Medium (39.8%)
- ❋ Growth: 8.8%
- ❋ Annual Job Openings: 6,470
- ❋ Self-Employed: 0.0%

**Considerations for Job Outlook:** Budgetary constraints are among the reasons job growth may slow; however, continued automation of library systems should allow these workers to perform some tasks previously done by librarians, thereby increasing employment of technicians. Opportunities should be best for technicians with specialized training.

**Assist librarians by helping readers in the use of library catalogs, databases, and indexes to locate books and other materials and by answering questions that require only brief consultation of standard reference. Compile records; sort and shelve books; remove or repair damaged books; register patrons; check materials in and out of the circulation process. Replace materials in shelving area (stacks) or files. Includes bookmobile drivers who operate bookmobiles or light trucks that pull trailers to specific locations on a predetermined schedule and assist with providing services in mobile libraries.** Reserve, circulate, renew, and discharge books and other materials. Enter and update patrons' records on computers. Provide assistance to teachers and students by locating materials and helping to complete special projects. Guide patrons in finding and using library resources, including reference materials, audiovisual equipment, computers, and electronic resources. Answer routine reference inquiries and refer patrons needing further assistance to librarians. Train other staff, volunteers, or student assistants, and schedule and supervise their work. Sort books, publications, and other items according to procedure and return them to shelves, files, or other designated storage areas. Conduct reference searches, using printed materials and in-house and online databases. Deliver and retrieve items throughout the library by hand or using pushcart. Take actions to halt disruption of library activities by problem patrons. Process interlibrary loans for patrons. Process print and non-print library materials to prepare them for inclusion in library collections.

Retrieve information from central databases for storage in a library's computer. Organize and maintain periodicals and reference materials. Compile and maintain records relating to circulation, materials, and equipment. Collect fines and respond to complaints about fines. Issue identification cards to borrowers. Verify bibliographical data for materials, including author, title, publisher, publication date, and edition. Review subject matter of materials to be classified and select classification numbers and headings according to classification systems. Send out notices about lost or overdue books. Prepare order slips for materials to be acquired, checking prices and figuring costs. Design, customize, and maintain databases, Web pages, and local area networks. Operate and maintain audiovisual equipment such as projectors, tape recorders, and videocassette recorders. File catalog cards according to system used.

**Education/Training Required:** Postsecondary vocational training. **Education and Training Program:** Library and Archives Assisting. **Knowledge/Courses**—Clerical, Computers and Electronics, Law and Government, Economics and Accounting, English Language.

**Personality Type:** Conventional-Social-Enterprising. **Career Cluster:** 05 Education and Training. **Career Pathway:** 5.2 Professional Support Services. **Other Jobs in This Pathway:** Educational, Guidance, School, and Vocational Counselors; Librarians; Library Assistants, Clerical.

**Skills**—Service Orientation, Programming, Management of Material Resources, Equipment Maintenance, Reading Comprehension, Learning Strategies, Management of Personnel Resources, Instructing.

**Work Environment:** Indoors; sitting; repetitive motions.

# Licensed Practical and Licensed Vocational Nurses

- ❋ Annual Earnings: $40,380
- ❋ Earnings Growth Potential: Low (26.5%)
- ❋ Growth: 20.6%
- ❋ Annual Job Openings: 39,130
- ❋ Self-Employed: 1.2%

**Considerations for Job Outlook:** An aging population is expected to boost demand for nursing services. Job prospects are expected to be very good, especially in employment settings that serve older populations.

**Care for ill, injured, convalescent, or disabled persons in hospitals, nursing homes, clinics, private homes, group**

homes, and similar institutions. **May work under the supervision of a registered nurse. Licensing required.** Administer prescribed medications or start intravenous fluids, recording times and amounts on patients' charts. Observe patients, charting and reporting changes in patients' conditions, such as adverse reactions to medication or treatment, and taking any necessary actions. Provide basic patient care and treatments such as taking temperatures or blood pressures, dressing wounds, treating bedsores, giving enemas or douches, rubbing with alcohol, massaging, or performing catheterizations. Sterilize equipment and supplies, using germicides, sterilizer, or autoclave. Answer patients' calls and determine how to assist them. Work as part of a health-care team to assess patient needs, plan and modify care, and implement interventions. Measure and record patients' vital signs, such as height, weight, temperature, blood pressure, pulse, and respiration. Collect samples such as blood, urine, and sputum from patients and perform routine laboratory tests on samples. Prepare patients for examinations, tests, or treatments and explain procedures. Assemble and use equipment such as catheters, tracheotomy tubes, and oxygen suppliers. Evaluate nursing intervention outcomes, conferring with other health-care team members as necessary. Record food and fluid intake and output. Help patients with bathing, dressing, maintaining personal hygiene, moving in bed, or standing and walking. Apply compresses, ice bags, and hot water bottles. Inventory and requisition supplies and instruments. Clean rooms and make beds. Supervise nurses' aides and assistants. Make appointments, keep records, and perform other clerical duties in doctors' offices and clinics. In private home settings, provide medical treatment and personal care, such as cooking for patients, keeping their rooms orderly, seeing that patients are comfortable and in good spirits, and instructing family members in simple nursing tasks. Set up equipment and prepare medical treatment rooms.

**Education/Training Required:** Postsecondary vocational training. **Education and Training Program:** Licensed Practical/Vocational Nurse Training. **Knowledge/Courses**—Psychology, Medicine and Dentistry, Therapy and Counseling, Biology, Philosophy and Theology, Customer and Personal Service.

**Personality Type:** Social-Realistic. **Career Cluster:** 08 Health Science. **Career Pathway:** 8.1 Therapeutic Services. **Other Jobs in This Pathway:** Clinical Psychologists; Community and Social Service Specialists, All Other; Counseling Psychologists; Dental Assistants; Dental Hygienists; Dentists, General; Health Technologists and Technicians, All Other; Healthcare Support Workers, All Other; Home Health Aides; Low Vision Therapists, Orientation

and Mobility Specialists, and Vision Rehabilitation Therapists; Massage Therapists; Medical and Clinical Laboratory Technicians; Medical and Health Services Managers; Medical Scientists, Except Epidemiologists; Medical Secretaries; Occupational Therapists; Ophthalmic Medical Technologists; Pharmacists; Pharmacy Technicians; Radiologic Technologists; School Psychologists; Social and Human Service Assistants; Speech-Language Pathologists; Speech-Language Pathology Assistants; Substance Abuse and Behavioral Disorder Counselors; others.

**Skills**—Science, Social Perceptiveness, Service Orientation, Operation and Control, Persuasion, Negotiation, Speaking, Time Management.

**Work Environment:** Indoors; standing; walking and running; using hands; repetitive motions; noise; contaminants; cramped work space; exposed to disease or infections.

# Life, Physical, and Social Science Technicians, All Other

- ❋ Annual Earnings: $43,350
- ❋ Earnings Growth Potential: Medium (40.9%)
- ❋ Growth: 13.3%
- ❋ Annual Job Openings: 3,640
- ❋ Self-Employed: 1.6%

**Considerations for Job Outlook:** About average employment growth is projected.

**This occupation includes all life, physical, and social science technicians not listed separately.** Because this is a highly diverse occupation, no data is available for some information topics.

**Education/Training Required:** Associate degree. **Education and Training Program:** Science Technologies/Technicians, Other.

**Career Clusters:** 08 Health Science; 13 Manufacturing. **Career Pathways:** 8.1 Therapeutic Services; 13.2 Manufacturing Production Process Development. **Other Jobs in These Pathways:** Clinical Psychologists; Community and Social Service Specialists, All Other; Counseling Psychologists; Dental Assistants; Dental Hygienists; Dentists, General; Electrical Engineering Technicians; Healthcare Support Workers, All Other; Home Health Aides; Licensed Practical and Licensed Vocational Nurses; Low Vision Therapists, Orientation and Mobility Specialists, and Vision Rehabilitation Therapists; Massage Therapists; Medical and Clinical Laboratory Technicians; Medical and Health Services Managers; Medical Scientists, Except Epidemiologists; Medical Secretaries; Occupational Therapists; Pharmacists; Pharmacy Technicians; Radiologic Technologists; School Psychologists; Social and Human Service Assistants; Speech-Language Pathologists; Speech-Language Pathology Assistants; Substance Abuse and Behavioral Disorder Counselors; others.

## Job Specialization: Precision Agriculture Technicians

**Apply geospatial technologies, including geographic information systems (GIS) and Global Positioning System (GPS), to agricultural production and management activities, such as pest scouting, site-specific pesticide application, yield mapping, and variable-rate irrigation. May use computers to develop and analyze maps and remote sensing images to compare physical topography with data on soils, fertilizer, pests or weather.** Collect information about soil and field attributes, yield data, or field boundaries, using field data recorders and basic geographic information systems (GIS). Create, layer, and analyze maps showing precision agricultural data such as crop yields, soil characteristics, input applications, terrain, drainage patterns and field management history. Document and maintain records of precision agriculture information. Compile and analyze geospatial data to determine agricultural implications of factors such as soil quality, terrain, field productivity, fertilizers, and weather conditions. Divide agricultural fields into georeferenced zones based on soil characteristics and production potentials. Develop soil sampling grids or identify sampling sites, using geospatial technology, for soil testing on characteristics such as nitrogen, phosphorus, and potassium content, pH, and micronutrients. Compare crop yield maps with maps of soil test data, chemical application patterns, or other information to develop site-specific crop management plans. Apply knowledge of government regulations when making agricultural recommendations. Recommend best crop varieties and seeding rates for specific field areas, based on analysis of geospatial data. Draw and read maps such as soil, contour, and plat maps. Process and analyze data from harvester monitors to develop yield maps. Demonstrate the uses and applications of geospatial technology, such as Global Positioning System (GPS), geographic information systems (GIS), automatic tractor guidance systems, variable rate chemical input applicators, surveying equipment, and computer mapping software. Program farm equipment, such as variable-rate planting equipment and pesticide sprayers, based on input

from crop scouting and analysis of field condition variability. Analyze remote sensing imagery to identify relationships between soil quality, crop canopy densities, light reflectance and weather history.

**Education/Training Required:** Moderate-term on-the-job training. **Education and Training Program:** Agricultural Mechanics and Equipment/Machine Technology. **Knowledge/Courses**—Food Production, Geography, Biology, Chemistry, Sales and Marketing, Mechanical.

**Personality Type:** Realistic-Investigative-Conventional. **Career Cluster:** 01 Agriculture, Food, and Natural Resources. **Career Pathways:** 1.2 Plant Systems; 1.3 Animal Systems. **Other Jobs in These Pathways:** Agricultural Technicians; Animal Breeders; Animal Scientists; Animal Trainers; Biochemists and Biophysicists; Biologists; Economists; Environmental Economists; Farm and Home Management Advisors; First-Line Supervisors of Landscaping, Lawn Service, and Groundskeeping Workers; First-Line Supervisors of Retail Sales Workers; Floral Designers; Food Science Technicians; Food Scientists and Technologists; Geneticists; Grounds Maintenance Workers, All Other; Landscaping and Groundskeeping Workers; Nonfarm Animal Caretakers; Pesticide Handlers, Sprayers, and Applicators, Vegetation; Retail Salespersons; Soil and Plant Scientists; Tree Trimmers and Pruners; Veterinarians.

**Skills**—Equipment Maintenance, Repairing, Science, Troubleshooting, Equipment Selection, Operations Analysis, Quality Control Analysis, Operation and Control.

**Work Environment:** Outdoors; very hot or cold.

## Job Specialization: Quality Control Analysts

**Conduct tests to determine quality of raw materials, bulk intermediate and finished products. May conduct stability sample tests.** Train other analysts to perform laboratory procedures and assays. Perform visual inspections of finished products. Serve as a technical liaison between quality control and other departments, vendors, or contractors. Participate in internal assessments and audits as required. Identify and troubleshoot equipment problems. Evaluate new technologies and methods to make recommendations regarding their use. Ensure that lab cleanliness and safety standards are maintained. Develop and qualify new testing methods. Coordinate testing with contract laboratories and vendors. Write technical reports or documentation such as deviation reports, testing protocols, and trend analyses. Write or revise standard quality control operating procedures. Supply quality control data necessary for regulatory submissions. Receive and inspect raw materials. Review data from contract laboratories to ensure accuracy and regulatory compliance. Prepare or review required method transfer documentation including technical transfer protocols or reports. Perform validations or transfers of analytical methods in accordance with applicable policies or guidelines. Participate in out-of-specification and failure investigations and recommend corrective actions. Monitor testing procedures to ensure that all tests are performed according to established item specifications, standard test methods, or protocols. Investigate or report questionable test results. Interpret test results, compare them to established specifications and control limits, and make recommendations on appropriateness of data for release. Identify quality problems and recommend solutions. Evaluate analytical methods and procedures to determine how they might be improved. Complete documentation needed to support testing procedures including data capture forms, equipment logbooks, or inventory forms. Calibrate, validate, or maintain laboratory equipment. Compile laboratory test data and perform appropriate analyses.

**Education/Training Required:** Postsecondary vocational training. **Education and Training Program:** Quality Control Technology/Technician. **Knowledge/Courses**—No data available.

**Personality Type:** Conventional-Investigative-Realistic. **Career Cluster:** 13 Manufacturing. **Career Pathway:** 13.2 Manufacturing Production Process Development. **Other Jobs in This Pathway:** Biofuels Processing Technicians; Biomass Plant Technicians; Chemical Plant and System Operators; Chemical Technicians; Electrical Engineering Technicians; Electromechanical Equipment Assemblers; Environmental Science and Protection Technicians, Including Health; Fabric and Apparel Patternmakers; Farm and Home Management Advisors; Fashion Designers; Hydroelectric Plant Technicians; Life, Physical, and Social Science Technicians, All Other; Methane/Landfill Gas Generation System Technicians; Nuclear Monitoring Technicians; Textile, Apparel, and Furnishings Workers, All Other.

**Skills**—No data available.

**Work Environment:** No data available.

## Job Specialization: Remote Sensing Technicians

**Apply remote sensing technologies to assist scientists in areas such as natural resources, urban planning, and homeland security. May prepare flight plans and sensor configurations for flight trips.** Participate in the planning and development of mapping projects. Maintain records of survey data. Document methods used and write technical reports containing information collected. Develop specialized computer software routines to customize and integrate image analysis. Collect verification data on the ground using equipment such as global positioning receivers, digital cameras, and notebook computers. Verify integrity and accuracy of data contained in remote sensing image analysis systems. Prepare documentation and presentations including charts, photos, or graphs. Operate airborne remote sensing equipment such as survey cameras, sensors, and scanners. Monitor raw data quality during collection and make equipment corrections as necessary. Merge scanned images or build photo mosaics of large areas using image processing software. Integrate remotely sensed data with other geospatial data. Evaluate remote sensing project requirements to determine the types of equipment or computer software necessary to meet project requirements such as specific image types and output resolutions. Develop and maintain geospatial information databases. Correct raw data for errors due to factors such as skew and atmospheric variation. Calibrate data collection equipment. Consult with remote sensing scientists, surveyors, cartographers, or engineers to determine project needs. Adjust remotely sensed images for optimum presentation by using software to select image displays, define image set categories, or choose processing routines. Manipulate raw data to enhance interpretation, either on the ground or during remote sensing flights. Collect geospatial data using technologies such as aerial photography, light and radio wave detection systems, digital satellites, and thermal energy systems.

**Education/Training Required:** Associate degree. **Education and Training Programs:** Geographic Information Science and Cartography; Signal/Geospatial Intelligence. **Knowledge/Courses**—No data available.

**Personality Type:** Realistic-Investigative-Conventional. **Career Cluster:** 11 Information Technology. **Career Pathway:** 11.2 Information Support Services. **Other Jobs in This Pathway:** Computer and Information Systems Managers; Computer Numerically Controlled Machine Tool Programmers, Metal and Plastic; Computer Operators; Remote Sensing Scientists and Technologists.

**Skills**—No data available.

**Work Environment:** No data available.

# Loan Officers

- ❋ Annual Earnings: $56,490
- ❋ Earnings Growth Potential: High (45.2%)
- ❋ Growth: 10.1%
- ❋ Annual Job Openings: 6,880
- ❋ Self-Employed: 3.7%

**Considerations for Job Outlook:** Overall economic expansion and population growth are expected to increase employment of these workers. However, increased automation through the use of the Internet loan application will temper employment growth. Good job opportunities are expected.

**Evaluate, authorize, or recommend approval of commercial, real estate, or credit loans. Advise borrowers on financial status and methods of payments. Includes mortgage loan officers and agents, collection analysts, loan servicing officers, and loan underwriters.** Meet with applicants to obtain information for loan applications and to answer questions about the process. Approve loans within specified limits and refer loan applications outside those limits to management for approval. Analyze applicants' financial status, credit, and property evaluations to determine feasibility of granting loans. Explain to customers the different types of loans and credit options that are available, as well as the terms of those services. Obtain and compile copies of loan applicants' credit histories, corporate financial statements, and other financial information. Review and update credit and loan files. Review loan agreements to ensure that they are complete and accurate according to policy. Compute payment schedules. Stay abreast of new types of loans and other financial services and products to better meet customers' needs. Submit applications to credit analysts for verification and recommendation. Handle customer complaints and take appropriate action to resolve them. Work with clients to identify their financial goals and to find ways of reaching those goals. Confer with underwriters to aid in resolving mortgage application problems. Negotiate payment arrangements with customers who have delinquent loans. Market bank products to individuals and firms, promoting bank services that may meet customers' needs. Supervise loan personnel. Set credit policies, credit lines, procedures, and standards in conjunction with senior managers. Provide special services such as investment banking for clients with more specialized needs. Analyze potential loan markets and develop referral networks to locate prospects for loans. Prepare reports to send to customers whose accounts are delinquent and forward irreconcilable accounts for collector action. Arrange for maintenance and liquidation of delinquent properties. Interview, hire, and train new employees. Petition courts to transfer titles and deeds of collateral to banks.

**Education/Training Required:** Bachelor's degree. **Education and Training Programs:** Credit Management; Finance, General. **Knowledge/Courses**—Economics and Accounting, Sales and Marketing, Law and Government, English Language, Mathematics, Customer and Personal Service.

**Personality Type:** Conventional-Enterprising-Social. **Career Cluster:** 06 Finance. **Career Pathways:** 6.1 Financial and Investment Planning; 6.3 Banking and Related Services. **Other Jobs in These Pathways:** Bill and Account Collectors; Budget Analysts; Credit Analysts; Credit Authorizers; Credit Checkers; Financial Analysts; Financial Managers, Branch or Department; Financial Quantitative Analysts; Financial Specialists, All Other; Fraud Examiners, Investigators and Analysts; Investment Underwriters; Loan Counselors; Loan Interviewers and Clerks; New Accounts Clerks; Personal Financial Advisors; Risk Management Specialists; Sales Agents, Financial Services; Sales Agents, Securities and Commodities; Securities and Commodities Traders; Securities, Commodities, and Financial Services Sales Agents; Tellers; Title Examiners, Abstractors, and Searchers; Treasurers and Controllers.

**Skills**—Mathematics, Service Orientation, Speaking, Operations Analysis, Writing, Judgment and Decision Making, Reading Comprehension, Active Listening.

**Work Environment:** Indoors; sitting; repetitive motions.

# Logisticians

- ❋ Annual Earnings: $70,800
- ❋ Earnings Growth Potential: Medium (38.5%)
- ❋ Growth: 19.5%
- ❋ Annual Job Openings: 4,190
- ❋ Self-Employed: 0.0%

**Considerations for Job Outlook:** Faster-than-average employment growth is projected.

**Analyze and coordinate the logistical functions of a firm or organization. Responsible for the entire life cycle of a product, including acquisition, distribution, internal allocation, delivery, and final disposal of resources.** Maintain and develop positive business relationships with a customer's key personnel involved in or directly relevant to a logistics activity. Develop an understanding of customers' needs and take actions to ensure that such needs are met. Direct availability and allocation of materials, supplies, and finished products. Collaborate with other departments as necessary to meet customer requirements, to take advantage of sales opportunities, or, in the case of shortages, to minimize negative impacts on a business. Protect and control proprietary materials. Review logistics performance with customers against targets, benchmarks, and service agreements. Develop and implement technical project management tools such as plans, schedules, and responsibility and compliance matrices. Direct team activities, establishing task priorities, scheduling and tracking work assignments, providing guidance, and ensuring the availability of resources. Report project plans, progress, and results. Direct and support the compilation and analysis of technical source data necessary for product development. Explain proposed solutions to customers, management, or other interested parties through written proposals and oral presentations. Provide project management services, including the provision and analysis of technical data. Develop proposals that include documentation for estimates. Plan, organize, and execute logistics support activities such as maintenance planning, repair analysis, and test equipment recommendations. Participate in the assessment and review of design alternatives and design change proposal impacts. Support the development of training materials and technical manuals. Stay informed of logistics technology advances and apply appropriate technology in order to improve logistics processes. Redesign the movement of goods in order to maximize value and minimize costs.

**Education/Training Required:** Bachelor's degree. **Education and Training Programs:** Logistics, Materials, and Supply Chain Management; Operations Management and Supervision; Transportation/Mobility Management. **Knowledge/Courses**—Telecommunications, Geography, Computers and Electronics, Economics and Accounting, Administration and Management, Public Safety and Security.

**Personality Type:** Enterprising-Conventional. **Career Clusters:** 04 Business, Management, and Administration; 16 Transportation, Distribution, and Logistics. **Career Pathways:** 4.1 Management; 16.2 Logistics, Planning, and Management Services. **Other Jobs in These Pathways:** Brownfield Redevelopment Specialists and Site Managers; Business Continuity Planners; Business Operations Specialists, All Other; Chief Executives; Chief Sustainability Officers; Compliance Managers; Computer and Information Systems Managers; Construction Managers; Customs Brokers; Energy Auditors; First-Line Supervisors of Office and Administrative Support Workers; General and Operations Managers; Investment Fund Managers; Loss Prevention Managers; Management Analysts; Managers, All Other; Public Relations Specialists; Regulatory Affairs Managers; Sales Managers; Security Management Specialists; Security Managers; Supply Chain Managers; Sustainability Specialists; Wind Energy Operations Managers; Wind Energy Project Managers; others.

**Skills**—Operations Analysis, Programming, Management of Personnel Resources, Coordination, Monitoring, Systems Evaluation, Systems Analysis, Persuasion.

**Work Environment:** Indoors; sitting.

# Job Specialization: Logistics Analysts

**Analyze product delivery or supply chain processes to identify or recommend changes. May manage route activity including invoicing, electronic bills, and shipment tracing.** Identify opportunities for inventory reductions. Monitor industry standards, trends, or practices to identify developments in logistics planning or execution. Enter logistics-related data into databases. Develop and maintain payment systems to ensure accuracy of vendor payments. Determine packaging requirements. Develop and maintain freight rate databases for use by supply chain departments to determine the most economical modes of transportation. Contact potential vendors to determine material availability. Contact carriers for rates or schedules. Communicate with and monitor service providers, such as ocean carriers, air freight forwarders, global consolidators, customs brokers, and trucking companies. Track product flow from origin to final delivery. Write or revise standard operating procedures for logistics processes. Review procedures such as distribution and inventory management to ensure maximum efficiency and minimum cost. Recommend improvements to existing or planned logistics processes. Provide ongoing analyses in areas such as transportation costs, parts procurement, back orders, and delivery processes. Prepare reports on logistics performance measures. Manage systems to ensure that pricing structures adequately reflect logistics costing. Monitor inventory transactions at warehouse facilities to assess receiving, storage, shipping, or inventory integrity. Maintain databases of logistics information. Maintain logistics records in accordance with corporate policies. Develop and maintain models for logistics uses, such as cost estimating and demand forecasting. Confer with logistics management teams to determine ways to optimize service levels, maintain supply-chain efficiency, and minimize cost. Compute reporting metrics, such as on-time delivery rates, order fulfillment rates, and inventory turns.

**Education/Training Required:** Bachelor's degree. **Education and Training Programs:** Logistics, Materials, and Supply Chain Management; Operations Management and Supervision; Transportation/Mobility Management. **Knowledge/Courses**—No data available.

**Personality Type:** Conventional-Enterprising-Investigative. **Career Clusters:** 04 Business, Management, and Administration; 16 Transportation, Distribution, and Logistics. **Career Pathways:** 4.1 Management; 16.3 Warehousing and Distribution Center Operations. **Other Jobs in These Pathways:** Brownfield Redevelopment Specialists and Site Managers; Business Continuity Planners; Business Operations Specialists, All Other; Chief Executives; Chief Sustainability Officers; Compliance Managers; Computer and Information Systems Managers; Construction Managers; Customs Brokers; Energy Auditors; First-Line Supervisors of Office and Administrative Support Workers; General and Operations Managers; Investment Fund Managers; Loss Prevention Managers; Management Analysts; Managers, All Other; Regulatory Affairs Managers; Sales Managers; Security Management Specialists; Security Managers; Shipping, Receiving, and Traffic Clerks; Supply Chain Managers; Sustainability Specialists; Wind Energy Operations Managers; Wind Energy Project Managers; others.

**Skills**—No data available.

**Work Environment:** No data available.

## Job Specialization: Logistics Engineers

**Design and analyze operational solutions for projects such as transportation optimization, network modeling, process and methods analysis, cost containment, capacity enhancement, routing and shipment optimization, and information management.** Propose logistics solutions for customers. Prepare production strategies and conceptual designs for production facilities. Interview key staff or tour facilities to identify efficiency-improvement, cost-reduction, or service-delivery opportunities. Direct the work of logistics analysts. Design plant distribution centers. Develop specifications for equipment, tools, facility layouts, or material-handling systems. Review contractual commitments, customer specifications, or related information to determine logistics and support requirements. Prepare or validate documentation on automated logistics or maintenance-data reporting and management information systems. Identify cost-reduction and process-improvement opportunities. Identify or develop business rules and standard operating procedures to streamline operating processes. Develop metrics, internal analysis tools, or key performance indicators for business units within logistics. Develop and maintain cost estimates, forecasts, or cost models. Determine feasibility of designing new facilities or modifying existing facilities, based on such factors as cost, available space, schedule, technical requirements, and ergonomics. Determine logistics support requirements, such as facility details, staffing needs, and safety or maintenance plans. Conduct logistics studies and analyses, such as time studies, zero-base analyses, rate analyses, network analyses, flow-path analyses, and supply chain analyses. Analyze and interpret logistics data involving customer service, forecasting, procurement, manufacturing, inventory, transportation, or warehousing. Provide logistics technology and information for effective and efficient support of product, equipment, or system manufacturing or service. Provide facility and capacity planning analyses for distribution and transportation functions in logistics. Evaluate effectiveness of current or future logistical processes.

**Education/Training Required:** Bachelor's degree. **Education and Training Programs:** Logistics, Materials, and Supply Chain Management; Operations Management and Supervision; Transportation/Mobility Management. **Knowledge/Courses**—No data available.

**Personality Type:** Investigative-Conventional-Realistic. **Career Clusters:** 04 Business, Management, and Administration; 16 Transportation, Distribution, and Logistics. **Career Pathways:** 4.1 Management; 16.2 Logistics, Planning, and Management Services. **Other Jobs in These Pathways:** Brownfield Redevelopment Specialists and Site Managers; Business Continuity Planners; Business Operations Specialists, All Other; Chief Executives; Chief Sustainability Officers; Compliance Managers; Computer and Information Systems Managers; Construction Managers; Customs Brokers; Energy Auditors; First-Line Supervisors of Office and Administrative Support Workers; General and Operations Managers; Investment Fund Managers; Loss Prevention Managers; Management Analysts; Managers, All Other; Public Relations Specialists; Regulatory Affairs Managers; Sales Managers; Security Management Specialists; Security Managers; Supply Chain Managers; Sustainability Specialists; Wind Energy Operations Managers; Wind Energy Project Managers; others.

**Skills**—No data available.

**Work Environment:** No data available.

## Management Analysts

- ❈ Annual Earnings: $78,160
- ❈ Earnings Growth Potential: High (43.8%)
- ❈ Growth: 23.9%
- ❈ Annual Job Openings: 30,650
- ❈ Self-Employed: 25.8%

**Considerations for Job Outlook:** Organizations are expected to rely increasingly on outside expertise in an effort to maintain competitiveness and improve performance. Keen competition is expected. Opportunities are expected to be best for those who have a graduate degree, specialized expertise, and ability in salesmanship and public relations.

**Conduct organizational studies and evaluations, design systems and procedures, conduct work simplifications and measurement studies, and prepare operations and procedures manuals to assist management in operating more efficiently and effectively. Includes program analysts and management consultants.** Gather and organize information on problems or procedures. Analyze data gathered and develop solutions or alternative methods of proceeding. Confer with personnel concerned to ensure successful functioning of newly implemented systems or procedures. Develop and implement records management program for filing, protection, and retrieval of records and assure compliance with program. Review forms and reports and confer with management and users about format, distribution, and purpose and to identify problems and improvements. Document findings of study and prepare recommendations for implementation of new systems, procedures, or organizational changes. Interview personnel and conduct on-site observation to ascertain unit functions; work performed; and methods, equipment, and personnel used. Prepare manuals and train workers in use of new forms, reports, procedures, or equipment according to organizational policy. Design, evaluate, recommend, and approve changes of forms and reports. Plan study of work problems and procedures, such as organizational change, communications, information flow, integrated production methods, inventory control, or cost analysis. Recommend purchase of storage equipment and design area layout to locate equipment in space available.

**Education/Training Required:** Work experience plus degree. **Education and Training Programs:** Business Administration and Management, General; Business/Commerce, General. **Knowledge/Courses**—Personnel and Human Resources, Clerical, Sales and Marketing, Economics and Accounting, Customer and Personal Service, Administration and Management.

**Personality Type:** Investigative-Enterprising-Conventional. **Career Cluster:** 04 Business, Management, and Administration. **Career Pathway:** 4.1 Management. **Other Jobs in This Pathway:** Administrative Services Managers; Brownfield Redevelopment Specialists and Site Managers; Business Continuity Planners; Business Operations Specialists, All Other; Chief Executives; Chief Sustainability Officers; Compliance Managers; Computer and Information Systems Managers; Construction Managers; Customs Brokers; Energy Auditors; First-Line Supervisors of Office and Administrative Support Workers; General and Operations Managers; Investment Fund Managers; Loss Prevention Managers; Managers, All Other; Public Relations Specialists; Regulatory Affairs Managers; Sales Managers; Security Management Specialists; Security Managers; Supply Chain Managers; Sustainability Specialists; Wind Energy Operations Managers; Wind Energy Project Managers; others.

**Skills**—Operations Analysis, Systems Evaluation, Systems Analysis, Science, Judgment and Decision Making, Management of Material Resources, Writing, Management of Personnel Resources.

**Work Environment:** Indoors; sitting.

## Managers, All Other

- ❈ Annual Earnings: $96,450
- ❈ Earnings Growth Potential: High (48.2%)
- ❈ Growth: 7.3%
- ❈ Annual Job Openings: 29,750
- ❈ Self-Employed: 57.1%

**Considerations for Job Outlook:** About average employment growth is projected.

**This occupation includes all managers not listed separately.** Because this is a highly diverse occupation, no data is available for some information topics.

**Education/Training Required:** Work experience in a related occupation. **Education and Training Program:** Business/Commerce, General.

**Career Clusters:** 03 Arts, Audio/Video Technology, and Communications; 04 Business, Management, and Administration; 07 Government and Public Administration; 09 Hospitality and Tourism; 10 Human Services; 16 Transportation, Distribution, and Logistics. **Career Pathways:** 3.1 Audio and Video Technology and Film; 3.4 Performing Arts; 4.1 Management; 4.2 Business, Financial Management, and Accounting; 7.1 Governance; 7.7 Public

Management and Administration; 9.3 Travel and Tourism; 10.3 Family and Community Services; 16.2 Logistics, Planning, and Management Services. **Other Jobs in These Pathways:** Accountants; Auditors; Bookkeeping, Accounting, and Auditing Clerks; Brownfield Redevelopment Specialists and Site Managers; Business Continuity Planners; Business Operations Specialists, All Other; Childcare Workers; Compliance Managers; Construction Managers; Customs Brokers; Energy Auditors; First-Line Supervisors of Office and Administrative Support Workers; General and Operations Managers; Investment Fund Managers; Loss Prevention Managers; Management Analysts; Nannies; Personal Care Aides; Regulatory Affairs Managers; Security Management Specialists; Security Managers; Supply Chain Managers; Sustainability Specialists; Wind Energy Operations Managers; Wind Energy Project Managers; others.

## Job Specialization: Brownfield Redevelopment Specialists and Site Managers

**Participate in planning and directing cleanup and redevelopment of contaminated properties for reuse. Does not include properties sufficiently contaminated to qualify as Superfund sites.** Review or evaluate environmental remediation project proposals. Review or evaluate designs for contaminant treatment or disposal facilities. Provide training on hazardous material or waste cleanup procedures and technologies. Provide expert witness testimony on issues such as soil, air, or water contamination and associated cleanup measures. Prepare reports or presentations to communicate brownfield redevelopment needs, status, or progress. Negotiate contracts for services or materials needed for environmental remediation. Prepare and submit permit applications for demolition, cleanup, remediation, or construction projects. Maintain records of decisions, actions, and progress related to environmental redevelopment projects. Inspect sites to assess environmental damage or monitor cleanup progress. Plan or implement brownfield redevelopment projects to ensure safety, quality, and compliance with applicable standards or requirements. Identify environmental contamination sources. Estimate costs for environmental cleanup and remediation of land redevelopment projects. Develop or implement plans for revegetation of brownfield sites. Design or implement plans for surface or ground water remediation. Design or implement plans for structural demolition and debris removal. Design or implement measures to improve the water, air, and soil quality of military test sites, abandoned mine land, or other contaminated sites. Design or conduct environmental restoration

studies. Coordinate the disposal of hazardous waste. Coordinate on-site activities for environmental cleanup or remediation projects to ensure compliance with environmental laws, standards, regulations, or other requirements. Conduct quantitative risk assessments for human health, environmental, or other risks. Conduct feasibility or cost-benefit studies for environmental remediation projects.

**Education/Training Required:** Bachelor's degree. **Education and Training Program:** Hazardous Materials Management and Waste Technology/Technician. **Knowledge/Courses**—No data available.

**Personality Type:** No data available. **Career Cluster:** 04 Business, Management, and Administration. **Career Pathways:** 4.1 Management; 4.2 Business, Financial Management, and Accounting. **Other Jobs in These Pathways:** Accountants; Auditors; Billing and Posting Clerks; Bookkeeping, Accounting, and Auditing Clerks; Business Continuity Planners; Business Operations Specialists, All Other; Compliance Managers; Construction Managers; Customs Brokers; Energy Auditors; Financial Managers, Branch or Department; First-Line Supervisors of Office and Administrative Support Workers; General and Operations Managers; Investment Fund Managers; Loss Prevention Managers; Management Analysts; Managers, All Other; Regulatory Affairs Managers; Security Management Specialists; Security Managers; Supply Chain Managers; Sustainability Specialists; Treasurers and Controllers; Wind Energy Operations Managers; Wind Energy Project Managers; others.

**Skills**—No data available.

**Work Environment:** No data available.

## Job Specialization: Compliance Managers

**Plan, direct, or coordinate activities of an organization to ensure compliance with ethical or regulatory standards.** Verify that software technology is in place to adequately provide oversight and monitoring in all required areas. Serve as a confidential point of contact for employees to communicate with management, seek clarification on issues or dilemmas, or report irregularities. Maintain documentation of compliance activities such as complaints received and investigation outcomes. Consult with corporate attorneys as necessary to address difficult legal compliance issues. Discuss emerging compliance issues with management or employees. Collaborate with human resources departments to ensure the implementation of consistent disciplinary action strategies in cases of compliance standard violations. Advise internal management or business partners on the implementation and operation of compliance programs. Review communications such as securities sales advertising to ensure there are no violations of standards or regulations. Provide employee training on compliance related topics, policies, or procedures. Report violations of compliance or regulatory standards to duly authorized enforcement agencies as appropriate or required. Provide assistance to internal and external auditors in compliance reviews. Prepare management reports regarding compliance operations and progress. Oversee internal reporting systems such as corporate compliance hotlines and inform employees about these systems. Monitor compliance systems to ensure their effectiveness. Identify compliance issues that require follow-up or investigation. Keep informed regarding pending industry changes, trends, and best practices and assess the potential impact of these changes on organizational processes. Disseminate written policies and procedures related to compliance activities. File appropriate compliance reports with regulatory agencies. Design or implement improvements in communication, monitoring, or enforcement of compliance standards.

**Education/Training Required:** Work experience plus degree. **Education and Training Program:** Business Administration and Management, General. **Knowledge/Courses**—No data available.

**Personality Type:** Conventional-Enterprising-Realistic. **Career Clusters:** 04 Business, Management, and Administration; 07 Government and Public Administration. **Career Pathways:** 4.1 Management; 4.2 Business, Financial Management, and Accounting; 7.1 Governance. **Other Jobs in These Pathways:** Accountants; Auditors; Billing and Posting Clerks; Bookkeeping, Accounting, and Auditing Clerks; Brownfield Redevelopment Specialists and Site Managers; Business Continuity Planners; Business Operations Specialists, All Other; Construction Managers; Customs Brokers; Energy Auditors; Financial Managers, Branch or Department; First-Line Supervisors of Office and Administrative Support Workers; General and Operations Managers; Investment Fund Managers; Loss Prevention Managers; Management Analysts; Managers, All Other; Regulatory Affairs Managers; Security Management Specialists; Security Managers; Supply Chain Managers; Sustainability Specialists; Treasurers and Controllers; Wind Energy Operations Managers; Wind Energy Project Managers; others.

**Skills**—No data available.

**Work Environment:** No data available.

## Job Specialization: Investment Fund Managers

**Plan, direct, or coordinate investment strategy or operations for a large pool of liquid assets supplied by institutional investors or individual investors.** Prepare for and respond to regulatory inquiries. Verify regulatory compliance of transaction reporting. Hire and evaluate staff. Direct activities of accounting or operations departments. Develop, implement, or monitor security valuation policies. Attend investment briefings or consult financial media to stay abreast of relevant investment markets. Review offering documents or marketing materials to ensure regulatory compliance. Perform or evaluate research, such as detailed company and industry analyses, to inform financial forecasting, decision making, or valuation. Present investment information, such as product risks, fees, and fund performance statistics. Monitor financial or operational performance of individual investments to ensure portfolios meet risk goals. Monitor regulatory or tax law changes to ensure fund compliance or to capitalize on development opportunities. Meet with investors to determine investment goals or to discuss investment strategies. Identify group and individual target investors for a specific fund. Develop, or direct development of, offering documents or marketing materials. Evaluate the potential of new product developments or market opportunities according to factors such as business plans, technologies, and market potential. Develop and implement fund investment policies and strategies. Select and direct the execution of trades. Analyze acquisitions to ensure conformance with strategic goals or regulatory requirements. Manage investment funds to maximize return on client investments. Select specific investments or investment mixes for purchase by an investment fund.

**Education/Training Required:** Work experience plus degree. **Education and Training Program:** Investments and Securities. **Knowledge/Courses**—No data available.

**Personality Type:** Enterprising-Conventional. **Career Cluster:** 04 Business, Management, and Administration. **Career Pathways:** 4.1 Management; 4.2 Business, Financial Management, and Accounting. **Other Jobs in These Pathways:** Accountants; Auditors; Billing and Posting Clerks; Bookkeeping, Accounting, and Auditing Clerks; Brownfield Redevelopment Specialists and Site Managers; Business Continuity Planners; Business Operations Specialists, All Other; Compliance Managers; Construction Managers; Customs Brokers; Energy Auditors; Financial Managers, Branch or Department; First-Line Supervisors of Office and Administrative Support Workers; General and Operations Managers; Loss Prevention Managers; Management

Analysts; Managers, All Other; Regulatory Affairs Managers; Security Management Specialists; Security Managers; Supply Chain Managers; Sustainability Specialists; Treasurers and Controllers; Wind Energy Operations Managers; Wind Energy Project Managers; others.

**Skills**—No data available.

**Work Environment:** No data available.

## Job Specialization: Loss Prevention Managers

**Plan and direct policies, procedures, or systems to prevent the loss of assets. Determine risk exposure or potential liability, and develop risk control measures.** Review loss-prevention exception reports and cash discrepancies to ensure adherence to guidelines. Perform cash audits and deposit investigations to fully account for store cash. Provide recommendations and solutions in crisis situations such as workplace violence, protests, and demonstrations. Monitor and review paperwork procedures and systems to prevent error-related shortages. Maintain databases such as bad check logs, reports on multiple offenders, and alarm activation lists. Investigate or interview individuals suspected of shoplifting or internal theft. Direct installation of covert surveillance equipment, such as security cameras. Advise retail establishments on development of loss-investigation procedures. Visit stores to ensure compliance with company policies and procedures. Verify correct use and maintenance of physical security systems, such as closed-circuit television, merchandise tags, and burglar alarms. Train loss prevention staff, retail managers, or store employees on loss control and prevention measures. Supervise surveillance, detection, or criminal processing related to theft and criminal cases. Recommend improvements in loss prevention programs, staffing, scheduling, or training. Perform or direct inventory investigations in response to shrink results outside of acceptable ranges. Hire or supervise loss-prevention staff. Maintain documentation of all loss prevention activity. Coordinate theft and fraud investigations involving career criminals or organized group activities. Direct loss prevention audit programs including target store audits, maintenance audits, safety audits, or electronic article surveillance (EAS) audits. Develop and maintain partnerships with federal, state, or local law enforcement agencies or members of the retail loss prevention community. Coordinate or conduct internal investigations of problems such as employee theft and violations of corporate loss prevention policies.

**Education/Training Required:** Bachelor's degree. **Education and Training Program:** Security and Loss Prevention Services. **Knowledge/Courses**—No data available.

**Personality Type:** Enterprising-Conventional. **Career Cluster:** 04 Business, Management, and Administration. **Career Pathways:** 4.1 Management; 4.2 Business, Financial Management, and Accounting. **Other Jobs in These Pathways:** Accountants; Auditors; Billing and Posting Clerks; Bookkeeping, Accounting, and Auditing Clerks; Brownfield Redevelopment Specialists and Site Managers; Business Continuity Planners; Business Operations Specialists, All Other; Compliance Managers; Construction Managers; Customs Brokers; Energy Auditors; Financial Managers, Branch or Department; First-Line Supervisors of Office and Administrative Support Workers; General and Operations Managers; Investment Fund Managers; Management Analysts; Managers, All Other; Regulatory Affairs Managers; Security Management Specialists; Security Managers; Supply Chain Managers; Sustainability Specialists; Treasurers and Controllers; Wind Energy Operations Managers; Wind Energy Project Managers; others.

**Skills**—No data available.

**Work Environment:** No data available.

## Job Specialization: Regulatory Affairs Managers

**Plan, direct, or coordinate production activities of an organization to ensure compliance with regulations and standard operating procedures.** Direct the preparation and submission of regulatory agency applications, reports, or correspondence. Review all regulatory agency submission materials to ensure timeliness, accuracy, comprehensiveness, and compliance with regulatory standards. Provide regulatory guidance to departments or development project teams regarding design, development, evaluation, or marketing of products. Formulate or implement regulatory affairs policies and procedures to ensure that regulatory compliance is maintained or enhanced. Manage activities such as audits, regulatory agency inspections, and product recalls. Communicate regulatory information to multiple departments and ensure that information is interpreted correctly. Develop regulatory strategies and implementation plans for the preparation and submission of new products. Provide responses to regulatory agencies regarding product information or issues. Maintain current knowledge of relevant regulations including proposed and final rules. Investigate product complaints and prepare documentation and submissions to appropriate regulatory agencies as necessary. Review materials such as marketing literature and user manuals to ensure that regulatory agency requirements are met. Implement or monitor complaint processing systems to ensure effective and timely resolution of all complaint investigations. Represent organizations before domestic or international regulatory agencies on major policy matters or decisions regarding company products. Oversee documentation efforts to ensure compliance with domestic and international regulations and standards. Participate in the development or implementation of clinical trial protocols. Develop and maintain standard operating procedures or local working practices. Establish regulatory priorities or budgets and allocate resources and workloads. Train staff in regulatory policies or procedures.

**Education/Training Required:** Work experience plus degree. **Education and Training Program:** Business Administration and Management, General. **Knowledge/Courses**—Biology, Medicine and Dentistry, Law and Government, Chemistry, Clerical, Personnel and Human Resources.

**Personality Type:** Enterprising-Conventional. **Career Clusters:** 04 Business, Management, and Administration; 07 Government and Public Administration. **Career Pathways:** 4.1 Management; 4.2 Business, Financial Management, and Accounting; 7.1 Governance; 7.6 Regulation. **Other Jobs in These Pathways:** Accountants; Auditors; Billing and Posting Clerks; Bookkeeping, Accounting, and Auditing Clerks; Brownfield Redevelopment Specialists and Site Managers; Business Continuity Planners; Business Operations Specialists, All Other; Compliance Managers; Construction Managers; Customs Brokers; Energy Auditors; Financial Managers, Branch or Department; First-Line Supervisors of Office and Administrative Support Workers; General and Operations Managers; Investment Fund Managers; Loss Prevention Managers; Management Analysts; Managers, All Other; Security Management Specialists; Security Managers; Supply Chain Managers; Sustainability Specialists; Treasurers and Controllers; Wind Energy Operations Managers; Wind Energy Project Managers; others.

**Skills**—Operations Analysis, Systems Evaluation, Management of Personnel Resources, Systems Analysis, Negotiation, Coordination, Writing, Science.

**Work Environment:** Indoors; sitting.

## Job Specialization: Security Managers

**Direct an organization's security functions, including physical security and safety of employees, facilities, and assets.** Write or review security-related documents, such as incident reports, proposals, and tactical or strategic initiatives. Train subordinate security professionals or other organization members in security rules and procedures. Plan security for special and high-risk events. Review financial reports to ensure efficiency and quality of security operations. Develop budgets for security operations. Order security-related supplies and equipment as needed. Coordinate security operations or activities with public law enforcement, fire and other agencies. Attend meetings, professional seminars, or conferences to keep abreast of changes in executive legislative directives or new technologies impacting security operations. Assist in emergency management and contingency planning. Arrange for or perform executive protection activities. Respond to medical emergencies, bomb threats, fire alarms, or intrusion alarms, following emergency response procedures. Recommend security procedures for security call centers, operations centers, domains, asset classification systems, system acquisition, system development, system maintenance, access control, program models, or reporting tools. Prepare reports or make presentations on internal investigations, losses, or violations of regulations, policies and procedures. Identify, investigate, or resolve security breaches. Monitor security policies, programs or procedures to ensure compliance with internal security policies, licensing requirements, or applicable government security requirements, policies, and directives. Conduct, support, or assist in governmental reviews, internal corporate evaluations, or assessments of the overall effectiveness of the facilities security processes. Conduct physical examinations of property to ensure compliance with security policies and regulations. Communicate security status, updates, and actual or potential problems, using established protocols.

**Education/Training Required:** Work experience plus degree. **Education and Training Program:** Security and Loss Prevention Services. **Knowledge/Courses**—No data available.

**Personality Type:** No data available. **Career Cluster:** 04 Business, Management, and Administration. **Career Pathways:** 4.1 Management; 4.2 Business, Financial Management, and Accounting. **Other Jobs in These Pathways:** Accountants; Auditors; Billing and Posting Clerks; Bookkeeping, Accounting, and Auditing Clerks; Brownfield Redevelopment Specialists and Site Managers; Business Continuity Planners; Business Operations Specialists, All Other; Compliance Managers; Construction Managers; Customs Brokers; Energy Auditors; Financial Managers, Branch or Department; First-Line Supervisors of Office and Administrative Support Workers; General and Operations Managers; Investment Fund Managers; Loss Prevention

Managers; Management Analysts; Managers, All Other; Regulatory Affairs Managers; Security Management Specialists; Supply Chain Managers; Sustainability Specialists; Treasurers and Controllers; Wind Energy Operations Managers; Wind Energy Project Managers; others.

**Skills**—No data available.

**Work Environment:** No data available.

## Job Specialization: Supply Chain Managers

**Direct, or coordinate production, purchasing, warehousing, distribution, or financial forecasting services and activities to limit costs and improve accuracy, customer service and safety. Examine existing procedures and opportunities for streamlining activities to meet product distribution needs. Direct the movement, storage, and processing of inventory.** Select transportation routes to maximize economy by combining shipments and consolidating warehousing and distribution. Diagram supply chain models to help facilitate discussions with customers. Develop material costs forecasts or standard cost lists. Assess appropriate material handling equipment needs and staffing levels to load, unload, move, or store materials. Appraise vendor manufacturing ability through on-site visits and measurements. Negotiate prices and terms with suppliers, vendors, or freight forwarders. Monitor supplier performance to assess ability to meet quality and delivery requirements. Monitor forecasts and quotas to identify changes or to determine their effect on supply chain activities. Meet with suppliers to discuss performance metrics, to provide performance feedback, or to discuss production forecasts or changes. Implement new or improved supply chain processes. Collaborate with other departments, such as procurement, engineering, and quality assurance, to identify or qualify new suppliers. Document physical supply chain processes, such as workflows, cycle times, position responsibilities, and system flows. Develop and implement procedures or systems to evaluate and select suppliers. Design and implement plant warehousing strategies for production materials or finished products. Confer with supply chain planners to forecast demand or create supply plans that ensure availability of materials and products. Define performance metrics for measurement, comparison, or evaluation of supply chain factors such as product cost and quality. Analyze inventories to determine how to increase inventory turns, reduce waste, or optimize customer service. Analyze information about supplier performance and procurement program success. Participate in the coordination

of engineering changes, product line extensions, or new product launches to ensure orderly and timely transitions in material and production flow.

**Education/Training Required:** Work experience plus degree. **Education and Training Program:** Logistics, Materials, and Supply Chain Management. **Knowledge/Courses**—Production and Processing, Transportation, Economics and Accounting, Administration and Management, Geography, Sales and Marketing.

**Personality Type:** Enterprising-Conventional. **Career Clusters:** 04 Business, Management, and Administration; 09 Hospitality and Tourism; 10 Human Services; 16 Transportation, Distribution, and Logistics. **Career Pathways:** 4.1 Management; 4.2 Business, Financial Management, and Accounting; 9.3 Travel and Tourism; 10.3 Family and Community Services; 16.2 Logistics, Planning, and Management Services. **Other Jobs in These Pathways:** Accountants; Auditors; Bookkeeping, Accounting, and Auditing Clerks; Brownfield Redevelopment Specialists and Site Managers; Business Continuity Planners; Business Operations Specialists, All Other; Childcare Workers; Compliance Managers; Construction Managers; Customs Brokers; Energy Auditors; First-Line Supervisors of Office and Administrative Support Workers; General and Operations Managers; Investment Fund Managers; Loss Prevention Managers; Management Analysts; Managers, All Other; Nannies; Personal Care Aides; Regulatory Affairs Managers; Security Management Specialists; Security Managers; Sustainability Specialists; Wind Energy Operations Managers; Wind Energy Project Managers; others.

**Skills**—Management of Material Resources, Management of Financial Resources, Systems Evaluation, Negotiation, Monitoring, Management of Personnel Resources, Systems Analysis, Complex Problem Solving.

**Work Environment:** Indoors; sitting.

## Job Specialization: Wind Energy Operations Managers

**Manage wind field operations, including personnel, maintenance activities, financial activities, and planning.** Train, or coordinate the training of, employees in operations, safety, environmental issues, or technical issues. Track and maintain records for wind operations, such as site performance, downtime events, parts usage, and substation events. Provide technical support to wind field customers, employees, or subcontractors. Manage warranty repair or replacement services. Order parts, tools, or equipment needed to maintain, restore, or improve wind field operations. Maintain operations records, such as work orders, site inspection forms, or other documentation. Negotiate or review and approve wind farm contracts. Recruit or select wind operations employees, contractors, or subcontractors. Monitor and maintain records of daily facility operations. Estimate costs associated with operations, including repairs and preventive maintenance. Establish goals, objectives, or priorities for wind field operations. Develop relationships and communicate with customers, site managers, developers, land owners, authorities, utility representatives, or residents. Develop processes and procedures for wind operations, including transitioning from construction to commercial operations. Prepare wind field operational budgets. Supervise employees or subcontractors to ensure quality of work or adherence to safety regulations or policies. Oversee the maintenance of wind field equipment or structures, such as towers, transformers, electrical collector systems, roadways, and other site assets.

**Education/Training Required:** Work experience plus degree. **Education and Training Program:** Energy Management and Systems Technology/Technician. **Knowledge/Courses**—No data available.

**Personality Type:** No data available. **Career Cluster:** 04 Business, Management, and Administration. **Career Pathways:** 4.1 Management; 4.2 Business, Financial Management, and Accounting. **Other Jobs in These Pathways:** Accountants; Auditors; Billing and Posting Clerks; Bookkeeping, Accounting, and Auditing Clerks; Brownfield Redevelopment Specialists and Site Managers; Business Continuity Planners; Business Operations Specialists, All Other; Compliance Managers; Construction Managers; Customs Brokers; Energy Auditors; Financial Managers, Branch or Department; First-Line Supervisors of Office and Administrative Support Workers; General and Operations Managers; Investment Fund Managers; Loss Prevention Managers; Management Analysts; Managers, All Other; Regulatory Affairs Managers; Security Management Specialists; Security Managers; Supply Chain Managers; Sustainability Specialists; Treasurers and Controllers; Wind Energy Project Managers; others.

**Skills**—No data available.

**Work Environment:** No data available.

## Job Specialization: Wind Energy Project Managers

**Lead or manage the development and evaluation of potential wind energy business opportunities, including environmental studies, permitting, and proposals. May also manage construction of projects.** Supervise the work of subcontractors or consultants to ensure quality and conformance to specifications or budgets. Prepare requests for proposals (RFPs) for wind project construction or equipment acquisition. Manage site assessments or environmental studies for wind fields. Lead or support negotiations involving tax agreements or abatements, power purchase agreements, land use, or interconnection agreements. Update schedules, estimates, forecasts, or budgets for wind projects. Review or evaluate proposals or bids to make recommendations regarding awarding of contracts. Provide verbal or written project status reports to project teams, management, subcontractors, customers, or owners. Review civil design, engineering, or construction technical documentation to ensure compliance with applicable government or industrial codes, standards, requirements, or regulations. Provide technical support for the design, construction, or commissioning of wind farm projects. Prepare wind project documentation, including diagrams or layouts. Manage wind project costs to stay within budget limits. Develop scope of work for wind project functions, such as design, site assessment, environmental studies, surveying, and field support services. Coordinate or direct development, energy assessment, engineering, or construction activities to ensure that wind project needs and objectives are met. Prepare, or assist in the preparation of, applications for environmental, building, or other required permits. Create wind energy project plans, including project scope, goals, tasks, resources, schedules, costs, contingencies, and other project information.

**Education/Training Required:** Work experience plus degree. **Education and Training Program:** Energy Management and Systems Technology/Technician. **Knowledge/Courses**—No data available.

**Personality Type:** No data available. **Career Cluster:** 04 Business, Management, and Administration. **Career Pathways:** 4.1 Management; 4.2 Business, Financial Management, and Accounting. **Other Jobs in These Pathways:** Accountants; Auditors; Billing and Posting Clerks; Bookkeeping, Accounting, and Auditing Clerks; Brownfield Redevelopment Specialists and Site Managers; Business Continuity Planners; Business Operations Specialists, All Other; Compliance Managers; Construction Managers; Customs Brokers; Energy Auditors; Financial Managers,

Branch or Department; First-Line Supervisors of Office and Administrative Support Workers; General and Operations Managers; Investment Fund Managers; Loss Prevention Managers; Management Analysts; Managers, All Other; Regulatory Affairs Managers; Security Management Specialists; Security Managers; Supply Chain Managers; Sustainability Specialists; Treasurers and Controllers; Wind Energy Operations Managers; others.

**Skills**—No data available.

**Work Environment:** No data available.

# Manicurists and Pedicurists

- ❋ Annual Earnings: $19,650
- ❋ Earnings Growth Potential: Very low (16.9%)
- ❋ Growth: 18.8%
- ❋ Annual Job Openings: 2,530
- ❋ Self-Employed: 32.0%

**Considerations for Job Outlook:** A larger population and increasing demand for personal appearance services, especially skin care, are expected to create jobs for these workers. Prospects should be good, especially for job seekers who have formal training.

**Clean and shape customers' fingernails and toenails. May polish or decorate nails.** Clean and sanitize tools and work environment. Schedule client appointments and accept payments. Remove previously applied nail polish, using liquid remover and swabs. Clean customers' nails in soapy water, using swabs, files, and orange sticks. Shape and smooth ends of nails, using scissors, files, and emery boards. Apply undercoat and clear or colored polish onto nails with brush. Advise clients on nail care and use of products and colors. Assess the condition of clients' hands, remove dead skin from the hands, and massage them. Soften nail cuticles with water and oil; push back cuticles, using cuticle knife; and trim cuticles, using scissors or nippers. Brush powder and solvent onto nails and paper forms to maintain nail appearance and to extend nails; then remove forms and shape and smooth nail edges, using rotary abrasive wheel. Maintain supply inventories and records of client services. Treat nails to repair or improve strength and resilience by wrapping or provide treatment to nail biters. Roughen surfaces of fingernails, using abrasive wheel. Promote and sell nail care products. Attach paper forms to tips of customers' fingers to support and shape artificial nails. Polish nails, using powdered polish and buffer. Whiten underside of nails with white paste or pencil. Decorate clients' nails by piercing them or attaching ornaments or designs.

**Education/Training Required:** Postsecondary vocational training. **Education and Training Programs:** Cosmetology/Cosmetologist Training, General; Nail Technician/Specialist and Manicurist Training. **Knowledge/Courses**—Sales and Marketing, Chemistry, Customer and Personal Service.

**Personality Type:** Realistic-Enterprising-Social. **Career Cluster:** 10 Human Services. **Career Pathway:** 10.4 Personal Care Services. **Other Jobs in This Pathway:** Barbers; Embalmers; Funeral Attendants; Funeral Service Managers; Hairdressers, Hairstylists, and Cosmetologists; Laundry and Dry-Cleaning Workers; Makeup Artists, Theatrical and Performance; Pressers, Textile, Garment, and Related Materials; Sewers, Hand; Sewing Machine Operators; Shampooers; Skincare Specialists; Tailors, Dressmakers, and Custom Sewers; Textile Bleaching and Dyeing Machine Operators and Tenders.

**Skills**—Management of Financial Resources.

**Work Environment:** Indoors; sitting; using hands; repetitive motions; contaminants; exposed to disease or infections; hazardous conditions.

# Market Research Analysts and Marketing Specialists

- ❋ Annual Earnings: $60,570
- ❋ Earnings Growth Potential: High (44.9%)
- ❋ Growth: 28.1%
- ❋ Annual Job Openings: 13,730
- ❋ Self-Employed: 6.8%

**Considerations for Job Outlook:** Demand for market research is expected as businesses strive to increase sales and as governments rely on survey research to form public policy. Opportunities should be best for job seekers who have a doctoral degree and strong quantitative skills.

**Research market conditions in local, regional, or national areas to determine potential sales of a product or service. May gather information on competitors, prices, sales, and methods of marketing and distribution. May use survey results to create a marketing campaign based on regional preferences and buying habits.** Collect and analyze data on customer demographics, preferences, needs, and buying habits to identify potential markets and factors affecting product demand. Prepare reports of findings, illustrating data graphically and translating complex findings into written text. Measure and assess customer and employee satisfaction. Forecast and track marketing and sales trends, analyzing collected data. Seek and provide information to help companies determine their position in the marketplace. Measure the effectiveness of marketing, advertising, and communications programs and strategies. Conduct research on consumer opinions and marketing strategies, collaborating with marketing professionals, statisticians, pollsters, and other professionals. Attend staff conferences to provide management with information and proposals concerning the promotion, distribution, design, and pricing of company products or services. Gather data on competitors and analyze their prices, sales, and method of marketing and distribution. Monitor industry statistics and follow trends in trade literature. Devise and evaluate methods and procedures for collecting data, such as surveys, opinion polls, or questionnaires, or arrange to obtain existing data. Develop and implement procedures for identifying advertising needs. Direct trained survey interviewers.

**Education/Training Required:** Bachelor's degree. **Education and Training Programs:** Apparel and Textile Marketing Management; Consumer Merchandising/Retailing Management; International Marketing; Marketing Research; Marketing, Other; Marketing/Marketing Management, General. **Knowledge/Courses**—Sales and Marketing, Clerical, Sociology and Anthropology, Economics and Accounting, Computers and Electronics, Personnel and Human Resources.

**Personality Type:** Investigative-Enterprising-Conventional. **Career Cluster:** 04 Business, Management, and Administration. **Career Pathways:** 4.1 Management; 14.5 Marketing Information Management and Research; 15.2 Science and Mathematics. **Other Jobs in These Pathways:** Brownfield Redevelopment Specialists and Site Managers; Business Continuity Planners; Business Operations Specialists, All Other; Chief Executives; Chief Sustainability Officers; Compliance Managers; Computer and Information Systems Managers; Construction Managers; Customs Brokers; Energy Auditors; First-Line Supervisors of Office and Administrative Support Workers; First-Line Supervisors of Retail Sales Workers; General and Operations Managers; Investment Fund Managers; Loss Prevention Managers; Management Analysts; Managers, All Other; Regulatory Affairs Managers; Sales Managers; Security Management Specialists; Security Managers; Supply Chain Managers; Sustainability Specialists; Wind Energy Operations Managers; Wind Energy Project Managers; others.

**Skills**—Programming, Systems Analysis, Operations Analysis, Systems Evaluation, Reading Comprehension, Management of Financial Resources, Mathematics, Writing.

**Work Environment:** Indoors; sitting.

# Marketing Managers

- ❋ Annual Earnings: $112,800
- ❋ Earnings Growth Potential: High (48.8%)
- ❋ Growth: 12.5%
- ❋ Annual Job Openings: 5,970
- ❋ Self-Employed: 4.1%

**Considerations for Job Outlook:** Job growth is expected to result from companies' need to distinguish their products and services in an increasingly competitive marketplace. Keen competition is expected.

**Determine the demand for products and services offered by firms and their competitors and identify potential customers. Develop pricing strategies with the goal of maximizing firms' profits or shares of the market while ensuring that firms' customers are satisfied. Oversee product development or monitor trends that indicate the need for new products and services.** Formulate, direct, and coordinate marketing activities and policies to promote products and services, working with advertising and promotion managers. Identify, develop, and evaluate marketing strategies, based on knowledge of establishment objectives, market characteristics, and cost and markup factors. Direct the hiring, training, and performance evaluations of marketing and sales staff and oversee their daily activities. Evaluate the financial aspects of product development, such as budgets, expenditures, research and development appropriations, and return-on-investment and profit-loss projections. Develop pricing strategies, balancing firm objectives and customer satisfaction. Compile lists describing product or service offerings. Initiate market research studies and analyze their findings. Use sales forecasting and strategic planning to ensure the sale and profitability of products, lines, or services, analyzing business developments and monitoring market trends. Coordinate and participate in promotional activities and trade shows, working with developers, advertisers, and production managers to market products and services. Consult with buying personnel to gain advice regarding the types of products or services expected to be in demand. Conduct economic and commercial surveys to identify potential markets for products and services. Select products and accessories to be displayed at trade or special production shows. Negotiate contracts with vendors and distributors to manage product distribution, establishing distribution networks and developing distribution strategies. Consult with product development personnel on product specifications such as design, color, and packaging. Advise businesses and other groups on local, national, and international factors affecting the buying and selling of products and services. Confer with legal staff to resolve problems such as copyright infringement and royalty sharing with outside producers and distributors.

**Education/Training Required:** Work experience plus degree. **Education and Training Programs:** Apparel and Textile Marketing Management; Consumer Merchandising/Retailing Management; International Marketing; Marketing Research; Marketing, Other; Marketing/Marketing Management, General. **Knowledge/Courses**—Sales and Marketing, Customer and Personal Service, Personnel and Human Resources, Communications and Media, Economics and Accounting, Sociology and Anthropology.

**Personality Type:** Enterprising-Conventional. **Career Cluster:** 14 Marketing, Sales, and Service. **Career Pathways:** 14.1 Management and Entrepreneurship; 14.2 Professional Sales and Marketing; 14.5 Marketing Information Management and Research. **Other Jobs in These Pathways:** Cashiers; Counter and Rental Clerks; Door-To-Door Sales Workers, News and Street Vendors, and Related Workers; Driver/Sales Workers; Energy Brokers; First-Line Supervisors of Non-Retail Sales Workers; First-Line Supervisors of Retail Sales Workers; Hotel, Motel, and Resort Desk Clerks; Marking Clerks; Online Merchants; Order Fillers, Wholesale and Retail Sales; Parts Salespersons; Property, Real Estate, and Community Association Managers; Real Estate Sales Agents; Reservation and Transportation Ticket Agents and Travel Clerks; Retail Salespersons; Sales and Related Workers, All Other; Sales Managers; Sales Representatives, Services, All Other; Sales Representatives, Wholesale and Manufacturing, Except Technical and Scientific Products; Sales Representatives, Wholesale and Manufacturing, Technical and Scientific Products; Solar Sales Representatives and Assessors; Stock Clerks—Stockroom, Warehouse, or Storage Yard; Stock Clerks, Sales Floor; Telemarketers; others.

**Skills**—Management of Financial Resources, Operations Analysis, Persuasion, Management of Material Resources, Negotiation, Systems Evaluation, Management of Personnel Resources, Systems Analysis.

**Work Environment:** Indoors; sitting.

# Marriage and Family Therapists

* Annual Earnings: $45,720
* Earnings Growth Potential: High (47.8%)
* Growth: 14.5%
* Annual Job Openings: 950
* Self-Employed: 5.9%

**Considerations for Job Outlook:** Increasing demand for services provided by counselors is expected to result in employment growth. But growth will vary by specialty and will be faster for mental health, substance abuse and behavioral disorder, and rehabilitation counselors than for counselors of other specialties. Opportunities should be favorable, particularly in rural areas.

**Diagnose and treat mental and emotional disorders, whether cognitive, affective, or behavioral, within the context of marriage and family systems. Apply psychotherapeutic and family systems theories and techniques in the delivery of professional services to individuals, couples, and families for the purpose of treating such diagnosed nervous and mental disorders.** Ask questions that will help clients identify their feelings and behaviors. Counsel clients on concerns such as unsatisfactory relationships, divorce and separation, child rearing, home management, and financial difficulties. Encourage individuals and family members to develop and use skills and strategies for confronting their problems in a constructive manner. Maintain case files that include activities, progress notes, evaluations, and recommendations. Collect information about clients, using techniques such as testing, interviewing, discussion, and observation. Develop and implement individualized treatment plans addressing family relationship problems. Determine whether clients should be counseled or referred to other specialists in such fields as medicine, psychiatry, and legal aid. Confer with clients in order to develop plans for post-treatment activities. Confer with other counselors to analyze individual cases and to coordinate counseling services. Follow up on results of counseling programs and clients' adjustments to determine effectiveness of programs. Provide instructions to clients on how to obtain help with legal, financial, and other personal issues. Contact doctors, schools, social workers, juvenile counselors, law enforcement personnel, and others to gather information in order to make recommendations to courts for the resolution of child custody or visitation disputes. Provide public education and consultation to other professionals or groups regarding counseling services, issues, and methods. Supervise other counselors, social service staff, and assistants. Provide family counseling and treatment services to inmates participating in substance abuse programs. Write evaluations of parents and children for use by courts deciding divorce and custody cases, testifying in court if necessary.

**Education/Training Required:** Master's degree. **Education and Training Programs:** Clinical Pastoral Counseling/ Patient Counseling; Marriage and Family Therapy/Counseling; Social Work. **Knowledge/Courses**—Therapy and Counseling, Psychology, Philosophy and Theology, Sociology and Anthropology, Medicine and Dentistry, Customer and Personal Service.

**Personality Type:** Social-Artistic-Investigative. **Career Cluster:** 10 Human Services. **Career Pathways:** 10.2 Counseling and Mental Health Services; 10.3 Family and Community Services. **Other Jobs in These Pathways:** Chief Executives; Child, Family, and School Social Workers; Childcare Workers; Clergy; Clinical Psychologists; Counseling Psychologists; Directors, Religious Activities and Education; Eligibility Interviewers, Government Programs; Health Educators; Healthcare Social Workers; Legislators; Managers, All Other; Mental Health and Substance Abuse Social Workers; Mental Health Counselors; Music Directors; Nannies; Personal Care Aides; Probation Officers and Correctional Treatment Specialists; Protective Service Workers, All Other; Recreation Workers; School Psychologists; Social and Community Service Managers; Social Workers, All Other; Substance Abuse and Behavioral Disorder Counselors; Supply Chain Managers; others.

**Skills**—Social Perceptiveness, Science, Operations Analysis, Active Listening, Service Orientation, Systems Evaluation, Systems Analysis, Speaking.

**Work Environment:** Indoors; sitting.

# Massage Therapists

- ❋ Annual Earnings: $34,900
- ❋ Earnings Growth Potential: High (48.5%)
- ❋ Growth: 18.9%
- ❋ Annual Job Openings: 3,950
- ❋ Self-Employed: 57.2%

**Considerations for Job Outlook:** Growing demand for massage services to help improve health and wellness is expected to create jobs for massage therapists. Opportunities for entry-level workers should be good. Job seekers with experience and licensure or certification should have the best prospects.

**Massage customers for hygienic or remedial purposes.** Confer with clients about their medical histories and any problems with stress or pain to determine whether massage would be helpful. Apply finger and hand pressure to specific points of the body. Massage and knead the muscles and soft tissues of the human body to provide courses of treatment for medical conditions and injuries or wellness maintenance. Maintain treatment records. Provide clients with guidance and information about techniques for postural improvement and stretching, strengthening, relaxation, and rehabilitative exercises. Assess clients' soft tissue condition, joint quality and function, muscle strength, and range of motion. Develop and propose client treatment plans that specify which types of massage are to be used. Refer clients to other types of therapists when necessary. Use complementary aids, such as infrared lamps, wet compresses, ice, and whirlpool baths, to promote clients' recovery, relaxation, and well-being. Treat clients in own offices or travel to clients' offices and homes. Consult with other health-care professionals such as physiotherapists, chiropractors, physicians, and psychologists to develop treatment plans for clients. Prepare and blend oils and apply the blends to clients' skin.

**Education/Training Required:** Postsecondary vocational training. **Education and Training Programs:** Asian Bodywork Therapy; Massage Therapy/Therapeutic Massage; Somatic Bodywork; Somatic Bodywork and Related Therapeutic Services, Other. **Knowledge/Courses**—Therapy and Counseling, Psychology, Sales and Marketing, Medicine and Dentistry, Chemistry, English Language.

**Personality Type:** Social-Realistic. **Career Cluster:** 08 Health Science. **Career Pathway:** 8.1 Therapeutic Services. **Other Jobs in This Pathway:** Clinical Psychologists; Community and Social Service Specialists, All Other; Counseling Psychologists; Dental Assistants; Dental Hygienists; Dentists, General; Health Technologists and Technicians, All Other; Healthcare Support Workers, All Other; Home Health Aides; Licensed Practical and Licensed Vocational Nurses; Low Vision Therapists, Orientation and Mobility Specialists, and Vision Rehabilitation Therapists; Medical and Clinical Laboratory Technicians; Medical and Health Services Managers; Medical Scientists, Except Epidemiologists; Medical Secretaries; Occupational Therapists; Ophthalmic Medical Technologists; Pharmacists; Pharmacy Technicians; Radiologic Technologists; School Psychologists; Social and Human Service Assistants; Speech-Language Pathologists; Speech-Language Pathology Assistants; Substance Abuse and Behavioral Disorder Counselors; others.

**Skills**—Operations Analysis, Science, Persuasion, Service Orientation, Critical Thinking, Active Listening, Speaking, Social Perceptiveness.

**Work Environment:** Indoors; standing; using hands; repetitive motions.

# Materials Engineers

- ❋ Annual Earnings: $83,120
- ❋ Earnings Growth Potential: Medium (37.8%)
- ❋ Growth: 9.3%
- ❋ Annual Job Openings: 810
- ❋ Self-Employed: 0.0%

**Considerations for Job Outlook:** Marine engineers and naval architects are expected to have employment growth of 6 percent from 2008–2018, slower than the average for all occupations. Continued demand for naval vessels and recreational small craft should more than offset the long-term decline in the domestic design and construction of large oceangoing vessels. Good prospects are expected for marine engineers and naval architects because of growth in employment, the need to replace workers who retire or take other jobs, and the limited number of students pursuing careers in this occupation.

**Evaluate materials and develop machinery and processes to manufacture materials for use in products that must meet specialized design and performance specifications. Develop new uses for known materials. Includes those working with composite materials or specializing in one type of material, such as graphite, metal and metal alloys, ceramics and glass, plastics and polymers, and naturally occurring materials.** Analyze product failure data and laboratory test results in order to determine causes of problems and develop solutions. Monitor material performance and evaluate material deterioration. Supervise the work of technologists, technicians, and other engineers and scientists. Design and direct the testing and/or control of processing procedures. Evaluate technical specifications and economic factors relating to process or product design objectives. Conduct or supervise tests on raw materials or finished products in order to ensure their quality. Perform managerial functions such as preparing proposals and budgets, analyzing labor costs, and writing reports. Solve problems in a number of engineering fields, such as mechanical, chemical, electrical, civil, nuclear, and aerospace. Plan and evaluate new projects, consulting with other engineers and corporate executives as necessary. Review new product plans and make recommendations for material selection based on design objectives, such as strength, weight, heat resistance, electrical conductivity, and cost. Design processing plants and equipment. Modify properties of metal alloys, using thermal and mechanical treatments. Guide technical staff engaged in developing materials for specific uses in projected products or devices. Plan and implement laboratory operations for the purpose of developing material and fabrication procedures that meet cost, product specification, and performance standards. Determine appropriate methods for fabricating and joining materials. Conduct training sessions on new material products, applications, or manufacturing methods for customers and their employees. Supervise production and testing processes in industrial settings such as metal refining facilities, smelting or foundry operations, or non-metallic materials production operations. Write for technical magazines, journals, and trade association publications. Replicate the characteristics of materials and their components with computers.

**Education/Training Required:** Bachelor's degree. **Education and Training Programs:** Ceramic Sciences and Engineering; Materials Engineering; Metallurgical Engineering. **Knowledge/Courses**—Engineering and Technology, Chemistry, Physics, Design, Mathematics, Mechanical.

**Personality Type:** Investigative-Realistic-Enterprising. **Career Cluster:** 15 Science, Technology, Engineering, and Mathematics. **Career Pathway:** 15.1 Engineering and Technology. **Other Jobs in This Pathway:** Architectural and Engineering Managers; Automotive Engineers; Biochemical Engineers; Biofuels/Biodiesel Technology and Product Development Managers; Civil Engineers; Cost Estimators; Electrical Engineers; Electronics Engineers, Except Computer; Energy Engineers; Engineers, All Other; Fuel Cell Engineers; Human Factors Engineers and Ergonomists; Industrial Engineers; Manufacturing Engineers; Mechanical Engineers; Mechatronics Engineers; Microsystems Engineers; Nanosystems Engineers; Photonics Engineers; Radio Frequency Identification Device Specialists; Robotics Engineers; Solar Energy Systems Engineers; Transportation Engineers; Validation Engineers; Wind Energy Engineers; others.

**Skills**—Science, Operations Analysis, Mathematics, Technology Design, Active Learning, Systems Analysis, Systems Evaluation, Management of Financial Resources.

**Work Environment:** Indoors; sitting; noise; contaminants.

# Materials Scientists

- ❋ Annual Earnings: $84,720
- ❋ Earnings Growth Potential: High (45.9%)
- ❋ Growth: 11.9%
- ❋ Annual Job Openings: 440
- ❋ Self-Employed: 0.3%

**Considerations for Job Outlook:** Manufacturing companies' outsourcing of research and development and testing operations is expected to limit employment growth for these scientists.

**Research and study the structures and chemical properties of various natural and manmade materials, including metals, alloys, rubber, ceramics, semiconductors, polymers, and glass. Determine ways to strengthen or combine materials or develop new materials with new or specific properties for use in a variety of products and applications.** Plan laboratory experiments to confirm feasibility of processes and techniques used in the production of materials having special characteristics. Confer with customers in order to determine how materials can be tailored to suit their needs. Conduct research into the structures and properties of materials such as metals, alloys, polymers, and ceramics to obtain information that could be used to develop new products or enhance existing ones. Prepare reports of materials study findings for the use of other scientists and requestors. Devise testing methods to evaluate the effects of various conditions on particular materials. Determine ways to strengthen or combine materials or develop new materials with new or specific properties for use in a variety of products and applications. Recommend materials for reliable performance in various environments. Test individual parts and products to ensure that manufacturer and governmental quality and safety standards are met. Visit suppliers of materials or users of products to gather specific information. Research methods of processing, forming, and firing materials to develop such products as ceramic fillings for teeth, unbreakable dinner plates, and telescope lenses. Study the nature, structure, and physical properties of metals and their alloys and their responses to applied forces. Monitor production processes to ensure that equipment is used efficiently and that projects are completed within appropriate time frames and budgets. Test material samples for tolerance under tension, compression, and shear to determine the cause of metal failures. Test metals to determine whether they meet specifications of mechanical strength; strength-weight ratio; ductility; magnetic and electrical properties; and resistance to abrasion, corrosion, heat, and cold. Teach in colleges and universities.

**Education/Training Required:** Bachelor's degree. **Education and Training Program:** Materials Science. **Knowledge/Courses**—Chemistry, Engineering and Technology, Mathematics, Physics, Production and Processing, Administration and Management.

**Personality Type:** Investigative-Realistic. **Career Cluster:** 15 Science, Technology, Engineering, and Mathematics. **Career Pathway:** 15.2 Science and Mathematics. **Other Jobs in This Pathway:** Architectural and Engineering Managers; Biochemists and Biophysicists; Biofuels/Biodiesel Technology and Product Development Managers; Bioinformatics Scientists; Biological Scientists, All Other; Biologists; Biostatisticians; Chemists; Clinical Data Managers; Clinical Research Coordinators; Community and Social Service Specialists, All Other; Dietitians and Nutritionists; Education, Training, and Library Workers, All Other; Geneticists; Geoscientists, Except Hydrologists and Geographers; Medical Scientists, Except Epidemiologists; Molecular and Cellular Biologists; Natural Sciences Managers; Operations Research Analysts; Physical Scientists, All Other; Social Scientists and Related Workers, All Other; Statisticians; Survey Researchers; Transportation Planners; Water Resource Specialists; others.

**Skills**—Science, Operations Analysis, Reading Comprehension, Writing, Mathematics, Complex Problem Solving, Active Learning, Critical Thinking.

**Work Environment:** Indoors; sitting; noise; hazardous conditions.

# Mathematical Science Teachers, Postsecondary

- ❋ Annual Earnings: $65,710
- ❋ Earnings Growth Potential: High (46.4%)
- ❋ Growth: 15.1%
- ❋ Annual Job Openings: 1,000
- ❋ Self-Employed: 0.2%

**Considerations for Job Outlook:** Enrollments in postsecondary institutions are expected to continue rising as more people attend college and as workers return to school to update their skills. Opportunities for part-time or temporary positions should be favorable, but significant competition exists for tenure-track positions.

**Teach courses pertaining to mathematical concepts, statistics, and actuarial science and to the application of original and standardized mathematical techniques in**

solving specific problems and situations. Evaluate and grade students' classwork, assignments, and papers. Compile, administer, and grade examinations or assign this work to others. Prepare and deliver lectures to undergraduate and/or graduate students on topics such as linear algebra, differential equations, and discrete mathematics. Prepare course materials such as syllabi, homework assignments, and handouts. Maintain student attendance records, grades, and other required records. Maintain regularly scheduled office hours to advise and assist students. Plan, evaluate, and revise curricula, course content, and course materials and methods of instruction. Initiate, facilitate, and moderate classroom discussions. Select and obtain materials and supplies such as textbooks. Keep abreast of developments in their field by reading current literature, talking with colleagues, and participating in professional conferences. Advise students on academic and vocational curricula and on career issues. Collaborate with colleagues to address teaching and research issues. Serve on academic or administrative committees that deal with institutional policies, departmental matters, and academic issues. Participate in student recruitment, registration, and placement activities. Perform administrative duties such as serving as department head. Conduct research in a particular field of knowledge and publish findings in books, professional journals, and/or electronic media. Supervise undergraduate and/or graduate teaching, internship, and research work. Act as advisers to student organizations. Participate in campus and community events. Write grant proposals to procure external research funding. Compile bibliographies of specialized materials for outside reading assignments. Provide professional consulting services to government and/or industry.

**Education/Training Required:** Doctoral degree. **Education and Training Programs:** Algebra and Number Theory; Analysis and Functional Analysis; Applied Mathematics, General; Business Statistics; Geometry/Geometric Analysis; Logic; Mathematical Statistics and Probability; Mathematics and Statistics, Other; Mathematics, General; Mathematics, Other; Statistics, General; Topology and Foundations. **Knowledge/Courses**—Mathematics, Education and Training, Physics, Computers and Electronics, English Language, Communications and Media.

**Personality Type:** Social-Investigative-Artistic. **Career Cluster:** 15 Science, Technology, Engineering, and Mathematics. **Career Pathway:** 15.2 Science and Mathematics. **Other Jobs in This Pathway:** Architectural and Engineering Managers; Biochemists and Biophysicists; Biofuels/Biodiesel Technology and Product Development Managers; Bioinformatics Scientists; Biological Scientists, All Other; Biologists; Biostatisticians; Chemists; Clinical Data Managers; Clinical Research Coordinators; Community and Social Service Specialists, All Other; Dietitians and Nutritionists; Education, Training, and Library Workers, All Other; Geneticists; Geoscientists, Except Hydrologists and Geographers; Medical Scientists, Except Epidemiologists; Molecular and Cellular Biologists; Natural Sciences Managers; Operations Research Analysts; Physical Scientists, All Other; Social Scientists and Related Workers, All Other; Statisticians; Survey Researchers; Transportation Planners; Water Resource Specialists; 37 other postsecondary teaching occupations; others.

**Skills**—Mathematics, Writing, Learning Strategies, Instructing, Reading Comprehension, Systems Evaluation, Active Learning, Speaking.

**Work Environment:** Indoors; sitting; standing.

# Mathematicians

- ❋ Annual Earnings: $99,380
- ❋ Earnings Growth Potential: High (46.8%)
- ❋ Growth: 22.4%
- ❋ Annual Job Openings: 150
- ❋ Self-Employed: 0.0%

**Considerations for Job Outlook:** Technological advances are expected to expand applications of mathematics, leading to employment growth of mathematicians. Competition is expected to be keen. Jobseekers with a strong background in math and a related discipline should have the best prospects.

**Conduct research in fundamental mathematics or in application of mathematical techniques to science, management, and other fields. Solve or direct solutions to problems in various fields by mathematical methods.** Apply mathematical theories and techniques to the solution of practical problems in business, engineering, the sciences, or other fields. Develop computational methods for solving problems that occur in areas of science and engineering or that come from applications in business or industry. Maintain knowledge in the field by reading professional journals, talking with other mathematicians, and attending professional conferences. Perform computations and apply methods of numerical analysis to data. Develop mathematical or statistical models of phenomena to be used for analysis or for computational simulation. Assemble sets of assumptions and explore the consequences of each set. Address the relationships of quantities, magnitudes, and forms through the use of numbers and symbols. Develop new principles and new relationships between existing mathematical principles to advance mathematical science. Design, analyze, and decipher encryption systems designed to transmit military, political, financial, or law-enforcement-related information in code. Conduct research to extend mathematical knowledge in traditional areas, such as algebra, geometry, probability, and logic.

**Education/Training Required:** Doctoral degree. **Education and Training Programs:** Algebra and Number Theory; Analysis and Functional Analysis; Applied Mathematics, General; Applied Mathematics, Other; Computational Mathematics; Geometry/Geometric Analysis; Logic; Mathematical Statistics and Probability; Mathematics and Statistics, Other; Mathematics, General; Mathematics, Other; Topology and Foundations. **Knowledge/Courses**—Mathematics, Physics, Computers and Electronics, Engineering and Technology, English Language.

**Personality Type:** Investigative-Conventional-Artistic. **Career Cluster:** 15 Science, Technology, Engineering, and Mathematics. **Career Pathway:** 15.2 Science and Mathematics. **Other Jobs in This Pathway:** Architectural and Engineering Managers; Biochemists and Biophysicists; Biofuels/Biodiesel Technology and Product Development Managers; Bioinformatics Scientists; Biological Scientists, All Other; Biologists; Biostatisticians; Chemists; Clinical Data Managers; Clinical Research Coordinators; Community and Social Service Specialists, All Other; Dietitians and Nutritionists; Education, Training, and Library Workers, All Other; Geneticists; Geoscientists, Except Hydrologists and Geographers; Medical Scientists, Except Epidemiologists; Molecular and Cellular Biologists; Natural Sciences Managers; Operations Research Analysts; Physical Scientists, All Other; Social Scientists and Related Workers, All Other; Statisticians; Survey Researchers; Transportation Planners; Water Resource Specialists; others.

**Skills**—Mathematics, Science, Active Learning, Programming, Reading Comprehension, Complex Problem Solving, Critical Thinking, Systems Analysis.

**Work Environment:** Indoors; sitting.

# Mechanical Engineers

- ❋ Annual Earnings: $78,160
- ❋ Earnings Growth Potential: Low (35.3%)
- ❋ Growth: 6.0%
- ❋ Annual Job Openings: 7,570
- ❋ Self-Employed: 2.3%

**Considerations for Job Outlook:** Materials engineers are expected to have employment growth of 9 percent from

2008–2018, about as fast as the average for all occupations. Growth should result from increased use of composite and other nontraditional materials developed through biotechnology and nanotechnology research. As manufacturing firms contract for their materials engineering needs, most employment growth is expected in professional, scientific, and technical services industries.

**Perform engineering duties in planning and designing tools, engines, machines, and other mechanically functioning equipment. Oversee installation, operation, maintenance, and repair of such equipment as centralized heat, gas, water, and steam systems.** Read and interpret blueprints, technical drawings, schematics, and computer-generated reports. Confer with engineers and other personnel to implement operating procedures, resolve system malfunctions, and provide technical information. Research and analyze customer design proposals, specifications, manuals, and other data to evaluate the feasibility, cost, and maintenance requirements of designs or applications. Specify system components or direct modification of products to ensure conformance with engineering design and performance specifications. Research, design, evaluate, install, operate, and maintain mechanical products, equipment, systems, and processes to meet requirements, applying knowledge of engineering principles. Investigate equipment failures and difficulties to diagnose faulty operation and to make recommendations to maintenance crew. Assist drafters in developing the structural design of products, using drafting tools, computer-assisted design (CAD), or drafting equipment and software. Provide feedback to design engineers on customer problems and needs. Oversee installation, operation, maintenance, and repair to ensure that machines and equipment are installed and functioning according to specifications. Conduct research that tests and analyzes the feasibility, design, operation, and performance of equipment, components, and systems. Recommend design modifications to eliminate machine or system malfunctions. Develop and test models of alternate designs and processing methods to assess feasibility, operating condition effects, possible new applications, and necessity of modification. Develop, coordinate, and monitor all aspects of production, including selection of manufacturing methods, fabrication, and operation of product designs. Estimate costs and submit bids for engineering, construction, or extraction projects and prepare contract documents.

**Education/Training Required:** Bachelor's degree. **Education and Training Program:** Mechanical Engineering. **Knowledge/Courses**—Design, Engineering and Technology, Physics, Mechanical, Production and Processing, Mathematics.

**Personality Type:** Investigative-Realistic-Conventional. **Career Cluster:** 15 Science, Technology, Engineering, and Mathematics. **Career Pathway:** 15.1 Engineering and Technology. **Other Jobs in This Pathway:** Architectural and Engineering Managers; Automotive Engineers; Biochemical Engineers; Biofuels/Biodiesel Technology and Product Development Managers; Civil Engineers; Cost Estimators; Education, Training, and Library Workers, All Other; Electrical Engineers; Electronics Engineers, Except Computer; Energy Engineers; Engineers, All Other; Fuel Cell Engineers; Human Factors Engineers and Ergonomists; Industrial Engineers; Manufacturing Engineers; Mechatronics Engineers; Microsystems Engineers; Nanosystems Engineers; Photonics Engineers; Radio Frequency Identification Device Specialists; Robotics Engineers; Solar Energy Systems Engineers; Transportation Engineers; Validation Engineers; Wind Energy Engineers; others.

**Skills**—Technology Design, Science, Mathematics, Installation, Operations Analysis, Programming, Quality Control Analysis, Troubleshooting.

**Work Environment:** Indoors; sitting; noise.

## Job Specialization: Automotive Engineers

**Develop new or improved designs for vehicle structural members, engines, transmissions and other vehicle systems, using computer-assisted design technology. Direct building, modification, and testing of vehicle and components.** Read current literature, attend meetings or conferences, and talk with colleagues to stay abreast of new technology and competitive products. Establish production or quality control standards. Prepare and present technical or project status reports. Develop or implement operating methods and procedures. Write, review, or maintain engineering documentation. Conduct research studies to develop new concepts in the field of automotive engineering. Coordinate production activities with other functional units such as procurement, maintenance, and quality control. Provide technical direction to other engineers or engineering support personnel. Perform failure, variation, or root cause analyses. Develop or integrate control feature requirements. Develop engineering specifications and cost estimates for automotive design concepts. Develop calibration methodologies, test methodologies, or tools. Conduct automotive design reviews. Calibrate vehicle systems, including control algorithms and other software systems. Build models for algorithm and control feature verification testing. Alter or modify designs to obtain specified

functional and operational performance. Design or analyze automobile systems in areas such as aerodynamics, alternate fuels, ergonomics, hybrid power, brakes, transmissions, steering, calibration, safety, and diagnostics. Conduct or direct system-level automotive testing. Design control systems or algorithms for purposes such as automotive energy management, emissions management, and increased operational safety or performance.

**Education/Training Required:** Bachelor's degree. **Education and Training Program:** Mechanical Engineering. **Knowledge/Courses**—No data available.

**Personality Type:** No data available. **Career Cluster:** 15 Science, Technology, Engineering, and Mathematics. **Career Pathway:** 15.1 Engineering and Technology. **Other Jobs in This Pathway:** Architectural and Engineering Managers; Biochemical Engineers; Biofuels/Biodiesel Technology and Product Development Managers; Civil Engineers; Cost Estimators; Education, Training, and Library Workers, All Other; Electrical Engineers; Electronics Engineers, Except Computer; Energy Engineers; Engineers, All Other; Fuel Cell Engineers; Human Factors Engineers and Ergonomists; Industrial Engineers; Manufacturing Engineers; Mechanical Engineers; Mechatronics Engineers; Microsystems Engineers; Nanosystems Engineers; Photonics Engineers; Radio Frequency Identification Device Specialists; Robotics Engineers; Solar Energy Systems Engineers; Transportation Engineers; Validation Engineers; Wind Energy Engineers; others.

**Skills**—No data available.

**Work Environment:** No data available.

## Job Specialization: Fuel Cell Engineers

**Design, evaluate, modify, and construct fuel cell components and systems for transportation, stationary, or portable applications.** Write technical reports or proposals related to engineering projects. Read current literature, attend meetings or conferences, and talk with colleagues to stay abreast of new technology and competitive products. Prepare test stations, instrumentation, or data acquisition systems for use in specific tests. Plan or implement cost reduction or product improvement projects in collaboration with other engineers, suppliers, support personnel, or customers. Coordinate engineering or test schedules with departments outside engineering, such as manufacturing. Validate design of fuel cells, fuel cell components, or fuel cell systems. Authorize the release of parts or subsystems for production. Simulate or model fuel cell, motor, or other system information using simulation software programs. Recommend or implement changes to fuel cell system design. Provide technical consultation or direction related to the development or production of fuel cell systems. Plan or conduct experiments to validate new materials, optimize startup protocols, reduce conditioning time, or examine contaminant tolerance. Manage hybrid system architecture, including sizing of components such as fuel cells, energy storage units, and electric drives, for fuel cell battery hybrids. Integrate electric drive subsystems with other vehicle systems to optimize performance or mitigate faults. Identify and define the vehicle and system integration challenges for fuel cell vehicles. Fabricate prototypes of fuel cell components, assemblies, stacks, or systems. Develop fuel cell materials and fuel cell test equipment. Conduct post-service or failure analyses, using electromechanical diagnostic principles and procedures. Design or implement fuel cell testing or development programs. Conduct fuel cell testing projects, using fuel cell test stations, analytical instruments, or electrochemical diagnostics, such as cyclic voltammetry, impedance spectroscopy, and hydrogen pumps.

**Education/Training Required:** Bachelor's degree. **Education and Training Program:** Mechanical Engineering. **Knowledge/Courses**—No data available.

**Personality Type:** No data available. **Career Cluster:** 15 Science, Technology, Engineering, and Mathematics. **Career Pathway:** 15.1 Engineering and Technology. **Other Jobs in This Pathway:** Architectural and Engineering Managers; Automotive Engineers; Biochemical Engineers; Biofuels/Biodiesel Technology and Product Development Managers; Civil Engineers; Cost Estimators; Education, Training, and Library Workers, All Other; Electrical Engineers; Electronics Engineers, Except Computer; Energy Engineers; Engineers, All Other; Human Factors Engineers and Ergonomists; Industrial Engineers; Manufacturing Engineers; Mechanical Engineers; Mechatronics Engineers; Microsystems Engineers; Nanosystems Engineers; Photonics Engineers; Radio Frequency Identification Device Specialists; Robotics Engineers; Solar Energy Systems Engineers; Transportation Engineers; Validation Engineers; Wind Energy Engineers; others.

**Skills**—No data available.

**Work Environment:** No data available.

# Medical and Clinical Laboratory Technicians

- ❋ Annual Earnings: $36,280
- ❋ Earnings Growth Potential: Low (33.3%)
- ❋ Growth: 16.1%
- ❋ Annual Job Openings: 5,460
- ❋ Self-Employed: 0.2%

**Considerations for Job Outlook:** Employment of these workers is expected to rise as the volume of laboratory tests continues to increase with population growth and the development of new tests. Excellent opportunities are expected.

**Perform routine medical laboratory tests for the diagnosis, treatment, and prevention of disease. May work under the supervision of a medical technologist.** Conduct chemical analyses of bodily fluids, such as blood and urine, using microscope or automatic analyzer to detect abnormalities or diseases, and enter findings into computer. Set up, adjust, maintain, and clean medical laboratory equipment. Analyze the results of tests and experiments to ensure conformity to specifications, using special mechanical and electrical devices. Analyze and record test data to issue reports that use charts, graphs and narratives. Conduct blood tests for transfusion purposes and perform blood counts. Perform medical research to further control and cure disease. Obtain specimens, cultivating, isolating, and identifying microorganisms for analysis. Examine cells stained with dye to locate abnormalities. Collect blood or tissue samples from patients, observing principles of asepsis to obtain blood sample. Consult with a pathologist to determine a final diagnosis when abnormal cells are found. Inoculate fertilized eggs, broths, or other bacteriological media with organisms. Cut, stain, and mount tissue samples for examination by pathologists. Supervise and instruct other technicians and laboratory assistants. Prepare standard volumetric solutions and reagents to be combined with samples, following standardized formulas or experimental procedures. Prepare vaccines and serums by standard laboratory methods, testing for virus inactivity and sterility. Test raw materials, processes, and finished products to determine quality and quantity of materials or characteristics of a substance.

**Education/Training Required:** Associate degree. **Education and Training Programs:** Blood Bank Technology Specialist Training; Clinical/Medical Laboratory Assistant Training; Clinical/Medical Laboratory Technician; Hematology Technology/Technician; Histologic Technician Training. **Knowledge/Courses**—Chemistry, Medicine and

M

Dentistry, Biology, Mechanical, Computers and Electronics, Production and Processing.

**Personality Type:** Realistic-Investigative-Conventional. **Career Cluster:** 08 Health Science. **Career Pathways:** 8.1 Therapeutic Services; 8.2 Diagnostics Services. **Other Jobs in These Pathways:** Clinical Psychologists; Counseling Psychologists; Cytogenetic Technologists; Cytotechnologists; Dental Assistants; Dental Hygienists; Dentists, General; Emergency Medical Technicians and Paramedics; Endoscopy Technicians; Healthcare Support Workers, All Other; Histotechnologists and Histologic Technicians; Home Health Aides; Licensed Practical and Licensed Vocational Nurses; Massage Therapists; Medical and Clinical Laboratory Technologists; Medical and Health Services Managers; Medical Assistants; Medical Secretaries; Pharmacists; Pharmacy Technicians; Radiologic Technologists; School Psychologists; Social and Human Service Assistants; Speech-Language Pathologists; Speech-Language Pathology Assistants; others.

**Skills**—Science, Equipment Maintenance, Equipment Selection, Troubleshooting, Repairing, Operation and Control, Quality Control Analysis, Operation Monitoring.

**Work Environment:** Indoors; standing; walking and running; using hands; repetitive motions; noise; contaminants; exposed to disease or infections; hazardous conditions.

# Medical and Clinical Laboratory Technologists

- ❋ Annual Earnings: $56,130
- ❋ Earnings Growth Potential: Low (30.9%)
- ❋ Growth: 11.9%
- ❋ Annual Job Openings: 5,330
- ❋ Self-Employed: 0.2%

**Considerations for Job Outlook:** Employment of these workers is expected to rise as the volume of laboratory tests continues to increase with population growth and the development of new tests. Excellent opportunities are expected.

**Perform complex medical laboratory tests for diagnosis, treatment, and prevention of disease. May train or supervise staff.** Conduct chemical analysis of bodily fluids, including blood, urine, and spinal fluid, to determine presence of normal and abnormal components. Analyze laboratory findings to check the accuracy of the results. Enter data from analysis of medical tests and clinical results into computer for storage. Operate, calibrate, and maintain equipment used in quantitative and qualitative analysis, such as spectrophotometers, calorimeters, flame photometers, and computer-controlled analyzers. Establish and monitor quality assurance programs and activities to ensure the accuracy of laboratory results. Set up, clean, and maintain laboratory equipment. Provide technical information about test results to physicians, family members, and researchers. Supervise, train, and direct lab assistants, medical and clinical laboratory technicians and technologists, and other medical laboratory workers engaged in laboratory testing. Collect and study blood samples to determine the number of cells, their morphology, or their blood group, blood type, and compatibility for transfusion purposes, using microscopic techniques. Analyze samples of biological material for chemical content or reaction. Cultivate, isolate, and assist in identifying microbial organisms, and perform various tests on these microorganisms. Obtain, cut, stain, and mount biological material on slides for microscopic study and diagnosis, following standard laboratory procedures. Select and prepare specimen and media for cell culture, using aseptic technique and knowledge of medium components and cell requirements. Develop, standardize, evaluate, and modify procedures, techniques, and tests used in the analysis of specimens and in medical laboratory experiments. Harvest cell cultures at optimum time based on knowledge of cell cycle differences and culture conditions. Conduct medical research under direction of microbiologist or biochemist.

**Education/Training Required:** Bachelor's degree. **Education and Training Programs:** Clinical Laboratory Science/ Medical Technology/Technologist; Clinical/Medical Laboratory Science and Allied Professions, Other; Cytogenetics/Genetics/Clinical Genetics Technology/Technologist; Cytotechnology/Cytotechnologist; Histologic Technology/ Histotechnologist; Renal/Dialysis Technologist/Technician. **Knowledge/Courses**—Biology, Chemistry, Medicine and Dentistry, Mechanical, Clerical, Mathematics.

**Personality Type:** Investigative-Realistic-Conventional. **Career Cluster:** 08 Health Science. **Career Pathway:** 8.2 Diagnostics Services. **Other Jobs in This Pathway:** Ambulance Drivers and Attendants, Except Emergency Medical Technicians; Anesthesiologist Assistants; Cardiovascular Technologists and Technicians; Cytogenetic Technologists; Cytotechnologists; Diagnostic Medical Sonographers; Emergency Medical Technicians and Paramedics; Endoscopy Technicians; Health Diagnosing and Treating Practitioners, All Other; Health Technologists and Technicians, All Other; Healthcare Practitioners and Technical Workers, All Other; Histotechnologists and Histologic Technicians; Medical and Clinical Laboratory Technicians; Medical and Health Services Managers; Medical Assistants;

Medical Equipment Preparers; Neurodiagnostic Technologists; Nuclear Medicine Technologists; Ophthalmic Laboratory Technicians; Physical Scientists, All Other; Physician Assistants; Radiologic Technicians; Radiologic Technologists; Surgical Technologists; Veterinary Assistants and Laboratory Animal Caretakers; others.

**Skills**—Science, Equipment Selection, Equipment Maintenance, Quality Control Analysis, Programming, Operation Monitoring, Troubleshooting, Operation and Control.

**Work Environment:** Indoors; standing; using hands; repetitive motions; noise; contaminants; exposed to disease or infections; hazardous conditions.

## Job Specialization: Cytogenetic Technologists

**Analyze chromosomes found in biological specimens such as amniotic fluids, bone marrow, and blood to aid in the study, diagnosis, or treatment of genetic diseases.** Develop and implement training programs for trainees, medical students, resident physicians or post-doctoral fellows. Stain slides to make chromosomes visible for microscopy. Summarize test results and report to appropriate authorities. Select or prepare specimens and media for cell cultures using aseptic techniques, knowledge of medium components, or cell nutritional requirements. Select banding methods to permit identification of chromosome pairs. Identify appropriate methods of specimen collection, preservation, or transport. Prepare slides of cell cultures following standard procedures. Select appropriate methods of preparation and storage of media to maintain potential of hydrogen (pH), sterility, or ability to support growth. Harvest cell cultures using substances such as mitotic arrestants, cell releasing agents, and cell fixatives. Create chromosome images using computer imaging systems. Determine optimal time sequences and methods for manual or robotic cell harvests. Examine chromosomes found in biological specimens to detect abnormalities. Recognize and report abnormalities in the color, size, shape, composition, or pattern of cells. Communicate test results or technical information to patients, physicians, family members, or researchers. Prepare biological specimens such as amniotic fluids, bone marrow, tumors, chorionic villi, and blood, for chromosome examinations. Count numbers of chromosomes and identify the structural abnormalities by viewing culture slides through microscopes, light microscopes, or photomicroscopes. Arrange and attach chromosomes in numbered pairs on karyotype charts, using standard genetics laboratory practices and nomenclature, to identify normal or abnormal chromosomes. Analyze chromosomes found in biological specimens to aid diagnoses and treatments for genetic diseases such as congenital birth defects, fertility problems, and hematological disorders. Input details of specimens into logs or computer systems.

**Education/Training Required:** Bachelor's degree. **Education and Training Programs:** Clinical Laboratory Science/Medical Technology/Technologist; Cytogenetics/Genetics/Clinical Genetics Technology/Technologist. **Knowledge/Courses**—Biology, Chemistry, Medicine and Dentistry, Education and Training.

**Personality Type:** Investigative-Realistic-Conventional. **Career Cluster:** 08 Health Science. **Career Pathway:** 8.2 Diagnostics Services. **Other Jobs in This Pathway:** Ambulance Drivers and Attendants, Except Emergency Medical Technicians; Anesthesiologist Assistants; Cardiovascular Technologists and Technicians; Cytotechnologists; Diagnostic Medical Sonographers; Emergency Medical Technicians and Paramedics; Endoscopy Technicians; Health Diagnosing and Treating Practitioners, All Other; Health Technologists and Technicians, All Other; Healthcare Practitioners and Technical Workers, All Other; Histotechnologists and Histologic Technicians; Medical and Clinical Laboratory Technicians; Medical and Clinical Laboratory Technologists; Medical and Health Services Managers; Medical Assistants; Medical Equipment Preparers; Neurodiagnostic Technologists; Nuclear Medicine Technologists; Ophthalmic Laboratory Technicians; Physical Scientists, All Other; Physician Assistants; Radiologic Technicians; Radiologic Technologists; Surgical Technologists; Veterinary Assistants and Laboratory Animal Caretakers; others.

**Skills**—Science, Reading Comprehension, Writing, Active Learning, Speaking, Mathematics, Instructing, Active Listening.

**Work Environment:** Indoors; sitting; using hands; repetitive motions; contaminants; exposed to disease or infections; hazardous conditions.

## Job Specialization: Cytotechnologists

**Stain, mount, and study cells to detect evidence of cancer, hormonal abnormalities, and other pathological conditions following established standards and practices.** Examine cell samples to detect abnormalities in the color, shape, or size of cellular components and patterns. Examine specimens using microscopes to evaluate specimen quality. Prepare and analyze samples, such as Papanicolaou (PAP) smear body fluids and fine needle aspirations

(FNAs), to detect abnormal conditions. Provide patient clinical data or microscopic findings to assist pathologists in the preparation of pathology reports. Assist pathologists or other physicians to collect cell samples such as by fine needle aspiration (FNA) biopsies. Examine specimens to detect abnormal hormone conditions. Document specimens by verifying patients' and specimens' information. Maintain effective laboratory operations by adhering to standards of specimen collection, preparation, or laboratory safety. Perform karyotyping or organizing of chromosomes according to standardized ideograms. Prepare cell samples by applying special staining techniques, such as chromosomal staining, to differentiate cells or cell components. Submit slides with abnormal cell structures to pathologists for further examination. Adjust, maintain, or repair laboratory equipment such as microscopes. Assign tasks or coordinate task assignments to ensure adequate performance of laboratory activities. Attend continuing education programs that address laboratory issues.

**Education/Training Required:** Bachelor's degree. **Education and Training Programs:** Clinical Laboratory Science/ Medical Technology/Technologist; Cytotechnology/Cytotechnologist. **Knowledge/Courses**—Biology, Medicine and Dentistry, Chemistry, Clerical, Law and Government.

**Personality Type:** Investigative-Realistic. **Career Cluster:** 08 Health Science. **Career Pathway:** 8.2 Diagnostics Services. **Other Jobs in This Pathway:** Ambulance Drivers and Attendants, Except Emergency Medical Technicians; Anesthesiologist Assistants; Cardiovascular Technologists and Technicians; Cytogenetic Technologists; Diagnostic Medical Sonographers; Emergency Medical Technicians and Paramedics; Endoscopy Technicians; Health Diagnosing and Treating Practitioners, All Other; Health Technologists and Technicians, All Other; Healthcare Practitioners and Technical Workers, All Other; Histotechnologists and Histologic Technicians; Medical and Clinical Laboratory Technicians; Medical and Clinical Laboratory Technologists; Medical and Health Services Managers; Medical Assistants; Medical Equipment Preparers; Neurodiagnostic Technologists; Nuclear Medicine Technologists; Ophthalmic Laboratory Technicians; Physical Scientists, All Other; Physician Assistants; Radiologic Technicians; Radiologic Technologists; Surgical Technologists; Veterinary Assistants and Laboratory Animal Caretakers; others.

**Skills**—Science, Mathematics, Reading Comprehension, Writing, Operation Monitoring, Judgment and Decision Making, Learning Strategies, Instructing.

**Work Environment:** Indoors; sitting; using hands; repetitive motions; contaminants; exposed to disease or infections; hazardous conditions.

# Job Specialization: Histotechnologists and Histologic Technicians

**Prepare histologic slides from tissue sections for microscopic examination and diagnosis by pathologists. May assist in research studies.** Cut sections of body tissues for microscopic examination using microtomes. Embed tissue specimens into paraffin wax blocks or infiltrate tissue specimens with wax. Freeze tissue specimens. Mount tissue specimens on glass slides. Stain tissue specimens with dyes or other chemicals to make cell details visible under microscopes. Examine slides under microscopes to ensure tissue preparation meets laboratory requirements. Identify tissue structures or cell components to be used in the diagnosis, prevention, or treatment of diseases. Operate computerized laboratory equipment to dehydrate, decalcify, or microincinerate tissue samples. Perform electron microscopy or mass spectrometry to analyze specimens. Perform procedures associated with histochemistry to prepare specimens for immunofluorescence or microscopy. Maintain laboratory equipment such as microscopes, mass spectrometers, microtomes, immunostainers, tissue processors, embedding centers, and water baths. Prepare or use prepared tissue specimens for teaching, research or diagnostic purposes. Supervise histology laboratory activities. Teach students or other staff.

**Education/Training Required:** Associate degree. **Education and Training Programs:** Clinical Laboratory Science/ Medical Technology/Technologist; Clinical/Medical Laboratory Science and Allied Professions, Other; Cytogenetics/Genetics/Clinical Genetics Technology/Technologist; Cytotechnology/Cytotechnologist; Histologic Technology/ Histotechnologist; Renal/Dialysis Technologist/Technician. **Knowledge/Courses**—Biology, Chemistry, Medicine and Dentistry, Production and Processing, Mechanical, Education and Training.

**Personality Type:** Realistic-Investigative-Conventional. **Career Cluster:** 08 Health Science. **Career Pathway:** 8.2 Diagnostics Services. **Other Jobs in This Pathway:** Ambulance Drivers and Attendants, Except Emergency Medical Technicians; Anesthesiologist Assistants; Cardiovascular Technologists and Technicians; Cytogenetic Technologists; Cytotechnologists; Diagnostic Medical Sonographers; Emergency Medical Technicians and Paramedics; Endoscopy Technicians; Health Diagnosing and Treating

Practitioners, All Other; Health Technologists and Technicians, All Other; Healthcare Practitioners and Technical Workers, All Other; Medical and Clinical Laboratory Technicians; Medical and Clinical Laboratory Technologists; Medical and Health Services Managers; Medical Assistants; Medical Equipment Preparers; Neurodiagnostic Technologists; Nuclear Medicine Technologists; Ophthalmic Laboratory Technicians; Physical Scientists, All Other; Physician Assistants; Radiologic Technicians; Radiologic Technologists; Surgical Technologists; Veterinary Assistants and Laboratory Animal Caretakers; others.

**Skills**—Science, Equipment Maintenance, Equipment Selection, Repairing, Operation and Control, Troubleshooting, Mathematics, Operation Monitoring.

**Work Environment:** Indoors; sitting; using hands; repetitive motions; contaminants; exposed to disease or infections; hazardous conditions.

# Medical and Health Services Managers

- ❋ Annual Earnings: $84,270
- ❋ Earnings Growth Potential: Medium (39.1%)
- ❋ Growth: 16.0%
- ❋ Annual Job Openings: 9,940
- ❋ Self-Employed: 6.0%

**Considerations for Job Outlook:** The health-care industry is expected to continue growing and diversifying, requiring managers increasingly to run business operations. Opportunities should be good, especially for jobseekers who have work experience in health care and strong business management skills.

**Plan, direct, or coordinate medicine and health services in hospitals, clinics, managed care organizations, public health agencies, or similar organizations.** Conduct and administer fiscal operations, including accounting, planning budgets, authorizing expenditures, establishing rates for services, and coordinating financial reporting. Direct, supervise, and evaluate work activities of medical, nursing, technical, clerical, service, maintenance, and other personnel. Maintain communication between governing boards, medical staff, and department heads by attending board meetings and coordinating interdepartmental functioning. Review and analyze facility activities and data to aid planning and cash and risk management and to improve service utilization. Plan, implement, and administer programs and services in a health-care or medical facility, including personnel administration, training, and coordination of medical, nursing, and physical plant staff. Direct or conduct recruitment, hiring, and training of personnel. Establish work schedules and assignments for staff, according to workload, space, and equipment availability. Maintain awareness of advances in medicine, computerized diagnostic and treatment equipment, data processing technology, government regulations, health insurance changes, and financing options. Monitor the use of diagnostic services, inpatient beds, facilities, and staff to ensure effective use of resources and assess the need for additional staff, equipment, and services. Develop and maintain computerized record management systems to store and process data such as personnel activities and information and to produce reports. Establish and evaluate objectives and evaluative operational criteria for units they manage. Prepare activity reports to inform management of the status and implementation plans of programs, services, and quality initiatives. Inspect facilities and recommend building or equipment modifications to ensure emergency readiness and compliance with access, safety, and sanitation regulations. Develop and implement organizational policies and procedures for the facility or medical unit.

**Education/Training Required:** Work experience plus degree. **Education and Training Programs:** Community Health and Preventive Medicine; Health and Medical Administrative Services, Other; Health Information/Medical Records Administration/Administrator; Health Services Administration; Health Unit Manager/Ward Supervisor Training; Health/Health Care Administration/Management; Hospital and Health Care Facilities Administration/Management; Public Health, General. **Knowledge/Courses**—Economics and Accounting, Personnel and Human Resources, Administration and Management, Sales and Marketing, Medicine and Dentistry, Law and Government.

**Personality Type:** Enterprising-Conventional-Social. **Career Cluster:** 08 Health Science. **Career Pathways:** 8.1 Therapeutic Services; 8.2 Diagnostics Services; 8.3 Health Informatics. **Other Jobs in These Pathways:** Cytogenetic Technologists; Cytotechnologists; Dental Assistants; Dental Hygienists; Emergency Medical Technicians and Paramedics; Endoscopy Technicians; Engineers, All Other; Executive Secretaries and Executive Administrative Assistants; First-Line Supervisors of Office and Administrative Support Workers; Healthcare Support Workers, All Other; Histotechnologists and Histologic Technicians; Home Health Aides; Licensed Practical and Licensed Vocational Nurses;

Medical and Clinical Laboratory Technologists; Medical Assistants; Medical Records and Health Information Technicians; Medical Secretaries; Pharmacists; Pharmacy Technicians; Physical Therapists; Public Relations Specialists; Radiologic Technologists; Receptionists and Information Clerks; Social and Human Service Assistants; Speech-Language Pathology Assistants; others.

**Skills**—Management of Financial Resources, Operations Analysis, Management of Material Resources, Science, Management of Personnel Resources, Systems Evaluation, Coordination, Time Management.

**Work Environment:** Indoors; sitting; exposed to disease or infections.

# Medical Assistants

- ❋ Annual Earnings: $28,860
- ❋ Earnings Growth Potential: Low (27.9%)
- ❋ Growth: 33.9%
- ❋ Annual Job Openings: 21,780
- ❋ Self-Employed: 0.0%

**Considerations for Job Outlook:** Technological advances in medicine and the aging of the population will create demand for health care, and doctors are expected to hire more assistants in response. Prospects should be excellent, especially for job seekers with certification.

**Perform administrative and certain clinical duties under the direction of physicians. Administrative duties may include scheduling appointments, maintaining medical records, billing, and coding for insurance purposes. Clinical duties may include taking and recording vital signs and medical histories, preparing patients for examination, drawing blood, and administering medications as directed by physician.** Record patients' medical history, vital statistics, and information such as test results in medical records. Prepare treatment rooms for patient examinations, keeping the rooms neat and clean. Interview patients to obtain medical information and measure their vital signs, weights, and heights. Authorize drug refills and provide prescription information to pharmacies. Clean and sterilize instruments and dispose of contaminated supplies. Prepare and administer medications as directed by a physician. Show patients to examination rooms and prepare them for the physician. Explain treatment procedures, medications, diets, and physicians' instructions to patients. Help physicians examine and treat patients, handing them instruments

and materials or performing such tasks as giving injections or removing sutures. Collect blood, tissue, or other laboratory specimens, log the specimens, and prepare them for testing. Perform routine laboratory tests and sample analyses. Contact medical facilities or departments to schedule patients for tests or admission. Operate X-ray, electrocardiogram (EKG), and other equipment to administer routine diagnostic tests. Change dressings on wounds. Set up medical laboratory equipment. Perform general office duties such as answering telephones, taking dictation, or completing insurance forms. Greet and log in patients arriving at office or clinic. Schedule appointments for patients. Inventory and order medical, lab, or office supplies and equipment. Keep financial records and perform other bookkeeping duties, such as handling credit and collections and mailing monthly statements to patients.

**Education/Training Required:** Moderate-term on-the-job training. **Education and Training Programs:** Allied Health and Medical Assisting Services, Other; Anesthesiologist Assistant Training; Chiropractic Assistant/Technician Training; Medical Administrative/Executive Assistant and Medical Secretary Training; Medical Insurance Coding Specialist/Coder Training; Medical Office Assistant/Specialist Training; Medical Office Management/Administration; Medical Reception/Receptionist; Medical/Clinical Assistant Training; Ophthalmic Technician/Technologist Training; Optometric Technician/Assistant Training; Orthoptics/Orthoptist. **Knowledge/Courses**—Medicine and Dentistry, Clerical, Psychology, Therapy and Counseling, Customer and Personal Service, Public Safety and Security.

**Personality Type:** Social-Conventional-Realistic. **Career Cluster:** 08 Health Science. **Career Pathways:** 8.2 Diagnostics Services; 8.3 Health Informatics. **Other Jobs in These Pathways:** Clinical Psychologists; Cytogenetic Technologists; Cytotechnologists; Editors; Emergency Medical Technicians and Paramedics; Endoscopy Technicians; Engineers, All Other; Executive Secretaries and Executive Administrative Assistants; First-Line Supervisors of Office and Administrative Support Workers; Health Technologists and Technicians, All Other; Histotechnologists and Histologic Technicians; Medical and Clinical Laboratory Technicians; Medical and Clinical Laboratory Technologists; Medical and Health Services Managers; Medical Records and Health Information Technicians; Medical Secretaries; Medical Transcriptionists; Mental Health Counselors; Physical Therapists; Public Relations Specialists; Radiologic Technologists; Receptionists and Information Clerks; Rehabilitation Counselors; Substance Abuse and Behavioral Disorder Counselors; Surgical Technologists; others.

**Skills**—Service Orientation, Active Listening, Science, Speaking, Social Perceptiveness, Negotiation, Operation Monitoring, Monitoring.

**Work Environment:** Indoors; standing; walking and running; using hands; repetitive motions; exposed to disease or infections.

# Medical Equipment Repairers

- ❋ Annual Earnings: $44,490
- ❋ Earnings Growth Potential: High (41.5%)
- ❋ Growth: 27.2%
- ❋ Annual Job Openings: 2,320
- ❋ Self-Employed: 16.4%

**Considerations for Job Outlook:** An increased demand for health-care services and the growing complexity of medical equipment are projected to result in greater need for these repairers. Excellent job prospects are expected. Job seekers who have an associate degree should have the best prospects.

**Test, adjust, or repair biomedical or electromedical equipment.** Inspect and test malfunctioning medical and related equipment following manufacturers' specifications, using test and analysis instruments. Examine medical equipment and facility's structural environment and check for proper use of equipment to protect patients and staff from electrical or mechanical hazards and to ensure compliance with safety regulations. Disassemble malfunctioning equipment and remove, repair, and replace defective parts such as motors, clutches, or transformers. Keep records of maintenance, repair, and required updates of equipment. Perform preventive maintenance or service such as cleaning, lubricating, and adjusting equipment. Test and calibrate components and equipment, following manufacturers' manuals and troubleshooting techniques and using hand tools, power tools, and measuring devices. Explain and demonstrate correct operation and preventive maintenance of medical equipment to personnel. Study technical manuals and attend training sessions provided by equipment manufacturers to maintain current knowledge. Plan and carry out work assignments, using blueprints, schematic drawings, technical manuals, wiring diagrams, and liquid and air flow sheets, following prescribed regulations, directives, and other instructions as required. Solder loose connections, using soldering iron. Test, evaluate, and classify excess or in-use medical equipment and determine serviceability, condition, and disposition in accordance with regulations. Research catalogs and repair part lists to locate sources for repair parts, requisitioning parts and recording their receipt.

Evaluate technical specifications to identify equipment and systems best suited for intended use and possible purchase based on specifications, user needs, and technical requirements. Contribute expertise to develop medical maintenance standard operating procedures.

**Education/Training Required:** Associate degree. **Education and Training Program:** Biomedical Technology/Technician. **Knowledge/Courses**—Mechanical, Engineering and Technology, Physics, Telecommunications, Computers and Electronics, Chemistry.

**Personality Type:** Realistic-Investigative-Conventional. **Career Cluster:** 13 Manufacturing. **Career Pathway:** 13.3 Maintenance, Installation, and Repair. **Other Jobs in This Pathway:** Aircraft Mechanics and Service Technicians; Automotive Specialty Technicians; Biological Technicians; Civil Engineering Technicians; Computer, Automated Teller, and Office Machine Repairers; Electrical and Electronic Equipment Assemblers; Electrical and Electronics Repairers, Commercial and Industrial Equipment; Electrical Engineering Technicians; Electrical Engineering Technologists; Electromechanical Engineering Technologists; Electronics Engineering Technicians; Electronics Engineering Technologists; Engineering Technicians, Except Drafters, All Other; Fuel Cell Technicians; Helpers—Installation, Maintenance, and Repair Workers; Industrial Engineering Technologists; Industrial Machinery Mechanics; Installation, Maintenance, and Repair Workers, All Other; Manufacturing Engineering Technologists; Manufacturing Production Technicians; Mapping Technicians; Mechanical Engineering Technologists; Mobile Heavy Equipment Mechanics, Except Engines; Telecommunications Line Installers and Repairers; Tire Repairers and Changers; others.

**Skills**—Equipment Maintenance, Repairing, Troubleshooting, Equipment Selection, Quality Control Analysis, Operation and Control, Installation, Operation Monitoring.

**Work Environment:** Indoors; standing; using hands; noise; bright or inadequate lighting; contaminants; cramped work space; exposed to disease or infections; hazardous conditions; hazardous equipment; minor burns, cuts, bites, or stings.

# Medical Records and Health Information Technicians

❋ Annual Earnings: $32,350
❋ Earnings Growth Potential: Low (34.3%)
❋ Growth: 20.3%
❋ Annual Job Openings: 7,030
❋ Self-Employed: 0.0%

**Considerations for Job Outlook:** Employment of these workers is expected to grow as the number of elderly—a demographic group with a higher incidence of injury and illness—increases. Job prospects should be best for technicians who have strong skills in technology and computer software.

**Compile, process, and maintain medical records of hospital and clinic patients in a manner consistent with medical, administrative, ethical, legal, and regulatory requirements of the heath-care system.** Protect the security of medical records to ensure that confidentiality is maintained. Review records for completeness, accuracy, and compliance with regulations. Retrieve patient medical records for physicians, technicians, or other medical personnel. Release information to persons and agencies according to regulations. Plan, develop, maintain, and operate a variety of health record indexes and storage and retrieval systems to collect, classify, store, and analyze information. Enter data such as demographic characteristics, history and extent of disease, diagnostic procedures, and treatment into computer. Process and prepare business and government forms. Compile and maintain patients' medical records to document condition and treatment and to provide data for research or cost control and care improvement efforts. Process patient admission and discharge documents. Assign the patient to diagnosis-related groups (DRGs), using appropriate computer software. Transcribe medical reports. Identify, compile, abstract, and code patient data, using standard classification systems. Resolve or clarify codes and diagnoses with conflicting, missing, or unclear information by consulting with doctors or others or by participating in the coding team's regular meetings. Compile medical care and census data for statistical reports on diseases treated, surgeries performed, or use of hospital beds. Post medical insurance billings. Train medical records staff. Prepare statistical reports, narrative reports, and graphic presentations of information such as tumor registry data for use by hospital staff, researchers, or other users. Manage the department and supervise clerical workers, directing and controlling activities of personnel in the medical records department.

Develop in-service educational materials. Consult classification manuals to locate information about disease processes.

**Education/Training Required:** Associate degree. **Education and Training Programs:** Health Information/Medical Records Technology/Technician; Medical Insurance Coding Specialist/Coder Training. **Knowledge/Courses**—Clerical, Law and Government, Customer and Personal Service.

**Personality Type:** Conventional-Enterprising. **Career Cluster:** 08 Health Science. **Career Pathway:** 8.3 Health Informatics. **Other Jobs in This Pathway:** Clinical Psychologists; Dental Laboratory Technicians; Editors; Engineers, All Other; Executive Secretaries and Executive Administrative Assistants; Fine Artists, Including Painters, Sculptors, and Illustrators; First-Line Supervisors of Office and Administrative Support Workers; Health Educators; Medical and Health Services Managers; Medical Appliance Technicians; Medical Assistants; Medical Secretaries; Medical Transcriptionists; Mental Health Counselors; Occupational Health and Safety Specialists; Occupational Health and Safety Technicians; Physical Therapists; Psychiatric Aides; Psychiatric Technicians; Public Relations Specialists; Receptionists and Information Clerks; Recreational Therapists; Rehabilitation Counselors; Substance Abuse and Behavioral Disorder Counselors; Therapists, All Other; others.

**Skills**—None met the criteria.

**Work Environment:** Indoors; sitting; using hands; repetitive motions; exposed to disease or infections.

# Medical Scientists, Except Epidemiologists

❋ Annual Earnings: $76,700
❋ Earnings Growth Potential: High (45.8%)
❋ Growth: 40.4%
❋ Annual Job Openings: 6,620
❋ Self-Employed: 2.5%

**Considerations for Job Outlook:** New discoveries in biological and medical science are expected to create strong employment growth for these workers. Medical scientists with both doctoral and medical degrees should have the best opportunities.

**Conduct research dealing with the understanding of human diseases and the improvement of human health. Engage in clinical investigation or other research, production, technical writing, or related activities.** Conduct research to develop methodologies, instrumentation, and procedures for medical application, analyzing data and presenting findings. Plan and direct studies to investigate human or animal disease, preventive methods, and treatments for disease. Follow strict safety procedures when handling toxic materials to avoid contamination. Evaluate effects of drugs, gases, pesticides, parasites, and microorganisms at various levels. Teach principles of medicine and medical and laboratory procedures to physicians, residents, students, and technicians. Prepare and analyze organ, tissue, and cell samples to identify toxicity, bacteria, or microorganisms or to study cell structure. Standardize drug dosages, methods of immunization, and procedures for manufacture of drugs and medicinal compounds. Investigate cause, progress, life cycle, or mode of transmission of diseases or parasites. Confer with health department, industry personnel, physicians, and others to develop health safety standards and public health improvement programs. Study animal and human health and physiological processes. Consult with and advise physicians, educators, researchers, and others regarding medical applications of physics, biology, and chemistry. Use equipment such as atomic absorption spectrometers, electron microscopes, flow cytometers, and chromatography systems.

**Education/Training Required:** Doctoral degree. **Education and Training Programs:** Anatomy; Biochemistry; Biomedical Sciences, General; Biophysics; Biostatistics; Cardiovascular Science; Cell Physiology; Cell/Cellular Biology and Histology; Endocrinology; Environmental Toxicology; Epidemiology; Exercise Physiology; Human/Medical Genetics; Immunology; Medical Microbiology and Bacteriology; Medical Science; Molecular Biology; Molecular Pharmacology; Molecular Physiology; Molecular Toxicology; Neuropharmacology; Oncology and Cancer Biology; Pathology/Experimental Pathology; Pharmacology; Pharmacology and Toxicology; Pharmacology and Toxicology, Other; Physiology, General; Physiology, Pathology, and Related Sciences, Other; Reproductive Biology; Toxicology; Vision Science/Physiological Optics. **Knowledge/Courses**—Biology, Medicine and Dentistry, Chemistry, Communications and Media, Personnel and Human Resources, Mathematics.

**Personality Type:** Investigative-Realistic-Artistic. **Career Clusters:** 08 Health Science; 15 Science, Technology, Engineering, and Mathematics. **Career Pathways:** 8.1 Therapeutic Services; 15.2 Science and Mathematics. **Other Jobs in These Pathways:** Architectural and Engineering Managers; Biofuels/Biodiesel Technology and Product Development Managers; Clinical Psychologists; Community and Social Service Specialists, All Other; Counseling Psychologists; Dental Assistants; Dental Hygienists; Dentists, General;

Education, Training, and Library Workers, All Other; Healthcare Support Workers, All Other; Home Health Aides; Licensed Practical and Licensed Vocational Nurses; Low Vision Therapists, Orientation and Mobility Specialists, and Vision Rehabilitation Therapists; Massage Therapists; Medical and Clinical Laboratory Technicians; Medical and Health Services Managers; Medical Secretaries; Occupational Therapists; Pharmacists; Pharmacy Technicians; Radiologic Technologists; School Psychologists; Social and Human Service Assistants; Speech-Language Pathologists; Speech-Language Pathology Assistants; others.

**Skills**—Science, Operations Analysis, Reading Comprehension, Mathematics, Systems Evaluation, Instructing, Complex Problem Solving, Systems Analysis.

**Work Environment:** Indoors; sitting; using hands.

# Medical Secretaries

- ❋ Annual Earnings: $30,530
- ❋ Earnings Growth Potential: Low (30.5%)
- ❋ Growth: 26.6%
- ❋ Annual Job Openings: 18,900
- ❋ Self-Employed: 1.4%

**Considerations for Job Outlook:** Projected employment growth varies by occupational specialty. Faster-than-average growth is expected for medical secretaries and legal secretaries; average growth for executive secretaries and administrative assistants; and slower than average growth for secretaries other than legal, medical, or executive, who account for most of the workers in these specialties. Many opportunities are expected.

**Perform secretarial duties, using specific knowledge of medical terminology and hospital, clinical, or laboratory procedures.** Answer telephones and direct calls to appropriate staff. Schedule and confirm patient diagnostic appointments, surgeries, and medical consultations. Greet visitors, ascertain purpose of visit, and direct them to appropriate staff. Operate office equipment, such as voice mail messaging systems, and use word processing, spreadsheet, and other software applications to prepare reports, invoices, financial statements, letters, case histories, and medical records. Complete insurance and other claim forms. Interview patients to complete documents, case histories, and forms such as intake and insurance forms. Receive and route messages and documents such as laboratory results to appropriate staff. Compile and record medical charts, reports, and correspondence, using typewriter or personal computer. Transmit correspondence and medical records by mail, e-mail, or fax. Maintain medical records, technical library documents, and correspondence files. Perform various clerical and administrative functions, such as ordering and maintaining an inventory of supplies. Perform bookkeeping duties, such as credits and collections, preparing and sending financial statements and bills, and keeping financial records. Transcribe recorded messages and practitioners' diagnoses and recommendations into patients' medical records. Arrange hospital admissions for patients. Prepare correspondence and assist physicians or medical scientists with preparation of reports, speeches, articles, and conference proceedings.

**Education/Training Required:** Moderate-term on-the-job training. **Education and Training Programs:** Medical Administrative/Executive Assistant and Medical Secretary Training; Medical Insurance Specialist/Medical Biller Training; Medical Office Assistant/Specialist Training. **Knowledge/Courses**—Clerical, Medicine and Dentistry, Customer and Personal Service, Computers and Electronics, Economics and Accounting.

**Personality Type:** Conventional-Social. **Career Cluster:** 08 Health Science. **Career Pathways:** 8.1 Therapeutic Services; 8.3 Health Informatics. **Other Jobs in These Pathways:** Clinical Psychologists; Counseling Psychologists; Dental Assistants; Dental Hygienists; Editors; Engineers, All Other; Executive Secretaries and Executive Administrative Assistants; First-Line Supervisors of Office and Administrative Support Workers; Healthcare Support Workers, All Other; Home Health Aides; Licensed Practical and Licensed Vocational Nurses; Medical and Clinical Laboratory Technicians; Medical and Health Services Managers; Medical Assistants; Medical Records and Health Information Technicians; Pharmacists; Pharmacy Technicians; Physical Therapists; Public Relations Specialists; Radiologic Technologists; Receptionists and Information Clerks; Rehabilitation Counselors; School Psychologists; Social and Human Service Assistants; Speech-Language Pathology Assistants; others.

**Skills**—Service Orientation, Active Listening, Speaking.

**Work Environment:** Indoors; sitting; repetitive motions; exposed to disease or infections.

# Meeting, Convention, and Event Planners

* Annual Earnings: $45,260
* Earnings Growth Potential: Medium (40.1%)
* Growth: 15.6%
* Annual Job Openings: 2,140
* Self-Employed: 5.9%

**Considerations for Job Outlook:** Increased globalization is expected to heighten demand for face-to-face meetings, contributing to employment growth of the workers who plan such meetings. Opportunities should be best for job seekers who have a bachelor's degree and some related experience.

**Coordinate activities of staff and convention personnel to make arrangements for group meetings and conventions.** Monitor event activities to ensure compliance with applicable regulations and laws, satisfaction of participants, and resolution of any problems that arise. Confer with staffs at chosen event sites to coordinate details. Inspect event facilities to ensure that they conform to customer requirements. Coordinate services for events, such as accommodation and transportation for participants, facilities, catering, signage, displays, special needs requirements, printing, and event security. Consult with customers to determine objectives and requirements for events such as meetings, conferences, and conventions. Meet with sponsors and organizing committees to plan scope and format of events, to establish and monitor budgets, or to review administrative procedures and event progress. Review event bills for accuracy, and approve payments. Evaluate and select providers of services according to customer requirements. Arrange the availability of audio-visual equipment, transportation, displays, and other event needs. Plan and develop programs, agendas, budgets, and services according to customer requirements. Negotiate contracts with such service providers and suppliers as hotels, convention centers, and speakers. Maintain records of event aspects, including financial details. Conduct post-event evaluations to determine how future events could be improved. Organize registration of event participants. Hire, train, and supervise volunteers and support staff required for events. Read trade publications, attend seminars, and consult with other meeting professionals to keep abreast of meeting management standards and trends. Direct administrative details such as financial operations, dissemination of promotional materials, and responses to inquiries. Promote conference, convention, and trade show services by performing tasks such as meeting with professional and trade associations and producing brochures and other publications. Develop event topics and choose featured speakers.

**Education/Training Required:** Bachelor's degree. **Education and Training Program:** Selling Skills and Sales Operations. **Knowledge/Courses**—Sales and Marketing, Clerical, Customer and Personal Service, English Language, Economics and Accounting, Administration and Management.

**Personality Type:** Enterprising-Conventional-Social. **Career Cluster:** 14 Marketing, Sales, and Service. **Career Pathway:** 14.2 Professional Sales and Marketing. **Other Jobs in This Pathway:** Cashiers; Counter and Rental Clerks; Door-To-Door Sales Workers, News and Street Vendors, and Related Workers; Driver/Sales Workers; Energy Brokers; First-Line Supervisors of Non-Retail Sales Workers; First-Line Supervisors of Retail Sales Workers; Hotel, Motel, and Resort Desk Clerks; Marketing Managers; Marking Clerks; Online Merchants; Order Fillers, Wholesale and Retail Sales; Parts Salespersons; Property, Real Estate, and Community Association Managers; Real Estate Sales Agents; Reservation and Transportation Ticket Agents and Travel Clerks; Retail Salespersons; Sales and Related Workers, All Other; Sales Representatives, Services, All Other; Sales Representatives, Wholesale and Manufacturing, Except Technical and Scientific Products; Sales Representatives, Wholesale and Manufacturing, Technical and Scientific Products; Solar Sales Representatives and Assessors; Stock Clerks—Stockroom, Warehouse, or Storage Yard; Stock Clerks, Sales Floor; Telemarketers; others.

**Skills**—Operations Analysis, Management of Financial Resources, Management of Material Resources, Negotiation, Systems Evaluation, Service Orientation, Time Management, Persuasion.

**Work Environment:** Indoors; sitting; noise.

# Mental Health and Substance Abuse Social Workers

* Annual Earnings: $38,600
* Earnings Growth Potential: Low (34.7%)
* Growth: 19.5%
* Annual Job Openings: 6,130
* Self-Employed: 2.2%

**Considerations for Job Outlook:** The rapidly increasing elderly population is expected to spur demand for social services. Job prospects should be favorable because of the need to replace the many workers who are leaving the occupation permanently.

**Assess and treat individuals with mental, emotional, or substance abuse problems, including abuse of alcohol, tobacco, and/or other drugs. Activities may include individual and group therapy, crisis intervention, case management, client advocacy, prevention, and education.** Counsel clients in individual and group sessions to assist them in dealing with substance abuse, mental and physical illness, poverty, unemployment, or physical abuse. Interview clients, review records, and confer with other professionals to evaluate mental or physical condition of client or patient. Collaborate with counselors, physicians, and nurses to plan and coordinate treatment, drawing on social work experience and patient needs. Monitor, evaluate, and record client progress with respect to treatment goals. Refer patient, client, or family to community resources for housing or treatment to assist in recovery from mental or physical illness, following through to ensure service efficacy. Counsel and aid family members to assist them in understanding, dealing with, and supporting the client or patient. Modify treatment plans according to changes in client status. Plan and conduct programs to prevent substance abuse, to combat social problems, or to improve health and counseling services in community. Supervise and direct other workers who provide services to clients or patients. Develop or advise on social policy and assist in community development. Conduct social research to advance knowledge in the social work field.

**Education/Training Required:** Master's degree. **Education and Training Program:** Clinical/Medical Social Work. **Knowledge/Courses**—Therapy and Counseling, Psychology, Sociology and Anthropology, Philosophy and Theology, Customer and Personal Service, Education and Training.

**Personality Type:** Social-Investigative-Artistic. **Career Cluster:** 10 Human Services. **Career Pathway:** 10.2 Counseling and Mental Health Services. **Other Jobs in This Pathway:** Clergy; Clinical Psychologists; Counseling Psychologists; Counselors, All Other; Directors, Religious Activities and Education; Epidemiologists; Health Educators; Healthcare Social Workers; Marriage and Family Therapists; Mental Health Counselors; Music Directors; Psychologists, All Other; Recreation Workers; Religious Workers, All Other; School Psychologists; Substance Abuse and Behavioral Disorder Counselors.

**Skills**—Social Perceptiveness, Science, Operations Analysis, Service Orientation, Learning Strategies, Active Learning, Persuasion, Negotiation.

**Work Environment:** Indoors; sitting; repetitive motions; noise; exposed to disease or infections.

# Mental Health Counselors

- ✴ Annual Earnings: $38,150
- ✴ Earnings Growth Potential: Medium (36.6%)
- ✴ Growth: 24.0%
- ✴ Annual Job Openings: 5,010
- ✴ Self-Employed: 6.1%

**Considerations for Job Outlook:** Increasing demand for services provided by counselors is expected to result in employment growth. But growth will vary by specialty and will be faster for mental health, substance abuse and behavioral disorder, and rehabilitation counselors than for counselors of other specialties. Opportunities should be favorable, particularly in rural areas.

**Counsel with emphasis on prevention. Work with individuals and groups to promote optimum mental health. May help individuals deal with addictions and substance abuse; family, parenting, and marital problems; suicide; stress management; problems with self-esteem; and issues associated with aging and mental and emotional health.** Maintain confidentiality of records relating to clients' treatment. Guide clients in the development of skills and strategies for dealing with their problems. Encourage clients to express their feelings and discuss what is happening in their lives and help them to develop insight into themselves and their relationships. Prepare and maintain all required treatment records and reports. Counsel clients and patients, individually and in group sessions, to assist in overcoming dependencies, adjusting to life, and making changes. Collect information about clients through interviews, observation, and tests. Act as client advocates to coordinate required services or to resolve emergency problems in crisis situations. Develop and implement treatment plans based on clinical experience and knowledge. Collaborate with other staff members to perform clinical assessments and develop treatment plans. Evaluate clients' physical or mental condition based on review of client information. Meet with families, probation officers, police, and other interested parties to exchange necessary information during the treatment process. Refer patients, clients, or family members to community resources or to specialists as necessary. Evaluate the effectiveness of counseling programs and clients' progress in resolving identified problems and moving towards defined objectives. Counsel family members to assist them in understanding, dealing with, and supporting clients or patients. Plan, organize, and lead structured programs of counseling, work, study, recreation, and social activities for clients. Modify treatment activities and approaches as needed

to comply with changes in clients' status. Learn about new developments in their field by reading professional literature, attending courses and seminars, and establishing and maintaining contact with other social service agencies. Discuss with individual patients their plans for life after leaving therapy.

**Education/Training Required:** Master's degree. **Education and Training Programs:** Clinical/Medical Social Work; Mental and Social Health Services and Allied Professions, Other; Mental Health Counseling/Counselor; Substance Abuse/Addiction Counseling. **Knowledge/Courses**—Therapy and Counseling, Psychology, Sociology and Anthropology, Philosophy and Theology, Customer and Personal Service, Medicine and Dentistry.

**Personality Type:** Social-Investigative-Artistic. **Career Clusters:** 08 Health Science; 10 Human Services. **Career Pathways:** 8.3 Health Informatics; 10.2 Counseling and Mental Health Services. **Other Jobs in These Pathways:** Clergy; Clinical Psychologists; Counseling Psychologists; Directors, Religious Activities and Education; Editors; Engineers, All Other; Executive Secretaries and Executive Administrative Assistants; First-Line Supervisors of Office and Administrative Support Workers; Health Educators; Healthcare Social Workers; Medical and Health Services Managers; Medical Assistants; Medical Records and Health Information Technicians; Medical Secretaries; Medical Transcriptionists; Mental Health and Substance Abuse Social Workers; Physical Therapists; Psychiatric Aides; Psychiatric Technicians; Public Relations Specialists; Receptionists and Information Clerks; Recreation Workers; Rehabilitation Counselors; School Psychologists; Substance Abuse and Behavioral Disorder Counselors; others.

**Skills**—Science, Social Perceptiveness, Active Listening, Operations Analysis, Service Orientation, Systems Evaluation, Persuasion, Systems Analysis.

**Work Environment:** Indoors; sitting.

# Microbiologists

- ✴ Annual Earnings: $65,920
- ✴ Earnings Growth Potential: Medium (40.6%)
- ✴ Growth: 12.2%
- ✴ Annual Job Openings: 750
- ✴ Self-Employed: 2.6%

**Considerations for Job Outlook:** Biotechnological research and development should continue to drive job growth. Doctoral degree holders are expected to face competition for research positions in academia.

**Investigate the growth, structure, development, and other characteristics of microscopic organisms, such as bacteria, algae, or fungi. Includes medical microbiologists who study the relationship between organisms and disease or the effects of antibiotics on microorganisms.** Investigate the relationship between organisms and disease including the control of epidemics and the effects of antibiotics on microorganisms. Prepare technical reports and recommendations based upon research outcomes. Supervise biological technologists and technicians and other scientists. Provide laboratory services for health departments, for community environmental health programs, and for physicians needing information for diagnosis and treatment. Use a variety of specialized equipment such as electron microscopes, gas chromatographs, and high pressure liquid chromatographs, electrophoresis units, thermocyclers, fluorescence activated cell sorters and phosphoimagers. Examine physiological, morphological, and cultural characteristics, using microscopes, to identify and classify microorganisms in human, water, and food specimens. Study growth, structure, development, and general characteristics of bacteria and other microorganisms to understand their relationships to human, plant, and animal health. Isolate and maintain cultures of bacteria or other microorganisms in prescribed or developed media, controlling moisture, aeration, temperature, and nutrition. Observe action of microorganisms upon living tissues of plants, higher animals, and other microorganisms, and on dead organic matter. Study the structure and function of human, animal, and plant tissues, cells, pathogens, and toxins. Conduct chemical analyses of substances such as acids, alcohols, and enzymes. Monitor and perform tests on water, food, and the environment to detect harmful microorganisms or to obtain information about sources of pollution, contamination, or infection. Develop new products and procedures for sterilization, food and pharmaceutical supply preservation, or microbial contamination detection. Research use of bacteria and microorganisms to develop vitamins, antibiotics, amino acids, grain alcohol, sugars, and polymers.

**Education/Training Required:** Doctoral degree. **Education and Training Programs:** Biochemistry and Molecular Biology; Cell/Cellular Biology and Anatomical Sciences, Other; Microbiology, General; Soil Microbiology; Structural Biology. **Knowledge/Courses**—Biology, Chemistry, Medicine and Dentistry, English Language, Education and Training, Mathematics.

**Personality Type:** Investigative-Realistic. **Career Cluster:** 15 Science, Technology, Engineering, and Mathematics. **Career Pathway:** 15.2 Science and Mathematics. **Other Jobs in This Pathway:** Architectural and Engineering Managers; Biochemists and Biophysicists; Biofuels/Biodiesel Technology and Product Development Managers; Bioinformatics Scientists; Biological Scientists, All Other; Biologists; Biostatisticians; Chemists; Clinical Data Managers; Clinical Research Coordinators; Community and Social Service Specialists, All Other; Dietitians and Nutritionists; Education, Training, and Library Workers, All Other; Geneticists; Geoscientists, Except Hydrologists and Geographers; Medical Scientists, Except Epidemiologists; Molecular and Cellular Biologists; Natural Sciences Managers; Operations Research Analysts; Physical Scientists, All Other; Social Scientists and Related Workers, All Other; Statisticians; Survey Researchers; Transportation Planners; Water Resource Specialists; others.

**Skills**—Science, Active Learning, Mathematics, Programming, Reading Comprehension, Learning Strategies, Operations Analysis, Writing.

**Work Environment:** Indoors; sitting; using hands; exposed to disease or infections; hazardous conditions.

# Middle School Teachers, Except Special and Career/Technical Education

- ❋ Annual Earnings: $51,960
- ❋ Earnings Growth Potential: Low (32.7%)
- ❋ Growth: 15.3%
- ❋ Annual Job Openings: 25,110
- ❋ Self-Employed: 0.0%

**Considerations for Job Outlook:** Enrollment from 2008–2018 is expected to grow more slowly than in recent years. Prospects are usually better in urban and rural areas, for bilingual teachers, and for math and science teachers.

**Teach students in public or private schools in one or more subjects at the middle, intermediate, or junior high level, which falls between elementary and senior high school as defined by applicable state laws and regulations.** Establish and enforce rules for behavior and procedures for maintaining order among the students for whom they are responsible. Adapt teaching methods and instructional materials to meet students' varying needs and interests. Instruct through lectures, discussions, and demonstrations in one or more subjects such as English, mathematics, or social studies. Prepare, administer, and grade tests and assignments to evaluate students' progress. Establish clear objectives for all lessons, units, and projects and communicate these objectives to students. Plan and conduct activities for a balanced program of instruction, demonstration, and work time that provides students with opportunities to observe, question, and investigate. Maintain accurate, complete, and correct student records as required by laws, district policies, and administrative regulations. Observe and evaluate students' performance, behavior, social development, and physical health. Assign lessons and correct homework. Prepare materials and classrooms for class activities. Enforce all administration policies and rules governing students. Confer with parents or guardians, other teachers, counselors, and administrators to resolve students' behavioral and academic problems. Prepare students for later grades by encouraging them to explore learning opportunities and to persevere with challenging tasks. Prepare objectives and outlines for courses of study, following curriculum guidelines or requirements of states and schools. Guide and counsel students with adjustment or academic problems or special academic interests. Meet with parents and guardians to discuss their children's progress and to determine their priorities for their children and their resource needs. Meet with other professionals to discuss individual students' needs and progress. Prepare and implement remedial programs for students requiring extra help.

**Education/Training Required:** Bachelor's degree. **Education and Training Programs:** Art Teacher Education; Computer Teacher Education; English/Language Arts Teacher Education; Family and Consumer Sciences/Home Economics Teacher Education; Foreign Language Teacher Education; Health Occupations Teacher Education; Health Teacher Education; History Teacher Education; Junior High/Intermediate/Middle School Education and Teaching; Mathematics Teacher Education; Music Teacher Education; Physical Education Teaching and Coaching; Reading Teacher Education; Science Teacher Education/General Science Teacher Education; Social Science Teacher Education; Social Studies Teacher Education; Teacher Education and Professional Development, Specific Subject Areas, Other; Technology Teacher Education/Industrial Arts Teacher Education. **Knowledge/Courses**—History and Archeology, Education and Training, Sociology and Anthropology, Fine Arts, Philosophy and Theology, English Language.

**Personality Type:** Social-Artistic. **Career Cluster:** 05 Education and Training. **Career Pathway:** 5.3 Teaching/Training. **Other Jobs in This Pathway:** Adult Basic and Secondary Education and Literacy Teachers and Instructors;

Athletes and Sports Competitors; Audio-Visual and Multimedia Collections Specialists; Career/Technical Education Teachers, Middle School; Career/Technical Education Teachers, Secondary School; Chemists; Coaches and Scouts; Dietitians and Nutritionists; Elementary School Teachers, Except Special Education; Fitness Trainers and Aerobics Instructors; Historians; Instructional Coordinators; Instructional Designers and Technologists; Interpreters and Translators; Kindergarten Teachers, Except Special Education; Librarians; Physicists; Preschool Teachers, Except Special Education; Recreation Workers; Secondary School Teachers, Except Special and Career/Technical Education; Self-Enrichment Education Teachers; Teacher Assistants; Teachers and Instructors, All Other; Tutors.

**Skills**—Learning Strategies, Instructing, Negotiation, Writing, Social Perceptiveness, Reading Comprehension, Active Listening, Systems Evaluation.

**Work Environment:** Indoors; standing; noise.

## Mining and Geological Engineers, Including Mining Safety Engineers

- ✸ Annual Earnings: $82,870
- ✸ Earnings Growth Potential: Medium (40.9%)
- ✸ Growth: 15.3%
- ✸ Annual Job Openings: 260
- ✸ Self-Employed: 0.0%

**Considerations for Job Outlook:** Mining and geological engineers, including mining safety engineers, are expected to have employment growth of 15 percent from 2008–2018, faster than the average for all occupations. Following a lengthy period of decline, strong growth in demand for minerals is expected to create some employment growth over the 2008–2018 period. Moreover, many currently employed mining engineers are approaching retirement age, a factor that should create additional job openings. Furthermore, relatively few schools offer mining engineering programs, resulting in good job opportunities for graduates. The best opportunities may require frequent travel or even living overseas for extended periods as mining operations around the world recruit graduates of U.S. mining engineering programs.

**Determine the location and plan the extraction of coal, metallic ores, nonmetallic minerals, and building materials such as stone and gravel. Work involves conducting preliminary surveys of deposits or undeveloped mines**

and planning their development; examining deposits or mines to determine whether they can be worked at a profit; making geological and topographical surveys; evolving methods of mining best suited to character, type, and size of deposits; and supervising mining operations. Inspect mining areas for unsafe structures, equipment, and working conditions. Select locations and plan underground or surface mining operations, specifying processes, labor usage, and equipment that will result in safe, economical, and environmentally sound extraction of minerals and ores. Examine maps, deposits, drilling locations, or mines to determine the location, size, accessibility, contents, value, and potential profitability of mineral, oil, and gas deposits. Supervise and coordinate the work of technicians, technologists, survey personnel, engineers, scientists, and other mine personnel. Prepare schedules, reports, and estimates of the costs involved in developing and operating mines. Monitor mine production rates to assess operational effectiveness. Design, implement, and monitor the development of mines, facilities, systems, or equipment. Select or develop mineral location, extraction, and production methods based on factors such as safety, cost, and deposit characteristics. Prepare technical reports for use by mining, engineering, and management personnel. Implement and coordinate mine safety programs, including the design and maintenance of protective and rescue equipment and safety devices. Test air to detect toxic gases and recommend measures to remove them, such as installation of ventilation shafts. Design, develop, and implement computer applications for use in mining operations such as mine design, modeling, or mapping or for monitoring mine conditions. Select or devise materials-handling methods and equipment to transport ore, waste materials, and mineral products efficiently and economically. Devise solutions to problems of land reclamation and water and air pollution, such as methods of storing excavated soil and returning exhausted mine sites to natural states. Lay out, direct, and supervise mine construction operations, such as the construction of shafts and tunnels. Evaluate data to develop new mining products, equipment, or processes.

**Education/Training Required:** Bachelor's degree. **Education and Training Program:** Mining and Mineral Engineering. **Knowledge/Courses**—Engineering and Technology, Design, Physics, Geography, Building and Construction, Chemistry.

**Personality Type:** Investigative-Realistic-Enterprising. **Career Cluster:** 15 Science, Technology, Engineering, and Mathematics. **Career Pathway:** 15.1 Engineering and Technology. **Other Jobs in This Pathway:** Architectural and Engineering Managers; Automotive Engineers; Biochemical Engineers; Biofuels/Biodiesel Technology and Product Development Managers; Civil Engineers; Cost Estimators; Electrical Engineers; Electronics Engineers, Except Computer; Energy Engineers; Engineers, All Other; Fuel Cell Engineers; Human Factors Engineers and Ergonomists; Industrial Engineers; Manufacturing Engineers; Mechanical Engineers; Mechatronics Engineers; Microsystems Engineers; Nanosystems Engineers; Photonics Engineers; Radio Frequency Identification Device Specialists; Robotics Engineers; Solar Energy Systems Engineers; Transportation Engineers; Validation Engineers; Wind Energy Engineers; others.

**Skills**—Programming, Management of Financial Resources, Science, Operations Analysis, Mathematics, Technology Design, Management of Material Resources, Systems Evaluation.

**Work Environment:** More often indoors than outdoors; sitting.

# Mixing and Blending Machine Setters, Operators, and Tenders

* Annual Earnings: $32,870
* Earnings Growth Potential: Medium (36.5%)
* Growth: 15.5%
* Annual Job Openings: 4,610
* Self-Employed: 1.4%

**Considerations for Job Outlook:** Faster-than-average employment growth is projected.

**Set up, operate, or tend machines to mix or blend materials such as chemicals, tobacco, liquids, color pigments, or explosive ingredients.** Weigh or measure materials, ingredients, and products to ensure conformance to requirements. Test samples of materials or products to ensure compliance with specifications by using test equipment. Start machines to mix or blend ingredients, then allow them to mix for specified times. Dump or pour specified amounts of materials into machinery and equipment. Operate or tend machines to mix or blend any of a wide variety of materials, such as spices, dough batter, tobacco, fruit juices, chemicals, livestock feed, food products, color pigments, or explosive ingredients. Observe production and monitor equipment to ensure safe and efficient operation. Stop mixing or blending machines when specified product qualities are obtained, then open valves and start pumps to transfer mixtures. Collect samples of materials or products for laboratory testing. Use hand tools or other devices to add or mix chemicals and ingredients for processing. Examine materials, ingredients, or products visually or with hands to ensure conformance to established standards. Record operational and production data on specified forms. Transfer materials, supplies, and products between work areas, using moving equipment and hand tools. Tend accessory equipment such as pumps and conveyors to move materials or ingredients through production processes. Read work orders to determine production specifications and information. Compound and process ingredients or dyes according to formulas. Unload mixtures into containers or onto conveyors for further processing. Clean and maintain equipment with hand tools. Dislodge and clear jammed materials or other items from machinery and equipment with hand tools. Open valves to drain slurry from mixers into storage tanks.

**Education/Training Required:** Moderate-term on-the-job training. **Education and Training Program:** Agricultural and Food Products Processing. **Knowledge/Courses**—Production and Processing, Chemistry, Mechanical, Physics, Mathematics, Public Safety and Security.

**Personality Type:** Realistic-Conventional-Investigative. **Career Cluster:** 13 Manufacturing. **Career Pathway:** 13.1 Production. **Other Jobs in This Pathway:** Assemblers and Fabricators, All Other; Cabinetmakers and Bench Carpenters; Coating, Painting, and Spraying Machine Setters, Operators, and Tenders; Computer-Controlled Machine Tool Operators, Metal and Plastic; Cost Estimators; Cutting, Punching, and Press Machine Setters, Operators, and Tenders, Metal and Plastic; First-Line Supervisors of Mechanics, Installers, and Repairers; First-Line Supervisors of Production and Operating Workers; Geothermal Technicians; Grinding, Lapping, Polishing, and Buffing Machine Tool Setters, Operators, and Tenders, Metal and Plastic; Helpers—Production Workers; Machine Feeders and Offbearers; Machinists; Molding, Coremaking, and Casting Machine Setters, Operators, and Tenders, Metal and Plastic; Packaging and Filling Machine Operators and Tenders; Packers and Packagers, Hand; Paper Goods Machine Setters, Operators, and Tenders; Production Workers, All Other; Recycling and Reclamation Workers; Recycling Coordinators; Sheet Metal Workers; Solderers and Brazers; Structural Metal Fabricators and Fitters; Team Assemblers; Welders, Cutters, and Welder Fitters; others.

**Skills**—Equipment Maintenance, Operation and Control, Repairing, Quality Control Analysis, Operation Monitoring, Troubleshooting, Equipment Selection, Science.

**Work Environment:** More often outdoors than indoors; standing; walking and running; using hands; bending or twisting the body; repetitive motions; noise; very hot or cold; contaminants; cramped work space; high places; hazardous conditions; hazardous equipment; minor burns, cuts, bites, or stings.

# Mobile Heavy Equipment Mechanics, Except Engines

* Annual Earnings: $44,830
* Earnings Growth Potential: Low (33.7%)
* Growth: 8.7%
* Annual Job Openings: 3,770
* Self-Employed: 5.8%

**Considerations for Job Outlook:** Continued expansion of the industries that use heavy mobile equipment, such as agriculture and energy exploration and mining, should lead to additional jobs for these workers. Opportunities should be good for job seekers who have experience or formal training.

**Diagnose, adjust, repair, or overhaul mobile mechanical, hydraulic, and pneumatic equipment, such as cranes, bulldozers, graders, and conveyors, used in construction, logging, and surface mining.** Test mechanical products and equipment after repair or assembly to ensure proper performance and compliance with manufacturers' specifications. Repair and replace damaged or worn parts. Diagnose faults or malfunctions to determine required repairs, using engine diagnostic equipment such as computerized test equipment and calibration devices. Operate and inspect machines or heavy equipment to diagnose defects. Dismantle and reassemble heavy equipment, using hoists and hand tools. Clean, lubricate, and perform other routine maintenance work on equipment and vehicles. Examine parts for damage or excessive wear, using micrometers and gauges. Read and understand operating manuals, blueprints, and technical drawings. Schedule maintenance for industrial machines and equipment and keep equipment service records. Overhaul and test machines or equipment to ensure operating efficiency. Assemble gear systems and align frames and gears. Fit bearings to adjust, repair, or overhaul mobile mechanical, hydraulic, and pneumatic equipment. Weld or solder broken parts and structural members, using electric or gas welders and soldering tools. Clean parts by spraying them with grease solvent or immersing them in tanks of solvent. Adjust, maintain, and repair or replace subassemblies, such as transmissions and crawler heads, using hand tools, jacks, and cranes. Adjust and maintain industrial machinery, using control and regulating devices. Fabricate needed parts or items from sheet metal. Direct workers who are assembling or disassembling equipment or cleaning parts.

**Education/Training Required:** Long-term on-the-job training. **Education and Training Programs:** Agricultural Mechanics and Equipment/Machine Technology; Heavy Equipment Maintenance Technology/Technician. **Knowledge/Courses**—Mechanical, Physics, Building and Construction, Engineering and Technology, Design, Transportation.

**Personality Type:** Realistic-Conventional. **Career Clusters:** 01 Agriculture, Food, and Natural Resources; 13 Manufacturing. **Career Pathways:** 1.4 Power Structure and Technical Systems; 13.3 Maintenance, Installation, and Repair. **Other Jobs in These Pathways:** Aircraft Mechanics and Service Technicians; Automotive Specialty Technicians; Biological Technicians; Civil Engineering Technicians; Computer, Automated Teller, and Office Machine Repairers; Electrical and Electronic Equipment Assemblers; Electrical and Electronics Repairers, Commercial and Industrial Equipment; Electrical Engineering Technicians; Electrical Engineering Technologists; Electromechanical Engineering Technologists; Electronics Engineering Technicians; Electronics Engineering Technologists; Engineering Technicians, Except Drafters, All Other; Fuel Cell Technicians; Helpers—Installation, Maintenance, and Repair Workers; Industrial Engineering Technologists; Industrial Machinery Mechanics; Installation, Maintenance, and Repair Workers, All Other; Manufacturing Engineering Technologists; Manufacturing Production Technicians; Mapping Technicians; Mechanical Engineering Technologists; Nanotechnology Engineering Technicians; Telecommunications Line Installers and Repairers; Tire Repairers and Changers; others.

**Skills**—Repairing, Equipment Maintenance, Troubleshooting, Installation, Equipment Selection, Quality Control Analysis, Operation and Control, Operation Monitoring.

**Work Environment:** Outdoors; standing; walking and running; kneeling, crouching, stooping, or crawling; using hands; bending or twisting the body; repetitive motions; noise; very hot or cold; bright or inadequate lighting; contaminants; cramped work space; whole-body vibration; high places; hazardous conditions; hazardous equipment; minor burns, cuts, bites, or stings.

# Morticians, Undertakers, and Funeral Directors

* ❋ Annual Earnings: $54,330
* ❋ Earnings Growth Potential: High (44.9%)
* ❋ Growth: 11.9%
* ❋ Annual Job Openings: 960
* ❋ Self-Employed: 12.8%

**Considerations for Job Outlook:** Projected employment growth reflects overall expansion of the death-care services industry, due to the aging of the population. Job opportunities are expected to be good.

**Perform various tasks to arrange and direct funeral services, such as coordinating transportation of bodies to mortuaries for embalming, interviewing families or other authorized people to arrange details, selecting pallbearers, procuring officials for religious rites, and providing transportation for mourners.** Consult with families or friends of the deceased to arrange funeral details such as obituary notice wording, casket selection, and plans for services. Obtain information needed to complete legal documents such as death certificates and burial permits. Oversee the preparation and care of the remains of people who have died. Contact cemeteries to schedule the opening and closing of graves. Provide information on funeral service options, products, and merchandise, and maintain a casket display area. Offer counsel and comfort to bereaved families and friends. Close caskets and lead funeral corteges to churches or burial sites. Arrange for clergy members to perform needed services. Provide or arrange transportation between sites for the remains, mourners, pallbearers, clergy, and flowers. Perform embalming duties as necessary. Direct preparations and shipment of bodies for out-of-state burial. Discuss and negotiate prearranged funerals with clients. Inform survivors of benefits for which they may be eligible. Maintain financial records, order merchandise, and prepare accounts. Plan placement of caskets at funeral sites, and place and adjust lights, fixtures, and floral displays. Arrange for pallbearers, and inform pallbearers and honorary groups of their duties. Receive and usher people to their seats for services. Plan, schedule, and coordinate funerals, burials, and cremations, arranging details such as floral delivery and the time and place of services. Manage funeral home operations, including the hiring, training, and supervision of embalmers, funeral attendants, or other staff. Clean funeral home facilities and grounds. Participate in community activities for funeral home promotion or other purposes.

**Education/Training Required:** Associate degree. **Education and Training Program:** Funeral Service and Mortuary Science, General. **Knowledge/Courses**—Philosophy and Theology, Therapy and Counseling, Chemistry, Customer and Personal Service, Biology, Economics and Accounting.

**Personality Type:** Enterprising-Social-Conventional. **Career Cluster:** 10 Human Services. **Career Pathway:** 10.4 Personal Care Services. **Other Jobs in This Pathway:** Barbers; Embalmers; Funeral Attendants; Funeral Service Managers; Hairdressers, Hairstylists, and Cosmetologists; Laundry and Dry-Cleaning Workers; Makeup Artists, Theatrical and Performance; Manicurists and Pedicurists; Pressers, Textile, Garment, and Related Materials; Sewers, Hand; Sewing Machine Operators; Shampooers; Skincare Specialists; Tailors, Dressmakers, and Custom Sewers; Textile Bleaching and Dyeing Machine Operators and Tenders.

**Skills**—Management of Financial Resources, Social Perceptiveness, Management of Material Resources, Service Orientation, Management of Personnel Resources, Persuasion, Negotiation, Speaking.

**Work Environment:** More often indoors than outdoors; standing; using hands; contaminants; exposed to disease or infections.

# Multimedia Artists and Animators

- ❋ Annual Earnings: $58,510
- ❋ Earnings Growth Potential: High (42.2%)
- ❋ Growth: 14.2%
- ❋ Annual Job Openings: 2,890
- ❋ Self-Employed: 60.1%

**Considerations for Job Outlook:** Demand for digital and multimedia artwork is expected to drive growth. Competition should be keen for certain kinds of jobs. Multimedia artists and animators should have better opportunities than other artists.

**Create special effects, animation, or other visual images, using film, video, computers, or other electronic tools and media, for use in products or creations such as computer games, movies, music videos, and commercials.** Design complex graphics and animation, using independent judgment, creativity, and computer equipment. Create two-dimensional and three-dimensional images depicting objects in motion or illustrating a process, using computer animation or modeling programs. Make objects or characters appear lifelike by manipulating light, color, texture, shadow, and transparency or manipulating static images to give the illusion of motion. Apply story development, directing, cinematography, and editing to animation to create storyboards that show the flow of the animation and map out key scenes and characters. Assemble, typeset, scan, and produce digital camera-ready art or film negatives and printer's proofs. Script, plan, and create animated narrative sequences under tight deadlines, using computer software and hand-drawing techniques. Create basic designs, drawings, and illustrations for product labels, cartons, direct mail, or television. Create pen-and-paper images to be scanned, edited, colored, textured, or animated by computer. Develop briefings, brochures, multimedia presentations, Web pages, promotional products, technical illustrations, and computer artwork for use in products, technical manuals, literature, newsletters, and slide shows. Use models to simulate the behavior of animated objects in the finished sequence. Create and install special effects as required by the script, mixing chemicals and fabricating needed parts from wood, metal, plaster, and clay. Participate in design and production of multimedia campaigns, handling budgeting and scheduling and assisting with such responsibilities as production coordination, background design, and progress tracking. Convert real objects to animated objects through modeling, using techniques such as optical scanning. Implement and maintain configuration control systems.

**Education/Training Required:** Bachelor's degree. **Education and Training Programs:** Animation, Interactive Technology, Video Graphics and Special Effects; Drawing; Graphic Design; Intermedia/Multimedia; Painting; Printmaking; Web Page, Digital/Multimedia and Information Resources Design. **Knowledge/Courses**—Fine Arts, Communications and Media, Design, Computers and Electronics, Sales and Marketing, English Language.

**Personality Type:** Artistic-Investigative. **Career Clusters:** 03 Arts, Audio/Video Technology, and Communications; 11 Information Technology. **Career Pathways:** 3.1 Audio and Video Technology and Film; 3.2 Printing Technology; 3.3 Visual Arts; 11.1 Network Systems. **Other Jobs in These Pathways:** Agents and Business Managers of Artists, Performers, and Athletes; Art Directors; Artists and Related Workers, All Other; Audio and Video Equipment Technicians; Broadcast Technicians; Camera Operators, Television, Video, and Motion Picture; Choreographers; Commercial and Industrial Designers; Computer and Information Systems Managers; Craft Artists; Data Entry Keyers; Designers, All Other; Desktop Publishers; Fashion Designers; Film and Video Editors; Fine Artists, Including Painters, Sculptors, and Illustrators; Graphic Designers; Interior Designers; Managers, All Other; Media and Communication Equipment Workers, All Other; Media and Communication

Workers, All Other; Painting, Coating, and Decorating Workers; Photographers; Proofreaders and Copy Markers; Technical Directors/Managers; others.

**Skills**—Technology Design, Programming, Management of Financial Resources, Coordination, Management of Material Resources, Negotiation, Active Listening, Systems Evaluation.

**Work Environment:** Indoors; sitting; using hands; repetitive motions.

# Museum Technicians and Conservators

* Annual Earnings: $37,310
* Earnings Growth Potential: Low (34.5%)
* Growth: 25.6%
* Annual Job Openings: 610
* Self-Employed: 1.9%

**Considerations for Job Outlook:** Employment growth for museum technicians should be strong as museum attendance levels remain high. Keen competition is expected.

**Prepare specimens, such as fossils, skeletal parts, lace, and textiles, for museum collection and exhibits. May restore documents or install, arrange, and exhibit materials.** Install, arrange, assemble, and prepare artifacts for exhibition, ensuring the artifacts' safety, reporting their status and condition, and identifying and correcting any problems with the setup. Coordinate exhibit installations, assisting with design; constructing displays, dioramas, display cases, and models; and ensuring the availability of necessary materials. Determine whether objects need repair and choose the safest and most effective method of repair. Clean objects, such as paper, textiles, wood, metal, glass, rock, pottery, and furniture, using cleansers, solvents, soap solutions, and polishes. Prepare artifacts for storage and shipping. Supervise and work with volunteers. Present public programs and tours. Specialize in particular materials or types of object, such as documents and books, paintings, decorative arts, textiles, metals, or architectural materials. Recommend preservation procedures, such as control of temperature and humidity, to curatorial and building staff. Classify and assign registration numbers to artifacts and supervise inventory control. Direct and supervise curatorial and technical staff in the handling, mounting, care, and storage of art objects. Perform on-site fieldwork, which may involve interviewing people, inspecting and identifying artifacts, note-taking, viewing sites and collections, and repainting

exhibition spaces. Repair, restore, and reassemble artifacts, designing and fabricating missing or broken parts, to restore them to their original appearance and prevent deterioration. Prepare reports on the operation of conservation laboratories, documenting the condition of artifacts, treatment options, and the methods of preservation and repair used. Study object documentation or conduct standard chemical and physical tests to ascertain the object's age, composition, original appearance, need for treatment or restoration, and appropriate preservation method.

**Education/Training Required:** Bachelor's degree. **Education and Training Programs:** Art History, Criticism and Conservation; Museology/Museum Studies; Public/Applied History. **Knowledge/Courses**—Fine Arts, History and Archeology, Chemistry, Design, English Language, Clerical.

**Personality Type:** Realistic-Artistic. **Career Clusters:** 03 Arts, Audio/Video Technology, and Communications; 15 Science, Technology, Engineering, and Mathematics. **Career Pathways:** 3.1 Audio and Video Technology and Film; 15.2 Science and Mathematics. **Other Jobs in These Pathways:** Architectural and Engineering Managers; Biofuels/Biodiesel Technology and Product Development Managers; Bioinformatics Scientists; Biological Scientists, All Other; Biologists; Broadcast Technicians; Chemists; Clinical Research Coordinators; Commercial and Industrial Designers; Community and Social Service Specialists, All Other; Dietitians and Nutritionists; Education, Training, and Library Workers, All Other; Geoscientists, Except Hydrologists and Geographers; Graphic Designers; Managers, All Other; Media and Communication Workers, All Other; Medical Scientists, Except Epidemiologists; Multimedia Artists and Animators; Natural Sciences Managers; Operations Research Analysts; Photographers; Social Scientists and Related Workers, All Other; Technical Directors/Managers; Transportation Planners; Water Resource Specialists; others.

**Skills**—Science, Technology Design, Writing, Installation, Management of Material Resources, Quality Control Analysis, Systems Evaluation, Systems Analysis.

**Work Environment:** Indoors; sitting; using hands; noise; contaminants.

# Music Directors and Composers

❋ Annual Earnings: $45,970
❋ Earnings Growth Potential: Very high (52.8%)
❋ Growth: 10.0%
❋ Annual Job Openings: 1,620
❋ Self-Employed: 36.2%

**Considerations for Job Outlook:** Most new wage-and-salary jobs are expected to be in religious organizations. Self-employed musicians should have slower than average employment growth. Keen competition is expected for full-time positions.

## Job Specialization: Music Composers and Arrangers

**Write and transcribe musical scores.** Copy parts from scores for individual performers. Transpose music from one voice or instrument to another to accommodate particular musicians. Use computers and synthesizers to compose, orchestrate, and arrange music. Write changes directly into compositions, or use computer software to make changes. Confer with producers and directors to define the nature and placement of film or television music. Guide musicians during rehearsals, performances, or recording sessions. Study original pieces of music to become familiar with them prior to making any changes. Study films or scripts to determine how musical scores can be used to create desired effects or moods. Write music for commercial mediums, including advertising jingles or film soundtracks. Accept commissions to create music for special occasions. Arrange music composed by others, changing the music to achieve desired effects. Write musical scores for orchestras, bands, choral groups, or individual instrumentalists or vocalists, using knowledge of music theory and of instrumental and vocal capabilities. Score compositions so that they are consistent with instrumental and vocal capabilities such as ranges and keys, using knowledge of music theory. Apply elements of music theory to create musical and tonal structures, including harmonies and melodies. Collaborate with other colleagues such as copyists to complete final scores. Determine voices, instruments, harmonic structures, rhythms, tempos, and tone balances required to achieve the effects desired in musical compositions. Experiment with different sounds and types and pieces of music, using synthesizers and computers as necessary to test and evaluate ideas. Explore and develop musical ideas based on sources such as imagination or sounds in the environment. Rewrite original musical scores in different musical styles by changing rhythms, harmonies, or tempos.

**Education/Training Required:** Work experience plus degree. **Education and Training Programs:** Conducting; Music Performance, General; Music Theory and Composition; Music, Other; Musicology and Ethnomusicology; Religious/Sacred Music; Voice and Opera. **Knowledge/Courses**—Fine Arts, Communications and Media, Computers and Electronics, Sales and Marketing, Production and Processing, Design.

**Personality Type:** Artistic-Enterprising. **Career Cluster:** 03 Arts, Audio/Video Technology, and Communications. **Career Pathway:** 3.4 Performing Arts. **Other Jobs in This Pathway:** Actors; Artists and Related Workers, All Other; Choreographers; Craft Artists; Dancers; Designers, All Other; Directors- Stage, Motion Pictures, Television, and Radio; Entertainers and Performers, Sports and Related Workers, All Other; Managers, All Other; Music Directors; Musicians, Instrumental; Poets, Lyricists and Creative Writers; Producers; Program Directors; Set and Exhibit Designers; Singers; Talent Directors; Technical Directors/Managers.

**Skills**—Operations Analysis, Writing, Coordination, Active Listening, Complex Problem Solving, Programming, Speaking.

**Work Environment:** Indoors; sitting; using hands; repetitive motions.

## Job Specialization: Music Directors

**Direct and conduct instrumental or vocal performances by musical groups such as orchestras or choirs.** Study scores to learn the music in detail, and to develop interpretations. Consider such factors as ensemble size and abilities, availability of scores, and the need for musical variety in order to select music to be performed. Use gestures to shape the music being played, communicating desired tempo, phrasing, tone, color, pitch, volume, and other performance aspects. Engage services of composers to write scores. Plan and implement fund-raising and promotional activities. Coordinate and organize tours, or hire touring companies to arrange concert dates, venues, accommodations, and transportation for longer tours. Confer with clergy to select music for church services. Transcribe musical compositions and melodic lines to adapt them to a particular group, or to create a particular musical style. Audition and select performers for musical presentations. Meet with composers to discuss interpretations of their works. Conduct guest soloists in addition to ensemble members. Collaborate with music librarians to ensure availability of scores. Assign and review staff work in such areas as scoring, arranging, copying music, and vocal coaching. Position members within groups to obtain balance among instrumental or vocal sections. Plan and schedule rehearsals and performances, and arrange details such as locations, accompanists, and instrumentalists. Meet with soloists and concertmasters to discuss and prepare for performances. Direct groups at rehearsals and live or recorded performances in order to achieve desired effects such as tonal and harmonic balance, dynamics, rhythm, and tempo. Perform administrative tasks such as applying for grants, developing budgets, negotiating contracts, and designing and printing programs and other promotional materials.

**Education/Training Required:** Work experience plus degree. **Education and Training Programs:** Conducting; Music Performance, General; Music Theory and Composition; Music, Other; Musicology and Ethnomusicology; Religious/Sacred Music; Voice and Opera. **Knowledge/Courses**—Fine Arts, Philosophy and Theology, Education and Training, History and Archeology, Communications and Media, Personnel and Human Resources.

**Personality Type:** Artistic-Enterprising-Social. **Career Clusters:** 03 Arts, Audio/Video Technology, and Communications; 10 Human Services. **Career Pathways:** 3.4 Performing Arts; 10.2 Counseling and Mental Health Services. **Other Jobs in These Pathways:** Actors; Clergy; Clinical Psychologists; Counseling Psychologists; Counselors, All Other; Directors- Stage, Motion Pictures, Television, and Radio; Directors, Religious Activities and Education; Entertainers and Performers, Sports and Related Workers, All Other; Health Educators; Healthcare Social Workers; Managers, All Other; Mental Health and Substance Abuse Social Workers; Mental Health Counselors; Music Composers and Arrangers; Musicians, Instrumental; Poets, Lyricists and Creative Writers; Producers; Program Directors; Recreation Workers; Religious Workers, All Other; School Psychologists; Singers; Substance Abuse and Behavioral Disorder Counselors; Talent Directors; Technical Directors/Managers; others.

**Skills**—Instructing, Systems Evaluation, Management of Personnel Resources, Monitoring, Systems Analysis, Learning Strategies, Management of Financial Resources, Persuasion.

**Work Environment:** Sitting; standing.

# Natural Sciences Managers

- ❋ Annual Earnings: $116,020
- ❋ Earnings Growth Potential: High (42.0%)
- ❋ Growth: 15.5%
- ❋ Annual Job Openings: 2,010
- ❋ Self-Employed: 0.0%

**Considerations for Job Outlook:** Employment is expected to grow along with that of the scientists and engineers these workers supervise. Prospects should be better in the rapidly growing areas of environmental and biomedical engineering and medical and environmental sciences.

**Plan, direct, or coordinate activities in such fields as life sciences, physical sciences, mathematics, and statistics and research and development in these fields.** Confer with scientists, engineers, regulators, and others to plan and review projects and to provide technical assistance. Develop client relationships and communicate with clients to explain proposals, present research findings, establish specifications, or discuss project status. Plan and direct research, development, and production activities. Prepare project proposals. Design and coordinate successive phases of problem analysis, solution proposals, and testing. Review project activities and prepare and review research, testing, and operational reports. Hire, supervise, and evaluate engineers, technicians, researchers, and other staff. Determine scientific and technical goals within broad outlines provided by top management and make detailed plans to accomplish these goals. Develop and implement policies, standards, and procedures for the architectural, scientific, and technical work performed to ensure regulatory compliance and operations enhancement. Develop innovative technology and train staff for its implementation. Provide for stewardship of plant and animal resources and habitats, studying land use; monitoring animal populations; and providing shelter, resources, and medical treatment for animals. Conduct own research in field of expertise. Recruit personnel and oversee the development and maintenance of staff competence. Advise and assist in obtaining patents or meeting other legal requirements. Prepare and administer budget, approve and review expenditures, and prepare financial reports. Make presentations at professional meetings to further knowledge in the field.

**Education/Training Required:** Work experience plus degree. **Education and Training Programs:** Acoustics; Analytical Chemistry; Anatomy; Animal Genetics; Animal Physiology; Astronomy; Astrophysics; Atmospheric Chemistry and Climatology; Atmospheric Physics and Dynamics; Atmospheric Sciences and Meteorology, General;

Atomic Physics; Biochemistry; Biological and Physical Sciences; Biology, General; Biometry; Biophysics; Biopsychology; Biostatistics; Biotechnology; Botany; Cell Biology and Histology; Chemistry, General; Ecology; Elementary Particle Physics; Entomology; Evolutionary Biology; Geochemistry; Geochemistry and Petrology; Geology/Earth Science, General; Geophysics and Seismology; Hydrology and Water Resources Science; Inorganic Chemistry; Marine Biology and Biological Oceanography; Meteorology; Microbiology, General; Molecular Biology; Natural Sciences; Nuclear Physics; Nutrition Sciences; Oceanography, Chemical and Physical; Optics; Organic Chemistry; Paleontology; Parasitology; Pathology; Pharmacology; Physical Chemistry; Physical Sciences; Physics, General; Planetary Astronomy and Science; Plant Genetics; Plant Pathology; Plant Physiology; Plasma and High-Temperature Physics; Polymer Chemistry; Radiation Biology; Science, Technology, and Society; Theoretical and Mathematical Physics; Toxicology; Virology; Zoology; others. **Knowledge/Courses**—Biology, Chemistry, Engineering and Technology, Law and Government, Administration and Management, Physics.

**Personality Type:** Enterprising-Investigative. **Career Clusters:** 04 Business, Management, and Administration; 15 Science, Technology, Engineering, and Mathematics. **Career Pathways:** 4.2 Business, Financial Management, and Accounting; 4.4 Business Analysis; 15.2 Science and Mathematics. **Other Jobs in These Pathways:** Accountants; Architectural and Engineering Managers; Auditors; Billing and Posting Clerks; Billing, Cost, and Rate Clerks; Biofuels/Biodiesel Technology and Product Development Managers; Bookkeeping, Accounting, and Auditing Clerks; Brownfield Redevelopment Specialists and Site Managers; Community and Social Service Specialists, All Other; Compliance Managers; Computer and Information Systems Managers; Education, Training, and Library Workers, All Other; Financial Analysts; Financial Managers, Branch or Department; Investment Fund Managers; Loss Prevention Managers; Managers, All Other; Payroll and Timekeeping Clerks; Regulatory Affairs Managers; Security Managers; Statement Clerks; Supply Chain Managers; Treasurers and Controllers; Wind Energy Operations Managers; Wind Energy Project Managers; others.

**Skills**—Science, Operations Analysis, Management of Financial Resources, Technology Design, Management of Personnel Resources, Mathematics, Time Management, Reading Comprehension.

**Work Environment:** Indoors; sitting; noise.

## Job Specialization: Clinical Research Coordinators

**Plan, direct, or coordinate clinical research projects. Direct the activities of workers engaged in clinical research projects to ensure compliance with protocols and overall clinical objectives. May evaluate and analyze clinical data.** Solicit industry-sponsored trials through contacts and professional organizations. Review scientific literature, participate in continuing education activities, or attend conferences and seminars to maintain current knowledge of clinical studies affairs and issues. Register protocol patients with appropriate statistical centers as required. Prepare for or participate in quality assurance audits conducted by study sponsors, federal agencies, or specially designated review groups. Participate in preparation and management of research budgets and monetary disbursements. Perform specific protocol procedures such as interviewing subjects, taking vital signs, and performing electrocardiograms. Interpret protocols and advise treating physicians on appropriate dosage modifications or treatment calculations based on patient characteristics. Develop advertising and other informational materials to be used in subject recruitment. Contact industry representatives to ensure equipment and software specifications necessary for successful study completion. Confer with health care professionals to determine the best recruitment practices for studies. Track enrollment status of subjects and document dropout information such as dropout causes and subject contact efforts. Review proposed study protocols to evaluate factors such as sample collection processes, data management plans, and potential subject risks. Record adverse event and side effect data and confer with investigators regarding the reporting of events to oversight agencies. Prepare study-related documentation such as protocol worksheets, procedural manuals, adverse event reports, institutional review board documents, and progress reports. Participate in the development of study protocols including guidelines for administration or data collection procedures. Oversee subject enrollment to ensure that informed consent is properly obtained and documented. Order drugs or devices necessary for study completion.

**Education/Training Required:** Work experience in a related occupation. **Education and Training Programs:** Biometry/Biometrics; Biostatistics; Biotechnology; Cell/Cellular Biology and Anatomical Sciences, Other; Immunology; Medical Microbiology and Bacteriology; Microbiology, General; Nutrition Sciences; Parasitology; Pathology/Experimental Pathology; Pharmacology; Statistics, General; Toxicology; Virology. **Knowledge/Courses**—No data available.

**Personality Type:** Enterprising-Investigative-Conventional. **Career Cluster:** 15 Science, Technology, Engineering, and Mathematics. **Career Pathway:** 15.2 Science and Mathematics. **Other Jobs in This Pathway:** Architectural and Engineering Managers; Biochemists and Biophysicists; Biofuels/Biodiesel Technology and Product Development Managers; Bioinformatics Scientists; Biological Scientists, All Other; Biologists; Biostatisticians; Chemists; Clinical Data Managers; Community and Social Service Specialists, All Other; Dietitians and Nutritionists; Education, Training, and Library Workers, All Other; Geneticists; Geoscientists, Except Hydrologists and Geographers; Medical Scientists, Except Epidemiologists; Molecular and Cellular Biologists; Natural Sciences Managers; Operations Research Analysts; Physical Scientists, All Other; Social Scientists and Related Workers, All Other; Statisticians; Survey Researchers; Transportation Planners; Water Resource Specialists; Zoologists and Wildlife Biologists; others.

**Skills**—No data available.

**Work Environment:** No data available.

## Job Specialization: Water Resource Specialists

**Design or implement programs and strategies related to water resource issues, such as supply, quality, and regulatory compliance issues.** Supervise teams of workers who capture water from wells and rivers. Review or evaluate designs for water detention facilities, storm drains, flood control facilities, or other hydraulic structures. Negotiate for water rights with communities or water facilities to meet water supply demands. Perform hydrologic, hydraulic, or water quality modeling. Compile water resource data, using geographic information systems (GIS) or global position systems (GPS) software. Compile and maintain documentation on the health of a body of water. Write proposals, project reports, informational brochures, or other documents on wastewater purification, water supply and demand, or other water resource subjects. Recommend new or revised policies, procedures, or regulations to support water resource or conservation goals. Provide technical expertise to assist communities in the development or implementation of storm water monitoring or other water programs. Present water resource proposals to government, public interest groups, or community groups. Identify methods for distributing purified wastewater into rivers, streams, or oceans. Monitor water use, demand, or quality in a particular geographic area. Identify and characterize specific causes or sources of water pollution. Develop plans to protect watershed health

or rehabilitate watersheds. Develop or implement standardized water monitoring and assessment methods. Conduct technical studies for water resources on topics such as pollutants and water treatment options. Conduct, or oversee the conduct of, investigations on matters such as water storage, wastewater discharge, pollutants, permits, or other compliance and regulatory issues. Conduct cost-benefit studies for watershed improvement projects or water management alternatives. Analyze storm water systems to identify opportunities for water resource improvements.

**Education/Training Required:** Work experience plus degree. **Education and Training Programs:** Geochemistry; Geological and Earth Sciences/Geosciences, Other; Geology/Earth Science, General; Hydrology and Water Resources Science; Oceanography, Chemical and Physical. **Knowledge/Courses**—No data available.

**Personality Type:** No data available. **Career Cluster:** 15 Science, Technology, Engineering, and Mathematics. **Career Pathway:** 15.2 Science and Mathematics. **Other Jobs in This Pathway:** Architectural and Engineering Managers; Biochemists and Biophysicists; Biofuels/Biodiesel Technology and Product Development Managers; Bioinformatics Scientists; Biological Scientists, All Other; Biologists; Biostatisticians; Chemists; Clinical Data Managers; Clinical Research Coordinators; Community and Social Service Specialists, All Other; Dietitians and Nutritionists; Education, Training, and Library Workers, All Other; Geneticists; Geoscientists, Except Hydrologists and Geographers; Medical Scientists, Except Epidemiologists; Molecular and Cellular Biologists; Natural Sciences Managers; Operations Research Analysts; Physical Scientists, All Other; Social Scientists and Related Workers, All Other; Statisticians; Survey Researchers; Transportation Planners; Zoologists and Wildlife Biologists; others.

**Skills**—No data available.

**Work Environment:** No data available.

## Network and Computer Systems Administrators

- ❀ Annual Earnings: $69,160
- ❀ Earnings Growth Potential: Medium (38.7%)
- ❀ Growth: 23.2%
- ❀ Annual Job Openings: 13,550
- ❀ Self-Employed: 0.8%

**Considerations for Job Outlook:** Employment of these workers should grow as organizations increasingly use network technologies. Job prospects are expected to be excellent.

**Install, configure, and support organizations' local area networks (LANs), wide area networks (WANs), and Internet systems or segments of network systems. Maintain network hardware and software. Monitor networks to ensure network availability to all system users and perform necessary maintenance to support network availability. May supervise other network support and client server specialists and plan, coordinate, and implement network security measures.** Perform data backups and disaster recovery operations. Maintain and administer computer networks and related computing environments including computer hardware, systems software, applications software, and all configurations. Plan, coordinate, and implement network security measures to protect data, software, and hardware. Operate master consoles to monitor the performance of computer systems and networks, and to coordinate computer network access and use. Perform routine network startup and shutdown procedures, and maintain control records. Design, configure, and test computer hardware, networking software and operating system software. Recommend changes to improve systems and network configurations, and determine hardware or software requirements related to such changes. Confer with network users about how to solve existing system problems. Monitor network performance to determine whether adjustments need to be made, and to determine where changes will need to be made in the future. Train people in computer system use. Load computer tapes and disks, and install software and printer paper or forms. Gather data pertaining to customer needs, and use the information to identify, predict, interpret, and evaluate system and network requirements. Analyze equipment performance records to determine the need for repair or replacement. Maintain logs related to network functions, as well as maintenance and repair records. Maintain an inventory of parts for emergency repairs. Coordinate with vendors and with company personnel to facilitate purchases. Diagnose, troubleshoot, and resolve hardware, software, or other network and system problems, and replace defective components when necessary. Configure, monitor, and maintain email applications or virus protection software. Research new technologies by attending seminars, reading trade articles, or taking classes, and implement or recommend the implementation of new technologies.

**Education/Training Required:** Bachelor's degree. **Education and Training Programs:** Network and System Administration/Administrator; System, Networking, and LAN/

WAN Management/Manager. **Knowledge/Courses—** Telecommunications, Computers and Electronics, Clerical, Administration and Management, Engineering and Technology.

**Personality Type:** Investigative-Realistic-Conventional. **Career Cluster:** 11 Information Technology. **Career Pathways:** 11.1 Network Systems; 11.2 Information Support Services; 11.4 Programming and Software Development. **Other Jobs in These Pathways:** Architectural and Engineering Managers; Bioinformatics Scientists; Computer and Information Systems Managers; Computer Hardware Engineers; Computer Numerically Controlled Machine Tool Programmers, Metal and Plastic; Computer Operators; Graphic Designers; Multimedia Artists and Animators; Remote Sensing Scientists and Technologists; Remote Sensing Technicians.

**Skills—**Programming, Equipment Maintenance, Troubleshooting, Equipment Selection, Technology Design, Repairing, Installation, Quality Control Analysis.

**Work Environment:** Indoors; sitting; using hands; repetitive motions; noise.

# Nonfarm Animal Caretakers

- ❀ Annual Earnings: $19,550
- ❀ Earnings Growth Potential: Very low (17.9%)
- ❀ Growth: 20.7%
- ❀ Annual Job Openings: 7,360
- ❀ Self-Employed: 26.5%

**Considerations for Job Outlook:** Pet owners purchasing more services—including grooming, boarding, and training—is expected to lead to employment growth for animal care and service workers. Emphasis on reducing animal abuse should also increase their employment in animal shelters. Excellent opportunities are expected.

**Feed, water, groom, bathe, exercise, or otherwise care for pets and other nonfarm animals, such as dogs, cats, ornamental fish or birds, zoo animals, and mice. Work in settings such as kennels, animal shelters, zoos, circuses, and aquariums. May keep records of feedings, treatments, and animals received or discharged. May clean, disinfect, and repair cages, pens, or fish tanks.** Feed and water animals according to schedules and feeding instructions. Clean, organize, and disinfect animal quarters such as pens, stables, cages, and yards and animal equipment such as saddles and bridles. Answer telephones and schedule appointments.

Examine and observe animals to detect signs of illness, disease, or injury. Respond to questions from patrons and provide information about animals, such as behavior, habitat, breeding habits, or facility activities. Provide treatment to sick or injured animals or contact veterinarians to secure treatment. Collect and record animal information such as weight, size, physical condition, treatments received, medications given, and food intake. Perform animal grooming duties such as washing, brushing, clipping, and trimming coats; cutting nails; and cleaning ears. Exercise animals to maintain their physical and mental health. Order, unload, and store feed and supplies. Mix food, liquid formulas, medications, or food supplements according to instructions, prescriptions, and knowledge of animal species. Clean and disinfect surgical equipment. Discuss with clients their pets' grooming needs. Observe and caution children petting and feeding animals in designated areas to ensure the safety of humans and animals. Find homes for stray or unwanted animals. Adjust controls to regulate specified temperature and humidity of animal quarters, nurseries, or exhibit areas. Anesthetize and inoculate animals, according to instructions. Transfer animals between enclosures to facilitate breeding, birthing, shipping, or rearrangement of exhibits. Install, maintain, and repair animal care facility equipment such as infrared lights, feeding devices, and cages. Train animals to perform certain tasks. Teach obedience classes. Sell pet food and supplies. Saddle and shoe animals.

**Education/Training Required:** Short-term on-the-job training. **Education and Training Programs:** Agricultural/ Farm Supplies Retailing and Wholesaling; Dog/Pet/Animal Grooming. **Knowledge/Courses**—Customer and Personal Service.

**Personality Type:** Realistic-Conventional. **Career Cluster:** 01 Agriculture, Food, and Natural Resources. **Career Pathways:** 1.1 Food Products and Processing Systems; 1.3 Animal Systems. **Other Jobs in These Pathways:** Agricultural Inspectors; Agricultural Technicians; Animal Breeders; Animal Scientists; Animal Trainers; Biologists; Buyers and Purchasing Agents, Farm Products; Chemical Technicians; Farm and Home Management Advisors; First-Line Supervisors of Office and Administrative Support Workers; Food and Tobacco Roasting, Baking, and Drying Machine Operators and Tenders; Food Batchmakers; Food Cooking Machine Operators and Tenders; Food Science Technicians; Food Scientists and Technologists; Geneticists; Graders and Sorters, Agricultural Products; Office Machine Operators, Except Computer; Pest Control Workers; Precision Agriculture Technicians; Veterinarians.

**Skills**—Installation, Management of Material Resources, Technology Design, Service Orientation, Science, Learning Strategies.

**Work Environment:** More often outdoors than indoors; standing; walking and running; using hands; noise; contaminants; minor burns, cuts, bites, or stings.

# Nuclear Engineers

- ❀ Annual Earnings: $99,920
- ❀ Earnings Growth Potential: Low (32.7%)
- ❀ Growth: 10.9%
- ❀ Annual Job Openings: 540
- ❀ Self-Employed: 0.0%

**Considerations for Job Outlook:** Nuclear engineers are expected to have employment growth of 11 percent from 2008–2018, about as fast as the average for all occupations. Most job growth will be in research and development and engineering services. Although no commercial nuclear power plants have been built in the United States for many years, increased interest in nuclear power as an energy source will spur demand for nuclear engineers to research and develop new designs for reactors. They also will be needed to work in defense-related areas, to develop nuclear medical technology, and to improve and enforce waste management and safety standards. Nuclear engineers are expected to have good employment opportunities because the small number of nuclear engineering graduates is likely to be in rough balance with the number of job openings.

**Conduct research on nuclear engineering problems or apply principles and theory of nuclear science to problems concerned with release, control, and utilization of nuclear energy and nuclear waste disposal.** Examine accidents to obtain data that can be used to design preventive measures. Monitor nuclear facility operations to identify any design, construction, or operation practices that violate safety regulations and laws or that could jeopardize the safety of operations. Keep abreast of developments and changes in the nuclear field by reading technical journals and by independent study and research. Perform experiments that will provide information about acceptable methods of nuclear material usage, nuclear fuel reclamation, and waste disposal. Design and oversee construction and operation of nuclear reactors and power plants and nuclear fuels reprocessing and reclamation systems. Design and develop nuclear equipment such as reactor cores, radiation shielding, and associated instrumentation and control mechanisms.

Initiate corrective actions or order plant shutdowns in emergency situations. Recommend preventive measures to be taken in the handling of nuclear technology, based on data obtained from operations monitoring or from evaluation of test results. Write operational instructions to be used in nuclear plant operation and nuclear fuel and waste handling and disposal. Conduct tests of nuclear fuel behavior and cycles and performance of nuclear machinery and equipment to optimize performance of existing plants. Direct operating and maintenance activities of operational nuclear power plants to ensure efficiency and conformity to safety standards. Synthesize analyses of test results and use the results to prepare technical reports of findings and recommendations. Prepare construction project proposals that include cost estimates and discuss proposals with interested parties such as vendors, contractors, and nuclear facility review boards. Analyze available data and consult with other scientists to determine parameters of experimentation and suitability of analytical models.

**Education/Training Required:** Bachelor's degree. **Education and Training Program:** Nuclear Engineering. **Knowledge/Courses**—Engineering and Technology, Physics, Design, Chemistry, Mathematics, Mechanical.

**Personality Type:** Investigative-Realistic-Conventional. **Career Cluster:** 15 Science, Technology, Engineering, and Mathematics. **Career Pathway:** 15.1 Engineering and Technology. **Other Jobs in This Pathway:** Architectural and Engineering Managers; Automotive Engineers; Biochemical Engineers; Biofuels/Biodiesel Technology and Product Development Managers; Civil Engineers; Cost Estimators; Electrical Engineers; Electronics Engineers, Except Computer; Energy Engineers; Engineers, All Other; Fuel Cell Engineers; Human Factors Engineers and Ergonomists; Industrial Engineers; Manufacturing Engineers; Mechanical Engineers; Mechatronics Engineers; Microsystems Engineers; Nanosystems Engineers; Photonics Engineers; Radio Frequency Identification Device Specialists; Robotics Engineers; Solar Energy Systems Engineers; Transportation Engineers; Validation Engineers; Wind Energy Engineers; others.

**Skills**—Operations Analysis, Science, Technology Design, Mathematics, Operation Monitoring, Troubleshooting, Quality Control Analysis, Systems Evaluation.

**Work Environment:** Indoors; sitting; exposed to radiation.

# Nuclear Medicine Technologists

* Annual Earnings: $68,560
* Earnings Growth Potential: Low (28.3%)
* Growth: 16.3%
* Annual Job Openings: 670
* Self-Employed: 0.8%

**Considerations for Job Outlook:** Job growth is expected to result from advancements in nuclear medicine and an increase in the number of older people requiring diagnostic procedures. Competition is expected to be keen.

**Prepare, administer, and measure radioactive isotopes in therapeutic, diagnostic, and tracer studies, using a variety of radioisotope equipment. Prepare stock solutions of radioactive materials and calculate doses to be administered by radiologists. Subject patients to radiation. Execute blood volume, red cell survival, and fat absorption studies, following standard laboratory techniques.** Detect and map radiopharmaceuticals in patients' bodies, using a camera to produce photographic or computer images. Administer radiopharmaceuticals or radiation intravenously to detect or treat diseases, using radioisotope equipment, under direction of a physician. Produce computer-generated or film images for interpretation by physicians. Calculate, measure, and record radiation dosages or radiopharmaceuticals received, used, and disposed, using computers and following physicians' prescriptions. Perform quality control checks on laboratory equipment and cameras. Maintain and calibrate radioisotope and laboratory equipment. Dispose of radioactive materials and store radiopharmaceuticals, following radiation safety procedures. Process cardiac function studies, using computers. Prepare stock radiopharmaceuticals, adhering to safety standards that minimize radiation exposure to workers and patients. Record and process results of procedures. Explain test procedures and safety precautions to patients and provide them with assistance during test procedures. Gather information on patients' illnesses and medical histories to guide choices of diagnostic procedures for therapies. Measure glandular activity, blood volume, red cell survival, and radioactivity of patient, using scanners, Geiger counters, scintillation counters, and other laboratory equipment. Train and supervise student or subordinate nuclear medicine technologists. Position radiation fields, radiation beams, and patients to allow for most effective treatment of patients' diseases, using computers. Add radioactive substances to biological specimens such as blood, urine, and feces to determine therapeutic drug or hormone levels. Develop treatment procedures for nuclear medicine treatment programs.

**Education/Training Required:** Associate degree. **Education and Training Programs:** Nuclear Medical Technology/Technologist; Radiation Protection/Health Physics Technician Training. **Knowledge/Courses**—Medicine and Dentistry, Biology, Chemistry, Physics, Customer and Personal Service, Therapy and Counseling.

**Personality Type:** Investigative-Realistic-Social. **Career Cluster:** 08 Health Science. **Career Pathways:** 8.1 Therapeutic Services; 8.2 Diagnostics Services. **Other Jobs in These Pathways:** Clinical Psychologists; Counseling Psychologists; Cytogenetic Technologists; Cytotechnologists; Dental Assistants; Dental Hygienists; Dentists, General; Emergency Medical Technicians and Paramedics; Endoscopy Technicians; Healthcare Support Workers, All Other; Histotechnologists and Histologic Technicians; Home Health Aides; Licensed Practical and Licensed Vocational Nurses; Massage Therapists; Medical and Clinical Laboratory Technicians; Medical and Clinical Laboratory Technologists; Medical and Health Services Managers; Medical Assistants; Medical Secretaries; Pharmacists; Pharmacy Technicians; Radiologic Technologists; School Psychologists; Social and Human Service Assistants; Speech-Language Pathology Assistants; others.

**Skills**—Science, Equipment Maintenance, Quality Control Analysis, Operation Monitoring, Repairing, Troubleshooting, Operation and Control, Service Orientation.

**Work Environment:** Indoors; standing; walking and running; using hands; contaminants; exposed to radiation; exposed to disease or infections; hazardous conditions.

# Nuclear Power Reactor Operators

- ❋ Annual Earnings: $75,650
- ❋ Earnings Growth Potential: Very low (23.2%)
- ❋ Growth: 18.9%
- ❋ Annual Job Openings: 270
- ❋ Self-Employed: 0.0%

**Considerations for Job Outlook:** Although annual energy use continues to grow in the United States, greater power plant efficiency is expected to temper employment gains resulting from that growth. Job opportunities should be excellent, however, because of the need to replace a large number of retiring workers.

**Control nuclear reactors.** Adjust controls to position rod and to regulate flux level, reactor period, coolant temperature, and rate of power flow, following standard procedures.

Respond to system or unit abnormalities, diagnosing the cause and recommending or taking corrective action. Monitor all systems for normal running conditions, performing activities such as checking gauges to assess output or assess the effects of generator loading on other equipment. Implement operational procedures such as those controlling startup and shutdown activities. Note malfunctions of equipment, instruments, or controls and report these conditions to supervisors. Monitor and operate boilers, turbines, wells, and auxiliary power plant equipment. Dispatch orders and instructions to personnel through radiotelephone or intercommunication systems to coordinate auxiliary equipment operation. Record operating data such as the results of surveillance tests. Participate in nuclear fuel element handling activities such as preparation, transfer, loading, and unloading. Conduct inspections and operations outside of control rooms as necessary. Direct reactor operators in emergency situations in accordance with emergency operating procedures. Authorize maintenance activities on units and changes in equipment and system operational status.

**Education/Training Required:** Long-term on-the-job training. **Education and Training Program:** Nuclear/Nuclear Power Technology/Technician. **Knowledge/Courses**—Physics, Chemistry, Engineering and Technology, Mechanical, Design, Mathematics.

**Personality Type:** Realistic-Conventional-Enterprising. **Career Cluster:** 13 Manufacturing. **Career Pathways:** 13.1 Production; 13.3 Maintenance, Installation, and Repair. **Other Jobs in These Pathways:** Assemblers and Fabricators, All Other; Automotive Specialty Technicians; Computer, Automated Teller, and Office Machine Repairers; Cost Estimators; Cutting, Punching, and Press Machine Setters, Operators, and Tenders, Metal and Plastic; Electrical and Electronic Equipment Assemblers; Electrical Engineering Technicians; Electronics Engineering Technicians; First-Line Supervisors of Mechanics, Installers, and Repairers; First-Line Supervisors of Production and Operating Workers; Geothermal Technicians; Helpers—Production Workers; Industrial Machinery Mechanics; Installation, Maintenance, and Repair Workers, All Other; Machinists; Packaging and Filling Machine Operators and Tenders; Packers and Packagers, Hand; Production Workers, All Other; Recycling and Reclamation Workers; Recycling Coordinators; Sheet Metal Workers; Solderers and Brazers; Team Assemblers; Telecommunications Line Installers and Repairers; Welders, Cutters, and Welder Fitters; others.

**Skills**—Operation and Control, Troubleshooting, Operation Monitoring, Science, Quality Control Analysis, Monitoring, Instructing, Mathematics.

**Work Environment:** Indoors; sitting; using hands; noise; exposed to radiation.

# Nursing Instructors and Teachers, Postsecondary

* Annual Earnings: $62,390
* Earnings Growth Potential: Medium (38.1%)
* Growth: 15.1%
* Annual Job Openings: 1,500
* Self-Employed: 0.2%

**Considerations for Job Outlook:** Enrollments in postsecondary institutions are expected to continue rising as more people attend college and as workers return to school to update their skills. Opportunities for part-time or temporary positions should be favorable, but significant competition exists for tenure-track positions.

**Demonstrate and teach patient care in classroom and clinical units to nursing students. Includes both teachers primarily engaged in teaching and those who do a combination of both teaching and research.** Initiate, facilitate, and moderate classroom discussions. Prepare and deliver lectures to undergraduate or graduate students on topics such as pharmacology, mental health nursing, and community health-care practices. Keep abreast of developments in their field by reading current literature, talking with colleagues, and participating in professional conferences. Prepare course materials such as syllabi, homework assignments, and handouts. Supervise students' laboratory and clinical work. Evaluate and grade students' classwork, laboratory and clinic work, assignments, and papers. Collaborate with colleagues to address teaching and research issues. Plan, evaluate, and revise curricula, course content, and course materials and methods of instruction. Assess clinical education needs and patient and client teaching needs, utilizing a variety of methods. Compile, administer, and grade examinations or assign this work to others. Advise students on academic and vocational curricula and on career issues. Maintain student attendance records, grades, and other required records. Maintain regularly scheduled office hours to advise and assist students. Supervise undergraduate or graduate teaching, internship, and research work. Conduct research in a particular field of knowledge and publish findings in professional journals, books, and/or electronic media. Participate in student recruitment, registration, and placement activities. Serve on academic or administrative committees that deal with institutional policies, departmental matters,

and academic issues. Coordinate training programs with area universities, clinics, hospitals, health agencies, and/or vocational schools. Compile bibliographies of specialized materials for outside reading assignments. Select and obtain materials and supplies such as textbooks and laboratory equipment. Participate in campus and community events. Write grant proposals to procure external research funding. Act as advisers to student organizations.

**Education/Training Required:** Doctoral degree. **Education and Training Program:** Pre-Nursing Studies. **Knowledge/Courses**—Therapy and Counseling, Sociology and Anthropology, Biology, Medicine and Dentistry, Philosophy and Theology, Psychology.

**Personality Type:** Social-Investigative. **Career Clusters:** 05 Education and Training; 08 Health Science. **Career Pathways:** 5.3 Teaching/Training; 8.1 Therapeutic Services. **Other Jobs in These Pathways:** Coaches and Scouts; Dental Assistants; Dental Hygienists; Elementary School Teachers, Except Special Education; Fitness Trainers and Aerobics Instructors; Healthcare Support Workers, All Other; Home Health Aides; Kindergarten Teachers, Except Special Education; Librarians; Licensed Practical and Licensed Vocational Nurses; Medical and Health Services Managers; Medical Secretaries; Middle School Teachers, Except Special and Career/Technical Education; Pharmacists; Pharmacy Technicians; Preschool Teachers, Except Special Education; Radiologic Technologists; Recreation Workers; Secondary School Teachers, Except Special and Career/Technical Education; Self-Enrichment Education Teachers; Social and Human Service Assistants; Speech-Language Pathology Assistants; Teacher Assistants; Tutors; 37 other postsecondary teaching occupations; others.

**Skills**—Instructing, Science, Writing, Learning Strategies, Speaking, Reading Comprehension, Active Learning, Active Listening.

**Work Environment:** Indoors; sitting; exposed to disease or infections.

# Occupational Health and Safety Specialists

* Annual Earnings: $64,660
* Earnings Growth Potential: Medium (40.0%)
* Growth: 11.2%
* Annual Job Openings: 2,490
* Self-Employed: 0.7%

**Considerations for Job Outlook:** These workers will be needed to ensure workplace safety in response to changing hazards, regulations, public expectations, and technology.

**Review, evaluate, and analyze work environments, and design programs and procedures to control, eliminate, and prevent diseases or injuries caused by chemical, physical, and biological agents or ergonomic factors.** Order suspension of activities that pose threats to workers' health and safety. Recommend measures to help protect workers from potentially hazardous work methods, processes, or materials. Investigate accidents to identify causes and to determine how such accidents might be prevented in the future. Investigate the adequacy of ventilation, exhaust equipment, lighting, and other conditions that could affect employee health, comfort, or performance. Develop and maintain hygiene programs such as noise surveys, continuous atmosphere monitoring, ventilation surveys, and asbestos management plans. Inspect and evaluate workplace environments, equipment, and practices in order to ensure compliance with safety standards and government regulations. Collaborate with engineers and physicians to institute control and remedial measures for hazardous and potentially hazardous conditions or equipment. Conduct safety training and education programs and demonstrate the use of safety equipment. Provide new-employee health and safety orientations and develop materials for these presentations. Collect samples of dust, gases, vapors, and other potentially toxic materials for analysis. Investigate health-related complaints and inspect facilities to ensure that they comply with public health legislation and regulations. Coordinate "right-to-know" programs regarding hazardous chemicals and other substances. Maintain and update emergency response plans and procedures. Develop and maintain medical monitoring programs for employees. Inspect specified areas to ensure the presence of fire prevention equipment, safety equipment, and first-aid supplies. Conduct audits at hazardous waste sites or industrial sites and participate in hazardous waste site investigations. Collect samples of hazardous materials or arrange for sample collection. Maintain inventories of hazardous materials and hazardous wastes, using waste tracking systems, to ensure that materials are handled properly.

**Education/Training Required:** Bachelor's degree. **Education and Training Programs:** Environmental Health; Industrial Safety Technology/Technician; Occupational Health and Industrial Hygiene; Occupational Safety and Health Technology/Technician; Quality Control and Safety Technologies/Technicians, Other. **Knowledge/Courses—** Chemistry, Biology, Physics, Engineering and Technology, Public Safety and Security, Building and Construction.

**Personality Type:** Investigative-Conventional. **Career Clusters:** 01 Agriculture, Food, and Natural Resources; 08 Health Science; 13 Manufacturing. **Career Pathways:** 1.6 Environmental Service Systems; 8.3 Health Informatics; 13.4 Quality Assurance. **Other Jobs in These Pathways:** Clinical Psychologists; Dental Laboratory Technicians; Editors; Engineers, All Other; Executive Secretaries and Executive Administrative Assistants; Fine Artists, Including Painters, Sculptors, and Illustrators; First-Line Supervisors of Office and Administrative Support Workers; Hazardous Materials Removal Workers; Health Educators; Inspectors, Testers, Sorters, Samplers, and Weighers; Medical and Health Services Managers; Medical Assistants; Medical Records and Health Information Technicians; Medical Secretaries; Medical Transcriptionists; Mental Health Counselors; Physical Therapists; Psychiatric Aides; Psychiatric Technicians; Public Relations Specialists; Receptionists and Information Clerks; Rehabilitation Counselors; Substance Abuse and Behavioral Disorder Counselors; Therapists, All Other; Water and Wastewater Treatment Plant and System Operators; others.

**Skills**—Science, Operations Analysis, Quality Control Analysis, Operation Monitoring, Persuasion, Troubleshooting, Systems Evaluation, Programming.

**Work Environment:** More often indoors than outdoors; sitting; noise; contaminants.

## Occupational Therapists

- ❋ Annual Earnings: $72,320
- ❋ Earnings Growth Potential: Low (32.4%)
- ❋ Growth: 25.6%
- ❋ Annual Job Openings: 4,580
- ❋ Self-Employed: 7.0%

**Considerations for Job Outlook:** Employment growth for occupational therapists should continue as the population ages and better medical technology increases the survival rates of people who become injured or ill. Job opportunities are expected be good.

**Assess, plan, organize, and participate in rehabilitative programs that help restore vocational, homemaking, and daily living skills, as well as general independence, to disabled persons.** Plan, organize, and conduct occupational therapy programs in hospital, institutional, or community settings to help rehabilitate those impaired because of illness, injury, or psychological or developmental problems. Test and evaluate patients' physical and mental abilities and analyze medical data to determine realistic rehabilitation goals for patients. Select activities that will help individuals learn work and life-management skills within limits of their mental and physical capabilities. Evaluate patients' progress and prepare reports that detail progress. Complete and maintain necessary records. Train caregivers to provide for the needs of patients during and after therapies. Recommend changes in patients' work or living environments, consistent with their needs and capabilities. Develop and participate in health promotion programs, group activities, or discussions to promote client health, facilitate social adjustment, alleviate stress, and prevent physical or mental disability. Consult with rehabilitation team to select activity programs and coordinate occupational therapy with other therapeutic activities. Plan and implement programs and social activities to help patients learn work and school skills and adjust to handicaps. Design and create, or requisition, special supplies and equipment such as splints, braces and computer-aided adaptive equipment. Conduct research in occupational therapy. Provide training and supervision in therapy techniques and objectives for students and nurses and other medical staff. Help clients improve decision making, abstract reasoning, memory, sequencing, coordination, and perceptual skills, using computer programs. Advise on health risks in the workplace and on health-related transition to retirement. Lay out materials such as puzzles, scissors, and eating utensils for use in therapy, and clean and repair these tools after therapy sessions. Provide patients with assistance in locating and holding jobs.

**Education/Training Required:** Master's degree. **Education and Training Program:** Occupational Therapy/Therapist. **Knowledge/Courses**—Therapy and Counseling, Psychology, Sociology and Anthropology, Medicine and Dentistry, Biology, Philosophy and Theology.

**Personality Type:** Social-Investigative. **Career Cluster:** 08 Health Science. **Career Pathway:** 8.1 Therapeutic Services. **Other Jobs in This Pathway:** Clinical Psychologists; Community and Social Service Specialists, All Other; Counseling Psychologists; Dental Assistants; Dental Hygienists; Dentists, General; Health Technologists and Technicians, All Other; Healthcare Support Workers, All Other; Home Health Aides; Licensed Practical and Licensed Vocational Nurses; Low Vision Therapists, Orientation and Mobility Specialists, and Vision Rehabilitation Therapists; Massage Therapists; Medical and Clinical Laboratory Technicians; Medical and Health Services Managers; Medical Scientists, Except Epidemiologists; Medical Secretaries; Ophthalmic Medical Technologists; Pharmacists; Pharmacy Technicians; Radiologic Technologists; School Psychologists; Social and Human Service Assistants; Speech-Language Pathologists; Speech-Language Pathology Assistants; Substance Abuse and Behavioral Disorder Counselors; others.

**Skills**—Operations Analysis, Science, Service Orientation, Social Perceptiveness, Active Listening, Writing, Learning Strategies, Instructing.

**Work Environment:** Indoors; standing; using hands; bending or twisting the body; exposed to disease or infections.

## Job Specialization: Low Vision Therapists, Orientation and Mobility Specialists, and Vision Rehabilitation Therapists

**Provide therapy to patients with visual impairments to improve their functioning in daily life activities. May train patients in activities such as computer use, communication skills, or home management skills.** Teach cane skills including cane use with a guide, diagonal techniques, and two-point touches. Refer clients to services, such as eye care, health care, rehabilitation, and counseling, to enhance visual and life functioning or when condition exceeds scope of practice. Provide consultation, support, or education to groups such as parents and teachers. Participate in professional development activities such as reading literature, continuing education, attending conferences, and collaborating with colleagues. Obtain, distribute, or maintain low vision devices. Design instructional programs to improve communication using devices such as slates and styluses, braillers, keyboards, adaptive handwriting devices, talking book machines, digital books, and optical character readers (OCRs). Collaborate with specialists, such as rehabilitation counselors, speech pathologists, and occupational therapists, to provide client solutions. Administer tests and interpret test results to develop rehabilitation plans for clients. Train clients to read or write Braille. Teach clients to travel independently using a variety of actual or simulated travel situations or exercises. Train clients to use tactile, auditory, kinesthetic, olfactory, and propioceptive information. Train clients to use adaptive equipment such as large print, reading stands, lamps, writing implements, software, and electronic devices. Monitor clients' progress to determine whether changes in rehabilitation plans are needed. Write reports or complete forms to document assessments, training, progress, or follow-up outcomes. Develop rehabilitation or instructional plans collaboratively with clients, based on results of assessments, needs, and goals. Assess clients' functioning in areas such as vision, orientation and mobility skills, social and emotional issues, cognition, physical abilities, and personal goals.

**Education/Training Required:** Master's degree. **Education and Training Program:** Occupational Therapy/Therapist. **Knowledge/Courses**—Therapy and Counseling, Psychology, Sociology and Anthropology, Education and Training, Transportation, Medicine and Dentistry.

**Personality Type:** Social-Investigative-Realistic. **Career Cluster:** 08 Health Science. **Career Pathway:** 8.1 Therapeutic Services. **Other Jobs in This Pathway:** Clinical Psychologists; Community and Social Service Specialists, All Other; Counseling Psychologists; Dental Assistants; Dental Hygienists; Dentists, General; Health Technologists and Technicians, All Other; Healthcare Support Workers, All Other; Home Health Aides; Licensed Practical and Licensed Vocational Nurses; Massage Therapists; Medical and Clinical Laboratory Technicians; Medical and Health Services Managers; Medical Scientists, Except Epidemiologists; Medical Secretaries; Occupational Therapists; Ophthalmic Medical Technologists; Pharmacists; Pharmacy Technicians; Radiologic Technologists; School Psychologists; Social and Human Service Assistants; Speech-Language Pathologists; Speech-Language Pathology Assistants; Substance Abuse and Behavioral Disorder Counselors; others.

**Skills**—Technology Design, Learning Strategies, Writing, Social Perceptiveness, Reading Comprehension, Service Orientation, Negotiation, Systems Evaluation.

**Work Environment:** More often outdoors than indoors; standing.

## Occupational Therapy Assistants

- ❋ Annual Earnings: $51,010
- ❋ Earnings Growth Potential: Low (35.1%)
- ❋ Growth: 29.8%
- ❋ Annual Job Openings: 1,180
- ❋ Self-Employed: 2.1%

**Considerations for Job Outlook:** Employment growth for occupational therapist assistants should continue as the population ages and better medical technology increases the survival rates of people who become injured or ill. Job prospects should be very good for assistants who have credentials.

**Assist occupational therapists in providing occupational therapy treatments and procedures. May, in accordance with state laws, assist in development of treatment plans, carry out routine functions, direct activity programs, and document the progress of treatments. Generally requires formal training.** Observe and record patients' progress, attitudes, and behavior and maintain this information in client records. Maintain and promote a positive attitude toward clients and their treatment programs. Monitor patients' performance in therapy activities, providing encouragement. Select therapy activities to fit patients' needs and capabilities. Instruct, or assist in instructing, patients and families in home programs, basic living skills, and the care and use of adaptive equipment. Evaluate the daily living skills and capacities of physically, developmentally, or emotionally disabled clients. Aid patients in dressing and grooming themselves. Implement, or assist occupational therapists with implementing, treatment plans designed to help clients function independently. Report to supervisors, verbally or in writing, on patients' progress, attitudes, and behavior. Alter treatment programs to obtain better results if treatment is not having the intended effect. Work under the direction of occupational therapists to plan, implement, and administer educational, vocational, and recreational programs that restore and enhance performance in individuals with functional impairments. Design, fabricate, and repair assistive devices and make adaptive changes to equipment and environments. Assemble, clean, and maintain equipment and materials for patient use. Teach patients how to deal constructively with their emotions. Perform clerical duties such as scheduling appointments, collecting data, and documenting health insurance billings. Transport patients to and from the occupational therapy work area. Demonstrate therapy techniques such as manual and creative arts or games. Order any needed educational or treatment supplies. Assist educational specialists or clinical psychologists in administering situational or diagnostic tests to measure client's abilities or progress.

**Education/Training Required:** Associate degree. **Education and Training Program:** Occupational Therapist Assistant Training. **Knowledge/Courses**—Psychology, Therapy and Counseling, Philosophy and Theology, Medicine and Dentistry, Sociology and Anthropology, Education and Training.

**Personality Type:** Social-Realistic. **Career Cluster:** 08 Health Science. **Career Pathway:** 8.1 Therapeutic Services. **Other Jobs in This Pathway:** Clinical Psychologists; Community and Social Service Specialists, All Other; Counseling Psychologists; Dental Assistants; Dental Hygienists; Dentists, General; Health Technologists and Technicians, All Other; Healthcare Support Workers, All Other; Home Health Aides; Licensed Practical and Licensed Vocational Nurses; Low Vision Therapists, Orientation and Mobility Specialists, and Vision Rehabilitation Therapists; Massage Therapists; Medical and Clinical Laboratory Technicians; Medical and Health Services Managers; Medical Scientists, Except Epidemiologists; Medical Secretaries; Occupational

Therapists; Pharmacists; Pharmacy Technicians; Radiologic Technologists; School Psychologists; Social and Human Service Assistants; Speech-Language Pathologists; Speech-Language Pathology Assistants; Substance Abuse and Behavioral Disorder Counselors; others.

**Skills**—Learning Strategies, Social Perceptiveness, Service Orientation, Negotiation, Instructing, Persuasion, Operation Monitoring, Writing.

**Work Environment:** Indoors; standing; using hands; noise; exposed to disease or infections.

# Office Clerks, General

- ❋ Annual Earnings: $26,610
- ❋ Earnings Growth Potential: Low (35.1%)
- ❋ Growth: 11.9%
- ❋ Annual Job Openings: 77,090
- ❋ Self-Employed: 0.4%

**Considerations for Job Outlook:** Employment growth is expected to be spurred by new technology that allows these clerks to perform tasks previously done by specialists. Numerous opportunities are expected.

**Perform duties too varied and diverse to be classified in any specific office clerical occupation requiring limited knowledge of office management systems and procedures. Clerical duties may be assigned in accordance with the office procedures of individual establishments and may include a combination of answering telephones, bookkeeping, typing or word processing, stenography, office machine operation, and filing.** Collect, count, and disburse money; do basic bookkeeping; and complete banking transactions. Communicate with customers, employees, and other individuals to answer questions, disseminate or explain information, take orders, and address complaints. Answer telephones, direct calls, and take messages. Compile, copy, sort, and file records of office activities, business transactions, and other activities. Complete and mail bills, contracts, policies, invoices, or checks. Operate office machines such as photocopiers and scanners, facsimile machines, voice mail systems, and personal computers. Compute, record, and proofread data and other information, such as records or reports. Maintain and update filing, inventory, mailing, and database systems, either manually or using a computer. Open, sort, and route incoming mail; answer correspondence; and prepare outgoing mail. Review files, records, and other documents to obtain information to respond to requests. Deliver messages and run errands. Inventory and order materials, supplies, and services. Complete work schedules, manage calendars, and arrange appointments. Process and prepare documents such as business or government forms and expense reports. Monitor and direct the work of lower-level clerks. Type, format, proofread, and edit correspondence and other documents from notes or dictating machines, using computers or typewriters. Count, weigh, measure, or organize materials. Train other staff members to perform work activities, such as using computer applications. Prepare meeting agendas, attend meetings, and record and transcribe minutes. Troubleshoot problems involving office equipment, such as computer hardware and software. Make travel arrangements for office personnel.

**Education/Training Required:** Short-term on-the-job training. **Education and Training Program:** General Office Occupations and Clerical Services. **Knowledge/Courses**—Clerical, Customer and Personal Service, Computers and Electronics.

**Personality Type:** Conventional-Enterprising-Realistic. **Career Cluster:** 04 Business, Management, and Administration. **Career Pathway:** 4.6 Administrative and Information Support. **Other Jobs in This Pathway:** Couriers and Messengers; Court Clerks; Court, Municipal, and License Clerks; Customer Service Representatives; Data Entry Keyers; Dispatchers, Except Police, Fire, and Ambulance; Executive Secretaries and Executive Administrative Assistants; File Clerks; Human Resources Assistants, Except Payroll and Timekeeping; Information and Record Clerks, All Other; Insurance Claims Clerks; Insurance Policy Processing Clerks; Interviewers, Except Eligibility and Loan; License Clerks; Mail Clerks and Mail Machine Operators, Except Postal Service; Office and Administrative Support Workers, All Other; Order Clerks; Patient Representatives; Postal Service Mail Carriers; Postal Service Mail Sorters, Processors, and Processing Machine Operators; Receptionists and Information Clerks; Secretaries and Administrative Assistants, Except Legal, Medical, and Executive; Shipping, Receiving, and Traffic Clerks; Switchboard Operators, Including Answering Service; Word Processors and Typists; others.

**Skills**—Management of Material Resources, Service Orientation, Active Listening, Management of Financial Resources, Reading Comprehension, Speaking.

**Work Environment:** Indoors; sitting; repetitive motions.

# Operating Engineers and Other Construction Equipment Operators

- ❋ Annual Earnings: $40,400
- ❋ Earnings Growth Potential: Low (34.5%)
- ❋ Growth: 12.0%
- ❋ Annual Job Openings: 11,820
- ❋ Self-Employed: 3.4%

**Considerations for Job Outlook:** Increased government spending on infrastructure is expected to generate employment growth for these workers. Operators who have varied expertise are expected to have the best prospects.

**Operate one or several types of power construction equipment, such as motor graders, bulldozers, scrapers, compressors, pumps, derricks, shovels, tractors, or front-end loaders, to excavate, move, and grade earth; erect structures; or pour concrete or other hard-surface pavement. May repair and maintain equipment in addition to other duties.** Learn and follow safety regulations. Take actions to avoid potential hazards and obstructions such as utility lines, other equipment, other workers, and falling objects. Adjust handwheels and depress pedals to control attachments such as blades, buckets, scrapers, and swing booms. Start engines; move throttles, switches, and levers; and depress pedals to operate machines such as bulldozers, trench excavators, road graders, and backhoes. Locate underground services, such as pipes and wires, prior to beginning work. Monitor operations to ensure that health and safety standards are met. Align machines, cutterheads, or depth gauge makers with reference stakes and guidelines or ground or position equipment by following hand signals of other workers. Load and move dirt, rocks, equipment, and materials, using trucks, crawler tractors, power cranes, shovels, graders, and related equipment. Drive and maneuver equipment equipped with blades in successive passes over working areas to remove topsoil, vegetation, and rocks and to distribute and level earth or terrain. Coordinate machine actions with other activities, positioning or moving loads in response to hand or audio signals from crew members. Operate tractors and bulldozers to perform such tasks as clearing land, mixing sludge, trimming backfills, and building roadways and parking lots. Repair and maintain equipment, making emergency adjustments or assisting with major repairs as necessary. Check fuel supplies at sites to ensure adequate availability. Connect hydraulic hoses, belts, mechanical linkages, or power take-off shafts to tractors. Operate loaders to pull out stumps, rip asphalt or concrete, rough-grade properties, bury refuse, or perform general cleanup. Select and fasten bulldozer blades

or other attachments to tractors, using hitches. Test atmosphere for adequate oxygen and explosive conditions when working in confined spaces.

**Education/Training Required:** Moderate-term on-the-job training. **Education and Training Programs:** Construction/Heavy Equipment/Earthmoving Equipment Operation; Mobile Crane Operation/Operator. **Knowledge/Courses**—Building and Construction, Mechanical, Engineering and Technology, Design, Production and Processing, Public Safety and Security.

**Personality Type:** Realistic-Conventional-Investigative. **Career Clusters:** 02 Architecture and Construction; 16 Transportation, Distribution, and Logistics. **Career Pathways:** 2.2 Construction; 16.1 Transportation Operations. **Other Jobs in These Pathways:** Automotive Master Mechanics; Bus Drivers, School or Special Client; Bus Drivers, Transit and Intercity; Cement Masons and Concrete Finishers; Construction Carpenters; Construction Laborers; Construction Managers; Cost Estimators; Drywall and Ceiling Tile Installers; Electricians; First-Line Supervisors of Construction Trades and Extraction Workers; First-Line Supervisors of Helpers, Laborers, and Material Movers, Hand; First-Line Supervisors of Transportation and Material-Moving Machine and Vehicle Operators; Heating and Air Conditioning Mechanics and Installers; Heavy and Tractor-Trailer Truck Drivers; Laborers and Freight, Stock, and Material Movers, Hand; Light Truck or Delivery Services Drivers; Painters, Construction and Maintenance; Pipe Fitters and Steamfitters; Plumbers; Refrigeration Mechanics and Installers; Roofers; Rough Carpenters; Solar Energy Installation Managers; Taxi Drivers and Chauffeurs; others.

**Skills**—Operation and Control, Repairing, Equipment Maintenance, Troubleshooting, Operation Monitoring, Quality Control Analysis, Equipment Selection, Installation.

**Work Environment:** Outdoors; sitting; using hands; repetitive motions; noise; very hot or cold; bright or inadequate lighting; contaminants; whole-body vibration; hazardous equipment; minor burns, cuts, bites, or stings.

# Operations Research Analysts

- ❋ Annual Earnings: $70,960
- ❋ Earnings Growth Potential: High (43.7%)
- ❋ Growth: 22.0%
- ❋ Annual Job Openings: 3,220
- ❋ Self-Employed: 0.2%

**Considerations for Job Outlook:** As technology advances and companies further emphasize efficiency, demand for operations research analysis should continue to grow. Excellent opportunities are expected, especially for those who have an advanced degree.

**Formulate and apply mathematical modeling and other optimizing methods, using a computer to develop and interpret information that assists management with decision making, policy formulation, or other managerial functions. May develop related software, service, or products. Frequently concentrates on collecting and analyzing data and developing decision support software. May develop and supply optimal time, cost, or logistics networks for program evaluation, review, or implementation.** Formulate mathematical or simulation models of problems, relating constants and variables, restrictions, alternatives, and conflicting objectives and their numerical parameters. Collaborate with others in the organization to ensure successful implementation of chosen problem solutions. Analyze information obtained from management in order to conceptualize and define operational problems. Perform validation and testing of models to ensure adequacy; reformulate models as necessary. Collaborate with senior managers and decision-makers to identify and solve a variety of problems and to clarify management objectives. Define data requirements; then gather and validate information, applying judgment and statistical tests. Study and analyze information about alternative courses of action in order to determine which plan will offer the best outcomes. Prepare management reports defining and evaluating problems and recommending solutions. Break systems into their component parts, assign numerical values to each component, and examine the mathematical relationships between them. Specify manipulative or computational methods to be applied to models. Observe the current system in operation and gather and analyze information about each of the parts of component problems, using a variety of sources. Design, conduct, and evaluate experimental operational models in cases where models cannot be developed from existing data. Develop and apply time and cost networks in order to plan, control, and review large projects. Develop business methods and procedures, including accounting systems, file systems, office systems, logistics systems, and production schedules.

**Education/Training Required:** Master's degree. **Education and Training Programs:** Management Science; Management Sciences and Quantitative Methods, Other; Operations Research. **Knowledge/Courses**—Mathematics, Engineering and Technology, Computers and Electronics,

Production and Processing, Economics and Accounting, Administration and Management.

**Personality Type:** Investigative-Conventional-Enterprising. **Career Clusters:** 04 Business, Management, and Administration; 15 Science, Technology, Engineering, and Mathematics. **Career Pathways:** 4.1 Management; 4.4 Business Analysis; 15.2 Science and Mathematics. **Other Jobs in These Pathways:** Brownfield Redevelopment Specialists and Site Managers; Business Continuity Planners; Business Operations Specialists, All Other; Chief Executives; Chief Sustainability Officers; Compliance Managers; Computer and Information Systems Managers; Construction Managers; Customs Brokers; Energy Auditors; First-Line Supervisors of Office and Administrative Support Workers; General and Operations Managers; Investment Fund Managers; Loss Prevention Managers; Management Analysts; Managers, All Other; Public Relations Specialists; Regulatory Affairs Managers; Sales Managers; Security Management Specialists; Security Managers; Supply Chain Managers; Sustainability Specialists; Wind Energy Operations Managers; Wind Energy Project Managers; others.

**Skills**—Operations Analysis, Science, Mathematics, Systems Evaluation, Systems Analysis, Programming, Complex Problem Solving, Active Learning.

**Work Environment:** Indoors; sitting.

# Opticians, Dispensing

* Annual Earnings: $32,940
* Earnings Growth Potential: Medium (36.0%)
* Growth: 13.4%
* Annual Job Openings: 2,020
* Self-Employed: 1.2%

**Considerations for Job Outlook:** Demand for vision correction will increase as the population ages. But projected employment growth for these workers should be moderated by the increasing prevalence of laser vision-correcting surgery. Very good job prospects are expected.

**Design, measure, fit, and adapt lenses and frames for client according to written optical prescription or specification. Assist client with selecting frames. Measure customer for size of eyeglasses and coordinate frames with facial and eye measurements and optical prescription. Prepare work order for optical laboratory containing instructions for grinding and mounting lenses in frames. Verify exactness of finished lens spectacles.**

**Adjust frame and lens position to fit client. May shape or reshape frames.** Measure clients' bridge and eye size, temple length, vertex distance, pupillary distance, and optical centers of eyes, using measuring devices. Verify that finished lenses are ground to specifications. Prepare work orders and instructions for grinding lenses and fabricating eyeglasses. Assist clients in selecting frames according to style and color and ensure that frames are coordinated with facial and eye measurements and optical prescriptions. Maintain records of customer prescriptions, work orders, and payments. Perform administrative duties such as tracking inventory and sales, submitting patient insurance information, and performing simple bookkeeping. Recommend specific lenses, lens coatings, and frames to suit client needs. Sell goods such as contact lenses, spectacles, sunglasses, and other goods related to eyes in general. Heat, shape, or bend plastic or metal frames to adjust eyeglasses to fit clients, using pliers and hands. Evaluate prescriptions in conjunction with clients' vocational and avocational visual requirements. Instruct clients in how to wear and care for eyeglasses. Determine clients' current lens prescriptions, when necessary, using lensometers or lens analyzers and clients' eyeglasses. Show customers how to insert, remove, and care for their contact lenses. Repair damaged frames. Obtain a customer's previous record or verify a prescription with the examining optometrist or ophthalmologist. Arrange and maintain displays of optical merchandise. Fabricate lenses to meet prescription specifications. Grind lens edges or apply coatings to lenses. Assemble eyeglasses by cutting and edging lenses and fitting the lenses into frames. Supervise the training of student opticians.

**Education/Training Required:** Long-term on-the-job training. **Education and Training Program:** Opticianry/Ophthalmic Dispensing Optician. **Knowledge/Courses—** Sales and Marketing, Clerical, Customer and Personal Service, Production and Processing, Economics and Accounting, Psychology.

**Personality Type:** Enterprising-Conventional-Realistic. **Career Cluster:** 08 Health Science. **Career Pathway:** 8.1 Therapeutic Services. **Other Jobs in This Pathway:** Clinical Psychologists; Community and Social Service Specialists, All Other; Counseling Psychologists; Dental Assistants; Dental Hygienists; Dentists, General; Health Technologists and Technicians, All Other; Healthcare Support Workers, All Other; Home Health Aides; Licensed Practical and Licensed Vocational Nurses; Low Vision Therapists, Orientation and Mobility Specialists, and Vision Rehabilitation Therapists; Massage Therapists; Medical and Clinical Laboratory Technicians; Medical and Health Services Managers; Medical Scientists, Except Epidemiologists; Medical Secretaries; Occupational Therapists; Pharmacists; Pharmacy Technicians; Radiologic Technologists; School Psychologists; Social and Human Service Assistants; Speech-Language Pathologists; Speech-Language Pathology Assistants; Substance Abuse and Behavioral Disorder Counselors; others.

**Skills—**Service Orientation, Technology Design, Negotiation, Instructing, Persuasion, Operations Analysis, Quality Control Analysis, Operation Monitoring.

**Work Environment:** Indoors; standing; using hands.

# Optometrists

* Annual Earnings: $94,990
* Earnings Growth Potential: High (47.8%)
* Growth: 24.4%
* Annual Job Openings: 2,010
* Self-Employed: 24.6%

**Considerations for Job Outlook:** An aging population and increasing insurance coverage for vision care are expected to lead to employment growth for optometrists. Excellent opportunities are expected.

**Diagnose, manage, and treat conditions and diseases of the human eye and visual system. Examine eyes and visual systems, diagnose problems or impairments, prescribe corrective lenses, and provide treatment. May prescribe therapeutic drugs to treat specific eye conditions.** Examine eyes, using observation, instruments, and pharmaceutical agents, to determine visual acuity and perception, focus, and coordination and to diagnose diseases and other abnormalities such as glaucoma or color blindness. Prescribe medications to treat eye diseases if state laws permit. Analyze test results and develop treatment plans. Prescribe, supply, fit, and adjust eyeglasses, contact lenses, and other vision aids. Educate and counsel patients on contact lens care, visual hygiene, lighting arrangements, and safety factors. Remove foreign bodies from eyes. Consult with and refer patients to ophthalmologist or other health care practitioners if additional medical treatment is determined necessary. Provide patients undergoing eye surgeries such as cataract and laser vision correction, with pre- and post-operative care. Prescribe therapeutic procedures to correct or conserve vision. Provide vision therapy and low vision rehabilitation.

**Education/Training Required:** First professional degree. **Education and Training Program:** Optometry (OD). **Knowledge/Courses—**Medicine and Dentistry, Biology, Therapy and Counseling, Physics, Sales and Marketing, Economics and Accounting.

**Personality Type:** Investigative-Social-Realistic. **Career Cluster:** 08 Health Science. **Career Pathway:** 8.1 Therapeutic Services. **Other Jobs in This Pathway:** Clinical Psychologists; Community and Social Service Specialists, All Other; Counseling Psychologists; Dental Assistants; Dental Hygienists; Dentists, General; Health Technologists and Technicians, All Other; Healthcare Support Workers, All Other; Home Health Aides; Licensed Practical and Licensed Vocational Nurses; Low Vision Therapists, Orientation and Mobility Specialists, and Vision Rehabilitation Therapists; Massage Therapists; Medical and Clinical Laboratory Technicians; Medical and Health Services Managers; Medical Scientists, Except Epidemiologists; Medical Secretaries; Occupational Therapists; Pharmacists; Pharmacy Technicians; Radiologic Technologists; School Psychologists; Social and Human Service Assistants; Speech-Language Pathologists; Speech-Language Pathology Assistants; Substance Abuse and Behavioral Disorder Counselors; others.

**Skills**—Science, Reading Comprehension, Management of Financial Resources, Operations Analysis, Quality Control Analysis, Management of Material Resources, Operation and Control, Service Orientation.

**Work Environment:** Indoors; sitting; using hands; exposed to disease or infections.

# Oral and Maxillofacial Surgeons

- ❋ Annual Earnings: $166,400+
- ❋ Earnings Growth Potential: Cannot be calculated
- ❋ Growth: 15.3%
- ❋ Annual Job Openings: 290
- ❋ Self-Employed: 28.1%

**Considerations for Job Outlook:** An increase in the elderly population—who often need complicated dental work—and expanded insurance coverage for dental procedures are expected to create job growth. Good prospects are expected from the need to replace the large number of dentists who are retiring.

**Perform surgery on mouth, jaws, and related head and neck structure to execute difficult and multiple extractions of teeth, to remove tumors and other abnormal growths, to correct abnormal jaw relations by mandibular or maxillary revision, to prepare mouth for insertion of dental prosthesis, or to treat fractured jaws.** Administer general and local anesthetics. Remove impacted, damaged, and non-restorable teeth. Evaluate the position of the wisdom teeth in order to determine whether problems exist currently or might occur in the future. Collaborate with other professionals such as restorative dentists and orthodontists in order to plan treatment. Perform surgery to prepare the mouth for dental implants and to aid in the regeneration of deficient bone and gum tissues. Remove tumors and other abnormal growths of the oral and facial regions, using surgical instruments. Treat infections of the oral cavity, salivary glands, jaws, and neck. Treat problems affecting the oral mucosa such as mouth ulcers and infections. Provide emergency treatment of facial injuries, including facial lacerations, intra-oral lacerations, and fractured facial bones. Perform surgery on the mouth and jaws in order to treat conditions such as cleft lip and palate and jaw growth problems. Restore form and function by moving skin, bone, nerves, and other tissues from other parts of the body in order to reconstruct the jaws and face. Perform minor cosmetic procedures such as chin and cheekbone enhancements and minor facial rejuvenation procedures including the use of Botox and laser technology. Treat snoring problems, using laser surgery.

**Education/Training Required:** First professional degree. **Education and Training Programs:** Oral and Maxillofacial Surgery Residency Program; Oral/Maxillofacial Surgery (Cert., MS, PhD). **Knowledge/Courses**—Medicine and Dentistry, Biology, Therapy and Counseling, Chemistry, Psychology, Personnel and Human Resources.

**Personality Type:** Realistic-Social-Investigative. **Career Cluster:** 08 Health Science. **Career Pathway:** 8.1 Therapeutic Services. **Other Jobs in This Pathway:** Clinical Psychologists; Counseling Psychologists; Dental Assistants; Dentists, All Other Specialists; Dental Hygienists; Dentists, General; Home Health Aides; Licensed Practical and Licensed Vocational Nurses; Low Vision Therapists, Orientation and Mobility Specialists, and Vision Rehabilitation Therapists; Massage Therapists; Medical and Clinical Laboratory Technicians; Medical and Health Services Managers; Medical Scientists, Except Epidemiologists; Medical Secretaries; Occupational Therapists; Orthodontists; Pharmacists; Pharmacy Technicians; Prosthodontists; Radiologic Technologists; School Psychologists; Social and Human Service Assistants; Speech-Language Pathologists; Speech-Language Pathology Assistants; Substance Abuse and Behavioral Disorder Counselors; others.

**Skills**—Science, Reading Comprehension, Operation and Control, Operations Analysis, Service Orientation, Complex Problem Solving, Active Learning, Critical Thinking.

**Work Environment:** Indoors; more often sitting than standing; using hands; bending or twisting the body; repetitive motions; exposed to disease or infections.

# Orthodontists

- ❋ Annual Earnings: $166,400+
- ❋ Earnings Growth Potential: Cannot be calculated
- ❋ Growth: 19.8%
- ❋ Annual Job Openings: 360
- ❋ Self-Employed: 28.1%

**Considerations for Job Outlook:** An increase in the elderly population—who often need complicated dental work—and expanded insurance coverage for dental procedures are expected to create job growth. Good prospects are expected from the need to replace the large number of dentists who are retiring.

**Examine, diagnose, and treat dental malocclusions and oral cavity anomalies. Design and fabricate appliances to realign teeth and jaws to produce and maintain normal function and to improve appearance.** Fit dental appliances in patients' mouths to alter the position and relationship of teeth and jaws and to realign teeth. Study diagnostic records such as medical/dental histories, plaster models of the teeth, photos of a patient's face and teeth, and X-rays to develop patient treatment plans. Diagnose teeth and jaw or other dental-facial abnormalities. Examine patients to assess abnormalities of jaw development, tooth position, and other dental-facial structures. Prepare diagnostic and treatment records. Adjust dental appliances periodically to produce and maintain normal function. Provide patients with proposed treatment plans and cost estimates. Instruct dental officers and technical assistants in orthodontic procedures and techniques. Coordinate orthodontic services with other dental and medical services. Design and fabricate appliances, such as space maintainers, retainers, and labial and lingual arch wires.

**Education/Training Required:** First professional degree. **Education and Training Programs:** Orthodontics Specialty; Orthodontics/Orthodontology. **Knowledge/Courses**—Medicine and Dentistry, Biology, Sales and Marketing, Economics and Accounting, Personnel and Human Resources, Customer and Personal Service.

**Personality Type:** Investigative-Realistic-Social. **Career Cluster:** 08 Health Science. **Career Pathway:** 8.1 Therapeutic Services. **Other Jobs in This Pathway:** Clinical Psychologists; Counseling Psychologists; Dental Assistants; Dental Hygienists; Dentists, All Other Specialists; Dentists, General; Home Health Aides; Licensed Practical and Licensed Vocational Nurses; Low Vision Therapists, Orientation and Mobility Specialists, and Vision Rehabilitation Therapists; Massage Therapists; Medical and Clinical Laboratory Technicians; Medical and Health Services Managers; Medical Scientists, Except Epidemiologists; Medical Secretaries; Occupational Therapists; Orthodontists; Pharmacists; Pharmacy Technicians; Prosthodontists; Radiologic Technologists; School Psychologists; Social and Human Service Assistants; Speech-Language Pathologists; Speech-Language Pathology Assistants; Substance Abuse and Behavioral Disorder Counselors; others.

**Skills**—Science, Operations Analysis, Instructing, Active Learning, Reading Comprehension, Writing, Management of Personnel Resources, Operation Monitoring.

**Work Environment:** Indoors; sitting; using hands; bending or twisting the body; repetitive motions; exposed to radiation; exposed to disease or infections.

# Orthotists and Prosthetists

- ❋ Annual Earnings: $65,060
- ❋ Earnings Growth Potential: High (48.2%)
- ❋ Growth: 15.4%
- ❋ Annual Job Openings: 210
- ❋ Self-Employed: 5.8%

**Considerations for Job Outlook:** Faster-than-average employment growth is projected.

**Assist patients with disabling conditions of limbs and spine or with partial or total absence of limb by fitting and preparing orthopedic braces or prostheses.** Examine, interview, and measure patients in order to determine their appliance needs and to identify factors that could affect appliance fit. Fit, test, and evaluate devices on patients and make adjustments for proper fit, function, and comfort. Instruct patients in the use and care of orthoses and prostheses. Design orthopedic and prosthetic devices based on physicians' prescriptions and examination and measurement of patients. Maintain patients' records. Make and modify plaster casts of areas that will be fitted with prostheses or orthoses for use in the device construction process. Select materials and components to be used, based on device design. Confer with physicians to formulate specifications and prescriptions for orthopedic or prosthetic devices. Repair, rebuild, and modify prosthetic and orthopedic appliances. Construct and fabricate appliances or supervise others who are constructing the appliances. Train and supervise orthopedic and prosthetic assistants and technicians and other support staff. Update skills and knowledge by attending conferences and seminars. Show and explain orthopedic and prosthetic appliances to health-care workers. Research new ways to construct and use orthopedic and prosthetic devices. Publish research findings and present them at conferences and seminars.

**Education/Training Required:** Bachelor's degree. **Education and Training Programs:** Assistive/Augmentative Technology and Rehabilitation Engineering; Orthotist/Prosthetist. **Knowledge/Courses**—Engineering and Technology, Medicine and Dentistry, Design, Therapy and Counseling, Production and Processing, Psychology.

**Personality Type:** Social-Realistic-Investigative. **Career Cluster:** 08 Health Science. **Career Pathway:** 8.3 Health Informatics. **Other Jobs in This Pathway:** Clinical Psychologists; Dental Laboratory Technicians; Editors; Engineers, All Other; Executive Secretaries and Executive Administrative Assistants; Fine Artists, Including Painters, Sculptors, and Illustrators; First-Line Supervisors of Office and Administrative Support Workers; Health Educators; Medical and Health Services Managers; Medical Appliance Technicians; Medical Assistants; Medical Records and Health Information Technicians; Medical Secretaries; Medical Transcriptionists; Mental Health Counselors; Occupational Health and Safety Specialists; Physical Therapists; Psychiatric Aides; Psychiatric Technicians; Public Relations Specialists; Receptionists and Information Clerks; Recreational Therapists; Rehabilitation Counselors; Substance Abuse and Behavioral Disorder Counselors; Therapists, All Other; others.

**Skills**—Operations Analysis, Technology Design, Science, Instructing, Service Orientation, Writing, Troubleshooting, Active Listening.

**Work Environment:** Indoors; standing; using hands; noise; contaminants; exposed to disease or infections; hazardous equipment; minor burns, cuts, bites, or stings.

# Painters, Construction and Maintenance

- ❋ Annual Earnings: $34,280
- ❋ Earnings Growth Potential: Low (34.5%)
- ❋ Growth: 7.0%
- ❋ Annual Job Openings: 10,650
- ❋ Self-Employed: 45.0%

**Considerations for Job Outlook:** Construction, remodeling, and maintenance of existing buildings and infrastructure will drive employment growth for these workers. Job prospects should be good because of the need to replace workers who leave these occupations permanently.

**Paint walls, equipment, buildings, bridges, and other structural surfaces with brushes, rollers, and spray guns. May remove old paint to prepare surfaces before painting. May mix colors or oils to obtain desired color or consistencies.** Cover surfaces with dropcloths or masking tape and paper to protect surfaces during painting. Fill cracks, holes, and joints with caulk, putty, plaster, or other fillers, using caulking guns or putty knives. Apply primers or sealers to prepare new surfaces such as bare wood or metal for finish coats. Apply paint, stain, varnish, enamel, and other finishes to equipment, buildings, bridges, and/or other structures, using brushes, spray guns, or rollers. Calculate amounts of required materials and estimate costs, based on surface measurements and/or work orders. Read work orders or receive instructions from supervisors or homeowners to determine work requirements. Erect scaffolding and swing gates, or set up ladders, to work above ground level. Remove fixtures such as pictures, door knobs, lamps, and electric switch covers prior to painting. Wash and treat surfaces with oil, turpentine, mildew remover, or other preparations, and sand rough spots to ensure that finishes will adhere properly. Mix and match colors of paint, stain, or varnish with oil and thinning and drying additives to obtain desired colors and consistencies. Remove old finishes by stripping, sanding, wire brushing, burning, or using water and/or abrasive blasting. Select and purchase tools and finishes for surfaces to be covered, considering durability, ease of handling, methods of application, and customers' wishes. Smooth surfaces, using sandpaper, scrapers, brushes, steel wool, and/or sanding machines. Polish final coats to specified finishes. Use special finishing techniques such as sponging, ragging, layering, or faux finishing. Waterproof buildings, using waterproofers and caulking. Cut stencils, and brush and spray lettering and decorations on surfaces. Spray or brush hot plastics or pitch onto surfaces. Bake finishes on painted and enameled articles, using baking ovens.

**Education/Training Required:** Moderate-term on-the-job training. **Education and Training Program:** Painting/Painter and Wall Coverer Training. **Knowledge/Courses**—Building and Construction, Transportation, Design, Customer and Personal Service, Production and Processing, Administration and Management.

**Personality Type:** Realistic-Conventional. **Career Cluster:** 02 Architecture and Construction. **Career Pathway:**

2.2 Construction. **Other Jobs in This Pathway:** Brickmasons and Blockmasons; Cement Masons and Concrete Finishers; Construction and Building Inspectors; Construction Carpenters; Construction Laborers; Construction Managers; Cost Estimators; Drywall and Ceiling Tile Installers; Electrical Power-Line Installers and Repairers; Electricians; Engineering Technicians, Except Drafters, All Other; Excavating and Loading Machine and Dragline Operators; First-Line Supervisors of Construction Trades and Extraction Workers; Heating and Air Conditioning Mechanics and Installers; Helpers—Carpenters; Helpers—Electricians; Helpers—Pipelayers, Plumbers, Pipefitters, and Steamfitters; Highway Maintenance Workers; Operating Engineers and Other Construction Equipment Operators; Pipe Fitters and Steamfitters; Plumbers; Refrigeration Mechanics and Installers; Roofers; Rough Carpenters; Solar Energy Installation Managers; others.

**Skills**—Operation and Control.

**Work Environment:** More often outdoors than indoors; standing; climbing; kneeling, crouching, stooping, or crawling; balancing; using hands; bending or twisting the body; repetitive motions; noise; contaminants; cramped work space; high places; hazardous conditions; minor burns, cuts, bites, or stings.

# Paralegals and Legal Assistants

- ❀ Annual Earnings: $46,680
- ❀ Earnings Growth Potential: Medium (36.9%)
- ❀ Growth: 28.1%
- ❀ Annual Job Openings: 10,400
- ❀ Self-Employed: 3.2%

**Considerations for Job Outlook:** Increased demand for accessible, cost-efficient legal services is expected to increase employment for paralegals, who may perform more tasks previously done by lawyers. Keen competition is expected. Experienced, formally trained paralegals should have the best job prospects.

**Assist lawyers by researching legal precedent, investigating facts, or preparing legal documents. Conduct research to support a legal proceeding, to formulate a defense, or to initiate legal action.** Prepare legal documents, including briefs, pleadings, appeals, wills, contracts, and real estate closing statements. Prepare affidavits or other documents, maintain document file, and file pleadings with court clerk. Gather and analyze research data, such as statutes; decisions;

and legal articles, codes, and documents. Investigate facts and law of cases to determine causes of action and to prepare cases. Call upon witnesses to testify at hearing. Direct and coordinate law office activity, including delivery of subpoenas. Arbitrate disputes between parties and assist in real estate closing process. Keep and monitor legal volumes to ensure that law library is up to date. Appraise and inventory real and personal property for estate planning.

**Education/Training Required:** Associate degree. **Education and Training Program:** Legal Assistant/Paralegal Training. **Knowledge/Courses**—Clerical, Law and Government, English Language, Computers and Electronics, Communications and Media.

**Personality Type:** Conventional-Investigative-Enterprising. **Career Cluster:** 12 Law, Public Safety, Corrections, and Security. **Career Pathway:** 12.5 Legal Services. **Other Jobs in This Pathway:** Administrative Law Judges, Adjudicators, and Hearing Officers; Arbitrators, Mediators, and Conciliators; Court Reporters; Farm and Home Management Advisors; Judges, Magistrate Judges, and Magistrates; Lawyers; Legal Secretaries; Legal Support Workers, All Other; Title Examiners, Abstractors, and Searchers.

**Skills**—Writing, Active Listening, Speaking, Service Orientation.

**Work Environment:** Indoors; sitting; repetitive motions.

# Personal Care Aides

- ❀ Annual Earnings: $19,640
- ❀ Earnings Growth Potential: Very low (18.7%)
- ❀ Growth: 46.0%
- ❀ Annual Job Openings: 47,780
- ❀ Self-Employed: 7.5%

**Considerations for Job Outlook:** Growth is expected to stem from a rise in the number of elderly people, an age group that relies increasingly on home care for assistance with daily activities. This growth, together with the need to replace workers who leave the occupation permanently, should result in excellent job prospects.

**Assist elderly or disabled adults with daily living activities at the person's home or in a daytime non-residential facility. Duties performed at a place of residence may include keeping house (making beds, doing laundry, washing dishes) and preparing meals. May provide meals and supervised activities at non-residential care facilities.**

May advise families, the elderly, and disabled on such things as nutrition, cleanliness, and household utilities. Perform health-care-related tasks, such as monitoring vital signs and medication, under the direction of registered nurses and physiotherapists. Administer bedside and personal care, such as ambulation and personal hygiene assistance. Prepare and maintain records of client progress and services performed, reporting changes in client condition to manager or supervisor. Perform housekeeping duties, such as cooking, cleaning, washing clothes and dishes, and running errands. Care for individuals and families during periods of incapacitation, family disruption, or convalescence, providing companionship, personal care, and help in adjusting to new lifestyles. Instruct and advise clients on issues such as household cleanliness, utilities, hygiene, nutrition, and infant care. Plan, shop for, and prepare nutritious meals or assist families in planning, shopping for, and preparing nutritious meals. Participate in case reviews, consulting with the team caring for the client, to evaluate the client's needs and plan for continuing services. Transport clients to locations outside the home, such as to physicians' offices or on outings, using a motor vehicle. Train family members to provide bedside care. Provide clients with communication assistance, typing their correspondence and obtaining information for them.

**Education/Training Required:** Short-term on-the-job training. **Education and Training Program:** Home Health Aide/Home Attendant Training. **Knowledge/Courses—** Therapy and Counseling, Psychology, Philosophy and Theology, Medicine and Dentistry, Transportation, Chemistry.

**Personality Type:** Social-Realistic-Conventional. **Career Cluster:** 10 Human Services. **Career Pathway:** 10.3 Family and Community Services. **Other Jobs in This Pathway:** Chief Executives; Child, Family, and School Social Workers; Childcare Workers; City and Regional Planning Aides; Counselors, All Other; Eligibility Interviewers, Government Programs; Farm and Home Management Advisors; Legislators; Managers, All Other; Marriage and Family Therapists; Nannies; Probation Officers and Correctional Treatment Specialists; Protective Service Workers, All Other; Social and Community Service Managers; Social Science Research Assistants; Social Scientists and Related Workers, All Other; Social Workers, All Other; Sociologists; Supply Chain Managers.

**Skills—**Service Orientation.

**Work Environment:** Standing; exposed to disease or infections.

# Personal Financial Advisors

* Annual Earnings: $64,750
* Earnings Growth Potential: High (49.6%)
* Growth: 30.1%
* Annual Job Openings: 8,530
* Self-Employed: 29.3%

**Considerations for Job Outlook:** Employment growth for these workers is projected as large numbers of baby boomers retire and need advice on managing their retirement accounts. In addition, widespread transition from traditional pension plans to individually managed retirement savings programs should also create jobs. Keen competition is expected in this relatively high-paying occupation.

**Advise clients on financial plans, using knowledge of tax and investment strategies, securities, insurance, pension plans, and real estate. Duties include assessing clients' assets, liabilities, cash flows, insurance coverages, tax statuses, and financial objectives to establish investment strategies.** Prepare and interpret for clients information such as investment performance reports, financial document summaries, and income projections. Recommend strategies clients can use to achieve their financial goals and objectives, including specific recommendations in such areas as cash management, insurance coverage, and investment planning. Build and maintain client bases, keeping current client plans up-to-date and recruiting new clients on an ongoing basis. Devise debt liquidation plans that include payoff priorities and timelines. Implement financial planning recommendations, or refer clients to someone who can assist them with plan implementation. Interview clients to determine their current incomes, expenses, insurance coverages, tax statuses, financial objectives, risk tolerances, and other information needed to develop financial plans. Monitor financial market trends to ensure that plans are effective, and to identify any necessary updates. Explain and document for clients the types of services that are to be provided, and the responsibilities to be taken by personal financial advisors. Explain to individuals and groups the details of financial assistance available to college and university students, such as loans, grants, and scholarships. Guide clients in the gathering of information such as bank account records, income tax returns, life and disability insurance records, pension plan information, and wills. Analyze financial information obtained from clients to determine strategies for meeting clients' financial objectives. Meet with clients' other advisors, including attorneys, accountants, trust officers, and investment bankers, to fully understand clients' financial goals and circumstances. Answer clients' questions about

P

the purposes and details of financial plans and strategies. Open accounts for clients, and disburse funds from account to creditors as agents for clients. Authorize release of financial aid funds to students.

**Education/Training Required:** Bachelor's degree. **Education and Training Programs:** Finance, General; Financial Planning and Services. **Knowledge/Courses**—Economics and Accounting, Sales and Marketing, Law and Government, Customer and Personal Service, Mathematics, Computers and Electronics.

**Personality Type:** Enterprising-Conventional-Social. **Career Cluster:** 06 Finance. **Career Pathway:** 6.1 Financial and Investment Planning. **Other Jobs in This Pathway:** Budget Analysts; Credit Analysts; Financial Analysts; Financial Managers, Branch or Department; Financial Quantitative Analysts; Financial Specialists, All Other; Fraud Examiners, Investigators and Analysts; Investment Underwriters; Loan Counselors; Risk Management Specialists; Sales Agents, Financial Services; Sales Agents, Securities and Commodities; Securities and Commodities Traders; Securities, Commodities, and Financial Services Sales Agents; Treasurers and Controllers.

**Skills**—Operations Analysis, Management of Financial Resources, Mathematics, Persuasion, Service Orientation, Speaking, Writing, Reading Comprehension.

**Work Environment:** Indoors; sitting.

# Pest Control Workers

- ❋ Annual Earnings: $30,340
- ❋ Earnings Growth Potential: Low (33.0%)
- ❋ Growth: 15.3%
- ❋ Annual Job Openings: 3,400
- ❋ Self-Employed: 7.3%

**Considerations for Job Outlook:** Demand for pest control services should grow as consumers desire improved living conditions and as the population increases in warmer states, where pests are more prevalent. Prospects should be good.

**Spray or release chemical solutions or toxic gases and set traps to kill pests and vermin, such as mice, termites, and roaches, that infest buildings and surrounding areas.** Record work activities performed. Inspect premises to identify infestation source and extent of damage to property, wall and roof porosity, and access to infested locations. Spray or dust chemical solutions, powders, or gases into rooms; onto clothing, furnishings, or wood; and over marshlands,

ditches, and catch-basins. Clean work site after completion of job. Direct or assist other workers in treatment and extermination processes to eliminate and control rodents, insects, and weeds. Drive truck equipped with power spraying equipment. Measure area dimensions requiring treatment, using rule; calculate fumigant requirements; and estimate cost for service. Post warning signs and lock building doors to secure area to be fumigated. Cut or bore openings in building or surrounding concrete, access infested areas, insert nozzle, and inject pesticide to impregnate ground. Study preliminary reports and diagrams of infested area and determine treatment type required to eliminate and prevent recurrence of infestation. Dig up and burn or spray weeds with herbicides. Set mechanical traps and place poisonous paste or bait in sewers, burrows, and ditches. Clean and remove blockages from infested areas to facilitate spraying procedure and provide drainage, using broom, mop, shovel, and rake. Position and fasten edges of tarpaulins over building and tape vents to ensure airtight environment and check for leaks.

**Education/Training Required:** Moderate-term on-the-job training. **Education and Training Program:** Agricultural/Farm Supplies Retailing and Wholesaling. **Knowledge/Courses**—Sales and Marketing, Chemistry, Biology, Customer and Personal Service, Building and Construction, Law and Government.

**Personality Type:** Realistic-Conventional. **Career Cluster:** 01 Agriculture, Food, and Natural Resources. **Career Pathway:** 1.1 Food Products and Processing Systems. **Other Jobs in This Pathway:** Agricultural Inspectors; Agricultural Technicians; Buyers and Purchasing Agents, Farm Products; Chemical Technicians; First-Line Supervisors of Office and Administrative Support Workers; Food and Tobacco Roasting, Baking, and Drying Machine Operators and Tenders; Food Batchmakers; Food Cooking Machine Operators and Tenders; Food Science Technicians; Food Scientists and Technologists; Graders and Sorters, Agricultural Products; Nonfarm Animal Caretakers; Office Machine Operators, Except Computer.

**Skills**—Equipment Selection, Repairing, Equipment Maintenance, Operation and Control, Troubleshooting, Mathematics, Persuasion, Systems Analysis.

**Work Environment:** More often outdoors than indoors; standing; walking and running; using hands; repetitive motions; very hot or cold; contaminants; cramped work space; hazardous conditions; minor burns, cuts, bites, or stings.

# Petroleum Engineers

- ❋ Annual Earnings: $114,080
- ❋ Earnings Growth Potential: High (44.4%)
- ❋ Growth: 18.4%
- ❋ Annual Job Openings: 860
- ❋ Self-Employed: 0.4%

**Considerations for Job Outlook:** Petroleum engineers are expected to have employment growth of 18 percent from 2008–2018, faster than the average for all occupations. Petroleum engineers increasingly will be needed to develop new resources, as well as new methods of extracting more from existing sources. Excellent opportunities are expected for petroleum engineers because the number of job openings is likely to exceed the relatively small number of graduates. Petroleum engineers work around the world, and in fact, the best employment opportunities may include some work in other countries.

**Devise methods to improve oil and gas well production and determine the need for new or modified tool designs. Oversee drilling and offer technical advice to achieve economical and satisfactory progress.** Assess costs and estimate the production capabilities and economic value of oil and gas wells to evaluate the economic viability of potential drilling sites. Monitor production rates and plan rework processes to improve production. Analyze data to recommend placement of wells and supplementary processes to enhance production. Specify and supervise well modification and stimulation programs to maximize oil and gas recovery. Direct and monitor the completion and evaluation of wells, well testing, or well surveys. Assist engineering and other personnel to solve operating problems. Develop plans for oil and gas field drilling and for product recovery and treatment. Maintain records of drilling and production operations. Confer with scientific, engineering, and technical personnel to resolve design, research, and testing problems. Write technical reports for engineering and management personnel. Evaluate findings to develop, design, or test equipment or processes. Assign work to staff to obtain maximum utilization of personnel. Interpret drilling and testing information for personnel. Design and implement environmental controls on oil and gas operations. Coordinate the installation, maintenance, and operation of mining and oilfield equipment. Supervise the removal of drilling equipment, the removal of any waste, and the safe return of land to structural stability when wells or pockets are exhausted. Inspect oil and gas wells to determine that installations are completed. Simulate reservoir performance for different recovery techniques, using computer models. Take samples to assess the amount and quality of oil, the depth at which resources lie, and the equipment needed to properly extract them. Coordinate activities of workers engaged in research, planning, and development. Design or modify mining and oilfield machinery and tools, applying engineering principles. Test machinery and equipment to ensure that it is safe and conforms to performance specifications.

**Education/Training Required:** Bachelor's degree. **Education and Training Program:** Petroleum Engineering. **Knowledge/Courses**—Engineering and Technology, Physics, Geography, Chemistry, Economics and Accounting, Design.

**Personality Type:** Investigative-Realistic-Conventional. **Career Cluster:** 15 Science, Technology, Engineering, and Mathematics. **Career Pathway:** 15.1 Engineering and Technology. **Other Jobs in This Pathway:** Architectural and Engineering Managers; Automotive Engineers; Biochemical Engineers; Biofuels/Biodiesel Technology and Product Development Managers; Civil Engineers; Cost Estimators; Electrical Engineers; Electronics Engineers, Except Computer; Energy Engineers; Engineers, All Other; Fuel Cell Engineers; Human Factors Engineers and Ergonomists; Industrial Engineers; Manufacturing Engineers; Mechanical Engineers; Mechatronics Engineers; Microsystems Engineers; Nanosystems Engineers; Photonics Engineers; Radio Frequency Identification Device Specialists; Robotics Engineers; Solar Energy Systems Engineers; Transportation Engineers; Validation Engineers; Wind Energy Engineers; others.

**Skills**—Science, Systems Evaluation, Management of Financial Resources, Management of Material Resources, Mathematics, Technology Design, Operation Monitoring, Systems Analysis.

**Work Environment:** Indoors; sitting.

# Pharmacists

- ❋ Annual Earnings: $111,570
- ❋ Earnings Growth Potential: Low (26.4%)
- ❋ Growth: 17.0%
- ❋ Annual Job Openings: 10,580
- ❋ Self-Employed: 0.6%

**Considerations for Job Outlook:** The increasing numbers of middle-aged and elderly people—who use more prescription drugs than younger people—should continue to spur employment growth for pharmacists. Job prospects are expected to be excellent.

**Compound and dispense medications, following prescriptions issued by physicians, dentists, or other authorized medical practitioners.** Review prescriptions to assure accuracy, to ascertain the needed ingredients, and to evaluate their suitability. Provide information and advice regarding drug interactions, side effects, dosage, and proper medication storage. Analyze prescribing trends to monitor patient compliance and to prevent excessive usage or harmful interactions. Order and purchase pharmaceutical supplies, medical supplies, and drugs, maintaining stock and storing and handling it properly. Maintain records such as pharmacy files; patient profiles; charge system files; inventories; control records for radioactive nuclei; and registries of poisons, narcotics, and controlled drugs. Provide specialized services to help patients manage conditions such as diabetes, asthma, smoking cessation, or high blood pressure. Advise customers on the selection of medication brands, medical equipment, and health-care supplies. Collaborate with other health-care professionals to plan, monitor, review, and evaluate the quality and effectiveness of drugs and drug regimens, providing advice on drug applications and characteristics. Compound and dispense medications as prescribed by doctors and dentists by calculating, weighing, measuring, and mixing ingredients or oversee these activities. Offer health promotion and prevention activities—for example, training people to use devices such as blood-pressure or diabetes monitors. Refer patients to other health professionals and agencies when appropriate. Prepare sterile solutions and infusions for use in surgical procedures, emergency rooms, or patients' homes. Plan, implement, and maintain procedures for mixing, packaging, and labeling pharmaceuticals according to policy and legal requirements to ensure quality, security, and proper disposal. Assay radiopharmaceuticals, verify rates of disintegration, and calculate the volume required to produce the desired results to ensure proper dosages.

**Education/Training Required:** First professional degree. **Education and Training Programs:** Clinical, Hospital, and Managed Care Pharmacy (MS, PhD); Industrial and Physical Pharmacy and Cosmetic Sciences (MS, PhD); Medicinal and Pharmaceutical Chemistry (MS, PhD); Natural Products Chemistry and Pharmacognosy (MS, PhD); Pharmaceutics and Drug Design (MS, PhD); Pharmacoeconomics/Pharmaceutical Economics (MS, PhD); Pharmacy (PharmD [USA], PharmD or BS/BPharm [Canada]); Pharmacy Administration and Pharmacy Policy and Regulatory Affairs (MS, PhD); Pharmacy, Pharmaceutical Sciences, and Administration, Other. **Knowledge/Courses**—Biology, Medicine and Dentistry, Chemistry, Therapy and Counseling, Psychology, Clerical.

**Personality Type:** Investigative-Conventional-Social. **Career Cluster:** 08 Health Science. **Career Pathways:** 8.1 Therapeutic Services; 8.5 Biotechnology Research and Development. **Other Jobs in These Pathways:** Clinical Psychologists; Community and Social Service Specialists, All Other; Counseling Psychologists; Dental Assistants; Dental Hygienists; Dentists, General; Health Technologists and Technicians, All Other; Healthcare Support Workers, All Other; Home Health Aides; Licensed Practical and Licensed Vocational Nurses; Low Vision Therapists, Orientation and Mobility Specialists, and Vision Rehabilitation Therapists; Massage Therapists; Medical and Clinical Laboratory Technicians; Medical and Health Services Managers; Medical Scientists, Except Epidemiologists; Medical Secretaries; Occupational Therapists; Ophthalmic Medical Technologists; Pharmacy Technicians; Radiologic Technologists; School Psychologists; Social and Human Service Assistants; Speech-Language Pathologists; Speech-Language Pathology Assistants; Substance Abuse and Behavioral Disorder Counselors; others.

**Skills**—Science, Operations Analysis, Reading Comprehension, Management of Material Resources, Active Listening, Writing, Instructing, Management of Financial Resources.

**Work Environment:** Indoors; standing; using hands; repetitive motions; exposed to disease or infections.

# Pharmacy Technicians

- ✳ Annual Earnings: $28,400
- ✳ Earnings Growth Potential: Low (30.1%)
- ✳ Growth: 30.6%
- ✳ Annual Job Openings: 18,200
- ✳ Self-Employed: 0.2%

**Considerations for Job Outlook:** Growth in the population of middle-aged and elderly people—who use more prescription drugs than younger people—should spur employment increases for these workers. Job prospects are expected to be good.

**Prepare medications under the direction of a pharmacist. May measure, mix, count out, label, and record amounts and dosages of medications.** Receive written prescription or refill requests and verify that information is complete and accurate. Maintain proper storage and security conditions for drugs. Answer telephones, responding to questions or requests. Fill bottles with prescribed medications and type and affix labels. Assist customers by answering simple questions, locating items, or referring them to the pharmacist for medication information. Price and file prescriptions that have been filled. Clean and help maintain equipment and work areas and sterilize glassware according to prescribed methods. Establish and maintain patient profiles, including lists of medications taken by individual patients. Order, label, and count stock of medications, chemicals, and supplies and enter inventory data into computer. Receive and store incoming supplies, verify quantities against invoices, and inform supervisors of stock needs and shortages. Transfer medication from vials to the appropriate number of sterile disposable syringes, using aseptic techniques. Under pharmacist supervision, add measured drugs or nutrients to intravenous solutions under sterile conditions to prepare intravenous (IV) packs. Supply and monitor robotic machines that dispense medicine into containers and label the containers. Prepare and process medical insurance claim forms and records. Mix pharmaceutical preparations according to written prescriptions. Operate cash registers to accept payment from customers. Compute charges for medication and equipment dispensed to hospital patients and enter data in computer. Deliver medications and pharmaceutical supplies to patients, nursing stations, or surgery. Price stock and mark items for sale. Maintain and merchandise home health-care products and services.

**Education/Training Required:** Moderate-term on-the-job training. **Education and Training Program:** Pharmacy Technician/Assistant Training. **Knowledge/Courses**—Medicine and Dentistry, Clerical, Computers and Electronics, Customer and Personal Service, Chemistry, Mathematics.

**Personality Type:** Conventional-Realistic. **Career Cluster:** 08 Health Science. **Career Pathway:** 8.1 Therapeutic Services. **Other Jobs in This Pathway:** Clinical Psychologists; Community and Social Service Specialists, All Other; Counseling Psychologists; Dental Assistants; Dental Hygienists; Dentists, General; Health Technologists and Technicians, All Other; Healthcare Support Workers, All Other; Home Health Aides; Licensed Practical and Licensed Vocational Nurses; Low Vision Therapists, Orientation and Mobility Specialists, and Vision Rehabilitation Therapists; Massage Therapists; Medical and Clinical Laboratory Technicians; Medical and Health Services Managers; Medical Scientists, Except Epidemiologists; Medical Secretaries; Occupational Therapists; Ophthalmic Medical Technologists; Pharmacists; Radiologic Technologists; School Psychologists; Social and Human Service Assistants; Speech-Language Pathologists; Speech-Language Pathology Assistants; Substance Abuse and Behavioral Disorder Counselors; others.

**Skills**—Management of Financial Resources, Service Orientation, Mathematics, Programming, Science, Active Listening.

**Work Environment:** Indoors; standing; walking and running; using hands; repetitive motions; exposed to disease or infections.

# Philosophy and Religion Teachers, Postsecondary

- ❋ Annual Earnings: $62,330
- ❋ Earnings Growth Potential: High (46.4%)
- ❋ Growth: 15.1%
- ❋ Annual Job Openings: 600
- ❋ Self-Employed: 0.2%

**Considerations for Job Outlook:** Enrollments in postsecondary institutions are expected to continue rising as more people attend college and as workers return to school to update their skills. Opportunities for part-time or temporary positions should be favorable, but significant competition exists for tenure-track positions.

**Teach courses in philosophy, religion, and theology.** Evaluate and grade students' classwork, assignments, and papers. Initiate, facilitate, and moderate classroom discussions. Prepare and deliver lectures to undergraduate and graduate students on topics such as ethics, logic, and contemporary religious thought. Prepare course materials such as syllabi, homework assignments, and handouts. Compile, administer, and grade examinations or assign this work to others. Keep abreast of developments in their field by reading current literature, talking with colleagues, and participating in professional conferences. Maintain student attendance records, grades, and other required records. Plan, evaluate, and revise curricula, course content, and course materials and methods of instruction. Maintain regularly scheduled office hours to advise and assist students. Select and obtain materials and supplies such as textbooks. Advise students on academic and vocational curricula and on career issues. Conduct research in a particular field of knowledge and publish findings in professional journals, books, or electronic media. Perform administrative duties such as serving as department head. Serve on academic or administrative committees that deal with institutional policies, departmental matters, and academic issues. Collaborate with colleagues to address teaching and research issues. Participate in campus and community events. Participate in student recruitment, registration, and placement activities. Compile bibliographies of specialized materials for outside reading assignments. Supervise undergraduate and graduate teaching, internship, and research work. Act as advisers to student organizations. Write grant proposals to procure external research funding. Provide professional consulting services to government or industry.

**Education/Training Required:** Doctoral degree. **Education and Training Programs:** Bible/Biblical Studies; Buddhist Studies; Christian Studies; Divinity/Ministry (BD, MDiv.); Ethics; Hindu Studies; Humanities/Humanistic Studies; Missions/Missionary Studies and Missiology; Pastoral Counseling and Specialized Ministries, Other; Pastoral Studies/Counseling; Philosophy; Philosophy and Religious Studies, Other; Philosophy, Other; Pre-Theology/Pre-Ministerial Studies; Rabbinical Studies (M.H.L./Rav); Religion/Religious Studies; Religious Education; Religious/Sacred Music; Talmudic Studies; Theological and Ministerial Studies, Other; Theology and Religious Vocations, Other; Theology/Theological Studies. **Knowledge/Courses—**Philosophy and Theology, History and Archeology, Sociology and Anthropology, Foreign Language, English Language, Education and Training.

**Personality Type:** Social-Artistic-Investigative. **Career Clusters:** 05 Education and Training; 10 Human Services. **Career Pathways:** 5.3 Teaching/Training; 10.2 Counseling and Mental Health Services. **Other Jobs in These Pathways:** Adult Basic and Secondary Education and Literacy Teachers and Instructors; Career/Technical Education Teachers, Secondary School; Clergy; Clinical Psychologists; Coaches and Scouts; Counseling Psychologists; Elementary School Teachers, Except Special Education; Fitness Trainers and Aerobics Instructors; Healthcare Social Workers; Instructional Coordinators; Instructional Designers and Technologists; Kindergarten Teachers, Except Special Education; Librarians; Mental Health and Substance Abuse Social Workers; Mental Health Counselors; Middle School Teachers, Except Special and Career/Technical Education; Preschool Teachers, Except Special Education; Recreation Workers; School Psychologists; Secondary School Teachers, Except Special and Career/Technical Education; Self-Enrichment Education Teachers; Substance Abuse and Behavioral Disorder Counselors; Teacher Assistants; Tutors; 37 other postsecondary teaching occupations; others.

**Skills—**Writing, Operations Analysis, Reading Comprehension, Learning Strategies, Speaking, Science, Critical Thinking, Active Listening.

**Work Environment:** Indoors; sitting.

# Photographers

- ❋ Annual Earnings: $29,130
- ❋ Earnings Growth Potential: Medium (40.4%)
- ❋ Growth: 11.5%
- ❋ Annual Job Openings: 4,800
- ❋ Self-Employed: 60.1%

**Considerations for Job Outlook:** Employment for some photographers is expected to increase as online publication of magazines expands, but other photographers are expected to be adversely affected by amateur photography and increased use of copyright-free photos. Competition should be keen.

**Photograph persons, subjects, merchandise, or other commercial products. May develop negatives and produce finished prints.** Take pictures of individuals, families, and small groups, either in studio or on location. Adjust apertures, shutter speeds, and camera focus based on a combination of factors such as lighting, field depth, subject motion, film type, and film speed. Use traditional or digital cameras, along with a variety of equipment such as tripods, filters, and flash attachments. Create artificial light, using flashes and reflectors. Determine desired images and picture composition; select and adjust subjects, equipment, and lighting to achieve desired effects. Scan photographs into computers for editing, storage, and electronic transmission. Test equipment prior to use to ensure that it is in good working order. Review sets of photographs to select the best work. Estimate or measure light levels, distances, and numbers of exposures needed, using measuring devices and formulas. Manipulate and enhance scanned or digital images to create desired effects, using computers and specialized software. Perform maintenance tasks necessary to keep equipment working properly. Perform general office duties such as scheduling appointments, keeping books, and ordering supplies. Consult with clients or advertising staff and study assignments to determine project goals, locations, and equipment needs. Select and assemble equipment and required background properties according to subjects, materials, and conditions. Enhance, retouch, and resize photographs and negatives, using airbrushing and other techniques. Set up, mount, or install photographic equipment and cameras. Produce computer-readable digital images from film, using flatbed scanners and photofinishing laboratories. Develop and print exposed film, using chemicals, touchup tools, and developing and printing equipment, or send film to photofinishing laboratories for processing. Direct activities of workers who are setting up photographic equipment.

**Education/Training Required:** Long-term on-the-job training. **Education and Training Programs:** Commercial Photography; Film/Video and Photographic Arts, Other; Photography; Photojournalism; Visual and Performing Arts, General. **Knowledge/Courses**—Sales and Marketing, Fine Arts, Clerical, Customer and Personal Service, Communications and Media, Production and Processing.

**Personality Type:** Artistic-Realistic. **Career Cluster:** 03 Arts, Audio/Video Technology, and Communications. **Career Pathways:** 3.1 Audio and Video Technology and Film; 3.3 Visual Arts; 3.5 Journalism and Broadcasting. **Other Jobs in These Pathways:** Agents and Business Managers of Artists, Performers, and Athletes; Art Directors; Audio and Video Equipment Technicians; Broadcast Technicians; Camera Operators, Television, Video, and Motion Picture; Commercial and Industrial Designers; Copy Writers; Directors—Stage, Motion Pictures, Television, and Radio; Editors; Film and Video Editors; Fine Artists, Including Painters, Sculptors, and Illustrators; Graphic Designers; Interior Designers; Managers, All Other; Media and Communication Workers, All Other; Multimedia Artists and Animators; Painting, Coating, and Decorating Workers; Producers; Program Directors; Public Relations Specialists; Radio and Television Announcers; Reporters and Correspondents; Talent Directors; Technical Directors/Managers; Technical Writers; others.

**Skills**—Operations Analysis, Science, Management of Personnel Resources, Technology Design, Operation and Control, Operation Monitoring, Social Perceptiveness, Negotiation.

**Work Environment:** More often indoors than outdoors; sitting; using hands.

# Physical Scientists, All Other

- ❋ Annual Earnings: $94,780
- ❋ Earnings Growth Potential: High (49.2%)
- ❋ Growth: 11.1%
- ❋ Annual Job Openings: 1,010
- ❋ Self-Employed: 10.9%

**Considerations for Job Outlook:** About average employment growth is projected.

**This occupation includes all physical scientists not listed separately.** Because this is a highly diverse occupation, no data is available for some information topics.

**Education/Training Required:** Bachelor's degree. **Education and Training Program:** Physical Sciences, Other.

**Career Clusters:** 08 Health Science; 15 Science, Technology, Engineering, and Mathematics. **Career Pathways:** 8.2 Diagnostics Services; 15.2 Science and Mathematics. **Other Jobs in These Pathways:** Anesthesiologist Assistants; Architectural and Engineering Managers; Biofuels/Biodiesel Technology and Product Development Managers; Biologists; Chemists; Community and Social Service Specialists, All Other; Cytogenetic Technologists; Cytotechnologists; Education, Training, and Library Workers, All Other; Emergency Medical Technicians and Paramedics; Endoscopy Technicians; Health Technologists and Technicians, All Other; Histotechnologists and Histologic Technicians; Medical and Clinical Laboratory Technicians; Medical and Clinical Laboratory Technologists; Medical and Health Services Managers; Medical Assistants; Medical Scientists, Except Epidemiologists; Neurodiagnostic Technologists; Operations Research Analysts; Physician Assistants; Radiologic Technicians; Radiologic Technologists; Surgical Technologists; Veterinary Assistants and Laboratory Animal Caretakers; others.

## Job Specialization: Remote Sensing Scientists and Technologists

**Apply remote sensing principles and methods to analyze data and solve problems in areas such as natural resource management, urban planning, and homeland security. May develop new analytical techniques and sensor systems or develop new applications for existing systems.** Analyze data acquired from aircraft, satellites, or ground-based platforms using statistical analysis software, image analysis software, or Geographic Information Systems (GIS). Manage or analyze data obtained from remote sensing systems to obtain meaningful results. Process aerial and satellite imagery to create products such as land-cover maps. Develop and build databases for remote sensing and related geospatial project information. Monitor quality of remote sensing data collection operations to determine if procedural or equipment changes are necessary. Attend meetings or seminars and read current literature to maintain knowledge of developments in the field of remote sensing. Prepare and deliver reports and presentations of geospatial project information. Conduct research into the application and enhancement of remote sensing technology. Discuss project goals, equipment requirements, and methodologies with colleagues and team members. Integrate other geospatial data sources into projects. Organize and maintain geospatial data and associated documentation. Participate in fieldwork as required. Design and implement strategies for collection, analysis, or display of geographic data. Collect supporting data such as climatic and field survey data to corroborate remote sensing data analyses. Develop new analytical techniques or sensor systems. Train technicians in the use of remote sensing technology. Direct all activity associated with implementation, operation, or enhancement of remote sensing hardware or software. Compile and format image data to increase its usefulness. Recommend new remote sensing hardware or software acquisitions. Direct installation and testing of new remote sensing hardware or software. Set up or maintain remote sensing data collection systems. Develop automated routines to correct for the presence of image distorting artifacts such as ground vegetation.

**Education/Training Required:** Bachelor's degree. **Education and Training Programs:** Geographic Information Science and Cartography; Signal/Geospatial Intelligence. **Knowledge/Courses**—Geography, Biology, Physics, Computers and Electronics, Engineering and Technology, Mathematics.

**Personality Type:** Realistic-Investigative. **Career Clusters:** 11 Information Technology; 12 Law, Public Safety, Corrections, and Security. **Career Pathways:** 11.2 Information Support Services; 12.4 Law Enforcement Services. **Other Jobs in These Pathways:** Bailiffs; Computer and Information Systems Managers; Computer Numerically Controlled Machine Tool Programmers, Metal and Plastic; Computer Operators; Correctional Officers and Jailers; Criminal Investigators and Special Agents; First-Line Supervisors of Police and Detectives; Forensic Science Technicians; Immigration and Customs Inspectors; Intelligence Analysts; Police Detectives; Police Identification and Records Officers; Police Patrol Officers; Remote Sensing Technicians; Sheriffs and Deputy Sheriffs.

**Skills**—Science, Operations Analysis, Mathematics, Writing, Systems Evaluation, Systems Analysis, Reading Comprehension, Complex Problem Solving.

**Work Environment:** Indoors; sitting.

# Physical Therapist Aides

- ❋ Annual Earnings: $23,680
- ❋ Earnings Growth Potential: Low (27.1%)
- ❋ Growth: 36.3%
- ❋ Annual Job Openings: 2,340
- ❋ Self-Employed: 1.3%

**Considerations for Job Outlook:** Projected growth stems from an expected increase in the elderly population and better medical technology that increases the survival rates of people who become injured or ill. Job opportunities should be good in settings that treat the elderly.

**Under close supervision of physical therapists or physical therapy assistants, perform delegated, selected, or routine tasks in specific situations. These duties include preparing patients and treatment areas.** Clean and organize work areas and disinfect equipment after treatment. Administer active and passive manual therapeutic exercises, therapeutic massages, and heat, light, sound, water, or electrical modality treatments such as ultrasound. Instruct, motivate, safeguard, and assist patients practicing exercises and functional activities, under direction of medical staff. Record treatment given and equipment used. Confer with physical therapy staff or others to discuss and evaluate patient information for planning, modifying, and coordinating treatment. Observe patients during treatment to compile and evaluate data on patients' responses and progress, and report to physical therapists. Secure patients into or onto therapy equipment. Change linens such as bed sheets and pillow cases. Transport patients to and from treatment areas, using wheelchairs or providing standing support. Arrange treatment supplies to keep them in order. Maintain equipment and furniture to keep it in good working condition, including performing the assembly and disassembly of equipment and accessories. Assist patients to dress, undress, and put on and remove supportive devices such as braces, splints, and slings. Perform clerical duties such as taking inventory, ordering supplies, answering telephones, taking messages, and filling out forms. Administer traction to relieve neck and back pain, using intermittent and static traction equipment. Schedule patient appointments with physical therapists and coordinate therapists' schedules. Train patients to use orthopedic braces, prostheses, or supportive devices. Measure patient's range-of-joint motion, body parts, and vital signs to determine effects of treatments or for patient evaluations. Participate in patient care tasks such as assisting with passing food trays, feeding residents, or bathing residents on bed rest. Fit patients for orthopedic braces, prostheses, or supportive devices, adjusting fit as needed.

**Education/Training Required:** Short-term on-the-job training. **Education and Training Program:** Physical Therapy Technician/Assistant Training. **Knowledge/Courses**—Medicine and Dentistry, Therapy and Counseling, Customer and Personal Service, Psychology, Public Safety and Security.

**Personality Type:** Social-Realistic. **Career Cluster:** 08 Health Science. **Career Pathway:** 8.1 Therapeutic Services. **Other Jobs in This Pathway:** Clinical Psychologists; Community and Social Service Specialists, All Other; Counseling Psychologists; Dental Assistants; Dental Hygienists; Dentists, General; Health Technologists and Technicians, All Other; Healthcare Support Workers, All Other; Home Health Aides; Licensed Practical and Licensed Vocational Nurses; Low Vision Therapists, Orientation and Mobility Specialists, and Vision Rehabilitation Therapists; Massage Therapists; Medical and Clinical Laboratory Technicians; Medical and Health Services Managers; Medical Scientists, Except Epidemiologists; Medical Secretaries; Occupational Therapists; Pharmacists; Pharmacy Technicians; Radiologic Technologists; School Psychologists; Social and Human Service Assistants; Speech-Language Pathologists; Speech-Language Pathology Assistants; Substance Abuse and Behavioral Disorder Counselors; others.

**Skills**—Technology Design, Operation and Control, Social Perceptiveness, Troubleshooting, Service Orientation, Operation Monitoring, Science, Learning Strategies.

**Work Environment:** Indoors; standing; walking and running; using hands; bending or twisting the body; repetitive motions; exposed to disease or infections.

## Physical Therapist Assistants

- ❊ Annual Earnings: $49,690
- ❊ Earnings Growth Potential: Medium (37.5%)
- ❊ Growth: 33.3%
- ❊ Annual Job Openings: 3,050
- ❊ Self-Employed: 1.3%

**Considerations for Job Outlook:** Projected growth stems from an expected increase in the elderly population and better medical technology that increases the survival rates of people who become injured or ill. Job opportunities should be good in settings that treat the elderly.

**Assist physical therapists in providing physical therapy treatments and procedures. May, in accordance with state laws, assist in the development of treatment plans, carry out routine functions, document the progress of treatment, and modify specific treatments in accordance with patient status and within the scope of treatment plans established by physical therapists. Generally requires formal training.** Instruct, motivate, safeguard, and assist patients as they practice exercises and functional activities.

Observe patients during treatments to compile and evaluate data on their responses and progress; provide results to physical therapists in person or through progress notes. Confer with physical therapy staffs or others to discuss and evaluate patient information for planning, modifying, and coordinating treatment. Transport patients to and from treatment areas, lifting and transferring them according to positioning requirements. Secure patients into or onto therapy equipment. Administer active and passive manual therapeutic exercises; therapeutic massages; aquatic physical therapy; and heat, light, sound, and electrical modality treatments such as ultrasound. Communicate with or instruct caregivers and family members on patient therapeutic activities and treatment plans. Measure patients' ranges-of-joint motion, body parts, and vital signs to determine effects of treatments or for patient evaluations. Monitor operation of equipment and record use of equipment and administration of treatment. Fit patients for orthopedic braces, prostheses, and supportive devices such as crutches. Train patients in the use of orthopedic braces, prostheses, or supportive devices. Clean work areas and check and store equipment after treatments. Assist patients to dress; undress; or put on and remove supportive devices such as braces, splints, and slings. Attend or conduct continuing education courses, seminars, or in-service activities. Perform clerical duties such as taking inventory, ordering supplies, answering telephones, taking messages, and filling out forms. Prepare treatment areas and electrotherapy equipment for use by physiotherapists. Administer traction to relieve neck and back pain, using intermittent and static traction equipment. Perform postural drainage, percussions, and vibrations and teach deep breathing exercises to treat respiratory conditions.

**Education/Training Required:** Associate degree. **Education and Training Program:** Physical Therapy Technician/Assistant Training. **Knowledge/Courses**—Therapy and Counseling, Medicine and Dentistry, Psychology, Biology, Customer and Personal Service, Education and Training.

**Personality Type:** Social-Realistic-Investigative. **Career Cluster:** 08 Health Science. **Career Pathway:** 8.1 Therapeutic Services. **Other Jobs in This Pathway:** Clinical Psychologists; Community and Social Service Specialists, All Other; Counseling Psychologists; Dental Assistants; Dental Hygienists; Dentists, General; Health Technologists and Technicians, All Other; Healthcare Support Workers, All Other; Home Health Aides; Licensed Practical and Licensed Vocational Nurses; Low Vision Therapists, Orientation and Mobility Specialists, and Vision Rehabilitation Therapists; Massage Therapists; Medical and Clinical Laboratory Technicians; Medical and Health Services Managers; Medical Scientists, Except Epidemiologists; Medical Secretaries;

Occupational Therapists; Pharmacists; Pharmacy Technicians; Radiologic Technologists; School Psychologists; Social and Human Service Assistants; Speech-Language Pathologists; Speech-Language Pathology Assistants; Substance Abuse and Behavioral Disorder Counselors; others.

**Skills**—Service Orientation, Quality Control Analysis, Social Perceptiveness, Science, Learning Strategies, Speaking, Reading Comprehension, Systems Evaluation.

**Work Environment:** Indoors; standing; walking and running; exposed to disease or infections.

# Physical Therapists

- ❋ Annual Earnings: $76,310
- ❋ Earnings Growth Potential: Low (29.7%)
- ❋ Growth: 30.3%
- ❋ Annual Job Openings: 7,860
- ❋ Self-Employed: 8.0%

**Considerations for Job Outlook:** Employment of physical therapists is expected to increase as the population ages and as better medical technology increases survival rates of people who become injured or ill. Job opportunities should be good in settings that treat primarily the elderly.

**Assess, plan, organize, and participate in rehabilitative programs that improve mobility, relieve pain, increase strength, and decrease or prevent deformity of patients suffering from disease or injury.** Perform and document initial exams, evaluating data to identify problems and determine diagnoses prior to interventions. Plan, prepare, and carry out individually designed programs of physical treatment to maintain, improve, or restore physical functioning; alleviate pain; and prevent physical dysfunction in patients. Record prognoses, treatments, responses, and progresses in patients' charts or enter information into computers. Identify and document goals, anticipated progresses, and plans for reevaluation. Evaluate effects of treatments at various stages and adjust treatments to achieve maximum benefits. Administer manual exercises, massages, or traction to help relieve pain, increase patient strength, or decrease or prevent deformity or crippling. Test and measure patients' strength, motor development and function, sensory perception, functional capacity, and respiratory and circulatory efficiency and record data. Instruct patients and families in treatment procedures to be continued at home. Confer with patients, medical practitioners, and appropriate others to plan, implement, and assess intervention programs. Review physicians' referrals and patients' medical records to help determine diagnoses and physical therapy treatments required. Obtain patients' informed consent to proposed interventions. Discharge patients from physical therapy when goals or projected outcomes have been attained and provide for appropriate follow-up care or referrals. Provide information to patients about proposed interventions, material risks, and expected benefits and any reasonable alternatives. Inform patients when diagnoses reveal findings outside the scope of physical therapy to treat and refer to appropriate practitioners. Direct, supervise, assess, and communicate with supportive personnel. Provide educational information about physical therapy and physical therapists, injury prevention, ergonomics, and ways to promote health. Refer clients to community resources and services.

**Education/Training Required:** Master's degree. **Education and Training Programs:** Kinesiotherapy/Kinesiotherapist; Physical Therapy/Therapist. **Knowledge/Courses**—Therapy and Counseling, Medicine and Dentistry, Psychology, Education and Training, Biology, Customer and Personal Service.

**Personality Type:** Social-Investigative-Realistic. **Career Cluster:** 08 Health Science. **Career Pathway:** 8.3 Health Informatics. **Other Jobs in This Pathway:** Clinical Psychologists; Dental Laboratory Technicians; Editors; Engineers, All Other; Executive Secretaries and Executive Administrative Assistants; Fine Artists, Including Painters, Sculptors, and Illustrators; First-Line Supervisors of Office and Administrative Support Workers; Health Educators; Medical and Health Services Managers; Medical Appliance Technicians; Medical Assistants; Medical Records and Health Information Technicians; Medical Secretaries; Medical Transcriptionists; Mental Health Counselors; Occupational Health and Safety Specialists; Occupational Health and Safety Technicians; Psychiatric Aides; Psychiatric Technicians; Public Relations Specialists; Receptionists and Information Clerks; Recreational Therapists; Rehabilitation Counselors; Substance Abuse and Behavioral Disorder Counselors; Therapists, All Other; others.

**Skills**—Science, Operations Analysis, Service Orientation, Instructing, Persuasion, Time Management, Social Perceptiveness, Reading Comprehension.

**Work Environment:** Indoors; standing; exposed to disease or infections.

# Physician Assistants

- ❋ Annual Earnings: $86,410
- ❋ Earnings Growth Potential: Low (33.5%)
- ❋ Growth: 39.0%
- ❋ Annual Job Openings: 4,280
- ❋ Self-Employed: 1.4%

**Considerations for Job Outlook:** Employment growth for these workers should be driven by an aging population and by health-care providers' increasing use of physician assistants to contain costs. Opportunities should be good, particularly in underserved areas.

**Under the supervision of physicians, provide health-care services typically performed by a physician. Conduct complete physicals, provide treatment, and counsel patients. May, in some cases, prescribe medication. Must graduate from an accredited educational program for physician assistants.** Examine patients to obtain information about their physical conditions. Obtain, compile, and record patient medical data, including health history, progress notes, and results of physical examinations. Interpret diagnostic test results for deviations from normal. Make tentative diagnoses and decisions about management and treatment of patients. Prescribe therapy or medication with physician approval. Administer or order diagnostic tests, such as X-ray, electrocardiogram, and laboratory tests. Instruct and counsel patients about prescribed therapeutic regimens, normal growth and development, family planning, emotional problems of daily living, and health maintenance. Perform therapeutic procedures such as injections, immunizations, suturing and wound care, and infection management. Provide physicians with assistance during surgery or complicated medical procedures. Visit and observe patients on hospital rounds or house calls, updating charts, ordering therapy, and reporting back to physicians. Supervise and coordinate activities of technicians and technical assistants. Order medical and laboratory supplies and equipment.

**Education/Training Required:** Master's degree. **Education and Training Program:** Physician Assistant Training. **Knowledge/Courses**—Medicine and Dentistry, Biology, Therapy and Counseling, Psychology, Chemistry, Sociology and Anthropology.

**Personality Type:** Social-Investigative-Realistic. **Career Cluster:** 08 Health Science. **Career Pathway:** 8.2 Diagnostics Services. **Other Jobs in This Pathway:** Ambulance Drivers and Attendants, Except Emergency Medical Technicians; Anesthesiologist Assistants; Cardiovascular Technologists and Technicians; Cytogenetic Technologists; Cytotechnologists; Diagnostic Medical Sonographers; Emergency Medical Technicians and Paramedics; Endoscopy Technicians; Health Diagnosing and Treating Practitioners, All Other; Health Technologists and Technicians, All Other; Healthcare Practitioners and Technical Workers, All Other; Histotechnologists and Histologic Technicians; Medical and Clinical Laboratory Technicians; Medical and Clinical Laboratory Technologists; Medical and Health Services Managers; Medical Assistants; Medical Equipment Preparers; Neurodiagnostic Technologists; Nuclear Medicine Technologists; Ophthalmic Laboratory Technicians; Physical Scientists, All Other; Radiologic Technicians; Radiologic Technologists; Surgical Technologists; Veterinary Assistants and Laboratory Animal Caretakers; others.

**Skills**—Science, Instructing, Service Orientation, Judgment and Decision Making, Social Perceptiveness, Reading Comprehension, Operations Analysis, Systems Evaluation.

**Work Environment:** Indoors; standing; using hands; exposed to disease or infections.

## Job Specialization: Anesthesiologist Assistants

**Assist anesthesiologists in the administration of anesthesia for surgical and non-surgical procedures. Monitor patient status and provide patient care during surgical treatment.** Verify availability of operating room supplies, medications, and gases. Provide clinical instruction, supervision or training to staff in areas such as anesthesia practices. Collect samples or specimens for diagnostic testing. Participate in seminars, workshops, or other professional activities to keep abreast of developments in anesthesiology. Collect and document patients' pre-anesthetic health histories. Provide airway management interventions including tracheal intubation, fiber optics, or ventilary support. Respond to emergency situations by providing cardiopulmonary resuscitation (CPR), basic cardiac life support (BLS), advanced cardiac life support (ACLS), or pediatric advanced life support (PALS). Monitor and document patients' progress during post-anesthesia period. Pretest and calibrate anesthesia delivery systems and monitors. Assist anesthesiologists in monitoring of patients including electrocardiogram (EKG), direct arterial pressure, central venous pressure, arterial blood gas, hematocrit, or routine measurement of temperature, respiration, blood pressure and heart rate. Assist in the provision of advanced life support techniques including those procedures using high frequency ventilation or intra-arterial cardiovascular assistance devices. Assist

P

anesthesiologists in performing anesthetic procedures such as epidural and spinal injections. Assist in the application of monitoring techniques such as pulmonary artery catheterization, electroencephalographic spectral analysis, echocardiography, and evoked potentials. Administer blood, blood products, or supportive fluids. Control anesthesia levels during procedures. Administer anesthetic, adjuvant, or accessory drugs under the direction of an anesthesiologist.

**Education/Training Required:** Master's degree. **Education and Training Program:** Physician Assistant Training. **Knowledge/Courses**—No data available.

**Personality Type:** Realistic-Social-Investigative. **Career Cluster:** 08 Health Science. **Career Pathway:** 8.2 Diagnostics Services. **Other Jobs in This Pathway:** Ambulance Drivers and Attendants, Except Emergency Medical Technicians; Cardiovascular Technologists and Technicians; Cytogenetic Technologists; Cytotechnologists; Diagnostic Medical Sonographers; Emergency Medical Technicians and Paramedics; Endoscopy Technicians; Health Diagnosing and Treating Practitioners, All Other; Health Technologists and Technicians, All Other; Healthcare Practitioners and Technical Workers, All Other; Histotechnologists and Histologic Technicians; Medical and Clinical Laboratory Technicians; Medical and Clinical Laboratory Technologists; Medical and Health Services Managers; Medical Assistants; Medical Equipment Preparers; Neurodiagnostic Technologists; Nuclear Medicine Technologists; Ophthalmic Laboratory Technicians; Physical Scientists, All Other; Physician Assistants; Radiologic Technicians; Radiologic Technologists; Surgical Technologists; Veterinary Assistants and Laboratory Animal Caretakers; others.

**Skills**—No data available.

**Work Environment:** No data available.

# Physicians and Surgeons

- ❀ Annual Earnings: $165,279
- ❀ Earnings Growth Potential: Very high (55.2%)
- ❀ Growth: 21.8%
- ❀ Annual Job Openings: 26,050
- ❀ Self-Employed: 11.7%

**Considerations for Job Outlook:** Employment growth is expected to be tied to increases in the aging population and in new medical technologies that allow more maladies to be diagnosed and treated. Job prospects should be very good, particularly in underserved areas.

# Job Specialization: Anesthesiologists

**Administer anesthetics during surgery or other medical procedures.** Administer anesthetic or sedation during medical procedures, using local, intravenous, spinal, or caudal methods. Monitor patient before, during, and after anesthesia and counteract adverse reactions or complications. Provide and maintain life support and airway management and help prepare patients for emergency surgery. Record type and amount of anesthesia and patient condition throughout procedure. Examine patient; obtain medical history; and use diagnostic tests to determine risk during surgical, obstetrical, and other medical procedures. Position patient on operating table to maximize patient comfort and surgical accessibility. Decide when patients have recovered or stabilized enough to be sent to another room or ward or to be sent home following outpatient surgery. Coordinate administration of anesthetics with surgeons during operation. Confer with other medical professionals to determine type and method of anesthetic or sedation to render patient insensible to pain. Coordinate and direct work of nurses, medical technicians, and other health-care providers. Order laboratory tests, X-rays, and other diagnostic procedures. Diagnose illnesses, using examinations, tests, and reports. Manage anesthesiological services, coordinating them with other medical activities and formulating plans and procedures. Provide medical care and consultation in many settings, prescribing medication and treatment and referring patients for surgery. Inform students and staff of types and methods of anesthesia administration, signs of complications, and emergency methods to counteract reactions. Schedule and maintain use of surgical suite, including operating, wash-up, and waiting rooms and anesthetic and sterilizing equipment. Instruct individuals and groups on ways to preserve health and prevent disease. Conduct medical research to aid in controlling and curing disease, to investigate new medications, and to develop and test new medical techniques.

**Education/Training Required:** First professional degree. **Education and Training Program:** Medicine (MD). **Knowledge/Courses**—Medicine and Dentistry, Biology, Chemistry, Psychology, Physics, Therapy and Counseling.

**Personality Type:** Investigative-Realistic-Social. **Career Cluster:** 08 Health Science. **Career Pathway:** 8.1 Therapeutic Services. **Other Jobs in This Pathway:** Clinical Psychologists; Community and Social Service Specialists, All Other; Counseling Psychologists; Dental Assistants; Dental Hygienists; Dentists, General; Health Technologists and Technicians, All Other; Healthcare Support Workers, All Other; Home Health Aides; Licensed Practical and

Licensed Vocational Nurses; Low Vision Therapists, Orientation and Mobility Specialists, and Vision Rehabilitation Therapists; Massage Therapists; Medical and Clinical Laboratory Technicians; Medical and Health Services Managers; Medical Scientists, Except Epidemiologists; Medical Secretaries; Occupational Therapists; Pharmacists; Pharmacy Technicians; Radiologic Technologists; School Psychologists; Social and Human Service Assistants; Speech-Language Pathologists; Speech-Language Pathology Assistants; Substance Abuse and Behavioral Disorder Counselors; 19 other physician occupations; others.

**Skills**—Science, Operation Monitoring, Reading Comprehension, Operations Analysis, Operation and Control, Judgment and Decision Making, Time Management, Management of Personnel Resources.

**Work Environment:** Indoors; more often sitting than standing; using hands; noise; contaminants; exposed to radiation; exposed to disease or infections; hazardous conditions.

## Job Specialization: Family and General Practitioners

**Diagnose, treat, and help prevent diseases and injuries that commonly occur in the general population.** Prescribe or administer treatment, therapy, medication, vaccination, and other specialized medical care to treat or prevent illness, disease, or injury. Order, perform, and interpret tests and analyze records, reports, and examination information to diagnose patients' condition. Monitor the patients' conditions and progress and re-evaluate treatments as necessary. Explain procedures and discuss test results or prescribed treatments with patients. Collect, record, and maintain patient information, such as medical history, reports, and examination results. Advise patients and community members concerning diet, activity, hygiene, and disease prevention. Refer patients to medical specialists or other practitioners when necessary. Direct and coordinate activities of nurses, students, assistants, specialists, therapists, and other medical staff. Coordinate work with nurses, social workers, rehabilitation therapists, pharmacists, psychologists, and other health-care providers. Deliver babies. Operate on patients to remove, repair, or improve functioning of diseased or injured body parts and systems. Plan, implement, or administer health programs or standards in hospital, business, or community for information, prevention, or treatment of injury or illness. Prepare reports for government or management of birth, death, and disease statistics; workforce evaluations; or medical status of individuals. Conduct research to study anatomy and develop or test

medications, treatments, or procedures to prevent or control disease or injury.

**Education/Training Required:** First professional degree. **Education and Training Programs:** Medicine (MD); Osteopathic Medicine/Osteopathy (DO). **Knowledge/Courses**—Medicine and Dentistry, Therapy and Counseling, Biology, Psychology, Sociology and Anthropology, Chemistry.

**Personality Type:** Investigative-Social. **Career Clusters:** 08 Health Science; 15 Science, Technology, Engineering, and Mathematics. **Career Pathways:** 8.1 Therapeutic Services; 15.2 Science and Mathematics. **Other Jobs in These Pathways:** Architectural and Engineering Managers; Biofuels/Biodiesel Technology and Product Development Managers; Clinical Psychologists; Community and Social Service Specialists, All Other; Counseling Psychologists; Dental Assistants; Dental Hygienists; Dentists, General; Education, Training, and Library Workers, All Other; Healthcare Support Workers, All Other; Home Health Aides; Licensed Practical and Licensed Vocational Nurses; Low Vision Therapists, Orientation and Mobility Specialists, and Vision Rehabilitation Therapists; Massage Therapists; Medical and Clinical Laboratory Technicians; Medical and Health Services Managers; Medical Scientists, Except Epidemiologists; Medical Secretaries; Pharmacists; Pharmacy Technicians; Radiologic Technologists; School Psychologists; Social and Human Service Assistants; Speech-Language Pathologists; Speech-Language Pathology Assistants; 19 other physician occupations; others.

**Skills**—Science, Operations Analysis, Judgment and Decision Making, Social Perceptiveness, Reading Comprehension, Service Orientation, Active Listening, Persuasion.

**Work Environment:** Indoors; standing; using hands; exposed to disease or infections.

## Job Specialization: Internists, General

**Diagnose and provide non-surgical treatment of diseases and injuries of internal organ systems. Provide care mainly for adults who have a wide range of problems associated with the internal organs.** Treat internal disorders, such as hypertension; heart disease; diabetes; and problems of the lung, brain, kidney, and gastrointestinal tract. Analyze records, reports, test results, or examination information to diagnose medical condition of patient. Prescribe or administer medication, therapy, and other specialized medical care to treat or prevent illness, disease, or injury. Provide and manage long-term, comprehensive medical care, including

P

diagnosis and non-surgical treatment of diseases, for adult patients in an office or hospital. Manage and treat common health problems, such as infections, influenza and pneumonia, as well as serious, chronic, and complex illnesses, in adolescents, adults, and the elderly. Monitor patients' conditions and progress and re-evaluate treatments as necessary. Collect, record, and maintain patient information, such as medical history, reports, and examination results. Make diagnoses when different illnesses occur together or in situations where the diagnosis may be obscure. Explain procedures and discuss test results or prescribed treatments with patients. Advise patients and community members concerning diet, activity, hygiene, and disease prevention. Refer patient to medical specialist or other practitioner when necessary. Immunize patients to protect them from preventable diseases. Advise surgeon of a patient's risk status and recommend appropriate intervention to minimize risk. Direct and coordinate activities of nurses, students, assistants, specialists, therapists, and other medical staff. Provide consulting services to other doctors caring for patients with special or difficult problems. Operate on patients to remove, repair, or improve functioning of diseased or injured body parts and systems. Plan, implement, or administer health programs in hospitals, businesses, or communities for prevention and treatment of injuries or illnesses.

**Education/Training Required:** First professional degree. **Education and Training Program:** Medicine (MD). **Knowledge/Courses**—Medicine and Dentistry, Biology, Therapy and Counseling, Psychology, Chemistry, Education and Training.

**Personality Type:** Investigative-Social-Realistic. **Career Cluster:** 08 Health Science. **Career Pathway:** 8.1 Therapeutic Services. **Other Jobs in This Pathway:** Clinical Psychologists; Community and Social Service Specialists, All Other; Counseling Psychologists; Dental Assistants; Dental Hygienists; Dentists, General; Health Technologists and Technicians, All Other; Healthcare Support Workers, All Other; Home Health Aides; Licensed Practical and Licensed Vocational Nurses; Low Vision Therapists, Orientation and Mobility Specialists, and Vision Rehabilitation Therapists; Massage Therapists; Medical and Clinical Laboratory Technicians; Medical and Health Services Managers; Medical Scientists, Except Epidemiologists; Medical Secretaries; Occupational Therapists; Pharmacists; Pharmacy Technicians; Radiologic Technologists; School Psychologists; Social and Human Service Assistants; Speech-Language Pathologists; Speech-Language Pathology Assistants; Substance Abuse and Behavioral Disorder Counselors; 19 other physician occupations; others.

**Skills**—Science, Operations Analysis, Reading Comprehension, Active Learning, Service Orientation, Complex Problem Solving, Systems Evaluation, Writing.

**Work Environment:** Indoors; standing; exposed to disease or infections.

## Job Specialization: Obstetricians and Gynecologists

**Diagnose, treat, and help prevent diseases of women, especially those affecting the reproductive system and the process of childbirth.** Care for and treat women during prenatal, natal, and post-natal periods. Explain procedures and discuss test results or prescribed treatments with patients. Treat diseases of female organs. Monitor patients' condition and progress and re-evaluate treatments as necessary. Perform cesarean sections or other surgical procedures as needed to preserve patients' health and deliver babies safely. Prescribe or administer therapy, medication, and other specialized medical care to treat or prevent illness, disease, or injury. Analyze records, reports, test results, or examination information to diagnose medical condition of patient. Collect, record, and maintain patient information, such as medical histories, reports, and examination results. Advise patients and community members concerning diet, activity, hygiene, and disease prevention. Refer patient to medical specialist or other practitioner when necessary. Consult with, or provide consulting services to, other physicians. Direct and coordinate activities of nurses, students, assistants, specialists, therapists, and other medical staff. Plan, implement, or administer health programs in hospitals, businesses, or communities for prevention and treatment of injuries or illnesses. Prepare government and organizational reports on birth, death, and disease statistics; workforce evaluations; or the medical status of individuals. Conduct research to develop or test medications, treatments, or procedures to prevent or control disease or injury.

**Education/Training Required:** First professional degree. **Education and Training Program:** Medicine (MD). **Knowledge/Courses**—Medicine and Dentistry, Therapy and Counseling, Biology, Psychology, Sociology and Anthropology, Chemistry.

**Personality Type:** Investigative-Social-Realistic. **Career Cluster:** 08 Health Science. **Career Pathway:** 8.1 Therapeutic Services. **Other Jobs in This Pathway:** Clinical Psychologists; Community and Social Service Specialists, All Other; Counseling Psychologists; Dental Assistants; Dental Hygienists; Dentists, General; Health Technologists and Technicians, All Other; Healthcare Support Workers,

All Other; Home Health Aides; Licensed Practical and Licensed Vocational Nurses; Low Vision Therapists, Orientation and Mobility Specialists, and Vision Rehabilitation Therapists; Massage Therapists; Medical and Clinical Laboratory Technicians; Medical and Health Services Managers; Medical Scientists, Except Epidemiologists; Medical Secretaries; Occupational Therapists; Pharmacists; Pharmacy Technicians; Radiologic Technologists; School Psychologists; Social and Human Service Assistants; Speech-Language Pathologists; Speech-Language Pathology Assistants; Substance Abuse and Behavioral Disorder Counselors; 19 other physician occupations; others.

**Skills**—Science, Operations Analysis, Reading Comprehension, Social Perceptiveness, Active Listening, Active Learning, Critical Thinking, Monitoring.

**Work Environment:** Indoors; standing; using hands; exposed to disease or infections.

## Job Specialization: Pediatricians, General

**Diagnose, treat, and help prevent children's diseases and injuries.** Examine patients or order, perform, and interpret diagnostic tests to obtain information on medical condition and determine diagnosis. Examine children regularly to assess their growth and development. Prescribe or administer treatment, therapy, medication, vaccination, and other specialized medical care to treat or prevent illness, disease, or injury in infants and children. Collect, record, and maintain patient information, such as medical history, reports, and examination results. Advise patients, parents or guardians, and community members concerning diet, activity, hygiene, and disease prevention. Treat children who have minor illnesses, acute and chronic health problems, and growth and development concerns. Explain procedures and discuss test results or prescribed treatments with patients and parents or guardians. Monitor patients' condition and progress and re-evaluate treatments as necessary. Plan and execute medical care programs to aid in the mental and physical growth and development of children and adolescents. Refer patient to medical specialist or other practitioner when necessary. Direct and coordinate activities of nurses, students, assistants, specialists, therapists, and other medical staff. Provide consulting services to other physicians. Plan, implement, or administer health programs or standards in hospital, business, or community for information, prevention, or treatment of injury or illness. Operate on patients to remove, repair, or improve functioning of diseased or injured body parts and systems. Conduct research to study anatomy and develop or test medications, treatments, or procedures to prevent or control disease or injury. Prepare reports for government or management of birth, death, and disease statistics; workforce evaluations; or medical status of individuals.

**Education/Training Required:** First professional degree. **Education and Training Program:** Medicine (MD). **Knowledge/Courses**—Medicine and Dentistry, Therapy and Counseling, Biology, Psychology, Chemistry, Sociology and Anthropology.

**Personality Type:** Investigative-Social. **Career Cluster:** 08 Health Science. **Career Pathway:** 8.1 Therapeutic Services. **Other Jobs in This Pathway:** Clinical Psychologists; Community and Social Service Specialists, All Other; Counseling Psychologists; Dental Assistants; Dental Hygienists; Dentists, General; Health Technologists and Technicians, All Other; Healthcare Support Workers, All Other; Home Health Aides; Licensed Practical and Licensed Vocational Nurses; Low Vision Therapists, Orientation and Mobility Specialists, and Vision Rehabilitation Therapists; Massage Therapists; Medical and Clinical Laboratory Technicians; Medical and Health Services Managers; Medical Scientists, Except Epidemiologists; Medical Secretaries; Occupational Therapists; Pharmacists; Pharmacy Technicians; Radiologic Technologists; School Psychologists; Social and Human Service Assistants; Speech-Language Pathologists; Speech-Language Pathology Assistants; Substance Abuse and Behavioral Disorder Counselors; 19 other physician occupations; others.

**Skills**—Science, Operations Analysis, Reading Comprehension, Systems Evaluation, Active Learning, Judgment and Decision Making, Service Orientation, Speaking.

**Work Environment:** Indoors; standing; using hands; exposed to disease or infections.

## Job Specialization: Physicians and Surgeons, All Other

**This occupation includes all physicians and surgeons not listed separately.** Because this is a highly diverse occupation, no data is available for some information topics.

**Education/Training Required:** First professional degree. **Education and Training Program:** Medicine (MD).

**Career Clusters:** 08 Health Science; 10 Human Services. **Career Pathways:** 8.1 Therapeutic Services; 10.2 Counseling and Mental Health Services. **Other Jobs in These Pathways:** Clergy; Clinical Psychologists; Community and Social Service Specialists, All Other; Counseling Psychologists;

Dental Assistants; Dental Hygienists; Dentists, General; Healthcare Social Workers; Healthcare Support Workers, All Other; Home Health Aides; Licensed Practical and Licensed Vocational Nurses; Massage Therapists; Medical and Clinical Laboratory Technicians; Medical and Health Services Managers; Medical Secretaries; Mental Health and Substance Abuse Social Workers; Mental Health Counselors; Pharmacists; Pharmacy Technicians; Radiologic Technologists; Recreation Workers; School Psychologists; Social and Human Service Assistants; Speech-Language Pathologists; Speech-Language Pathology Assistants; 19 other physician occupations; others.

## Job Specialization: Psychiatrists

**Diagnose, treat, and help prevent disorders of the mind.** Prescribe, direct, and administer psychotherapeutic treatments or medications to treat mental, emotional, or behavioral disorders. Analyze and evaluate patient data and test findings to diagnose nature and extent of mental disorders. Collaborate with physicians, psychologists, social workers, psychiatric nurses, or other professionals to discuss treatment plans and progress. Gather and maintain patient information and records, including social and medical histories obtained from patients, relatives, and other professionals. Design individualized care plans, using a variety of treatments. Counsel outpatients and other patients during office visits. Examine or conduct laboratory or diagnostic tests on patients to provide information on general physical conditions and mental disorders. Advise and inform guardians, relatives, and significant others of patients' conditions and treatments. Teach, take continuing education classes, attend conferences and seminars, and conduct research and publish findings to increase understanding of mental, emotional, and behavioral states and disorders. Review and evaluate treatment procedures and outcomes of other psychiatrists and medical professionals. Prepare and submit case reports and summaries to government and mental health agencies. Serve on committees to promote and maintain community mental health services and delivery systems.

**Education/Training Required:** First professional degree. **Education and Training Program:** Medicine (MD). **Knowledge/Courses**—Therapy and Counseling, Medicine and Dentistry, Psychology, Biology, Sociology and Anthropology, Philosophy and Theology.

**Personality Type:** Investigative-Social-Artistic. **Career Cluster:** 08 Health Science. **Career Pathway:** 8.1 Therapeutic Services. **Other Jobs in This Pathway:** Clinical Psychologists; Community and Social Service Specialists, All

Other; Counseling Psychologists; Dental Assistants; Dental Hygienists; Dentists, General; Health Technologists and Technicians, All Other; Healthcare Support Workers, All Other; Home Health Aides; Licensed Practical and Licensed Vocational Nurses; Low Vision Therapists, Orientation and Mobility Specialists, and Vision Rehabilitation Therapists; Massage Therapists; Medical and Clinical Laboratory Technicians; Medical and Health Services Managers; Medical Scientists, Except Epidemiologists; Medical Secretaries; Occupational Therapists; Pharmacists; Pharmacy Technicians; Radiologic Technologists; School Psychologists; Social and Human Service Assistants; Speech-Language Pathologists; Speech-Language Pathology Assistants; Substance Abuse and Behavioral Disorder Counselors; 19 other physician occupations; others.

**Skills**—Science, Social Perceptiveness, Operations Analysis, Persuasion, Negotiation, Service Orientation, Instructing, Judgment and Decision Making.

**Work Environment:** Indoors; sitting; exposed to disease or infections.

## Job Specialization: Surgeons

**Treat diseases, injuries, and deformities by invasive methods, such as manual manipulation, or by using instruments and appliances.** Analyze patient's medical history, medication allergies, physical condition, and examination results to verify operation's necessity and to determine best procedure. Operate on patients to correct deformities, repair injuries, prevent and treat diseases, or improve or restore patients' functions. Follow established surgical techniques during the operation. Prescribe preoperative and postoperative treatments and procedures, such as sedatives, diets, antibiotics, and preparation and treatment of the patient's operative area. Examine patient to provide information on medical condition and surgical risk. Diagnose bodily disorders and orthopedic conditions and provide treatments, such as medicines and surgeries, in clinics, hospital wards, and operating rooms. Direct and coordinate activities of nurses, assistants, specialists, residents, and other medical staff. Provide consultation and surgical assistance to other physicians and surgeons. Refer patient to medical specialist or other practitioners when necessary. Examine instruments, equipment, and operating room to ensure sterility. Prepare case histories. Manage surgery services, including planning, scheduling and coordination, determination of procedures, and procurement of supplies and equipment. Conduct research to develop and test surgical techniques that can improve operating procedures and outcomes.

**Education/Training Required:** First professional degree. **Education and Training Program:** Medicine (MD). **Knowledge/Courses**—Medicine and Dentistry, Biology, Therapy and Counseling, Psychology, Chemistry, Customer and Personal Service.

**Personality Type:** Investigative-Realistic-Social. **Career Cluster:** 08 Health Science. **Career Pathway:** 8.1 Therapeutic Services. **Other Jobs in This Pathway:** Clinical Psychologists; Community and Social Service Specialists, All Other; Counseling Psychologists; Dental Assistants; Dental Hygienists; Dentists, General; Health Technologists and Technicians, All Other; Healthcare Support Workers, All Other; Home Health Aides; Licensed Practical and Licensed Vocational Nurses; Low Vision Therapists, Orientation and Mobility Specialists, and Vision Rehabilitation Therapists; Massage Therapists; Medical and Clinical Laboratory Technicians; Medical and Health Services Managers; Medical Scientists, Except Epidemiologists; Medical Secretaries; Occupational Therapists; Pharmacists; Pharmacy Technicians; Radiologic Technologists; School Psychologists; Social and Human Service Assistants; Speech-Language Pathologists; Speech-Language Pathology Assistants; Substance Abuse and Behavioral Disorder Counselors; 19 other physician occupations; others.

**Skills**—Science, Reading Comprehension, Active Learning, Instructing, Operations Analysis, Judgment and Decision Making, Learning Strategies, Social Perceptiveness.

**Work Environment:** Indoors; standing; using hands; contaminants; exposed to radiation; exposed to disease or infections.

# Physicists

* Annual Earnings: $106,370
* Earnings Growth Potential: High (44.7%)
* Growth: 15.9%
* Annual Job Openings: 690
* Self-Employed: 0.0%

**Considerations for Job Outlook:** An increased focus on basic research, particularly that related to energy, is expected to drive employment growth for these workers. Prospects should be favorable for physicists in applied research, development, and related technical fields.

**Conduct research into phases of physical phenomena, develop theories and laws on basis of observation and experiments, and devise methods to apply laws and theories to industry and other fields.** Perform complex calculations as part of the analysis and evaluation of data, using computers. Describe and express observations and conclusions in mathematical terms. Analyze data from research conducted to detect and measure physical phenomena. Report experimental results by writing papers for scientific journals or by presenting information at scientific conferences. Design computer simulations to model physical data so that it can be better understood. Collaborate with other scientists in the design, development, and testing of experimental, industrial, or medical equipment, instrumentation, and procedures. Direct testing and monitoring of contamination of radioactive equipment and recording of personnel and plant area radiation exposure data. Observe the structure and properties of matter and the transformation and propagation of energy, using equipment such as masers, lasers, and telescopes, in order to explore and identify the basic principles governing these phenomena. Develop theories and laws on the basis of observation and experiments and apply these theories and laws to problems in areas such as nuclear energy, optics, and aerospace technology. Teach physics to students. Develop manufacturing, assembly, and fabrication processes of lasers, masers, and infrared and other light-emitting and light-sensitive devices. Conduct application evaluations and analyze results in order to determine commercial, industrial, scientific, medical, military, or other uses for electro-optical devices. Develop standards of permissible concentrations of radioisotopes in liquids and gases. Conduct research pertaining to potential environmental impacts of atomic energy–related industrial development in order to determine licensing qualifications. Advise authorities of procedures to be followed in radiation incidents or hazards and assist in civil defense planning.

**Education/Training Required:** Doctoral degree. **Education and Training Programs:** Acoustics; Astrophysics; Atomic/Molecular Physics; Condensed Matter and Materials Physics; Elementary Particle Physics; Health/Medical Physics; Nuclear Physics; Optics/Optical Sciences; Physics, General; Physics, Other; Plasma and High-Temperature Physics; Theoretical and Mathematical Physics. **Knowledge/Courses**—Physics, Mathematics, Engineering and Technology, Computers and Electronics, English Language, Telecommunications.

**Personality Type:** Investigative-Realistic. **Career Clusters:** 05 Education and Training; 15 Science, Technology, Engineering, and Mathematics. **Career Pathways:** 5.3 Teaching/Training; 15.2 Science and Mathematics. **Other Jobs in These Pathways:** Adult Basic and Secondary Education and Literacy Teachers and Instructors; Architectural and Engineering Managers; Biofuels/Biodiesel Technology and Product Development Managers; Biologists; Career/Technical

Education Teachers, Secondary School; Chemists; Coaches and Scouts; Community and Social Service Specialists, All Other; Education, Training, and Library Workers, All Other; Elementary School Teachers, Except Special Education; Fitness Trainers and Aerobics Instructors; Instructional Coordinators; Instructional Designers and Technologists; Kindergarten Teachers, Except Special Education; Librarians; Medical Scientists, Except Epidemiologists; Middle School Teachers, Except Special and Career/Technical Education; Operations Research Analysts; Preschool Teachers, Except Special Education; Recreation Workers; Secondary School Teachers, Except Special and Career/Technical Education; Self-Enrichment Education Teachers; Teacher Assistants; Teachers and Instructors, All Other; Tutors; others.

**Skills**—Science, Programming, Mathematics, Technology Design, Active Learning, Reading Comprehension, Learning Strategies, Writing.

**Work Environment:** Indoors; sitting.

# Physics Teachers, Postsecondary

- ❀ Annual Earnings: $77,610
- ❀ Earnings Growth Potential: High (44.4%)
- ❀ Growth: 15.1%
- ❀ Annual Job Openings: 400
- ❀ Self-Employed: 0.2%

**Considerations for Job Outlook:** Enrollments in postsecondary institutions are expected to continue rising as more people attend college and as workers return to school to update their skills. Opportunities for part-time or temporary positions should be favorable, but significant competition exists for tenure-track positions.

**Teach courses pertaining to the laws of matter and energy. Includes both teachers primarily engaged in teaching and those who do a combination of both teaching and research.** Evaluate and grade students' classwork, laboratory work, assignments, and papers. Prepare and deliver lectures to undergraduate and/or graduate students on topics such as quantum mechanics, particle physics, and optics. Compile, administer, and grade examinations or assign this work to others. Maintain student attendance records, grades, and other required records. Supervise students' laboratory work. Prepare course materials such as syllabi, homework assignments, and handouts. Maintain regularly scheduled office hours to advise and assist students. Supervise undergraduate and/or graduate teaching, internship, and research work.

Keep abreast of developments in their field by reading current literature, talking with colleagues, and participating in professional conferences. Plan, evaluate, and revise curricula, course content, and course materials and methods of instruction. Initiate, facilitate, and moderate classroom discussions. Conduct research in a particular field of knowledge and publish findings in professional journals, books, and/or electronic media. Advise students on academic and vocational curricula and on career issues. Select and obtain materials and supplies such as textbooks and laboratory equipment. Collaborate with colleagues to address teaching and research issues. Participate in student recruitment, registration, and placement activities. Serve on academic or administrative committees that deal with institutional policies, departmental matters, and academic issues. Write grant proposals to procure external research funding. Perform administrative duties such as serving as department head. Act as advisers to student organizations. Provide professional consulting services to government and/or industry. Compile bibliographies of specialized materials for outside reading assignments. Participate in campus and community events.

**Education/Training Required:** Doctoral degree. **Education and Training Programs:** Acoustics; Atomic/Molecular Physics; Condensed Matter and Materials Physics; Elementary Particle Physics; Nuclear Physics; Optics/Optical Sciences; Physics, General; Physics, Other; Plasma and High-Temperature Physics; Theoretical and Mathematical Physics. **Knowledge/Courses**—Physics, Mathematics, Chemistry, Engineering and Technology, Education and Training, Computers and Electronics.

**Personality Type:** Social-Investigative. **Career Cluster:** 15 Science, Technology, Engineering, and Mathematics. **Career Pathway:** 15.2 Science and Mathematics. **Other Jobs in This Pathway:** Architectural and Engineering Managers; Biochemists and Biophysicists; Biofuels/Biodiesel Technology and Product Development Managers; Bioinformatics Scientists; Biological Scientists, All Other; Biologists; Biostatisticians; Chemists; Clinical Data Managers; Clinical Research Coordinators; Community and Social Service Specialists, All Other; Dietitians and Nutritionists; Education, Training, and Library Workers, All Other; Geneticists; Geoscientists, Except Hydrologists and Geographers; Medical Scientists, Except Epidemiologists; Molecular and Cellular Biologists; Natural Sciences Managers; Operations Research Analysts; Physical Scientists, All Other; Social Scientists and Related Workers, All Other; Statisticians; Survey Researchers; Transportation Planners; Water Resource Specialists; 37 other postsecondary teaching occupations; others.

**Skills**—Science, Writing, Reading Comprehension, Speaking, Operations Analysis, Learning Strategies, Instructing, Active Listening.

**Work Environment:** Indoors; sitting.

# Pipelayers

* ❋ Annual Earnings: $34,800
* ❋ Earnings Growth Potential: Low (34.3%)
* ❋ Growth: 17.2%
* ❋ Annual Job Openings: 2,280
* ❋ Self-Employed: 12.4%

**Considerations for Job Outlook:** Employment of these workers is projected to increase due to new construction and renovation projects, as well as maintenance of existing pipe systems. Increasing emphasis on water conservation should require retrofitting to conserve water, leading to employment growth for plumbers. Workers with welding experience should have especially good opportunities.

**Lay pipe for storm or sanitation sewers, drains, and water mains. Perform any combination of these tasks: grade trenches or culverts, position pipe, or seal joints.** Check slopes for conformance to requirements, using levels or lasers. Cover pipes with earth or other materials. Cut pipes to required lengths. Connect pipe pieces and seal joints, using welding equipment, cement, or glue. Install and repair sanitary and stormwater sewer structures and pipe systems. Install and use instruments such as lasers, grade rods, and transit levels. Grade and level trench bases, using tamping machines and hand tools. Lay out pipe routes, following written instructions or blueprints and coordinating layouts with supervisors. Align and position pipes to prepare them for welding or sealing. Dig trenches to desired or required depths by hand or using trenching tools. Operate mechanized equipment such as pickup trucks, rollers, tandem dump trucks, front-end loaders, and backhoes. Train others in pipe-laying and provide supervision. Tap and drill holes into pipes to introduce auxiliary lines or devices. Locate existing pipes needing repair or replacement, using magnetic or radio indicators.

**Education/Training Required:** Moderate-term on-the-job training. **Education and Training Programs:** Pipefitting/Pipefitter and Sprinkler Fitter; Plumbing Technology/Plumber. **Knowledge/Courses**—Building and Construction, Mechanical.

**Personality Type:** Realistic. **Career Cluster:** 02 Architecture and Construction. **Career Pathway:** 2.2 Construction. **Other Jobs in This Pathway:** Brickmasons and Blockmasons; Cement Masons and Concrete Finishers; Construction and Building Inspectors; Construction Carpenters; Construction Laborers; Construction Managers; Cost Estimators; Drywall and Ceiling Tile Installers; Electrical Power-Line Installers and Repairers; Electricians; Engineering Technicians, Except Drafters, All Other; First-Line Supervisors of Construction Trades and Extraction Workers; Heating and Air Conditioning Mechanics and Installers; Helpers—Carpenters; Helpers—Electricians; Helpers—Pipelayers, Plumbers, Pipefitters, and Steamfitters; Highway Maintenance Workers; Operating Engineers and Other Construction Equipment Operators; Painters, Construction and Maintenance; Pipe Fitters and Steamfitters; Plumbers; Refrigeration Mechanics and Installers; Roofers; Rough Carpenters; Solar Energy Installation Managers; others.

**Skills**—Repairing, Operation and Control, Equipment Maintenance, Troubleshooting, Equipment Selection, Installation, Quality Control Analysis, Operation Monitoring.

**Work Environment:** Outdoors; standing; walking and running; using hands; bending or twisting the body; repetitive motions; noise; very hot or cold; bright or inadequate lighting; contaminants; cramped work space; whole-body vibration; hazardous equipment; minor burns, cuts, bites, or stings.

# Plumbers, Pipefitters, and Steamfitters

* ❋ Annual Earnings: $46,660
* ❋ Earnings Growth Potential: Medium (40.9%)
* ❋ Growth: 15.3%
* ❋ Annual Job Openings: 17,550
* ❋ Self-Employed: 12.3%

**Considerations for Job Outlook:** Employment of these workers is projected to increase due to new construction and renovation projects, as well as maintenance of existing pipe systems. Increasing emphasis on water conservation should require retrofitting to conserve water, leading to employment growth for plumbers. Workers with welding experience should have especially good opportunities.

## Job Specialization: Pipe Fitters and Steamfitters

**Lay out, assemble, install, and maintain pipe systems, pipe supports, and related hydraulic and pneumatic equipment for steam, hot water, heating, cooling, lubricating, sprinkling, and industrial production and processing systems.** Cut, thread, and hammer pipe to specifications, using tools such as saws, cutting torches, and pipe threaders and benders. Assemble and secure pipes, tubes, fittings, and related equipment according to specifications by welding, brazing, cementing, soldering, and threading joints. Attach pipes to walls, structures, and fixtures, such as radiators or tanks, using brackets, clamps, tools, or welding equipment. Inspect, examine, and test installed systems and pipelines, using pressure gauge, hydrostatic testing, observation, or other methods. Measure and mark pipes for cutting and threading. Lay out full scale drawings of pipe systems, supports, and related equipment, following blueprints. Plan pipe system layout, installation, or repair according to specifications. Select pipe sizes and types and related materials, such as supports, hangers, and hydraulic cylinders, according to specifications. Cut and bore holes in structures such as bulkheads, decks, walls, and mains prior to pipe installation, using hand and power tools. Modify, clean, and maintain pipe systems, units, fittings, and related machines and equipment, following specifications and using hand and power tools. Install automatic controls used to regulate pipe systems. Turn valves to shut off steam, water, or other gases or liquids from pipe sections, using valve keys or wrenches. Remove and replace worn components. Prepare cost estimates for clients. Inspect work sites for obstructions and to ensure that holes will not cause structural weakness. Operate motorized pumps to remove water from flooded manholes, basements, or facility floors. Dip nonferrous piping materials in a mixture of molten tin and lead to obtain a coating that prevents erosion or galvanic and electrolytic action.

**Education/Training Required:** Long-term on-the-job training. **Education and Training Programs:** Pipefitting/Pipefitter and Sprinkler Fitter; Plumbing and Related Water Supply Services, Other; Plumbing Technology/Plumber. **Knowledge/Courses**—Building and Construction, Mechanical, Physics, Design, Engineering and Technology, Chemistry.

**Personality Type:** Realistic-Conventional. **Career Cluster:** 02 Architecture and Construction. **Career Pathway:** 2.2 Construction. **Other Jobs in This Pathway:** Brickmasons and Blockmasons; Cement Masons and Concrete Finishers; Construction and Building Inspectors; Construction Carpenters; Construction Laborers; Construction Managers; Cost Estimators; Drywall and Ceiling Tile Installers; Electrical Power-Line Installers and Repairers; Electricians; Engineering Technicians, Except Drafters, All Other; Excavating and Loading Machine and Dragline Operators; First-Line Supervisors of Construction Trades and Extraction Workers; Heating and Air Conditioning Mechanics and Installers; Helpers—Carpenters; Helpers—Electricians; Helpers—Pipelayers, Plumbers, Pipefitters, and Steamfitters; Highway Maintenance Workers; Operating Engineers and Other Construction Equipment Operators; Painters, Construction and Maintenance; Plumbers; Refrigeration Mechanics and Installers; Roofers; Rough Carpenters; Solar Energy Installation Managers; others.

**Skills**—Repairing, Equipment Maintenance, Installation, Troubleshooting, Operation and Control, Quality Control Analysis, Operation Monitoring, Equipment Selection.

**Work Environment:** More often outdoors than indoors; standing; using hands; bending or twisting the body; repetitive motions; noise; very hot or cold; bright or inadequate lighting; contaminants; cramped work space; high places; hazardous conditions; hazardous equipment; minor burns, cuts, bites, or stings.

## Job Specialization: Plumbers

**Assemble, install, and repair pipes, fittings, and fixtures of heating, water, and drainage systems according to specifications and plumbing codes.** Measure, cut, thread, and bend pipe to required angles, using hand and power tools or machines such as pipe cutters, pipe-threading machines, and pipe-bending machines. Study building plans and inspect structures to assess material and equipment needs to establish the sequence of pipe installations and to plan installation around obstructions such as electrical wiring. Locate and mark the position of pipe installations, connections, passage holes, and fixtures in structures, using measuring instruments such as rulers and levels. Assemble pipe sections, tubing, and fittings, using couplings, clamps, screws, bolts, cement, plastic solvent, caulking, or soldering, brazing, and welding equipment. Fill pipes or plumbing fixtures with water or air and observe pressure gauges to detect and locate leaks. Install pipe assemblies, fittings, valves, appliances such as dishwashers and water heaters, and fixtures such as sinks and toilets, using hand and power tools. Direct workers engaged in pipe cutting and preassembly and installation of plumbing systems and components. Cut openings in structures to accommodate pipes and pipe fittings, using hand and power tools. Review blueprints and building codes and specifications to determine work details and procedures. Install underground storm, sanitary, and water piping systems and extend piping to connect fixtures and plumbing to these systems. Repair and maintain plumbing, replacing defective washers, replacing or mending broken pipes, and opening clogged drains. Keep records of assignments and produce detailed work reports. Hang steel supports from ceiling joists to hold pipes in place. Perform complex calculations and planning for special or very large jobs. Clear away debris in renovations. Install oxygen and medical gas in hospitals. Prepare written work cost estimates and negotiate contracts.

**Education/Training Required:** Long-term on-the-job training. **Education and Training Programs:** Pipefitting/ Pipefitter and Sprinkler Fitter; Plumbing and Related Water Supply Services, Other; Plumbing Technology/Plumber. **Knowledge/Courses**—Building and Construction, Physics, Mechanical, Design, Engineering and Technology, Customer and Personal Service.

**Personality Type:** Realistic-Conventional-Investigative. **Career Cluster:** 02 Architecture and Construction. **Career Pathway:** 2.2 Construction. **Other Jobs in This Pathway:** Brickmasons and Blockmasons; Cement Masons and Concrete Finishers; Construction and Building Inspectors; Construction Carpenters; Construction Laborers; Construction Managers; Cost Estimators; Drywall and Ceiling Tile Installers; Electrical Power-Line Installers and Repairers; Electricians; Engineering Technicians, Except Drafters, All Other; Excavating and Loading Machine and Dragline Operators; First-Line Supervisors of Construction Trades and Extraction Workers; Heating and Air Conditioning Mechanics and Installers; Helpers—Carpenters; Helpers—Electricians; Helpers—Pipelayers, Plumbers, Pipefitters, and Steamfitters; Highway Maintenance Workers; Operating Engineers and Other Construction Equipment Operators; Painters, Construction and Maintenance; Pipe Fitters and Steamfitters; Refrigeration Mechanics and Installers; Roofers; Rough Carpenters; Solar Energy Installation Managers; others.

**Skills**—Repairing, Equipment Maintenance, Installation, Troubleshooting, Equipment Selection, Operation and Control, Operation Monitoring, Quality Control Analysis.

**Work Environment:** More often outdoors than indoors; standing; walking and running; kneeling, crouching, stooping, or crawling; using hands; bending or twisting the body; repetitive motions; noise; very hot or cold; bright or inadequate lighting; contaminants; cramped work space; whole-body vibration; hazardous equipment; minor burns, cuts, bites, or stings.

# Podiatrists

- ❀ Annual Earnings: $118,030
- ❀ Earnings Growth Potential: Very high (57.5%)
- ❀ Growth: 9.0%
- ❀ Annual Job Openings: 320
- ❀ Self-Employed: 19.1%

**Considerations for Job Outlook:** Projected employment growth reflects a more active, older population that is sustaining a rising number of foot injuries. Opportunities for entry-level job seekers should be good for qualified applicants.

**Diagnose and treat diseases and deformities of the human foot.** Treat bone, muscle, and joint disorders affecting the feet. Diagnose diseases and deformities of the foot, using medical histories, physical examinations, X-rays, and laboratory test results. Prescribe medications, corrective devices, physical therapy, or surgery. Treat conditions such as corns, calluses, ingrown nails, tumors, shortened tendons, bunions, cysts, and abscesses by surgical methods. Advise patients about treatments and foot care techniques necessary for prevention of future problems. Refer patients to physicians when symptoms indicative of systemic disorders, such as arthritis or diabetes, are observed in feet and legs. Correct deformities by means of plaster casts and strapping. Make and fit prosthetic appliances. Perform administrative duties such as hiring employees, ordering supplies, and keeping records. Educate the public about the benefits of foot care through techniques such as speaking engagements, advertising, and other forums. Treat deformities, using mechanical methods, such as whirlpool or paraffin baths, and electrical methods, such as shortwave and low-voltage currents.

**Education/Training Required:** First professional degree. **Education and Training Program:** Podiatric Medicine/ Podiatry (DPM). **Knowledge/Courses**—Medicine and Dentistry, Biology, Therapy and Counseling, Sales and Marketing, Chemistry, Economics and Accounting.

**Personality Type:** Investigative-Social-Realistic. **Career Cluster:** 08 Health Science. **Career Pathway:** 8.1 Therapeutic Services. **Other Jobs in This Pathway:** Clinical Psychologists; Community and Social Service Specialists, All Other; Counseling Psychologists; Dental Assistants; Dental Hygienists; Dentists, General; Health Technologists and Technicians, All Other; Healthcare Support Workers, All Other; Home Health Aides; Licensed Practical and Licensed Vocational Nurses; Low Vision Therapists, Orientation and

P

Mobility Specialists, and Vision Rehabilitation Therapists; Massage Therapists; Medical and Clinical Laboratory Technicians; Medical and Health Services Managers; Medical Scientists, Except Epidemiologists; Medical Secretaries; Occupational Therapists; Pharmacists; Pharmacy Technicians; Radiologic Technologists; School Psychologists; Social and Human Service Assistants; Speech-Language Pathologists; Speech-Language Pathology Assistants; Substance Abuse and Behavioral Disorder Counselors; others.

**Skills**—Science, Management of Financial Resources, Active Learning, Technology Design, Management of Material Resources, Reading Comprehension, Service Orientation, Instructing.

**Work Environment:** Indoors; sitting; using hands; repetitive motions; contaminants; exposed to radiation; exposed to disease or infections.

# Police and Sheriff's Patrol Officers

- ❋ Annual Earnings: $53,540
- ❋ Earnings Growth Potential: Medium (40.8%)
- ❋ Growth: 8.7%
- ❋ Annual Job Openings: 22,790
- ❋ Self-Employed: 0.0%

**Considerations for Job Outlook:** Population growth is the main source of demand for police services. Overall, opportunities in local police departments should be favorable for qualified applicants.

## Job Specialization: Police Patrol Officers

**Patrol assigned areas to enforce laws and ordinances, regulate traffic, control crowds, prevent crime, and arrest violators.** Provide for public safety by maintaining order, responding to emergencies, protecting people and property, enforcing motor vehicle and criminal laws, and promoting good community relations. Monitor, note, report, and investigate suspicious persons and situations, safety hazards, and unusual or illegal activity in patrol area. Record facts to prepare reports that document incidents and activities. Identify, pursue, and arrest suspects and perpetrators of criminal acts. Patrol specific areas on foot, horseback, or motorized conveyance, responding promptly to calls for assistance. Review facts of incidents to determine whether

criminal acts or statute violations were involved. Investigate traffic accidents and other accidents to determine causes and to determine whether crimes have been committed. Render aid to accident victims and other persons requiring first aid for physical injuries. Testify in court to present evidence or act as witness in traffic and criminal cases. Photograph or draw diagrams of crime or accident scenes and interview principals and eyewitnesses. Relay complaint and emergency-request information to appropriate agency dispatchers. Evaluate complaint and emergency-request information to determine response requirements. Process prisoners and prepare and maintain records of prisoner bookings and prisoner statuses during booking and pre-trial processes. Monitor traffic to ensure motorists observe traffic regulations and exhibit safe driving procedures. Issue citations or warnings to violators of motor vehicle ordinances. Direct traffic flow and reroute traffic during emergencies. Inform citizens of community services and recommend options to facilitate longer-term problem resolution. Provide road information to assist motorists. Inspect public establishments to ensure compliance with rules and regulations. Act as official escorts at times, such as when leading funeral processions or firefighters.

**Education/Training Required:** Long-term on-the-job training. **Education and Training Programs:** Criminal Justice/Police Science; Criminalistics and Criminal Science. **Knowledge/Courses**—Psychology, Public Safety and Security, Law and Government, Customer and Personal Service, Therapy and Counseling, Sociology and Anthropology.

**Personality Type:** Realistic-Enterprising-Conventional. **Career Cluster:** 12 Law, Public Safety, Corrections, and Security. **Career Pathway:** 12.4 Law Enforcement Services. **Other Jobs in This Pathway:** Bailiffs; Correctional Officers and Jailers; Criminal Investigators and Special Agents; First-Line Supervisors of Police and Detectives; Forensic Science Technicians; Immigration and Customs Inspectors; Intelligence Analysts; Police Detectives; Police Identification and Records Officers; Remote Sensing Scientists and Technologists; Sheriffs and Deputy Sheriffs.

**Skills**—Negotiation, Persuasion, Service Orientation, Operation and Control, Social Perceptiveness, Active Listening, Critical Thinking, Coordination.

**Work Environment:** More often outdoors than indoors; sitting; using hands; noise; very hot or cold; bright or inadequate lighting; contaminants; exposed to disease or infections; hazardous equipment; minor burns, cuts, bites, or stings.

## Job Specialization: Sheriffs and Deputy Sheriffs

**Enforce law and order in rural or unincorporated districts or serve legal processes of courts. May patrol courthouse, guard court or grand jury, or escort defendants.** Drive vehicles or patrol specific areas to detect law violators, issue citations, and make arrests. Investigate illegal or suspicious activities. Verify that the proper legal charges have been made against law offenders. Execute arrest warrants, locating and taking persons into custody. Record daily activities and submit logs and other related reports and paperwork to appropriate authorities. Patrol and guard courthouses, grand jury rooms, or assigned areas to provide security, enforce laws, maintain order, and arrest violators. Notify patrol units to take violators into custody or to provide needed assistance or medical aid. Place people in protective custody. Serve statements of claims, subpoenas, summonses, jury summonses, orders to pay alimony, and other court orders. Take control of accident scenes to maintain traffic flow, to assist accident victims, and to investigate causes. Question individuals entering secured areas to determine their business, directing and rerouting individuals as necessary. Transport or escort prisoners and defendants en route to courtrooms, prisons or jails, attorneys' offices, or medical facilities. Locate and confiscate real or personal property, as directed by court order. Manage jail operations and tend to jail inmates.

**Education/Training Required:** Long-term on-the-job training. **Education and Training Programs:** Criminal Justice/Police Science; Criminalistics and Criminal Science. **Knowledge/Courses**—Public Safety and Security, Law and Government, Telecommunications, Psychology, Therapy and Counseling, Philosophy and Theology.

**Personality Type:** Enterprising-Realistic-Social. **Career Cluster:** 12 Law, Public Safety, Corrections, and Security. **Career Pathways:** 12.3 Security and Protective Services; 12.4 Law Enforcement Services. **Other Jobs in These Pathways:** Animal Control Workers; Bailiffs; Correctional Officers and Jailers; Criminal Investigators and Special Agents; Crossing Guards; First-Line Supervisors of Police and Detectives; First-Line Supervisors of Protective Service Workers, All Other; Forensic Science Technicians; Forest Firefighters; Gaming Surveillance Officers and Gaming Investigators; Immigration and Customs Inspectors; Intelligence Analysts; Lifeguards, Ski Patrol, and Other Recreational Protective Service Workers; Parking Enforcement Workers; Police Detectives; Police Identification and Records Officers; Police Patrol Officers; Police, Fire, and Ambulance Dispatchers; Private Detectives and Investigators; Remote Sensing Scientists and Technologists; Retail Loss Prevention Specialists; Security Guards; Transit and Railroad Police.

**Skills**—Negotiation, Social Perceptiveness, Persuasion, Service Orientation, Management of Personnel Resources, Critical Thinking, Time Management, Reading Comprehension.

**Work Environment:** More often outdoors than indoors; sitting; using hands; repetitive motions; noise; very hot or cold; bright or inadequate lighting; contaminants; cramped work space; exposed to disease or infections; hazardous equipment.

# Police, Fire, and Ambulance Dispatchers

- ❋ Annual Earnings: $35,370
- ❋ Earnings Growth Potential: Medium (36.9%)
- ❋ Growth: 17.8%
- ❋ Annual Job Openings: 3,840
- ❋ Self-Employed: 0.0%

**Considerations for Job Outlook:** The growing and aging population will increase demand for emergency services, leading to employment increases for these dispatchers. Job opportunities should be favorable.

**Receive complaints from public concerning crimes and police emergencies. Broadcast orders to police patrol units in vicinity of complaint to investigate. Operate radio, telephone, or computer equipment to receive reports of fires and medical emergencies and relay information or orders to proper officials.** Question callers about their locations and the nature of their problems to determine types of response needed. Receive incoming telephone or alarm system calls regarding emergency and non-emergency police and fire service, emergency ambulance service, information, and after-hours calls for departments within a city. Determine response requirements and relative priorities of situations and dispatch units in accordance with established procedures. Record details of calls, dispatches, and messages. Enter, update, and retrieve information from teletype networks and computerized data systems regarding such things as wanted persons, stolen property, vehicle registration, and stolen vehicles. Maintain access to and security of highly sensitive materials. Relay information and messages to and from emergency sites, to law enforcement agencies, and to all other individuals or groups requiring notification. Scan status charts and computer screens and contact emergency response field units to determine emergency units available for dispatch. Observe alarm registers and scan maps to determine whether a specific emergency is in the dispatch service area. Maintain files of information relating to emergency calls such as personnel rosters, and emergency call-out and pager files. Monitor various radio frequencies such as those used by public works departments, school security, and civil defense to keep apprised of developing situations. Learn material and pass required tests for certification. Read and effectively interpret small-scale maps and information from a computer screen to determine locations and provide directions. Answer routine inquiries and refer calls not requiring dispatches to appropriate departments and agencies. Test and adjust communication and alarm systems and report malfunctions to maintenance units. Provide emergency medical instructions to callers. Monitor alarm systems to detect emergencies such as fires and illegal entry into establishments.

**Education/Training Required:** Moderate-term on-the-job training. **Education and Training Programs:** No related CIP programs; this job is learned through moderate-term on-the-job training. **Knowledge/Courses**—Telecommunications, Customer and Personal Service, Clerical, Law and Government, Public Safety and Security, Psychology.

**Personality Type:** Conventional-Realistic-Enterprising. **Career Cluster:** 12 Law, Public Safety, Corrections, and Security. **Career Pathway:** 12.3 Security and Protective Services. **Other Jobs in This Pathway:** Animal Control Workers; Crossing Guards; First-Line Supervisors of Protective Service Workers, All Other; Forest Firefighters; Gaming Surveillance Officers and Gaming Investigators; Lifeguards, Ski Patrol, and Other Recreational Protective Service Workers; Parking Enforcement Workers; Private Detectives and Investigators; Retail Loss Prevention Specialists; Security Guards; Sheriffs and Deputy Sheriffs; Transit and Railroad Police.

**Skills**—Active Listening, Critical Thinking, Persuasion, Social Perceptiveness, Service Orientation, Operation and Control, Programming, Operations Analysis.

**Work Environment:** Indoors; sitting; using hands; repetitive motions; noise; contaminants.

# Political Science Teachers, Postsecondary

❋ Annual Earnings: $70,540
❋ Earnings Growth Potential: High (48.9%)
❋ Growth: 15.1%
❋ Annual Job Openings: 500
❋ Self-Employed: 0.2%

**Considerations for Job Outlook:** Enrollments in postsecondary institutions are expected to continue rising as more people attend college and as workers return to school to update their skills. Opportunities for part-time or temporary positions should be favorable, but significant competition exists for tenure-track positions.

**Teach courses in political science, international affairs, and international relations.** Initiate, facilitate, and moderate classroom discussions. Prepare and deliver lectures to undergraduate or graduate students on topics such as classical political thought, international relations, and democracy and citizenship. Evaluate and grade students' classwork, assignments, and papers. Compile, administer, and grade examinations or assign this work to others. Prepare course materials such as syllabi, homework assignments, and handouts. Keep abreast of developments in their field by reading current literature, talking with colleagues, and participating in professional conferences. Plan, evaluate, and revise curricula, course content, and course materials and methods of instruction. Maintain student attendance records, grades, and other required records. Maintain regularly scheduled office hours in order to advise and assist students. Advise students on academic and vocational curricula and on career issues. Select and obtain materials and supplies such as textbooks. Conduct research in a particular field of knowledge and publish findings in professional journals, books, and electronic media. Supervise undergraduate and graduate teaching, internship, and research work. Collaborate with colleagues to address teaching and research issues. Serve on academic or administrative committees that deal with institutional policies, departmental matters, and academic issues. Participate in student recruitment, registration, and placement activities. Participate in campus and community events. Compile bibliographies of specialized materials for outside reading assignments. Act as advisers to student organizations. Perform administrative duties such as serving as department head. Write grant proposals to procure external research funding. Provide professional consulting services to government and industry.

**Education/Training Required:** Doctoral degree. **Education and Training Programs:** American Government and Politics (United States); Humanities/Humanistic Studies; International Relations and Affairs; Political Science and Government, General; Political Science and Government, Other; Social Science Teacher Education. **Knowledge/Courses**—History and Archeology, Philosophy and Theology, Sociology and Anthropology, Geography, Law and Government, English Language.

**Personality Type:** Social-Enterprising-Artistic. **Career Clusters:** 05 Education and Training; 07 Government and Public Administration; 15 Science, Technology, Engineering, and Mathematics. **Career Pathways:** 5.3 Teaching/Training; 7.1 Governance; 7.4 Planning; 15.2 Science and Mathematics. **Other Jobs in These Pathways:** Administrative Services Managers; Architectural and Engineering Managers; Biofuels/Biodiesel Technology and Product Development Managers; Chief Executives; Chief Sustainability Officers; Coaches and Scouts; Compliance Managers; Elementary School Teachers, Except Special Education; Fitness Trainers and Aerobics Instructors; General and Operations Managers; Instructional Coordinators; Instructional Designers and Technologists; Kindergarten Teachers, Except Special Education; Librarians; Managers, All Other; Middle School Teachers, Except Special and Career/Technical Education; Preschool Teachers, Except Special Education; Recreation Workers; Regulatory Affairs Managers; Secondary School Teachers, Except Special and Career/Technical Education; Self-Enrichment Education Teachers; Social and Community Service Managers; Teacher Assistants; Tutors; 37 other postsecondary teaching occupations; others.

**Skills**—Science, Instructing, Writing, Speaking, Operations Analysis, Active Learning, Reading Comprehension, Learning Strategies.

**Work Environment:** Indoors; sitting.

# Political Scientists

- ❋ Annual Earnings: $107,420
- ❋ Earnings Growth Potential: Very high (54.6%)
- ❋ Growth: 19.4%
- ❋ Annual Job Openings: 280
- ❋ Self-Employed: 1.4%

**Considerations for Job Outlook:** Political scientists are expected to experience employment growth especially in nonprofit, political lobbying, and civic organizations.

Opportunities should be best for job seekers who have an advanced degree.

**Study the origin, development, and operation of political systems. Research a wide range of subjects, such as relations between the United States and foreign countries, the beliefs and institutions of foreign nations, or the politics of small towns or a major metropolis. May study topics such as public opinion, political decision making, and ideology. May analyze the structure and operation of governments, as well as various political entities. May conduct public opinion surveys, analyze election results, or analyze public documents.** Teach political science. Disseminate research results through academic publications, written reports, or public presentations. Identify issues for research and analysis. Develop and test theories, using information from interviews, newspapers, periodicals, case law, historical papers, polls, and/or statistical sources. Maintain current knowledge of government policy decisions. Collect, analyze, and interpret data such as election results and public opinion surveys; report on findings, recommendations, and conclusions. Interpret and analyze policies; public issues; legislation; and the operations of governments, businesses, and organizations. Evaluate programs and policies and make related recommendations to institutions and organizations. Write drafts of legislative proposals and prepare speeches, correspondence, and policy papers for governmental use. Forecast political, economic, and social trends. Consult with and advise government officials, civic bodies, research agencies, the media, political parties, and others concerned with political issues. Provide media commentary and/or criticism related to public policy and political issues and events.

**Education/Training Required:** Master's degree. **Education and Training Programs:** American Government and Politics (United States); Canadian Government and Politics; International Relations and Affairs; International/Global Studies; Political Science and Government, General; Political Science and Government, Other. **Knowledge/Courses**—History and Archeology, Law and Government, Philosophy and Theology, Sociology and Anthropology, Foreign Language, Geography.

**Personality Type:** Investigative-Artistic-Social. **Career Clusters:** 07 Government and Public Administration; 15 Science, Technology, Engineering, and Mathematics. **Career Pathways:** 7.1 Governance; 15.2 Science and Mathematics. **Other Jobs in These Pathways:** Administrative Services Managers; Architectural and Engineering Managers; Biofuels/Biodiesel Technology and Product Development Managers; Biologists; Chemists; Chief Executives;

Chief Sustainability Officers; Clinical Research Coordinators; Community and Social Service Specialists, All Other; Compliance Managers; Dietitians and Nutritionists; Education, Training, and Library Workers, All Other; General and Operations Managers; Legislators; Managers, All Other; Mapping Technicians; Medical Scientists, Except Epidemiologists; Natural Sciences Managers; Operations Research Analysts; Regulatory Affairs Managers; Reporters and Correspondents; Social and Community Service Managers; Storage and Distribution Managers; Surveying Technicians; Transportation Managers; others.

**Skills**—Science, Speaking, Writing, Critical Thinking, Active Listening, Active Learning, Systems Analysis, Reading Comprehension.

**Work Environment:** Indoors; sitting.

# Postal Service Mail Carriers

- ❀ Annual Earnings: $53,860
- ❀ Earnings Growth Potential: Low (28.5%)
- ❀ Growth: –1.1%
- ❀ Annual Job Openings: 10,720
- ❀ Self-Employed: 0.0%

**Considerations for Job Outlook:** Declining mail volume, along with automation, is expected to offset employment growth driven by the need to provide mail-delivery services to a growing population. Keen competition is expected. Opportunities are expected to be best in areas experiencing population growth.

**Sort mail for delivery. Deliver mail on established routes by vehicle or on foot.** Obtain signed receipts for registered, certified, and insured mail; collect associated charges; and complete any necessary paperwork. Sort mail for delivery, arranging it in delivery sequence. Deliver mail to residences and business establishments along specified routes by walking and/or driving, using a combination of satchels, carts, cars, and small trucks. Return to the post office with mail collected from homes, businesses, and public mailboxes. Turn in money and receipts collected along mail routes. Sign for cash-on-delivery and registered mail before leaving post offices. Record address changes and redirect mail for those addresses. Hold mail for customers who are away from delivery locations. Bundle mail in preparation for delivery or transportation to relay boxes. Leave notices telling patrons where to collect mail that could not be delivered. Meet schedules for the collection and return of mail. Return incorrectly addressed mail to senders. Maintain accurate records of deliveries. Answer customers' questions about postal services and regulations. Provide customers with change of address cards and other forms. Report any unusual circumstances concerning mail delivery, including the condition of street letter boxes. Register, certify, and insure parcels and letters. Travel to post offices to pick up the mail for routes and/or pick up mail from postal relay boxes. Enter change of address orders into computers that process forwarding address stickers. Complete forms that notify publishers of address changes. Sell stamps and money orders.

**Education/Training Required:** Short-term on-the-job training. **Education and Training Program:** General Office Occupations and Clerical Services. **Knowledge/Courses**—Transportation, Public Safety and Security.

**Personality Type:** Conventional-Realistic. **Career Cluster:** 04 Business, Management, and Administration. **Career Pathway:** 4.6 Administrative and Information Support. **Other Jobs in This Pathway:** Couriers and Messengers; Court Clerks; Court, Municipal, and License Clerks; Customer Service Representatives; Data Entry Keyers; Dispatchers, Except Police, Fire, and Ambulance; Executive Secretaries and Executive Administrative Assistants; File Clerks; Human Resources Assistants, Except Payroll and Timekeeping; Information and Record Clerks, All Other; Insurance Claims Clerks; Insurance Policy Processing Clerks; Interviewers, Except Eligibility and Loan; License Clerks; Mail Clerks and Mail Machine Operators, Except Postal Service; Office and Administrative Support Workers, All Other; Office Clerks, General; Order Clerks; Patient Representatives; Postal Service Mail Sorters, Processors, and Processing Machine Operators; Receptionists and Information Clerks; Secretaries and Administrative Assistants, Except Legal, Medical, and Executive; Shipping, Receiving, and Traffic Clerks; Switchboard Operators, Including Answering Service; Word Processors and Typists; others.

**Skills**—Operation and Control.

**Work Environment:** More often outdoors than indoors; standing; walking and running; using hands; bending or twisting the body; repetitive motions; noise; very hot or cold; bright or inadequate lighting; contaminants; minor burns, cuts, bites, or stings.

# Preschool Teachers, Except Special Education

- ❈ Annual Earnings: $25,700
- ❈ Earnings Growth Potential: Low (33.1%)
- ❈ Growth: 19.0%
- ❈ Annual Job Openings: 17,830
- ❈ Self-Employed: 1.4%

**Considerations for Job Outlook:** Continued emphasis on early childhood education is increasing the employment of preschool teachers. The need to replace workers who leave the occupation permanently should create good job opportunities.

**Instruct children (normally up to 5 years of age) in activities designed to promote social, physical, and intellectual growth needed for primary school in preschool, day care center, or other child development facility. May be required to hold state certification.** Provide a variety of materials and resources for children to explore, manipulate, and use, both in learning activities and in imaginative play. Attend to children's basic needs by feeding them, dressing them, and changing their diapers. Establish and enforce rules for behavior and procedures for maintaining order. Read books to entire classes or to small groups. Teach basic skills such as color, shape, number, and letter recognition; personal hygiene; and social skills. Organize and lead activities designed to promote physical, mental, and social development, such as games, arts and crafts, music, storytelling, and field trips. Observe and evaluate children's performance, behavior, social development, and physical health. Meet with parents and guardians to discuss their children's progress and needs, determine their priorities for their children, and suggest ways that they can promote learning and development. Identify children showing signs of emotional, developmental, or health-related problems and discuss them with supervisors, parents or guardians, and child development specialists. Enforce all administration policies and rules governing students. Prepare materials and classrooms for class activities. Serve meals and snacks in accordance with nutritional guidelines. Teach proper eating habits and personal hygiene. Assimilate arriving children to the school environment by greeting them, helping them remove outerwear, and selecting activities of interest to them. Adapt teaching methods and instructional materials to meet students' varying needs and interests. Establish clear objectives for all lessons, units, and projects and communicate those objectives to children. Demonstrate activities to children.

Arrange indoor and outdoor space to facilitate creative play, motor-skill activities, and safety.

**Education/Training Required:** Postsecondary vocational training. **Education and Training Programs:** Child Care and Support Services Management; Early Childhood Education and Teaching. **Knowledge/Courses**—Philosophy and Theology, Therapy and Counseling, Sociology and Anthropology, Geography, Customer and Personal Service, Psychology.

**Personality Type:** Social-Artistic. **Career Clusters:** 05 Education and Training; 10 Human Services. **Career Pathways:** 5.3 Teaching/Training; 10.1 Early Childhood Development and Services. **Other Jobs in These Pathways:** Adult Basic and Secondary Education and Literacy Teachers and Instructors; Athletes and Sports Competitors; Audio-Visual and Multimedia Collections Specialists; Career/Technical Education Teachers, Middle School; Career/Technical Education Teachers, Secondary School; Chemists; Coaches and Scouts; Dietitians and Nutritionists; Elementary School Teachers, Except Special Education; Farm and Home Management Advisors; Fitness Trainers and Aerobics Instructors; Historians; Instructional Coordinators; Instructional Designers and Technologists; Interpreters and Translators; Kindergarten Teachers, Except Special Education; Librarians; Middle School Teachers, Except Special and Career/Technical Education; Physicists; Recreation Workers; Secondary School Teachers, Except Special and Career/Technical Education; Self-Enrichment Education Teachers; Teacher Assistants; Teachers and Instructors, All Other; Tutors.

**Skills**—Learning Strategies, Social Perceptiveness, Service Orientation, Coordination, Monitoring, Time Management, Negotiation, Complex Problem Solving.

**Work Environment:** Indoors; standing; noise.

# Private Detectives and Investigators

- ❈ Annual Earnings: $42,870
- ❈ Earnings Growth Potential: Medium (39.9%)
- ❈ Growth: 22.0%
- ❈ Annual Job Openings: 1,930
- ❈ Self-Employed: 20.7%

**Considerations for Job Outlook:** Growth in employment of private detectives and investigators should result from heightened confidentiality and security concerns and from increased litigation. Keen competition is expected for most jobs.

**Detect occurrences of unlawful acts or infractions of rules in private establishments or seek, examine, and compile information for clients.** Question persons to obtain evidence for cases of divorce, child custody, or missing persons or information about an individual's character or financial status. Conduct private investigations on a paid basis. Confer with establishment officials, security departments, police, or postal officials to identify problems, provide information, and receive instructions. Observe and document activities of individuals to detect unlawful acts or to obtain evidence for cases, using binoculars and still or video cameras. Investigate companies' financial standings or locate funds stolen by embezzlers, using accounting skills. Monitor industrial or commercial properties to enforce conformance to establishment rules and to protect people or property. Search computer databases, credit reports, public records, tax and legal filings, and other resources to locate persons or to compile information for investigations. Write reports and case summaries to document investigations. Count cash and review transactions, sales checks, and register tapes to verify amounts and to identify shortages. Perform undercover operations such as evaluating employee performance and honesty by posing as customers or employees. Expose fraudulent insurance claims or stolen funds. Alert appropriate personnel to suspects' locations. Conduct background investigations of individuals, such as pre-employment checks, to obtain information about each individual's character, financial status, or personal history. Testify at hearings and court trials to present evidence. Warn troublemakers causing problems on establishment premises and eject them from premises when necessary. Obtain and analyze information on suspects, crimes, and disturbances to solve cases, identify criminal activity, and gather information for court cases. Apprehend suspects and release them to law-enforcement authorities or security personnel.

**Education/Training Required:** Work experience in a related occupation. **Education and Training Program:** Criminal Justice/Police Science. **Knowledge/Courses—** Clerical, Law and Government, Customer and Personal Service, Computers and Electronics, Sales and Marketing, Mathematics.

**Personality Type:** Enterprising-Conventional. **Career Cluster:** 12 Law, Public Safety, Corrections, and Security. **Career Pathway:** 12.3 Security and Protective Services. **Other Jobs in This Pathway:** Animal Control Workers; Crossing Guards; First-Line Supervisors of Protective Service Workers, All Other; Forest Firefighters; Gaming Surveillance Officers and Gaming Investigators; Lifeguards, Ski Patrol, and Other Recreational Protective Service Workers; Parking Enforcement Workers; Police, Fire, and Ambulance Dispatchers; Retail Loss Prevention Specialists; Security Guards; Sheriffs and Deputy Sheriffs; Transit and Railroad Police.

**Skills—**Service Orientation, Active Listening, Negotiation, Writing, Speaking, Critical Thinking, Persuasion, Social Perceptiveness.

**Work Environment:** More often outdoors than indoors; sitting; using hands; repetitive motions; noise; very hot or cold; bright or inadequate lighting; contaminants.

# Probation Officers and Correctional Treatment Specialists

- ❋ Annual Earnings: $47,200
- ❋ Earnings Growth Potential: Low (34.5%)
- ❋ Growth: 19.3%
- ❋ Annual Job Openings: 4,180
- ❋ Self-Employed: 0.3%

**Considerations for Job Outlook:** Many states are expected to emphasize alternatives to incarceration, such as probation. As a result, employment growth should be strong for these workers. Opportunities should be excellent.

**Provide social services to assist in rehabilitation of law offenders in custody or on probation or parole. Make recommendations for actions involving formulation of rehabilitation plan and treatment of offender, including conditional release and education and employment stipulations.** Prepare and maintain case folder for each assigned inmate or offender. Write reports describing offenders' progress. Inform offenders or inmates of requirements of conditional release, such as office visits, restitution payments, or educational and employment stipulations. Discuss with offenders how such issues as drug and alcohol abuse and anger management problems might have played roles in their criminal behavior. Gather information about offenders' backgrounds by talking to offenders, their families and friends, and other people who have relevant information. Develop rehabilitation programs for assigned offenders or inmates, establishing rules of conduct, goals, and objectives. Develop liaisons and networks with other parole officers, community agencies, staff in correctional institutions, psychiatric facilities, and after-care agencies to make plans for helping offenders with life adjustments. Arrange for medical, mental health, or substance abuse treatment services according to individual needs and court orders. Provide offenders or inmates with assistance in matters concerning detainers, sentences in other jurisdictions, writs, and applications for social assistance. Arrange for post-release services such as employment, housing, counseling, education, and social activities. Recommend remedial action or initiate court action when terms of probation or parole are not complied with. Interview probationers and parolees regularly to evaluate their progress in accomplishing goals and maintaining the terms specified in their probation contracts and rehabilitation plans. Supervise people on community-based sentences, including people on electronically monitored home detention. Assess the suitability of penitentiary inmates for release under parole and statutory release programs and submit recommendations to parole boards. Investigate alleged parole violations, using interviews, surveillance, and search and seizure.

**Education/Training Required:** Bachelor's degree. **Education and Training Program:** Social Work. **Knowledge/Courses**—Therapy and Counseling, Psychology, Sociology and Anthropology, Philosophy and Theology, Law and Government, Public Safety and Security.

**Personality Type:** Social-Enterprising-Conventional. **Career Cluster:** 10 Human Services. **Career Pathway:** 10.3 Family and Community Services. **Other Jobs in This Pathway:** Chief Executives; Child, Family, and School Social Workers; Childcare Workers; City and Regional Planning Aides; Counselors, All Other; Eligibility Interviewers, Government Programs; Farm and Home Management Advisors; Legislators; Managers, All Other; Marriage and Family Therapists; Nannies; Personal Care Aides; Protective Service Workers, All Other; Social and Community Service Managers; Social Science Research Assistants; Social Scientists and Related Workers, All Other; Social Workers, All Other; Sociologists; Supply Chain Managers.

**Skills**—Social Perceptiveness, Negotiation, Service Orientation, Persuasion, Monitoring, Critical Thinking, Speaking, Judgment and Decision Making.

**Work Environment:** More often indoors than outdoors; sitting; very hot or cold; exposed to disease or infections.

# Producers and Directors

❊ Annual Earnings: $68,440
❊ Earnings Growth Potential: Very high (53.0%)
❊ Growth: 9.8%
❊ Annual Job Openings: 4,040
❊ Self-Employed: 20.1%

**Considerations for Job Outlook:** Employment growth is expected to be driven by expanding film and television operations and an increase in production of online and mobile video content. Keen competition is expected.

## Job Specialization: Directors—Stage, Motion Pictures, Television, and Radio

**Interpret script, conduct rehearsals, and direct activities of cast and technical crew for stage, motion pictures, television, or radio programs.** Direct live broadcasts, films and recordings, or non-broadcast programming for public entertainment or education. Supervise and coordinate the work of camera, lighting, design, and sound crew members. Study and research scripts to determine how they should be directed. Cut and edit film or tape to integrate component parts into desired sequences. Collaborate with film and sound editors during the post-production process as films are edited and soundtracks are added. Confer with technical directors, managers, crew members, and writers to discuss details of production, such as photography, script, music, sets, and costumes. Plan details such as framing, composition, camera movement, sound, and actor movement for each shot or scene. Communicate to actors the approach, characterization, and movement needed for each scene in such a way that rehearsals and takes are minimized. Establish pace of programs and sequences of scenes according to time requirements and cast and set accessibility. Choose settings and locations for films and determine how scenes will be shot in these settings. Identify and approve equipment and elements required for productions, such as scenery, lights, props, costumes, choreography, and music. Compile scripts, program notes, and other material related to productions. Perform producers' duties such as securing financial backing, establishing and administering budgets, and recruiting cast and crew. Select plays or scripts for production and determine how material should be interpreted and performed. Compile cue words and phrases; cue announcers, cast members, and technicians during performances. Consult with writers, producers, or actors about script changes or "workshop" scripts, through rehearsal with writers and actors, to create final drafts. Collaborate with producers to hire crew members such as art directors, cinematographers, and costumer designers. Review film daily to check on work in progress and to plan for future filming.

**Education/Training Required:** Work experience plus degree. **Education and Training Programs:** Cinematography and Film/Video Production; Directing and Theatrical Production; Drama and Dramatics/Theatre Arts, General; Dramatic/Theatre Arts and Stagecraft, Other; Film/Cinema/Video Studies; Radio and Television. **Knowledge/Courses**—Communications and Media, Fine Arts, Telecommunications, Production and Processing, Computers and Electronics, Engineering and Technology.

**Personality Type:** Enterprising-Artistic. **Career Cluster:** 03 Arts, Audio/Video Technology, and Communications. **Career Pathways:** 3.4 Performing Arts; 3.5 Journalism and Broadcasting. **Other Jobs in These Pathways:** Actors; Artists and Related Workers, All Other; Audio and Video Equipment Technicians; Broadcast Technicians; Camera Operators, Television, Video, and Motion Picture; Copy Writers; Editors; Entertainers and Performers, Sports and Related Workers, All Other; Film and Video Editors; Managers, All Other; Media and Communication Workers, All Other; Music Composers and Arrangers; Music Directors; Musicians, Instrumental; Photographers; Poets, Lyricists and Creative Writers; Producers; Program Directors; Public Relations Specialists; Radio and Television Announcers; Reporters and Correspondents; Singers; Talent Directors; Technical Directors/Managers; Technical Writers; others.

**Skills**—Management of Personnel Resources, Management of Material Resources, Negotiation, Persuasion, Coordination, Speaking, Instructing, Time Management.

**Work Environment:** Indoors; sitting; using hands; repetitive motions; noise.

## Job Specialization: Producers

**Plan and coordinate various aspects of radio, television, stage, or motion picture production, such as selecting script; coordinating writing, directing, and editing; and arranging financing.** Coordinate the activities of writers, directors, managers, and other personnel throughout the production process. Monitor post-production processes to ensure accurate completion of all details. Perform management activities such as budgeting, scheduling, planning, and marketing. Determine production size, content, and budget, establishing details such as production schedules and management policies. Compose and edit scripts or provide

screenwriters with story outlines from which scripts can be written. Conduct meetings with staff to discuss production progress and to ensure production objectives are attained. Resolve personnel problems that arise during the production process by acting as liaisons between dissenting parties when necessary. Produce shows for special occasions, such as holidays or testimonials. Edit and write news stories from information collected by reporters. Write and submit proposals to bid on contracts for projects. Hire directors, principal cast members, and key production staff members. Arrange financing for productions. Select plays, scripts, books, or ideas to be produced. Review film, recordings, or rehearsals to ensure conformance to production and broadcast standards. Perform administrative duties such as preparing operational reports, distributing rehearsal call sheets and script copies, and arranging for rehearsal quarters. Obtain and distribute costumes, props, music, and studio equipment needed to complete productions. Negotiate contracts with artistic personnel, often in accordance with collective bargaining agreements. Maintain knowledge of minimum wages and working conditions established by unions or associations of actors and technicians. Plan and coordinate the production of musical recordings, selecting music and directing performers. Negotiate with parties, including independent producers and the distributors and broadcasters who will be handling completed productions.

**Education/Training Required:** Work experience plus degree. **Education and Training Programs:** Cinematography and Film/Video Production; Directing and Theatrical Production; Drama and Dramatics/Theatre Arts, General; Dramatic/Theatre Arts and Stagecraft, Other; Film/Cinema/Video Studies; Radio and Television. **Knowledge/Courses**—Communications and Media, Fine Arts, Clerical, Sales and Marketing, Telecommunications, English Language.

**Personality Type:** Enterprising-Artistic. **Career Cluster:** 03 Arts, Audio/Video Technology, and Communications. **Career Pathways:** 3.4 Performing Arts; 3.5 Journalism and Broadcasting. **Other Jobs in These Pathways:** Actors; Artists and Related Workers, All Other; Audio and Video Equipment Technicians; Broadcast Technicians; Camera Operators, Television, Video, and Motion Picture; Copy Writers; Directors—Stage, Motion Pictures, Television, and Radio; Editors; Entertainers and Performers, Sports and Related Workers, All Other; Film and Video Editors; Managers, All Other; Media and Communication Workers, All Other; Music Composers and Arrangers; Music Directors; Musicians, Instrumental; Photographers; Poets, Lyricists and Creative Writers; Program Directors; Public Relations

Specialists; Radio and Television Announcers; Reporters and Correspondents; Singers; Talent Directors; Technical Directors/Managers; Technical Writers; others.

**Skills**—Management of Financial Resources, Management of Material Resources, Coordination, Monitoring, Management of Personnel Resources, Time Management, Negotiation, Writing.

**Work Environment:** Indoors; sitting.

## Job Specialization: Program Directors

**Direct and coordinate activities of personnel engaged in preparation of radio or television station program schedules and programs such as sports or news.** Plan and schedule programming and event coverage based on broadcast length; time availability; and other factors such as community needs, ratings data, and viewer demographics. Monitor and review programming to ensure that schedules are met, guidelines are adhered to, and performances are of adequate quality. Direct and coordinate activities of personnel engaged in broadcast news, sports, or programming. Check completed program logs for accuracy and conformance with FCC rules and regulations and resolve program log inaccuracies. Establish work schedules and assign work to staff members. Coordinate activities between departments such as news and programming. Perform personnel duties such as hiring staff and evaluating work performance. Evaluate new and existing programming for suitability and to assess the need for changes, using information such as audience surveys and feedback. Develop budgets for programming and broadcasting activities and monitor expenditures to ensure that they remain within budgetary limits. Confer with directors and production staff to discuss issues such as production and casting problems, budgets, policies, and news coverage. Select, acquire, and maintain programs, music, films, and other needed materials and obtain legal clearances for their use as necessary. Monitor network transmissions for advisories concerning daily program schedules, program content, special feeds, or program changes. Develop promotions for current programs and specials. Prepare copy and edit tape so that material is ready for broadcasting. Develop ideas for programs and features that a station could produce. Participate in the planning and execution of fundraising activities. Review information about programs and schedules to ensure accuracy and provide such information to local media outlets as necessary. Read news, read or record public service and promotional announcements, and otherwise participate as a member of an on-air shift as required.

**Education/Training Required:** Work experience plus degree. **Education and Training Programs:** Cinematography and Film/Video Production; Directing and Theatrical Production; Drama and Dramatics/Theatre Arts, General; Dramatic/Theatre Arts and Stagecraft, Other; Film/Cinema/Video Studies; Radio and Television. **Knowledge/Courses**—Telecommunications, Communications and Media, Clerical, Computers and Electronics, Personnel and Human Resources, Engineering and Technology.

**Personality Type:** Enterprising-Conventional-Artistic. **Career Cluster:** 03 Arts, Audio/Video Technology, and Communications. **Career Pathways:** 3.4 Performing Arts; 3.5 Journalism and Broadcasting. **Other Jobs in These Pathways:** Actors; Artists and Related Workers, All Other; Audio and Video Equipment Technicians; Broadcast Technicians; Camera Operators, Television, Video, and Motion Picture; Copy Writers; Directors—Stage, Motion Pictures, Television, and Radio; Editors; Entertainers and Performers, Sports and Related Workers, All Other; Film and Video Editors; Managers, All Other; Media and Communication Workers, All Other; Music Composers and Arrangers; Music Directors; Musicians, Instrumental; Photographers; Poets, Lyricists and Creative Writers; Producers; Public Relations Specialists; Radio and Television Announcers; Reporters and Correspondents; Singers; Talent Directors; Technical Directors/Managers; Technical Writers; others.

**Skills**—Management of Financial Resources, Management of Material Resources, Operations Analysis, Management of Personnel Resources, Systems Evaluation, Systems Analysis, Instructing, Time Management.

**Work Environment:** Indoors; sitting; noise.

## Job Specialization: Talent Directors

**Audition and interview performers to select most appropriate talent for parts in stage, television, radio, or motion picture productions.** Review performer information such as photos, resumes, voice tapes, videos, and union membership in order to decide whom to audition for parts. Read scripts and confer with producers in order to determine the types and numbers of performers required for a given production. Select performers for roles or submit lists of suitable performers to producers or directors for final selection. Audition and interview performers in order to match their attributes to specific roles or to increase the pool of available acting talent. Maintain talent files that include information such as performers' specialties, past performances, and availability. Prepare actors for auditions by providing scripts and information about roles and casting requirements. Serve as liaisons between directors, actors, and agents. Attend or view productions in order to maintain knowledge of available actors. Negotiate contract agreements with performers, with agents, or between performers and agents or production companies. Contact agents and actors in order to provide notification of audition and performance opportunities and to set up audition times. Hire and supervise workers who help locate people with specified attributes and talents. Arrange for and/or design screen tests or auditions for prospective performers. Locate performers or extras for crowd and background scenes and stand-ins or photo doubles for actors by direct contact or through agents.

**Education/Training Required:** Long-term on-the-job training. **Education and Training Programs:** Cinematography and Film/Video Production; Directing and Theatrical Production; Drama and Dramatics/Theatre Arts, General; Dramatic/Theatre Arts and Stagecraft, Other; Film/Cinema/Video Studies; Radio and Television. **Knowledge/Courses**—Fine Arts, Communications and Media, Clerical, Computers and Electronics, Sales and Marketing, Telecommunications.

**Personality Type:** Enterprising-Artistic. **Career Cluster:** 03 Arts, Audio/Video Technology, and Communications. **Career Pathways:** 3.4 Performing Arts; 3.5 Journalism and Broadcasting. **Other Jobs in These Pathways:** Actors; Artists and Related Workers, All Other; Audio and Video Equipment Technicians; Broadcast Technicians; Camera Operators, Television, Video, and Motion Picture; Copy Writers; Directors—Stage, Motion Pictures, Television, and Radio; Editors; Entertainers and Performers, Sports and Related Workers, All Other; Film and Video Editors; Managers, All Other; Media and Communication Workers, All Other; Music Composers and Arrangers; Music Directors; Musicians, Instrumental; Photographers; Poets, Lyricists and Creative Writers; Producers; Program Directors; Public Relations Specialists; Radio and Television Announcers; Reporters and Correspondents; Singers; Technical Directors/Managers; Technical Writers; others.

**Skills**—Negotiation, Persuasion, Management of Personnel Resources, Speaking, Social Perceptiveness, Reading Comprehension, Monitoring, Management of Financial Resources.

**Work Environment:** Indoors; sitting; noise.

## Job Specialization: Technical Directors/Managers

**Coordinate activities of technical departments, such as taping, editing, engineering, and maintenance, to produce radio or television programs.** Direct technical aspects of newscasts and other productions, checking and switching between video sources and taking responsibility for the on-air product, including camera shots and graphics. Test equipment to ensure proper operation. Monitor broadcasts to ensure that programs conform to station or network policies and regulations. Observe pictures through monitors and direct camera and video staff concerning shading and composition. Act as liaisons between engineering and production departments. Supervise and assign duties to workers engaged in technical control and production of radio and television programs. Schedule use of studio and editing facilities for producers and engineering and maintenance staff. Confer with operations directors to formulate and maintain fair and attainable technical policies for programs. Operate equipment to produce programs or broadcast live programs from remote locations. Train workers in use of equipment such as switchers, cameras, monitors, microphones, and lights. Switch between video sources in a studio or on multi-camera remotes, using equipment such as switchers, video slide projectors, and video effects generators. Set up and execute video transitions and special effects such as fades, dissolves, cuts, keys, and supers, using computers to manipulate pictures as necessary. Collaborate with promotions directors to produce on-air station promotions. Discuss filter options, lens choices, and the visual effects of objects being filmed with photography directors and video operators. Follow instructions from production managers and directors during productions, such as commands for camera cuts, effects, graphics, and takes.

**Education/Training Required:** Long-term on-the-job training. **Education and Training Programs:** Cinematography and Film/Video Production; Directing and Theatrical Production; Drama and Dramatics/Theatre Arts, General; Dramatic/Theatre Arts and Stagecraft, Other; Film/Cinema/Video Studies; Radio and Television. **Knowledge/Courses**—Communications and Media, Telecommunications, Fine Arts, Engineering and Technology, Production and Processing, Computers and Electronics.

**Personality Type:** Enterprising-Realistic-Conventional. **Career Cluster:** 03 Arts, Audio/Video Technology, and Communications. **Career Pathways:** 3.1 Audio and Video Technology and Film; 3.4 Performing Arts; 3.5 Journalism and Broadcasting. **Other Jobs in These Pathways:** Actors; Audio and Video Equipment Technicians; Broadcast

Technicians; Commercial and Industrial Designers; Copy Writers; Directors—Stage, Motion Pictures, Television, and Radio; Editors; Entertainers and Performers, Sports and Related Workers, All Other; Graphic Designers; Managers, All Other; Media and Communication Workers, All Other; Multimedia Artists and Animators; Music Composers and Arrangers; Music Directors; Musicians, Instrumental; Photographers; Poets, Lyricists and Creative Writers; Producers; Program Directors; Public Relations Specialists; Radio and Television Announcers; Reporters and Correspondents; Singers; Talent Directors; Technical Writers; others.

**Skills**—Equipment Selection, Monitoring, Management of Personnel Resources, Coordination, Systems Analysis, Operation and Control, Instructing, Operation Monitoring.

**Work Environment:** Indoors; sitting; using hands.

# Production, Planning, and Expediting Clerks

- ❀ Annual Earnings: $42,220
- ❀ Earnings Growth Potential: Medium (39.5%)
- ❀ Growth: 1.5%
- ❀ Annual Job Openings: 7,410
- ❀ Self-Employed: 0.5%

**Considerations for Job Outlook:** Job openings are expected to arise from the need to replace workers who leave the occupation. Opportunities should be limited in manufacturing but better in industries with faster growth, such as wholesale trade and warehousing.

**Coordinate and expedite the flow of work and materials within or between departments of an establishment according to production schedules, inventory levels, costs, and production problems.** Examine documents, materials, and products, and monitor work processes to assess completeness, accuracy, and conformance to standards and specifications. Review documents such as production schedules, work orders, and staffing tables to determine personnel and materials requirements, and material priorities. Revise production schedules when required due to design changes, labor or material shortages, backlogs, or other interruptions, collaborating with management, marketing, sales, production, and engineering. Confer with department supervisors and other personnel to assess progress and discuss needed changes. Confer with establishment personnel, vendors, and customers to coordinate production and shipping activities, and to resolve complaints or eliminate delays. Record production data, including volume produced, consumption of raw materials, and quality control measures. Requisition and maintain inventories of materials and supplies necessary to meet production demands. Calculate figures such as required amounts of labor and materials, manufacturing costs, and wages, using pricing schedules, adding machines, calculators, or computers. Distribute production schedules and work orders to departments. Compile information such as production rates and progress, materials inventories, materials used, and customer information, so that status reports can be completed. Arrange for delivery, assembly, and distribution of supplies and parts to expedite flow of materials and meet production schedules. Contact suppliers to verify shipment details. Maintain files such as maintenance records, bills of lading, and cost reports. Plan production commitments and timetables for business units, specific programs, and/or jobs, using sales forecasts. Establish and prepare product construction directions and locations; information on required tools, materials, and equipment; numbers of workers needed; and cost projections.

**Education/Training Required:** Moderate-term on-the-job training. **Education and Training Program:** Parts, Warehousing, and Inventory Management Operations. **Knowledge/Courses**—Production and Processing, Clerical, Computers and Electronics, Administration and Management, Mathematics, Customer and Personal Service.

**Personality Type:** Conventional-Enterprising. **Career Cluster:** 16 Transportation, Distribution, and Logistics. **Career Pathway:** 16.3 Warehousing and Distribution Center Operations. **Other Jobs in This Pathway:** Logistics Analysts; Shipping, Receiving, and Traffic Clerks; Traffic Technicians.

**Skills**—Management of Material Resources, Negotiation, Management of Financial Resources, Reading Comprehension, Persuasion, Time Management, Programming, Speaking.

**Work Environment:** Indoors; sitting; noise; contaminants.

# Property, Real Estate, and Community Association Managers

- ❀ Annual Earnings: $51,480
- ❀ Earnings Growth Potential: High (49.1%)
- ❀ Growth: 8.4%
- ❀ Annual Job Openings: 7,800
- ❀ Self-Employed: 45.9%

P

**Considerations for Job Outlook:** Job growth is expected to be driven, in part, by a growing population and increasing use of third-party management companies for residential property oversight. Opportunities should be best for jobseekers who have a college degree and earn professional designation.

**Plan, direct, or coordinate selling, buying, leasing, or governance activities of commercial, industrial, or residential real estate properties.** Meet with prospective tenants to show properties, explain terms of occupancy, and provide information about local areas. Direct collection of monthly assessments; rental fees; and deposits and payment of insurance premiums, mortgage, taxes, and incurred operating expenses. Inspect grounds, facilities, and equipment routinely to determine necessity of repairs or maintenance. Investigate complaints, disturbances, and violations and resolve problems, following management rules and regulations. Manage and oversee operations, maintenance, administration, and improvement of commercial, industrial, or residential properties. Plan, schedule, and coordinate general maintenance, major repairs, and remodeling or construction projects for commercial or residential properties. Negotiate the sale, lease, or development of property and complete or review appropriate documents and forms. Maintain records of sales, rental or usage activity, special permits issued, maintenance and operating costs, or property availability. Determine and certify the eligibility of prospective tenants, following government regulations. Prepare detailed budgets and financial reports for properties. Direct and coordinate the activities of staff and contract personnel and evaluate their performance. Maintain contact with insurance carriers, fire and police departments, and other agencies to ensure protection and compliance with codes and regulations. Market vacant space to prospective tenants through leasing agents, advertising, or other methods. Solicit and analyze bids from contractors for repairs, renovations, and maintenance. Review rents to ensure that they are in line with rental markets. Prepare and administer contracts for provision of property services such as cleaning, maintenance, and security services. Purchase building and maintenance supplies, equipment, or furniture. Act as liaisons between on-site managers or tenants and owners.

**Education/Training Required:** Bachelor's degree. **Education and Training Program:** Real Estate. **Knowledge/ Courses**—Sales and Marketing, Clerical, Economics and Accounting, Building and Construction, Customer and Personal Service, Administration and Management.

**Personality Type:** Enterprising-Conventional. **Career Cluster:** 14 Marketing, Sales, and Service. **Career Pathway:** 14.2 Professional Sales and Marketing. **Other Jobs in This Pathway:** Cashiers; Counter and Rental Clerks; Door-To-Door Sales Workers, News and Street Vendors, and Related Workers; Driver/Sales Workers; Energy Brokers; First-Line Supervisors of Non-Retail Sales Workers; First-Line Supervisors of Retail Sales Workers; Hotel, Motel, and Resort Desk Clerks; Marketing Managers; Marking Clerks; Online Merchants; Order Fillers, Wholesale and Retail Sales; Parts Salespersons; Real Estate Sales Agents; Reservation and Transportation Ticket Agents and Travel Clerks; Retail Salespersons; Sales and Related Workers, All Other; Sales Representatives, Services, All Other; Sales Representatives, Wholesale and Manufacturing, Except Technical and Scientific Products; Sales Representatives, Wholesale and Manufacturing, Technical and Scientific Products; Solar Sales Representatives and Assessors; Stock Clerks—Stockroom, Warehouse, or Storage Yard; Stock Clerks, Sales Floor; Telemarketers; Wholesale and Retail Buyers, Except Farm Products; others.

**Skills**—Management of Financial Resources, Negotiation, Management of Personnel Resources, Persuasion, Operations Analysis, Management of Material Resources, Service Orientation, Writing.

**Work Environment:** More often indoors than outdoors; sitting.

## Prosthodontists

- ❋ Annual Earnings: $118,400
- ❋ Earnings Growth Potential: Very high (65.1%)
- ❋ Growth: 28.3%
- ❋ Annual Job Openings: 30
- ❋ Self-Employed: 27.9%

**Considerations for Job Outlook:** An increase in the elderly population—who often need complicated dental work— and expanded insurance coverage for dental procedures are expected to create job growth. Good prospects are expected from the need to replace the large number of dentists who are retiring.

**Construct oral prostheses to replace missing teeth and other oral structures to correct natural and acquired deformation of mouth and jaws; to restore and maintain oral function, such as chewing and speaking; and to improve appearance.** Replace missing teeth and associated oral structures with permanent fixtures, such as crowns and bridges, or removable fixtures, such as dentures. Fit prostheses to patients, making any necessary adjustments and modifications. Design and fabricate dental prostheses or supervise dental technicians and laboratory bench workers who construct the devices. Measure and take impressions of patients' jaws and teeth to determine the shape and size of dental prostheses, using face bows, dental articulators, recording devices, and other materials. Collaborate with general dentists, specialists, and other health professionals to develop solutions to dental and oral health concerns. Repair, reline, and/or rebase dentures. Restore function and aesthetics to traumatic injury victims or to individuals with diseases or birth defects. Use bonding technology on the surface of the teeth to change tooth shape or to close gaps. Treat facial pain and jaw joint problems. Place veneers onto teeth to conceal defects. Bleach discolored teeth to brighten and whiten them.

**Education/Training Required:** First professional degree. **Education and Training Programs:** Prosthodontics Specialty; Prosthodontics/Prosthodontology (Cert., MS, PhD). **Knowledge/Courses**—Medicine and Dentistry, Biology, Chemistry, Psychology, Engineering and Technology, Sales and Marketing.

**Personality Type:** Investigative-Realistic. **Career Cluster:** 08 Health Science. **Career Pathway:** 8.1 Therapeutic Services. **Other Jobs in This Pathway:** Clinical Psychologists; Counseling Psychologists; Dental Assistants; Dental Hygienists; Dentists, All Other Specialists; Dentists, General; Home Health Aides; Licensed Practical and Licensed Vocational Nurses; Low Vision Therapists, Orientation and Mobility Specialists, and Vision Rehabilitation Therapists; Massage Therapists; Medical and Clinical Laboratory Technicians; Medical and Health Services Managers; Medical Scientists, Except Epidemiologists; Medical Secretaries; Occupational Therapists; Pharmacists; Oral and Maxillofacial Surgeons; Orthodontists; Pharmacy Technicians; Radiologic Technologists; School Psychologists; Social and Human Service Assistants; Speech-Language Pathologists; Speech-Language Pathology Assistants; Substance Abuse and Behavioral Disorder Counselors; others.

**Skills**—Operations Analysis, Science, Technology Design, Social Perceptiveness, Service Orientation, Learning Strategies, Management of Personnel Resources, Instructing.

**Work Environment:** Indoors; more often sitting than standing; using hands; repetitive motions; noise; contaminants; cramped work space; exposed to radiation; exposed to disease or infections; hazardous conditions; hazardous equipment; minor burns, cuts, bites, or stings.

# Protective Service Workers, All Other

- ❋ Annual Earnings: $29,890
- ❋ Earnings Growth Potential: Medium (39.3%)
- ❋ Growth: 14.0%
- ❋ Annual Job Openings: 7,150
- ❋ Self-Employed: 0.2%

**Considerations for Job Outlook:** Faster-than-average employment growth is projected.

**This occupation includes all protective service workers not listed separately.** Because this is a highly diverse occupation, no data is available for some information topics.

**Education/Training Required:** Short-term on-the-job training. **Education and Training Program:** Protective Services Operations.

**Career Clusters:** 10 Human Services; 12 Law, Public Safety, Corrections, and Security. **Career Pathways:** 10.3 Family and Community Services; 12.1 Correction Services. **Other Jobs in These Pathways:** Chief Executives; Child, Family, and School Social Workers; Childcare Workers; City and Regional Planning Aides; Counselors, All Other; Eligibility Interviewers, Government Programs; Farm and Home Management Advisors; First-Line Supervisors of Correctional Officers; First-Line Supervisors of Police and Detectives; Legislators; Managers, All Other; Marriage and Family Therapists; Nannies; Personal Care Aides; Probation Officers and Correctional Treatment Specialists; Security Guards; Social and Community Service Managers; Social Science Research Assistants; Social Scientists and Related Workers, All Other; Social Workers, All Other; Sociologists; Supply Chain Managers.

## Job Specialization: Retail Loss Prevention Specialists

**Implement procedures and systems to prevent merchandise loss. Conduct audits and investigations of employee activity. May assist in developing policies, procedures, and systems for safeguarding assets.** Implement and monitor processes to reduce property and financial losses. Investigate known or suspected internal theft, external theft or vendor fraud. Collaborate with law enforcement agencies to report or investigate crimes. Conduct store audits to identify problem areas or procedural deficiencies. Direct work of contract security officers or other loss prevention agents.

Identify and report merchandise or stock shortages. Inspect buildings, equipment, or access points to determine security risks. Maintain documentation or reports on security-related incidents or investigations. Monitor compliance with standard operating procedures for loss prevention, physical security, or risk management. Perform covert surveillance of areas susceptible to loss, such loading docks, distribution centers, and warehouses. Prepare written reports on investigations. Recommend new or improved processes or equipment to reduce risk exposure. Train establishment personnel in loss prevention activities. Verify proper functioning of physical security systems, such as closed-circuit TVs, alarms, sensor tag systems, and locks. Testify in civil or criminal court proceedings. Apprehend shoplifters in accordance with guidelines. Conduct employee background investigations and review reports with operational or human resources managers. Coordinate with risk management, human resources, or other departments to assist in company programs, investigations, or training. Identify and report safety concerns to maintain a safe shopping and working environment. Recommend methods to reduce potential financial fraud losses. Respond to critical incidents, such as catastrophic events, violent weather, and civil disorders.

**Education/Training Required:** Associate degree. **Education and Training Program:** Security and Loss Prevention Services. **Knowledge/Courses**—No data available.

**Personality Type:** Enterprising-Conventional. **Career Cluster:** 12 Law, Public Safety, Corrections, and Security. **Career Pathway:** 12.3 Security and Protective Services. **Other Jobs in This Pathway:** Animal Control Workers; Crossing Guards; First-Line Supervisors of Protective Service Workers, All Other; Forest Firefighters; Gaming Surveillance Officers and Gaming Investigators; Lifeguards, Ski Patrol, and Other Recreational Protective Service Workers; Parking Enforcement Workers; Police, Fire, and Ambulance Dispatchers; Private Detectives and Investigators; Security Guards; Sheriffs and Deputy Sheriffs; Transit and Railroad Police.

**Skills**—No data available.

**Work Environment:** No data available.

# Psychologists, All Other

- ❀ Annual Earnings: $89,900
- ❀ Earnings Growth Potential: Very high (54.2%)
- ❀ Growth: 14.4%
- ❀ Annual Job Openings: 680
- ❀ Self-Employed: 32.8%

**Considerations for Job Outlook:** Employment growth is expected due to increased emphasis on mental health in a variety of specializations, including school counseling, depression, and substance abuse. Job seekers with a doctoral degree should have the best opportunities.

**This occupation includes all psychologists not listed separately.** Because this is a highly diverse occupation, no data is available for some information topics.

**Education/Training Required:** Master's degree. **Education and Training Program:** Psychology, Other.

**Career Clusters:** 08 Health Science; 10 Human Services; 15 Science, Technology, Engineering, and Mathematics. **Career Pathways:** 8.1 Therapeutic Services; 10.2 Counseling and Mental Health Services; 15.2 Science and Mathematics. **Other Jobs in These Pathways:** Architectural and Engineering Managers; Biofuels/Biodiesel Technology and Product Development Managers; Clergy; Clinical Psychologists; Counseling Psychologists; Dental Assistants; Dental Hygienists; Dentists, General; Healthcare Social Workers; Healthcare Support Workers, All Other; Home Health Aides; Licensed Practical and Licensed Vocational Nurses; Massage Therapists; Medical and Clinical Laboratory Technicians; Medical and Health Services Managers; Medical Secretaries; Mental Health and Substance Abuse Social Workers; Pharmacists; Pharmacy Technicians; Radiologic Technologists; Recreation Workers; School Psychologists; Social and Human Service Assistants; Speech-Language Pathologists; Speech-Language Pathology Assistants; others.

# Job Specialization: Neuropsychologists and Clinical Neuropsychologists

**Apply theories and principles of neuropsychology to diagnose and treat disorders of higher cerebral functioning.** Write or prepare detailed clinical neuropsychological reports using data from psychological or neuropsychological tests, self-report measures, rating scales, direct observations, or interviews. Provide psychotherapy, behavior therapy, or other counseling interventions to patients with neurological disorders. Provide education or counseling to individuals and families. Participate in educational programs, in-service training, or workshops to remain current in methods and techniques. Read current literature, talk with colleagues, and participate in professional organizations or conferences to keep abreast of developments in neuropsychology. Interview patients to obtain comprehensive medical histories. Identify and communicate risks associated with specific neurological surgical procedures such as epilepsy surgery. Educate and supervise practicum students, psychology interns, or hospital staff. Diagnose and treat conditions such as chemical dependency, alcohol dependency, Acquired Immune Deficiency Syndrome (AIDS) dementia, and environmental toxin exposure. Distinguish between psychogenic and neurogenic syndromes, two or more suspected etiologies of cerebral dysfunction, or between disorders involving complex seizures. Diagnose and treat neural and psychological conditions in medical and surgical populations such as patients with early dementing illness or chronic pain with a neurological basis. Design or implement rehabilitation plans for patients with cognitive dysfunction. Establish neurobehavioral baseline measures for monitoring progressive cerebral disease or recovery. Compare patients' progress before and after pharmacologic, surgical, or behavioral interventions. Diagnose and treat psychiatric populations for conditions such as somatoform disorder, dementias, and psychoses.

**Education/Training Required:** Doctoral degree. **Education and Training Program:** Physiological Psychology/Psychobiology. **Knowledge/Courses**—Therapy and Counseling, Psychology, Biology, Medicine and Dentistry, Sociology and Anthropology, Philosophy and Theology.

**Personality Type:** Investigative-Social-Artistic. **Career Cluster:** 15 Science, Technology, Engineering, and Mathematics. **Career Pathway:** 15.2 Science and Mathematics. **Other Jobs in This Pathway:** Architectural and Engineering Managers; Biochemists and Biophysicists; Biofuels/Biodiesel Technology and Product Development Managers; Bioinformatics Scientists; Biological Scientists, All Other; Biologists; Biostatisticians; Chemists; Clinical Data Managers; Clinical Research Coordinators; Community and Social Service Specialists, All Other; Dietitians and Nutritionists; Education, Training, and Library Workers, All Other; Geneticists; Geoscientists, Except Hydrologists and Geographers; Medical Scientists, Except Epidemiologists; Molecular and Cellular Biologists; Natural Sciences Managers; Operations Research Analysts; Physical Scientists, All Other; Social Scientists and Related Workers, All Other; Statisticians; Survey Researchers; Transportation Planners; Water Resource Specialists; others.

**Skills**—Science, Social Perceptiveness, Reading Comprehension, Active Learning, Writing, Learning Strategies, Systems Evaluation, Instructing.

**Work Environment:** Indoors; sitting; using hands; exposed to disease or infections.

# Psychology Teachers, Postsecondary

- ❋ Annual Earnings: $67,330
- ❋ Earnings Growth Potential: High (46.8%)
- ❋ Growth: 15.1%
- ❋ Annual Job Openings: 1,000
- ❋ Self-Employed: 0.2%

**Considerations for Job Outlook:** Enrollments in postsecondary institutions are expected to continue rising as more people attend college and as workers return to school to update their skills. Opportunities for part-time or temporary positions should be favorable, but significant competition exists for tenure-track positions.

**Teach courses in psychology, such as child, clinical, and developmental psychology and psychological counseling.** Prepare and deliver lectures to undergraduate and/or graduate students on topics such as abnormal psychology, cognitive processes, and work motivation. Evaluate and grade students' classwork, laboratory work, assignments, and papers. Initiate, facilitate, and moderate classroom discussions. Compile, administer, and grade examinations or assign this work to others. Keep abreast of developments in their field by reading current literature, talking with colleagues, and participating in professional conferences. Prepare course materials such as syllabi, homework assignments, and handouts. Plan, evaluate, and revise curricula, course content, and course materials and methods of instruction. Maintain student attendance records, grades, and other required records. Supervise undergraduate and/or graduate teaching, internship, and research work. Maintain regularly scheduled office hours to advise and assist students. Conduct research in a particular field of knowledge and publish findings in professional journals, books, and electronic media. Advise students on academic and vocational curricula and on career issues. Select and obtain materials and supplies such as textbooks. Collaborate with colleagues to address teaching and research issues. Serve on academic or administrative committees that deal with institutional policies, departmental matters, and academic issues. Compile bibliographies of specialized materials for outside reading assignments. Participate in student recruitment, registration, and placement activities. Supervise students' laboratory work. Perform administrative duties such as serving as department head. Act as advisers to student organizations. Write grant proposals to procure external research funding. Participate in campus and community events. Provide professional consulting services to government and industry.

**Education/Training Required:** Doctoral degree. **Education and Training Programs:** Humanities/Humanistic Studies; Marriage and Family Therapy/Counseling; Psychology Teacher Education; Psychology, General; Psychology, Other; Social Science Teacher Education. **Knowledge/Courses**—Therapy and Counseling, Psychology, Sociology and Anthropology, Philosophy and Theology, Education and Training, English Language.

**Personality Type:** Social-Investigative-Artistic. **Career Clusters:** 05 Education and Training; 08 Health Science; 10 Human Services; 12 Law, Public Safety, Corrections, and Security. **Career Pathways:** 5.3 Teaching/Training; 8.1 Therapeutic Services; 10.2 Counseling and Mental Health Services; 12.1 Correction Services. **Other Jobs in These Pathways:** Child, Family, and School Social Workers; Clergy; Coaches and Scouts; Dental Assistants; Elementary School Teachers, Except Special Education; Fitness Trainers and Aerobics Instructors; Healthcare Support Workers, All Other; Home Health Aides; Licensed Practical and Licensed Vocational Nurses; Medical and Health Services Managers; Medical Secretaries; Middle School Teachers, Except Special and Career/Technical Education; Pharmacists; Pharmacy Technicians; Preschool Teachers, Except Special Education; Radiologic Technologists; Recreation Workers; Secondary School Teachers, Except Special and Career/Technical Education; Security Guards; Self-Enrichment Education Teachers; Social and Human Service Assistants; Speech-Language Pathology Assistants; Teacher Assistants; Tutors; 37 other postsecondary teaching occupations; others.

**Skills**—Science, Learning Strategies, Instructing, Writing, Operations Analysis, Reading Comprehension, Active Learning, Speaking.

**Work Environment:** Indoors; sitting.

# Public Relations and Fundraising Managers

❋ Annual Earnings: $91,810
❋ Earnings Growth Potential: High (45.8%)
❋ Growth: 12.9%
❋ Annual Job Openings: 2,060
❋ Self-Employed: 0.0%

**Considerations for Job Outlook:** Job growth is expected to result from companies' need to distinguish their products and services in an increasingly competitive marketplace. Keen competition is expected.

**Plan and direct public relations programs designed to create and maintain a favorable public image for employer or client or, if engaged in fundraising, plan and direct activities to solicit and maintain funds for special projects and nonprofit organizations.** Identify main client groups and audiences and determine the best way to communicate publicity information to them. Write interesting and effective press releases, prepare information for media kits, and develop and maintain company Internet or intranet Web pages. Develop and maintain the company's corporate image and identity, which includes the use of logos and signage. Manage communications budgets. Manage special events such as sponsorship of races, parties introducing new products, or other activities the firm supports to gain public attention through the media without advertising directly. Draft speeches for company executives and arrange interviews and other forms of contact for them. Assign, supervise, and review the activities of public relations staff. Evaluate advertising and promotion programs for compatibility with public relations efforts. Establish and maintain effective working relationships with local and municipal government officials and media representatives. Confer with labor relations managers to develop internal communications that keep employees informed of company activities. Direct activities of external agencies, establishments, and departments that develop and implement communication strategies and information programs. Formulate policies and procedures related to public information programs, working with public relations executives. Respond to requests for information about employers' activities or status. Establish goals for soliciting funds, develop policies for collection and safeguarding of contributions, and coordinate disbursement of funds. Facilitate consumer relations or the relationship between parts of the company such as the managers and employees or different branch offices. Maintain company archives. Manage in-house communication courses. Produce films and other video products, regulate their distribution, and operate film library. Observe and report on social, economic, and political trends that might affect employers.

**Education/Training Required:** Work experience plus degree. **Education and Training Program:** Public Relations/Image Management. **Knowledge/Courses**—Sales and Marketing, Communications and Media, Customer and Personal Service, Personnel and Human Resources, English Language, Administration and Management.

**Personality Type:** Enterprising-Artistic. **Career Cluster:** 04 Business, Management, and Administration. **Career Pathway:** 4.1 Management. **Other Jobs in This Pathway:** Brownfield Redevelopment Specialists and Site Managers; Business Continuity Planners; Business Operations Specialists, All Other; Chief Executives; Chief Sustainability Officers; Compliance Managers; Computer and Information Systems Managers; Construction Managers; Customs Brokers; Energy Auditors; First-Line Supervisors of Office and Administrative Support Workers; General and Operations Managers; Investment Fund Managers; Loss Prevention Managers; Management Analysts; Managers, All Other; Public Relations Specialists; Regulatory Affairs Managers; Sales Managers; Security Management Specialists; Security Managers; Supply Chain Managers; Sustainability Specialists; Wind Energy Operations Managers; Wind Energy Project Managers; others.

**Skills**—Management of Financial Resources, Persuasion, Management of Material Resources, Negotiation, Management of Personnel Resources, Systems Evaluation, Systems Analysis, Coordination.

**Work Environment:** Indoors; sitting.

# Public Relations Specialists

- ❈ Annual Earnings: $52,090
- ❈ Earnings Growth Potential: High (41.3%)
- ❈ Growth: 24.0%
- ❈ Annual Job Openings: 13,130
- ❈ Self-Employed: 4.5%

**Considerations for Job Outlook:** As the business environment becomes increasingly globalized, the need for good public relations and communications is growing rapidly. Opportunities should be best for workers with knowledge of more than one language.

**Engage in promoting or creating goodwill for individuals, groups, or organizations by writing or selecting favorable publicity material and releasing it through various communications media. May prepare and arrange displays and make speeches.** Prepare or edit organizational publications for internal and external audiences, including employee newsletters and stockholders' reports. Respond to requests for information from the media or designate another appropriate spokesperson or information source. Establish and maintain cooperative relationships with representatives of community, consumer, employee, and public interest groups. Plan and direct development and communication of informational programs to maintain favorable public and stockholder perceptions of an organization's accomplishments and agenda. Confer with production and support personnel to produce or coordinate production of advertisements and promotions. Arrange public appearances, lectures, contests, or exhibits for clients to increase product and service awareness and to promote goodwill. Study the objectives, promotional policies, and needs of organizations to develop public relations strategies that will influence public opinion or promote ideas, products, and services. Consult with advertising agencies or staff to arrange promotional campaigns in all types of media for products, organizations, or individuals. Confer with other managers to identify trends and key group interests and concerns or to provide advice on business decisions. Coach client representatives in effective communication with the public and with employees. Prepare and deliver speeches to further public relations objectives. Purchase advertising space and time as required to promote client's product or agenda. Plan and conduct market and public opinion research to test products or determine potential for product success, communicating results to client or management.

**Education/Training Required:** Bachelor's degree. **Education and Training Programs:** Family and Consumer Sciences/Human Sciences Communication; Health Communication; Political Communication; Public Relations/Image Management; Speech Communication and Rhetoric. **Knowledge/Courses**—Communications and Media, Sales and Marketing, English Language, Geography, Computers and Electronics, Customer and Personal Service.

**Personality Type:** Enterprising-Artistic-Social. **Career Clusters:** 03 Arts, Audio/Video Technology, and Communications; 04 Business, Management, and Administration; 08 Health Science; 10 Human Services. **Career Pathways:** 3.5 Journalism and Broadcasting; 4.1 Management; 8.3 Health Informatics; 10.5 Consumer Services Career. **Other Jobs in These Pathways:** Brownfield Redevelopment Specialists and Site Managers; Business Continuity Planners; Business Operations Specialists, All Other; Compliance Managers; Construction Managers; Customs Brokers; Energy Auditors; Executive Secretaries and Executive Administrative Assistants; First-Line Supervisors of Office and Administrative Support Workers; First-Line Supervisors of Retail Sales Workers; General and Operations Managers; Investment Fund Managers; Loss Prevention Managers; Management Analysts; Managers, All Other; Medical Assistants; Medical Secretaries; Receptionists and Information Clerks; Regulatory Affairs Managers; Security Management Specialists; Security Managers; Supply Chain Managers; Sustainability Specialists; Wind Energy Operations Managers; Wind Energy Project Managers; others.

**Skills**—Operations Analysis, Social Perceptiveness, Negotiation, Writing, Systems Evaluation, Speaking, Persuasion, Time Management.

**Work Environment:** Indoors; sitting.

# Purchasing Agents, Except Wholesale, Retail, and Farm Products

* Annual Earnings: $56,580
* Earnings Growth Potential: Medium (38.0%)
* Growth: 13.9%
* Annual Job Openings: 11,860
* Self-Employed: 1.4%

**Considerations for Job Outlook:** Almost all of the growth is expected to be for purchasing agents, except wholesale, retail, and farm products, as more companies demand a greater number of goods and services.

**Purchase machinery, equipment, tools, parts, supplies, or services necessary for the operation of an establishment. Purchase raw or semi-finished materials for manufacturing.** Purchase the highest-quality merchandise at the lowest possible price and in correct amounts. Prepare purchase orders, solicit bid proposals, and review requisitions for goods and services. Research and evaluate suppliers based on price, quality, selection, service, support, availability, reliability, production and distribution capabilities, and the supplier's reputation and history. Analyze price proposals, financial reports, and other data and information to determine reasonable prices. Monitor and follow applicable laws and regulations. Negotiate, or renegotiate, and administer contracts with suppliers, vendors, and other representatives. Monitor shipments to ensure that goods come in on time and trace shipments and follow up on undelivered goods in the event of problems. Confer with staff, users, and vendors to discuss defective or unacceptable goods or services and determine corrective action. Evaluate and monitor contract performance to ensure compliance with contractual obligations and to determine need for changes. Maintain and review computerized or manual records of items purchased, costs, delivery, product performance, and inventories. Review catalogs, industry periodicals, directories, trade journals, and Internet sites and consult with other department personnel to locate necessary goods and services. Study sales records and inventory levels of current stock to develop strategic purchasing programs that facilitate employee access to supplies. Interview vendors and visit suppliers' plants and distribution centers to examine and learn about products, services, and prices. Arrange the payment of duty and freight charges. Hire, train, and/or supervise purchasing clerks, buyers, and expediters. Write and review product specifications, maintaining a working technical knowledge of the goods or services to be purchased. Monitor changes affecting supply and demand, tracking market conditions, price trends, or futures markets.

**Education/Training Required:** Long-term on-the-job training. **Education and Training Programs:** Insurance; Merchandising and Buying Operations; Sales, Distribution, and Marketing Operations, General. **Knowledge/Courses**—Clerical, Economics and Accounting, Production and Processing, Administration and Management, Computers and Electronics, Communications and Media.

**Personality Type:** Conventional-Enterprising. **Career Cluster:** 14 Marketing, Sales, and Service. **Career Pathway:** 14.3 Buying and Merchandising. **Other Jobs in This Pathway:** Retail Salespersons; Sales Representatives, Wholesale and Manufacturing, Except Technical and Scientific Products; Telemarketers; Wholesale and Retail Buyers, Except Farm Products.

**Skills**—Management of Financial Resources, Negotiation, Monitoring, Persuasion, Judgment and Decision Making, Speaking, Writing, Systems Evaluation.

**Work Environment:** Indoors; sitting; using hands; repetitive motions.

# Purchasing Managers

- ❋ Annual Earnings: $95,070
- ❋ Earnings Growth Potential: High (42.1%)
- ❋ Growth: 1.5%
- ❋ Annual Job Openings: 2,110
- ❋ Self-Employed: 3.6%

**Considerations for Job Outlook:** Almost all of the growth is expected to be for purchasing agents, except wholesale, retail, and farm products, as more companies demand a greater number of goods and services.

**Plan, direct, or coordinate the activities of buyers, purchasing officers, and related workers involved in purchasing materials, products, and services.** Maintain records of goods ordered and received. Locate vendors of materials, equipment, or supplies and interview them to determine product availability and terms of sales. Prepare and process requisitions and purchase orders for supplies and equipment. Control purchasing department budgets. Interview and hire staff and oversee staff training. Review purchase order claims and contracts for conformance to company policy. Analyze market and delivery systems to assess present and future material availability. Develop and implement purchasing and contract management instructions, policies, and procedures. Participate in the development of specifications for equipment, products, or substitute materials. Resolve vendor or contractor grievances and claims against suppliers. Represent companies in negotiating contracts and formulating policies with suppliers. Review, evaluate, and approve specifications for issuing and awarding bids. Direct and coordinate activities of personnel engaged in buying, selling, and distributing materials, equipment, machinery, and supplies. Prepare bid awards requiring board approval. Prepare reports regarding market conditions and merchandise costs. Administer online purchasing systems. Arrange for disposal of surplus materials.

**Education/Training Required:** Work experience plus degree. **Education and Training Program:** Purchasing, Procurement/Acquisitions and Contracts Management. **Knowledge/Courses**—Production and Processing, Economics and Accounting, Transportation, Administration and Management, Personnel and Human Resources, Sales and Marketing.

**Personality Type:** Enterprising-Conventional. **Career Cluster:** 04 Business, Management, and Administration. **Career Pathway:** 4.1 Management. **Other Jobs in This Pathway:** Brownfield Redevelopment Specialists and Site Managers; Business Continuity Planners; Business Operations Specialists, All Other; Chief Executives; Chief Sustainability Officers; Compliance Managers; Computer and Information Systems Managers; Construction Managers; Customs Brokers; Energy Auditors; First-Line Supervisors of Office and Administrative Support Workers; General and Operations Managers; Investment Fund Managers; Loss Prevention Managers; Management Analysts; Managers, All Other; Public Relations Specialists; Regulatory Affairs Managers; Sales Managers; Security Management Specialists; Security Managers; Supply Chain Managers; Sustainability Specialists; Wind Energy Operations Managers; Wind Energy Project Managers; others.

**Skills**—Management of Financial Resources, Management of Material Resources, Negotiation, Management of Personnel Resources, Persuasion, Systems Evaluation, Systems Analysis, Coordination.

**Work Environment:** Indoors; sitting.

# Radiation Therapists

- ❋ Annual Earnings: $74,980
- ❋ Earnings Growth Potential: Low (32.0%)
- ❋ Growth: 27.1%
- ❋ Annual Job Openings: 690
- ❋ Self-Employed: 0.0%

**Considerations for Job Outlook:** The increasing number of elderly people, who are more likely than younger people to need radiation treatment, is expected to lead to employment growth for these workers. Prospects are expected to be good; job seekers with a bachelor's degree should have the best opportunities.

**Provide radiation therapy to patients as prescribed by radiologists according to established practices and standards. Duties may include reviewing prescriptions and diagnoses; acting as liaisons with physicians and supportive care personnel; preparing equipment such as immobilization, treatment, and protection devices; and maintaining records, reports, and files. May assist in dosimetry procedures and tumor localization.** Position patients for treatment with accuracy according to prescription. Administer prescribed doses of radiation to specific body parts, using radiation therapy equipment according to established practices and standards. Check radiation therapy equipment to ensure proper operation. Review prescriptions, diagnoses, patient charts, and identification. Follow principles of radiation protection for patients, radiation

R

therapists, and others. Maintain records, reports, and files as required, including such information as radiation dosages, equipment settings, and patients' reactions. Conduct most treatment sessions independently, in accordance with long-term treatment plans and under general direction of patients' physicians. Enter data into computers and set controls to operate and adjust equipment and regulate dosages. Observe and reassure patients during treatments and report unusual reactions to physicians or turn equipment off if unexpected adverse reactions occur. Calculate actual treatment dosages delivered during each session. Check for side effects such as skin irritation, nausea, and hair loss to assess patients' reaction to treatment. Prepare and construct equipment such as immobilization, treatment, and protection devices. Educate, prepare, and reassure patients and their families by answering questions, providing physical assistance, and reinforcing physicians' advice regarding treatment reactions and post-treatment care. Provide assistance to other health care personnel during dosimetry procedures and tumor localization. Help physicians, radiation oncologists, and clinical physicists to prepare physical and technical aspects of radiation treatment plans, using information about patient conditions and anatomies. Photograph treated areas of patients and process film. Act as liaisons with medical physicists and supportive care personnel. Train and supervise student or subordinate radiotherapy technologists. Implement appropriate follow-up care plans.

**Education/Training Required:** Associate degree. **Education and Training Program:** Medical Radiologic Technology/Science—Radiation Therapist. **Knowledge/Courses**—Medicine and Dentistry, Biology, Physics, Psychology, Philosophy and Theology, Therapy and Counseling.

**Personality Type:** Social-Realistic-Conventional. **Career Cluster:** 08 Health Science. **Career Pathway:** 8.2 Diagnostics Services. **Other Jobs in This Pathway:** Ambulance Drivers and Attendants, Except Emergency Medical Technicians; Anesthesiologist Assistants; Cardiovascular Technologists and Technicians; Cytogenetic Technologists; Cytotechnologists; Diagnostic Medical Sonographers; Emergency Medical Technicians and Paramedics; Endoscopy Technicians; Health Diagnosing and Treating Practitioners, All Other; Health Technologists and Technicians, All Other; Healthcare Practitioners and Technical Workers, All Other; Histotechnologists and Histologic Technicians; Medical and Clinical Laboratory Technicians; Medical and Clinical Laboratory Technologists; Medical and Health Services Managers; Medical Assistants; Medical Equipment Preparers; Neurodiagnostic Technologists; Ophthalmic Laboratory Technicians; Physical Scientists, All Other;

Physician Assistants; Radiologic Technicians; Radiologic Technologists; Surgical Technologists; Veterinary Assistants and Laboratory Animal Caretakers; others.

**Skills**—Operation and Control, Equipment Selection, Equipment Maintenance, Science, Quality Control Analysis, Operation Monitoring, Troubleshooting, Repairing.

**Work Environment:** Indoors; standing; walking and running; using hands; bending or twisting the body; repetitive motions; contaminants; exposed to radiation; exposed to disease or infections.

# Radiologic Technologists

* Annual Earnings: $54,340
* Earnings Growth Potential: Low (32.8%)
* Growth: 17.2%
* Annual Job Openings: 6,800
* Self-Employed: 0.8%

**Considerations for Job Outlook:** As the population grows and ages, demand for diagnostic imaging is expected to increase. Job seekers who have knowledge of multiple technologies should have the best prospects.

**Take X-rays and CAT scans or administer nonradioactive materials into patient's bloodstream for diagnostic purposes. Includes technologists who specialize in other modalities, such as computed tomography and magnetic resonance. Includes workers whose primary duties are to demonstrate portions of the human body on X-ray film or fluoroscopic screen.** Review and evaluate developed X-rays, video tape, or computer generated information to determine if images are satisfactory for diagnostic purposes. Use radiation safety measures and protection devices to comply with government regulations and to ensure safety of patients and staff. Explain procedures and observe patients to ensure safety and comfort during scan. Operate or oversee operation of radiologic and magnetic imaging equipment to produce images of the body for diagnostic purposes. Position and immobilize patient on examining table. Position imaging equipment and adjust controls to set exposure time and distance, according to specification of examination. Key commands and data into computer to document and specify scan sequences, adjust transmitters and receivers, or photograph certain images. Monitor video display of area being scanned and adjust density or contrast to improve picture quality. Monitor patients' conditions and reactions, reporting abnormal signs to physician. Set up examination rooms, ensuring that all necessary equipment is ready. Prepare and administer oral or injected contrast media to patients. Take thorough and accurate patient medical histories. Remove and process film. Record, process and maintain patient data and treatment records, and prepare reports. Coordinate work with clerical personnel or other technologists. Demonstrate new equipment, procedures, and techniques to staff, and provide technical assistance. Provide assistance in dressing or changing seriously ill, injured, or disabled patients. Move ultrasound scanner over patient's body and watch pattern produced on video screen. Measure thickness of section to be radiographed, using instruments similar to measuring tapes. Operate fluoroscope to aid physician to view and guide wire or catheter through blood vessels to area of interest. Assign duties to radiologic staff to maintain patient flows and achieve production goals.

**Education/Training Required:** Associate degree. **Education and Training Programs:** Allied Health Diagnostic, Intervention, and Treatment Professions, Other; Medical Radiologic Technology/Science—Radiation Therapist; Radiologic Technology/Science—Radiographer. **Knowledge/Courses**—Medicine and Dentistry, Physics, Customer and Personal Service, Biology, Psychology, Chemistry.

**Personality Type:** Realistic-Social. **Career Cluster:** 08 Health Science. **Career Pathways:** 8.1 Therapeutic Services; 8.2 Diagnostics Services. **Other Jobs in These Pathways:** Clinical Psychologists; Counseling Psychologists; Cytogenetic Technologists; Cytotechnologists; Dental Assistants; Dental Hygienists; Dentists, General; Emergency Medical Technicians and Paramedics; Endoscopy Technicians; Healthcare Support Workers, All Other; Histotechnologists and Histologic Technicians; Home Health Aides; Licensed Practical and Licensed Vocational Nurses; Massage Therapists; Medical and Clinical Laboratory Technicians; Medical and Clinical Laboratory Technologists; Medical and Health Services Managers; Medical Assistants; Medical Secretaries; Pharmacists; Pharmacy Technicians; School Psychologists; Social and Human Service Assistants; Speech-Language Pathologists; Speech-Language Pathology Assistants; others.

**Skills**—Science, Operation and Control, Service Orientation, Operation Monitoring, Quality Control Analysis, Programming, Instructing, Social Perceptiveness.

**Work Environment:** Indoors; standing; walking and running; using hands; bending or twisting the body; repetitive motions; contaminants; exposed to radiation; exposed to disease or infections.

# Railroad Brake, Signal, and Switch Operators

* Annual Earnings: $47,670
* Earnings Growth Potential: Medium (37.2%)
* Growth: 9.4%
* Annual Job Openings: 1,070
* Self-Employed: 0.0%

**Considerations for Job Outlook:** Freight transportation and the occupations associated with it are expected to expand as global trade increases and as more goods are shipped by rail. Opportunities should be good for qualified job seekers because many workers, particularly at freight railroads, are expected to retire.

**Operate railroad track switches. Couple or uncouple rolling stock to make up or break up trains. Signal engineers by hand or by flagging. May inspect couplings, air hoses, journal boxes, and hand brakes.** Answer questions from passengers concerning train rules, stations, and timetable information. Monitor oil, air, and steam pressure gauges and make sure water levels are adequate. Open and close chute gates to load and unload cars. Repair and install rails and ties. Provide passengers with assistance entering and exiting trains. Place passengers' baggage in racks above seats on trains. Collect tickets, fares, and passes from passengers. Attach cables to cars being hoisted by cables or chains in mines, quarries, or industrial plants. Set flares, flags, lanterns, or torpedoes in front and at rear of trains during emergency stops to warn oncoming trains. Refuel and lubricate engines. Record numbers of cars available, numbers of cars sent to repair stations, and types of service needed. Operate and drive locomotives, diesel switch engines, dinkey engines, flatcars, and railcars in train yards and at industrial sites. Adjust controls to regulate air conditioning, heating, and lighting on trains for comfort of passengers. Watch for and relay traffic signals to start and stop cars during shunting. Observe signals from other crewmembers so that work activities can be coordinated. Pull or push track switches to reroute cars. Inspect tracks, cars, and engines for defects and to determine service needs, sending engines and cars for repairs as necessary. Signal locomotive engineers to start or stop trains when coupling or uncoupling cars, using hand signals, lanterns, or radio communication. Open and close ventilation doors. Ride atop cars that have been shunted and turn handwheels to control speeds or stop cars at specified positions. Receive oral or written instructions from yardmasters or yard conductors

R

indicating track assignments and cars to be switched. Climb ladders to tops of cars to set brakes. Connect air hoses to cars, using wrenches. Inspect couplings, air hoses, journal boxes, and handbrakes to ensure that they are securely fastened and functioning properly.

**Education/Training Required:** Moderate-term on-the-job training. **Education and Training Program:** Truck and Bus Driver Training/Commercial Vehicle Operator and Instructor Training. **Knowledge/Courses**—Transportation, Public Safety and Security, Mechanical, Law and Government.

**Personality Type:** Realistic-Conventional. **Career Cluster:** 16 Transportation, Distribution, and Logistics. **Career Pathway:** 16.1 Transportation Operations. **Other Jobs in This Pathway:** Airline Pilots, Copilots, and Flight Engineers; Automotive and Watercraft Service Attendants; Automotive Master Mechanics; Bus Drivers, School or Special Client; Bus Drivers, Transit and Intercity; Commercial Pilots; Crane and Tower Operators; First-Line Supervisors of Helpers, Laborers, and Material Movers, Hand; First-Line Supervisors of Transportation and Material-Moving Machine and Vehicle Operators; Freight and Cargo Inspectors; Heavy and Tractor-Trailer Truck Drivers; Laborers and Freight, Stock, and Material Movers, Hand; Light Truck or Delivery Services Drivers; Mates—Ship, Boat, and Barge; Motor Vehicle Operators, All Other; Operating Engineers and Other Construction Equipment Operators; Parking Lot Attendants; Pilots, Ship; Railroad Conductors and Yardmasters; Sailors and Marine Oilers; Ship and Boat Captains; Storage and Distribution Managers; Taxi Drivers and Chauffeurs; Transportation Managers; Transportation Workers, All Other; others.

**Skills**—Operation and Control, Troubleshooting, Operation Monitoring, Repairing, Quality Control Analysis, Equipment Maintenance, Equipment Selection.

**Work Environment:** Outdoors; standing; walking and running; using hands; bending or twisting the body; repetitive motions; noise; very hot or cold; bright or inadequate lighting; contaminants; cramped work space; whole-body vibration; hazardous conditions; hazardous equipment; minor burns, cuts, bites, or stings.

# Railroad Conductors and Yardmasters

- ❀ Annual Earnings: $49,770
- ❀ Earnings Growth Potential: Low (32.7%)
- ❀ Growth: 6.9%
- ❀ Annual Job Openings: 1,700
- ❀ Self-Employed: 0.0%

**Considerations for Job Outlook:** Freight transportation and the occupations associated with it are expected to expand as global trade increases and as more goods are shipped by rail. Opportunities should be good for qualified job seekers because many workers, particularly at freight railroads, are expected to retire.

**Conductors coordinate activities of train crew on passenger or freight train. Coordinate activities of switch-engine crew within yard of railroad, industrial plant, or similar location. Yardmasters coordinate activities of workers engaged in railroad traffic operations, such as the makeup or breakup of trains and yard switching, and review train schedules and switching orders.** Signal engineers to begin train runs, stop trains, or change speed, using telecommunications equipment or hand signals. Receive information regarding train or rail problems from dispatchers or from electronic monitoring devices. Direct and instruct workers engaged in yard activities, such as switching tracks, coupling and uncoupling cars, and routing inbound and outbound traffic. Keep records of the contents and destination of each train car and make sure that cars are added or removed at proper points on routes. Operate controls to activate track switches and traffic signals. Instruct workers to set warning signals in front and at rear of trains during emergency stops. Direct engineers to move cars to fit planned train configurations, combining or separating cars to make up or break up trains. Receive instructions from dispatchers regarding trains' routes, timetables, and cargoes. Review schedules, switching orders, way bills, and shipping records to obtain cargo loading and unloading information and to plan work. Confer with engineers regarding train routes, timetables, and cargoes and to discuss alternative routes when there are rail defects or obstructions. Arrange for the removal of defective cars from trains at stations or stops. Inspect each car periodically during runs. Observe yard traffic to determine tracks available to accommodate inbound and outbound traffic. Document and prepare reports of accidents, unscheduled stops, or delays. Confirm routes and destination information for freight cars. Supervise and coordinate crew activities to transport freight and passengers and to provide boarding, porter, maid, and meal services to passengers. Supervise workers in the inspection and maintenance of mechanical equipment to ensure efficient and safe train operation. Record departure and arrival times, messages, tickets and revenue collected, and passenger accommodations and destinations.

**Education/Training Required:** Moderate-term on-the-job training. **Education and Training Program:** Truck and Bus Driver Training/Commercial Vehicle Operator and Instructor Training. **Knowledge/Courses**—Transportation, Public Safety and Security, Mechanical.

**Personality Type:** Enterprising-Realistic-Conventional. **Career Cluster:** 16 Transportation, Distribution, and Logistics. **Career Pathway:** 16.1 Transportation Operations. **Other Jobs in This Pathway:** Airline Pilots, Copilots, and Flight Engineers; Automotive and Watercraft Service Attendants; Automotive Master Mechanics; Bus Drivers, School or Special Client; Bus Drivers, Transit and Intercity; Commercial Pilots; Crane and Tower Operators; First-Line Supervisors of Helpers, Laborers, and Material Movers, Hand; First-Line Supervisors of Transportation and Material-Moving Machine and Vehicle Operators; Freight and Cargo Inspectors; Heavy and Tractor-Trailer Truck Drivers; Laborers and Freight, Stock, and Material Movers, Hand; Light Truck or Delivery Services Drivers; Mates—Ship, Boat, and Barge; Motor Vehicle Operators, All Other; Operating Engineers and Other Construction Equipment Operators; Parking Lot Attendants; Pilots, Ship; Sailors and Marine Oilers; Ship and Boat Captains; Storage and Distribution Managers; Taxi Drivers and Chauffeurs; Transportation Inspectors; Transportation Managers; Transportation Workers, All Other; others.

**Skills**—Operation and Control, Management of Personnel Resources, Operation Monitoring, Quality Control Analysis, Coordination, Complex Problem Solving, Monitoring, Time Management.

**Work Environment:** Outdoors; sitting; using hands; noise; very hot or cold; bright or inadequate lighting; contaminants; hazardous conditions; hazardous equipment.

# Rail-Track Laying and Maintenance Equipment Operators

❋ Annual Earnings: $45,970
❋ Earnings Growth Potential: Low (34.4%)
❋ Growth: 14.8%
❋ Annual Job Openings: 650
❋ Self-Employed: 0.0%

**Considerations for Job Outlook:** Faster-than-average employment growth is projected.

**Lay, repair, and maintain track for standard or narrow-gauge railroad equipment used in regular railroad service or in plant yards, quarries, sand and gravel pits, and mines. Includes ballast-cleaning-machine operators and roadbed-tamping-machine operators.** Drive vehicles that automatically move and lay tracks or rails over sections of track to be constructed, repaired, or maintained. Operate track-wrench machines to tighten or loosen bolts at joints that hold ends of rails together. Clean, grade, and level ballast on railroad tracks. Dress and reshape worn or damaged railroad switch points and frogs, using portable power grinders. Push controls to close grasping devices on track or rail sections so that they can be raised or moved. Drive graders, tamping machines, brooms, and ballast cleaning/spreading machines to redistribute gravel and ballast between rails. Adjust controls of machines that spread, shape, raise, level, and align track according to specifications. Engage mechanisms that lay tracks or rails to specified gauges. Grind ends of new or worn rails to attain smooth joints, using portable grinders. Observe leveling indicator arms to verify levelness and alignment of tracks. Operate single- or multiple-head spike-driving machines to drive spikes into ties and secure rails. Operate single- or multiple-head spike pullers to pull old spikes from ties. Operate tie-adzing machines to cut ties and permit insertion of fishplates that hold rails. Drill holes through rails, tie plates, and fishplates for insertion of bolts and spikes, using power drills. Repair and adjust track switches, using wrenches and replacement parts. Spray ties, fishplates, and joints with oil to protect them from weathering. String and attach wire-guidelines machine to rails so that tracks or rails can be aligned or leveled. Cut rails to specified lengths, using rail saws. Patrol assigned track sections so that damaged or broken track can be located and reported. Paint railroad signs, such as speed limits and gate-crossing warnings. Lubricate machines, change oil, and fill hydraulic reservoirs to specified levels. Clean tracks and clear ice and snow from tracks and switch boxes. Clean and make minor repairs to machines and equipment.

R

**Education/Training Required:** Moderate-term on-the-job training. **Education and Training Program:** Construction/Heavy Equipment/Earthmoving Equipment Operation. **Knowledge/Courses**—Building and Construction, Mechanical, Transportation, Public Safety and Security.

**Personality Type:** Realistic. **Career Cluster:** 02 Architecture and Construction. **Career Pathway:** 2.2 Construction. **Other Jobs in This Pathway:** Brickmasons and Blockmasons; Cement Masons and Concrete Finishers; Construction and Building Inspectors; Construction Carpenters; Construction Laborers; Construction Managers; Cost Estimators; Drywall and Ceiling Tile Installers; Electrical Power-Line Installers and Repairers; Electricians; Engineering Technicians, Except Drafters, All Other; First-Line Supervisors of Construction Trades and Extraction Workers; Heating and Air Conditioning Mechanics and Installers; Helpers—Carpenters; Helpers—Electricians; Helpers—Pipelayers, Plumbers, Pipefitters, and Steamfitters; Highway Maintenance Workers; Operating Engineers and Other Construction Equipment Operators; Painters, Construction and Maintenance; Pipe Fitters and Steamfitters; Plumbers; Refrigeration Mechanics and Installers; Roofers; Rough Carpenters; Solar Energy Installation Managers; others.

**Skills**—Repairing, Equipment Maintenance, Troubleshooting, Operation and Control, Equipment Selection, Operation Monitoring, Quality Control Analysis, Installation.

**Work Environment:** Outdoors; standing; walking and running; using hands; bending or twisting the body; repetitive motions; noise; very hot or cold; bright or inadequate lighting; contaminants; whole-body vibration; hazardous conditions; hazardous equipment; minor burns, cuts, bites, or stings.

# Real Estate Brokers

- ✸ Annual Earnings: $54,910
- ✸ Earnings Growth Potential: Very high (53.5%)
- ✸ Growth: 8.6%
- ✸ Annual Job Openings: 3,080
- ✸ Self-Employed: 58.3%

**Considerations for Job Outlook:** A growing population is expected to require the services of real estate brokers, creating more jobs for these workers. People who are well-trained, ambitious, and socially and professionally active in their communities should have the best prospects.

**Operate real estate office or work for commercial real estate firm, overseeing real estate transactions. Other duties usually include selling real estate or renting properties and arranging loans.** Sell, for a fee, real estate owned by others. Obtain agreements from property owners to place properties for sale with real estate firms. Monitor fulfillment of purchase contract terms to ensure that they are handled in a timely manner. Compare a property with similar properties that have recently sold to determine its competitive market price. Act as an intermediary in negotiations between buyers and sellers over property prices and settlement details and during the closing of sales. Generate lists of properties for sale, their locations and descriptions, and available financing options, using computers. Maintain knowledge of real estate law; local economies; fair housing laws; and types of available mortgages, financing options, and government programs. Check work completed by loan officers, attorneys, and other professionals to ensure that it is performed properly. Arrange for financing of property purchases. Appraise property values, assessing income potential when relevant. Maintain awareness of current income tax regulations, local zoning, building and tax laws, and growth possibilities of the area where a property is located. Manage and operate real estate offices, handling associated business details. Supervise agents who handle real estate transactions. Rent properties or manage rental properties. Arrange for title searches of properties being sold. Give buyers virtual tours of properties in which they are interested, using computers. Review property details to ensure that environmental regulations are met. Develop, sell, or lease property used for industry or manufacturing. Maintain working knowledge of various factors that determine a farm's capacity to produce, including agricultural variables and proximity to market centers and transportation facilities.

**Education/Training Required:** Work experience in a related occupation. **Education and Training Program:** Real Estate. **Knowledge/Courses**—Sales and Marketing, Law and Government, Building and Construction, Customer and Personal Service, Personnel and Human Resources, Economics and Accounting.

**Personality Type:** Enterprising-Conventional. **Career Cluster:** 14 Marketing, Sales, and Service. **Career Pathway:** 14.2 Professional Sales and Marketing. **Other Jobs in This Pathway:** Cashiers; Counter and Rental Clerks; Door-To-Door Sales Workers, News and Street Vendors, and Related Workers; Driver/Sales Workers; Energy Brokers; First-Line Supervisors of Non-Retail Sales Workers; First-Line Supervisors of Retail Sales Workers; Hotel, Motel, and Resort Desk Clerks; Marketing Managers; Marking Clerks; Online Merchants; Order Fillers, Wholesale and Retail Sales; Parts

Salespersons; Property, Real Estate, and Community Association Managers; Real Estate Sales Agents; Reservation and Transportation Ticket Agents and Travel Clerks; Retail Salespersons; Sales and Related Workers, All Other; Sales Representatives, Services, All Other; Sales Representatives, Wholesale and Manufacturing, Except Technical and Scientific Products; Sales Representatives, Wholesale and Manufacturing, Technical and Scientific Products; Solar Sales Representatives and Assessors; Stock Clerks—Stockroom, Warehouse, or Storage Yard; Stock Clerks, Sales Floor; Telemarketers; others.

**Skills**—Negotiation, Persuasion, Judgment and Decision Making, Active Learning, Speaking, Management of Financial Resources, Reading Comprehension, Service Orientation.

**Work Environment:** More often indoors than outdoors; sitting.

# Real Estate Sales Agents

- ❇ Annual Earnings: $40,030
- ❇ Earnings Growth Potential: High (48.9%)
- ❇ Growth: 16.2%
- ❇ Annual Job Openings: 12,830
- ❇ Self-Employed: 58.3%

**Considerations for Job Outlook:** A growing population is expected to require the services of real estate agents, creating more jobs for these workers. People who are well-trained, ambitious, and socially and professionally active in their communities should have the best prospects.

**Rent, buy, or sell property for clients. Perform duties such as studying property listings, interviewing prospective clients, accompanying clients to property site, discussing conditions of sale, and drawing up real estate contracts. Includes agents who represent buyer.** Present purchase offers to sellers for consideration. Confer with escrow companies, lenders, home inspectors, and pest control operators to ensure that terms and conditions of purchase agreements are met before closing dates. Interview clients to determine what kinds of properties they are seeking. Prepare documents such as representation contracts, purchase agreements, closing statements, deeds, and leases. Coordinate property closings, overseeing signing of documents and disbursement of funds. Act as an intermediary in negotiations between buyers and sellers, generally representing one or the other. Promote sales of properties through advertisements, open houses, and participation in multiple listing services. Compare a property with similar properties that have recently sold to determine its competitive market price. Coordinate appointments to show homes to prospective buyers. Generate lists of properties that are compatible with buyers' needs and financial resources. Display commercial, industrial, agricultural, and residential properties to clients and explain their features. Arrange for title searches to determine whether clients have clear property titles. Review plans for new construction with clients, enumerating and recommending available options and features. Answer clients' questions regarding construction work, financing, maintenance, repairs, and appraisals. Accompany buyers during visits to and inspections of property, advising them on the suitability and value of the homes they are visiting. Inspect condition of premises and arrange for necessary maintenance or notify owners of maintenance needs. Advise sellers on how to make homes more appealing to potential buyers. Arrange meetings between buyers and sellers when details of transactions need to be negotiated. Advise clients on market conditions, prices, mortgages, legal requirements, and related matters.

**Education/Training Required:** Postsecondary vocational training. **Education and Training Program:** Real Estate. **Knowledge/Courses**—Sales and Marketing, Customer and Personal Service, Law and Government, Building and Construction, Economics and Accounting, Computers and Electronics.

**Personality Type:** Enterprising-Conventional. **Career Cluster:** 14 Marketing, Sales, and Service. **Career Pathway:** 14.2 Professional Sales and Marketing. **Other Jobs in This Pathway:** Cashiers; Counter and Rental Clerks; Door-To-Door Sales Workers, News and Street Vendors, and Related Workers; Driver/Sales Workers; Energy Brokers; First-Line Supervisors of Non-Retail Sales Workers; First-Line Supervisors of Retail Sales Workers; Hotel, Motel, and Resort Desk Clerks; Marketing Managers; Marking Clerks; Online Merchants; Order Fillers, Wholesale and Retail Sales; Parts Salespersons; Property, Real Estate, and Community Association Managers; Reservation and Transportation Ticket Agents and Travel Clerks; Retail Salespersons; Sales and Related Workers, All Other; Sales Representatives, Services, All Other; Sales Representatives, Wholesale and Manufacturing, Except Technical and Scientific Products; Sales Representatives, Wholesale and Manufacturing, Technical and Scientific Products; Solar Sales Representatives and Assessors; Stock Clerks—Stockroom, Warehouse, or Storage Yard; Stock Clerks, Sales Floor; Telemarketers; Wholesale and Retail Buyers, Except Farm Products; others.

R

**Skills**—Negotiation, Persuasion, Service Orientation, Systems Evaluation, Judgment and Decision Making, Mathematics, Speaking, Coordination.

**Work Environment:** More often indoors than outdoors; sitting.

# Receptionists and Information Clerks

* Annual Earnings: $25,240
* Earnings Growth Potential: Low (30.4%)
* Growth: 15.2%
* Annual Job Openings: 48,020
* Self-Employed: 0.8%

**Considerations for Job Outlook:** Although technology makes these workers more productive, many new jobs are expected as clerical work is consolidated and involves more tasks. Employment growth is expected in offices of physicians and other health practitioners and in the legal services, personal care services, construction, and management and technical consulting industries. Plentiful opportunities are expected.

**Answer inquiries and obtain information for general public, customers, visitors, and other interested parties. Provide information regarding activities conducted at establishment and location of departments, offices, and employees within organization.** Operate telephone switchboard to answer, screen, and forward calls, providing information, taking messages, and scheduling appointments. Receive payment and record receipts for services. Perform administrative support tasks such as proofreading, transcribing handwritten information, and operating calculators or computers to work with pay records, invoices, balance sheets, and other documents. Greet persons entering establishment, determine nature and purpose of visit, and direct or escort them to specific destinations. Hear and resolve complaints from customers and public. File and maintain records. Transmit information or documents to customers, using computer, mail, or facsimile machine. Schedule appointments and maintain and update appointment calendars. Analyze data to determine answers to questions from customers or members of the public. Provide information about establishment such as location of departments or offices, employees within the organization, or services provided. Keep a current record of staff members' whereabouts and availability. Collect, sort, distribute, and prepare mail, messages, and courier deliveries. Calculate and quote rates for tours, stocks, insurance policies, or other products and services. Take orders for merchandise or materials and send them to the proper departments to be filled. Process and prepare memos, correspondence, travel vouchers, or other documents. Schedule space and equipment for special programs and prepare lists of participants. Enroll individuals to participate in programs and notify them of their acceptance. Conduct tours or deliver talks describing features of public facility such as a historic site or national park. Perform duties such as taking care of plants and straightening magazines to maintain lobby or reception area.

**Education/Training Required:** Short-term on-the-job training. **Education and Training Programs:** General Office Occupations and Clerical Services; Health Unit Coordinator/Ward Clerk Training; Medical Reception/Receptionist; Receptionist Training. **Knowledge/Courses**—Clerical, Customer and Personal Service, Computers and Electronics, Communications and Media.

**Personality Type:** Conventional-Enterprising-Social. **Career Clusters:** 04 Business, Management, and Administration; 08 Health Science. **Career Pathways:** 4.6 Administrative and Information Support; 8.3 Health Informatics. **Other Jobs in These Pathways:** Customer Service Representatives; Data Entry Keyers; Dispatchers, Except Police, Fire, and Ambulance; Engineers, All Other; Executive Secretaries and Executive Administrative Assistants; File Clerks; First-Line Supervisors of Office and Administrative Support Workers; Information and Record Clerks, All Other; Insurance Claims Clerks; Insurance Policy Processing Clerks; Interviewers, Except Eligibility and Loan; Medical and Health Services Managers; Medical Assistants; Medical Records and Health Information Technicians; Medical Secretaries; Office and Administrative Support Workers, All Other; Office Clerks, General; Order Clerks; Patient Representatives; Physical Therapists; Postal Service Mail Carriers; Postal Service Mail Sorters, Processors, and Processing Machine Operators; Public Relations Specialists; Secretaries and Administrative Assistants, Except Legal, Medical, and Executive; Shipping, Receiving, and Traffic Clerks; others.

**Skills**—Service Orientation, Speaking, Active Listening.

**Work Environment:** Indoors; sitting; using hands; repetitive motions.

# Recreation and Fitness Studies Teachers, Postsecondary

❀ Annual Earnings: $57,650
❀ Earnings Growth Potential: High (50.0%)
❀ Growth: 15.1%
❀ Annual Job Openings: 600
❀ Self-Employed: 0.2%

**Considerations for Job Outlook:** Enrollments in postsecondary institutions are expected to continue rising as more people attend college and as workers return to school to update their skills. Opportunities for part-time or temporary positions should be favorable, but significant competition exists for tenure-track positions.

**Teach courses pertaining to recreation, leisure, and fitness studies, including exercise physiology and facilities management.** Evaluate and grade students' classwork, assignments, and papers. Maintain student attendance records, grades, and other required records. Prepare and deliver lectures to undergraduate and graduate students on topics such as anatomy, therapeutic recreation, and conditioning theory. Prepare course materials such as syllabi, homework assignments, and handouts. Maintain regularly scheduled office hours to advise and assist students. Compile, administer, and grade examinations or assign this work to others. Plan, evaluate, and revise curricula, course content, and course materials and methods of instruction. Initiate, facilitate, and moderate classroom discussions. Keep abreast of developments in their field by reading current literature, talking with colleagues, and participating in professional conferences. Advise students on academic and vocational curricula and on career issues. Participate in student recruitment, registration, and placement activities. Collaborate with colleagues to address teaching and research issues. Select and obtain materials and supplies such as textbooks. Participate in campus and community events. Serve on academic or administrative committees that deal with institutional policies, departmental matters, and academic issues. Compile bibliographies of specialized materials for outside reading assignments. Supervise undergraduate or graduate teaching, internship, and research work. Perform administrative duties such as serving as department heads. Prepare students to act as sports coaches. Conduct research in a particular field of knowledge and publish findings in professional journals, books, or electronic media. Act as advisers to student organizations. Write grant proposals to procure external research funding. Provide professional consulting services to government or industry.

**Education/Training Required:** Doctoral degree. **Education and Training Programs:** Health and Physical Education, General; Parks, Recreation, and Leisure Studies; Sport and Fitness Administration/Management. **Knowledge/Courses**—Education and Training, Philosophy and Theology, Therapy and Counseling, Psychology, Medicine and Dentistry, Sociology and Anthropology.

**Personality Type:** Social. **Career Clusters:** 01 Agriculture, Food, and Natural Resources; 05 Education and Training. **Career Pathways:** 1.5 Natural Resources Systems; 5.1 Administration and Administrative Support; 5.3 Teaching/Training. **Other Jobs in These Pathways:** Adult Basic and Secondary Education and Literacy Teachers and Instructors; Career/Technical Education Teachers, Secondary School; Climate Change Analysts; Coaches and Scouts; Education Administrators, Elementary and Secondary School; Education Administrators, Postsecondary; Elementary School Teachers, Except Special Education; Environmental Restoration Planners; Environmental Scientists and Specialists, Including Health; Fitness Trainers and Aerobics Instructors; Industrial Ecologists; Industrial Truck and Tractor Operators; Instructional Coordinators; Instructional Designers and Technologists; Kindergarten Teachers, Except Special Education; Librarians; Middle School Teachers, Except Special and Career/Technical Education; Preschool Teachers, Except Special Education; Recreation Workers; Refuse and Recyclable Material Collectors; Secondary School Teachers, Except Special and Career/Technical Education; Self-Enrichment Education Teachers; Teacher Assistants; Tutors; 37 other postsecondary teaching occupations; others.

**Skills**—Learning Strategies, Operations Analysis, Active Learning, Instructing, Science, Speaking, Active Listening, Writing.

**Work Environment:** More often indoors than outdoors; standing.

# Recreation Workers

❀ Annual Earnings: $22,260
❀ Earnings Growth Potential: Low (26.0%)
❀ Growth: 14.7%
❀ Annual Job Openings: 10,720
❀ Self-Employed: 9.0%

**Considerations for Job Outlook:** Growth will stem from people spending more time and money on recreation, but budget constraints may limit the number of new jobs. Applicants for part-time, seasonal, and temporary recreation jobs should have good opportunities, but competition will remain keen for full-time career positions.

**Conduct recreation activities with groups in public, private, or volunteer agencies or recreation facilities. Organize and promote activities such as arts and crafts, sports, games, music, dramatics, social recreation, camping, and hobbies, taking into account the needs and interests of individual members.** Enforce rules and regulations of recreational facilities to maintain discipline and ensure safety. Organize, lead, and promote interest in recreational activities such as arts, crafts, sports, games, camping, and hobbies. Manage the daily operations of recreational facilities. Administer first aid according to prescribed procedures and notify emergency medical personnel when necessary. Ascertain and interpret group interests, evaluate equipment and facilities, and adapt activities to meet participant needs. Greet new arrivals to activities, introducing them to other participants, explaining facility rules, and encouraging participation. Complete and maintain time and attendance forms and inventory lists. Explain principles, techniques, and safety procedures to participants in recreational activities and demonstrate use of materials and equipment. Evaluate recreation areas, facilities, and services to determine if they are producing desired results. Confer with management to discuss and resolve participant complaints. Supervise and coordinate the work activities of personnel, such as training staff members and assigning work duties. Meet and collaborate with agency personnel, community organizations, and other professional personnel to plan balanced recreational programs for participants. Schedule maintenance and use of facilities. Direct special activities or events such as aquatics, gymnastics, or performing arts. Meet with staff to discuss rules, regulations, and work-related problems. Provide for entertainment and set up related decorations and equipment. Encourage participants to develop their own activities and leadership skills through group discussions. Serve as liaison between park or recreation administrators and activity instructors. Evaluate staff performance, recording evaluations on appropriate forms. Oversee the purchase, planning, design, construction, and upkeep of recreation facilities and areas.

**Education/Training Required:** Bachelor's degree. **Education and Training Programs:** Health and Physical Education/Fitness, Other; Parks, Recreation, and Leisure Facilities Management; Parks, Recreation, and Leisure Studies; Parks, Recreation, Leisure, and Fitness Studies, Other; Sport and Fitness Administration/Management. **Knowledge/Courses**—Therapy and Counseling, Psychology, Sociology and Anthropology, Customer and Personal Service, Clerical, Sales and Marketing.

**Personality Type:** Social-Enterprising-Artistic. **Career Clusters:** 01 Agriculture, Food, and Natural Resources; 05 Education and Training; 10 Human Services. **Career Pathways:** 1.5 Natural Resources Systems; 5.3 Teaching/Training; 10.2 Counseling and Mental Health Services. **Other Jobs in These Pathways:** Adult Basic and Secondary Education and Literacy Teachers and Instructors; Career/Technical Education Teachers, Secondary School; Clergy; Clinical Psychologists; Coaches and Scouts; Counseling Psychologists; Elementary School Teachers, Except Special Education; Fitness Trainers and Aerobics Instructors; Healthcare Social Workers; Industrial Truck and Tractor Operators; Instructional Coordinators; Instructional Designers and Technologists; Kindergarten Teachers, Except Special Education; Librarians; Mental Health and Substance Abuse Social Workers; Mental Health Counselors; Middle School Teachers, Except Special and Career/Technical Education; Preschool Teachers, Except Special Education; Refuse and Recyclable Material Collectors; School Psychologists; Secondary School Teachers, Except Special and Career/Technical Education; Self-Enrichment Education Teachers; Teacher Assistants; Teachers and Instructors, All Other; Tutors; others.

**Skills**—Management of Material Resources, Management of Personnel Resources, Service Orientation, Social Perceptiveness, Learning Strategies, Instructing, Management of Financial Resources, Coordination.

**Work Environment:** More often indoors than outdoors; standing; noise; very hot or cold.

# Recreational Therapists

- ❋ Annual Earnings: $39,410
- ❋ Earnings Growth Potential: Medium (37.5%)
- ❋ Growth: 14.6%
- ❋ Annual Job Openings: 1,160
- ❋ Self-Employed: 0.1%

**Considerations for Job Outlook:** Employment growth for recreational therapists is expected to continue as the population ages and better medical technology increases the survival rates of people who become injured or ill.

**Plan, direct, or coordinate medically approved recreation programs for patients in hospitals, nursing homes, or other institutions. Activities include sports, trips, dramatics, social activities, and arts and crafts. May assess a patient condition and recommend appropriate**

**recreational activity.** Observe, analyze, and record patients' participation, reactions, and progress during treatment sessions, modifying treatment programs as needed. Develop treatment plan to meet needs of patient, based on needs assessment, patient interests, and objectives of therapy. Encourage clients with special needs and circumstances to acquire new skills and get involved in health-promoting leisure activities, such as sports, games, arts and crafts, and gardening. Counsel and encourage patients to develop leisure activities. Confer with members of treatment team to plan and evaluate therapy programs. Conduct therapy sessions to improve patients' mental and physical well-being. Instruct patient in activities and techniques, such as sports, dance, music, art, or relaxation techniques, designed to meet their specific physical or psychological needs. Obtain information from medical records, medical staff, family members, and the patients themselves to assess patients' capabilities, needs, and interests. Plan, organize, direct, and participate in treatment programs and activities to facilitate patients' rehabilitation, help them integrate into the community, and prevent further medical problems. Prepare and submit reports and charts to treatment team to reflect patients' reactions and evidence of progress or regression.

**Education/Training Required:** Bachelor's degree. **Education and Training Program:** Therapeutic Recreation/Recreational Therapy. **Knowledge/Courses**—Therapy and Counseling, Psychology, Sociology and Anthropology, Philosophy and Theology, Medicine and Dentistry, Fine Arts.

**Personality Type:** Social-Artistic. **Career Cluster:** 08 Health Science. **Career Pathway:** 8.3 Health Informatics. **Other Jobs in This Pathway:** Clinical Psychologists; Dental Laboratory Technicians; Editors; Engineers, All Other; Executive Secretaries and Executive Administrative Assistants; Fine Artists, Including Painters, Sculptors, and Illustrators; First-Line Supervisors of Office and Administrative Support Workers; Health Educators; Medical and Health Services Managers; Medical Appliance Technicians; Medical Assistants; Medical Records and Health Information Technicians; Medical Secretaries; Medical Transcriptionists; Mental Health Counselors; Occupational Health and Safety Specialists; Occupational Health and Safety Technicians; Physical Therapists; Psychiatric Aides; Psychiatric Technicians; Public Relations Specialists; Receptionists and Information Clerks; Rehabilitation Counselors; Substance Abuse and Behavioral Disorder Counselors; Therapists, All Other; others.

**Skills**—Service Orientation, Operations Analysis, Social Perceptiveness, Science, Persuasion, Negotiation, Coordination, Learning Strategies.

**Work Environment:** Indoors; standing; exposed to disease or infections.

# Job Specialization: Art Therapists

**Plan or conduct art therapy sessions or programs to improve clients' physical, cognitive, or emotional well-being.** Analyze data to determine the effectiveness of treatments or therapy approaches. Analyze or synthesize client data to draw conclusions or make recommendations for art therapy. Assess client needs or disorders, using drawing, painting, sculpting, or other artistic processes. Communicate client assessment findings and recommendations in oral, written, audio, video, or other forms. Conduct art therapy sessions providing guided self-expression experiences to help clients recover from or cope with cognitive, emotional, or physical impairments. Confer with other professionals on client's treatment team to develop, coordinate, or integrate treatment plans. Customize art therapy programs for specific client populations, such as those in schools, nursing homes, wellness centers, prisons, shelters, or hospitals. Design art therapy sessions or programs to meet client's goals or objectives. Develop individualized treatment plans that incorporate studio art therapy, counseling, or psychotherapy techniques. Establish goals or objectives for art therapy sessions in consultation with clients or site administrators. Instruct individuals or groups in the use of art media, such as paint, clay, or yarn. Interpret the artistic creations of clients to assess their functioning, needs, or progress. Observe and document client reactions, progress, or other outcomes related to art therapy. Photograph or videotape client artwork for inclusion in client records or for promotional purposes. Talk with clients during art or other therapy sessions to build rapport, acknowledge their progress, or reflect upon their reactions to the artistic process. Write treatment plans, case summaries, or progress or other reports related to individual clients or client groups. Conduct information sharing sessions, such as in-service workshops for other professionals, potential client groups, or the general community. Coordinate art showcases to display artwork produced by clients.

**Education/Training Required:** Master's degree. **Education and Training Program:** Art Therapy/Therapist Training. **Knowledge/Courses**—No data available.

**Personality Type:** No data available. **Career Cluster:** 08 Health Science. **Career Pathway:** 8.1 Therapeutic Services. **Other Jobs in This Pathway:** Clinical Psychologists; Community and Social Service Specialists, All Other; Counseling Psychologists; Dental Assistants; Dental Hygienists;

Dentists, General; Health Technologists and Technicians, All Other; Healthcare Support Workers, All Other; Home Health Aides; Licensed Practical and Licensed Vocational Nurses; Low Vision Therapists, Orientation and Mobility Specialists, and Vision Rehabilitation Therapists; Massage Therapists; Medical and Clinical Laboratory Technicians; Medical and Health Services Managers; Medical Scientists, Except Epidemiologists; Medical Secretaries; Occupational Therapists; Pharmacists; Pharmacy Technicians; Radiologic Technologists; School Psychologists; Social and Human Service Assistants; Speech-Language Pathologists; Speech-Language Pathology Assistants; Substance Abuse and Behavioral Disorder Counselors; others.

**Skills**—No data available.

**Work Environment:** No data available.

## Job Specialization: Music Therapists

**Plan, organize, or direct medically prescribed music therapy activities designed to positively influence patients' psychological or behavioral status.** Adapt existing or create new music therapy assessment instruments or procedures to meet an individual client's needs. Analyze data to determine the effectiveness of specific treatments or therapy approaches. Analyze or synthesize client data to draw conclusions or make recommendations for therapy. Assess client functioning levels, strengths, and areas of need in terms of perceptual, sensory, affective, communicative, musical, or other abilities. Communicate client assessment findings and recommendations in oral, written, audio, video, or other forms. Confer with professionals on client's treatment team to develop, coordinate, or integrate treatment plans. Customize treatment programs for specific client populations, such as hospice, psychiatric, or obstetrics populations. Design music therapy experiences to meet client's goals or objectives. Engage clients in music experiences to identify client responses to different styles of music, types of musical experiences, such as improvising or listening, or elements of music, such as tempo or harmony. Establish client goals or objectives for music therapy treatment, considering client needs, capabilities, interests, overall therapeutic program, coordination of treatment, or length of treatment. Gather diagnostic data from sources such as case documentation, observations of clients, or interviews of clients or family members. Improvise instrumentally, vocally, or physically to meet client's therapeutic needs. Observe and document client reactions, progress, or other outcomes related to music therapy. Plan or structure music therapy sessions to achieve appropriate transitions, pacing, sequencing, energy

level, or intensity in accordance with treatment plans. Play musical instruments, such as keyboard, guitar, or percussion instruments.

**Education/Training Required:** Bachelor's degree. **Education and Training Program:** Music Therapy/Therapist Training. **Knowledge/Courses**—No data available.

**Personality Type:** No data available. **Career Cluster:** 08 Health Science. **Career Pathway:** 8.1 Therapeutic Services. **Other Jobs in This Pathway:** Clinical Psychologists; Community and Social Service Specialists, All Other; Counseling Psychologists; Dental Assistants; Dental Hygienists; Dentists, General; Health Technologists and Technicians, All Other; Healthcare Support Workers, All Other; Home Health Aides; Licensed Practical and Licensed Vocational Nurses; Low Vision Therapists, Orientation and Mobility Specialists, and Vision Rehabilitation Therapists; Massage Therapists; Medical and Clinical Laboratory Technicians; Medical and Health Services Managers; Medical Scientists, Except Epidemiologists; Medical Secretaries; Occupational Therapists; Pharmacists; Pharmacy Technicians; Radiologic Technologists; School Psychologists; Social and Human Service Assistants; Speech-Language Pathologists; Speech-Language Pathology Assistants; Substance Abuse and Behavioral Disorder Counselors; others.

**Skills**—No data available.

**Work Environment:** No data available.

## Refuse and Recyclable Material Collectors

❋ Annual Earnings: $32,640
❋ Earnings Growth Potential: High (42.6%)
❋ Growth: 18.6%
❋ Annual Job Openings: 7,110
❋ Self-Employed: 11.8%

**Considerations for Job Outlook:** Improvements in technology are expected to increase productivity, holding employment stable. Good job prospects are expected from the need to replace the many workers leaving these occupations.

**Collect and dump refuse or recyclable materials from containers into truck. May drive truck.** Inspect trucks prior to beginning routes to ensure safe operating condition. Refuel trucks and add other necessary fluids, such as oil. Fill out any needed reports for defective equipment. Drive to disposal sites to empty trucks that have been filled.

Drive trucks along established routes through residential streets and alleys or through business and industrial areas. Operate equipment that compresses the collected refuse. Operate automated or semi-automated hoisting devices that raise refuse bins and dump contents into openings in truck bodies. Dismount garbage trucks to collect garbage and remount trucks to ride to the next collection point. Communicate with dispatchers concerning delays, unsafe sites, accidents, equipment breakdowns, and other maintenance problems. Keep informed of road and weather conditions to determine how routes will be affected. Tag garbage or recycling containers to inform customers of problems such as excess garbage or inclusion of items that are not permitted. Clean trucks and compactor bodies after routes have been completed. Sort items set out for recycling and throw materials into designated truck compartments. Organize schedules for refuse collection. Provide quotes for refuse collection contracts.

**Education/Training Required:** Short-term on-the-job training. **Education and Training Programs:** No related CIP programs; this job is learned through informal short-term on-the-job training. **Knowledge/Courses—**Transportation, Customer and Personal Service.

**Personality Type:** Realistic-Conventional. **Career Cluster:** 01 Agriculture, Food, and Natural Resources. **Career Pathway:** 1.5 Natural Resources Systems. **Other Jobs in This Pathway:** Climate Change Analysts; Conveyor Operators and Tenders; Derrick Operators, Oil and Gas; Engineering Technicians, Except Drafters, All Other; Environmental Economists; Environmental Restoration Planners; Environmental Science and Protection Technicians, Including Health; Environmental Scientists and Specialists, Including Health; Fishers and Related Fishing Workers; Forest and Conservation Technicians; Geological Sample Test Technicians; Geophysical Data Technicians; Helpers—Extraction Workers; Industrial Ecologists; Industrial Truck and Tractor Operators; Logging Equipment Operators; Mechanical Engineering Technicians; Park Naturalists; Range Managers; Recreation Workers; Rotary Drill Operators, Oil and Gas; Service Unit Operators, Oil, Gas, and Mining; Soil and Water Conservationists; Wellhead Pumpers; Zoologists and Wildlife Biologists; others.

**Skills—**Equipment Maintenance, Repairing, Operation and Control, Troubleshooting, Equipment Selection, Operation Monitoring, Quality Control Analysis.

**Work Environment:** Outdoors; more often sitting than standing; walking and running; using hands; bending or twisting the body; repetitive motions; noise; very hot or cold; contaminants; exposed to disease or infections; hazardous equipment; minor burns, cuts, bites, or stings.

# Registered Nurses

* Annual Earnings: $64,690
* Earnings Growth Potential: Low (31.7%)
* Growth: 22.2%
* Annual Job Openings: 103,900
* Self-Employed: 0.6%

**Considerations for Job Outlook:** Employment growth for registered nurses will be driven by the medical needs of an aging population. In addition, registered nurses are expected to provide more primary care as a low-cost alternative to physician-provided care. Job opportunities should be excellent.

**Assess patient health problems and needs, develop and implement nursing care plans, and maintain medical records. Administer nursing care to ill, injured, convalescent, or disabled patients. May advise patients on health maintenance and disease prevention or provide case management. Licensing or registration required. Includes advance practice nurses such as nurse practitioners, clinical nurse specialists, certified nurse midwives, and certified registered nurse anesthetists. Advanced practice nursing is practiced by RNs who have specialized formal, post-basic education and who function in highly autonomous and specialized roles.** Maintain accurate, detailed reports and records. Monitor, record and report symptoms and changes in patients' conditions. Record patients' medical information and vital signs. Modify patient treatment plans as indicated by patients' responses and conditions. Consult and coordinate with health care team members to assess, plan, implement and evaluate patient care plans. Order, interpret, and evaluate diagnostic tests to identify and assess patient's condition. Monitor all aspects of patient care, including diet and physical activity. Direct and supervise less skilled nursing or health care personnel or supervise a particular unit. Prepare patients for, and assist with, examinations and treatments. Observe nurses and visit patients to ensure proper nursing care. Assess the needs of individuals, families or communities, including assessment of individuals' home or work environments to identify potential health or safety problems. Instruct individuals, families and other groups on topics such as health education, disease prevention and childbirth, and develop health improvement programs. Prepare rooms, sterile instruments, equipment and supplies, and ensure that stock of supplies is maintained.

Inform physician of patient's condition during anesthesia. Administer local, inhalation, intravenous, and other anesthetics. Provide health care, first aid, immunizations and assistance in convalescence and rehabilitation in locations such as schools, hospitals, and industry. Perform physical examinations, make tentative diagnoses, and treat patients en route to hospitals or at disaster site triage centers. Conduct specified laboratory tests. Hand items to surgeons during operations. Prescribe or recommend drugs, medical devices or other forms of treatment, such as physical therapy, inhalation therapy, or related therapeutic procedures. Direct and coordinate infection control programs, advising and consulting with specified personnel about necessary precautions.

**Education/Training Required:** Associate degree. **Education and Training Programs:** Adult Health Nurse/Nursing; Clinical Nurse Specialist Training; Critical Care Nursing; Family Practice Nurse/Nursing; Maternal/Child Health and Neonatal Nurse/Nursing; Nurse Anesthetist Training; Nurse Midwife/Nursing Midwifery; Nursing Science; Occupational and Environmental Health Nursing; Pediatric Nurse/Nursing; Perioperative/Operating Room and Surgical Nurse/Nursing; Psychiatric/Mental Health Nurse/Nursing; Public Health/Community Nurse/Nursing; Registered Nursing/Registered Nurse Training. **Knowledge/Courses**—Medicine and Dentistry, Psychology, Therapy and Counseling, Biology, Philosophy and Theology, Sociology and Anthropology.

**Personality Type:** Social-Investigative-Conventional. **Career Cluster:** 08 Health Science. **Career Pathway:** 8.1 Therapeutic Services. **Other Jobs in This Pathway:** Clinical Psychologists; Community and Social Service Specialists, All Other; Counseling Psychologists; Dental Assistants; Dental Hygienists; Dentists, General; Health Technologists and Technicians, All Other; Healthcare Support Workers, All Other; Home Health Aides; Licensed Practical and Licensed Vocational Nurses; Low Vision Therapists, Orientation and Mobility Specialists, and Vision Rehabilitation Therapists; Massage Therapists; Medical and Clinical Laboratory Technicians; Medical and Health Services Managers; Medical Scientists, Except Epidemiologists; Medical Secretaries; Occupational Therapists; Pharmacists; Pharmacy Technicians; Radiologic Technologists; School Psychologists; Social and Human Service Assistants; Speech-Language Pathologists; Speech-Language Pathology Assistants; Substance Abuse and Behavioral Disorder Counselors; others.

**Skills**—Science, Social Perceptiveness, Quality Control Analysis, Service Orientation, Learning Strategies, Management of Material Resources, Coordination, Instructing.

**Work Environment:** Indoors; standing; walking and running; using hands; exposed to disease or infections.

## Job Specialization: Acute Care Nurses

**Provide advanced nursing care for patients with acute conditions such as heart attacks, respiratory distress syndrome, or shock. May care for pre- and post-operative patients or perform advanced, invasive diagnostic or therapeutic procedures.** Analyze the indications, contraindications, risk complications, and cost-benefit tradeoffs of therapeutic interventions. Diagnose acute or chronic conditions that could result in rapid physiological deterioration or life-threatening instability. Distinguish between normal and abnormal developmental and age-related physiological and behavioral changes in acute, critical, and chronic illness. Manage patients' pain relief and sedation by providing pharmacologic and non-pharmacologic interventions, monitoring patients' responses, and changing care plans accordingly. Interpret information obtained from electrocardiograms (EKGs) or radiographs (X-rays). Perform emergency medical procedures, such as basic cardiac life support (BLS), advanced cardiac life support (ACLS), and other condition stabilizing interventions. Assess urgent and emergent health conditions using both physiologically and technologically derived data. Adjust settings on patients' assistive devices such as temporary pacemakers. Assess the impact of illnesses or injuries on patients' health, function, growth, development, nutrition, sleep, rest, quality of life, or family, social, and educational relationships. Collaborate with members of multidisciplinary health care teams to plan, manage, or assess patient treatments. Discuss illnesses and treatments with patients and family members. Document data related to patients' care including assessment results, interventions, medications, patient responses, or treatment changes. Treat wounds or superficial lacerations. Set up, operate, or monitor invasive equipment and devices such as colostomy or tracheotomy equipment, mechanical ventilators, catheters, gastrointestinal tubes, and central lines. Obtain specimens or samples for laboratory work. Order, perform, or interpret the results of diagnostic tests and screening procedures based on assessment results, differential diagnoses, and knowledge about age, gender and health status of clients.

**Education/Training Required:** Associate degree. **Education and Training Program:** Critical Care Nursing.

**Knowledge/Courses**—Medicine and Dentistry, Therapy and Counseling, Psychology, Biology, Sociology and Anthropology, Philosophy and Theology.

**Personality Type:** Social-Investigative-Realistic. **Career Cluster:** 08 Health Science. **Career Pathway:** 8.1 Therapeutic Services. **Other Jobs in This Pathway:** Clinical Psychologists; Community and Social Service Specialists, All Other; Counseling Psychologists; Dental Assistants; Dental Hygienists; Dentists, General; Health Technologists and Technicians, All Other; Healthcare Support Workers, All Other; Home Health Aides; Licensed Practical and Licensed Vocational Nurses; Low Vision Therapists, Orientation and Mobility Specialists, and Vision Rehabilitation Therapists; Massage Therapists; Medical and Clinical Laboratory Technicians; Medical and Health Services Managers; Medical Scientists, Except Epidemiologists; Medical Secretaries; Occupational Therapists; Pharmacists; Pharmacy Technicians; Radiologic Technologists; School Psychologists; Social and Human Service Assistants; Speech-Language Pathologists; Speech-Language Pathology Assistants; Substance Abuse and Behavioral Disorder Counselors; others.

**Skills**—Science, Social Perceptiveness, Reading Comprehension, Operation Monitoring, Service Orientation, Systems Evaluation, Operation and Control, Active Learning.

**Work Environment:** Indoors; standing; walking and running; using hands; noise; contaminants; cramped work space; exposed to radiation; exposed to disease or infections.

## Job Specialization: Advanced Practice Psychiatric Nurses

**Provide advanced nursing care for patients with psychiatric disorders. May provide psychotherapy under the direction of a psychiatrist.** Teach classes in mental health topics such as stress reduction. Participate in activities aimed at professional growth and development including conferences or continuing education activities. Direct or provide home health services. Monitor the use and status of medical and pharmaceutical supplies. Develop practice protocols for mental health problems based on review and evaluation of published research. Develop, implement, or evaluate programs such as outreach activities, community mental health programs, and crisis situation response activities. Treat patients for routine physical health problems. Write prescriptions for psychotropic medications as allowed by state regulations and collaborative practice agreements. Refer patients requiring more specialized or complex treatment to psychiatrists, primary care physicians, or other medical specialists. Provide routine physical health screenings to detect or monitor problems such as heart disease and diabetes. Participate in treatment team conferences regarding diagnosis or treatment of difficult cases. Interpret diagnostic or laboratory tests such as electrocardiograms (EKGs) and renal functioning tests. Evaluate patients' behavior to formulate diagnoses or assess treatments. Develop and implement treatment plans. Monitor patients' medication usage and results. Educate patients and family members about mental health and medical conditions, preventive health measures, medications, or treatment plans. Distinguish between physiologically and psychologically based disorders and diagnose appropriately. Document patients' medical and psychological histories, physical assessment results, diagnoses, treatment plans, prescriptions, or outcomes. Consult with psychiatrists or other professionals when unusual or complex cases are encountered. Assess patients' mental and physical status based on the presenting symptoms and complaints.

**Education/Training Required:** Master's degree. **Education and Training Program:** Psychiatric/Mental Health Nurse Training/Nursing. **Knowledge/Courses**—Therapy and Counseling, Psychology, Medicine and Dentistry, Sociology and Anthropology, Philosophy and Theology, Biology.

**Personality Type:** Social-Investigative. **Career Cluster:** 08 Health Science. **Career Pathway:** 8.1 Therapeutic Services. **Other Jobs in This Pathway:** Clinical Psychologists; Community and Social Service Specialists, All Other; Counseling Psychologists; Dental Assistants; Dental Hygienists; Dentists, General; Health Technologists and Technicians, All Other; Healthcare Support Workers, All Other; Home Health Aides; Licensed Practical and Licensed Vocational Nurses; Low Vision Therapists, Orientation and Mobility Specialists, and Vision Rehabilitation Therapists; Massage Therapists; Medical and Clinical Laboratory Technicians; Medical and Health Services Managers; Medical Scientists, Except Epidemiologists; Medical Secretaries; Occupational Therapists; Pharmacists; Pharmacy Technicians; Radiologic Technologists; School Psychologists; Social and Human Service Assistants; Speech-Language Pathologists; Speech-Language Pathology Assistants; Substance Abuse and Behavioral Disorder Counselors; others.

**Skills**—Social Perceptiveness, Science, Negotiation, Service Orientation, Systems Evaluation, Persuasion, Learning Strategies, Reading Comprehension.

**Work Environment:** Indoors; sitting; exposed to disease or infections.

# Job Specialization: Clinical Nurse Specialists

**Plan, direct, or coordinate daily patient care activities in a clinical practice. Ensure adherence to established clinical policies, protocols, regulations, and standards.** Coordinate or conduct educational programs or in-service training sessions on topics such as clinical procedures. Observe, interview, and assess patients to identify care needs. Evaluate the quality and effectiveness of nursing practice or organizational systems. Provide direct care by performing comprehensive health assessments, developing differential diagnoses, conducting specialized tests, or prescribing medications or treatments. Provide specialized direct and indirect care to inpatients and outpatients within a designated specialty such as obstetrics, neurology, oncology, or neonatal care. Maintain departmental policies, procedures, objectives, or infection control standards. Collaborate with other health care professionals and service providers to ensure optimal patient care. Develop nursing service philosophies, goals, policies, priorities, or procedures. Develop, implement, or evaluate standards of nursing practice in specialty area such as pediatrics, acute care, and geriatrics. Develop or assist others in development of care and treatment plans. Make clinical recommendations to physicians, other health care providers, insurance companies, patients, or health care organizations. Plan, evaluate, or modify treatment programs based on information gathered by observing and interviewing patients, or by analyzing patient records. Present clients with information required to make informed health care and treatment decisions. Instruct nursing staff in areas such as the assessment, development, implementation and evaluation of disability, illness, management, technology, or resources. Direct or supervise nursing care staff in the provision of patient therapy. Identify training needs or conduct training sessions for nursing students or medical staff. Read current literature, talk with colleagues, or participate in professional organizations or conferences to keep abreast of developments in nursing.

**Education/Training Required:** Master's degree. **Education and Training Program:** Clinical Nurse Specialist Training. **Knowledge/Courses**—Medicine and Dentistry, Biology, Therapy and Counseling, Psychology, Sociology and Anthropology, Philosophy and Theology.

**Personality Type:** Enterprising-Social-Conventional. **Career Cluster:** 08 Health Science. **Career Pathways:** 8.1 Therapeutic Services; 8.3 Health Informatics. **Other Jobs in These Pathways:** Clinical Psychologists; Counseling Psychologists; Dental Assistants; Dental Hygienists; Editors; Engineers, All Other; Executive Secretaries and Executive Administrative Assistants; First-Line Supervisors of Office and Administrative Support Workers; Healthcare Support Workers, All Other; Home Health Aides; Licensed Practical and Licensed Vocational Nurses; Medical and Clinical Laboratory Technicians; Medical and Health Services Managers; Medical Assistants; Medical Records and Health Information Technicians; Medical Secretaries; Pharmacists; Pharmacy Technicians; Physical Therapists; Public Relations Specialists; Radiologic Technologists; Receptionists and Information Clerks; School Psychologists; Social and Human Service Assistants; Speech-Language Pathology Assistants; others.

**Skills**—Science, Operations Analysis, Instructing, Service Orientation, Negotiation, Persuasion, Judgment and Decision Making, Systems Evaluation.

**Work Environment:** Indoors; standing; using hands; noise; contaminants; exposed to radiation; exposed to disease or infections.

# Job Specialization: Critical Care Nurses

**Provide advanced nursing care for patients in critical or coronary care units.** Identify patients' age-specific needs and alter care plans as necessary to meet those needs. Provide post-mortem care. Evaluate patients' vital signs and laboratory data to determine emergency intervention needs. Perform approved therapeutic or diagnostic procedures based upon patients' clinical status. Administer blood and blood products, monitoring patients for signs and symptoms related to transfusion reactions. Administer medications intravenously, by injection, orally, through gastric tubes, or by other methods. Advocate for patients' and families' needs, or provide emotional support for patients and their families. Set up and monitor medical equipment and devices such as cardiac monitors, mechanical ventilators and alarms, oxygen delivery devices, transducers, and pressure lines. Monitor patients' fluid intake and output to detect emerging problems such as fluid and electrolyte imbalances. Monitor patients for changes in status and indications of conditions such as sepsis or shock and institute appropriate interventions. Assess patients' pain levels and sedation requirements. Assess patients' psychosocial status and needs including areas such as sleep patterns, anxiety, grief, anger, and support systems. Collaborate with other health care professionals to develop and revise treatment plans based on identified needs and assessment data. Collect specimens for laboratory tests. Compile and analyze data obtained from monitoring or diagnostic tests. Conduct pulmonary assessments to identify abnormal respiratory patterns or breathing sounds that indicate problems. Document patients' medical histories and assessment findings. Document patients' treatment plans, interventions, outcomes, or plan revisions. Identify patients who are at risk of complications due to nutritional status. Prioritize nursing care for assigned critically ill patients based on assessment data and identified needs.

**Education/Training Required:** Associate degree. **Education and Training Program:** Critical Care Nursing. **Knowledge/Courses**—Medicine and Dentistry, Biology, Psychology, Therapy and Counseling, Sociology and Anthropology, Philosophy and Theology.

**Personality Type:** Social-Investigative-Realistic. **Career Cluster:** 08 Health Science. **Career Pathway:** 8.1 Therapeutic Services. **Other Jobs in This Pathway:** Clinical Psychologists; Community and Social Service Specialists, All Other; Counseling Psychologists; Dental Assistants; Dental Hygienists; Dentists, General; Health Technologists and Technicians, All Other; Healthcare Support Workers, All Other; Home Health Aides; Licensed Practical and Licensed Vocational Nurses; Low Vision Therapists, Orientation and Mobility Specialists, and Vision Rehabilitation Therapists; Massage Therapists; Medical and Clinical Laboratory Technicians; Medical and Health Services Managers; Medical Scientists, Except Epidemiologists; Medical Secretaries; Occupational Therapists; Pharmacists; Pharmacy Technicians; Radiologic Technologists; School Psychologists; Social and Human Service Assistants; Speech-Language Pathologists; Speech-Language Pathology Assistants; Substance Abuse and Behavioral Disorder Counselors; others.

**Skills**—Science, Social Perceptiveness, Operation and Control, Operation Monitoring, Quality Control Analysis, Service Orientation, Monitoring, Learning Strategies.

**Work Environment:** Indoors; standing; walking and running; using hands; bending or twisting the body; noise; contaminants; cramped work space; exposed to radiation; exposed to disease or infections.

# Rehabilitation Counselors

- ❋ Annual Earnings: $32,350
- ❋ Earnings Growth Potential: Low (35.8%)
- ❋ Growth: 18.9%
- ❋ Annual Job Openings: 5,070
- ❋ Self-Employed: 5.7%

**Considerations for Job Outlook:** Increasing demand for services provided by counselors is expected to result in employment growth. But growth will vary by specialty and will be faster for mental health, substance abuse and behavioral disorder, and rehabilitation counselors than for counselors of other specialties. Opportunities should be favorable, particularly in rural areas.

**Counsel individuals to maximize the independence and employability of persons coping with personal, social, and vocational difficulties that result from birth defects, illness, disease, accidents, or the stress of daily life. Coordinate activities for residents of care and treatment facilities. Assess client needs and design and implement rehabilitation programs that may include personal and vocational counseling, training, and job placement.** Monitor and record clients' progress in order to ensure that goals and objectives are met. Confer with clients to discuss their options and goals so that rehabilitation programs and plans for accessing needed services can be developed. Prepare and maintain records and case files, including documentation such as clients' personal and eligibility information, services provided, narratives of client contacts, and relevant correspondence. Arrange for physical, mental, academic, vocational, and other evaluations to obtain information for assessing clients' needs and developing rehabilitation plans. Analyze information from interviews, educational and medical records, consultation with other professionals, and diagnostic evaluations to assess clients' abilities, needs, and eligibility for services. Develop rehabilitation plans that fit clients' aptitudes, education levels, physical abilities, and career goals. Maintain close contact with clients during job training and placements to resolve problems and evaluate placement adequacy. Locate barriers to client employment, such as inaccessible work sites, inflexible schedules, and transportation problems, and work with clients to develop strategies for overcoming these barriers. Develop and maintain relationships with community referral sources such as schools and community groups. Arrange for on-site job coaching or assistive devices such as specially equipped wheelchairs in order to help clients adapt to work or school environments. Confer with physicians, psychologists, occupational therapists, and other professionals to develop and implement client rehabilitation programs. Develop diagnostic procedures for determining clients' needs. Participate in job development and placement programs, contacting prospective employers, placing clients in jobs, and evaluating the success of placements.

**Education/Training Required:** Master's degree. **Education and Training Programs:** Assistive/Augmentative Technology and Rehabilitation Engineering; Vocational Rehabilitation Counseling/Counselor. **Knowledge/Courses**—Therapy and Counseling, Psychology,

R

Philosophy and Theology, Education and Training, Personnel and Human Resources, Sociology and Anthropology.

**Personality Type:** Social-Investigative. **Career Cluster:** 08 Health Science. **Career Pathway:** 8.3 Health Informatics. **Other Jobs in This Pathway:** Clinical Psychologists; Dental Laboratory Technicians; Editors; Engineers, All Other; Executive Secretaries and Executive Administrative Assistants; Fine Artists, Including Painters, Sculptors, and Illustrators; First-Line Supervisors of Office and Administrative Support Workers; Health Educators; Medical and Health Services Managers; Medical Appliance Technicians; Medical Assistants; Medical Records and Health Information Technicians; Medical Secretaries; Medical Transcriptionists; Mental Health Counselors; Occupational Health and Safety Specialists; Occupational Health and Safety Technicians; Physical Therapists; Psychiatric Aides; Psychiatric Technicians; Public Relations Specialists; Receptionists and Information Clerks; Recreational Therapists; Substance Abuse and Behavioral Disorder Counselors; Therapists, All Other; others.

**Skills**—Operations Analysis, Social Perceptiveness, Systems Analysis, Service Orientation, Science, Systems Evaluation, Learning Strategies, Monitoring.

**Work Environment:** More often indoors than outdoors; sitting; walking and running.

# Reservation and Transportation Ticket Agents and Travel Clerks

- ❀ Annual Earnings: $31,740
- ❀ Earnings Growth Potential: Medium (37.2%)
- ❀ Growth: 8.1%
- ❀ Annual Job Openings: 5,150
- ❀ Self-Employed: 2.3%

**Considerations for Job Outlook:** Increased use of online reservations systems and self-service ticketing machines are expected to reduce the number of workers needed for most routine services, but these agents and clerks will still provide in-person requests. Competition is expected.

**Make and confirm reservations and sell tickets to passengers and for large hotel or motel chains. May check baggage and direct passengers to designated concourse, pier, or track; make reservations; deliver tickets; arrange for visas; contact individuals and groups to inform them of package tours; or provide tourists with travel information, such as points of interest, restaurants, rates, and emergency service.** Plan routes, itineraries, and accommodation details and compute fares and fees, using schedules, rate books, and computers. Make and confirm reservations for transportation and accommodations, using telephones, faxes, mail, and computers. Prepare customer invoices and accept payment. Answer inquiries regarding such information as schedules, accommodations, procedures, and policies. Assemble and issue required documentation such as tickets, travel insurance policies, and itineraries. Determine whether space is available on travel dates requested by customers and assign requested spaces when available. Inform clients of essential travel information such as travel times, transportation connections, and medical and visa requirements. Maintain computerized inventories of available passenger space and provide information on space reserved or available. Confer with customers to determine their service requirements and travel preferences. Examine passenger documentation to determine destinations and to assign boarding passes. Provide boarding or disembarking assistance to passengers needing special assistance. Check baggage and cargo and direct passengers to designated locations for loading. Announce arrival and departure information, using public-address systems. Trace lost, delayed, or misdirected baggage for customers. Promote particular destinations, tour packages, and other travel services. Provide clients with assistance in preparing required travel documents and forms. Open and close information facilities and keep them clean during operation. Provide customers with travel suggestions and information such as guides, directories, brochures, and maps. Contact customers or travel agents to advise them of travel conveyance changes or to confirm reservations. Contact motel, hotel, resort, and travel operators to obtain current advertising literature.

**Education/Training Required:** Short-term on-the-job training. **Education and Training Programs:** Selling Skills and Sales Operations; Tourism and Travel Services Marketing Operations; Tourism Promotion Operations. **Knowledge/Courses**—Customer and Personal Service, Transportation, Sales and Marketing, Clerical.

**Personality Type:** Conventional-Enterprising-Social. **Career Clusters:** 09 Hospitality and Tourism; 14 Marketing, Sales, and Service. **Career Pathways:** 9.3 Travel and Tourism; 14.2 Professional Sales and Marketing. **Other Jobs in These Pathways:** Cashiers; Counter and Rental Clerks; Door-To-Door Sales Workers, News and Street Vendors, and Related Workers; Driver/Sales Workers; Energy Brokers; First-Line Supervisors of Non-Retail Sales Workers; First-Line Supervisors of Retail Sales Workers; Food Service Managers; Hotel, Motel, and Resort Desk Clerks;

Managers, All Other; Marking Clerks; Online Merchants; Order Fillers, Wholesale and Retail Sales; Parts Salespersons; Property, Real Estate, and Community Association Managers; Real Estate Sales Agents; Retail Salespersons; Sales Representatives, Services, All Other; Sales Representatives, Wholesale and Manufacturing, Except Technical and Scientific Products; Sales Representatives, Wholesale and Manufacturing, Technical and Scientific Products; Solar Sales Representatives and Assessors; Stock Clerks—Stockroom, Warehouse, or Storage Yard; Stock Clerks, Sales Floor; Supply Chain Managers; Telemarketers; others.

**Skills**—Service Orientation, Negotiation, Active Listening, Persuasion, Programming, Mathematics, Systems Evaluation, Speaking.

**Work Environment:** Indoors; sitting; using hands; repetitive motions; noise.

# Respiratory Therapists

* Annual Earnings: $54,280
* Earnings Growth Potential: Low (26.3%)
* Growth: 20.9%
* Annual Job Openings: 4,140
* Self-Employed: 0.0%

**Considerations for Job Outlook:** Growth of the elderly population is expected to increase employment for these workers, especially as they take on additional duties related to case management, disease prevention, and emergency care. Opportunities are expected to be very good.

**Assess, treat, and care for patients with breathing disorders. Assume primary responsibility for all respiratory care modalities, including the supervision of respiratory therapy technicians. Initiate and conduct therapeutic procedures; maintain patient records; and select, assemble, check, and operate equipment.** Set up and operate devices such as mechanical ventilators, therapeutic gas administration apparatus, environmental control systems, and aerosol generators, following specified parameters of treatment. Provide emergency care, including artificial respiration, external cardiac massage, and assistance with cardiopulmonary resuscitation. Determine requirements for treatment, such as type, method, and duration of therapy; precautions to be taken; and medication and dosages, compatible with physicians' orders. Monitor patient's physiological responses to therapy, such as vital signs, arterial blood gases, and blood chemistry changes, and consult with physician if adverse reactions occur. Read prescription, measure arterial blood gases, and review patient information to assess patient condition. Work as part of a team of physicians, nurses, and other health-care professionals to manage patient care. Enforce safety rules and ensure careful adherence to physicians' orders. Maintain charts that contain patients' pertinent identification and therapy information. Inspect, clean, test, and maintain respiratory therapy equipment to ensure equipment is functioning safely and efficiently, ordering repairs when necessary. Educate patients and their families about their conditions and teach appropriate disease management techniques, such as breathing exercises and the use of medications and respiratory equipment. Explain treatment procedures to patients to gain cooperation and allay fears. Relay blood analysis results to a physician. Perform pulmonary function and adjust equipment to obtain optimum results in therapy. Perform bronchopulmonary drainage and assist or instruct patients in performance of breathing exercises. Demonstrate respiratory care procedures to trainees and other health-care personnel. Teach, train, supervise, and utilize the assistance of students, respiratory therapy technicians, and assistants. Make emergency visits to resolve equipment problems.

**Education/Training Required:** Associate degree. **Education and Training Program:** Respiratory Care Therapy/Therapist. **Knowledge/Courses**—Medicine and Dentistry, Biology, Customer and Personal Service, Therapy and Counseling, Psychology, Chemistry.

**Personality Type:** Social-Investigative-Realistic. **Career Cluster:** 08 Health Science. **Career Pathway:** 8.1 Therapeutic Services. **Other Jobs in This Pathway:** Clinical Psychologists; Community and Social Service Specialists, All Other; Counseling Psychologists; Dental Assistants; Dental Hygienists; Dentists, General; Health Technologists and Technicians, All Other; Healthcare Support Workers, All Other; Home Health Aides; Licensed Practical and Licensed Vocational Nurses; Low Vision Therapists, Orientation and Mobility Specialists, and Vision Rehabilitation Therapists; Massage Therapists; Medical and Clinical Laboratory Technicians; Medical and Health Services Managers; Medical Scientists, Except Epidemiologists; Medical Secretaries; Occupational Therapists; Pharmacists; Pharmacy Technicians; Radiologic Technologists; School Psychologists; Social and Human Service Assistants; Speech-Language Pathologists; Speech-Language Pathology Assistants; Substance Abuse and Behavioral Disorder Counselors; others.

**Skills**—Science, Repairing, Equipment Maintenance, Equipment Selection, Operation and Control, Operation Monitoring, Quality Control Analysis, Service Orientation.

R

**Work Environment:** Indoors; standing; walking and running; using hands; repetitive motions; contaminants; exposed to radiation; exposed to disease or infections.

# Retail Salespersons

- ❋ Annual Earnings: $20,670
- ❋ Earnings Growth Potential: Very low (22.0%)
- ❋ Growth: 8.3%
- ❋ Annual Job Openings: 162,690
- ❋ Self-Employed: 3.4%

**Considerations for Job Outlook:** As the population grows and retail sales increase, employment of these workers is expected to grow. Opportunities are expected to be good.

**Sell merchandise, such as furniture, motor vehicles, appliances, or apparel, in a retail establishment.** Greet customers and ascertain what each customer wants or needs. Open and close cash registers, performing tasks such as counting money; separating charge slips, coupons, and vouchers; balancing cash drawers; and making deposits. Maintain knowledge of current sales and promotions, policies regarding payment and exchanges, and security practices. Compute sales prices and total purchases and receive and process cash or credit payment. Watch for and recognize security risks and thefts and know how to prevent or handle these situations. Maintain records related to sales. Recommend, select, and help locate or obtain merchandise based on customer needs and desires. Answer questions regarding the store and its merchandise. Describe merchandise and explain use, operation, and care of merchandise to customers. Prepare sales slips or sales contracts. Ticket, arrange, and display merchandise to promote sales. Place special orders or call other stores to find desired items. Demonstrate use or operation of merchandise. Clean shelves, counters, and tables. Exchange merchandise for customers and accept returns. Bag or package purchases and wrap gifts. Help customers try on or fit merchandise. Inventory stock and requisition new stock. Prepare merchandise for purchase or rental. Sell or arrange for delivery, insurance, financing, or service contracts for merchandise. Estimate and quote trade-in allowances. Estimate cost of repair or alteration of merchandise. Estimate quantity and cost of merchandise required, such as paint or floor covering. Rent merchandise to customers.

**Education/Training Required:** Short-term on-the-job training. **Education and Training Programs:** Floriculture/Floristry Operations and Management; Retailing and Retail Operations; Sales, Distribution, and Marketing Operations, General; Selling Skills and Sales Operations. **Knowledge/Courses**—Sales and Marketing, Customer and Personal Service, Communications and Media, Psychology.

**Personality Type:** Enterprising-Conventional. **Career Clusters:** 01 Agriculture, Food, and Natural Resources; 14 Marketing, Sales, and Service. **Career Pathways:** 1.2 Plant Systems; 14.2 Professional Sales and Marketing; 14.3 Buying and Merchandising. **Other Jobs in These Pathways:** Cashiers; Counter and Rental Clerks; Door-To-Door Sales Workers, News and Street Vendors, and Related Workers; Driver/Sales Workers; Energy Brokers; First-Line Supervisors of Landscaping, Lawn Service, and Groundskeeping Workers; First-Line Supervisors of Non-Retail Sales Workers; First-Line Supervisors of Retail Sales Workers; Hotel, Motel, and Resort Desk Clerks; Landscaping and Groundskeeping Workers; Marketing Managers; Marking Clerks; Online Merchants; Order Fillers, Wholesale and Retail Sales; Parts Salespersons; Property, Real Estate, and Community Association Managers; Purchasing Agents, Except Wholesale, Retail, and Farm Products; Real Estate Sales Agents; Sales Representatives, Services, All Other; Sales Representatives, Wholesale and Manufacturing, Except Technical and Scientific Products; Sales Representatives, Wholesale and Manufacturing, Technical and Scientific Products; Solar Sales Representatives and Assessors; Stock Clerks—Stockroom, Warehouse, or Storage Yard; Stock Clerks, Sales Floor; Telemarketers; others.

**Skills**—Persuasion, Negotiation, Service Orientation, Technology Design, Active Listening, Instructing.

**Work Environment:** Indoors; standing; walking and running.

# Sailors and Marine Oilers

- ❋ Annual Earnings: $36,260
- ❋ Earnings Growth Potential: Medium (38.4%)
- ❋ Growth: 11.7%
- ❋ Annual Job Openings: 1,790
- ❋ Self-Employed: 0.0%

**Considerations for Job Outlook:** Job growth is expected to stem from increasing tourism and from growth in offshore oil and gas production. Employment is also projected to increase in and around major port cities due to growing international trade. Opportunities should be excellent as the need to replace workers, particularly officers, generates many job openings.

Stand watch to look for obstructions in path of vessels; measure water depths; turn wheels on bridges; or use emergency equipment as directed by captains, mates, or pilots. Break out, rig, overhaul, and store cargo-handling gear, stationary rigging, and running gear. Perform a variety of maintenance tasks to preserve the painted surface of ships and to maintain line and ship equipment. Must hold government-issued certification and tankerman certification when working aboard liquid-carrying vessels. Provide engineers with assistance in repairing and adjusting machinery. Attach hoses and operate pumps to transfer substances to and from liquid cargo tanks. Give directions to crew members engaged in cleaning wheelhouses and quarterdecks. Load or unload materials from vessels. Lower and man lifeboats when emergencies occur. Participate in shore patrols. Read pressure and temperature gauges or displays and record data in engineering logs. Record in ships' logs data such as weather conditions and distances traveled. Stand by wheels when ships are on automatic pilot and verify accuracy of courses, using magnetic compasses. Steer ships under the direction of commanders or navigating officers or direct helmsmen to steer, following designated courses. Chip and clean rust spots on decks, superstructures, and sides of ships, using wire brushes and hand or air chipping machines. Relay specified signals to other ships, using visual signaling devices such as blinker lights and semaphores. Splice and repair ropes, wire cables, and cordage, using marlinespikes, wirecutters, twine, and hand tools. Paint or varnish decks, superstructures, lifeboats, or sides of ships. Overhaul lifeboats and lifeboat gear and lower or raise lifeboats with winches or falls. Operate, maintain, and repair ship equipment such as winches, cranes, derricks, and weapons systems. Measure depths of water in shallow or unfamiliar waters, using leadlines, and telephone or shout depth information to vessel bridges. Maintain ships' engines under direction of ships' engineering officers. Lubricate machinery, equipment, and engine parts such as gears, shafts, and bearings. Handle lines to moor vessels to wharfs, to tie up vessels to other vessels, or to rig towing lines. Examine machinery to verify specified pressures and lubricant flows. Clean and polish wood trim, brass, and other metal parts. Break out, rig, and stow cargo-handling gear, stationary rigging, and running gear.

**Education/Training Required:** Short-term on-the-job training. **Education and Training Program:** Marine Transportation Services, Other. **Knowledge/Courses**—Mechanical, Transportation, Public Safety and Security, Engineering and Technology, Geography, Production and Processing.

**Personality Type:** Realistic-Conventional. **Career Cluster:** 16 Transportation, Distribution, and Logistics. **Career**

**Pathway:** 16.1 Transportation Operations. **Other Jobs in This Pathway:** Airline Pilots, Copilots, and Flight Engineers; Automotive and Watercraft Service Attendants; Automotive Master Mechanics; Bus Drivers, School or Special Client; Bus Drivers, Transit and Intercity; Commercial Pilots; Crane and Tower Operators; First-Line Supervisors of Helpers, Laborers, and Material Movers, Hand; First-Line Supervisors of Transportation and Material-Moving Machine and Vehicle Operators; Freight and Cargo Inspectors; Heavy and Tractor-Trailer Truck Drivers; Laborers and Freight, Stock, and Material Movers, Hand; Light Truck or Delivery Services Drivers; Mates—Ship, Boat, and Barge; Motor Vehicle Operators, All Other; Operating Engineers and Other Construction Equipment Operators; Parking Lot Attendants; Pilots, Ship; Railroad Conductors and Yardmasters; Ship and Boat Captains; Storage and Distribution Managers; Taxi Drivers and Chauffeurs; Transportation Inspectors; Transportation Managers; Transportation Workers, All Other; others.

**Skills**—Repairing, Equipment Maintenance, Operation and Control, Troubleshooting, Equipment Selection, Operation Monitoring, Quality Control Analysis, Technology Design.

**Work Environment:** More often outdoors than indoors; standing; walking and running; balancing; using hands; bending or twisting the body; noise; very hot or cold; bright or inadequate lighting; contaminants; cramped work space; whole-body vibration; high places; hazardous conditions; hazardous equipment.

# Sales Engineers

- ❀ Annual Earnings: $87,390
- ❀ Earnings Growth Potential: Medium (40.6%)
- ❀ Growth: 8.8%
- ❀ Annual Job Openings: 3,500
- ❀ Self-Employed: 0.0%

**Considerations for Job Outlook:** Projected job growth will stem from the increasing variety and technical nature of goods and services to be sold. Competition is expected. Prospects should be best for job seekers with excellent interpersonal skills and communication, math, and science aptitude.

**Sell business goods or services, the selling of which requires a technical background equivalent to a baccalaureate degree in engineering.** Plan and modify product configurations to meet customer needs. Confer with customers and engineers to assess equipment needs and to determine system requirements. Collaborate with sales teams to understand customer requirements, to promote the sale of company products, and to provide sales support. Secure and renew orders and arrange delivery. Develop, present, or respond to proposals for specific customer requirements, including request for proposal responses and industry-specific solutions. Sell products requiring extensive technical expertise and support for installation and use, such as material handling equipment, numerical-control machinery, and computer systems. Diagnose problems with installed equipment. Prepare and deliver technical presentations that explain products or services to customers and prospective customers. Recommend improved materials or machinery to customers, documenting how such changes will lower costs or increase production. Provide technical and non-technical support and services to clients or other staff members regarding the use, operation, and maintenance of equipment. Research and identify potential customers for products or services. Visit prospective buyers at commercial, industrial, or other establishments to show samples or catalogs and to inform them about product pricing, availability, and advantages. Create sales or service contracts for products or services. Arrange for demonstrations or trial installations of equipment. Keep informed on industry news and trends; products; services; competitors; relevant information about legacy, existing, and emerging technologies; and the latest product-line developments. Attend company training seminars to become familiar with product lines. Provide information needed for the development of custom-made machinery. Develop sales plans to introduce products in new markets. Write technical documentation for products. Identify resale opportunities and support them to achieve sales plans.

**Education/Training Required:** Bachelor's degree. **Education and Training Program:** Selling Skills and Sales Operations. **Knowledge/Courses**—Sales and Marketing, Engineering and Technology, Design, Physics, Computers and Electronics, Customer and Personal Service.

**Personality Type:** Enterprising-Realistic-Investigative. **Career Cluster:** 14 Marketing, Sales, and Service. **Career Pathway:** 14.2 Professional Sales and Marketing. **Other Jobs in This Pathway:** Cashiers; Counter and Rental Clerks; Door-To-Door Sales Workers, News and Street Vendors, and Related Workers; Driver/Sales Workers; Energy Brokers; First-Line Supervisors of Non-Retail Sales Workers; First-Line Supervisors of Retail Sales Workers; Hotel, Motel, and Resort Desk Clerks; Marketing Managers; Marking Clerks; Online Merchants; Order Fillers, Wholesale and Retail Sales; Parts Salespersons; Property, Real

Estate, and Community Association Managers; Real Estate Sales Agents; Reservation and Transportation Ticket Agents and Travel Clerks; Retail Salespersons; Sales and Related Workers, All Other; Sales Representatives, Services, All Other; Sales Representatives, Wholesale and Manufacturing, Except Technical and Scientific Products; Sales Representatives, Wholesale and Manufacturing, Technical and Scientific Products; Solar Sales Representatives and Assessors; Stock Clerks—Stockroom, Warehouse, or Storage Yard; Stock Clerks, Sales Floor; Telemarketers; others.

**Skills**—Technology Design, Persuasion, Negotiation, Systems Evaluation, Systems Analysis, Troubleshooting, Active Learning, Judgment and Decision Making.

**Work Environment:** Indoors; sitting; repetitive motions.

# Sales Managers

* Annual Earnings: $98,530
* Earnings Growth Potential: High (49.3%)
* Growth: 14.9%
* Annual Job Openings: 12,660
* Self-Employed: 4.2%

**Considerations for Job Outlook:** Job growth is expected to result from companies' need to distinguish their products and services in an increasingly competitive marketplace. Keen competition is expected.

**Direct the actual distribution or movement of products or services to customers. Coordinate sales distribution by establishing sales territories, quotas, and goals, and establish training programs for sales representatives. Analyze sales statistics gathered by staff to determine sales potential and inventory requirements and monitor customer preferences.** Resolve customer complaints regarding sales and service. Oversee regional and local sales managers and their staffs. Plan and direct staffing, training, and performance evaluations to develop and control sales and service programs. Determine price schedules and discount rates. Review operational records and reports to project sales and determine profitability. Monitor customer preferences to determine focus of sales efforts. Prepare budgets and approve budget expenditures. Confer or consult with department heads to plan advertising services and to secure information on equipment and customer specifications. Direct and coordinate activities involving sales of manufactured products, services, commodities, real estate, or other subjects of sale. Confer with potential customers regarding equipment needs and advise customers on types of equipment to purchase. Direct foreign sales and service outlets of an organization. Advise dealers and distributors on policies and operating procedures to ensure functional effectiveness of businesses. Visit franchised dealers to stimulate interest in establishment or expansion of leasing programs. Direct clerical staff to keep records of export correspondence, bid requests, and credit collections and to maintain current information on tariffs, licenses, and restrictions. Direct, coordinate, and review activities in sales and service accounting and recordkeeping and in receiving and shipping operations. Assess marketing potential of new and existing store locations, considering statistics and expenditures. Represent company at trade association meetings to promote products.

**Education/Training Required:** Work experience plus degree. **Education and Training Programs:** Business Administration and Management, General; Business/Commerce, General; Consumer Merchandising/Retailing Management; Marketing, Other; Marketing/Marketing Management, General. **Knowledge/Courses**—Sales and Marketing, Personnel and Human Resources, Economics and Accounting, Administration and Management, Customer and Personal Service, Psychology.

**Personality Type:** Enterprising-Conventional. **Career Clusters:** 04 Business, Management, and Administration; 10 Human Services; 14 Marketing, Sales, and Service. **Career Pathways:** 4.1 Management; 10.5 Consumer Services Career; 14.1 Management and Entrepreneurship; 14.4 Marketing Communications and Promotion. **Other Jobs in These Pathways:** Brownfield Redevelopment Specialists and Site Managers; Business Continuity Planners; Business Operations Specialists, All Other; Chief Executives; Chief Sustainability Officers; Compliance Managers; Computer and Information Systems Managers; Construction Managers; Customs Brokers; Energy Auditors; First-Line Supervisors of Office and Administrative Support Workers; First-Line Supervisors of Retail Sales Workers; General and Operations Managers; Investment Fund Managers; Loss Prevention Managers; Management Analysts; Managers, All Other; Public Relations Specialists; Regulatory Affairs Managers; Security Management Specialists; Security Managers; Supply Chain Managers; Sustainability Specialists; Wind Energy Operations Managers; Wind Energy Project Managers; others.

**Skills**—Management of Financial Resources, Management of Personnel Resources, Management of Material Resources, Systems Evaluation, Persuasion, Monitoring, Negotiation, Systems Analysis.

**Work Environment:** Indoors; sitting.

# Sales Representatives, Services, All Other

- ❈ Annual Earnings: $50,620
- ❈ Earnings Growth Potential: High (49.2%)
- ❈ Growth: 13.9%
- ❈ Annual Job Openings: 22,810
- ❈ Self-Employed: 3.7%

**Considerations for Job Outlook:** Faster-than-average employment growth is projected.

**This occupation includes all services sales representatives not listed separately.** Because this is a highly diverse occupation, no data is available for some information topics.

**Education/Training Required:** Work experience in a related occupation. **Education and Training Program:** Selling Skills and Sales Operations.

**Career Cluster:** 14 Marketing, Sales, and Service. **Career Pathway:** 14.2 Professional Sales and Marketing. **Other Jobs in This Pathway:** Cashiers; Counter and Rental Clerks; Door-To-Door Sales Workers, News and Street Vendors, and Related Workers; Driver/Sales Workers; Energy Brokers; First-Line Supervisors of Non-Retail Sales Workers; First-Line Supervisors of Retail Sales Workers; Hotel, Motel, and Resort Desk Clerks; Marketing Managers; Marking Clerks; Online Merchants; Order Fillers, Wholesale and Retail Sales; Parts Salespersons; Property, Real Estate, and Community Association Managers; Real Estate Sales Agents; Reservation and Transportation Ticket Agents and Travel Clerks; Retail Salespersons; Sales and Related Workers, All Other; Sales Representatives, Wholesale and Manufacturing, Except Technical and Scientific Products; Sales Representatives, Wholesale and Manufacturing, Technical and Scientific Products; Solar Sales Representatives and Assessors; Stock Clerks—Stockroom, Warehouse, or Storage Yard; Stock Clerks, Sales Floor; Telemarketers; Wholesale and Retail Buyers, Except Farm Products; others.

## Job Specialization: Energy Brokers

**Purchase or sell energy for customers.** Purchase or sell energy or energy derivatives for customers. Contact prospective buyers or sellers of power to arrange transactions. Create product packages based on assessment of customers' or potential customers' needs. Educate customers and answer customer questions related to the buying or selling of energy, energy markets, or alternative energy sources. Explain contracts and related documents to customers. Forecast energy supply and demand to minimize the cost of meeting load demands and to maximize the value of supply resources. Negotiate prices and contracts for energy sales or purchases. Price energy based on market conditions. Analyze customer bills and utility rate structures to select optimal rate structures for customers. Develop and deliver proposals or presentations on topics such as the purchase and sale of energy. Facilitate the delivery or receipt of wholesale power or retail load scheduling. Monitor the flow of energy in response to changes in consumer demand.

**Education/Training Required:** Work experience in a related occupation. **Education and Training Program:** Specialized Merchandising, Sales, and Marketing Operations, Other. **Knowledge/Courses**—No data available.

**Personality Type:** Enterprising-Conventional. **Career Cluster:** 14 Marketing, Sales, and Service. **Career Pathway:** 14.2 Professional Sales and Marketing. **Other Jobs in This Pathway:** Cashiers; Counter and Rental Clerks; Door-To-Door Sales Workers, News and Street Vendors, and Related Workers; Driver/Sales Workers; First-Line Supervisors of Non-Retail Sales Workers; First-Line Supervisors of Retail Sales Workers; Hotel, Motel, and Resort Desk Clerks; Marketing Managers; Marking Clerks; Online Merchants; Order Fillers, Wholesale and Retail Sales; Parts Salespersons; Property, Real Estate, and Community Association Managers; Real Estate Sales Agents; Reservation and Transportation Ticket Agents and Travel Clerks; Retail Salespersons; Sales and Related Workers, All Other; Sales Representatives, Services, All Other; Sales Representatives, Wholesale and Manufacturing, Except Technical and Scientific Products; Sales Representatives, Wholesale and Manufacturing, Technical and Scientific Products; Solar Sales Representatives and Assessors; Stock Clerks—Stockroom, Warehouse, or Storage Yard; Stock Clerks, Sales Floor; Telemarketers; Wholesale and Retail Buyers, Except Farm Products; others.

**Skills**—No data available.

**Work Environment:** No data available.

# Sales Representatives, Wholesale and Manufacturing, Except Technical and Scientific Products

- ❀ Annual Earnings: $52,440
- ❀ Earnings Growth Potential: High (48.6%)
- ❀ Growth: 6.6%
- ❀ Annual Job Openings: 45,790
- ❀ Self-Employed: 3.7%

**Considerations for Job Outlook:** Continued expansion in the variety and number of goods sold is expected to lead to additional jobs for these workers. Prospects should be best for job seekers with a college degree, technical expertise, and interpersonal skills.

**Sell goods for wholesalers or manufacturers to businesses or groups of individuals. Work requires substantial knowledge of items sold.** Answer customers' questions about products, prices, availability, product uses, and credit terms. Recommend products to customers based on customers' needs and interests. Contact regular and prospective customers to demonstrate products, explain product features, and solicit orders. Estimate or quote prices, credit or contract terms, warranties, and delivery dates. Consult with clients after sales or contract signings to resolve problems and to provide ongoing support. Prepare drawings, estimates, and bids that meet specific customer needs. Provide customers with product samples and catalogs. Identify prospective customers by using business directories, following leads from existing clients, participating in organizations and clubs, and attending trade shows and conferences. Arrange and direct delivery and installation of products and equipment. Monitor market conditions; product innovations; and competitors' products, prices, and sales. Negotiate details of contracts and payments and prepare sales contracts and order forms. Perform administrative duties, such as preparing sales budgets and reports, keeping sales records, and filing expense account reports. Obtain credit information about prospective customers. Forward orders to manufacturers. Check stock levels and reorder merchandise as necessary. Plan, assemble, and stock product displays in retail stores or make recommendations to retailers regarding product displays, promotional programs, and advertising. Negotiate with retail merchants to improve product exposure such as shelf positioning and advertising. Train customers' employees to operate and maintain new equipment. Buy products from manufacturers or brokerage firms and distribute them to wholesale and retail clients.

**Education/Training Required:** Work experience in a related occupation. **Education and Training Programs:** Apparel and Accessories Marketing Operations; Business, Management, Marketing, and Related Support Services, Other; Fashion Merchandising; General Merchandising, Sales, and Related Marketing Operations, Other; Insurance; Sales, Distribution, and Marketing Operations, General; Special Products Marketing Operations; Specialized Merchandising, Sales, and Marketing Operations, Other. **Knowledge/Courses**—Sales and Marketing, Economics and Accounting, Customer and Personal Service, Transportation, Mathematics, Production and Processing.

**Personality Type:** Conventional-Enterprising. **Career Cluster:** 14 Marketing, Sales, and Service. **Career Pathways:** 14.2 Professional Sales and Marketing; 14.3 Buying and Merchandising. **Other Jobs in These Pathways:** Cashiers; Counter and Rental Clerks; Door-To-Door Sales Workers, News and Street Vendors, and Related Workers; Driver/Sales Workers; Energy Brokers; First-Line Supervisors of Non-Retail Sales Workers; First-Line Supervisors of Retail Sales Workers; Hotel, Motel, and Resort Desk Clerks; Marketing Managers; Marking Clerks; Online Merchants; Order Fillers, Wholesale and Retail Sales; Parts Salespersons; Property, Real Estate, and Community Association Managers; Purchasing Agents, Except Wholesale, Retail, and Farm Products; Real Estate Sales Agents; Reservation and Transportation Ticket Agents and Travel Clerks; Retail Salespersons; Sales and Related Workers, All Other; Sales Representatives, Services, All Other; Sales Representatives, Wholesale and Manufacturing, Technical and Scientific Products; Solar Sales Representatives and Assessors; Stock Clerks—Stockroom, Warehouse, or Storage Yard; Stock Clerks, Sales Floor; Telemarketers; others.

**Skills**—Negotiation, Persuasion, Service Orientation, Critical Thinking, Operations Analysis, Social Perceptiveness, Active Listening, Speaking.

**Work Environment:** Outdoors; more often sitting than standing; walking and running; noise; contaminants.

## Sales Representatives, Wholesale and Manufacturing, Technical and Scientific Products

* Annual Earnings: $73,710
* Earnings Growth Potential: High (50.2%)
* Growth: 9.7%
* Annual Job Openings: 14,230
* Self-Employed: 3.6%

**Considerations for Job Outlook:** Continued expansion in the variety and number of goods sold is expected to lead to additional jobs for these workers. Prospects should be best for job seekers with a college degree, technical expertise, and interpersonal skills.

**Sell goods for wholesalers or manufacturers where technical or scientific knowledge is required in such areas as biology, engineering, chemistry, and electronics that is normally obtained from at least two years of postsecondary education.** Contact new and existing customers to discuss their needs and to explain how these needs could be met by specific products and services. Answer customers' questions about products, prices, availability, product uses, and credit terms. Quote prices, credit terms, and other bid specifications. Emphasize product features based on analyses of customers' needs and on technical knowledge of product capabilities and limitations. Negotiate prices and terms of sales and service agreements. Maintain customer records, using automated systems. Identify prospective customers by using business directories, following leads from existing clients, participating in organizations and clubs, and attending trade shows and conferences. Prepare sales contracts for orders obtained and submit orders for processing. Select the correct products or assist customers in making product selections based on customers' needs, product specifications, and applicable regulations. Collaborate with colleagues to exchange information such as selling strategies and marketing information. Prepare sales presentations and proposals that explain product specifications and applications. Provide customers with ongoing technical support. Demonstrate and explain the operation and use of products. Inform customers of estimated delivery schedules, service contracts, warranties, or other information pertaining to purchased products. Attend sales and trade meetings and read related publications in order to obtain information about market conditions, business trends, and industry developments. Visit establishments to evaluate needs and to promote product or service sales. Complete expense reports, sales reports, and other paperwork. Initiate sales campaigns and follow marketing plan guidelines in order to meet sales and production expectations. Recommend ways for customers to alter product usage in order to improve production. Complete product and development training as required.

**Education/Training Required:** Work experience in a related occupation. **Education and Training Programs:** Business, Management, Marketing, and Related Support Services, Other; Selling Skills and Sales Operations. **Knowledge/Courses**—Sales and Marketing, Customer and Personal Service, Production and Processing, Administration and Management, Transportation, Computers and Electronics.

**Personality Type:** Enterprising-Conventional. **Career Cluster:** 14 Marketing, Sales, and Service. **Career Pathway:** 14.2 Professional Sales and Marketing. **Other Jobs in This Pathway:** Cashiers; Counter and Rental Clerks; Door-To-Door Sales Workers, News and Street Vendors, and Related Workers; Driver/Sales Workers; Energy Brokers; First-Line Supervisors of Non-Retail Sales Workers; First-Line Supervisors of Retail Sales Workers; Hotel, Motel, and Resort Desk Clerks; Marketing Managers; Marking Clerks; Online Merchants;

Order Fillers, Wholesale and Retail Sales; Parts Salespersons; Property, Real Estate, and Community Association Managers; Real Estate Sales Agents; Reservation and Transportation Ticket Agents and Travel Clerks; Retail Salespersons; Sales and Related Workers, All Other; Sales Representatives, Services, All Other; Sales Representatives, Wholesale and Manufacturing, Except Technical and Scientific Products; Solar Sales Representatives and Assessors; Stock Clerks—Stockroom, Warehouse, or Storage Yard; Stock Clerks, Sales Floor; Telemarketers; Wholesale and Retail Buyers, Except Farm Products; others.

**Skills**—Persuasion, Negotiation, Management of Financial Resources, Management of Material Resources, Active Listening, Speaking, Reading Comprehension, Instructing.

**Work Environment:** Indoors; sitting.

## Job Specialization: Solar Sales Representatives and Assessors

**Contact new or existing customers to determine their solar equipment needs, suggest systems or equipment, or estimate costs.** Generate solar energy customer leads to develop new accounts. Prepare proposals, quotes, contracts, or presentations for potential solar customers. Select solar energy products, systems, or services for customers based on electrical energy requirements, site conditions, price, or other factors. Assess sites to determine suitability for solar equipment, using equipment such as tape measures, compasses, and computer software. Calculate potential solar resources or solar array production for a particular site considering issues such as climate, shading, and roof orientation. Create customized energy management packages to satisfy customer needs. Develop marketing or strategic plans for sales territories. Gather information from prospective customers to identify their solar energy needs. Prepare or review detailed design drawings, specifications, or lists related to solar installations. Provide customers with information such as quotes, orders, sales, shipping, warranties, credit, funding options, incentives, or tax rebates. Provide technical information about solar power, solar systems, equipment, and services to potential customers or dealers. Take quote requests or orders from dealers or customers. Demonstrate use of solar and related equipment to customers or dealers.

**Education/Training Required:** Work experience in a related occupation. **Education and Training Programs:** Business, Management, Marketing, and Related Support Services, Other; Selling Skills and Sales Operations. **Knowledge/Courses**—No data available.

**Personality Type:** No data available. **Career Cluster:** 14 Marketing, Sales, and Service. **Career Pathway:** 14.2 Professional Sales and Marketing. **Other Jobs in This Pathway:** Cashiers; Counter and Rental Clerks; Door-To-Door Sales Workers, News and Street Vendors, and Related Workers; Driver/Sales Workers; Energy Brokers; First-Line Supervisors of Non-Retail Sales Workers; First-Line Supervisors of Retail Sales Workers; Hotel, Motel, and Resort Desk Clerks; Marketing Managers; Marking Clerks; Online Merchants; Order Fillers, Wholesale and Retail Sales; Parts Salespersons; Property, Real Estate, and Community Association Managers; Real Estate Sales Agents; Reservation and Transportation Ticket Agents and Travel Clerks; Retail Salespersons; Sales and Related Workers, All Other; Sales Representatives, Services, All Other; Sales Representatives, Wholesale and Manufacturing, Except Technical and Scientific Products; Sales Representatives, Wholesale and Manufacturing, Technical and Scientific Products; Stock Clerks—Stockroom, Warehouse, or Storage Yard; Stock Clerks, Sales Floor; Telemarketers; Wholesale and Retail Buyers, Except Farm Products; others.

**Skills**—No data available.

**Work Environment:** No data available.

## Secondary School Teachers, Except Special and Career/Technical Education

- ❋ Annual Earnings: $53,230
- ❋ Earnings Growth Potential: Low (34.2%)
- ❋ Growth: 8.9%
- ❋ Annual Job Openings: 41,240
- ❋ Self-Employed: 0.0%

**Considerations for Job Outlook:** Enrollment from 2008–2018 is expected to grow more slowly than in recent years. Prospects are usually better in urban and rural areas, for bilingual teachers, and for math and science teachers.

**Instruct students in secondary public or private schools in one or more subjects at the secondary level, such as English, mathematics, or social studies. May be designated according to subject matter specialty, such as typing instructors, commercial teachers, or English teachers.** Establish and enforce rules for behavior and procedures for maintaining order among the students for whom they are responsible. Instruct through lectures, discussions, and demonstrations in one or more subjects such as English, mathematics, or social studies. Establish clear objectives for all lessons, units, and projects and communicate those objectives to students. Prepare, administer, and grade tests and assignments to evaluate students' progress. Prepare materials and classrooms for class activities. Adapt teaching methods and instructional materials to meet students' varying needs and interests. Assign and grade classwork and homework. Maintain accurate and complete student records as required by laws, district policies, and administrative regulations. Enforce all administration policies and rules governing students. Observe and evaluate students' performance, behavior, social development, and physical health. Plan and conduct activities for a balanced program of instruction, demonstration, and work time that provides students with opportunities to observe, question, and investigate. Prepare students for later grades by encouraging them to explore learning opportunities and to persevere with challenging tasks. Guide and counsel students with adjustment and/or academic problems or special academic interests. Instruct and monitor students in the use and care of equipment and materials to prevent injuries and damage. Prepare for assigned classes and show written evidence of preparation upon request of immediate supervisors. Meet with parents and guardians to discuss their children's progress and to determine their priorities for their children and their resource needs. Confer with parents or guardians, other teachers, counselors, and administrators in order to resolve students' behavioral and academic problems. Use computers, audiovisual aids, and other equipment and materials to supplement presentations.

**Education/Training Required:** Bachelor's degree. **Education and Training Programs:** Agricultural Teacher Education; Art Teacher Education; Biology Teacher Education; Business Teacher Education; Chemistry Teacher Education; Computer Teacher Education; Drama and Dance Teacher Education; Driver and Safety Teacher Education; English/Language Arts Teacher Education; Family and Consumer Sciences/Home Economics Teacher Education; Foreign Language Teacher Education; French Language Teacher Education; Geography Teacher Education; German Language Teacher Education; Health Occupations Teacher Education; Health Teacher Education; History Teacher Education; Junior High/Intermediate/Middle School Education and Teaching; Latin Teacher Education; Mathematics Teacher Education; Music Teacher Education; Physical Education Teaching and Coaching; Physics Teacher Education; Reading Teacher Education; Sales and Marketing Operations/Marketing and Distribution Teacher Education; Science Teacher Education; Secondary Education and

Teaching; Social Science Teacher Education; Social Studies Teacher Education; Spanish Language Teacher Education; Speech Teacher Education; Teacher Education, Multiple Levels; Technology Teacher Education/Industrial Arts Teacher Education; others. **Knowledge/Courses—** History and Archeology, Philosophy and Theology, Sociology and Anthropology, Fine Arts, Education and Training, Therapy and Counseling.

**Personality Type:** Social-Artistic-Enterprising. **Career Cluster:** 05 Education and Training. **Career Pathway:** 5.3 Teaching/Training. **Other Jobs in This Pathway:** Adult Basic and Secondary Education and Literacy Teachers and Instructors; Athletes and Sports Competitors; Audio-Visual and Multimedia Collections Specialists; Career/Technical Education Teachers, Middle School; Career/Technical Education Teachers, Secondary School; Chemists; Coaches and Scouts; Dietitians and Nutritionists; Elementary School Teachers, Except Special Education; Fitness Trainers and Aerobics Instructors; Historians; Instructional Coordinators; Instructional Designers and Technologists; Interpreters and Translators; Kindergarten Teachers, Except Special Education; Librarians; Middle School Teachers, Except Special and Career/Technical Education; Physicists; Preschool Teachers, Except Special Education; Recreation Workers; Self-Enrichment Education Teachers; Teacher Assistants; Teachers and Instructors, All Other; Tutors.

**Skills—**Learning Strategies, Systems Evaluation, Instructing, Social Perceptiveness, Service Orientation, Writing, Speaking, Judgment and Decision Making.

**Work Environment:** Indoors; standing.

# Secretaries and Administrative Assistants, Except Legal, Medical, and Executive

- ❋ Annual Earnings: $30,830
- ❋ Earnings Growth Potential: Medium (36.1%)
- ❋ Growth: 4.6%
- ❋ Annual Job Openings: 36,550
- ❋ Self-Employed: 1.3%

**Considerations for Job Outlook:** Projected employment growth varies by occupational specialty. Faster-than-average growth is expected for medical secretaries and legal secretaries; average growth for executive secretaries and administrative assistants; and slower-than-average growth for secretaries other than legal, medical, or executive, who account for most of the workers in these specialties. Many opportunities are expected.

**Perform routine clerical and administrative functions such as drafting correspondence, scheduling appointments, organizing and maintaining paper and electronic files, or providing information to callers.** Operate office equipment such as fax machines, copiers, and phone systems and use computers for spreadsheet, word-processing, database management, and other applications. Answer telephones and give information to callers, take messages, or transfer calls to appropriate individuals. Greet visitors and callers, handle their inquiries, and direct them to the appropriate persons according to their needs. Set up and maintain paper and electronic filing systems for records, correspondence, and other material. Locate and attach appropriate files to incoming correspondence requiring replies. Open, read, route, and distribute incoming mail and other material and prepare answers to routine letters. Complete forms in accordance with company procedures. Make copies of correspondence and other printed material. Review work done by others to check for correct spelling and grammar, ensure that company format policies are followed, and recommend revisions. Compose, type, and distribute meeting notes, routine correspondence, and reports. Learn to operate new office technologies as they are developed and implemented. Maintain scheduling and event calendars. Schedule and confirm appointments for clients, customers, or supervisors. Manage projects and contribute to committee and team work. Mail newsletters, promotional material, and other information. Order and dispense supplies. Conduct searches to find needed information, using such sources as the Internet. Provide services to customers, such as order placement and account information. Collect and disburse funds from cash accounts and keep records of collections and disbursements. Prepare and mail checks. Establish work procedures and schedules and keep track of the daily work of clerical staff. Coordinate conferences and meetings. Take dictation in shorthand or by machine and transcribe information. Arrange conferences, meetings, and travel reservations for office personnel.

**Education/Training Required:** Moderate-term on-the-job training. **Education and Training Programs:** Administrative Assistant and Secretarial Science, General; Executive Assistant/Executive Secretary Training. **Knowledge/Courses**—Clerical, Customer and Personal Service, Economics and Accounting, Computers and Electronics, English Language, Personnel and Human Resources.

**Personality Type:** Conventional-Enterprising. **Career Cluster:** 04 Business, Management, and Administration. **Career Pathway:** 4.6 Administrative and Information Support. **Other Jobs in This Pathway:** Couriers and Messengers; Court Clerks; Court, Municipal, and License Clerks; Customer Service Representatives; Data Entry Keyers; Dispatchers, Except Police, Fire, and Ambulance; Executive Secretaries and Executive Administrative Assistants; File Clerks; Human Resources Assistants, Except Payroll and Timekeeping; Information and Record Clerks, All Other; Insurance Claims Clerks; Insurance Policy Processing Clerks; Interviewers, Except Eligibility and Loan; License Clerks; Mail Clerks and Mail Machine Operators, Except Postal Service; Office and Administrative Support Workers, All Other; Office Clerks, General; Order Clerks; Patient Representatives; Postal Service Mail Carriers; Postal Service Mail Sorters, Processors, and Processing Machine Operators; Receptionists and Information Clerks; Shipping, Receiving, and Traffic Clerks; Switchboard Operators, Including Answering Service; Word Processors and Typists; others.

**Skills**—Service Orientation, Management of Financial Resources, Writing, Time Management, Management of Material Resources, Active Listening, Reading Comprehension, Speaking.

**Work Environment:** Indoors; sitting; repetitive motions.

# Securities, Commodities, and Financial Services Sales Agents

- ✸ Annual Earnings: $70,190
- ✸ Earnings Growth Potential: Very high (55.4%)
- ✸ Growth: 9.3%
- ✸ Annual Job Openings: 12,680
- ✸ Self-Employed: 15.4%

**Considerations for Job Outlook:** Consolidation of the financial industry is expected to inhibit employment growth. Individuals' ability to manage their own investments online is likely to reduce the need for brokers. Job competition should be keen.

**Buy and sell securities in investment and trading firms or call upon businesses and individuals to sell financial services. Provide financial services, such as loan, tax, and securities counseling. May advise securities customers about such things as stocks, bonds, and market conditions.** No task data available.

**Education/Training Required:** Bachelor's degree. **Education and Training Programs:** Business and Personal/Financial Services Marketing Operations; Financial Planning and Services; Investments and Securities. **Knowledge/Courses**—No data available.

**Personality Type:** No data available. **Career Cluster:** 06 Finance. **Career Pathway:** 6.1 Financial and Investment Planning. **Other Jobs in This Pathway:** Budget Analysts; Credit Analysts; Financial Analysts; Financial Managers, Branch or Department; Financial Quantitative Analysts; Financial Specialists, All Other; Fraud Examiners, Investigators and Analysts; Investment Underwriters; Loan Counselors; Personal Financial Advisors; Risk Management Specialists; Sales Agents, Financial Services; Sales Agents, Securities and Commodities; Securities and Commodities Traders; Treasurers and Controllers.

**Skills**—No data available.

**Work Environment:** No data available.

## Job Specialization: Sales Agents, Securities and Commodities

**Buy and sell securities in investment and trading firms and develop and implement financial plans for individuals, businesses, and organizations.** Complete sales order tickets and submit for processing of client requested transactions. Interview clients to determine clients' assets, liabilities, cash flow, insurance coverage, tax status, and financial objectives. Record transactions accurately and keep clients informed about transactions. Develop financial plans based on analysis of clients' financial status and discuss financial options with clients. Review all securities transactions to ensure accuracy of information and ensure that trades conform to regulations of governing agencies. Offer advice on the purchase or sale of particular securities. Relay buy or sell orders to securities exchanges or to firm trading departments. Identify potential clients, using advertising campaigns, mailing lists, and personal contacts. Review financial periodicals, stock and bond reports, business publications, and other material to identify potential investments for clients and to keep abreast of trends affecting market conditions. Contact prospective customers to determine customer needs, present information, and explain available services. Prepare documents needed to implement plans selected by clients. Analyze market conditions to determine optimum times to execute securities transactions. Explain stock market terms and trading practices to clients. Inform and advise concerned parties regarding fluctuations and securities transactions affecting plans or accounts. Calculate costs for

billings and commissions purposes. Supply the latest price quotes on any security, as well as information on the activities and financial positions of the corporations issuing these securities. Prepare financial reports to monitor client or corporate finances. Read corporate reports and calculate ratios to determine best prospects for profit on stock purchases and to monitor client accounts.

**Education/Training Required:** Bachelor's degree. **Education and Training Programs:** Business and Personal/Financial Services Marketing Operations; Financial Planning and Services; Investments and Securities. **Knowledge/Courses**—Economics and Accounting, Customer and Personal Service, Sales and Marketing, Clerical, Law and Government, Mathematics.

**Personality Type:** Enterprising-Conventional. **Career Cluster:** 06 Finance. **Career Pathway:** 6.1 Financial and Investment Planning. **Other Jobs in This Pathway:** Budget Analysts; Credit Analysts; Financial Analysts; Financial Managers, Branch or Department; Financial Quantitative Analysts; Financial Specialists, All Other; Fraud Examiners, Investigators and Analysts; Investment Underwriters; Loan Counselors; Personal Financial Advisors; Risk Management Specialists; Sales Agents, Financial Services; Securities and Commodities Traders; Securities, Commodities, and Financial Services Sales Agents; Treasurers and Controllers.

**Skills**—Systems Analysis, Persuasion, Systems Evaluation, Management of Financial Resources, Reading Comprehension, Judgment and Decision Making, Service Orientation, Negotiation.

**Work Environment:** Indoors; sitting.

## Job Specialization: Sales Agents, Financial Services

**Sell financial services such as loan, tax, and securities counseling to customers of financial institutions and business establishments.** Determine customers' financial services needs and prepare proposals to sell services that address these needs. Contact prospective customers to present information and explain available services. Sell services and equipment, such as trusts, investments, and check processing services. Prepare forms or agreements to complete sales. Develop prospects from current commercial customers, referral leads, and sales and trade meetings. Review business trends in order to advise customers regarding expected fluctuations. Make presentations on financial services to groups to attract new clients. Evaluate costs and revenue of agreements to determine continued profitability.

**Education/Training Required:** Bachelor's degree. **Education and Training Programs:** Business and Personal/Financial Services Marketing Operations; Financial Planning and Services; Investments and Securities. **Knowledge/Courses**—Sales and Marketing, Economics and Accounting, Customer and Personal Service, Law and Government, Mathematics, Personnel and Human Resources.

**Personality Type:** Enterprising-Conventional. **Career Cluster:** 06 Finance. **Career Pathway:** 6.1 Financial and Investment Planning. **Other Jobs in This Pathway:** Budget Analysts; Credit Analysts; Financial Analysts; Financial Managers, Branch or Department; Financial Quantitative Analysts; Financial Specialists, All Other; Fraud Examiners, Investigators and Analysts; Investment Underwriters; Loan Counselors; Personal Financial Advisors; Risk Management Specialists; Sales Agents, Securities and Commodities; Securities and Commodities Traders; Securities, Commodities, and Financial Services Sales Agents; Treasurers and Controllers.

**Skills**—Persuasion, Systems Evaluation, Mathematics, Negotiation, Service Orientation, Active Learning, Systems Analysis, Speaking.

**Work Environment:** Indoors; sitting.

## Job Specialization: Securities and Commodities Traders

**Buy and sell securities and commodities to transfer debt, capital, or risk. Establish and negotiate unit prices and terms of sale.** Buy or sell stocks, bonds, commodity futures, foreign currencies, or other securities at stock exchanges on behalf of investment dealers. Agree on buying or selling prices at optimal levels for clients. Make bids and offers to buy or sell securities. Analyze target companies and investment opportunities to inform investment decisions. Develop and maintain supplier and customer relationships. Devise trading, option, and hedge strategies. Identify opportunities and develop channels for purchase or sale of securities or commodities. Inform other traders, managers, or customers of market conditions, including volume, price, competition, and dynamics. Monitor markets and positions. Process paperwork for special orders, including margin and option purchases. Receive sales order tickets and inspect forms to determine accuracy of information. Report all positions or trading results. Review securities transactions to ensure conformance to regulations. Track and analyze factors that affect price movement, such as trade policies, weather conditions, political developments, and supply-and-demand

changes. Write and sign sales order confirmation forms to record and approve security transactions. Audit accounts and correct errors. Make transportation arrangements for sold or purchased commodities. Prepare financial reports, such as reviews of portfolio positions. Reconcile account-related statements, such as quarterly and annual statements and confirmations. Report deficiencies in account payments, securities deliveries, or documentation requirements to avoid rule violations. Supervise support staff and ensure proper execution of contracts.

**Education/Training Required:** Bachelor's degree. **Education and Training Programs:** Business and Personal/Financial Services Marketing Operations; Financial Planning and Services; Investments and Securities. **Knowledge/Courses**—No data available.

**Personality Type:** Enterprising-Conventional. **Career Cluster:** 06 Finance. **Career Pathway:** 6.1 Financial and Investment Planning. **Other Jobs in This Pathway:** Budget Analysts; Credit Analysts; Financial Analysts; Financial Managers, Branch or Department; Financial Quantitative Analysts; Financial Specialists, All Other; Fraud Examiners, Investigators and Analysts; Investment Underwriters; Loan Counselors; Personal Financial Advisors; Risk Management Specialists; Sales Agents, Financial Services; Sales Agents, Securities and Commodities; Securities, Commodities, and Financial Services Sales Agents; Treasurers and Controllers.

**Skills**—No data available.

**Work Environment:** No data available.

## Security and Fire Alarm Systems Installers

- ❋ Annual Earnings: $38,500
- ❋ Earnings Growth Potential: Low (35.4%)
- ❋ Growth: 24.8%
- ❋ Annual Job Openings: 2,780
- ❋ Self-Employed: 6.3%

**Considerations for Job Outlook:** Much-faster-than-average employment growth is projected.

**Install, program, maintain, and repair security and fire alarm wiring and equipment. Ensure that work is in accordance with relevant codes.** Examine systems to locate problems such as loose connections or broken insulation. Test backup batteries, keypad programming, sirens, and all security features in order to ensure proper functioning, and to diagnose malfunctions. Mount and fasten control panels, door and window contacts, sensors, and video cameras, and attach electrical and telephone wiring in order to connect components. Install, maintain, or repair security systems, alarm devices, and related equipment, following blueprints of electrical layouts and building plans. Inspect installation sites and study work orders, building plans, and installation manuals in order to determine materials requirements and installation procedures. Feed cables through access holes, roof spaces, and cavity walls to reach fixture outlets; then position and terminate cables, wires and strapping. Adjust sensitivity of units based on room structures and manufacturers' recommendations, using programming keypads. Test and repair circuits and sensors, following wiring and system specifications. Drill holes for wiring in wall studs, joists, ceilings, and floors. Demonstrate systems for customers, and explain details such as the causes and consequences of false alarms. Consult with clients to assess risks and to determine security requirements. Keep informed of new products and developments. Mount raceways and conduits, and fasten wires to wood framing, using staplers. Prepare documents such as invoices and warranties. Provide customers with cost estimates for equipment installation. Order replacement parts.

**Education/Training Required:** Postsecondary vocational training. **Education and Training Programs:** Electrician; Security System Installation, Repair, and Inspection Technology/Technician. **Knowledge/Courses**—Telecommunications, Building and Construction, Mechanical, Computers and Electronics, Public Safety and Security, Design.

**Personality Type:** Realistic-Conventional. **Career Cluster:** 02 Architecture and Construction. **Career Pathways:** 2.2 Construction; 2.3 Maintenance/Operations. **Other Jobs in These Pathways:** Brickmasons and Blockmasons; Cement Masons and Concrete Finishers; Construction and Building Inspectors; Construction Carpenters; Construction Laborers; Construction Managers; Cost Estimators; Drywall and Ceiling Tile Installers; Electrical Power-Line Installers and Repairers; Electricians; Engineering Technicians, Except Drafters, All Other; First-Line Supervisors of Construction Trades and Extraction Workers; Heating and Air Conditioning Mechanics and Installers; Helpers—Carpenters; Helpers—Electricians; Helpers—Pipelayers, Plumbers, Pipefitters, and Steamfitters; Highway Maintenance Workers; Operating Engineers and Other Construction Equipment Operators; Painters, Construction and Maintenance; Pipe Fitters and Steamfitters; Plumbers; Refrigeration Mechanics and Installers; Roofers; Rough Carpenters; Solar Energy Installation Managers; others.

**Skills**—Installation, Repairing, Equipment Maintenance, Troubleshooting, Operation and Control, Equipment Selection, Quality Control Analysis, Operation Monitoring.

**Work Environment:** More often indoors than outdoors; standing; climbing; using hands; repetitive motions; noise; very hot or cold; bright or inadequate lighting; contaminants; cramped work space; high places.

# Security Guards

- ❋ Annual Earnings: $23,920
- ❋ Earnings Growth Potential: Low (28.4%)
- ❋ Growth: 14.2%
- ❋ Annual Job Openings: 37,390
- ❋ Self-Employed: 1.3%

**Considerations for Job Outlook:** Concern about crime, vandalism, and terrorism are expected to result in increased demand for security services. This increased demand, along with the need to replace workers leaving the occupation permanently, should result in favorable job opportunities.

**Guard, patrol, or monitor premises to prevent theft, violence, or infractions of rules.** Monitor and authorize entrance and departure of employees, visitors, and other persons to guard against theft and maintain security of premises. Write reports of daily activities and irregularities, such as equipment or property damage, theft, presence of unauthorized persons, or unusual occurrences. Call police or fire departments in cases of emergency, such as fire or presence of unauthorized persons. Answer alarms and investigate disturbances. Circulate among visitors, patrons, or employees to preserve order and protect property. Patrol industrial or commercial premises to prevent and detect signs of intrusion and ensure security of doors, windows, and gates. Escort or drive motor vehicle to transport individuals to specified locations or to provide personal protection. Operate detecting devices to screen individuals and prevent passage of prohibited articles into restricted areas. Answer telephone calls to take messages, answer questions, and provide information during nonbusiness hours or when switchboard is closed. Warn persons of rule infractions or violations and apprehend or evict violators from premises, using force when necessary. Inspect and adjust security systems, equipment, or machinery to ensure operational use and to detect evidence of tampering. Monitor and adjust controls that regulate building systems, such as air conditioning, furnace, or boiler.

**Education/Training Required:** Short-term on-the-job training. **Education and Training Programs:** Securities

Services Administration/Management; Security and Loss Prevention Services. **Knowledge/Courses**—Public Safety and Security.

**Personality Type:** Realistic-Conventional-Enterprising. **Career Cluster:** 12 Law, Public Safety, Corrections, and Security. **Career Pathways:** 12.1 Correction Services; 12.3 Security and Protective Services. **Other Jobs in These Pathways:** Animal Control Workers; Child, Family, and School Social Workers; Crossing Guards; First-Line Supervisors of Correctional Officers; First-Line Supervisors of Police and Detectives; First-Line Supervisors of Protective Service Workers, All Other; Forest Firefighters; Gaming Surveillance Officers and Gaming Investigators; Lifeguards, Ski Patrol, and Other Recreational Protective Service Workers; Parking Enforcement Workers; Police, Fire, and Ambulance Dispatchers; Private Detectives and Investigators; Protective Service Workers, All Other; Retail Loss Prevention Specialists; Sheriffs and Deputy Sheriffs; Transit and Railroad Police.

**Skills**—Operation and Control.

**Work Environment:** More often indoors than outdoors; standing; walking and running; using hands; noise; contaminants.

# Self-Enrichment Education Teachers

- ❋ Annual Earnings: $36,340
- ❋ Earnings Growth Potential: High (48.3%)
- ❋ Growth: 32.0%
- ❋ Annual Job Openings: 12,030
- ❋ Self-Employed: 17.3%

**Considerations for Job Outlook:** Demand for self-enrichment education will increase as more people embrace lifelong learning or seek to acquire or improve skills that make them more attractive to prospective employers. Opportunities should be favorable.

**Teach or instruct courses other than those that normally lead to an occupational objective or degree. Courses may include self-improvement, nonvocational, and nonacademic subjects. Teaching may or may not take place in a traditional educational institution.** Adapt teaching methods and instructional materials to meet students' varying needs and interests. Conduct classes, workshops, and demonstrations and provide individual instruction to teach topics and skills such as cooking, dancing, writing, physical

fitness, photography, personal finance, and flying. Monitor students' performance to make suggestions for improvement and to ensure that they satisfy course standards, training requirements, and objectives. Observe students to determine qualifications, limitations, abilities, interests, and other individual characteristics. Instruct students individually and in groups, using various teaching methods such as lectures, discussions, and demonstrations. Establish clear objectives for all lessons, units, and projects and communicate those objectives to students. Instruct and monitor students in use and care of equipment and materials to prevent injury and damage. Prepare students for further development by encouraging them to explore learning opportunities and to persevere with challenging tasks. Prepare materials and classrooms for class activities. Enforce policies and rules governing students. Plan and conduct activities for a balanced program of instruction, demonstration, and work time that provides students with opportunities to observe, question, and investigate. Prepare instructional program objectives, outlines, and lesson plans. Maintain accurate and complete student records as required by administrative policy. Participate in publicity planning and student recruitment. Plan and supervise class projects, field trips, visits by guest speakers, contests, or other experiential activities and guide students in learning from those activities. Attend professional meetings, conferences, and workshops in order to maintain and improve professional competence. Meet with other instructors to discuss individual students and their progress.

**Education/Training Required:** Work experience in a related occupation. **Education and Training Program:** Adult and Continuing Education and Teaching. **Knowledge/Courses**—Fine Arts, Education and Training, Psychology, Customer and Personal Service, Sales and Marketing, Administration and Management.

**Personality Type:** Social-Artistic-Enterprising. **Career Cluster:** 05 Education and Training. **Career Pathway:** 5.3 Teaching/Training. **Other Jobs in This Pathway:** Adult Basic and Secondary Education and Literacy Teachers and Instructors; Athletes and Sports Competitors; Audio-Visual and Multimedia Collections Specialists; Career/Technical Education Teachers, Middle School; Career/Technical Education Teachers, Secondary School; Chemists; Coaches and Scouts; Dietitians and Nutritionists; Elementary School Teachers, Except Special Education; Fitness Trainers and Aerobics Instructors; Historians; Instructional Coordinators; Instructional Designers and Technologists; Interpreters and Translators; Kindergarten Teachers, Except Special Education; Librarians; Middle School Teachers, Except Special and Career/Technical Education; Physicists; Preschool Teachers, Except Special Education; Recreation Workers;

Secondary School Teachers, Except Special and Career/Technical Education; Teacher Assistants; Teachers and Instructors, All Other; Tutors.

**Skills**—Operations Analysis, Learning Strategies, Instructing, Persuasion, Active Learning, Speaking, Technology Design, Social Perceptiveness.

**Work Environment:** Indoors; standing.

# Septic Tank Servicers and Sewer Pipe Cleaners

- ❈ Annual Earnings: $33,570
- ❈ Earnings Growth Potential: Medium (36.2%)
- ❈ Growth: 23.8%
- ❈ Annual Job Openings: 1,320
- ❈ Self-Employed: 4.5%

**Considerations for Job Outlook:** Much-faster-than-average employment growth is projected.

**Clean and repair septic tanks, sewer lines, or drains. May patch walls and partitions of tank, replace damaged drain tile, or repair breaks in underground piping.** Drive trucks to transport crews, materials, and equipment. Communicate with supervisors and other workers, using equipment such as wireless phones, pagers, or radio telephones. Prepare and keep records of actions taken, including maintenance and repair work. Operate sewer cleaning equipment, including power rodders, high velocity water jets, sewer flushers, bucket machines, wayne balls, and vac-alls. Ensure that repaired sewer line joints are tightly sealed before backfilling begins. Withdraw cables from pipes and examine them for evidence of mud, roots, grease, and other deposits indicating broken or clogged sewer lines. Install rotary knives on flexible cables mounted on machine reels according to the diameters of pipes to be cleaned. Measure excavation sites, using plumbers' snakes, tapelines, or lengths of cutting heads within sewers, and mark areas for digging. Locate problems, using specially designed equipment, and mark where digging must occur to reach damaged tanks or pipes. Start machines to feed revolving cables or rods into openings, stopping machines and changing knives to conform to pipe sizes. Clean and repair septic tanks; sewer lines; or related structures such as manholes, culverts, and catch basins. Service, adjust, and make minor repairs to equipment, machines, and attachments. Inspect manholes to locate sewer line stoppages. Cut damaged sections of pipe with cutters; remove broken sections from ditches; and replace pipe sections, using pipe sleeves. Dig out sewer lines manually, using shovels. Break asphalt and other pavement so that pipes can be accessed, using airhammers, picks, and shovels. Cover repaired pipes with dirt and pack backfilled excavations, using air and gasoline tampers. Requisition or order tools and equipment. Rotate cleaning rods manually, using turning pins. Clean and disinfect domestic basements and other areas flooded by sewer stoppages. Tap mainline sewers to install sewer saddles. Update sewer maps and manhole charts.

**Education/Training Required:** Moderate-term on-the-job training. **Education and Training Program:** Plumbing Technology/Plumber. **Knowledge/Courses**—Building and Construction, Mechanical, Sales and Marketing, Transportation, Production and Processing, Customer and Personal Service.

**Personality Type:** Realistic. **Career Cluster:** 02 Architecture and Construction. **Career Pathway:** 2.2 Construction. **Other Jobs in This Pathway:** Brickmasons and Blockmasons; Cement Masons and Concrete Finishers; Construction and Building Inspectors; Construction Carpenters; Construction Laborers; Construction Managers; Cost Estimators; Drywall and Ceiling Tile Installers; Electrical Power-Line Installers and Repairers; Electricians; Engineering Technicians, Except Drafters, All Other; First-Line Supervisors of Construction Trades and Extraction Workers; Heating and Air Conditioning Mechanics and Installers; Helpers—Carpenters; Helpers—Electricians; Helpers—Pipelayers, Plumbers, Pipefitters, and Steamfitters; Highway Maintenance Workers; Operating Engineers and Other Construction Equipment Operators; Painters, Construction and Maintenance; Pipe Fitters and Steamfitters; Plumbers; Refrigeration Mechanics and Installers; Roofers; Rough Carpenters; Solar Energy Installation Managers; others.

**Skills**—Repairing, Equipment Maintenance, Troubleshooting, Operation and Control, Equipment Selection, Installation, Management of Material Resources, Operation Monitoring.

**Work Environment:** Outdoors; standing; walking and running; using hands; bending or twisting the body; repetitive motions; noise; very hot or cold; bright or inadequate lighting; contaminants; cramped work space; exposed to disease or infections; hazardous equipment; minor burns, cuts, bites, or stings.

## Set and Exhibit Designers

- ❋ Annual Earnings: $46,680
- ❋ Earnings Growth Potential: High (45.2%)
- ❋ Growth: 16.5%
- ❋ Annual Job Openings: 510
- ❋ Self-Employed: 26.2%

**Considerations for Job Outlook:** Faster-than-average employment growth is projected.

**Design special exhibits and movie, television, and theater sets. May study scripts, confer with directors, and conduct research to determine appropriate architectural styles.** Examine objects to be included in exhibits to plan where and how to display them. Acquire, or arrange for acquisition of, specimens or graphics required to complete exhibits. Prepare rough drafts and scale working drawings of sets, including floor plans, scenery, and properties to be constructed. Confer with clients and staff to gather information about exhibit space, proposed themes and content, timelines, budgets, materials, and promotion requirements. Estimate set- or exhibit-related costs, including materials, construction, and rental of props or locations. Develop set designs based on evaluation of scripts, budgets, research information, and available locations. Direct and coordinate construction, erection, or decoration activities to ensure that sets or exhibits meet design, budget, and schedule requirements. Inspect installed exhibits for conformance to specifications and satisfactory operation of special effects components. Plan for location-specific issues such as space limitations, traffic flow patterns, and safety concerns. Submit plans for approval and adapt plans to serve intended purposes or to conform to budget or fabrication restrictions. Prepare preliminary renderings of proposed exhibits, including detailed construction, layout, and material specifications and diagrams relating to aspects such as special effects and lighting. Select and purchase lumber and hardware necessary for set construction. Collaborate with those in charge of lighting and sound so that those production aspects can be coordinated with set designs or exhibit layouts. Research architectural and stylistic elements appropriate to the time period to be depicted, consulting experts for information as necessary. Design and produce displays and materials that can be used to decorate windows, interior displays, or event locations such as streets and fairgrounds. Coordinate the removal of sets, props, and exhibits after productions or events are complete.

**Education/Training Required:** Bachelor's degree. **Education and Training Programs:** Design and Applied Arts, Other; Design and Visual Communications, General; Illustration; Technical Theatre/Theatre Design and Technology. **Knowledge/Courses**—Fine Arts, Design, History and Archeology, Communications and Media, Sociology and Anthropology, Computers and Electronics.

**Personality Type:** Artistic-Realistic. **Career Cluster:** 03 Arts, Audio/Video Technology, and Communications. **Career Pathways:** 3.1 Audio and Video Technology and Film; 3.3 Visual Arts; 3.4 Performing Arts. **Other Jobs in These Pathways:** Actors; Art Directors; Audio and Video Equipment Technicians; Broadcast Technicians; Camera Operators, Television, Video, and Motion Picture; Commercial and Industrial Designers; Directors—Stage, Motion Pictures, Television, and Radio; Entertainers and Performers, Sports and Related Workers, All Other; Film and Video Editors; Graphic Designers; Interior Designers; Managers, All Other; Media and Communication Workers, All Other; Multimedia Artists and Animators; Music Composers and Arrangers; Music Directors; Musicians, Instrumental; Painting, Coating, and Decorating Workers; Photographers; Poets, Lyricists and Creative Writers; Producers; Program Directors; Singers; Talent Directors; Technical Directors/Managers; others.

**Skills**—Management of Financial Resources, Operations Analysis, Management of Material Resources, Mathematics, Equipment Selection, Management of Personnel Resources, Technology Design, Time Management.

**Work Environment:** Indoors; sitting; using hands.

## Sheet Metal Workers

- ❋ Annual Earnings: $41,710
- ❋ Earnings Growth Potential: Medium (40.1%)
- ❋ Growth: 6.5%
- ❋ Annual Job Openings: 5,170
- ❋ Self-Employed: 5.2%

**Considerations for Job Outlook:** Employment of sheet metal workers in the construction industry is expected to increase along with building activity. But employment is likely to decline somewhat in manufacturing, due to increased automation and the movement of some work abroad. Opportunities should be particularly good for job seekers who have apprenticeship training or who are certified welders.

**Fabricate, assemble, install, and repair sheet metal products and equipment, such as ducts, control boxes,**

drainpipes, and furnace casings. **Work may involve any of the following: setting up and operating fabricating machines to cut, bend, and straighten sheet metal; shaping metal over anvils, blocks, or forms, using hammer; operating soldering and welding equipment to join sheet metal parts; and inspecting, assembling, and smoothing seams and joints of burred surfaces.** Determine project requirements, including scope, assembly sequences, and required methods and materials, according to blueprints, drawings, and written or verbal instructions. Lay out, measure, and mark dimensions and reference lines on material such as roofing panels according to drawings or templates, using calculators, scribes, dividers, squares, and rulers. Maneuver completed units into position for installation and anchor the units. Convert blueprints into shop drawings to be followed in the construction and assembly of sheet metal products. Install assemblies such as flashing, pipes, tubes, heating and air conditioning ducts, furnace casings, rain gutters, and downspouts in supportive frameworks. Select gauges and types of sheet metal or non-metallic material according to product specifications. Drill and punch holes in metal for screws, bolts, and rivets. Fasten seams and joints together with welds, bolts, cement, rivets, solder, caulks, metal drive clips, and bonds to assemble components into products or to repair sheet metal items. Fabricate or alter parts at construction sites, using shears, hammers, punches, and drills. Finish parts, using hacksaws and hand, rotary, or squaring shears. Trim, file, grind, deburr, buff, and smooth surfaces, seams, and joints of assembled parts, using hand tools and portable power tools. Maintain equipment, making repairs and modifications when necessary. Shape metal material over anvils, blocks, or other forms, using hand tools. Transport prefabricated parts to construction sites for assembly and installation. Develop and lay out patterns that use materials most efficiently, using computerized metalworking equipment to experiment with different layouts. Inspect individual parts, assemblies, and installations for conformance to specifications and building codes, using measuring instruments such as calipers, scales, and micrometers. Secure metal roof panels in place and interlock and fasten grooved panel edges.

**Education/Training Required:** Long-term on-the-job training. **Education and Training Program:** Sheet Metal Technology/Sheetworking. **Knowledge/Courses**—Building and Construction, Mechanical, Design, Engineering and Technology, Production and Processing, Physics.

**Personality Type:** Realistic. **Career Cluster:** 13 Manufacturing. **Career Pathway:** 13.1 Production. **Other Jobs in This Pathway:** Assemblers and Fabricators, All Other; Cabinetmakers and Bench Carpenters; Coating, Painting, and Spraying Machine Setters, Operators, and Tenders; Computer-Controlled Machine Tool Operators, Metal and Plastic; Cost Estimators; Cutting, Punching, and Press Machine Setters, Operators, and Tenders, Metal and Plastic; First-Line Supervisors of Mechanics, Installers, and Repairers; First-Line Supervisors of Production and Operating Workers; Geothermal Technicians; Grinding, Lapping, Polishing, and Buffing Machine Tool Setters, Operators, and Tenders, Metal and Plastic; Helpers—Production Workers; Machine Feeders and Offbearers; Machinists; Mixing and Blending Machine Setters, Operators, and Tenders; Molding, Coremaking, and Casting Machine Setters, Operators, and Tenders, Metal and Plastic; Packaging and Filling Machine Operators and Tenders; Packers and Packagers, Hand; Paper Goods Machine Setters, Operators, and Tenders; Production Workers, All Other; Recycling and Reclamation Workers; Recycling Coordinators; Solderers and Brazers; Structural Metal Fabricators and Fitters; Team Assemblers; Welders, Cutters, and Welder Fitters; others.

**Skills**—Repairing, Equipment Maintenance, Installation, Equipment Selection, Quality Control Analysis, Technology Design, Mathematics, Troubleshooting.

**Work Environment:** Outdoors; standing; walking and running; using hands; bending or twisting the body; repetitive motions; noise; very hot or cold; bright or inadequate lighting; contaminants; cramped work space; high places; hazardous equipment; minor burns, cuts, bites, or stings.

## Ship Engineers

- ❋ Annual Earnings: $65,880
- ❋ Earnings Growth Potential: High (42.1%)
- ❋ Growth: 18.6%
- ❋ Annual Job Openings: 700
- ❋ Self-Employed: 0.0%

**Considerations for Job Outlook:** Job growth is expected to stem from increasing tourism and from growth in offshore oil and gas production. Employment is also projected to increase in and around major port cities due to growing international trade. Opportunities should be excellent as the need to replace workers, particularly officers, generates many job openings.

**Supervise and coordinate activities of crew engaged in operating and maintaining engines; boilers; deck machinery; and electrical, sanitary, and refrigeration equipment aboard ship.** Record orders for changes in ship speed and direction, and note gauge readings and test data, such as revolutions per minute and voltage output, in engineering logs and bellbooks. Install engine controls, propeller shafts, and propellers. Perform and participate in emergency drills as required. Fabricate engine replacement parts such as valves, stay rods, and bolts, using metalworking machinery. Operate and maintain off-loading liquid pumps and valves. Maintain and repair engines, electric motors, pumps, winches and other mechanical and electrical equipment, or assist other crew members with maintenance and repair duties. Maintain electrical power, heating, ventilation, refrigeration, water, and sewerage. Monitor and test operations of engines and other equipment so that malfunctions and their causes can be identified. Monitor engine, machinery, and equipment indicators when vessels are underway, and report abnormalities to appropriate shipboard staff. Start engines to propel ships, and regulate engines and power transmissions to control speeds of ships, according to directions from captains or bridge computers. Order and receive engine rooms' stores such as oil and spare parts; maintain inventories and record usage of supplies. Act as liaisons between ships' captains and shore personnel to ensure that schedules and budgets are maintained and that ships are operated safely and efficiently. Clean engine parts, and keep engine rooms clean. Supervise the activities of marine engine technicians engaged in the maintenance and repair of mechanical and electrical marine vessels, and inspect their work to ensure that it is performed properly. Maintain complete records of engineering department activities, including machine operations. Perform general marine vessel maintenance and repair work such as repairing leaks, finishing interiors, refueling, and maintaining decks.

**Education/Training Required:** Work experience in a related occupation. **Education and Training Program:** Marine Maintenance/Fitter and Ship Repair Technology/Technician. **Knowledge/Courses**—Mechanical, Building and Construction, Engineering and Technology, Transportation, Chemistry, Public Safety and Security.

**Personality Type:** Realistic-Conventional-Enterprising. **Career Cluster:** 16 Transportation, Distribution, and Logistics. **Career Pathway:** 16.1 Transportation Operations. **Other Jobs in This Pathway:** Airline Pilots, Copilots, and Flight Engineers; Automotive and Watercraft Service Attendants; Automotive Master Mechanics; Bus Drivers, School or Special Client; Bus Drivers, Transit and Intercity; Commercial Pilots; Crane and Tower Operators; First-Line Supervisors of Helpers, Laborers, and Material Movers, Hand; First-Line Supervisors of Transportation and Material-Moving Machine and Vehicle Operators; Freight and Cargo Inspectors; Heavy and Tractor-Trailer Truck Drivers; Laborers and Freight, Stock, and Material Movers, Hand; Light Truck or Delivery Services Drivers; Mates—Ship, Boat, and Barge; Motor Vehicle Operators, All Other; Operating Engineers and Other Construction Equipment Operators; Parking Lot Attendants; Pilots, Ship; Railroad Conductors and Yardmasters; Sailors and Marine Oilers; Ship and Boat Captains; Storage and Distribution Managers; Taxi Drivers and Chauffeurs; Transportation Managers; Transportation Workers, All Other; others.

**Skills**—Repairing, Equipment Maintenance, Troubleshooting, Equipment Selection, Operation and Control, Operation Monitoring, Quality Control Analysis, Science.

**Work Environment:** Outdoors; standing; using hands; noise; very hot or cold; bright or inadequate lighting; contaminants; cramped work space; whole-body vibration; high places; hazardous conditions; hazardous equipment; minor burns, cuts, bites, or stings.

## Skincare Specialists

- ❋ Annual Earnings: $28,920
- ❋ Earnings Growth Potential: Medium (40.9%)
- ❋ Growth: 37.8%
- ❋ Annual Job Openings: 2,030
- ❋ Self-Employed: 31.9%

**Considerations for Job Outlook:** A larger population and increasing demand for personal appearance services, especially skin care, are expected to create jobs for these workers. Prospects should be good, especially for job seekers who have formal training.

**Provide skin care treatments to face and body to enhance an individual's appearance.** Sterilize equipment and clean work areas. Keep records of client needs and preferences and the services provided. Demonstrate how to clean and care for skin properly and recommend skin-care regimens. Examine clients' skin, using magnifying lamps or visors when necessary, to evaluate skin condition and appearance. Select and apply cosmetic products such as creams, lotions, and tonics. Cleanse clients' skin with water, creams, or lotions. Treat the facial skin to maintain and improve its appearance, using specialized techniques and products such as peels and masks. Refer clients to medical personnel for treatment of serious skin problems. Determine which products or colors will improve clients' skin quality and appearance. Perform simple extractions to remove blackheads. Provide facial and body massages. Remove body and facial hair by applying wax. Apply chemical peels in order to reduce fine lines and age spots. Advise clients about colors and types of makeup and instruct them in makeup application techniques. Sell makeup to clients. Collaborate with plastic surgeons and dermatologists to provide patients with preoperative and postoperative skin care. Give manicures and pedicures and apply artificial nails. Tint eyelashes and eyebrows.

**Education/Training Required:** Postsecondary vocational training. **Education and Training Programs:** Cosmetology/Cosmetologist Training, General; Facial Treatment Specialist/Facialist Training. **Knowledge/Courses**—Sales and Marketing, Chemistry, Customer and Personal Service.

**Personality Type:** Enterprising-Social-Realistic. **Career Cluster:** 10 Human Services. **Career Pathway:** 10.4 Personal Care Services. **Other Jobs in This Pathway:** Barbers; Embalmers; Funeral Attendants; Funeral Service Managers; Hairdressers, Hairstylists, and Cosmetologists; Laundry and Dry-Cleaning Workers; Makeup Artists, Theatrical and Performance; Manicurists and Pedicurists; Pressers, Textile, Garment, and Related Materials; Sewers, Hand; Sewing Machine Operators; Shampooers; Tailors, Dressmakers, and Custom Sewers; Textile Bleaching and Dyeing Machine Operators and Tenders.

**Skills**—Service Orientation.

**Work Environment:** Indoors; standing; using hands; bending or twisting the body; repetitive motions.

# Social and Community Service Managers

- ❀ Annual Earnings: $57,950
- ❀ Earnings Growth Potential: Medium (40.8%)
- ❀ Growth: 13.8%
- ❀ Annual Job Openings: 4,820
- ❀ Self-Employed: 3.1%

**Considerations for Job Outlook:** Faster-than-average employment growth is projected.

**Plan, organize, or coordinate the activities of a social service program or community outreach organization. Oversee the program or organization's budget and policies regarding participant involvement, program requirements, and benefits. Work may involve directing social workers, counselors, or probation officers.** Establish and maintain relationships with other agencies and organizations in community to meet community needs and to ensure that services are not duplicated. Prepare and maintain records

and reports, such as budgets, personnel records, or training manuals. Direct activities of professional and technical staff members and volunteers. Evaluate the work of staff and volunteers to ensure that programs are of appropriate quality and that resources are used effectively. Establish and oversee administrative procedures to meet objectives set by boards of directors or senior management. Participate in the determination of organizational policies regarding such issues as participant eligibility, program requirements, and program benefits. Research and analyze member or community needs to determine program directions and goals. Speak to community groups to explain and interpret agency purposes, programs, and policies. Recruit, interview, and hire or sign up volunteers and staff. Represent organizations in relations with governmental and media institutions. Plan and administer budgets for programs, equipment, and support services. Analyze proposed legislation, regulations, or rule changes to determine how agency services could be impacted. Act as consultants to agency staff and other community programs regarding the interpretation of program-related federal, state, and county regulations and policies. Implement and evaluate staff training programs. Direct fundraising activities and the preparation of public relations materials.

**Education/Training Required:** Bachelor's degree. **Education and Training Programs:** Business Administration and Management, General; Business, Management, Marketing, and Related Support Services, Other; Business/Commerce, General; Community Organization and Advocacy; Entrepreneurship/Entrepreneurial Studies; Human Services, General; Non-Profit/Public/Organizational Management; Public Administration. **Knowledge/Courses**—Therapy and Counseling, Psychology, Sociology and Anthropology, Philosophy and Theology, Personnel and Human Resources, Customer and Personal Service.

**Personality Type:** Enterprising-Social. **Career Clusters:** 04 Business, Management, and Administration; 07 Government and Public Administration; 10 Human Services. **Career Pathways:** 4.1 Management; 7.1 Governance; 7.7 Public Management and Administration; 10.3 Family and Community Services. **Other Jobs in These Pathways:** Brownfield Redevelopment Specialists and Site Managers; Business Continuity Planners; Business Operations Specialists, All Other; Chief Executives; Chief Sustainability Officers; Childcare Workers; Compliance Managers; Construction Managers; Customs Brokers; Energy Auditors; First-Line Supervisors of Office and Administrative Support Workers; General and Operations Managers; Investment Fund Managers; Loss Prevention Managers; Management Analysts; Managers, All Other; Nannies; Personal Care Aides; Regulatory Affairs Managers; Security Management

Specialists; Security Managers; Supply Chain Managers; Sustainability Specialists; Wind Energy Operations Managers; Wind Energy Project Managers; others.

**Skills**—Management of Financial Resources, Management of Personnel Resources, Management of Material Resources, Systems Evaluation, Operations Analysis, Social Perceptiveness, Systems Analysis, Learning Strategies.

**Work Environment:** Indoors; sitting.

# Social and Human Service Assistants

- ❀ Annual Earnings: $28,200
- ❀ Earnings Growth Potential: Low (33.4%)
- ❀ Growth: 22.6%
- ❀ Annual Job Openings: 15,390
- ❀ Self-Employed: 0.3%

**Considerations for Job Outlook:** As the elderly population grows, demand for the services provided by these workers is expected to increase. Opportunities are expected to be excellent, particularly for job seekers with some postsecondary education, such as a certificate or associate degree in a related subject.

**Assist professionals from a wide variety of fields such as psychology, rehabilitation, or social work to provide client services, as well as support for families. May assist clients in identifying available benefits and social and community services and help clients obtain them. May assist social workers with developing, organizing, and conducting programs to prevent and resolve problems relevant to substance abuse, human relationships, rehabilitation, or adult daycare.** Keep records and prepare reports for owner or management concerning visits with clients. Submit reports and review reports or problems with superior. Interview individuals and family members to compile information on social, educational, criminal, institutional, or drug histories. Provide information and refer individuals to public or private agencies or community services for assistance. Consult with supervisors concerning programs for individual families. Advise clients regarding food stamps, child care, food, money management, sanitation, or housekeeping. Oversee day-to-day group activities of residents in institution. Visit individuals in homes or attend group meetings to provide information on agency services, requirements, and procedures. Monitor free, supplementary meal program to ensure cleanliness of facility and that eligibility guidelines are met for persons receiving meals. Meet with youth groups to acquaint them with consequences of delinquent acts. Assist in planning of food budgets, using charts and sample budgets. Transport and accompany clients to shopping areas or to appointments, using automobiles. Assist in locating housing for displaced individuals. Observe and discuss meal preparation and suggest alternate methods of food preparation. Observe clients' food selections and recommend alternative economical and nutritional food choices. Explain rules established by owner or management, such as sanitation and maintenance requirements or parking regulations. Care for children in clients' homes during clients' appointments. Inform tenants of facilities such as laundries and playgrounds. Assist clients with preparation of forms such as tax or rent forms. Demonstrate use and care of equipment for tenants' use.

**Education/Training Required:** Moderate-term on-the-job training. **Education and Training Program:** Mental and Social Health Services and Allied Professions, Other. **Knowledge/Courses**—Therapy and Counseling, Philosophy and Theology, Psychology, Customer and Personal Service, Sociology and Anthropology, Clerical.

**Personality Type:** Conventional-Social-Enterprising. **Career Cluster:** 08 Health Science. **Career Pathway:** 8.1 Therapeutic Services. **Other Jobs in This Pathway:** Clinical Psychologists; Community and Social Service Specialists, All Other; Counseling Psychologists; Dental Assistants; Dental Hygienists; Dentists, General; Health Technologists and Technicians, All Other; Healthcare Support Workers, All Other; Home Health Aides; Licensed Practical and Licensed Vocational Nurses; Low Vision Therapists, Orientation and Mobility Specialists, and Vision Rehabilitation Therapists; Massage Therapists; Medical and Clinical Laboratory Technicians; Medical and Health Services Managers; Medical Scientists, Except Epidemiologists; Medical Secretaries; Occupational Therapists; Ophthalmic Medical Technologists; Pharmacists; Pharmacy Technicians; Radiologic Technologists; School Psychologists; Speech-Language Pathologists; Speech-Language Pathology Assistants; Substance Abuse and Behavioral Disorder Counselors; others.

**Skills**—Social Perceptiveness, Service Orientation, Active Listening, Science, Learning Strategies, Systems Analysis, Speaking, Persuasion.

**Work Environment:** Indoors; sitting.

# Social Science Research Assistants

- ❋ Annual Earnings: $37,230
- ❋ Earnings Growth Potential: High (42.6%)
- ❋ Growth: 17.8%
- ❋ Annual Job Openings: 1,270
- ❋ Self-Employed: 1.5%

**Considerations for Job Outlook:** Faster-than-average employment growth is projected.

**Assist social scientists in laboratory, survey, and other social research. May perform publication activities, laboratory analysis, quality control, or data management. Normally these individuals work under the direct supervision of social scientists and assist in those activities that are more routine.** Code data in preparation for computer entry. Provide assistance in the design of survey instruments such as questionnaires. Prepare, manipulate, and manage extensive databases. Prepare tables, graphs, fact sheets, and written reports summarizing research results. Obtain informed consent of research subjects and/or their guardians. Edit and submit protocols and other required research documentation. Screen potential subjects in order to determine their suitability as study participants. Conduct Internet-based and library research. Supervise the work of survey interviewers. Perform descriptive and multivariate statistical analyses of data, using computer software. Recruit and schedule research participants. Develop and implement research quality control procedures. Track research participants, and perform any necessary follow-up tasks. Verify the accuracy and validity of data entered in databases; correct any errors. Track laboratory supplies and expenses such as participant reimbursement. Provide assistance with the preparation of project-related reports, manuscripts, and presentations. Present research findings to groups of people. Perform needs assessments and/or consult with clients in order to determine the types of research and information that are required. Allocate and manage laboratory space and resources. Design and create special programs for tasks such as statistical analysis and data entry and cleaning. Perform data entry and other clerical work as required for project completion. Administer standardized tests to research subjects, and/or interview them in order to collect research data. Collect specimens such as blood samples, as required by research projects.

**Education/Training Required:** Associate degree. **Education and Training Program:** Social Sciences, General. **Knowledge/Courses**—Psychology, Sociology and Anthropology, Clerical, Computers and Electronics, English Language, Communications and Media.

**Personality Type:** Conventional-Investigative. **Career Cluster:** 10 Human Services. **Career Pathway:** 10.3 Family and Community Services. **Other Jobs in This Pathway:** Chief Executives; Child, Family, and School Social Workers; Childcare Workers; City and Regional Planning Aides; Counselors, All Other; Eligibility Interviewers, Government Programs; Farm and Home Management Advisors; Legislators; Managers, All Other; Marriage and Family Therapists; Nannies; Personal Care Aides; Probation Officers and Correctional Treatment Specialists; Protective Service Workers, All Other; Social and Community Service Managers; Social Scientists and Related Workers, All Other; Social Workers, All Other; Sociologists; Supply Chain Managers.

**Skills**—Programming, Science, Mathematics, Reading Comprehension, Quality Control Analysis, Management of Financial Resources, Technology Design, Operations Analysis.

**Work Environment:** Indoors; sitting.

## Job Specialization: City and Regional Planning Aides

**Compile data from various sources, such as maps, reports, and field and file investigations, for use by city planner in making planning studies.** Participate in and support team planning efforts. Prepare reports, using statistics, charts, and graphs, to illustrate planning studies in areas such as population, land use, or zoning. Research, compile, analyze, and organize information from maps, reports, investigations, and books for use in reports and special projects. Provide and process zoning and project permits and applications. Respond to public inquiries and complaints. Serve as liaison between planning department and other departments and agencies. Inspect sites and review plans for minor development permit applications. Conduct interviews, surveys, and site inspections concerning factors that affect land usage, such as zoning, traffic flow, and housing. Prepare, maintain, and update files and records, including land use data and statistics. Prepare, develop, and maintain maps and databases. Perform clerical duties such as composing, typing, and proofreading documents; scheduling appointments and meetings; handling mail; and posting public notices. Perform code enforcement tasks.

**Education/Training Required:** Associate degree. **Education and Training Program:** Social Sciences, General. **Knowledge/Courses**—Geography, History and

Archeology, Design, Law and Government, Building and Construction, Sociology and Anthropology.

**Personality Type:** Conventional-Realistic. **Career Cluster:** 10 Human Services. **Career Pathway:** 10.3 Family and Community Services. **Other Jobs in This Pathway:** Chief Executives; Child, Family, and School Social Workers; Childcare Workers; Counselors, All Other; Eligibility Interviewers, Government Programs; Farm and Home Management Advisors; Legislators; Managers, All Other; Marriage and Family Therapists; Nannies; Personal Care Aides; Probation Officers and Correctional Treatment Specialists; Protective Service Workers, All Other; Social and Community Service Managers; Social Science Research Assistants; Social Scientists and Related Workers, All Other; Social Workers, All Other; Sociologists; Supply Chain Managers.

**Skills**—Science, Systems Analysis, Negotiation, Mathematics, Systems Evaluation, Writing, Speaking, Time Management.

**Work Environment:** Indoors; sitting.

# Social Scientists and Related Workers, All Other

- ❋ Annual Earnings: $74,620
- ❋ Earnings Growth Potential: High (41.8%)
- ❋ Growth: 22.4%
- ❋ Annual Job Openings: 2,380
- ❋ Self-Employed: 1.5%

**Considerations for Job Outlook:** Much-faster-than-average employment growth is projected.

**This occupation includes all social scientists and related workers not listed separately.** Because this is a highly diverse occupation, no data is available for some information topics.

**Education/Training Required:** Master's degree. **Education and Training Program:** Social Sciences, Other.

**Career Clusters:** 10 Human Services; 15 Science, Technology, Engineering, and Mathematics. **Career Pathways:** 10.3 Family and Community Services; 15.2 Science and Mathematics. **Other Jobs in These Pathways:** Anthropologists; Archeologists; Architectural and Engineering Managers; Archivists; Astronomers; Atmospheric and Space Scientists; Biochemists and Biophysicists; Biofuels/Biodiesel Technology and Product Development Managers; Bioinformatics Scientists; Biological Scientists, All Other; Biologists; Biostatisticians; Cartographers and Photogrammetrists; Chemists; Chief Executives; Child, Family, and School Social Workers; Childcare Workers; City and Regional Planning Aides; Clinical Data Managers; Clinical Research Coordinators; Community and Social Service Specialists, All Other; Counselors, All Other; Curators; Dietitians and Nutritionists; Economists; Education, Training, and Library Workers, All Other; Eligibility Interviewers, Government Programs; Environmental Economists; Epidemiologists; others.

# Job Specialization: Transportation Planners

**Prepare studies for proposed transportation projects. Gather, compile, and analyze data. Study the use and operation of transportation systems. Develop transportation models or simulations.** Prepare or review engineering studies or specifications. Represent jurisdictions in the legislative and administrative approval of land development projects. Prepare necessary documents to obtain project approvals or permits. Direct urban traffic counting programs. Develop or test new methods and models of transportation analysis. Define or update information such as urban boundaries and classification of roadways. Analyze transportation-related consequences of federal and state legislative proposals. Analyze information from traffic counting programs. Review development plans for transportation system effects, infrastructure requirements, or compliance with applicable transportation regulations. Prepare reports and recommendations on transportation planning. Produce environmental documents, such as environmental assessments and environmental impact statements. Participate in public meetings or hearings to explain planning proposals, to gather feedback from those affected by projects, or to achieve consensus on project designs. Document and evaluate transportation project needs and costs. Develop design ideas for new or improved transport infrastructure, such as junction improvements, pedestrian projects, bus facilities, and car parking areas. Develop computer models to address transportation planning issues. Design transportation surveys to identify areas of public concern. Analyze and interpret data from traffic modeling software, geographic information systems, or associated databases. Collaborate with engineers to research, analyze, or resolve complex transportation design issues. Recommend transportation system improvements or projects, based on economic, population, land-use or traffic projections. Define regional or local transportation planning problems and priorities. Analyze information related to transportation, such as land use policies, environmental impact of projects, or long-range planning needs.

**Education/Training Required:** Master's degree. **Education and Training Program:** City/Urban, Community and Regional Planning. **Knowledge/Courses**—No data available.

**Personality Type:** Investigative-Conventional-Realistic. **Career Cluster:** 15 Science, Technology, Engineering, and Mathematics. **Career Pathway:** 15.2 Science and Mathematics. **Other Jobs in This Pathway:** Architectural and Engineering Managers; Biochemists and Biophysicists; Biofuels/Biodiesel Technology and Product Development Managers; Bioinformatics Scientists; Biological Scientists, All Other; Biologists; Biostatisticians; Chemists; Clinical Data Managers; Clinical Research Coordinators; Community and Social Service Specialists, All Other; Dietitians and Nutritionists; Education, Training, and Library Workers, All Other; Geneticists; Geoscientists, Except Hydrologists and Geographers; Medical Scientists, Except Epidemiologists; Molecular and Cellular Biologists; Natural Sciences Managers; Operations Research Analysts; Physical Scientists, All Other; Social Scientists and Related Workers, All Other; Statisticians; Survey Researchers; Water Resource Specialists; Zoologists and Wildlife Biologists; others.

**Skills**—No data available.

**Work Environment:** No data available.

# Social Work Teachers, Postsecondary

- ❋ Annual Earnings: $63,090
- ❋ Earnings Growth Potential: High (43.6%)
- ❋ Growth: 15.1%
- ❋ Annual Job Openings: 300
- ❋ Self-Employed: 0.2%

**Considerations for Job Outlook:** Enrollments in postsecondary institutions are expected to continue rising as more people attend college and as workers return to school to update their skills. Opportunities for part-time or temporary positions should be favorable, but significant competition exists for tenure-track positions.

**Teach courses in social work.** Initiate, facilitate, and moderate classroom discussions. Evaluate and grade students' classwork, assignments, and papers. Prepare and deliver lectures to undergraduate or graduate students on topics such as family behavior, child and adolescent mental health, and

social intervention evaluation. Keep abreast of developments in their field by reading current literature, talking with colleagues, and participating in professional conferences. Supervise students' laboratory work and fieldwork. Conduct research in a particular field of knowledge and publish findings in professional journals, books, or electronic media. Prepare course materials such as syllabi, homework assignments, and handouts. Maintain regularly scheduled office hours to advise and assist students. Supervise undergraduate or graduate teaching, internship, and research work. Plan, evaluate, and revise curricula, course content, and course materials and methods of instruction. Collaborate with colleagues and with community agencies to address teaching and research issues. Compile, administer, and grade examinations or assign this work to others. Advise students on academic and vocational curricula and on career issues. Maintain student attendance records, grades, and other required records. Write grant proposals to procure external research funding. Serve on academic or administrative committees that deal with institutional policies, departmental matters, and academic issues. Perform administrative duties such as serving as department head. Compile bibliographies of specialized materials for outside reading assignments. Select and obtain materials and supplies such as textbooks and laboratory equipment. Participate in student recruitment, registration, and placement activities. Participate in campus and community events. Provide professional consulting services to government and industry. Act as advisers to student organizations.

**Education/Training Required:** Doctoral degree. **Education and Training Programs:** Clinical/Medical Social Work; Social Work; Teacher Education and Professional Development, Specific Subject Areas, Other. **Knowledge/Courses**—Therapy and Counseling, Sociology and Anthropology, Psychology, Philosophy and Theology, Education and Training, English Language.

**Personality Type:** Social-Investigative. **Career Clusters:** 05 Education and Training; 10 Human Services. **Career Pathways:** 5.3 Teaching/Training; 10.2 Counseling and Mental Health Services; 10.3 Family and Community Services. **Other Jobs in These Pathways:** Chief Executives; Child, Family, and School Social Workers; Childcare Workers; Clergy; Clinical Psychologists; Coaches and Scouts; Counseling Psychologists; Elementary School Teachers, Except Special Education; Fitness Trainers and Aerobics Instructors; Healthcare Social Workers; Kindergarten Teachers, Except Special Education; Librarians; Managers, All Other; Middle School Teachers, Except Special and Career/Technical Education; Nannies; Personal Care Aides; Preschool Teachers, Except Special Education; Recreation Workers;

School Psychologists; Secondary School Teachers, Except Special and Career/Technical Education; Self-Enrichment Education Teachers; Supply Chain Managers; Teacher Assistants; Tutors; 37 other postsecondary teaching occupations; others.

**Skills**—Instructing, Writing, Active Learning, Learning Strategies, Speaking, Reading Comprehension, Active Listening, Systems Evaluation.

**Work Environment:** Indoors; sitting.

# Sociologists

❋ Annual Earnings: $72,360
❋ Earnings Growth Potential: Medium (39.2%)
❋ Growth: 22.0%
❋ Annual Job Openings: 200
❋ Self-Employed: 0.0%

**Considerations for Job Outlook:** Employment growth of sociologists in a variety of fields is tied to expected demand for their research and analytical skills. Opportunities should be best for job seekers who have an advanced degree.

**Study human society and social behavior by examining the groups and social institutions that people form, as well as various social, religious, political, and business organizations. May study the behavior and interaction of groups, trace their origin and growth, and analyze the influence of group activities on individual members.** Analyze and interpret data in order to increase the understanding of human social behavior. Prepare publications and reports containing research findings. Plan and conduct research to develop and test theories about societal issues such as crime, group relations, poverty, and aging. Collect data about the attitudes, values, and behaviors of people in groups, using observation, interviews, and review of documents. Develop, implement, and evaluate methods of data collection, such as questionnaires or interviews. Teach sociology. Direct work of statistical clerks, statisticians, and others who compile and evaluate research data. Consult with and advise individuals such as administrators, social workers, and legislators regarding social issues and policies, as well as the implications of research findings. Collaborate with research workers in other disciplines. Develop approaches to the solution of groups' problems based on research findings in sociology and related disciplines. Observe group interactions and role affiliations to collect data, identify problems, evaluate progress, and determine the need for additional change. Develop problem intervention procedures, utilizing techniques such as interviews, consultations, role-playing, and participant observation of group interactions.

**Education/Training Required:** Master's degree. **Education and Training Programs:** Criminology; Demography and Population Studies; Sociology; Urban Studies/Affairs. **Knowledge/Courses**—Sociology and Anthropology, Philosophy and Theology, History and Archeology, Psychology, English Language, Mathematics.

**Personality Type:** Investigative-Artistic-Social. **Career Clusters:** 10 Human Services; 15 Science, Technology, Engineering, and Mathematics. **Career Pathways:** 10.3 Family and Community Services; 15.2 Science and Mathematics. **Other Jobs in These Pathways:** Architectural and Engineering Managers; Biofuels/Biodiesel Technology and Product Development Managers; Biologists; Chemists; Chief Executives; Child, Family, and School Social Workers; Childcare Workers; Clinical Research Coordinators; Community and Social Service Specialists, All Other; Dietitians and Nutritionists; Education, Training, and Library Workers, All Other; Eligibility Interviewers, Government Programs; Legislators; Managers, All Other; Medical Scientists, Except Epidemiologists; Nannies; Natural Sciences Managers; Operations Research Analysts; Personal Care Aides; Probation Officers and Correctional Treatment Specialists; Protective Service Workers, All Other; Social and Community Service Managers; Social Workers, All Other; Supply Chain Managers; Water Resource Specialists; others.

**Skills**—Science, Reading Comprehension, Writing, Speaking, Mathematics, Active Listening, Learning Strategies, Active Learning.

**Work Environment:** Indoors; sitting.

# Sociology Teachers, Postsecondary

❋ Annual Earnings: $64,810
❋ Earnings Growth Potential: High (45.4%)
❋ Growth: 15.1%
❋ Annual Job Openings: 500
❋ Self-Employed: 0.2%

**Considerations for Job Outlook:** Enrollments in postsecondary institutions are expected to continue rising as more people attend college and as workers return to school to update their skills. Opportunities for part-time or temporary positions should be favorable, but significant competition exists for tenure-track positions.

**Teach courses in sociology.** Evaluate and grade students' classwork, assignments, and papers. Prepare and deliver lectures to undergraduate and graduate students on topics such as race and ethnic relations, measurement and data collection, and workplace social relations. Initiate, facilitate, and moderate classroom discussions. Prepare course materials such as syllabi, homework assignments, and handouts. Compile, administer, and grade examinations or assign this work to others. Keep abreast of developments in their field by reading current literature, talking with colleagues, and participating in professional conferences. Maintain student attendance records, grades, and other required records. Maintain regularly scheduled office hours in order to advise and assist students. Plan, evaluate, and revise curricula, course content, and course materials and methods of instruction. Advise students on academic and vocational curricula and on career issues. Collaborate with colleagues to address teaching and research issues. Conduct research in a particular field of knowledge and publish findings in professional journals, books, or electronic media. Select and obtain materials and supplies such as textbooks and laboratory equipment. Supervise undergraduate and graduate teaching, internship, and research work. Serve on academic or administrative committees that deal with institutional policies, departmental matters, and academic issues. Participate in student recruitment, registration, and placement activities. Perform administrative duties such as serving as department head. Supervise students' laboratory work and fieldwork. Write grant proposals to procure external research funding. Act as advisers to student organizations. Compile bibliographies of specialized materials for outside reading assignments. Participate in campus and community events. Provide professional consulting services to government and industry.

**Education/Training Required:** Doctoral degree. **Education and Training Programs:** Humanities/Humanistic Studies; Social Science Teacher Education; Sociology. **Knowledge/Courses**—Sociology and Anthropology, Philosophy and Theology, History and Archeology, Education and Training, English Language, Geography.

**Personality Type:** Social-Investigative-Artistic. **Career Clusters:** 05 Education and Training; 15 Science, Technology, Engineering, and Mathematics. **Career Pathways:** 5.3 Teaching/Training; 15.2 Science and Mathematics. **Other Jobs in These Pathways:** Adult Basic and Secondary Education and Literacy Teachers and Instructors; Architectural and Engineering Managers; Biofuels/Biodiesel Technology and Product Development Managers; Biologists; Career/Technical Education Teachers, Secondary School; Chemists; Coaches and Scouts; Community and Social Service

Specialists, All Other; Education, Training, and Library Workers, All Other; Elementary School Teachers, Except Special Education; Fitness Trainers and Aerobics Instructors; Instructional Coordinators; Instructional Designers and Technologists; Kindergarten Teachers, Except Special Education; Librarians; Medical Scientists, Except Epidemiologists; Middle School Teachers, Except Special and Career/Technical Education; Operations Research Analysts; Preschool Teachers, Except Special Education; Recreation Workers; Secondary School Teachers, Except Special and Career/Technical Education; Self-Enrichment Education Teachers; Teacher Assistants; Tutors; 37 other postsecondary teaching occupations; others.

**Skills**—Science, Learning Strategies, Writing, Instructing, Active Learning, Operations Analysis, Speaking, Reading Comprehension.

**Work Environment:** Indoors; sitting.

# Software Developers, Applications

- Annual Earnings: $87,790
- Earnings Growth Potential: Medium (38.1%)
- Growth: 34.0%
- Annual Job Openings: 21,840
- Self-Employed: 2.7%

**Considerations for Job Outlook:** Employment is expected to increase as businesses and other organizations continue to demand newer, more sophisticated software products. As a result of rapid growth, job prospects for software engineers should be excellent. The need to replace workers who leave the occupation is expected to generate numerous openings for programmers.

**Develop, create, and modify general computer applications software or specialized utility programs. Analyze user needs and develop software solutions. Design software or customize software for client use with the aim of optimizing operational efficiency. May analyze and design databases within an application area, working individually or coordinating database development as part of a team.** Confer with systems analysts, engineers, programmers and others to design system and to obtain information on project limitations and capabilities, performance requirements and interfaces. Modify existing software to correct errors, allow it to adapt to new hardware, or to improve its performance. Analyze user needs and software requirements to determine feasibility of design within time and cost constraints. Consult with customers about software system design and maintenance. Coordinate software system installation and monitor equipment functioning to ensure specifications are met. Design, develop and modify software systems, using scientific analysis and mathematical models to predict and measure outcome and consequences of design. Develop and direct software system testing and validation procedures, programming, and documentation. Analyze information to determine, recommend, and plan computer specifications and layouts, and peripheral equipment modifications. Supervise the work of programmers, technologists and technicians and other engineering and scientific personnel. Obtain and evaluate information on factors such as reporting formats required, costs, and security needs to determine hardware configuration. Determine system performance standards. Train users to use new or modified equipment. Store, retrieve, and manipulate data for analysis of system capabilities and requirements. Specify power supply requirements and configuration. Recommend purchase of equipment to control dust, temperature, and humidity in area of system installation.

**Education/Training Required:** Bachelor's degree. **Education and Training Programs:** Computer Graphics; Computer Science; Computer Software and Media Applications, Other; Data Modeling/Warehousing and Database Administration; Modeling, Virtual Environments and Simulation; Web Page, Digital/Multimedia, and Information Resources Design. **Knowledge/Courses**—Computers and Electronics, Mathematics, Engineering and Technology, Design, English Language.

**Personality Type:** Investigative-Realistic-Conventional. **Career Cluster:** 11 Information Technology. **Career Pathways:** 8.3 Health Informatics; 11.1 Network Systems; 11.2 Information Support Services; 11.3 Interactive Media; 11.4 Programming and Software Development; 13.3 Maintenance, Installation, and Repair; 15.2 Science and Mathematics. **Other Jobs in These Pathways:** Architectural and Engineering Managers; Automotive Specialty Technicians; Biofuels/Biodiesel Technology and Product Development Managers; Clinical Psychologists; Computer and Information Systems Managers; Computer, Automated Teller, and Office Machine Repairers; Electrical and Electronic Equipment Assemblers; Electrical Engineering Technicians; Electronics Engineering Technicians; Engineers, All Other; Executive Secretaries and Executive Administrative Assistants; First-Line Supervisors of Office and Administrative Support Workers; Graphic Designers; Helpers—Installation, Maintenance, and Repair Workers; Industrial Machinery Mechanics; Installation, Maintenance, and Repair Workers, All Other; Medical and Health Services Managers;

Medical Assistants; Medical Records and Health Information Technicians; Medical Secretaries; Mobile Heavy Equipment Mechanics, Except Engines; Physical Therapists; Public Relations Specialists; Receptionists and Information Clerks; Telecommunications Line Installers and Repairers; others.

**Skills**—Programming, Troubleshooting, Technology Design, Systems Evaluation, Operations Analysis, Mathematics, Systems Analysis, Quality Control Analysis.

**Work Environment:** Indoors; sitting; repetitive motions.

# Software Developers, Systems Software

- ❋ Annual Earnings: $94,180
- ❋ Earnings Growth Potential: Low (35.2%)
- ❋ Growth: 30.4%
- ❋ Annual Job Openings: 15,340
- ❋ Self-Employed: 2.7%

**Considerations for Job Outlook:** Employment is expected to increase as businesses and other organizations continue to demand newer, more sophisticated software products. As a result of rapid growth, job prospects for software engineers should be excellent. The need to replace workers who leave the occupation is expected to generate numerous openings for programmers.

**Research, design, develop, and test operating systems-level software, compilers, and network distribution software for medical, industrial, military, communications, aerospace, business, scientific, and general computing applications. Set operational specifications and formulate and analyze software requirements. Apply principles and techniques of computer science, engineering, and mathematical analysis.** Modify existing software to correct errors, to adapt it to new hardware or to upgrade interfaces and improve performance. Design and develop software systems, using scientific analysis and mathematical models to predict and measure outcome and consequences of design. Consult with engineering staff to evaluate interface between hardware and software, develop specifications and performance requirements and resolve customer problems. Analyze information to determine, recommend and plan installation of a new system or modification of an existing system. Develop and direct software system testing and validation procedures. Direct software programming and development of documentation. Consult with customers or other departments on project status, proposals and technical issues such as software system design and maintenance. Advise customer about, or perform, maintenance of software system. Coordinate installation of software system. Monitor functioning of equipment to ensure system operates in conformance with specifications. Store, retrieve, and manipulate data for analysis of system capabilities and requirements. Confer with data processing and project managers to obtain information on limitations and capabilities for data processing projects. Prepare reports and correspondence concerning project specifications, activities and status. Evaluate factors such as reporting formats required, cost constraints, and need for security restrictions to determine hardware configuration. Supervise and assign work to programmers, designers, technologists and technicians and other engineering and scientific personnel. Train users to use new or modified equipment. Utilize microcontrollers to develop control signals, implement control algorithms and measure process variables such as temperatures, pressures and positions. Recommend purchase of equipment to control dust, temperature, and humidity in area of system installation. Specify power supply requirements and configuration.

**Education/Training Required:** Bachelor's degree. **Education and Training Programs:** Computer Graphics; Computer Science; Computer Software and Media Applications, Other; Data Modeling/Warehousing and Database Administration; Modeling, Virtual Environments and Simulation; Web Page, Digital/Multimedia, and Information Resources Design. **Knowledge/Courses—**Computers and Electronics, Engineering and Technology, Design, Telecommunications, Mathematics, Communications and Media.

**Personality Type:** Investigative-Conventional-Realistic. **Career Cluster:** 11 Information Technology. **Career Pathways:** 11.1 Network Systems; 11.2 Information Support Services; 11.3 Interactive Media; 11.4 Programming and Software Development. **Other Jobs in These Pathways:** Architectural and Engineering Managers; Bioinformatics Scientists; Computer and Information Systems Managers; Computer Hardware Engineers; Computer Numerically Controlled Machine Tool Programmers, Metal and Plastic; Computer Operators; Graphic Designers; Multimedia Artists and Animators; Remote Sensing Scientists and Technologists; Remote Sensing Technicians.

**Skills—**Programming, Technology Design, Operations Analysis, Science, Equipment Selection, Quality Control Analysis, Systems Evaluation, Mathematics.

**Work Environment:** Indoors; sitting; repetitive motions.

# Soil and Plant Scientists

- ❋ Annual Earnings: $57,340
- ❋ Earnings Growth Potential: Medium (40.0%)
- ❋ Growth: 15.5%
- ❋ Annual Job Openings: 700
- ❋ Self-Employed: 12.3%

**Considerations for Job Outlook:** Job growth is expected to stem primarily from efforts to increase the quantity and quality of food for a growing population and to balance output with protection and preservation of soil, water, and ecosystems. Opportunities should be good for agricultural and food scientists in almost all fields.

**Conduct research in breeding, physiology, production, yield, and management of crops and agricultural plants, their growth in soils, and control of pests or study the chemical, physical, biological, and mineralogical composition of soils as they relate to plant or crop growth. May classify and map soils and investigate effects of alternative practices on soil and crop productivity.** Communicate research and project results to other professionals and the public or teach related courses, seminars or workshops. Provide information and recommendations to farmers and other landowners regarding ways in which they can best use land, promote plant growth, and avoid or correct problems such as erosion. Investigate responses of soils to specific management practices to determine the use capabilities of soils and the effects of alternative practices on soil productivity. Develop methods of conserving and managing soil that can be applied by farmers and forestry companies. Conduct experiments to develop new or improved varieties of field crops, focusing on characteristics such as yield, quality, disease resistance, nutritional value, or adaptation to specific soils or climates. Investigate soil problems and poor water quality to determine sources and effects. Study soil characteristics to classify soils on the basis of factors such as geographic location, landscape position, and soil properties. Develop improved measurement techniques, soil conservation methods, soil sampling devices, and related technology. Conduct experiments investigating how soil forms and changes and how it interacts with land-based ecosystems and living organisms. Identify degraded or contaminated soils and develop plans to improve their chemical, biological, and physical characteristics. Survey undisturbed and disturbed lands for classification, inventory, mapping, environmental impact assessments, environmental protection planning, and conservation and reclamation planning. Plan and supervise land conservation and reclamation programs for industrial development projects and waste management programs for composting and farming. Perform chemical analyses of the microorganism content of soils to determine microbial reactions and chemical mineralogical relationships to plant growth.

**Education/Training Required:** Bachelor's degree. **Education and Training Programs:** Agricultural and Horticultural Plant Breeding; Agriculture, General; Horticultural Science; Plant Protection and Integrated Pest Management; Plant Sciences, General; Plant Sciences, Other; Range Science and Management; Soil Chemistry and Physics; Soil Microbiology; Soil Science and Agronomy, General. **Knowledge/Courses**—Biology, Food Production, Geography, Chemistry, Physics, Communications and Media.

**Personality Type:** Investigative-Realistic. **Career Cluster:** 01 Agriculture, Food, and Natural Resources. **Career Pathway:** 1.2 Plant Systems. **Other Jobs in This Pathway:** Agricultural Technicians; Animal Scientists; Biochemists and Biophysicists; Biologists; Economists; Environmental Economists; Farm and Home Management Advisors; First-Line Supervisors of Landscaping, Lawn Service, and Groundskeeping Workers; First-Line Supervisors of Retail Sales Workers; Floral Designers; Food Science Technicians; Food Scientists and Technologists; Geneticists; Grounds Maintenance Workers, All Other; Landscaping and Groundskeeping Workers; Pesticide Handlers, Sprayers, and Applicators, Vegetation; Precision Agriculture Technicians; Retail Salespersons; Tree Trimmers and Pruners.

**Skills**—Science, Operations Analysis, Mathematics, Reading Comprehension, Systems Analysis, Writing, Systems Evaluation, Speaking.

**Work Environment:** More often indoors than outdoors; sitting.

## Speech-Language Pathologists

- ✳ Annual Earnings: $66,920
- ✳ Earnings Growth Potential: Low (35.8%)
- ✳ Growth: 18.5%
- ✳ Annual Job Openings: 4,380
- ✳ Self-Employed: 9.0%

**Considerations for Job Outlook:** The aging population, better medical technology that increases the survival rates of people who become injured or ill, and growing enrollments in elementary and secondary schools are expected to increase employment of these workers. Job prospects are expected to be favorable.

**Assess and treat persons with speech, language, voice, and fluency disorders. May select alternative communication systems and teach their use. May perform research related to speech and language problems.** Monitor patients' progress and adjust treatments accordingly. Evaluate hearing and speech/language test results and medical or background information to diagnose and plan treatment for speech, language, fluency, voice, and swallowing disorders. Administer hearing or speech and language evaluations, tests, or examinations to patients to collect information on type and degree of impairments, using written and oral tests and special instruments. Record information on the initial evaluation, treatment, progress, and discharge of clients. Develop and implement treatment plans for problems such as stuttering, delayed language, swallowing disorders, and inappropriate pitch or harsh voice problems based on own assessments and recommendations of physicians, psychologists, or social workers. Develop individual or group programs in schools to deal with speech or language problems. Instruct clients in techniques for more effective communication, including sign language, lip reading, and voice improvement. Teach clients to control or strengthen tongue, jaw, face muscles, and breathing mechanisms. Develop speech exercise programs to reduce disabilities. Consult with and advise educators or medical staff on speech or hearing topics, such as communication strategies or speech and language stimulation. Instruct patients and family members in strategies to cope with or avoid communication-related misunderstandings. Design, develop, and employ alternative diagnostic or communication devices and strategies. Conduct lessons and direct educational or therapeutic games to assist teachers dealing with speech problems. Refer clients to additional medical or educational services if needed. Participate in conferences or training or publish research results to share knowledge of new hearing or speech disorder treatment methods or technologies. Communicate with nonspeaking students, using sign language or computer technology.

**Education/Training Required:** Master's degree. **Education and Training Programs:** Audiology/Audiologist and Speech-Language Pathology/Pathologist; Communication Disorders Sciences and Services, Other; Communication Disorders, General; Communication Sciences and Disorders, General; Speech-Language Pathology/Pathologist. **Knowledge/Courses**—Therapy and Counseling, English Language, Psychology, Sociology and Anthropology, Education and Training, Medicine and Dentistry.

**Personality Type:** Social-Investigative-Artistic. **Career Cluster:** 08 Health Science. **Career Pathway:** 8.1 Therapeutic Services. **Other Jobs in This Pathway:** Clinical

Psychologists; Community and Social Service Specialists, All Other; Counseling Psychologists; Dental Assistants; Dental Hygienists; Dentists, General; Health Technologists and Technicians, All Other; Healthcare Support Workers, All Other; Home Health Aides; Licensed Practical and Licensed Vocational Nurses; Low Vision Therapists, Orientation and Mobility Specialists, and Vision Rehabilitation Therapists; Massage Therapists; Medical and Clinical Laboratory Technicians; Medical and Health Services Managers; Medical Scientists, Except Epidemiologists; Medical Secretaries; Occupational Therapists; Ophthalmic Medical Technologists; Pharmacists; Pharmacy Technicians; Radiologic Technologists; School Psychologists; Social and Human Service Assistants; Speech-Language Pathology Assistants; Substance Abuse and Behavioral Disorder Counselors; others.

**Skills**—Science, Learning Strategies, Social Perceptiveness, Writing, Monitoring, Systems Evaluation, Active Learning, Technology Design.

**Work Environment:** Indoors; sitting; noise; exposed to disease or infections.

# Statisticians

- ❋ Annual Earnings: $72,830
- ❋ Earnings Growth Potential: High (46.3%)
- ❋ Growth: 13.1%
- ❋ Annual Job Openings: 960
- ❋ Self-Employed: 2.8%

**Considerations for Job Outlook:** As data processing becomes faster and more efficient, employers are expected to need statisticians to analyze data. Projected employment growth for biostatisticians is related to the need for workers who can conduct research and clinical trials.

**Engage in the development of mathematical theory or apply statistical theory and methods to collect, organize, interpret, and summarize numerical data to provide usable information. May specialize in fields such as bio-statistics, agricultural statistics, business statistics, economic statistics, or other fields.** Report results of statistical analyses, including information in the form of graphs, charts, and tables. Process large amounts of data for statistical modeling and graphic analysis, using computers. Identify relationships and trends in data, as well as any factors that could affect the results of research. Analyze and interpret statistical data in order to identify significant differences in relationships among sources of information. Prepare data for processing by organizing information, checking

for any inaccuracies, and adjusting and weighting the raw data. Evaluate the statistical methods and procedures used to obtain data in order to ensure validity, applicability, efficiency, and accuracy. Evaluate sources of information in order to determine any limitations in terms of reliability or usability. Plan data collection methods for specific projects and determine the types and sizes of sample groups to be used. Design research projects that apply valid scientific techniques and utilize information obtained from baselines or historical data in order to structure uncompromised and efficient analyses. Develop an understanding of fields to which statistical methods are to be applied in order to determine whether methods and results are appropriate. Supervise and provide instructions for workers collecting and tabulating data. Apply sampling techniques or utilize complete enumeration bases in order to determine and define groups to be surveyed. Adapt statistical methods in order to solve specific problems in many fields, such as economics, biology, and engineering. Develop and test experimental designs, sampling techniques, and analytical methods. Examine theories, such as those of probability and inference, in order to discover mathematical bases for new or improved methods of obtaining and evaluating numerical data.

**Education/Training Required:** Master's degree. **Education and Training Programs:** Applied Mathematics, General; Biostatistics; Business Statistics; Mathematical Statistics and Probability; Mathematics, General; Statistics, General; Statistics, Other. **Knowledge/Courses**—Mathematics, Computers and Electronics, English Language, Law and Government, Education and Training.

**Personality Type:** Conventional-Investigative. **Career Clusters:** 04 Business, Management, and Administration; 15 Science, Technology, Engineering, and Mathematics. **Career Pathways:** 4.2 Business Financial Management and Accounting; 15.2 Science and Mathematics. **Other Jobs in These Pathways:** Accountants; Architectural and Engineering Managers; Auditors; Billing and Posting Clerks; Billing, Cost, and Rate Clerks; Biofuels/Biodiesel Technology and Product Development Managers; Bookkeeping, Accounting, and Auditing Clerks; Brownfield Redevelopment Specialists and Site Managers; Community and Social Service Specialists, All Other; Compliance Managers; Education, Training, and Library Workers, All Other; Financial Analysts; Financial Managers, Branch or Department; Investment Fund Managers; Loss Prevention Managers; Managers, All Other; Medical Scientists, Except Epidemiologists; Payroll and Timekeeping Clerks; Regulatory Affairs Managers; Security Managers; Statement Clerks; Supply Chain Managers; Treasurers and Controllers; Wind Energy Operations Managers; Wind Energy Project Managers; others.

**Skills**—Programming, Mathematics, Science, Operations Analysis, Active Learning, Reading Comprehension, Critical Thinking, Learning Strategies.

**Work Environment:** Indoors; sitting; using hands; repetitive motions.

## Job Specialization: Biostatisticians

**Develop and apply biostatistical theory and methods to the study of life sciences.** Write research proposals or grant applications for submission to external bodies. Teach graduate or continuing education courses or seminars in biostatistics. Read current literature, attend meetings or conferences, and talk with colleagues to keep abreast of methodological or conceptual developments in fields such as biostatistics, pharmacology, life sciences, and social sciences. Prepare statistical data for inclusion in reports to data monitoring committees, federal regulatory agencies, managers, or clients. Prepare articles for publication or presentation at professional conferences. Calculate sample size requirements for clinical studies. Determine project plans, timelines, or technical objectives for statistical aspects of biological research studies. Assign work to biostatistical assistants or programmers. Write program code to analyze data using statistical analysis software. Write detailed analysis plans and descriptions of analyses and findings for research protocols or reports. Plan or direct research studies related to life sciences. Prepare tables and graphs to present clinical data or results. Monitor clinical trials or experiments to ensure adherence to established procedures or to verify the quality of data collected. Draw conclusions or make predictions based on data summaries or statistical analyses. Develop or use mathematical models to track changes in biological phenomena such as the spread of infectious diseases. Design surveys to assess health issues. Develop or implement data analysis algorithms. Design research studies in collaboration with physicians, life scientists, or other professionals. Design or maintain databases of biological data. Collect data through surveys or experimentation. Analyze archival data such as birth, death, and disease records. Review clinical or other medical research protocols and recommend appropriate statistical analyses. Provide biostatistical consultation to clients or colleagues.

**Education/Training Required:** Master's degree. **Education and Training Programs:** Applied Mathematics, General; Biostatistics; Business Statistics; Mathematical Statistics and Probability; Mathematics, General; Statistics, General; Statistics, Other. **Knowledge/Courses**—Mathematics, Biology, Computers and Electronics, Medicine and Dentistry, English Language, Education and Training.

**Personality Type:** Investigative-Conventional. **Career Cluster:** 15 Science, Technology, Engineering, and Mathematics. **Career Pathway:** 15.2 Science and Mathematics. **Other Jobs in This Pathway:** Architectural and Engineering Managers; Biochemists and Biophysicists; Biofuels/Biodiesel Technology and Product Development Managers; Bioinformatics Scientists; Biological Scientists, All Other; Biologists; Chemists; Clinical Data Managers; Clinical Research Coordinators; Community and Social Service Specialists, All Other; Dietitians and Nutritionists; Education, Training, and Library Workers, All Other; Geneticists; Geoscientists, Except Hydrologists and Geographers; Medical Scientists, Except Epidemiologists; Molecular and Cellular Biologists; Natural Sciences Managers; Operations Research Analysts; Physical Scientists, All Other; Social Scientists and Related Workers, All Other; Statisticians; Survey Researchers; Transportation Planners; Water Resource Specialists; Zoologists and Wildlife Biologists; others.

**Skills**—Programming, Science, Mathematics, Writing, Reading Comprehension, Operations Analysis, Active Learning, Instructing.

**Work Environment:** Indoors; sitting.

## Job Specialization: Clinical Data Managers

**Apply knowledge of health care and database management to analyze clinical data, and to identify and report trends.** Read technical literature and participate in continuing education or professional associations to maintain awareness of current database technology and best practices. Provide support and information to functional areas such as marketing, clinical monitoring, and medical affairs. Prepare appropriate formatting to datasets as requested. Evaluate processes and technologies, and suggest revisions to increase productivity and efficiency. Develop technical specifications for data management programming and communicate needs to information technology staff. Develop or select specific software programs for various research scenarios. Contribute to the compilation, organization, and production of protocols, clinical study reports, regulatory submissions, or other controlled documentation. Write work instruction manuals, data capture guidelines, or standard operating procedures. Track the flow of work forms including in-house data flow or electronic forms transfer. Train staff on technical procedures or software program usage. Supervise the work of data management project staff. Prepare data analysis listings and activity, performance, or progress reports. Perform quality control audits to ensure accuracy, completeness, or proper usage of clinical systems and data. Monitor work productivity or quality to ensure compliance with standard operating procedures. Generate data queries based on validation checks or errors and omissions identified during data entry to resolve identified problems. Design and validate clinical databases including designing or testing logic checks. Confer with end users to define or implement clinical system requirements such as data release formats, delivery schedules, and testing protocols. Analyze clinical data using appropriate statistical tools. Process clinical data including receipt, entry, verification, or filing of information.

**Education/Training Required:** Bachelor's degree. **Education and Training Programs:** Applied Mathematics, General; Biostatistics; Business Statistics; Mathematical Statistics and Probability; Mathematics, General; Statistics, General; Statistics, Other. **Knowledge/Courses**—Medicine and Dentistry, Biology, Clerical, Administration and Management, Computers and Electronics.

**Personality Type:** Conventional-Investigative. **Career Cluster:** 15 Science, Technology, Engineering, and Mathematics. **Career Pathway:** 15.2 Science and Mathematics. **Other Jobs in This Pathway:** Architectural and Engineering Managers; Biochemists and Biophysicists; Biofuels/Biodiesel Technology and Product Development Managers; Bioinformatics Scientists; Biological Scientists, All Other; Biologists; Biostatisticians; Chemists; Clinical Research Coordinators; Community and Social Service Specialists, All Other; Dietitians and Nutritionists; Education, Training, and Library Workers, All Other; Geneticists; Geoscientists, Except Hydrologists and Geographers; Medical Scientists, Except Epidemiologists; Molecular and Cellular Biologists; Natural Sciences Managers; Operations Research Analysts; Physical Scientists, All Other; Social Scientists and Related Workers, All Other; Statisticians; Survey Researchers; Transportation Planners; Water Resource Specialists; Zoologists and Wildlife Biologists; others.

**Skills**—Programming, Mathematics, Operations Analysis, Technology Design, Systems Evaluation, Systems Analysis, Instructing, Writing.

**Work Environment:** Indoors; sitting; repetitive motions.

# Stock Clerks and Order Fillers

* Annual Earnings: $21,290
* Earnings Growth Potential: Very low (23.3%)
* Growth: 7.2%
* Annual Job Openings: 56,260
* Self-Employed: 0.3%

**Considerations for Job Outlook:** Steady growth is expected, especially in retail trade where workers handling individual items and small quantities make job tasks difficult to automate. Job prospects should be good because of the need to replace workers who leave the occupation.

## Job Specialization: Marking Clerks

**Print and attach price tickets to articles of merchandise using one or several methods, such as marking price on tickets by hand or using ticket-printing machine.** Put price information on tickets, marking by hand or using ticket-printing machine. Compare printed price tickets with entries on purchase orders to verify accuracy and notify supervisor of discrepancies. Pin, paste, sew, tie, or staple tickets, tags, or labels to article. Record number and types of articles marked and pack articles in boxes. Mark selling price by hand on boxes containing merchandise. Record price, buyer, and grade of product on tickets attached to products auctioned. Keep records of production, returned goods, and related transactions. Indicate item size, style, color, and inspection results on tags, tickets, and labels, using rubber stamp or writing instrument. Change the price of books in a warehouse.

**Education/Training Required:** Short-term on-the-job training. **Education and Training Program:** Retailing and Retail Operations. **Knowledge/Courses**—Production and Processing, Sales and Marketing, Mathematics.

**Personality Type:** Conventional-Realistic-Enterprising. **Career Cluster:** 14 Marketing, Sales, and Service. **Career Pathway:** 14.2 Professional Sales and Marketing. **Other Jobs in This Pathway:** Cashiers; Counter and Rental Clerks; Door-To-Door Sales Workers, News and Street Vendors, and Related Workers; Driver/Sales Workers; Energy Brokers; First-Line Supervisors of Non-Retail Sales Workers; First-Line Supervisors of Retail Sales Workers; Hotel, Motel, and Resort Desk Clerks; Marketing Managers; Online Merchants; Order Fillers, Wholesale and Retail Sales; Parts Salespersons; Property, Real Estate, and Community Association Managers; Real Estate Sales Agents; Reservation and Transportation Ticket Agents and Travel Clerks; Retail Salespersons; Sales and Related Workers, All Other; Sales Representatives, Services, All Other; Sales Representatives, Wholesale and Manufacturing, Except Technical and Scientific Products; Sales Representatives, Wholesale and Manufacturing, Technical and Scientific Products; Solar Sales Representatives and Assessors; Stock Clerks—Stockroom, Warehouse, or Storage Yard; Stock Clerks, Sales Floor; Telemarketers; Wholesale and Retail Buyers, Except Farm Products; others.

**Skills**—None met the criteria.

**Work Environment:** Indoors; standing; walking and running; using hands; bending or twisting the body; repetitive motions.

## Job Specialization: Order Fillers, Wholesale and Retail Sales

**Fill customers' mail and telephone orders from stored merchandise in accordance with specifications on sales slips or order forms.** Read orders to ascertain catalog numbers, sizes, colors, and quantities of merchandise. Obtain merchandise from bins or shelves. Compute prices of items or groups of items. Complete order receipts. Keep records of outgoing orders. Place merchandise on conveyors leading to wrapping areas. Requisition additional materials, supplies, and equipment.

**Education/Training Required:** Short-term on-the-job training. **Education and Training Program:** Retailing and Retail Operations. **Knowledge/Courses**—Sales and Marketing.

**Personality Type:** Conventional-Realistic. **Career Cluster:** 14 Marketing, Sales, and Service. **Career Pathway:** 14.2 Professional Sales and Marketing. **Other Jobs in This Pathway:** Cashiers; Counter and Rental Clerks; Door-To-Door Sales Workers, News and Street Vendors, and Related Workers; Driver/Sales Workers; Energy Brokers; First-Line Supervisors of Non-Retail Sales Workers; First-Line Supervisors of Retail Sales Workers; Hotel, Motel, and Resort Desk Clerks; Marketing Managers; Marking Clerks; Online Merchants; Parts Salespersons; Property, Real Estate, and Community Association Managers; Real Estate Sales Agents; Reservation and Transportation Ticket Agents and Travel Clerks; Retail Salespersons; Sales and Related Workers, All Other; Sales Representatives, Services, All Other; Sales Representatives, Wholesale and Manufacturing, Except Technical and Scientific Products; Sales Representatives, Wholesale and Manufacturing, Technical and Scientific Products; Solar Sales

Representatives and Assessors; Stock Clerks—Stockroom, Warehouse, or Storage Yard; Stock Clerks, Sales Floor; Telemarketers; Wholesale and Retail Buyers, Except Farm Products; others.

**Skills**—None met the criteria.

**Work Environment:** Indoors; standing; using hands; repetitive motions; noise; contaminants.

## Job Specialization: Stock Clerks, Sales Floor

**Receive, store, and issue sales floor merchandise. Stock shelves, racks, cases, bins, and tables with merchandise and arrange merchandise displays to attract customers. May periodically take physical count of stock or check and mark merchandise.** Answer customers' questions about merchandise and advise customers on merchandise selection. Itemize and total customer merchandise selection at checkout counter, using cash register, and accept cash or charge card for purchases. Take inventory or examine merchandise to identify items to be reordered or replenished. Pack customer purchases in bags or cartons. Stock shelves, racks, cases, bins, and tables with new or transferred merchandise. Receive, open, unpack, and issue sales floor merchandise. Clean display cases, shelves, and aisles. Compare merchandise invoices to items actually received to ensure that shipments are correct. Requisition merchandise from supplier based on available space, merchandise on hand, customer demand, or advertised specials. Transport packages to customers' vehicles. Stamp, attach, or change price tags on merchandise, referring to price list. Design and set up advertising signs and displays of merchandise on shelves, counters, or tables to attract customers and promote sales.

**Education/Training Required:** Short-term on-the-job training. **Education and Training Program:** Retailing and Retail Operations.

**Personality Type:** Conventional-Realistic-Enterprising. **Career Cluster:** 14 Marketing, Sales, and Service. **Career Pathway:** 14.2 Professional Sales and Marketing. **Other Jobs in This Pathway:** Cashiers; Counter and Rental Clerks; Door-To-Door Sales Workers, News and Street Vendors, and Related Workers; Driver/Sales Workers; Energy Brokers; First-Line Supervisors of Non-Retail Sales Workers; First-Line Supervisors of Retail Sales Workers; Hotel, Motel, and Resort Desk Clerks; Marketing Managers; Marking Clerks; Online Merchants; Order Fillers, Wholesale and Retail Sales; Parts Salespersons; Property, Real Estate, and Community Association Managers; Real Estate

Sales Agents; Reservation and Transportation Ticket Agents and Travel Clerks; Retail Salespersons; Sales and Related Workers, All Other; Sales Representatives, Services, All Other; Sales Representatives, Wholesale and Manufacturing, Except Technical and Scientific Products; Sales Representatives, Wholesale and Manufacturing, Technical and Scientific Products; Solar Sales Representatives and Assessors; Stock Clerks—Stockroom, Warehouse, or Storage Yard; Telemarketers; Wholesale and Retail Buyers, Except Farm Products; others.

**Skills**—None met the criteria.

**Work Environment:** Indoors; standing; walking and running; kneeling, crouching, stooping, or crawling; using hands; bending or twisting the body; repetitive motions.

## Job Specialization: Stock Clerks— Stockroom, Warehouse, or Storage Yard

**Receive, store, and issue materials, equipment, and other items from stockroom, warehouse, or storage yard. Keep records and compile stock reports.** Receive and count stock items and record data manually or by using computer. Pack and unpack items to be stocked on shelves in stockrooms, warehouses, or storage yards. Verify inventory computations by comparing them to physical counts of stock and investigate discrepancies or adjust errors. Store items in an orderly and accessible manner in warehouses, tool rooms, supply rooms, or other areas. Mark stock items, using identification tags, stamps, electric marking tools, or other labeling equipment. Clean and maintain supplies, tools, equipment, and storage areas to ensure compliance with safety regulations. Determine proper storage methods, identification, and stock location based on turnover, environmental factors, and physical capabilities of facilities. Keep records on the use and damage of stock or stock handling equipment. Examine and inspect stock items for wear or defects, reporting any damage to supervisors. Provide assistance or direction to other stockroom, warehouse, or storage yard workers. Dispose of damaged or defective items or return them to vendors. Drive trucks to pick up incoming stock or to deliver parts to designated locations. Prepare and maintain records and reports of inventories, price lists, shortages, shipments, expenditures, and goods used or issued. Sell materials, equipment, and other items from stock in retail settings. Issue or distribute materials, products, parts, and supplies to customers or co-workers based on information from incoming requisitions. Advise retail customers or internal users on the appropriateness of parts, supplies, or materials requested. Purchase new or additional stock or prepare documents that provide for such purchases. Compile, review, and maintain data from contracts, purchase orders, requisitions, and other documents to assess supply needs. Confer with engineering and purchasing personnel and vendors regarding stock procurement and availability.

**Education/Training Required:** Short-term on-the-job training. **Education and Training Program:** Retailing and Retail Operations.

**Personality Type:** Realistic-Conventional. **Career Cluster:** 14 Marketing, Sales, and Service. **Career Pathway:** 14.2 Professional Sales and Marketing. **Other Jobs in This Pathway:** Cashiers; Counter and Rental Clerks; Door-To-Door Sales Workers, News and Street Vendors, and Related Workers; Driver/Sales Workers; Energy Brokers; First-Line Supervisors of Non-Retail Sales Workers; First-Line Supervisors of Retail Sales Workers; Hotel, Motel, and Resort Desk Clerks; Marketing Managers; Marking Clerks; Online Merchants; Order Fillers, Wholesale and Retail Sales; Parts Salespersons; Property, Real Estate, and Community Association Managers; Real Estate Sales Agents; Reservation and Transportation Ticket Agents and Travel Clerks; Retail Salespersons; Sales and Related Workers, All Other; Sales Representatives, Services, All Other; Sales Representatives, Wholesale and Manufacturing, Except Technical and Scientific Products; Sales Representatives, Wholesale and Manufacturing, Technical and Scientific Products; Solar Sales Representatives and Assessors; Stock Clerks, Sales Floor; Telemarketers; Wholesale and Retail Buyers, Except Farm Products; others.

**Skills**—Management of Material Resources, Persuasion, Negotiation, Service Orientation.

**Work Environment:** Indoors; standing; walking and running; using hands; bending or twisting the body; repetitive motions; contaminants.

## Structural Iron and Steel Workers

* Annual Earnings: $44,540
* Earnings Growth Potential: Medium (40.9%)
* Growth: 12.4%
* Annual Job Openings: 2,020
* Self-Employed: 5.1%

**Considerations for Job Outlook:** Opportunities are expected iron and metal workers to arise from the need to build new structures and from the need to maintain, repair, and replace existing ones. Job prospects should be best in the South and the West due to their growing populations.

**Raise, place, and unite iron or steel girders, columns, and other structural members to form completed structures or structural frameworks. May erect metal storage tanks and assemble prefabricated metal buildings.** Read specifications and blueprints to determine the locations, quantities, and sizes of materials required. Verify vertical and horizontal alignment of structural-steel members, using plumb bobs, laser equipment, transits, and/or levels. Connect columns, beams, and girders with bolts, following blueprints and instructions from supervisors. Hoist steel beams, girders, and columns into place, using cranes, or signal hoisting equipment operators to lift and position structural-steel members. Bolt aligned structural-steel members in position for permanent riveting, bolting, or welding into place. Ride on girders or other structural-steel members to position them or use rope to guide them into position. Fabricate metal parts, such as steel frames, columns, beams, and girders, according to blueprints or instructions from supervisors. Pull, push, or pry structural-steel members into approximate positions for bolting into place. Cut, bend, and weld steel pieces, using metal shears, torches, and welding equipment. Fasten structural-steel members to hoist cables, using chains, cables, or rope. Assemble hoisting equipment and rigging such as cables, pulleys, and hooks to move heavy equipment and materials. Force structural-steel members into final positions, using turnbuckles, crowbars, jacks, and hand tools. Erect metal and precast concrete components for structures such as buildings, bridges, dams, towers, storage tanks, fences, and highway guard rails. Unload and position prefabricated steel units for hoisting as needed. Drive drift pins through rivet holes to align rivet holes in structural-steel members with corresponding holes in previously placed members. Dismantle structures and equipment. Insert sealing strips, wiring, insulating material, ladders, flanges, gauges, and valves, depending on types of structures being assembled. Catch hot rivets in buckets and insert rivets in holes, using tongs. Place blocks under reinforcing bars used to reinforce floors.

**Education/Training Required:** Long-term on-the-job training. **Education and Training Programs:** Construction Trades, Other; Metal Building Assembly/Assembler. **Knowledge/Courses**—Building and Construction, Engineering and Technology, Mechanical, Production and Processing, Design, Physics.

**Personality Type:** Realistic-Investigative-Conventional. **Career Cluster:** 02 Architecture and Construction. **Career Pathway:** 2.2 Construction. **Other Jobs in This Pathway:**

Brickmasons and Blockmasons; Cement Masons and Concrete Finishers; Construction and Building Inspectors; Construction Carpenters; Construction Laborers; Construction Managers; Cost Estimators; Drywall and Ceiling Tile Installers; Electrical Power-Line Installers and Repairers; Electricians; Engineering Technicians, Except Drafters, All Other; First-Line Supervisors of Construction Trades and Extraction Workers; Heating and Air Conditioning Mechanics and Installers; Helpers—Carpenters; Helpers—Electricians; Helpers—Pipelayers, Plumbers, Pipefitters, and Steamfitters; Highway Maintenance Workers; Operating Engineers and Other Construction Equipment Operators; Painters, Construction and Maintenance; Pipe Fitters and Steamfitters; Plumbers; Refrigeration Mechanics and Installers; Roofers; Rough Carpenters; Solar Energy Installation Managers; others.

**Skills**—Equipment Selection, Operation and Control, Repairing, Equipment Maintenance, Quality Control Analysis, Installation, Troubleshooting, Operation Monitoring.

**Work Environment:** Outdoors; standing; climbing; walking and running; balancing; using hands; bending or twisting the body; repetitive motions; noise; very hot or cold; bright or inadequate lighting; contaminants; cramped work space; whole-body vibration; high places; hazardous conditions; hazardous equipment; minor burns, cuts, bites, or stings.

# Substance Abuse and Behavioral Disorder Counselors

* Annual Earnings: $38,120
* Earnings Growth Potential: Low (35.2%)
* Growth: 21.0%
* Annual Job Openings: 3,550
* Self-Employed: 6.0%

**Considerations for Job Outlook:** Increasing demand for services provided by counselors is expected to result in employment growth. But growth will vary by specialty and will be faster for mental health, substance abuse and behavioral disorder, and rehabilitation counselors than for counselors of other specialties. Opportunities should be favorable, particularly in rural areas.

**Counsel and advise individuals with alcohol; tobacco; drug; or other problems, such as gambling and eating disorders. May counsel individuals, families, or groups or engage in prevention programs.** Counsel clients and patients individually and in group sessions to assist in overcoming dependencies, adjusting to life, and making changes. Complete and maintain accurate records and reports regarding the patients' histories and progress, services provided, and other required information. Develop client treatment plans based on research, clinical experience, and client histories. Review and evaluate clients' progress in relation to measurable goals described in treatment and care plans. Interview clients, review records, and confer with other professionals to evaluate individuals' mental and physical condition and to determine their suitability for participation in a specific program. Intervene as advocate for clients or patients to resolve emergency problems in crisis situations. Provide clients or family members with information about addiction issues and about available services and programs, making appropriate referrals when necessary. Modify treatment plans to comply with changes in client status. Coordinate counseling efforts with mental health professionals and other health professionals such as doctors, nurses, and social workers. Attend training sessions to increase knowledge and skills. Plan and implement follow-up and aftercare programs for clients to be discharged from treatment programs. Conduct chemical dependency program orientation sessions. Counsel family members to assist them in understanding, dealing with, and supporting clients or patients. Participate in case conferences and staff meetings. Act as liaisons between clients and medical staff. Coordinate activities with courts, probation officers, community services, and other post-treatment agencies. Confer with family members or others close to clients to keep them informed of treatment planning and progress. Instruct others in program methods, procedures, and functions. Follow progress of discharged patients to determine effectiveness of treatments.

**Education/Training Required:** Bachelor's degree. **Education and Training Programs:** Clinical/Medical Social Work; Mental and Social Health Services and Allied Professions, Other; Substance Abuse/Addiction Counseling. **Knowledge/Courses**—Therapy and Counseling, Psychology, Sociology and Anthropology, Philosophy and Theology, Education and Training, Clerical.

**Personality Type:** Social-Artistic-Investigative. **Career Clusters:** 08 Health Science; 10 Human Services. **Career Pathways:** 8.1 Therapeutic Services; 8.3 Health Informatics; 10.2 Counseling and Mental Health Services. **Other Jobs in These Pathways:** Clergy; Clinical Psychologists; Counseling Psychologists; Dental Assistants; Dental Hygienists; Engineers, All Other; Executive Secretaries and Executive Administrative Assistants; First-Line Supervisors of Office and Administrative Support Workers; Healthcare Support Workers, All Other; Home Health Aides; Licensed Practical and Licensed Vocational Nurses; Medical and Clinical Laboratory Technicians; Medical and Health Services Managers; Medical Assistants; Medical Records and Health Information Technicians; Medical Secretaries; Pharmacists; Pharmacy Technicians; Physical Therapists; Public Relations Specialists; Radiologic Technologists; Receptionists and Information Clerks; Recreation Workers; Social and Human Service Assistants; Speech-Language Pathology Assistants; others.

**Skills**—Social Perceptiveness, Service Orientation, Persuasion, Learning Strategies, Active Listening, Negotiation, Monitoring, Systems Analysis.

**Work Environment:** Indoors; sitting.

# Subway and Streetcar Operators

- Annual Earnings: $56,880
- Earnings Growth Potential: Medium (36.4%)
- Growth: 18.8%
- Annual Job Openings: 390
- Self-Employed: 0.0%

**Considerations for Job Outlook:** Freight transportation and the occupations associated with it are expected to expand as global trade increases and as more goods are shipped by rail. Opportunities should be good for qualified job seekers because many workers, particularly at freight railroads, are expected to retire.

**Operate subway or elevated suburban train with no separate locomotive or electric-powered streetcar to transport passengers. May handle fares.** Operate controls to open and close transit vehicle doors. Drive and control rail-guided public transportation such as subways; elevated trains; and electric-powered streetcars, trams, or trolleys in order to transport passengers. Monitor lights indicating obstructions or other trains ahead and watch for car and truck traffic at crossings to stay alert to potential hazards. Direct emergency evacuation procedures. Regulate vehicle speed and the time spent at each stop in order to maintain schedules. Report delays, mechanical problems, and emergencies to supervisors or dispatchers, using radios. Make announcements to passengers, such as notifications of upcoming stops or schedule delays. Complete reports, including shift summaries and incident or accident reports. Greet passengers; provide information; and answer questions concerning fares, schedules, transfers, and routings. Attend meetings on driver and passenger safety in order to learn ways in which job performance might be affected. Collect fares from passengers and issue change and transfers. Record transactions and coin receptor readings in order to verify the amount of money collected.

**Education/Training Required:** Moderate-term on-the-job training. **Education and Training Program:** Truck and Bus Driver Training/Commercial Vehicle Operator and Instructor Training. **Knowledge/Courses**—Transportation, Public Safety and Security, Customer and Personal Service, Telecommunications, Mechanical, Communications and Media.

**Personality Type:** Realistic-Conventional. **Career Cluster:** 16 Transportation, Distribution, and Logistics. **Career Pathway:** 16.1 Transportation Operations. **Other Jobs in This Pathway:** Airline Pilots, Copilots, and Flight Engineers; Automotive and Watercraft Service Attendants; Automotive Master Mechanics; Bus Drivers, School or Special Client; Bus Drivers, Transit and Intercity; Commercial Pilots; Crane and Tower Operators; First-Line Supervisors of Helpers, Laborers, and Material Movers, Hand; First-Line Supervisors of Transportation and Material-Moving Machine and Vehicle Operators; Freight and Cargo Inspectors; Heavy and Tractor-Trailer Truck Drivers; Laborers and Freight, Stock, and Material Movers, Hand; Light Truck or Delivery Services Drivers; Mates—Ship, Boat, and Barge; Motor Vehicle Operators, All Other; Operating Engineers and Other Construction Equipment Operators; Parking Lot Attendants; Pilots, Ship; Railroad Conductors and Yardmasters; Sailors and Marine Oilers; Ship and Boat Captains; Storage and Distribution Managers; Taxi Drivers and Chauffeurs; Transportation Managers; Transportation Workers, All Other; others.

**Skills**—Operation and Control, Operation Monitoring, Equipment Maintenance, Repairing, Troubleshooting, Equipment Selection, Management of Financial Resources, Quality Control Analysis.

**Work Environment:** Outdoors; sitting; using hands; repetitive motions; noise; very hot or cold; bright or inadequate lighting; contaminants; hazardous conditions.

# Supervisors of Construction and Extraction Workers

❋ Annual Earnings: $58,680
❋ Earnings Growth Potential: Medium (38.3%)
❋ Growth: 15.4%
❋ Annual Job Openings: 24,220
❋ Self-Employed: 19.0%

**Considerations for Job Outlook:** Faster-than-average employment growth is projected.

**Directly supervise and coordinate activities of construction or extraction workers.** Examine and inspect work progress, equipment, and construction sites to verify safety and to ensure that specifications are met. Read specifications such as blueprints to determine construction requirements and to plan procedures. Estimate material and worker requirements to complete jobs. Supervise, coordinate, and schedule the activities of construction or extractive workers. Confer with managerial and technical personnel, other departments, and contractors in order to resolve problems and to coordinate activities. Coordinate work activities with other construction project activities. Locate, measure, and mark site locations and placement of structures and equipment, using measuring and marking equipment. Order or requisition materials and supplies. Record information such as personnel, production, and operational data on specified forms and reports. Assign work to employees based on material and worker requirements of specific jobs. Provide assistance to workers engaged in construction or extraction activities, using hand tools and equipment. Train workers in construction methods, operation of equipment, safety procedures, and company policies. Analyze worker and production problems and recommend solutions such as improving production methods or implementing motivational plans. Arrange for repairs of equipment and machinery. Suggest or initiate personnel actions such as promotions, transfers, and hires.

**Education/Training Required:** Work experience in a related occupation. **Education and Training Programs:** Blasting/Blaster; Building/Construction Finishing, Management, and Inspection, Other; Building/Construction Site Management/Manager; Building/Home/Construction Inspection/Inspector; Building/Property Maintenance; Carpentry/Carpenter; Concrete Finishing/Concrete Finisher; Construction Trades, Other; Drywall Installation/Drywaller; Electrical and Power Transmission Installation/Installer, General; Electrical and Power Transmission

Installers, Other; Electrician; Glazier Training; Lineworker; Masonry/Mason Training; Painting/Painter and Wall Coverer Training; Plumbing Technology/Plumber; Roofer Training; Well Drilling/Driller. **Knowledge/Courses—**Building and Construction, Mechanical, Design, Engineering and Technology, Production and Processing, Public Safety and Security.

**Personality Type:** Enterprising-Realistic-Conventional. **Career Cluster:** 02 Architecture and Construction. **Career Pathway:** 2.2 Construction. **Other Jobs in This Pathway:** Brickmasons and Blockmasons; Cement Masons and Concrete Finishers; Construction and Building Inspectors; Construction Carpenters; Construction Laborers; Construction Managers; Cost Estimators; Drywall and Ceiling Tile Installers; Electrical Power-Line Installers and Repairers; Electricians; Engineering Technicians, Except Drafters, All Other; Excavating and Loading Machine and Dragline Operators; Heating and Air Conditioning Mechanics and Installers; Helpers—Carpenters; Helpers—Electricians; Helpers—Pipelayers, Plumbers, Pipefitters, and Steamfitters; Highway Maintenance Workers; Operating Engineers and Other Construction Equipment Operators; Painters, Construction and Maintenance; Pipe Fitters and Steamfitters; Plumbers; Refrigeration Mechanics and Installers; Roofers; Rough Carpenters; Solar Energy Installation Managers; others.

**Skills**—Equipment Selection, Management of Personnel Resources, Equipment Maintenance, Operation and Control, Quality Control Analysis, Operations Analysis, Management of Material Resources, Troubleshooting.

**Work Environment:** Outdoors; standing; using hands; noise; very hot or cold; bright or inadequate lighting; contaminants; hazardous equipment.

## Job Specialization: Solar Energy Installation Managers

**Direct work crews installing residential or commercial solar photovoltaic or thermal systems.** Plan and coordinate installations of photovoltaic (PV) solar and solar thermal systems to ensure conformance to codes. Supervise solar installers, technicians, and subcontractors for solar installation projects to ensure compliance with safety standards. Assess potential solar installation sites to determine feasibility and design requirements. Assess system performance or functionality at the system, subsystem, and component levels. Coordinate or schedule building inspections for solar installation projects. Monitor work of contractors and subcontractors to ensure projects conform to plans,

specifications, schedules, or budgets. Perform start-up of systems for testing or customer implementation. Provide technical assistance to installers, technicians, or other solar professionals in areas such as solar electric systems, solar thermal systems, electrical systems, and mechanical systems. Visit customer sites to determine solar system needs, requirements, or specifications. Develop and maintain system architecture, including all piping, instrumentation, or process flow diagrams. Estimate materials, equipment, and personnel needed for residential or commercial solar installation projects. Evaluate subcontractors or subcontractor bids for quality, cost, and reliability. Identify means to reduce costs, minimize risks, or increase efficiency of solar installation projects. Prepare solar installation project proposals, quotes, budgets, or schedules. Purchase or rent equipment for solar energy system installation.

**Education/Training Required:** Work experience in a related occupation. **Education and Training Programs:** Blasting/Blaster; Building/Construction Finishing, Management, and Inspection, Other; Building/Construction Site Management/Manager; Building/Home/Construction Inspection/Inspector; Building/Property Maintenance; Carpentry/Carpenter; Concrete Finishing/Concrete Finisher; Construction Trades, Other; Drywall Installation/Drywaller; Electrical and Power Transmission Installation/Installer, General; Electrical and Power Transmission Installers, Other; Electrician; Glazier Training; Lineworker; Masonry/Mason Training; Painting/Painter and Wall Coverer Training; Plumbing Technology/Plumber; Roofer Training; Well Drilling/Driller. **Knowledge/Courses—**No data available.

**Personality Type:** No data available. **Career Cluster:** 02 Architecture and Construction. **Career Pathway:** 2.2 Construction. **Other Jobs in This Pathway:** Brickmasons and Blockmasons; Cement Masons and Concrete Finishers; Construction and Building Inspectors; Construction Carpenters; Construction Laborers; Construction Managers; Cost Estimators; Drywall and Ceiling Tile Installers; Electrical Power-Line Installers and Repairers; Electricians; Engineering Technicians, Except Drafters, All Other; Excavating and Loading Machine and Dragline Operators; First-Line Supervisors of Construction Trades and Extraction Workers; Heating and Air Conditioning Mechanics and Installers; Helpers—Carpenters; Helpers—Electricians; Helpers—Pipelayers, Plumbers, Pipefitters, and Steamfitters; Highway Maintenance Workers; Operating Engineers and Other Construction Equipment Operators; Painters, Construction and Maintenance; Pipe Fitters and Steamfitters; Plumbers; Refrigeration Mechanics and Installers; Roofers; Rough Carpenters; others.

**Skills**—No data available.

**Work Environment:** No data available.

# Surgical Technologists

- ❋ Annual Earnings: $39,920
- ❋ Earnings Growth Potential: Low (29.6%)
- ❋ Growth: 25.3%
- ❋ Annual Job Openings: 4,630
- ❋ Self-Employed: 0.2%

**Considerations for Job Outlook:** Employment growth for these workers is expected as a growing and aging population has more surgeries and as advances allow technologists to assist surgeons more often. Job opportunities should be best for technologists who are certified.

**Assist in operations under the supervision of surgeons, registered nurses, or other surgical personnel. May help set up operating rooms; prepare and transport patients for surgery; adjust lights and equipment; pass instruments and other supplies to surgeons and surgeons' assistants; hold retractors; cut sutures; and help count sponges, needles, supplies, and instruments.** Count sponges, needles, and instruments before and after operations. Maintain a proper sterile field during surgical procedures. Hand instruments and supplies to surgeons and surgeons' assistants, hold retractors and cut sutures, and perform other tasks as directed by surgeons during operations. Prepare patients for surgery, including positioning patients on operating tables and covering them with sterile surgical drapes to prevent exposure. Scrub arms and hands and assist surgical teams to scrub and put on gloves, masks, and surgical clothing. Wash and sterilize equipment, using germicides and sterilizers. Monitor and continually assess operating room conditions, including needs of the patient and surgical team. Prepare dressings or bandages and apply or assist with their application following surgeries. Clean and restock operating rooms, gathering and placing equipment and supplies and arranging instruments according to instructions such as those found on a preference card. Operate, assemble, adjust, or monitor sterilizers, lights, suction machines, and diagnostic equipment to ensure proper operation. Prepare, care for, and dispose of tissue specimens taken for laboratory analysis. Provide technical assistance to surgeons, surgical nurses, and anesthesiologists. Maintain supply of fluids such as plasma, saline, blood, and glucose for use during operations. Maintain files and records of surgical procedures. Observe patients' vital signs to assess physical condition. Order surgical supplies.

**Education/Training Required:** Postsecondary vocational training. **Education and Training Programs:** Pathology/Pathologist Assistant Training; Surgical Technology/Technologist. **Knowledge/Courses**—Medicine and Dentistry, Biology, Psychology, Chemistry, Therapy and Counseling, Customer and Personal Service.

**Personality Type:** Realistic-Social-Conventional. **Career Cluster:** 08 Health Science. **Career Pathway:** 8.2 Diagnostics Services. **Other Jobs in This Pathway:** Ambulance Drivers and Attendants, Except Emergency Medical Technicians; Anesthesiologist Assistants; Cardiovascular Technologists and Technicians; Cytogenetic Technologists; Cytotechnologists; Diagnostic Medical Sonographers; Emergency Medical Technicians and Paramedics; Endoscopy Technicians; Health Diagnosing and Treating Practitioners, All Other; Health Technologists and Technicians, All Other; Healthcare Practitioners and Technical Workers, All Other; Histotechnologists and Histologic Technicians; Medical and Clinical Laboratory Technicians; Medical and Clinical Laboratory Technologists; Medical and Health Services Managers; Medical Assistants; Medical Equipment Preparers; Neurodiagnostic Technologists; Nuclear Medicine Technologists; Ophthalmic Laboratory Technicians; Physical Scientists, All Other; Physician Assistants; Radiologic Technicians; Radiologic Technologists; Veterinary Assistants and Laboratory Animal Caretakers; others.

**Skills**—Equipment Maintenance, Equipment Selection, Operation Monitoring, Repairing, Quality Control Analysis, Operation and Control, Management of Material Resources, Coordination.

**Work Environment:** Indoors; standing; using hands; bending or twisting the body; repetitive motions; contaminants; exposed to radiation; exposed to disease or infections; hazardous conditions; hazardous equipment; minor burns, cuts, bites, or stings.

# Survey Researchers

- ❋ Annual Earnings: $36,050
- ❋ Earnings Growth Potential: High (48.2%)
- ❋ Growth: 30.3%
- ❋ Annual Job Openings: 1,340
- ❋ Self-Employed: 6.7%

**Considerations for Job Outlook:** Demand for market research is expected as businesses strive to increase sales and as governments rely on survey research to form public policy. Opportunities should be best for job seekers who have a doctoral degree and strong quantitative skills.

Design or conduct surveys. May supervise interviewers who conduct the survey in person or over the telephone. May present survey results to client. Prepare and present summaries and analyses of survey data, including tables, graphs, and fact sheets that describe survey techniques and results. Consult with clients in order to identify survey needs and any specific requirements, such as special samples. Analyze data from surveys, old records, and/or case studies, using statistical software programs. Review, classify, and record survey data in preparation for computer analysis. Conduct research in order to gather information about survey topics. Conduct surveys and collect data, using methods such as interviews, questionnaires, focus groups, market analysis surveys, public opinion polls, literature reviews, and file reviews. Collaborate with other researchers in the planning, implementation, and evaluation of surveys. Direct and review the work of staff members, including survey support staff and interviewers who gather survey data. Monitor and evaluate survey progress and performance, using sample disposition reports and response rate calculations. Produce documentation of the questionnaire development process, data collection methods, sampling designs, and decisions related to sample statistical weighting. Determine and specify details of survey projects, including sources of information, procedures to be used, and the design of survey instruments and materials. Support, plan, and coordinate operations for single or multiple surveys. Direct updates and changes in survey implementation and methods. Hire and train recruiters and data collectors. Write training manuals to be used by survey interviewers.

**Education/Training Required:** Bachelor's degree. **Education and Training Programs:** Applied Economics; Business/Managerial Economics; Economics, General; Marketing Research. **Knowledge/Courses**—Administration and Management, Sociology and Anthropology, Mathematics, Economics and Accounting, Personnel and Human Resources, Clerical.

**Personality Type:** Investigative-Conventional-Enterprising. **Career Clusters:** 04 Business, Management, and Administration; 14 Marketing, Sales, and Service; 15 Science, Technology, Engineering, and Mathematics. **Career Pathways:** 4.1 Management; 14.5 Marketing Information Management and Research; 15.2 Science and Mathematics. **Other Jobs in These Pathways:** Brownfield Redevelopment Specialists and Site Managers; Business Continuity Planners; Business Operations Specialists, All Other; Chief Executives; Chief Sustainability Officers; Compliance Managers; Computer and Information Systems Managers; Construction Managers; Customs Brokers; Energy Auditors; First-Line Supervisors of Office and Administrative Support Workers; First-Line Supervisors of Retail Sales Workers; General and Operations Managers; Investment Fund Managers; Loss Prevention Managers; Management Analysts; Managers, All Other; Regulatory Affairs Managers; Sales Managers; Security Management Specialists; Security Managers; Supply Chain Managers; Sustainability Specialists; Wind Energy Operations Managers; Wind Energy Project Managers; others.

**Skills**—Programming, Mathematics, Writing, Science, Reading Comprehension, Learning Strategies, Speaking, Management of Financial Resources.

**Work Environment:** Indoors; sitting; noise.

# Surveying and Mapping Technicians

- ❋ Annual Earnings: $37,900
- ❋ Earnings Growth Potential: Medium (38.1%)
- ❋ Growth: 20.4%
- ❋ Annual Job Openings: 2,940
- ❋ Self-Employed: 5.6%

**Considerations for Job Outlook:** Increasing demand for geographic information should be the main source of employment growth. Job seekers with a bachelor's degree and strong technical skills should have favorable prospects.

## Job Specialization: Mapping Technicians

**Calculate mapmaking information from field notes and draw and verify accuracy of topographical maps.** Check all layers of maps to ensure accuracy, identifying and marking errors and making corrections. Determine scales, line sizes, and colors to be used for hard copies of computerized maps, using plotters. Monitor mapping work and the updating of maps to ensure accuracy, the inclusion of new and/or changed information, and compliance with rules and regulations. Identify and compile database information to create maps in response to requests. Produce and update overlay maps to show information boundaries, water locations, and topographic features on various base maps and at different scales. Trace contours and topographic details to generate maps that denote specific land and property locations and geographic attributes. Lay out and match aerial photographs in sequences in which they were taken and identify any areas missing from photographs. Compare topographical features and contour lines with images from aerial photographs, old maps, and other reference materials to verify the accuracy of their identification. Compute and measure scaled distances between reference points to establish relative positions of adjoining prints and enable the creation of photographic mosaics. Research resources such as survey maps and legal descriptions to verify property lines and to obtain information needed for mapping. Form three-dimensional images of aerial photographs taken from different locations, using mathematical techniques and plotting instruments. Enter GPS data, legal deeds, field notes, and land survey reports into GIS workstations so that information can be transformed into graphic land descriptions such as maps and drawings. Analyze aerial photographs to detect and interpret significant military, industrial, resource, or topographical data. Redraw and correct maps, such as revising parcel maps to reflect tax code area changes, using information from official records and surveys.

**Education/Training Required:** Moderate-term on-the-job training. **Education and Training Programs:** Geographic Information Science and Cartography; Surveying Technology/Surveying. **Knowledge/Courses**—Geography, Design, Computers and Electronics, Engineering and Technology, Mathematics, Clerical.

**Personality Type:** Conventional-Realistic. **Career Clusters:** 07 Government and Public Administration; 13 Manufacturing. **Career Pathways:** 7.1 Governance; 13.3 Maintenance, Installation, and Repair. **Other Jobs in These Pathways:** Administrative Services Managers; Aircraft Mechanics and Service Technicians; Automotive Specialty Technicians; Biological Technicians; Chief Executives; Chief Sustainability Officers; Civil Engineering Technicians; Compliance Managers; Computer, Automated Teller, and Office Machine Repairers; Electrical and Electronic Equipment Assemblers; Electrical and Electronics Repairers, Commercial and Industrial Equipment; Electrical Engineering Technicians; Electronics Engineering Technicians; General and Operations Managers; Helpers—Installation, Maintenance, and Repair Workers; Industrial Machinery Mechanics; Installation, Maintenance, and Repair Workers, All Other; Managers, All Other; Mobile Heavy Equipment Mechanics, Except Engines; Regulatory Affairs Managers; Social and Community Service Managers; Storage and Distribution Managers; Telecommunications Line Installers and Repairers; Tire Repairers and Changers; Transportation Managers; others.

**Skills**—Programming, Mathematics, Quality Control Analysis, Management of Personnel Resources, Learning Strategies, Instructing, Operation and Control, Writing.

**Work Environment:** Indoors; sitting; using hands; repetitive motions.

# Job Specialization: Surveying Technicians

**Adjust and operate surveying instruments such as theodolite and electronic distance-measuring equipment and compile notes, make sketches, and enter data into computers.** Perform calculations to determine Earth curvature corrections, atmospheric impacts on measurements, traverse closures and adjustments, azimuths, level runs, and placement of markers. Record survey measurements and descriptive data using notes, drawings, sketches, and inked tracings. Search for section corners, property irons, and survey points. Position and hold the vertical rods, or targets, that theodolite operators use for sighting to measure angles, distances, and elevations. Lay out grids and determine horizontal and vertical controls. Compare survey computations with applicable standards to determine adequacy of data. Set out and recover stakes, marks, and other monumentation. Conduct surveys to ascertain the locations of natural features and man-made structures on Earth's surface, underground, and underwater, using electronic distance-measuring equipment and other surveying instruments. Direct and supervise work of subordinate members of surveying parties. Compile information necessary to stake projects for construction, using engineering plans. Prepare topographic and contour maps of land surveyed, including site features and other relevant information, such as charts, drawings, and survey notes. Place and hold measuring tapes when electronic distance-measuring equipment is not used. Collect information needed to carry out new surveys using source maps, previous survey data, photographs, computer records, and other relevant information. Operate and manage land-information computer systems, performing tasks such as storing data, making inquiries, and producing plots and reports. Run rods for benches and cross-section elevations. Perform manual labor, such as cutting brush for lines, carrying stakes, rebar, and other heavy items, and stacking rods. Maintain equipment and vehicles used by surveying crews. Provide assistance in the development of methods and procedures for conducting field surveys.

**Education/Training Required:** Moderate-term on-the-job training. **Education and Training Programs:** Geographic Information Science and Cartography; Surveying Technology/Surveying. **Knowledge/Courses**—Geography, Design, Building and Construction, Mathematics, Law and Government, Engineering and Technology.

**Personality Type:** Realistic-Conventional. **Career Clusters:** 02 Architecture and Construction; 07 Government and Public Administration. **Career Pathways:** 2.1 Design/Pre-Construction; 7.1 Governance. **Other Jobs in These Pathways:** Administrative Services Managers; Architects, Except Landscape and Naval; Architectural and Engineering Managers; Architectural Drafters; Chief Executives; Chief Sustainability Officers; Civil Drafters; Civil Engineering Technicians; Compliance Managers; Electrical Drafters; Electronic Drafters; Engineering Technicians, Except Drafters, All Other; Engineers, All Other; General and Operations Managers; Geodetic Surveyors; Interior Designers; Legislators; Managers, All Other; Mapping Technicians; Mechanical Drafters; Regulatory Affairs Managers; Reporters and Correspondents; Social and Community Service Managers; Storage and Distribution Managers; Transportation Managers; others.

**Skills**—Equipment Maintenance, Operation and Control, Repairing, Science, Equipment Selection, Mathematics, Troubleshooting, Operation Monitoring.

**Work Environment:** More often outdoors than indoors; standing; walking and running; using hands; noise; very hot or cold; contaminants; hazardous equipment; minor burns, cuts, bites, or stings.

# Surveyors

- ❀ Annual Earnings: $54,880
- ❀ Earnings Growth Potential: High (43.9%)
- ❀ Growth: 14.9%
- ❀ Annual Job Openings: 2,330
- ❀ Self-Employed: 2.5%

**Considerations for Job Outlook:** Increasing demand for geographic information should be the main source of employment growth. Job seekers with a bachelor's degree and strong technical skills should have favorable prospects.

**Make exact measurements and determine property boundaries. Provide data relevant to the shape, contour, gravitation, location, elevation, or dimension of land or land features on or near Earth's surface for engineering, mapmaking, mining, land evaluation, construction, and other purposes.** Verify the accuracy of survey data including measurements and calculations conducted at survey sites. Calculate heights, depths, relative positions, property lines, and other characteristics of terrain. Search legal records, survey records, and land titles to obtain information about property boundaries in areas to be surveyed. Prepare and maintain sketches, maps, reports, and legal descriptions of surveys to describe, certify, and assume liability for work performed. Direct or conduct surveys to establish legal boundaries for properties, based on legal deeds and titles. Prepare or supervise preparation of all data, charts, plots, maps, records, and documents related to surveys. Write descriptions of property boundary surveys for use in deeds, leases, or other legal documents. Compute geodetic measurements and interpret survey data to determine positions, shapes, and elevations of geomorphic and topographic features. Determine longitudes and latitudes of important features and boundaries in survey areas using theodolites, transits, levels, and satellite-based global positioning systems (GPS). Record the results of surveys including the shape, contour, location, elevation, and dimensions of land or land features. Coordinate findings with the work of engineering and architectural personnel, clients, and others concerned with projects. Establish fixed points for use in making maps, using geodetic and engineering instruments. Train assistants and helpers, and direct their work in such activities as performing surveys or drafting maps. Plan and conduct ground surveys designed to establish baselines, elevations, and other geodetic measurements. Adjust surveying instruments to maintain their accuracy. Analyze survey objectives and specifications to prepare survey proposals or to direct others in survey proposal preparation. Develop criteria for survey methods and procedures.

**Education/Training Required:** Bachelor's degree. **Education and Training Program:** Surveying Technology/Surveying. **Knowledge/Courses**—Geography, Design, Building and Construction, History and Archeology, Engineering and Technology, Law and Government.

**Personality Type:** Realistic-Conventional-Investigative. **Career Cluster:** 02 Architecture and Construction. **Career Pathway:** 2.1 Design/Pre-Construction. **Other Jobs in This Pathway:** Architects, Except Landscape and Naval; Architectural and Engineering Managers; Architectural Drafters; Cartographers and Photogrammetrists; Civil Drafters; Civil Engineering Technicians; Drafters, All Other; Electrical Drafters; Electronic Drafters; Engineering Technicians, Except Drafters, All Other; Engineers, All Other; Geodetic Surveyors; Interior Designers; Landscape Architects; Mechanical Drafters; Surveying Technicians.

**Skills**—Science, Equipment Selection, Mathematics, Repairing, Equipment Maintenance, Management of Personnel Resources, Operation Monitoring, Quality Control Analysis.

**Work Environment:** More often outdoors than indoors; standing; walking and running; using hands; noise; very hot or cold; hazardous equipment; minor burns, cuts, bites, or stings.

## Job Specialization: Geodetic Surveyors

**Measure large areas of Earth's surface, using satellite observations, global navigation satellite systems (GNSS), light detection and ranging (LIDAR), or related sources.** Review existing standards, controls, or equipment used, recommending changes or upgrades as needed. Provide training and interpretation in the use of methods or procedures for observing and checking controls for geodetic and plane coordinates. Plan or direct the work of geodetic surveying staff, providing technical consultation as needed. Distribute compiled geodetic data to government agencies or the general public. Read current literature, talk with colleagues, continue education, or participate in professional organizations or conferences to keep abreast of developments in technology, equipment, or systems. Verify the mathematical correctness of newly collected survey data. Request additional survey data when field collection errors occur or engineering surveying specifications are not maintained. Prepare progress or technical reports. Maintain databases of geodetic and related information including coordinate, descriptive, or quality assurance data. Compute, retrace, or adjust existing surveys of features such as highway alignments, property boundaries, utilities, control, and other surveys to match other measurements and to ensure accuracy and continuity of data used in engineering, surveying, or construction projects. Compute horizontal and vertical coordinates of control networks using direct leveling or other geodetic survey techniques such as triangulation, trilateration, and traversing to establish features of the earth's surface. Calculate the exact horizontal and vertical position of points on the earth's surface. Analyze control or survey data to ensure adherence to project specifications or land survey standards. Assess the quality of control data to determine the need for additional survey data for engineering, construction, or other projects.

**Education/Training Required:** Bachelor's degree. **Education and Training Program:** Surveying Technology/ Surveying. **Knowledge/Courses**—Geography, Physics, Mathematics, Engineering and Technology, Computers and Electronics, Design.

**Personality Type:** Investigative-Conventional-Realistic. **Career Cluster:** 02 Architecture and Construction. **Career Pathway:** 2.1 Design/Pre-Construction. **Other Jobs in This Pathway:** Architects, Except Landscape and Naval; Architectural and Engineering Managers; Architectural Drafters; Cartographers and Photogrammetrists; Civil Drafters; Civil Engineering Technicians; Drafters, All Other; Electrical Drafters; Electronic Drafters; Engineering Technicians, Except Drafters, All Other; Engineers, All Other; Interior Designers; Landscape Architects; Mechanical Drafters; Surveying Technicians.

**Skills**—Mathematics, Programming, Science, Equipment Selection, Quality Control Analysis, Operation and Control, Writing, Management of Personnel Resources.

**Work Environment:** More often outdoors than indoors; standing; using hands; very hot or cold.

## Tapers

- ❊ Annual Earnings: $45,490
- ❊ Earnings Growth Potential: Medium (39.6%)
- ❊ Growth: 13.0%
- ❊ Annual Job Openings: 900
- ❊ Self-Employed: 18.8%

**Considerations for Job Outlook:** Projected employment growth is likely to stem from increases in new construction and remodeling. Overall job prospects are expected to be good, especially for experienced workers.

**Seal joints between sheets of plasterboard or other wallboard to prepare wall surfaces for painting or papering.** Sand rough spots of dried cement between applications of compounds. Remove extra compound after surfaces have been covered sufficiently. Press paper tape over joints to embed tape into sealing compound and to seal joints. Mix sealing compounds by hand or with portable electric mixers. Install metal molding at wall corners to secure wallboards. Check adhesives to ensure that they will work and will remain durable. Apply texturizing compounds and primers to walls and ceilings before final finishing, using trowels, brushes, rollers, or spray guns. Sand or patch nicks or cracks in plasterboard or wallboard. Apply additional coats to fill in holes and make surfaces smooth. Use mechanical applicators that spread compounds and embed tape in one operation. Spread sealing compound between boards or panels and over cracks, holes, and nail and screw heads, using trowels, broadknives, or spatulas. Spread and smooth cementing material over tape, using trowels or floating machines to blend joints with wall surfaces. Select the correct sealing compound or tape. Countersink nails or screws below surfaces of walls before applying sealing compounds, using hammers or screwdrivers.

**Education/Training Required:** Moderate-term on-the-job training. **Education and Training Program:** Construction Trades, Other. **Knowledge/Courses**—Building and Construction, Design, Public Safety and Security.

**Personality Type:** Realistic. **Career Cluster:** 02 Architecture and Construction. **Career Pathway:** 2.2 Construction. **Other Jobs in This Pathway:** Brickmasons and Blockmasons; Cement Masons and Concrete Finishers; Construction and Building Inspectors; Construction Carpenters; Construction Laborers; Construction Managers; Cost Estimators; Drywall and Ceiling Tile Installers; Electrical Power-Line Installers and Repairers; Electricians; Engineering Technicians, Except Drafters, All Other; First-Line Supervisors of Construction Trades and Extraction Workers; Heating and Air Conditioning Mechanics and Installers; Helpers—Carpenters; Helpers—Electricians; Helpers—Pipelayers, Plumbers, Pipefitters, and Steamfitters; Highway Maintenance Workers; Operating Engineers and Other Construction Equipment Operators; Painters, Construction and Maintenance; Pipe Fitters and Steamfitters; Plumbers; Refrigeration Mechanics and Installers; Roofers; Rough Carpenters; Solar Energy Installation Managers; others.

**Skills**—Repairing, Equipment Selection, Installation, Equipment Maintenance.

**Work Environment:** Standing; climbing; walking and running; kneeling, crouching, stooping, or crawling; balancing; using hands; bending or twisting the body; repetitive motions; noise; contaminants; cramped work space; high places.

# Tax Examiners and Collectors, and Revenue Agents

- ❋ Annual Earnings: $49,360
- ❋ Earnings Growth Potential: Medium (40.2%)
- ❋ Growth: 13.0%
- ❋ Annual Job Openings: 3,520
- ❋ Self-Employed: 2.3%

**Considerations for Job Outlook:** Employment growth of revenue agents and tax collectors should remain strong. The Federal Government is expected to increase its tax enforcement efforts, but demand for these workers' services is expected to be adversely affected by the automation of examiners' tasks and outsourcing of collection duties to private agencies.

**Determine tax liability or collect taxes from individuals or business firms according to prescribed laws and regulations.** Collect taxes from individuals or businesses according to prescribed laws and regulations. Maintain knowledge of tax code changes and of accounting procedures and theory to properly evaluate financial information. Maintain records for each case, including contacts, telephone numbers, and actions taken. Confer with taxpayers or their representatives to discuss the issues, laws, and regulations involved in returns and to resolve problems with returns. Contact taxpayers by mail or telephone to address discrepancies and to request supporting documentation. Send notices to taxpayers when accounts are delinquent. Notify taxpayers of any overpayment or underpayment and either issue a refund or request further payment. Conduct independent field audits and investigations of income tax returns to verify information or to amend tax liabilities. Review filed tax returns to determine whether claimed tax credits and deductions are allowed by law. Review selected tax returns to determine the nature and extent of audits to be performed on them. Enter tax return information into computers for processing. Examine accounting systems and records to determine whether accounting methods used were appropriate and in compliance with statutory provisions. Process individual and corporate income tax returns and sales and excise tax returns. Impose payment deadlines on delinquent taxpayers and monitor payments to ensure that deadlines are met. Check tax forms to verify that names and taxpayer identification numbers are correct, that computations have been performed correctly, or that amounts match those on supporting documentation. Examine and analyze tax assets and liabilities to determine resolution of delinquent tax problems. Recommend criminal prosecutions or civil penalties. Determine appropriate methods of debt settlement, such as offers of compromise, wage garnishment, or seizure and sale of property.

**Education/Training Required:** Bachelor's degree. **Education and Training Programs:** Accounting; Taxation. **Knowledge/Courses**—Law and Government, Customer and Personal Service, Economics and Accounting, Computers and Electronics, Clerical, Mathematics.

**Personality Type:** Conventional-Enterprising. **Career Cluster:** 07 Government and Public Administration. **Career Pathway:** 7.5 Revenue and Taxation. **Other Jobs in This Pathway:** Financial Examiners; Tax Preparers.

**Skills**—Programming, Reading Comprehension, Mathematics, Active Learning, Operations Analysis, Judgment and Decision Making, Negotiation, Active Listening.

**Work Environment:** Indoors; sitting; repetitive motions.

# Taxi Drivers and Chauffeurs

- ❋ Annual Earnings: $22,440
- ❋ Earnings Growth Potential: Low (26.6%)
- ❋ Growth: 15.5%
- ❋ Annual Job Openings: 7,730
- ❋ Self-Employed: 26.3%

**Considerations for Job Outlook:** Growth in tourism and business travel is expected to lead to employment increases for these workers. Job opportunities are expected to be plentiful.

**Drive automobiles, vans, or limousines to transport passengers. May occasionally carry cargo.** Test vehicle equipment such as lights, brakes, horns, or windshield wipers to ensure proper operation. Notify dispatchers or company mechanics of vehicle problems. Drive taxicabs, limousines, company cars, or privately owned vehicles to transport passengers. Follow regulations governing taxi operation and ensure that passengers follow safety regulations. Pick up passengers at prearranged locations, at taxi stands, or by cruising streets in high-traffic areas. Perform routine vehicle maintenance such as regulating tire pressure and adding gasoline, oil, and water. Communicate with dispatchers by radio, telephone, or computer to exchange information and receive requests for passenger service. Record name, date, and taxi identification information on trip sheets, along with trip information such as time and place of pickup and dropoff and total fee. Complete accident reports when necessary. Provide passengers with assistance entering and exiting vehicles and help them with any luggage. Arrange to pick up particular customers or groups on a regular schedule. Vacuum and clean interiors and wash and polish exteriors of automobiles. Pick up or meet employers according to requests, appointments, or schedules. Operate vans with special equipment such as wheelchair lifts to transport people with special needs. Collect fares or vouchers from passengers and make change or issue receipts as necessary. Determine fares based on trip distances and times, using taximeters and fee schedules, and announce fares to passengers. Perform minor vehicle repairs such as cleaning spark plugs or take vehicles to mechanics for servicing. Turn the taximeter on when passengers enter the cab and turn it off when they reach the final destination. Report to taxicab services or garages to receive vehicle assignments. Perform errands for customers or employers, such as delivering or picking up mail and packages.

**Education/Training Required:** Short-term on-the-job training. **Education and Training Program:** Truck and Bus Driver Training/Commercial Vehicle Operator and Instructor Training. **Knowledge/Courses**—Transportation, Psychology.

**Personality Type:** Realistic-Enterprising. **Career Cluster:** 16 Transportation, Distribution, and Logistics. **Career Pathway:** 16.1 Transportation Operations. **Other Jobs in This Pathway:** Airline Pilots, Copilots, and Flight Engineers; Automotive and Watercraft Service Attendants; Automotive Master Mechanics; Bus Drivers, School or Special Client; Bus Drivers, Transit and Intercity; Commercial Pilots; Crane and Tower Operators; First-Line Supervisors of Helpers, Laborers, and Material Movers, Hand; First-Line Supervisors of Transportation and Material-Moving Machine and Vehicle Operators; Freight and Cargo Inspectors; Heavy and Tractor-Trailer Truck Drivers; Laborers and Freight, Stock, and Material Movers, Hand; Light Truck or Delivery Services Drivers; Mates—Ship, Boat, and Barge; Motor Vehicle Operators, All Other; Operating Engineers and Other Construction Equipment Operators; Parking Lot Attendants; Pilots, Ship; Railroad Conductors and Yardmasters; Sailors and Marine Oilers; Ship and Boat Captains; Storage and Distribution Managers; Transportation Inspectors; Transportation Managers; Transportation Workers, All Other; others.

**Skills**—Operation and Control, Operation Monitoring, Service Orientation.

**Work Environment:** Outdoors; sitting; noise; very hot or cold; contaminants.

# Teacher Assistants

- ❋ Annual Earnings: $23,220
- ❋ Earnings Growth Potential: Low (28.9%)
- ❋ Growth: 10.3%
- ❋ Annual Job Openings: 41,270
- ❋ Self-Employed: 0.2%

**Considerations for Job Outlook:** An increase in the numbers of students in special education and students who are not native speakers of English is expected to create jobs for teacher assistants. Opportunities should be favorable.

Perform duties that are instructional in nature or deliver direct services to students or parents. Serve in a position for which a teacher or another professional has ultimate responsibility for the design and implementation of educational programs and services. Provide extra assistance to students with special needs, such as non-English-speaking students or those with physical and mental disabilities. Tutor and assist children individually or in small groups to help them master assignments and to reinforce learning concepts presented by teachers. Supervise students in classrooms, halls, cafeterias, school yards, and gymnasiums or on field trips. Enforce administration policies and rules governing students. Observe students' performance and record relevant data to assess progress. Discuss assigned duties with classroom teachers to coordinate instructional efforts. Instruct and monitor students in the use and care of equipment and materials to prevent injuries and damage. Present subject matter to students under the direction and guidance of teachers, using lectures, discussions, or supervised role-playing methods. Organize and label materials and display students' work in a manner appropriate for their eye levels and perceptual skills. Distribute tests and homework assignments and collect them when they are completed. Type, file, and duplicate materials. Distribute teaching materials such as textbooks, workbooks, papers, and pencils to students. Use computers, audiovisual aids, and other equipment and materials to supplement presentations. Attend staff meetings and serve on committees as required. Prepare lesson materials, bulletin board displays, exhibits, equipment, and demonstrations. Carry out therapeutic regimens such as behavior modification and personal development programs under the supervision of special education instructors, psychologists, or speech-language pathologists. Provide disabled students with assistive devices, supportive technology, and assistance accessing facilities such as restrooms. Assist in bus loading and unloading. Take class attendance and maintain attendance records. Grade homework and tests, and compute and record results, using answer sheets or electronic marking devices. **Education/Training Required:** Short-term on-the-job training. **Education and Training Programs:** Teacher Assistant/Aide Training; Teaching Assistant/Aide Training, Other. **Knowledge/Courses**—Geography, History and Archeology, Psychology, Therapy and Counseling, Sociology and Anthropology, English Language.

**Personality Type:** Social-Conventional. **Career Cluster:** 05 Education and Training. **Career Pathway:** 5.3 Teaching/Training. **Other Jobs in This Pathway:** Adult Basic and Secondary Education and Literacy Teachers and Instructors; Athletes and Sports Competitors; Audio-Visual and Multimedia Collections Specialists; Career/Technical Education Teachers, Middle School; Career/Technical Education Teachers, Secondary School; Chemists; Coaches and Scouts; Dietitians and Nutritionists; Elementary School Teachers, Except Special Education; Fitness Trainers and Aerobics Instructors; Historians; Instructional Coordinators; Instructional Designers and Technologists; Interpreters and Translators; Kindergarten Teachers, Except Special Education; Librarians; Middle School Teachers, Except Special and Career/Technical Education; Physicists; Preschool Teachers, Except Special Education; Recreation Workers; Secondary School Teachers, Except Special and Career/Technical Education; Self-Enrichment Education Teachers; Teachers and Instructors, All Other; Tutors.

**Skills**—Learning Strategies, Technology Design, Programming, Persuasion, Instructing.

**Work Environment:** Indoors; standing; noise.

# Teachers and Instructors, All Other

- ❋ Annual Earnings: $29,820
- ❋ Earnings Growth Potential: Medium (40.5%)
- ❋ Growth: 14.7%
- ❋ Annual Job Openings: 22,570
- ❋ Self-Employed: 20.6%

**Considerations for Job Outlook:** Faster-than-average employment growth is projected.

**This occupation includes all teachers and instructors not listed separately.** Because this is a highly diverse occupation, no data is available for some information topics.

**Education/Training Required:** Bachelor's degree. **Education and Training Program:** Education, Other.

**Career Cluster:** 05 Education and Training. **Career Pathway:** 5.3 Teaching/Training. **Other Jobs in This Pathway:** Adult Basic and Secondary Education and Literacy Teachers and Instructors; Athletes and Sports Competitors; Audio-Visual and Multimedia Collections Specialists; Career/Technical Education Teachers, Middle School; Career/Technical Education Teachers, Secondary School; Chemists; Coaches and Scouts; Dietitians and Nutritionists; Elementary School Teachers, Except Special Education; Fitness Trainers and Aerobics Instructors; Historians; Instructional Coordinators; Instructional Designers and Technologists; Interpreters and Translators; Kindergarten Teachers, Except Special Education; Librarians; Middle School Teachers,

Except Special and Career/Technical Education; Physicists; Preschool Teachers, Except Special Education; Recreation Workers; Secondary School Teachers, Except Special and Career/Technical Education; Self-Enrichment Education Teachers; Teacher Assistants; Tutors.

## Job Specialization: Tutors

**Provide non-classroom, academic instruction to students on an individual or small-group basis for proactive or remedial purposes.** Travel to students' homes, libraries, or schools to conduct tutoring sessions. Schedule tutoring appointments with students or their parents. Research or recommend textbooks, software, equipment, or other learning materials to complement tutoring. Prepare and facilitate tutoring workshops, collaborative projects, or academic support sessions for small groups of students. Participate in training and development sessions to improve tutoring practices or learn new tutoring techniques. Organize tutoring environment to promote productivity and learning. Monitor student performance or assist students in academic environments, such as classrooms, laboratories, or computing centers. Review class material with students by discussing text, working solutions to problems, or reviewing worksheets or other assignments. Provide feedback to students using positive reinforcement techniques to encourage, motivate, or build confidence in students. Prepare lesson plans or learning modules for tutoring sessions according to students' needs and goals. Maintain records of students' assessment results, progress, feedback, or school performance, ensuring confidentiality of all records. Identify, develop, or implement intervention strategies, tutoring plans, or individualized education plans (IEPs) for students. Develop teaching or training materials, such as handouts, study materials, or quizzes. Communicate students' progress to students, parents or teachers in written progress reports, in person, by phone, or by email. Collaborate with students, parents, teachers, school administrators, or counselors to determine student needs, develop tutoring plans, or assess student progress. Assess students' progress throughout tutoring sessions. Administer, proctor, or score academic or diagnostic assessments. Teach students study skills, note-taking skills, and test-taking strategies.

**Education/Training Required:** Short-term on-the-job training. **Education and Training Programs:** Adult Literacy Tutor/Instructor Training; Teaching Assistants/Aides, Other, Training. **Knowledge/Courses**—No data available.

**Personality Type:** No data available. **Career Cluster:** 05 Education and Training. **Career Pathway:** 5.3 Teaching/

Training. **Other Jobs in This Pathway:** Adult Basic and Secondary Education and Literacy Teachers and Instructors; Athletes and Sports Competitors; Audio-Visual and Multimedia Collections Specialists; Career/Technical Education Teachers, Middle School; Career/Technical Education Teachers, Secondary School; Chemists; Coaches and Scouts; Dietitians and Nutritionists; Elementary School Teachers, Except Special Education; Fitness Trainers and Aerobics Instructors; Historians; Instructional Coordinators; Instructional Designers and Technologists; Interpreters and Translators; Kindergarten Teachers, Except Special Education; Librarians; Middle School Teachers, Except Special and Career/Technical Education; Physicists; Preschool Teachers, Except Special Education; Recreation Workers; Secondary School Teachers, Except Special and Career/Technical Education; Self-Enrichment Education Teachers; Teacher Assistants; Teachers and Instructors, All Other.

**Skills**—No data available.

**Work Environment:** No data available.

## Technical Writers

* Annual Earnings: $63,280
* Earnings Growth Potential: High (41.3%)
* Growth: 18.2%
* Annual Job Openings: 1,680
* Self-Employed: 2.0%

**Considerations for Job Outlook:** Fast growth is expected because of the need for technical writers to explain an increasing number of scientific and technical products. Prospects should be good, especially for workers with strong technical and communication skills. Competition will be keen for some jobs.

**Write technical materials, such as equipment manuals, appendices, or operating and maintenance instructions. May assist in layout work.** Organize material and complete writing assignment according to set standards regarding order, clarity, conciseness, style, and terminology. Maintain records and files of work and revisions. Edit, standardize, or make changes to material prepared by other writers or establishment personnel. Confer with customer representatives, vendors, plant executives, or publisher to establish technical specifications and to determine subject material to be developed for publication. Review published materials and recommend revisions or changes in scope, format, content, and methods of reproduction and binding. Select photographs, drawings, sketches, diagrams, and charts to illustrate material. Study drawings, specifications, mockups, and product samples to integrate and delineate technology, operating procedure, and production sequence and detail. Interview production and engineering personnel and read journals and other material to become familiar with product technologies and production methods. Observe production, developmental, and experimental activities to determine operating procedure and detail. Arrange for typing, duplication, and distribution of material. Assist in laying out material for publication. Analyze developments in specific field to determine need for revisions in previously published materials and development of new material. Review manufacturer's and trade catalogs, drawings, and other data relative to operation, maintenance, and service of equipment. Draw sketches to illustrate specified materials or assembly sequence.

**Education/Training Required:** Bachelor's degree. **Education and Training Programs:** Business/Corporate Communications; Speech Communication and Rhetoric. **Knowledge/Courses**—Communications and Media, Clerical, English Language, Computers and Electronics, Education and Training, Engineering and Technology.

**Personality Type:** Artistic-Investigative-Conventional. **Career Clusters:** 03 Arts, Audio/Video Technology, and Communications; 04 Business, Management, and Administration. **Career Pathways:** 3.5 Journalism and Broadcasting; 4.5 Marketing. **Other Jobs in These Pathways:** Advertising Sales Agents; Audio and Video Equipment Technicians; Broadcast News Analysts; Broadcast Technicians; Camera Operators, Television, Video, and Motion Picture; Copy Writers; Directors—Stage, Motion Pictures, Television, and Radio; Editors; Film and Video Editors; Media and Communication Workers, All Other; Photographers; Producers; Program Directors; Public Address System and Other Announcers; Public Relations Specialists; Radio and Television Announcers; Reporters and Correspondents; Sound Engineering Technicians; Talent Directors; Technical Directors/Managers.

**Skills**—Writing, Reading Comprehension, Active Learning, Speaking, Critical Thinking, Operations Analysis, Complex Problem Solving, Active Listening.

**Work Environment:** Indoors; sitting; using hands; repetitive motions.

# Telecommunications Equipment Installers and Repairers, Except Line Installers

❋ Annual Earnings: $54,710
❋ Earnings Growth Potential: High (43.0%)
❋ Growth: –0.2%
❋ Annual Job Openings: 3,560
❋ Self-Employed: 4.0%

**Considerations for Job Outlook:** Telecommunications companies providing many new services, such as faster Internet connections and video on demand, are expected to result in employment growth for these workers. But better equipment will require less maintenance work, slowing employment growth. Prospects should be best for job seekers with computer skills and training in electronics.

**Set up, rearrange, or remove switching and dialing equipment used in central offices. Service or repair telephones and other communication equipment on customers' properties. May install equipment in new locations or install wiring and telephone jacks in buildings under construction.** Note differences in wire and cable colors so that work can be performed correctly. Test circuits and components of malfunctioning telecommunications equipment to isolate sources of malfunctions, using test meters, circuit diagrams, polarity probes, and other hand tools. Test repaired, newly installed, or updated equipment to ensure that it functions properly and conforms to specifications, using test equipment and observation. Drive crew trucks to and from work areas. Inspect equipment on a regular basis to ensure proper functioning. Repair or replace faulty equipment such as defective and damaged telephones, wires, switching system components, and associated equipment. Remove and remake connections to change circuit layouts, following work orders or diagrams. Demonstrate equipment to customers, explain how it is to be used, and respond to any inquiries or complaints. Analyze test readings, computer printouts, and trouble reports to determine equipment repair needs and required repair methods. Adjust or modify equipment to enhance equipment performance or to respond to customer requests. Remove loose wires and other debris after work is completed. Request support from technical service centers when on-site procedures fail to solve installation or maintenance problems. Communicate with bases, using telephones or two-way radios, to receive instructions or technical advice or to report equipment status. Assemble and install communication equipment such as data and telephone communication lines, wiring, switching equipment, wiring frames, power apparatus, computer systems, and networks. Collaborate with other workers to locate and correct malfunctions. Review manufacturers' instructions, manuals, technical specifications, building permits, and ordinances to determine communication equipment requirements and procedures. Test connections to ensure that power supplies are adequate and that communications links function.

**Education/Training Required:** Postsecondary vocational training. **Education and Training Program:** Communications Systems Installation and Repair Technology. **Knowledge/Courses**—Telecommunications, Mechanical, Computers and Electronics, Engineering and Technology, Design, Public Safety and Security.

**Personality Type:** Realistic-Investigative-Conventional. **Career Cluster:** 03 Arts, Audio/Video Technology, and Communications. **Career Pathway:** 3.6 Telecommunications. **Other Jobs in This Pathway:** Broadcast Technicians; Communications Equipment Operators, All Other; Electronic Home Entertainment Equipment Installers and Repairers; Film and Video Editors; Media and Communication Workers, All Other; Radio Mechanics; Radio Operators; Radio, Cellular, and Tower Equipment Installers and Repairers; Sound Engineering Technicians.

**Skills**—Installation, Repairing, Equipment Maintenance, Troubleshooting, Equipment Selection, Quality Control Analysis, Operation and Control, Programming.

**Work Environment:** More often outdoors than indoors; standing; using hands; bending or twisting the body; repetitive motions; noise; very hot or cold; bright or inadequate lighting; contaminants; cramped work space; high places; hazardous conditions; hazardous equipment; minor burns, cuts, bites, or stings.

# Telecommunications Line Installers and Repairers

- ❋ Annual Earnings: $50,850
- ❋ Earnings Growth Potential: High (47.1%)
- ❋ Growth: 0.9%
- ❋ Annual Job Openings: 2,790
- ❋ Self-Employed: 2.1%

**Considerations for Job Outlook:** Despite declines in some of the industries that employ these workers, some growth is expected as cities and the overall population expand and create a need for power and communications lines. Very good opportunities are expected as more workers in the electrical power industry near retirement age than workers in other industries.

**String and repair telephone and television cable, including fiber optics and other equipment for transmitting messages or television programming.** Travel to customers' premises to install, maintain, and repair audio and visual electronic reception equipment and accessories. Inspect and test lines and cables, recording and analyzing test results to assess transmission characteristics and locate faults and malfunctions. Splice cables, using hand tools, epoxy, or mechanical equipment. Measure signal strength at utility poles, using electronic test equipment. Set up service for customers, installing, connecting, testing, and adjusting equipment. Place insulation over conductors and seal splices with moisture-proof covering. Access specific areas to string lines and install terminal boxes, auxiliary equipment, and appliances, using bucket trucks or by climbing poles and ladders or entering tunnels, trenches, or crawl spaces. String cables between structures and lines from poles, towers, or trenches and pull lines to proper tension. Install equipment such as amplifiers and repeaters to maintain the strength of communications transmissions. Lay underground cable directly in trenches or string it through conduits running through trenches. Pull up cable by hand from large reels mounted on trucks; then pull lines through ducts by hand or with winches. Clean and maintain tools and test equipment. Explain cable service to subscribers after installation and collect any installation fees that are due. Compute impedance of wires from poles to houses to determine additional resistance needed for reducing signals to desired levels. Use a variety of construction equipment to complete installations, including digger derricks, trenchers, and cable plows. Dig trenches for underground wires and cables. Dig holes for power poles, using power augers or shovels; set poles in place with cranes; and hoist poles upright, using winches. Fill and tamp holes, using cement, earth, and tamping devices. Participate in the construction and removal of telecommunication towers and associated support structures.

**Education/Training Required:** Long-term on-the-job training. **Education and Training Program:** Communications Systems Installation and Repair Technology. **Knowledge/Courses**—Telecommunications, Building and Construction, Engineering and Technology, Customer and Personal Service, Design, Transportation.

**Personality Type:** Realistic-Enterprising. **Career Cluster:** 13 Manufacturing. **Career Pathway:** 13.3 Maintenance, Installation, and Repair. **Other Jobs in This Pathway:** Aircraft Mechanics and Service Technicians; Automotive

Specialty Technicians; Biological Technicians; Civil Engineering Technicians; Computer, Automated Teller, and Office Machine Repairers; Electrical and Electronic Equipment Assemblers; Electrical and Electronics Repairers, Commercial and Industrial Equipment; Electrical Engineering Technicians; Electrical Engineering Technologists; Electromechanical Engineering Technologists; Electronics Engineering Technicians; Electronics Engineering Technologists; Engineering Technicians, Except Drafters, All Other; Fuel Cell Technicians; Helpers—Installation, Maintenance, and Repair Workers; Industrial Engineering Technologists; Industrial Machinery Mechanics; Installation, Maintenance, and Repair Workers, All Other; Manufacturing Engineering Technologists; Manufacturing Production Technicians; Mapping Technicians; Mechanical Engineering Technologists; Mobile Heavy Equipment Mechanics, Except Engines; Nanotechnology Engineering Technicians; Tire Repairers and Changers; others.

**Skills**—Troubleshooting, Equipment Maintenance, Repairing, Operation and Control, Equipment Selection, Quality Control Analysis, Operation Monitoring, Installation.

**Work Environment:** Outdoors; standing; walking and running; kneeling, crouching, stooping, or crawling; using hands; bending or twisting the body; repetitive motions; noise; very hot or cold; bright or inadequate lighting; contaminants; cramped work space; high places; hazardous conditions; hazardous equipment; minor burns, cuts, bites, or stings.

# Tellers

- ❋ Annual Earnings: $24,100
- ❋ Earnings Growth Potential: Very low (22.3%)
- ❋ Growth: 6.2%
- ❋ Annual Job Openings: 28,440
- ❋ Self-Employed: 0.1%

**Considerations for Job Outlook:** Banks opening branches in a variety of locations, such as grocery stores, should result in some employment growth. Favorable job prospects are expected.

**Receive and pay out money. Keep records of money and negotiable instruments involved in a financial institution's various transactions.** Balance currency, coin, and checks in cash drawers at ends of shifts and calculate daily transactions, using computers, calculators, or adding machines. Cash checks and pay out money after verifying that signatures are correct, that written and numerical amounts agree, and that accounts have sufficient funds. Receive checks and cash for deposit, verify amounts, and check accuracy of deposit slips. Examine checks for endorsements and to verify other information such as dates, bank names, identification of the persons receiving payments, and the legality of the documents. Enter customers' transactions into computers to record transactions and issue computer-generated receipts. Count currency, coins, and checks received, by hand or using currency-counting machine, to prepare them for deposit or shipment to branch banks or the Federal Reserve Bank. Identify transaction mistakes when debits and credits do not balance. Prepare and verify cashier's checks. Arrange monies received in cash boxes and coin dispensers according to denomination. Process transactions such as term deposits, retirement savings plan contributions, automated teller transactions, night deposits, and mail deposits. Receive mortgage, loan, or public utility bill payments, verifying payment dates and amounts due. Resolve problems or discrepancies concerning customers' accounts. Explain, promote, or sell products or services such as travelers' checks, savings bonds, money orders, and cashier's checks, using computerized information about customers to tailor recommendations. Perform clerical tasks such as typing, filing, and microfilm photography. Monitor bank vaults to ensure cash balances are correct. Order a supply of cash to meet daily needs. Sort and file deposit slips and checks. Receive and count daily inventories of cash, drafts, and travelers' checks. Process and maintain records of customer loans. Count, verify, and post armored car deposits.

**Education/Training Required:** Short-term on-the-job training. **Education and Training Program:** Banking and Financial Support Services. **Knowledge/Courses**—Sales and Marketing, Customer and Personal Service, Economics and Accounting, Clerical, Public Safety and Security, Computers and Electronics.

**Personality Type:** Conventional-Enterprising. **Career Cluster:** 06 Finance. **Career Pathway:** 6.3 Banking and Related Services. **Other Jobs in This Pathway:** Bill and Account Collectors; Credit Analysts; Credit Authorizers; Credit Checkers; Loan Counselors; Loan Interviewers and Clerks; New Accounts Clerks; Title Examiners, Abstractors, and Searchers.

**Skills**—Service Orientation, Mathematics, Active Listening, Instructing.

**Work Environment:** Indoors; more often sitting than standing; using hands; repetitive motions.

# Tile and Marble Setters

- ❈ Annual Earnings: $38,110
- ❈ Earnings Growth Potential: High (43.0%)
- ❈ Growth: 14.3%
- ❈ Annual Job Openings: 3,070
- ❈ Self-Employed: 35.1%

**Considerations for Job Outlook:** Expected employment gains for these workers will arise from growing population and resulting increases in building and renovating structures. Job openings are also expected from the need to replace workers who leave the occupations permanently.

**Apply hard tile, marble, and wood tile to walls, floors, ceilings, and roof decks.** Align and straighten tile, using levels, squares, and straightedges. Determine and implement the best layout to achieve a desired pattern. Cut and shape tile to fit around obstacles and into odd spaces and corners, using hand- and power-cutting tools. Finish and dress the joints and wipe excess grout from between tiles, using damp sponge. Apply mortar to tile back, position the tile, and press or tap with trowel handle to affix tile to base. Mix, apply, and spread plaster, concrete, mortar, cement, mastic, glue, or other adhesives to form a bed for the tiles, using brush, trowel, and screed. Prepare cost and labor estimates based on calculations of time and materials needed for project. Measure and mark surfaces to be tiled, following blueprints. Level concrete and allow to dry. Build underbeds and install anchor bolts, wires, and brackets. Prepare surfaces for tiling by attaching lath or waterproof paper or by applying a cement mortar coat onto a metal screen. Study blueprints and examine surface to be covered to determine amount of material needed. Cut, surface, polish, and install marble and granite or install pre-cast terrazzo, granite, or marble units. Install and anchor fixtures in designated positions, using hand tools. Cut tile backing to required size, using shears. Remove any old tile, grout, and adhesive, using chisels and scrapers, and clean the surface carefully. Lay and set mosaic tiles to create decorative wall, mural, and floor designs. Assist customers in selection of tile and grout. Remove and replace cracked or damaged tile. Measure and cut metal lath to size for walls and ceilings, using tin snips. Select and order tile and other items to be installed, such as bathroom accessories, walls, panels, and cabinets, according to specifications. Mix and apply mortar or cement to edges and ends of drain tiles to seal halves and joints. Spread mastic or other adhesive base on roof deck to form base for promenade tile, using serrated spreader.

**Education/Training Required:** Long-term on-the-job training. **Education and Training Program:** Masonry/Mason Training. **Knowledge/Courses**—Building and Construction, Design, Mechanical.

**Personality Type:** Realistic-Conventional-Artistic. **Career Cluster:** 02 Architecture and Construction. **Career Pathway:** 2.2 Construction. **Other Jobs in This Pathway:** Brickmasons and Blockmasons; Cement Masons and Concrete Finishers; Construction and Building Inspectors; Construction Carpenters; Construction Laborers; Construction Managers; Cost Estimators; Drywall and Ceiling Tile Installers; Electrical Power-Line Installers and Repairers; Electricians; Engineering Technicians, Except Drafters, All Other; First-Line Supervisors of Construction Trades and Extraction Workers; Heating and Air Conditioning Mechanics and Installers; Helpers—Carpenters; Helpers—Electricians; Helpers—Pipelayers, Plumbers, Pipefitters, and Steamfitters; Highway Maintenance Workers; Operating Engineers and Other Construction Equipment Operators; Painters, Construction and Maintenance; Pipe Fitters and Steamfitters; Plumbers; Refrigeration Mechanics and Installers; Roofers; Rough Carpenters; Solar Energy Installation Managers; others.

**Skills**—Equipment Maintenance, Equipment Selection, Repairing, Troubleshooting, Operation and Control, Mathematics, Operation Monitoring, Technology Design.

**Work Environment:** Standing; kneeling, crouching, stooping, or crawling; using hands; bending or twisting the body; repetitive motions; noise; very hot or cold; bright or inadequate lighting; contaminants; cramped work space; hazardous equipment; minor burns, cuts, bites, or stings.

# Training and Development Managers

- ❈ Annual Earnings: $89,170
- ❈ Earnings Growth Potential: High (43.4%)
- ❈ Growth: 11.9%
- ❈ Annual Job Openings: 1,010
- ❈ Self-Employed: 0.6%

**Considerations for Job Outlook:** Efforts to recruit and retain employees, the growing importance of employee training, and new legal standards are expected to increase employment of these workers. College graduates and those with certification should have the best opportunities.

Plan, direct, or coordinate the training and develop-ment activities and staff of organizations. Conduct ori-entation sessions and arrange on-the-job training for new hires. Evaluate instructor performance and the effective-ness of training programs, providing recommendations for improvement. Develop testing and evaluation procedures. Conduct or arrange for ongoing technical training and per-sonal development classes for staff members. Confer with management and conduct surveys to identify training needs based on projected production processes, changes, and other factors. Develop and organize training manuals, multimedia visual aids, and other educational materials. Plan, develop, and provide training and staff development programs, using knowledge of the effectiveness of methods such as class-room training, demonstrations, on-the-job training, meet-ings, conferences, and workshops. Analyze training needs to develop new training programs or modify and improve exist-ing programs. Review and evaluate training and apprentice-ship programs for compliance with government standards. Train instructors and supervisors in techniques and skills for training and dealing with employees. Coordinate established courses with technical and professional courses provided by community schools and designate training procedures. Pre-pare training budget for department or organization.

**Education/Training Required:** Work experience plus degree. **Education and Training Program:** Human Resources Development. **Knowledge/Courses**—Educa-tion and Training, Personnel and Human Resources, Soci-ology and Anthropology, Sales and Marketing, Therapy and Counseling, English Language.

**Personality Type:** Enterprising-Social. **Career Clusters:** 04 Business, Management, and Administration; 05 Educa-tion and Training. **Career Pathway:** 4.3 Human Resources. **Other Jobs in This Pathway:** Human Resources Specialists.

**Skills**—Management of Financial Resources, Learning Strategies, Management of Personnel Resources, Instructing, Systems Evaluation, Management of Material Resources, Systems Analysis, Speaking.

**Work Environment:** Indoors; sitting.

# Training and Development Specialists

- ❋ Annual Earnings: $54,160
- ❋ Earnings Growth Potential: High (42.6%)
- ❋ Growth: 23.3%
- ❋ Annual Job Openings: 10,710
- ❋ Self-Employed: 1.6%

**Considerations for Job Outlook:** Efforts to recruit and retain employees, the growing importance of employee training, and new legal standards are expected to increase employment of these workers. College graduates and those with certification should have the best opportunities.

**Conduct training and development programs for employees.** Keep up with developments in area of expertise by reading current journals, books and magazine articles. Present information, using a variety of instructional tech-niques and formats such as role playing, simulations, team exercises, group discussions, videos and lectures. Schedule classes based on availability of classrooms, equipment, and instructors. Organize and develop, or obtain, training pro-cedure manuals and guides and course materials such as handouts and visual materials. Offer specific training pro-grams to help workers maintain or improve job skills. Mon-itor, evaluate and record training activities and program effectiveness. Attend meetings and seminars to obtain infor-mation for use in training programs, or to inform manage-ment of training program status. Coordinate recruitment and placement of training program participants. Evaluate training materials prepared by instructors, such as outlines, text, and handouts. Develop alternative training methods if expected improvements are not seen. Assess training needs through surveys, interviews with employees, focus groups, or consultation with managers, instructors or customer rep-resentatives. Screen, hire, and assign workers to positions based on qualifications. Select and assign instructors to con-duct training. Devise programs to develop executive poten-tial among employees in lower-level positions. Design, plan, organize and direct orientation and training for employ-ees or customers of industrial or commercial establishment. Negotiate contracts with clients, including desired training outcomes, fees and expenses. Supervise instructors, evaluate instructor performance, and refer instructors to classes for skill development. Monitor training costs to ensure budget is not exceeded, and prepare budget reports to justify expen-ditures. Refer trainees to employer relations representatives, to locations offering job placement assistance, or to appro-priate social services agencies if warranted.

**Education/Training Required:** Work experience plus degree. **Education and Training Program:** Human Resources Development. **Knowledge/Courses**—Education and Training, Sociology and Anthropology, Sales and Marketing, Clerical, Personnel and Human Resources, Psychology.

**Personality Type:** Social-Artistic-Conventional. **Career Clusters:** 04 Business, Management, and Administration; 05 Education and Training. **Career Pathway:** 4.3 Human Resources. **Other Jobs in This Pathway:** Human Resources Specialists.

**Skills**—Operations Analysis, Learning Strategies, Science, Instructing, Systems Evaluation, Management of Material Resources, Writing, Management of Financial Resources.

**Work Environment:** Indoors; sitting.

# Transportation Inspectors

- ❈ Annual Earnings: $57,640
- ❈ Earnings Growth Potential: High (46.3%)
- ❈ Growth: 18.3%
- ❈ Annual Job Openings: 1,130
- ❈ Self-Employed: 4.2%

**Considerations for Job Outlook:** Faster-than-average employment growth is projected.

**Inspect equipment or goods in connection with the safe transport of cargo or people. Includes rail transport inspectors, such as freight inspectors, car inspectors, rail inspectors, and other nonprecision inspectors of other types of transportation vehicles.** No task data available.

**Education/Training Required:** Work experience in a related occupation. **Education and Training Programs:** No related CIP programs; this job is learned through work experience in a related occupation. **Knowledge/Courses**—No data available.

**Personality Type:** No data available. **Career Cluster:** 16 Transportation, Distribution, and Logistics. **Career Pathway:** 16.1 Transportation Operations. **Other Jobs in This Pathway:** Airline Pilots, Copilots, and Flight Engineers; Automotive and Watercraft Service Attendants; Automotive Master Mechanics; Bus Drivers, School or Special Client; Bus Drivers, Transit and Intercity; Commercial Pilots; Crane and Tower Operators; First-Line Supervisors of Helpers, Laborers, and Material Movers, Hand; First-Line Supervisors of Transportation and Material-Moving Machine and Vehicle Operators; Freight and Cargo Inspectors; Heavy and Tractor-Trailer Truck Drivers; Laborers and Freight, Stock, and Material Movers, Hand; Light Truck or Delivery Services Drivers; Mates—Ship, Boat, and Barge; Motor Vehicle Operators, All Other; Operating Engineers and Other Construction Equipment Operators; Parking Lot Attendants; Pilots, Ship; Railroad Conductors and Yardmasters; Sailors and Marine Oilers; Ship and Boat Captains; Storage and Distribution Managers; Taxi Drivers and Chauffeurs; Transportation Managers; Transportation Workers, All Other; others.

**Skills**—No data available.

**Work Environment:** No data available.

# Job Specialization: Aviation Inspectors

**Inspect aircraft, maintenance procedures, air navigational aids, air traffic controls, and communications equipment to ensure conformance with federal safety regulations.** Inspect work of aircraft mechanics performing maintenance, modification, or repair and overhaul of aircraft and aircraft mechanical systems to ensure adherence to standards and procedures. Start aircraft and observe gauges, meters, and other instruments to detect evidence of malfunctions. Examine aircraft access plates and doors for security. Examine landing gear, tires, and exteriors of fuselage, wings, and engines for evidence of damage or corrosion and to determine whether repairs are needed. Prepare and maintain detailed repair, inspection, investigation, and certification records and reports. Inspect new, repaired, or modified aircraft to identify damage or defects and to assess airworthiness and conformance to standards, using checklists, hand tools, and test instruments. Examine maintenance records and flight logs to determine if service and maintenance checks and overhauls were performed at prescribed intervals. Recommend replacement, repair, or modification of aircraft equipment. Recommend changes in rules, policies, standards, and regulations based on knowledge of operating conditions, aircraft improvements, and other factors. Issue pilots' licenses to individuals meeting standards. Investigate air accidents and complaints to determine causes. Observe flight activities of pilots to assess flying skills and to ensure conformance to flight and safety regulations. Conduct flight test programs to test equipment, instruments, and systems under a variety of conditions, using both manual and automatic controls. Approve or deny issuance of certificates of airworthiness. Analyze training programs and conduct oral and written examinations to ensure the competency of persons operating, installing, and repairing aircraft equipment.

Schedule and coordinate in-flight testing programs with ground crews and air traffic control to ensure availability of ground tracking, equipment monitoring, and related services.

**Education/Training Required:** Work experience in a related occupation. **Education and Training Program:** Aircraft Powerplant Technology/Technician. **Knowledge/ Courses**—Mechanical, Physics, Transportation, Chemistry, Design, Law and Government.

**Personality Type:** Realistic-Conventional-Investigative. **Career Cluster:** 16 Transportation, Distribution, and Logistics. **Career Pathways:** 16.1 Transportation Operations; 16.5 Transportation Systems/Infrastructure Planning, Management, and Regulation. **Other Jobs in These Pathways:** Airline Pilots, Copilots, and Flight Engineers; Automotive and Watercraft Service Attendants; Automotive Master Mechanics; Bus Drivers, School or Special Client; Bus Drivers, Transit and Intercity; Commercial Pilots; Crane and Tower Operators; First-Line Supervisors of Helpers, Laborers, and Material Movers, Hand; First-Line Supervisors of Transportation and Material-Moving Machine and Vehicle Operators; Freight and Cargo Inspectors; Heavy and Tractor-Trailer Truck Drivers; Laborers and Freight, Stock, and Material Movers, Hand; Light Truck or Delivery Services Drivers; Mates—Ship, Boat, and Barge; Motor Vehicle Operators, All Other; Operating Engineers and Other Construction Equipment Operators; Parking Lot Attendants; Pilots, Ship; Railroad Conductors and Yardmasters; Sailors and Marine Oilers; Ship and Boat Captains; Storage and Distribution Managers; Taxi Drivers and Chauffeurs; Transportation Managers; Transportation Workers, All Other; others.

**Skills**—Science, Equipment Maintenance, Troubleshooting, Repairing, Operation and Control, Equipment Selection, Quality Control Analysis, Operation Monitoring.

**Work Environment:** More often indoors than outdoors; sitting; noise.

# Job Specialization: Freight and Cargo Inspectors

**Inspect the handling, storage, and stowing of freight and cargoes.** Prepare and submit reports after completion of freight shipments. Inspect shipments to ensure that freight is securely braced and blocked. Record details about freight conditions, handling of freight, and any problems encountered. Advise crews in techniques of stowing dangerous and heavy cargo. Observe loading of freight to ensure that crews comply with procedures. Recommend remedial procedures to correct any violations found during inspections. Inspect loaded cargo, cargo lashed to decks or in storage facilities, and cargo handling devices to determine compliance with health and safety regulations and need for maintenance. Measure ships' holds and depths of fuel and water in tanks, using sounding lines and tape measures. Notify workers of any special treatment required for shipments. Direct crews to reload freight or to insert additional bracing or packing as necessary. Check temperatures and humidities of shipping and storage areas to ensure that they are at appropriate levels to protect cargo. Determine cargo transportation capabilities by reading documents that set forth cargo loading and securing procedures, capacities, and stability factors. Read draft markings to determine depths of vessels in water. Issue certificates of compliance for vessels without violations. Write certificates of admeasurement that list details such as designs, lengths, depths, and breadths of vessels, and methods of propulsion. Calculate gross and net tonnage, hold capacities, volumes of stored fuel and water, cargo weights, and ship stability factors, using mathematical formulas. Post warning signs on vehicles containing explosives or flammable or radioactive materials. Measure heights and widths of loads to ensure they will pass over bridges or through tunnels on scheduled routes. Time rolls of ships, using stopwatches. Determine types of licenses and safety equipment required, and compute applicable fees such as tolls and wharfage fees.

**Education/Training Required:** Work experience in a related occupation. **Education and Training Programs:** No related CIP programs; this job is learned through work experience in a related occupation. **Knowledge/Courses**—Transportation, Engineering and Technology, Public Safety and Security, Physics, Geography, Mechanical.

**Personality Type:** Realistic-Conventional. **Career Cluster:** 16 Transportation, Distribution, and Logistics. **Career Pathways:** 16.1 Transportation Operations; 16.5 Transportation Systems/Infrastructure Planning, Management, and Regulation. **Other Jobs in These Pathways:** Airline Pilots, Copilots, and Flight Engineers; Automotive and Watercraft Service Attendants; Automotive Master Mechanics; Bus Drivers, School or Special Client; Bus Drivers, Transit and Intercity; Commercial Pilots; Crane and Tower Operators; First-Line Supervisors of Helpers, Laborers, and Material Movers, Hand; First-Line Supervisors of Transportation and Material-Moving Machine and Vehicle Operators; Heavy and Tractor-Trailer Truck Drivers; Laborers and Freight, Stock, and Material Movers, Hand; Light Truck or Delivery Services Drivers; Mates—Ship, Boat, and Barge; Motor Vehicle Operators, All Other; Operating Engineers and Other Construction Equipment Operators; Parking Lot Attendants; Pilots, Ship; Railroad Conductors and Yardmasters; Sailors and Marine Oilers; Ship and Boat Captains; Storage and Distribution Managers; Taxi Drivers and Chauffeurs; Transportation Inspectors; Transportation Managers; Transportation Workers, All Other; others.

**Skills**—Operation and Control, Quality Control Analysis, Operation Monitoring, Science, Management of Personnel Resources, Troubleshooting, Writing, Judgment and Decision Making.

**Work Environment:** More often outdoors than indoors; standing; noise; very hot or cold; bright or inadequate lighting; contaminants; cramped work space; high places; hazardous equipment.

## Job Specialization: Transportation Vehicle, Equipment, and Systems Inspectors, Except Aviation

**Inspect and monitor transportation equipment, vehicles, or systems to ensure compliance with regulations and safety standards.** Conduct vehicle or transportation equipment tests, using diagnostic equipment. Investigate and make recommendations on carrier requests for waiver of federal standards. Prepare reports on investigations or inspections and actions taken. Issue notices and recommend corrective actions when infractions or problems are found. Investigate incidents or violations such as delays, accidents, and equipment failures. Investigate complaints regarding safety violations. Inspect repairs to transportation vehicles and equipment to ensure that repair work was performed properly. Examine transportation vehicles, equipment, or systems to detect damage, wear, or malfunction. Inspect vehicles and other equipment for evidence of abuse, damage, or mechanical malfunction. Examine carrier operating rules, employee qualification guidelines, and carrier training and testing programs for compliance with regulations or safety standards. Inspect vehicles or equipment to ensure compliance with rules, standards, or regulations.

**Education/Training Required:** Work experience in a related occupation. **Education and Training Programs:** No related CIP programs; this job is learned through work experience in a related occupation. **Knowledge/Courses**—Mechanical, Transportation, Public Safety and Security, Engineering and Technology, Administration and Management, Physics.

**Personality Type:** Realistic-Conventional-Investigative. **Career Cluster:** 16 Transportation, Distribution, and

Logistics. **Career Pathways:** 16.1 Transportation Operations; 16.5 Transportation Systems/Infrastructure Planning, Management, and Regulation. **Other Jobs in These Pathways:** Airline Pilots, Copilots, and Flight Engineers; Automotive and Watercraft Service Attendants; Automotive Master Mechanics; Bus Drivers, School or Special Client; Bus Drivers, Transit and Intercity; Commercial Pilots; Crane and Tower Operators; First-Line Supervisors of Helpers, Laborers, and Material Movers, Hand; First-Line Supervisors of Transportation and Material-Moving Machine and Vehicle Operators; Freight and Cargo Inspectors; Heavy and Tractor-Trailer Truck Drivers; Laborers and Freight, Stock, and Material Movers, Hand; Light Truck or Delivery Services Drivers; Mates—Ship, Boat, and Barge; Motor Vehicle Operators, All Other; Operating Engineers and Other Construction Equipment Operators; Parking Lot Attendants; Pilots, Ship; Railroad Conductors and Yardmasters; Sailors and Marine Oilers; Ship and Boat Captains; Storage and Distribution Managers; Taxi Drivers and Chauffeurs; Transportation Managers; Transportation Workers, All Other; others.

**Skills**—Equipment Maintenance, Repairing, Troubleshooting, Science, Operation and Control, Quality Control Analysis, Operation Monitoring, Equipment Selection.

**Work Environment:** Outdoors; standing; walking and running; using hands; bending or twisting the body; repetitive motions; noise; very hot or cold; bright or inadequate lighting; contaminants; cramped work space; hazardous equipment; minor burns, cuts, bites, or stings.

## Transportation, Storage, and Distribution Managers

- ❋ Annual Earnings: $80,210
- ❋ Earnings Growth Potential: High (41.8%)
- ❋ Growth: –5.3%
- ❋ Annual Job Openings: 2,740
- ❋ Self-Employed: 3.4%

**Considerations for Job Outlook:** Employment is projected to decline slowly.

## Job Specialization: Logistics Managers

**Plan, direct, or coordinate purchasing, warehousing, distribution, forecasting, customer service, or planning services. Manage logistics personnel and logistics systems**

**and direct daily operations.** Train shipping department personnel in roles and responsibilities regarding global logistics strategies. Maintain metrics, reports, process documentation, customer service logs, and training or safety records. Recommend purchase of new or improved technology, such as automated systems. Implement specific customer requirements, such as internal reporting and customized transportation metrics. Resolve problems concerning transportation, logistics systems, imports and exports, or customer issues. Develop risk management programs to ensure continuity of supply in emergency scenarios. Plan and implement improvements to internal or external logistics systems and processes. Recommend optimal transportation modes, routing, equipment, or frequency. Participate in carrier management processes, such as selection, qualification, and performance evaluation. Negotiate transportation rates and services. Monitor product import or export processes to ensure compliance with regulatory or legal requirements. Establish or monitor specific supply chain-based performance measurement systems. Ensure carrier compliance with company policies and procedures for product transit and delivery. Direct distribution center operation to ensure achievement of cost, productivity, accuracy, or timeliness objectives. Design models for use in evaluating logistics programs and services. Create policies and procedures for logistics activities. Collaborate with other departments to integrate logistics with business systems and processes, such as customer sales, order management, accounting, and shipping. Analyze the financial impact of proposed logistics changes, such as routing, shipping modes, product volumes and mixes, and carriers. Supervise the work of logistics specialists, planners, or schedulers. Plan and implement material flow management systems to meet production requirements.

**Education/Training Required:** Work experience plus degree. **Education and Training Program:** Logistics, Materials, and Supply Chain Management. **Knowledge/Courses**—No data available.

**Personality Type:** Enterprising-Conventional. **Career Clusters:** 04 Business, Management, and Administration; 16 Transportation, Distribution, and Logistics. **Career Pathways:** 4.1 Management; 4.2 Business, Financial Management, and Accounting; 16.2 Logistics, Planning, and Management Services. **Other Jobs in These Pathways:** Accountants; Auditors; Bookkeeping, Accounting, and Auditing Clerks; Brownfield Redevelopment Specialists and Site Managers; Business Continuity Planners; Business Operations Specialists, All Other; Compliance Managers; Construction Managers; Customs Brokers; Energy Auditors; Financial Managers, Branch or Department; First-Line Supervisors of Office and Administrative Support Workers; General and Operations Managers; Investment Fund Managers; Loss Prevention Managers; Management Analysts; Managers, All Other; Regulatory Affairs Managers; Security Management Specialists; Security Managers; Supply Chain Managers; Sustainability Specialists; Treasurers and Controllers; Wind Energy Operations Managers; Wind Energy Project Managers; others.

**Skills**—No data available.

**Work Environment:** No data available.

# Job Specialization: Storage and Distribution Managers

**Plan, direct, and coordinate the storage and distribution operations within organizations or the activities of organizations that are engaged in storing and distributing materials and products.** Prepare and manage departmental budgets. Supervise the activities of workers engaged in receiving, storing, testing, and shipping products or materials. Interview, select, and train warehouse and supervisory personnel. Plan, develop, and implement warehouse safety and security programs and activities. Prepare or direct preparation of correspondence; reports; and operations, maintenance, and safety manuals. Issue shipping instructions and provide routing information to ensure that delivery times and locations are coordinated. Review invoices, work orders, consumption reports, and demand forecasts to estimate peak delivery periods and to issue work assignments. Confer with department heads to coordinate warehouse activities such as production, sales, records control, and purchasing. Inspect physical conditions of warehouses, vehicle fleets, and equipment and order testing, maintenance, repair, or replacement as necessary. Schedule and monitor air or surface pickup, delivery, or distribution of products or materials. Respond to customers' or shippers' questions and complaints regarding storage and distribution services. Develop and document standard and emergency operating procedures for receiving, handling, storing, shipping, or salvaging products or materials. Develop and implement plans for facility modification or expansion such as equipment purchase or changes in space allocation or structural design. Track and trace goods while they are en route to their destinations, expediting orders when necessary. Negotiate with carriers, warehouse operators, and insurance company representatives for services and preferential rates. Arrange for necessary shipping documentation and contact customs officials to effect release of shipments. Evaluate freight costs and the inventory costs associated with transit times to ensure that costs are appropriate. Advise sales and billing departments of transportation charges for customers' accounts.

**Education/Training Required:** Work experience in a related occupation. **Education and Training Programs:** Aeronautics/Aviation/Aerospace Science and Technology, General; Aviation/Airway Management and Operations; Business Administration and Management, General; Business/Commerce, General; Logistics, Materials, and Supply Chain Management; Public Administration; Transportation/Mobility Management. **Knowledge/Courses**—Transportation, Personnel and Human Resources, Production and Processing, Administration and Management, Economics and Accounting, Psychology.

**Personality Type:** Enterprising-Conventional. **Career Clusters:** 04 Business, Management, and Administration; 07 Government and Public Administration; 16 Transportation, Distribution, and Logistics. **Career Pathways:** 4.1 Management; 7.1 Governance; 16.1 Transportation Operations; 16.2 Logistics, Planning, and Management Services. **Other Jobs in These Pathways:** Automotive Master Mechanics; Brownfield Redevelopment Specialists and Site Managers; Bus Drivers, School or Special Client; Business Continuity Planners; Business Operations Specialists, All Other; Compliance Managers; Construction Managers; Customs Brokers; Energy Auditors; First-Line Supervisors of Office and Administrative Support Workers; General and Operations Managers; Heavy and Tractor-Trailer Truck Drivers; Investment Fund Managers; Laborers and Freight, Stock, and Material Movers, Hand; Light Truck or Delivery Services Drivers; Loss Prevention Managers; Management Analysts; Managers, All Other; Regulatory Affairs Managers; Security Management Specialists; Security Managers; Supply Chain Managers; Sustainability Specialists; Wind Energy Operations Managers; Wind Energy Project Managers; others.

**Skills**—Management of Financial Resources, Management of Material Resources, Operations Analysis, Management of Personnel Resources, Negotiation, Coordination, Operation and Control, Systems Evaluation.

**Work Environment:** Indoors; standing.

## Job Specialization: Transportation Managers

**Plan, direct, and coordinate the transportation operations within an organization or the activities of organizations that provide transportation services.** Direct activities related to dispatching, routing, and tracking transportation vehicles such as aircraft and railroad cars. Plan, organize, and manage the work of subordinate staff to ensure that the work is accomplished in a manner consistent with organizational requirements. Direct investigations to verify and resolve customer or shipper complaints. Serve as contact persons for all workers within assigned territories. Implement schedule and policy changes. Collaborate with other managers and staff members to formulate and implement policies, procedures, goals, and objectives. Monitor operations to ensure that staff members comply with administrative policies and procedures, safety rules, union contracts, and government regulations. Promote safe work activities by conducting safety audits, attending company safety meetings, and meeting with individual staff members. Develop criteria, application instructions, procedural manuals, and contracts for federal and state public transportation programs. Monitor spending to ensure that expenses are consistent with approved budgets. Direct and coordinate, through subordinates, activities of operations department to obtain use of equipment, facilities, and human resources. Direct activities of staff performing repairs and maintenance to equipment, vehicles, and facilities. Conduct investigations in cooperation with government agencies to determine causes of transportation accidents and to improve safety procedures. Analyze expenditures and other financial information to develop plans, policies, and budgets for increasing profits and improving services. Negotiate and authorize contracts with equipment and materials suppliers and monitor contract fulfillment. Supervise workers assigning tariff classifications and preparing billing. Set operations policies and standards, including determination of safety procedures for the handling of dangerous goods.

**Education/Training Required:** Work experience in a related occupation. **Education and Training Programs:** Aeronautics/Aviation/Aerospace Science and Technology, General; Aviation/Airway Management and Operations; Business Administration and Management, General; Business/Commerce, General; Logistics, Materials, and Supply Chain Management; Public Administration; Transportation/Mobility Management. **Knowledge/Courses**—Transportation, Geography, Production and Processing, Personnel and Human Resources, Administration and Management, Economics and Accounting.

**Personality Type:** Enterprising-Conventional. **Career Clusters:** 04 Business, Management, and Administration; 07 Government and Public Administration; 16 Transportation, Distribution, and Logistics. **Career Pathways:** 4.1 Management; 7.1 Governance; 16.1 Transportation Operations; 16.2 Logistics, Planning, and Management Services. **Other Jobs in These Pathways:** Automotive Master

Mechanics; Brownfield Redevelopment Specialists and Site Managers; Bus Drivers, School or Special Client; Business Continuity Planners; Business Operations Specialists, All Other; Compliance Managers; Construction Managers; Customs Brokers; Energy Auditors; First-Line Supervisors of Office and Administrative Support Workers; General and Operations Managers; Heavy and Tractor-Trailer Truck Drivers; Investment Fund Managers; Laborers and Freight, Stock, and Material Movers, Hand; Light Truck or Delivery Services Drivers; Loss Prevention Managers; Management Analysts; Managers, All Other; Regulatory Affairs Managers; Security Management Specialists; Security Managers; Supply Chain Managers; Sustainability Specialists; Wind Energy Operations Managers; Wind Energy Project Managers; others.

**Skills**—Management of Financial Resources, Systems Evaluation, Negotiation, Systems Analysis, Management of Material Resources, Social Perceptiveness, Management of Personnel Resources, Time Management.

**Work Environment:** Indoors; sitting.

# Tree Trimmers and Pruners

- ❀ Annual Earnings: $30,450
- ❀ Earnings Growth Potential: Low (33.9%)
- ❀ Growth: 26.3%
- ❀ Annual Job Openings: 1,720
- ❀ Self-Employed: 22.7%

**Considerations for Job Outlook:** Demand for lawn care and landscaping services is expected to grow, resulting in employment growth for these workers. Job prospects are expected to be good. Opportunities for year-round work should be best in regions with temperate climates.

**Cut away dead or excess branches from trees or shrubs to maintain right-of-way for roads, sidewalks, or utilities or to improve appearance, health, and value of trees. Prune or treat trees or shrubs, using handsaws, pruning hooks, shears, and clippers. May use truck-mounted lifts and power pruners. May fill cavities in trees to promote healing and prevent deterioration.** Supervise others engaged in tree trimming work and train lower-level employees. Transplant and remove trees and shrubs and prepare trees for moving. Operate shredding and chipping equipment and feed limbs and brush into the machines. Remove broken limbs from wires, using hooked extension poles. Prune, cut down, fertilize, and spray trees as directed by tree surgeons. Spray trees to treat diseased or unhealthy trees, including mixing chemicals and calibrating spray equipment. Clean, sharpen, and lubricate tools and equipment. Clear sites, streets, and grounds of woody and herbaceous materials such as tree stumps and fallen trees and limbs. Load debris and refuse onto trucks and haul it away for disposal. Inspect trees to determine whether they have diseases or pest problems. Cut away dead and excess branches from trees or clear branches around power lines, using climbing equipment or buckets of extended truck booms, and/or chainsaws, hooks, handsaws, shears, and clippers. Collect debris and refuse from tree trimming and removal operations into piles, using shovels, rakes, or other tools. Operate boom trucks, loaders, stump chippers, brush chippers, tractors, power saws, trucks, sprayers, and other equipment and tools. Apply tar or other protective substances to cut surfaces to seal them and to protect them from fungi and insects. Climb trees, using climbing hooks and belts, or climb ladders to gain access to work areas. Split logs or wooden blocks into bolts, pickets, posts, or stakes, using hand tools such as ax wedges, sledgehammers, and mallets. Cable, brace, tie, bolt, stake, and guy trees and branches to provide support. Trim jagged stumps, using saws or pruning shears. Trim, top, and reshape trees to achieve attractive shapes or to remove low-hanging branches. Water, root-feed, and fertilize trees. Harvest tanbark by cutting rings and slits in bark and stripping bark from trees, using spuds or axes. Install lightning protection on trees.

**Education/Training Required:** Short-term on-the-job training. **Education and Training Program:** Applied Horticulture/Horticultural Business Services, Other. **Knowledge/Courses**—Biology, Mechanical, Transportation, Physics, Public Safety and Security, Sales and Marketing.

**Personality Type:** Realistic. **Career Cluster:** 01 Agriculture, Food, and Natural Resources. **Career Pathway:** 1.2 Plant Systems. **Other Jobs in This Pathway:** Agricultural Technicians; Animal Scientists; Biochemists and Biophysicists; Biologists; Economists; Environmental Economists; Farm and Home Management Advisors; First-Line Supervisors of Landscaping, Lawn Service, and Groundskeeping Workers; First-Line Supervisors of Retail Sales Workers; Floral Designers; Food Science Technicians; Food Scientists and Technologists; Geneticists; Grounds Maintenance Workers, All Other; Landscaping and Groundskeeping Workers; Pesticide Handlers, Sprayers, and Applicators, Vegetation; Precision Agriculture Technicians; Retail Salespersons; Soil and Plant Scientists.

**Skills**—Operation and Control, Equipment Maintenance, Repairing, Operation Monitoring, Troubleshooting, Equipment Selection, Quality Control Analysis, Management of Personnel Resources.

**Work Environment:** Outdoors; standing; climbing; walking and running; balancing; using hands; bending or twisting the body; repetitive motions; noise; very hot or cold; bright or inadequate lighting; contaminants; cramped work space; whole-body vibration; high places; hazardous conditions; hazardous equipment; minor burns, cuts, bites, or stings.

## Urban and Regional Planners

* Annual Earnings: $63,040
* Earnings Growth Potential: Low (35.9%)
* Growth: 19.0%
* Annual Job Openings: 1,470
* Self-Employed: 0.0%

**Considerations for Job Outlook:** State and local governments are expected to hire urban and regional planners to help manage population growth and commercial development. Private businesses, mainly architecture and engineering firms, will also hire these workers to deal with storm water management, environmental regulation, and other concerns. Job prospects should be best for job seekers with a master's degree.

**Develop comprehensive plans and programs for use of land and physical facilities of local jurisdictions such as towns, cities, counties, and metropolitan areas.** Design, promote, and administer government plans and policies affecting land use, zoning, public utilities, community facilities, housing, and transportation. Hold public meetings and confer with government, social scientists, lawyers, developers, the public, and special interest groups to formulate and develop land use or community plans. Recommend approval, denial, or conditional approval of proposals. Determine the effects of regulatory limitations on projects. Assess the feasibility of proposals and identify necessary changes. Create, prepare, or requisition graphic and narrative reports on land use data, including land area maps overlaid with geographic variables such as population density. Conduct field investigations, surveys, impact studies, or other research to compile and analyze data on economic, social, regulatory, and physical factors affecting land use. Advise planning officials on project feasibility, cost-effectiveness, regulatory conformance, and possible alternatives. Discuss with planning officials the purpose of land use projects such as transportation, conservation, residential, commercial, industrial, and community use. Keep informed about economic and legal issues involved in zoning codes, building codes, and environmental regulations. Mediate community disputes and assist in developing alternative plans and recommendations for programs or projects. Coordinate work with economic consultants and architects during the formulation of plans and the design of large pieces of infrastructure. Review and evaluate environmental impact reports pertaining to private and public planning projects and programs. Supervise and coordinate the work of urban planning technicians and technologists. Investigate property availability.

**Education/Training Required:** Master's degree. **Education and Training Program:** City/Urban, Community and Regional Planning. **Knowledge/Courses**—Geography, History and Archeology, Transportation, Design, Law and Government, Building and Construction.

**Personality Type:** Investigative-Enterprising-Artistic. **Career Cluster:** 07 Government and Public Administration. **Career Pathway:** 7.4 Planning. **Other Jobs in This Pathway:** Political Science Teachers, Postsecondary.

**Skills**—Systems Analysis, Management of Financial Resources, Operations Analysis, Science, Systems Evaluation, Judgment and Decision Making, Mathematics, Programming.

**Work Environment:** Indoors; sitting; noise.

## Ushers, Lobby Attendants, and Ticket Takers

* Annual Earnings: $18,560
* Earnings Growth Potential: Very low (14.9%)
* Growth: 13.7%
* Annual Job Openings: 8,190
* Self-Employed: 1.4%

**Considerations for Job Outlook:** Faster-than-average employment growth is projected.

**Assist patrons at entertainment events by performing duties such as collecting admission tickets and passes from patrons, assisting in finding seats, searching for lost articles, and locating such facilities as restrooms and telephones.** Sell and collect admission tickets and passes from patrons at entertainment events. Greet patrons attending entertainment events. Examine tickets or passes to verify authenticity, using criteria such as color and date issued. Guide patrons to exits or provide other instructions or assistance in case of emergency. Maintain order and ensure adherence to safety rules. Provide assistance with patrons' special needs, such as helping those with wheelchairs. Direct patrons to restrooms, concession stands, and telephones. Refuse admittance to undesirable persons or persons without tickets or passes. Settle seating disputes and help solve other customer concerns. Assist patrons in finding seats, lighting the way with flashlights if necessary. Search for lost articles or for parents of lost children. Count and record number of tickets collected. Operate refreshment stands during intermission or obtain refreshments for press box patrons during performances. Verify credentials of patrons desiring entrance into press-box and permit only authorized persons to enter. Distribute programs to patrons. Schedule and manage volunteer usher corps. Work with others to change advertising displays. Manage inventory and sale of artist merchandise. Give door checks to patrons who are temporarily leaving establishments. Manage informational kiosk and display of event signs and posters. Page individuals wanted at the box office.

**Education/Training Required:** Short-term on-the-job training. **Education and Training Programs:** No related CIP programs; this job is learned through short-term on-the-job training.

**Personality Type:** Social-Conventional-Enterprising. **Career Cluster:** 09 Hospitality and Tourism. **Career Pathway:** 9.4 Recreation, Amusements, and Attractions. **Other Jobs in This Pathway:** Amusement and Recreation Attendants; Baggage Porters and Bellhops; Concierges; Costume Attendants; Entertainment Attendants and Related Workers, All Other; Farm and Home Management Advisors; Gaming and Sports Book Writers and Runners; Gaming Dealers; Gaming Service Workers, All Other; Locker Room, Coatroom, and Dressing Room Attendants; Lodging Managers; Motion Picture Projectionists; Personal Care and Service Workers, All Other.

**Skills**—Service Orientation.

**Work Environment:** Indoors; standing; using hands; repetitive motions.

# Veterinarians

- ❀ Annual Earnings: $82,040
- ❀ Earnings Growth Potential: Medium (39.2%)
- ❀ Growth: 32.9%
- ❀ Annual Job Openings: 3,020
- ❀ Self-Employed: 6.9%

**Considerations for Job Outlook:** Growth in the pet population and pet owners' increased willingness to pay for intensive veterinary care and treatment are projected to create significantly more jobs for veterinarians. Excellent job opportunities are expected.

**Diagnose and treat diseases and dysfunctions of animals. May engage in a particular function, such as research and development, consultation, administration, technical writing, sale or production of commercial products, or rendering of technical services to commercial firms or other organizations. Includes veterinarians who inspect livestock.** Examine animals to detect and determine the nature of diseases or injuries. Treat sick or injured animals by prescribing medication, setting bones, dressing wounds, or performing surgery. Inoculate animals against various diseases such as rabies and distemper. Collect body tissue, feces, blood, urine, or other body fluids for examination and analysis. Operate diagnostic equipment such as radiographic and ultrasound equipment and interpret the resulting images. Advise animal owners regarding sanitary measures, feeding, and general care necessary to promote health of animals. Educate the public about diseases that can be spread from animals to humans. Train and supervise workers who handle and care for animals. Provide care to a wide range of animals or specialize in a particular species, such as horses or exotic birds. Euthanize animals. Establish and conduct quarantine and testing procedures that prevent the spread of diseases to other animals or to humans and that comply with applicable government regulations. Conduct postmortem studies and analyses to determine the causes of animals' deaths. Perform administrative duties such as scheduling appointments, accepting payments from clients, and maintaining business records. Drive mobile clinic vans to farms so that health problems can be treated or prevented. Direct the overall operations of animal hospitals, clinics, or mobile services to farms. Specialize in a particular type of treatment such as dentistry, pathology, nutrition, surgery, microbiology, or internal medicine. Inspect and test horses, sheep, poultry, and other animals to detect the presence of communicable diseases. Research diseases to which animals could be susceptible. Plan and execute animal nutrition and reproduction programs. Inspect animal housing facilities to determine their cleanliness and adequacy. Determine the effects of drug therapies, antibiotics, or new surgical techniques by testing them on animals.

**Education/Training Required:** First professional degree. **Education and Training Programs:** Comparative and Laboratory Animal Medicine; Laboratory Animal Medicine; Large Animal/Food Animal and Equine Surgery and Medicine; Small/Companion Animal Surgery and Medicine; Theriogenology; Veterinary Anatomy; Veterinary Anesthesiology; Veterinary Dentistry; Veterinary Dermatology;

Veterinary Emergency and Critical Care Medicine; Veterinary Infectious Diseases; Veterinary Internal Medicine; Veterinary Medicine; Veterinary Microbiology; Veterinary Microbiology and Immunobiology; Veterinary Nutrition; Veterinary Ophthalmology; Veterinary Pathology; Veterinary Pathology and Pathobiology; Veterinary Physiology; Veterinary Practice; Veterinary Preventive Medicine; Veterinary Preventive Medicine Epidemiology and Public Health; Veterinary Radiology; Veterinary Sciences/Veterinary Clinical Sciences, General; Veterinary Surgery; Veterinary Toxicology; Veterinary Toxicology and Pharmacology; Zoological Medicine; others. **Knowledge/Courses**—Medicine and Dentistry, Biology, Chemistry, Therapy and Counseling, Sales and Marketing, Personnel and Human Resources.

**Personality Type:** Investigative-Realistic. **Career Clusters:** 01 Agriculture, Food, and Natural Resources; 08 Health Science. **Career Pathways:** 1.3 Animal Systems; 8.1 Therapeutic Services. **Other Jobs in These Pathways:** Biologists; Clinical Psychologists; Community and Social Service Specialists, All Other; Counseling Psychologists; Dental Assistants; Dental Hygienists; Dentists, General; Healthcare Support Workers, All Other; Home Health Aides; Licensed Practical and Licensed Vocational Nurses; Low Vision Therapists, Orientation and Mobility Specialists, and Vision Rehabilitation Therapists; Massage Therapists; Medical and Clinical Laboratory Technicians; Medical and Health Services Managers; Medical Scientists, Except Epidemiologists; Medical Secretaries; Nonfarm Animal Caretakers; Occupational Therapists; Pharmacists; Pharmacy Technicians; Radiologic Technologists; School Psychologists; Social and Human Service Assistants; Speech-Language Pathologists; Speech-Language Pathology Assistants; others.

**Skills**—Science, Operations Analysis, Reading Comprehension, Active Learning, Instructing, Service Orientation, Writing, Judgment and Decision Making.

**Work Environment:** Indoors; standing; using hands; noise; contaminants; exposed to radiation; exposed to disease or infections; minor burns, cuts, bites, or stings.

# Veterinary Assistants and Laboratory Animal Caretakers

- ❋ Annual Earnings: $22,040
- ❋ Earnings Growth Potential: Low (25.2%)
- ❋ Growth: 22.8%
- ❋ Annual Job Openings: 2,550
- ❋ Self-Employed: 3.0%

**Considerations for Job Outlook:** Much-faster-than-average employment growth is projected.

**Feed, water, and examine pets and other nonfarm animals for signs of illness, disease, or injury in laboratories and animal hospitals and clinics. Clean and disinfect cages and work areas and sterilize laboratory and surgical equipment. May provide routine post-operative care, administer medication orally or topically, or prepare samples for laboratory examination under the supervision of veterinary or laboratory animal technologists or technicians, veterinarians, or scientists.** Monitor animals recovering from surgery and notify veterinarians of any unusual changes or symptoms. Administer anesthetics during surgery and monitor the effects on animals. Clean, maintain, and sterilize instruments and equipment. Administer medication, immunizations, and blood plasma to animals as prescribed by veterinarians. Provide emergency first aid to sick or injured animals. Clean and maintain kennels, animal holding areas, examination and operating rooms, and animal loading/unloading facilities to control the spread of disease. Hold or restrain animals during veterinary procedures. Perform routine laboratory tests or diagnostic tests such as taking and developing X-rays. Fill medication prescriptions. Collect laboratory specimens such as blood, urine, and feces for testing. Examine animals to detect behavioral changes or clinical symptoms that could indicate illness or injury. Assist veterinarians in examining animals to determine the nature of illnesses or injuries. Prepare surgical equipment and pass instruments and materials to veterinarians during surgical procedures. Perform enemas, catheterization, ear flushes, intravenous feedings, and gavages. Prepare feed for animals according to specific instructions such as diet lists and schedules. Exercise animals and provide them with companionship. Record information relating to animal genealogy, feeding schedules, appearance, behavior, and breeding. Educate and advise clients on animal health-care, nutrition, and behavior problems. Perform hygiene-related duties such as clipping animals' claws and cleaning and polishing teeth. Prepare examination or treatment rooms by stocking them with appropriate supplies. Provide assistance with euthanasia of animals and disposal of corpses. Perform office reception duties such as scheduling appointments and helping customers. Dust, spray, or bathe animals to control insect pests. Write reports, maintain research information, and perform clerical duties.

**Education/Training Required:** Short-term on-the-job training. **Education and Training Program:** Veterinary/Animal Health Technology/Technician and Veterinary Assistant. **Knowledge/Courses**—Biology, Medicine and

Dentistry, Chemistry, Sales and Marketing, Clerical, Customer and Personal Service.

**Personality Type:** Realistic-Social-Investigative. **Career Cluster:** 08 Health Science. **Career Pathway:** 8.2 Diagnostics Services. **Other Jobs in This Pathway:** Ambulance Drivers and Attendants, Except Emergency Medical Technicians; Anesthesiologist Assistants; Cardiovascular Technologists and Technicians; Cytogenetic Technologists; Cytotechnologists; Diagnostic Medical Sonographers; Emergency Medical Technicians and Paramedics; Endoscopy Technicians; Health Diagnosing and Treating Practitioners, All Other; Health Technologists and Technicians, All Other; Healthcare Practitioners and Technical Workers, All Other; Histotechnologists and Histologic Technicians; Medical and Clinical Laboratory Technicians; Medical and Clinical Laboratory Technologists; Medical and Health Services Managers; Medical Assistants; Medical Equipment Preparers; Neurodiagnostic Technologists; Nuclear Medicine Technologists; Ophthalmic Laboratory Technicians; Physical Scientists, All Other; Physician Assistants; Radiologic Technicians; Radiologic Technologists; Surgical Technologists; others.

**Skills**—Science, Management of Financial Resources, Management of Material Resources, Service Orientation, Operations Analysis, Mathematics, Operation and Control.

**Work Environment:** Indoors; standing; walking and running; kneeling, crouching, stooping, or crawling; using hands; bending or twisting the body; repetitive motions; noise; contaminants; exposed to radiation; exposed to disease or infections; minor burns, cuts, bites, or stings.

# Veterinary Technologists and Technicians

- ❋ Annual Earnings: $29,710
- ❋ Earnings Growth Potential: Low (31.0%)
- ❋ Growth: 35.8%
- ❋ Annual Job Openings: 4,850
- ❋ Self-Employed: 0.2%

**Considerations for Job Outlook:** Increases in the pet population and in advanced veterinary care are expected to create employment growth for these workers. Excellent job opportunities are expected.

**Perform medical tests in a laboratory environment for use in the treatment and diagnosis of diseases in animals. Prepare vaccines and serums for prevention of diseases.**

**Prepare tissue samples; take blood samples; and execute laboratory tests such as urinalysis and blood counts. Clean and sterilize instruments and materials and maintain equipment and machines.** Administer anesthesia to animals, under the direction of a veterinarian, and monitor animals' responses to anesthetics so that dosages can be adjusted. Care for and monitor the condition of animals recovering from surgery. Prepare and administer medications, vaccines, serums, and treatments as prescribed by veterinarians. Perform laboratory tests on blood, urine, and feces, such as urinalyses and blood counts, to assist in the diagnosis and treatment of animal health problems. Administer emergency first aid, such as performing emergency resuscitation or other life-saving procedures. Collect, prepare, and label samples for laboratory testing, culture, or microscopic examination. Clean and sterilize instruments, equipment, and materials. Provide veterinarians with the correct equipment and instruments as needed. Fill prescriptions, measuring medications and labeling containers. Prepare animals for surgery, performing such tasks as shaving surgical areas. Take animals into treatment areas and assist with physical examinations by performing such duties as obtaining temperature, pulse, and respiration data. Observe the behavior and condition of animals and monitor their clinical symptoms. Take and develop diagnostic radiographs, using X-ray equipment. Maintain laboratory, research, and treatment records, as well as inventories of pharmaceuticals, equipment, and supplies. Give enemas and perform catheterizations, ear flushes, intravenous feedings, and gavages. Prepare treatment rooms for surgery. Maintain instruments, equipment, and machinery to ensure proper working condition. Perform dental work such as cleaning, polishing, and extracting teeth. Clean kennels, animal holding areas, surgery suites, examination rooms, and animal loading/unloading facilities to control the spread of disease. Provide information and counseling regarding issues such as animal health care, behavior problems, and nutrition. Provide assistance with animal euthanasia and the disposal of remains.

**Education/Training Required:** Associate degree. **Education and Training Program:** Veterinary/Animal Health Technology/Technician and Veterinary Assistant. **Knowledge/Courses**—Biology, Medicine and Dentistry, Chemistry, Customer and Personal Service, Mathematics, Clerical.

**Personality Type:** Realistic-Investigative. **Career Cluster:** 08 Health Science. **Career Pathway:** 8.1 Therapeutic Services. **Other Jobs in This Pathway:** Clinical Psychologists; Community and Social Service Specialists, All Other; Counseling Psychologists; Dental Assistants; Dental Hygienists; Dentists, General; Health Technologists and Technicians, All Other; Healthcare Support Workers, All Other; Home

Health Aides; Licensed Practical and Licensed Vocational Nurses; Low Vision Therapists, Orientation and Mobility Specialists, and Vision Rehabilitation Therapists; Massage Therapists; Medical and Clinical Laboratory Technicians; Medical and Health Services Managers; Medical Scientists, Except Epidemiologists; Medical Secretaries; Occupational Therapists; Pharmacists; Pharmacy Technicians; Radiologic Technologists; School Psychologists; Social and Human Service Assistants; Speech-Language Pathologists; Speech-Language Pathology Assistants; Substance Abuse and Behavioral Disorder Counselors; others.

**Skills**—Science, Equipment Maintenance, Equipment Selection, Operation and Control, Quality Control Analysis, Service Orientation, Troubleshooting, Critical Thinking.

**Work Environment:** Indoors; standing; walking and running; using hands; bending or twisting the body; repetitive motions; noise; contaminants; exposed to radiation; exposed to disease or infections; minor burns, cuts, bites, or stings.

# Vocational Education Teachers, Postsecondary

- ❋ Annual Earnings: $48,210
- ❋ Earnings Growth Potential: High (42.3%)
- ❋ Growth: 15.1%
- ❋ Annual Job Openings: 4,000
- ❋ Self-Employed: 0.2%

**Considerations for Job Outlook:** Enrollments in postsecondary institutions are expected to continue rising as more people attend college and as workers return to school to update their skills. Opportunities for part-time or temporary positions should be favorable, but significant competition exists for tenure-track positions.

**Teach or instruct vocational or occupational subjects at the postsecondary level (but at less than the baccalaureate) to students who have graduated or left high school. Includes correspondence school instructors; industrial, commercial, and government training instructors; and adult education teachers and instructors who prepare persons to operate industrial machinery and equipment and transportation and communications equipment. Teaching may take place in public or private schools whose primary business is education or in a school associated with an organization whose primary business is other than education.** Supervise and monitor students' use of tools and equipment. Observe and evaluate students' work to determine progress, provide feedback, and make suggestions for improvement. Present lectures and conduct discussions to increase students' knowledge and competence, using visual aids such as graphs, charts, videotapes, and slides. Administer oral, written, or performance tests to measure progress and to evaluate training effectiveness. Prepare reports and maintain records such as student grades, attendance rolls, and training activity details. Supervise independent or group projects, field placements, laboratory work, or other training. Determine training needs of students or workers. Provide individualized instruction and tutorial or remedial instruction. Conduct on-the-job training, classes, or training sessions to teach and demonstrate principles, techniques, procedures, and methods of designated subjects. Develop curricula and plan course content and methods of instruction. Prepare outlines of instructional programs and training schedules and establish course goals. Integrate academic and vocational curricula so that students can obtain a variety of skills. Develop teaching aids such as instructional software, multimedia visual aids, or study materials. Select and assemble books, materials, supplies, and equipment for training, courses, or projects. Advise students on course selection, career decisions, and other academic and vocational concerns. Participate in conferences, seminars, and training sessions to keep abreast of developments in the field and integrate relevant information into training programs. Serve on faculty and school committees concerned with budgeting, curriculum revision, and course and diploma requirements. Review enrollment applications and correspond with applicants to obtain additional information. Arrange for lectures by experts in designated fields.

**Education/Training Required:** Work experience in a related occupation. **Education and Training Programs:** Agricultural Teacher Education; Business Teacher Education; Health Occupations Teacher Education; Sales and Marketing Operations/Marketing and Distribution Teacher Education; Teacher Education and Professional Development, Specific Subject Areas, Other; Technical Teacher Education; Technology Teacher Education/Industrial Arts Teacher Education; Trade and Industrial Teacher Education. **Knowledge/Courses**—Education and Training, Therapy and Counseling, Psychology, Computers and Electronics, Sales and Marketing, Design.

**Personality Type:** Social-Realistic. **Career Cluster:** 05 Education and Training. **Career Pathway:** 5.3 Teaching/Training. **Other Jobs in This Pathway:** Adult Basic and Secondary Education and Literacy Teachers and Instructors; Athletes and Sports Competitors; Audio-Visual and Multimedia Collections Specialists; Career/Technical Education Teachers, Middle School; Career/Technical Education Teachers, Secondary School; Chemists; Coaches and Scouts;

Dietitians and Nutritionists; Elementary School Teachers, Except Special Education; Fitness Trainers and Aerobics Instructors; Historians; Instructional Coordinators; Instructional Designers and Technologists; Interpreters and Translators; Kindergarten Teachers, Except Special Education; Librarians; Middle School Teachers, Except Special and Career/Technical Education; Physicists; Preschool Teachers, Except Special Education; Recreation Workers; Secondary School Teachers, Except Special and Career/Technical Education; Self-Enrichment Education Teachers; Teacher Assistants; Tutors; 37 other postsecondary teaching occupations.

**Skills**—Instructing, Learning Strategies, Writing, Operations Analysis, Speaking, Active Learning, Monitoring, Reading Comprehension.

**Work Environment:** Indoors; standing; using hands.

# Water and Wastewater Treatment Plant and System Operators

- ❋ Annual Earnings: $40,770
- ❋ Earnings Growth Potential: Medium (39.0%)
- ❋ Growth: 19.8%
- ❋ Annual Job Openings: 4,690
- ❋ Self-Employed: 0.0%

**Considerations for Job Outlook:** Growth in the population, especially in suburban areas, is expected to boost demand for water and wastewater-treatment services. Job opportunities should be excellent.

**Operate or control an entire process or system of machines, often through the use of control boards, to transfer or treat water or liquid waste.** Add chemicals such as ammonia, chlorine, or lime to disinfect and deodorize water and other liquids. Operate and adjust controls on equipment to purify and clarify water, process or dispose of sewage, and generate power. Inspect equipment or monitor operating conditions, meters, and gauges to determine load requirements and detect malfunctions. Collect and test water and sewage samples, using test equipment and color analysis standards. Record operational data, personnel attendance, or meter and gauge readings on specified forms. Maintain, repair, and lubricate equipment, using hand tools and power tools. Clean and maintain tanks and filter beds, using hand tools and power tools. Direct and coordinate plant workers engaged in routine operations and maintenance activities.

**Education/Training Required:** Long-term on-the-job training. **Education and Training Program:** Water Quality and Wastewater Treatment Management and Recycling Technology/Technician. **Knowledge/Courses**—Physics, Building and Construction, Mechanical, Biology, Chemistry, Engineering and Technology.

**Personality Type:** Realistic-Conventional. **Career Cluster:** 01 Agriculture, Food, and Natural Resources. **Career Pathway:** 1.6 Environmental Service Systems. **Other Jobs in This Pathway:** Environmental Engineering Technicians; Hazardous Materials Removal Workers; Occupational Health and Safety Specialists.

**Skills**—Repairing, Equipment Maintenance, Troubleshooting, Operation and Control, Equipment Selection, Operation Monitoring, Quality Control Analysis, Systems Evaluation.

**Work Environment:** Outdoors; standing; climbing; walking and running; kneeling, crouching, stooping, or crawling; using hands; bending or twisting the body; repetitive motions; noise; very hot or cold; bright or inadequate lighting; contaminants; cramped work space; exposed to disease or infections; hazardous conditions; hazardous equipment; minor burns, cuts, bites, or stings.

# Writers and Authors

- ❋ Annual Earnings: $55,420
- ❋ Earnings Growth Potential: High (48.4%)
- ❋ Growth: 14.8%
- ❋ Annual Job Openings: 5,420
- ❋ Self-Employed: 69.4%

**Considerations for Job Outlook:** Projected job growth for these workers stems from increased use of online media and growing demand for Web-based information. But print publishing is expected to continue weakening. Job competition should be keen.

## Job Specialization: Copy Writers

**Write advertising copy for use by publication or broadcast media to promote sale of goods and services.** Write advertising copy for use by publication, broadcast, or Internet media to promote the sale of goods and services. Present drafts and ideas to clients. Discuss the product, advertising themes and methods, and any changes that should be made in advertising copy with the client. Consult with sales, media, and marketing representatives to obtain information on product or service and discuss style and length of advertising copy. Vary language and tone of messages based on product and medium. Edit or rewrite existing copy as necessary and submit copy for approval by supervisor. Write to customers in their terms and on their level so that the advertiser's sales message is more readily received. Write articles; bulletins; sales letters; speeches; and other related informative, marketing, and promotional material. Invent names for products and write the slogans that appear on packaging, brochures, and other promotional material. Review advertising trends, consumer surveys, and other data regarding marketing of goods and services to determine the best way to promote products. Develop advertising campaigns for a wide range of clients, working with an advertising agency's creative director and art director to determine the best way to present advertising information. Conduct research and interviews to determine which of a product's selling features should be promoted.

**Education/Training Required:** Bachelor's degree. **Education and Training Programs:** Broadcast Journalism; Business/Corporate Communications; Communication, Journalism, and Related Programs, Other; Family and Consumer Sciences/Human Sciences Communication; Journalism; Mass Communication/Media Studies; Playwriting and Screenwriting; Speech Communication and Rhetoric. **Knowledge/Courses**—Sales and Marketing, Communications and Media, English Language, Clerical, Computers and Electronics, Administration and Management.

**Personality Type:** Enterprising-Artistic. **Career Cluster:** 03 Arts, Audio/Video Technology, and Communications. **Career Pathway:** 3.5 Journalism and Broadcasting. **Other Jobs in This Pathway:** Audio and Video Equipment Technicians; Broadcast News Analysts; Broadcast Technicians; Camera Operators, Television, Video, and Motion Picture; Directors—Stage, Motion Pictures, Television, and Radio; Editors; Film and Video Editors; Media and Communication Workers, All Other; Photographers; Producers; Program Directors; Public Address System and Other Announcers; Public Relations Specialists; Radio and Television Announcers; Reporters and Correspondents; Sound Engineering Technicians; Talent Directors; Technical Directors/Managers; Technical Writers.

**Skills**—Writing, Persuasion, Reading Comprehension, Negotiation, Operations Analysis, Active Listening, Management of Personnel Resources, Speaking.

**Work Environment:** Indoors; sitting.

## Job Specialization: Poets, Lyricists and Creative Writers

**Create original written works, such as scripts, essays, prose, poetry, or song lyrics, for publication or performance.** Revise written material to meet personal standards and to satisfy needs of clients, publishers, directors, or producers. Choose subject matter and suitable form to express personal feelings and experiences or ideas or to narrate stories or events. Plan project arrangements or outlines and organize material accordingly. Prepare works in appropriate format for publication and send them to publishers or producers. Follow appropriate procedures to get copyrights for completed work. Write fiction or nonfiction prose such as short stories, novels, biographies, articles, descriptive or critical analyses, and essays. Develop factors such as themes, plots, characterizations, psychological analyses, historical environments, action, and dialogue to create material. Confer with clients, editors, publishers, or producers to discuss changes or revisions to written material. Conduct research to obtain factual information and authentic detail, using sources such as newspaper accounts, diaries, and interviews. Write narrative, dramatic, lyric, or other types of poetry for publication. Attend book launches and publicity events or conduct public readings. Write words to fit musical compositions, including lyrics for operas, musical plays, and choral works. Adapt text to accommodate musical requirements of composers and singers. Teach writing classes. Write humorous material for publication or for performances such as comedy routines, gags, and comedy shows. Collaborate with other writers on specific projects.

**Education/Training Required:** Bachelor's degree. **Education and Training Programs:** Broadcast Journalism; Business/Corporate Communications; Communication, Journalism, and Related Programs, Other; Family and Consumer Sciences/Human Sciences Communication; Journalism; Mass Communication/Media Studies; Playwriting and Screenwriting; Speech Communication and Rhetoric. **Knowledge/Courses**—Fine Arts, Communications and Media, Philosophy and Theology, Sociology and Anthropology, Sales and Marketing, History and Archeology.

**Personality Type:** Artistic-Investigative. **Career Cluster:** 03 Arts, Audio/Video Technology, and Communications. **Career Pathway:** 3.4 Performing Arts. **Other Jobs in This Pathway:** Actors; Artists and Related Workers, All Other; Choreographers; Craft Artists; Dancers; Designers, All Other; Directors—Stage, Motion Pictures, Television, and Radio; Entertainers and Performers, Sports and Related Workers, All Other; Managers, All Other; Music Composers and Arrangers; Music Directors; Musicians, Instrumental;

Producers; Program Directors; Set and Exhibit Designers; Singers; Talent Directors; Technical Directors/Managers.

**Skills**—Writing, Reading Comprehension, Active Learning, Management of Financial Resources, Persuasion, Active Listening, Social Perceptiveness, Negotiation.

**Work Environment:** Indoors; sitting; using hands; repetitive motions.

# Zoologists and Wildlife Biologists

- ❋ Annual Earnings: $57,430
- ❋ Earnings Growth Potential: Medium (37.9%)
- ❋ Growth: 12.8%
- ❋ Annual Job Openings: 880
- ❋ Self-Employed: 2.6%

**Considerations for Job Outlook:** Biotechnological research and development should continue to drive job growth. Doctoral degree holders are expected to face competition for research positions in academia.

**Study the origins, behavior, diseases, genetics, and life processes of animals and wildlife. May specialize in wildlife research and management, including the collection and analysis of biological data to determine the environmental effects of present and potential use of land and water areas.** Study animals in their natural habitats, assessing effects of environment and industry on animals, interpreting findings, and recommending alternative operating conditions for industry. Inventory or estimate plant and wildlife populations. Analyze characteristics of animals to identify and classify them. Make recommendations on management systems and planning for wildlife populations and habitat, consulting with stakeholders and the public at large to explore options. Disseminate information by writing reports and scientific papers or journal articles and by making presentations and giving talks for schools, clubs, interest groups, and park interpretive programs. Study characteristics of animals such as origin, interrelationships, classification, life histories and diseases, development, genetics, and distribution. Perform administrative duties such as fundraising, public relations, budgeting, and supervision of zoo staff. Organize and conduct experimental studies with live animals in controlled or natural surroundings. Oversee the care and distribution of zoo animals, working with curators and zoo directors to determine the best way to contain animals, maintain their habitats, and manage facilities. Coordinate preventive programs to control the outbreak of wildlife diseases. Prepare collections of preserved specimens or microscopic slides for species identification and study of development or disease. Raise specimens for study and observation or for use in experiments. Collect and dissect animal specimens and examine specimens under microscope.

**Education/Training Required:** Bachelor's degree. **Education and Training Programs:** Animal Behavior and Ethology; Animal Physiology; Cell/Cellular Biology and Anatomical Sciences, Other; Ecology; Entomology; Wildlife Biology; Wildlife, Fish, and Wildlands Science and Management; Zoology/Animal Biology; Zoology/Animal Biology, Other. **Knowledge/Courses**—Biology, Geography, Clerical, Chemistry, Computers and Electronics, Education and Training.

**Personality Type:** Investigative-Realistic. **Career Clusters:** 01 Agriculture, Food, and Natural Resources; 15 Science, Technology, Engineering, and Mathematics. **Career Pathways:** 1.5 Natural Resources Systems; 15.2 Science and Mathematics. **Other Jobs in These Pathways:** Architectural and Engineering Managers; Biofuels/Biodiesel Technology and Product Development Managers; Biologists; Chemists; Climate Change Analysts; Clinical Research Coordinators; Community and Social Service Specialists, All Other; Conveyor Operators and Tenders; Dietitians and Nutritionists; Education, Training, and Library Workers, All Other; Engineering Technicians, Except Drafters, All Other; Environmental Restoration Planners; Environmental Scientists and Specialists, Including Health; Fishers and Related Fishing Workers; Industrial Ecologists; Industrial Truck and Tractor Operators; Logging Equipment Operators; Mechanical Engineering Technicians; Medical Scientists, Except Epidemiologists; Natural Sciences Managers; Operations Research Analysts; Recreation Workers; Refuse and Recyclable Material Collectors; Service Unit Operators, Oil, Gas, and Mining; Water Resource Specialists; others.

**Skills**—Science, Writing, Reading Comprehension, Systems Evaluation, Systems Analysis, Time Management, Mathematics, Operation and Control.

**Work Environment:** More often indoors than outdoors; sitting.

# APPENDIX

# Definitions of Skills and Knowledge/ Courses Referenced in This Book

| Definitions of Skills | |
|---|---|
| Skill Name | Definition |
| Active Learning | Working with new material or information to grasp its implications. |
| Active Listening | Listening to what other people are saying and asking questions as appropriate. |
| Complex Problem Solving | Identifying complex problems, reviewing the options, and implementing solutions. |
| Coordination | Adjusting actions in relation to others' actions. |
| Critical Thinking | Using logic and analysis to identify the strengths and weaknesses of different approaches. |
| Equipment Maintenance | Performing routine maintenance and determining when and what kind of maintenance is needed. |
| Equipment Selection | Determining the kind of tools and equipment needed to do a job. |
| Installation | Installing equipment, machines, wiring, or programs to meet specifications. |
| Instructing | Teaching others how to do something. |
| Judgment and Decision Making | Weighing the relative costs and benefits of a potential action. |

## Definitions of Skills

| Skill Name | Definition |
| --- | --- |
| Learning Strategies | Using multiple approaches when learning or teaching new things. |
| Management of Financial Resources | Determining how money will be spent to get the work done and accounting for these expenditures. |
| Management of Material Resources | Obtaining and seeing to the appropriate use of equipment, facilities, and materials needed to do certain work. |
| Management of Personnel Resources | Motivating, developing, and directing people as they work; identifying the best people for the job. |
| Mathematics | Using mathematics to solve problems. |
| Monitoring | Assessing how well one is doing when learning or doing something. |
| Negotiation | Bringing others together and trying to reconcile differences. |
| Operation and Control | Controlling operations of equipment or systems. |
| Operation Monitoring | Watching gauges, dials, or other indicators to make sure a machine is working properly. |
| Operations Analysis | Analyzing needs and product requirements to create a design. |
| Persuasion | Persuading others to approach things differently. |
| Programming | Writing computer programs for various purposes. |
| Quality Control Analysis | Evaluating the quality or performance of products, services, or processes. |
| Reading Comprehension | Understanding written sentences and paragraphs in work-related documents. |
| Repairing | Repairing machines or systems, using the needed tools. |
| Science | Using scientific methods to solve problems. |
| Service Orientation | Actively looking for ways to help people. |
| Social Perceptiveness | Being aware of others' reactions and understanding why they react the way they do. |
| Speaking | Talking to others to effectively convey information. |
| Systems Analysis | Determining how a system should work and how changes will affect outcomes. |

*(continued)*

*(continued)*

## Definitions of Skills

| Skill Name | Definition |
| --- | --- |
| Systems Evaluation | Looking at many indicators of system performance and taking into account their accuracy. |
| Technology Design | Generating or adapting equipment and technology to serve user needs. |
| Time Management | Managing one's own time and the time of others. |
| Troubleshooting | Determining what is causing an operating error and deciding what to do about it. |
| Writing | Communicating effectively with others in writing as indicated by the needs of the audience. |

## Definitions of Knowledge/Courses

| Knowledge/Course Name | Definition |
| --- | --- |
| Administration and Management | Knowledge of principles and processes involved in business and organizational planning, coordination, and execution. This includes strategic planning, resource allocation, manpower modeling, leadership techniques, and production methods. |
| Biology | Knowledge of plant and animal living tissue, cells, organisms, and entities, including their functions, interdependencies, and interactions with each other and the environment. |
| Building and Construction | Knowledge of materials, methods, and the appropriate tools to construct objects, structures, and buildings. |
| Chemistry | Knowledge of the composition, structure, and properties of substances and of the chemical processes and transformations that they undergo. This includes uses of chemicals and their interactions, danger signs, production techniques, and disposal methods. |
| Clerical Studies | Knowledge of administrative and clerical procedures and systems such as word-processing systems, filing and records management systems, stenography and transcription, forms, design principles, and other office procedures and terminology. |

# Definitions of Knowledge/Courses

| Knowledge/Course Name | Definition |
| --- | --- |
| Communications and Media | Knowledge of media production, communication, and dissemination techniques and methods, including alternative ways to inform and entertain via written, oral, and visual media. |
| Computers and Electronics | Knowledge of electric circuit boards, processors, chips, and computer hardware and software, including applications and programming. |
| Customer and Personal Service | Knowledge of principles and processes for providing customer and personal services, including needs assessment techniques, quality service standards, alternative delivery systems, and customer satisfaction evaluation techniques. |
| Design | Knowledge of design techniques, principles, tools, and instruments involved in the production and use of precision technical plans, blueprints, drawings, and models. |
| Economics and Accounting | Knowledge of economic and accounting principles and practices, the financial markets, banking, and the analysis and reporting of financial data. |
| Education and Training | Knowledge of instructional methods and training techniques, including curriculum design principles, learning theory, group and individual teaching techniques, design of individual development plans, and test design principles. |
| Engineering and Technology | Knowledge of equipment, tools, and mechanical devices and their uses to produce motion, light, power, technology, and other applications. |
| English Language | Knowledge of the structure and content of the English language, including the meaning and spelling of words, rules of composition, and grammar. |
| Fine Arts | Knowledge of theory and techniques required to produce, compose, and perform works of music, dance, visual arts, drama, and sculpture. |
| Food Production | Knowledge of techniques and equipment for planting, growing, and harvesting of food for consumption, including crop rotation methods, animal husbandry, and food storage/handling techniques. |

*(continued)*

*(continued)*

| Definitions of Knowledge/Courses | |
|---|---|
| Knowledge/Course Name | Definition |
| Foreign Language | Knowledge of the structure and content of a foreign (non-English) language, including the meaning and spelling of words, rules of composition and grammar, and pronunciation. |
| Geography | Knowledge of various methods for describing the location and distribution of land, sea, and air masses, including their physical locations, relationships, and characteristics. |
| History and Archeology | Knowledge of past historical events and their causes, indicators, and impact on particular civilizations and cultures. |
| Law and Government | Knowledge of laws, legal codes, court procedures, precedents, government regulations, executive orders, agency rules, and the democratic political process. |
| Mathematics | Knowledge of numbers and their operations and interrelationships, including arithmetic, algebra, geometry, calculus, and statistics and their applications. |
| Mechanical Devices | Knowledge of machines and tools, including their designs, uses, benefits, repair, and maintenance. |
| Medicine and Dentistry | Knowledge of the information and techniques needed to diagnose and treat injuries, diseases, and deformities. This includes symptoms, treatment alternatives, drug properties and interactions, and preventive health-care measures. |
| Personnel and Human Resources | Knowledge of policies and practices involved in personnel/human resource functions. This includes recruitment, selection, training, and promotion regulations and procedures; compensation and benefits packages; labor relations and negotiation strategies; and personnel information systems. |
| Philosophy and Theology | Knowledge of different philosophical systems and religions, including their basic principles, values, ethics, ways of thinking, customs, and practices and their impact on human culture. |
| Physics | Knowledge and prediction of physical principles, laws, and applications, including air, water, material dynamics, light, atomic principles, heat, electric theory, earth formations, and meteorological and related natural phenomena. |

# Definitions of Knowledge/Courses

| Knowledge/Course Name | Definition |
|---|---|
| Production and Processing | Knowledge of inputs, outputs, raw materials, waste, quality control, costs, and techniques for maximizing the manufacture and distribution of goods. |
| Psychology | Knowledge of human behavior and performance, mental processes, psychological research methods, and the assessment and treatment of behavioral and affective disorders. |
| Public Safety and Security | Knowledge of weaponry; public safety; security operations, rules, regulations, precautions, and prevention; and the protection of people, data, and property. |
| Sales and Marketing | Knowledge of principles and methods involved in showing, promoting, and selling products or services. This includes marketing strategies and tactics, product demonstration and sales techniques, and sales control systems. |
| Sociology and Anthropology | Knowledge of group behavior and dynamics; societal trends and influences; and cultures and their history, migrations, ethnicity, and origins. |
| Telecommunications | Knowledge of transmission, broadcasting, switching, control, and operation of telecommunications systems. |
| Therapy and Counseling | Knowledge of information and techniques needed to rehabilitate physical and mental ailments and to provide career guidance, including alternative treatments, rehabilitation equipment and its proper use, and methods to evaluate treatment effects. |
| Transportation | Knowledge of principles and methods for moving people or goods by air, rail, sea, or road, including their relative costs, advantages, and limitations. |

# Index

## C

**D**

**E**

*Best Jobs for the 21st Century © JIST Works*